THE INTERNATIONAL ENCYCLOPEDIA OF AIRCRAFT

First published in 1991 by Oriole Publishing Ltd for W H Smith Ltd

Conception and production by Thema GmbH, Munich
English edition prepared by The Book Creation Company Ltd, London
Manufactured in Italy, by Officine Grafiche De Agostini, Novara, Italy

ISBN: 1-870318-45-5

CONTENTS

Chapter 1

BOMBERS

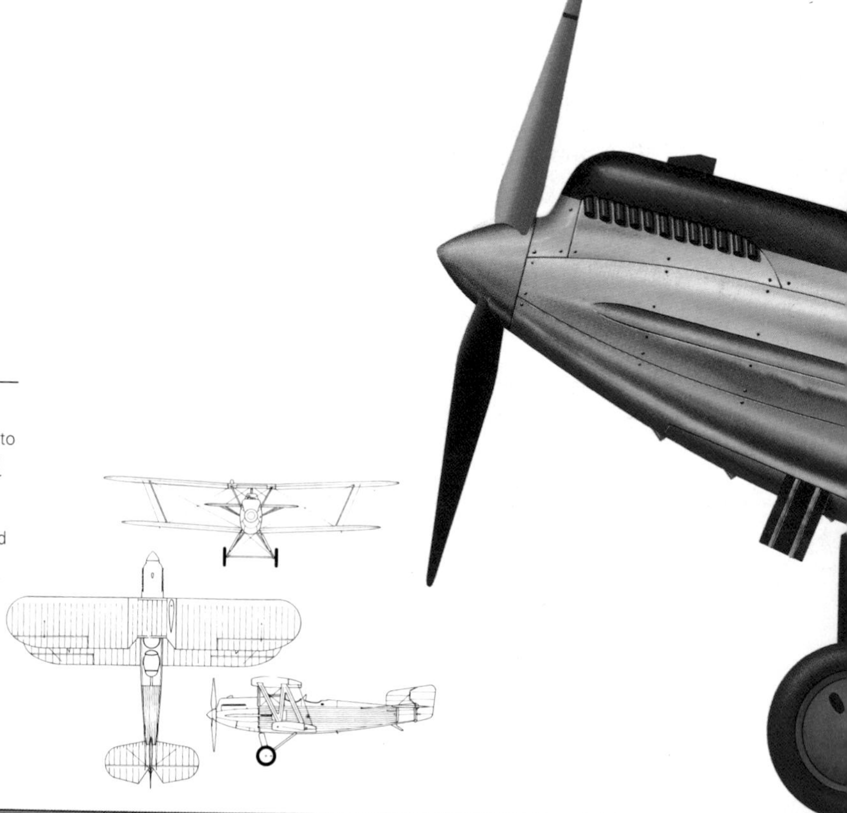

Fairey Fox

In its Fox the company produced an extremely elegant biplane day bomber whose combination of a powerful engine and clean lines produced performance sparkling enough to outpace contemporary fighters: noteworthy features in the streamlining were the low-drag engine installation, the elimination of the previously standard Scarff ring mounting in favour of a Fairey high-speed mounting for the rear machine-gun, and the elimination of all non-essential protuberances. The first Fox flew in January 1925, and was so impressive that an immediate order was placed for enough aircraft to equip No.12 Squadron. This unit received its Foxes in August 1926, operating them until their replacement by Harts in 1931. Total production was curtailed by financial restrictions to just 28 aircraft, of which some were re-engined with Rolls-Royce Kestrels under the designation Fox Mk IA.

Specification: Fairey Fox Mk I two-seat light day bomber
Span: 11.58m (38ft 0in)
Length: 9.50m (31ft 2in)
Powerplant: 1×Fairey Felix (Curtiss D-12), 358kW (480hp)
Armament: 2×7.7-mm (0.303-in) machine-guns plus provision for up to 209kg (460lb) of bombs carried externally
Max T/O weight: 1867kg (4,117lb)
Max speed: 156.5mph at sea level
Operational range: 500 miles

de Havilland/Westland D.H.9A

The D.H.9A was one of the most important aircraft used by the British in World War I, and as a modern type of proven combat capability it was retained in large-scale service after that war. Some 885 of these improved D.H.9s were built, 390 of them by Westland, the design parent for the variant. More than 300 D.H.9As were post-war deliveries, the last being ordered in 1927. By comparison with its predecessor, the D.H.9A had a larger wing, a revised fuselage and a Liberty or 280-kW (375-hp) Rolls-Royce Eagle VIII inline engine. D.H.9As served with home and overseas squadrons, remaining the mainstay of the former until the advent of the Fawn and of the latter until the arrival of the Wapiti and Fairey IIIF. Home-based squadrons totalled 12 including Auxiliary Air Force squadrons after that service's creation in 1925, and several flying training schools also flew the type.

Specification: de Havilland/Westland D.H.9A two-seat light day bomber
Span: 14.02m (46ft 0in)
Length: 9.14m (30ft 0in)
Powerplant: 1×Liberty 12, 298kW (400hp)
Armament: 2 or 3×7.7-mm (0.303-in) machine-guns plus provision for up to 299kg (660lb) of bombs carried internally and externally
Max T/O weight: 2107kg (4,645lb)
Max speed: 120mph at 10,000 ft
Operational endurance: 5 hours 45 minutes

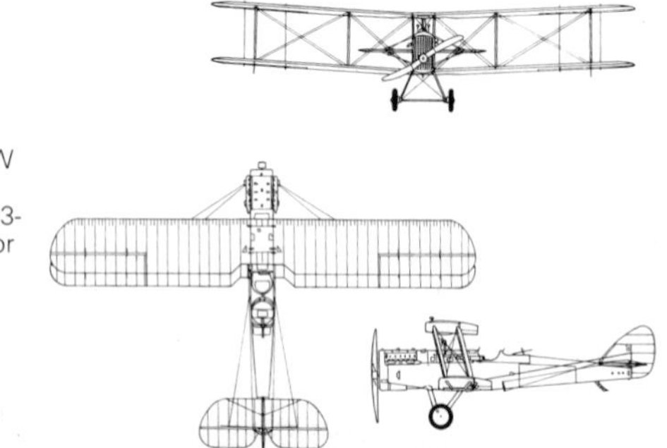

de Havilland D.H.10 Amiens

The D.H.10 was just too late to see operational service in World War I, only eight having been delivered by the time of the Armistice. The type first flew in March 1918 with two 179-kW (240-hp) BHP engines driving pusher propellers, though the tractor layout became standard with the 268-kW (360-hp) Eagle-engined second prototype. Orders totalled 1,291, but only 220 were completed as D.H.10A Amiens Mk III bombers with the Liberty engine. The first operator unit was No.104 Squadron of the Independent Air Force, and after the Armistice the sole home-based RAF unit to fly the type was No.120 Squadron, which used its Amiens for delivery of mail between the UK and the British occupation forces in Germany during 1919. The type also served with two overseas squadrons, one in Egypt and the other in India.

Specification: de Havilland D.H.10A Amiens Mk III three/four-seat day light bomber
Span: 19.96m (65ft 6in)
Length: 12.08m (39ft 7.5in)
Powerplant: 2×Liberty 12, 298kW (400hp) each
Armament: 2 or 4×7.7-mm (0.303-in) machine-guns plus provision for up to 408kg (900lb) of bombs carried internally
Max T/O weight: 4082kg (9,000lb)
Max speed: 112.5mph at 10,000 ft
Operational endurance: 6 hours

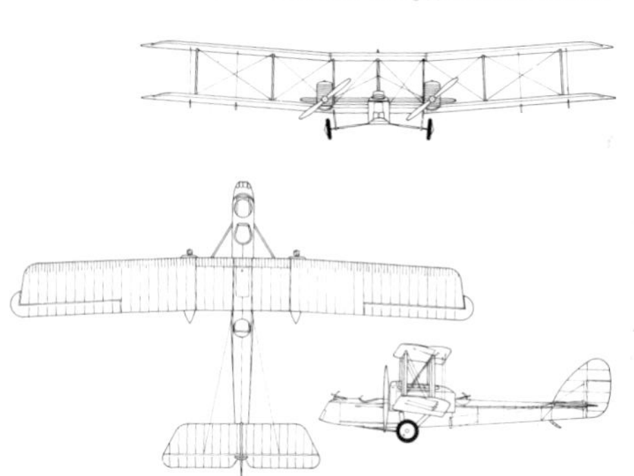

A Fairey Fox Mk I of No. 12 Squadron, the only RAF unit to operate this high speed light bomber. This Curtiss D-12 (Fairey Felix) engined Fox wears the distinctive fox's mask insignia of No. 12 on its fin. When it entered service in August 1926, the Fox was faster than any RAF fighter.

Fairey Fawn

The Fawn was the first completely new light day bomber to enter service with the RAF during the 1920s. The type was a landplane development of the experimental Pintail amphibian, and was initially conceived as a reconnaissance type. The Fawn Mk I prototype flew in March 1923 as a slab-sided biplane with clumsy main landing arrangement, and was followed by two Fawn Mk II prototypes with a lengthened fuselage for better longitudinal stability. The Mk II variant proved suitable, and in 1923 some 48 were ordered for delivery from January 1924. There followed 20 Fawn Mk IIIs, and production ceased in 1926. In 1924 all six home-based day bomber regular squadrons operated the D.H.9A, and the Fawns re-equipped three of these (Nos 11, 12 and 100 Squadrons) while also forming the equipment of two later units (Nos 503 and 602 Squadrons).

Specification: Fairey Fawn Mk III two-seat light day bomber
Span: 15.21 m (49 ft 11 in)
Length: 9.78 m (32 ft 1 in)
Powerplant: 1×Napier Lion II, 350 kW (470 hp)
Armament: 2×7.7-mm (0.303-in) machine-guns plus provision for up to 209 kg (460 lb) of bombs carried externally
Max T/O weight: 2646 kg (5,834 lb)
Max speed: 114 mph at sea level
Operational range: 650 miles

Avro Aldershot

The Aldershot was one of the first new bombers developed for the RAF after World War I, and made its initial flight in 1922 as a large biplane of mixed construction with folding three-bay wings and wide-track divided landing gear braced to the underside of the lower wings just inboard of the fold line. The type was evaluated against the de Havilland Derby and selected for small-scale production. The 15 Aldershot Mk III production aircraft were ordered in 1923, and began to equip No.99 Squadron from April 1924. This was the only operational Aldershot unit, for the Air Ministry at this time decided to abandon the single-engined 'heavy' bomber, and from 1926 the Aldershots were replaced by Handley Page Hyderabads. There was also an ambulance version known as the Andover.

Specification: Avro Aldershot three-seat day and night bomber
Span: 20.73 m (68 ft 0 in)
Length: 13.72 m (45 ft 0 in)
Powerplant: 1×Rolls-Royce Condor III, 485 kW (650 hp)
Armament: 1×7.7-mm (0.303-in) machine-gun plus provision for up to 907 kg (2,000 lb) of bombs carried internally
Max T/O weight: 5967 kg (10,950 lb)
Max speed: 110 mph at sea level
Operational range: 652 miles

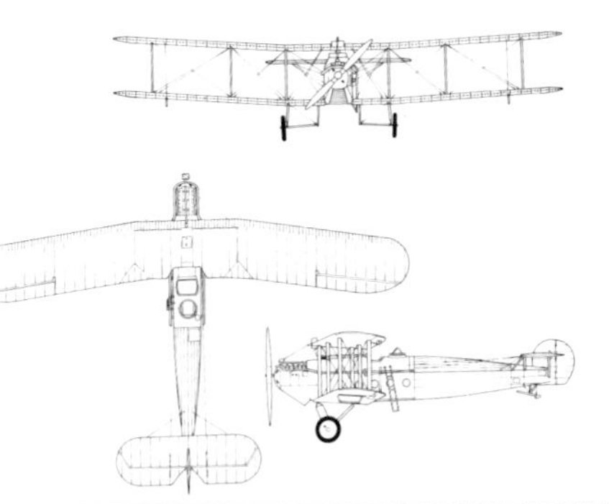

Hawker Hart

Specification: Hawker Hart two-seat light day bomber
Span: 11.35 m (37 ft 3 in)
Length: 8.94 m (29 ft 4 in)
Powerplant: 1×Rolls-Royce Kestrel IB, 239 kW (525 hp), or Kestrel X(DR), 380 kW (510 hp)
Armament: 2×7.7-mm (0.303-in) machine-guns plus provision for up to 227 kg (500 lb) of bombs carried externally
Max T/O weight: 2066 kg (4,554 lb)
Max speed: 184 mph at optimum altitude
Operational range: 470 miles

The Hart was one of the RAF's most important and versatile aircraft of the 1930s, and first flew in June 1928 as a clean biplane whose appearance was in every respect 'right'. The type was selected as the service's standard light day bomber in preference to Avro and Fairey competitors. Production started with an order for 15 aircraft, and these formed the equipment of No.33 Squadron from January 1930. Total production of the Hart for the RAF reached about 460 aircraft including communications, Indian and desert variants. Hart bombers were produced by Hawker (94), Armstrong Whitworth (149) and Vickers (112). These 265 aircraft were the mainstay of seven regular and eight Auxiliary Air Force squadrons up to 1936, when they were phased out in favour of the Hind, and were extremely popular for their useful combination of performance and manoeuvrability.

Hawker Horsley

The Horsley was an ungainly aeroplane, a fact explained by the type's design for the dual roles of torpedo and day bombing. The prototype was first flown in 1925 with a chin radiator and landing gear of the divided type braced to the lower longerons and the undersurface of the lower wings outboard of the inner interplane struts. Production amounted to 112 aircraft in all-wooden Horsley Mk I and composite but finally all-metal Horsley Mk II variants. The Horsley began to enter service in 1927, initially replacing Fawns as bombers in Nos 11 and 100 Squadrons. Torpedo use started in June 1928 with No.36 Squadron at Donibristle in Scotland, where No. 100 Squadron was also based later in the same role. The Horsley bombers served with a total of five home-based squadrons, and the final aircraft in the Wessex Bombing Area (those of No.504 Squadron) were replaced only in February 1934.

Specification: Hawker Horsley two-seat light day bomber and torpedo bomber
Span: 17.22 m (56 ft 6 in)
Length: 11.84 m (38 ft 10 in)
Powerplant: 1×Rolls-Royce Condor IIIA, 496 kW (665 hp)
Armament: 2×7.7-mm (0.303-in) machine-guns plus provision for up to 680 kg (1,500 lb) of bombs or 1×975-kg (2,150-lb) torpedo carried externally
Max T/O weight: 3538 kg (7,800 lb) as a bomber or 4205 kg (9,271 lb) as a torpedo bomber
Max speed: 126 mph at optimum altitude
Operational endurance: 10 hours

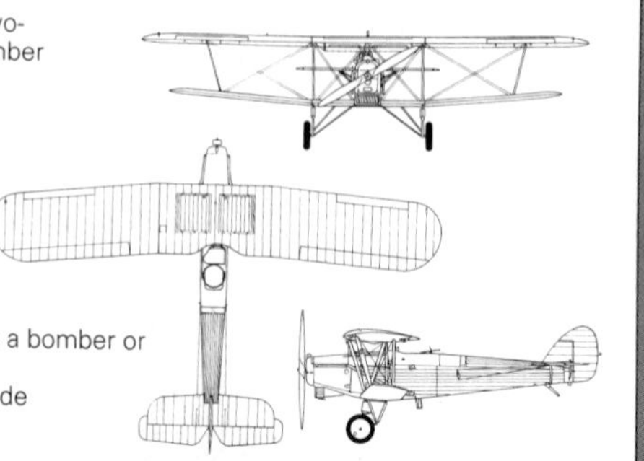

Westland Wapiti

The Wapiti was developed as a D.H.9A successor, and to keep costs as low as possible many D.H.9A components were used. The first example flew in March 1927, and after exhaustive trials an initial batch of 25 Wapiti Mk Is was ordered with the 313-kW (420-hp) Jupiter VI radial plus wooden wings and rear fuselage. These were trialled in the Middle East, and the Wapiti Mk II became the mount for home-based squadrons: this variant had an all-metal structure and a 343-kW (460-hp) Jupiter VI. Total Wapiti production for the RAF was about 500 up to August 1932, and other variants were the Mk IIA with the Jupiter VIII or XFa, the Mk V with a longer fuselage and strengthened landing gear, and the Mk VI dual-control trainer. Wapitis served with nine home-based Auxiliary Air Force squadrons up to 1937, and also had an impressive record with 11 overseas squadrons as 'imperial policing' aircraft.

Specification: Westland Wapiti Mk IIA two-seat general-purpose aeroplane
Span: 14.15 m (46 ft 5 in)
Length: 9.65 m (31 ft 8 in)
Powerplant: 1×Bristol Jupiter XFa, 373 kW (500 hp)
Armament: 2×7.7-mm (0.303-in) machine-guns plus provision for up to 227 kg (500 lb) of bombs carried externally
Max T/O weight: 2449 kg (5,400 lb)
Max speed: 160 mph at 12,000 ft
Operational range: 310 miles

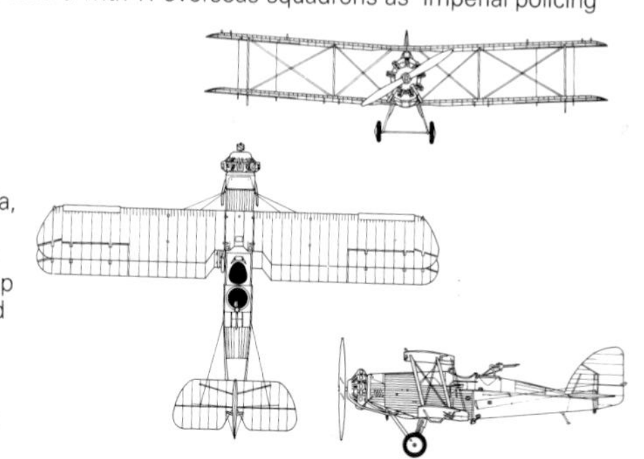

Heavily influenced by the Fairey Fox, the Hawker Hart was designed as a high-speed light day bomber, relying on speed to evade enemy defences. This aircraft wears the markings of No. 33 Squadron, the first Hart unit, which was based successively at Eastchurch, Bicester and Upper Heyford. The versatile Hart served with seven home-based bomber squadrons, eight auxiliary units and with a handful of squadrons in India and the Middle East.

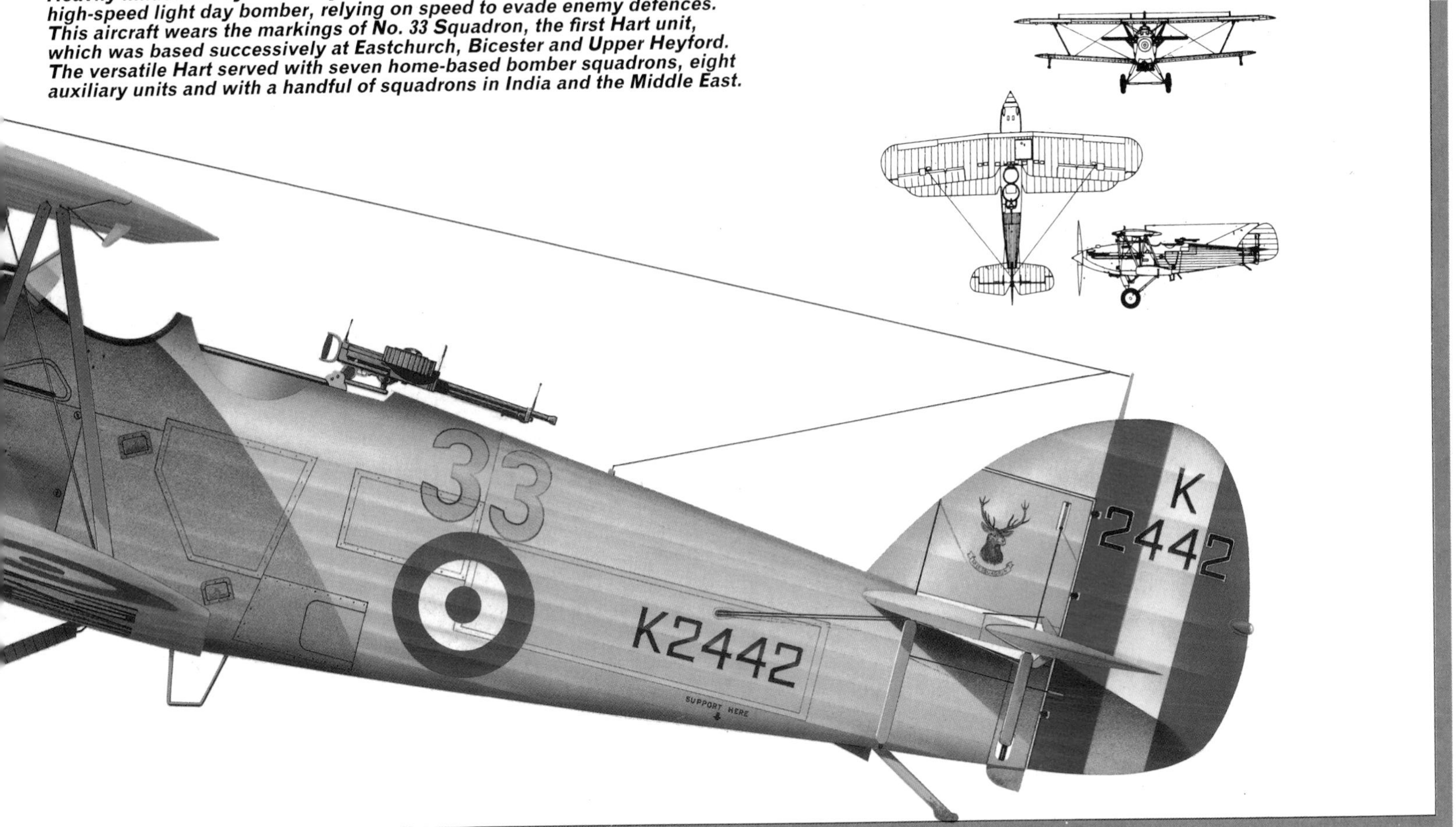

Vickers Vildebeest

Called Vildebeeste up to 1934, this elderly biplane torpedo bomber was forced to serve right into 1942 by delays in fielding a monoplane replacement. The type was designed as a Horsley replacement and first flew in April 1928 with a Jupiter radial, later replaced by an uncowled Pegasus I, driving a two-blade wooden propeller. The Vildebeest Mk I began to join No.100 Squadron in 1933, and was subsequently joined by the Vildebeest Mk II with the 492-kW (660-hp) Pegasus IIM3 radial, and by the Vildebeest Mk III with a modified rear cockpit and permanent third seat. The final model was the Vildebeest Mk IV with a Perseus radial in a long-chord cowling and driving a three-blade metal propeller. The Vildebeest equipped three home-based squadrons, and about 100 of the 194 production aircraft were still in service with home and overseas squadrons at the outbreak of World War II.

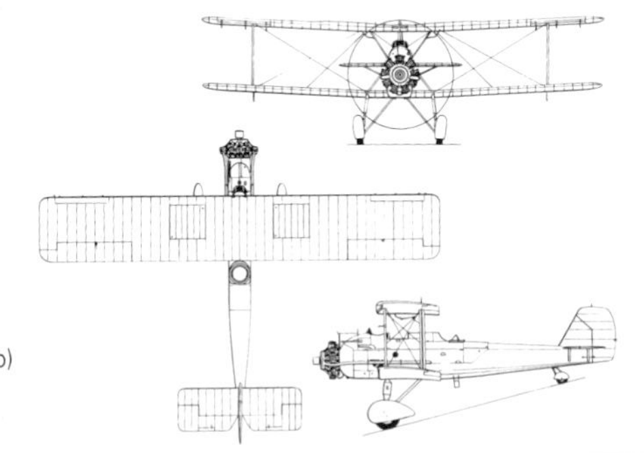

Specification: Vickers Vildebeest Mk IV three-seat torpedo bomber
Span: 14.935 m (49 ft 0 in)
Length: 11.48 m (37 ft 8 in)
Powerplant: 1×Bristol Perseus VIII, 615 kW (825 hp)
Armament: 2×7.7-mm (0.303-in) machine-guns plus provision for 1×457-mm (18-in) torpedo or up to 454 kg (1,000 lb) of bombs carried externally
Max T/O weight: 3856 kg (8,500 lb)
Max speed: 156 mph at optimum altitude
Operational range: 630 miles

Westland Wallace

In 1931 Westland produced a private-venture development of the Wapiti as the P.V.6 or Wapiti Mk VII with a Pegasus VII radial, a longer fuselage and a revised landing gear arrangement with spatted wheels. The prototype proved sufficiently better than the Wapiti for 12 Wallace Mk I conversions to be ordered: powered by 425-kW (570-hp) Pegasus IIM3 engines, these entered service in 1933 with No.501 Squadron, an RAF Special Reserve (later Auxiliary Air Force) unit. Another 56 such conversions followed before the advent of the Wallace Mk II with the Pegasus IV engine and an enclosed cockpit. Wallace Mk II production totalled 104, the last being delivered in October 1936. The type was used only by four AAF squadrons and the AA Co-Operation Flight. Later aircraft were used for target-towing, and 83 were still on charge at the outbreak of World War II, the last being retired in 1943.

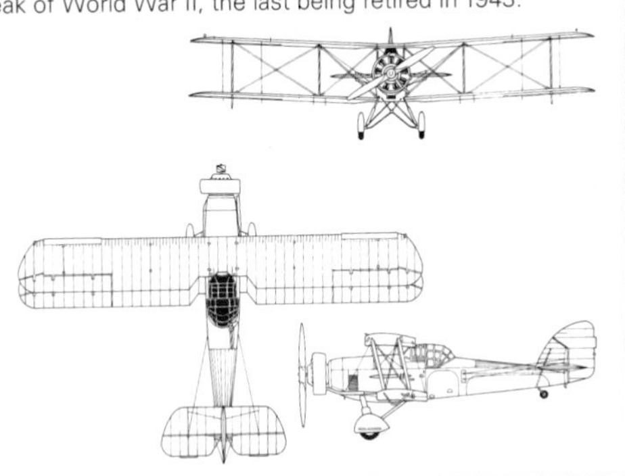

Specification: Westland Wallace Mk II two-seat general-purpose aeroplane and light day bomber
Span: 14.15 m (46 ft 5 in)
Length: 10.41 m (34 ft 2 in)
Powerplant: 1×Bristol Pegasus IV, 507 kW (680 hp)
Armament: 2×7.7-mm (0.303-in) machine-guns plus provision for up to 263 kg (580 lb) of bombs carried externally
Max T/O weight: 2608 kg (5,750 lb)
Max speed: 158 mph at 15,000 ft
Operational range: 470 miles

Hawker Hind

The Hind was a developed version of the Hart and first flew in September 1934. Monoplane bombers such as the Battle and Blenheim were already in the offing, so the Hind was essentially an interim type that served the RAF well in the days of its expansion in the mid-1930s. Compared with the Hart, the Hind had a number of detail refinements as well as a supercharged engine, a cutaway gunner's position and a tailwheel instead of a skid. The first production aeroplane flew in September 1935, and by the time the line closed in September 1938 some 503 Hind bombers had been built excluding 25 two-seat trainers for the use of the RAF Volunteer Reserve, which also received 139 similar conversions. The first Hind unit was No.21 Squadron from December 1935, and a total of 30 regular and 13 auxiliary squadrons operated the type, which was phased out of first-line service in mid-1939.

Specification: Hawker Hind two-seat light day bomber
Span: 11.35 m (37 ft 3 in)
Length: 9.02 m (29 ft 7 in)
Powerplant: 1×Rolls-Royce Kestrel V, 477 kW (640 hp)
Armament: 2×7.7-mm (0.303-in) machine-guns plus provision for up to 227 kg (500 lb) of bombs carried externally
Max T/O weight: 2403 kg (5,298 lb)
Max speed: 186 mph at 16,400 ft
Operational range: 430 miles

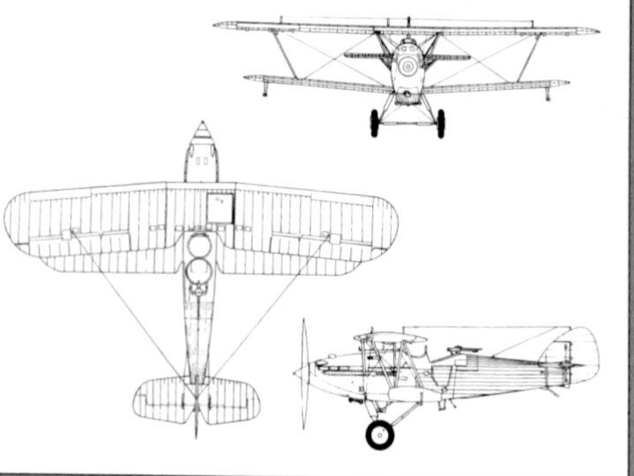

Bristol Blenheim

The technical spur to the development of the Blenheim was the Type 142 high-speed monoplane six-passenger transport built for Lord Rothermere. This completely outstripped contemporary British biplane fighters in speed, and the military Type 142M was soon planned as a high-speed day bomber to replace the Hind. The Air Ministry ordered 150 Blenheim Mk I bombers 'off the drawing board', and the initial two aircraft were used for prototype trials. The first of these flew in June 1936, the first full service example following in November of the same year. The Blenheim Mk I was a clean stressed-skin monoplane with flaps and tailwheel landing gear whose main units retracted into the engine nacelles. Mk I production totalled 1,134 up to 1939: No.137 Squadron was first to receive the type in March 1937, and eventually a total of 17 home bomber squadrons operated the Blenheim Mk I.

Specification: Bristol Blenheim Mk I three-seat light day bomber
Span: 17.17 m (56 ft 3 in)
Length: 12.12 m (39 ft 9 in)
Powerplant: 2×Bristol Mercury VIII, 626 kW (840 hp) each
Armament: 2×7.7-mm (0.303-in) machine-guns plus provision for up to 454 kg (1,000 lb) of bombs carried internally
Max T/O weight: 5670 kg (12,500 lb)
Max speed: 260 mph at optimum altitude
Operational range: 1,125 miles

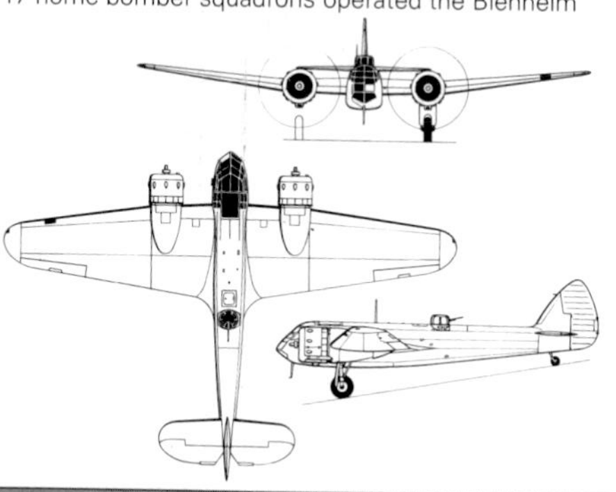

Vickers Wellesley

The Wellesley prototype was built as a private venture using the Vickers-developed geodetic structure, and first flew in June 1935 as a somewhat ungainly machine with its ring-cowled radial engine installation looking like a nose-mounted afterthought. The type's long and efficient wings conferred excellent range performance, and as the Wellesley conformed to the Air Ministry's 1935 general-purpose specification, an initial order for 96 Wellesley Mk Is was placed, the figure eventually rising to 176. These could be equipped as bombers with two strut-mounted underwing containers for the disposable load. The Wellesley Mk I began to enter service with No.76 Squadron in April 1937, and the type equipped six home-based squadrons as well as four overseas squadrons, but by the outbreak of World War II only four Wellesleys were left in Bomber Command.

Specification: Vickers Wellesley Mk I two-seat general-purpose monoplane and light day bomber
Span: 22.73 m (74 ft 7 in)
Length: 11.96 m (39 ft 3 in)
Powerplant: 1×Bristol Pegasus XX, 690 kW (925 hp)
Armament: 2×7.7-mm (0.303-in) machine-guns plus provision for up to 907 kg (2,000 lb) of bombs carried internally
Max T/O weight: 5035 kg (11,100 lb)
Max speed: 228 mph at 19,680 ft
Operational range: 1,110 miles

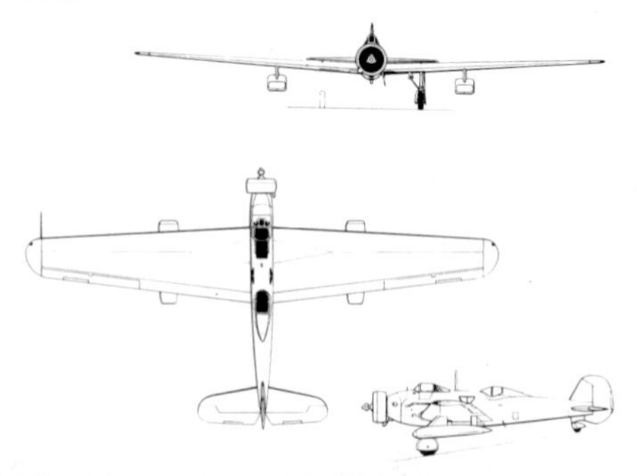

Fairey Battle

The Battle resulted from the RAF's need for a modern light bomber to replace its Hawker biplane bombers at a time that the service was expanding rapidly. Though a fairly modern stressed-skin monoplane, in combat the Battle betrayed its over-hasty rush into service by revealing itself to be underpowered, undergunned and lacking in development potential. These factors were not appreciated when the prototype first flew in March 1936, of course, and an initial order was placed for 655 aircraft, later swollen to 2,185 as the shadow factory scheme came on stream. The first Battle Mk I flew in 1937, and the type was soon operated by No.63 Squadron. Such was the pace of production that a year later no fewer than 15 squadrons flew the type, of which the RAF had more than 1,000 on charge with 18 regular and two auxiliary squadrons at the outbreak of World War II.

Specification: Fairey Battle Mk I three-seat light day bomber
Span: 16.46 m (54 ft 0 in)
Length: 12.85 m (41 ft 1.75 in)
Powerplant: 1×Rolls-Royce Merlin I, II, III or V, 768 kW (1,030 hp)
Armament: 2×7.7-mm (0.303-in) machine-guns plus provision for up to 454 kg (1,000 lb) of bombs carried internally
Max T/O weight: 4895 kg (10,792 lb)
Max speed: 241 mph at 13,000 ft
Operational range: 1,050 miles

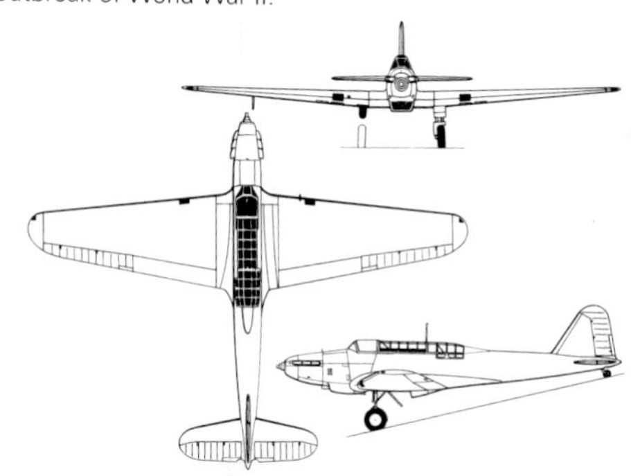

Handley Page Harrow

The Harrow was one of the RAF's first generation of monoplane bombers, and though never used in combat by Bomber Command it played a significant part in the training of bomber crews. The Harrow was based on the H.P.51 troop transport, and first flew in October 1936 some 14 months after 100 had been ordered 'off the drawing board'. The 38 Harrow Mk I bombers had the 619-kW (830-hp) Pegasus X radial, and were followed by the 62 Harrow Mk IIs with greater power and improved defensive armament. Production ended in December 1937, 11 months after the type had begun to enter service with No. 214 Squadron. By the time production ceased another four squadrons (Nos 37, 75, 115 and 215) had equipped with the type, and with some Whitley squadrons these formed Bomber Command's main strength until well into 1939. At the outbreak of war the type was retired to the transport role.

Specification: Handley Page Harrow Mk II five-seat heavy bomber
Span: 26.95 m (88 ft 5 in)
Length: 25.04 m (82 ft 2 in)
Powerplant: 2×Bristol Pegasus XX, 690 kW (925 hp) each
Armament: 4×7.7-mm (0.303-in) machine-guns plus provision for up to 1361 kg (3,000 lb) of bombs carried internally
Max T/O weight: 10433 kg (23,000 lb)
Max speed: 200 mph at 10,000 ft
Operational range: 1,250 miles

Armstrong Whitworth Whitley

The Whitley was a Bomber Command mainstay in the period leading up to World War II. The Whitley was chosen as the Command's new primary bomber in August 1935 even though the first prototype flew only in March 1936. Production started with 34 Whitley Mk Is with two 593-kW (795-hp) Tiger IX radials. The first Whitley unit was No. 10 Squadron, which accepted its first aircraft in March 1937. Next came 46 Whitley Mk II aircraft with dihedralled outer wings and 686-kW (920-hp) Tiger VIII engines, and 80 Whitley Mk IIIs with a retractable 'dustbin' turret in the ventral position. With the Mk IV the Whitley gained a four-gun power-operated rear turret, and the engine changed to the Rolls-Royce Merlin inline: the 40 Mk IVs and Mk IVAs had the 768- and 854-kW (1,030- and 1,145-hp) Merlin IV and X respectively. In September 1939 six Whitley squadrons were operational.

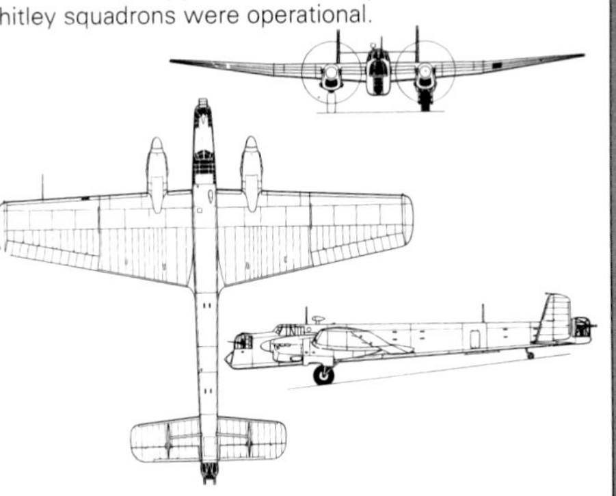

Specification: Armstrong Whitworth Whitley Mk I five-seat long-range night bomber
Span: 25.60 m (84 ft 0 in)
Length: 21.11 m (69 ft 3 in)
Powerplant: 2×Armstrong Siddeley Tiger IX, 593 kW (795 hp) each
Armament: 2×7.7-mm (0.303-in) machine-guns plus provision for up to 1524 kg (3,360 lb) of bombs carried internally
Max T/O weight: 9824 kg (21,660 lb)
Max speed: 183 mph at 16,400 ft
Operational range: 1,250 miles

Vickers Wellington

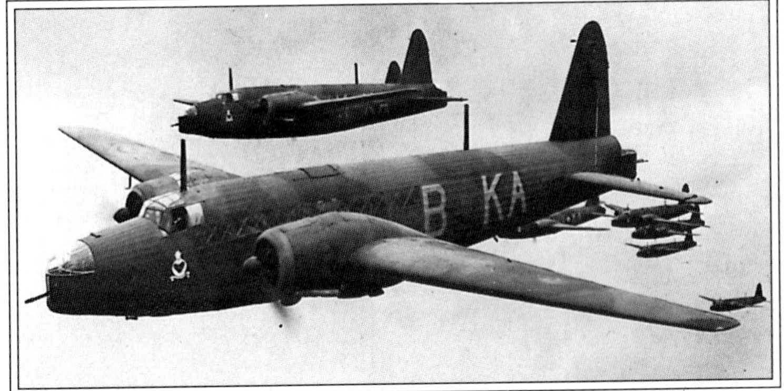

The Wellington was designed in response to a 1932 specification, and made use of Vickers' special geodetic construction pioneered in the Wellesley for exceptional strength. The type first flew in June 1936, and though it had been planned to fit Rolls-Royce Goshawk inlines or Bristol Mercury radials the engine selected was the Pegasus. The variant that entered service with No. 99 Squadron in October 1938 was the Wellington Mk I, of which 181 were built with Pegasus XX radials. By the outbreak of war Bomber Command had six operational Wellington squadrons, and the other variants developed before the war were the Mk IA with a Nash and Thompson turret, the Mk IC with the ventral turret replaced by beam guns, the Mk II with 853-kW (1,145-hp) Rolls-Royce Merlin X inlines and the Mk III with 1025-kW (1,375-hp) Bristol Hercules III radials.

Specification: Vickers Wellington Mk IC five/six-seat long-range medium night bomber
Span: 26.26 m (86 ft 2 in)
Length: 19.68 m (64 ft 7 in)
Powerplant: 2×Bristol Pegasus XVIII, 746 kW (1,000 hp) each
Armament: 6×7.7-mm (0.303-in) machine-guns plus provision for up to 2041 kg (4,500 lb) of bombs carried internally
Max T/O weight: 12928 kg (28,500 lb)
Max speed: 235 mph at 15,500 ft
Operational range: 2,550 miles

Bristol Bombay

The Bombay was a large high-wing monoplane with ungainly fixed landing gear, and its configuration is explained largely by its design to a specification calling for a 24-troop personnel transport that could double as a bomber. The Type 130 prototype first flew in June 1935 with Pegasus X radials driving fixed-pitch propellers, and amongst its more notable features was a very strong wing of multi-spar steel strip construction. With Bristol already overtaxed by Blenheim construction, the Bombay was transferred to Short & Harland in Northern Ireland and the first of 50 Bombay Mk I production aircraft flew in March 1939 with variable-pitch propellers. Some were used to ferry supplies to France between the autumn of 1939 and the spring of 1940, but the type was operated mainly by four Middle Eastern squadrons primarily as a transport, though some night raids against Benghazi were flown in 1940.

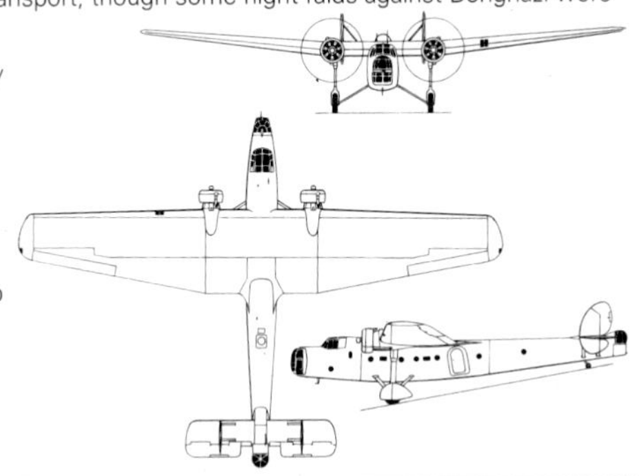

Specification: Bristol Bombay Mk I three-seat bomber and transport aeroplane
Span: 29.18 m (95 ft 9 in)
Length: 21.11 m (69 ft 3 in)
Powerplant: 2×Bristol Pegasus XXII, 753 kW (1,010 hp) each
Armament: 2×7.7-mm (0.303-in) machine-guns plus provision for up to 907 kg (2,000 lb) of bombs carried externally
Max T/O weight: 9072 kg (20,000 lb)
Max speed: 192 mph at 6,500 ft
Operational range: 880 miles

Handley Page Heyford

Specification: Handley Page Heyford Mk IA four-seat heavy night bomber
Span: 22.86m (75ft 0in)
Length: 17.68m (58ft 0in)
Powerplant: 2×Rolls-Royce Kestrel IIIS or IIIS5, 429kW (575hp) each
Armament: 3×7.7-mm (0.303-in) machine-guns plus provision for up to 1588kg (3,500lb) of bombs carried internally
Max T/O weight: 7666kg (16,900lb)
Max speed: 142mph at 13,000ft
Operational range: 920 miles with a 726-kg (1,600-lb) bombload

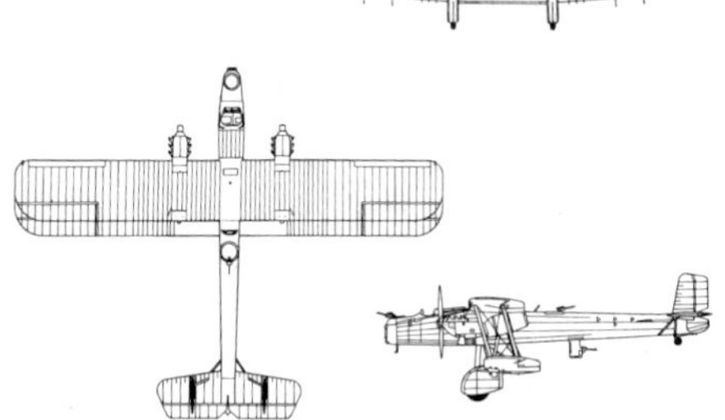

The Heyford was the RAF's last biplane heavy bomber, an unusual type with the fuselage attached to the undersurface of the upper wing and the centre section of the lower wing thickened for internal carriage of the bombload. The long main landing gear units were attached at their upper ends to the engine nacelles, while the wheel spats were attached at their rear to the lower-wing centre section. The Heyford prototype flew in June 1930, and production of 124 aircraft up to July 1936 comprised 38 Mk Is and Mk IAs, 16 Mk IIs with de-rated Kestrel VI engines, and 70 Mk IIIs with fully rated Kestrel VI engines and four-blade propellers. The type entered service in November 1933, and equipped a total of 11 squadrons before being phased out from 1937, removed from first-line service in 1939 and finally declared obsolete in July 1941.

Handley Page O/400

The O/400 was the RAF's standard heavy bomber, a development of the O/100 that had been planned in 1914 as a 'bloody paralyser' to a far-sighted naval requirement. By comparison with the O/100 the type had more power, detail improvements and the fuel relocated from the two engine nacelles to the fuselage, from where it was pumped to an upper-wing centre section tank for gravity feed to the two inline engines. The type was in service with seven Independent Air Force squadrons (Nos 58, 97, 15, 207, 214, 215 and 216) just before the end of the war, and remained in limited service in the period immediately after the war until replaced by the de Havilland D.H.10 Amiens and the Vickers Vimy. The O/400 had a slightly longer post-war career in Egypt, where it served with Nos 70 and 216 Squadrons up to 1920.

Specification: Handley Page O/400 four-seat heavy bomber
Span: 30.48m (100ft 0in)
Length: 19.16m (62ft 10.25in)
Powerplant: 2×Rolls-Royce Eagle VIII, 268kW (360hp) each
Armament: 3 to 5×7.7-mm (0.303-in) machine-guns plus provision for up to 907kg (2,000lb) of bombs carried internally
Max T/O weight: 6360kg (14,022lb)
Max speed: 97.5mph at sea level
Operational endurance: 8 hours

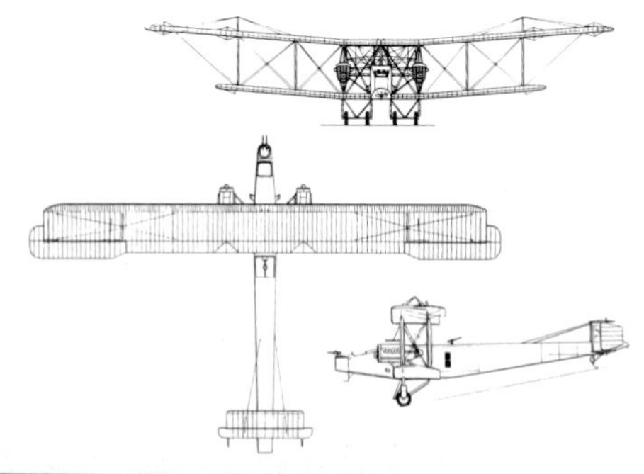

Handley Page V/1500

The V/1500 was the largest British bomber of World War I, and also the first British machine of its type with four engines (two push/pull pairs located between the wings). The prototype was created to provide a capability to bomb Berlin from bases in East Anglia, and first flew in May 1918. Some 255 aircraft were ordered, but only three were operational with No. 166 Squadron at the time of World War I's end, and only about 32 were completed by the parent company, Beardmore in Scotland and Harland and Wolff in Northern Ireland. Only three squadrons (Nos 166, 167 and 274) ever received the type, which made some notable long-distance flights including the bombing of Kabul in 1919 from bases in India. The type disappeared from service in the early 1920s when its was appreciated that the smaller Vimy could undertake the same basic role at lower manpower and operating costs.

Specification: Handley Page V/1500 five/seven-seat long-range heavy bomber
Span: 38.41m (126ft 0in)
Length: 19.51m (64ft 0in)
Powerplant: 4×Rolls-Royce Eagle VIII, 280kW (375hp) each
Armament: 4 or 8×7.7-mm (0.303-in) machine-guns plus provision for up to 3402kg (7,500lb) of bombs carried internally
Max T/O weight: 13608kg (30,000lb)
Max speed: 99mph at 6,500ft
Operational range: 1,300 miles

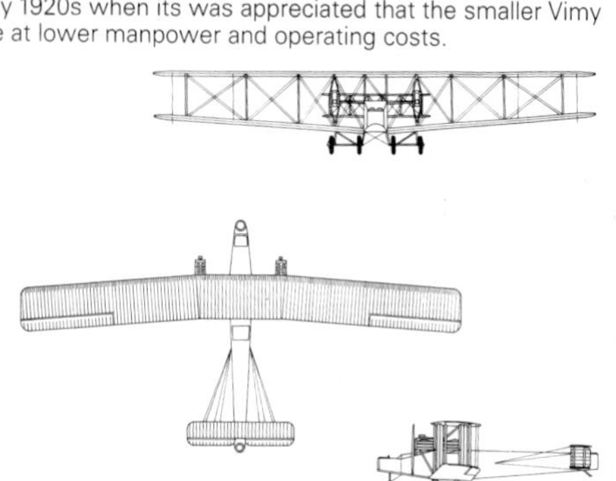

Wearing the traditional Nivo dark green night bomber finish, this Handley Page Heyford also proudly sports the winged arrow insignia of No. 10 Squadron, based at Boscombe Down. The last of the RAF's biplane heavy bombers, the Heyford served from November 1933 until 1939, with 11 bomber squadrons. The Heyford's bombload was carried in the bulged centre section of the lower wing, where it was easily accessible to armourers.

Vickers Vimy

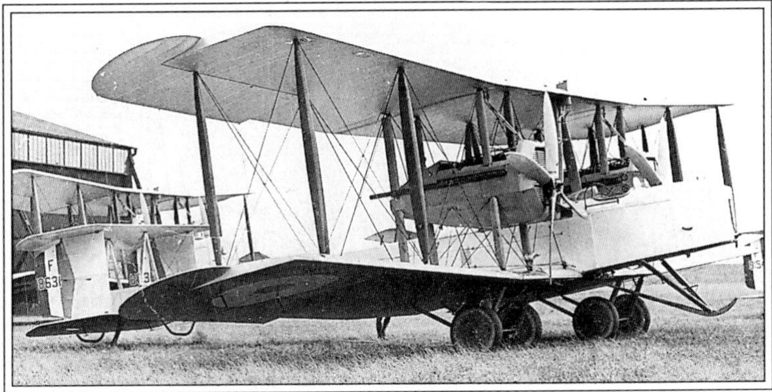

The Vimy was one of three new-generation bombers with which the RAF planned to take the air war to Germany in 1919. The end of World War I aborted this plan, but unlike its partners the Vimy went on to a successful post-war career. The type first flew in November 1917, and the main production version was the Vimy Mk IV with Eagle VIII engines. Large contracts were cancelled at the end of the war but total Vimy Mk IV production amounted to 240, the last batch of 30 being ordered in 1925. The type entered service in July 1919 with No. 58 Squadron in Egypt, home to another three squadrons; the type was retired from Middle Eastern service in August 1926 after operating the Cairo-Baghdad air mail service. Five home-based squadrons operated the Vimy, which was replaced as a first-line bomber by the Virginia during 1924 and 1925 but remained operational with No. 502 Squadron until January 1929.

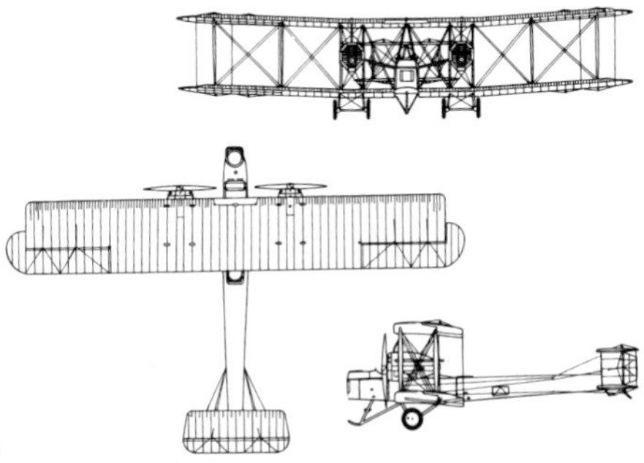

Specification: Vickers Vimy Mk IV three-seat heavy night bomber
Span: 20.75 m (68 ft 1 in)
Length: 13.27 m (43 ft 6.5 in)
Powerplant: 2×Rolls-Royce Eagle VIII, 268 kW (360 hp) each
Armament: 2×7.7-mm (0.303-in) machine-guns plus provision for up to 1123 kg (2,476 lb) of bombs carried internally
Max T/O weight: 5647 kg (12,500 lb)
Max speed: 103 mph at 6,500 ft
Operational range: about 900 miles

Vickers Virginia

Remaining in service from 1924 to 1937, the Virginia was a real mainstay of the RAF bomber capability. The prototype first flew in November 1922 and the type began to enter service as the Virginia Mk III, replacing the Vimy bombers of Nos 7 and 58 Squadrons, the first of eight regular and two auxiliary squadrons to operate the type. Total production of the Virginia series was 124, and while the Mks III to VI had dihedral on the lower wings and unswept outer wings, the Mks VII to X had sweptback outer panels and dihedral on both upper and lower wings. The Mk IX introduced a tail gun position, while the Mk X had a primary structure of metal and introduced leading-edge slats and a tailwheel in place of the original skid. The type was finally replaced as a bomber by the Heyford and Whitley, surviving aircraft being relegated to parachute training.

Specification: Vickers Virginia Mk X four-seat heavy night bomber
Span: 26.72 m (87 ft 8 in)
Length: 18.97 m (62 ft 2.75 in)
Powerplant: 2×Napier Lion V, 425 kW (570 hp) each
Armament: 3×7.7-mm (0.303-in) machine-guns plus provision for up to 1452 kg (3,200 lb) of bombs carried internally
Max T/O weight: 7983 kg (17,600 lb)
Max speed: 108 mph at 4,920 ft
Operational range: 985 miles

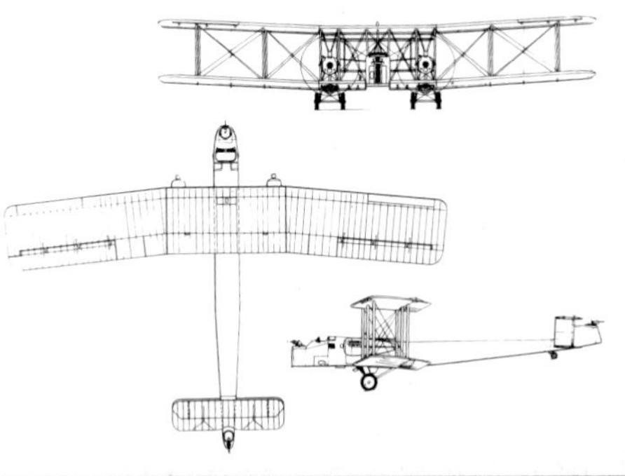

Boulton Paul Overstrand

Specification: Boulton Paul Overstrand Mk I five-seat medium day bomber
Span: 21.95 m (72 ft 0 in)
Length: 14.02 m (46 ft 0 in)
Powerplant: 2×Bristol Pegasus IIM3, 432 kW (580 hp) each
Armament: 3×7.7-mm (0.303-in) machine-guns plus provision for up to 726 kg (1,600 lb) of bombs carried internally
Max T/O weight: 5443 kg (12,000 lb)
Max speed: 153 mph at 6,500 ft
Operational range: 545 miles

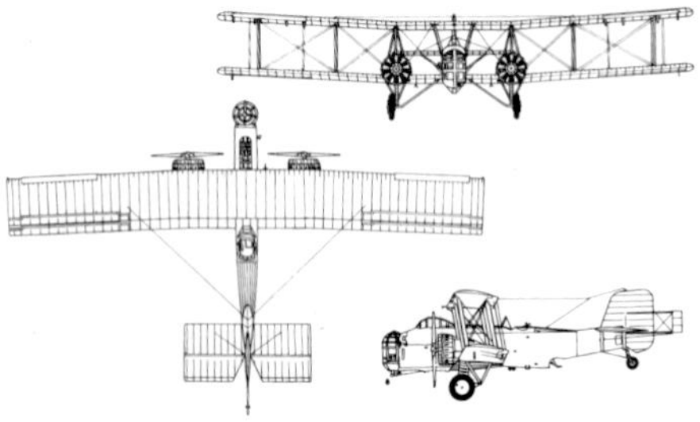

The Overstrand was a straight-forward but far-sighted development of the Sidestrand with more-powerful engines in low-drag Townend ring cowlings for greater performance with an increased bombload, an enclosed and heated cockpit, a shielded dorsal position, an autopilot and perhaps most importantly of all a fully enclosed nose turret. The first Overstrand flew in 1933 and was a Sidestrand conversion with 414-kW (555-hp) Pegasus IM3 engines. The only production variant was the Overstrand Mk I, and 24 of this model were produced to replace the Sidestrands of No. 101 Squadron at Bicester from December 1934; four Overstrands were also allocated to No. 144 Squadron. From 1937 the Overstrand was replaced by the Bristol Blenheim, the obsolescent aircraft going on to serve as gunnery trainers up to 1941. The planned Superstrand with retractable landing gear remained only a project.

Handley Page Hyderabad

The Hyderabad was a military derivative of the W.8 which first flew in December 1919 as one of the first purpose-designed airliners. The Hyderabad was the company's response to a 1922 bomber specification, and when it took to the air in October 1923 it was the world's first large aeroplane with automatic leading-edge slats. Such slats were not incorporated into the Hyderabad Mk I production type, which was also the RAF's last all-wooden heavy bomber. Delivery of the 38 aircraft was slow, No. 99 Squadron receiving its Hyderabads from December 1925 but No. 10 Squadron re-equipping only from January 1928. Hyderabads were also flown by two Auxiliary Air Force units, Nos 502 and 503 Squadrons. The bomber was withdrawn from first-line service in 1930 and from AAF service in 1933, and the type was declared obsolete in 1934.

Specification: Handley Page Hyderabad Mk I four-seat heavy night bomber
Span: 22.86 m (75 ft 0 in)
Length: 18.03 m (59 ft 2 in)
Powerplant: 2×Napier Lion IIB or V, 338.5 kW (454 hp) each
Armament: 3×7.7-mm (0.303-in) machine-guns plus provision for up to 499 kg (1,100 lb) of bombs carried internally
Max T/O weight: 6164 kg (13,590 lb)
Max speed: 109 mph at sea level
Operational range: 500 miles

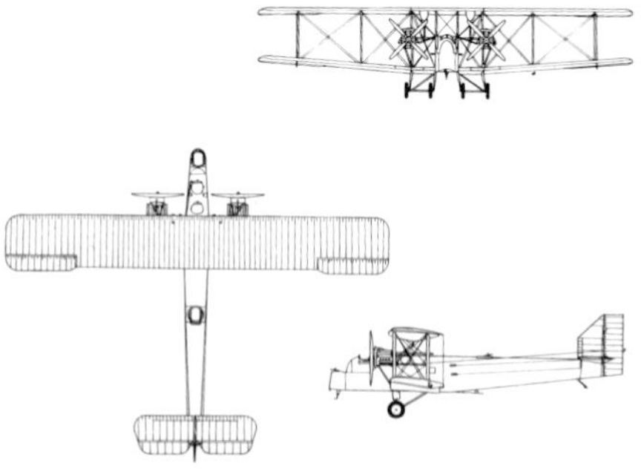

Boulton Paul Sidestrand

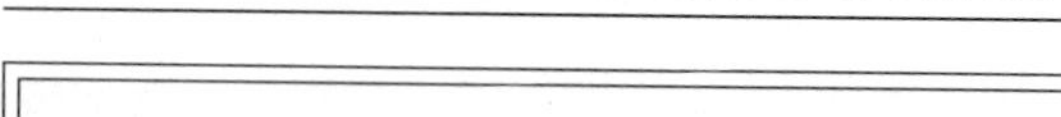

Boulton Paul used its experience with the unsuccessful Bourges and Bugle twin-engined bombers in developing the Sidestrand, a type that first flew in 1926 and displayed almost fighter-like agility as a result of its great strength and well-balanced, powerful controls including the distinctive servo-actuated rudder. The aeroplane was designed for Napier Lion inline engines, but always flew with Jupiter radials. The RAF decided to order the type as its first medium bomber, and when the type became operational with No. 101 Squadron at Bircham Newton during April 1928 it also became the first RAF twin-engined bomber to enter service since World War I. Production totalled just 18 aircraft: the Mk II had ungeared Jupiter VI engines and the Mk III geared Jupiter VIIIF engines. The Sidestrand was replaced by the Overstrand in December 1934.

Specification: Boulton Paul Sidestrand Mk III three/four-seat medium day bomber
Span: 21.92 m (71 ft 11 in)
Length: 14.02 m (46 ft 0 in)
Powerplant: 2×Bristol Jupiter VIIIF, 343 kW (460 hp) each
Armament: 3×7.7-mm (0.303-in) machine-guns plus provision for up to 476 kg (1,050 lb) of bombs carried internally
Max T/O weight: 4627 kg (10,200 lb)
Max speed: 140.5 mph at 10,000 ft
Operational range: 500 miles

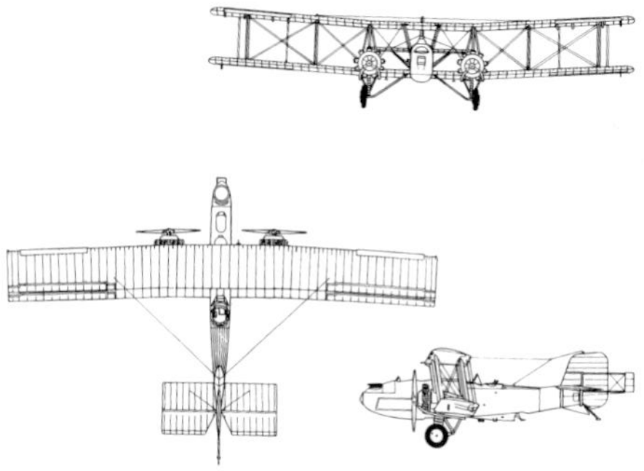

No. 101 Squadron was the only RAF squadron to be fully equipped with Boulton Paul Overstrands, moving them from Bircham Newton to Andover and then to Bicester, where four aircraft split off to form No. 144 Squadron.

Handley Page Hinaidi

The Hinaidi was a structural rather than aerodynamic development of the Hyderabad (with a primary structure of metal rather than wood in the main production variant) and with Jupiter radials in place of the Lion inlines for slightly better performance with a usefully increased warload. The two Hinaidi prototypes were Hyderabad conversions and thus retained a wooden structure, and first flew in March 1927. The 12 new-build Hinaidi Mk Is retained the Hyderabad's wooden construction, and were complemented by seven Hyderabad conversions before the advent of the metal-structured Hinaidi Mk II, of which 33 were built up to 1932. The first Hinaidi unit was No. 99 Squadron, which received its aircraft from October 1929. There followed No. 10 Squadron, together with Nos 502 and 503 Squadrons of the Auxiliary Air Force. Hinaidis were replaced by Heyfords from 1933, and declared obsolete during 1937. The Clive was a transport version for Indian service.

Specification: Handley Page Hinaidi Mk II four-seat heavy night bomber
Span: 22.86 m (75 ft 0 in)
Length: 18.03 m (59 ft 2 in)
Powerplant: 2×Bristol Jupiter VIII, 328 kW (440 hp) each
Armament: 3×7.7-mm (0.303-in) machine-guns plus provision for up to 657 kg (1,448 lb) of bombs carried internally
Max T/O weight: 6577 kg (14,500 lb)
Max speed: 122.5 mph at sea level
Operational range: 850 miles

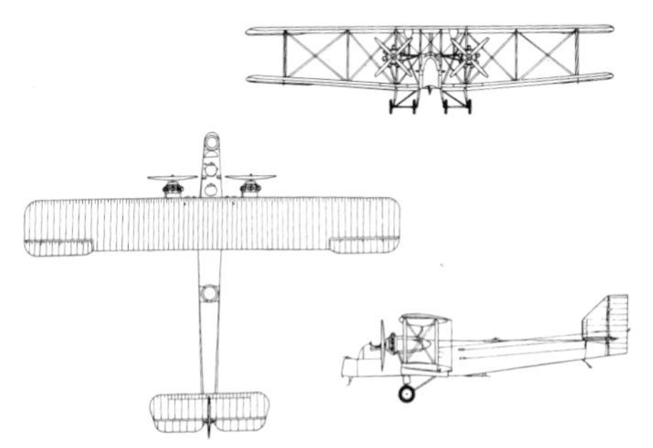

Fairey Hendon

The Hendon has the distinction of having been the first all-metal low-wing cantilever monoplane to enter RAF squadron service. The type was designed to the same specification as the Handley Page Heyford, and first flew as the Fairey Night Bomber (later Hendon Mk I) in November 1931 with a pair of 343-kW (460-hp) Bristol Jupiter X radials, though it was later re-engined with 358-kW (580-hp) Kestrel IIIS inlines. The type was particularly notable for its thick wing and careful streamlining, the latter extending to the large fairings over the main landing gear units. Production amounted to 14 Hendon Mk IIs between September 1936 and March 1937, these aircraft forming the equipment of No. 38 Squadron, from which a flight was detached to create No. 115 Squadron. The type was obsolescent as it entered service, and was replaced by the Vickers Wellington in mid-1939.

Specification: Fairey Hendon Mk II five-seat heavy night bomber
Span: 31.01 m (101 ft 9 in)
Length: 18.52 m (60 ft 9 in)
Powerplant: 2×Rolls-Royce Kestrel VI, 447 kW (600 hp) each
Armament: 3×7.7-mm (0.303-in) machine-guns plus provision for up to 753 kg (1,660 lb) of bombs carried internally
Max T/O weight: 9072 kg (20,000 lb)
Max speed: 155 mph at 15,000 ft
Operational range: 1,360 miles

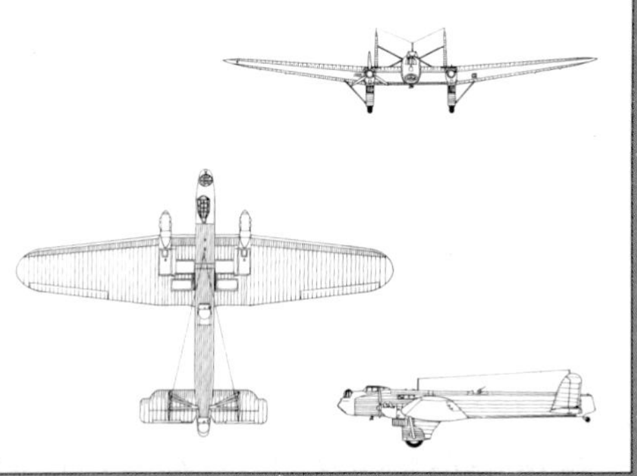

Boeing B-17 Flying Fortress

Mainstay of US daylight precision bombing operations in Europe, and also widely used in other theatres and roles, the B-17 was a high-altitude heavy bomber and first flew as the Model 299 (unofficially XB-17) in July 1935. The type was followed by 13 Y1B-17 (B-17) and one Y1B-17A (B-17A) pre-production aircraft and by small batches of B-17B, B-17C and B-17D evaluation aircraft. The first true service model was thus the B-17E (512 built) with the definitive tail and the better defensive armament of one 7.62-mm (0.3-in) and 12 12.7-mm (0.5-in) machine-guns. There followed 3,405 essentially similar B-17Fs with a frameless Plexiglas nose and finally, in the bomber sequence, 8,680 examples of the B-17G with further improved defensive capability including a new chin turret, a revised tail turret, staggered waist gun positions and provision for additional armament.

Although outnumbered by the B-24, the B-17 is the most famous of the USAAF heavies. The mainstay of the daylight bombing effort over Europe, the Flying Fortress gained its name through its phenomenal array of defensive armament, necessary to fly safely in the same skies as Luftwaffe fighters.

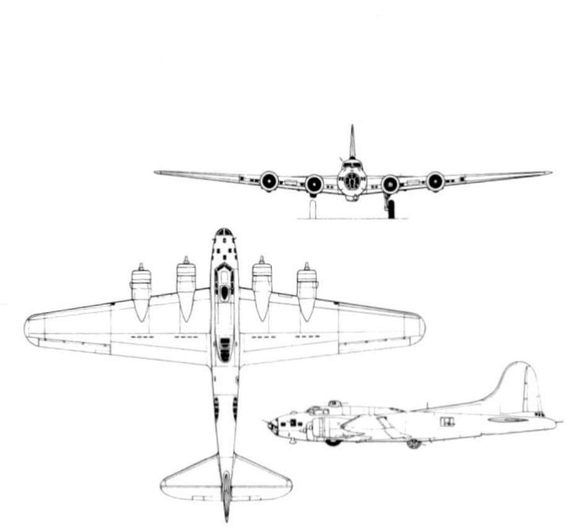

Boeing B-29 Superfortress

Best known as the aeroplane that brought World War II to an end with the atom bombing of Hiroshima and Nagasaki in August 1945, the B-29 had already brought Japan to its knees in a sustained campaign of bombing against cities, industrial areas and communications. The type entered service only in late 1943 after a first flight by the XB-29 in September 1942. Designed for the long-range strategic role with high performance, remotely controlled gun barbettes and pressurization of the crew compartments, the B-29 was in every way an exceptional but complex aeroplane whose development required three prototypes and 14 YB-29 pre-production aircraft before the first of 2,458 B-29s was delivered. The only other two wartime bomber variants were the B-29A (1,119 built with a revised wing and four-gun forward dorsal barbette) and the B-29B (311 built with increased bombload and defensive armament restricted to just the tail turret).

Specification: Boeing B-29 Superfortress 11-seat strategic heavy bomber
Span: 43.05 m (141 ft 3 in)
Length: 30.18 m (99 ft 0 in)
Powerplant: 4×Wright R-3350-23, 1491 kW (2,000 hp) each
Armament: 10×12.7-mm (0.5-in) machine-guns in forward and aft dorsal and ventral barbettes and a tail turret, plus provision for up to 9072 kg (20,000 lb) of bombs carried internally
Max T/O weight: 56250 kg (124,000 lb)
Max speed: 358 mph at 25,000 ft
Operational range: 3,250 miles

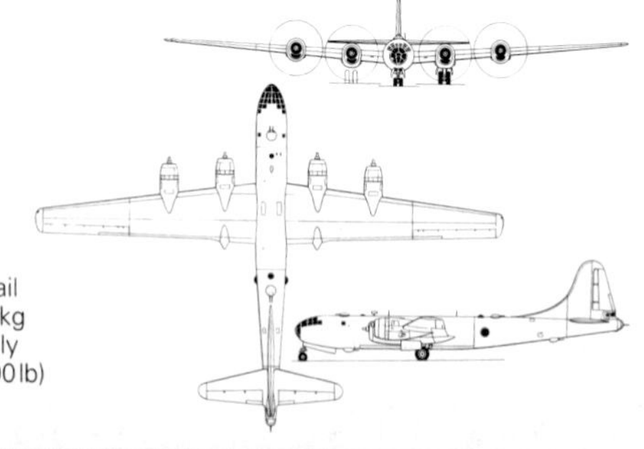

Consolidated B-24 Liberator

Though planned only in 1939, the B-24 was built in larger numbers (18,482 in all) than any other US aeroplane of World War II, and served in many roles with both main US services as well as those of several Allies. The type was designed to offer performance superior to that of the B-17, including speed, ceiling and range respectively of more than 300 mph, 35,000 ft and 3,000 miles. A high aspect ratio wing was chosen for low drag, and the XB-24 flew in December 1939. Improved features were evaluated in 25 YB-24, B-24A and B-24C aircraft, while full-scale production began with the B-24D and modified B-24E, of which 2,738 and 791 were built. The 430 B-24Gs introduced a nose turret, and the 3,100 B-24Hs were similar. The B-24J was an improved B-24H, and 6,678 were built. Finally came 1,667 B-24Ls and 2,593 B-24Ms based on the B-24J. There were also experimental and naval variants.

Specification: Consolidated B-24J Liberator 8/12-seat strategic heavy bomber
Span: 33.53 m (110 ft 0 in)
Length: 20.47 m (67 ft 2 in)
Powerplant: 4×Pratt & Whitney R-1830-65, 895 kW (1,200 hp) each
Armament: 10×12.7-mm (0.5-in) machine-guns in nose, dorsal, ventral, waist and tail positions, plus provision for up to 3992 kg (8,000 lb) of bombs carried internally
Max T/O weight: 29484 kg (65,000 lb)
Max speed: 300 mph at 30,000 ft
Operational range: 2,100 miles

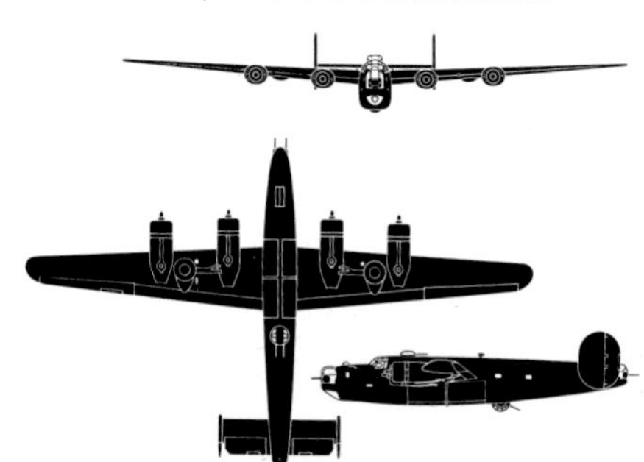

At first disliked on account of its high wing loading and tricycle undercarriage, the Marauder became a major medium bomber, seeing much action in Europe and the Mediterranean. During the Normandy landings it was particularly active, blasting German defences to allow the invasion force to land safely.

Douglas B-18 Bolo

The B-18 was developed in 1935 to meet a US Army requirement for a bomber to replace the Martin B-10. Powered by two 693-kW (930-hp) R-1820-45 radials, the DB-1 prototype used the engines, wings and tail unit of the DC-2 airliner married to a deep and capacious fuselage of new design with single defensive guns in the nose, dorsal and ventral positions. The type was ordered into production as the B-18, these 134 aircraft carrying 2948 kg (6,500 lb) rather than 1996 kg (4,400 lb) of bombs. Further procurement covered 217 B-18As with greater power, a pointed but extensively glazed nose, and a revised dorsal gun position; the Canadians took 20 as Digby Mk Is. Relegated as bombers in 1942, many survivors were modified as transports while 124 B-18As were modified as anti-submarine aircraft, two going to Brazil as B-18Cs and the others remaining in US hands as B-18Ds.

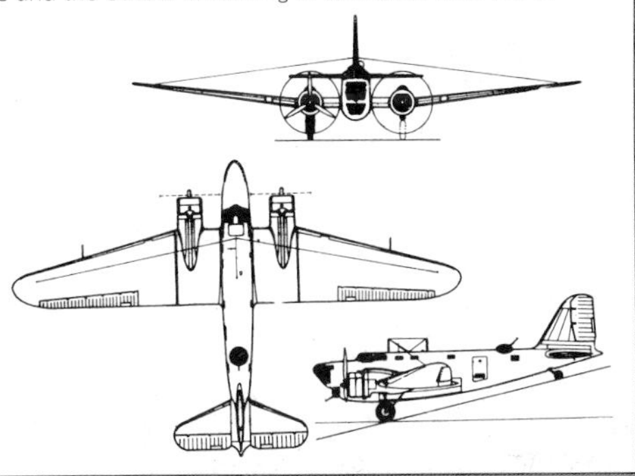

Specification: Boeing B-18A Bolo six-seat medium bomber
Span: 27.28 m (89 ft 6 in)
Length: 17.62 m (57 ft 10 in)
Powerplant: 2×Wright R-1820-53, 746 kW (1,000 hp) each
Armament: 3×7.62-mm (0.3-in) machine-guns in nose, dorsal and ventral positions, plus provision for 2948 kg (6,500 lb) of bombs carried internally
Max T/O weight: 12552 kg (27,673 lb)
Max speed: 215 mph at 10,000 ft
Operational range: 900 miles

Douglas B-23 Dragon

The B-23 was in essence a heavily refined version of the B-18, developed via the proposed B-22 with a more streamlined fuselage, a considerably larger vertical tail, more-powerful engines mounted on the wings of the DC-3 airliner and, for the first time in an American bomber, a tail gun position with a single 12.7-mm (0.5-in) weapon to complement the single smaller weapons in the nose, dorsal and ventral positions. Unusually, the type was ordered 'off the drawing board' when late in 1938 the B-18A contract was amended so that the last 32 were delivered as B-23s. The first flew in July 1939, and the type served briefly as a coastal patrol bomber in the Pacific before being relegated to training in 1942. Twelve were converted as UC-67 transports and glider tugs in that same year.

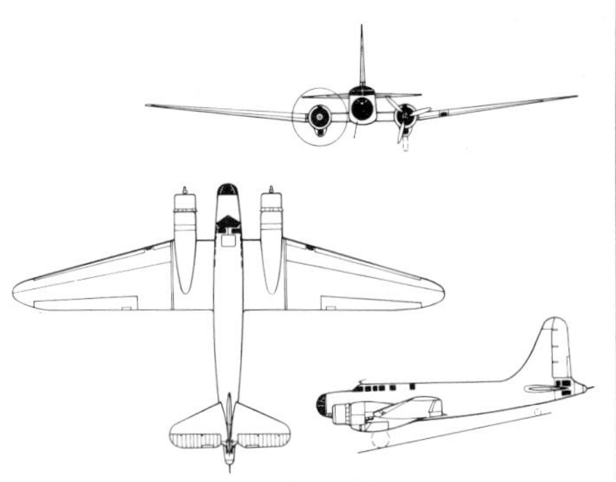

Specification: Douglas B-23 Dragon four/five-seat medium bomber
Span: 28.04 m (92 ft 0 in)
Length: 17.78 m (58 ft 4 in)
Powerplant: 2×Wright R-2600-3, 1193 kW (1,600 hp) each
Armament: 1×12.7-mm (0.5-in) and 3×7.62-mm (0.3-in) machine-guns, plus provision for up to 1996 kg (4,400 lb) of bombs carried internally
Max T/O weight: 13835 kg (30,500 lb)
Max speed: 282 mph at 12,000 ft
Operational range: 1,455 miles

Lockheed A-28 and A-29 Hudson

One of the few civil aircraft that has successfully made the transition to a combat role, the Lockheed 14 Super Electra formed the basis of the Hudson coastal patrol bomber produced to meet British requirements. After direct purchases by the RAF, the type was included in the scope of the Lend-Lease arrangement. As a first step the USAAF ordered 52 A-28s basically similar to the Hudson Mk I with Pratt & Whitney R-1830-45 radials, and these were allocated to the UK. There followed 450 A-28As with convertible interiors for trooping, and these too went to the UK. Production then switched to the A-29 with Wright engines, and the 416 of these for the UK were joined by 384 convertible A-29As. Specifically US models were the AT-18 version of the A-29A with a dorsal turret for gunnery training, and the AT-18B navigation trainer: totals were 217 and 83 respectively.

Specification: Lockheed A-29 four-seat light attack bomber and maritime patrol aeroplane
Span: 19.96 m (65 ft 6 in)
Length: 13.51 m (44 ft 4 in)
Powerplant: 2×Wright R-1820-87, 895 kW (1,200 hp) each
Armament: 5×7.62-mm (0.3-in) machine-guns in dorsal and ventral positions, and in fixed nose mountings, plus provision for up to 726 kg (1,600 lb) of bombs carried under the wings
Max T/O weight: 9526 kg (21,000 lb)
Max speed: 253 mph at 15,000 ft
Operational range: 1,550 miles

North American B-25 Mitchell

Ordered 'off the drawing board' in September 1939 for service in 1941, the B-25 proved itself an outstanding tactical medium bomber, and was widely used by the Allies as well as by the USAAF and, to a lesser extent, the US Navy. The NA-40 first prototype flew in January 1939, and was followed by 24 B-25s used mainly for evaluation. The first fully operational variant was the B-25A, of which 40 were built. Production then rose steeply in models such as the B-25B (119 built with dorsal and ventral turrets but no tail gunner), B-25C (1,619 with different engines and external bomb racks), the basically similar B-25D (2,290), B-25G (405 with a 75-mm/2.95-in nose gun), B-25H (1,000 with revised armament and no dorsal turret), B-25J (4,318 with provision for heavier bombs and, in later models, a solid nose with eight heavy machine-guns). There were several experimental developments.

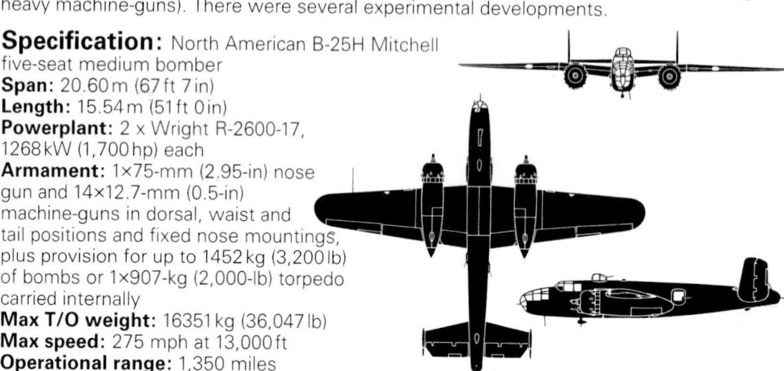

Specification: North American B-25H Mitchell five-seat medium bomber
Span: 20.60 m (67 ft 7 in)
Length: 15.54 m (51 ft 0 in)
Powerplant: 2 x Wright R-2600-17, 1268 kW (1,700 hp) each
Armament: 1×75-mm (2.95-in) nose gun and 14×12.7-mm (0.5-in) machine-guns in dorsal, waist and tail positions and fixed nose mountings, plus provision for up to 1452 kg (3,200 lb) of bombs or 1×907-kg (2,000-lb) torpedo carried internally
Max T/O weight: 16351 kg (36,047 lb)
Max speed: 275 mph at 13,000 ft
Operational range: 1,350 miles

North American A-36 Invader

Though now little known or appreciated, the A-36 was in fact the first variant of the celebrated P-51 Mustang fighter to see service with the USAAF. Developed with the company designation NA-97 as a variant of the basic P-51 (USAAF equivalent of the RAF's Mustang Mk IA) with a wing-mounted armament of six machine-guns in place of the four 20-mm cannon, the A-36A production model was planned for the ground-attack and dive-bombing roles with two underwing bomb racks and, uniquely in Mustang variants, hydraulically operated dive brakes above and below the wings. The first example flew in September 1942, and production of all 500 was completed by March 1943. The A-36A received its operational blooding in the invasions of Sicily and Italy during July and September 1943.

Specification: North American A-36A Invader single-seat ground-attack fighter and dive-bomber
Span: 11.34 m (37 ft 0.25 in)
Length: 9.83 m (32 ft 3 in)
Powerplant: 1×Allison V-1710-87, 988 kW (1,325 hp)
Armament: 6×12.7-mm (0.5-in) machine-guns, plus provision for 2×227-kg (500-lb) bombs carried under the wings
Max T/O weight: 4536 kg (10,000 lb)
Max speed: 310 mph at 10,000 ft
Operational range: 550 miles

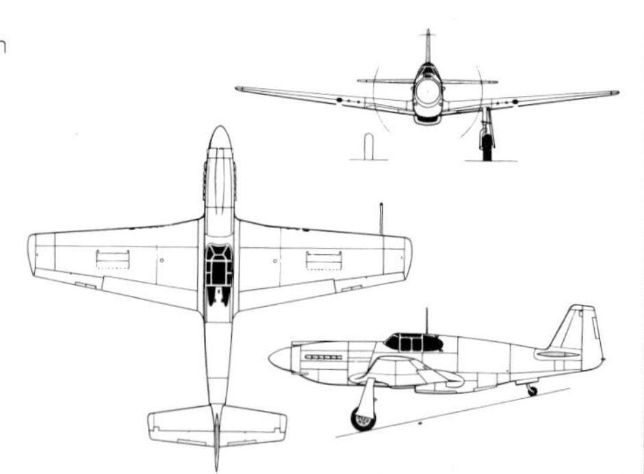

Vultee A-35 Vengeance

In 1940 the UK ordered from the USA the Vultee V-72, which was placed in limited service as the Vengeance Mk I dive-bomber. After the implementation of the Lend-Lease Act in March 1941 the type was designated A-31 for procurement purposes, though the 243 repossessed by the USAAF were designated V-72 as the aeroplane had not been type-classified for US service. Six V-72s were then used for development purposes as one XA-31A/B and five YA-31Cs, leading to the A-35. The USAAF then received 100 examples of an improved Vengeance Mk I as the A-35 with the 1193-kW (1,600-hp) R-2600-19, 99 of them being redesignated as A-35A when retrofitted with four 12.7-mm (0.5-in) wing guns, and 831 examples of the A-35B with increased armament and a more powerful engine. The USAAF never used the A-35 in its planned role, most being assigned to target-towing and other secondary roles.

Specification: Vultee A-35B Vengeance two-seat dive-bomber
Span: 14.63 m (48 ft 0 in)
Length: 12.11 m (39 ft 9 in)
Powerplant: 1×Wright R-2600-13, 1268 kW (1,700 hp)
Armament: 7×12.7-mm (0.5-in) machine-guns (six fixed in wings and one in rear cockpit), plus provision for up to 907 kg (2,000 lb) of bombs carried internally
Max T/O weight: 7440 kg (16,400 lb)
Max speed: 279 mph at 13,500 ft
Operational range: 2,300 miles

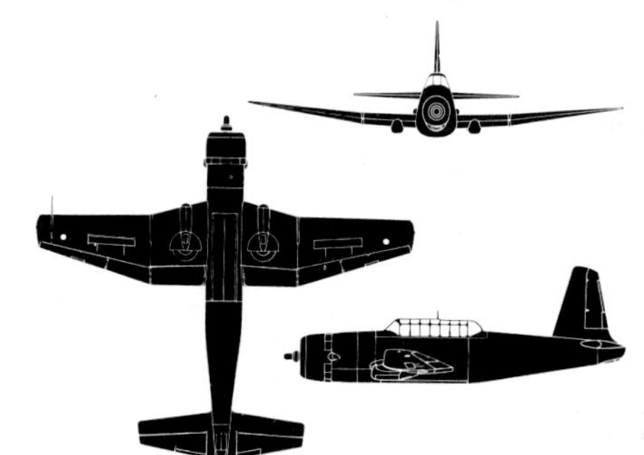

Boeing XB-15

First flown in October 1937 after its original designation had been altered from XBLR-1 to XB-15, the sole Model 294 resulted from a 1933 USAAC requirement for a bomber with an 8050-km (5,000-mile) range and thus able to strike from continental US bases at forces invading Alaska or Hawaii. The Boeing design won the sole contract from a Martin contender, and as befitted its advanced role the aeroplane featured many innovative features, including wing crawlways to allow engine adjustments or repairs in flight, two auxiliary power units to provide electrical power, bunks and, for the first time in an American military aeroplane, a flight engineer. The type was designed for 1491-kW (2,000-hp) engines whose non-availability meant the use of lower-powered engines and much degraded performance. The type was operated in World War II as the XC-105 freight transport with a large side door.

Specification: Boeing XB-15 experimental six/eight-seat heavy long-range bomber
Span: 45.42 m (149 ft 0 in)
Length: 26.70 m (87 ft 7 in)
Powerplant: 4×Pratt & Whitney R-1830-11, 746 kW (1,000 hp) each
Armament: 4×12.7-mm (0.5-in) and 4×7.62-mm (0.3-in) machine-guns plus provision for up to 5443 kg (12,000 lb) of bombs carried internally
Max T/O weight: 32070 kg (70,700 lb)
Max speed: 195 mph at optimum altitude
Operational range: 5,130 miles

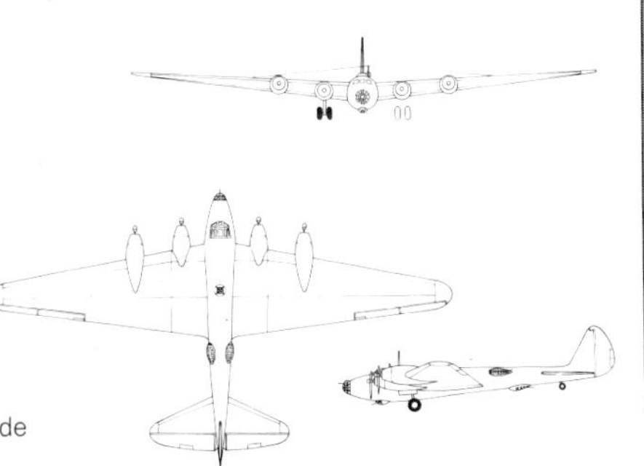

Boeing B-17 Flying Fortress

Resulting from a USAAC requirement of 1934 for a bomber able to deliver a 907-kg (2,000-lb) bombload over a radius of 3540 km (2,200 miles) at speeds up to 250 mph, the Model 299 (unofficially XB-17) first flew in July 1935 with 559-kW (750-hp) Pratt & Whitney R-1690-S1E-G radials. Despite this aeroplane's crash in October 1935, the USAAC ordered 13 YB-17s (later Y1B-17s) with 694-kW (930-hp) Wright GR-1820-39 engines and minor modifications; 12 aircraft were later designated B-17, while the 13th aeroplane was fitted with turbocharged engines and became the sole B-17A. Further small batches were used for continued evaluation, and comprised 39 B-17Bs with R-1820-65s plus larger flaps and rudder, 38 B-17Cs with self-sealing tanks and enhanced gun armament, and 42 B-17Ds with better armour, cowl flaps and a revised electrical system. The following B-17E was the first mass-production variant.

Specification: Boeing B-17C Flying Fortress nine-seat long-range heavy bomber
Span: 31.62 m (103 ft 9 in)
Length: 20.70 m (67 ft 11 in)
Powerplant: 4×Wright R-1820-65, 895 kW (1,200 hp) each
Armament: 1×7.62-mm (0.3-in) and 6×12.7-mm (0.5-in) machine-guns plus provision for up to 4761 kg (10,496 lb) of bombs carried internally
Max T/O weight: 22520 kg (49,650 lb)
Max speed: 291 mph at 25,000 ft
Operational range: 3,400 miles

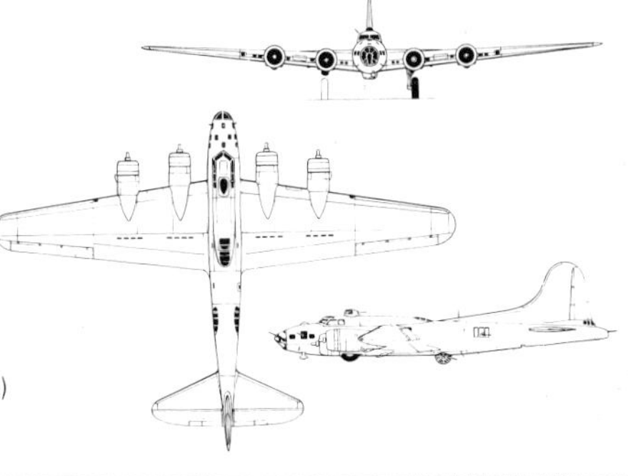

Douglas XB-19

Design of this large aeroplane began in 1935 as an exercise in the development of large bombers, in this instance with a planned powerplant of six 1193-kW (1,600-hp) Allison XV-3420-1 inline engines to provide greater payload and performance than possible with the Boeing XB-15. The sole aeroplane was originally designated the XBLR-2. The whole programme was seriously delayed by its complexity, lack of adequate funding and problems with the engines, with the result that the first flight was not made in 1938 as planned: in fact construction began only a few weeks before the scheduled first-flight date, and the type was recast with four R-3350 radials and the designation XB-19. The resulting aeroplane was a low-wing monoplane of stressed-skin construction with tricycle landing gear, and finally flew in June 1941. The aeroplane was finally used as a transport with Allison V-3420-11 inlines and the designation XB-19A.

Specification: Douglas XB-19 experimental 16/24-seat heavy strategic bomber
Span: 64.62 m (212 ft 0 in)
Length: 40.34 m (132 ft 4 in)
Powerplant: 4×Wright R-3350-5, 1491 kW (2,000 hp) each
Armament: 2×37-mm (1.48-in) cannon, 5×12.7-mm (0.5-in) and 4×7.62-mm (0.3-in) machine-guns plus provision for up to 16829 kg (37,100 lb) of bombs carried internally
Max T/O weight: 73482 kg (162,000 lb)
Max speed: 224 mph at 15,700 ft
Operational range: 5,200 miles

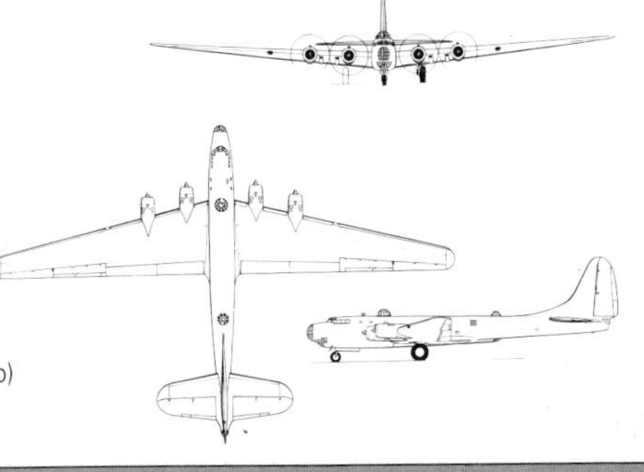

Douglas B-23 Dragon

The B-23 was basically an extensively developed version of the B-18 developed via the projected B-22 with a better streamlined fuselage, a considerably larger vertical tail, more powerful engines mounted on the stronger wings of the DC-3 airliner, fully retractable landing gear and, for the first time in an American bomber, a tail gun position with a single 12.7-mm (0.5-in) weapon to complement the single 7.62-mm (0.3-in) machine-guns in the nose, dorsal and ventral positions. Unusually for the USAAC, the type was ordered 'off the drawing board' when late in 1938 the B-18A contract was amended so that the last 32 were delivered as B-23s. The first B-23 flew in July 1939, and though performance and operational capabilities were markedly superior to those of the B-18, production was confined to just these 32 machines as the new Boeing B-17E offered considerably greater payload and performance.

Specification: Douglas B-23 Dragon four/five-seat medium bomber
Span: 28.04 m (92 ft 0 in)
Length: 17.79 m (58 ft 4.75 in)
Powerplant: 2×Wright R-2600-3, 1193 kW (1,600 hp) each
Armament: 1×12.7-mm (0.5-in) and 3×7.62-mm (0.3-in) machine-guns plus provision for up to 1996 kg (4,400 lb) of bombs carried internally
Max T/O weight: 14696 kg (32,400 lb)
Max speed: 282 mph at 12,000 ft
Operational range: 1,400 miles

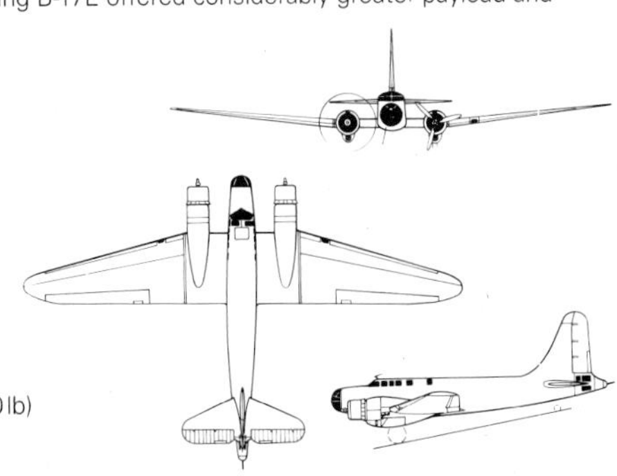

Aichi D3A

Known to the Allies as the 'Val', the D3A was the most important dive-bomber in service with the Imperial Japanese Navy at the beginning of World War II. It was Japan's first all-metal, low-wing, monoplane dive-bomber, and was inspired by German machines such as the Heinkel He 66, He 70 and He 74. The first prototype flew in January 1938 with a 529-kW (710-hp) Nakajima Hikari 1 radial, and extensive development was necessary before the D3A1 began to enter service in late 1940 at land bases, as well as on aircraft-carriers. Some 477 aircraft were built up to 1942, when the D3A2 entered production for better all-round performance with the 969-kW (1,300-hp) Kinsei 54 radial. Between 1942 and 1944 some 815 D3A2s were built, and many of these outclassed aircraft were pressed into service as *kamikaze* platforms.

Specification: Aichi D3A1 carrierborne and land-based two-seat dive-bomber
Span: 14.365 m (47 ft 2 in)
Length: 10.195 m (33 ft 5.5 in)
Powerplant: 1×Mitsubishi Kinsei 44, 798 kW (1,070 hp)
Armament: 3×0.303-in (7.7-mm) machine-guns, plus provision for 1×250-kg (551-lb) bomb carried under the fuselage and 2×60-kg (132-lb) bombs carried under the wings
Loaded weight: 3650 kg (8,047 lb)
Max speed: 240 mph at 9,845 ft
Operational range: 915 miles

Aichi B7A Ryusei

Known to the Japanese as the Ryusei (shooting star) and to the Allies as the 'Grace', the B7A was planned to a 1941 requirement for a single aeroplane to replace the B6N torpedo-bomber and D4Y dive-bomber. Aichi was ordered to use the powerful but troublesome Homare radial, and the flight trials from May 1942 were plagued by engine problems. When the engine was working properly the B7A had sparkling performance, and large orders were placed. The rear-firing 7.92-mm (0.312-in) machine-gun and 1342-kW (1,800-hp) Homare 11 of the nine B7A1s were replaced in the 105 B7A2 production aircraft by a larger calibre gun and more powerful Homare 12, but production was ended when the main factory was destroyed by an earthquake in May 1945. The B7A3 Ryusei-KAI would have used the 1640-kW (2,200-hp) Mitsubishi MK9A for improved performance.

Specification: Aichi B7A2 Ryusei carrierborne and land-based two-seat torpedo- and dive-bomber
Span: 14.40 m (47 ft 3 in)
Length: 11.49 m (37 ft 8.25 in)
Powerplant: 1×Nakajima NK9C Homare 12, 1361 kW (1,825 hp)
Armament: 2×20-mm cannon and 1×13-mm (0.51-in) machine- gun, plus provision for 1×800-kg (1,764-lb) torpedo or up to 800 kg (1,764 lb) of bombs carried internally
Max T/O weight: 6500 kg (14,330 lb)
Max speed: 352 mph at 21,490 ft
Operational range: 1,151 miles

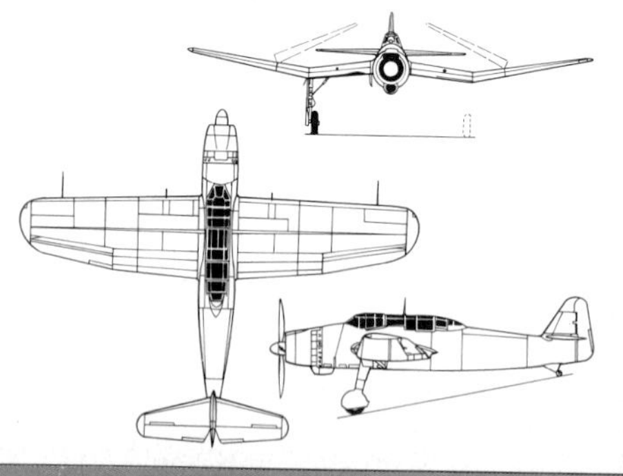

Kawasaki Ki-48

Known to the Allies as the 'Lily', the Ki-48 was widely used by the Imperial Japanese Army between 1940 and 1944, but was never more than moderately successful. The type was planned in 1938 after the Japanese had encountered the Soviets' formidable Tupolev SB-2, and first flew in prototype form in July 1939. Tail flutter problems had to be eradicated before the Ki-48-Ia was placed in production, the first such aircraft being delivered in July 1940 with 708-kW (950-hp) Ha-25 radials. Some 557 Ki-48-Ia and improved -Ib bombers were produced up to June 1942 when the Ki-48-II appeared with greater power and better protection for the fuel tanks, crew and ammunition. Up to October 1944 1,408 Ki-48-IIs were built in -IIa bomber, -IIb dive-bomber and -IIc bomber variants, the last having much enhanced defensive armament.

Specification: Kawasaki Ki-48-IIb land-based four-seat light bomber and dive-bomber
Span: 17.45 m (57 ft 3 in)
Length: 12.75 m (41 ft 10 in)
Powerplant: 2×Nakajima Ha-115 (Army Type 1), 857 kW (1,150 hp) each
Armament: 3×7.92-mm (0.312-in) machine-guns, plus provision for up to 800 kg (1,764 lb) of bombs carried internally
Max T/O weight: 6750 kg (14,881 lb)
Max speed: 314 mph at 18,375 ft
Operational range: 1,491 miles

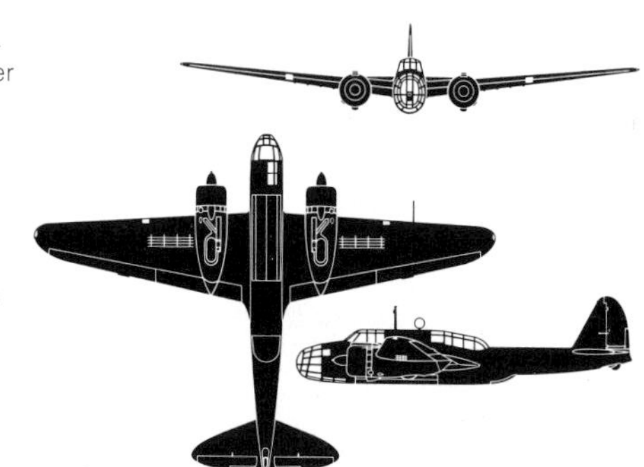

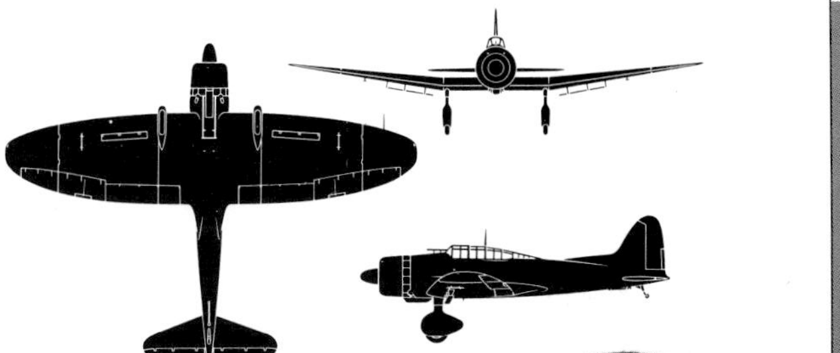

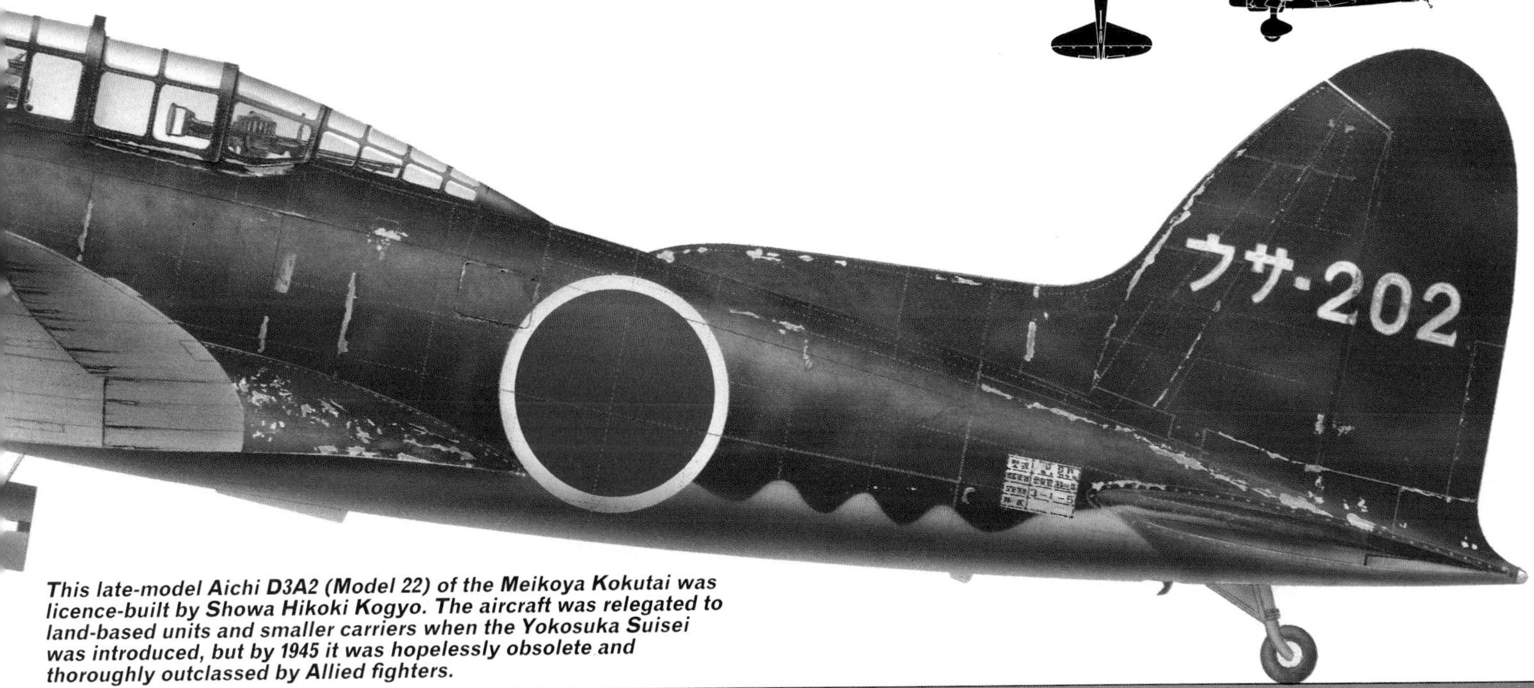

This late-model Aichi D3A2 (Model 22) of the Meikoya Kokutai was licence-built by Showa Hikoki Kogyo. The aircraft was relegated to land-based units and smaller carriers when the Yokosuka Suisei was introduced, but by 1945 it was hopelessly obsolete and thoroughly outclassed by Allied fighters.

Mitsubishi G3M

Notorious as the bombers primarily responsible for sinking the British capital ships HMS *Repulse* and HMS *Prince of Wales*, the G3M was known to the Allies as the 'Nell'. The type was planned as a long-range fleet support bomber, and first flew in July 1935 with 447-kW (600-hp) Hiro Type 91 radials. Some 21 prototypes and pre-production aircraft were built with the Type 1, and later the Kinsei 2 radial, before production aircraft was ordered during 1936 of the G3M1 with the 678-kW (910-hp) Kinsei 3. These 34 aircraft were followed at Mitsubishi by 343 G3M2 Model 21s and 238 G3M2 Model 22s up to 1941. Nakajima made 412 G3M2 Model 22s and G3M3s between 1941 and 1943. The Model 21 had the Kinsei 42 with inferior altitude rating to the Kinsei 45 of the Model 22, and the G3M3 the 969-kW (1,300-hp) Kinsei 51 and improved defensive armament of the Model 22. There was also an L3Y transport version.

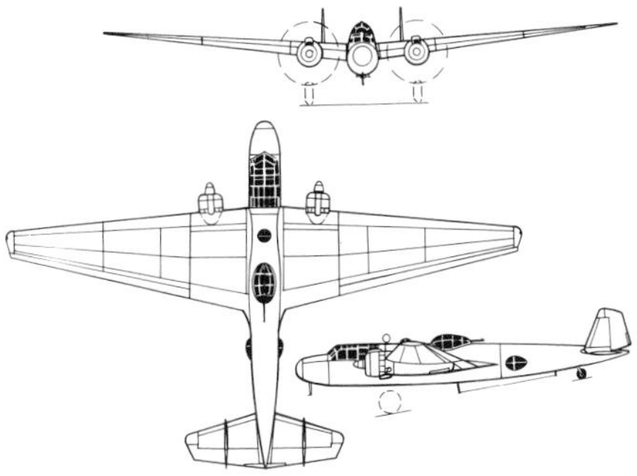

Specification: Mitsubishi G3M2 Model 22 land-based seven-seat fleet support bomber
Span: 25.00 m (82 ft 0.25 in)
Length: 16.45 m (51 ft 11.5 in)
Powerplant: 2×Mitsubishi Kinsei 45, 802 kW (1,075 hp) each
Armament: 1×20-mm cannon and 4×0.303-in (7.7-mm) machine-guns, plus provision for 1×800-kg (1,764-lb) torpedo or up to 800 kg (1,764 lb) of bombs carried externally
Loaded weight: 8000 kg (17,637 lb)
Max speed: 232 mph at 13,715 ft
Operational range: 2,722 miles

Mitsubishi Ki-21

Entering service in September 1938 and obsolescent by December 1941, the Imperial Japanese Army bomber known to the Allies as the 'Sally' continued in first-line service throughout World War II. The Ki-21 was designed in 1936 as a heavy bomber, though all such Japanese aircraft were light (at best medium) bombers by Allied standards. The prototype flew in December 1936 with 615-kW (825-hp) Mitsubishi Ha-6 radials. The type was accepted for production with Ha-5 engines as the Ki-21-Ia (143 built), followed by 120 Ki-21-Ib bombers with improved defences, and 160 Ki-21-Ic bombers with more fuel and still better defensive armament; Nakajima added 351 of all three variants. The 590 Ki-21-IIa bombers had more power, and the 688 Ki-21-IIb bombers introduced a dorsal turret. Many Ki-21-Is were converted as MC-21 transports.

Specification: Mitsubishi Ki-21-IIb land-based five-seat heavy bomber
Span: 22.50 m (73 ft 9.75 in)
Length: 16.00 m (52 ft 6 in)
Powerplant: 2×Mitsubishi Ha-101 (Army Type 100), 1118 kW (1,500 hp) each
Armament: 1×12.7-mm (0.5-in) and 5×0.303-in (7.7-mm) machine-guns, plus provision for up to 1000 kg (2,205 lb) of bombs carried internally
Max T/O weight: 10610 kg (23,391 lb)
Max speed: 302 mph at 15,485 ft
Operational range: 1,680 miles

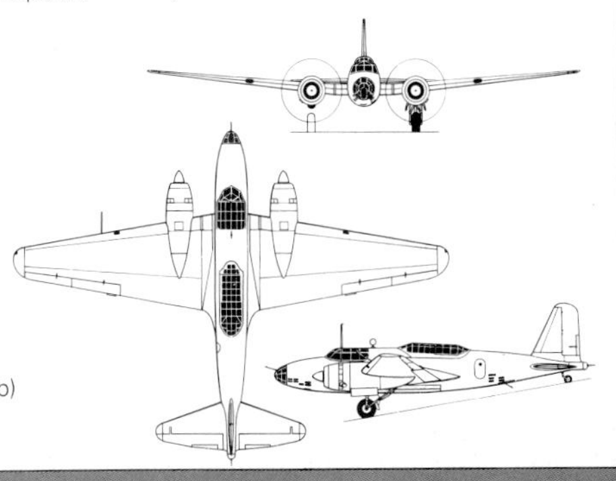

Mitsubishi G4M Hamaki

This early Mitsubishi G4M1 'Betty' served with the 1st Chutai of the Takao Kokutai, and served at the almost impregnable fortress of Rabaul in the northern half of New Britain. The unit suffered heavy losses during the war, and was eventually reformed as the 753rd Kokutai. It was nicknamed the 'One-Shot Lighter' by Allied and Hameki (Cigar) by Japanese pilots.

Known to the Allies as the 'Betty', the G4M was built in larger numbers than any other Japanese bomber, and served very widely right up to the end of World War II. Designed in 1937 as a land-based attack bomber of exceptional performance, the G4M was successful in the early stages of the war but then suffered catastrophic losses when the typically Japanese failings of a light structure and lack of protection were exploited by Allied fighters. Total production was 2,446 between 1939 and August 1945, and the main variants were the initial G4M1 (1,200 built), the G4M2 with aerodynamic improvements and 1342-kW (1,800-hp) Kasei 21 radials for better altitude performance (1,152), the better-protected G4M3 with 1361-kW (1,825-hp) Kasei 25b radials (60) and the disastrous G6M1 escort version with 1141-kW (1,530-hp) Kasei 11 radials (30).

Mitsubishi Ki-67 Hiryu

The Hiryu (flying dragon) was known to the Allies as the 'Peggy', and though operational for only the last 11 months of the war proved itself the best Imperial Japanese Army 'heavy' bomber of World War II, and was also developed as a glider tug, heavy fighter, interceptor, reconnaissance aircraft, suicide bomber and torpedo-bomber. The type was designed in 1941 as successor to the Ki-49. The first prototype flew in December 1942, and many prototypes and pre-production aircraft were used to explore the design's multiple capabilities: only in December 1943 was the design frozen and Mitsubishi instructed to begin production of the Ki-67-I as a heavy and torpedo-bomber. The highest priority was allocated to production, but only 698 aircraft had been completed by the end of the war, later aircraft having better defensive armament.

Specification: Mitsubishi Ki-67-I Hiryu land-based six/eight-seat heavy bomber
Span: 22.50 m (73 ft 9.75 in)
Length: 18.70 m (61 ft 4.25 in)
Powerplant: 2×Mitsubishi Ha-104 (Army Type 4), 1417 kW (1,900 hp) each
Armament: 1×20-mm cannon and 5×12.7-mm (0.5-in) machine-guns, plus provision for 1×800- or 1070-kg (1,764- or 2,359-lb) torpedo or up to 800 kg (1,764 lb) of bombs carried internally
Loaded weight: 13765 kg (30,347 lb)
Max speed: 334 mph at 19,980 ft
Operational range: 2,360 miles

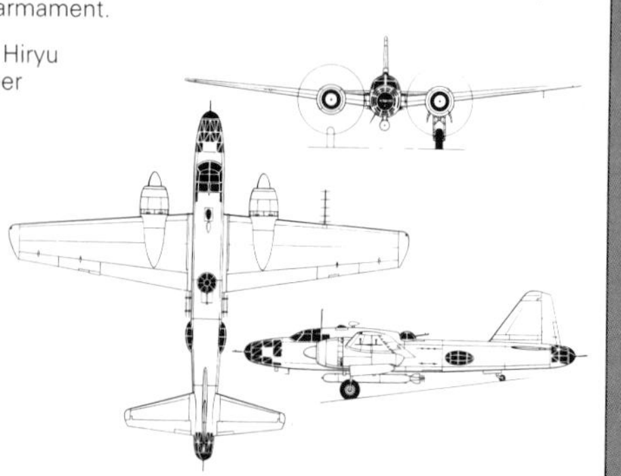

Nakajima B5N

Best known for its part in the Japanese attack on Pearl Harbor in December 1941, the torpedo-bomber known to the Allies as the 'Kate' was planned in 1936 to match the capabilities of Japan's new aircraft-carriers and the offensive tactical policy planned for them. The first prototype flew in January 1937 with a 596-kW (800-hp) Hikari 2 radial, replaced in the B5N1 initial production variant by a 626-kW (840-hp) Hikari 3. These early aircraft were used as conventional light bombers over China, and were then converted into B5N1-K trainers. In 1939 the B5N1 was replaced in production by the B5N2 with greater power. Production lasted to 1943, and amounted in all to 1,149 aircraft. Obsolete by 1943, the B5N2s were then used for anti-ship and anti-submarine patrol with radar and magnetic anomaly detection gear respectively.

Specification: Nakajima B5N2 carrierborne and land-based three-seat torpedo-bomber
Span: 15.518 m (50 ft 11 in)
Length: 10.30 m (33 ft 9.5 in)
Powerplant: 1×Nakajima NK1B Sakae 11, 746 kW (1,000 hp)
Armament: 1×0.303-in (7.7-mm) machine-gun, plus provision for 1×800-kg (1,764-lb) torpedo or up to 800 kg (1,764 lb) of bombs carried externally
Max T/O weight: 4100 kg (9,039 lb)
Max speed: 235 mph at 11,810 ft
Operational range: 1,237 miles

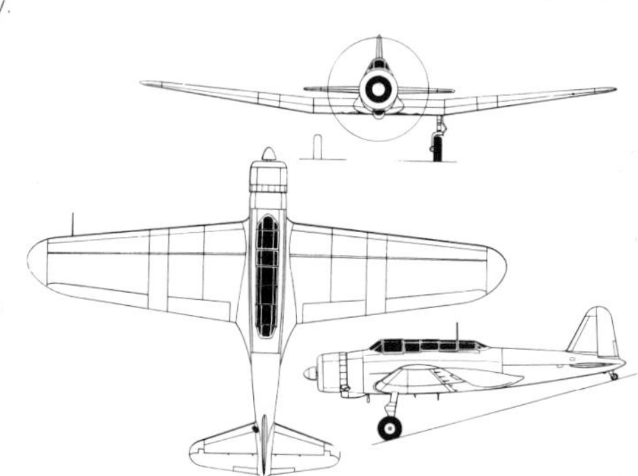

Specification: Mitsubishi G4M1 land-based seven-seat attack bomber
Span: 25.00 m (82 ft 0.25 in)
Length: 20.00 m (65 ft 7.5 in)
Powerplant: 2×Mitsubishi MK4E Kasei 15, 1141 kW (1,530 hp)
Armament: 1×20-mm cannon and 4×0.303-in (7.7-mm) machine-guns, plus provision for 1×800-kg (1,764-lb) torpedo or 800 kg (1,764 lb) of bombs carried semi-internally
Loaded weight: 9500 kg (20,944 lb)
Max speed: 266 mph at 13,780 ft
Operational range: 3,749 miles

Nakajima B6N Tenzan

The Tenzan (heavenly mountain) was known to the Allies as the 'Jill', and was planned in 1939 as successor to the obsolescent B5N with a similar airframe offering superior performance through use of considerably greater power. The prototype flew in spring 1941 with 1394-kW (1,870-hp) Nakajima Mamoru 11 radials and displayed adequate performance. But the design suffered from a number of engineering defects whose remedy occupied the time to the end of 1942. After two years of testing the B6N was finally accepted for production as the B6N1: 133 such aircraft were built between February and July 1943. Nakajima had meanwhile been formed to abandon production of the Mamoru and the B6N was therefore recast with a Mitsubishi radial as the B6N2. Production of this model totalled 1,133 aircraft, and the type was also used for the reconnaissance and *kamikaze* roles.

Specification: Nakajima B6N2 Tenzan carrierborne and land-based three-seat torpedo-bomber
Span: 14.894 m (48 ft 10.5 in)
Length: 10.865 m (35 ft 7.75 in)
Powerplant: 1×Mitsubishi MK4T Kasei 25, 1379 kW (1,850 hp)
Armament: 1×13-mm (0.51-in) machine-gun and 1×0.303-in (7.7-mm) machine-gun, plus provision for 1×800-kg (1,764-lb) torpedo or up to 800 kg (1,764 lb) of bombs carried externally
Max T/O weight: 5650 kg (12,456 lb)
Max speed: 299 mph at 16,075 ft
Operational range: 1,892 miles

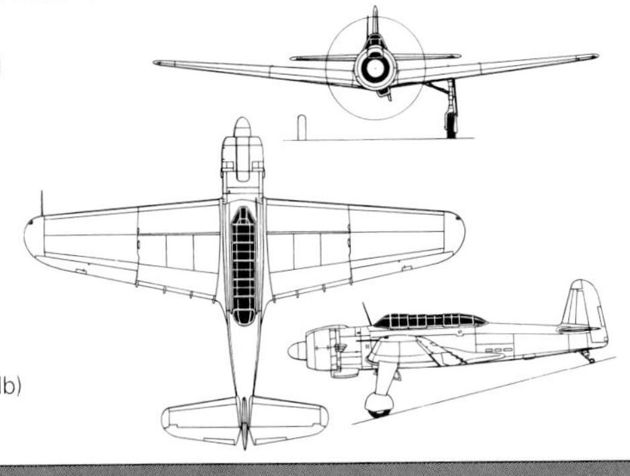

Nakajima G8N Renzan

The Renzan (mountain range) was known to the Allies as the 'Rita', and was one of the few four-engined bombers developed by Japan. The type originated from a 1943 requirement for a G4M replacement with greater bombload, performance and, most importantly, defensive armament and protection. In this last capacity the G8N1 had power-operated nose, tail, dorsal and ventral cannon turrets plus protection for the crew, fuel tanks and other vital components. The design was optimized for ease of production, and the first prototype flew in October 1944. By this time, however, a reassessment of the Imperial Japanese Navy's role combined with a critical shortage of light alloys to force cancellation of the programme in mid-1945 after the completion of just four prototypes.

Specification: Nakajima G8N1 Renzan land-based 10-seat heavy bomber prototype
Span: 32.54 m (106 ft 9 in)
Length: 22.935 m (75 ft 3 in)
Powerplant: 4×Nakajima NK9K-L Homare 24, 1491 kW (2,000 hp) each
Armament: 6×20-mm cannon and 4×13-mm (0.51-in) machine-guns, plus provision for up to 4000 kg (8,818 lb) of bombs carried internally
Max T/O weight: 32150 kg (70,879 lb)
Max speed: 368 mph at 26,245 ft
Operational range: 4,639 miles

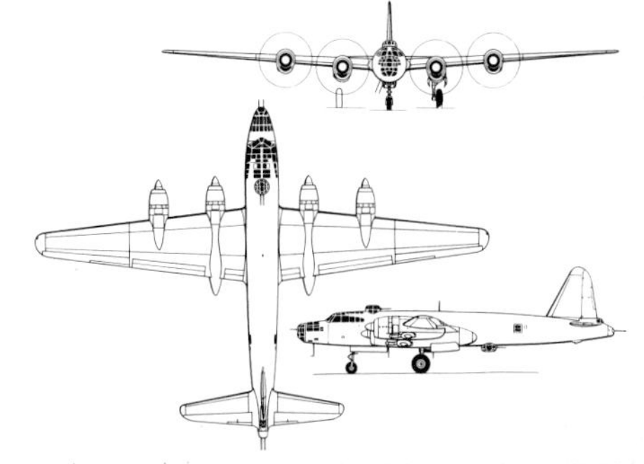

Nakajima Ki-49 Donryu

The Donryu (storm dragon), known to the Allies as the 'Helen', was a good design built only in limited numbers (819 in all), and overshadowed by larger numbers of the Ki-21 and by the superior capabilities of the Ki-67. The type originated from a 1938 requirement for a Ki-21 heavy bomber replacement, and first flew in August 1939 with 708-kW (950-hp) Nakajima Ha-5 KAI radials. Later prototypes and pre-production aircraft introduced the 932-kW (1,250-hp) Nakajima Ha-41 radials. The Ki-49-I (129 built) was accepted for production in March 1941. From August 1942 delivery was made of 617 Ki-49-II improved bombers with greater power, better self-sealing tanks, rearranged armour and heavier defensive armament. The Ki-49-III had 1804-kW (2,420-hp) Nakajima Ha-117s for improved performance, but only six were built before the end of the war.

Specification: Nakajima Ki-49-II land-based eight-seat heavy bomber
Span: 20.424 m (67 ft 0 in)
Length: 16.50 m (54 ft 1.75 in)
Powerplant: 2×Nakajima Ha-109 (Army Type 2), 1118 kW (1,500 hp)
Armament: 1×20-mm cannon, 3×12.7-mm (0.5-in) machine-guns and 2×0.303-in (7.7-mm) machine-guns, plus provision for up to 1000 kg (2,205 lb) of bombs carried internally
Max T/O weight: 11400 kg (25,133 lb)
Max speed: 306 mph at 16,405 ft
Operational range: 1,833 miles

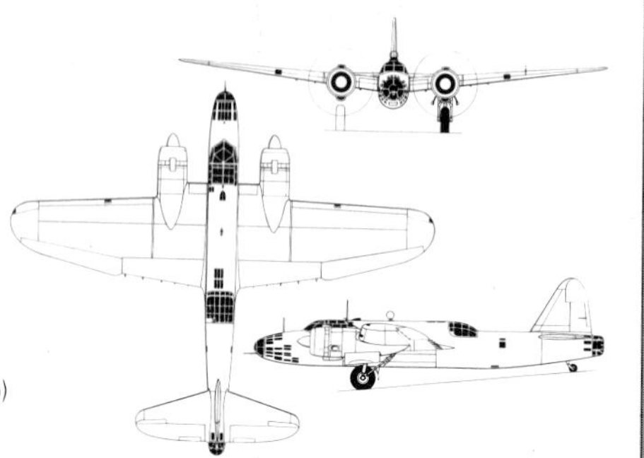

Nakajima Kikka

The Kikka (orange blossom) was designed from September 1944 after receipt in Japan of reports about the Messerschmitt Me 262. The design was modelled aerodynamically on the German aeroplane, and planned as an attack bomber with folding wings to allow the type's concealment in caves and tunnels. The powerplant originally planned was a pair of 200-kg (441-lb) thrust Tsu-11 Campini-type jets, but these were supplanted by 340-kg (750-lb) thrust Ne-12 turbojets and then Ne-20s modelled on the German BMW 003. The first prototype flew on 7 August 1945 (one day after the nuclear bombing of Hiroshima), and a second flight was aborted four days later by incorrect installation of the RATO units needed for take-off. A second prototype had been completed, and 18 other aircraft were under construction at the end of the war.

Specification: Nakajima Kikka land-based single-seat attack bomber prototype
Span: 10.00 m (32 ft 9.75 in)
Length: 8.125 m (26 ft 8 in)
Powerplant: 2×Ne-20, 475 kg (1,047 lb) st each
Armament: 1×500- or 800-kg (1,102- or 1,764-lb) bomb carried externally
Max T/O weight: 4080 kg (8,995 lb)
Max speed: 433 mph at 32,810 ft
Operational range: 586 miles

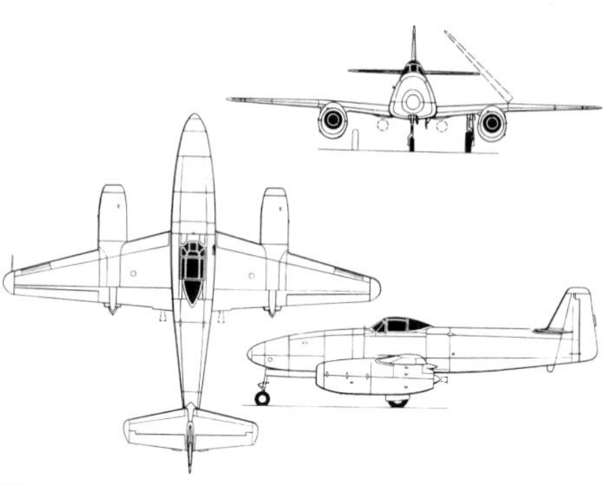

Yososuka D4Y Suisei

Developed as a D3A replacement, the Suisei (comet) was known to the Allies as the 'Judy', and was unusual in being developed with both radial and inline engines for carrierborne and land-based operations respectively. The design was strongly influenced by the Heinkel He 118, which the Japanese at one time planned to build under licence, but the result was an aeroplane smaller but of higher performance than the German aeroplane. The prototype flew in December 1940 with a 717-kW (960-hp) Daimler-Benz DB 600G inline. Production totalled 2,038 in four main variants: the D4Y1 dive-bomber (and D4Y1-C reconnaissance variant) with the 895-kW (1,200-hp) Aichi AE1A Atsuta 12 inline, the D4Y2 dive-bomber (and D4Y2-S night-fighter variant) with the 1044-kW (1,400-hp) Atsuta 32, the D4Y3 dive-bomber with the Kinsei radial, and the D4Y4 *kamikaze* aeroplane with the Kinsei 62.

Specification: Aichi D4Y3 Suisei carrierborne and land-based two-seat dive-bomber and reconnaissance aeroplane
Span: 11.50 m (37 ft 8.75 in)
Length: 10.22 m (33 ft 6.5 in)
Powerplant: 1×Mitsubishi MK8P Kinsei 62, 1163 kW (1,560 hp)
Armament: 3×0.303-in (7.7-mm) machine-guns, plus provision for up to 560 kg (1,234 lb) of bombs carried externally
Max T/O weight: 4657 kg (10,267 lb)
Max speed: 357 mph at 19,950 ft
Operational range: 1,896 miles

Yokosuka P1Y Ginga

The Ginga (milky way) was known to the Allies as the 'Frances'. Designed primarily as a high-speed bomber, it also served as a night-fighter, reconnaissance aeroplane and torpedo-bomber. The design was originated in 1940 by the Yokosuka Naval Air Depot, with manufacture entrusted to Nakajima. Powered by two 1357-kW (1,820-hp) Homare 11 radials, the prototype flew in August 1943 and displayed good performance but severe system problems. The first variant was the P1Y1 and its P1Y1-S Byakko (white lightning) night-fighter derivative with two pairs of obliquely forward- and upward-firing 20-mm cannon: 996 were built by Nakajima. The P1Y2 variant was produced by Kawanishi to the extent of 96 aircraft: powered by the 1379-kW (1,850-hp) Mitsubishi Kasei 25 radial, the P1Y2 was partnered by a P1Y2-S Kyokko (aurora) night-fighter.

Specification: Yokosuka P1Y1 Ginga land-based three-seat attack and torpedo-bomber
Span: 20.00 m (65 ft 7.5 in)
Length: 15.00 m (49 ft 2.5 in)
Powerplant: 2×Nakajima NK9C Homare 12, 1361 kW (1,825 hp)
Armament: 2×20-mm cannon, plus provision for 1×800-kg (1,764-lb) torpedo or up to 1000 kg (2,205 lb) of bombs carried internally
Max T/O weight: 13500 kg (29,762 lb)
Max speed: 340 mph at 19,355 ft
Operational range: 3,338 miles

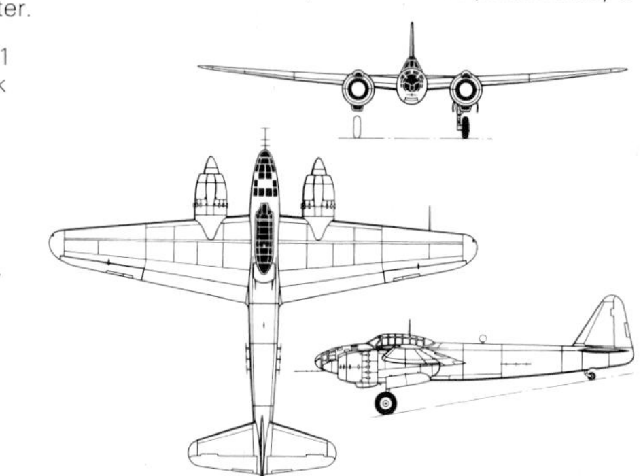

Tupolev SB-2

This was the USSR's most important light bomber at the beginning of World War II, and between 1936 and 1940 had acquitted itself well in the Spanish Civil War and against the Finns and Japanese. The type was developed as the ANT-40 with the 544-kW (730-hp) M-25 and 619-kW (830-hp) M-100 radials, the latter being chosen for the SB-2 initial production model with M-100 or M-100A engines driving fixed- or variable-pitch propellers. Production of the series eventually totalled 6,937, and apart from the baseline SB-2 the main military variants were the SB-2bis with 716-kW (960-hp) M-103 inlines and increased fuel capacity, the SB-RK (otherwise Archangelskii Ar-2) dive-bomber of which some 200 were built with reduced wing area and 820-kW (1,100-hp) M-105R inlines, and the B.71 Czech-built model of which 111 were built by Aero and Avia with 641-kW (860-hp) Hispano-Suiza HS 12Ydrs inlines.

Specification: Tupolev SB-2
three-seat light bomber
Span: 20.33 m (66 ft 8.5 in)
Length: 12.57 m (41 ft 2.75 in)
Powerplant: 2×M-100, 619 kW (830 hp) each
Armament: 4×7.62-mm (0.3-in) machine-guns plus provision for up to 1000 kg (2,205 lb) of bombs carried internally
Max T/O weight: 5628 kg (12,407 lb)
Max speed: 255 mph at 13,125 ft
Operational range: 746 miles

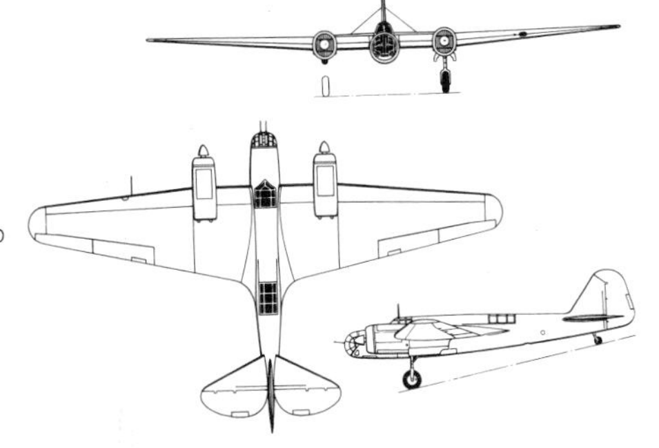

Tupolev TB-3

This was one of the true pioneers of the 'modern' heavy bomber concept when first flown in 1930 as the ANT-6 extrapolation of the twin-engined ANT-4 (TB-1) with four 447-kW (600-hp) Curtiss Conqueror inlines, later replaced by a quartet of 544-kW (730-hp) BMW VI inlines. This vast all-metal monoplane with fixed landing gear then entered production as the TB-3, and the 817 aircraft featured progressively more-powerful engines ranging from the initial 533-kW (715-hp) M-17F via the 619-kW (830-hp) M-34R, 671-kW (900-hp) M-34FRN and 723-kW (970-hp) AM-34RN to the ultimate 895-kW (1,200-hp) AM-34FRNV. The use of these most powerful engines allowed an increase in bombload to 5800 kg (12,787 lb) at certain sacrifice of defensive firepower, but after early and only limited employment as night bombers in 1941 these obsolete aircraft were adapted successfully and usefully for the transport role with the designation G-2.

Specification: Tupolev TB-3
four/six-seat heavy bomber
Span: 41.80 m (137 ft 1.7 in)
Length: 24.40 m (80 ft 0.7 in)
Powerplant: 4×AM-34RN, 723 kW (970 hp) each
Armament: 6×7.62-mm (0.3-in) machine-guns plus provision for up to 4000 kg (8,818 lb) of bombs carried internally and externally
Max T/O weight: 19500 kg (42,990 lb)
Max speed: 179 mph at 13,125 ft
Operational range: 1,939 miles

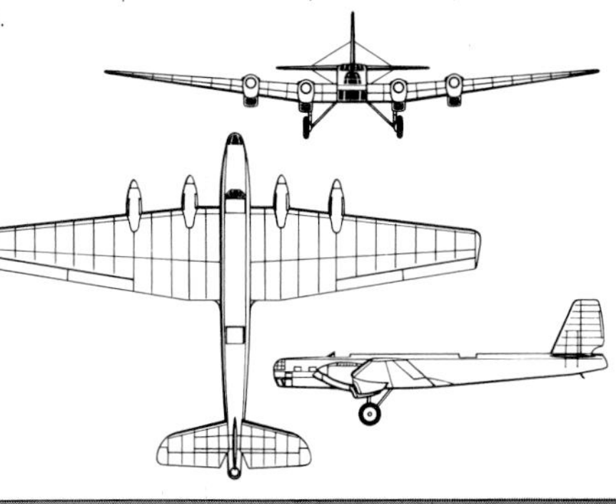

Tupolev Tu-2

The Tu-2 was one of the finest attack bombers of World War II. The type first flew as the three-seat ANT-58 prototype with two 1044-kW (1,400-hp) Mikulin AM-37 inlines and was developed then into a four-seater with a stretched fuselage: this latter was trialled as the ANT-59 with AM-37s and the ANT-60 with 1103-kW (1,480-hp) ASh-82 radials. The latter led to the Tu-2 initial production model with ASh-82 or ASh-82FNV radials and a bombload of 2000 kg (4,409 lb). Wartime production amounted to about 1,000 within an overall figure of 2,500+, and variants included the Tu-2S with more power, a heavier bombload and a single heavy machine-gun instead of twin rifle-calibre guns in the dorsal and ventral positions; the Tu-2D long-range bomber; and the Tu-2R (or Tu-6) reconnaissance aeroplane. Post-war developments were the Tu-2Sh ground-attack, Tu-2T torpedo, Tu-2U trainer and Tu-1 escort fighter aircraft.

Specification: Tupolev Tu-2S
four-seat attack bomber
Span: 18.86 m (61 ft 10.5 in)
Length: 13.80 m (45 ft 3.3 in)
Powerplant: 2×Shvetsov ASh-82FNV, 1379 kW (1,850 hp) each
Armament: 2×20-mm cannon and 3×12.7-mm (0.5-in) machine-guns plus provision for up to 3000 kg (6,614 lb) of bombs carried internally
Max T/O weight: 11450 kg (25,243 lb)
Max speed: 342 mph at 18,700 ft
Operational range: 1,300 miles

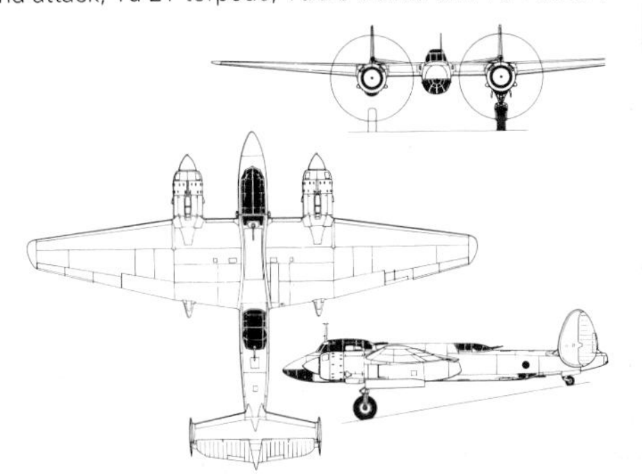

Yakovlev Yak-2 and Yak-4

The Yak-2 was the production variant of the BB-22 prototype built with two 716-kW (960-hp) M-103 inlines as a high-speed reconnaissance fighter. The type was then pressed into unsuccessful service as a short-range bomber. The designation Yak-4 was initially applied to the Yak-2 variant with the M-105 inline engine, but continued development resulted in a somewhat different aeroplane with revised accommodation putting the crew under a single glasshouse canopy, additional armour provision and a redesigned rear fuselage to give the gunner better fields of fire. This type began to enter production in 1940 and comprised most of the 600 or so aircraft built. The Yak-4's service career was short, probably because of structural problems, and the sole variant was the R-12 reconnaissance aeroplane produced by converting Yak-4 bombers.

Specification: Yakovlev Yak-4
two-seat light attack bomber
Span: 14.00 m (45 ft 11.1 in)
Length: 10.17 m (33 ft 4.5 in)
Powerplant: 2×Klimov M-105, 783 kW (1,050 hp) each
Armament: 3×7.62-mm (0.3-in) machine-guns plus provision for up to 600 kg (1,323 lb) of bombs carried internally and externally
Max T/O weight: 5200 kg (11,465 lb)
Max speed: 335 mph at 16,405 ft
Operational range: 497 miles

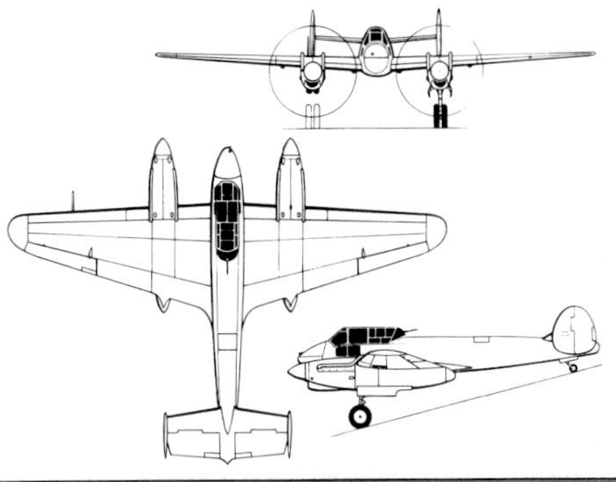

Ilyushin Il-10

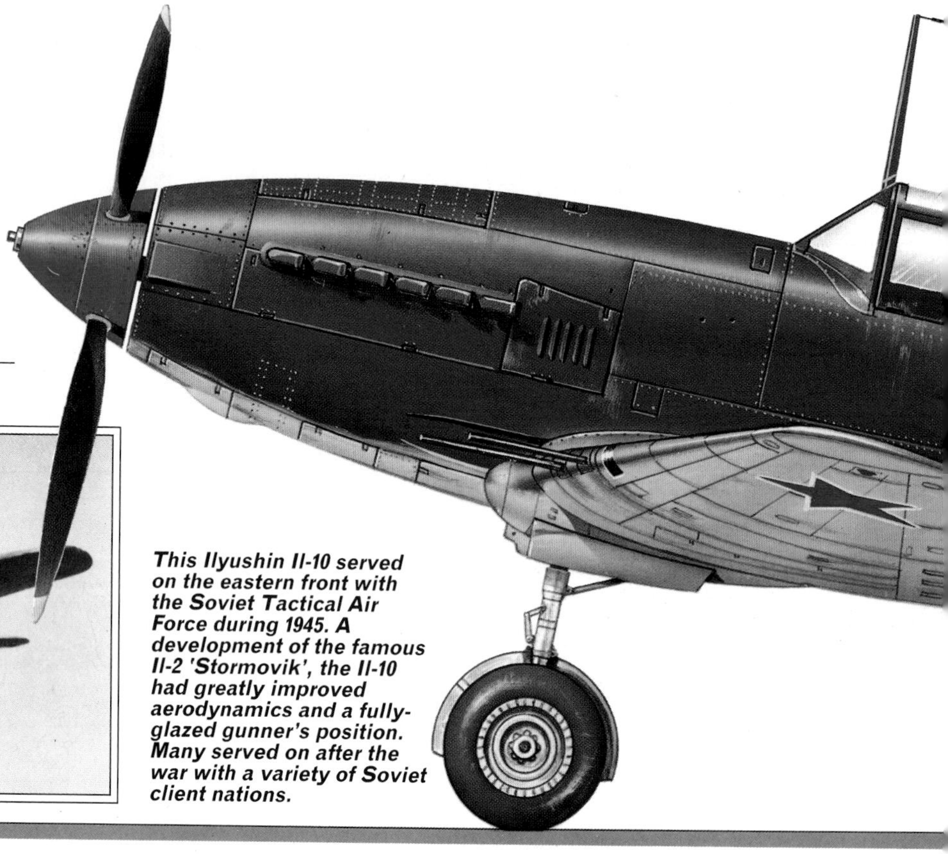

This Ilyushin Il-10 served on the eastern front with the Soviet Tactical Air Force during 1945. A development of the famous Il-2 'Stormovik', the Il-10 had greatly improved aerodynamics and a fully-glazed gunner's position. Many served on after the war with a variety of Soviet client nations.

Ilyushin Il-2

The 36,150 or so Il-2s built between 1941 and 1945 are eloquent testimony to the Soviets' commitment to tactical air support. The type started life as a pair of TsKB-55 two-seat prototypes each powered by the 1007-kW (1,350-hp) M-35A inline, followed by the single-seat KsKB-57 with two 20-mm cannon and two machine-guns rather than four wing-mounted machine-guns. Powered by the 1193-kW (1,600-hp) AM-38, the KsKB-57 was followed by the similar Il-2 production model. The Il-2M introduced the 1267.5-kW (1,700-hp) AM-38A as well as 23- rather than 20-mm cannon, but was found to lack adequate rear protection and was replaced by the definitive Il-2M3 with a dorsal gunner and further improved armament; this in turn spawned an anti-tank model with 37-mm cannon and provision for 200 anti-tank bomblets. Lesser variants were the Il-2T torpedo-bomber and the Il-2U two-seat conversion trainer.

Specification: Ilyushin Il-2M3 two-seat ground-attack aeroplane
Span: 14.60 m (47 ft 10.75 in)
Length: 11.60 m (38 ft 0.5 in)
Powerplant: 1×Mikulin AM-38F, 1320 kW (1,770 hp)
Armament: 2×23-mm cannon, 1×12.7-mm (0.5-in) and 2×7.62-mm (0.3-in) machine-guns plus provision for up to 600 kg (1,321 lb) of bombs carried internally or 8×82 rockets carried under the wings
Max T/O weight: 6360 kg (14,021 lb)
Max speed: 251 mph at 4,920 ft
Operational range: 475 miles

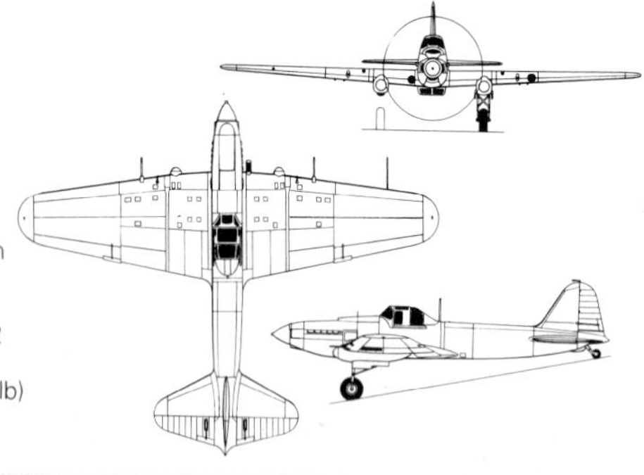

Ilyushin DB-3 and Il-4

Built between 1937 and 1944 to the extent of some 6,800 aircraft, the DB-3 was the USSR's main long-range medium bomber throughout World War II despite its obsolescence in the conflict's closing stages. The KsKB-26 and TsKB-30 prototypes pioneered the 596.5- and 570-kW (800- and 765-hp) Gnome-Rhone 14K and M-85 radials respectively. The TsKB-30 paved the way for the DB-3B initial production model with a bluff nose and M-85 or, in later aircraft, 716-kW (960-hp) M-86 radials: 1,528 of these aircraft were built including a few DB-PT twin-float seaplane torpedo-bomber prototypes. The DB-3F was an improved model with a longer and more tapered nose powered by two 708-kW (950-hp) M-87A or, in the redesigned Il-4 version, M-88B radials. This version had improved performance and better protection (both gun and armour), and production totalled 5,256 aircraft.

Specification: Ilyushin Il-4 three-seat long-range medium bomber
Span: 21.44 m (70 ft 4 in)
Length: 14.80 m (48 ft 6.7 in)
Powerplant: 2×M-88B, 820 kW (1,100 hp) each
Armament: 3×12.7- or 7.62-mm (0.5- or 0.3-in) machine-guns plus provision for 2500 kg (5,512 lb) of bombs carried internally and externally, or 1000 kg (2,205 lb) of bombs carried internally and 1×940-kg (2,072-lb) torpedo carried externally
Max T/O weight: 10300 kg (22,707 lb)
Max speed: 261 mph at 19,685 ft
Operational range: 2,361 miles

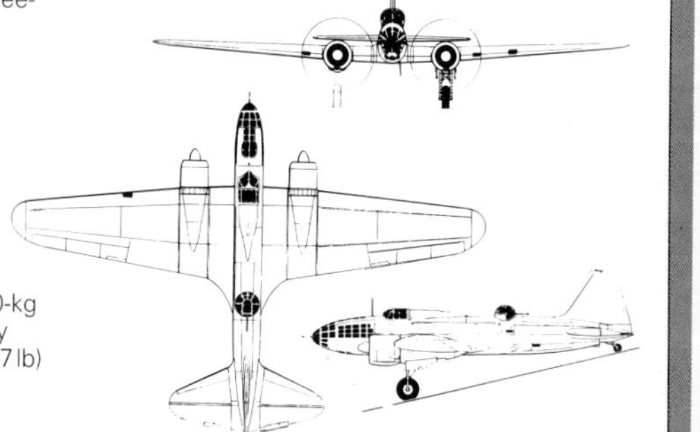

Specification: Ilyushin Il-10 two-seat ground-attack aeroplane
Span: 13.40m (43ft 11.5in)
Length: 11.20m (36ft 9in)
Powerplant: 1×Mikulin AM-42, 1491kW (2,000hp)
Armament: 2×23-mm cannon, 1×12.7-mm (0.5-in) machine-gun and 2×7.62-mm (0.3-in) machine-guns plus provision for up to 400kg (882lb) of bombs carried internally and 8×82- or 132-mm (3.2- or 5.2-in) rockets carried under the wings
Max T/O weight: 6536kg (14,409lb)
Max speed: 315 mph at sea level
Operational range: 621 miles

In 1944 the Soviet air force evaluated as an Il-2 successor the generally similar Il-8 with the 1491-kW (2,000-hp) AM-42 inline, four wing cannon and provision for 1000kg (2,205lb) of bombs but then opted for the altogether superior Il-10 that entered combat in February 1945. This retained a distinct family likeness to the Il-2 but was somewhat smaller, considerably more agile and fitted for an alternative wing armament of four cannon at the expense of slightly reduced bombload. Production amounted to some 6,960 aircraft including post-war production in the USSR and Czechoslovakia, the latter's version being the Avia B.33. Post-war developments were the Il-10M with a redesigned and more angular wing, a modified tailplane and other improvements.

Douglas A-20 Boston

Although the USSR is generally reluctant to admit the fact, its use of Lend-Lease aircraft supplied by the USA and to a lesser extent by the UK played a significant part in Soviet air operations during World War II. Typical of the aircraft supplied is the Boston and Havoc series, of whose total production nearly half was delivered to the USSR: the USA reserved some 3,125 DB-7B, DB-73, DB-7C, A-20B, A-20C, A-20G, A-20H and A-20K aircraft for the USSR, and of these 2,901 were accepted. The Soviets fully appreciated the basic type's performance and tricycle landing gear but were less impressed by the defensive armament, not infrequently adding a dorsal turret with a 12.7-mm (0.5-in) machine-gun in place of the manually operated guns of early aircraft. The aircraft were used for tactical support and anti-shipping strike along the full length of the Eastern Front.

Specification: Douglas A-20G Havoc three-seat light bomber and tactical support aeroplane
Span: 18.69m (61ft 4in)
Length: 14.63m (48ft 0in)
Powerplant: 2×Wright R-2600-63, 1193kW (1,600hp) each
Armament: up to 11×12.7-mm (0.5-in) machine-guns plus provision for up to 1814kg (4,000lb) of bombs carried internally
Max T/O weight: 12338kg (27,200lb)
Max speed: 339 mph at 12,400ft
Operational range: 1,090 miles

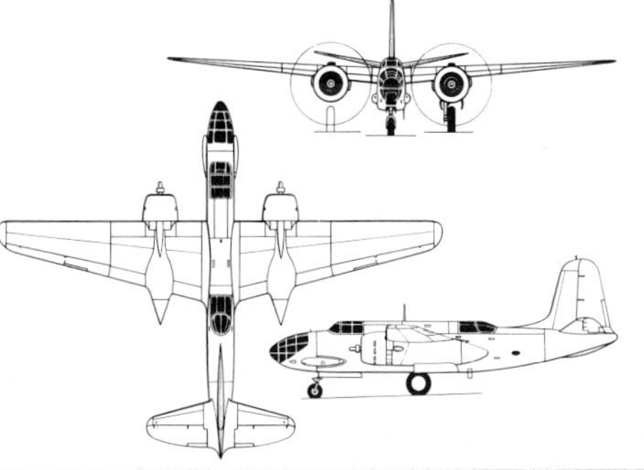

North American B-25 Mitchell

Though delivered in considerably smaller numbers (862 aircraft of the B-25B, B-25D, B-25G and B-25J variants), the Mitchell was nonetheless a welcome addition to the tactical air strength of the USSR and saw extensive and valuable service from the epic Battle of Stalingrad to the final Battle of Berlin. As with the Boston/Havoc series, the Soviets appreciated the performance and tricycle landing gear of the Mitchell, but also approved more strongly of the diverse offensive armament options combined with a more potent defensive arrangement. Both the Havoc and the Mitchell included in their gun armaments provision for heavy machine-guns in blistered fairings on the side of the forward fuselage, and this feature was particularly favoured by the Soviets, whose tactics included a close approach to a target suppressed by machine-gun fire before the bombs were released.

Specification: North American B-25J Mitchell five-seat medium bomber and ground-attack aeroplane
Span: 20.60m (67ft 7in)
Length: 15.54m (51ft 0in)
Powerplant: 2×Wright R-2600-13, 1267.5kW (1,700hp) each
Armament: up to 18×12.7-mm (0.5-in) machine-guns plus provision for 1452kg (3,200lb) of bombs or 1×907-kg (2,000-lb) torpedo carried internally and 8×127-mm (5-in) rockets carried under the wings
Max T/O weight: 16351kg (36,047lb)
Max speed: 275 mph at 13,000ft
Operational range: 1,350 miles

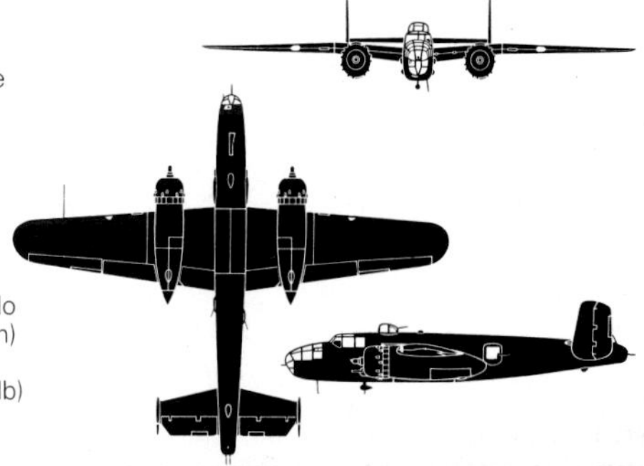

Petlyakov Pe-2

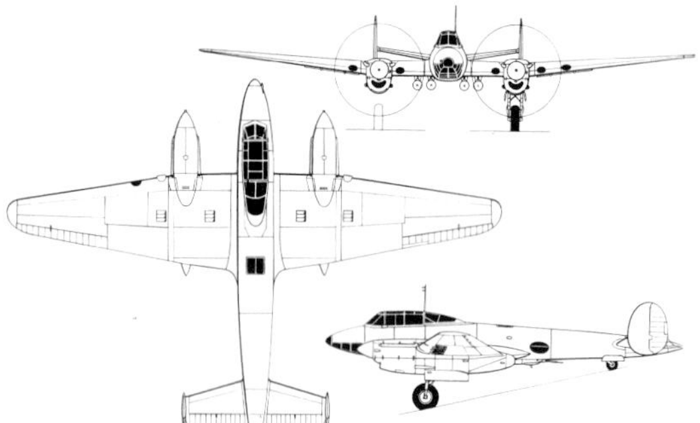

Petlyakov Pe-8

The Pe-8 was the most important Soviet heavy bomber of World War II, but production was a mere 81 aircraft because of the USSR's overwhelming industrial and operational emphasis on tactical air operations. The type first flew as the ANT-42 and was eventually fitted with a supercharging system in which the air flow for all four 820-kW (1,100-hp) M-105 engines was handled by a fuselage-mounted supercharger powered by its own M-100 engine. Another interesting feature a turret in the lower rear of each inboard nacelle to provide lower-hemisphere protection. The initial Pe-8 production aircraft were similar to the ANT-42 apart from their AM-35A engines, but later aircraft switched to the Shvetsov ASh-82FN radial without the nacelle turrets, and some aircraft had Charomskii M-30B diesels. Only limited use was made of these potentially useful aircraft.

Specification: Petlyakov Pe-8 10-seat heavy bomber
Span: 39.94 m (131 ft 0.5 in)
Length: 22.47 m (73 ft 8.7 in)
Powerplant: 4×Mikulin AM-35A, 1007 kW (1,350 hp) each
Armament: 2×20-mm cannon, 2×12.7-mm (0.5-in) machine-guns and 2×7.62-mm (0.3-in) machine-guns plus provision for up to 4000 kg (8,818 lb) of bombs carried internally
Max T/O weight: 33325 kg (73,469 lb)
Max speed: 272 mph at 24,935 ft
Operational range: 2,920 miles

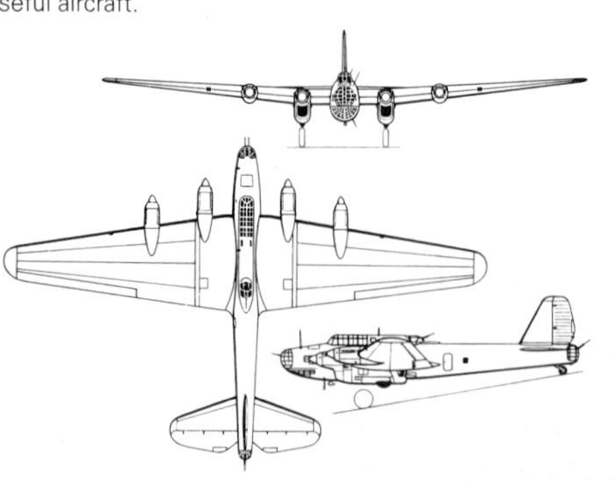

Polikarpov U-2

More than 40,000 examples of the U-2 and its variants were built, making this the world's most prolific aeroplane type ever, but the type still remains relatively little known even with its later designation Po-2. The U-2 was designed as a simple trainer with engines in the power range from 75 to 112 kW (100 to 150 hp) for civil and military operators, and first flew in February 1928. This sturdy biplane proved remarkably successful and adaptable, and a number of pre-war trainer, ambulance and light transport variants were produced. During World War II the U-2 was developed into the U-2VS night harassment or nuisance raider type to keep the Germans from resting, and proved so effective that the Germans adopted a similar concept using their own primary trainers. The U-2NAK was a night observation counterpart to the U-2VS.

Specification: Polikarpov U-2VS two/three-seat night harassment or nuisance raider aeroplane
Span: 11.40 m (37 ft 5 in)
Length: 8.15 m (26 ft 9 in)
Powerplant: 1×M-11, 75 kW (100 hp)
Armament: 1×7.62-mm (0.3-in) machine-gun plus provision for 250 kg (550 lb) or 82-mm (3.2-in) rockets carried under the wings
Max T/O weight: 1195 kg (2,634 lb)
Max speed: 93 mph at sea level
Operational range: 329 miles

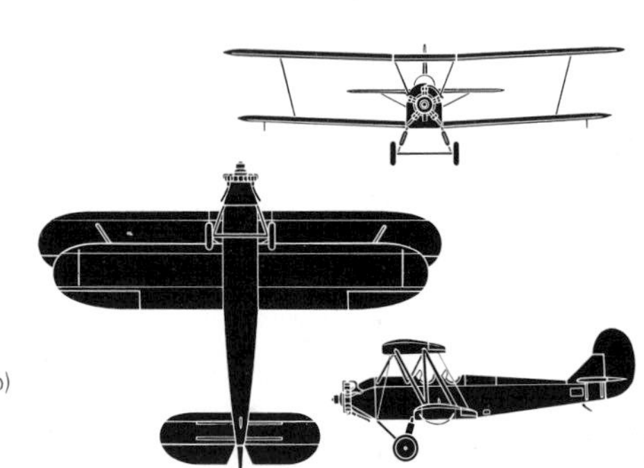

The Pe-2 was the USSR's counterpart to the British Mosquito and German Ju 88 as a multi-role type, but was conceived as a dive-bomber. Production amounted to 11,427 including two prototypes each of the VI-100 and PB-100 high-altitude bomber and dive-bomber versions with two 820-kW (1,100-hp) M-105R inlines. The Pe-2 was very similar to the PB-100 with its extensively glazed nose, dihedral tailplane and underwing dive-brakes, though later aircraft had 902-kW (1,210-hp) VK-105RF engines, a dorsal turret in the Pe-2FT version, and reduced nose glazing. Variants of this highly successful basic type included the Pe-2I (or Pe-2M) fighter-bomber with two 23-mm nose cannon and 1208-kW (1,620-hp) VK-107A engines in extended-span wings, the Pe-2R photo-reconnaissance variant with additional fuel, the Pe-2UT conversion trainer with tandem seating under a revised canopy, and the Pe-3 multi-role fighter.

Specification: Petlyakov Pe-2FT three/four-seat dive-bomber
Span: 17.16 m (56 ft 3.5 in)
Length: 12.66 m (41 ft 6.5 in)
Powerplant: 2×Klimov VK-105RF, 902 kW (1,210 hp) each
Armament: 2×7.62-mm (0.3-in) and 3×12.7-mm (0.5-in) machine-guns plus provision for up to 1200 kg (2,645 lb) of bombs carried internally and externally
Max T/O weight: 8520 kg (18,783 lb)
Max speed: 360 mph at 13,125 ft
Operational range: 817 miles

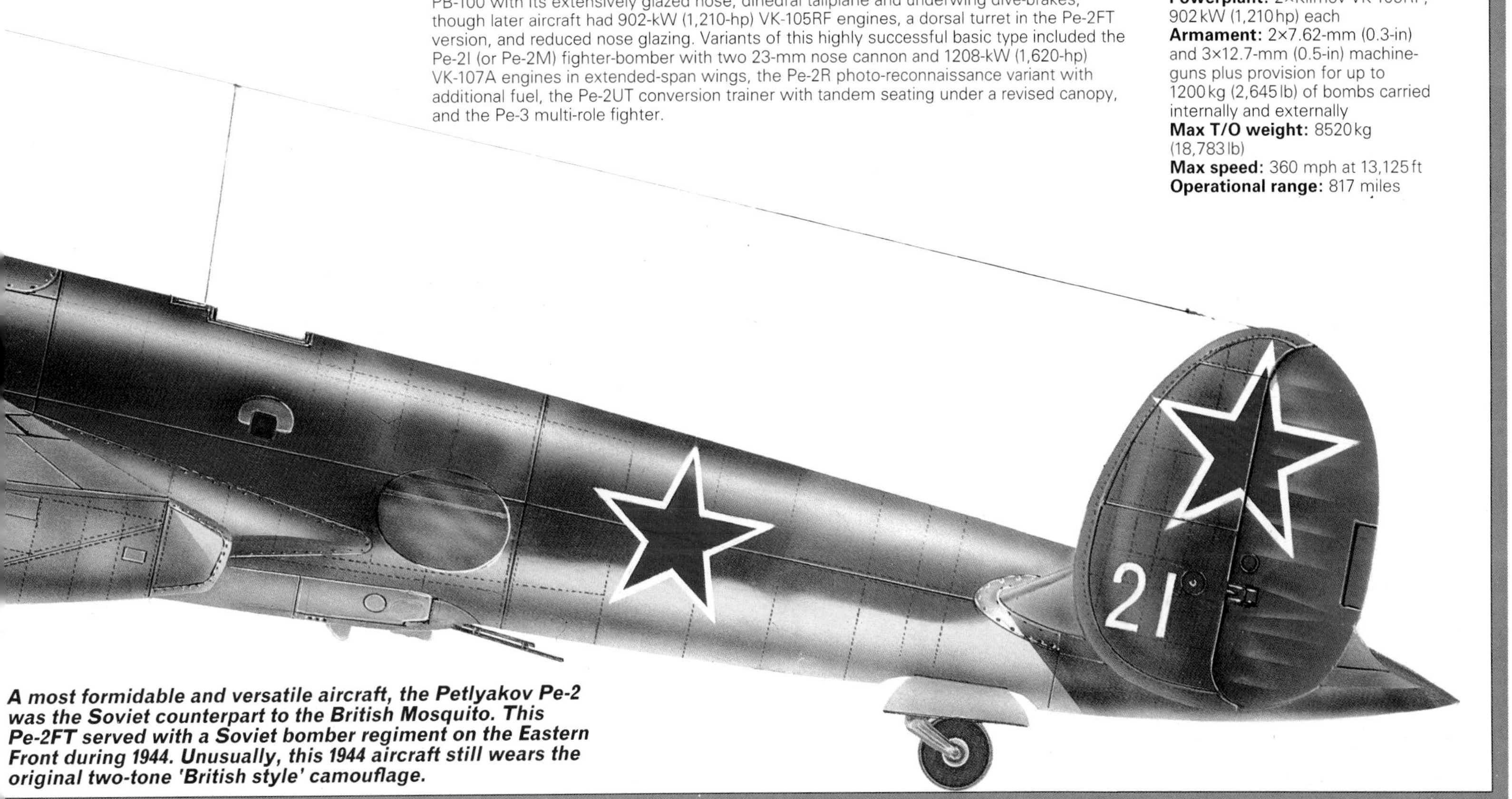

A most formidable and versatile aircraft, the Petlyakov Pe-2 was the Soviet counterpart to the British Mosquito. This Pe-2FT served with a Soviet bomber regiment on the Eastern Front during 1944. Unusually, this 1944 aircraft still wears the original two-tone 'British style' camouflage.

Sukhoi Su-2

The Su-2 was designed as a short-range bomber on the basis of the Tupolev ANT-51, and first flew during 1940 as the BB. Despite increased armour and armament, the extra power of the 708-kW (950-hp) M-87A, M-87B and M-88 radials used in the three prototypes secured better performance than had been possible with the ANT-51, and production was inaugurated of the BB-1 (later redesignated Su-2) with the 708-kW (950-hp) M-88 or 746-kW (1,000-hp) M-88B radial. The last production aircraft in a run of slightly more than 500 had the 1044-kW (1,400-hp) ASh-82, but even this considerable boost in power did little to improve performance to the level that could allow the Su-2 to cope with the attentions of German fighters, and losses were so severe that in 1942 the type was relegated to second-line tasks despite the USSR's immensely pressing need for combat aircraft.

Specification: Sukhoi Su-2 two-seat light reconnaissance bomber and ground-attack aeroplane
Span: 14.30 m (46 ft 11 in)
Length: 10.25 m (33 ft 7.5 in)
Powerplant: 1×M-88B, 746 kW (1,000 hp)
Armament: 5 or 6×7.62-mm (0.3-in) machine-guns plus provision for up to 600 kg (1,323 lb) of bombs carried internally and externally, or 10×82-mm (3.2-in) rockets or 8×132-mm (5.2-in) rockets carried under the wings
Max T/O weight: 4375 kg (9,645 lb)
Max speed: 286 mph at 16,405 ft
Operational range: 746 miles

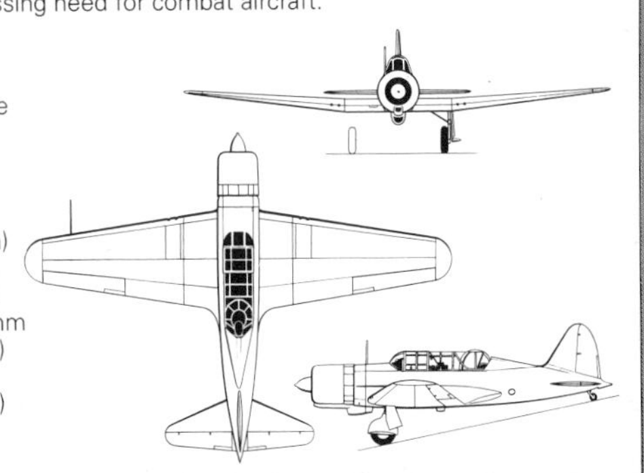

Sukhoi Su-6

The Su-6 was developed as Aeroplane 81 in competition with the Il-2, and emerged for its first flight in April 1941 as a large single-seater with the most powerful radial engine available. But with the single-seat Il-2 in production Sukhoi was instructed to develop the Su-6(A) concept into a two-seater, the Su-6(2A) with a dorsal gunner and heavier forward-firing armament in the form of two 37- rather than 23-mm cannon to provide an anti-tank capability. With its greater power, better protection and heavier armament the Su-6(2A) was deemed superior to the Il-2M3 but no serious consideration was given to disrupting the all-important Ilyushin production programme. Sukhoi's final effort to secure production was the Su-6(2A/M-42), a much revised variant with the 1491-kW (2,000-hp) Mikulin AM-42 inline and a revised wing, but this variant was deemed inferior to the Il-8 and Il-10.

Specification: Sukhoi Su-6(2A) two-seat ground-attack and anti-tank aeroplane
Span: 13.50 m (44 ft 3.5 in)
Length: 9.243 m (30 ft 4 in)
Powerplant: 1×Shvetsov ASh-71F, 1640 kW (2,200 hp)
Armament: 2×37-mm cannon, 1×12.7-mm (0.5-in) machine-gun and 2×7.62-mm (0.3-in) machine-guns plus provision for 400 kg (882 lb) of bombs carried internally or 10×82- or 132-mm (3.2- or 5.2-in) rockets carried under the wings
Max T/O weight: 5534 kg (12,200 lb)
Max speed: 319 mph at 8,200 ft
Operational range: 605 miles

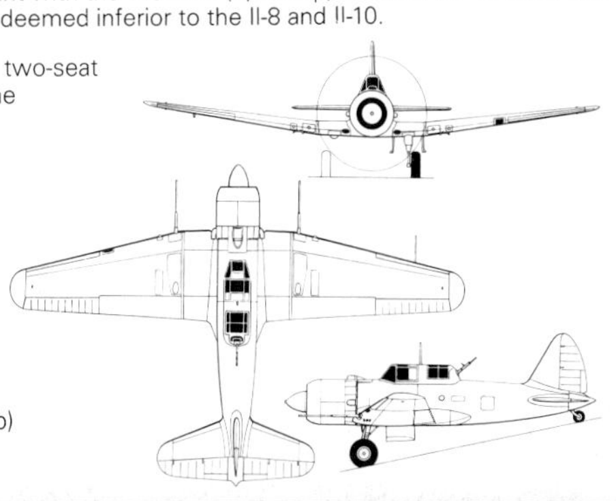

Dornier Do 217

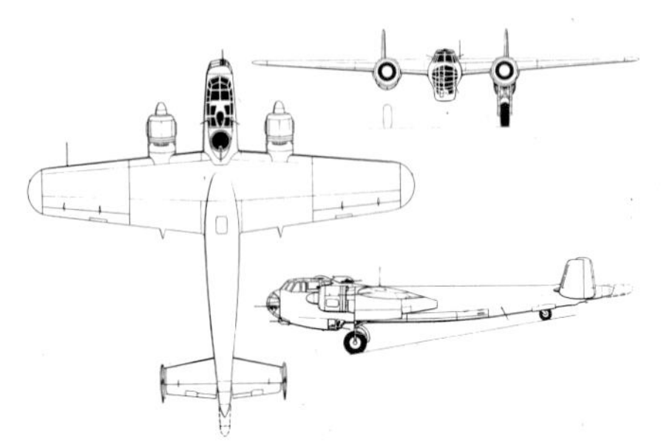

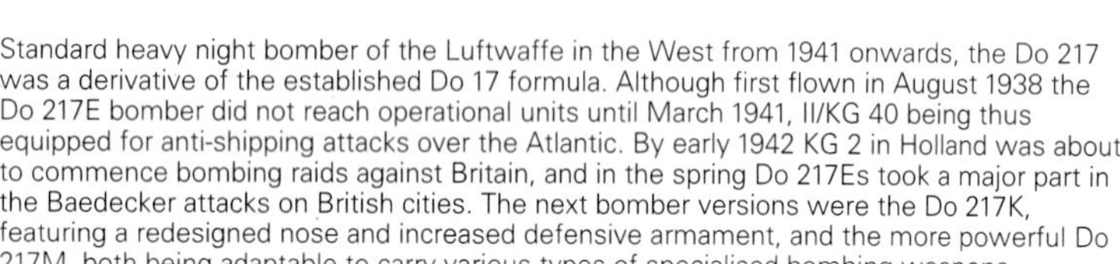

Standard heavy night bomber of the Luftwaffe in the West from 1941 onwards, the Do 217 was a derivative of the established Do 17 formula. Although first flown in August 1938 the Do 217E bomber did not reach operational units until March 1941, II/KG 40 being thus equipped for anti-shipping attacks over the Atlantic. By early 1942 KG 2 in Holland was about to commence bombing raids against Britain, and in the spring Do 217Es took a major part in the Baedecker attacks on British cities. The next bomber versions were the Do 217K, featuring a redesigned nose and increased defensive armament, and the more powerful Do 217M, both being adaptable to carry various types of specialised bombing weapons.

Arado Ar 234

A shoulder-wing twin-engine aircraft, the Ar 234 was the world's first jet bomber to achieve combat status. It was radical in many respects, being equipped with nosewheel landing gear – after early tests with a jettisonable three-wheel trolley had been discontinued – and a catapult ejector seat for the pilot. The Ar 234B-1 reconnaissance version carried up to four cameras and appeared in June 1944, followed by the Ar 234B-2 bomber, which equipped with three-axis autopilot and BZA bombing computer, could carry up to 2000 kg (4,410 lb) of bombs externally. The bomber started combat operations with elements of KG 76 during the Ardennes campaign of December 1944.

Specification: Arado Ar 234B-2 single-seat twin-jet bomber
Powerplant: two 890-kg (1,962-lb) thrust Junker Jumo 004B turbojets
Span: 14.10 m (46 ft 3½ in)
Length: 12.64 m (41 ft 5½ in)
Height: 4.30 m (14 ft 1½ in)
Wing area: 26.40 m² (284.18 sq ft)
Take-off weight: 9450 kg (20,833 lb)
Maximum speed: 740 km/h (460 mph)
Ceiling: 32,810 ft (10000 m)
Range: 1630 km (1,013 miles)
Armament: up to two 1000-kg (2,204 lb) bombs carried externally under engine nacelles

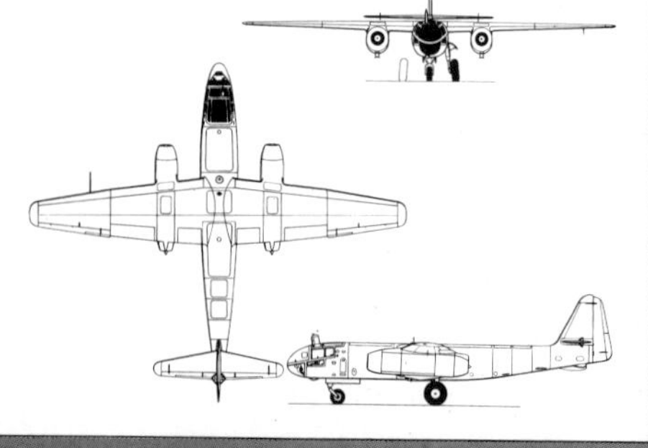

Dornier Do 17/Do 215

Most widely used German medium bomber at the outbreak of war, the Do 17 was a twin-engine shoulder-wing aircraft whose four-man crew was concentrated in the nose. The standard bomber version was the Do 17Z-2 which equipped four Kampfgeschwader and several other Kampfgruppen during the first year of the war, and saw widespread action during the Battles of France and Britain. It was of extremely clean design and possessed a moderately good performance on modest engine power, although by the end of 1940 it was outmoded, being withdrawn from service as a bomber to undertake other roles.

Specification: Dornier Do 17Z-2 twin-engined medium bomber with four-man crew
Powerplant: two 746-kW (1,000-hp) Bramo 323P radial engines
Span: 18.0 m (59 ft 0½ in)
Length: 15.79 m (51 ft 9½ in)
Height: 4.55 m (14 ft 11¼ in)
Wing area: 55.0 m² (592.0 sq ft)
Take-off weight: 8590 kg (18,940 lb)
Maximum speed: 345 km/h (214 mph)
Ceiling: 26,904 ft (8200 m)
Range: 1160 km (721 miles)
Armament: bomb load of up to 1000 kg (2,205 lb) and up to eight 7.9-mm (0.31-inch) machine-guns

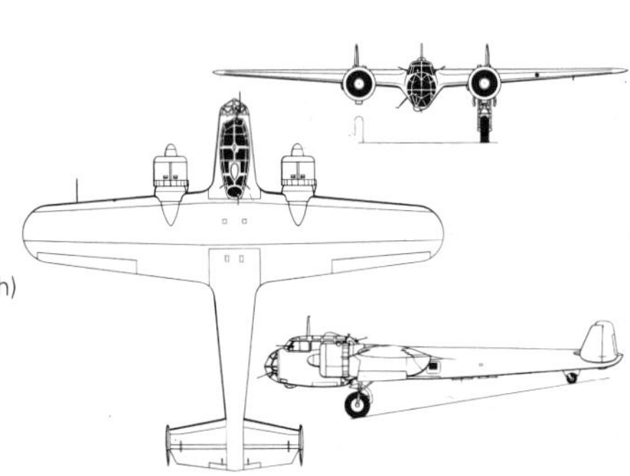

Specification: Dornier Do 217E-2 four-crew heavy bomber
Powerplant: 1179-kW (1,580-hp) BMW 801ML 14-cylinder radials
Span: 19.0 m (62 ft 4 in)
Length: 18.2 m (59 ft 8½ in)
Height: 5.03 m (16 ft 6 in)
Wing area: 57.0 m² (613.5 sq ft)
Take-off weight: 15000 kg (33,070 lb)
Maximum speed: 515 km/h (320 mph)
Ceiling: 29,530 ft (9000 m)
Range: 2300 km (1,430 miles)
Armament: one 15-mm, two 13-mm and seven 7.9-mm machine-guns, and up to 4000 kg (8,818 lb) of bombs carried internally and externally

This Dornier Do-217 E-4/R-19 bears the markings of the 9/KG 2, a bomber unit based in Sösterburg and Schiphol in the late summer of 1942. The KG 2 was one of the few bomber units still in the West – the majority had already been transferred to other operational sites. The model shown here was one of the first of the unit's three planes to have an MG-81Z machine-gun built into the rear tail section.

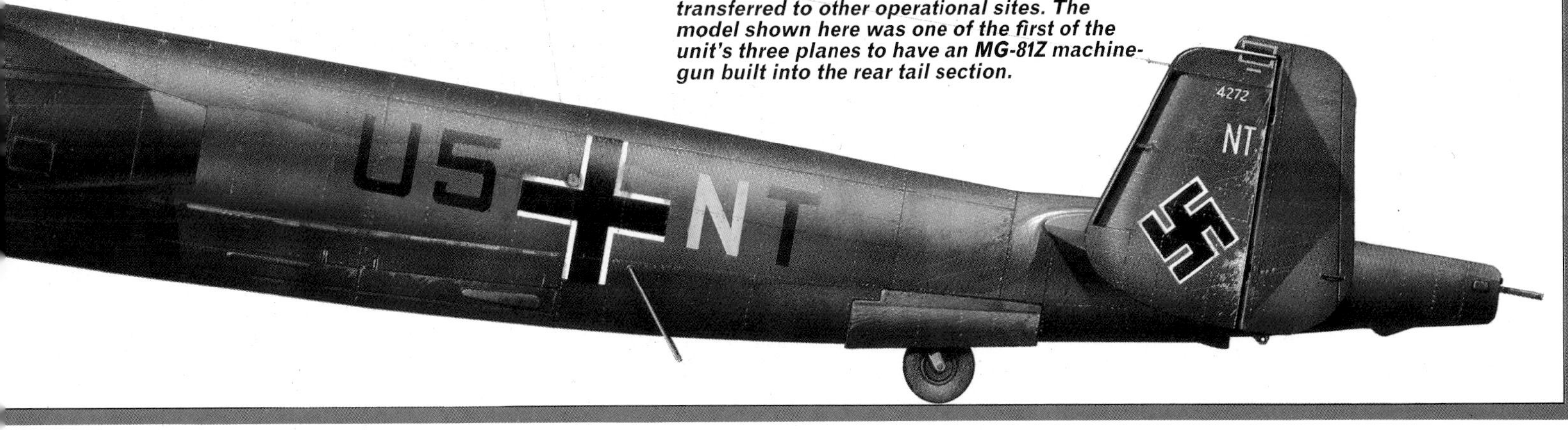

Dornier Do 317

Ultimate derivative of the Do 17 design, the Do 317 was intended to meet a requirement for an advanced high-speed high altitude heavy bomber capable of attacking any part of the British Isles from French bases, and to employ two 1984-kW (2,660-hp) 24-cylinder DB604 engines. Temporarily shelved in 1940, one pressurised prototype Do 317V1 was completed, characterised by unusual triangular fins and rudders. Five subsequent prototypes were completed under the designation Do 217R without pressurisation and came to be used operationally by III/KG 40 late in 1944, each aircraft carrying a single Hs 293 rocket-propelled, radio-controlled winged bomb. No subsequent production was undertaken.

Specification: Dornier Do 317B (projected) four-crew high altitude heavy bomber with pressure cabin
Powerplant: two 2074-kW (2,870-hp) DB610A/B 24-cylinder engines
Span: 26.0 m (85 ft 3½ in)
Length: 16.8 m (55 ft 1½ in)
Height: 5.45 m (17 ft 10½ in)
Take-off weight: 24020 kg (52,910 lb)
Maximum speed: 670 km/h (416 mph)
Ceiling: 34,500 ft (10510 m)
Range: 3600 km (2,237 miles)
Armament: one 20-mm, four 13-mm and two 7.9-mm guns, and up to 5605 kg (12,346 lb) of bombs internally and externally

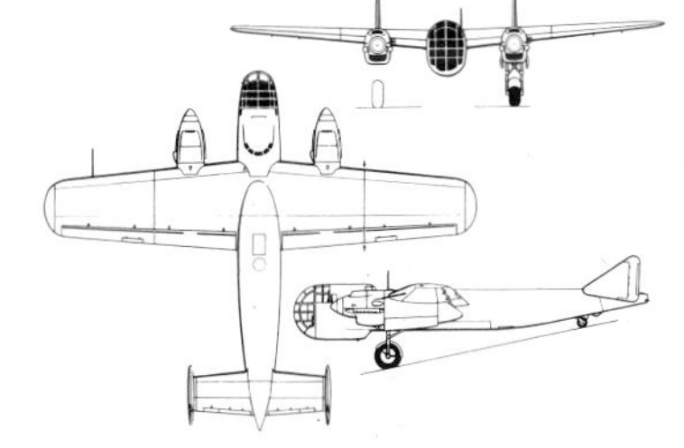

Focke-Wulf Fw 190G

Although conceived as a fast night-bomber capable of striking at fixed targets remote from the ground battle, the Fw 190G variant of the famous fighter first entered service as a ground support fighter-bomber in North Africa in February 1943, and soon after joined fast fighter-bomber Gruppen on the Eastern Front. Capable of carrying a single heavy bomb of 1800 kg (3,790 lb) under the fuselage, or up to six smaller fragmentation bombs under fuselage and wings, the G-1 and G-3 were used to telling effect against Allied aircraft, armour and infantry concentrations. Only in the final stages of the war were they flown in near-suicidal bombing attacks against such targets as headquarters and bridges.

Specification: Focke-Wulf Fw 190G-1 single-seat attack and ground-support fighter-bomber
Powerplant: one 1268-kW (1,700-hp) BMW 801D-2 14-cylinder radial
Span: 10.5 m (34 ft 5½ in)
Length: 8.84 m (29 ft 0 in)
Height: 3.96 m (13 ft 0 in)
Wing area: 18.3 m² (197 sq ft)
Maximum weight: 6630 kg (14,600 lb)
Ceiling: 36,100 ft (11000 m)
Range: 805 km (500 miles)
Armament: two 20-mm cannon and up to 1800 kg (3,790 lb) of bombs under fuselage and/or wings

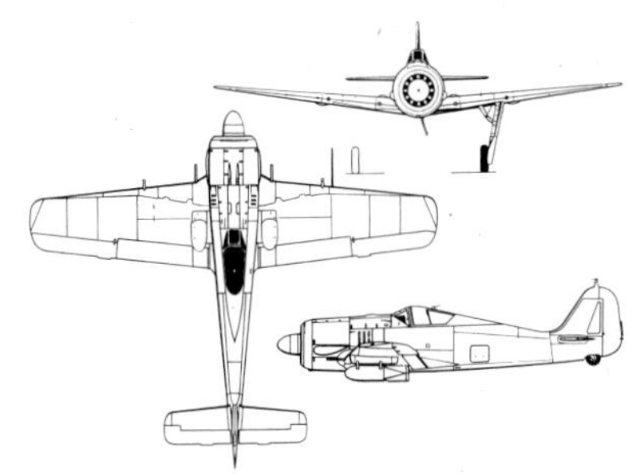

Heinkel He 111

A Heinkel He 111P-2 from the 55th Bomber Wing, which was stationed at Villacoublay in the autumn of 1940 for night raids on British towns. Its unit markings and trim markings were blacked ou with a temporary night camouflage. Over 7,300 of these bombers were built during World War II.

Operationally tested in the Spanish Civil War, the He 111 was the best of Germany's heavy bombers in the first half of World War II. Standard wartime version was the He 111H, which eventually equipped 13 bomber Geschwader and six other bomber Gruppen. Also widely used as a pathfinder with special radio aids and for shipping attacks, He 111s served on every wartime front from the Arctic to Africa and from the Atlantic to Iraq. Of robust low-wing layout, He 111s carried torpedoes, Hs 293 missiles, V-1 flying bombs and, after German abandoning of strategic bombing, the aircraft was used as a transport and glider tug. The He 111Z was a five-engine "twin He 111H" glider tug development.

Heinkel He 177

A belated attempt to introduce a realistic four-engine strategic bomber, the He 177 was a large aircraft employing twin coupled engines in two nacelles, and first joined operational Luftwaffe units in mid-1942. With a large bomb bay and high-aspect ratio wing, the He 177A was a good weightlifter but suffered constant mechanical and structural problems and seldom engaged in true strategic raids in the West, being mainly used in shipping attacks, though KG 1 flew 87 He 177s in a memorable raid on Velikye Luki in the East in mid-1944. He 177 operations petered out owing to the Luftwaffe's lack of fuel; one aircraft was however being modified to carry Germany's atomic bomb at the end of the war.

Specification: Heinkel He 177A-1/R1 Greif five-crew heavy bomber
Powerplant: two 2010-kW, 2,700-hp DB606 (four DB601) 24-cylinder inline engine in annular cowlings
Span: 31.43 m (103 ft 1½ in)
Length: 20.04 m (66 ft 11 in)
height: 6.39 m (20 ft 11½ in)
Wing area: 510 m² (1,098 sq ft)
Take-off weight: 30000 kg (66,140 lb)
Maximum speed: 510 km/h (317 mph)
Ceiling: 22,966 ft (7000 m)
Range: 3200 km (1,990 miles)
Armament: one 20-mm, two 13-mm and three 7.9-mm guns; up to 5600 kg (12,346 lb) of bombs (short range)

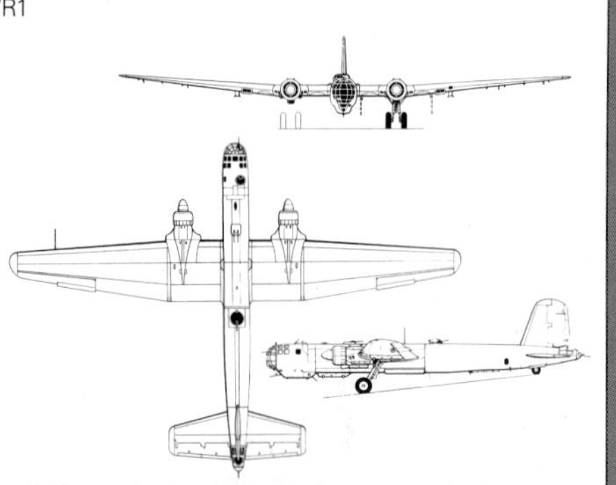

Heinkel He 274

During investigations to eradicate engine problems on the He 177, Heinkel tendered proposals for a bomber with four separate engines, an enlarged wing and twin fins and rudders, but employing the He 177's fuselage. This, the He 274, commenced manufacture at Suresnes, France, in 1943 but the prototype He 274V1, though almost complete, had not flown when the Allies captured the factory in 1944. German attempts to destroy it were only partly successful and the French later repaired it and re-designated it the AAS 01A, and it was eventually flown. No German efforts were made to continue with the bomber, which would have been able to deliver a worthwhile bombload from the tropopause.

Specification: Heinkel He 274A (projected) four-crew high-altitude heavy bomber
Powerplant: four turbocharged 1380-kW (1,850-hp) DB603A-2 engines
Span: 44.2 m (145 ft 0 in)
Length: 23.8 m (78 ft 1½ in)
Height: 5.5 m (18 ft 0½ in)
Wing area: 170.0 m² (1,830 sq ft)
Maximum weight: 38045 kg (83,800 lb)
Maximum speed: 580 km/h (360 mph)
Ceiling: 46,920 ft (14300 m)
Range: 2850 km (1,770 miles)
Armament: five 13-mm machine-guns and maximum bomb load of 4000 kg (8,820 lb) carried internally

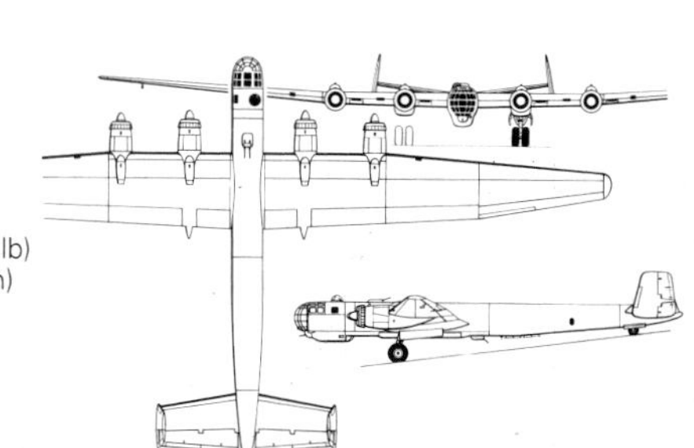

Specification: Heinkel He 111H-16 five-crew heavy bomber
Powerplant: two 1007 kg (1,350-hp) Jumo 211F-2 inline engines
Span: 22.6 m (74 ft 1½ in)
Length: 16.4 m (53 ft 9 in)
Height: 4.0 m (13 ft 1½ in)
Take-off weight: 14000 kg (30,865 lb)
Maximum speed: 435 km/h (270 mph)
Ceiling: 27,800 ft (8500 m
Range: 1960 km (1,210 miles)
Armament: one 20-mm, two 13-mm and four 7.9-mm guns; up to 2500 kg (5,510 lb) of bombs, or one 2180-kg (4,796-lb) FZG-76 (V1) flying bomb, one Hs 293 or two torpedoes

Heinkel He 277

An aircraft of much closer similarity to the basic but troublesome He 177 was the He 277, which featured four separate DB603 engines but retained the same wing, fuselage and tail of the earlier design. Although Goering forbade Heinkel from pursuing the He 277 it was Hitler who demanded an aircraft capable of flying heavy raids on Britain and insisted on all-out work on the aircraft. The prototype He 277V1 first flew late in 1943 and was followed by nine other aircraft, the He 277V2 and eight production He 277B-5/R2, all of which featured twin fins and rudders. More powerful versions were proposed but the entire programme was abandoned in 1944 when Germany switched almost all aircraft output to fighters.

Specification: Heinkel He 277B-5/R-2 seven-crew heavy bomber
Powerplant: four 1380-kW (1,850-hp) DB603A 12-cylinder engines
Span: 31.43 m (103 ft 1½ in)
Length: 22.15 m (72 ft 8 in)
Height: 6.67 m (21 ft 10½ in)
Wing area: 100.0 m² (1,076 sq ft)
Maximum weight: 44490 kg (98,105 lb)
Maximum speed: 570 km/h (354 mph)
Ceiling: 49,210 ft (15000 m)
Maximum range: 6000 km (3,728 miles)
Armament: one 20-mm, two 13-mm and eight 7.9-mm guns, and bombload of up to 4500 kg (9,900 lb)

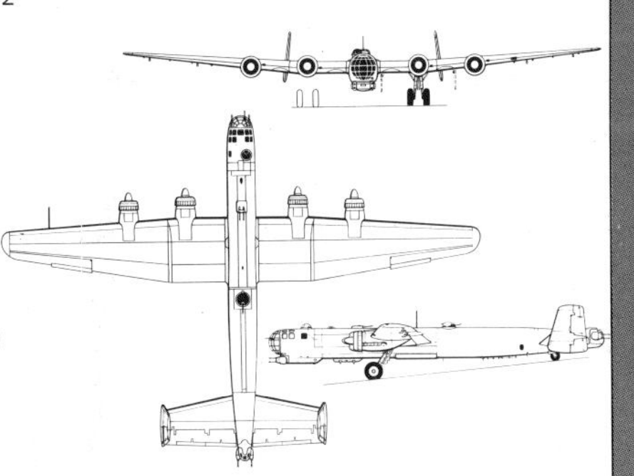

Junkers Ju 87

Forever remembered as a component of Hitler's Blitzkrieg, the crank-winged Ju 87 served its apprenticeship in Spain before equipping the Luftwaffe's *Stukaverband*, ultimately joining a total of some 20 dive-bomber Gruppen on every front of the European war. Early wartime versions were the Ju 87B and the long-range Ju 87R, capable of carrying a 1000-kg (2,200-lb) bomb; these were followed by the Ju 87D with improved Jumo 211J engine and improved armour and armament. The specialist Ju 87G anti-tank aircraft was armed with a pair of underwing 40-mm guns. The Ju 87 dive bomber was a precise weapon when used against shipping, airfield and factories, but was extremely vulnerable to fighter attack.

Specification: Junkers Ju 87B-2 two-crew dive-bomber
Powerplant: one 746-kW (1,000-hp) Junkers Jumo 211A in-line engine
Span: 13.8 m (45 ft 3½ in)
Length: 10.8 m (35 ft 5½ in)
Height: 3.9 m (12 ft 9½ in)
Wing area: 31.9 m² (343 sq ft)
Take-off weight: 4250 kg (9,321 lb)
Maximum speed: 380 km/h (237 mph)
Ceiling: 26,248 ft (8000 m)
Range: 600 km (372 miles)
Armament: one or two 7.9-mm machine-guns in rear cockpit, and a single bomb of up to 1000 kg or one 500-kg bomb and light underwing bombs

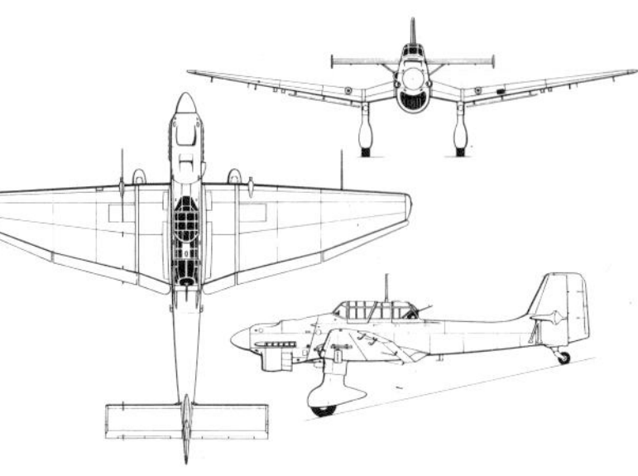

Junkers Ju 88

Employed in many roles, the Ju 88 entered service with the Luftwaffe in 1939 and remained in the front line until VE-day. A mid-wing all-metal aircraft, it was fast, manoeuvrable and popular among its crews, being employed both as a dive bomber and a level medium bomber capable of carrying a useful bomb load. It fought throughout the battles of conquest in 1939 and 1940, and was widely used in the Battle of Britain, the Balkans, Mediterranean and on the Eastern Front. The basic bomber was the Ju 88A (including anti-shipping variants), and culminated in the fast Ju 88S which had a top speed of 615 km/h (382 mph). Redundant Ju 88s became the lower components of the Mistel composite weapon.

Specification: Junkers Ju 88A-4 four-crew dive or level medium bomber
Powerplant: two 1000-kW (1,340-hp) Junkers Jumo 211J-1 engines
Span: 20.0 m (65 ft 7½ in)
Length: 14.4 m (47 ft 2½ in)
Height: 4.85 m (15 ft 11 in)
Wing area: 54.5 m² (587 sq ft)
Maxiumum weight: 14000 kg (30,870 lb)
Maximum speed: 470 km/h (280 mph)
Ceiling: 26,900 ft (8200 m)
Maximum range: 2730 km (1,696 miles)
Armament: up to seven 7.9-mm machine-guns and bomb load of up to four 500-kg (1,100-lb) bombs

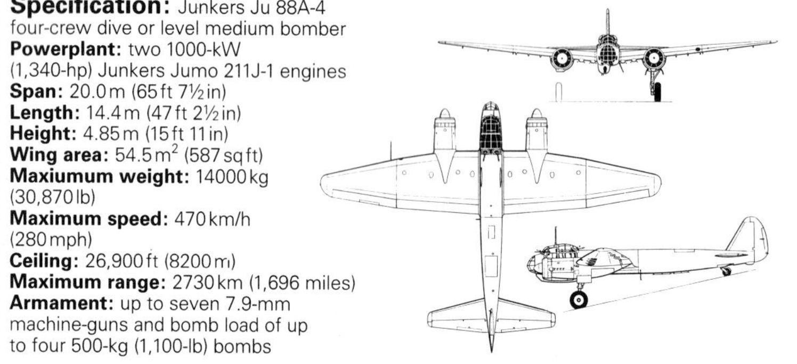

Junkers Ju 188

A straightforward development of the Ju 88E, with enlarged wings and vertical tail, improved crew accommodation and more powerful engines, the Ju 188E joined the German night bomber force in the summer of 1943. With bomb capacity increased to 3000 kg (6,615 lb) and improved defensive armament, this version proved a highly efficient bomber and a redoubtable opponent. Reconnaissance sub-variants were the 188D, F and H, and during 1944 the A, E, G and S bombers were fairly widely used, the G being capable of lifting 3300 kg (7,275 lb) of bombs, and the unarmed S, with GM-1 nitrous oxide injection, possessing a top speed of 686 km/h (426 mph) – at least comparable with the fastest Mosquito.

Specification: Junkers Ju 188E-1 four-crew fast medium bomber
Powerplant: 1194-kW (1,600-hp) BMW 801ML air-cooled radials
Span: 22.0 m (72 ft 2 in)
Length: 14.95 m (48 ft 0½ in)
Height: 4.44 m (14 ft 6½ in)
Wing area: 56.0 m² (603 sq ft)
Take-off weight: 15508 kg (31,989 lb)
Maximum speed: 500 km/h (310 mph)
Ceiling: 30,513 ft (9300 m)
Range: 1950 km (1,210 miles)
Armament: one 20-mm, one 13-mm and up to four 7.9-mm guns, and bombs or torpedoes up to 3000 kg (6,615 lb) weight

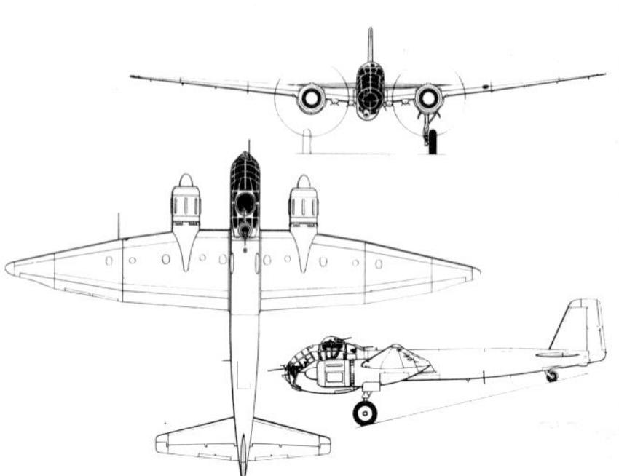

Junkers Ju 288

Intended as a replacement for the Ju 88, the radical Ju 288 was a completely new design with 1194-kW (1,600-hp) BMW 801MA radials and twin vertical tail surfaces and twin mainwheel landing gear, being flown in prototype form in January 1941. Originally planned to carry a 5000-kg (11,025-lb) bomb load, this had to be considerably reduced following handling problems. Progressively more powerful engines were flown as well as remotely-located gun armament. When many of Germany's bombers (including the Ju 288) were cancelled in 1943, the Ju 288 was pursued in the ground attack role using such huge single-shot guns as the 35.56-cm Gerat 104 Munchhausen weapon, but production was not achieved.

Specification: Junkers Ju 288C-1 (projected) four-crew high-speed medium bomber
Powerplant: two 2200-kW (2,950-hp) DB610 24-cylinder engines
Span: 22.66 m (74 ft 4 in)
Length: 18.15 m (59 ft 6½ in)
Wing area: 65.0 m² (700 sq ft)
Take-off weight: 21390 kg (47,165 lb)
Maximum speed: 655 km/h (407 mph)
Ceiling: 34,110 ft (10400 m)
Range: 2600km (1,615 miles)
Armament: three or five 15-mm guns in nose, dorsal and tail barbettes, and up to three 1000-kg (2,200-lb) bombs stowed internally

Messerschmitt Me 264

The four-engine Me 264 was conceived in 1941 as a transatlantic bomber to be based in France and capable of bombing America's east coast cities. Of clean, shoulder-wing configuration the prototype flew in December 1942, production examples being intended to be capable of carrying up to 3000 kg (6,615 lb) of bombs on a 45-hour flight, for which 25250 litres (5,555 Imp gal) of fuel and six assisted take-off rockets would be required. When America entered the war the bomber requirement was advanced beyond the Me 264's capabilities and the six-engine Me 264B, as well as the Ju 390 and Ta 400, came to be developed. Only the Ju 390 ever made a test flight which took it close to the American coast.

Specification: Messerschmitt Me 264A (V3) six-crew, long-range bomber-reconnaissance aircraft
Powerplant: four 1268-kW (1,700-hp) BMW 801G 14-cylinder radials
Span: 43.0 m (141 ft 3 in)
Length: 20.9 m (68 ft 7 in)
Height: 6.78 m (22 ft 3 in)
Wing area: 127.7 m² (1,370 sq ft)
Take-off weight: 45540 kg (100,416 lb)
Maximum speed: 470 km/h (292 mph)
Ceiling: 8000 m (26,240 ft)
Range: 15,000 km (9,325 miles)
Armament: up to 3000 kg (6,615 lb) of bombs and two 20-mm cannon and four 13-mm machine-guns

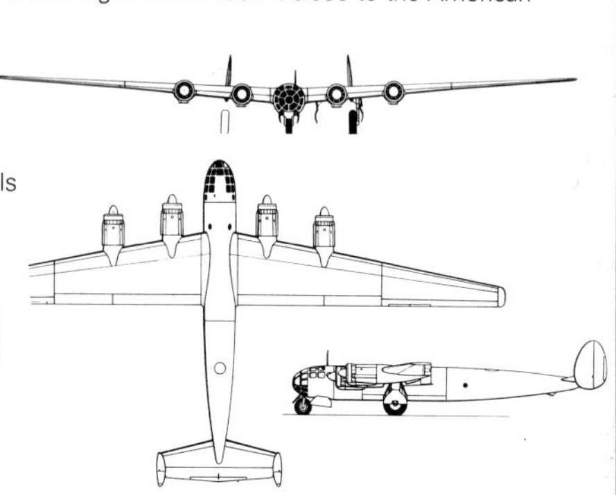

Martin Baltimore

The Baltimore was developed from the Maryland to a specifically British requirement, and when it first flew in June 1941 had greater power for higher performance and a deepened fuselage allowing crew members to change places in flight. The type began to enter service in January 1942, and was used only in the Mediterranean theatre. Baltimore Mk I and Mk II production totalled 50 and 100 respectively, these variants having single or twin Vickers 'K' guns in the dorsal position. The 250 Baltimore Mk IIIs had a two- or four-gun dorsal turret. Further aircraft were Lend-Lease aircraft, and included 281 Baltimore Mk IIIAs with two 12.7-mm (0.5-in) guns in the dorsal turret, 294 generally similar Baltimore Mk IVs, and 600 Baltimore Mk Vs with more power and 12.7-mm (0.5-in) wing guns in place of the 7.7-mm (0.303-in) weapons of earlier models.

Specification: Martin Baltimore Mk III four-seat light bomber
Span: 18.69 m (61 ft 4 in)
Length: 14.77 m (48 ft 5.75 in)
Powerplant: 2×Wright R-2600-19, 1238 kW (1,660 hp) each
Armament: 8 or 10×0.303-in (7.7-mm) machine-guns in a four-gun fixed wing installation, two- or four-gun dorsal turret and two-gun ventral position, plus provision for up to 907 kg (2,000 lb) of bombs carried internally
Max T/O weight: 10433 kg (23,000 lb)
Max speed: 302 mph at 11,000 ft
Operational range: 950 miles

Martin Marauder

Though very widely employed by the USAAF, the B-26 Marauder medium bomber was not widely employed by the RAF, five Mediterranean squadrons being equipped with the type from August 1942. The first model used by the RAF was the Marauder Mk I, and these 77 aircraft were Lend-Lease B-26As with the original 19.81-m (65-ft) span wings. Then came the Marauder Mk IA, these 19 aircraft being equivalent to the USAAF's B-26B with greater power and used by a Bahamas-based operational conversion unit. Subsequent deliveries included 100 Marauder Mk IIs (B-26Cs with longer-span wings) and 350 Marauder Mk IIIs (200 B-26Fs with greater wing incidence and 150 B-26Gs with different equipment). Many of these British aircraft were passed on to the South African Air Force, which deployed five squadrons with this type in the Mediterranean and Italy.

Specification: Martin Marauder Mk III five-seat medium bomber
Span: 21.64 m (71 ft 0 in)
Length: 17.53 m (57 ft 6 in)
Powerplant: 2×Pratt & Whitney R-2800-43, 1491 kW (2,000 hp) each
Armament: 11×12.7-mm (0.5-in) machine-guns in nose installation (four fixed and one trainable), twin-gun dorsal and tail turrets, and single-gun waist positions, plus provision for up to 1814 kg (4,000 lb) of bombs carried internally
Max T/O weight: 17328 kg (38,200 lb)
Max speed: 305 mph at 15,000 ft
Operational range: 1,200 miles

Short Stirling

The Stirling was the RAF's first four-engined heavy bomber of World War II, and resulted from a 1936 requirement. Though in many respects a good aeroplane, the Stirling was operationally hampered in speed, ceiling and payload by its small wing, whose span had been dictated by the maximum opening of RAF hangars at the time the design was being planned. The first Stirling flew in May 1939, and the type began to enter service in August 1940. The 756 Stirling Mk Is had 1189-kW (1,595-hp) Hercules XI radials, the two experimental Stirling Mk IIs had 1193-kW (1,600-hp) Wright R-2600 Cyclones, and the 875 Stirling Mk IIIs featured increased power and a revised dorsal turret. The Stirling was used as a bomber between February 1942 and September 1944, but from late 1943 was usefully developed as a glider tug and paratroop transport.

Specification: Short Stirling Mk III seven/eight-seat heavy night bomber
Span: 30.20 m (99 ft 1 in)
Length: 26.50 m (87 ft 3 in)
Powerplant: 4×Bristol Hercules XVI, 1230 kW (1,650 hp) each
Armament: 8×0.303-in (7.7-mm) machine-guns in twin-gun nose and dorsal turrets, and four-gun tail turret, plus provision for up to 6350 kg (14,000 lb) of bombs carried internally
Max T/O weight: 31790 kg (70,000 lb)
Max speed: 270 mph at 14,500 ft
Operational range: 2,010 miles with 1588-kg (3,500-lb) bombload

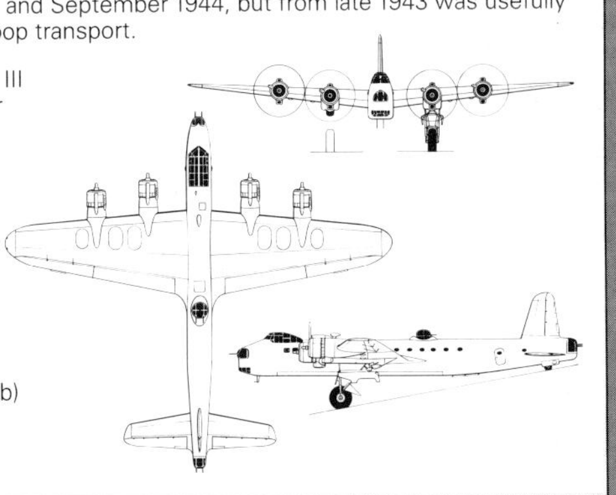

Vickers Wellington

The RAF's most successful twin-engined bomber of World War II, the Wellington bore the main weight of the night bomber offensive until the advent of the four-engined bombers. The type resulted from a 1932 specification, was designed for Vickers geodetic construction, first flew in June 1936 and entered service in 1938. The 181 Wellington Mk Is were followed by 187 Wellington Mk IAs with revised nose and tail turrets, and by 2,685 Wellington Mk ICs with the ventral turret replaced by beam guns. The 401 Wellington Mk IIs had 854-kW (1,145-hp) Merlin X inlines, and the next model was the Wellington Mk III, of which 1,519 were built with four-gun tail turrets and Bristol Hercules III or XI radials. The 220 Wellington Mk IVs had two 783-kW (1,050-hp) Pratt & Whitney Wasp radials, while the 64 high-altitude Wellington Mk VIs had 1193-kW (1,600-hp) Merlin 60s or 62s.

Specification: Vickers Wellington Mk IC five/six-seat medium bomber
Span: 26.26 m (86 ft 2 in)
Length: 19.68 m (64 ft 7 in)
Powerplant: 2×Bristol Pegasus XVIII, 746 kW (1,000 hp) each
Armament: 6×0.303-in (7.7-mm) machine-guns in twin-gun nose and tail turrets, and single-gun beam positions, plus provision for up to 2041 kg (4,500 lb) of bombs carried internally
Max T/O weight: 12928 kg (28,500 lb)
Max speed: 235 mph at 15,500 ft
Operational range: 2,550 miles with 454-kg (1,000-lb) bombload

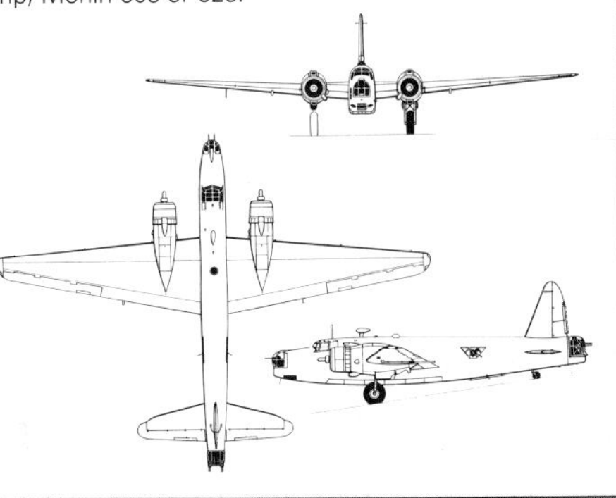

Avro Lancaster

The Lancaster is justly celebrated as the UK's most important heavy bomber of World War II. The type started life as the Manchester Mk III, a four-engined derivative of that unhappy bomber. Carrying the triple empennage of the Manchester, the Lancaster first flew in January 1941 and began to enter service early in 1942. Production of the Lancaster Mk I totalled 3,444, 33 of these being converted as Lancaster B.Mk I (Specials) with an enlarged bomb bay for the 9979-kg (22,000-lb) 'Grand Slam' bomb. The Lancaster B.Mk III was similar to the Mk I apart from its American-built Merlin engines, and 3,020 were built excluding the 430 similar Lancaster B.Mk Xs produced in Canada. Other variants were 300 Lancaster Mk IIs with Bristol Hercules VI or XVI radials, and 180 Lancaster B.Mk VII with a Martin dorsal turret carrying two 12.7-mm (0.5-in) guns.

Specification: Avro Lancaster Mk I seven-seat heavy night bomber
Span: 31.09 m (102 ft 0 in)
Length: 21.18 m (69 ft 6 in)
Powerplant: 4×Rolls-Royce Merlin 24, 1223 kW (1,640 hp) each
Armament: 8 or 10×0.303-in (7.7-mm) machine-guns in twin-gun nose, dorsal and eventually deleted ventral turrets, and four-gun tail turret, plus provision for up to 8185 kg (18,000 lb) of bombs carried internally
Max T/O weight: 31752 kg (70,000 lb)
Max speed: 287 mph at 11,500 ft
Operational range: 1,660 miles with 6350-kg (14,000-lb) bombload

Armstrong Whitworth Whitley

One of the three mainstays of RAF Bomber Command in 1939, the Whitley was designed to meet a 1934 specification and first flew in March 1936. The first 80 aircraft were delivered as 34 Whitley Mk Is with 593-kW (795-hp) Armstrong Siddeley Tiger IX radials and 46 Whitley Mk IIs with 686-kW (920-hp) Tiger VIIIs. There followed the Whitley Mk III (80 built) with powered nose turrets, a ventral 'dustbin' turret and revised bomb racks. The Whitley Mk IV introduced the Merlin inline and a power-operated tail turret: the 33 Mk IVs had two 768-kW (1,030-hp) Merlin IVs and the seven Mk IVAs two 854-kW (1,145-hp) Merlin Xs. The final bomber variant was the Whitley Mk V, of which 1,466 were built with a nose lengthened by 0.38 m (15 in) and straight leading edges to its fins. The Whitley was retired from Bomber Command in April 1942.

Specification: Armstrong Whitworth Whitley Mk V five-seat heavy night bomber
Span: 25.60 m (84 ft 0 in)
Length: 21.11 m (69 ft 3 in)
Powerplant: 2×Rolls-Royce Merlin X, 854 kW (1,145 hp) each
Armament: 5×0.303-in (7.7-mm) machine-guns in single-gun nose and four-gun tail turrets, plus provision for up to 3175 kg (7,000 lb) of bombs carried internally
Max T/O weight: 15196 kg (35,000 lb)
Max speed: 230 mph at 16,400 ft
Operational range: 1,650 miles with 1361-kg (3,000-lb) bombload

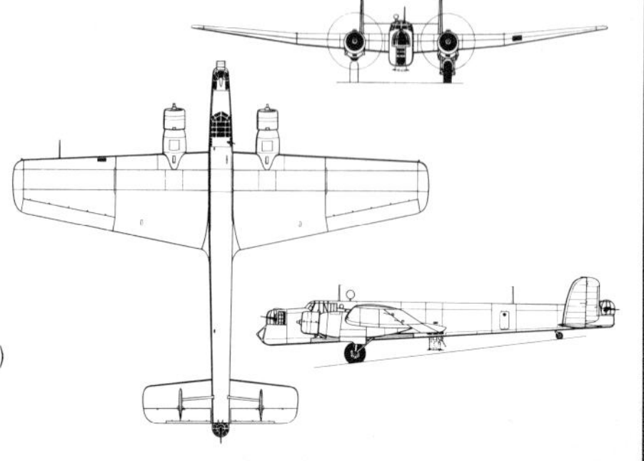

Avro Manchester

Though much had been expected of the Manchester, which resulted from a 1936 medium bomber requirement, the type proved a failure and thus a great disappointment in service. The fault lay not with the airframe, which went on to form the basis of the superlative Lancaster, but with an engine type that was rushed into service before all its problems had been eliminated. The Manchester first flew in July 1939 with endplate vertical tail surfaces, a distinctive third fin being added above the rear fuselage after flight trials. Only 20 of the initial Manchester Mk I were built before production switched to the Manchester Mk IA with larger endplate surfaces on a tailplane span increased from 6.71 to 10.06 m (22 to 33 ft). Total production amounted to 200 aircraft, and these served from November 1940 to mid-1942.

Specification: Avro Manchester Mk IA seven-seat medium night bomber
Span: 27.46 m (90 ft 1 in)
Length: 20.98 m (68 ft 10 in)
Powerplant: 2×Rolls-Royce Vulture I, 1312 kW (1,760 hp) each
Armament: 8×0.303-in (7.7-mm) machine-guns in twin-gun nose and ventral (later dorsal) turrets, and four-gun tail turret, plus provision for up to 4695 kg (10,350 lb) of bombs carried internally
Max T/O weight: 25402 kg (56,000 lb)
Max speed: 265 mph at 17,000 ft
Operational range: 1,630 miles with 3629-kg (8,000-lb) bombload

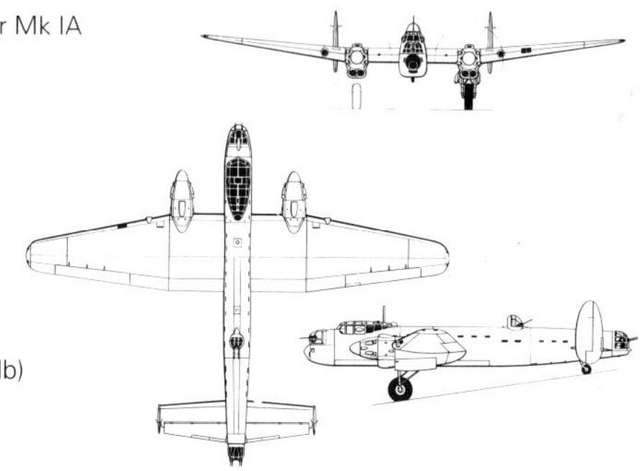

The Avro Lancaster was undoubtedly the RAF's greatest bomber of World War II, and by far the most important instrument of 'Bertie' Harris's policy of mass night attacks on German cities. This particular aircraft is a Lancaster I shown in the markings of No. 207 Sqn, although R5852 went on to serve later with No. 83 Sqn before being written off after overshooting a landing on 10 September 1942.

Boeing Fortress

First flown in April 1935 and the most famous of US bombers in World War II, the B-17 Flying Fortress was also used in limited numbers by the RAF. The designation Fortress Mk I was applied to 20 B-17Cs received in spring 1941, but for a variety of reasons (frozen guns, unserviceable bombsights, inadequate defensive armament etc) these were unsuccessful in their intended Northern European role as bombers and relegated, after a short tour in the Middle East, to the maritime reconnaissance role. Next came 19 Fortress Mk IIs and 45 Fortress Mk IIAs equivalent respectively to the B-17F and B-17E, and these served exclusively with Coastal Command. Finally there were 85 Fortress Mk IIIs equivalent to the B-17G, and though these served with Bomber Command it was with No.100 Group in the electronic countermeasures rather than bomber role.

Specification: Boeing Fortress Mk I 10-seat heavy day bomber
Span: 31.64 m (103 ft 9.5 in)
Length: 20.69 m (67 ft 10.5 in)
Powerplant: 4 x Wright R-1820-G205A, 895 kW (1,200 hp) each
Armament: 1×7.62-mm (0.3-in) machine-gun in nose and 6×12.7-mm (0.5-in) machine-guns in two-gun dorsal and ventral positions, and single-gun waist positions, plus provision for up to 4761 kg (10,496 lb) of bombs carried internally
Max T/O weight: 20625 kg (45,670 lb)
Max speed: 320 mph at 20,000 ft
Operational range: 2,400 miles with 1814-kg (4,000-lb) bombload

Bristol Blenheim

Developed from the Type 142 high-speed transport, the Blenheim first flew in June 1936 and was ordered into large-scale production. Some 1,365 Blenheim Mk Is were built, this variant having a short nose and 626-kW (840-hp) Mercury VIIIs. By 1939 the Mk Is had generally been replaced in home-based squadrons by the improved Blenheim Mk IV, but continued to perform usefully in other theatres. The Mk IV introduced a longer nose, more power and, as the war progressed, an undernose gun position. Production of 3,961 included 676 produced in Canada with the name Bolingbroke. The last version was the Blenheim Mk V high-altitude bomber, which saw only very limited operational service. The type was powered by 708-kW (950-hp) Mercury XXXs, and 942 were built in Mk VA bomber, Mk VB (originally Bisley) ground-attack, Mk VC trainer and Mk VD tropicalised versions.

Specification: Bristol Blenheim Mk IV three-seat light bomber
Span: 17.17 m (56 ft 4 in)
Length: 12.98 m (42 ft 7 in)
Powerplant: 2×Bristol Mercury XV, 686 kW (925 hp) each
Armament: 5×0.303-in (7.7-mm) machine-guns in single-gun nose installation (fixed) and twin-gun undernose and dorsal turrets, plus provision for up to 454 kg (1,000 lb) of bombs carried internally and 145 kg (320 lb) of bombs carried externally
Normal T/O weight: 6532 kg (14,400 lb)
Max speed: 266 mph at 11,800 ft
Operational range: 1,460 miles

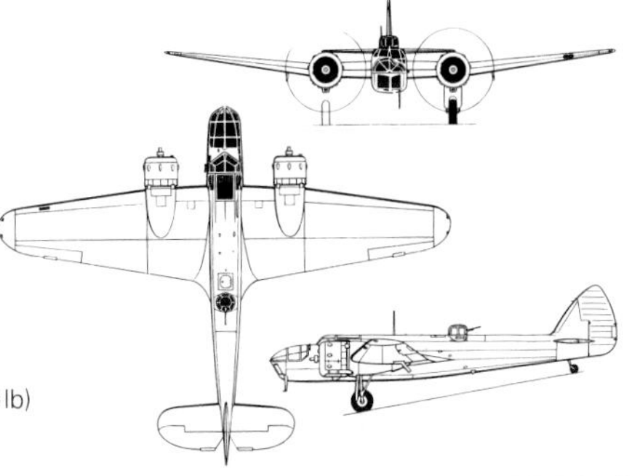

Handley Page Halifax

One of the first batch of production Halifaxes delivered to the RAF in the winter of 1940-41, L9530 is shown in the markings of RAF No. 76 Sqn in Bomber Command's No. 4 Group at Middleton St George. The crest was added by the pilot, Christopher Cheshire, brother of the more famous Leonard Cheshire. It is shown with all bomb doors open and the projections aft of the trailing edge just outboard of the centre section are fuel-jettison pipes.

Though not as celebrated as the Lancaster, the Halifax was also an extremely important night bomber and resulted from the 1936 specification that led to the Manchester. The design was recast for a quartet of Merlins, and the prototype first flew in October 1939. The Halifax entered service in November 1940. The initial model was the Halifax Mk I, of which 84 were built in Series I, II and III subvariants with Merlin Xs, greater weight and more fuel respectively. Then came 1,977 Halifax Mk IIs based on the Mk I Series III with Merlin XXs or XXIIs and, in some aircraft, a four-gun dorsal turret; the 904 Halifax Mk Vs were very similar to the Mk IIs. The 2,091 Halifax Mk IIIs changed to radial engines, and the last two bomber variants retained this arrangement, the 467 Halifax Mk VIs having Hercules 100s and more fuel, and the 35 Halifax Mk VIIs having Hercules XVIs.

Consolidated Liberator

The Liberator was more successful than the Fortress in RAF service though it, too, made its greatest impact in the maritime role. The initial model, used for maritime patrol and transport, was the Liberator Mk I (26 including LB-30A transports) equivalent to the B-24A. Next came the Liberator Mk II bomber (126 including LB-30 transports) equivalent to the B-24C, followed by the Liberator Mk III (156 including some Mk IIIAs with anti-ship radar in place of the ventral turret) equivalent to the B-24D. The designation Liberator Mk IV was allocated to the proposed B-24E delivery. The next model was thus the Liberator Mk V (112), a B-24D version with more fuel, used mainly for maritime reconnaissance. Deliveries of the B-24H and B-24J totalled 1,668 Liberator Mk VIs and Mk VIIIs for the bomber and maritime reconnaissance roles.

Specification: Consolidated Liberator B.Mk VI eight-seat heavy day bomber
Span: 33.53 m (110 ft 0 in)
Length: 20.45 m (67 ft 1 in)
Powerplant: 4×Pratt & Whitney R-1830-43/65, 895 kW (1,200 hp) each
Armament: 10×12.7-mm (0.5-in) machine-guns in twin-gun nose, dorsal, ventral and tail turrets, and single-gun waist positions, plus provision for up to 5806 kg (12,800 lb) of bombs carried internally
Max T/O weight: 28123 kg (62,000 lb)
Max speed: 270 mph at 20,000 ft
Operational range: 2,290 miles

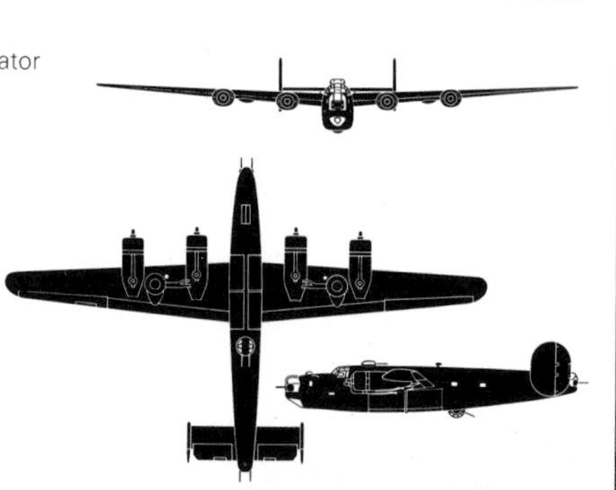

de Havilland Mosquito

With the Ju 88 the most versatile aeroplane of World War II, the Mosquito was built of a ply/balsa sandwich material and designed as a high-speed bomber without defensive armament. First flown in December 1940 for service from May 1942, the Mosquito proved itself in variants of ever improving capability. The first bomber variant was the Mosquito B.Mk IV, of which 273 built with Merlin 21s and four 227-kg (500-lb) bombs or one 1814-kg (4,000-lb) bomb. The Mosquito B.Mk VII was a Canadian model of which 25 were built with Packard-built Merlin 31s. Then came the Mosquito B.Mk IX, of which 54 were built with Merlin 72s and additional 454 kg (1,000 lb) of bombload; the Mosquito B.Mk XVI, of which 1,200 were built, was a Mk IX variant with a pressurised cabin. The 45 Canadian-built Mosquito Mk XXs had American equipment, and were followed by 225 Mosquito B.Mk 25s with Merlin 225s.

Specification: de Havilland Mosquito B.Mk XVI two-seat high-altitude light bomber
Span: 16.51 m (54 ft 2 in)
Length: 13.56 m (44 ft 6 in)
Powerplant: 2×Rolls-Royce Merlin 72, 1253 kW (1,680 hp) each
Armament: provision for up to 4×227-kg (500-lb) bombs carried internally and 2×227-kg (500-lb) bombs carried externally, or 1×1814-kg (4,000-lb) bomb carried internally
Max T/O weight: 10433 kg (23,000 lb)
Max speed: 408 mph at 26,000 ft
Operational range: 1,485 miles

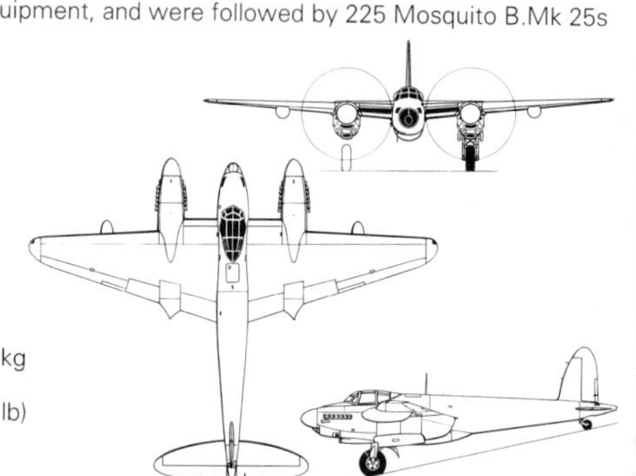

pecification: Handley Page Halifax k III seven-seat heavy night bomber
pan: 30.12 m (98 ft 10 in)
ength: 21.82 m (71 ft 7 in)
owerplant: 4×Bristol Hercules VI, 1204 kW (1,615 hp) each
rmament: 9×0.303-in (7.7-mm) achine-guns in single-gun nose osition and four-gun dorsal and tail rrets, and 1×12.7-mm (0.5-in) in otional ventral position, plus ovision for up to 5897 kg (13,000 lb) f bombs carried internally
lax T/O weight: 29484 kg (65,000 lb)
lax speed: 282 mph at 13,500 ft
perational range: 1,985 miles

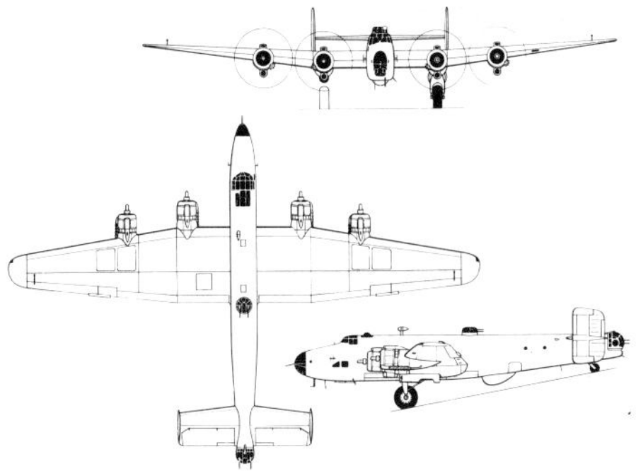

Douglas Boston

Boston was the name given by the British to the DB-7 light bomber that served with the US Army as the A-20. The Boston Mk I and Mk II were 20 DB-7s and 146 DB-7Bs taken over from French orders for use respectively as trainers and, after conversion, Havoc Mk I night-fighters. The first bomber variant was thus the Boston Mk III, of which 781 were received from the summer of 1941 as ex-French DB-7B and US A-20C aircraft with Wright R-2600 rather than the earlier types' Pratt & Whitney R-1830 radials. At this stage Lend-Lease came into operation and Bostons were more closely akin to their US counterparts: the 200 Boston Mk IIIAs were in effect A-20Cs that standardised USAAF and RAF requirements, the 169 Boston Mk IVs were A-20Gs with a dorsal turret, and the 90 Boston Mk Vs were A-20Ks with a transparent 'bombardier' nose.

Specification: Douglas Boston Mk III four-seat light attack bomber
Span: 18.69 m (61 ft 4 in)
Length: 14.40 m (47 ft 3 in)
Powerplant: 2×Wright R-2600-A5B, 1193 kW (1,600 hp) each
Armament: 8×0.303-in (7.7-mm) machine-guns in four-gun nose installation (fixed) and twin-gun dorsal and ventral positions, plus provision for up to 907 kg (2,000 lb) of bombs carried internally
Max T/O weight: 11340 kg (25,000 lb)
Max speed: 304 mph at 13,000 ft
Operational range: 1,020 miles with maximum bombload

Handley Page Hampden

Last and speediest of the RAF's pre-war bombers, the Hampden was operationally disappointing and was at a tactical disadvantage because the exceptionally slim 'pod-and-boom' fuselage prevented the interchange of crew members in flight. The Hampden resulted from a 1932 requirement and first flew in June 1936, entering service in late 1938. Production amounted to 1,430 Hampden Mk Is including 160 built in Canada. These operated by day during 1939 and 1940, but their losses meant relegation to a scarcely more successful night role; as a result 141 were converted to Hampden TB.Mk I torpedo bombers for use by Coastal Command with one 457-mm (18-in) torpedo and two 227-kg (50-lb) bombs. There was also a Hereford variant with 746-kW (1,000-hp) Napier Dagger VIII H-type inlines, but these 100 aircraft were not used operationally.

Specification: Handley Page Hampden Mk I four-seat medium bomber
Span: 21.08 m (69 ft 2 in)
Length: 16.33 m (53 ft 7 in)
Powerplant: 2×Bristol Pegasus XVIII, 731 kW (980 hp) each
Armament: 6×0.303-in (7.7-mm) machine-guns in single-gun nose (fixed and trainable) installations, and twin-gun dorsal and ventral positions, plus provision for up to 1814 kg (4,000 lb) of bombs carried internally
Max T/O weight: 9526 kg (21,000 lb)
Max speed: 265 mph at 15,500 ft
Operational range: 1,885 miles with 907-kg (2,000-lb) bombload

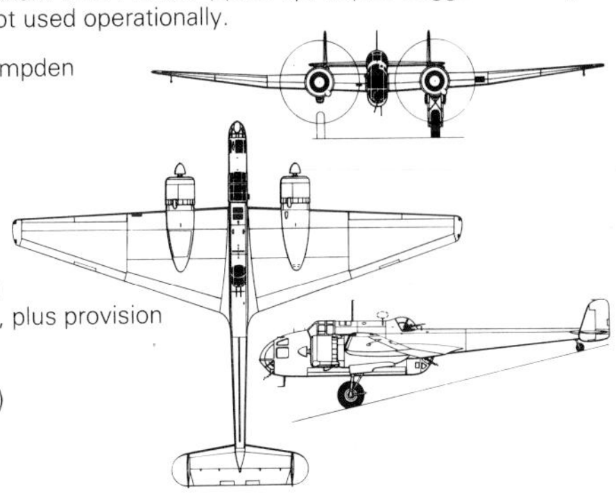

Savoia-Marchetti S.M.79

Specification: Savoia-Marchetti S.M.79-I Sparviero four/five-seat medium bomber
Span: 21.20 m (69 ft 6.7 in)
Length: 15.80 m (51 ft 10 in)
Powerplant: 3×Alfa Romeo 126 RC 34, 582 kW (780 hp) each
Armament: 3×12.7-mm (0.5-in) and 1×7.7-mm (0.303-in) machine-guns plus provision for up to 1250 kg (2,756 lb) of bombs carried internally
Max T/O weight: 10480 kg (23,100 lb)
Max speed: 267 mph at 13,125 ft
Operational range: 1,180 miles

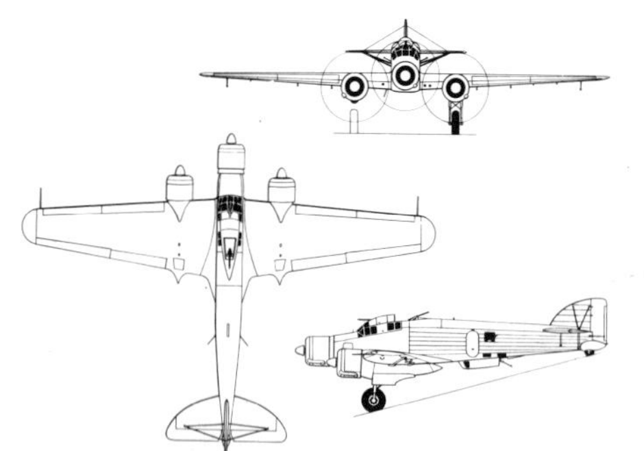

This Savoia Marchetti S.M.79 Sparviero served with the 205a Squadriglia at Milis, Sardinia, and was active in the battle to counter the Allied invasion of Sicily. The green mice insignia was adapted from the badge carried by the pre-war record breaking Sparvieros. Thirty-six of these aircraft remained serviceable when Italy capitulated, and most flew South to join the Italian Co-Belligerent Air Force.

CRDA Cant Z.501 Gabbiano

The Gabbiano (seagull) was a long-range reconnaissance bomber flying-boat, and first flew in February 1934 as a commendably clean parasol-wing monoplane with parallel bracing struts from which projected the two stabilizing floats. The type was powered by a 671-kW (900-hp) Isotta-Fraschini Asso XI inline located on the centre section of the wing in an extended nacelle that also provided accommodation for the flight engineer, who was also provided with a defensive machine-gun. There were two other machine-gun positions, that in the bow often being converted later into an unarmed observer's position. The Gabbiano had excellent range and began to enter service in 1937, some 202 aircraft having been delivered by the time of Italy's entry into World War II during June 1940. Production continued into 1943 and reached 445 aircraft, many remaining in service into 1950.

Specification: CRDA Cant Z.501 Gabbiano four/five-seat reconnaissance bomber flying-boat
Span: 22.50 m (73 ft 10 in)
Length: 14.30 m (46 ft 11 in)
Powerplant: 1×Isotta-Fraschini Asso XI, 671 kW (900 hp)
Armament: 2 or 3×7.7-mm (0.303-in) machine-guns plus provision for up to 640 kg (1,411 lb) of bombs carried under the wing struts
Max T/O weight: 7035 kg (15,510 lb)
Max speed: 171 mph at 8,200 ft
Operational range: 1,491 miles

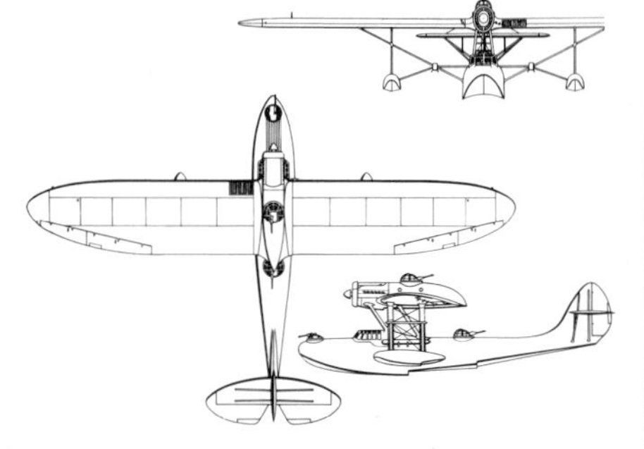

Caproni-Bergamaschi Ca.135

The prototype of the Ca.135 was first flown in 1935, and was a commendably clean design with two 596.5-kW (800-hp) Isotta-Fraschini Asso XI inlines plus retractable ventral and dorsal turrets. Initial production was undertaken for Spain (14 Ca.135 tipo Spagna aircraft with 623-kW/836-hp Asso XI RC 40 engines) and Peru (32 Ca.135 tipo Peru aircraft with revised armament and 671-kW/900-hp Asso XI RC 40 engines; the Spanish aircraft were not delivered, and after being re-engined with the 746-kW (1,000-hp) Fiat A.80 RC 41 with the designation Ca.135/A.80 they were used by the Italian air force as bomber trainers. The main variant was the Ca.135bis, of which the Hungarian air force received about 100. This switched to radial engines, and amongst other changes was a modified and lengthened nose as well as further revised armament.

Specification: Caproni-Bergamaschi Ca.135bis four-seat medium bomber
Span: 18.80 m (61 ft 8.25 in)
Length: 14.38 m (47 ft 2 in)
Powerplant: 2×Piaggio P.XI RC 40, 746 kW (1,000 hp) each
Armament: 3×12.7-mm (0.5-in) or 1×12.7-mm (0.5-in) and 2×7.7-mm (0.303-in) machine-guns plus provision for 1600 kg (3,527 lb) of bombs carried internally
Max T/O weight: 9600 kg (21,164 lb)
Max speed: 273 mph at 15,750 ft
Operational range: 1,240 miles

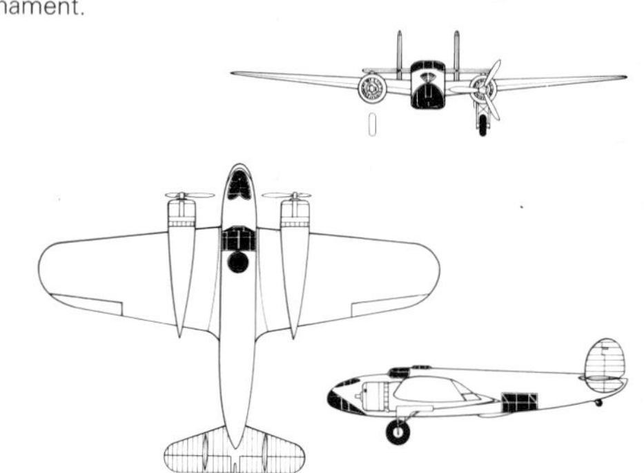

The Sparviero (sparrowhawk) was Italy's most important bomber of World War II, and first flew in 1934 as an eight-passenger civil transport evolution of the S.M.81. The type's performance and payload commended development as a medium bomber, however, resulting in the S.M.79-I for Italy and the twin-engined S.M.79B for export with a redesigned glazed nose and a variety of engine types. The S.M.79C, JR, K and T were limited-number versions for special requirements, and the next Italian air force variant was the S.M.79-II torpedo bomber with two 768-kW (1,030-hp) Fiat A.80 RC 41 engines and provision for two 450-mm (17.7-in) torpedoes; the S.M.79-III was an improved version without the ventral gondola but with heavier nose armament. Production of the bombers totalled some 1,230, and there were also three S.M.83 10-passenger transport derivatives.

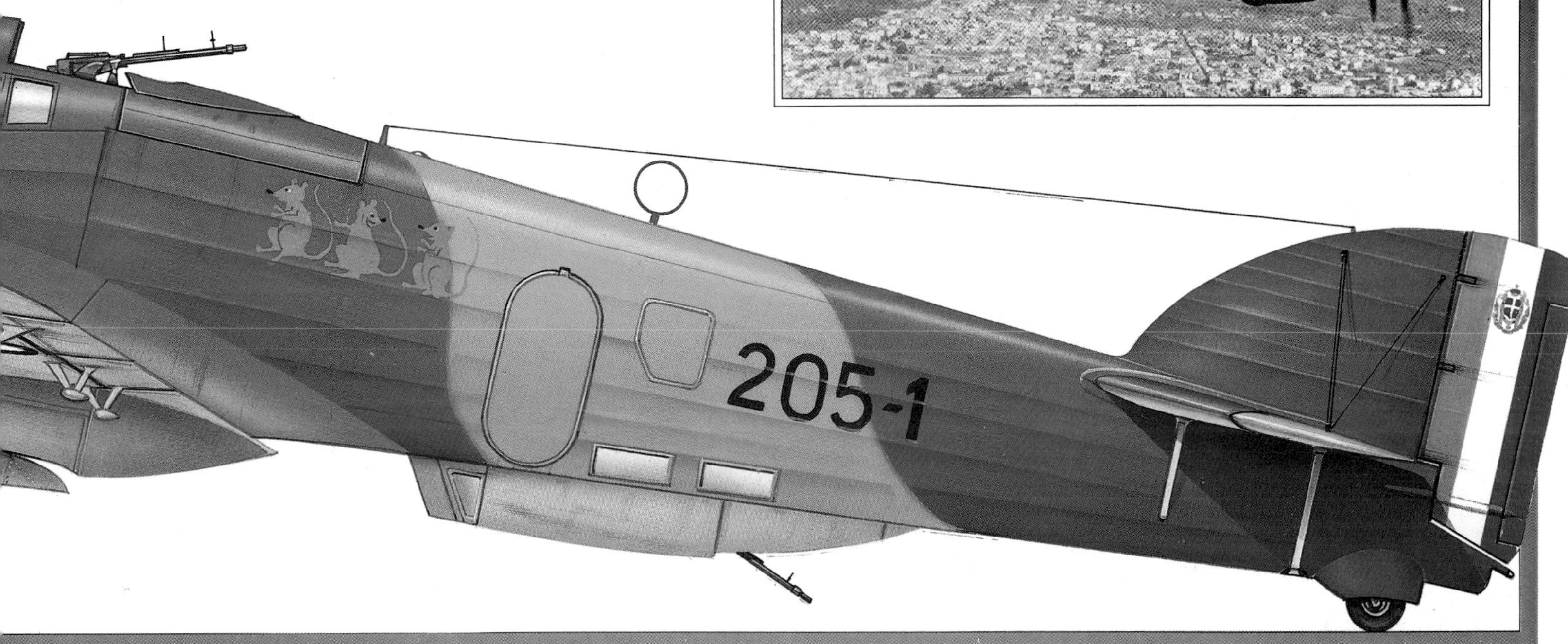

Savoia-Marchetti S.M.81 Pipistrello

Despite its later type number, the Pipistrello (bat) was the predecessor of the S.M.79 and first flew in 1935 as the bomber counterpart of the S.M.73 transport. The type has Italy's favoured tri-motor powerplant configuration and fixed tailwheel landing gear. The type was built to the extent of 535 aircraft with Gnome-Rhone 14K, Alfa Romeo 125 RC 35 or 126 RC 34, or Piaggio P.X RC 35 radials, and served as a bomber and reconnaissance type in the Abyssinian and Spanish wars of the late 1930s. At the time of Italy's entry into World War II during June 1940 some 300 such aircraft equipped 14 *gruppi*, soon switching to less arduous tasks such as freighting, 18-troop transport, glider-towing and anti-submarine patrol. The only variant was a single S.M.81B with two 626-kW (840-hp) Isotta-Fraschini Asso RC engines and the nose revised for a glazed bombardier position.

Specification: Savoia-Marchetti S.M.81 Pipistrello six-seat medium bomber and reconnaissance aeroplane
Span: 24.00 m (78 ft 9 in)
Length: 17.80 m (58 ft 4.75 in)
Powerplant: 3×Piaggio P.X RC 35, 522 kW (700 hp) each
Armament: 5×7.7-mm (0.303-in) machine-guns plus provision for up to 2000 kg (4,409 lb) of bombs carried internally
Max T/O weight: 9300 kg (20,503 lb)
Max speed: 211 mph at 3,280 ft
Operational range: 1,243 miles

Breda Ba.65

The Ba.65 ground-attack aeroplane was developed from the Ba.64 and first flew in September 1935 with a 746-kW (1,000-hp) Fiat A.80 RC 81 radial. It was a type of which the Italians expected great things, but proved to be a complete failure. Though the fuselage had the appearance of a semi-monocoque type, it was in fact based on a steel-tube frame covered with alloy sheet, which was also used for most of the wing. The first 81 production aircraft were extraordinarily given a lower-powered engine in the form of a licence-built Gnome-Rhome 14K of only 671 kW (900 hp), and were single-seaters. There followed 137 examples of the Ba.65bis, an improved attack model with the A.80 RC 41 engine. Some of these were produced in two-seat form with a dorsal gunner in an open position or in a small manually operated turret. The type was also exported to Chile, Iraq and Portugal.

Specification: Breda Ba.65/A.80 single-seat attack aeroplane
Span: 12.10 m (39 ft 8.5 in)
Length: 9.30 m (30 ft 6.25 in)
Powerplant: 1×Fiat A.80 RC 41, 746 kW (1,000 hp)
Armament: 2×12.7-mm (0.5-in) and 2×7.7-mm (0.303-in) machine-guns plus provision for up to 300 kg (661 lb) of bombs carried internally and 200 kg (441 lb) of bombs carried under the wings
Max T/O weight: 2950 kg (6,504 lb)
Max speed: 267 mph at 16,405 ft
Operational range: 342 miles

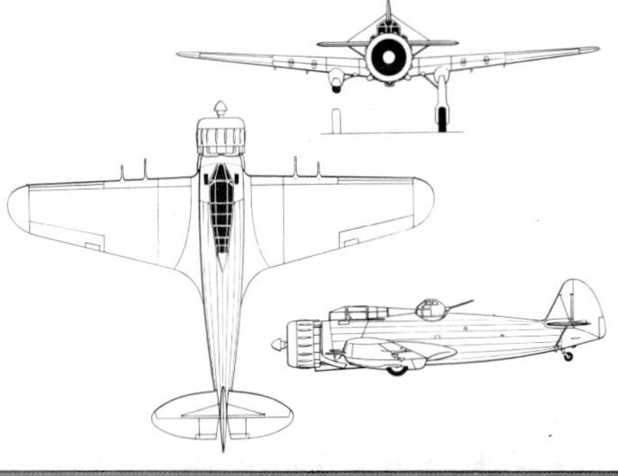

Fiat BR.20 Cicogna

The Cicogna (stork) was first flown in February 1936. Though the type was immediately trumpeted by fascist Italian propaganda as one of the ultimate medium bombers, the type was really indifferent in performance and capability. The initial BR.20 production model was powered by 746-kW (1,000-hp) Fiat A.80 RC 41 engines, and in addition to a bombload of 1600 kg (3,527 lb) carried a defensive armament of one 12.7-mm (0.5-in) and two 7.7-mm (0.303-in) machine-guns. Production amounted to 320 aircraft, including 85 for Japan, before the appearance of the BR.20M with a modified nose and armament. These 264 aircraft were in turn followed by 15 of the BR.20bis final development with 932-kW (1,250-hp) Fiat A.82 RC 42S engines, a redesigned nose, a power-operated dorsal turret and two 7.7-mm (0.303-in) machine-guns in lateral blisters.

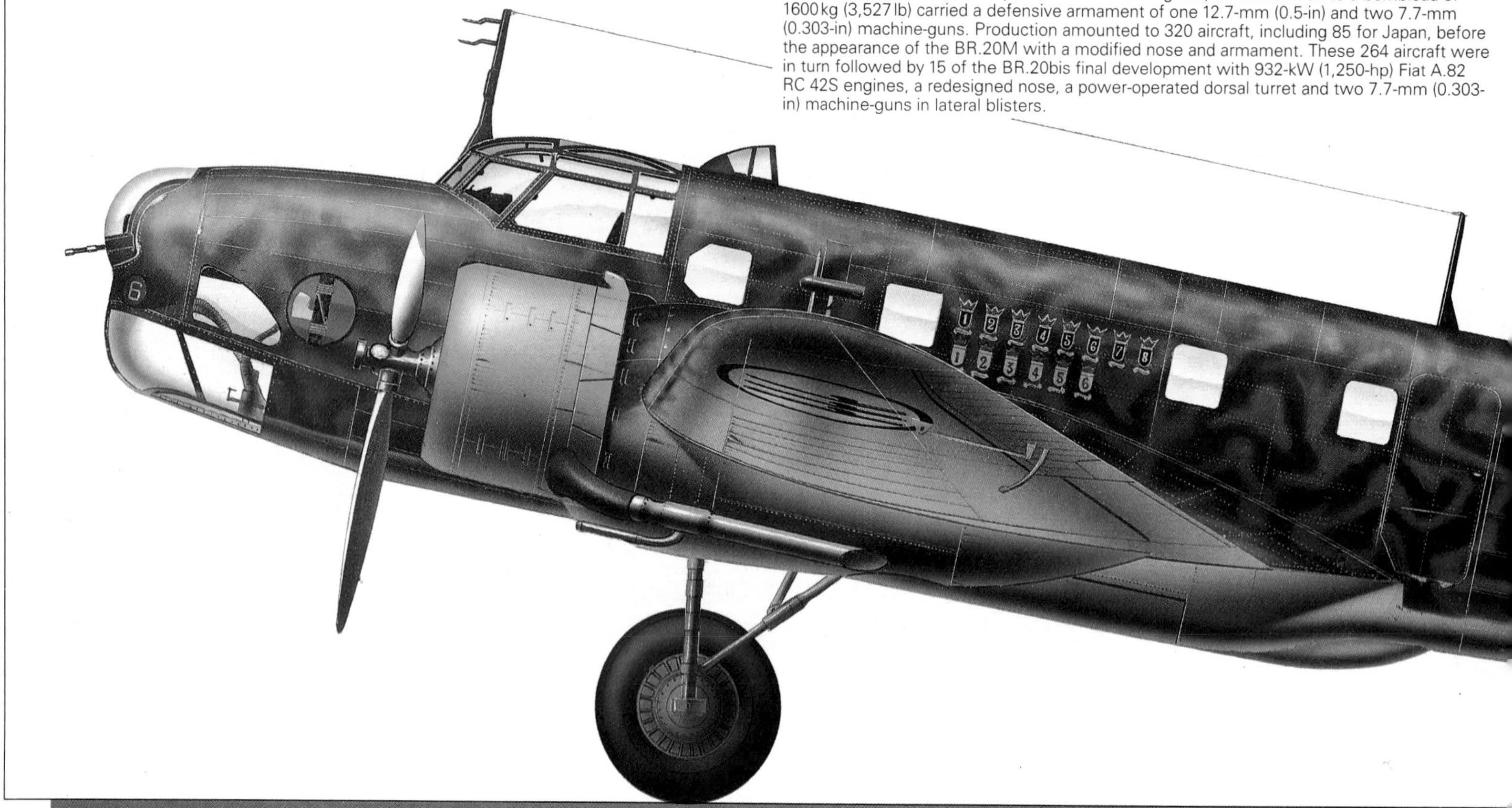

Caproni-Bergamaschi Ca.309 Ghibli

The Ghibli (desert wind) was a light bomber and reconnaissance aeroplane developed from the Ca.306 Borea (north wind) six-passenger light transport. The Ca.309 was intended for policing work in Africa, and therefore it mattered not at all that it retained the fixed but nicely faired tailwheel landing gear of its civil predecessor. The seven Ca.306s were followed by 78 Ca.309 Serie I to V light bombers delivered between 1936 and 1938. Between 1940 and 1944 these were supplemented by 165 examples of the Ca.309 Serie VI close-support bombers with a modified nose and forward-firing armament bolstered by one or two 20-mm cannon. As the obsolescence of these aircraft became apparent they were used increasingly as light transport and communications aircraft, bringing the wheel back full circle to the Ca.306 initial model.

Specification: Caproni-Bergamaschi Ca.309 Ghibli three-seat light bomber and reconnaissance aeroplane
Span: 16.20 m (53 ft 1.75 in)
Length: 13.30 m (43 ft 7.6 in)
Powerplant: 2×Alfa Romeo 115-I, 149 kW (200 hp) each
Armament: 3×7.7-mm (0.303-in) machine-guns plus provision for up to 335 kg (740 lb) of bombs carried under the wings
Max T/O weight: 2930 kg (6,459 lb)
Max speed: 162 mph at optimum altitude
Operational range: 932 miles

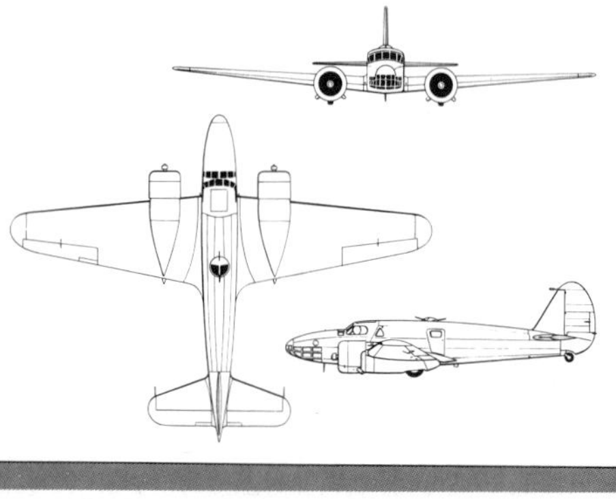

Breda Ba.88 Lince

The Lince (lynx) was another attack type of which great things were claimed but which was an operational disaster. The type first flew in October 1936 with a single vertical tail and two 671-kW (900-hp) Gnome-Rhone 14K radials, and in 1937 set two speed-over-distance world records. But this performance was not maintained in the 148 operational aircraft of the initial production batch, which had twin endplate vertical surfaces, Piaggio P.XI RC 40 radials and a dorsal turret. The type was designed for the attack, bomber and reconnaissance roles, and as early aircraft proved total failures because of the weight of their operational equipment many later aircraft were sent straight from the production line to the scrapyard. Production was completed by three Ba.88M dive-bombers with 626-kW (840-hp) Fiat A.74 RC 38 radials, one more machine-gun in the nose, and a wing increased in span by 2.0 m (6 ft 6.75 in).

Specification: Breda Ba.88 Lince two-seat attack, bomber and reconnaissance aeroplane
Span: 15.60 m (51 ft 2.25 in)
Length: 10.79 m (35 ft 4.75 in)
Powerplant: 2×Piaggio P.XI RC 40, 746 kW (1,000 hp) each
Armament: 1×7.7-mm (0.303-in) and 3×12.7-mm (0.5-in) machine-guns plus provision for 1000 kg (2,205 lb) of bombs carried internally or 3×200 kg (441 lb) bombs carried under the fuselage
Max T/O weight: 6750 kg (14,881 lb)
Max speed: 304 mph at 13,125 ft
Operational range: 1,020 miles

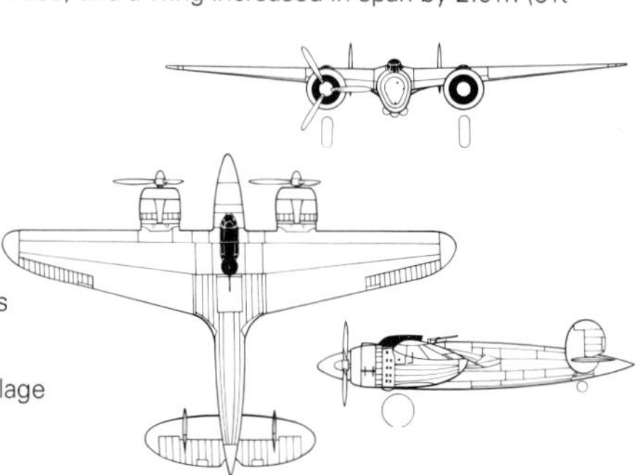

Specification: Fiat BR.20M Cicogna five-seat medium bomber
Span: 21.56 m (70 ft 8.75 in)
Length: 16.68 m (54 ft 8 in)
Powerplant: 2×Fiat A.80 RC 41, 746 kW (1,000 hp) each
Armament: 1×12.7-mm (0.5-in) and 2×7.7-mm (0.303-in) machine-guns plus provision for up to 1600 kg (3,527 lb) of bombs carried internally
Max T/O weight: 10100 kg (22,270 lb)
Max speed: 273 mph at sea level
Operational range: 1,709 miles

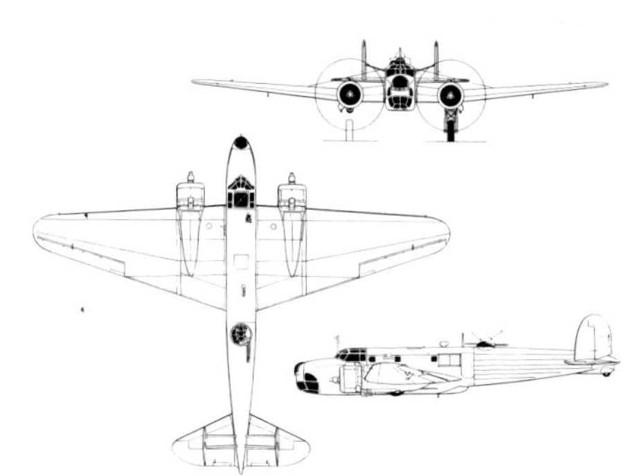

This Fiat BR.20M Cicogna (stork) wears the markings of 3 Squadriglia, 13 Stormo, and was based at Pugli, in Southern Italy during April 1941, before moving to North Africa. This aircraft's bomb log shows that it made eight missions over England during the Battle of Britain, and six daylight raids over Greece.

CRDA Cant Z.1007B Alcione

The Alcione (kingfisher) was one of Italy's best medium bombers of World War II, and began life as the Z.1007 that first flew in March 1937 with three 615-kW (825-hp) Isotta-Fraschini Asso XI inlines. Some 34 production aircraft were built to the same standard, but Cant then produced the redesigned and slightly enlarged Z.1007bis with revised armament and more power in the form of three radials. This entered production in nine series, the first three having a single vertical tail surface and the last six being revised with endplate surfaces on a tailplane possessing marked dihedral. The only other variant was the Z.1007ter with three 858-kW (1,150-hp) Piaggio P.XIX radials and a reduced bombload of 1000 kg (2,205 lb) for higher performance including a maximum speed of 311 mph. Total production of the Z.1007bis and Z.1007ter was 526.

Specification: CRDA Cant Z.1007bis Alcione five-seat medium bomber
Span: 24.80 m (81 ft 4.25 in)
Length: 18.35 m (60 ft 2.5 in)
Powerplant: 3×Piaggio P.XI R2C 40, 746 kW (1,000 hp) each
Armament: 2×12.7-mm (0.5-in) and 2×7.7-mm (0.303-in) machine-guns plus provision for up to 1200 kg (2,646 lb) of bombs carried internally or 1000 kg (2,205 lb) of bombs carried externally
Max T/O weight: 13620 kg (30,027 lb)
Max speed: 289 mph at 13,125 ft
Operational range: 1,087 miles with maximum internal bombload

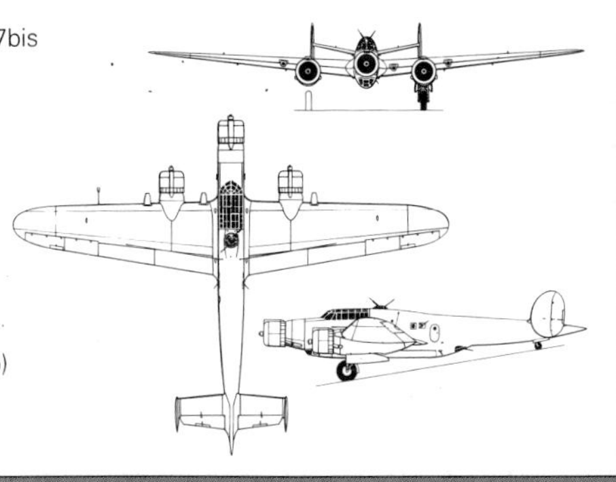

CRDA Cant Z.506B Airone

The Airone (heron) was developed as a reconnaissance bomber floatplane on the basis of the Z.506A 14-passenger airliner, itself a derivative of the Z.505 mailplane. Production of the Z.506B military version began in 1937, and eventually totalled 324. By comparison with the civil types the Z.506B had a stepped upper fuselage line for the cockpit, a dorsal turret, and a ventral gondola accommodating the long weapon bay between a forward observer/aimer position and aft gunner's position. The type remained basically unaltered through its production life, minor modifications being a different dorsal turret and the addition of two waist gun positions. Some Z.506B bombers were converted to Z.506S air/sea rescue floatplanes, and in 1936 there appeared the prototype of the Z.508 landplane heavy bomber derivative that set several records but was not put into production.

Specification: CRDA Cant Z.506B Airone four/five-seat reconnaissance bomber floatplane
Span: 26.50 m (86 ft 11.25 in)
Length: 19.25 m (63 ft 1.75 in)
Powerplant: 3×Alfa Romeo 126 RC 34, 559 kW (750 hp) each
Armament: 1×12.7-mm (0.5-in) and 2 or 4×7.7-mm (0.303-in) machine-guns plus provision for up to 1200 kg (2,646 lb) of bombs or 1×torpedo carried internally
Max T/O weight: 12300 kg (27,117 lb)
Max speed: 227 mph at optimum altitude
Operational range: 1,705 miles

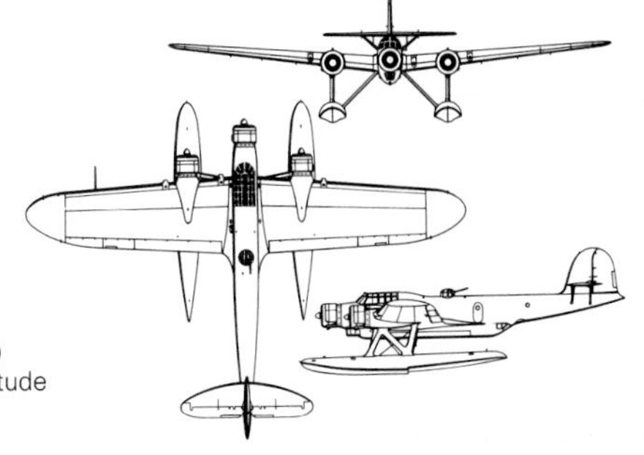

Caproni-Bergamaschi Ca.310

The Libeccio (south-west wind) was produced in parallel with the Ca.309, and while retaining the same basic airframe was fitted with more-powerful engines and retractable landing gear for greatly enhanced warload and performance. The prototype first flew in February 1937, and total production of an extensive and diverse family amounted to more than 1,600 aircraft. The main bomber variants were the Ca.310, the Ca.310bis for Yugoslavia with an unstepped nose, the similar Ca.311 for Italy, the Ca.311bis with a stepped nose and heavier gun armament, the Ca.312 with Piaggio P.XVI RC 35 radials, the Ca.312bis for Norway with an unstepped nose, the Ca.313 with Isotta-Fraschini Asso 120 IRCC 40 engines and developed in a large number of role-specialised subvariants, and the Ca.314 with Isotta-Fraschini Delta RC 35 engines and developed yet again in a number of role-specialised subvariants.

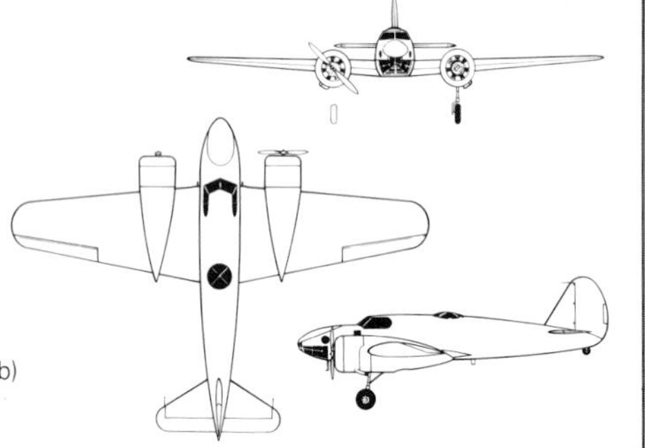

Specification: Caproni-Bergamaschi Ca.310 Libeccio three-seat light bomber and reconnaissance aeroplane
Span: 16.20 m (53 ft 1.75 in)
Length: 12.20 m (40 ft 0.25 in)
Powerplant: 2×Piaggio P.VII C 35, 350 kW (470 hp) each
Armament: 3×7.7-mm (0.303-in) machine-guns plus provision for up to 400 kg (882 lb) of bombs carried under the wings
Max T/O weight: 4650 kg (10,252 lb)
Max speed: 227 mph at 9,845 ft
Operational range: 1,025 miles

Savoia-Marchetti S.M.82 Marsupiale

Yet another tri-motor bomber/transport, the Marsupiale (marsupial) was first flown in 1938 as a development of the S.M.75 with a deeper fuselage. The S.M.75 was itself a derivative of the S.M.73 with larger dimensions, greater power and retractable landing gear. Production totalled about 400 aircraft, of which only 12 were in service at the time of Italy's entry into World War II during June 1940. The type was somewhat underpowered and therefore lacked the performance for effective use as a first-line bomber: so while wartime exigencies on occasion demanded such use, the type was operated mainly in the trooping and freight transport roles, in which it could carry 40 men and 400 kg (8,818 lb) respectively. The type remained in service after the war as a transport, those aircraft used in this role generally being re-engined with 898.5-kW (1,215-hp) Pratt & Whitney Twin Wasp radials.

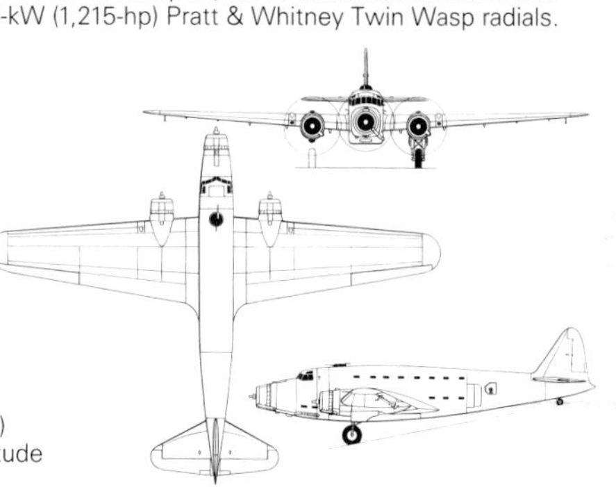

Specification: Savoia-Marchetti S.M.82 Marsupiale four/five-seat medium bomber and transport aeroplane
Span: 29.68 m (97 ft 4.5 in)
Length: 22.90 m (75 ft 1.7 in)
Powerplant: 3×Alfa Romeo 128 RC 21, 708 kW (950 hp) each
Armament: 1×12.7-mm (0.5-in) and 4×7.7-mm (0.303-in) machine-guns plus provision for up to 4000 kg (8,818 lb) of bombs carried internally
Max T/O weight: 17820 kg (39,386 lb)
Max speed: 230 mph at optimum altitude
Operational range: 1,864 miles

Piaggio P.108

The P.108 first flew in 1939 as a development of the P.50-II with Piaggio P.XII RC 35 engines, and became Italy's sole four-engined bomber of World War II. The type was planned in four main versions, but the only one to enter military service was the P.108B heavy bomber, of which about 20 pre-production and production examples were built with distinctive triple-stepped upper nose contours. Some of these were converted for the night bomber role with flame-dampers and a revised nose in which the turret was removed and the amount of glazing reduced. Other variants were the single P.108A anti-ship variant with a nose-mounted 102-mm (4-in) gun, 24 P.108C airliners with accommodation for 32 passengers (or 56 troops when impressed for military service), the single P.108M upgraded bomber with a nose armament of one 20-mm cannon and four 7.7-mm (0.303-in) machine-guns, and the single P.108T military freighter.

Specification: Piaggio P.108B seven-seat heavy bomber
Span: 32.00 m (104 ft 11.75 in)
Length: 22.29 m (73 ft 1.5 in)
Powerplant: 4×Piaggio P.XII RC 35, 1119 kW (1,500 hp) each
Armament: 8×12.7-mm (0.5-in) machine-guns plus provision for up to 3500 kg (7,716 lb) of bombs carried internally
Max T/O weight: 29885 kg (65,885 lb)
Max speed: 267 mph at 13,780 ft
Operational range: 2,187 miles

Fiat RS.14

The RS.14 was designed as a long-range reconnaissance bomber floatplane, and first flew in May 1939 with 626-kW (840-hp) Fiat A.74 RC 38 engines as the RS.14A all-metal monoplane. The type was of very clean lines with the floats attached to the underside of the engine nacelles and lower fuselage by trim struts of low-drag design. The overall cleanliness of the design was marred only slightly in the bombing role of the RS.14B production version by a dorsal turret and a shallow ventral gondola (or rather tray) for the weapon load. Production amounted to 184 aircraft including small numbers of the RS.14C air/sea rescue variant without the ventral tray. The AS.14 was a landplane attack derivative with retractable landing gear, armour and a forward-firing armament of one 37-mm cannon and four 12.7-mm (0.5-in) machine-guns. The type had good performance, but flew only in prototype form.

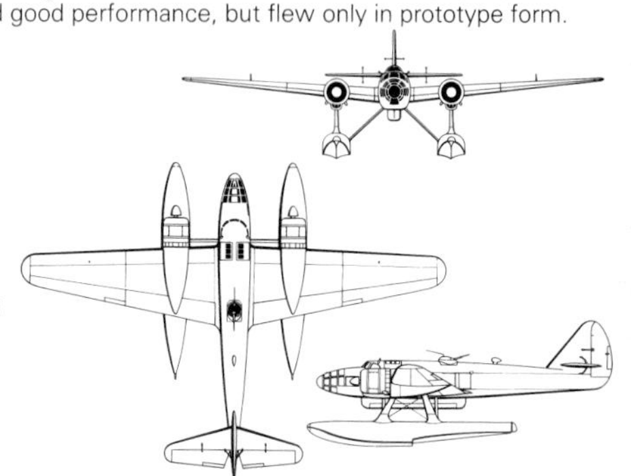

Specification: Fiat RS.14B five-seat bomber and reconnaissance floatplane
Span: 19.54 m (64 ft 1 in)
Length: 14.10 m (46 ft 3 in)
Powerplant: 2×Fiat A.74 RC 38, 649 kW (870 hp) each
Armament: 1×12.7-mm (0.5-in) and 2×7.7-mm (0.303-in) machine-guns plus provision for up to 400 kg (882 lb) of bombs carried internally
Max T/O weight: 8000 kg (17,637 lb)
Max speed: 254 mph at 13,125 ft
Operational range: 1,553 miles

Tupolev Tu-26 'Backfire'

The appearance in 1969 of this supersonic swing-wing strategic medium bomber caused little surprise among Western observers as it was suspected that the fixed-wing Tu-22 'Blinder' had failed to meet Soviet long-range bombing requirements. The 'Backfire-A', which served in relatively small numbers in the mid-1970s, retained the Tu-22's fairings aft of the wings to house the landing gear, but these were eliminated in the extended-span 'Backfire-B', a version that depended for true long range strategic operations on inflight refuelling. 'Backfire-C', identified in 1984, features modified-ramp engine air intakes. Present in-service strength (including the naval air arm) is about 350 aircraft.

Specification: Tupolev Tu-26 'Backfire-B' four-seat supersonic strategic bomber
Span: 34.45 m (113 ft 0 in) spread, 26.21 m (86 ft 0 in) swept
Length: 42.00 m (137 ft 10 in)
Powerplant: 2×Kuznetsov(?) turbofans, 20000 kg (44,092 lb) st each
Armament: two 23-mm cannon in tail barbette, plus up to 12000 kg (26,455 lb) of disposable ordnance
Max speed: Mach 2.0 at 36,090 ft
Operational range: 3,420 miles

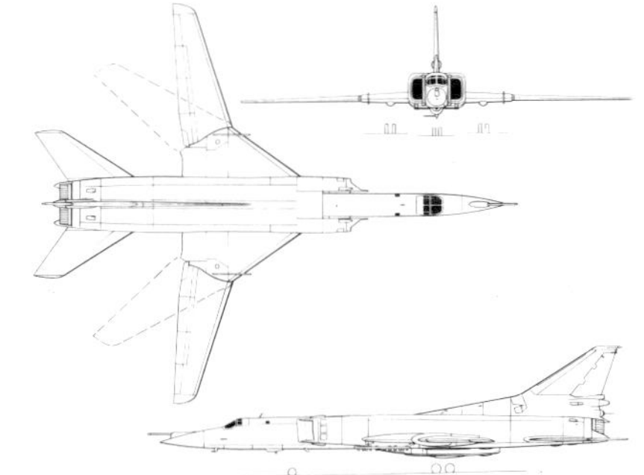

Tupolev Tu-80/85 'Barge'

Intended to advance the basic Tu-4/Boeing B-29A design, the Tu-80 was first flown in November 1949 with redesigned nose and enlarged vertical tail surface. Soviet 23-mm cannon replaced the former heavy machine-gun armament and speed was increased to 404 mph. Production was not undertaken of either this or the Tu-85, a further development of the Tu-4 of which three prototypes (one structural test airframe) were built. The Tu-85 featured engines of considerably increased power which bestowed a substantially improved performance. However, accelerated development of turbojets and turboprops in the USSR in the early 1950s brought an end to the Tu-80/85 programmes.

Specification: Tupolev Tu-85 'Barge' 16-seat long-range heavy bomber prototype
Span: 55.94 m (183 ft 6.3 in)
Length: 39.31 m (128 ft 11.6 in)
Powerplant: 4×Dobrynin VD-4k, 4,3000 hp each
Armament: 10×23-mm cannon in tail, dorsal and ventral turrets, plus up to 20000 kg (44,092 lb) of free-fall bombs
Max speed: 413 mph at 32,810 ft
Operational range: 7,450 miles

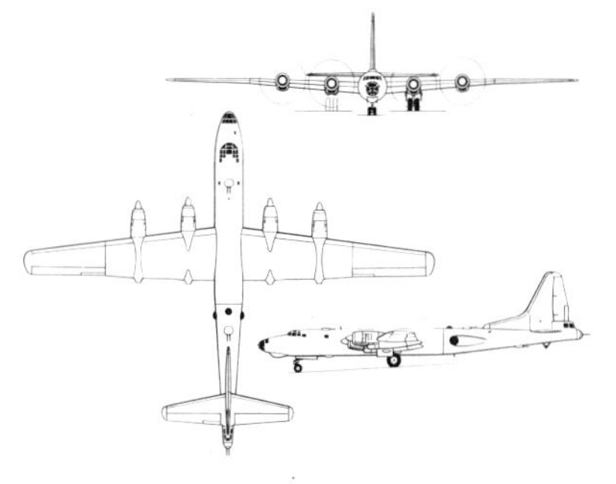

Tupolev Tu-? 'Blackjack'

Thought to be entering operational service in 1988, this large swing-wing Tupolev strategic bomber is currently known in the West only by its NATO reporting name 'Blackjack-A'. Featuring low-set wings with large fixed gloved sections, the aircraft is powered by four afterburning turbofans in a pair of rectangular underwing nacelles. Related to, but not directly developed from the Tu-26 'Backfire', 'Blackjack' is expected to carry AS-15 'Kent' cruise missiles or a mix of missiles and bombs, and achieves its very long range by employing subsonic cruise for much of the sortie. It is thought likely that the USSR anticipates a total production of about 100 examples.

Specification: Tupolev Tu-? 'Blackjack-A' four/five-seat strategic bomber
Span: 52.00 m (170 ft 7 in)
Length: 50.65 m (166 ft 2 in)
Powerplant: 4×turbofans,23000 kg (50,705 lb) st each
Armament: up to 16500 kg (36,376 lb) of disposable stores
Max speed: Mach 2.1 at high altitide
Operational range: 9,500 miles

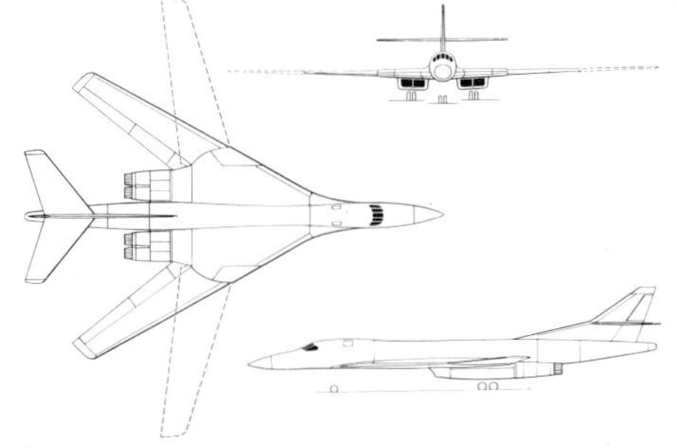

Yakovlev Yak-28 'Brewer'

Introduced to replace the first-generation Il-28 jet medium bomber, the supersonic Yak-28 featured sharply swept parallel-chord wing with twin turbojets in large underslung wing nacelles. Having first flown in about 1961 it was first seen in numbers in 1969. An unusual feature was the twin-wheel tandem main landing gear units which retracted into the front and rear fuselage, with small balancing wheel units retracting into wingtip fairings. The pilot was accommodated under a fighter-type sliding canopy, the navigator/bomb aimer being placed in a long, slim glazed nose. Bombing radar was housed in a large radome under the nose. The bomb load was housed in an internal fuselage bay.

Specification: Yakovlev Yak-28 'Brewer-C' two-seat strike supersonic strike and attack aircraft
Span: 12.95 m (42 ft 6 in)
Length: 22.30 m (73 ft 2 in)
Powerplant: 2×Tumanskii R-11F, 6200 kg (13,668 lb) st each
Armament: up to 2000 kg (4,409 lb) of disposable stores
Max speed: Mach 1.11 at 32,810 ft
Operational range: 1,000 miles

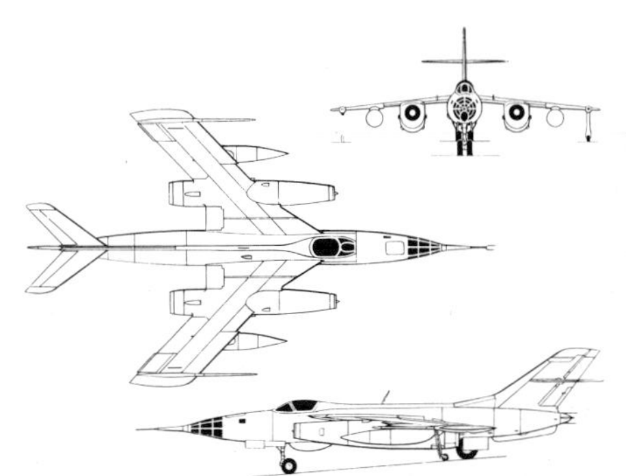

Ilyushin Il-28 'Beagle'

First flown on 8 July 1948 and shown publicly two years later, the Il-28 first generation twin-jet tactical bomber with shoulder-set unswept wing proved to be a competent, adaptable and very widely-used aircraft in service in a score of communist-bloc air forces for quarter of a century. With centrifugal-flow turbojets in underslung wing nacelles, the Il-28 featured swept tail surfaces and nosewheel landing gear. Employed for many years as a tactical bomber by numerous VVS regiments, it was equipped with rudimentary bombing radar, and the tail gunner doubled as a radio operator. A training version was the Il-28U 'Mascot', and licence was undertaken in Czechoslovakia, Poland and China.

Specification: Ilyushin Il-28 'Beagle' three-seat tactical bomb
Span: 21.45 m (70 ft 4.5 in)
Length: 17.45 m (57 ft 3 in)
Powerplant: 2×Klimov VK-1A, 2700 kg (5,952 lb) st each
Armament: 4×23-mm cannon (two in tail turret and two fixed i nose) plus up to 1000 kg (2,205 l of free-fall bombs
Max speed: 560 mph at 14,765 f
Operational range: 1,490 miles

Ilyushin Il-54 'Blowlamp'

An imaginative development of the Il-28 'Beagle' subsonic tactical jet bomber, the Il-54 introduced a sharply swept wing whilst retaining the swept tail surfaces of the previous design. First flown in 1955, this transonic aircraft broke new ground in a number of respects, not least with its bicycle main landing gear with wing tip-mounted balancing wheels. Nevertheless the presence of wing fences and fuselage strakes suggests that aerodynamic and control problems were encountered, and one suspects that the large main landing gear units proved unwieldy. It did not progress beyond the prototype stage, although it was identified by the NATO reporting name 'Blowlamp'.

Specification: Ilyushin Il-54 'Blowlamp' three-seat transonic bomber prototype
Span: 17.85 m (58 ft 4.75 in)
Length: 21.8 m (71 ft 6.25 in)
Powerplant: 2×Lyul'ka AI-7, 6500 kg (14,330 lb) st each
Armament: 2×23-mm cannon in tail turret, plus up to 6000 kg (13,228 lb) of free-fall bombs
Max speed: 715 mph at sea level
Operational range: 870 miles

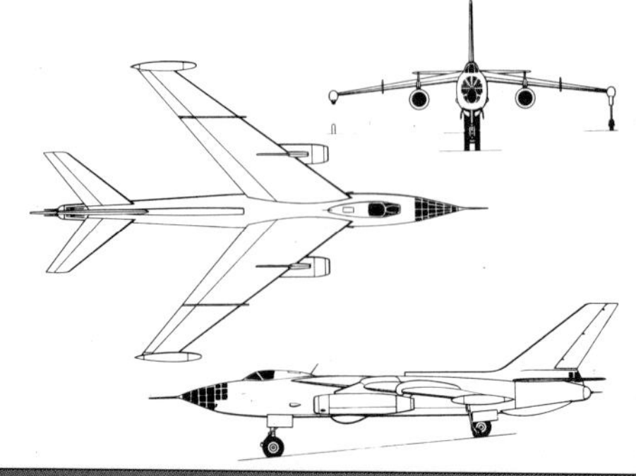

Myasishchyev M-4 'Bison-A'

First Soviet four-turbojet strategic bomber, the M-4 'Bison' was first seen in prototype form in 1954 and probably entered service in about 1959. With moderately-swept flying surfaces the engines were buried in the wing roots and, because of its poor operating ceiling with bomb load, it was heavily defended with five turrets each with twin 23-mm cannon. About 60 'Bisons' remained in service in 1980, but since then roughly half of these have been converted into tankers, while the 'Bison-B ' and 'Bison-C' have served as long-range maritime reconnaissance aircraft. The tankers, with fuselage-mounted hose and reel unit, fly in support of Tu-26 'Backfire' and Tu-95 'Bear' strategic bombers.

Specification: Myasishchyev M-4 'Bison-A' 9/11-seat strategic bomber
Span: 50.48 m (165 ft 7.5 in)
Length: 47.20 m (154 ft 10 in)
Powerplant: 4×Mikulin AM-3D, 9500 kg (20,943 lb) st each
Armament: 10×23-mm cannon in dorsal, ventral and tail positions, plus up to 9000 kg (19,841 lb) of free fall bombs
Max speed: 621 mph at high altitude
Operational range: 6,650 miles

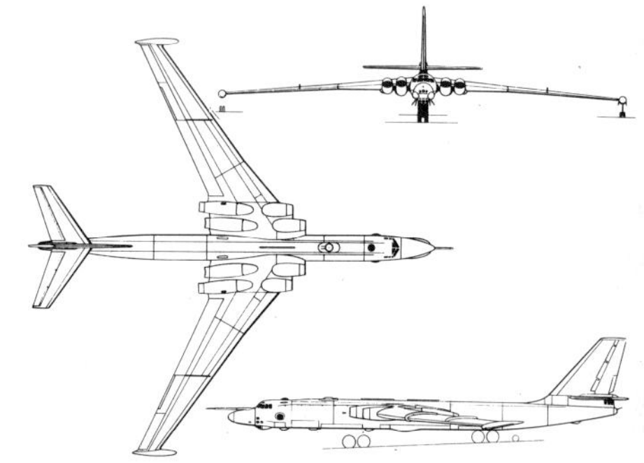

*The Ilyushin Il-28 known by the **NATO** codename 'Beagle', was also known as the 'Soviet Canberra', thanks to its durability and adaptability. Like the Canberra, many Il-28s were put into support service once their active service was over; this Finnish air force target-tower was an example.*

Myasishchyev M-50 'Bounder'

Although this aircraft never achieved operational status, it is included on account of its advanced design concept, employing a shoulder-set delta wing, two of the Koliesov turbojets being mounted under the wings and the others at the wing tips. It employed tandem main landing gear units each with four wheels, and wing-mounted balancing twin-wheel units. The three crew members were located in a forward cabin, leaving the long slender fuselage unrestricted for bomb and fuel accommodation. First flown in about 1960, the M-50 was almost certainly influenced in concept by the American Convair B-58 Hustler delta-wing supersonic bomber which had first flown in 1956.

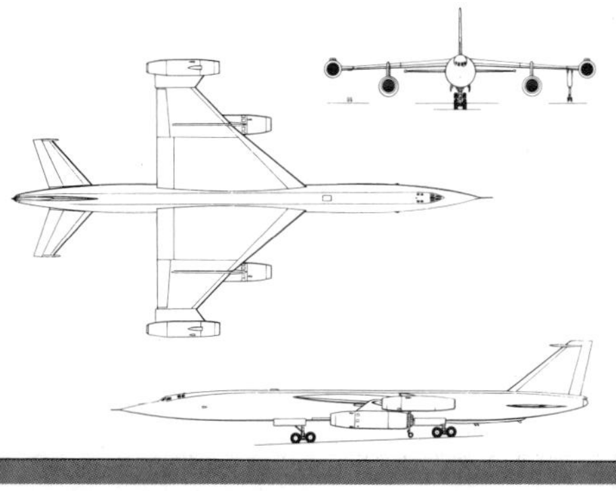

Specification: Myasishchyev M-50 'Bounder' three-seat supersonic medium bomber prototype
Span: 37.0 m (121 ft 4.7 in)
Length: 57.0 m (187 ft 0 in)
Powerplant: 4×Koliesov ND-7F or VD-7F, 18000 kg (39,6783 lb) st each
Armament: up to 13500 kg (29,722 lb) of free-fall bombs carried internally
Max speed: Mach 1.83 at high altitude
Operational range: 3,730 miles

Sukhoi Su-24 'Fencer'

A shoulder-set swing-wing strike aircraft which entered combat service in December 1974, the Su-24 currently equips five or six regiments of the Soviet air force; more than 500 are believed to be in service. Capable of Mach 1.2 at low level, 'Fencer' is said to feature terrain avoidance radar, nav/attack radar of the pulse Doppler type, and a laser rangefinder and marked target seeker. 'Fencer-A' and 'Fencer-B', originally identified, appear to have differed only in rear fuselage structure, but 'Fencer-C' with new nose-mounted sensor probes appears to possess upgraded electronics, 'Fencer-D' has a refulling probe, 'Fencer-E' is the electronic warfare model and 'Fencer-F' is a reconnaissance variant.

Specification: Sukhoi Su-24 'Fencer-C' two-seat strike and attack aircraft
Span: 17.50 m (57 ft 5 in) spread, 10.50 m (324 ft 5.5 in) swept
Length: 21.29 m (69 ft 10 in)
Powerplant: 2×Lyul'ka AL-21F-3, 11200 kg (24,691 lb) st each
Armament: 1 or 2×30-mm cannon, plus 11000 kg (24,250 lb) of disposable stores
Max speed: Mach 2.4 at 36,090 ft
Operational range: 1,615 miles

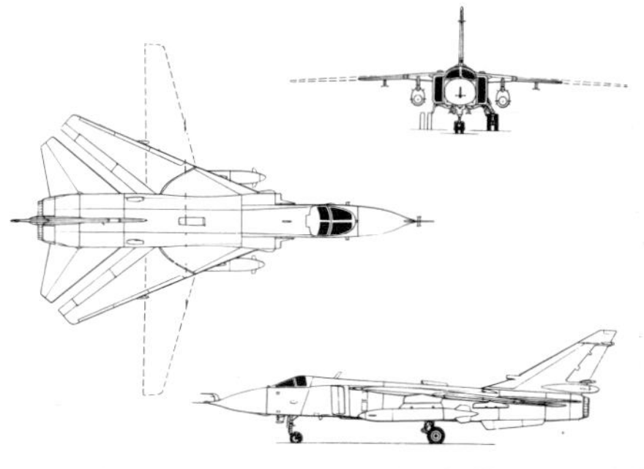

Tupolev Tu-95/142 'Bear'

Basically employing 1950s technology, the Tu-95 'Bear-A' four-propjet swept-wing strategic heavy bomber entered service in 1956 equipped with 'Short Horn' bombing/navigation and 'Bee Hind' tail warning radar. 'Bear-B' followed, capable of carrying an AS-3 'Kangaroo' stand-off weapon and equipped with 'Crown Drum' nose radar; 'Bear-C' was a dual-role variant for Elint and reconnaissance, but retaining the AS-3 provision. The next strategic bomber version was the 'Bear-G' with 'Down-Beat' attack radar, normally armed with a pair of AS-4 'Kitchen' air-to-surface missiles. Latest estimates suggest that about 150 'Bear-H' aircraft are serving with Soviet Strategic Aviation, each carrying two or four AS-15 'Kent' cruise missiles.

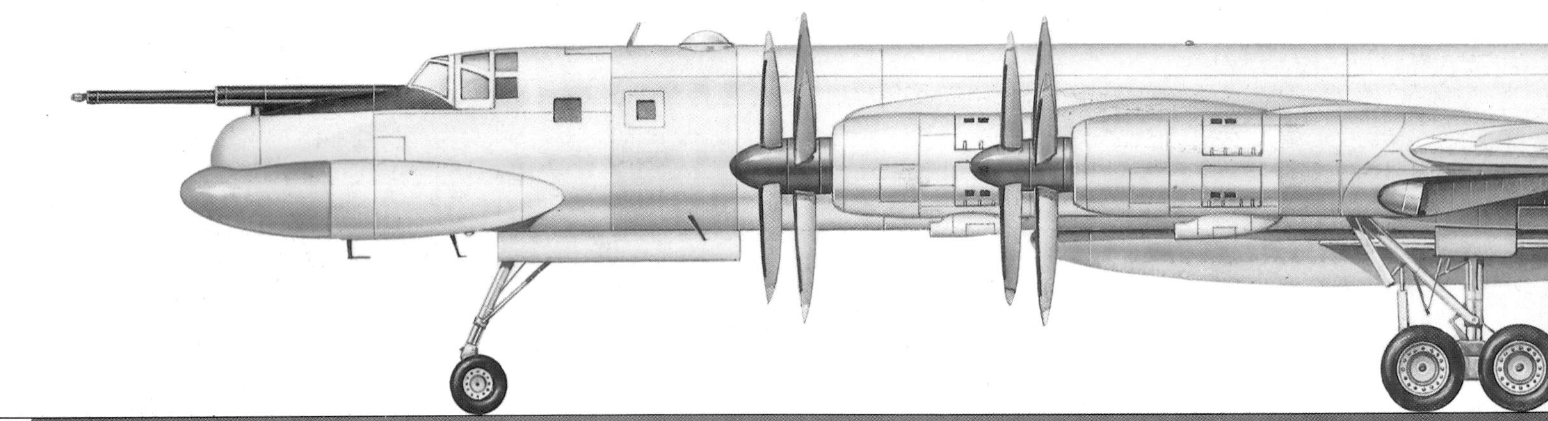

Sukhoi T-100

This strange, futuristic-looking aircraft was a bomber project that was initiated in the early 1960s, probably drawing inspiration from the North American XB-70 Valkyrie. A slender cylindrical fuselage sat atop a double-delta wing with the engines mounted in nacelles underneath. The engine area also housed the tricycle landing gear and presumably the weapon bay. Small canard foreplanes were attached behind the cockpit and a drooped nose allowed the pilot forward vision when lowered. When raised, the only available windows were a small panel on each side, repeated for the weapon systems operator/navigator behind. Using titanium heavily in the structure, the T-100 is known to have had a quadruplex flight control system. It made its first flight on 22 August 1972, but the programme was quickly overtaken by changing operational requirements.

Specification: Sukhoi T-100 two-seat strategic bomber prototype

No figures relating to the T-100 have been released, and the published photographs make estimates difficult
Armament: free fall nuclear weapons
Maximum speed: Mach 2.8

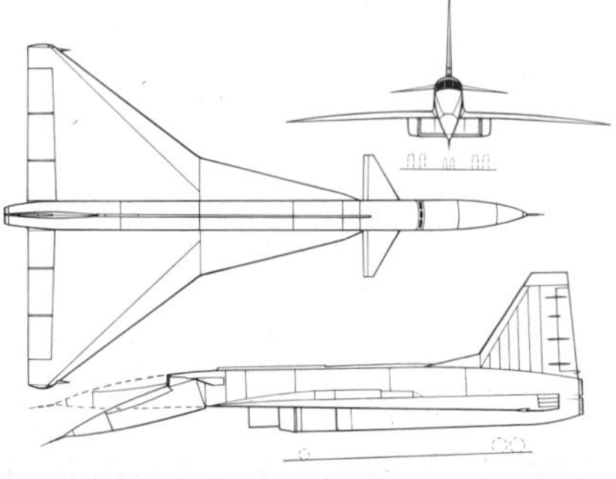

Tupolev Tu-4 'Bull'

Copied from three USAAF B-29A Superfortress heavy bombers which force-landed in Soviet territory in 1944, the Tu-4 was put into widespread production in the USSR, being first flown there on 3 July 1947. Some 420 examples were built in all by 1952, serving as strategic bombers with the Soviet Long-Range Aviation. The Tu-4 differed from the American aircraft in omitting the pressurised tunnel for crew passage amidships, bag-type fuel tanks in place of integral cells, UBT machine-gun armament and Shvetsov radial engines. Although the Tu-4 represented a big advance over genuine Soviet indigenous designs, the Soviet aircraft was inferior to the B-29 on account of greater weight.

Specification: Tupolev Tu-4 'Bull' 9/10-seat long-range heavy bomber
Span: 43.05 m (141 ft 4 in)
Length: 30.18 m (99 ft 0.2 in)
Powerplant: 4×Shvetsov ASh-73TK, 2,400 hp each
Armament: 10 12.7-mm (0.5 in) machine-guns in tail, dorsal and ventral turrets, plus up to 8000 kg (17,637 lb) of free-fall bombs
Max speed: 347 mph at 32,810 ft
Operational range: 3,170 miles

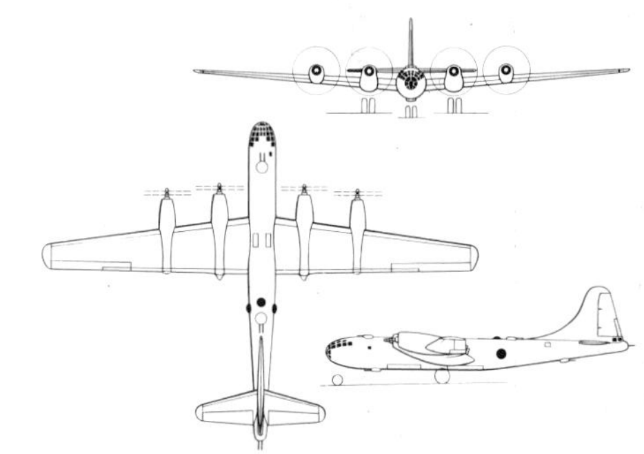

Specification: Tupolev Tu-95 'Bear-A' 10-seat strategic heavy bomber
Span: 51.10 m (167 ft 7.75 in)
Length: 47.50 m (155 ft 10 in)
Powerplant: 4×Kuznetsov NK-12MV, 14,795 ehp each
Armament: 6×23-mm cannon in tail, dorsal and ventral turrets, plus up to 20000 kg (44,092 lb) of disposable ordnance
Max speed: 528 mph at 29,530 ft
Operational range: 7,800 miles

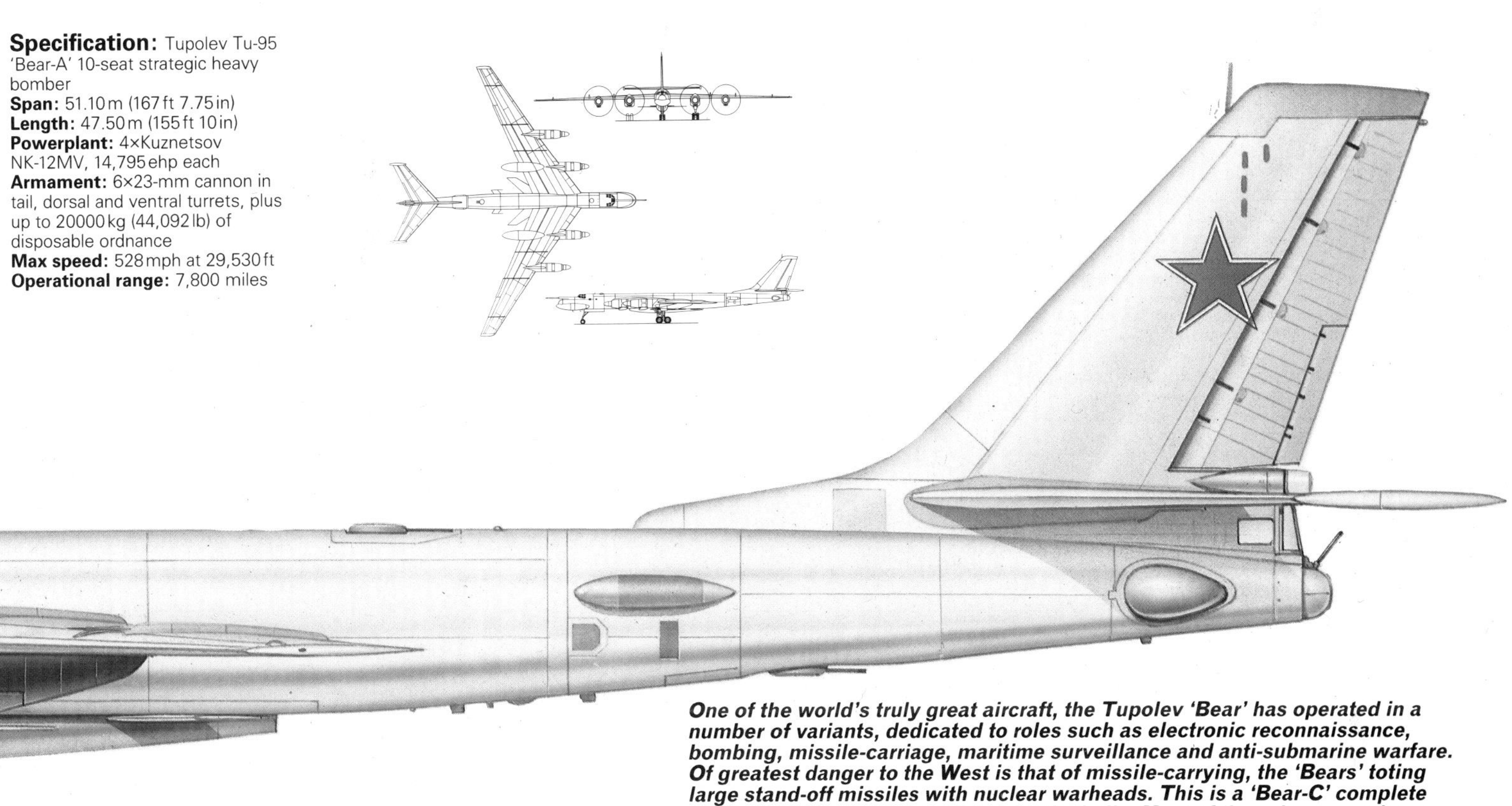

One of the world's truly great aircraft, the Tupolev 'Bear' has operated in a number of variants, dedicated to roles such as electronic reconnaissance, bombing, missile-carriage, maritime surveillance and anti-submarine warfare. Of greatest danger to the West is that of missile-carrying, the 'Bears' toting large stand-off missiles with nuclear warheads. This is a 'Bear-C' complete with AS-3 'Kangaroo' missile under the belly. Most of these have now been reworked as 'Bear-Gs' for AS-4 'Kitchen' carriage, or as electronic surveillance platforms.

Tupolev Tu-14 'Bosun'

Originating a design rival for the same first-generation jet bomber requirement that produced the successful Il-28, the Tu-14 attracted the interest of the Soviet naval air arm. Selecting a rather larger design formula than Ilyushin, the Tupolev design bureau produced a series of prototypes (Tu-72/73) powered by three turbojets, but when twin-jet derivatives (Tu-79/81) appeared with more powerful Klimov VK-1 engines this version was selected for production for the naval air arm as the Tu-14 bomber, the Tu-14R reconnaissance aircraft and the Tu-14T torpedo bomber; about 200 were produced and service began in 1950. The NATO reporting name was 'Bosun' for all three versions.

Specification: Tupolev Tu-14 'Bosun' three-seat naval medium and (-14T) torpedo bomber
Span: 21.686 m (71 ft 1.75 in)
Length: 21.69 m (71 ft 2 in)
Powerplant: 2×Klimov VK-1, 2700 kg (5,952 lb) st each
Armament: 2×23-mm cannon in tail turret, plus up to 3000 kg (6,614 lb) of free-fall bombs or (-14T) two torpedoes
Max speed: 525 mph at 16,405 ft
Operational range: 1,870 miles

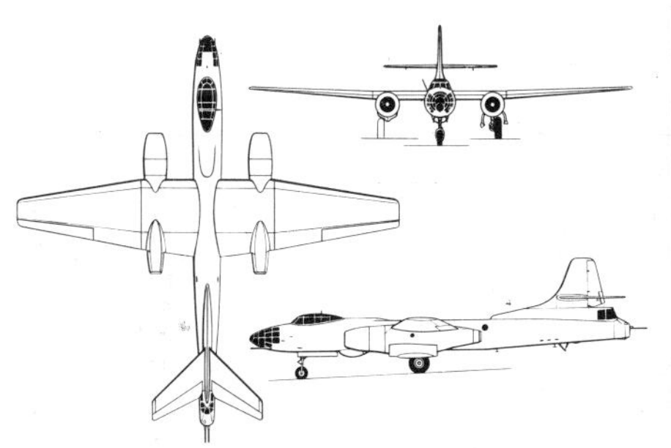

Tupolev Tu-16 'Badger'

Long-serving swept-wing subsonic strategic bomber, the Tu-16 first entered DA service in 1955, since when about 2,000 have been built and almost a dozen variants have been identified. The original 'Badger-A' (and similar 'B') carried conventional or nuclear free-fall bombs; these were followed by the 'C' anti-shipping version armed with AS-2 'Kipper' or AS-6 'Kingfish' missiles, the 'D', 'E' and 'F' reconnaissance aircraft, the 'G' bomber usually armed with AS-5 'Kelt' or AS-6 air-to-surface missiles, the 'H' escort (chaff-dispensing) or stand-off bomber, the 'J' and 'K' ECM aircraft, and the 'L' with advanced electronics. More than 300 of the later versions remain in Soviet service, and variants have been exported to Egypt, Indonesia, Iraq and Libya.

Specification: Tupolev Tu-16 'Badger-A' six-seat medium bomber
Span: 32.93 m (108 ft 0.5 in)
Length: 36.25 m (118 ft 11.25 in)
Powerplant: 2×Mikulin AM-3M, 9500 kg (20,944 lb) st each
Armament: 7×23-mm cannon (one fixed in nose and two each in tail, dorsal and ventral turrets), plus up to 10000 kg (22,046 lb) of disposable ordnance
Max speed: 615 mph at 19,685 ft
Operational range: 4,570 miles

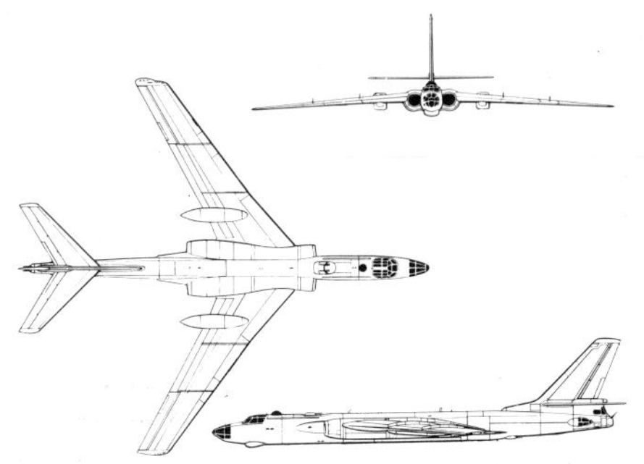

Boeing B-47 Stratojet

Resulting from the USAAF's 1944 requirement for a high-speed medium bomber, the classic and highly successful Stratojet evolved through a number of interim concepts with straight and then swept wings. After digesting German research, the designers finally fixed on flexible, 35° swept wings with suspended engine pods, and a tandem main landing gear arrangement under the fuselage. The XB-47 flew in December 1947 with Allison J35-A-2 turbojets, but from the second prototype all B-47s had the J47. The 10 B-47As were lead-in aircraft, and were followed by 399 strengthened B-47Bs with more fuel and provision for inflight-refuelling, and by 1,241 B-47Es with more power, ejector seats, a drag-chute, and cannon rather than machine-guns in the tail. There were also RB-47E, RB-47H and RB-47K reconnaissance models, and a number of experimental and special-purpose variants.

This B-47 Stratojet of the 380th Bomb Wing (Medium), based at Plattsburgh AFB, New York, is depicted in the markings worn during rotational 'Reflex Action' duty at RAF Brize Norton. The white undersides were applied to reflect nuclear flash. The red tail stripe was the squadron colour, and a squadron badge would have been carried on the starboard side of the nose. To port is the 'mailed fist' crest of Strategic Air Command.

Northrop B-35 and B-49

The B-35 flying wing bomber was planned from 1941 to carry 4536 kg (10,000 lb) of bombs over a radius of 8050 km (5,000 miles) and so able to attack Germany and Japan from bases in US territory. The XB-35 prototype first flew in June 1946 with four 2423-kW (3,250-hp) Pratt & Whitney R-4360 radials driving pusher contraprops for a speed of 350 mph. Span was 52.43 m (172 ft) and maximum weight 94802 kg (209,000 lb) and, though performance was good, problems were met with the propellers, which were replaced on the second prototype and 13 pre-production YB-35s by single-rotation units. Production of 200 B-35As was then cancelled in favour of a higher-speed but shorter-range variant with jet propulsion. This YB-35B was redesignated YB-49 and first flew in October 1947. The programme was cancelled after the loss of two YB-49s in mid-air explosions.

Specification: Northrop YB-49
seven-seat strategic heavy bomber prototype
Span: 52.43 m (172 ft 0 in)
Length: 16.18 m (53 ft 1 in)
Powerplant: 8×Allison J35-A-5, 1814 kg (4,000 lb) st each
Armament: 2×12.7-mm (0.5-in) machine-guns in tail position, plus provision for 16965 kg (37,400 lb) of bombs carried internally
Max T/O weight: 96617 kg (213,000 lb)
Max speed: 520 mph at 30,000 ft
Operational range: 2,800 miles with 4536-kg (10,000-lb) bombload

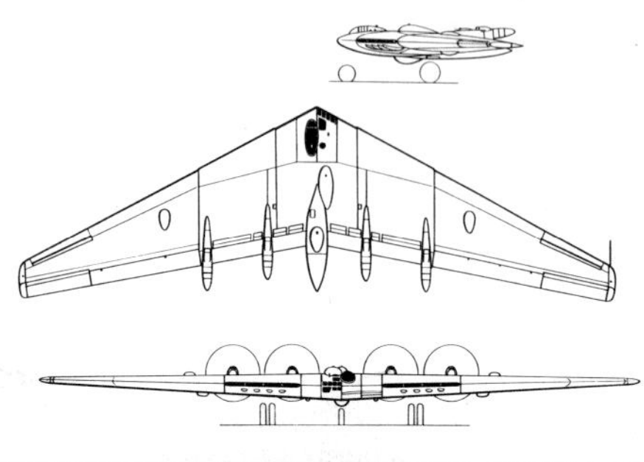

Convair B-36

Still one of the largest aircraft ever to have flown, the B-36 was developed to meet the same basic requirement as the B-35 and also had pusher engines, though in this instance married to a conventional layout. The XB-36 flew in August 1946 and was followed by one YB-36 with a raised cockpit and main landing gear units with four-wheel bogies, and by 22 B-36As with R-4360-25 engines but no armament. The operational versions were 73 B-36Bs with 2610-kW (3,500-hp) R-4360-41 radials, 86 B-36Ds (including 64 conversions) with four turbojets in two underwing pods for greater speed, 24 RB-36D strategic reconnaissance aircraft (including seven B-36B conversions), 22 RB-36Es (all conversions), 34 B-36Fs with more powerful R-3460-53 radials, 24 RB-36Fs with more fuel, 83 B-36Hs and 73 RB-36Hs with improved flightdecks, and 33 B-36Js with more fuel and strengthened landing gear.

Specification: Convair B-36J
15-seat strategic heavy bomber
Span: 70.10 m (230 ft 0 in)
Length: 49.40 m (162 ft 1 in)
Powerplant: 6×Pratt & Whitney R-4360-53, 2833 kW (3,800 hp) each, and 4×General Electric J47-GE-19, 2359 kg (5,200 lb) st each
Armament: 12×20-mm cannon in 6×remote-control barbettes, plus provision for up to 39010 kg (86,000 lb) of bombs internally
Max T/O weight: 185976 kg (410,000 lb)
Max speed: 411 mph at 36,400 ft
Operational range: 6,800 miles with a 4536-kg (10,000-lb) bombload

Specification: Boeing B-47E-II Stratojet three-seat strategic medium bomber
Span: 35.36 m (116 ft 0 in)
Length: 33.48 m (109 ft 10 in)
Powerplant: 6×General Electric J47-GE-25/25A, 2722 kg (6,000 lb) st each
Armament: 2×20-mm cannon in a remote-control tail barbette, plus provision for up to 9072 kg (20,000 lb) of bombs carried internally
Max T/O weight: 93759 kg (206,700 lb)
Max speed: 606 mph at 16,300 ft
Operational range: 4,000 miles

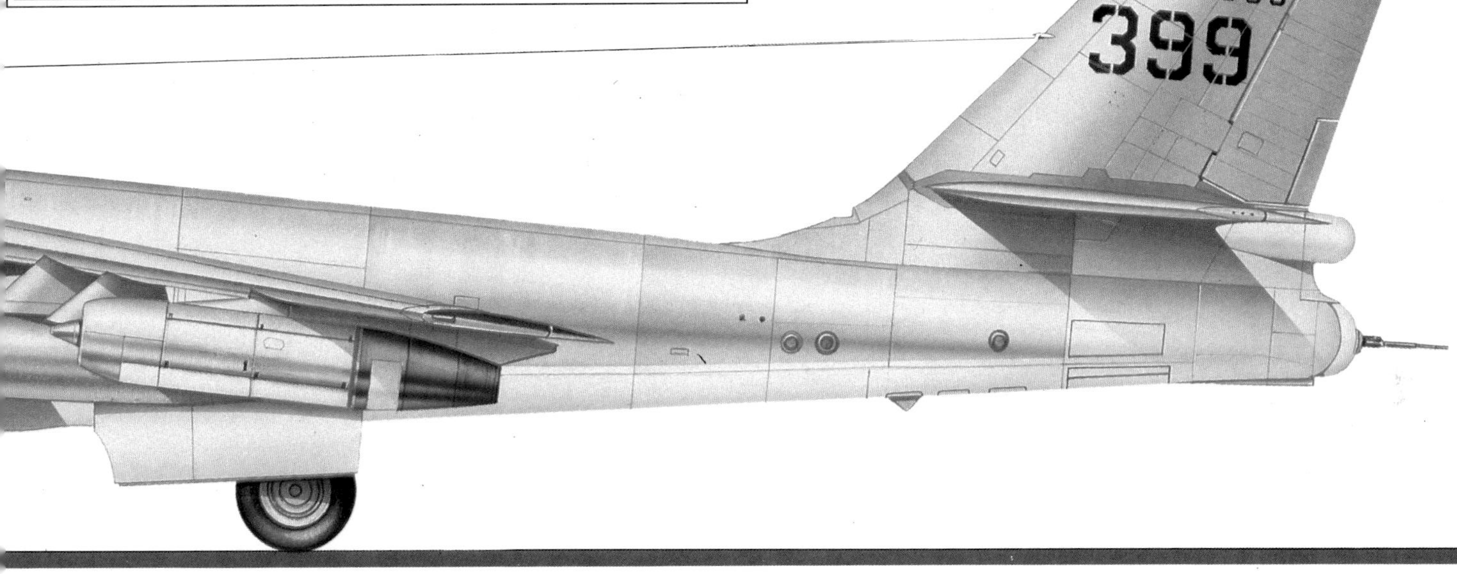

North American *B-45 Tornado*

The B-45 was the USA's first four-engine jet bomber to fly (as the XB-45 in March 1947), and was essentially an interim type that applied jet propulsion to the piston-engine bomber concept with two pilots, a bombardier and a tail gunner. The B-45A initially had Allison J35-A-11 turbojets, but these were later changed to 1814-kg (4,000-lb) thrust J47-GE-9s. These 96 aircraft were to have been followed by the B-45B with a new radar and fire-control system, but this was not procured so the next variant was the B-45C, of which only 10 were built. This was designed for tactical use and had a strengthened airframe and canopy, allowing a 9072-kg (20,000-lb) increase in weight with large tiptanks. The final production model was the RB-45C 12-camera reconnaissance variant, of which 33 were built.

Specification: North American B-45C Tornado four-seat tactical light bomber
Span: 27.13 m (89 ft 0 in) without tiptanks
Length: 22.96 m (75 ft 4 in)
Powerplant: 4×General Electric J47-GE-13/15, 2359 kg (5,200 lb) st each
Armament: 2×12.7-mm (0.5-in) machine-guns in a tail turret, plus provision for up to 9979 kg (22,000 lb) of bombs carried internally
Max T/O weight: 51235 kg (112,952 lb)
Max speed: 579 mph at sea level
Operational range: 1,910 miles

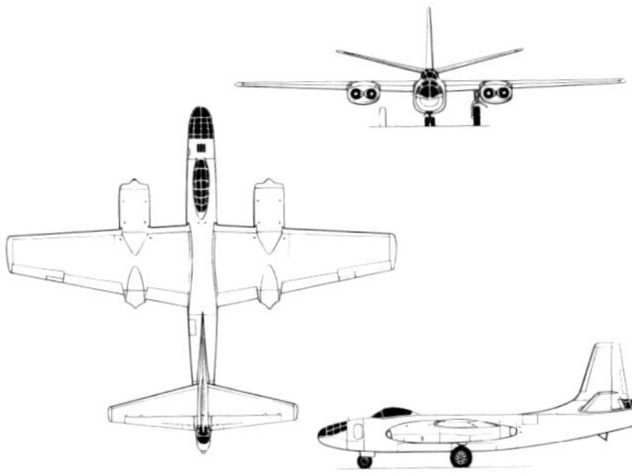

Convair B-46

The B-46 was one of four designs submitted in response to the USAAF's April 1944 requirement for a medium bomber with a tactical radius of 1610 km (1,000 miles), a speed of 500 mph or more, and a service ceiling of 40,000 ft or more. The Convair design was of superb aerodynamic cleanliness, but was essentially piston-engined in concept translated to jet propulsion by the use of paired engines in underwing pods. The sole XB-46 first flew in April 1947, and after manufacturer's trials was flown to Wright Field for service evaluation. These showed a sea-level speed of 491 mph and a climb to 35,000 ft in 19 minutes, together with excellent handling characteristics. But the XB-46 was clearly inferior to the Boeing XB-47 in concept and development potential, and therefore failed to secure a production order.

Specification: Convair XB-46 three-seat medium bomber
Span: 34.44 m (113 ft 0 in)
Length: 32.23 m (105 ft 9 in)
Powerplant: 4×General Electric J35-C-3, 1814 kg (4,000 lb) st each
Armament: 2×12.7-mm (0.5-in) machine-guns in a remote-control tail barbette, plus provision for up to 9979 kg (22,000 lb) of bombs carried internally
Normal T/O weight: 41278 kg (91,000 lb)
Max speed: 545 mph at 15,000 ft
Operational range: 2,870 miles with a 3629-kg (8,000-lb) bombload

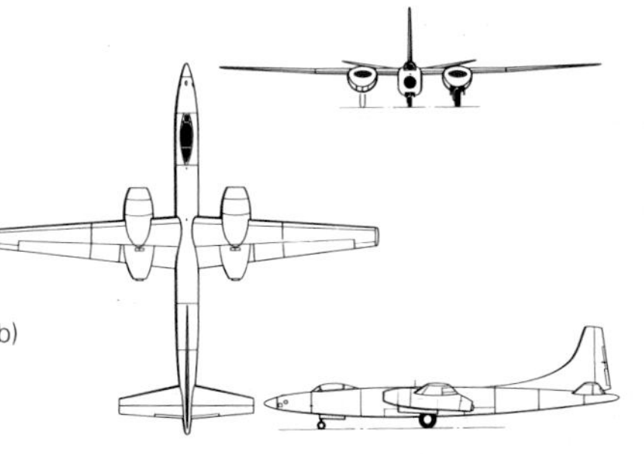

Convair B-58 Hustler

One of the most ambitious warplanes ever attempted, the B-58 was planned as a supersonic bomber with a 18.90-m (62-ft) jettisonable pod for fuel and a single nuclear weapon, escape pods for the crew, an area-ruled fuselage, a large delta wing supporting four podded engines, and extensive use of honeycomb sandwich skin panels. The first XB-58 flew in November 1956, and the advanced nature of the whole programme is shown by the fact that the two XB-58 prototypes were followed by 28 more YB-58A pre-production and service evaluation aircraft. Some of the latter were later upgraded as RB-58A strategic reconnaissance aircraft, and others as TB-58A dual-control conversion trainers. The operational bomber was the B-58A, of which 86 were built with provision for a dual pod in which the larger segment contained fuel and the smaller segment a number of advanced sensors or the weapons.

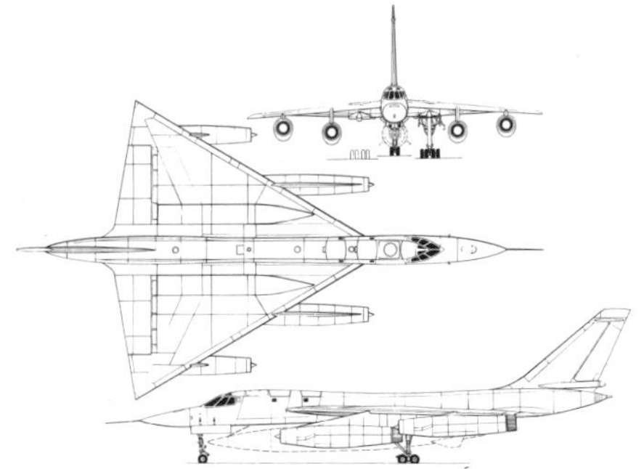

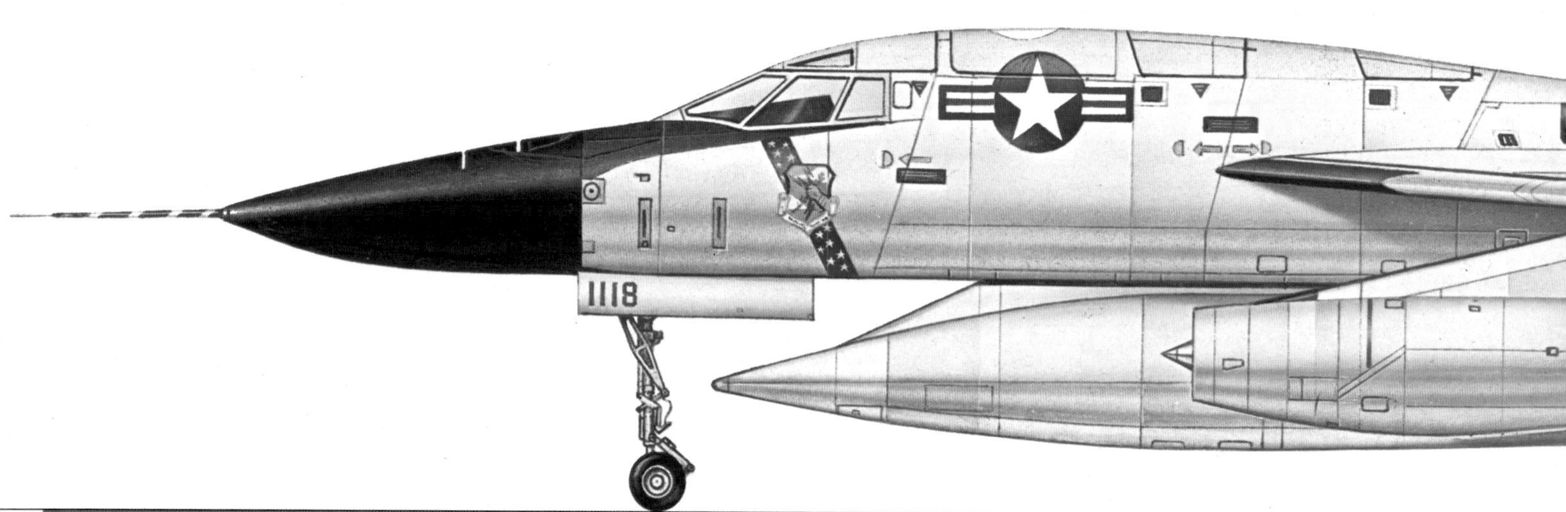

Martin B-48

Comparable in concept to the Convair B-46 but with six rather than four turbojets and less-refined aerodynamics, the B-48 was again planned to meet the USAAF's 1944 medium bomber requirement, and first flew in June 1947 as the XB-48. The engines were located in podded triplets, one under each wing, but the additional power could not compensate for the greater weight and higher drag of the airframe, and performance was well below that demanded by the Air Force, the standard 3629-kg (8,000-lb) bombload being carried over a range of only 2,500 miles. A second prototype was used in the service evaluation, which made it clear that there was no real purpose in pursuing development of the type beyond the prototype stage.

Specification: Martin XB-48 three-seat medium bomber prototype
Span: 33.02 m (108 ft 4 in)
Length: 26.14 m (85 ft 9 in)
Powerplant: 6×General Electric J35-A-5, 2087 kg (4,600 lb) st each
Armament: 1×20-mm cannon in a remote-control tail barbette, plus provision for up to 9072 kg (20,000 lb) of bombs carried internally
Normal T/O weight: 46358 kg (102,200 lb)
Max speed: 495 mph at 15,000 ft
Operational range: 2,500 miles with a 3629-kg (8,000-lb) bombload

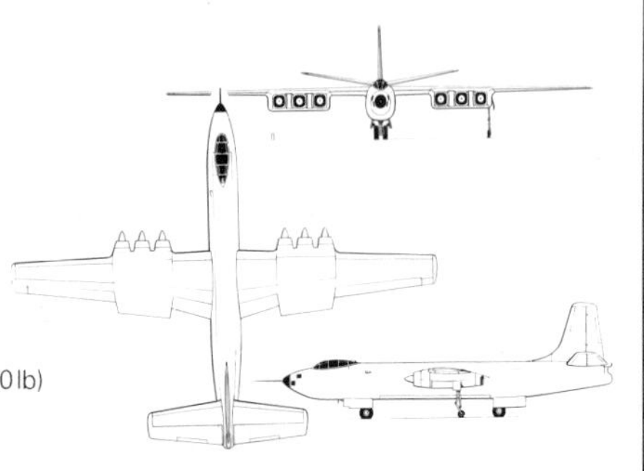

Boeing B-50 Superfortress

In 1944 Pratt & Whitney re-engined a standard B-29A with R-4360 radials in place of the normal Wright R-3350s under the designation XB-44, and this more powerful version was placed in production during 1945 as the B-29D. The designation was revised to B-50 before deliveries began, and other major modifications were a taller vertical tail, a stronger but lighter wing structure, upgraded landing gear, hydraulic nosewheel steering and hydraulic rudder boost. The first production model was the B-50A, and the 79 aircraft of this variant were followed by 45 examples of the B-50B, of which all but one were later revised for inflight-refuelling, and 222 examples of the B-50D with two fixed underwing tanks, a one-piece nose moulding of Plexiglas and a new forward upper turret. Aircraft were converted as RB-50 reconnaissance, TB-50 trainer and jet-boosted KB-50 tanker aircraft.

Specification: Boeing B-50D Superfortress 10-seat strategic medium bomber
Span: 43.05 m (141 ft 3 in)
Length: 30.18 m (99 ft 0 in)
Powerplant: 4×Pratt & Whitney R-4360-35/35A/51, 2610 kW (3,500 hp) each
Armament: 1×20-mm cannon and 12×12.7-mm (0.5-in) machine-guns in 5×turrets, plus provision for up to 9072 kg (20,000 lb) of bombs carried internally
Max T/O weight: 78473 kg (173,000 lb)
Max speed: 380 mph at 25,000 ft
Operational range: 4,900 miles

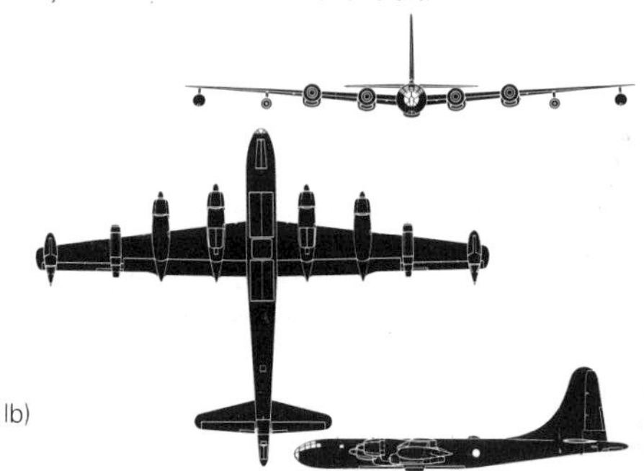

Specification: Convair B-58A Hustler three-seat supersonic strategic medium bomber
Span: 17.32 m (56 ft 10 in)
Length: 29.49 m (96 ft 9 in)
Powerplant: 4×General Electric J79-GE-5A, 7076 kg (15,600 lb) st each
Armament: 1×20-mm multi-barrel cannon in a remote-control tail barbette, plus provision for nuclear or conventional weapons in the jettisonable pod
Max T/O weight: 73936 kg (163,000 lb)
Max speed: Mach 2.1 at 40,000 ft
Operational range: 2,000 miles

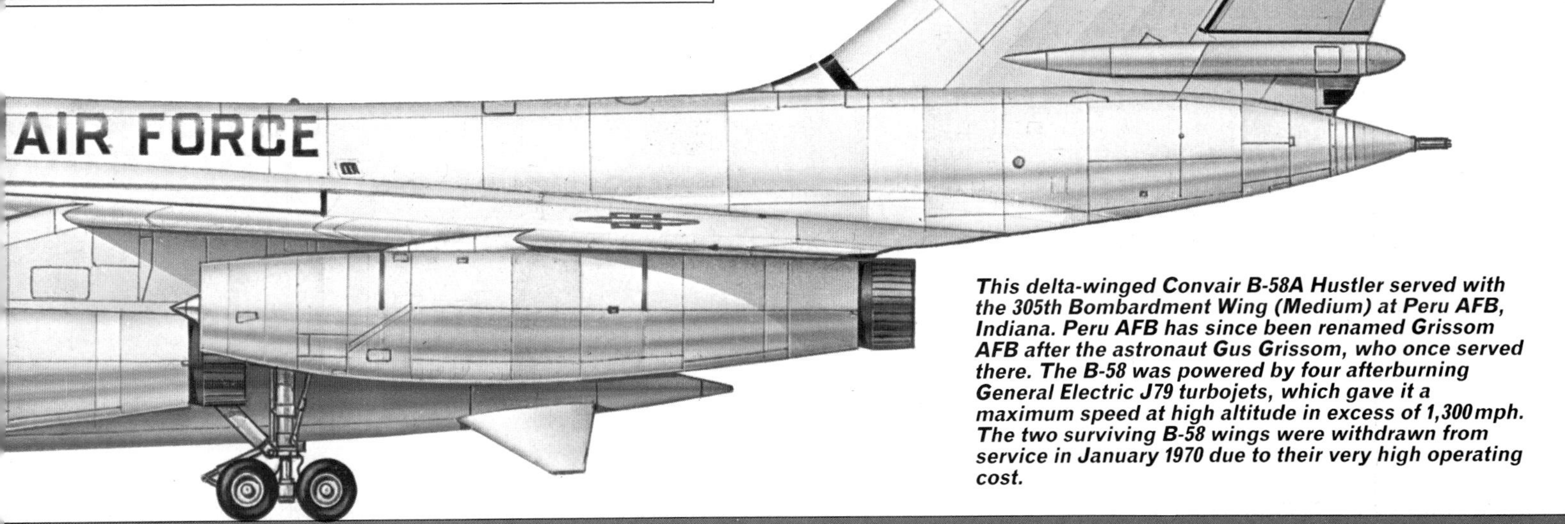

This delta-winged Convair B-58A Hustler served with the 305th Bombardment Wing (Medium) at Peru AFB, Indiana. Peru AFB has since been renamed Grissom AFB after the astronaut Gus Grissom, who once served there. The B-58 was powered by four afterburning General Electric J79 turbojets, which gave it a maximum speed at high altitude in excess of 1,300 mph. The two surviving B-58 wings were withdrawn from service in January 1970 due to their very high operating cost.

Martin B-51

Designed in competition with the Douglas B-42/43 Mixmaster series as successor to the Douglas A-26 Invader in the high-speed attack and interdiction role, the XA-45 was a radical design based on a long fuselage fitted with a variable-incidence 35° swept wing, a swept T-tail, tandem landing gear, and three turbojets mounted as a pair under the forward fuselage and the third in the tail. During the design phase the type was redesignated XB-51 and two prototypes were ordered, the first of these flying in October 1949. During trials the type proved to have good performance but poor handling, and production plans were cancelled. The production variant would have featured a nose very heavy armament of eight 20-mm cannon in addition to the bombload.

Specification: Martin XB-51 two-seat attack bomber prototype
Span: 16.15 m (53 ft 0 in)
Length: 24.38 m (80 ft 0 in)
Powerplant: 3×General Electric J47-GE-7/13, 2640 kg (5,820 lb) st each
Armament: provision for 4717 kg (10,400 lb) of bombs carried internally
Normal T/O weight: 25367 kg (55,923 lb)
Max speed: 645 mph at sea level
Operational range: 1,613 miles

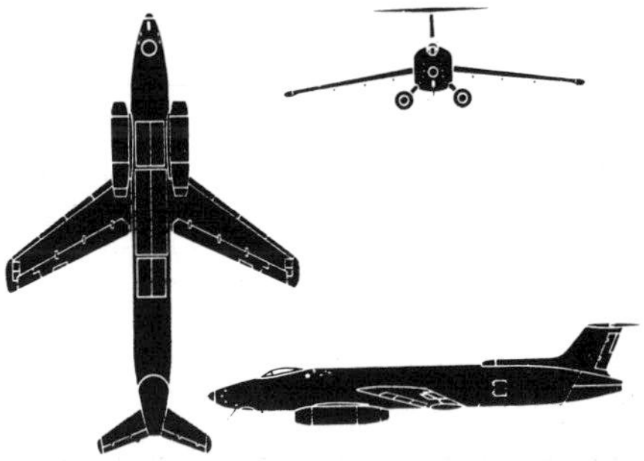

Martin B-57

The B-57 was the licence-built US version of the English Electric Canberra, and the first combat type of non-American design to be accepted for US service after World War II. The first Martin-built aircraft were eight B-57As similar to the Canberra B.Mk 2 but re-engineered and with Wright turbojets: the first flew in July 1953. The 67 RB-57As were similar but carried cameras in an aft bay. Next came 202 B-57B night intruders with tandem seating and revised armament including eight machine-guns or four cannon; variants were the RB-57B reconnaissance conversions, EB-57B ECM conversions, 38 B-57C transition trainers, and 68 B-57E target tugs. The 20 RB-57Ds were high-altitude reconnaissance platforms with 48.76-m (107.5-ft) span wings and J57-P-37A turbojets, and the 12 RB-57Fs had 37.19-m (122-ft) wings and TF33-P-11 turbofans.

Specification: Martin B-57B two-seat night intruder and tactical light bomber
Span: 19.51 m (64 ft 0 in)
Length: 19.96 m (65 ft 6 in)
Powerplant: 2×Wright J65-W-5, 3266 kg (7,200 lb) st each
Armament: 8×12.7-mm (0.5-in) machine-guns or 4×20-mm cannon, plus provision for 16×rockets carried under the wings and 2722 kg (6,000 lb) of bombs carried internally
Max T/O weight: 24948 kg (55,000 lb)
Max speed: 582 mph at 40,000 ft
Operational range: 2,300 miles

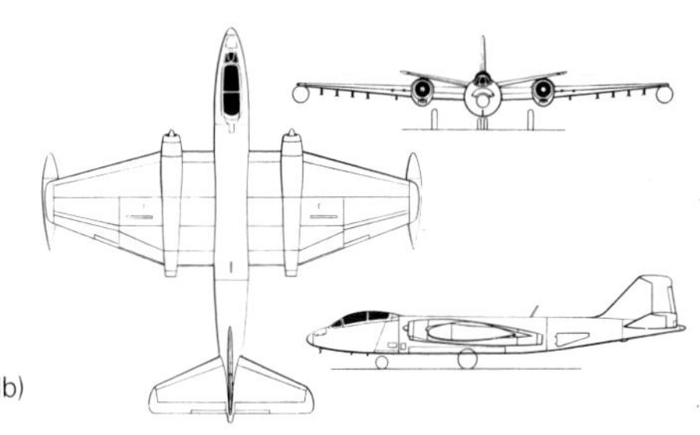

Boeing B-52 Stratofortress

Designed from 1945 as a turbine-engined successor to the B-36 strategic bomber, the mighty B-52 was planned with 20° sweep and turboprops before maturing as a 'big brother' to the B-47 with 35° sweep, podded pairs of turbojets and inflight-refuelling capability for global reach. The XB-52 flew six months after the YB-52's initial flight in April 1952. The three B-52As introduced a raised cockpit, and were followed by 50 fully operational B-52Bs (including 27 RB-52Bs), 35 higher-weight B-52Cs, 170 similar B-52Ds, 100 B-52Es with improved electronics, 89 B-52Fs with greater power, 193 B-52Gs with a shorter vertical tail, a remote-control tail barbette, underwing tanks and integral wing tankage, and 102 B-52Hs with 7258-kg (16,000-lb) thrust Pratt & Whitney TF33-P-1 turbofans for greater range. B-52G/Hs still serve with improved systems and cruise missiles.

Specification: Boeing B-52G Stratofortress six-seat strategic heavy bomber
Span: 56.39 m (185 ft 0 in)
Length: 48.03 m (157 ft 7 in)
Powerplant: 8×Pratt & Whitney J57-P-43W, 5080 kg (11,200 lb) st each
Armament: 4×12.7-mm (0.5-in) machine-guns in a remote-control tail barbette, plus provision for 22680 kg (50,000 lb) of bombs or other stores
Max T/O weight: 221357+ kg (488,000+ lb)
Max speed: 595 mph at optimum altitude
Operational range: 7,500+ miles

Convair B-60

To compete with the B-52 in the race to provide the USAF with a turbojet-powered successor to the B-36 in the heavy strategic bombing role, Convair proposed a relatively simple modification to the B-36 with eight turbojets in four podded pairs under 35° swept wings. The type was planned as the YB-36G with basically the same fuselage and wing centre section as the B-36, to which were married a revised nose section, new outer wing panels and swept tail surfaces. The landing gear was strengthened and the fuel capacity increased, and in this form two YB-60s were ordered. The first machine flew in April 1952, but clearly possessed less development potential than the B-52, and it failed to secure a production order.

Specification: Convair YB-60 10-seat strategic heavy bomber prototype
Span: 62.70 m (206 ft 0 in)
Length: 52.12 m (171 ft 0 in)
Powerplant: 8×Pratt & Whitney J57-P-3, 3992 kg (8,800 lb) st each
Armament: 2×20-mm cannon in a remote-control tail barbette, plus provision for an unrevealed weight of bombs carried internally
Max T/O weight: 163296 kg (360,000 lb)
Max speed: 520 mph at 45,000 ft
Operational range: 8,000 miles

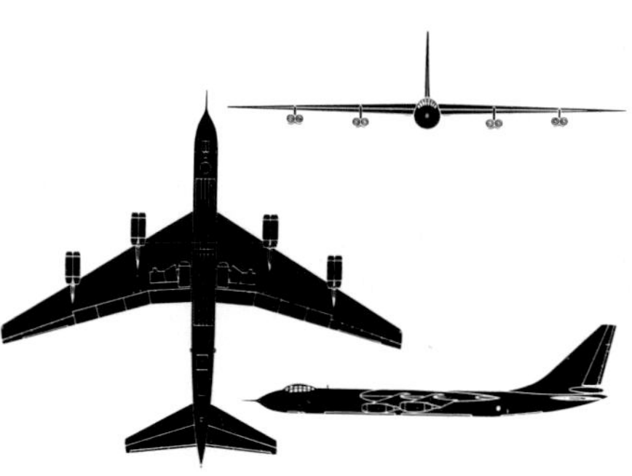

Douglas B-66 Destroyer

The B-66 was evolved from the US Navy's A3D (A-3) Skywarrior to provide the USAF with a tactical light bomber and reconnaissance platform. Much redesign (including provision for inflight-refuelling) was necessary, and the new Allison J71 turbojet was adopted. Five RB-66As were ordered as pre-production night reconnaissance aircraft, the first flying in June 1954. There followed 175 RB-66Bs, of which the last 30 were completed as RB-66Cs with electronic rather than optical reconnaissance gear. The only pure bomber variant was the B-66B designed for operation at higher weights, and the first of 72 was delivered in March 1956. Some 13 were later modified to B-66E standard with improved equipment, and the last production model was the WB-66D weather reconnaissance variant of which 36 were built. Several electronic warfare variants were produced as conversions.

Specification: Douglas B-66B Destroyer three-seat tactical light bomber
Span: 22.10 m (72 ft 6 in)
Length: 22.91 m (75 ft 2 in)
Powerplant: 2×Allison J71-A-13, 4536 kg (10,000 lb) st each
Armament: 2×20-mm cannon in a remote-control tail barbette, plus provision for up to 6804 kg (15,000 lb) of bombs carried internally
Max T/O weight: 37649 kg (83,000 lb)
Max speed: 594 mph at 36,000 ft
Operational range: 1,500 miles

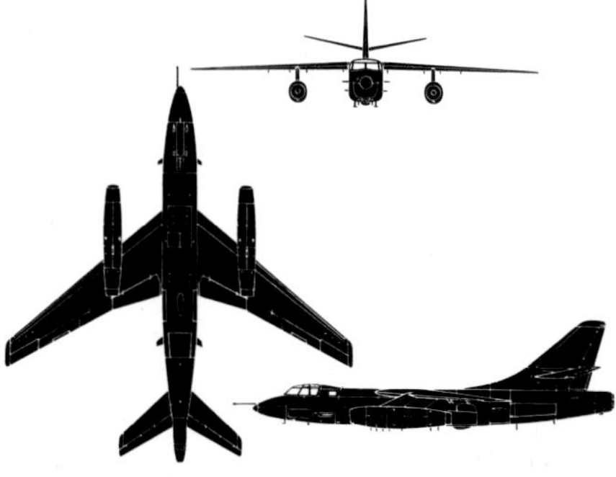

North American B-70 Valkyrie

Designed as a highly supersonic successor to the B-52 in the high-altitude strategic heavy bombing role, the B-70 Valkyrie was an extraordinarily ambitious design built largely of stainless steel with a delta main wing whose tips folded down in the air to -65° to improve supersonic stability, twin vertical tail surfaces and canard foreplanes. The crew was accommodated in a pressure capsule, and each man was provided with a separate escape capsule. The first of two XB-70A prototypes flew in September 1964 and, though there were a large number of teething problems, all who flew the type commended its performance. But by this time the fallacy of high-altitude bombing in face of SAMs was clear, and the programme was cancelled in 1964. The two prototypes were used for experimental flying, the second XB-70A being destroyed in a mid-air collision during June 1966.

Specification: North American XB-70A Valkyrie four-seat supersonic strategic heavy bomber prototype
Span: 32.00 m (105 ft 0 in)
Length: 59.89 m (196 ft 6 in)
Powerplant: 6×General Electric J93-GE-3, 12338 kg (27,200 lb) st each
Armament: provision for up to 14×thermonuclear bombs carried internally
Max T/O weight: 249476 kg (550,000 lb)
Max speed: Mach 3.08 at high altitude
Operational range: 5,000 miles

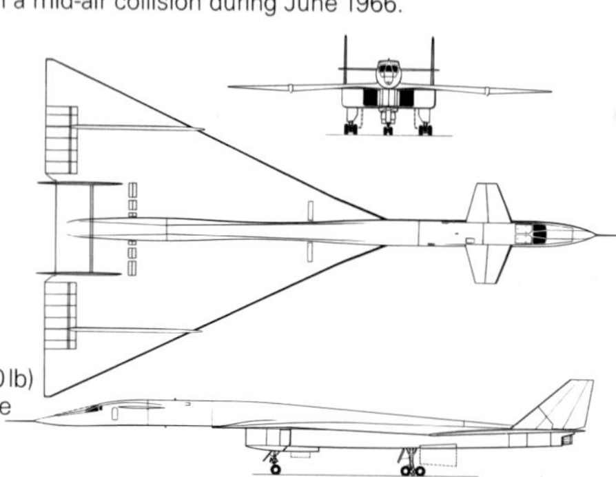

Avro Vulcan B.Mk 2

With increased engine power available, from 1956 the Vulcan's designers produced a more effective wing: this had four-section elevons rather than the outboard ailerons and inboard elevons of the Vulcan B.Mk 1, while the combination of greater span and increased outboard chord produced a reduced thickness/chord ratio. The wing was test flown on the prototype Vulcan B.Mk 1, the first Vulcan B.Mk 2 following in August 1958. The type began to enter service in 1960 with 7711-kg (17,000-lb) Olympus Mk 200 engines for greater ceiling with a weightier warload, and from 1962 the aircraft were modified for carriage of the 'Blue Steel' stand-off missile. From 1966 the development of effective SAMs by the USSR forced the RAF to recast the Vulcan B.Mk 2 in the low-level role with terrain-following radar, and the type was retired in 1982 after small-scale operations in the Falklands War.

Specification: Avro Vulcan B.Mk 2 five-seat long-range strategic bomber
Span: 33.83 m (111 ft 0 in)
Length: 32.15 m (105 ft 6 in)
Powerplant: 4×Rolls-Royce (Bristol Siddeley) Olympus Mk 301, 9072 kg (20,000 lb) st each
Armament: provision for up to 9526 kg (21,000 lb) of bombs carried internally
Max T/O weight: about 113400 kg (250,000 lb)
Max speed: 640 mph at high altitude
Operational range: 4,600 miles

BAC (English Electric) TSR.2

Cancelled in 1965 for political reasons just as its complex systems were beginning to reach initial maturity, the TSR.2 was an extraordinarily ambitious design of enormous potential. The type was planned from 1955 as an all-weather Canberra replacement able to operate supersonically in all weathers at high- or low-level in the tactical strike and reconnaissance roles. The design was aerodynamically advanced, and a leap forward in airframe, avionics, engine and equipment technologies. The integrated nav/attack system (based on an inertial system, computer and radar for automatic low-level flight with data displayed on the pilot's HUD) also offered great potential, but was one of the features most difficult to develop. The first TSR.2 flew in September 1964, but only this of four completed prototypes actually got into the air.

Specification: British Aircraft Corporation TSR.2 two-seat tactical strike and reconnaissance prototype
Span: 11.28 m (37 ft 0 in)
Length: 27.13 m (89 ft 0 in)
Powerplant: 2×Bristol Siddeley Olympus Mk 22R, 8891 kg (19,600 lb) st each
Armament: provision for up to 2722 kg (6,000 lb) of disposable stores carried internally, and for 1814 kg (4,000 lb) of disposable stores carried on 4×underwing hardpoints
Max T/O weight: 43545 kg (96,000 lb)
Max speed: Mach 2.25 at high altitude
Operational range: 2,300 miles

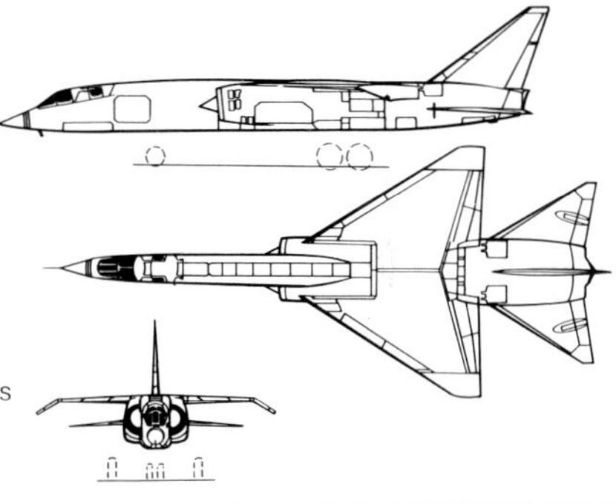

Blackburn Buccaneer

After sorry tale of cancellations (the BAC TSR.2, General Dynamics F-111K and Anglo-French Variable-Geometry concept) in its effort to find a low-level strike and reconnaissance platform, the RAF somewhat reluctantly accepted most of the Royal Navy's surplus Buccaneer S.Mk 2s. Some 70 of these were modified to RAF standards as Buccaneer S.Mk 2As, proving themselves quite exceptional in the transonic low-level role. Further modifications turned these aircraft into Buccaneer S.Mk 2Bs with underwing provision for three AJ168 Martel anti-radar missiles and their associated data-link pod, and a bulged bomb bay door able to accommodate an extra fuel tank. So successful was the Buccaneer, moreover, that the RAF ordered 43 new-production S.Mk 2B aircraft, and a useful force remains in service to this day in the over-water strike role.

Specification: Blackburn Buccaneer S.Mk 2B two-seat strike and reconnaissance aeroplane
Span: 13.41 m (44 ft 0 in)
Length: 19.33 m (63 ft 5 in)
Powerplant: 2×Rolls-Royce Spey RB168 Mk 101, 5105 kg (11,255 lb) st each
Armament: provision for up to 1814 kg (4,000 lb) of disposable stores carried internally, and for up to 5443 kg (12,000 lb) of disposable stores carried on 4×underwing hardpoints
Max T/O weight: 28123 kg (62,000 lb)
Max speed: 646 mph at 200 ft
Operational range: 2,300 miles

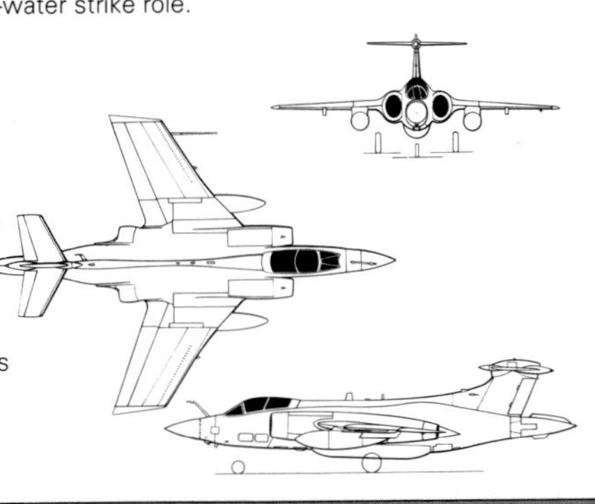

Panavia Tornado

Developed as a STOL multi-role type by a British, Italian and West German consortium, the superb Tornado IDS first flew in August 1974 as a compact type offering excellent payload/range performance combined with high outright performance and superb field performance through its variable-geometry wings, high-lift devices and potent powerplant with automatically scheduled inlets and nozzles. The type began to enter British service as the Tornado GR.Mk 1 and Tornado GR.Mk 1T dual-control trainer in 1980. The Tornado is cleared for an exceptional diversity of weapons, and these can be delivered with pinpoint accuracy after a low-level supersonic approach under control of the sophisticated nav/attack system working through a 'fly-by-wire' control system for the rudder and 'tailerons', the latter supplemented at low speed by wing-mounted spoilers.

Specification: Panavia Tornado GR.Mk 1 two-seat variable-geometry interdictor, strike and reconnaissance aeroplane
Span: 13.91 m (45 ft 7.5 in) spread and 8.60 m (28 ft 2.5 in) swept
Length: 16.72 m (54 ft 10.25 in)
Powerplant: 2×Turbo-Union RB199-34R Mk 103, 7620 kg (16,800 lb) st each
Armament: 2×27-mm cannon, plus provision for up to 9000 kg (19,840 lb) of disposable stores carried on 7×external hardpoints
Max T/O weight: 27215 kg (60,000 lb)
Max speed: Mach 2.2+ at 36,000 ft
Operational range: 1,725 miles

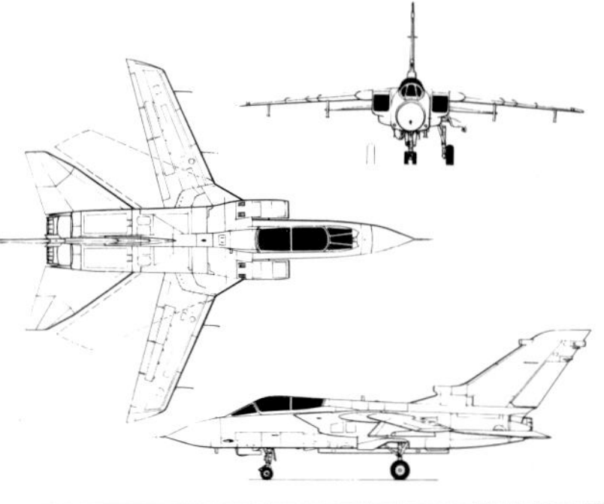

Vickers Valiant

Developed during 1948 as a private venture intermediate in capability between the Lincoln and the Victor/Vulcan package being developed to replace it, the Valiant offered such low risks that a specification was written round it and two prototypes ordered. The first of these flew in May 1951 and was quickly lost in an accident, the second prototype then assuming the main weight of development. Five pre-production aircraft were followed by 107 production aircraft between 1954 and 1957. The most important of these were the Valiant B.Mk 1 bombers that served with 10 Bomber Command squadrons. Other models were 11 Valiant B(PR).Mk 1 reconnaissance aircraft, 14 Valiant B(PR)K.Mk 1 multi-role bomber, reconnaissance and tanker aircraft, and 48 Valiant B(K).Mk 1 dual-role bombers and tankers with additional transfer fuel. All Valiants were withdrawn in January 1965 because of fatigue problems.

Specification: Vickers Valiant B.Mk 1 five-seat long-range strategic bomber
Span: 34.85 m (114 ft 4 in)
Length: 32.99 m (108 ft 3 in)
Powerplant: 4×Rolls-Royce Avon Mk 201, 4536 kg (10,000 lb) st each
Armament: provision for up to 9526 kg (21,000 lb) of disposable stores carried internally
Max T/O weight: 79378 kg (175,000 lb)
Max speed: 567 mph at high altitude
Operational range: 3,450 miles

This Vickers Valiant of No. 214 Squadron, based at RAF Marham during the early 1960s, is wearing the overall white colour scheme with toned-down markings that is typical of the period. This unusual scheme was designed to protect the aircraft by reflecting and not absorbing the 'flash' from a nuclear explosion. The Valiant's main role was strategic nuclear strike.

Avro Lancaster

Because of delays with its successor, the Lancaster remained in service after the war mainly in variants such as the Lancaster B.Mk 1, B.Mk 3 (with Packard-built Merlin 28, 38 or 224 engines) and B.Mk 7 with revised armament. Limited development of the bomber continued, particularly in the longer-range F.E. (Far East) subvariants, but the main effort was devoted to roles such as photo-reconnaissance (Lancaster PR.Mk 1 conversion of the B.Mk 1), air/sea rescue (Lancaster ASR.Mk 3 conversions by Cunliffe-Own with an airdropped lifeboat), and maritime reconnaissance (Lancaster GR.Mk 3 conversions of the ASR.Mk 3, later redesignated Lancaster MR.Mk 3). Canadian-built Lancaster B.Mk 10s were converted for similar roles as the Lancaster 10-P, Lancaster 10-SR and Lancaster 10-MR (later Lancaster 10-MP). The last Lancaster was retired in 1953.

Specification: Avro Lancaster B.Mk 7 (F.E.) seven-seat long-range heavy bomber
Span: 31.09 m (102 ft 0 in)
Length: 21.48 m (70 ft 5.5 in)
Powerplant: 4×Rolls-Royce Merlin 24, 1223 kW (1,640 hp) each
Armament: 4×12.7-mm (0.5-in) machine-guns in twin-gun dorsal and tail turrets, 2×7.62-mm (0.303-in) machiner-guns in nose turret, plus provision for up to 9979 kg 22,000 lb) of bombs carried internally
Max T/O weight: 32659 kg (72,000 lb)
Max speed: 287 mph at 11,500 ft
Operational range: 1,660 miles with 6350-kg (14,000-lb) bombload

de Havilland Mosquito

At the end of World War II the Mosquito served Bomber Command in substantial numbers, most of the aircraft being Mosquito B.Mk XVIs of the 11 squadrons of No.8 Group (otherwise the Light Night Striking Force). First flown in November 1943, this had two-stage Merlin 70-series engines, a pressurised cabin for cruise at 40,000 ft and, though conceived for a 1361-kg (3,000-lb) bombload, generally the 1814-kg (4,000-lb) bombload made possible by bulged bomb bay doors. Some 1,200 B.Mk XVIs were built, and these formed the mainstay of the RAF's postwar light bomber force with the Mosquito B.Mk 35, of which 122 were built by Airspeed for service with squadrons of the British Air Forces of Occupation (Germany) and the 2nd Tactical Air Force. This improved B.Mk XVI first flew in March 1945, and some were modified with improved bombsights and aids such as Rebecca and Gee H Mk 2.

Specification: de Havilland Mosquito B.Mk 35 two-seat light bomber
Span: 16.50 m (54 ft 2 in)
Length: 12.43 m (40 ft 9.5 in)
Powerplant: 2×Rolls-Royce Merlin 113A/114A, 1260 kW (1,690 hp) each
Armament: provision for up to 1814 kg (4,000 lb) of bombs carried internally
Max T/O weight: 11431 kg (25,200 lb)
Max speed: 425 mph at high altitude
Operational range: 2,050 miles with 907-kg (2,000-lb) bombload

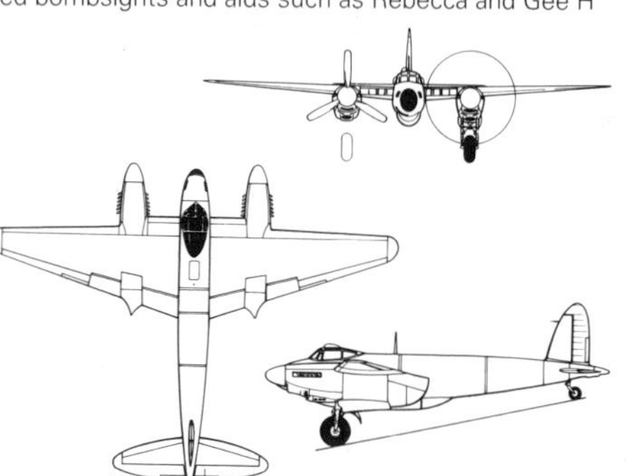

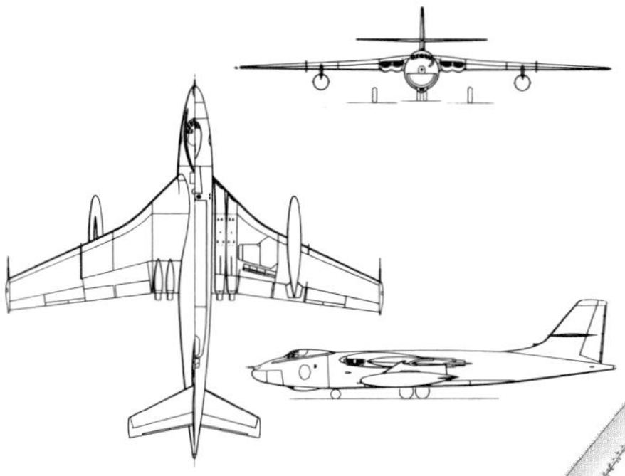

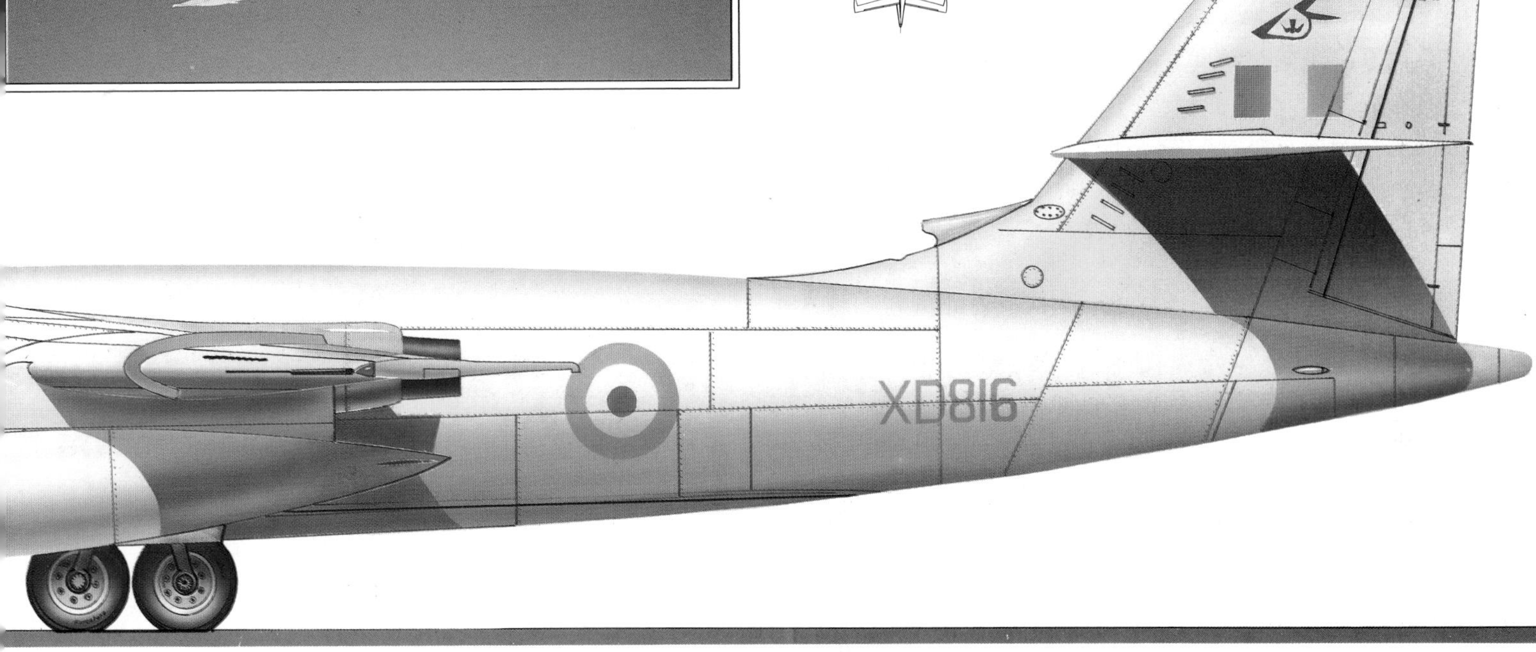

Avro Lincoln

The Lincoln was the Lancaster's successor, and was designed to a 1943 specification for a high-altitude bomber with a longer wing and fuselage, revised bomb bay defensive armament, and a modified nose. The type was mooted first as the Lancaster B.Mk IV and B.Mk V with Merlin 85 and Merlin 68 engines respectively, but was subsequently redesignated Lincoln B.Mk 1 and B.Mk 2. The prototype flew in June 1944 but the type was just too late for World War II service. Production amounted to 82 B.Mk 1s and 446 B.Mk 2s, conversions of B.Mk 2s to B.Mk 1 standard being designated B.Mk 4. The Canadian version would have been the Lincoln B.Mk 15, of which one was completed, while the Australian models were the Lincoln B.Mk 30 (54 built) and the Lincoln MR.Mk 31 maritime reconnaissance version with a nose lengthened by 1.98 m (6 ft 6 in) for radar and two operators (19 built).

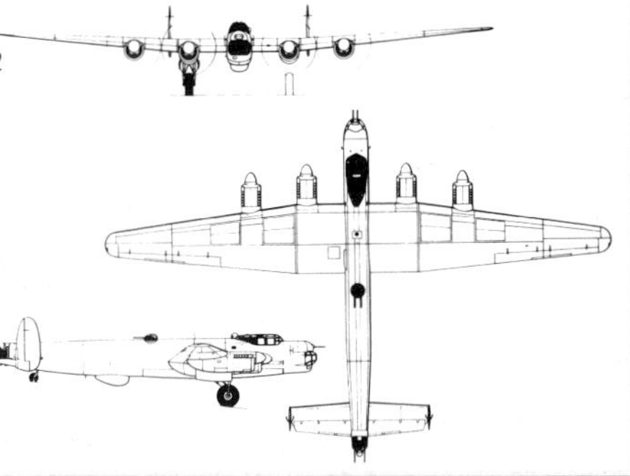

Specification: Avro Lincoln B.Mk 2 seven-seat long-range heavy bomber
Span: 36.58 m (120 ft 0 in)
Length: 23.85 m (78 ft 3 in)
Powerplant: 4×Packard-built Rolls-Royce Merlin 68, 68A or 300, 1305 kW (1,750 hp) each
Armament: 2×20-mm cannon in dorsal turret and 4×12.7-mm (0.5-in) machine-guns in twin-gun nose and tail turrets, plus provision for up to 6350 kg (14,000 lb) of bombs carried internally
Max T/O weight: 37195 kg (82,000 lb)
Max speed: 305 mph at 19,000 ft
Operational range: 2,800 miles

Boeing Washington

The Washington was the first US aircraft to enter British service after World War II, and was allocated to the UK in 1950 as part of the USA's military aid programme pending the arrival of the UK's first indigenously designed jet-powered bombers. The 88 Washington B.Mk 1s were used to supplement the obsolescent Lincoln force in the long-range strategic role, and were all ex-USAF B-29s and slightly longer-span B-29As, de-cocooned after storage in the Arizona desert and extensively refurbished before delivery to the RAF, which much appreciated the type's altitude performance, relative quiet and pressurised crew accommodation. The Washington was eventually phased out in favour of the English Electric Canberra, all but a few Sigint conversions being returned to the USA by the end of 1954.

Specification: Boeing Washington Mk 1 10-seat long-range heavy bomber7
Span: 43.05 m (141 ft 3 in)
Length: 30.18 m (99 ft 0 in)
Powerplant: 4×Wright R-3350-23/23A/41, 1641 kW (2,200 hp) each
Armament: 11×12.7-mm (0.5-in) machine-guns in two-gun fuselage barbettes and three-gun tail turret, plus provision for up to 9072 kg (20,000 lb) of bombs carried internally
Max T/O weight: 63504 kg (140,000 lb)
Max speed: 350 mph at 25,000 ft
Operational range: 2,850 miles

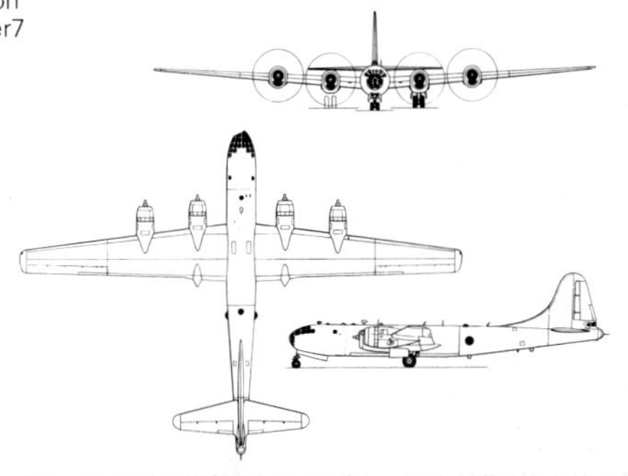

Handley Page Victor B.Mk 2

The Victor B.Mk 2 that began to enter service in 1962 was a considerably more capable type than the B.Mk 1. Amongst its features were a re-engineered airframe with longer-span wings and drag-reducing 'Kuchemann carrot' trailing-edge fairings, provision for the 'Blue Steel' stand-off missile, turbofans in place of the original Armstrong Siddeley Sapphire turbojets, provision for inflight-refuelling, and much enhanced ECM. The type first flew in February 1959 and immediately revealed far superior range performance as well as better operational characteristics. Only 30 Victor B.Mk 2s were built up to May 1963, and these served with two squadrons of Bomber Command, which became Strike Command in April 1968. From 1964 the Victor B.Mk 2 was used in the low-level role, and between 1973 and 1975 the last 20 were modified as Victor K.Mk 2 three-point inflight-refuelling tankers.

Specification: Handley Page Victor B.Mk 2 five-seat long-range strategic bomber
Span: 36.58 m (120 ft 0 in)
Length: 35.05 m (114 ft 11 in)
Powerplant: 4×Rolls-Royce Conway Mk 103, 7938 kg (17,500 lb) st each
Armament: provision for up to 15876 kg (35,000 lb) of disposable stores carried internally
Max T/O weight: 105689 kg (233,000 lb)
Max speed: 640 mph at 36,000 ft
Operational range: 4,600 miles

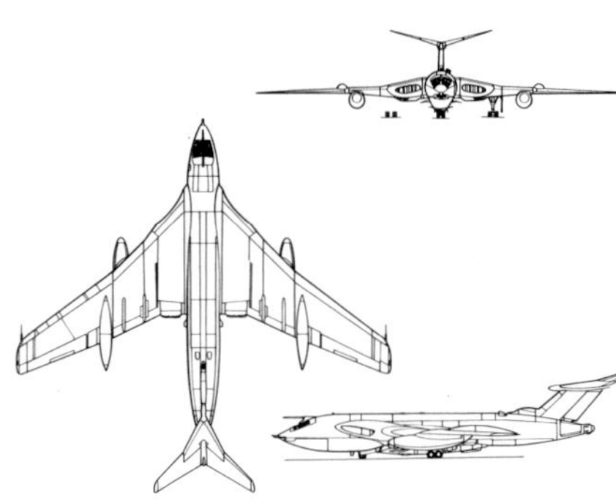

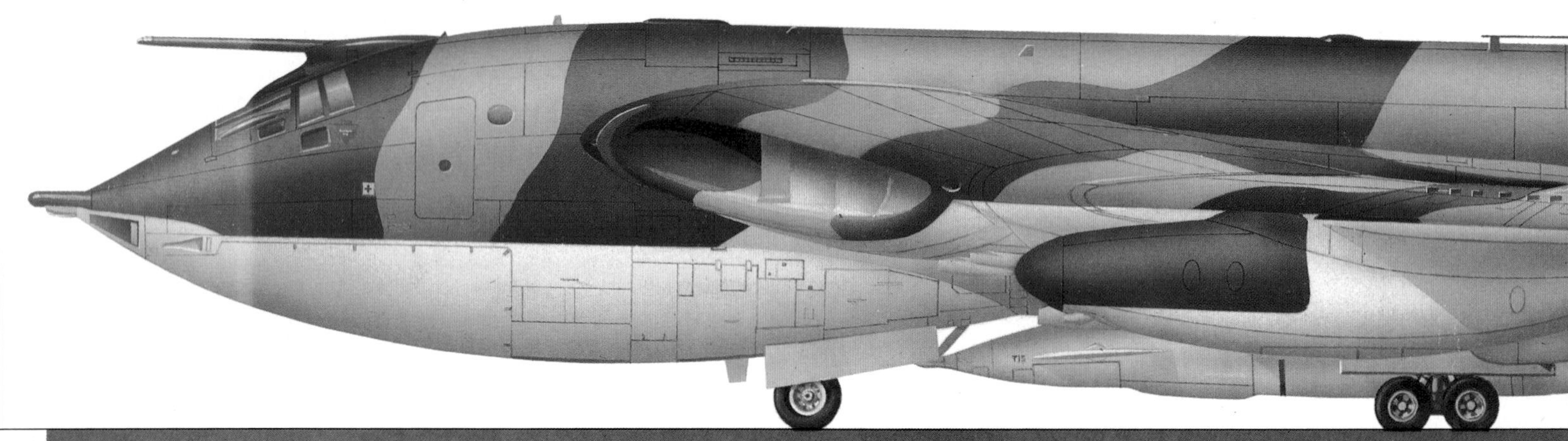

English Electric Canberra B.Mk 2/6

The Canberra was conceived in response to a 1945 requirement and first flew in May 1949. Though eventually developed into a large number of other forms, the Canberra was planned as a tactical light bomber whose low aspect ratio wing would provide fuel economy and a high ceiling, and also helped to provide the Canberra with considerable agility. The first production version was the Canberra B.Mk 2 with Avon Mk 101s and a crew of three for visual bombing (a crew of two for radar bombing had been planned), and this began to enter service in 1951. These 430 aircraft were followed by the Canberra B.Mk 6 with Avon Mk 109s and more fuel for better performance and greater range; production totalled 103. The two types served to 1970, and were gradually shifted from European operations with 35 squadrons to Near and Far Eastern operations with four and one squadrons respectively.

Specification: English Electric Canberra B.Mk 2 three-seat light bomber
Span: 19.49 m (63 ft 11.5 in)
Length: 19.96 m (65 ft 6 in)
Powerplant: 2×Rolls-Royce Avon Mk 101, 2948 kg (6,500 lb) st each
Armament: provision for up to 2722 kg (6,000 lb) of disposable stores carried internally
Max T/O weight: 20865 kg (46,000 lb)
Max speed: 570 mph at 40,000 ft
Operational range: 2,660 miles

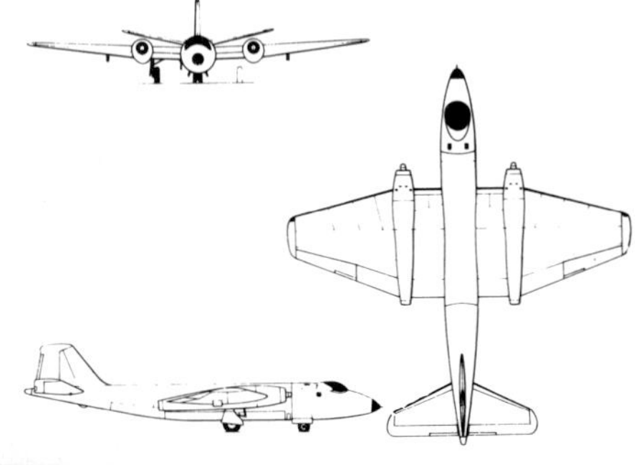

Short Sperrin

Designed to a 1946 specification for a Lincoln replacement, the Sperrin was intended for high-speed carriage of conventional or nuclear weapons for delivery from a bombing altitude of 45,000 ft. There was to be no defensive armament, bombing was to be undertaken either by radar or visually, and the airframe was to employ neither new materials nor novel concepts so that production and maintenance would be easy. The forward fuselage accommodated the pressurised crew compartment and the massive bombing radar, and the four engines were located, somewhat unusually, in over-and-under pairs on the unswept wings. The first S.A.4 Sperrin prototype was flown in August 1951, by which time the official decision had been taken to produce the more advanced Vickers Valiant rather than the Sperrin. The two prototypes were used for trials purposes.

Specification: Short Sperrin five-seat long-range medium bomber prototype
Span: 33.22 m (109 ft 0 in)
Length: 31.15 m (102 ft 2.5 in)
Powerplant: 4×Rolls-Royce Avon RA7, 3402 kg (7,500 lb) st each
Armament: provision for up to 9072 kg (20,000 lb) of bombs carried internally
Max T/O weight: 52164 kg (115,000 lb)
Max speed: 564 mph at high altitude
Operational range: 3,680 miles

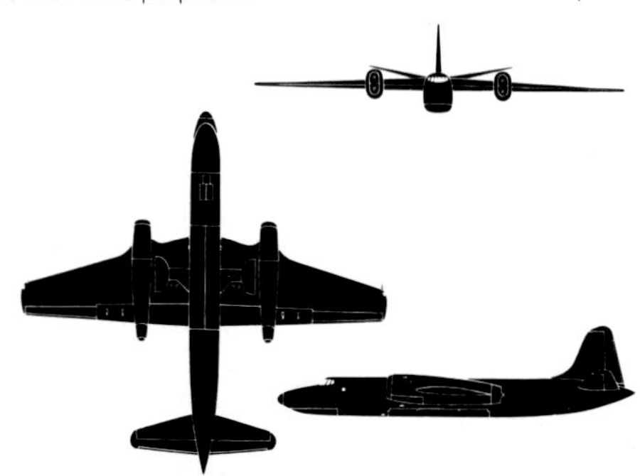

A Handley Page Victor B.Mk 2R of the Wittering wing, whose yellow lion insignia adorns the fin. Camouflage was introduced from 1965, when the V-Force switched to the low-level role, and squadron badges were abandoned when centralised servicing was introduced some time later. The two squadrons of the Wittering wing, Nos 100 and 139, were the only units equipped with the Victor B.Mk 2, and were armed with the Avro Blue Steel stand-off nuclear missile.

Avro Vulcan B.Mk 1

Stemming from a 1947 requirement for a long-range strategic platform able to operate at high speed and high altitude, the Vulcan was the world's first delta-winged bomber to reach operational service, but before this the performance of the layout was thoroughly explored in a series of Type 707 scaled-down test aircraft. The Type 698 prototype flew in August 1952, and the Vulcan B.Mk 1 began to enter service in 1957 with considerably more power and compound leading-edge sweep. From 1959 many Vulcan B.Mk 1s were revised for an inflight-refuelling capability, and from 1961 most surviving aircraft were upgraded to B.Mk 1A standard with more power and ECM in a rear-fuselage bulge projecting aft of the rudder. The last of the 45 Vulcan B.Mk 1s was delivered in April 1957, and the type served with six squadrons of RAF Bomber Command until phased out in the mid-1960s.

Specification: Avro Vulcan B.Mk 1 five-seat long-range strategic bomber
Span: 30.18 m (99 ft 0 in)
Length: 29.59 m (97 ft 1 in)
Powerplant: 4×Rolls-Royce (Bristol Siddeley) Olympus Mk 101, 4990 kg (11,000 lb) st each
Armament: provision for up to 9526 kg (21,000 lb) of bombs carried internally
Max T/O weight: about 77111 kg (170,000 lb)
Max speed: 620 mph at high altitude
Operational range: about 3,000 miles

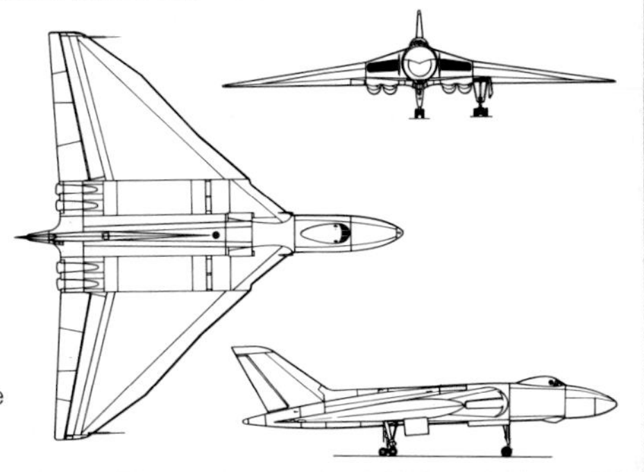

Handley Page Victor B.Mk 1

Designed to the same specification as the Vulcan for a long-range high-altitude bomber, the Victor was a completely different aeroplane of exceptional technical interest using 'crescent' flying surfaces married to an area-ruled fuselage with a bulged forward section for the crew and radar. Though first flown in December 1952, the Victor B.Mk 1 did not enter service until 1957, when it was already obsolescent as an operational type. Serving with four Bomber Command squadrons, most of the 50 aircraft were upgraded in service with an inflight-refuelling capability and the ability to carry underwing drop tanks, and surviving aircraft were later improved to B.Mk 1A standard with enhanced ECM. As the B.Mk 1 was supplanted in bomber service by the B.Mk 2 variant, aircraft were converted to Victor K.Mk 1A two- or three-point inflight-refuelling tankers for use by three squadrons.

Specification: Handley Page Victor B.Mk 1 five-seat long-range strategic bomber
Span: 33.53 m (110 ft 0 in)
Length: 35.05 m (114 ft 11 in)
Powerplant: 4×Armstrong Siddeley Sapphire Mk 200, 4990 kg (11,000 lb) st each
Armament: provision for up to 15876 kg (35,000 lb) of disposable stores carried internally
Max T/O weight: 81647 kg (180,000 lb)
Max speed: 640 mph at 36,000 ft
Operational range: 2,700 miles

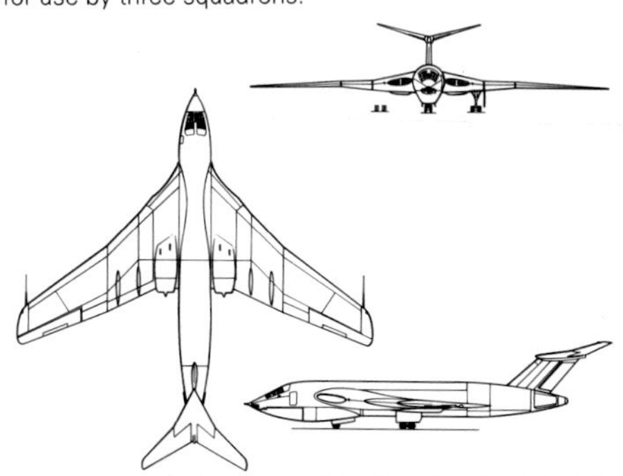

Chapter 2

FIGHTERS

Sopwith F.1 Camel

In terms of aircraft destroyed (1,294) the Camel was the best British fighter of World War I, and 5,490 examples were built. The type was derived conceptually from the Pup, and began to enter service in mid-1917. The nickname Camel resulted from the forward-fuselage hump over the two machine-guns. Power was provided by any of four rotaries in the range from 75 to 112-kW (100 to 150-hp), and the concentration of the major masses (engine, fuel, armament and pilot) round the centre of gravity in the forward fuselage gave the fighter exceptional agility, though the turning characteristics were tricky enough to cause all but experienced pilots some acute handling problems. There was also a naval 2F.1 version with a single gun, reduced span and a detachable tail.

Specification: Sopwith F.1 Camel single-seat fighter
Span: 8.53 m (28 ft 0 in)
Length: 5.715 m (18 ft 9 in)
Powerplant: 1×Clerget 9Z, 97-kW (130-hp)
Armament: 2×7.7-mm (0.303-in) Vickers machine-guns, plus provision for 4×11.3-kg bombs
Max speed: 115 mph at 6,500 ft
Operational endurance: 2 hours 30 minutes

Airco D.H.2

Forming the equipment of the first British single-seat fighter squadron, the D.H.2 was introduced in 1916 as a sturdy biplane to counter the Fokker E-series A. Pusher configuration was selected as the UK lacked a gun interrupter gear; the original mounting allowed elevation of the gun, but this was soon turned into a fixed mounting as pilots learned to aim the complete aeroplane at the target, using the highly responsive controls to wring the best performance out of this nimble machine. Production amounted to some 400 aircraft, and from spring 1916 the D.H.2 was instrumental in defeating the 'Fokker Scourge' and thereby giving the British air superiority. For lack of a replacement the type soldiered on into mid-1917.

Specification: Airco D.H.2 single-seat fighter
Span: 8.61 m (28 ft 3 in)
Length: 7.68 m (25 ft 2.5 in)
Powerplant: 1×Gnome Monosoupape, 75-kW (100-hp)
Armament: 1×7.7-mm (0.303-in) Lewis machine-gun
Max speed: 93 mph at sea level
Operational endurance: 2 hours 45 minutes

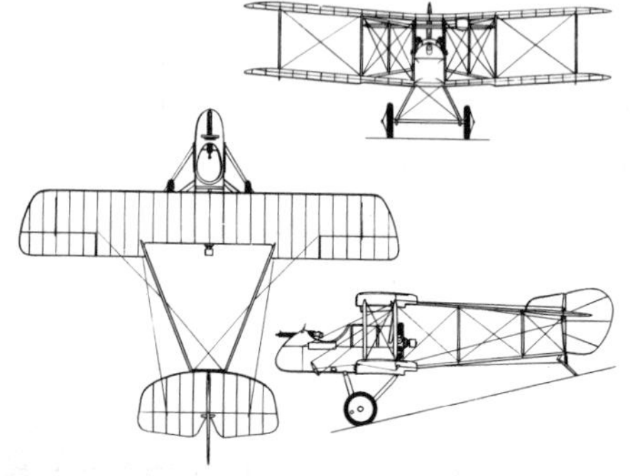

Bristol F.2B Fighter

The Bristol Fighter was the most successful two-seat fighter of World War I, and was built to the extent of 4,470 aircraft between 1916 and 1926. This biplane type was developed as the R.2A reconnaissance machine, but offered such performance with the 142-kW (190-hp) Rolls-Royce Falcon that it became the F.2A fighter. Early operations in 1917 were not fruitful, but as soon as pilots began to handle this high-performance yet agile machine like a single-seater, with a gunner to deal with flank and rear targets or attackers, the definitive F.2B began to rack up impressive combat results, especially when powered by the Falcon III. The USA planned to build 2,000 Fighters with a Liberty engine, but these plans were curtailed by the end of the war.

Specification: Bristol F.2B Fighter two-seat fighter
Span: 11.96 m (39 ft 3 in)
Length: 7.87 m (25 ft 10 in)
Powerplant: 1×Rolls-Royce Falcon III, 205-kW (275-hp)
Armament: 2 or 3×0.303-in (7.7-mm) machine-guns (one fixed and one or two trainable), plus up to 109-kg (240-lb) of bombs
Max speed: 125 mph at sea level
Operational endurance: 3 hours

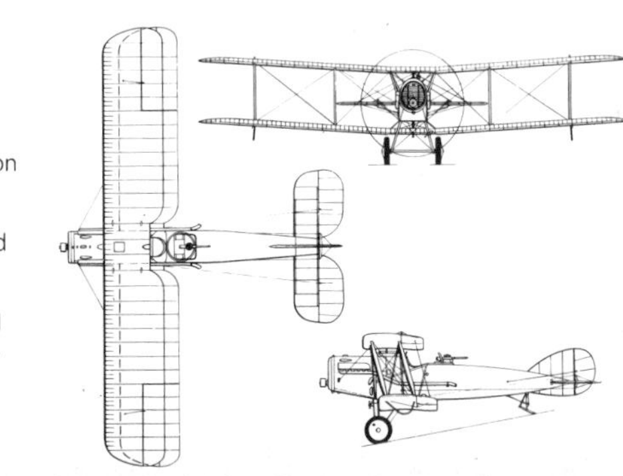

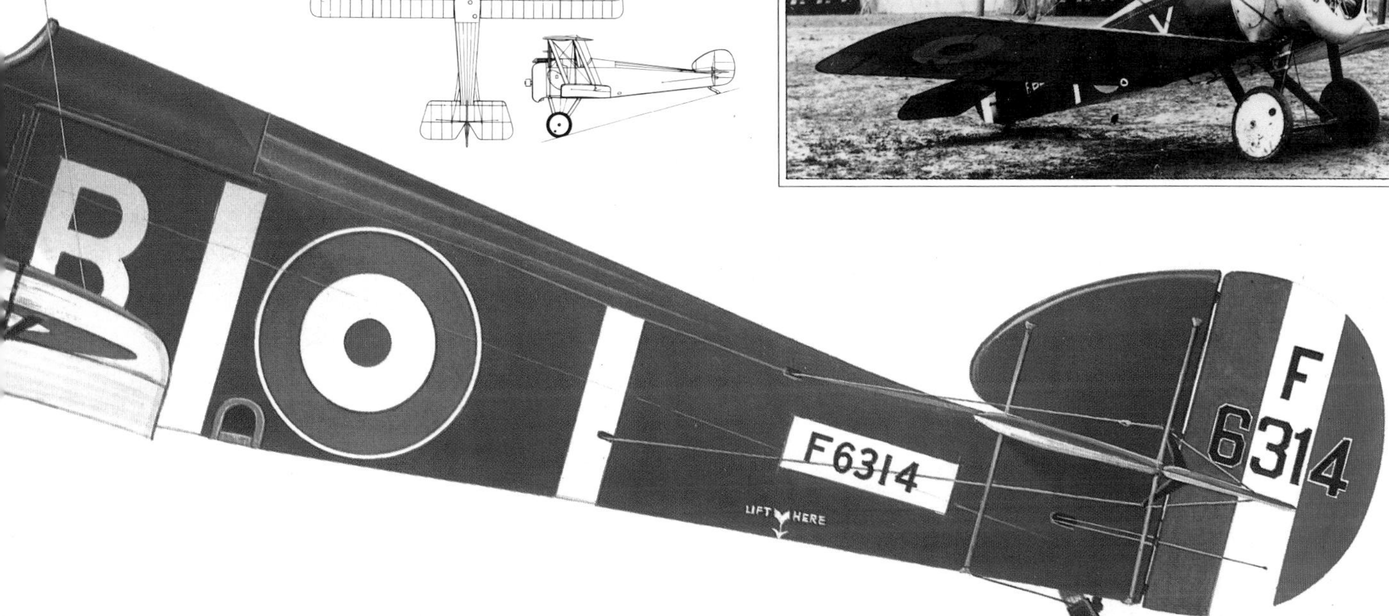

A Sopwith Camel of 'B' Flight, No. 210 Squadron, based at St Omer on the Western Front. The squadron's Camels scored many victories during the desperate fighting of April and May 1918.

Royal Aircraft Factory S.E.5a

Rivalling the Camel for the honour of being the finest British fighter of World War I, the S.E.5a lacked the agility of the Camel but had better performance and was a more stable gun platform of the type favoured by aces such as 'Mick' Mannock. The S.E.5 with a 112-kW (150-hp) Hispano-Suiza appeared in service during spring 1917, and was followed in early summer by the S.E.5a with 149-kW (200-hp) Hispano-Suiza and later the similarly-rated Viper, which gave the S.E.5a altitude performance to match that of the Fokker D VII. The armament fit was perhaps an anachronistic feature, being an interrupted Vickers in the engine decking and an uninterrupted Lewis above the centre section. Total production amounted to 5,205, American plans for another 1,000 being cancelled at the Armistice.

Specification: Royal Aircraft Factory S.E.5a single-seat fighter
Span: 8.115 m (26 ft 7.5 in)
Length: 6.375 m (20 ft 11 in)
Powerplant: 1×Wolseley Viper, 149-kW (200-hp)
Armament: 2×7.7-mm (0.303-in) machine-guns (one Vickers and one Lewis)
Max speed: 138 mph at sea level
Operational endurance: 3 hours

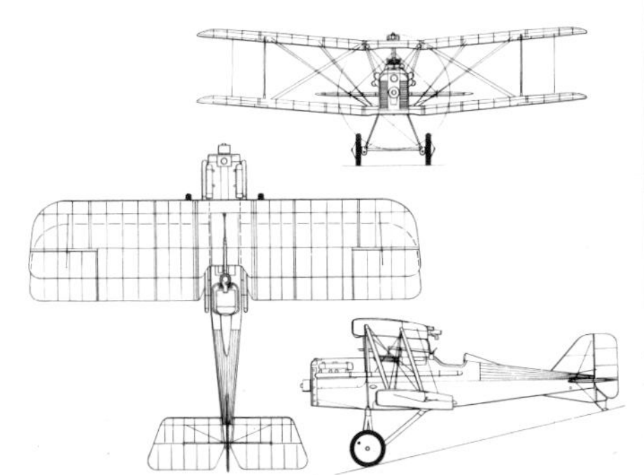

Sopwith Pup

So named for its development from the 1½-Strutter, the Pup was a delightful fighter with viceless handling characteristics and modestly good performance on its low-powered engine. There was nothing exceptional about the Pup's design, which was nevertheless beautifully balanced, and from the time of its service debut in late summer 1916, the type began to make its mark against significantly more powerful German adversaries through use of its greater agility. This resulted, in part, from a low wing loading, which also contributed to the Pup's good performance at altitude. Production amounted to 1,770, and among the Pup's distinctions is the first landing by an aeroplane on the flightdeck of a ship under way. Beardmore developed a W.B.III variant for carrier operations with folding wings and retractable undercarriage.

Specification: Sopwith Pup single-seat fighter
Span: 8.08 m (26 ft 6 in)
Length: 5.89 m (19 ft 3.75 in)
Powerplant: 1×Le Rhône, 60-kW (80-hp)
Armament: 1×7.7-mm (0.303-in) Vickers or Lewis machine-gun, plus provision for 8×Le Prieur rockets
Max speed: 111 mph at sea level
Operational endurance: 3 hours

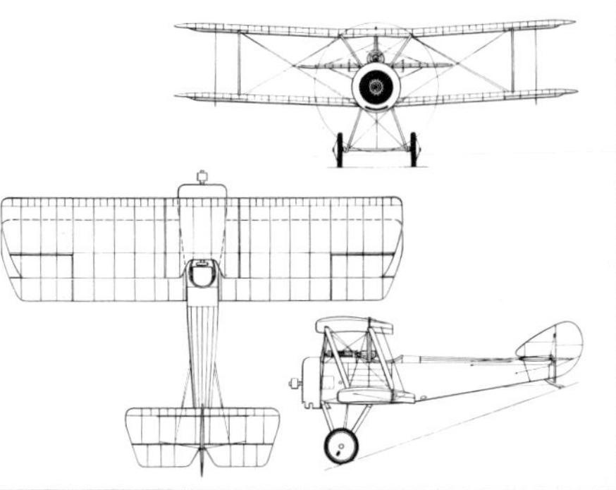

Fokker Dr I

Perhaps the best known German fighter of World War I because it was flown by such aces as Manfred von Richthofen, the Dr I was an indifferent performer in all aspects of air combat but climb and agility, in which it possessed almost legendary capability. The Dr I was inspired by the Sopwith Triplane, but took the triplane formula to extremes in maximising wing area while minimising overall span. Designed by Reinhold Platz, the Dr I had a rotary engine, a steel-tube fuselage and virtually cantilever wings of wooden construction with ply skinning over their forward surfaces. The type entered service in August 1917, and 420 were built up to May 1918, by which time its low performance was a distinct liability in the hands of all but the most capable of pilots flying purely defensive sorties.

Specification: Fokker Dr I single-seat fighter
Span: 7.19 m (23 ft 7.1 in)
Length: 5.77 m (18 ft 11.1 in)
Powerplant: 1×Oberursel UR II or Thulin-built Le Rhône, 82-kW (110-hp)
Armament: 2×7.9-mm (0.312-in) MG 08/15 machine-guns
Max speed: 103 mph at 13,125 ft
Operational endurance: 1 hour 30 minutes

Fokker D VII

The Fokker D VII was the best German fighter of World War I, and served between April and November 1918. The type had good but not exceptional performance, its well-justified reputation depending on its high-altitude agility and its enormous strength. The controls were beautifully balanced, and at altitude the D VII could 'hang' on its propeller in the climb to fire at aircraft above it. Strength was derived from the welded steel-tube fuselage (with metal and ply skinning) and biplane deep-section wooden wings (with leading-edge ply skinning). The latter were effectively cantilever units, but had struts for additional strength. The D VII was delivered with a 119-kW (160-hp) Mercedes D III engine or higher-powered BMW, and production totalled 412 Fokker machines plus more from Albatros.

Specification: Fokker D VII single-seat fighter
Span: 8.90 m (29 ft 3.5 in)
Length: 6.95 m (22 ft 9.75 in)
Powerplant: 1×BMW III, 138-kW (185-hp)
Armament: 2×7.9-mm (0.312-in) MG 08/15 machine-guns
Max speed: 124 mph at sea level
Operational endurance: 1 hour 30 minutes

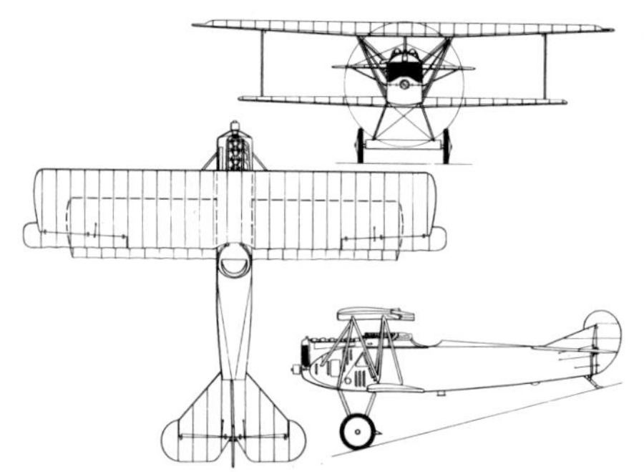

Sopwith Triplane

The Triplane was a novel solution to the problem faced by the designers of fighters in late 1916: larger wings were required to keep down wing loading (and thus maintain climb performance) for increasingly powerful fighters, but such wings reduced agility and the pilot's fields of vision. The Sopwith solution in a Pup successor was division of the required area into three narrow wings, with consequent advantages in strength, agility and vision. The aeroplane that made use of the solution was the Triplane, which began to enter service with the RNAS in February 1917. The Triplane possessed a rate of climb unmatched by any of the more powerful German fighters of the period. Production amounted to 140 aircraft that served only in 1917.

Specification: Sopwith Triplane single-seat fighter
Span: 8.08 m (26 ft 6 in)
Length: 5.74 m (18 ft 10 in)
Powerplant: 1×Clerget 9Z, 97-kW (130-hp)
Armament: 1×7.7-mm (0.303-in) Vickers machine-gun
Max speed: 113 mph at 6,500 ft
Operational endurance: 2 hours 45 minutes

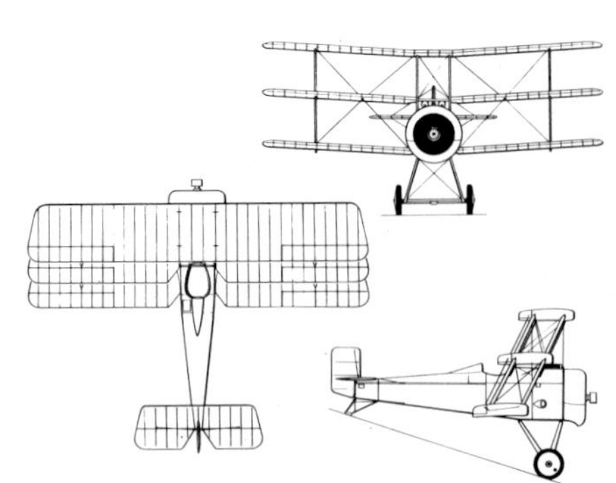

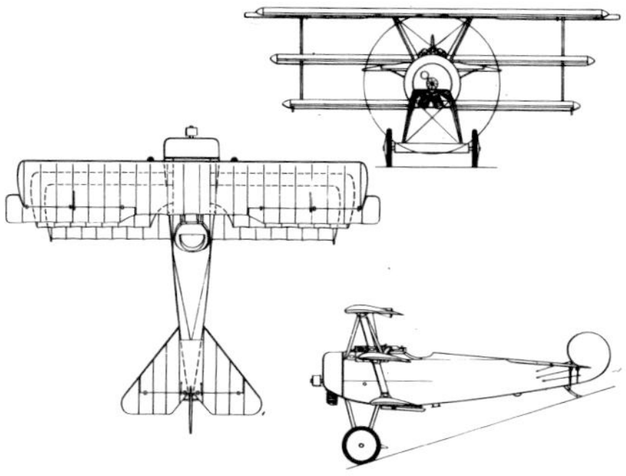

This Fokker Dr 1 triplane was flown in May 1917 by Leutnant Pippart, commander of JaSta (squadron) 19, based at Balatre. Its unit markings are yellow and black stripes on the tailplane, and personal markings are painted in white on the fuselage.

Albatros D V

Caught on the technical hop by the appearance of new Allied fighters such as the Sopwith Camel, the Germans responded with the Albatros D V, a development of the D I, D II and D III with an oval semi-monocoque fuselage, a top wing lowered to improve the pilot's field of vision, a rounded rudder and a slightly more powerful engine driving a propeller with a larger and better streamlined spinner. The D V (and D Va with modified aileron controls) lacked the performance to match the new Allied machines, but was rushed into extensive production for service from May 1917 to the end of the war. The type was moderately successful when flown by experienced pilots, but had an alarming tendency to shed its lower wings in a dive.

Specification: Albatros D V single-seat fighter
Span: 9.05 m (29 ft 8.25 in)
Length: 7.33 m (24 ft 0.6 in)
Powerplant: 1×Mercedes D IIIa, 134-kW (180-hp)
Armament: 2×7.92-mm (0.312-in) MG 08/15 machine-guns
Max speed: 116 mph at 3,280 ft
Operational endurance: 2 hours

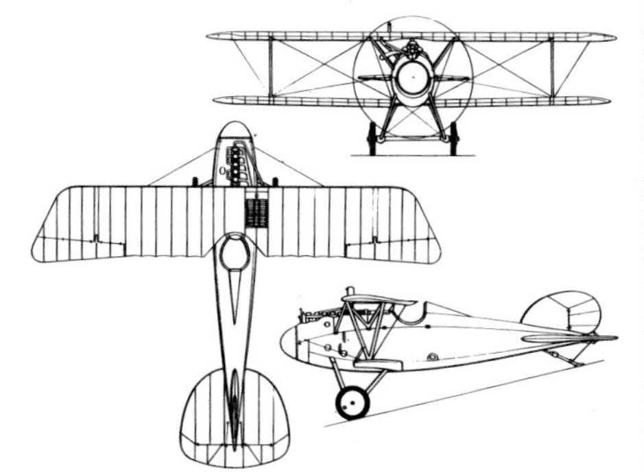

Fokker E III

When it appeared in the late summer of 1915, the Fokker E I was the world's first true fighter, for despite its poor performance and indifferent monoplane structure (derived from its M.5k unarmed predecessor) it was armed with a machine-gun enabled to fire directly forward through the propeller disc by the world's first practical interrupter gear. The E I (few built) was underpowered, and succeeded by the E II with greater power (23 built) and then by the definitive E III (between 120 and 150 built) with the same engine but a number of detail improvements. This was the aircraft of the 1915/6 'Fokker Scourge' in which these poor aircraft prevailed because of their armament and the skill of their pilots. Allied developments prompted the E IV with two guns and greater power, but this lacked any real agility.

Specification: Fokker E III single-seat fighter
Span: 9.52 m (31 ft 2.75 in)
Length: 7.20 m (23 ft 7.5 in)
Powerplant: 1×Oberursel U I, 75-kW (100-hp)
Armament: 1×7.9-mm (0.312-in) Parabellum or MG 08/15 machine-gun
Max speed: 87.5 mph at sea level
Operational endurance: 1 hour 30 minutes

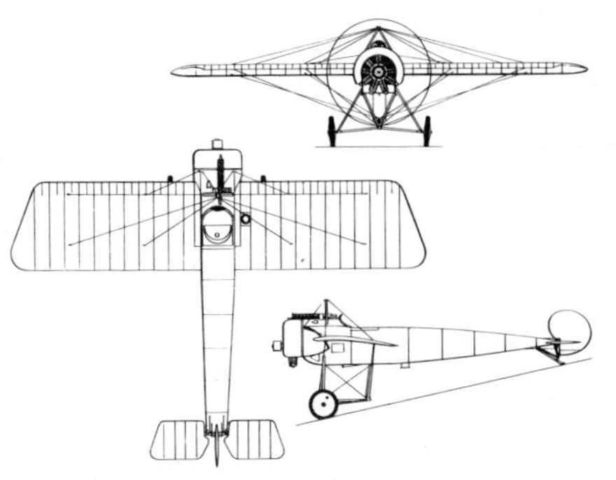

Royal Aircraft Factory S.E.5

Specification: Royal Aircraft Factory S.E.5a single-seat fighter and ground-attack aeroplane
Span: 8.12 m (26 ft 7.5 in)
Length: 6.38 m (20 ft 11 in)
Powerplant: 1×Wolseley W.4A Viper, 149 kW (200 hp)
Armament: 2×7.7-mm (0.303-in) machine-guns plus provision for up to 4×11.3-kg (25-lb) bombs carried under the fuselage
Max T/O weight: 880 kg (1,940 lb)
Max speed: 138 mph at sea level
Operational endurance: 2 hours 30 minutes

The S.E.5 was developed at much the same time as the Camel and first flew in December 1916. The design concept was basically different from that of the Camel, the use of a powerful static engine in a substantial airframe helping to ensure that the aeroplane had high performance, was easy to fly and was also an excellent gun platform for the odd combination of one interrupted Vickers gun and, located above the upper wing, one uninterrupted Lewis gun. The S.E.5 was powered by a 112-kW (150-hp) Hispano-Suiza, and the 82 production aircraft began to enter service in April 1917. Further development of the engine increased power to 149 kW (200 hp), and with this engine the fighter became the S.E.5a, of which 5,121 were built for service from mid-1917. The engine was insufficiently developed, however, and most aircraft had the Wolseley Viper, and such aircraft were flown by many aces.

Vickers F.B.5 Gunbus

In 1913 Vickers produced one of the earliest British armed aircraft as the Experimental Fighting Biplane No.1, but this crashed on its first take-off. The same basic configuration, with a pusher engine between the struts supporting the empennage so that the gunner could be accommodated in the front seat of the central nacelle, was used in the following E.F.B.2, 3 and 4. The last was built to the extent of six naval aircraft, and was the precursor of the army's Fighting Biplane No.5. So convinced was Vickers that war was imminent in mid-1914 that it decided to produce 50 such aircraft in anticipation of orders. Deliveries to the army began in late 1914, and the type began to reach squadrons in France during February 1915. Production totalled 119 in the UK, with another 99 (including some F.B.9s) in France, and the type was withdrawn as totally obsolete in mid-1916.

Specification: Vickers F.B.5 Gunbus two-seat fighter and ground-attack aeroplane
Span: 11.13 m (36 ft 6 in)
Length: 8.28 m (27 ft 2 in)
Powerplant: 1×Clerget 9, 82 kW (110 hp)
Armament: 1×7.7-mm (0.303-in) machine-gun plus provision for light bombs carried under the fuselage
Max T/O weight: 930 kg (2,050 lb)
Max speed: 70 mph at 5,000 ft
Operational endurance: 4 hours 30 minutes

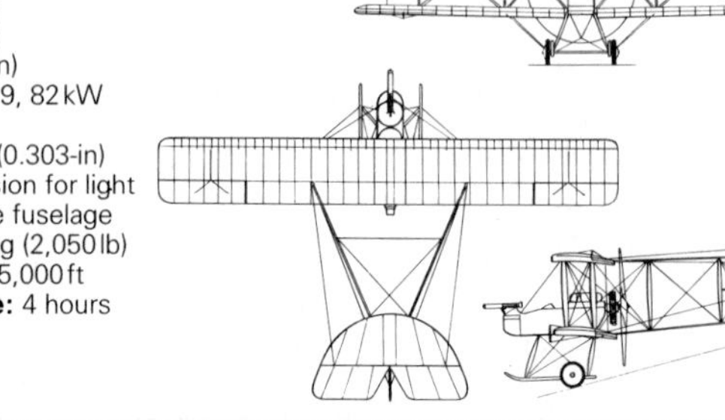

Bristol Scout

The Scout was an attractive type developed from the S.B.5 monoplane ordered by an Italian but cancelled in 1913. To the fuselage of this aeroplane the company added biplane wings and a revised tail to produce the Scout A. Two similar Scout Bs with provision for rifle armament paved the way for the Scout C, of which 161 were built between November 1914 and March 1916: 87 for the army with 60-kW (80-hp) Le Rhone rotary and 74 for the navy with the 60-kW Gnome rotary. The final variant was the Scout D with revised fuel and oil tanks, and in later aircraft new wings with greater dihedral, ailerons of shorter span and provision for an overwing Lewis gun. The aircraft were delivered in four subvariants with Gnome or Le Rhone rotaries, the army receiving 130 between February and September 1916, and the navy accepting 80 between April and December 1916. The type remained operational into mid-1917.

Specification: Bristol Scout D single-seat fighter
Span: 8.33 m (27 ft 4 in)
Length: 6.02 m (19 ft 9 in)
Powerplant: 1×Le Rhone 9, 60 kW (80 hp)
Armament: 1×7.7-mm (0.303-in) machine-gun
Max T/O weight: 567 kg (1,250 lb)
Max speed: 100 mph at sea level
Operational endurance: 2 hours 30 minutes

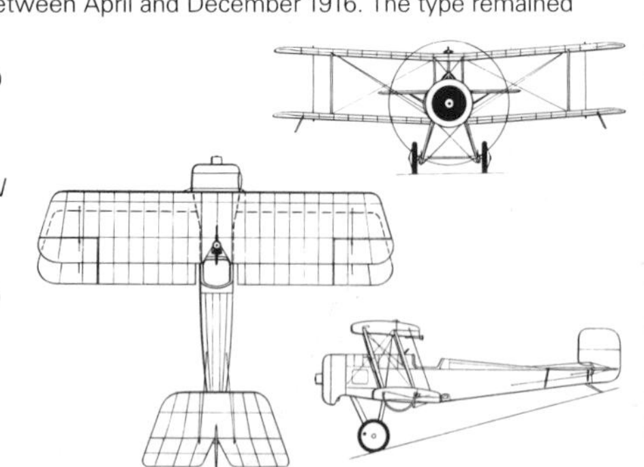

With the introduction of the S.E.5a in mid-1917, the Royal Flying Corps had a fighter equal to the best German machines. At last a British fighter carried two machine-guns and could match the firepower of the Albatross series fighters, and its powerful 200-hp engine gave it an advantage over most German opponents. By late 1917 most RFC fighter squadrons were equipped either with S.E.5as or Sopwith Camels.

Royal Aircraft Factory F.E.2b

Despite a size and payload capability that later allowed the type to be used as a night bomber, the F.E.2 was schemed as a fighter whose use of a pusher powerplant (located between the booms that stretched back from the wings to support the tail unit) allowed the design of a large central nacelle with accommodation for two including a forward-seated gunner with good fields of fire. The prototype first flew in January 1915, and was followed by 12 F.E.2a production aircraft with the 75-kW (100-hp) Green engine which proved so inadequate that the aircraft were re-engined to F.E.2b standard with the 89.5-kW (120-hp) Beardmore. The F.E.2b began to enter service late in 1915, and production totalled 1,927 aircraft that served with 16 squadrons on the Western Front and five squadrons for home defence. About 300 F.E.2d aircraft were built with the 186-kW (250-hp) Rolls-Royce Mk III for better performance, and some F.E.2 aircraft remained operational to the end of the war.

Specification: Royal Aircraft Factory F.E.2b two-seat fighter and utility aeroplane
Span: 14.55 m (47 ft 9 in)
Length: 9.83 m (32 ft 3 in)
Powerplant: 1×Beardmore, 89.5 kW (120 hp)
Armament: 1 or 2×7.7-mm (0.303-in) machine-guns
Max T/O weight: 1347 kg (2,970 lb)
Max speed: 80.5 mph at sea level
Operational endurance: 3 hours

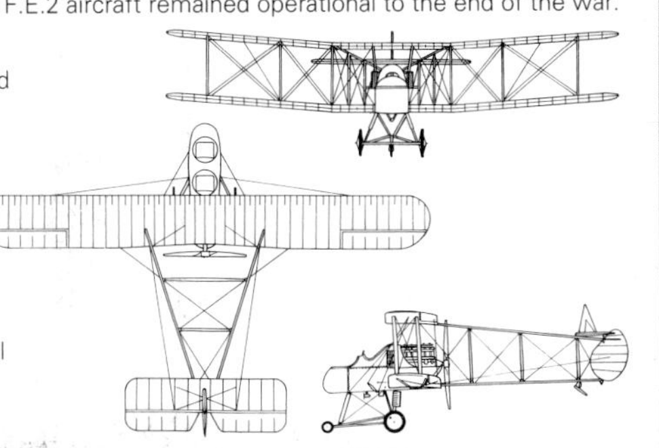

Airco D.H.2

Faced with the task of designing a fighter able to deal with the Fokker E types, Geoffrey de Havilland circumvented the problem created by the British lack of an effective gun interrupter gear by creating a nimble biplane with a pusher engine that left the nose of the central nacelle free for a machine-gun installation. The prototype D.H.2 flew in June 1915 with gun mountings on each side of the nacelle to give the pilot a choice of armament locations. The cumbersome nature of this arrangement led to a central location that allowed the gun to be elevated and depressed, though a fixed installation soon became the norm. The D.H.2 began to enter service in January 1916, and after pilots had mastered its tricky handling the D.H.2 began to prove its worth. Production totalled 400, and despite its rapid obsolescence from autumn 1916 it was March 1917 before replacement began.

Specification: Airco D.H.2 single-seat fighter
Span: 8.61 m (28 ft 3 in)
Length: 7.68 m (25 ft 2.5 in)
Powerplant: 1×Gnome Monosoupape, 75 kW (100 hp), or Le Rhone 9, 82 kW (110 hp)
Armament: 1×7.7-mm (0.303-in) machine-gun
Max T/O weight: 654 kg (1,441 lb)
Max speed: 93 mph at sea level
Operational endurance: 2 hours 45 minutes

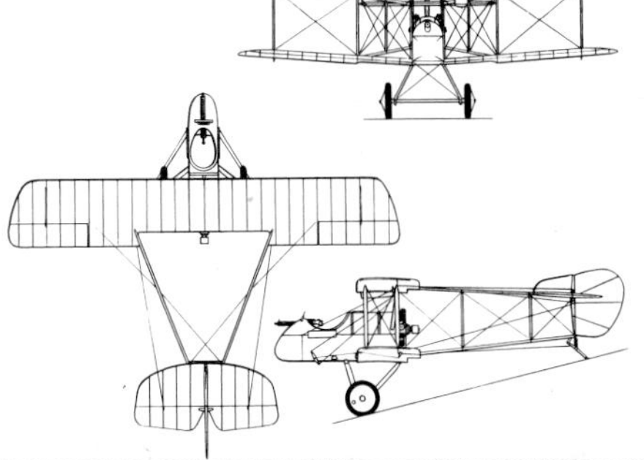

Sopwith 7F.1 Snipe

Specification: Sopwith 7F.1 Snipe Mk I single-seat fighter and ground-attack aeroplane
Span: 9.17 m (30 ft 1 in)
Length: 6.02 m (19 ft 9 in)
Powerplant: 1×Bentley B.R.2, 172 kW (230 hp)
Armament: 2×7.7-mm (0.303-in) machine-guns plus provision for up to 4×11.3-kg (25-lb) bombs carried under the fuselage
Max T/O weight: 916 kg (2,020 lb)
Max speed: 121 mph at 10,000 ft
Operational endurance: 3 hours

The Snipe was designed round the new 172-kW (230-hp) Bentley B.R.2 rotary engine as successor to the Camel, and in its prototype form with the 112-kW (150-hp) Bentley B.R.1 bore a strong external resemblance to its predecessor. The first prototype flew late in 1917, and was followed by the second and third prototypes with a modified vertical tail (small fin and horn-balanced rudder) and two- rather than one-bay wings of revised structure. Two more prototypes followed before the Snipe Mk I was accepted for production. The type entered service in the summer of 1918, and though its performance was no better than that of the Camel except in climb, the Snipe had Camel-type agility without the earlier fighter's tricky handling. Production of 1,800 aircraft was ordered, but only 100 had been delivered by November 1918 and production into 1919 resulted in a total of only 497 aircraft that served until 1926.

Sopwith 1½ Strutter

Believed to have been thus nicknamed for the fact that its cabane struts appeared to be interplane struts cut in half, the 1½ Strutter was the first British aeroplane fitted with an interrupted gun, complemented by a trainable gun in the rear cockpit. First flown in December 1915 with an 82-kW (110-hp) Clerget rotary, the type resulted from a naval requirement and showed such capability that large-scale production was undertaken with the naval and army designations Admiralty Type 9700 and Two-Seater respectively. The type was produced in two- and single-seat forms, the latter being a bomber operated almost exclusively by the navy. Deliveries began in spring 1916, and total British production of 1,513 1½ Strutters was complemented by about 4,500 French-built aircraft. Replacement with more agile fighters of higher performance began in July 1917.

Specification: Sopwith 1½ Strutter two-seat fighter
Span: 10.21 m (33 ft 6 in)
Length: 7.97 m (25 ft 3 in)
Powerplant: 1×Clerget 9, 97 kW (130 hp)
Armament: 2×7.7-mm (0.303-in) machine-guns
Max T/O weight: 974 kg (2,150 lb)
Max speed: 100 mph at 6,500 ft
Operational endurance: 3 hours 45 minutes

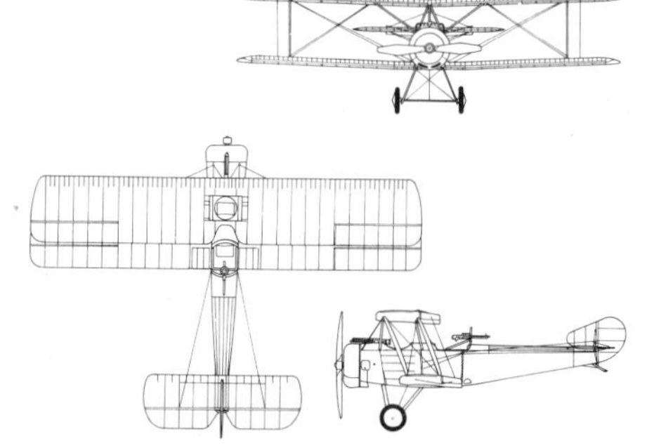

Royal Aircraft Factory F.E.8

Designed at much the same time as the D.H.2, for lack of a gun interrupter gear the F.E.8 adopted a basically similar configuration: a central nacelle accommodating the nose-mounted gun (initially in a remotely controlled installation in the lower nose where it was inaccessible to the pilot for the clearance of stoppages or changing of ammunition drums), the pilot, fuel and pusher engine between four booms that stretched back from the wings to support the empennage. The prototype flew in October 1915. Orders for the F.E.8 totalled 297 including the two prototypes, but only 182 were delivered før service from August 1916. The type was pleasant to fly but less nimble than the D.H.2, and by the summer of 1917 all F.E.8s had been withdrawn from first-line service. Most aircraft were powered by the Gnome rotary, but small numbers were flown with 82-kW (110-hp) Clerget or Le Rhone rotaries.

Specification: Royal Aircraft Factory F.E.8 single-seat fighter
Span: 9.60 m (31 ft 5 in)
Length: 7.21 m (23 ft 8 in)
Powerplant: 1×Gnome Monosoupape, 75 kW (100 hp)
Armament: 1×7.7-mm (0.303-in) machine-gun
Max T/O weight: 610 kg (1,345 lb)
Max speed: 94 mph at sea level
Operational endurance: 2 hours 30 minutes

The Sopwith Snipe was designed to provide the formidable manoeuvrability of the Camel but to be much easier to fly. Given that the RFC lost over 14,000 men in training accidents – more than in action – this was a very important consideration. A handful entered service during the climactic summer of 1918, but the war was over before it could have a significant impact.

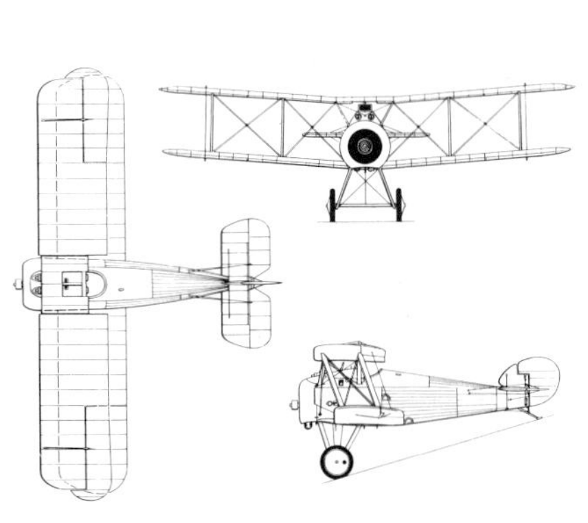

Sopwith Pup

Known formally as the Admiralty Type 9901, this delightful aeroplane is better known by the nickname it received as the scaled-down single-seat 'pup' of the 1.5-Strutter. The first of six prototypes flew early in 1916 with the 60-kW (80-hp) Clerget 7, later replaced by a Clerget 9 of the same power. This latter was used in production aircraft together with identically rated Gnome and Le Rhone rotaries, and in some of the aircraft earmarked for home defence against Zeppelins and bombers the 75-kW (100-hp) Gnome Monosoupape. Deliveries began in September 1916 to army and navy squadrons, and despite the type's low power and thus its no more than adequate performance the Pup proved a real winner, for its viceless handling and good agility enabled it to tackle German fighters that had more-powerful engines and double its firepower. Some 1,770 Pups were built, and these were withdrawn from the summer of 1917.

Specification: Sopwith Pup single-seat fighter and ground-attack aeroplane
Span: 8.08 m (26 ft 6 in)
Length: 6.04 m (19 ft 9.75 in)
Powerplant: 1×Le Rhone 9, 60 kW (80 hp)
Armament: 1×7.7-mm (0.303-in) machine-gun plus provision for up to 4×11.3-kg (25-lb) bombs carried under the fuselage or 8×Le Prieur rockets carried on the interplane struts
Max T/O weight: 556 kg (1,225 lb)
Max speed: 111.5 mph at sea level
Operational endurance: 3 hours

Sopwith Triplane

In an effort to provide a fighter with the Pup's agility and tractability with improved fields of vision and generally better performance, Sopwith came up with the remarkable Triplane, which retained the Pup's fuselage and empennage in combination with a more powerful engine and a cellule of three narrow-chord wings to provide all the desired features, including higher speed and a better rate of climb. The prototype first flew in May 1916, and deliveries began at the end of the year. The type was ordered by the army and navy but operated only by the latter, which exchanged its 60 SPAD S.7s for the army's 266 Triplanes at army request. In fact only about 140 Triplanes were built, and their success is attested by the fact that no fewer than 15 German manufacturers produced triplane fighter designs in direct response. Proposals for static-engined British variants resulted only in prototypes.

Specification: Sopwith Triplane single-seat fighter
Span: 8.08 m (26 ft 6 in)
Length: 5.74 m (18 ft 10 in)
Powerplant: 1×Clerget 9, 97 kW (130 hp)
Armament: 1 or 2×7.7-mm (0.303-in) machine-guns
Max T/O weight: 699 kg (1,541 lb)
Max speed: 117 mph at 5,000 ft
Operational endurance: 2 hours 45 minutes

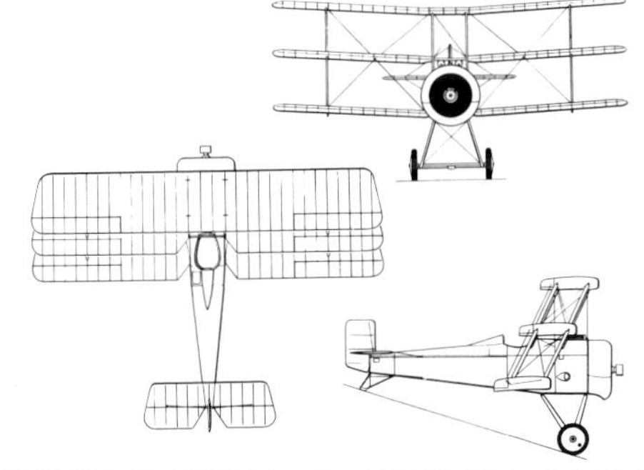

Bristol F.2 Fighter

In March 1916 Bristol completed the design of the R.2A with the 89-kW (120-hp) Beardmore as replacement for the R.E.8 two-seat reconnaissance aeroplane, and this was later transformed into the R.2B by the adoption of the 112-kW (150-hp) Hispano-Suiza engine and sesquiplane wings. The type was then recast as a fighter and the F.2A prototype flew in September 1916. Production F.2A aircraft were powered by the Rolls-Royce Falcon, and began to enter service in February 1917. Crews initially used their Fighters as ordinary two-seaters and flew defensively, and it was only when they learned the tricks of flying their mounts offensively that the type began to prove highly successful. The main production version was the F.2B that introduced a more powerful engine with more fuel, a covered lower-wing centre section, and structural revision to the fuselage to improve the pilot's fields of vision. Some 3,100 were built.

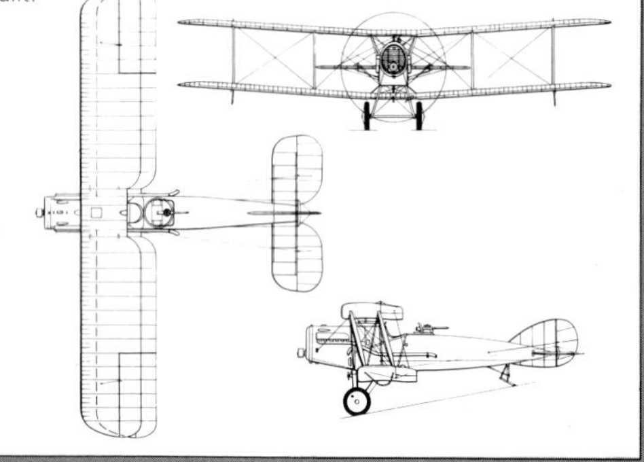

Specification: Bristol F.2B Fighter two-seat fighter and ground-attack aeroplane
Span: 11.96 m (39 ft 3 in)
Length: 7.87 m (25 ft 10 in)
Powerplant: 1×Rolls-Royce Falcon III, 205 kW (275 hp)
Armament: 2 or 3×7.7-mm (0.303-in) machine-guns plus provision for 12×9.1-kg (20-lb) bombs carried under the wings
Max T/O weight: 1474 kg (3,250 lb)
Max speed: 123 mph at 5,000 ft
Operational endurance: 3 hours

Airco D.H.5

The D.H.2 had offered its pilot an excellent field of vision, and in designing the D.H.5 as its replacement with a tractor engine and interrupted gun, de Havilland chose backward stagger of the wings to give the pilot equally good fields of vision. In other respects the D.H.5 was thoroughly conventional, with a wire-braced wooden structure, fabric covering and fixed tailskid landing gear. The first example flew late in 1916, and despite performance considerably lower than that of the contemporary Pup an order was placed for 400 aircraft, of which the first began to enter service in May 1917. Only five squadrons received the type, whose indifferent air-combat capability led to rapid relegation to the ground-attack role. Here the D.H.5 proved far more suitable, and orders for another 150 were placed, though not all had been built before the type was withdrawn at the end of 1917.

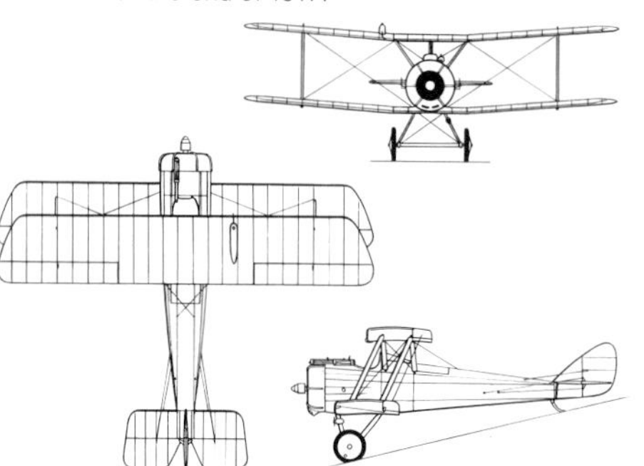

Specification: Airco D.H.5 single-seat fighter and ground-attack aeroplane
Span: 7.82 m (25 ft 8 in)
Length: 6.71 m (22 ft 0 in)
Powerplant: 1×Le Rhone 9, 82 kW (110 hp)
Armament: 1×7.7-mm (0.303-in) machine-gun and provision for up to 4×11.3-kg (25-lb) bombs carried under the fuselage
Max T/O weight: 677 kg (1,492 lb)
Max speed: 102 mph at 10,000 ft
Operational endurance: 2 hours 45 minutes

Sopwith F.1 and 2F.1 Camel

The Camel was the most successful British fighter of World War I, Camel pilots shooting down more than 3,000 aircraft. The type was a linear descendant of the Pup with a sturdier airframe, considerably more powerful engine and an armament of two interrupted guns in a forward fuselage hump that contributed to the type's nickname. The first of three (possibly four) prototypes flew in January 1917 with an 82-kW (110-hp) Clerget rotary and immediately displayed the Camel's great virtue and failing: almost incredible agility and distinctly tricky handling. Service deliveries began in June 1917, and production totalled 5,490 aircraft with engines increasing in power to 112 kW (150 hp). There were several experimental developments, but the only other production version was the navalised 2F.1 with a two-part fuselage and shorter-span wings.

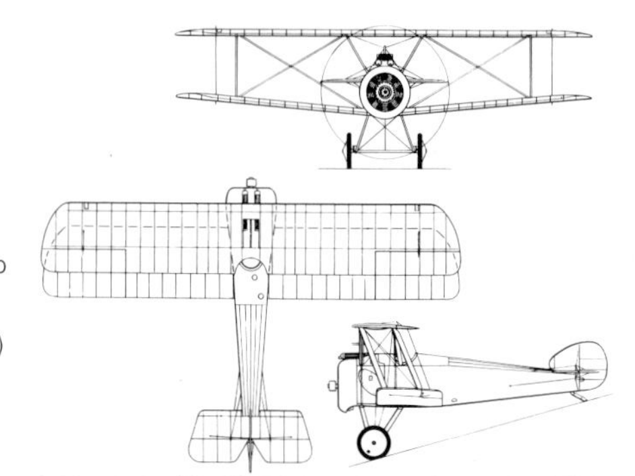

Specification: Sopwith F.1 Camel single-seat fighter and ground-attack aeroplane
Span: 8.53 m (28 ft 0 in)
Length: 5.72 m (18 ft 9 in)
Powerplant: 1×Clerget 9, 97 kW (130 hp)
Armament: 2×7.7-mm (0.303-in) machine-guns plus provision for up to 4×11.3-kg (25-lb) bombs carried under the fuselage
Max T/O weight: 659 kg (1,453 lb)
Max speed: 115 mph at 6,500 ft
Operational endurance: 2 hours 30 minutes

Sopwith 5F.1 Dolphin

Unlike earlier Sopwith fighters the Dolphin was powered by a static engine, and the deep fuselage virtually filled the gap between the backward-staggered wings so that the pilot sat with his head protruding through a gap in the upper-wing centre section for superb fields of vision in the upper hemisphere. The prototype flew in May 1917 with a 149-kW (200-hp) Hispano-Suiza geared engine, and the same powerplant was used in the Dolphin Mk I that began to enter service late in 1917. Problems with the geared engine then led to the Dolphin Mk III with a direct-drive version of the same engine, and the designation Dolphin Mk II was used for a few aircraft with a 224-kW (300-hp) Hispano-Suiza direct-drive engine. Production totalled 1,532, but only 621 were issued to operational squadrons, which disliked the Dolphin's unusual stalling characteristics and the vulnerability of the pilot in a nose-over landing accident.

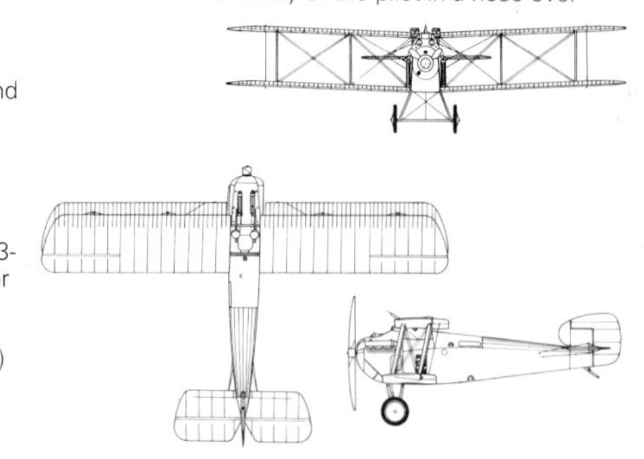

Specification: Sopwith 5F.1 Dolphin Mk I single-seat fighter and ground-attack aeroplane
Span: 9.91 m (32 ft 6 in)
Length: 6.78 m (22 ft 3 in)
Powerplant: 1×Hispano-Suiza 8, 149 kW (200 hp)
Armament: 3 or 4×7.7-mm (0.303-in) machine-guns plus provision for up to 4×11.3-kg (25-lb) bombs carried under the fuselage
Max T/O weight: 911 kg (2,008 lb)
Max speed: 112 mph at 10,000 ft
Operational endurance: about 1 hour 45 minutes

Fokker D VII

To compete in Germany's first single-seat fighter competition during January 1918, Fokker produced its V 11 prototype, which used many Dr I structural and design features in a biplane layout with a 119-kW (160-hp) Mercedes D.III inline engine. The type displayed sparkling performance and agility, and the D VII production model began to enter service in April, initially with the D.III engine but later with the BMW III for improved performance at altitude. By the end of World War I more than 700 D VIIs had been delivered, and the type won enormous approval and respect from German and Allied pilots for its agility as well as its good performance and handling even at high altitude. Another important feature was its capacity to hang on its propeller, allowing pilots to fire upward when other fighters would have stalled and entered a spin. There were many variants, none produced in quantity.

Specification: Fokker D VII single-seat fighter
Span: 8.90 m (29 ft 2.5 in)
Length: 6.95 m (22 ft 9.5 in)
Powerplant: 1×BMW III, 138 kW (185 hp)
Armament: 2×7.92-mm (0.312-in) LMG 08/15 machine-guns
Max T/O weight: 880 kg (1,940 lb)
Max speed: 124 mph at 3,280 ft
Operational endurance: 1 hour 30 minutes

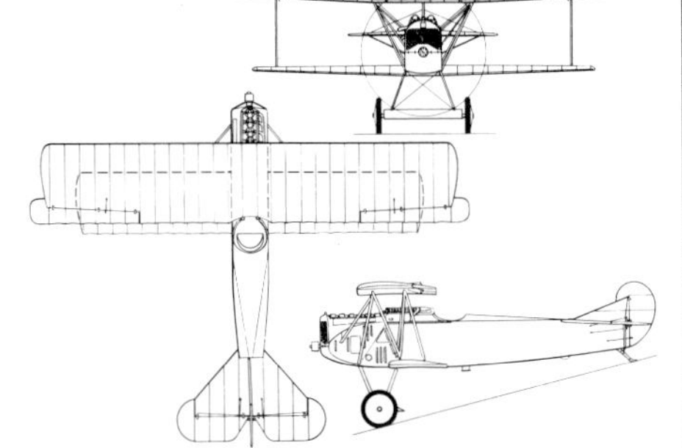

LFG (Roland) D VI

The D VI followed the D II series and, built for the January 1918 German fighter competition, was the most elegant design evolved by the manufacturer. The type had a clinker-built fuselage, with overlapping planks laid over an internal framework, and the lower wing was supported just under the fuselage by a small 'keel'. The type was powered by the 119-kW (160-hp) Mercedes D.III inline, and was redesignated D VIa when the D VIb was produced with a different engine because of Mercedes engine shortages. Development added features such as a ventral fin under a revised tail unit, and small-scale production was undertaken to provide an alternative should production of the Fokker D VII be interrupted for any reason. A few D VIs were used over the Western Front, while others went to the German navy for the defence of seaplane bases.

Specification: LFG (Roland) D VIb single-seat fighter
Span: 9.40 m (30 ft 10 in)
Length: 6.30 m (20 ft 8 in)
Powerplant: 1×Benz Bz.IIIa, 149 kW (200 hp)
Armament: 2×7.92-mm (0.312-in) LMG 08/15 machine-guns
Max T/O weight: 860 kg (1,896 lb)
Max speed: 114 mph at optimum altitude
Operational endurance: 2 hours

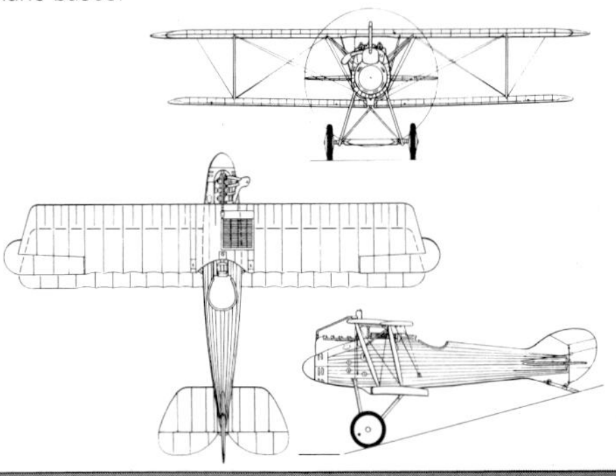

Fokker D VIII

For the Germans' second fighter competition in April 1918 Fokker produced the V26 prototype with the fuselage and empennage of the D VI married to a rotary engine and parasol wing of thick-section cantilever construction and plywood-covered wooden structure, supported above the fuselage on each side by a forward tripod of short struts and an aft single long strut. In the trials the type displayed such excellent take-off, climb and agility characteristics that it was ordered straight into production as the E V. In service these early aircraft were regarded with some suspicion after engine lubrication and wing structural problems, but after these had been eradicated the fighter re-entered production as the D VIII and became very popular. Only a small number of aircraft reached operational units before the end of World War I, their surprisingly high performance proving most useful.

Specification: Fokker D VIII single-seat fighter
Span: 8.35 m (27 ft 4.75 in)
Length: 5.85 m (19 ft 2.25 in)
Powerplant: 1×Oberursel U.II, 82 kW (110 hp)
Armament: 2×7.92-mm (0.312-in) LMG 08/15 machine-guns
Max T/O weight: 605 kg (1,334 lb)
Max speed: 127 mph at sea level
Operational endurance: 1 hour 30 minutes

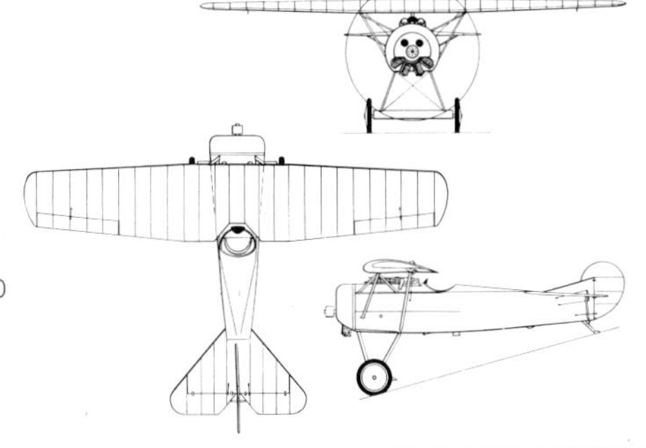

Siemens-Schuckert D IV

Siemens-Schuckert began the construction of aircraft in World War I, and its first fighter was the D I modelled on the Nieuport 11, a French machine. Via the D II prototype the manufacturer then moved to a completely German design, ordered late in 1917 as the D III equal-span biplane with the 119-kW (160-hp) Siemens-Halske Sh.III rotary engine whose diameter dictated the circular section of the compact fuselage that tapered sharply into the empennage with its large tailplane and angular vertical surfaces. After the teething problems of this engine had been cured, the 50 D IIIs matured as extremely fast-climbing interceptors whose other performance figures were low. The D III was followed by the D IV, which introduced much aerodynamic refinement for slightly higher speed and still better climb rate. A total of 280 was ordered, but less than 140 D IVs were completed, most entering service after August 1918.

Specification: Siemens-Schuckert D IV single-seat fighter
Span: 8.35 m (27 ft 4.75 in)
Length: 5.70 m (18 ft 8.5 in)
Powerplant: 1×Siemens-Halske Sh.IIIa, 119 kW (160 hp)
Armament: 2×7.92-mm (0.312-in) LMG 08/15 machine-guns
Max T/O weight: 735 kg (1,620 lb)
Max speed: 119 mph at optimum altitude
Operational endurance: 2 hours

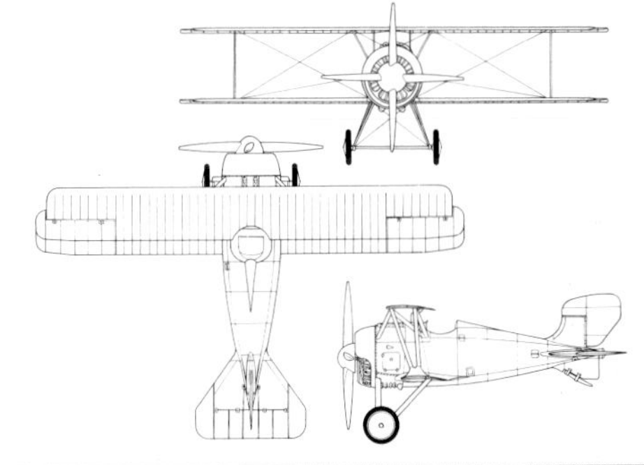

Albatros D V

In an effort to keep its basic fighter design competitive with the Allied fighters that began to appear during 1917, Albatros developed a much improved version of the D III with a fuselage of deeper, elliptical cross-section to reduce drag and thus boost performance, a factor in which the larger-diameter propeller spinner played its part. Other changes were further reduction in the height of the upper wing above the fuselage, a revised rudder, a pilot's headrest that was often removed, and a different aileron control system. The D V entered service in May 1917, and was soon joined by the D Va that reverted to the upper wing and aileron control system of the D III. Very large-scale production of both variants was undertaken, but the design was outmoded and could not match the latest Allied fighters. The lower wing was also weak, and tended to break away in a steep dive.

Specification: Albatros D V single-seat fighter
Span: 9.05 m (29 ft 8.25 in)
Length: 7.33 m (24 ft 0.5 in)
Powerplant: 1×Mercedes D.IIIa, 134 to 149 kW (180 to 200 hp) depending on compression ratio
Armament: 2×7.92-mm (0.312-in) LMG 08/15 machine-guns
Max T/O weight: 937 kg (2,066 lb)
Max speed: 116 mph at optimum altitude
Operational endurance: 2 hours

Halberstadt D II

The Halberstadt D-series of single-seat fighters was developed from the unarmed B II reconnaissance two-seater, inheriting that type's considerable structural strength. The D I appeared late in 1915 with a single interrupted gun and a powerplant comprising one 75-kW (100-hp) Mercedes D.I inline engine. The production model, of which few were built, was the D II with the more powerful Mercedes D.II engine and a wing radiator in place of the original nose-mounted unit. These served for a few months from June 1916 before being supplanted by the D III, which differed mainly in its larger horn-balanced ailerons and as powerplant one 89-kW (120-hp) Argus As.II inline. A few D IVs were produced for Turkey with twin guns and the 112-kW (150-hp) Benz Bz.III, and the D V of 1917 was a refined type with a more streamlined plywood-covered fuselage and the As.II engine.

Specification: Halberstadt D II single-seat fighter
Span: 8.80 m (29 ft 10.5 in)
Length: 7.30 m (23 ft 11.5 in)
Powerplant: 1×Mercedes D.II, 89 kW (120 hp)
Armament: 1×7.92-mm (0.312-in) LMG 08/15 machine-gun
Max T/O weight: 730 kg (1,610 lb)
Max speed: 93 mph at optimum altitude
Operational endurance: 2 hours

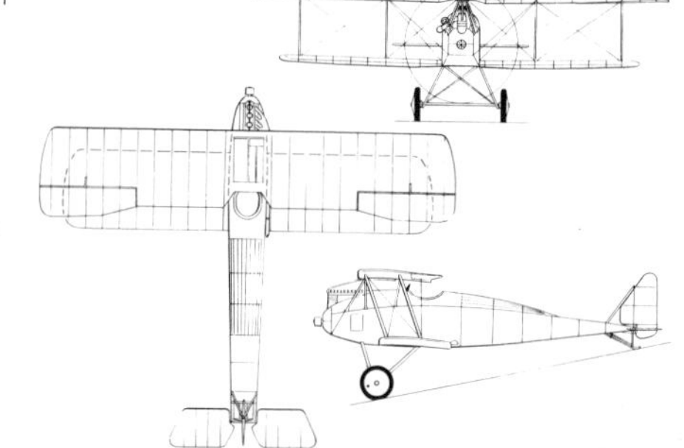

Albatros D II

The Fokker E-series fighters were obsolescent by the spring of 1916, and as part of the German effort to find a successor Albatros developed the D I that first flew in August 1916 with a well streamlined plywood-covered fuselage, equal-chord biplane wings and a Benz Bz.III or Mercedes D.III inline engine whose 112 or 119 kW (150 or 160 hp) allowed the installation of two guns without serious degradation of the fighter's high performance. The type was soon in service, and proved superior in all important respects to current Allied fighters. The sole criticism levelled at the type was the location of the upper wing, which impaired the pilot's upward field of vision, and in the definitive D II the wing was lowered, the D.III engine standardised and, in later aircraft, the fuselage ear-type radiators exchanged for a faired radiator in the upper-wing centre section.

Specification: Albatros D II single-seat fighter
Span: 8.50 m (27 ft 10.75 in)
Length: 7.40 m (24 ft 3.25 in)
Powerplant: 1×Mercedes D.III, 119 kW (160 hp)
Armament: 2×7.92-mm (0.312-in) LMG 08.15 machine-guns
Max T/O weight: 888 kg (1,958 lb)
Max speed: 109 mph at optimum altitude
Operational endurance: 1 hour 30 minutes

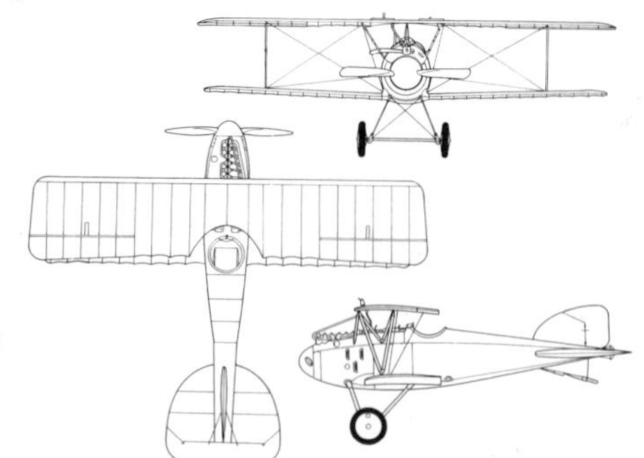

This Albatros D V wears the red-edged green tail markings of Jasta 5, one of the Imperial Air Service's elite fighter units on the Western Front. This included such aces as Paul Baumer and Hans von Hippel. The multi-pointed star emblem on the fuselage side proclaims this to be the mount of a less well known pilot, Leutnant Klein. The aircraft, like many Albatros Scouts, has an unpainted wooden fuselage.

Fokker E III

The Eindecker (monoplane) was a version of the M.5k general-purpose aeroplane fitted with a forward-firing machine-gun and interrupter gear to prevent bullets from hitting propeller blade(s). The inspiration for this otherwise combat aeroplane was Roland Garros's Morane-Saulnier Type L, which came down behind the German lines on 19 April 1915 and was then found to be fitted with a gun and steel deflector plates. The Eindecker entered production as the E I with the 60-kW (80-hp) Oberursel U.0 rotary, and was the world's first true fighter. The E I was soon superseded by the generally similar E II with the 75-kW (100-hp) U.I rotary for improved performance and then by the definitive E III with detail modifications. The final attempt to wring extra capability out of the basic design was the overweight E IV with two guns and the 119-kW (160-hp) U.III rotary. Total E-series production was about 300 aircraft.

Specification: Fokker E III
single-seat fighter
Span: 9.50 m (31 ft 2.75 in)
Length: 7.20 m (23 ft 7.5 in)
Powerplant: 1×Oberursel U.I, 75 kW (100 hp)
Armament: 1×7.92-mm (0.312-in) LMG 08/15 machine-gun
Max T/O weight: 610 kg (1,345 lb)
Max speed: 87 mph at sea level
Operational endurance: 1 hour 30 minutes

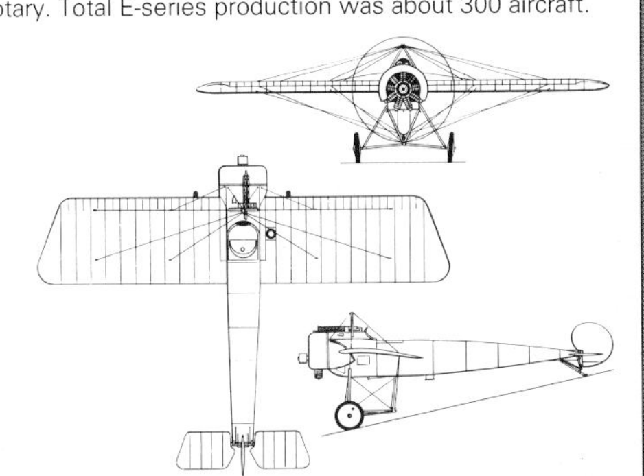

Fokker D III

To replace its E-series monoplanes, in the summer of 1916 Fokker evolved the D I biplane fighter from its M.18z prototype. Production followed, but as the type was powered only by an 89-kW (120-hp) Mercedes D.II inline engine it was soon outclassed by Allied fighters even when revised into the D IV with slightly greater size and the 119-kW (160-hp) Mercedes D.III engine. The D II appeared later than the D I but was derived from the earlier M.17z prototype. The D II had shorter wings and a longer fuselage, and as it was powered by a 75-kW (100-hp) Oberursel U.I rotary engine it was lighter and more manoeuvrable than the D I. In an effort to maintain an edge over Allied fighters, the succeeding D III had more power, a fuselage based on that of the D II, D I wings and an armament of two machine-guns. The final D V was a refined version of the D III with the U.I engine, and was used as a trainer.

Specification: Fokker D III
single-seat fighter
Span: 9.05 m (29 ft 8.25 in)
Length: 6.30 m (20 ft 8 in)
Powerplant: 1×Oberursel U.III, 119 kW (160 hp)
Armament: 1 or 2×7.92-mm (0.312-in) LMG 08/15 machine-guns
Max T/O weight: 710 kg (1,565 lb)
Max speed: 99 mph at sea level
Operational endurance: 1 hour 30 minutes

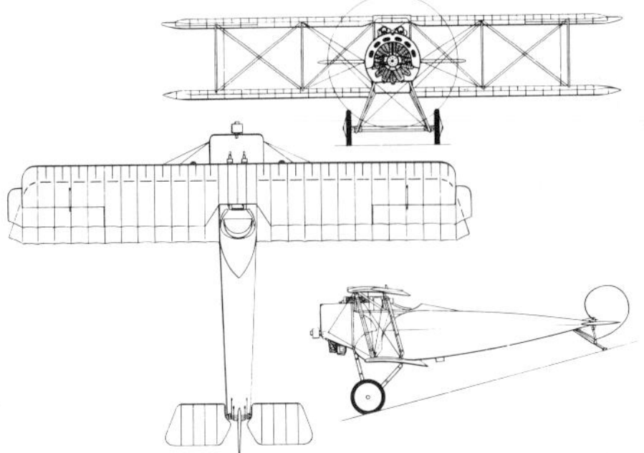

Pfalz D XII

The last Pfalz design to be built in numbers was the D XII fighter, a type designed for the second German fighter competition held in May 1918. In layout the type was a sturdy twin-bay biplane with a plywood-covered semi-monocoque fuselage, a large tailplane and horn-balanced control surfaces. The prototype first flew with the Mercedes D.IIIa inline, but in the competition examples were flown with the Mercedes D.III and BMW III engines. The D XII was ordered into production mainly as an insurance against problems with the Fokker D VIII, and was generally used by Bavarian units. After initial disappointment that they had not received the Fokker fighter, these units soon came to appreciate the very real virtues of the Pfalz machine, which were adequate performance, good agility and extreme strength. Production totalled some 200 aircraft.

A Pfalz D XII in typical late war markings, with a camouflaged fuselage and lozenge-pattern camouflage on the upper surfaces. The black and white tail denotes the Bavarian Jasta 16. The Pfalz D XII was an excellent fighting scout, in some respects better than the contemporary Fokker D VII, which was built in larger numbers and was thus more widely known.

Albatros D III

As soon as the D II was in production, its designer turned to a more advanced version intended to offer considerably improved manoeuvrability. The result was the D III that retained the fuselage and empennage of the D II but added a version of the D.III engine with a higher compression ratio for slightly more power, and adopted a new wing cellule without stagger. The wings comprised a longer-span upper wing with raked tips and a narrow-chord lower wing in a sesquiplane arrangement with V-layout interplane struts. At the same time the radiator was shifted from the centre section to the starboard wing so that a bullet puncture would not result in the pilot being scalded. The D III entered service in the spring of 1917, and was produced in large numbers to become the decisive fighter over the Western Front between that time and the autumn of the same year.

Specification: Albatros D III single-seat fighter
Span: 9.05 m (29 ft 8.25 in)
Length: 7.33 m (24 ft 0.5 in)
Powerplant: 1×Mercedes D.IIIa, 127 or 130 kW (170 or 175 hp)
Armament: 2×7.92-mm (0.312-in) LMG 08/15 machine-guns
Max T/O weight: 886 kg (1,953 lb)
Max speed: 109 mph at 3,280 ft
Operational endurance: 2 hours

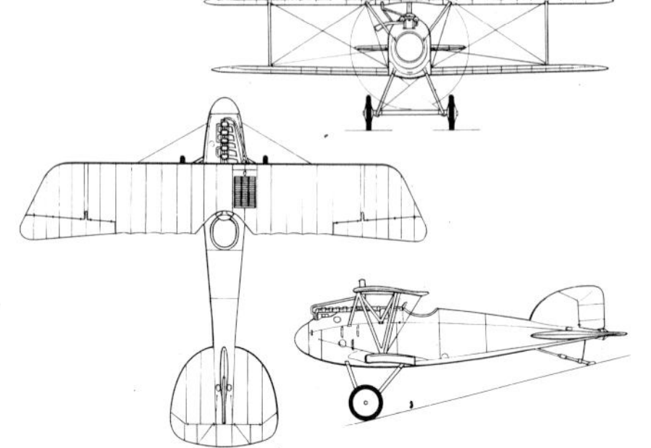

Pfalz D III

The Pfalz E-series of monoplane fighters was produced in parallel with the Fokker E-series, and the manufacturer then built the LFG (Roland) D I and D II fighters under licence. In the summer of 1917 Pfalz flew the prototype of its own D III fighter, which drew heavily on Roland design and construction practices. The type was an unequal-span biplane with an almost sesquiplane layout, a fuselage of very clean lines, and a 119-kW (160-hp) Mercedes D.III inline in a commendably low-drag installation. The D III entered service in the autumn of 1917, mainly with Bavarian units, and was complemented from 1918 by the D IIIa with a more powerful engine. It has often been claimed that the type was unpopular, but this is difficult to understand as Allied pilots rated a captured example highly. The type was better balanced and more manoeuvrable than the Albatros D V, and production totalled more than 600 machines.

Specification: Pfalz D IIIa single-seat fighter
Span: 9.40 m (30 ft 10 in)
Length: 6.95 m (22 ft 9.5 in)
Powerplant: 1×Mercedes D.IIIa, 134 kW (180 hp)
Armament: 2×7.92-mm (0.312-in) LMG 08/15 machine-guns
Max T/O weight: 935 kg (2,061 lb)
Max speed: 103 mph at 9,845 ft
Operational endurance: about 2 hours

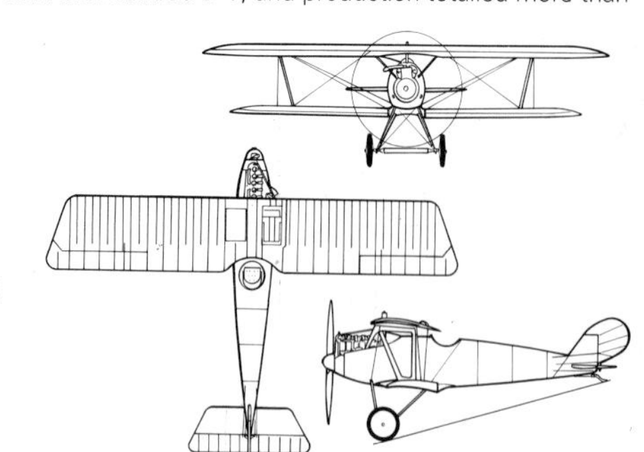

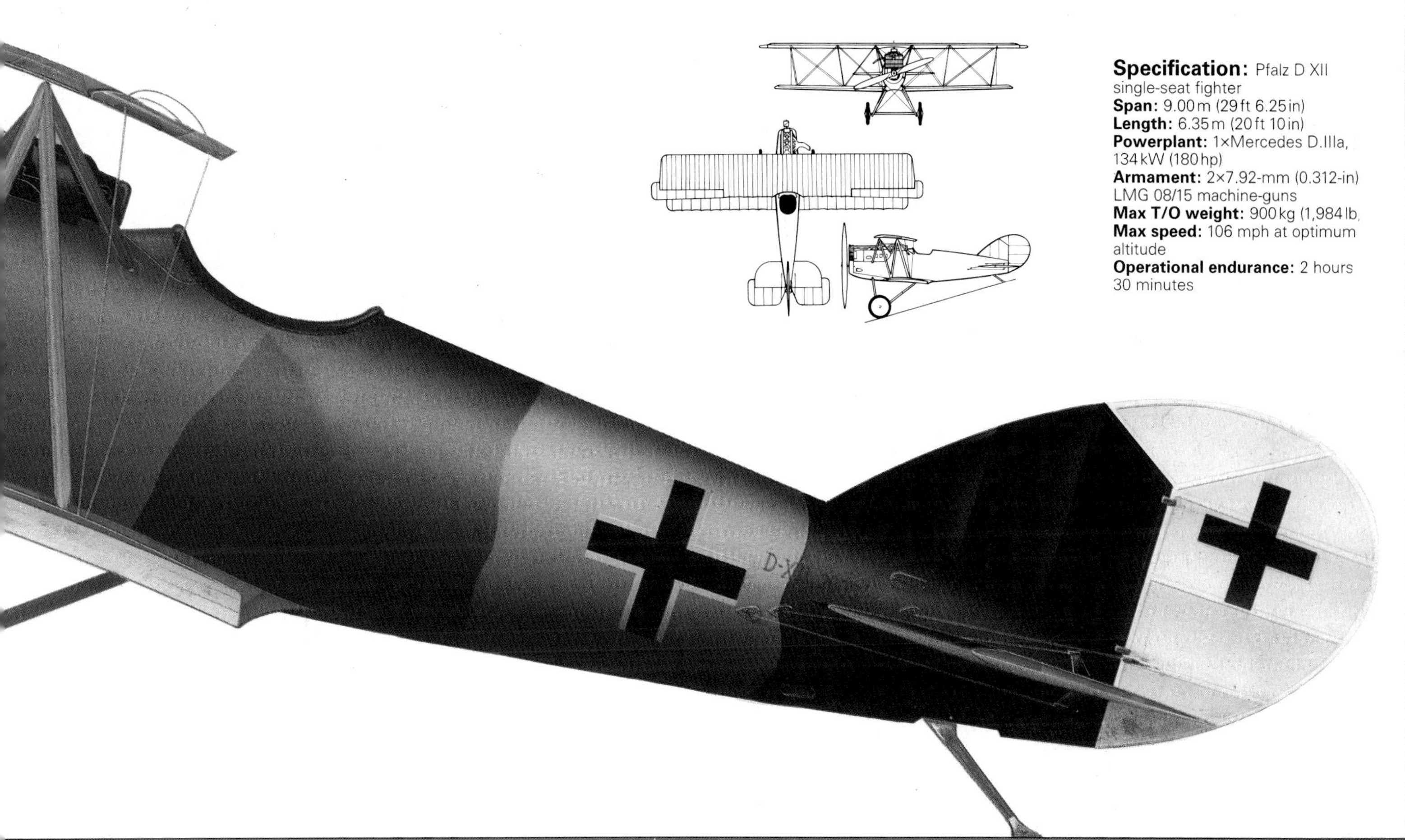

Specification: Pfalz D XII single-seat fighter
Span: 9.00 m (29 ft 6.25 in)
Length: 6.35 m (20 ft 10 in)
Powerplant: 1×Mercedes D.IIIa, 134 kW (180 hp)
Armament: 2×7.92-mm (0.312-in) LMG 08/15 machine-guns
Max T/O weight: 900 kg (1,984 lb)
Max speed: 106 mph at optimum altitude
Operational endurance: 2 hours 30 minutes

Fokker Dr I

Impressed with the climb rate and agility of the Sopwith Triplane in spring 1917, German fighter pilots called for a German equivalent. Of the crop of prototypes that appeared, the best was the Fokker V 3 with a fabric-covered welded steel tube fuselage, a large triangular tailplane, the standard 'comma' rudder without a fixed fin, and cantilever plywood/fabric-covered wooden wings. These last vibrated badly in flight, and the V 4 introduced lightweight interplane struts as well as aerodynamic improvements. This variant entered production in summer 1917 as the F I, a designation soon changed to Dr I. Production of 300 aircraft lasted to May 1918. The type acquired a high reputation, but hindsight indicates that this is a reflection not of the type's performance, which was only indifferent because of its low-powered engine, but of the skill of the aces who flew this agile fighter.

Specification: Fokker Dr I single-seat fighter
Span: 7.20 m (23 ft 7.5 in)
Length: 5.77 m (18 ft 11.25 in)
Powerplant: 1×Oberursel Ur.II or Thulin-built Le Rhone 9, 82 kW (110 hp)
Armament: 2×7.92-mm (0.312-in) MG 08/15 machine-guns
Max T/O weight: 585 kg (1,290 lb)
Max speed: 103 mph at 13,125 ft
Operational endurance: 1 hour 30 minutes

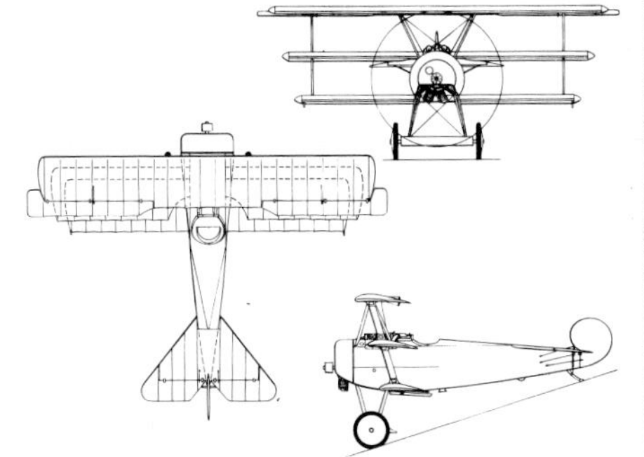

LFG (Roland) D II

The D I was in essence the C II two-seater scaled down as a single-seat fighter. The type was nicknamed Haifisch (shark) for its deep fuselage with the slightly swept upper wing attached directly to it. The D I first flew in July 1916, and was produced in small numbers. The definitive version was the D II, which retained the same 119-kW (160-hp) Mercedes D.III engine but featured a number of drag-reducing revisions as well as a modified empennage. The D II began to enter service early in 1917, and was complemented by the D IIa with a more powerful engine. The D II and D IIa were not popular in service, pilots complaining about lack of vision and heavy controls. The D III introduced a revised and shallower fuselage over which the upper-wing centre section was supported on cabane struts, but only a few were built. The single D V prototype had a more refined fuselage structure.

Specification: LFG (Roland) D IIa single-seat fighter
Span: 8.94 m (29 ft 4 in)
Length: 6.93 m (22 ft 9 in)
Powerplant: 1×Argus As.III, 134 kW (180 hp)
Armament: 2×7.92-mm (0.312-in) LMG 08/15 machine-guns
Max T/O weight: 795 kg (1,753 lb)
Max speed: 112.5 mph at optimum altitude
Operational endurance: 2 hours

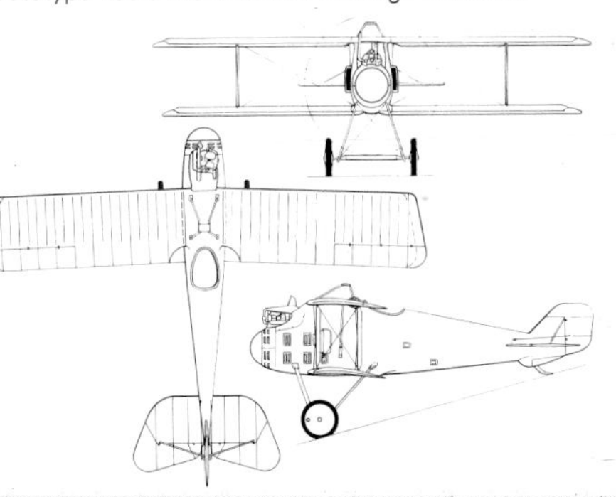

Bristol Bulldog

Possessing what represented the first significant advance in fighter speed for about 10 years, the metal-structured Bulldog, with customary two-gun armament, joined home-base RAF fighter squadrons (commencing with No. 3) in May 1929. Despite being handicapped by the unwieldy, air-cooled Jupiter radial, it went on to serve with a total of 11 squadrons, surviving in service until 1936. Only briefly, during the Abyssinian crisis of 1935, did a single squadron serve overseas. Long remembered for its scintillating Hendon displays, the Bulldog was however unforgiving of careless handling; the later Mk IIA had improved rudder, strengthened landing gear and a tailwheel.

Specification: Bristol Bulldog IIA single-seat interceptor fighter biplane
Powerplant: one 366-kW (490-hp) Bristol Jupiter VIIIF radial
Span: 10.34 m (33 ft 11 in)
Length: 7.62 m (25 ft 0 in)
Height: 3.00 m (9 ft 10 in)
Wing area: 29.90 m^2 (306.5 sq ft)
Take-off weight: 1590 kg (3,503 lb)
Max speed: 174 mph
Ceiling: 27,000 ft
Range: 295 miles
Armament: two nose-mounted 7.7-mm (0.303-in) synchronised Vickers machine-guns

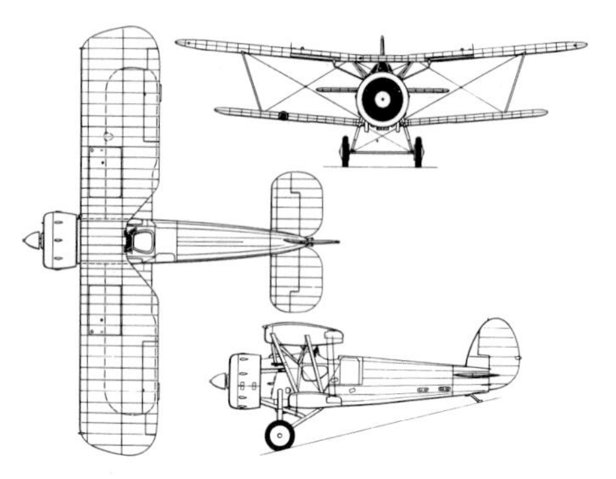

Armstrong Whitworth Siskin

Developed from the predominantly wooden Siddeley Siskin biplane with ABC Dragonfly radial, the Armstrong Whitworth Siskin III was of composite wood and steel strip construction and was powered by a 14-cylinder two-row Jaguar III radial. Characterised by Vee interplane struts between wings of unequal span and armed with a pair of synchronised machine-guns, the Siskin III (57 built) served with Nos 41 and 111 Squadrons from May 1924, and was joined in 1927 by the Siskin IIIA (348 built) of all-metal structure. Powered by a Jaguar IV, the Mark IIIA served with Nos 1, 17, 19, 25, 29, 32, 41, 43, 54, 56 and 111 Squadrons until the early 1930s. Dual-control Siskin IIIDC trainers (47 built) also served.

Specification: Armstrong Whitworth Siskin IIIA single-seat single-engine biplane interceptor
Powerplant: one 313-kW (420-hp) Armstrong Siddeley Jaguar IV radial
Span: 10.10 m (33 ft 2 in)
Length: 7.72 m (25 ft 4 in)
Height: 3.09 m (10 ft 2 in)
Wing area: 27.22 m^2 (293.18 sq ft)
Take-off weight: 1367 kg (3,012 lb)
Maximum speed: 156 mph
Ceiling: 27,000 ft
Range: 225 miles
Armament: two nose-mounted synchronised 7.7-mm (0.303-in) Vickers machine-guns

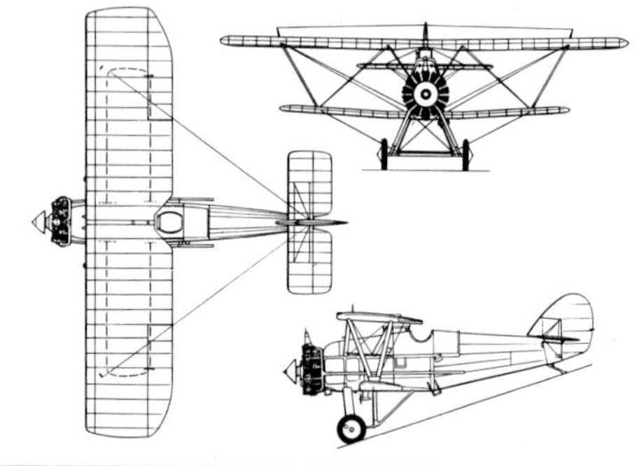

The Bristol F2.B Fighter

Despite its ungainly appearance, the two-seat Bristol Fighter was scarcely more than 20 per cent bigger and heavier than the single-seat scouts of the late-World War I period. In the post-war era the "Brisfit" came to be employed as what would later be termed a ground-support fighter, simply because in overseas theatres the RAF had few air defence responsibilities. In the 1920s it served with four army co-operation squadrons and three in Germany. In the Middle East and on India's North West Frontier the Bristol Fighter flew with a total of 10 army co-operation squadrons, often carrying 100-lb (45-kg) bombs under the wings, until finally replaced by Westland Wapitis in 1931.

Specification: Bristol F2.B Fighter two-seat general purpose and ground support fighter.
Powerplant: one 179-kW (240-hp) Rolls-Royce Falcon III engine
Span: 11.99 m (39 ft 4 in)
Length: 7.87 m (25 ft 10 in)
Height: 2.97 m (9 ft 9 in)
Wing area: 37.74 m^2 (406 sq ft)
Take-off weight: 1176 kg (2,590 lb)
Max speed: 126 mph
Ceiling: 20,000 ft
Range: 290 miles
Armament: one 7.7-mm (0.303-in) Vickers and one Lewis machine-gun; two 100-lb (45-kg) bombs underwing

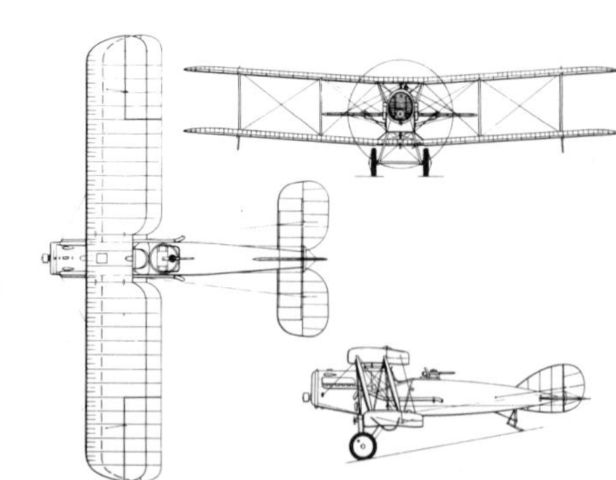

This Bristol Bulldog IIa wears the broken blue band insignia of No. 32 Squadron. Red tailfin and wheels signify that the aircraft belongs to the commander of 'A Flight'. At one time the Bulldog equipped two thirds of the RAF's Fighter Squadrons.

Gloster Gamecock

Replacing the Siskin IIIA on RAF squadrons, the Gamecock was the last fighter to employ wooden construction throughout, an expedient forced up the Service by the universal shortage of metal-working tradesmen. It employed the nine-cylinder Bristol Jupiter radial which, by 1926, was a more reliable and less costly engine than the Jaguar, and represented an all-round improvement in the Grebe fighter. It was extremely popular among its pilots as being highly manoeuvrable and will long be remembered for the many delightful aerobatic displays given at Hendon. Gamecocks were not finally withdrawn from service until July 1931, after a total of 82 had been produced; they served on five squadrons.

Specification: Gloster Gamecock I single-seat interceptor fighter biplane
Powerplant: one 317-kW (425-hp) Bristol Jupiter VI radial
Span: ;9.08 m (29 ft 9½ in)
Length: 7.90 m (25 ft 11 in)
Height: 2.95 m (9 ft 8 in)
Wing area: 24.9 m^2 (264 sq ft)
Take-off weight: 1300 kg (2,863 lb)
Max speed: 155 mph
Ceiling: 25,000 ft
Range: 260 miles
Armament: two nose-mounted 7.7-mm (0.303-in) synchronised Vickers machine-guns

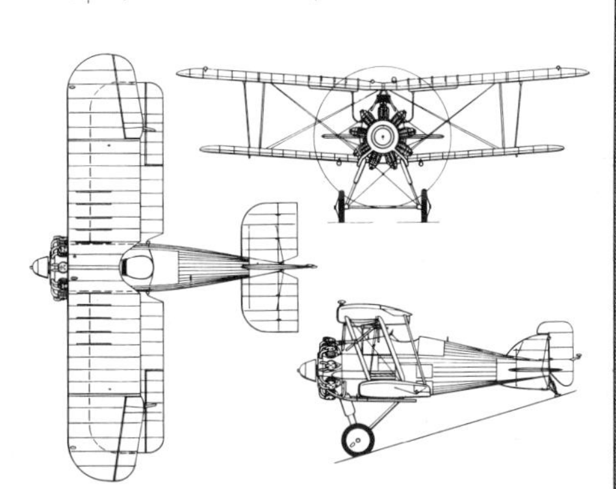

Gloster Gauntlet

Specification F.7/30, issued in 1930, called for a fighter with four-gun armament and a 400 km/h (250-mph) top speed, it being generally expected this would be met by an inline engine-powered aircraft, possibly a monoplane. Owing to the failure of the favoured Goshawk engine the radial-powered two-bay Gauntlet biplane emerged the successful contender, its speed, though not meeting the target, representing a big advance. Flown in Gauntlet configuration in October 1932, the prototype was followed by 228 production examples which served with 20 RAF and AAF fighter squadrons, being eventually withdrawn from service early in World War II. The Mk II employed an improved Hawker metal construction.

Specification: Gloster Gauntlet II single-seat two-bay biplane interceptor fighter
Powerplant: one 481-kW (645-hp) Bristol Mercury VIS2 radial
Span: 9.99 m (32 ft 9½ in)
Length: 7.98 m (26 ft 2 in)
Height: 3.25 m (10 ft 4 in)
Wing area: 29.26 m^2 (315 sq ft)
Take-off weight: 1802 kg (3,970 lb)
Max speed: 230 mph
Ceiling: 33,500 ft
Range: 460 miles
Armament: two nose-mounted 7.7-mm (0.303-in) synchronised Vickers mchine-guns

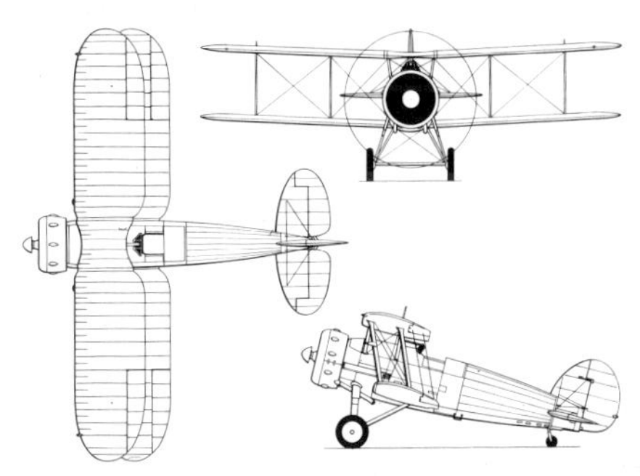

Hawker Fury

The quintessential British biplane interceptor, the beautiful Fury I (118 built) first flew in 1929 and joined No. 43 Squadron at Tangmere in May 1931, followed by Nos. 1 and 25 nine months later. First RAF fighter with a speed of over 200 mph, the Fury demonstrated the designer's skill in close-cowling the Kestrel (emulated by the Merlin in the Hurricane and Spitfire). It was joined in service by the Fury II (113 built with Kestrel VI, wheel spats and a speed of 223 mph) in November 1936, equipping four squadrons in the years immediately before World War II. A similar though independently developed design was the Nimrod fleet fighter, of which 81 were produced.

Specification: Hawker Fury I single-seat single-bay biplane interceptor fighter
Powerplant: one 392-kW (525-hp) Rolls-Royce Kestrel IIS inline
Span: 9.14 m (30 ft 0 in)
Length: 8.14 m (26 ft 8½ in)
Height: 3.10 m (10 ft 2 in)
Wing area: 23.44 m^2 (252 sq ft)
Take-off weight: 1584 kg (3,490 lb)
Max speed: 207 mph
Ceiling: 28,000 ft
Range: 305 miles
Armament: two nose mounted 7.7-mm (0.303-in) synchronised Vickers machine-guns

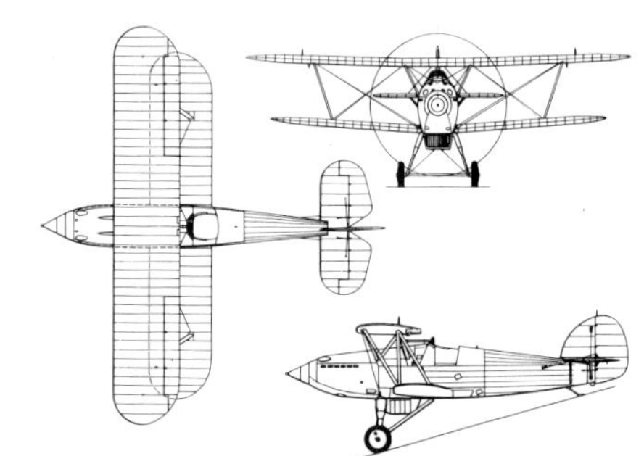

The sleek and graceful Hawker Fury provided an incredible contrast to its rival, the pugnacious-looking, snub-nosed Bristol Bulldog. Both aircraft were designed as replacements for the ageing Siskins and Gamecocks in service with Fighter Command. The beautiful Fury was faster than the Bulldog, but was never bought in such large numbers. Both were superb aerobatic mounts, and both were loved by their pilots, but the Fury Squadrons always enjoyed something of an elite reputation. This aircraft was flown by the 'A' Flight commander of the Tangmere based No. 43 Squadron, the famous 'Fighting Cocks'.

Gloster Gladiator

A direct development of the Gauntlet, the single-bay Gladiator was finally adjudged winner of the F.7/30 competition, being flown in September 1934 and rewarded with large production contracts (443 for the RAF and 60 for the FAA as the Sea Gladiator). Provided with enclosed cockpit, landing flaps on upper and lower wings, and cantilever landing gear, the four-gun Gladiator subsequently served with 32 RAF and AAF squadrons, also fighting in the Middle East well into World War II. The Mk II was powered by a Mercury VIIIA engine driving a three-blade Fairey propeller and was equipped for desert service. The Sea Gladiator featured arrester hook and survival dinghy.

Specification: Gloster Gladiator I single-seat single-bay biplane interceptor fighter
Powerplant: one 627-kW (840-hp) Bristol Mercury IX radial
Span: 9.83 m (32 ft 3 in)
Length: 8.36 m (27 ft 5 in)
Heigth: 3.15 m (10 ft 4 in)
Wing area: 30.00 m^2 (323 sq ft)
Take-off weight: 2157 kg (4,750 lb)
Max speed: 253 mph
Ceiling: 33,000 ft
Range: 490 miles
Armament: two nose-mounted and two wing mounted 7.7-mm (0.303-in) Browning machine-guns

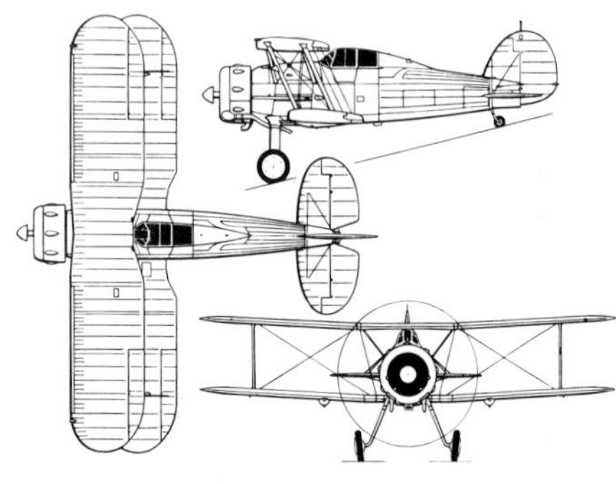

Gloster Grebe

The Grebe fighter was a development (by way of the experimental Grouse) of the Nieuport Nighthawk; it was however a single-bay biplane with wings of unequal span, and was powered by the Jaguar engine which was currently favoured by the RAF. Three prototypes were designated Grebe Is, and were followed by 112 production Mk IIs, the first deliveries being made to No. 25 Squadron in October 1924, replacing Snipes, followed by Nos 19, 29, 32 and 56 Squadrons, all home-based. Among trials with Grebes were those involving air-launching from the airship R.33. Severe wing flutter caused a number of early accidents and was largely cured by adding vee struts to brace the upper wing tips.

Specification: Gloster Grebe II single-seat interceptor fighter biplane
Powerplant: one 298-kW (400-hp) Armstrong Siddeley Jaguar IV radial
Span: 8.94 m (29 ft 4 in)
Length: 6.17 m (20 ft 3 in)
Height: 2.82 m (9 ft 3 in)
Wing area: 23.95 m^2 (254 sq ft)
Take-off weight: 1187 kg (2,614 lb)
Max speed: 152 mph
Ceiling: 23,000 ft
Range: 240 miles
Armament: two nose-mounted 7.7-mm (0.303-in) synchronised Vickers machine-guns

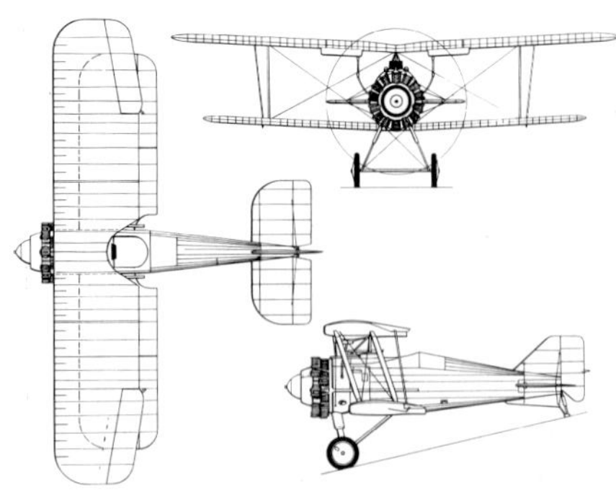

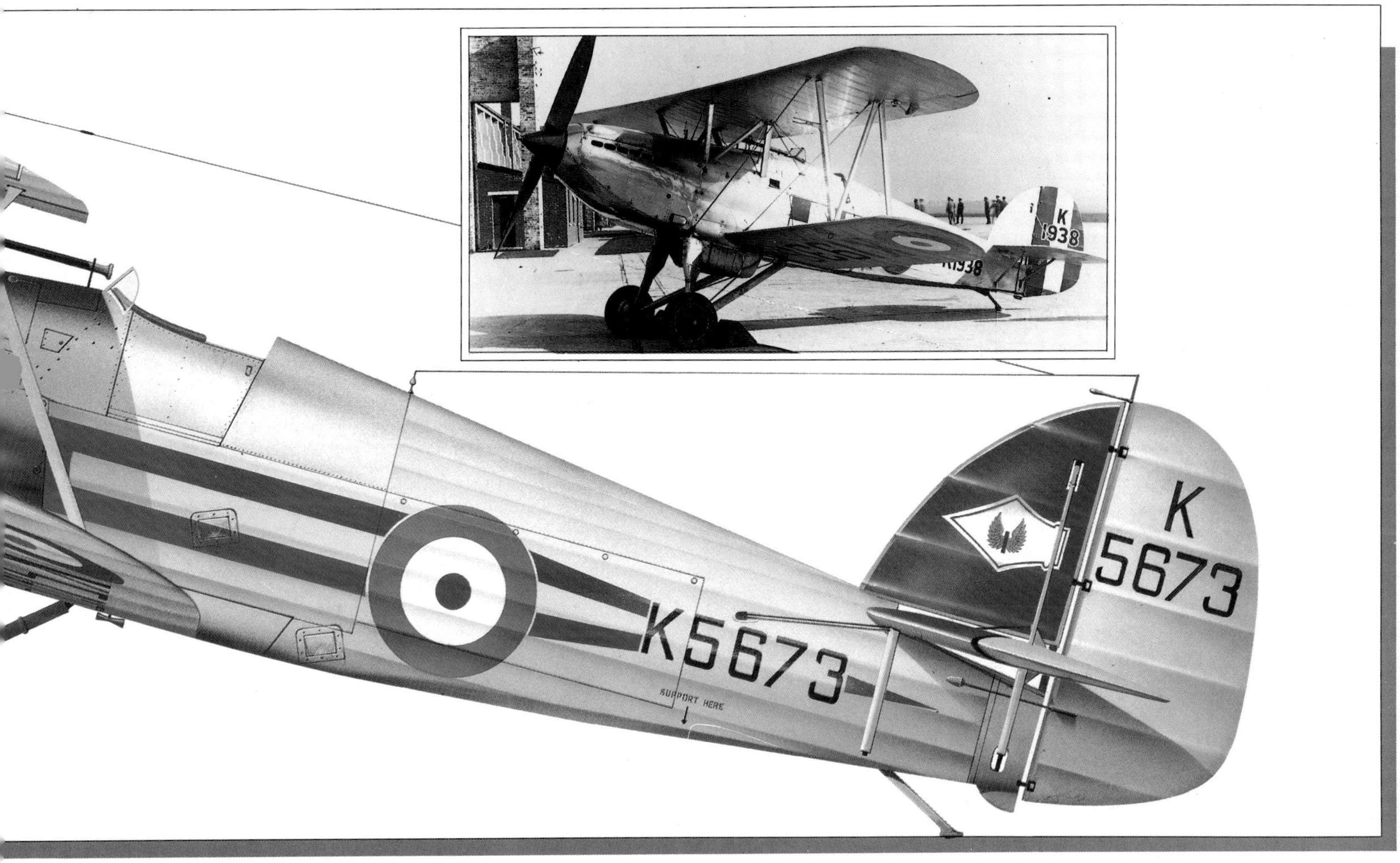

Hawker Demon

The appearance in service in 1930 of the Hart light bomber with a speed higher than the fastest fighter (the Bulldog) prompted the Air Ministry to order a fighter version of the Hart. This, the two-seat, three-gun Demon, entered service with No. 23 Squadron in May 1931 and, although not as fast as the single-seat Fury, then joining the RAF, proved very popular and eventually equipped 14 RAF and AAF fighter squadrons in the UK and the Middle East (serving with Nos 23, 41, 64 and 74 Squadrons in the Mediterranean during the Abyssinian crisis). Late production aircraft, built by, Boulton Paul, were equipped with "lobster-back" shield to protect the rear cockpit gunner. Production totalled 239.

Specification: Hawker Demon I two-seat fighter biplane
Powerplant: one 418-kW (560-hp) Rolls-Royce Kestrel V(DR) inline
Span: 11.35 m (37 ft 3 in)
Length: 9.02 m (29 ft 7 in)
Height: 3.18 m (10 ft 5 in)
Wing area: 32.31 m² (348 sq ft)
Take-off weight: 2119 kg (4,668 lb)
Max speed: 182 mph
Ceiling: 27,500 ft
Range: 450 miles
Armament: two nose-mounted 7.7-mm (0.303-in) Vickers and one 7.7-mm (0.303-in) Lewis machine-gun in rear cockpit

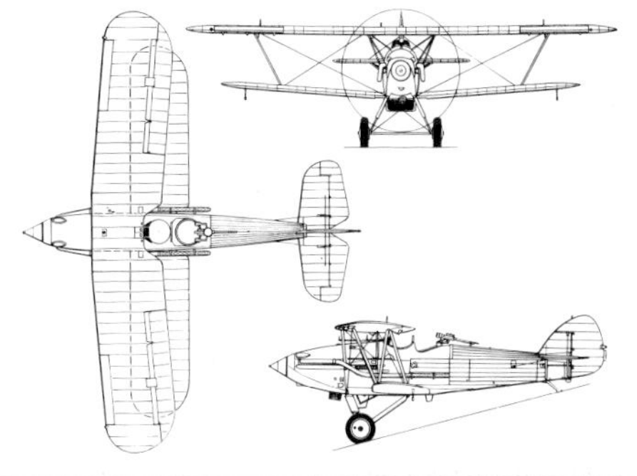

Hawker Hurricane I *(pre-war)*

The first RAF monoplane interceptor with retractable undercarriage and a top speed of over 300 mph, the Hurricane was first flown on 6 November 1935 and first entered service with No. 111 Squadron in December 1937. Armed with eight machine-guns, early examples featured fabric-covered wings and two-blade wooden propellers. Almost a year ahead of the Spitfire, Hurricanes were selected as the cornerstone of Fighter Command in 1939 and, by the outbreak of war, with 497 already built, equipped 17 squadrons. By that date improved versions with three-blade variable pitch propellers and metal-clad wings were being introduced, while tropical trials and test with cannon armament were in progress.

Specification: Hawker Hurricane I (pre-war) single-seat, single-engine interceptor monoplane
Powerplant: one 768-kW (1,030-hp) Rolls-Royce Merlin III liquid-cooled inline engine
Span: 12.19 m (40 ft 0 in)
Length: 9.58 m (31 ft 5 in)
Height: 4.00 m (13 ft 1½ in)
Wing area: 23.55 m² (257.5 sq ft)
Take-off weight: 2996 kg (6,000 lb)
Max speed: 316 mph
Ceiling: 33,200 ft
Range: 460 miles
Armament: eight wing-mounted 7.7-mm (0.303-in) machine-guns

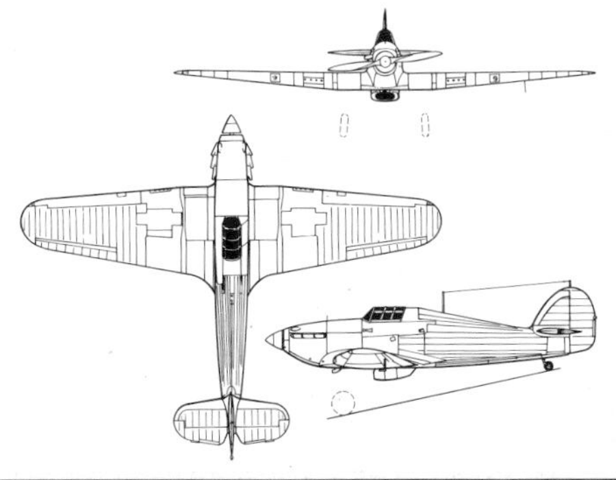

Hawker Woodcock

A single-bay biplane development of the unsuccessful Woodcock I, W.G. Carter's Mk II Woodcock nevertheless perpetuated the wooden-structured, two-gun, radial-powered World War I scout formula and was therefore little advanced from the Snipe. It did however constitute the means by which the Hawker company survived in the mid-1920s. Woodcocks were moreover the first purpose-designed night fighters to join the RAF, serving with No. 3 Squadron at Upavon from October 1925 and No. 17 the following April, these squadrons being responsible for the night defence of the industrial Midlands from possible attack by France. Sixty-three were built before they were replaced in service in 1928 by Gloster Gamecocks.

Specification: Hawker Woodcock II single-seat night interceptor fighter
Powerplant: one 313-kW (420-hp) Bristol Jupiter IV nine-cylinder air-cooled radial
Span: 9.91 m (32 ft 6 in)
Length: 7.09 m (23 ft 3 in)
Height: 3.12 m (10 ft 3 in)
Wing area: 32. 16 m^2 (346 sq ft)
Take-off weight: 1380 kg (3,040 lb)
Max speed: 138 mph
Ceiling: 20,000 ft
Range: 280 miles
Armament: two 7.7-mm (0.303-in) synchronised Vickers machine-guns

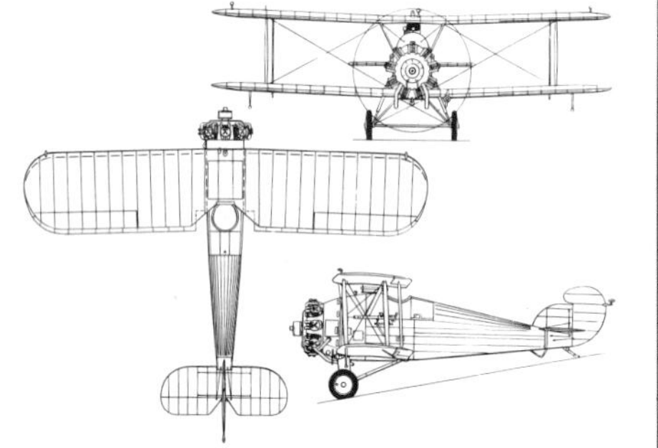

Nieuport Nighthawk

A little-remembered post-World War I fighter, the Nighthawk was important on account of employing a rigid radial in place of the former customary rotary engines. Successful contender for the RAF Type I SS fighter requirement, and designed largely by H.P. Folland, the Nighthawk was rewarded with a small production contract for the Gloucestershire Company (later Gloster Aircraft Co) and four such aircraft, two with Jaguar and two with Jupiter engines, served with the Snipes of No. 1 Squadron in Mesopotamia for comparative evaluation in 1923-4. Of all-wood construction, the Nighthawk represented the transition from Folland's wartime SE.5A to his post-war Gloster Grebe and Gamecock fighters.

Specification: Nieuport Nighthawk single-seat fighter biplane
Powerplant: one 242-kW (325-hp) Siddeley Jaguar II or 287-kW (385-hp) Bristol Jupiter III radial
Span: 8.53 m (28 ft 0 in)
Length: 5.49 m (18 ft 0 in)
Height: 2.74 m (9 ft 0 in)
Wing area: 25.46 m^2 (270 sq ft)
Take-off weight: 1158 kg (2,550 lb)
Max speed: 150 mph*
Ceiling: 24,900 ft*
RAnge: 310 miles*
Armament: two nose-mounted 7.7-mm (0.303-in) Vickers machine-guns
*with Jaguar engine

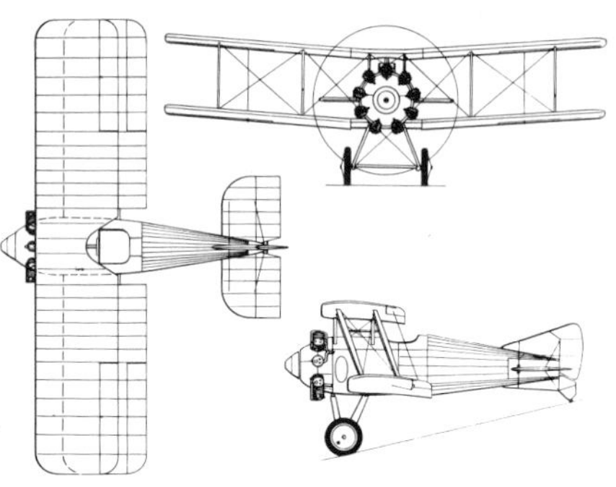

Sopwith Snipe

The classic fighting scout of the late World War I period, the Sopwith Snipe was retained in RAF service after the Armistice to constitute almost its sole home-base fighter equipment for several years. The two-gun Snipe equipped 11 home-based squadrons and four overseas, though for a time (1920-2) the No. 25 Squadron Snipes represented the only fighter defence of the UK. Possessed of nimble manoeuvrability, the aircraft was of all-wood construction and featured two-bay wings of equal span. Snipes survived with home-based squadrons until August 1926 when replaced by Gamecocks, and in Iraq for a further three months, although two-seat trainers continued to serve until 1928.

Specification: Sopwith 7.1 Snipe single-seat biplane fighter
Powerplant: one 172-kW (230-hp) nine-cylinder air-cooled rotary engine
Span: 9.17 m m(30 ft 1 in)
Length: 6.02 m (19 ft 9 in)
Height: 2.67 m (8 ft 9 in)
Wing area: 25.11 m^2 (270 sq ft)
Take-off weight: 917 kg (2,020 lb)
Max speed: 121 mph
Ceiling: 20,000 ft
Range: 240 miles
Armament: two nose-mounted synchronised 7.7-mm (0.303-in) machine-guns; eight light bombs

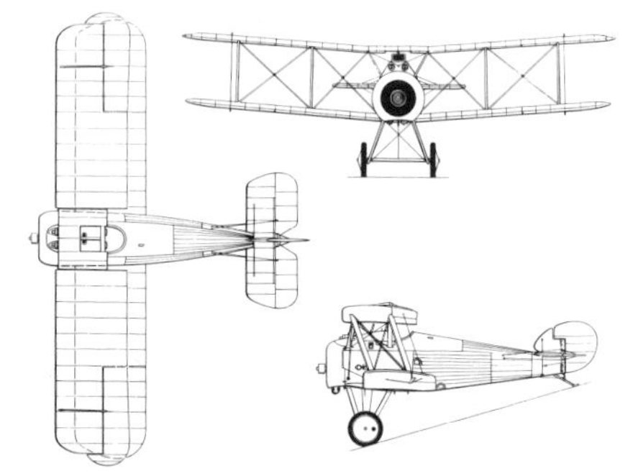

Supermarine Spitfire I *(pre-war)*

Influenced by his successful Schneider Trophy seaplanes, R.J. Mitchell produced his classic Spitfire design to meet a 1934 fighter requirement, the prototype being first flown in March 1936 and soon afterwards fitted with eight wing guns. Of metal stressed-skin construction (with fabric-covered control surfaces), the Spitfire was of exceptionally clean lines with elliptical wings and outward-retracting landing gear. First service deliveries were to No. 19 Squadron at Duxford in August 1938, but did not become fully operational until early 1939. By the outbreak of war nine squadrons had been fully equipped; early Merlin IIs with wooden propellers were being replaced by Merlin IIIs and three-blade props.

Specification: Supermarine Spitfire I (pre-war) single-seat single-engine interceptor monoplane
Powerplant: one 768-kW (1,030-hp) Rolls-Royce Merlin III liquid-cooled inline engine
Span: 11.23 m (36 ft 10 in)
Length: 9.12 m (29 ft 11 in)
Height: 3.02 m (9 ft 11 in)
Wing area: 22.49 m^2 (242 sq ft)
Take-off weight: 2626 kg (5,784 lb)
Max speed: 355 mph
Ceiling: 34,000 ft
Range: 510 miles
Armament: eight wing-mounted 7.7-mm (0.303-in) machine-guns

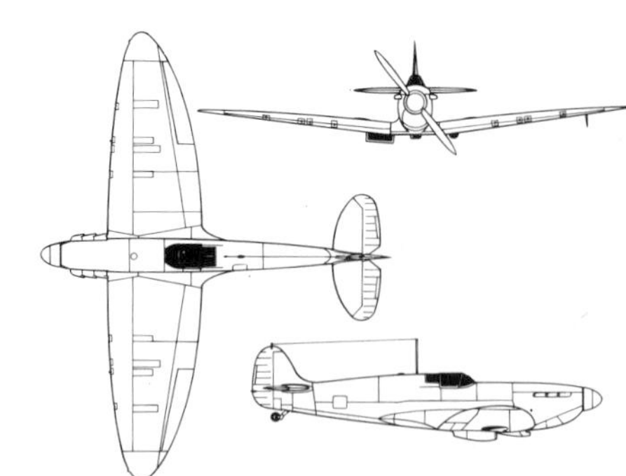

Boeing F3B

In its effort to produce a successor to the F2B-1, Boeing developed the Model 74 prototype that was trialled as a seaplane with one central and two stabilising outrigger floats. The type was evaluated as the XF3B-1 but rejected, and on return to Boeing was then revised fairly radically with a lengthened version of basically the same fuselage, a new tail unit and landing gear, and a completely revised wing cellule with slightly swept upper wings and unswept lower wings that diverged from earlier Boeing practice in being of parallel chord. This Model 77 was first flown in February 1928 and proved admirable in performance and handling. The US Navy ordered a total of 74 such F3B-1 aircraft, and these began to enter service from August 1938 on board the carriers *Langley, Lexington* and *Saratoga in the hands of squadrons VF-2B, VF-3B, VB-1B and VB-2B.*

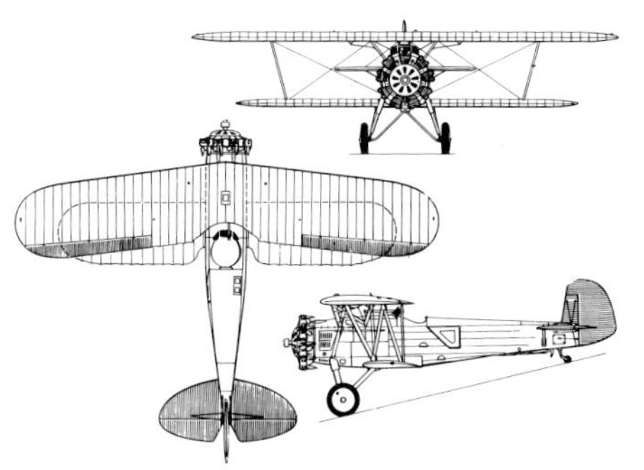

Specification: Boeing F3B-1 single-seat carrierborne fighter
Span: 10.06 m (33 ft 0 in)
Length: 7.57 m (24 ft 10 in)
Powerplant: 1×Pratt & Whitney R-1340-80 Wasp, 317 kW (425 hp)
Armament: 1×12.7-mm (0.5-in) and 1×7.62-mm (0.3-in) machine-guns plus provision for up to 5×11.3-kg (25-lb) bombs carried under the fuselage and wings
Max T/O weight: 1336 kg (2,945 lb)
Max speed: 157 mph at sea level
Operational range: 340 miles

Grumman F2F

Such was the performance of the FF-1 that Grumman began immediately to think of a comparable but smaller single-seat fighter with aerodynamically refined lines. This resulted in the XF2F-1 that first flew in October 1933 with a neatly cowled 466-kW (625-hp) XR-1535-44 Twin Wasp as a trim biplane with fabric-covered metal biplane wings, a metal semi-monocoque fuselage, an enclosed cockpit and fully retractable landing gear. The type's performance was outstanding, and an order was placed for 54 F2F-1 production aircraft. These were delivered between January and October 1935 for use by squadrons VF-2B on board the *Lexington* and VF-3B on board the *Ranger*; the latter became VF-7B and VF-5 on board the *Yorktown* and *Wasp* respectively. The type was supplanted by the F3F in 1939 and was then relegated to shore stations as a gunnery trainer.

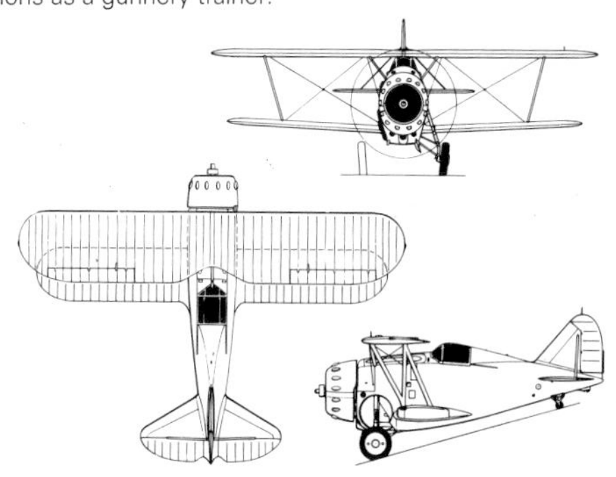

Specification: Grumman F2F-1 single-seat carrierborne fighter and fighter-bomber
Span: 8.69 m (28 ft 6 in)
Length: 6.53 m (21 ft 5 in)
Powerplant: 1×Pratt & Whitney R-1535-72 Twin Wasp, 485 kW (650 hp)
Armament: 2×7.62-mm (0.3-in) machine-guns plus provision for 2×52.6-kg (116-lb) bombs carried under the wings
Max T/O weight: 1745 kg (3,847 lb)
Max speed: 238 mph at 7,500 ft
Operational range: 985 miles

Brewster F2A Buffalo

Though of considerable importance in historical terms as the US Navy's first 'modern' all-metal monoplane fighter, the F2A was in all objective respects an indifferent type that resulted from a 1936 requirement. The XF2A-1 first flew in December 1937 with the 708-kW (950-hp) Wright XR-1820-22 radial, and amongst its features were an enclosed cockpit, hydraulic flaps and landing gear whose main units retracted inwards until the wheels were housed in the lower sides of the portly fuselage. Some 54 F2A-1 aircraft were ordered with the 701-kW (940-hp) R-1820-34 and a larger fin, the first of these entering service in January 1939 with squadron VF-3 on the *Saratoga*: only 10 were placed in service, the others being declared surplus and passed to Finland. Next came 43 F2A-2s with the R-1820-40, and finally 108 F2A-3s with a bulletproof windscreen and more armour.

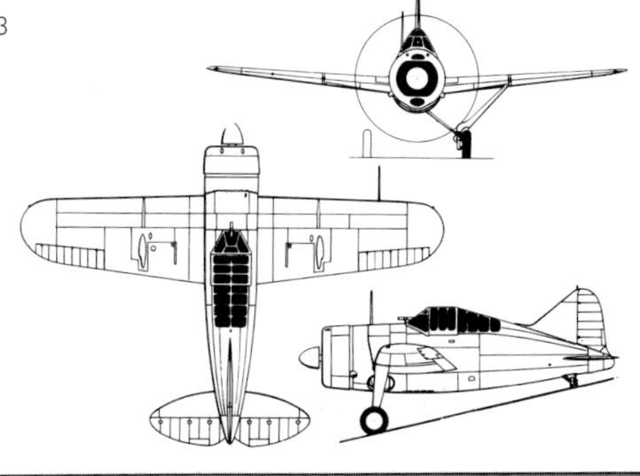

Specification: Brewster F2A-3 single-seat carrierborne and land-based fighter and fighter-bomber
Span: 10.67 m (35 ft 0 in)
Length: 8.03 m (26 ft 4 in)
Powerplant: 1×Wright R-1820-40 Cyclone, 895 kW (1,200 hp)
Armament: 4×12.7-mm (0.5-in) machine-guns plus provision for 2×45-kg (100-lb) bombs carried under the wings
Max T/O weight: 3247 kg (7,159 lb)
Max speed: 321 mph at 16,500 ft
Operational range: 965 miles

Grumman F4F Wildcat

As development of the F2A monoplane fighter began, the US Navy contracted for the XF4F-1 advanced biplane fighter in case the monoplane was a failure. This contract was later cancelled and replaced by the XF4F-2 monoplane prototype. The XF4F-2 flew in September 1937 with a 783-kW (1,050-hp) R-1830-66 radial, and though faster than the XF2A it was in other respects inferior. The US Navy realised the Grumman type's potential, though, and ordered the aeroplane to be revised as the XF4F-3. This flew in March 1939 with the XR-1830-76, increased wing span and area, a revised tail and modified armament. A second XF4F-3 prototype introduced a reprofiled fin and a higher tailplane position, and this formed the basis of the F4F-3 production model, of which 78 were ordered in August 1939 with deliveries beginning in August 1940 at the start of a great career in World War II.

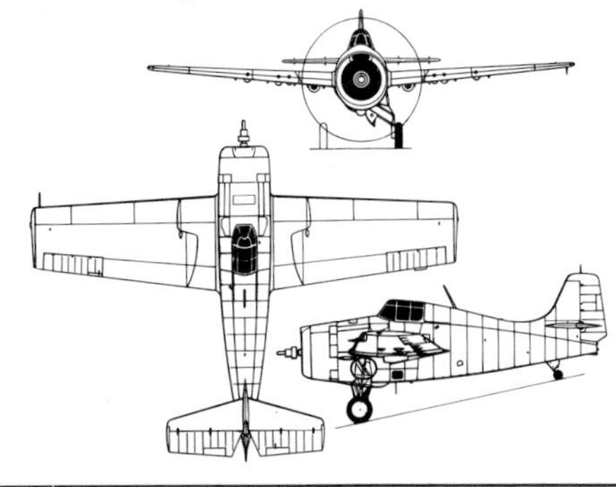

Specification: Grumman F4F-3 single-seat carrierborne and shore-based fighter
Span: 11.58 m (38 ft 0 in)
Length: 8.76 m (28 ft 9 in)
Powerplant: 1×Pratt & Whitney R-1830-36 Twin Wasp, 895 kW (1,200 hp)
Armament: 4×12.7-mm (0.5-in) machine-guns
Max T/O weight: 2665 kg (5,876 lb)
Max speed: 325 mph at 19,400 ft
Operational range: 900 miles

Boeing F4B

Specification: Boeing F4B-4 single-seat carrierborne fighter
Span: 9.14 m (30 ft 0 in)
Length: 6.12 m (20 ft 1 in)
Powerplant: 1×Pratt & Whitney R-1340-16 Wasp, 410 kW (550 hp)
Armament: 2×7.62-mm (0.3-in) machine-guns
Max T/O weight: 1638 kg (3,611 lb)
Max speed: 188 mph at 6,000 ft
Operational range: 370 miles

Vought VE-7S

First flown in the summer of 1918, the VE-7 was the first product of the Lewis & Vought Corporation, and resembled a scaled-down D.H.4 with the engine installation of the SPAD S.7. The type proved excellent, and was ordered into what was, for the period, large-scale production (128 aircraft). Though designed as a two-seat advanced trainer, the type had good performance and agility, and was therefore used in several fighter forms. These were the VE-7S single-seat fighter with one Vickers (later Browning) machine-gun (one aeroplane), the VE-7SF variant of the VE-7S with British emergency flotation gear (64 aircraft), and the VE-7SH seaplane fighter with the single central and two underwing stabilising floats of the VE-7H unarmed two-seat trainer and observation variant (VE-7SF conversions). The VE-7 remained in first-line service up to 1926.

Specification: Vought VE-7SF single-seat fighter
Span: 10.40 m (34 ft 1.5 in)
Length: 7.44 m (24 ft 5 in)
Powerplant: 1×Wright E-2, 134 kW (180 hp)
Armament: 1×7.7-mm (0.303-in) or 7.62-mm (0.3-in) machine-gun
Max T/O weight: 953 kg (2,100 lb)
Max speed: 117 mph at sea level
Operational range: 291 miles

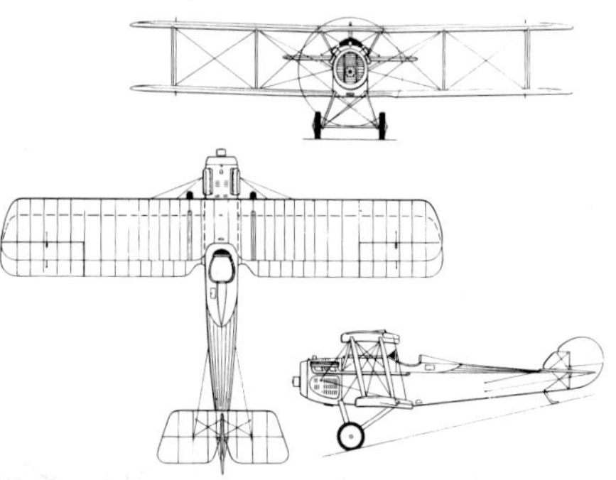

Boeing FB

The FB was the naval version of the US Army's PW-9, which had first flown in June 1923 as an unequal-span biplane of mixed construction and powered by a 324-kW (435-hp) Curtiss D-12 inline. Naval orders began with 14 FB-1s for use as landplanes by the US Marines, which received only 10 examples from December 1924. The 11th and 12th aircraft became FB-2s with the 380-kW (510-hp) Packard 1A-1500 inline, a through-axle and an arrester hook. The 13th aeroplane was identical to the FB-2s apart from its twin-float landing gear, and was the sole FB-3. The final aeroplane also had twin floats and was used for trials with a radial engine: with the 336-kW (450-hp) Wright P-1 it was the FB-4, the designation changing to FB-6 when the 298-kW (400-hp) Pratt & Whitney R-1340 Wasp was fitted. The only other production variant was the FB-5, of which 27 were delivered with the 2A-1500 engine.

Specification: Boeing FB-5 single-seat carrierborne fighter
Span: 9.75 m (32 ft 0 in)
Length: 7.24 m (23 ft 9 in)
Powerplant: 1×Packard 2A-1500, 388 kW (520 hp)
Armament: 2×7.62-mm (0.3-in) machine-guns
Max T/O weight: 1474 kg (3,249 lb)
Max speed: 176 mph at sea level
Operational range: 420 miles

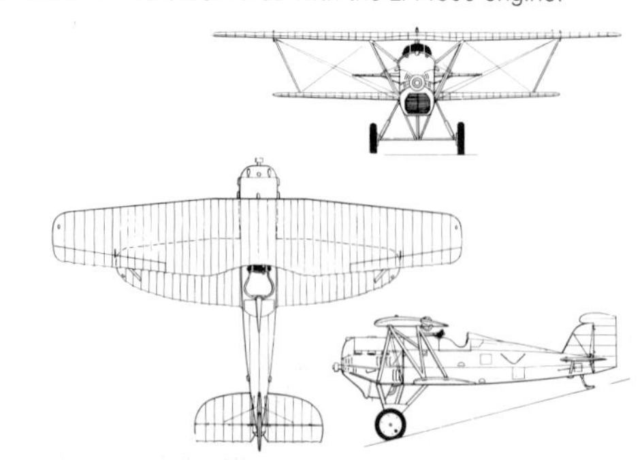

In 1928 Boeing flew two similar prototypes designed to provide an F3B successor: the Model 83 had spreader-bar landing gear and an arrester hook, while the Model 89 had divided main landing gear units and an underfuselage attachment for one 249-kg (550-lb) bomb. The aircraft were evaluated as XF4B-1s, and the US Navy then ordered 27 examples of the F4B-1 based on the Model 89 but with the Model 83's arrester hook. Deliveries began in May 1929, and production of the series in its various land- and sea-based variants totalled 586. Later models for the US Navy included 46 F4B-2s based on the Army's P-12C with spreader-bar landing gear, a tailwheel and narrow-chord cowling ring, 21 F4B-3s based on the P-12E with a semi-monocoque fuselage, and 92 generally similar F4B-4s with a larger fin. In 1940 surplus P-12s were transferred from the Army to the Navy with the designation F4B-4A.

This aircraft wears the Felix the Cat emblem that is today associated with VF-31 'Tomcatters', equipped with F-14 Tomcats. Pre-war, the badge was used by VF-6, and is seen here on one of that squadron's Boeing F4B-4 fighters. The aircraft served aboard the USS Saratoga during 1935. The black cowling, fuselage and band and chevron mark it as belonging to the leader of No. 4 Section.

Curtiss F6C

This member of the prolific Hawk series of fighters started with the F6C-1, of which the US Navy ordered nine examples in 1925 for landplane use by the US Marines' squadron VF-9M. Five were delivered as such with the Curtiss D-12, the other four becoming F6C-2s with arrester hooks and strengthening for carrier operations by squadron VF-2, and in 1927 the navy took 35 examples of the F6C-3, which was similar to the F6C-2 and served with the carrier-based squadron VF-5S (later VB-1B) on board the *Lexington* and the US Marines' shore-based squadron VF-8M. With the F6C-4, of which 31 were built for squadron VF-2B on board the *Langley*, the Navy switched to the 313-kW (420-hp) Pratt & Whitney Wasp radial. There were also F6C-5 to -7 experimental and racing models, and when retired from carrier service in 1930 the surviving production aircraft passed to the US Marines for service into the early 1930s.

Specification: Curtiss F6C-4
single-seat carrierborne and shore-based fighter and fighter-bomber
Span: 11.43 m (37 ft 6 in)
Length: 6.86 m (22 ft 6 in)
Powerplant: 1×Pratt & Whitney R-1340 Wasp, 306 kW (410 hp)
Armament: 2×7.62-mm (0.3-in) machine-guns plus provision for light bombs carried under the wings
Max T/O weight: 1438 kg (3,171 lb)
Max speed: 155 mph at sea level
Operational range: 340 miles

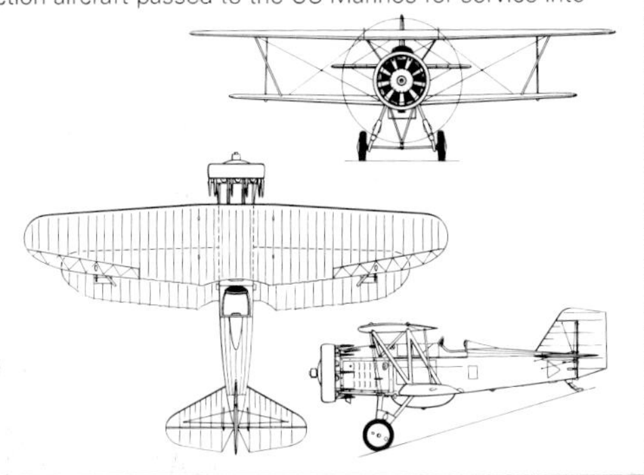

Vought FU

From the VE-7 and its up-engined VE-9 observation partner the company developed the UO observation aeroplane, in which an aerodynamically refined VE airframe was mated with successively more powerful engines ending from 1927 with the 164-kW (220-hp) Wright J-5 Whirlwind. The type had originally been schemed as a fighter, but the success of the VE-7 in this role led to the development of the aeroplane for observation in variants up to the UO-5. In 1926, however, the US Navy required an interim fighter floatplane for catapult launch from battleships, and such a variant was developed with a supercharged engine as the UO-3 but then redesignated FU-1. Production of 20 aircraft was completed in 1927, but the type remained in first-line service with squadron VF-2B for only one year, thereafter being converted as the FU-2 utility aeroplane.

Specification: Vought FU-1
single-seat ship-based fighter floatplane
Span: 10.46 m (34 ft 4 in)
Length: 8.65 m (28 ft 4.5 in)
Powerplant: 1×Wright J-5 Whirlwind, 164 kW (220 hp)
Armament: 2×7.62-mm (0.3-in) machine-guns
Max T/O weight: 1258 kg (2,774 lb)
Max speed: 122 mph at sea level
Operational range: 410 miles

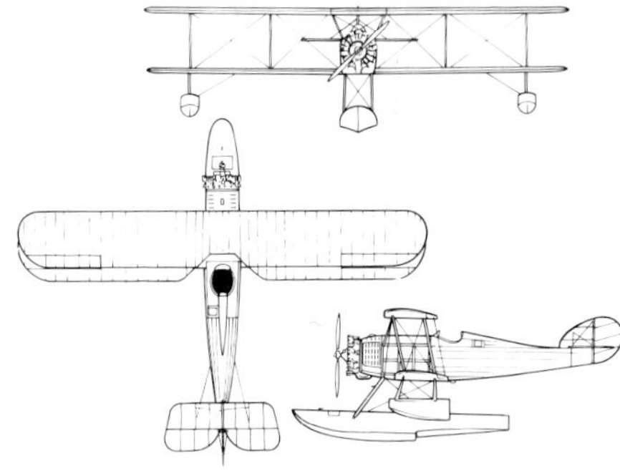

Grumman F3F

The F3F was an evolutionary development of the F2F to overcome the latter's handling deficiencies, which included directional instability and a tendency to tighten in a spin, as well as to improve manoeuvrability. The XF3F-1 prototype was thus slightly larger than its predecessor in span and length, and featured a number of aerodynamic refinements. The type first flew in March 1935, and despite the loss of the first machine in a dive-recovery test and severe damage to the second in a flat-spin accident, the trials were completed satisfactorily and an order for 54 F3F-1 aircraft was placed. These were delivered from January 1936 and served with squadrons VF-5B and VF-6B on board the *Ranger* and *Saratoga* respectively. Later developments were the F3F-2 with a supercharged engine driving a controllable-pitch propeller (81 built), and the F3F-3 with drag reductions (27 built).

A Grumman F3F-2 of VMF-1 (Marine Fighter Squadron 1) based at Quantico during 1937. The portly-looking F3F-2 was bought in large numbers by the US Navy and US Marine Corps, and the aircraft served until 1940, when it was replaced by Brewster Buffalo and Grumman Wildcat monoplanes. The F2F and F3F were the first US Navy fighters to feature an enclosed cockpit and a retractable undercarriage.

Curtiss F7C Seahawk

After the US Navy decided that radial engines should be used in carrierborne aircraft for their reduced vulnerability and simpler maintenance, Curtiss produced a private-enterprise fighter prototype with such an engine. This Model 43 first flew in February 1927, and featured a sturdy biplane wing cellule with a sweptback upper wing and straight lower wing, divided main landing gear units, and fuel tanks located outside the main fuselage structure but inside the aerodynamic fairings on each side of the fuselage. The type was evaluated as the XF7C-1, and 17 production aircraft were then ordered with the designation F7C-1: by comparison with the prototype these had greater span and, being intended only as landplanes, had no provision for alternative float landing gear. Deliveries began in August 1927, and the aircraft were used by squadron VF-5M of the US Marines based at Quantico.

Specification: Curtiss F7C-1 Seahawk single-seat shore-based fighter
Span: 9.34 m (32 ft 8 in)
Length: 6.88 m (22 ft 0.9 in)
Powerplant: 1×Pratt & Whitney R-1340 Wasp, 336 kW (450 hp)
Armament: 2×7.62-mm (0.3-in) machine-guns
Max T/O weight: 1262 kg (2,782 lb)
Max speed: 155 mph at sea level
Operational range: 355 miles

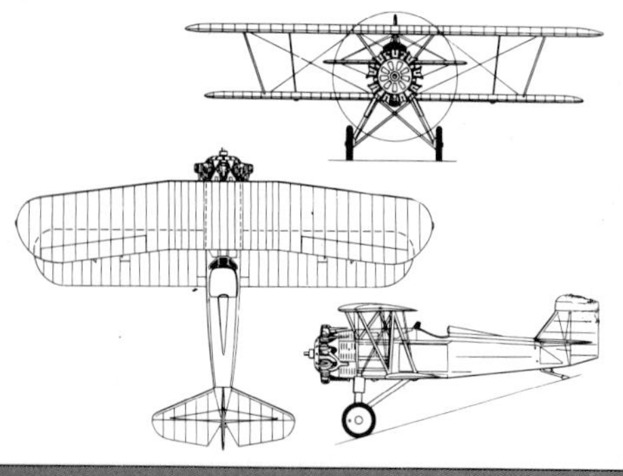

Boeing F2B

Boeing's Model 69 prototype was based on the Model 15 and had wings of less unequal span, but failed to secure the anticipated US Army production contract. The type was then revised with a Wasp radial and flown in November 1926 as the XF2B-1 naval prototype. Trials of radial engines in the FB-4/6 had already demonstrated the superiority of the air-cooled radial over the water-cooled inline for carrierborne aircraft, and the combination of such an engine with the Model 69 airframe resulted in an excellent fighter. By comparison with the prototype, the F2B-1 production type had no propeller spinner and introduced a balanced rudder, and some 32 such aircraft were delivered from January 1928 for use by squadrons VF-1B and VB-2B on board the carrier *Saratoga* in the fighter and bomber roles respectively. A small number of Model 69-B export aircraft were built.

Specification: Boeing F2B-1 single-seat carrierborne fighter
Span: 9.17 m (30 ft 1 in)
Length: 6.98 m (22 ft 11 in)
Powerplant: 1×Pratt & Whitney R-1340-B Wasp, 317 kW (425 hp)
Armament: 1×12.7-mm (0.5-in) and 1×7.62-mm (0.3-in) machine-guns plus provision for up to 5×11.3-kg (25-lb) bombs carried under the fuselage and wings
Max T/O weight: 1272 kg (2,805 lb)
Max speed: 158 mph at sea level
Operational range: 315 miles

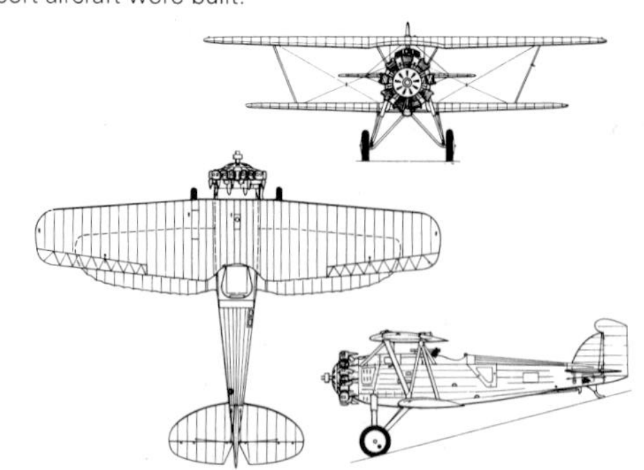

Specification: Grumman F3F-3 single-seat carrierborne and shore-based fighter
Span: 9.75 m (32 ft 0 in)
Length: 7.06 m (23 ft 2 in)
Powerplant: 1×Wright R-1820-22 Cyclone, 708 kW (950 hp)
Armament: 2×7.62-mm (0.3-in) machine-guns
Max T/O weight: 2175 kg (4,795 lb)
Max speed: 264 mph at 15,200 ft
Operational range: 980 miles

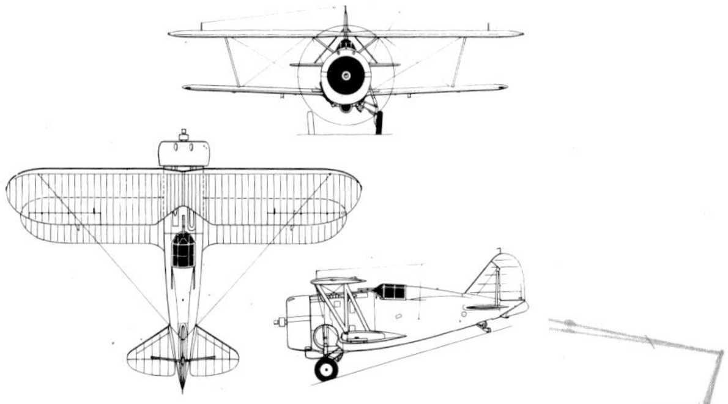

Curtiss F9F Sparrowhawk

This trim fighter was thoroughly typical of the Hawk series in its layout and construction, but was highly unusual in being used for the onboard protection of US Navy airships. The type resulted from a 1930 requirement for a carrier fighter small enough not to need folding wings, and flew in 1931 as the XF9C-1. This was rejected for its planned role because its small size limited capabilities to an unacceptable degree, but this diminutive size came into its own when the Navy decided to procure a fighter that could be carried by an airship fitted with the trapeze required to launch and recover hook-fitted fighters. Trials of the XF9C-2 proved successful, and six F9C-2 production aircraft were delivered in 1932. The *Akron* was lost in 1933 without aircraft on board, and the Sparrowhawk served with the *Macon* until she too was lost in 1935 with four F9C-2s in her hangar.

Specification: Curtiss F9C-2 Sparrowhawk single-seat airship-borne fighter
Span: 7.77 m (25 ft 6 in)
Length: 6.13 m (20 ft 1.5 in)
Powerplant: 1×Wright R-975-E Whirlwind, 327 kW (438 hp)
Armament: 2×7.62-mm (0.3-in) machine-guns
Max T/O weight: 1261 kg (2,779 lb)
Max speed: 176 mph at 4,000 ft
Operational range: 297 miles

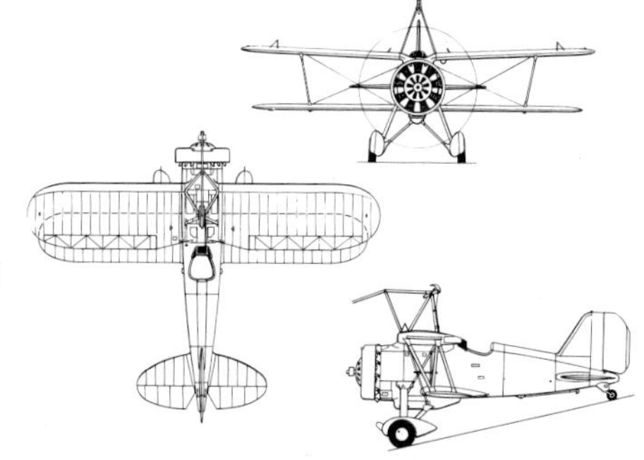

Grumman FF

The FF resulted from the US Navy's first contract with Grumman, and was a two-seat fighter that introduced retractable landing gear to American naval service. The XFF-1 first flew in December 1931 with a 459-kW (616-hp) R-1820-E radial enclosed in a narrow-chord ring cowl, and its most distinctive features were the 'glasshouse' canopy and the oddly deep fuselage sweeping up sharply in front of the lower wing to provide accommodation for the retracted mainwheels. Trials confirmed that the type was faster than contemporary single-seaters, and an order was placed for 27 FF-1 fighters. These were delivered in 1933 and equipped squadron VF-5B on board the *Lexington*. As they became obsolete later in the 1930s, 25 of the aircraft were revised as FF-2 dual-control fighter trainers. The SF-1 was a scout version of which 33 were delivered with more fuel and reduced armament.

Specification: Grumman FF-1 two-seat carrierborne fighter
Span: 10.52 m (34 ft 6 in)
Length: 7.47 m (24 ft 6 in)
Powerplant: 1×Wright R-1820-78 Cyclone, 522 kW (700 hp)
Armament: 3×7.62-mm (0.3-in) machine-guns plus provision for 2×52.6-kg (116-lb) bombs carried under the wings
Max T/O weight: 2106 kg (4,643 lb)
Max speed: 201 mph at 8,000 ft
Operational range: 732 miles

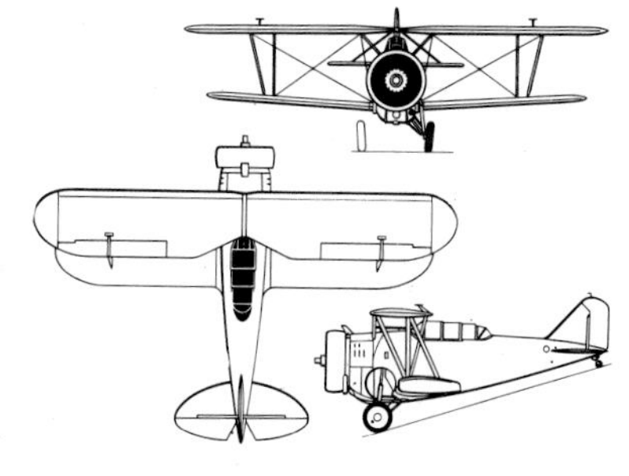

Republic P-47 Thunderbolt

The P-47 was a logical development of the P-43, and was a massive aeroplane with a considerably more powerful engine and a rear-fuselage turbocharger installation. The result was one of World War II's most important fighters, which flew in May 1941 as the XP-47B. The initial production model was the P-47B, of which 171 were built. These were followed by 602 P-47Cs with provision for a ventral drop tank, and by 12,559 P-47Ds with a paddle-bladed propeller, steadily increasing armament, additional fuel and, in later examples, a cut-down rear fuselage and 360° vision bubble canopy. Other variants were the Curtiss-produced P-47G (354 built), the P-47M high-power version of the P-47D (130 built) with the 2088-kW (2,800-hp) R-2800-57(C), and the P-47N long-range model (1,816 built) for service in the Pacific theatre.

Seversky P-35

In 1935 Seversky produced the private-venture SEV-2XP, a two-seat fighter with fixed landing gear. This was later rebuilt as the SEV-1XP single-seater with semi-retractable gear. First flown with a 634-kW (850-hp) Wright R-1820-G5, this was later redesignated SEV-7 when fitted with the 708-kW (950-hp) Pratt & Whitney R-1830-9 and a revised vertical tail. The fighter was tested by the USAAC as the Model AP-1, and at the end of 1936 an order was placed for 77 P-35s with one 12.7-mm (0.5-in) and one 7.62-mm (0.3-in) machine-gun mounted in the engine cowling. For export the company developed the EP-1-06 version with the R-1830-45 radial and revised armament. The Swedish air force ordered 120 with the designation J9: deliveries were affected by a 1940 US government embargo, and the last 60 were delivered to the USAAC with the designation P-35A.

Specification: Republic (Seversky) P-35A single-seat fighter
Span: 10.97 m (36 ft 0 in)
Length: 8.18 m (26 ft 10 in)
Powerplant: 1×Pratt & Whitney R-1830-45, 783 kW (1,050 hp)
Armament: 2×12.7-mm (0.5-in) machine-guns and two 7.62-mm (0.3-in) machine-guns
Max T/O weight: 3050 kg (6,723 lb)
Max speed: 290 mph at 12,000 ft
Operational range: 950 miles

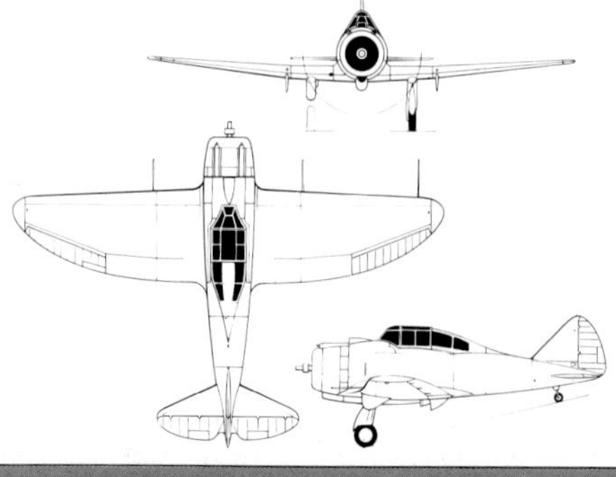

Curtiss P-36 Hawk

Designed at the same time as the P-35, the Curtiss Model 75 first flew in May 1935 and was evaluated as the Model 75A with the 671-kW (900-hp) Wright R-1670-5. There followed three service test Y1P-36 (Model 75E) aircraft with increased glazing, a retractable tailwheel and the 708-kW (950-hp) R-1830-13, and these were redesignated P-36 at the end of successful trials. Some 180 P-36As followed with the fully rated 783-kW (1,050-hp) R-1830-13 and improved armament (one 12.7-mm/0.5-in and one 7.62-mm/0.3-in cowling gun rather than two rifle-calibre guns). Later models were 30 P-36Cs with the 895-kW (1,200-hp) R-1830-17 and two wing guns, and the P-36G: 30 of these were ordered by Norway but seized before delivery for US service. There were several experimental variants, and a large number of export orders for the fixed-gear Hawk 75, retractable gear Hawk 75A and Mohawk variants.

Specification: Curtiss P-36C Hawk single-seat fighter
Span: 11.38 m (37 ft 4 in)
Length: 8.69 m (28 ft 6 in)
Powerplant: 1×Wright R-1830-17, 895 kW (1,200 hp)
Armament: 1×12.7-mm (0.5-in) machine-gun and 3×7.62-mm (0.3-in) machine-guns
Max T/O weight: 3243 kg (6,150 lb)
Max speed: 311 mph at 10,000 ft
Operational range: 820 miles

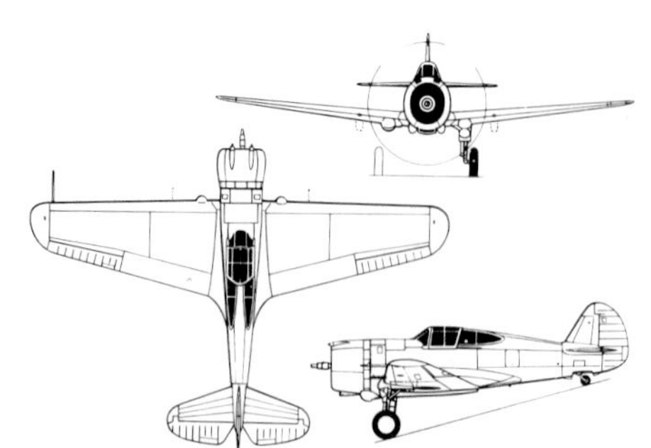

Although mainly used as an air-to-air fighter during its early career, the P-47 Thunderbolt developed a superb talent for ground attack, particularly after the Normandy landings. Together with RAF Typhoons, the P-47 cleared the way for the advancing Allied armies. This P-47D belonged to the 86th Fighter Group, flying ground attack missions and bomber escort missions in Italy in late 1944.

Specification: Republic P-47D-25 Thunderbolt single-seat fighter and fighter-bomber
Span: 12.43 m (40 ft 9.5 in)
Length: 11.01 m (36 ft 1.75 in)
Powerplant: 1×Pratt & Whitney R-2800-59, 1890 kW (2,535 hp)
Armament: 8×12.7-mm (0.5-in) machine-guns, plus provision for up to 1134 kg (2,500 lb) of bombs carried externally or 10×127-mm (5-in) rockets carried under the wings
Max T/O weight: 8800 kg (19,400 lb)
Max speed: 428 mph at 30,000 ft
Operational range: 475 miles

Lockheed P-38 Lightning

Resulting from a 1937 specification for a high-altitude fighter, the Lockheed 22 was the company's first combat aeroplane and flew in January 1939 as the XP-38. Though the type clearly had great promise, the advanced nature of the design and its turbocharged engines meant considerable development effort through 13 YP-38s and 30 P-38As before the initial combat-capable variants appeared as the P-38D (36 built) and P-38E (210) with a nose armament of four machine-guns and one 37- or 20-mm cannon respectively. Production then moved to 537 tropicalised P-38Fs with more power, 1,082 P-38Gs with provision for a 907-kg (2,000-lb) bombload, 601 P-38Hs with upgraded turbocharging, 2,970 P-38Js with improvements including chin radiators and in the last 1,400 machines increased tankage, 3,943 P-38Ls with more power and underwing rocket capability, and P-38M two-seat night-fighter conversions of the P-38L.

Specification: Lockheed P-38J Lightning single-seat long-range fighter and fighter-bomber
Span: 15.85 m (52 ft 0 in)
Length: 11.52 m (37 ft 10 in)
Powerplant: 2×Allison V-1710-89/91, 1062 kW (1,425 hp) each
Armament: 1×20-mm cannon and 4×12.7-mm (0.5-in) machine-guns, plus provision for up to 2×227-, 454- or 726-kg (500-, 1,000- or 1,600-lb) bombs or 10×127-mm (5-in) rockets
Max T/O weight: 9798 kg (21,600 lb)
Max speed: 414 mph at 25,000 ft
Operational range: 2,260 miles

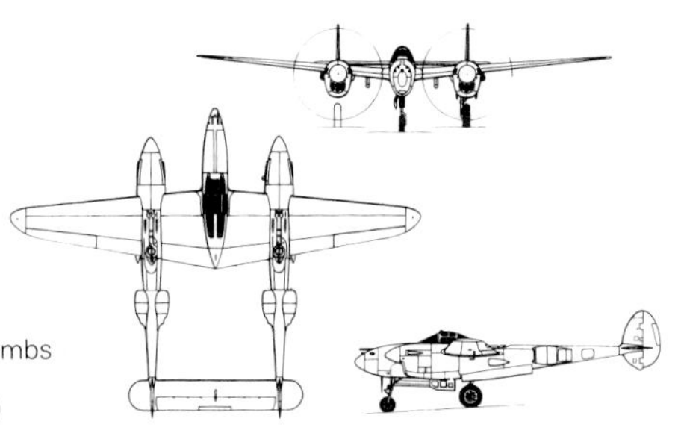

Bell P-39 Airacobra

The P-39 was an ingenious but ultimately unsuccessful fighter that sought to increase agility by locating the engine on the centre of gravity (behind the pilot), thereby leaving the nose for a 37-mm cannon and the nose unit for the tricycle landing gear. The XP-39 prototype flew in April 1938 and was followed by 13 YP-39 service test aircraft. Production was ordered with the designation P-45, but this was then altered to P-39 so that the first 20 aircraft were P-39Cs. Later production included 863 P-39Ds with self-sealing tanks, 229 P-39Fs with an Aeroproducts rather than Curtiss propeller, 25 P-39Js with the -59 engine, 2,545 P-39K/M/Ns with -63/83/85 engines, 250 P-39Ls with a Curtiss propeller, and 4,905 P-39Qs destined mostly for the USSR as ground-attack aircraft. Some 179 Airacobra Mk Is repossessed from the UK were designated P-400.

Specification: Bell P-39D Airacobra single-seat interceptor and fighter-bomber
Span: 10.36 m (34 ft 0 in)
Length: 9.19 m (30 ft 2 in)
Powerplant: 1×Allison V-1710-35, 857 kW (1,150 hp)
Armament: 1×37-mm cannon, 2×12.7-mm (0.5-in) machine-guns and 4×7.62-mm (0.3-in) machine-guns, plus provision for 1×227-kg (500-lb) bomb carried under the fuselage
Max T/O weight: 3720 kg (8,200 lb)
Max speed: 35 mph at 5,000 ft
Operational range: 800 miles

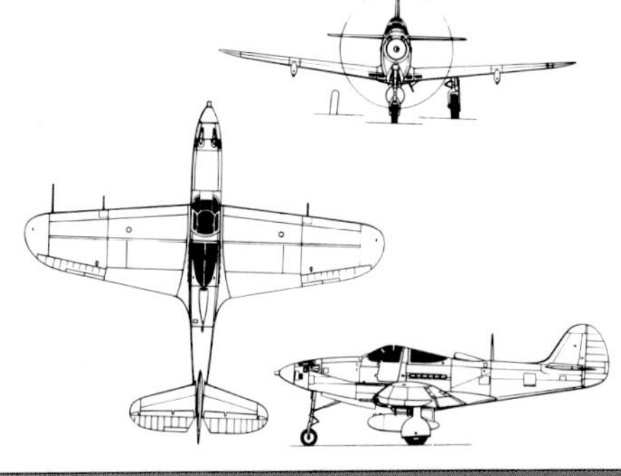

Northrop P-61 Black Widow

The P-61 was the USAAF's first purpose-designed night-fighter, and emerged as a large twin-boom aeroplane of distinctly aggressive appearance with radar in the nose of the central nacelle, which was surmounted by a low-drag cannon barbette. The first XP-61 flew in May 1942, followed by a second prototype and 13 YP-61 service test aircraft. Production of 200 P-61As was ordered, only the first 37 of these having the cannon barbette that was then deleted because of buffet problems. Later aircraft had underwing hardpoints for drop tanks or bombs, and these were standard on the 450 P-61Bs, of which the last 250 reintroduced the dorsal barbette. The final production variant was the P-61C, of which just 41 were built with 2088-kW (2,800-hp) R-2800-73 engines. Some 36 F-15A Reporter (later redesignated RF-61C) reconnaissance aircraft were also built.

By the time of its arrival in service in 1944, the Black Widow did not have that much to do; the night bomber threat for which it had been designed had virtually evaporated. Nevertheless, the big but sweet-handling monster notched up an impressive combat record in the last year of the war. This example is a P-61B, complete with seven Japanese kills from the Pacific theatre.

Curtiss P-40 Warhawk

The P-40 was in essence the P-36 revised for an inline engine, the XP-40 prototype being a converted P-36A that first flew in its revised guise during October 1938. Production versions were the initial P-40 (199 built), the P-40B (131) with two extra guns, the P-40C (193) with a redesigned fuel system, the P-40D (22) with shorter fuselage and landing gear, the P-40E (2,320) version of the P-40D with two extra guns, the P-40F (1,311) with a V-1650-1 Merlin, the P-40K (1,300) version of the P-40F with a V-1710-73, the P-40L (700) version of the P-40F with two guns removed, the P-40M (600) with a V-1710-81, and the P-40N (5,219) with a lightweight structure. The type was used mostly in the low-level and ground-attack roles: many were delivered under Lend-Lease to the USSR, China and the British empire, the last operating the type with the names Tomahawk and Kittyhawk.

Specification: Curtiss P-40N-20 Warhawk single-seat fighter and fighter-bomber
Span: 11.38 m (37 ft 4 in)
Length: 10.16 m (33 ft 4 in)
Powerplant: 1×Allison V-1710-81/99/115, 1014 kW (1,360 hp)
Armament: 6×12.7-mm (0.5-in) machine-guns, plus provision for 1×227-kg (500-lb) bomb carried under the fuselage
Max T/O weight: 4014 kg (8,850 lb)
Max speed: 378 mph at 10,500 ft
Operational range: 240 miles

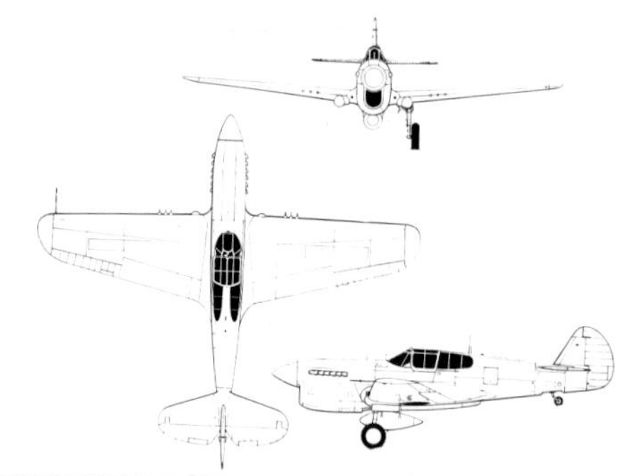

Republic P-43 Lancer

In 1939 a single P-35 was revised as the Model AP-4 with a lowered canopy and turbocharged engine, and trialed under the designation XP-41. In 1940 Republic (successor to Seversky) received an order for 13 YP-43 service test aircraft with inward-retracting main landing gear units. These were followed by production aircraft in the form of 54 P-43s with the R-1830-47 engine and an armament of two heavy machine-guns in the cowling and two rifle-calibre guns in the wings. Other deliveries were 80 similar P-43As with the R-1830-49 engine, and 125 P-43A-1s with a different engine and modified armament, the latter including drop loads for the fighter-bomber role. Most P-43A-1s were delivered to China, and other Lancers were revised for reconnaissance with rear-fuselage cameras under the designations P-43B/C/D/E depending on the specific camera fit.

Specification: Republic P-43A-1 Lancer single-seat fighter and fighter-bomber
Span: 10.97 m (36 ft 0 in)
Length: 8.68 m (28 ft 6 in)
Powerplant: 1×Pratt & Whitney R-1830-57, 895 kW (1,200 hp)
Armament: 4×12.7-mm (0.5-in) machine-guns, plus provision for 91 kg (200 lb) of bombs carried under the wings
Max T/O weight: 3847 kg (8,480 lb)
Max speed: 356 mph at 20,000 ft
Operational range: 800 miles

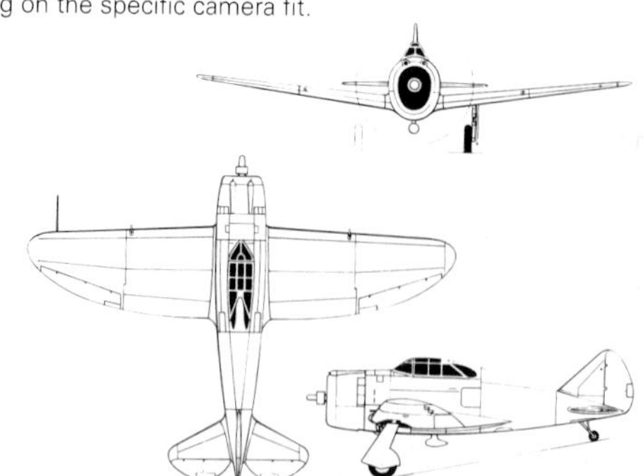

Specification: Northrop P-61B Black Widow three-seat night-fighter and intruder aeroplane
Span: 20.12 m (66 ft 0 in)
Length: 15.11 m (49 ft 7 in)
Powerplant: 2×Pratt & Whitney R-2800-65, 1491 kW (2,000 hp) each
Armament: 4×20-mm cannon and 4×12.7-mm (0.5-in) machine-guns, plus provision for up to 4×726-kg (1,600-lb) bombs carried under the wings
Max T/O weight: 17240 kg (38,000 lb)
Max speed: 366 mph at 20,000 ft
Operational range: 3,000 miles

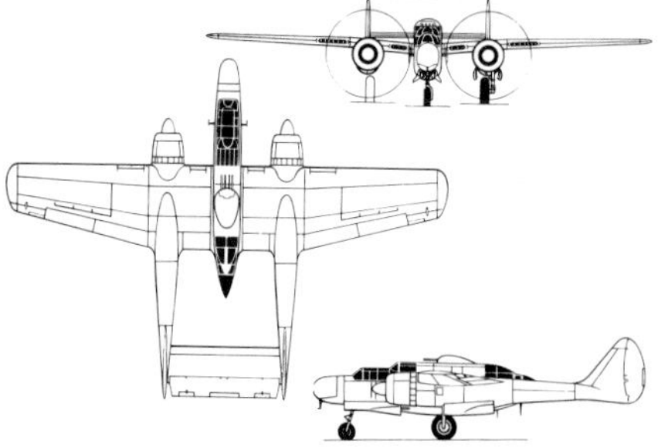

North American *P-51 Mustang*

Probably the finest fighter of World War II, the Mustang resulted from a British specification and first flew as the NA-73X in October 1940 with the Allison V-1710 engine. Two Mustang Mk Is were evaluated by the USAAC as XP-51s, and with official interest thus sparked the type was accepted for US service. The first 57 P-51s were aircraft to a British order requisitioned by the USAAF, while orders covered 275 P-51As with four 12.7-mm (0.5-in) wing guns, 1,988 P-51Bs with a Packard-built Merlin engine and provision for bombs, 1,750 P-51Cs with a bubble canopy, 7,966 P-51Ds with more power, two more guns and a dorsal fin, 555 P-51Hs with a longer fuselage and taller tail, and 1,337 P-51Ks with an Aeroproducts propeller. The Mustang was the outstanding escort fighter of the war with the aid of drop tanks, and in its Merlin-engined forms was an exceptional all-round fighter.

Specification: North American P-51D Mustang long-range fighter and fighter-bomber
Span: 11.89 m (37 ft 0.25 in)
Length: 9.85 m (32 ft 3.25 in)
Powerplant: 1×Packard (Rolls-Royce) V-1650-7 Merlin, 1126 kW (1,510 hp)
Armament: 6×12.7-mm (0.5-in) machine-guns, plus provision for 907 kg (2,000 lb) of bombs or 6×127-mm (5-in) rockets carried under the wings
Max T/O weight: 5262 kg (11,600 lb)
Max speed: 437 mph at 25,000 ft
Operational range: 950 miles

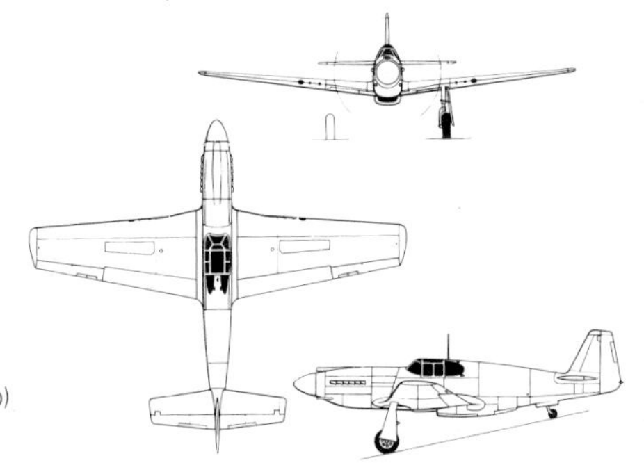

Curtiss P-60

From the P-40 Curtiss developed the XP-46 with an 857-kW (1,150-hp) Allison V-1710-39 engine, smaller dimensions and inward-retracting main landing gear units. This proved disappointing, but was used as the basis for the XP-53 with laminar-flow wings and a 1193-kW (1,600-hp) Continental XIV-1430-3 engine. Neither prototype was completed, one of them being used instead for the XP-60 with a Packard-built Merlin engine, replaced in the XP-60A by a V-1710-75 with General Electric turbocharger. The planned 474 P-60As were then cancelled as underpowered, and the type was thereafter used for development: the XP-60B had a Wright turbocharger; the XP-60C had the 1491-kW (2,000-hp) R-2800-53 radial with contraprops; the XP-60D had a 969-kW (1,300-hp) V-1650-3 driving a four-blade propeller; and the XP-60E had an R-2800-10 driving a four-blade propeller.

Specification: Curtiss XP-60E single-seat interceptor prototype
Span: 12.59 m (41 ft 4 in)
Length: 10.34 m (33 ft 11 in)
Powerplant: 1×Pratt & Whitney R-2800-10, 1491 kW (2,000 hp)
Armament: 4×12.7-mm (0.5-in) machine-guns
Max T/O weight: 5225 kg (11,520 lb)
Max speed: 405 mph at 15,000 ft
Operational range: 315 miles

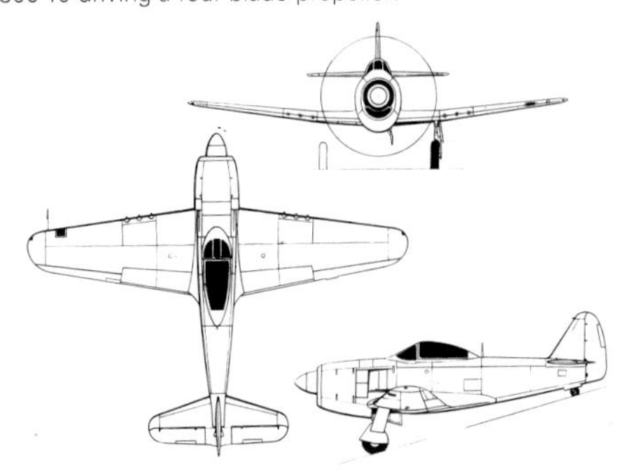

Bell P-63 Kingcobra

The P-63 resulted from the experimental XP-39E with clipped-tip wings of laminar-flow section, and was the only US fighter to enter flight-test and large-scale production in World War II. The XP-39E design was further refined as the XP-63, which first flew in December 1942. Both XP-63 prototype fighters were lost, the following XP-63A being equipped as a fighter-bomber to the standard of the P-63A. Some 1,725 of this model were followed by 1,227 P-63Cs with additional armour, a ventral fin and the 1126-kW (1,510-hp) V-1710-117. A single P-63D with a bubble canopy and V-1710-109 engine was followed by 13 P-63Es with the standard canopy; 2,930 P-63Es were cancelled. The last 'mass production' variant was the P-63F with a redesigned vertical tail and the V-1710-135 engine: only two were delivered. Other variants were the RP-63C and RP-63G manned targets.

Specification: Bell P-63A Kingcobra single-seat fighter and fighter-bomber
Span: 11.63 m (38 ft 4 in)
Length: 9.95 m (32 ft 8 in)
Powerplant: 1×Allison V-1710-93, 988 kW (1,325 hp)
Armament: 1×37-mm cannon and four 12.7-mm (0.5-in) machine-guns, plus provision for up to 3×227-kg (500-lb) bombs carried externally
Max T/O weight: 4763 kg (10,500 lb)
Max speed: 361 mph at 5,000 ft
Operational range: 450 miles

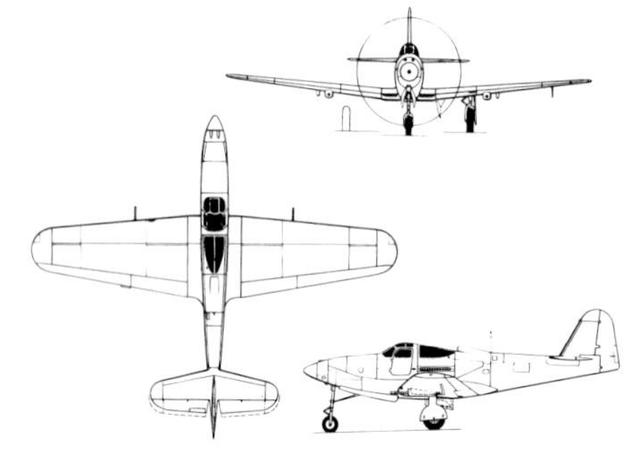

Douglas P-70 Havoc

In 1942 an A-20B light attack bomber was converted as the XP-70, prototype for the USAAF's first radar-equipped night-fighter: this had R-2600-11 engines, a 'solid' nose housing the British radar, and a ventral pack with four 20-mm forward-firing cannon. With the concept validated by flight trials, the USAAF ordered the conversion of 59 A-20s to P-70 standard as operational trainers. These aircraft paved the way for the P-70A operational model: this had a revised nose with the radar and six 12.7-mm (0.5-in) machine-guns, and its variants were the 13 P-70A-1s and 26 P-70A-2s converted respectively from A-20C and A-20G bombers. There was also a single P-70B-1 conversion of an A-20G with the six nose guns blistered on the fuselage sides, and several P-70B-2 night-fighter trainers converted from A-20G and A-20J bombers.

Specification: Douglas P-70 Havoc two-seat night-fighter
Span: 18.69 m (61 ft 4 in)
Length: 14.63 m (48 ft 0 in)
Powerplant: 2×Wright R-2600-11, 1193 kW (1,600 hp)
Armament: 4×20-mm cannon
Max T/O weight: 9645 kg (21,264 lb)
Max speed: 329 mph at 14,000 ft
Operational range: 1,060 miles

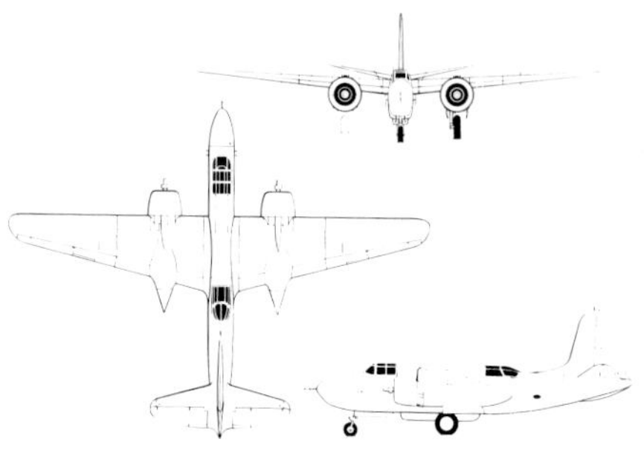

General Motors P-75 Eagle

In 1942 the USAAF issued a specification for a fast-climbing interceptor, and General Motors responded with a mid-engined proposal melding the most powerful available engine with a new fuselage and major components of existing aircraft (a gull-wing arrangement using the outer wings of the P-51, the tail unit of the A-24 and the landing gear of the F4U). Revision of the design led to the adoption of a straight wing using the outer panels of the P-40. Two XP-75 prototypes were complemented by six XP-75A prototypes for the escort role with a bubble canopy, and an order for 2,500 P-75As was placed. The first XP-75 flew in November 1943, all eight prototypes being available by spring 1944. The programme then ran into trouble, resulting in redesign of the tail unit, and the USAAF decided in September 1944 to cancel the programme. By that time five P-75As had been built.

Specification: General Motors (Fisher Body Division) XP-75A single-seat escort fighter prototype
Span: 15.04 m (49 ft 4 in)
Length: 12.32 m (40 ft 5 in)
Powerplant: 1×Allison V-3420-23, 2151 kW (2,885 hp)
Armament: (P-75A) 4×12.7-mm (0.5-in) machine-guns and 6×7.62-mm (0.3-in) machine-guns, plus provision for 2×227-kg (500-lb) bombs carried under the wings
Max T/O weight: 8260 kg (18,210 lb)
Max speed: 433 mph at 20,000 ft
Operational range: 2,050 miles

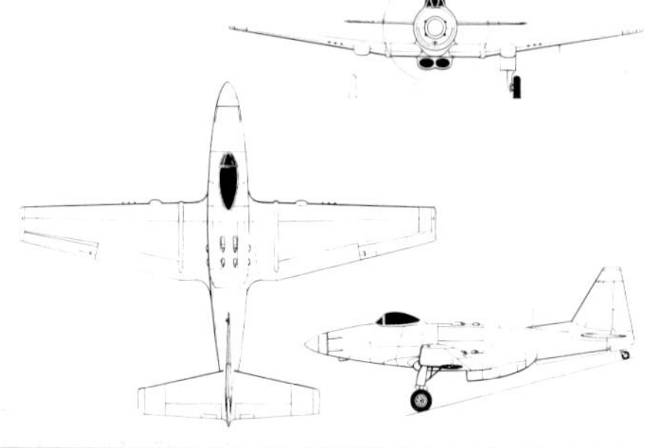

Bell P-77

The XP-77 was an attempt to produce a fighter making minimal demand on the so-called 'strategic' light alloys. Comparable aircraft were developed by the British, French and Italians, but the American concept used a supercharged powerplant offering only 373 kW (500 hp). The original Tri-4 proposal of October 1941 was expected to reach 410 mph at 27,000 ft at a weight of 1225 kg (2,700 lb) with an armament of two 20-mm cannon and two 12.7-mm (0.5-in) machine-guns. Procurement of six XP-77s was authorised in August 1942, this D-6 variant having an unsupercharged engine and provision for a 147-kg (325-lb) drop load. The first XP-77 flew as late as April 1944, and such were the apparent development problems of this basically wooden type at a point in the war when 'strategic' materials were in abundant supply that the programme was cancelled after the construction of only two prototypes.

Specification: Bell XP-77 single-seat fighter-bomber prototype
Span: 8.38 m (27 ft 6 in)
Length: 6.97 m (22 ft 10.5 in)
Powerplant: 1×Ranger XV-770-7, 388 kW (520 hp)
Armament: 2×12.7-mm (0.5-in) machine-guns, plus provision for 147 kg (325 lb) of bombs carried under the fuselage
Max T/O weight: 1827 kg (4,028 lb)
Max speed: 330 mph at 4,000 ft
Operational range: 550 miles

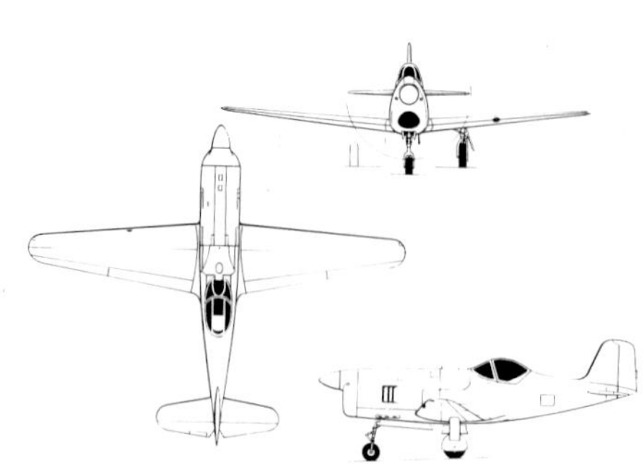

Nakajima Ki-27

Land-based counterpart to the A5M, the Ki-27 had fixed landing gear and was known to the Allies as the 'Nate'. The type began to enter service in 1937. Total production amounted to 3,399 aircraft, and the Ki-27 remained in front-line service up to the end of 1942, when it was gradually supplanted by the Ki-43. The prototype flew in October 1936, and the initial Ki-27a production variant was basically similar apart from the use of an Ha-1b radial with a higher rating at altitude, plus a metal-faired cockpit canopy. The Ki-27a was followed by the Ki-27b with a number of detail improvements, most notably the reintroduction of a clear-view canopy and provision for a small bomb load in the ground-attack role. A lightweight Ki-27 KAI was produced in prototype form, but was overtaken by the Ki-43.

Specification: Nakajima Ki-27b single-seat land-based fighter
Span: 11.31 m (37 ft 1.25 in)
Length: 7.53 m (24 ft 8.5 in)
Powerplant: 1×Nakajima Ha-1b (Army Type 97), 582 kW (780 hp)
Armament: 2×7.7-mm (0.303-in) machine-guns, plus up to four 25-kg (55-lb) bombs carried externally
Loaded weight: 1790 kg (3,946 lb)
Max speed: 292 mph at 11,480 ft
Operational range: 1,060 miles

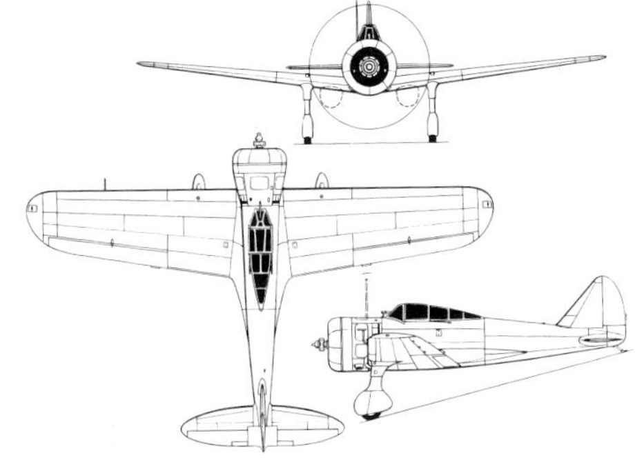

Nakajima Ki-44 Shoki

The Shoki (demon) was known to the Allies as the 'Tojo', and though based conceptually on the Ki-43 was an altogether heavier machine whose virtues of high speed and good climb rate were initially disliked by Japanese army pilots who preferred the exceptional agility of the Ki-43. The type was the army's first dedicated interceptor, and flew in August 1940. The initial Ki-44-I was produced in small numbers with machine-gun armament and the 932-kW (1,250-hp) Nakajima Ha-41 engine, though the first definitive version was the upengined Ki-44-II that graduated in three variants from mixed machine-gun via heavy machine-gun to cannon armament. The final model was the Ki-44-III with the 1491-kW (2,000-hp) Ha-145 engine and larger flying surfaces. Production amounted to 1,225 aircraft.

Specification: Nakajima Ki-44-IIb Shoki single-seat land-based interceptor fighter
Span: 9.45 m (31 ft 0 in)
Length: 8.75 m (28 ft 10 in)
Powerplant: 1×Nakajima Ha-109 (Army Type 2), 1133 kW (1,520 hp)
Armament: 4×12.7-mm (0.5-in) machine-guns
Max T/O weight: 2993 kg (6,598 lb)
Max speed: 376 mph at 17,060 ft
Operational range: 1,056 miles

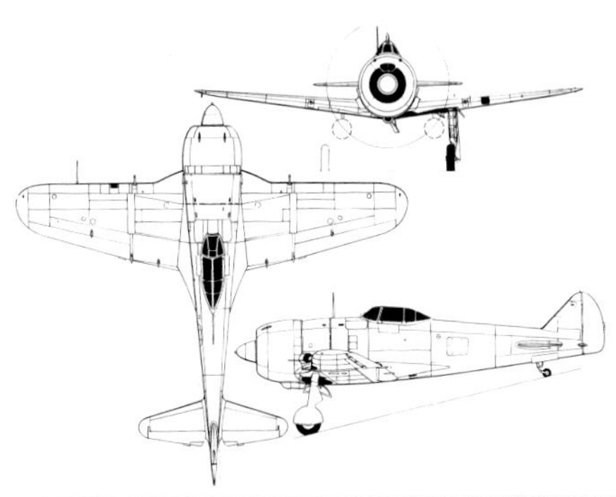

Nakajima Ki-84 Hayate

The Hayate (gale) was known to the Allies as the 'Frank', and was the army's best mass-production fighter of World War II. The type was planned as successor to the Ki-43 with better protection and heavier armament, and first flew in March 1943. The Ki-84-I began to enter service in the summer of 1944 with any of several Ha-45 engine variants in the 1417-kW (1,900-hp) class plus an armament of four 20-mm cannon or, in the Ki-84-Ic bomber destroyer version, two 20-mm and two 30-mm cannon. Production was beset by a number of problems, and Nakajima introduced a variant identified as the Ki-84-II with a partially wood structure. Total production was 3,514 including experimental variants such as the Ki-84-III turbocharged high-altitude model, all-wood Ki-106, part-steel Ki-113, Ki-116 with 1118-kW (1,500-hp) Mitsubishi Ha-33 engine, and Ki-117 high-altitude version.

Specification: Nakajima Ki-84-Ia Hayate single-seat land-based fighter and fighter-bomber
Span: 11.238 m (36 ft 10.5 in)
Length: 9.92 m (32 ft 6.5 in)
Powerplant: 1×Nakajima Ha-45 (Army Type 4), 1417 kW (1,900 hp)
Armament: 2×20-mm cannon and 2×12.7-mm (0.5-in) machine-guns, plus up to 500 kg (1,102 lb) of bombs carried externally
Max T/O weight: 3890 kg (8,576 lb)
Max speed: 392 mph at 20,080 ft
Operational range: 1,053 miles

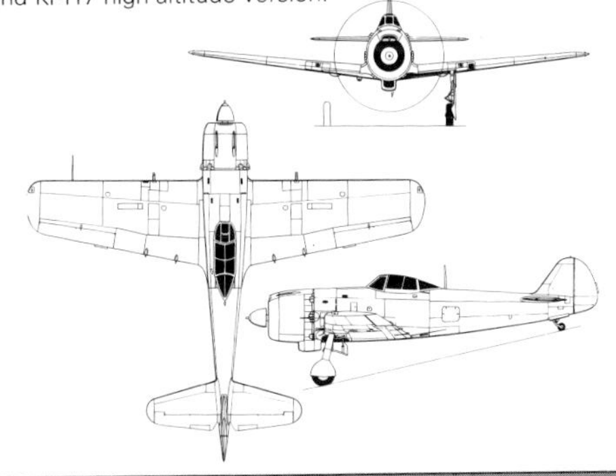

Nakajima J1N Gekko

The Gekko (moonlight) was known to the Allies as the 'Irving', and was planned in 1938 as a long-range heavy or escort fighter, with twin-engine powerplant. The prototype first flew in May 1941, and was then developed as the J1N1-C reconnaissance aeroplane. But as Japan's situation began to worsen several aircraft were modified as J1N1-C (later J1N1-R) night-fighters, including some redesignated J1N1-F with a 20-mm cannon in a dorsal turret. Further development produced the J1N1-S with radar and obliquely arranged cannon (pairs firing forwards both upwards and downwards) radar, as well as the J1N-1Sa with the downward-firing cannon deleted. The -S variants had an unstepped rear fuselage, and sometimes carried a searchlight in place of radar. Total J1N1 production was 479.

Specification: Nakajima J1N1-S Gekko two-seat land-based night-fighter
Span: 16.98 m (55 ft 8.5 in)
Length: 12.77 m (41 ft 10.75 in)
Powerplant: 2×Nakajima NK1F Sakae 21, 843 kW (1,130 hp) each
Armament: 4×20-mm cannon
Max T/O weight: 8184 kg (18,043 lb)
Max speed: 315 mph at 19,160 ft
Operational range: 2,348 miles

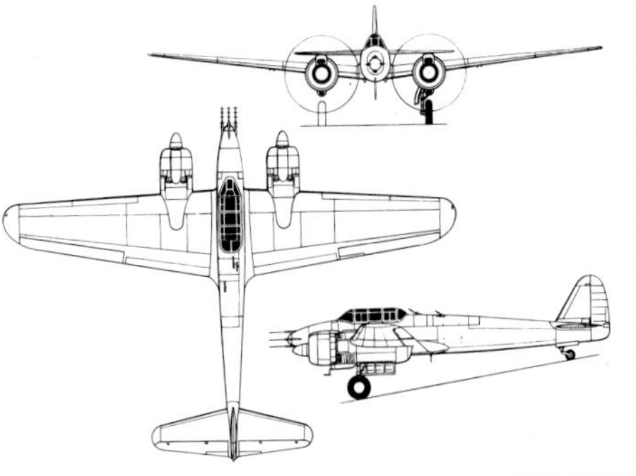

Kawasaki Ki-61 Hien

The Hien (Swallow) was Japan's only major fighter of World War II with an inline engine. The first prototype flew in December 1941, and the Ki-61-I began to enter service with army squadrons in the summer of 1942. Production totalled 3,078 aircraft in variants such as the Ki-61-Ia and -Ib with differing armaments, the Ki-61-I KAIc with underwing hardpoints and Japanese rather than German cannon, the Ki-61-I KAId with 30- rather than 20-mm cannon. Next came the Ki-61-II series with the 1118-kW (1,500-hp) Kawasaki Ha-140 for better performance at altitude and, in the Ki-61-II KAI, a longer fuselage and heavier armament including four 20-mm cannon. The few Ki-61-IIs were to have been followed by the Ki-61-III with cut-down rear fuselage and 360° vision canopy. The type was known to the Allies as the 'Tony'.

Specification: Kawasaki Ki-61-Ib single-seat land-based fighter and fighter-bomber
Span: 12.00m (39ft 4.5in)
Length: 8.75m (28ft 8.5in)
Powerplant: 1×Kawasaki Ha-40 (Army Type 2), 876kW (1,175hp)
Armament: 3×20-mm cannon and 2×12.7-mm (0.5-in) machine-guns or 4×12.7-mm (0.5-in) machine-guns, plus up to 500kg (1,102lb) of bombs carried externally
Max T/O weight: 3250kg (7,175lb)
Max speed: 368mph at 15,945ft
Operational range: 684 miles

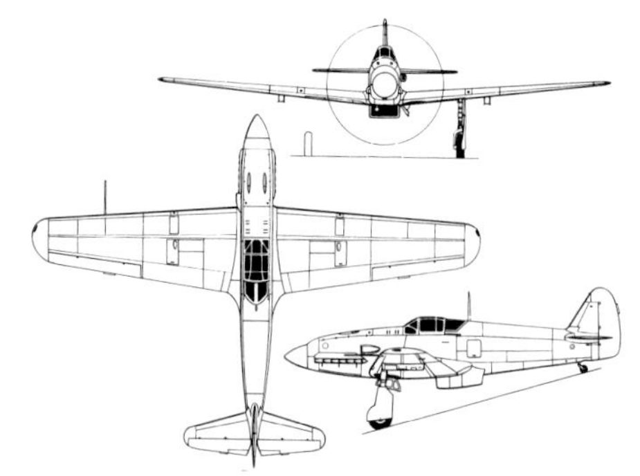

Kawasaki Ki-45 Toryu

The Toryu (Dragon slayer) was one of the best night-fighters available to the Imperial Japanese Army in World War II, and the design dated back to the twin-engine Ki-38 of 1937. The type first flew in 1939, but development was protracted by the army's insistence on modifications and the type entered production only in October 1941 as the Ki-45-KAIa heavy fighter. The type entered service in 1942 with a variety of armaments and later with Ha-102 rather than 708-kW (950-hp) Ha-25 engines, and a derivative was the Ki-45-KAIb ground-attack and anti-ship fighter with revised armament including a 37- or 75-mm cannon. The dedicated night-fighter was the Ki-45-KAIc with obliquely forward-firing cannon, and this spawned a Ki-45-KAId anti-shipping variant. The type was known to the Allies as the 'Nick', and production totalled 1,701.

Specification: Kawasaki Ki-45-KAIc Toryu two-seat land-based night-fighter
Span: 15.02m (49ft 3.25in)
Length: 11.00m (36ft 1in)
Powerplant: 2×Mitsubishi Ha-102 (Army Type 1), 805kW (1,080hp) each
Armament: 1×37-mm cannon, 2×20-mm cannon and (in early aircraft) 1×7.92-mm (0.312-in) machine-gun
Loaded weight: 5500kg (12,125lb)
Max speed: 340mph at 22,965ft
Operational range: 1,243 miles

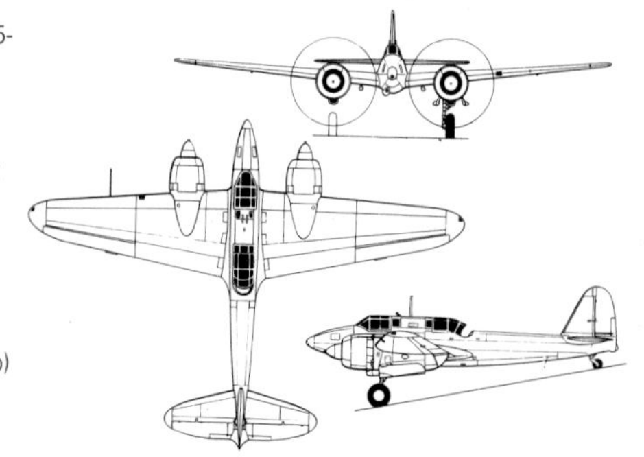

Kawasaki Ki-100

Shortage of Ha-140 engines for the Ki-61-II prompted the 1944 decision to engine 275 stockpiled airframes with the Ha 112 radial in a revised forward fuselage, and the first such combination was flown in February 1945. The result was one of the army's finest fighters of World War II, and this Ki-100-Ia interceptor and bomber destroyer began to enter service in March 1945 as a home-defence fighter. Another 121 aircraft were built, 118 as Ki-100-Ib fighters with a cut-down rear fuselage plus 360° vision cockpit enclosure, and three Ki-100-III prototypes with the 1118-kW (1,500-hp) Ha-112-Ru turbocharged engine for better performance at altitude. Despite its primary interception role, the Ki-100 could also be used effectively as a fighter-bomber.

Specification: Kawasaki Ki-100-Ib single-seat land-based interceptor fighter and fighter-bomber
Span: 12.00m (39ft 4.5in)
Length: 8.82m (28ft 11.25in)
Powerplant: 1×Mitsubishi Ha-112-II (Army Type 4), 1118kW (1,500hp)
Armament: 2×20-mm cannon and 2×12.7-mm (0.5-in) machine-guns, plus up to 500kg (1,102lb) of bombs carried externally
Loaded weight: 3495kg (7,705lb)
Max speed: 332mph at 32,810ft
Operational range: 1,367 miles

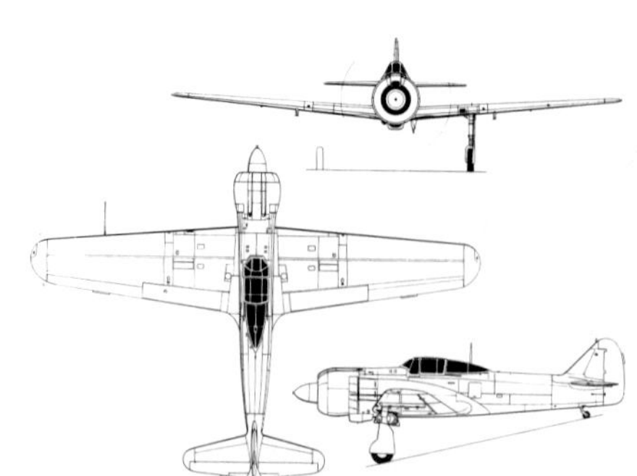

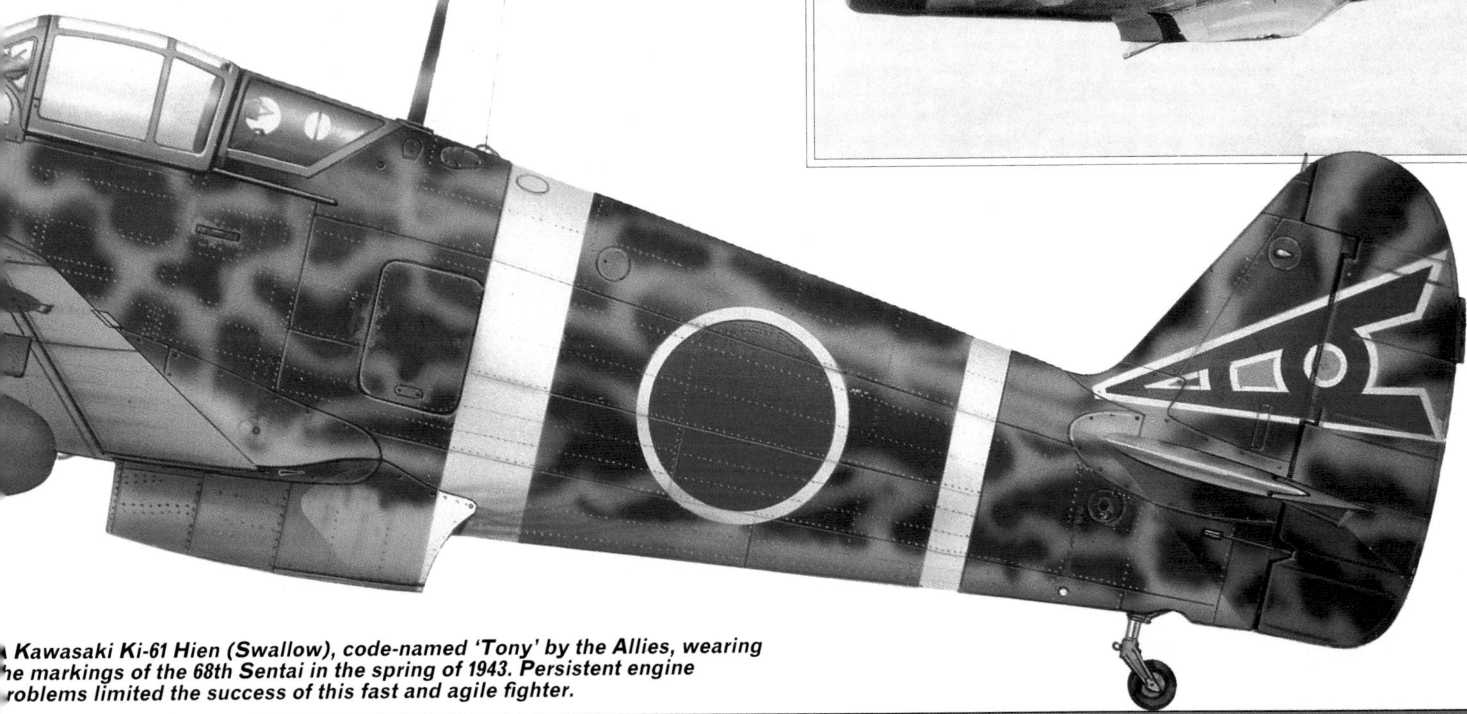

Kawasaki Ki-61 Hien (Swallow), code-named 'Tony' by the Allies, wearing he markings of the 68th Sentai in the spring of 1943. Persistent engine roblems limited the success of this fast and agile fighter.

Kawanishi N1K1-J Shiden

The Shiden (violet lightning) was one of the best land-based fighters available to the Imperial Japanese Navy late in World War II, and stemmed most unusually from the N1K1 floatplane fighter that first flew in August 1942. Design of the N1K1-J with conventional landing gear began in November 1942, the prototype flying in July 1943 and the type entering service in early 1944 to gain the Allied name 'George 11'. Production amounted to 1,007 in three differently armed variants before the advent of the radically improved N1K2-J Shiden-KAI ('George 21') with parts reduced by one-third to save some 225 kg (496 lb) in weight. The wing was dropped from mid- to low-set position, and the type's already formidable climb and agility were improved in these 428 aircraft.

Specification: Kawanishi N1K2-J Shiden-KAI single-seat land-based fighter and fighter-bomber
Span: 12.00 m (39 ft 4.5 in)
Length: 9.345 m (30 ft 8 in)
Powerplant: 1×Nakajima NK9H Homare 21, 1484 kW (1,990 hp)
Armament: 4×20-mm cannon, plus up to 500 kg (1,102 lb) of bombs carried externally
Max T/O weight: 4860 kg (10,714 lb)
Max speed: 369 mph at 18,375 ft
Operational range: 1,488 miles

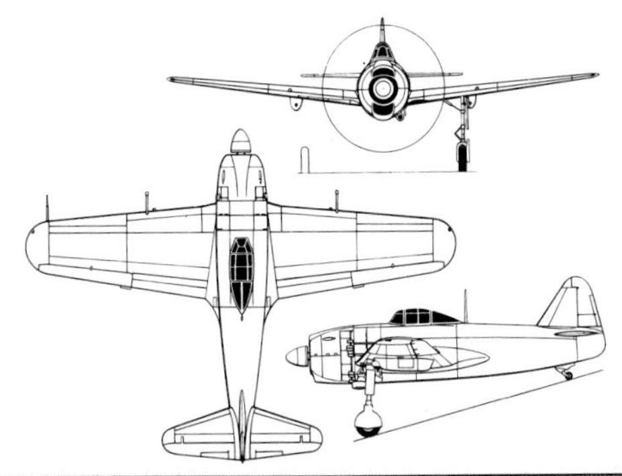

Mitsubishi Ki-46

The Ki-46 was known to the Allies as the 'Dinah', and was designed as a high-performance reconnaissance aeroplane. The type had exceptionally clean lines and first flew in November 1939, thereafter being built as the Ki-46-I with 671-kW (900-hp) Ha-26-I engines, the Ki-46-II with 805-kW (1,080-hp) Ha-102 engines and the refined Ki-46-III with a better streamlined forward fuselage, more fuel and greater power. The last was a quite exceptional aeroplane, and was further developed in 1942 as the Ki-46-III KAI interceptor with armament in place of cameras. The Ki-46-III KAI proved to have poor climb, and the type was developed more usefully as the Ki-46-IIIb ground-attack aeroplane without the Ki-46-III KAI's obliquely forward-firing 37-mm cannon. It is not known how many of the 609 Ki-46-IIIs were converted as armed aircraft.

Specification: Mitsubishi Ki-46-III KAI two-seat land-based interceptor fighter
Span: 14.70 m (48 ft 2.75 in)
Length: 11.49 m (37 ft 8.25 in)
Powerplant: 2×Mitsubishi HA-112-II (Army Type 4), 1118 kW (1,500 hp) each
Armament: 2×20-mm cannon and 1×37-mm cannon
Loaded weight: 6228 kg (13,730 lb)
Max speed: 391 mph at 19,685 ft
Operational range: 1,243 miles plus 1-hour combat endurance

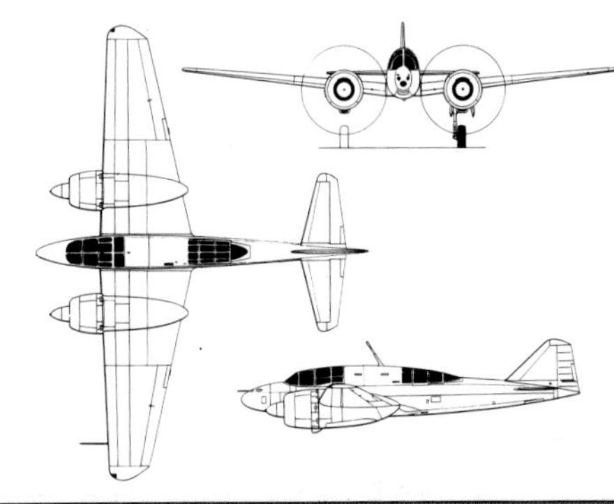

Nakajima Ki-43 Hayabusa

Specification: Nakajima Ki-43-IIb Hayabusa single-seat land-based fighter
Span: 10.84 m (35 ft 6.75 in)
Length: 8.92 m (29 ft 3.25 in)
Powerplant: 1×Nakajima Ha-115 (Army Type 1), 857 kW (1,150 hp)
Armament: 2×12.7-mm (0.5-in) machine-guns, plus up to 500 kg (1,102 lb) of bombs carried externally
Max T/O weight: 2925 kg (6,450 lb)
Max speed: 329 mph at 13,125 ft
Operational range: 1,095 miles

The Hayabusa (peregrine falcon) was known to the Allies as the 'Oscar', and though overtaken in performance by other Imperial Japanese Army fighters quite early in World War II it remained numerically the Army's most important fighter of the War: production amounted to 5,919 including the prototype that first flew in January 1939. The type began to enter service in autumn 1941, and the initial Ki-43-I with two machine-guns and the 731-kW (980-hp) Nakajima Ha-25 engine was followed in late 1942 by the Ki-43-II with more power and greater firepower. Variants were the Ki-43-IIa with clipped wings, the Ki-43-IIb with detail refinements, and the Ki-43-II KAI with individual exhaust stacks. The final variant was the Ki-43-III with the 917-kW (1,230-hp) Ha-115-II engine.

Mitsubishi J2M Raiden

The Raiden (thunderbolt) was known to the Allies as the 'Jack', and was a naval fighter planned to succeed the A6M in the interceptor role. Designed by the A6M team, the J2M was basically a good fighter that failed to deliver its initial promise because of structural, engine and production failings, with the result that production reached only about 500 aircraft from a planned total of several thousands. The J2M1 prototype flew in March 1942 and was followed by the Kasei 23a-powered J2M2 production model with two 20-mm cannon and two 7.7-mm (0.303-in) machine-guns, the J2M3 with better armament, the J2M3a with homogeneous cannon armament, the experimental J2M4 high-altitude fighter, the J2M5 with the 1357-kW (1,820-hp) Kasei 26a and blister canopy, and the J2M7 development of the J2M3 with the Kasei 26.

Specification: Mitsubishi J2M3 Raiden single-seat land-based interceptor fighter
Span: 10.80 m (35 ft 5.25 in)
Length: 9.94 m (32 ft 7.5 in)
Powerplant: 1×Mitsubishi MK4R-A Kasei 23a, 1342 kW (1,800 hp)
Armament: 4×20-mm cannon, plus up to 120 kg (264 lb) of bombs carried externally
Max T/O weight: 3683 kg (8,120 lb)
Max speed: 365 mph at 17,390 ft
Operational range: 1,180 miles

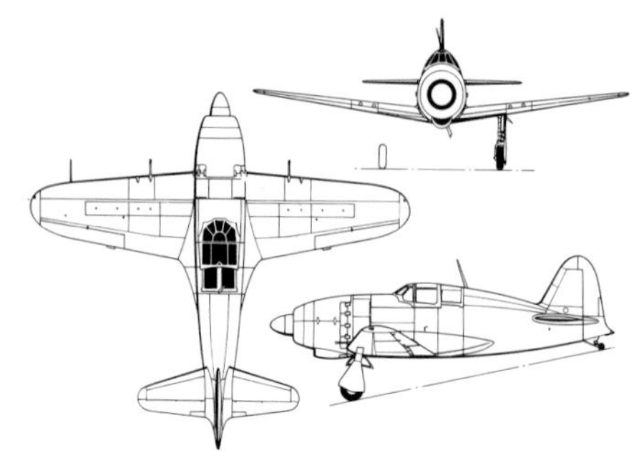

Mitsubishi A5M

Known to the Allies as the 'Claude', this attractive low-wing aeroplane was the Imperial Japanese Navy's first monoplane fighter, the fixed but spatted landing gear not seriously affecting performance while reducing weight and simplifying both manufacture and maintenance. Prototypes were trialled in 1935 with an assortment of wing planforms and engines before the A5M1 model entered service in 1936 with the 436-kW (585-hp) Kotobuki 2. In 1937 there appeared the A5M2 with greater power and, in the A5M2b variant, an enclosed cockpit. The A5M3 was an experimental model with the 455-kW (610-hp) Hispano-Suiza 12Xcrs inline and an engine-mounted 20-mm cannon, while the definitive variant was the A5M4 together with its A5M4-K trainer variant. Production totalled 1,094, and the A5M4 remained in service into late 1942.

Specification: Mitsubishi A5M4 single-seat carrierborne and land-based fighter
Span: 11.00 m (36 ft 1.25 in)
Length: 7.565 m (24 ft 9.25 in)
Powerplant: 1×Nakajima Kotobuki 41 KAI, 585 kW (785 hp)
Armament: 2×7.7-mm (0.303-in) machine-guns, plus up to 60 kg (132 lb) of bombs carried externally
Loaded weight: 1671 kg (3,684 lb)
Max speed: 270 mph at 9,845 ft
Operational range: 746 miles

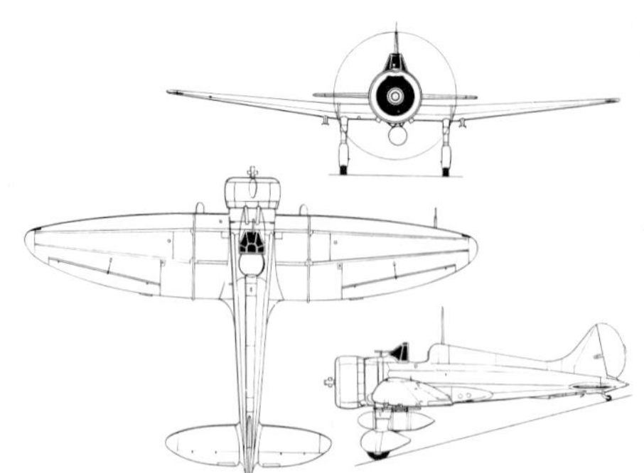

This Nakajima Ki-43-III-Ko Hayabusa (peregrine falcon) was flown by the 48th Sentai during the summer of 1945. By 1945 the 'Oscar' was underpowered and under-armed, but its agility earned it a place on the production line until the Japanese surrender.

Mitsubishi A6M Reisen

Known to the Japanese as the Reisen (zero fighter) and to the Allies as the 'Zeke', the A6M was the A5M's successor and one of the decisive weapons of World War II's early stages. The prototype flew in April 1939, and production up to the end of the War amounted to some 10,450 fighters with wheeled landing gear. The A6M2 entered service in summer 1940, and for the first time in a carrier fighter offered performance equal to or better than that of land-based fighters. The A6M2 was powered by the 708-kW (950-hp) Sakae 12, and later models with greater firepower and protection were the A6M3 with the 843-kW (1,130-hp) Sakae 21, the experimental A6M4 with turbocharged engine, the A6M5 with detail improvements, the A6M6 with the water/methanol-boosted Sakae 31 and self-sealing tanks, the A6M7 dive-bomber and the A6M8 with the 1163-kW (1,560-hp) Mitsubishi Kinsei 62.

Specification: Mitsubishi A6M5 Model 52 Reisen single-seat carrierborne and land-based fighter and fighter-bomber
Span: 11.00 m (36 ft 1 in)
Length: 9.12 m (29 ft 11 in)
Powerplant: 1×Nakajima NK1F Sakae 21, 843 kW (1,130 hp)
Armament: 2×20-mm cannon and 2×7.7-mm (0.303-in) machine-guns, plus up to 120 kg (264 lb) of bombs carried externally
Loaded weight: 2733 kg (6,025 lb)
Max speed: 351 mph at 19,685 ft
Operational range: 1,194 miles

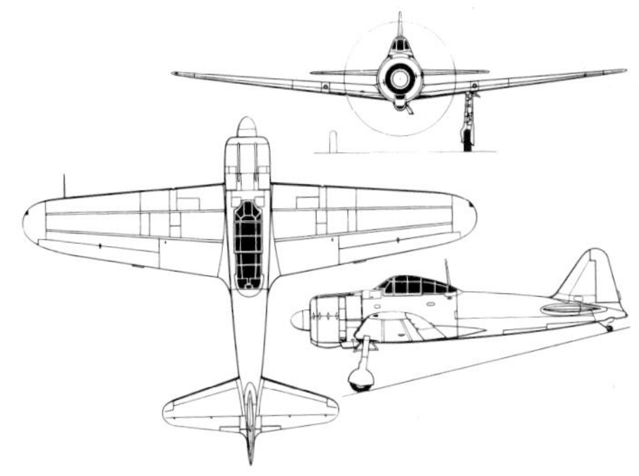

Mitsubishi J8M Shusui

The Shusui (swinging sword) was spurred by the threat of the US Army Air Force's Boeing B-29 Superfortress strategic bomber. The Imperial forces responded with a requirement for a fast-climbing interceptor, and it was thought that this could be satisfied by production of Germany's Messerschmitt Me 163 Komet rocket-powered fighter. However, the submarine carrying one Komet and the blueprints was sunk, leaving Japan with just one Walter HWK 109 rocket engine and an instruction manual for the Komet. From these the Japanese produced their own version as the army's Ki-200 and navy's J8M. After gliding trials the J8M1 was launched on its first powered flight in July 1945, crashing after engine failure. Production was under way at the end of the War, but only seven aircraft had been completed.

Specification: Mitsubishi J8M1 Shusui single-seat land-based point-defence interceptor fighter
Span: 9.50 m (31 ft 2 in)
Length: 6.05 m (19 ft 10.25 in)
Powerplant: 1×Toko Ro 2 (KR10), 1500 kg (3,307 lb)
Armament: 2×30-mm cannon
Loaded weight: 3885 kg (8,565 lb)
Max speed: 559 mph at 32,810 ft
Powered endurance: 5 minutes 30 seconds

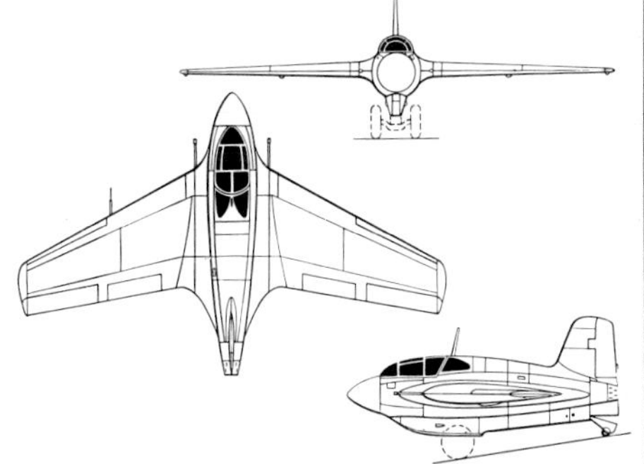

Lavochkin La-5

In the later part of 1941 Lavochkin re-engined a LaGG-3 with an ASh-82A radial, and when first flown in 1942 this proved some 25 mph faster than the Messerschmitt Bf 109F at low level. The type completely fulfilled the Soviets' new requirement for a fast-climbing but highly manoeuvrable low-level interceptor, and was ordered into production as the La-5 with the 992-PkW (1,330-hp) ASh-82F. Entering service in summer 1942, the type proved immediately successful and, in later form, introduced a cut-down rear fuselage so that a framed but 360° vision canopy could be fitted. In 1943 an improved model began to appear: this La-5FN had more power, more fuel and strengthened landing gear. There was also a La-5UTI two-seat conversion trainer. Production was in the order of 10,000, and the type was vital in wresting air superiority from the Germans in 1943/44.

Specification:
Lavochkin La-5FN single-seat fighter and fighter-bomber
Span: 9.80 m (32 ft 1.75 in)
Length: 8.67 m (28 ft 5.3 in)
Powerplant: 1×Shvetsov ASh-82FN, 1215 kW (1,630 hp)
Armament: 2×20- or 23-mm cannon, plus provision for 2×150-kg (331-lb) bombs or 6×82-mm (3.2-in) rockets carried under the wings
Normal T/O weight: 3402 kg (7,500 lb)
Max speed: 403 mph at 21,325 ft
Operational range: 475 miles

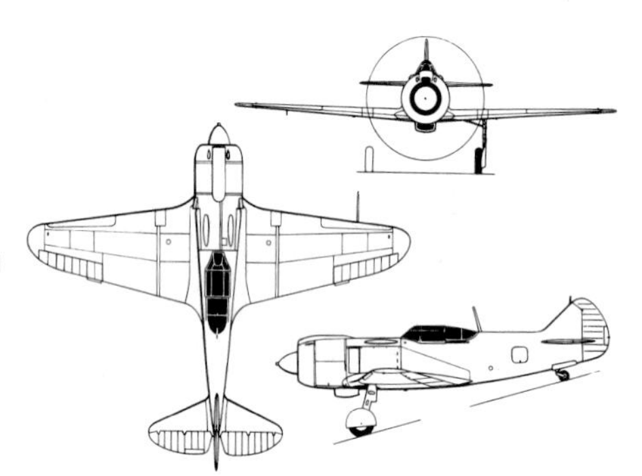

Lavochkin-Gorbunov-Gudkov LaGG-3

A single I-22 (LaGG-1) prototype with an 820-kW (1,100-hp) M-105P inline was built to meet the requirements of a 1938 requirement for a new fighter, and this all-wood design first flew in March 1939. The type was generally impressive and, with controllability and strengthening features proved in the I-301 prototype, entered production in 1940 and service in 1941 as the LaGG-3. This had armament revised from the LaGG-1's single 23-mm VYa cannon and twin 7.62-mm (0.3-in) ShKAS machine-guns to any of six differing fits of 20- and 23-mm cannon plus 12.7-mm (0.5-in) and 7.62-mm machine-guns. The type was notable for its ruggedness: the fuselage was built up of birch frames covered with plastic-impregnated plywood, the wings had the same type of surface over a two-spar structure, and the metal-framed control surfaces were fabric-covered. Production totalled 6,527.

Specification: Lavochkin-Gorbunov-Gudkov LaGG-3 single-seat fighter and fighter-bomber
Span: 9.80 m (32 ft 1.75 in)
Length: 8.82 m (28 ft 11.25 in)
Powerplant: 1×Klimov VK-105PF, 902 kW (1,210 hp)
Armament: typically 1×20-mm cannon and 2×12.7-mm (0.5-in) machine-guns, plus provision for 2×100-kg (100-lb) and 4×25-kg (55-lb) bombs or 6×82-mm (3.2-in) rockets carried under the wings
Max T/O weight: 3280 kg (7,231 lb)
Max speed: 348 mph at 16,405 ft
Operational range: 404 miles

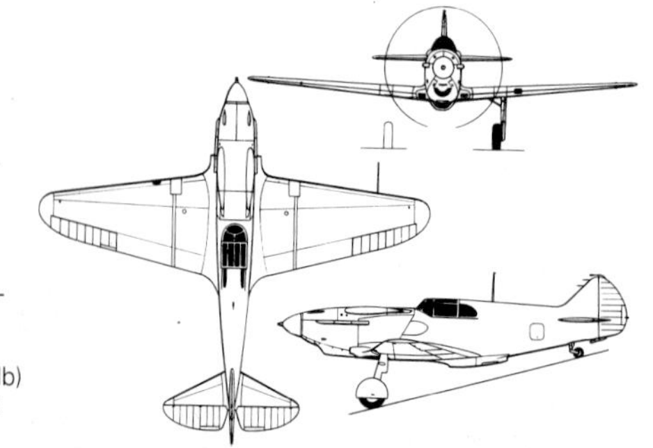

Lavochkin La-7

Though a logical extension of the La-5, the La-7 was designed as a pure interceptor to complement rather than replace the La-5. The type had metal longerons and spars, considerably more power, a cleaned-up airframe for reduced drag, and heavier armament. First flown in November 1943 and found to be outstanding, the La-7 entered service in May 1944 and was built to the extent of 5,753 aircraft by the time production ended in early 1946. There was also an La-7UTI two-seat trainer, and several experimental variants included the high-altitude La-7TK with twin turbochargers, the La-7ASh-71 with a 1491-kW (2,000-hp) engine, the La-7ASh-83 with a 1417-kW (1,900-hp) lightweight engine, the high-altitude La-7R with an RD-1 liquid-fuelled rocket engine in the tail, and La-7S or La-7PuVRD with two underwing ramjets.

Specification: Lavochkin La-7 single-seat interceptor fighter and fighter-bomber
Span: 9.80 m (32 ft 1.75 in)
Length: 8.60 m (28 ft 2.5 in)
Powerplant: 1×Shvetsov ASh-82FNV, 1379 kW (1,850 hp)
Armament: 2 or 3×20-mm cannon, plus provision for 2×100-kg (220-lb) bombs or 6×82-mm (3.2-in) rockets carried under the wings
Normal T/O weight: 3260 kg (7,187 lb)
Max speed: 423 mph at 22,310 ft
Operational range: 395 miles

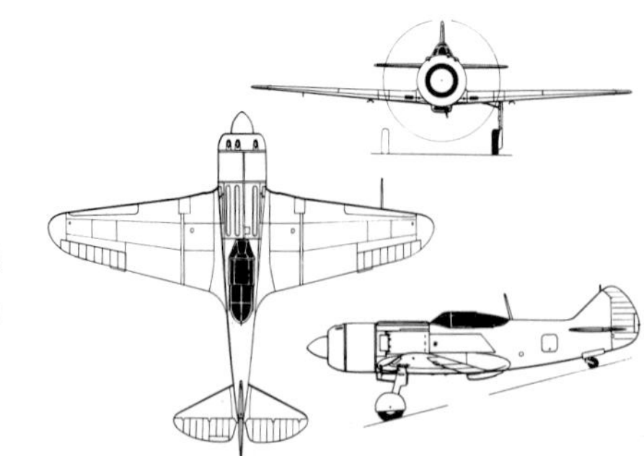

The La-5 entered production in July 1942 and by the end of the year no fewer than 1,182 had been completed. The first large-scale use of the La-5 was in the fighting around Stalingrad in November 1942, and it also saw extensive service during the great armoured battles around Kursk in July 1943.

Mikoyan-Gurevich MiG-1

Although not successful in operational terms, the MiG-1 has the distinction of having pioneered the USSR's wartime generation of low-wing monoplane fighters with a liquid-cooled engine and retractable landing gear. Designed in the same programme that led to the LaGG-1 and Yak-1, the I-200 (initially I-61) prototype flew in April 1940 after a design and prototype construction phase that had taken only three months. A speed of 373 mph was returned at 22,965 ft, and the type was ordered into production as the mixed-construction MiG-1 (wooden outer wings, rear fuselage and tail combined with a metal centre section and forward fuselage). Production amounted to only 100 aircraft generally unsuitable for combat because of the type's extremely difficult handling characteristics, and attrition was so high that few remained to face the Germans in summer 1941.

Specification: Mikoyan-Gurevich MiG-1 single-seat fighter and fighter-bomber
Span: 10.30 m (33 ft 9.5 in)
Length: 8.16 m (26 ft 9.25 in)
Powerplant: 1×Mikulin AM-35A, 1007 kW (1,350 hp)
Armament: 1×12.7-mm (0.5-in) and 2×7.62-mm (0.3-in) machine-guns, plus provision for 2×100-kg (220-lb) bombs or 6×82-mm (3.2-in) rockets carried under the wings
Max T/O weight: 3305 kg (7,286 lb)
Max speed: 390 mph at 22,965 ft
Operational range: 464 miles

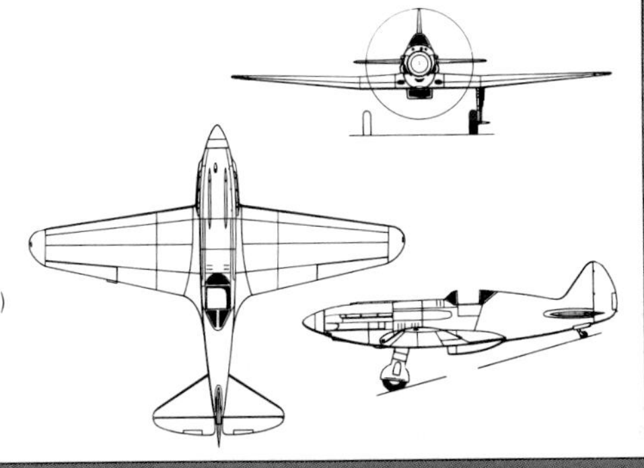

Mikoyan-Gurevich MiG-3

The MiG-3 was modelled closely on the MiG-1 but extensively modified in an effort to overcome the problems associated with the earlier fighter's performance and handling. Amongst the numerous system and component modifications were replacement of the side-opening canopy by a rear-sliding unit, additional fuel, increased outer wing dihedral, a different propeller and larger tyres. No real attempt was made, however, to remedy the main defect, namely the short fuselage that located the tail too close to the wings for adequate longitudinal stability. The MiG-3 followed the 100th MiG-1 on the assembly line and began to enter service in mid-1941. Production totalled 3,322 and, after poor success in the low/medium-altitude fighting in which its heavy engine and poor manoeuvrability left it at a severe disadvantage, the MiG-3 was relegated to secondary tasks by 1942.

Specification: Mikoyan-Gurevich MiG-3 single-seat fighter and fighter-bomber
Span: 10.30 m (33 ft 9.5 in)
Length: 8.255 m (27 ft 1 in)
Powerplant: 1×Mikulin AM-35A, 1007 kW (1,350 hp)
Armament: 1×12.7-mm (0.5-in) and 2×7.62-mm (0.3-in) machine-guns, plus provision for 2×100-kg (220-lb) bombs or 6×82-mm (3.2-in) rockets carried under the wings
Normal T/O weight: 3350 kg (7,385 lb)
Max speed: 398 mph at 22,965 ft
Operational range: 743 miles

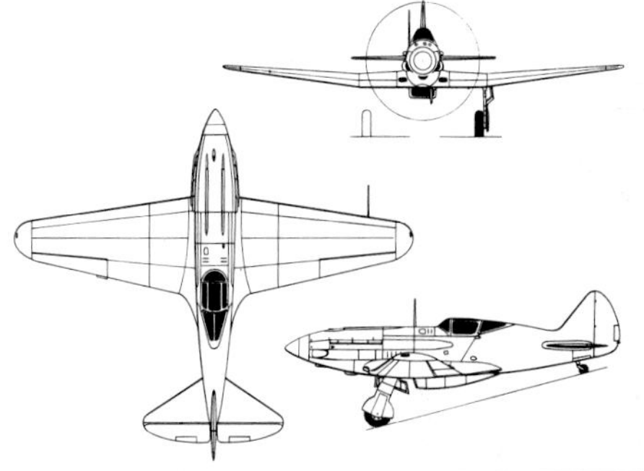

Yakovlev Yak-9

Developed in parallel with the Yak-3, the Yak-9 was a development of the Yak-7DI with metal-sparred wings for greater fuel capacity and longer range. The Yak-9 entered production in mid-1942, and by 1944 outnumbered all other Soviet fighters combined. The type remained in production until after the war, 16,769 being built in many variants: the Yak-9B fighter-bomber with 600-kg (1,323-lb) external load, the longer-ranged Yak-9D, the Yak-9DD escort fighter with drop tanks, the anti-tank Yak-9DK with a 45-mm nose cannon, the post-war Yak-9P with 1230-kW (1,650-hp) VK-107A engine, the Yak-9PVO night interceptor, the Yak-9R reconnaissance version, the anti-tank Yak-9T-37 and Yak-9T-45 with 37- and 45-mm nose cannon respectively, the upgraded Yak-9U with VK-107A engine and an all-metal structure, the Yak-9UF reconnaissance aeroplane, and the Yak-9UT trainer.

Specification: Yakovlev Yak-9D single-seat long-range fighter
Span: 9.74 m (31 ft 11.5 in)
Length: 8.50 m (27 ft 10.7 in)
Powerplant: 1×Klimov VK-105PF-2/3, 925 kW (1,240 hp)
Armament: 1×20-mm cannon and 1×12.7-mm (0.5-in) machine-gun
Normal T/O weight: 3115 kg (6,867 lb)
Max speed: 373 mph at 9,845 ft
Operational range: 826 miles

Petlyakov Pe-3

The Pe-2 was the USSR's most outstanding tactical bomber of World War II, a versatile twin-engine type that began to reach units service in early in 1941 and served throughout the war. The high performance of the Pe-2 suggested early in the type's development career that a heavy fighter version would offer useful capabilities, and this resulted in the Pe-3 first flown early in 1941 as a day and night interceptor with more potent gun armament and additional fuel in the small bomb bay. Only 23 such aircraft were built with an armament of two 20-mm cannon plus two 12.7-mm (0.5-in) and two 7.62-mm (0.3-in) machine-guns in the nose as well as one 12.7-mm weapon in a dorsal turret. Later in 1941 some 300 Pe-3bis fighters were built for the night-fighter role with revised armament and a gun camera or, in the Pe-2R reconnaissance fighter variant, vertical and oblique cameras.

Specification: Petlyakov Pe-3bis two-seat night-fighter
Span: 17.16 m (56 ft 3.6 in)
Length: 12.78 m (41 ft 11 in)
Powerplant: 2×Klimov VK-105RA, 820 kW (1,100 hp) each
Armament: 2×20-mm cannon, 3×12.7-mm (0.5-in) machine-guns and 2×7.62-mm (0.3-in) machine-guns, plus provision for 3×100-kg (220-lb) bombs carried internally and 8×82- or 132-mm (3.2- or 5.2-in) rockets carried under the wings
Max T/O weight: (Pe-2) 7536 kg (16,614 lb)
Max speed: (Pe-2) 336 mph at 13,125 ft
Operational range: (Pe-2) 817 miles

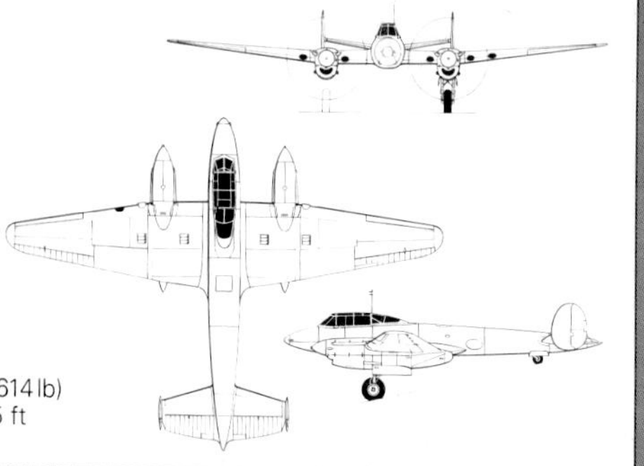

Polikarpov I-15

The I-15 was a logical development of the I-5 sesquiplane fighter of 1930 with single interplane struts, cantilever main landing gear legs, more power and, to provide the pilot with better vision, a gulled centre-section to the upper wing. Design began in the summer of 1932, and the mixed-construction TsKB-3 prototype flew in October 1933 with a Wright Cyclone radial whose 529-kW (710-hp) M-25 licence-built version powered the 270 definitive production aircraft after the first 404 had made do with the 358-kW (480-hp) M-22 and the next 59 with imported Cyclones. In January 1937 there flew the first I-15bis (otherwise I-152) with a conventional upper wing and a more powerful engine with long-chord cowling rather than the I-15's short-chord ring. Production totalled 2,408, and both types saw limited but useful service during Germany's 1941 invasion of the USSR.

Specification: Polikarpov I-15bis single-seat fighter and fighter-bomber
Span: 10.20 m (33 ft 5.5 in)
Length: 6.33 m (20 ft 9.25 in)
Powerplant: 1×M-25B, 559 kW (750 hp)
Armament: 4×7.62-mm (0.3-in) machine-guns, plus provision for 2×50-kg (110-lb) bombs or 6×82-mm (3.2-in) rockets
Max T/O weight: 1900 kg (4,189 lb)
Max speed: 230 mph at 9,845 ft
Operational range: 329 miles:

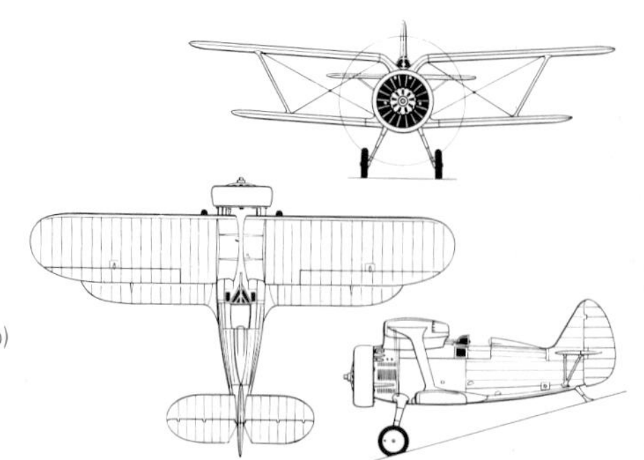

Of the 37,000 Yakovlev fighters produced during the war, the vast majority were Yak-9s. It was of primitive construction, having a wooden wing, welded steel fuselage and mixed aluminium panels and fabric covering, but proved to be a highly manoeuvrable and versatile fighter often seen as the Soviet Spitfire. This aircraft was one of those flying with the Free French Normandie-Niémen regiment in 1944.

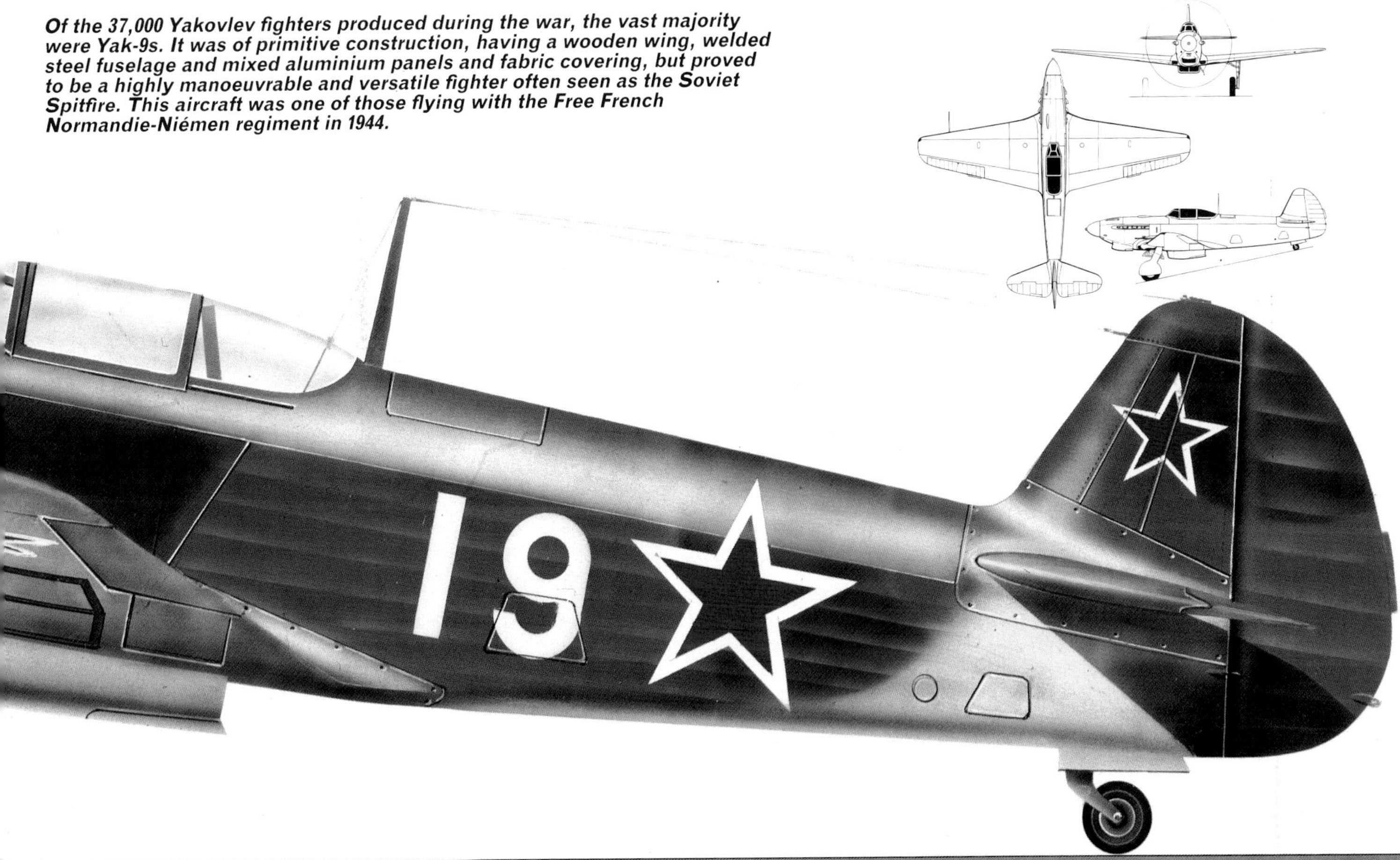

Polikarpov I-153

Developed from July 1937 as the I-15ter for a first flight in summer 1938 and service in early 1939, the I-153 was essentially the gull-winged I-15 with more powerful armament and retractable landing gear, the latter helping to make the I-153 the fastest biplane fighter ever to see operational service. Production totalled 3,437, and the initial I-153 was powered in its earlier form by the 559-kW (750-hp) M-25V, later examples with the M-62 radial often being of the I-153BS variant with four 12.7-mm (0.5-in) machine-guns in place of the earlier model's quartet of rifle-calibre guns. There was also an I-153P variant produced in small numbers with two 20-mm cannon. Experimental versions were the I-153V with a pressure cabin, the I-153V-TKGK with a rubberized fabric pressure cabin and twin turbochargers, and the I-153DM with two underwing ramjets.

Specification: Polikarpov I-153 single-seat fighter and fighter-bomber
Span: 10.00 m (32 ft 9.5 in)
Length: 6.17 m (20 ft 2.9 in)
Powerplant: 1×M-62, 746 kW (1,000 hp)
Armament: 4×7.62- or 12.7-mm (0.3- or 0.5-in) machine-guns, plus provision for 2×50-kg (110-lb) bombs or 6/8 82-mm (3.2-in) rockets carried under the wings
Max T/O weight: 2110 kg (4,652 lb)
Max speed: 275 mph at 16,405 ft
Operational range: 547 miles

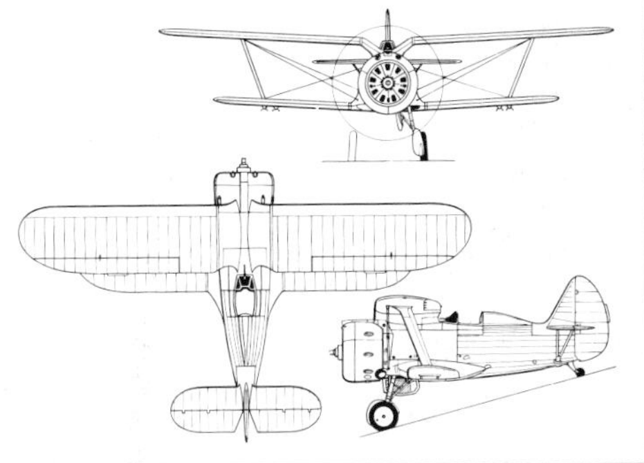

Polikarpov I-16

The I-16 was developed with the I-15 to meet a 1932 decision to build a fighter arm using a mix of agile biplanes and fast monoplanes. The TsKB-12 prototype flew in December 1933, and despite marginal handling was ordered into production with the 358-kW (480-hp) M-22. The I-16 Type 1 began to enter service in 1935 as the world's first low-wing monoplane fighter with flaps and retractable landing gear. About 7,005 fighters were built in variants such as the Type 4 with a 541-kW (750-hp) Wright Cyclone, Type 5 with a 522-kW (700-hp) M-25, strengthened Type 6 with an M-25A engine, Type 10 with an M-25V engine and heavier armament, Type 17 with two cannon in the wings, Type 18 with an 686-kW (920-hp) M-62, Type 24 with an M-63 engine, and the late-production Types 28 to 30 built with old tooling. Some 1,639 UTI-4 (plus small numbers of early UTI-2 and UTI-3) trainers were also built.

Specification: Polikarpov I-16 Type 24 single-seat fighter and fighter-bomber
Span: 9.00 m (29 ft 6.3 in)
Length: 6.13 m (20 ft 1.25 in)
Powerplant: 1×Shvetsov M-63, 820 kW (1,100 hp)
Armament: 2×20-mm cannon and 2×7.62-mm (0.3-in) machine-guns, plus provision for 2×chemical containers or 6×82-mm (3.2-in) rockets carried under the wings
Max T/O weight: 2095 kg (4,619 lb)
Max speed: 326 mph at sea level
Operational range: 435 miles

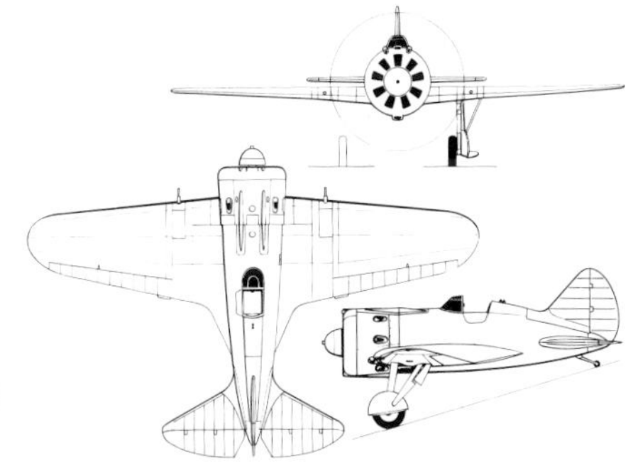

Polikarpov I-17

Designed and built in a mere eight months for a first flight in September 1934, the TsKB-15 prototype was conceived as an advanced fighter with a liquid-cooled engine for comparison with the radial-engined TsKB-12. The prototype was otherwise known as the I-17-1 and powered by a 567-kW (760-hp) Hispano-Suiza 12Ybrs. The concept was certainly advanced and the armament of two 20-mm cannon and two 7.62-mm (0.3-in) machine-guns particularly impressive for the period; but the structure was overly complicated and therefore both heavy and difficult to mass produce. The TsKB-19 (I-17-2) had inward- rather than outward-retracting main landing gear units, one cannon and four machine-guns, and a licence-built 12Y engine, the Klimov M-100. The TsKB-33 (I-17-3) had evaporative engine cooling and only three machine-guns. It is possible that a few I-17-2 production aircraft were built.

Specification: Polikarpov I-17-2 single-seat fighter prototype
Span: 10.00 m (32 ft 9.7 in)
Length: 8.80 m (28 ft 10.5 in)
Powerplant: 1×Klimov M-100A, 641 kW (860 hp)
Armament: 1×20-mm cannon and 4×7.62-mm (0.3-in) machine-guns, plus provision for 2×50-kg (110-lb) bombs carried under the wings
Normal T/O weight: 1950 kg (4,299 lb)
Max speed: 305 mph at sea level
Operational range: 491 miles

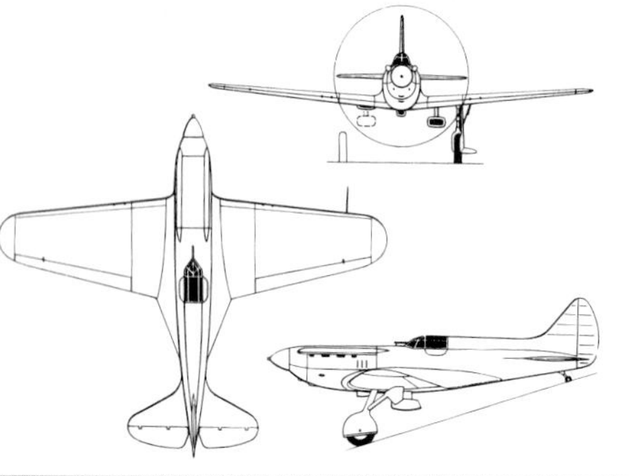

Yakovlev Yak-1

A contemporary of the LaGG-1 and MiG-1, the Yak-1 was the production version of the I-26 prototype that first flew in January 1940 on a 783-kW (1,050-hp) M-105P inline engine, and was Yakovlev's first fighter. A considerable development effort was required to turn the I-26 into an effective fighter: the 64 Yak-1s produced by the end of 1940 with three different armament options and other differences may be considered pre-production rather than true production machines. Production thereafter increased rapidly, the main variants being the definitive Yak-1 with the 820-kW (1,100-hp) VK-105PA engine, the Yak-1B with cut-down rear fuselage and 360° vision canopy, and the reduced-weight Yak-1M. From early 1942 the aircraft had a more pointed wing of slightly greater span. Production was completed in summer 1943 after the delivery of 8,721 aircraft.

Specification: Yakovlev Yak-1M single-seat fighter and fighter-bomber
Span: 10.25 m (33 ft 7.5 in)
Length: 8.48 m (27 ft 9.85 in)
Powerplant: 1×Klimov VK-105PF, 880 kW (1,180 hp)
Armament: 1×20-mm cannon and 2×7.62-mm (0.3-in) machine-guns, plus provision for 2×100-kg (220-lb) bombs or 6×82-mm (3.2-in) rockets carried under the wings
Normal T/O weight: 2660 kg (5,864 lb)
Max speed: 404 mph at 14,765 ft
Operational range: 559 miles

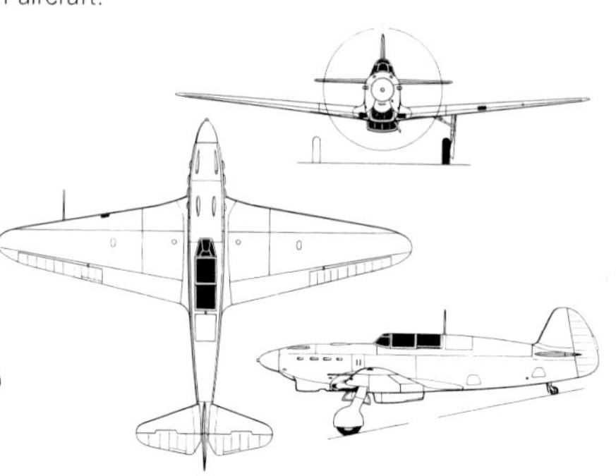

Yakovlev Yak-3

The Yak-3 resulted from a requirement of late 1941 calling for a short-range dogfighter and close-support fighter. Possibly the most agile monoplane of World War II, the Yak-3 was much delayed by official concentration on other types and by problems with the chosen VK-107 engine. The programme thus got fully under way only in August 1943, and was in essence the fuselage of the Yak-1M with the cut-down decking and canopy of the Yak-1B, a new wing and, finally, a VK-105. The prototype flew in late 1943 and deliveries began in July of the same year. Production tempo rose with astonishing speed: 4,848 had been completed by May 1945, when production ceased. Experimental variants included the anti-tank Yak-3T with one 37-mm and two 20-mm cannon, the Yak-3P with three 20-mm cannon, and the Yak-3UTI with a low-powered ASh-21 engine leading to the Yak-11 trainer.

Specification: Yakovlev Yak-3 single-seat fighter
Span: 9.20 m (30 ft 2.25 in)
Length: 8.49 m (27 ft 10.25 in)
Powerplant: 1×Klimov VK-105PF-2, 969 kW (1,300 hp)
Armament: 1×20-mm cannon and 2×12.7-mm (0.5-in) machine-guns
Normal T/O weight: 2660 kg (5,864 lb)
Max speed: 410 mph at 10,500 ft
Operational range: 440 miles

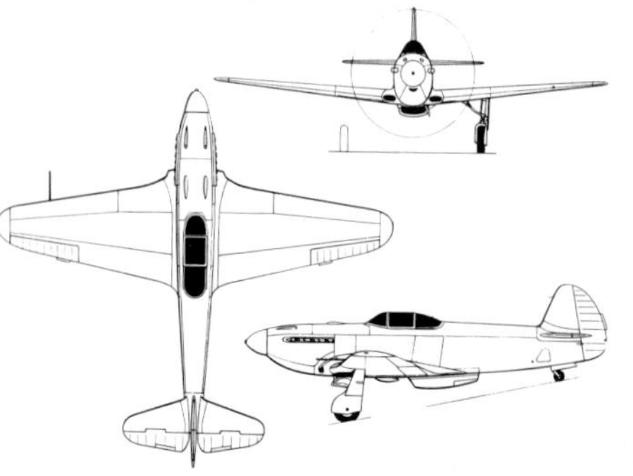

Yakovlev Yak-7

The Yak-7 was initially a two-seat trainer and liaison aeroplane based on the I-26, but its outstanding handling qualities commended the type's development as a single-seat fighter, which flew in prototype form during June 1941. Thereafter the two types were produced in parallel, the two-seater as the Yak-7V (later UTI-26, with armament reduced to just a single machine-gun) and the single-seater as the Yak-7A. Production rose rapidly, and from late 1941 the Yak-7A was replaced by the Yak-7B with the original 10-m (32.81-ft) span wing and considerably improved equipment standards. Production lasted to spring 1943, deliveries amounting to 6,399 including about 5,000 Yak-7Bs. There were several experimental models such as the long-range Yak-7DI with extra fuel capacity and alloy rather than wooden spars, and the Yak-7PVRD with two underwing ramjets.

Specification: Yakovlev Yak-7B single-seat fighter and fighter-bomber
Span: 10.00 m (32 ft 9.7 in)
Length: 8.475 m (27 ft 9.7 in)
Powerplant: 1×Klimov VK-105PF, 925 kW (1,240 hp)
Armament: 1×20-mm cannon and 2×12.7-mm (0.5-in) machine-guns, plus provision for 2×100-kg (220-lb) bombs or 6×82-mm (3.2-in) rockets carried under the wings
Normal T/O weight: 3040 kg (6,702 lb)
Max speed: 354 mph at 11,810 ft
Operational range: 510 miles

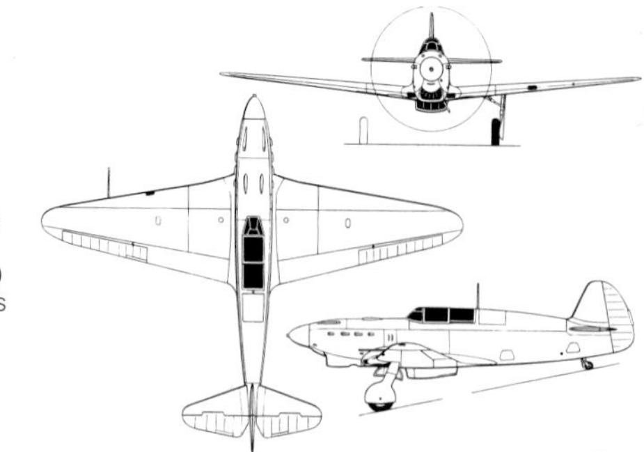

Dewoitine D.520

As early as 1940 the Italians began to appreciate that their biplane fighters and even their first-generation monoplane fighters were only of limited use against the best British aircraft. In November 1942 the Germans took over unoccupied France, in the process capturing 246 D.520s. Most of these were used by the Germans not altogether successfully as fighter trainers, but included in the number disbursed to Germany's allies were 60 to Italy. As the Italian programme for the development and production of new inline-engined machines was well behind schedule, these ex-French machines were gratefully received and allocated to single squadrons of the 13°, 22°, 24° and 167° Gruppi for use as second-line fighters (largely in defence of Naples and central Italy) and also as fighter trainers.

Specification: Dewoitine D.520 single-seat fighter
Span: 10.20 m (33 ft 5.5 in)
Length: 8.76 m (28 ft 8.75 in)
Powerplant: 1× Hispano-Suiza 12Y 45, 686 kW (920 hp)
Armament: 1×20-mm cannon and 4×7.5-mm (0.295-in) machine-guns
Normal T/O weight: 2783 kg (6,134 lb)
Max speed: 332 mph at 19,685 ft
Operational range: 553 miles

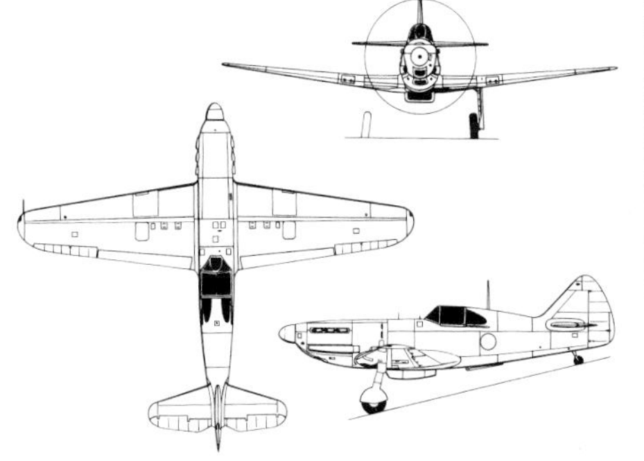

Supermarine Spitfire F.Mk V

The technical poverty of the Italian co-belligerent air force from late 1943 forced the Allies to provide modern equipment if their Italian allies were to be of any practical use. These Italian units were operated mostly over the Balkans, and from October 1944 the 20° Gruppo of the 61° Stormo received some 33 examples of the Spitfire F.Mk VB, the variant with a wing armament of two cannon and four rifle-calibre machine-guns. These were well used aircraft before the Italians received them, but nonetheless performed with some considerable distinction in the trying tactical and geographical conditions into which they were thrown. The Spitfire remained in Italian service up to 1952, post-war deliveries for the 5° and 51° Stormi being of the Spitfire F.Mk IX variant with the Merlin 63 engine.

Specification: Supermarine Spitfire LF.Mk VB single-seat fighter and fighter-bomber
Span: 9.80 m (32 ft 2 in) with clipped wings
Length: 9.11 m (29 ft 11 in)
Powerplant: 1×Rolls-Royce Merlin 40M, 50M or 55M, 1096 kW (1,470 hp)
Armament: 2×20-mm cannon and 4×7.7-mm (0.303-in) machine-guns plus provision for 227 kg (500 lb) of bombs under the fuselage or wings
Normal T/O weight: 3016 kg (6,650 lb)
Max speed: 357 mph at 6,000 ft
Operational range: 470 miles

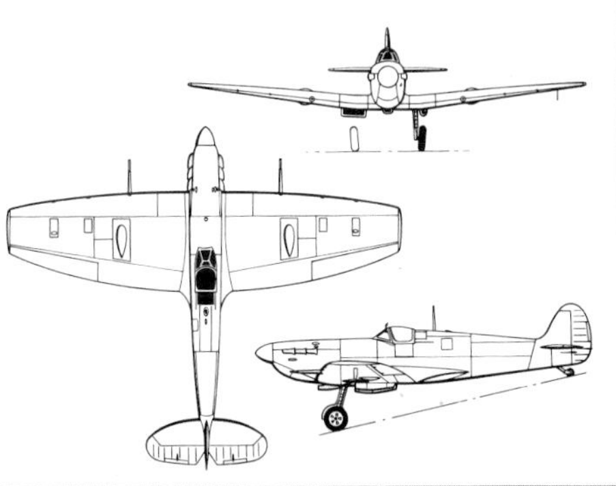

Messerschmitt Bf 109

Given the poverty of its ally's fighter arm in the mid-war years, Germany felt it was in its own interest to bolster the Italian air force with numbers of fairly advanced fighters. The obvious candidate was the Bf 109, and initial deliveries comprised sufficient Bf 109F fighter-bombers (in F-4/B and F-4/R1 variants) for the 3° and 150° Gruppi (Wings). Despite the fact that Italy's fighter production capability was centred in northern Italy, where the fascist state was revived after Italy's armistice with the Allies in September 1943, further reinforcement was necessary in 1944: the Italians thus received the upengined and upgunned Bf 109G model in the form of 28 G-6, 97 G-10 and four G-12 variants. And right at the end of the war final German deliveries amounted to 19 examples of the Bf 109K-4 with more power and armament as well as a pressurised cockpit.

Specification: Messerschmitt Bf 109K-4 single-seat fighter
Span: 9.97 m (32 ft 8.5 in)
Length: 8.85 m (29 ft 0.5 in)
Powerplant: 1×Daimler-Benz DB 605ASCM, 1491 kW (2,000 hp)
Armament: 1×30-mm and 2×15-mm cannon
Max T/O weight: 3600 kg (7,937 lb)
Max speed: 452 mph at 19,685 ft
Operational range: 366 miles

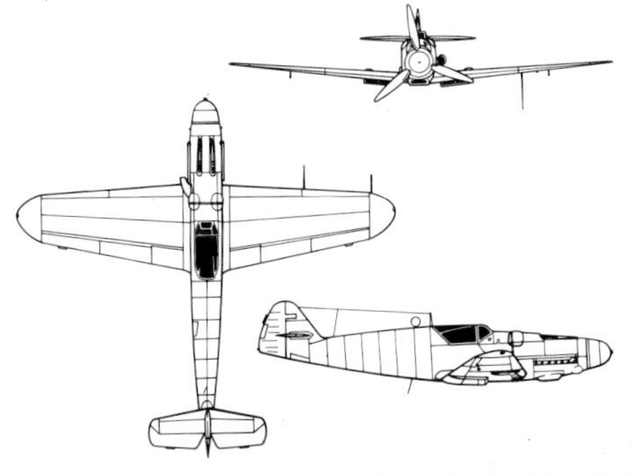

Bell P-39 Airacobra

With most Italian fighter production in the hands of the fascist state in northern Italy after the armistice of September 1943, the Allies had to provide the co-belligerent Italians of the south with any modern equipment, including fighters. Several Italian fighter squadrons were tasked with fighter-bomber support of the Yugoslav partisans during 1944, and these units were provided with 149 examples of the P-39 Airacobra. The two variants involved were the P-39N with the V-1710-85 engine and the P-39Q with the mixed machine-gun battery of earlier models replaced by a homogenous battery (two 12.7-mm/0.5-in guns in the nose cowling and single guns in the blister under each wing). Late aircraft also introduced a four- rather than three-blade propeller, and had altered fuel capacity and armour protection. The type was retired only in 1951.

Specification: Bell P-39N Airacobra single-seat fighter and fighter-bomber
Span: 10.36 m (34 ft 0 in)
Length: 9.19 m (30 ft 2 in)
Powerplant: 1×Allison V-1710-85, 895 kW (1,200 hp)
Armament: 1×37-mm cannon, 2×12.7-mm (0.5-in) machine-guns and 4×7.62-mm (0.3-in) machine-guns plus provision for 1×227-kg (500-lb) bomb carried under the fuselage
Max T/O weight: 3720 kg (8,200 lb)
Max speed: 399 mph at 9,700 ft
Operational range: 750 miles

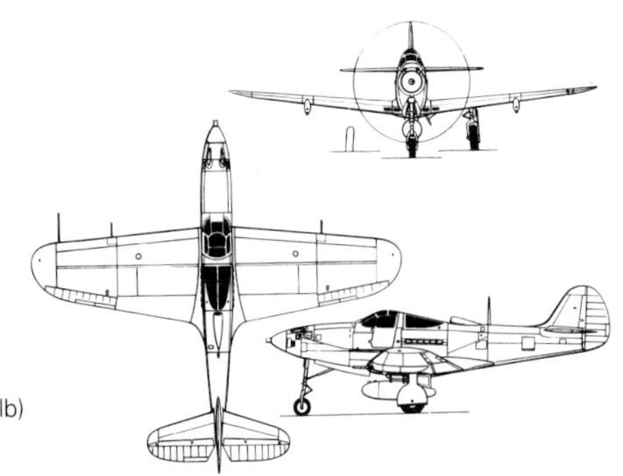

Fiat CR.42 Falco

The CR.42 first flew in 1936 as a developed version of the CR.32 with a more advanced structure and a radial engine. This was Italy's last biplane fighter, and though an exceptional example of its genre it was overshadowed by British monoplane fighters. Production totalled at least 1,780, and variants included the initial CR.42 Falco (falcon) with one 12.7-mm (0.5-in) and one 7.7-mm (0.303-in) machine-guns for Belgian, Hungarian and Italian orders, the CR.42AS close-support fighter with underwing bombs, the CR.42bis with two 12.7-mm (0.5-in) machine-guns ordered by Sweden as the J 11, the CR.42CN limited night-fighter conversion of the CR.42 with two underwing searchlights, and the CR.42ter version of the CR.42bis with two additional 12.7-mm (0.5-in) machine-guns. Experimental models were the CR.42B with a 753.kW (1,010-hp) Daimler-Benz DB 601 inline for a speed of 323mph, and the ICR.42 floatplane fighter.

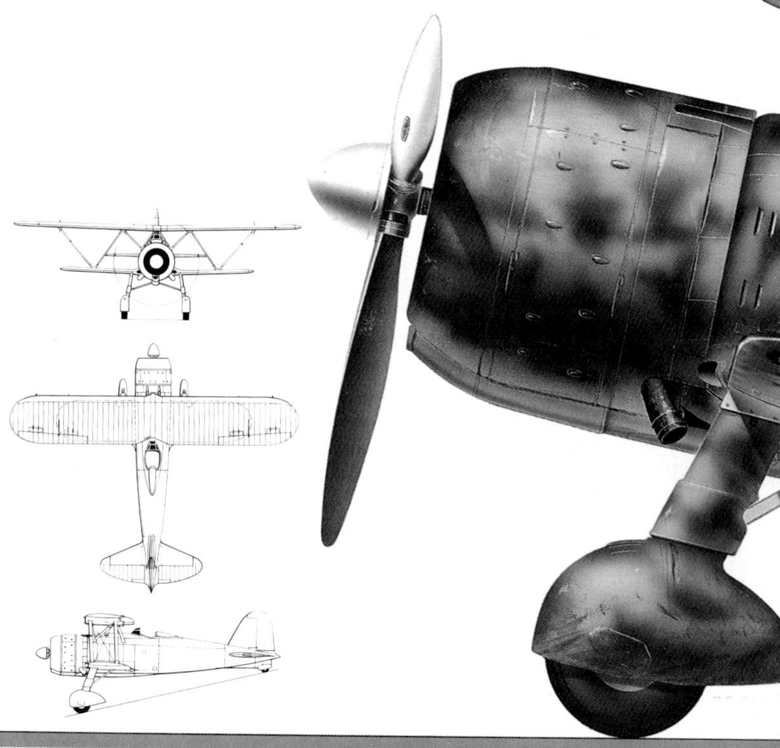

Fiat CR.32

Italy's most important fighter of the late 1930s, the CR.32 biplane was first flown in August 1933 as a development of the CR.30 using the same type of metal/fabric-covered all-metal structure and Warren-type interplane bracing but with smaller overall dimensions plus improved performance and agility. The initial CR.32 had the 447-kW (600-hp) Fiat A.30 RAbis inline and two 7.7-mm (0.303-in) machine-guns, and these 350 aircraft were followed by 283 examples of the CR.32bis close-support version. Next came 150 examples of an improved CR.32, the CR.32ter with revised landing gear and improved equipment, and the final aircraft were 337 CR.32quater fighters essentially similar to the CR.32ter but with a lightened structure and updated equipment. The type suffered heavily in combat with British monoplane fighters.

Specification: Fiat CR.32bis single-seat fighter and light close-support aeroplane
Span: 9.50 m (31 ft 2.25 in)
Length: 7.47 m (24 ft 6 in)
Powerplant: 1×Fiat A.30 RAbis, 447 kW (600 hp)
Armament: 2×12.7-mm (0.5-in) and two 7.7-mm (0.303-in) machine-guns plus provision for 100 kg (220 lb) of bombs carried under the fuselage
Normal T/O weight: 1975 kg (4,350 lb)
Max speed: 224 mph at 9,845 ft
Operational range: 466 miles

Ambrosini S.A.I.207

At the conceptual level the lightweight inline-engined fighter of basically wooden construction appealed to the Italians because of the limited demands it made on scarce industrial facilities and structural resources. One of the more interesting results was the S.A.I.207 developed from the pre-war S.A.I.7 sports monoplane with a 209-kW (280-hp) Hirth HM.508D engine. From this was developed a prototype fighter trainer with a similarly rated Isotta-Fraschini Beta RC 10 inline, and then the S.A.I.107 fighter prototype with a 403-kW (540-hp) Isotta-Fraschini Gamma inline. Orders were placed for 2,000 examples of the S.A.I.207 production version, but only 13 pre-production aircraft were completed, the order then being switched to the improved S.A.I.403 Dardo (dart) with improved armament and the 559-kW (750-hp) Isotta-Fraschini Delta RC 21/60; only a prototype S.A.I.403 was completed.

Specification: Ambrosini S.A.I.207 single-seat lightweight interceptor fighter
Span: 9.00 m (29 ft 6.3 in)
Length: 8.02 m (26 ft 3.75 in)
Powerplant: 1×Isotta-Fraschini Delta RC 40, 559 kW (750 hp)
Armament: 2×12.7-mm (0.5-in) machine-guns
Max T/O weight: 2415 kg (5,324 lb)
Max speed: 398 mph at 14,765 ft
Operational range: 590 miles

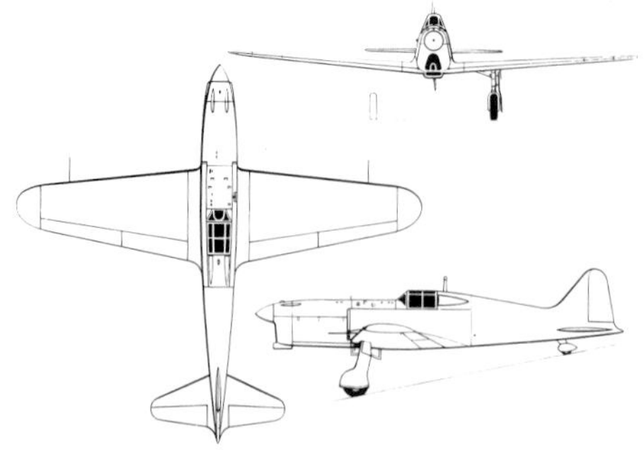

Specification: Fiat CR.42AS Falco single-seat fighter and light close-support aeroplane
Span: 9.70 m (31 ft 9.75 in)
Length: 8.26 m (27 ft 1 in)
Powerplant: 1×Fiat A.74 RC 38, 626 kW (840 hp)
Armament: 2×12.7-mm (0.5-in) machine-guns plus provision for up to 200 kg (441 lb) of bombs carried under the wings
Normal T/O weight: 2295 kg (5,060 lb)
Max speed: 280 mph at 17,485 ft
Operational range: 480 miles

'his aircraft belonged to the 4° Stormo as indicated by the white horse 'Cavallino Rampante' badge on the fuselage and wears the mailed leg mblem of the 97ª Squadriglia on its tail fin. It also wears the Fasces mblem below the cockpit. This particular unit was based at Benin in ibya and took part in the North African campaign, later moving to ollum.

Fiat G.50 Freccia

First flown in February 1937, the Freccia (arrow) was Italy's first attempt to produce an all-metal 'modern' monoplane fighter with retractable landing gear and an enclosed cockpit, though pilot opposition led to the retrofit of a semi-enclosed cockpit on the aircraft of the initial production series. These 246 aircraft had two 12.7-mm (0.5-in) machine-guns, and were followed by 421 examples of the G.50bis with greater fuel capacity, improved radio and a modified wing. Production of the G.50B unarmed two-seat trainer totalled 108, and the same basic airframe formed the basis of the G.50bis/A two-seat carrierborne fighter with four 12.7-mm (0.5-in) machine-guns. This latter was flown only in prototype form, and other prototypes (G.50ter, G.50V, G.51 and G.52) were developed round imported German inlines or their Italian licence-built versions. The basic type was also exported to Croatia and Finland.

Specification: Fiat G.50bis Freccia single-seat fighter and fighter-bomber
Span: 10.90 m (36 ft 0.75 in)
Length: 7.80 m (25 ft 7 in)
Powerplant: 1×Fiat A.74 RC 38, 626 kW (840 hp)
Armament: 2×12.7-mm (0.5-in) machine-guns plus provision for up to 300 kg (661 lb) of bombs carried under the wings
Normal T/O weight: 2522 kg (5,560 lb)
Max speed: 293 mph at 14,765 ft
Operational range: 420 miles

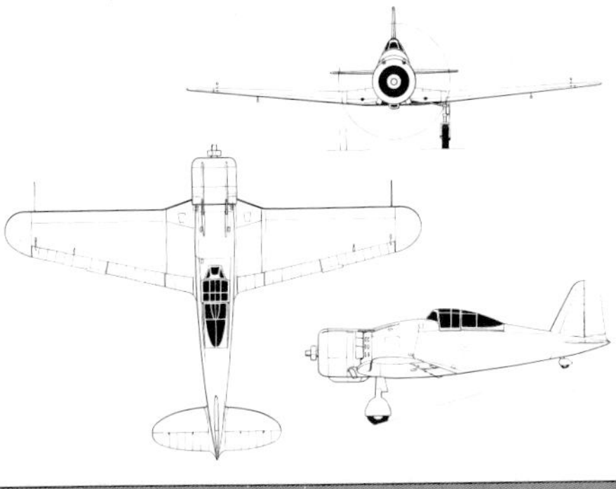

Macchi MC.200 Saetta

The Saetta (lightning) was in most respects an admirable fighter with beautiful handling and great agility, but was tactically hampered by the modest performance and light armament imposed by its low-powered radial in a high-drag installation. The first prototype flew in December 1937 with an enclosed cockpit and retractable tailwheel, both of these features being disliked by most service pilots and therefore eliminated from the MC.200A1 initial production model, which in its MC.200A2 late form acquired two 7.7-mm (0.303-in) machine-guns in the wings. Production amounted to 1,153 aircraft in 25 series, and other variants were the MC.200AS tropicalised fighter and the MC.200CB able to operate as a fighter-bomber with 320 kg (706 lb) of bombs or as a long-range escort fighter with drop tanks. The MC.201 variant was to have had the 746-kW (1,000-hp) Fiat A.76 RC 40 in a modified fuselage.

Specification: Macchi MC.200 Saetta single-seat interceptor fighter
Span: 10.58 m (34 ft 8.7 in)
Length: 8.19 m (26 ft 10.5 in)
Powerplant: 1×Fiat A.74 RC 38, 649 kW (870 hp)
Armament: 2×12.7-mm (0.5-in) machine-guns and (later aircraft) 2×7.7-mm (0.303-in) machine-guns
Normal T/O weight: 2200 kg (4,850 lb)
Max speed: 312 mph at 14,765 ft
Operational range: 540 miles

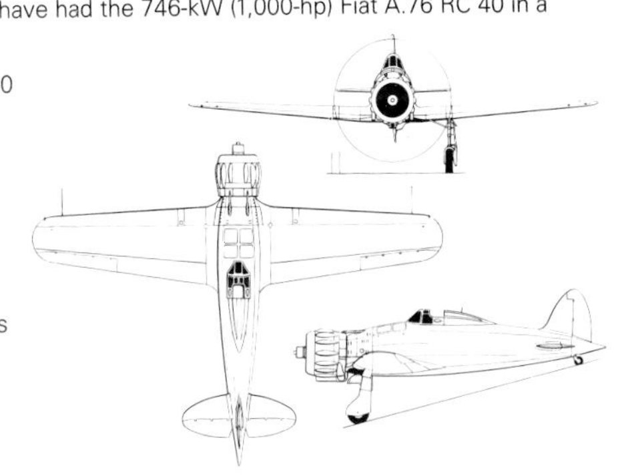

Macchi MC.202 Folgore

Specification: Macchi MC.202 Folgore single-seat fighter
Span: 10.58 m (34 ft 8.7 in)
Length: 8.85 m (29 ft 0.5 in)
Powerplant: 1×Alfa Romeo AR.1000 RC 41-1 Monsone, 876 kW (1,175 hp)
Armament: 2×12.7-mm (0.5-in) machine-guns and (later aircraft) 2×7.7-mm (0.303-in) machine-guns
Normal T/O weight: 2937 kg (6,475 lb)
Max speed: 370 mph at 16,405 ft
Operational range: 475 miles

In common with several other Italian radial-engined fighters of the period, the MC.200 was given a new lease of life by the installation of an inline engine of German origins and offering reduced drag as well as considerably more power. The Folgore (thunderbolt) was first flown in August 1940 with a DB 601A-1 and a retractable tailwheel, and proved wholly superior to the MC.200. Production amounted to some 1,100 aircraft in 11 series, and power was provided by imported or licence-built engines. Later aircraft featured increased armament with the addition of two rifle-calibre wing machine-guns. Variants used in small numbers were the tropicalised MC.202AS and the dual-role MC.202CB that could be used as a fighter-bomber with 320 kg (706 lb) of bombs under the wings or as a long-range escort fighter with underwing drop tanks. The type was also trialled as the MC.200D with a chin radiator.

Caproni-Reggiane Re.2000 Falco I

Bearing a marked similarity to the Seversky P-35, the Re.2000 first flew in 1938 as competitor to the Macchi MC.200. The latter was ordered for the Italian air force, but the Falco (falcon) was placed in production for export as the Re.2000 Serie 1 with minor modifications: deliveries totalled 157 aircraft including 70 for Hungary (local designation Heja I, with Heja II for the licence-built variant with a 735-kW/986-hp WMK 14 radial) and 60 for Sweden (local designation J 20). Variants were the Re.2000 Serie 2 shipborne fighter for the Italian navy (10 Serie 1 conversions with the 764-kW/1,025-hp P.XIbis radial) and the Re.2000 Serie 3 long-range fighter with additional internal fuel and provision for an auxiliary tank or 2000-kg (4,405-lb) bomb load (12 Serie 1 conversions).

Specification: Caproni-Reggiane Re.2000 Serie 1 Falco I single-seat fighter
Span: 11.00 m (36 ft 1 in)
Length: 7.99 m (26 ft 2.5 in)
Powerplant: 1×Piaggio P.XI RC 40, 735 kW (986 hp)
Armament: 2×12.7-mm (0.5-in) machine-guns
Normal T/O weight: 2595 kg (5,722 lb)
Max speed: 329 mph at 16,405 ft
Operational range: 870 miles

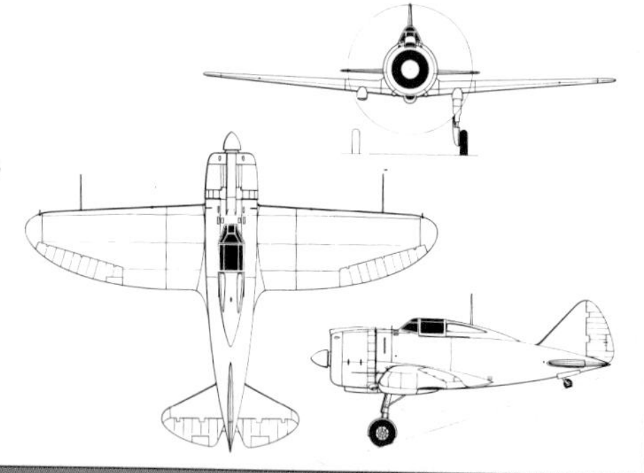

Fiat G.55 Centauro

The Centauro (centaur) was a development of the G.50 with a Daimler-Benz DB 605A-1 inline built under licence in Italy. The type evolved from the DB 601-powered G.50V, and was first flown in the spring of 1942. Flight trials confirmed that this was an excellent fighter, but production was slow to start and only a few of the eventual total of 200 aircraft had been delivered before Italy's armistice with the Allies in September 1943. Most G.55s thus fought with the fascist air arm on the German side in northern Italy. Three prototypes and eight pre-production aircraft were followed by about 185 G.55 Series 1 fighters. There were also about 10 examples of the G.55S torpedo strike fighter, but none of the G.55 Serie 2 bomber destroyer with five 20-mm cannon. After the war 85 more aircraft were delivered as G.55A single-seat fighter trainers and G.55B two-seat advanced trainers.

Specification: Fiat G.55 Serie 1 Centauro single-seat fighter and fighter-bomber
Span: 11.85 m (38 ft 10.5 in)
Length: 9.37 m (30 ft 9 in)
Powerplant: 1×Fiat RA.1050 RC 58 Tifone, 1100 kW (1,475 hp)
Armament: 3×20-mm cannon and 2×12.7-mm (0.5-in) machine-guns plus provision for up to 320 kg (706 lb) of bombs carried under the wings
Normal T/O weight: 3520 kg (7,760 lb)
Max speed: 385 mph at 22,965 ft
Operational range: 1,025 miles

Identified as an aircraft of the 22° Gruppo by the* Spauracchio *(scarecrow) device on the fuselage band, and by the numerals as belonging to the 369ª Squadriglia, this mid-series M.C.202 was based at Capodichino, Naples as part of the 53° Stormo CT at the time of the invasion of Sicily in July 1943. Although its maximum speed of 373 mph (600 km/h) was adequate to match Allied fighters of the Spitfire Mk V's generation, the purpose of deploying aircraft such as the M.C.202 to defend Italian cities from attacks by Allied bombers was questionable as their light armament was quite inadequate for the role of bomber-destroyer.

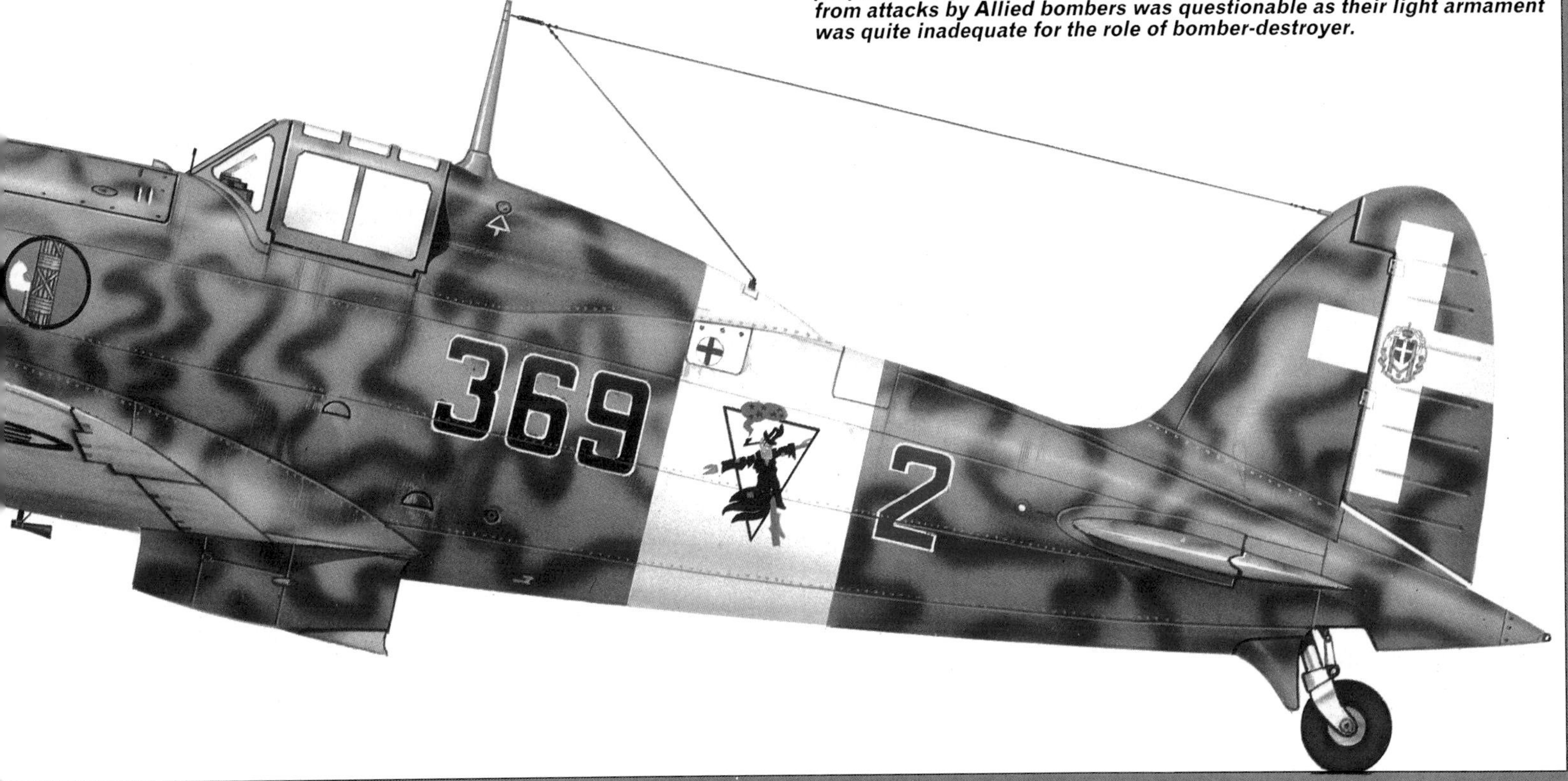

Macchi MC.205V Veltro

With the Veltro (greyhound) the line of direct development from the MC.200 reached its apogee to produce a superb fighter. The type first flew in April 1942 with a licence-built DB 605A-1 in an airframe derived from that of the MC.202. The type proved outstanding in performance and handling right from the start, but was again slow to enter production. Most of the 262 MC.205V production aircraft served with the fascist Italian and German air arms up to the end of the war, later aircraft having two 20-mm cannon in place of the two rifle-calibre wing machine-guns to provide for the first time a genuinely effective armament. A variant that failed to enter production was the MC.205N Orione high-altitude fighter with increased-span wings and an armament of one 20-mm cannon and four 12.7-mm (0.5-in) machine-guns in the N-1 variant or three cannon and two machine-guns in the N-2 variant.

Specification: Macchi MC.205V Veltro single-seat fighter and fighter-bomber
Span: 10.58 m (34 ft 8.7 in)
Length: 8.85 m (29 ft 0.5 in)
Powerplant: 1×Fiat RA.1050 RC 58 Tifone, 1100 kW (1,475 hp)
Armament: 2×12.7-mm (0.5-in) and two 7.7-mm (0.303-in) machine-guns plus provision for up to 320 kg (706 lb) of bombs carried under the wings
Normal T/O weight: 3224 kg (7,108 lb)
Max speed: 399 mph at 23,620 ft
Operational range: 646 miles

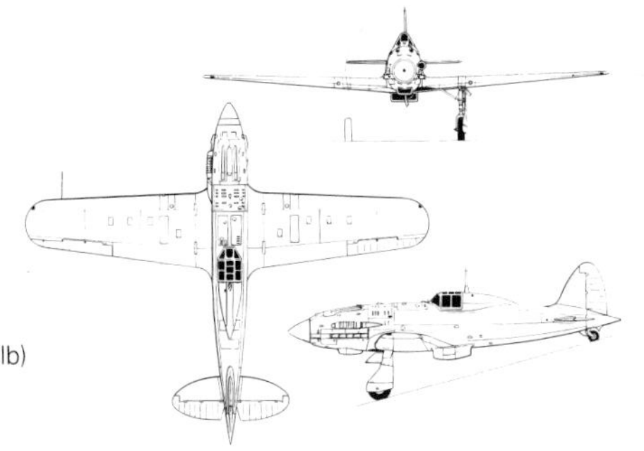

Caproni-Reggiane *Re.2001 Falco II*

It was quickly appreciated that the Re.2000's main limitation was its large but comparatively low-powered radial, and in 1941 there appeared the Re.2001 Falco II with a 783-kW (1,050-hp) Daimler-Benz DB 601A-1 inline, redesigned canopy and revised wing. The type was used in a large development programme with other engines, and the total of 237 aircraft included 224 production aircraft in two fighter, one fighter-bomber and one night-fighter series. There followed 227 Re.2002 Ariete (ram) fighter-bombers with the 880-kW (1,180-hp) Piaggio P.XIX RC 45 radial, and finally 37 Re.2005 Sagittario (archer) fighters with the licence-built DB 605A-1 inline and wide-track inward-retracting rather than narrow-track outward-retracting landing gear and other improvements to produce a genuinely high-performance type. The Re.2005 first flew in September 1942.

Specification: Caproni-Reggiane Re.2005 Sagittario single-seat fighter and fighter-bomber
Span: 11.00 m (36 ft 1 in)
Length: 8.73 m (28 ft 7.75 in)
Powerplant: 1×Fiat RA.1050 RC 58 Tifone, 1100 kW (1,475 hp)
Armament: 3×20-mm cannon and 2×12.7-mm (0.5-in) machine-guns plus provision for 1000 kg (2,205 lb) of bombs carried under the wings
Normal T/O weight: 3610 kg (7,960 lb)
Max speed: 421 mph at 6,560 ft
Operational range: 777 miles

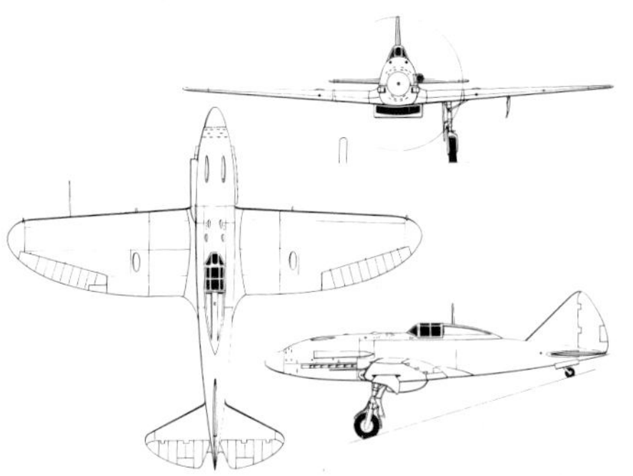

Supermarine **Spitfire** (Merlin-engine)

Specification: Supermarine Spitfire Mk IX single-seat fighter and fighter-bomber
Span: 11.22 m (36 ft 10 in)
Length: 9.46 m (31 ft 0 in)
Powerplant: 1×Rolls-Royce Merlin 63, 1230 kW (1,650 hp)
Armament: 2×20-mm cannon and 4×0.303-in (7.7-mm) machine-guns plus provision for 454 kg (1,000 lb) of bombs carried externally
Max T/O weight: 4309 kg (9,500 lb)
Max speed: 408 mph at 25,000 ft
Operational range: 980 miles

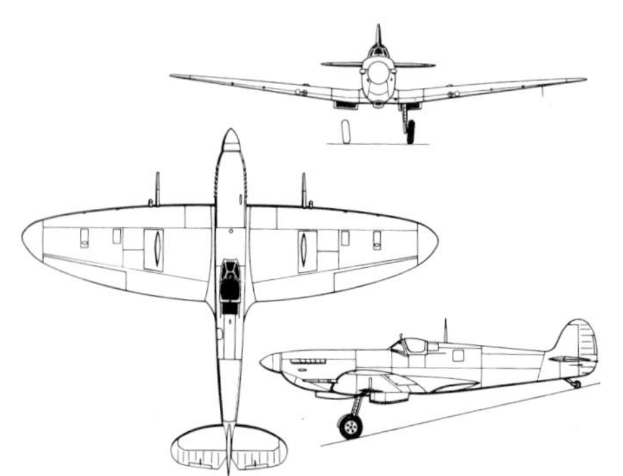

The most celebrated British fighter of World War II and the only one to remain in production right through the War, the Spitfire first flew in March 1936 and displayed impressive performance. The type was not really designed for mass production and was hampered by its narrow-track landing gear, but entered production for service in 1938. Mk Is had the 768-kW (1,030-hp) Merlin III and eight 0.303-in (7.7-mm) machine-guns, and were redesignated Mk IA when the Mk IB appeared with two 20-mm cannon and four machine-guns. Subsequent variants were the Mk IIA/B with the 876-kW (1,175-hp) Merlin XII, the Mk VA, B and universal-winged C with the 1096-kW (1,470-hp) Merlin 45, 50 or 55 in high-, medium- and low-altitude versions, the high-altitude Mks VI and VII, the tropical Mk VIII, the upgraded and multi-version Mk IX, and the Mk XVI version of the Mk IX with US-built Merlin.

Gloster Gladiator

The Gladiator was the UK's last production biplane fighter. The type first flew in 1934 and was an evolutionary development of the Gauntlet with greater power, cantilever main landing gear legs, trailing-edge flaps and an enclosed cockpit. The type was ordered for the RAF as the Gladiator Mk I and entered service in January 1937; a naval version was ordered for the Fleet Air Arm as the Sea Gladiator and began to enter service in February 1939. The Sea Gladiator and improved Gladiator Mk II were each powered by the Mercury VIIIA. Production ended in spring 1940 after 768 aircraft, including small export quantities. The Gladiator was used to telling effect against the Italians in the Mediterranean theatre up to the end of 1941. Small numbers served in the UK and Norway.

Specification: Gloster Gladiator Mk I single-seat fighter
Span: 9.83 m (32 ft 3 in)
Length: 8.36 m (27 ft 5 in)
Powerplant: 1×Bristol Mercury IX, 626 kW (840 hp)
Armament: 4×0.303-in (7.7-mm) machine-guns
Max T/O weight: 2083 kg (4,592 lb)
Max speed: 253 mph at 14,500 ft
Operational range: 428 miles

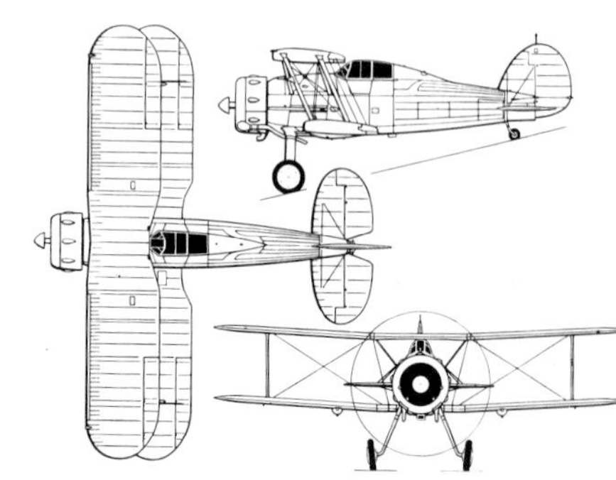

Hawker Hurricane

The Hurricane was the RAF's first low-wing monoplane fighter with retractable landing gear, and was an extremely robust type that bore the brunt of the RAF's fighter operations up to 1941. The prototype flew in November 1935, and the type began to enter service as the Hurricane Mk I in December 1937. The Hurricane's simple structure aided rapid production, and by the beginning of World War II some 500 were in service with 18 squadrons. The Mk I was followed in mid-1940 by the Mk II with the 954-kW (1,280-hp) Merlin XX, and this was developed in variants such as Mk IIA (eight machine-guns), Mk IIB (12 machine-guns), Mk IIC (four 20-mm cannon), Mk IID (two 40-mm cannon for tank-busting) and Mk IIB/C 'Hurribomber' variants with two 113-kg (250-lb) bombs. The Mk IV had a 'universal' wing for different armaments. Production totalled 14,232.

Specification: Hawker Hurricane Mk I single-seat fighter
Span: 12.19 m (40 ft 0 in)
Length: 9.55 m (31 ft 4 in)
Powerplant: 1×Rolls-Royce Merlin II, 768 kW (1,030 hp)
Armament: 8×0.303-in (7.7-mm) machine-guns
Max T/O weight: 2820 kg (6,218 lb)
Max speed: 308 mph at 10,000 ft
Operational range: 525 miles

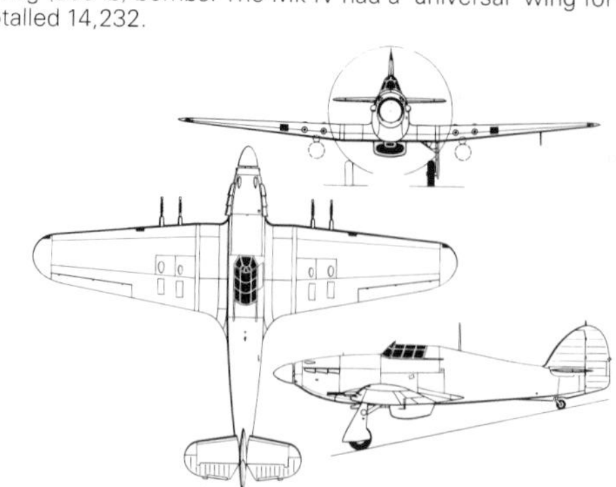

is Vickers-Supermarine Spitfire VIII served with 452 Squadron of RAAF. Following their 'Flying Circus' and 'Ramrod' excursions m Kenley and Redhill, the Squadron returned to Australia, where y were given new Spitfire VIIIs for further attack and defence trols. This mark of Spitfire was designed around the two-stage rlin 61 engine; it had a retractable tailwheel and pointed rudder.

Bristol Blenheim

First flown in June 1936 as a medium bomber, the Blenheim was powered by two 626-kW (9840-hp) Mercury VIIIs and possessed the speed for conversion into an interim night-fighter. The Mk IF had AI Mk III or IV radar and a belly pack with four forward-firing machine-guns. In 1939 the short-nose Blenheim I was superseded by the long-nose Blenheim IV, and this, too, was developed, becoming the Mk IVF long-range fighter, which lacked the radar of the Mk IF but retained the ventral gun pack in addition to the bomber's standard armament (one fixed forward-firing gun and one dorsal turret gun). The type lacked the speed, agility and strength to 'mix it' with enemy single-seat fighters and soon disappeared from front-line service. About 200 Mk I and an unknown number of Mk IV conversions were made.

Specification: Bristol Blenheim Mk IVF two-seat long-range fighter
Span: 17.17 m (56 ft 4 in)
Length: 12.98 m (42 ft 7 in)
Powerplant: 2×Bristol Mercury XV, 686 kW (920 hp)
Armament: 6×0.303-in (7.7-mm) machine-guns
Max T/O weight: 6580 kg (14,500 lb)
Max speed: 260 mph at 12,000 ft
Operational range: 1,460 miles

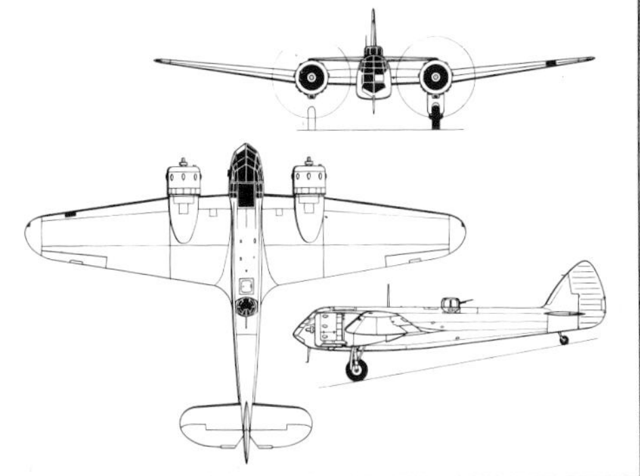

Boulton Paul Defiant

First flown in August 1937, the Defiant pioneered a new concept: a fighter with its gun battery grouped into a power-operated turret rather than fixed in the fuselage and/or wings. The Defiant Mk I began to enter service in 1940, and initially scored against German opponents who failed to appreciate its novel armament disposition. As soon as the Germans knew of the Defiant's lack of forward firepower plus indifferent performance and agility, losses began to mount and the Defiant was switched to night-fighting, the Defiant NF.Mk IA having AI Mk IV radar. The 723 Defiant Mk Is were followed by 210 Defiant Mk IIs with the 939-kW (1,260-hp) Merlin XX engine, and these were later converted to night-fighters and then to target tugs. The Defiant TT.Mk I was the Mk II built (140 aircraft) as a target tug.

Specification: Boulton Paul Defiant Mk I two-seat fighter
Span: 11.99 m (39 ft 4 in)
Length: 10.77 m (35 ft 5 in)
Powerplant: 1×Rolls-Royce Merlin III, 770 kW (1,030 hp)
Armament: 4×0.303-in (7.7-mm) machine-guns
Max T/O weight: 3900 kg (8,600 lb)
Max speed: 304 mph at 17,000 ft
Operational range: 465 miles

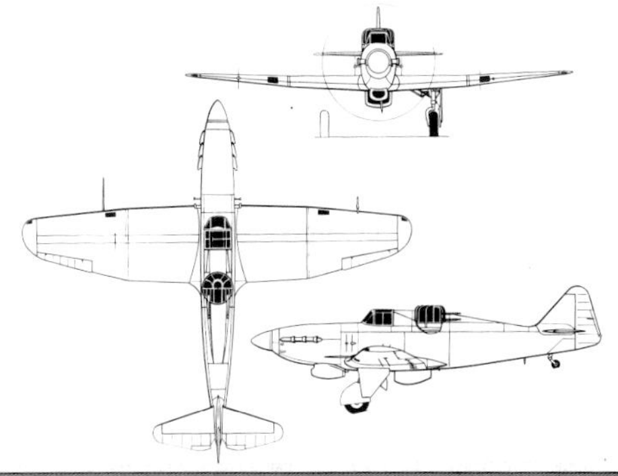

Hawker Typhoon

Specification: Hawker Typhoon Mk IB single-seat fighter and ground-attack/fighter-bomber
Span: 12.67 m (41 ft 7 in)
Length: 9.74 m (31 ft 7.5 in)
Powerplant: 1×Napier Sabre IIC, 1685 kW (2,260 hp)
Armament: 4×20-mm cannon plus provision for 2×454-kg (1,000-lb) bombs or 8×rockets under the wings
Max T/O weight: 6341 kg (13,980 lb)
Max speed: 412 mph at 19,000 ft
Operational range: 510 miles

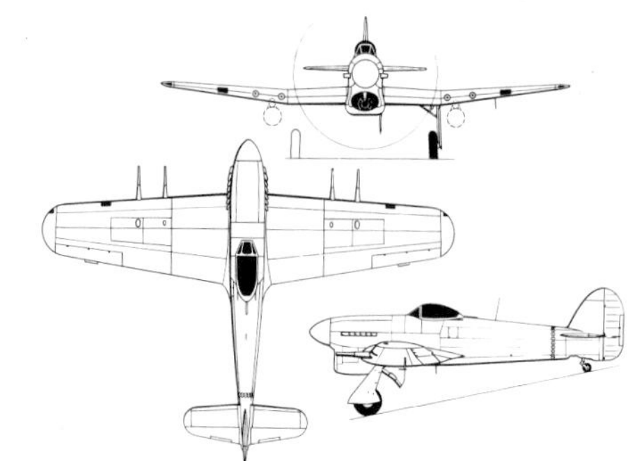

Bristol Beaufighter

One of World War II's classic twin-engined fighters, the Beaufighter was evolved from the Beaufort torpedo bomber and first flew in July 1939. The type entered service in September 1940, the first variant being the Mk IF night-fighter with radar and the Mk IC coastal version with extra radio equipment. The Mk IIF was a night-fighter with 954-kW (1,280-hp) Rolls-Royce Merlin XX inlines, and the next production model was the Mk VI with 1193-kW (1,600-hp Hercules VI radials and produced in night-fighting and coastal versions with radar and torpedo capability respectively. The Mk VI (ITF) had eight rockets in place of the wing guns, the TF.Mk X was an uprated Mk VI, the Mk XIC lacked torpedo capability and the TF.Mk 21 was the Australian-built Mk X. Production totalled 5,918.

Specification: Bristol Beaufighter TF.Mk X two- or three-seat anti-shipping attack fighter
Span: 17.63 m (57 ft 10 in)
Length: 12.70 m (41 ft 8 in)
Powerplant: 2×Bristol Hercules XVII, 1320 kW (1,770 hp)
Armament: 4×20-mm cannon and 1×0.303-in (7.7-mm) machine-gun, plus provision for 1×torpedo under the fuselage and 2×113-kg (250-lb) bombs or 8×41-kg (90-lb) rockets under the wings
Max T/O weight: 11521 kg (25,400 lb)
Max speed: 303 mph at 13,000 ft
Operational range: 1,470 miles

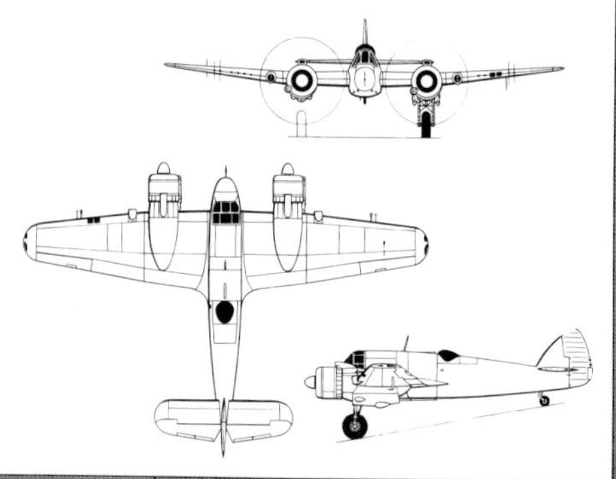

Westland Whirlwind

Designed from 1935 as a long-range fighter, the Whirlwind was schemed round the Peregrine engine that ultimately proved too troublesome to maintain in production, and this is one of the reasons for the early demise of what was for its time a promising fighter that offered its pilot a very good field of vision. The prototype first flew in October 1938 and showed good performance, and production fighters began to enter service in June 1940 after a troublesome development period. The Whirlwind's handling was good and its low-altitude performance excellent, so the type was used primarily for low-altitude intrusion during 1941 and 1942. The latter year saw the retrofitting of bomb racks onto the survivors of the 112 Whirlwinds built, making them useful fighter-bombers.

Specification: Westland Whirlwind single-seat fighter and fighter-bomber
Span: 13.72 m (45 ft 0 in)
Length: 9.90 m (32 ft 6 in)
Powerplant: 2×Rolls-Royce Peregrine I, 660 kW (885 hp) each
Armament: 4×20-mm cannon plus provision for 2×113- or 227-kg (250- or 500-lb) bombs under the wings
Max T/O weight: 5171 kg (11,400 lb)
Max speed: 360 mph at 15,000 ft
Operational range: 800 miles

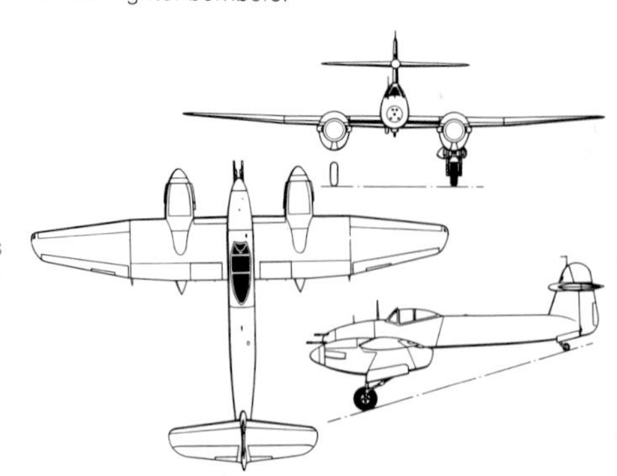

The Typhoon was schemed in 1937 as successor to the Hurricane and began life in parallel with the Tornado, which used the same airframe in combination with a Rolls-Royce Vulture engine. The Typhoon first flew in February 1940 and displayed extremely impressive performance with an armament of 12 0.303-in (7.7-mm) machine-guns. The Vulture engine was not successful and the Tornado was cancelled, while the Typhoon was ordered into production as the Mk IA with machine-gun armament and the 1566-kW (2,100-hp) Sabre I, followed by the more numerous Mk IB with four 20-mm cannon. The Typhoon was a disappointment at altitude but it proved to be an exceptional fighter-bomber specialising in anti-tank work. Production totalled 3,270 including prototype numbers of the reconnaissance FR.Mk IB and night-fighting NF.Mk IB.

This Typhoon served with 56 and 609 Squadrons before a brief career as an aerobatic aircraft. It was one of 15 planes built by Hawker, the rest were subcontracted to Gloster. This plane still has its original cockpit cover, while markings on the underside of the wings are to prevent confusion with the Bf 109 or the Fw 190. The four 20-mm guns and eight rockets made the Typhoon a successful anti-tank plane.

de Havilland Mosquito

The Mosquito was conceived as an unarmed high-speed bomber of largely wooden construction, and first flew in November 1940. By this time the type would clearly possess such phenomenal capabilities that it was developed in virtually separate streams as an unarmed bomber, an unarmed reconnaissance type, a radar-carrying night-fighter, and a potent fighter-bomber within an overall production total of 7,785 Mosquitoes. The major night-fighter variants were the NF.Mk II, NF.Mk XIII, NF.Mk XVII, NF.Mk XIX, NF.Mk 30 and post-war NF.Mk 36 with steadily improved radar and greater power. The fighter-bomber series included the FB.Mk VI, FB.Mk XVIII with a 57-mm gun in place of the four 20-mm cannon, FB.Mk 26 built in Canada, TR.Mk 37 Sea Mosquito torpedo fighter built in Canada and FB.Mk 40 post-war version built in Australia.

Specification: de Havilland Mosquito FB.Mk VI two-seat long-range fighter-bomber
Span: 16.51 m (54 ft 2 in)
Length: 12.34 m (40 ft 6 in)
Powerplant: 2×Rolls-Royce Merlin 25, 1219 kW (1,635 hp)
Armament: 4×20-mm cannon and 4×7.7-mm (0.303-in) machine-guns, plus provision for 4×113- or 227-kg (250- or 500-lb) bombs carried internally and externally and, on some aircraft, 8×27-kg (60-lb) rockets under the wings
Max T/O weight: 10096 kg (22,258 lb)
Max speed: 380 mph at 13,000 ft
Operational range: 1,885 miles

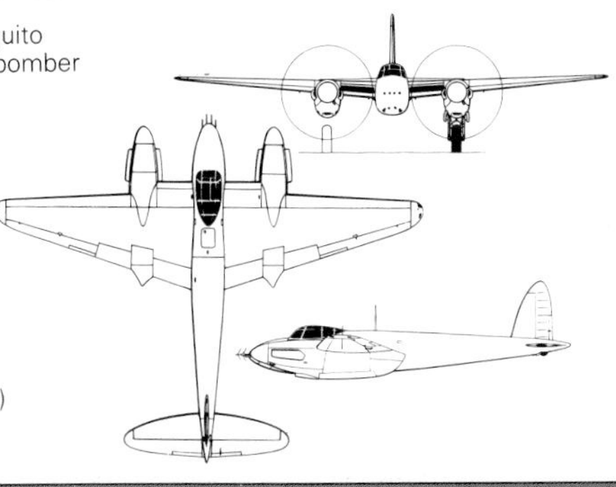

Supermarine Spitfire (Griffon-engine)

One of the features of the Spitfire was its ability to use extra power for increased performance without serious degradation of handling, and this resulted in a series with the larger and more potent Griffon engine. The first production variant was the F.Mk XII with the 1294-kW (1,735-hp) Griffon III or IV, but this was soon supplemented by the F.Mk XIV equivalent of the Mk VIII with the Griffon 65 engine, the F.Mk XVIII with additional fuel and other detail improvements including a modified wing, the F.Mk 21 with revised wing shape and the Griffon 61, the F.Mk 22 with a 360° vision canopy and the post-war F.Mk 24. Total production of the Spitfire amounted to 20,351, of which the Griffon-engined variants were in a severe minority despite their superior performance.

Specification: Supermarine Spitfire F.Mk 21 single-seat fighter and fighter-bomber
Span: 11.25 m (36 ft 11 in)
Length: 9.96 m (32 ft 8 in)
Powerplant: 1×Rolls-Royce Griffon 61, 1528 kW (2,050 hp)
Armament: 4×20-mm cannon plus provision for 1×227-kg (500-lb) and 2×113-kg (250-lb) bombs carried externally
Max T/O weight: 4173 kg (9,200 lb)
Max speed: 454 mph at 26,000 ft
Operational range: 880 miles

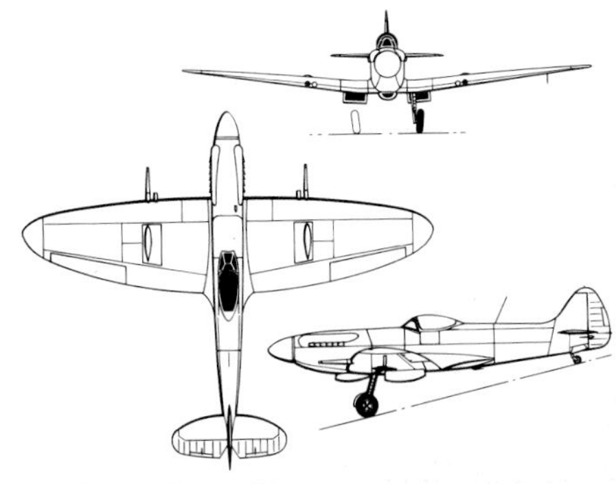

Hawker Tempest

Another great fighter from the drawing board of Sydney Camm, the Tempest was planned as an improved Typhoon with a thinner wing, 360° vision cockpit canopy and more power to provide superior all-round performance. Prototypes were ordered with Bristol Centaurus radials, Rolls-Royce Griffon inlines and Napier Sabre inlines, the first flying in September 1942. The first variant to enter service in January 1944, and the only one to see service in World War II, was the Sabre-engined Tempest F.Mk V, of which 800 were built. Then came the Tempest F.Mk II with the 1864-kW (2,500-hp) Centaurus V or VI, of which 450 were built for postwar service, and finally the Tempest F.Mk VI with the 2013-kW (2,700-hp) Sabre VA, of which 142 were built, again for post-war service. Total production was 1,418.

Specification: Hawker Tempest F.Mk V single-seat fighter and fighter-bomber
Span: 12.50 m (41 ft 0 in)
Length: 10.26 m (33 ft 8 in)
Powerplant: 1×Napier Sabre IIC, 1685 kW (2,260 hp)
Armament: 4×20-mm cannon plus provision for 2×454-kg (1,000-lb) bombs or 8×rockets under the wings
Max T/O weight: 5897 kg (13,000 lb)
Max speed: 426 mph at 18,500 ft
Operational range: 1,530 miles

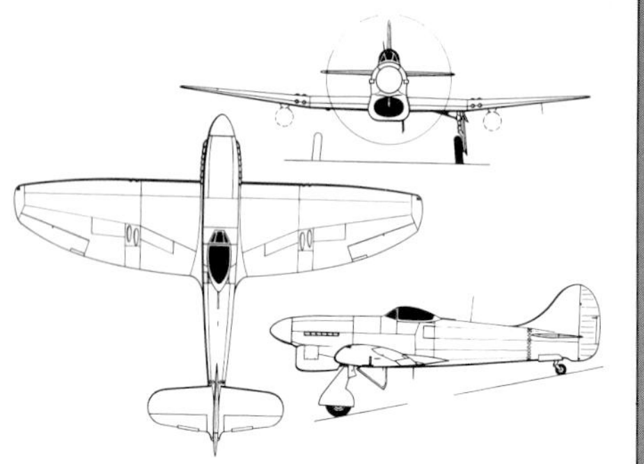

Gloster Meteor

The Meteor was the UK's first and the Allies' only jet fighter to enter operational service in World War II. The design capitalised on Gloster's experience with the UK's first jet-powered aeroplane, the E.28/39, and the first Meteor flew in March 1943. The prototypes were flown with an assortment of Halford, Metrovick and Whittle engines, but the 771-kg (1,700-lb) st Rolls-Royce Welland I was selected for the production Meteor F.Mk I. The first production Meteor was supplied to the USA in exchange for a Bell P-59 Airacomet, and only 16 of the 20 Meteor F.Mk Is entered service from July 1944, making their debut against German V-1 flying bombs launched against southern England. The improved Meteor Mk III began to enter service at the beginning of 1945, the first 15 of the 280 built being powered by Welland turbojets. Development and large-scale production continued after the war.

Specification: Gloster Meteor F.Mk III single-seat fighter
Span: 13.11 m (43 ft 0 in)
Length: 12.57 m (41 ft 3 in)
Powerplant: 2×Rolls-Royce Derwent I, 907 kg (2,000 lb) st each
Armament: 4×20-mm cannon
Max T/O weight: 6033 kg (13,300 lb)
Max speed: 493 mph at 30,000 ft
Operational range: 1,340 miles

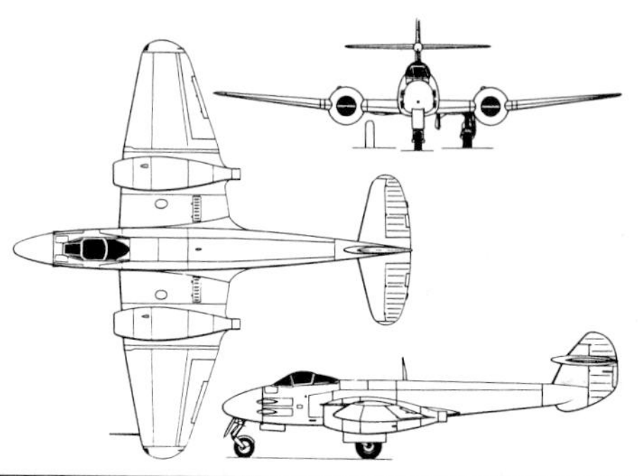

Miles M.20

The M.20 resulted from a fear that production of current fighters might not match losses in the Battle of Britain, and was designed and built in a mere 65 days for a first flight in September 1940. The design was optimized for ease of construction with fixed landing gear and no hydraulics, and wherever possible used standard parts such as the power egg of the Beaufighter Mk II and a number of items from the Miles Master advanced trainer. The primary structure was of wood with a wooden covering, and the M.20 was fitted with one of the world's first 360° vision cockpit canopies. Despite the fixed landing gear, overall performance was adequate and range excellent. The armament was standard, but with an ammunition capacity higher than those of the Hurricane and Spitfire. The Mk II was a naval version, but neither type entered production.

Specification: Miles M.20 single-seat fighter prototype
Span: 10.54 m (34 ft 7 in)
Length: 9.35 m (30 ft 8 in)
Powerplant: 1×Rolls-Royce Merlin XX, 1089 kW (1,460 hp)
Armament: 8×0.303-in (7.7-mm) machine-guns
Max T/O weight: 3629 kg (8,000 lb)
Max speed: 345 mph at 20,400 ft
Operational range: 1,200 miles

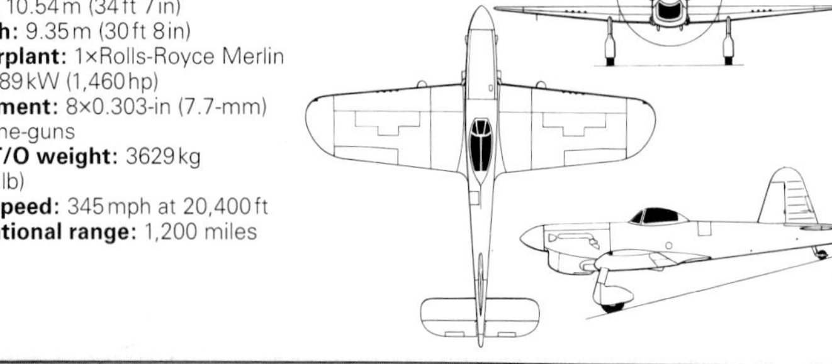

Martin-Baker M.B.3 and M.B.5

Designed to meet a 1939 specification for a fighter capable of 400 mph at 15,000 ft and possessing a service ceiling of 35,000 ft, the M.B.3 was developed for ease of construction, simplicity of maintenance and perfection of handling in the air and on the ground. Wide-track landing gear provided ground stability, a battery of six 20-mm cannon generated enormous firepower, and the 1506-kW (2,020-hp) Napier Sabre II provided a maximum speed of 415 mph at 20,000 ft. The first M.B.3 flew in August 1942, but development was abandoned in favour of the M.B.5 powered by a Griffon. The M.B.5 was conceptually a more advanced aircraft, and first flew in May 1944. The M.B.5 was a quite outstanding aeroplane and has a fair claim to being the best piston-engined fighter ever built, but was not ordered into production.

Specification: Martin-Baker M.B.5 single-seat interceptor fighter prototype
Span: 10.67 m (35 ft 0 in)
Length: 11.51 m (37 ft 9 in)
Powerplant: 1×Rolls-Royce Griffon 83, 1745 kW (2,340 hp)
Armament: 6×20-mm cannon
Max T/O weight: 5484 kg (12,090 lb)
Max speed: 460 mph at 20,000 ft
Operational range: not known

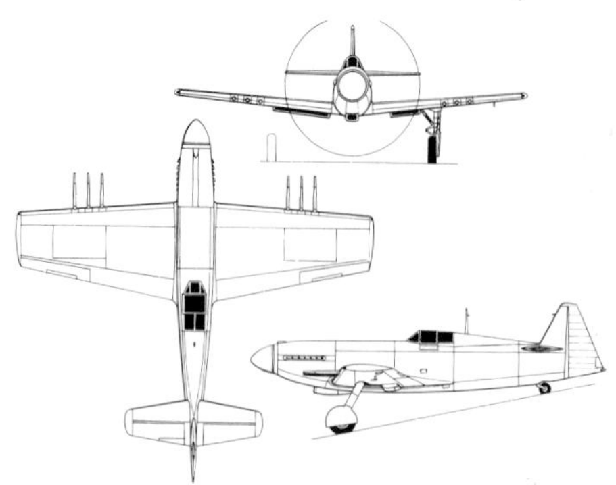

Israel Aircraft Industries **Kfir**

To replace the Mirage III IAI developed the Kfir (lion cub) retaining the same basic airframe as the Nesher but revised to accommodate the wider and more powerful J79 turbojet and fitted with a suite of advanced Israeli electronics. First displayed in 1975, the Kfir was placed in production in its initial Kfir-C1 form for two squadrons, but was soon overtaken by the Kfir-C2 with fixed canard foreplanes for enhanced agility; there is also a Kfir-TC2 two-seat variant. In 1983 the company introduced the Kfir-C7 and its Kfir-TC7 two-seat version, the latter designed for the advanced combat role rather than training. The latest versions have greater power, a revised 'hands on throttle and stick' cockpit, capability for 'smart' weapons, inflight-refuelling capability, and improved electronics. Israel currently deploys some 200 or more Kfirs in one attack and three air-defence squadrons.

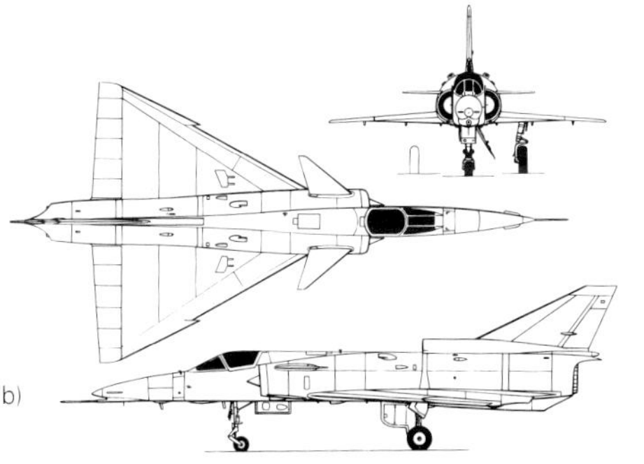

Specification: Israel Aircraft Industries Kfir-C2 single-seat interceptor and ground-attack aeroplane
Span: 8.22 m (26 ft 11.6 in)
Length: 15.65 m (51 ft 4.5 in)
Powerplant: 1×General Electric J79-J1E, 8119 kg (17,900 lb) st
Armament: 2×30-mm cannon plus provision for up to 5775 kg (12,731 lb) of disposable stores carried on 5×underfuselage and 4×underwing hardpoints
Max T/O weight: 16200 kg (35,714 lb)
Max speed: Mach 2.3 mph at 36,090 ft
Operational range: 954 miles

McDonnell Douglas **F-15 Eagle**

In the aftermath of the 1973 'Yom Kippur War' the Israeli air force thought hard about its aircraft needs, and in addition to the planned Lavi suggested the purchase of the Phantom II's US successor, the F-15 Eagle, as an air superiority and long-range strike aeroplane for two squadrons. An initial 25 aircraft were ordered in the form of 23 F-15A single- and two F-15B two-seaters. These were delivered from December 1976, but a subsequent request for 25 more Eagles was trimmed by the USA to just 15. Of these first-generation Eagles the Israeli air force has 35 F-15As and two F-15Bs, and these have seen combat service over Lebanon during 1982 and subsequently. The Middle Eastern situation remained sufficiently precarious for the USA to reconsider Israel's position, and current orders encompass 16 second-generation aircraft in the form of 11 F-15C single- and five F-15D two-seaters.

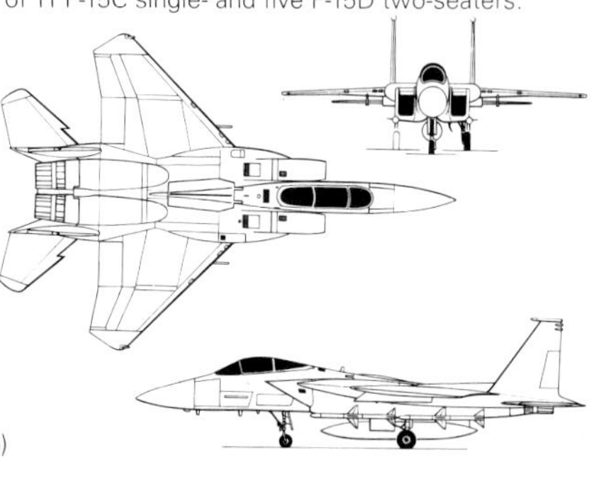

Specification: McDonnell Douglas F-15C Eagle single-seat air superiority and attack fighter
Span: 13.05 m (42 ft 9.75 in)
Length: 19.43 m (63 ft 9 in)
Powerplant: 2×Pratt & Whitney F100-P-100, 10864 kg (23,950 lb) st each
Armament: 1×20-mm rotary-barrel cannon plus provision for up to 7248 kg (16,000 lb) of disposable stores carried on 4×tangential, 3×underfuselage and 2×underwing hardpoints
Max T/O weight: 30845 kg (68,000 lb)
Max speed: Mach 2.5
Operational range: 2,878+ miles

GD F-16 Fighting Falcon

As a dogfighting and attack fighter to complement the F-15 Israel selected the F-16 Fighting Falcon for use by three and ultimately more squadrons. The Israeli order for 75 F-16A single- and F-16B two-seaters was placed in August 1978, and was accelerated by the cancellation of the Iranian order after the fall of the Shah in 1979: the first F-16s were delivered in December 1979. Like the F-15s these have been extensively used in combat, the larger dorsal fairings of these Israeli aircraft suggesting that combat experience had led to the introduction of more-extensive electronics, probably of Israeli manufacture. There are currently 63 F-16As and eight F-16Bs, plus 51 improved F-16C single- and 24 F-16D two-seaters from later orders. The F-16 is the most important Israeli warplane, and current orders for 75 aircraft include advanced types to fill the gap left by the Lavi's cancellation.

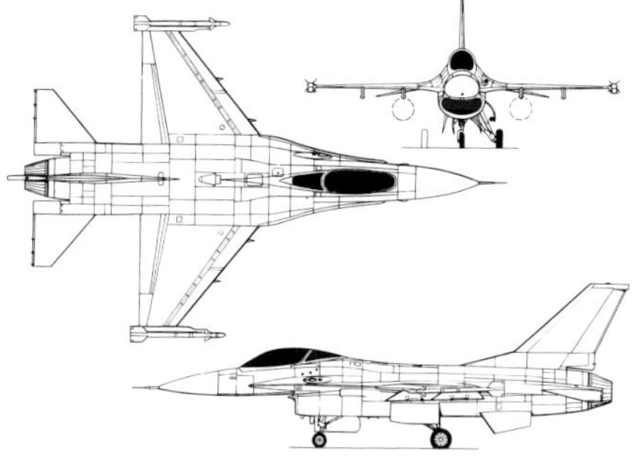

Specification: General Dynamics F-16A Fighting Falcon single-seat air combat and close support fighter
Span: 9.45 m (31 ft 0 in) excluding missiles
Length: 15.09 m (49 ft 4.9 in)
Powerplant: 1×Pratt & Whitney F100-P-200, 11340 kg (25,000 lb) st
Armament: 1×20-mm rotary-barrel cannon plus provision for up to 6893 kg (15,200 lb) of disposable stores carried on 1×underfuselage, 6×underwing and 2×wingtip hardpoints
Max T/O weight: 16057 kg (35,400 lb)
Max speed: Mach 2+ at 40,000 ft
Operational range: 1,370 miles

Israel Aircraft Industries **Lavi**

To undertake the whole gamut of air-combat tasks in replacement of most of its current warplanes Israel decided in the late 1970s to produce a highly advanced type whose indigenous production would free the country of other nations' export restrictions. The type was designated Lavi (young lion) and designed with US financial as well as technical aid, emerging in 1986 as a fascinating and potentially excellent canard design of the relaxed-stability type controlled by a fly-by-wire system and using a high proportion of composites in its structure. The Israeli electronics were of the most advanced types with full capabilities in the air-to-air and air-to-ground arenas using a wide assortment of weapons. US and Israeli fears about the financial basis of the programme finally combined, however, and in August 1987 it was announced that the programme was being cancelled in March 1988.

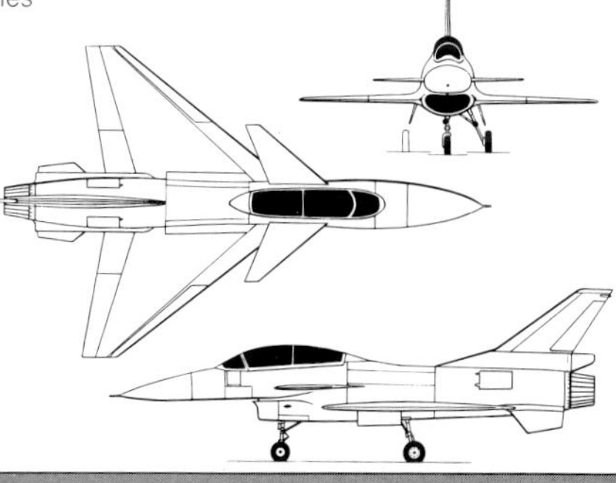

Specification: Israel Aircraft Industries Lavi single-seat multi-role fighter
Span: 8.78 m (28 ft 9.7 in)
Length: 14.57 m (47 ft 9.6 in)
Powerplant: 1×Beth Shemeth-built Pratt & Whitney PW1120, 9400 kg (20,723 lb) st
Armament: 1×30-mm cannon plus provision for up to 7250+ kg (15,983+ lb) of disposable stores carried on 3×underfuselage, 4×underwing and 2×wingtip hardpoints
Max T/O weight: 19300 kg (42,549 lb)
Max speed: Mach 1.85 mph at optimum altitude
Operational range: 2,300 miles

Avia S.199

On its creation in 1948 Israel possessed only the most rudimentary of air forces, and cast its net wide for men and materiel. One of the best sources of supply was Czechoslovakia, from which Israel bought 84 fighters in 1948-49. Some 26 of these were S.199s, Czech derivatives of the Messerschmitt Bf 109G-14 produced at the previously German-controlled factories at Catovice and Letnany. The standard airframe was combined with the only available engine, the Jumo 211F. The result was dubbed Mezec (mule) by Czech pilots for its dismal handling characteristics including tricky take-off and landing performance, sluggish acceleration, and over-sensitive controls in the air. The aircraft were dismantled for air transport to Israel from Zatec via Corsica to Ramad David air force base, and all arrived safely for re-assembly and issue to No.101 Squadron. This Operation 'Balak' lasted from May to 12 August 1948.

Specification: Avia S.199 single-seat fighter
Span: 9.92 m (32 ft 6.5 in)
Length: 9.10 m (29 ft 10.25 in)
Powerplant: 1×Junkers Jumo 211F, 1007 kW (1,350 hp)
Armament: 2×20-mm cannon and 2×13.1-mm (0.52-in) machine-guns
Max T/O weight: 3500 kg (7,716 lb)
Max speed: 366 mph at 19,685 ft
Operational range: 528 miles

Identified by the more bulbous cowling round the engine, the Avia S.199 was a hastily-created fighter matching the Bf 109G airframe to the Jumo 211 engine. The result was not a success, but in its desperation the nascent Israeli air force took 25, enough to equip one squadron. These formed Israel's only air defence during the nation's first months of existence, but soon Spitfires and other types were acquired.

Supermarine Spitfire

As part of its 84-aircraft deal with Czechoslovakia in 1946 Israel acquired 58 Spitfire LF.Mk IXE fighters from the 76 that had been allocated to the Czech air force between the end of World War II and the descent of the 'Iron Curtain' in 1948 . In Operation 'Velvetta' these were flown to Ekron air force base in Israel from Kanovica, and six aircraft were lost to forced landing before refuelling rights were obtained at Podgorica in Yugoslavia, and the total that reached Israel was thus 52. The Israelis far preferred the Spitfires to the S.199s, and rebuilt another five Mk IX machines from abandoned British or crashed Egyptian aircraft. In 1950-51 the Israeli air force received an extra 50 LF.Mk IXs from the Italian air force. Some 30 surviving aircraft were finally reconditioned and in 1954 sold to Burma as the Israeli air force began to re-equip with jet fighters.

Specification: Supermarine Spitfire LF.Mk IXE single-seat fighter and fighter-bomber
Span: 9.80 m (32 ft 2 in)
Length: 9.56 m (31 ft 4.5 in)
Powerplant: 1×Rolls-Royce Merlin 70, 1100 kW (1,475 hp)
Armament: 2×20-mm cannon and 2×12.7-mm (0.5-in) machine-guns plus provision for 1×227-kg (500-lb) bomb carried under the fuselage and 2×113-kg (250-lb) bombs carried under the wings
Max T/O weight: 3629 kg (8,000 lb)
Max speed: 404 mph at 21,000 ft
Operational range: 434 miles

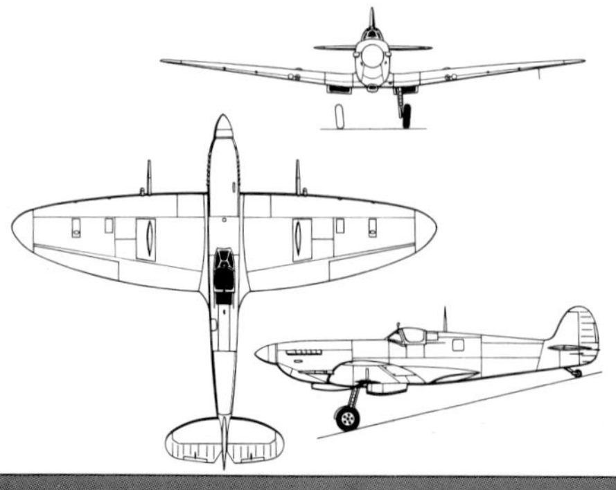

North American P-51D Mustang

By the early 1950s the Israeli air force was avid to re-equip its fighter arm with jet aircraft, but found both funding and sources of supply difficult. Initial plans were made to acquire British and French types, but as an interim measure it was decided to bolster the current strength of the Spitfire-equipped fighter arm with 25 P-51D Mustangs bought from the Swedish air force. The Mustang did not long remain in service, but was the primary fighter of the Israeli air force at the time that the latter was being 'professionalised' as Israel's first line of defence. It is of great historical importance to note that it was with the Mustang and de Havilland Mosquito that the 'new' Israeli air arm developed its primary concept of using multi-role fighters in the interception and ground-attack roles to maximise the tactical capabilities of its limited aircraft strength.

Specification: North American P-51D Mustang single-seat fighter and fighter-bomber
Span: 11.28 m (37 ft 0.25 in)
Length: 9.83 m (32 ft 3 in)
Powerplant: 1×Packard V-1650-7 Merlin, 1264 kW (1,695 hp)
Armament: 6×12.7-mm (0.5-in) machine-guns plus provision for 2×454-kg (1,000-lb) bombs or 6×127-mm (5-in) rockets carried under the wings
Max T/O weight: 5488 kg (12,100 lb)
Max speed: 437 mph at 25,000 ft
Operational range: 2,080 miles

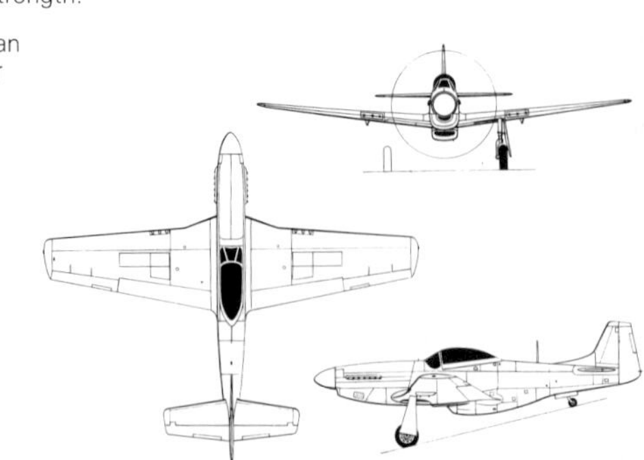

Dassault M.D.450 Ouragan

Israel's first jet fighter was the Gloster Meteor, and to supplement this essentially interim type Israel late in 1955 ordered 24 Dassault Mystère IICs and 24 Canadair CL-13B Sabre Mk 6s. The Canadian government was afraid of exacerbating the tense Middle Eastern situation and cancelled the Sabre order. Israel decided instead to take the Mystère IVA, but was faced with the problem of finding a stopgap until this more advanced type was ready: the type selected was another Dassault design, the Ouragan (hurricane), of which enough were ordered to equip five ground-attack squadrons. Some 24 were new aircraft from Dassault but at least another 42 were diverted from French air force stocks, and it is thought that at least 75 Ouragans were acquired. All were delivered with great speed in 1955, and the type played an important part in the 1956 and 1967 wars against the Arabs.

Specification: Dassault M.D.450 Ouragan single-seat fighter and fighter-bomber
Span: 12.29 m (40 ft 3.75 in) without tiptanks
Length: 10.74 m (35 ft 2.75 in)
Powerplant: 1×Hispano Suiza-built Rolls-Royce Nene Mk 104B, 2270 kg (5,004 lb) st
Armament: 4×20-mm cannon plus provision for 2×454-kg (1,000-lb) bombs or 16×105-mm (4.13-in) rockets carried under the wings
Max T/O weight: 7900 kg (17,416 lb)
Max speed: 584 mph at sea level
Operational range: 560 miles

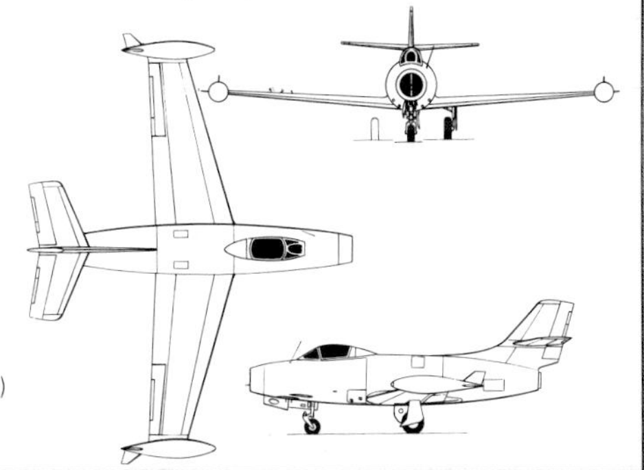

Dassault M.D.452 Mystère IVA

With the collapse of its Mystère IIC/Sabre Mk 6 procurement plan in 1955 the Israeli air force opted for a larger number of the considerably improved Mystère IVA with more highly swept flying surfaces of thinner section, a longer and finer fuselage, and more power. The Israelis' initial order covered 45 of these aircraft, but it is thought that 60 or perhaps slightly more aircraft were delivered from 1956 for the equipment of three squadrons. These operated mainly in the interceptor role at the beginning of their careers, but were gradually shifted to the close support task as more modern aircraft (including 24 Super Mystère B-2s) became available in the pure fighter role. Eight Mystère IVAs were lost in the 1967 Arab-Israeli war, and 27 survivors fought in the 1973 war before retirement in the 1970s.

Specification: Dassault M.D.452 Mystere IVA fighter and fighter-bomber
Span: 11.12 m (36 ft 5.75 in)
Length: 12.85 m (42 ft 2 in)
Powerplant: 1×Hispano-Suiza Verdon 350, 3500 kg (7,716 lb) st
Armament: 2×30-mm cannon plus provision for up to 907 kg (2,000 lb) of disposable stores carried on 4×underwing hardpoints
Max T/O weight: 9500 kg (20,950 lb)
Max speed: 696 mph at sea level
Operational range: 820 miles

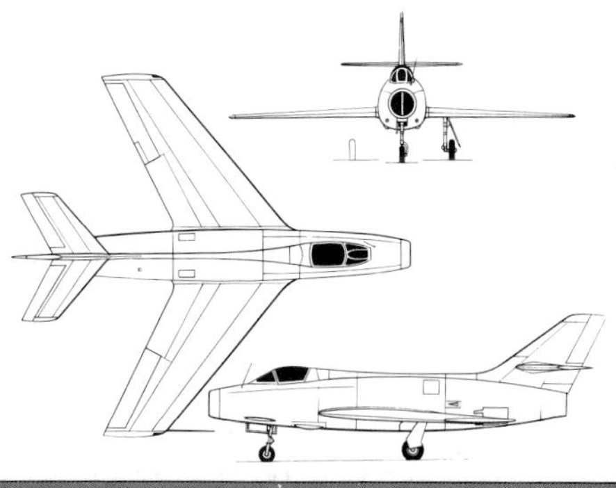

Sud-Ouest S.O.4050 Vautour

The big Vautour was selected in 1956 as the Israeli air force's successor to the de Havilland Mosquito in the long-range attack role as it provided a counter to the Arabs' Ilyushin Il-28 light jet bombers. The version chosen was the Vautour II-A, an attack model closely similar to the more numerous Vautour II-N two-seat all-weather night and attack fighter apart from its single-seat accommodation. Some 300 of the variant had been ordered for the French air force, but ultimately a mere 30 were built, and 19 of these were exported to Israel from 1960. Israel also received 5 Vautour II-Ns in 1960, these were equipped with nose radar for the night fighter role. The Vautours were particularly important in the pre-emptive attack with which Israel launched the 1967 war, striking at airfields as far apart as Iraq and at Luxor in Upper Egypt.

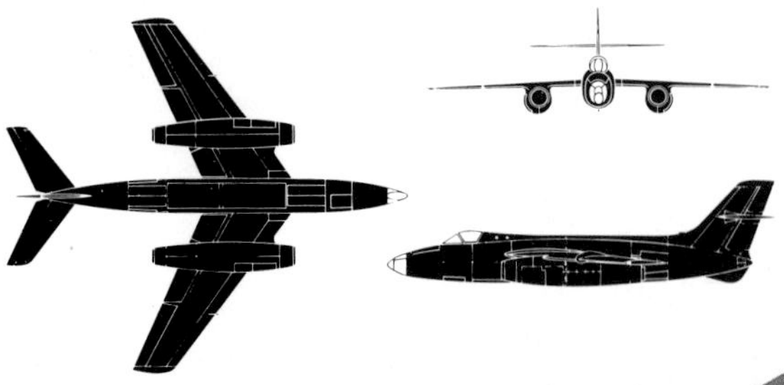

Specification: Société Nationale des Constructions Aéronautiques du Sud-Ouest S.O.4050 Vautour II-A single-seat tactical fighter
Span: 15.09 m (46 ft 9.5 in)
Length: 15.57 m (51 ft 1 in)
Powerplant: 2×SNECMA Atar 1201E-3, 3500 kg (7,716 lb) each
Armament: 4×30-mm cannon plus provision for up to 10×bombs or 240×rockets carried internally and 2×450-kg (992-lb) bombs or 76×rockets carried under the wings
Max T/O weight: 20000 kg (44,092 lb)
Max speed: 687 mph at sea level
Operational range: 2,485 miles

Dassault Mirage III

To provide a definitive solution to its need for a supersonic interceptor, filled in the short term by the Super Mystère B-2, Israel maintained its now well established French connection in ordering the Mirage III, a delta-winged interceptor with Mach 2 performance and, just as importantly so far as the Israelis were concerned, a powerful ground-attack facility. Orders covered 72 examples of the Mirage IIICJ interceptor and five examples of the Mirage IIIBj tandem two-seat conversion and continuation trainer. These aircraft were delivered in the mid-1960s as the equipment of three squadrons, and were decisive in the 1967 war: they spearheaded the pre-emptive strike against the Arab air forces' airfields with 'dibber' and conventional bombs, and then completely overwhelmed the few Arab aircraft that survived to take to the air in the 'Six-Day War'.

Specification: Dassault Mirage IIICJ single-seat interceptor and ground-attack fighter
Span: 8.22 m (26 ft 11.6 in)
Length: 14.75 m (48 ft 5 in)
Powerplant: 1×SNECMA Atar 9C, 6000 kg (13,228 lb) st
Armament: 2×30-mm cannon plus provision for up to 2268 kg (5,000 lb) of disposable stores carried on 1×underfuselage and 4×underwing hardpoints
Max T/O weight: 12700 kg (27,998 lb)
Max speed: Mach 2+ at 36,090 ft
Operational range: 1,492 miles

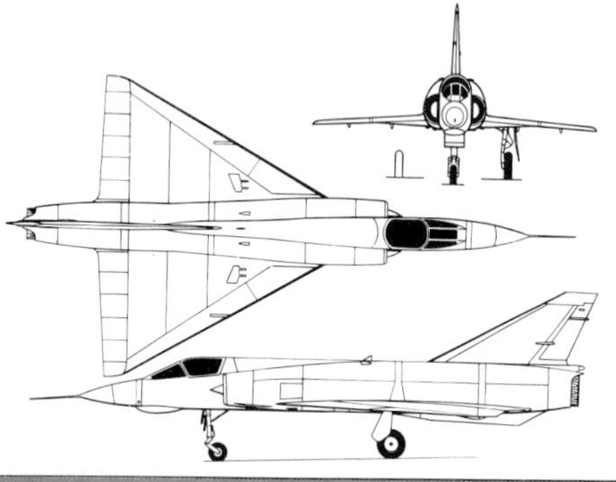

Israel Aircraft Industries Nesher

Israel decided that the Mirage III's electronics were too sophisticated for the clear weather conditions of the Middle East, and therefore asked Dassault to develop a radarless, and thus cheaper, version. This emerged as the Mirage 5, of which Israel ordered 50 with the designation Mirage 5J. France embargoed the delivery of the aircraft after the 1968 'Six-Day War', but Israel had foreseen such an eventuality and had started the design of a more sophisticated adaptation of the Mirage IIIC for the interception and ground-attack roles. In the short term, however, Israel's air force required replacements for aircraft lost in the 1967 war and IAI responded with the rapid design of a Mirage 5 type as the Nesher (eagle) based on the reverse-engineered airframe of the Mirage IIICJ and design details secured by espionage. About 60 were built, some later being exported as Daggers.

Specification: Israel Aircraft Industries Nesher single-seat fighter and ground-attack aeroplane
Span: 8.22 m (26 ft 11.6 in)
Length: 14.75 m (48 ft 5 in)
Powerplant: 1×SNECMA Atar 9C, 6000 kg (13,228 lb) st
Armament: 2×30-mm cannon plus provision for up to 4000 kg (8,814 lb) of disposable stores carried on 1×underfuselage and 6×underwing hardpoints
Max T/O weight: 13700 kg (30,200 lb)
Max speed: Mach 2.2 at 36,090 ft
Operational range: 1,608 miles with a 2000-kg (4,409-lb) warload

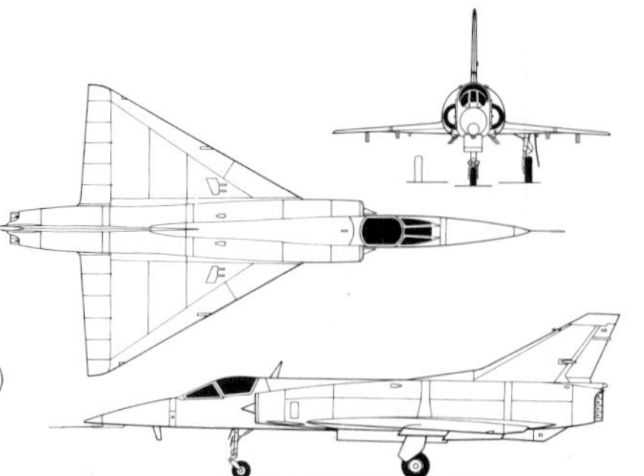

The single-seat Vautour IIA was procured by Israel for long-range attack duties. Later Vautour IIN (illustrated) night fighters were purchased, these having intercept radar in the nose and a second seat for the radar operator. Many survived in secondary roles such as ECM long enough to receive this modern gaudy camouflage.

McDonnell Douglas **A-4 Skyhawk II**

Apart from the USA, Israel has been the world's largest operator of the A-4 attack aeroplane. The type was ordered in the aftermath of the 1967 'Six-Day War' that revealed the need for a dedicated close support aeroplane, and deliveries of at least 258 single- and two-seat Skyhawks included 90 A-4H single- and 10 TA-4H two-seaters together with 117 A-4N single-seaters ordered by Israel, plus a minimum of 28 A-4E and 13 A-4M single-seaters delivered as emergency attrition replacements during the 1973 'Yom Kippur War'. In this latter war the Skyhawks were a decisive weapon in the Sinai and Golan campaigns, and since that time have been extensively refurbished and indeed improved with Israeli electronics and lengthened jetpipes to reduce the efficiency of the heat-seeking missiles used by Arab ground forces. Current strength is thought to be 40+ A/TA-4H and 70+ A-4N aircraft in three squadrons.

Specification: McDonnell Douglas A-4N Skyhawk II single-seat attack aeroplane
Span: 8.38 m (27 ft 6 in)
Length: 12.29 m (40 ft 3.75 in) excluding probe
Powerplant: 1×Pratt & Whitney J52-P-408A, 5443 kg (11,200 lb) st
Armament: 2×30-mm cannon plus provision for up to 4153 kg (9,155 lb) of disposable stores carried on 1×underfuselage and 4×underweing hardpoints
Max T/O weight: 11113 kg (24,500 lb)
Max speed: 670 mph at sea level
Operational range: 2,000 miles

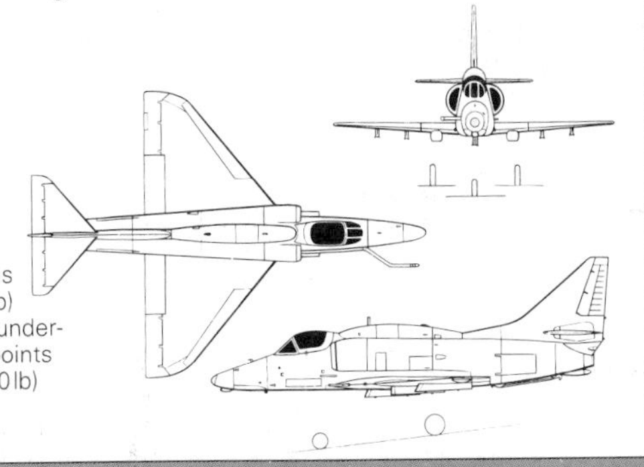

McDonnell Douglas **F-4 Phantom II**

The 1967 'Six-Day War' revealed to the Israeli air force the need for a new fighter, and the type selected was almost inevitably the great Phantom II in its F-4E multi-role and RF-4E reconnaissance versions. An initial order for 44 F-4Es and six RF-4Es was placed, these being delivered from September 1969. Deliveries then totalled at least 144 F-4Es and 12 RF-4Es, including a minimum of 58 ex-US Air Force F-4Es transferred as attrition replacements during the 1973 'Yom Kippur War'. Current Israeli strength is 113 F-4Es and 15 RF-4Es in five squadrons, and all of these are to be upgraded or even remanufactured to the more potent Super Phantom (or Phantom 2000) standard in an IAI programme with completely revised electrics, a new electronic suite including radar and advanced cockpit displays, structural strengthening and other operational enhancements.

Specification: McDonnell Douglas F-4E Phantom II two-seat multi-role fighter
Span: 11.77 m (38 ft 7.5 in)
Length: 19.20 m (63 ft 0 in)
Powerplant: 2×General Electric J79-GE-17A, 8119 kg (17,900 lb) st each
Armament: 1×20-mm rotary-barrel cannon plus provision for up to 7257 kg (16,000 lb) of disposable stores carried on 4×underfuselage weapon stations and 1×underfuselage and 4×underwing hardpoints
Max T/O weight: 28030 kg (61,795 lb)
Max speed: Mach 2.17 at 36,000 ft
Operational range: 1,424 miles

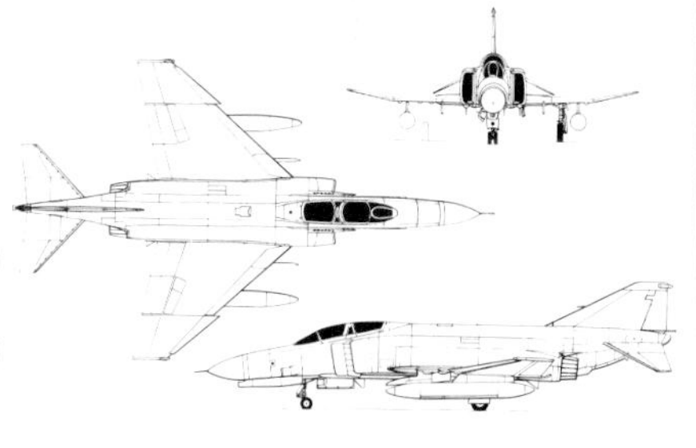

GD F-16 Fighting Falcon

Winner of a competition (against the YF-17) for a highly manoeuvrable lightweight fighter in January 1975, the F-16 became the subject of very large production and licence contracts, the USAF alone ordering 1,985 aircraft. Other F-16 purchasers include Belgium (160), Denmark (58), Egypt (80), Israel (150), South Korea (36), the Netherlands (213), Norway (72), Pakistan (40), and Venezuela (24) – these figures including two-seat trainers. Advanced equipment includes inertial and TACAN navigators, pulse-Doppler range and angle track radar, central air data and fire-control computers. The flying control system includes flight control computer, fly-by-wire system and automatic leading- and trailing-edge flaps.

Convair F-102 Delta Dagger

Third member of the century-series of American supersonic interceptors, the F-102 delta-wing all-weather fighter first flew as the YF-102 prototype on 24 October 1953 – itself a development of the earlier XF-92A research aircraft. The production F-102A made considerable use of large structural forgings to achieve great strength in its very thin delta wing; other advanced features included honeycomb-bonded elevons, area-ruled fuselage, and Falcon AAMs and their associated fire-control system. With the arrival of more advanced interceptors, F-102s re-equipped Air National Guard squadrons and served until replaced in the 1960s by the F-106. Production totalled 889 aircraft.

Specification: Convair F-102A Delta Dagger single-seat all-weather interceptor
Span: 11.62 m (38 ft 1.5 in)
Length: 20.84 m (68 ft 4.5 in)
Powerplant: 1×Pratt & Whitney J57-P-35, 7711 kg (17,000 lb) st
Armament: 6×GAR-1D (AIM-4) Falcon AAMs and 70-mm (2.75-in) unguided rockets
Max speed: Mach 1.25 at altitude
Operational range: 1,350 miles

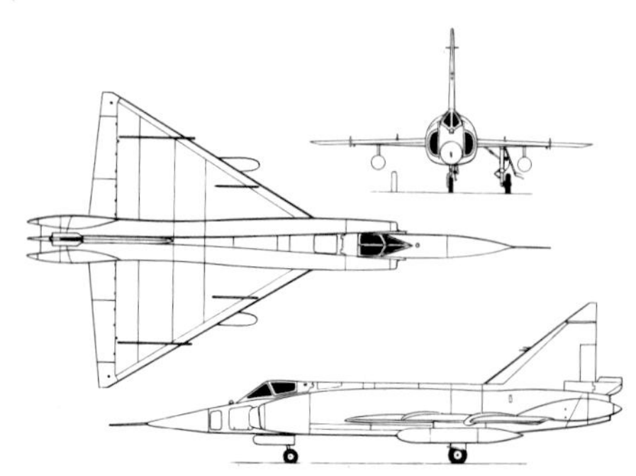

Convair F-106 Delta Dart

Following service-entry delays with the F-102A, the USAF began examination of a developed version (initially termed the F-102B) to meet its ultimate interceptor requirement. This became the J75-powered F-106 Delta Dart, a Mach 2.3 fighter intended to carry a single Douglas AIR-2A Genie or AIR-2B Super Genie nuclear rocket and four Hughes AIM-4F/G Falcon AAMs. Problems with the Hughes MA-1 fire-control system almost resulted in cancellation of the project, but in the event 277 F-106A single-seaters and 63 two-seat combat trainers were built before production ran out in 1960. By dint of updating programmes the F-106 remained an effective interceptor, surviving on ANG squadrons until the late 1980s.

Specification: Convair F-106A Delta Dart single-seat all-weather interceptor
Span: 11.67 m (38 ft 3.5 in)
Length: 21.56 m (70 ft 8.5 in)
Powerplant: 1×Pratt & Whitney J75-P-17, 11113 kg (24,500 lb) st
Armament: 1×20-mm cannon or AIR-2 Genie nuclear-tipped rocket and 4×AIM-4 AAMs
Max speed: Mach 2.3 at 36,000 ft
Operational range: 1,533 miles

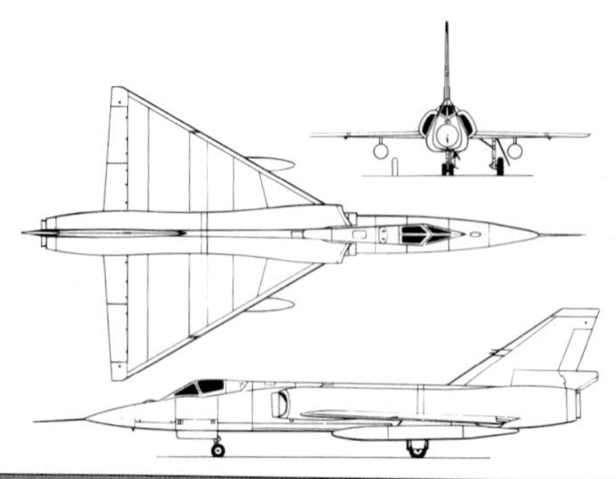

Specification: General Dynamics F-16C Fighting Falcon air-combat and multi-role fighter
Span: 9.45 m (31 ft 0 in)
Length: 15.09 m (49 ft 6 in)
Powerplant: 1×Pratt & Whitney F100-P-200, 10814 kg (23,840 lb) st
Armament: 1×20-mm rotary barrel cannon, 2×AIM-9 Sidewinder AAMs and up to 9276 kg (20,450 lb) of disposable stores
Max speed: Mach 2.1+ at altitude
Operational range: 1,260 miles

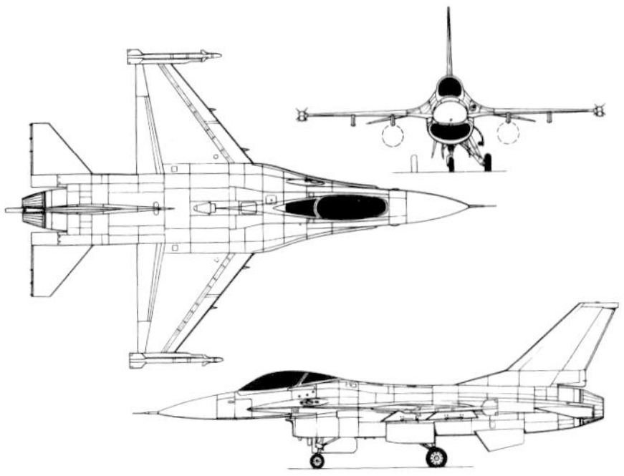

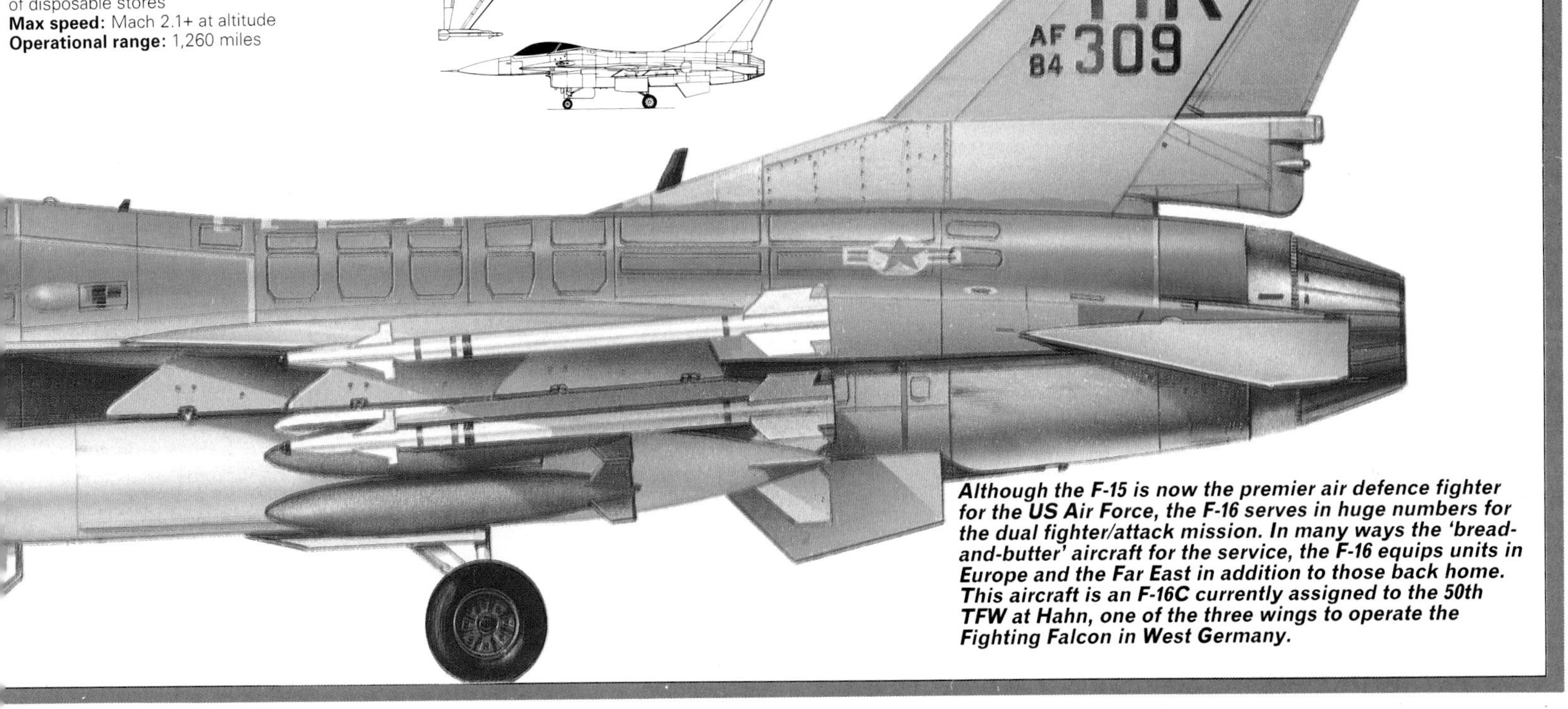

Although the F-15 is now the premier air defence fighter for the US Air Force, the F-16 serves in huge numbers for the dual fighter/attack mission. In many ways the 'bread-and-butter' aircraft for the service, the F-16 equips units in Europe and the Far East in addition to those back home. This aircraft is an F-16C currently assigned to the 50th TFW at Hahn, one of the three wings to operate the Fighting Falcon in West Germany.

Lockheed YF-12A

The designation YF-12A covered three interceptor fighter test-bed aircraft first flown on 7 August 1963 and developed alongside the largely CIA-funded A-12 strategic reconnaissance platform. With two special-fuelled turbo-ramjets, the two-seat YF-12A possessed a maximum cruise speed of Mach 3.35 at high altitude (limited by kinetic heating) and featured long-range Hughes ASG-18 pulse-Doppler fire control radar in the nose and up to eight advanced AAMs; an infrared sensor/tracker system was also included. The first YF-12A, together with two others, pursued a test programme until November 1979, and remains one of the most advanced interceptors ever developed.

Specification: Lockheed YF-12A two-seat interceptor
Span: 16.94 m (55 ft 7 in)
Length: 30.98 m (101 ft 8 in)
Powerplant: 2×Pratt & Whitney J58 (JT11D-20B), 14755 kg (32,500 lb) st each
Armament: 8×Hughes GAR-9 (AIM-47A) AAMs carried internally
Max speed: Mach 3.35 at altitude
Operational range: 2,500 miles

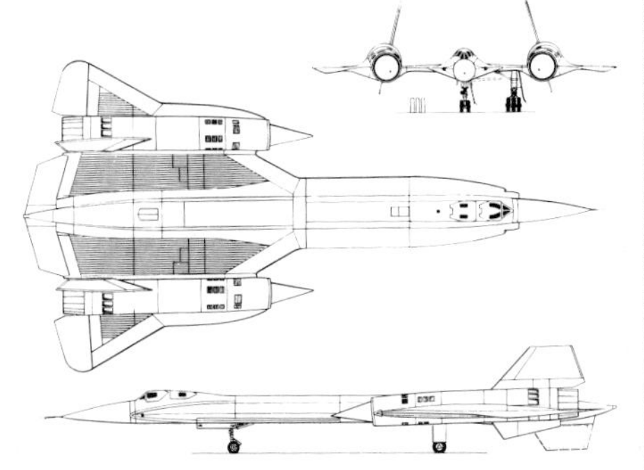

Lockheed F-104 Starfighter

First flown in prototype form as the XF-104 on 28 February 1954, the Starfighter was one of the world's first genuine Mach 2 fighters but failed to achieve widespread service with American air forces, several squadrons being equipped with F-104As, Bs, Cs and Ds at the end of the decade. It did, however, enter licence production in Europe as the F-104G, a total of 947 being built by consortiums in West Germany, the Netherlands, Belgium and Italy; it was also built in Canada as the CF-104 and in Japan as the F-104J. Characterised by very short, thin, unswept wings, the Starfighter features a multi-purpose NASARR radar system, bombing computer, air data computer and fully-automatic inertial navigation system.

Specification: Lockheed F-104G Starfighter single-seat multi-role fighter
Span: 6.68 m (21 ft 11 in)
Length: 16.69 m (54 ft 9 in)
Powerplant: 1×General Electric J79-GE-11A, 7167 kg (15,800 lb) st
Armament: 1×20-mm rotary barrel cannon, 2×AIM-9 Sidewinder AAMs and up to 1955 kg (4,310 lb) of disposable stores
Max speed: Mach 2.2 at altitude
Operational range: 1,520 miles

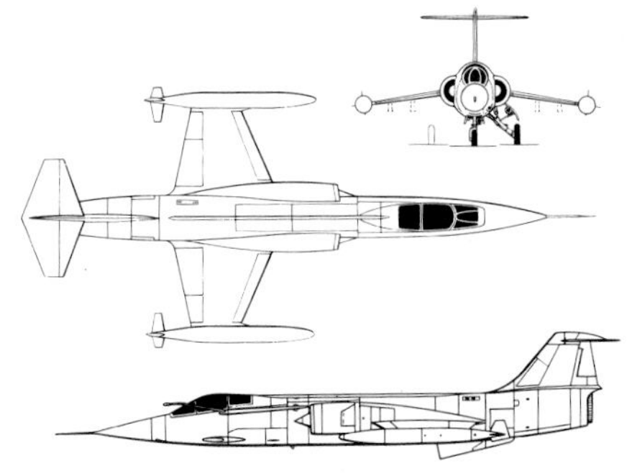

McDonnell F-4 Phantom II

A total of 5,057 F-4 Phantom IIs had been built when production of this, one of the finest all-round aircraft ever designed, ended in 1979. First developed as a carrier fighter for the US Navy, the XF4H-1 was flown in May 1958. The naval F-4A and B (fighter and strike fighter) aircraft were followed by the F-4C, D and E for the USAF, the last-named introducing more powerful engines, smaller APQ-120 radar, manoeuvring wing slats and 20-mm multi-barrel cannon. F-4s of the USAF, USN and USMC were heavily committed with distinction throughout the Vietnam war. Licence production and export of F-4s was undertaken to numerous nations, early British aircraft (F-4K and M) being powered by Rolls-Royce Speys.

McDonnell F-101 Voodoo

Resulting from a 1946 USAF demand for a long-range escort fighter (which produced the McDonnell XF-88 in 1947), the F-101 was designed as an escort fighter for SAC's B-36 intercontinental bomber. SAC participation was withdrawn before the F-101's first flight in September 1954, and the F-101A entered service as a long-range fighter with limited nuclear strike ability with TAC early in 1957, but its front-line service was shortlived, the subsequent RF-101B/C reconnaissance versions being the long-life variants. A strengthened fighter version, with nuclear LABS delivery system, was the F-101C, but only 47 were produced for TAC. The last surviving Canadian CF-101s were retired late in 1984.

Specification: McDonnell F-101B Voodoo two-seat all-weather long-range interceptor
Span: 12.09 m (39 ft 8 in)
Length: 20.54 m (67 ft 4.5 in)
Powerplant: 2×Pratt & Whitney J57-P-55, 6749 kg (14,880 lb) st each
Armament: 2×GAR-2 Genie nuclear-tipped rockets and 4×AIM-4 Falcon AAMs, or 6×AIM-4 AAMs
Max speed: Mach 1.85 at altitude
Operational range: 1,550 miles

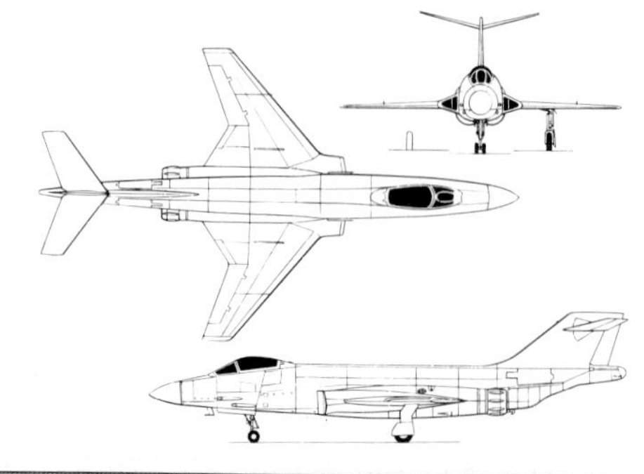

McDonnell F-15 Eagle

First flown in 1972, the F-15 multi-role fighter established itself as one of the best aircraft in its class in the world, with outstanding performance, manoeuvrability and load-carrying ability. The F-15A and B single- and two-seat aircraft (respectively) were superseded by the improved F-15C and D in the early 1980s, introducing FAST packs for additional fuel, avionics and cameras. Currently entering USAF service (with orders for 392 aircraft) is the strengthened F-15E long-range adverse-weather dual-role fighter, employing new high resolution APG-70 radar plus FLIR and LANTIRN pods. F-15s have entered service with Israeli, Saudi and Japanese air forces, and a STOL version is under development.

Specification: McDonnell Douglas F-15E Eagle two-seat dual-role fighter
Span: 13.05 m (42 ft 9.5 in)
Length: 19.43 m (63 ft 9 in)
Powerplant: 2×General Electric F110, 12701 kg (28,000 lb) st each
Armament: 1×20-mm six-barrel rotary cannon and up to 10660 kg (23,500 lb) of disposable stores
Max speed: Mach 2.54 at altitude
Ferry range: 3,570 miles

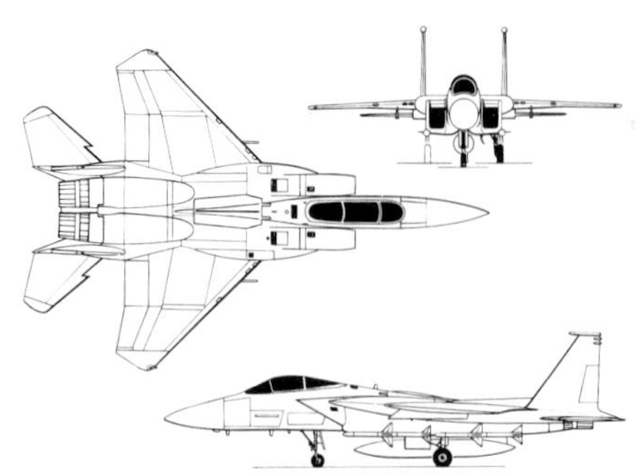

Specification: McDonnell Douglas F-4E Phantom II two-seat multi-role fighter
Span: 11.79 m (38 ft 5 in)
Length: 19.20 m (63 ft 0 in)
Powerplant: 2×General Electric J79-GE-17, 8119 kg (17,900 lb) st each
Armament: 1×20-mm cannon and up to 7258 kg (16,000 lb) of disposable stores
Max speed: Mach 2.17 at altitude
Operational range: 1,410 miles

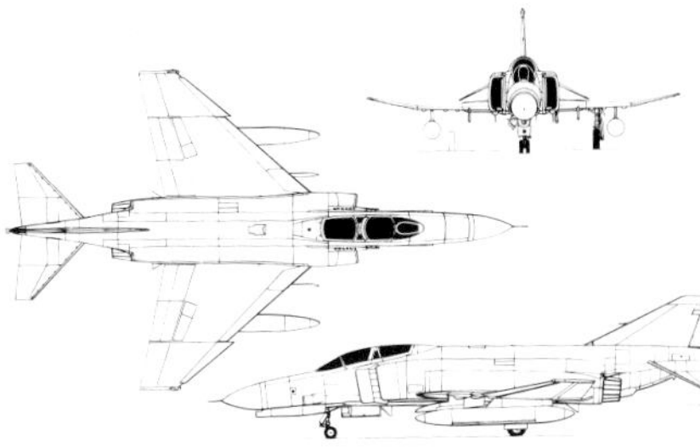

One of the world's most successful warplane designs, the Phantom held the position of the USAF's most important fighter through the late 1960s and 1970s. The war in South East Asia saw it involved in air-to-air and air-to-ground fighting, excelling at both. This F-4E served with the 388th TFW at Korat in Thailand.

NA F-100 Super Sabre

The world's first operational supersonic fighter, the F-100 derived from the basic F-86 transonic interceptor and featured 45° swept wing, being first flown in April 1953. Early F-100As suffered inertia roll-yaw coupling, this fault being overcome by extending the fin and wing tips in the F-100C fighter-bomber which featured eight wing hardpoints for external stores. The F-100D, with nuclear capability, introduced LABS and provision for ECM systems, served extensively in Vietnam performing attack, FAC and EW roles; it afterwards equipped US ANG units until 1980. A total of 1,274 F-100Ds was produced, and versions also served with the air forces of Denmark, France, Taiwan and Turkey.

Specification: North American F-100D Super Sabre single-seat attack fighter
Span: 11.82 m (38 ft 9.5 in)
Length: 14.36 m (47 ft 1.5 in)
Powerplant: 1×Pratt & Whitney J57-P-21A, 7711 kg (17,000 lb) st
Armament: 4×20-mm cannon and up to 3402 kg (7,000 lb) of disposable stores
Max speed: Mach 1.31 at 35,000 ft
Operational range: 600 miles

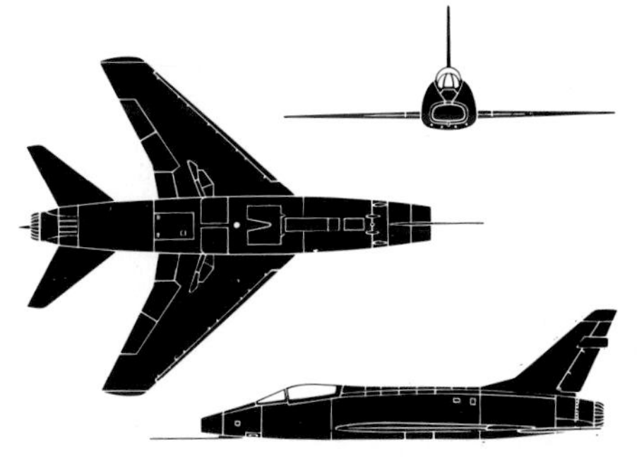

North American YF-107A

Initially designated the F-100B, this advanced fighter-bomber development of the Super Sabre was powered by a single afterburning Pratt & Whitney turbojet with bifurcated variable-wedge dorsal intake immediately aft of the cockpit. Three prototypes were produced, the first being flown on 10 September 1956, the aircraft featuring spoiler ailerons and a single-piece all-moving fin (later adopted in the A3J Vigilante attack bomber). Four 20-mm cannon were located in the lower sides of the nose and a central store – either bomb or fuel tank – was carried, semi-recessed under the fuselage. Although the prototypes frequently exceeded Mach 2 the whole project was cancelled in 1957 in favour of the F-105.

Specification: North American YF-107A single-seat fighter-bomber
Span: 11.15 m (36 ft 7 in)
Length: 18.54 m (60 ft 10 in)
Powerplant: 1×Pratt & Whitney J75-P-9, 11113 kg (24,500 lb) st
Armament: 4×20-mm cannon and 5443 kg (12,000 lb) of disposable stores
Max speed: Mach 2.25 at altitude
Operational range: not revealed

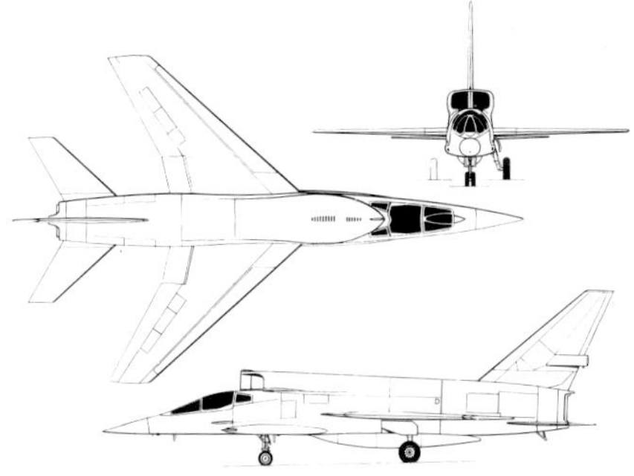

Northrop F-5 and Tiger II

More than 2,000 F-5s were still flying in January 1987 when production (for more than 30 world air forces) ended. A single-seat derivative of the T-38 Talon trainer, the original N-156C flew in July 1959, this being developed into the F-5A and B Freedom Fighter lightweight, inexpensive supersonic fighters for export to US allies. Currently in widespread service are the F-5E and F Tiger II with auto-manoeuvring leading- and trailing-edge flaps. Latest equipment in USAF examples, employed as 'aggressors' to simulate Soviet fighters, includes APQ-159 multi-mode radar with off-boresight target acquisition and track-while-scan. Licence production has been undertaken in Spain (CASA) and Canada (Canadair).

Specification: Northrop F-5E Tiger II single-seat lightweight fighter
Span: 8.13 m (26 ft 8 in)
Length: 14.45 m (47 ft 4.5 in)
Powerplant: 2×General Electric J85-GE-11B, 2268 kg (5,000 lb) st each
Armament: 2×20-mm cannon; 2×AIM-9 AAMs and up to 3175 kg (7,000 lb) of disposable stores
Max speed: Mach 1.64 at 36,000 ft
Operational range: 1,543 miles

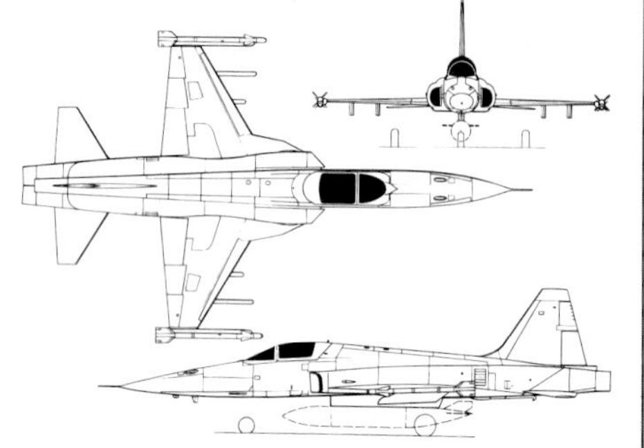

Northrop YF-17 Cobra

Produced as a private venture as the Northrop P-600, the Cobra was tendered to the USAF's competition for a lightweight fighter in 1974, but in the following year was defeated by the General Dynamics YF-16 Fighting Falcon. The YF-17As had been flown in June and August 1974 and, following the USAF's competition, they underwent prolonged evaluation by the US Navy, which had previously issued a requirement for a combat/strike fighter. In due course the Cobra was selected for development by McDonnell Douglas and Northrop as the F/A-18 Hornet. It was of unusual appearance featuring twin outward-canted vertical tail surfaces and wing-root leading-edge extensions extending along the sides of the nose.

Specification: Northrop YF-17A Cobra single-seat lightweight fighter
Span: 10.67 m (35 ft 0 in)
Length: 15.85 m (52 ft 0 in)
Powerplant: 2×General Electric YJ101, 6804 kg (15,000 lb) st each
Armament: 2×20-mm cannon and 2×AIM-9 Sidewinder AAMs
Max speed: Mach 2.1 at altitude
Operational range: not revealed

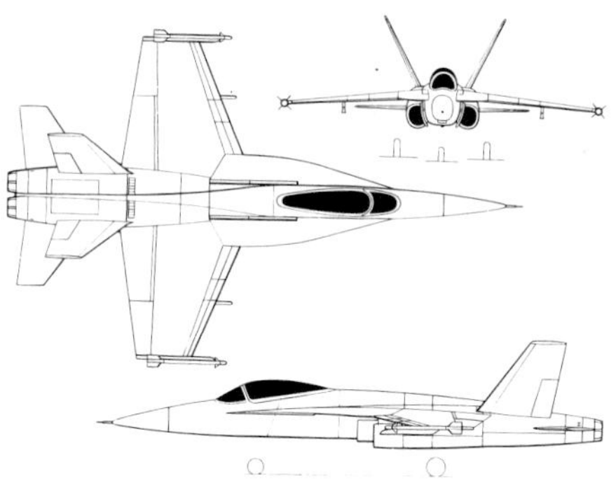

Northrop F-20 Tigershark

Victim of two prototype losses in the early 1980s, the F-20 was a single-engine derivative of the F-5E Tiger fighter and fully met all design promises but failed to attract customers. With 80 per cent more thrust than the F-5E, the F-20 possesses a genuine Mach 2 performance and features a wide range of modern avionics including APG-67 look-up/look-down multi-mode radar, digital signal processing, solid-state digital mission computer, HUD, ALR-46 radar warning receiver, ALE-40 and ALQ-171 countermeasures systems. Weapon compatibility was completed with a wide range of missiles and it is still just possible that this relatively low-cost aircraft will attract an overseas market.

Specification: Northrop F-20 Tigershark single-seat fighter
Span: 8.13 m (26 ft 8 in)
Length: 14.42 m (47 ft 3.5 in)
Powerplant: 1×General Electric F404-GE-100, 8172 kg (18,000 lb) st
Armament: 2×20-mm cannon and up to 4082 kg (9,000 lb) of disposable ordnance
Max speed: Mach 2.1 at altitude
Ferry range: 2,165 miles

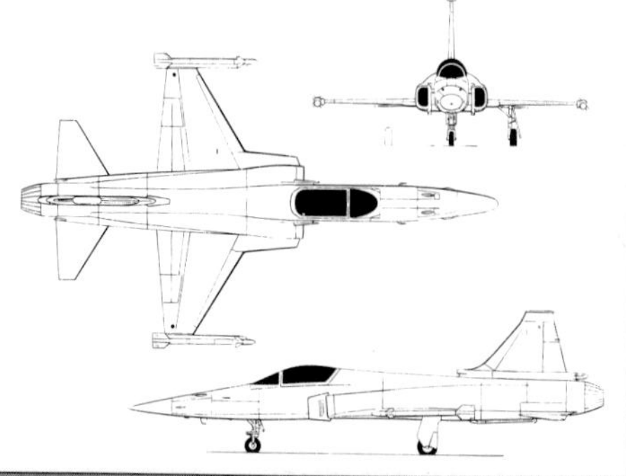

Republic F-105 Thunderchief

First flown in 1955, the F-105 suffered long delays resulting from USAF vacillation. The first production version, the single-seat F-105B, joined TAC in August 1958 and was followed by the F-105D in 1961. A highly effective strike fighter with tactical nuclear capability, the 'Thud' was widely employed in low-level strikes in Vietnam, initially carrying heavy loads of iron bombs. In the late 1960s it was performing the hazardous 'Wild Weasel' role, and employed Shrike and Standard ARMs in efforts to neutralise the hostile surface-to-air missile concentrations. Its weapon system centred upon the NASARR monopulse multi-mode radar, Doppler and ASG-19 armament control system. The F-105 was retired in 1984.

Specification: Republic F-105D Thunderchief single-seat fighter-bomber
Span: 10.64 m (34 ft 10.5 in)
Length: 19.63 m (64 ft 4.5 in)
Powerplant: 1×Pratt & Whitney J75-P-19W, 11113 kg (24,500 lb) st
Armament: 1×20-mm six-barrel rotary cannon and up to 5443 kg (12,000 lb) of disposable stores
Max speed: Mach 2.08 at altitude
Operational range: 2,207 miles

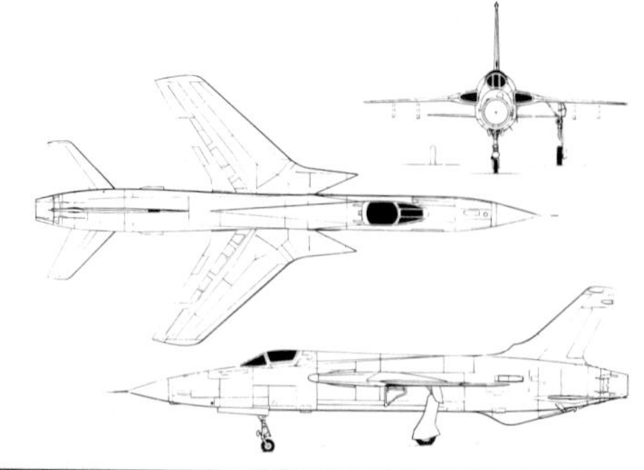

Mikoyan-Gurevich MiG-19 'Farmer'

Certainly Europe's and possibly the world's first genuinely supersonic fighter to fly, the MiG-19 was a stupendous technical achievement generally superior to its US counterpart, the F-100 Super Sabre. Developed as Aeroplane SM and flown in prototype form (probably in October 1952) as the I-350, the type featured 58° leading-edge sweep on the long and very thin wings, twin afterburning engines and a tailplane set on the fuselage rather than the fin. Other prototypes followed with alternative Tumanskii engine fits, the 3040-kg (6,702-lb) AM-5F being selected for the production MiG-19F. About 2,500 aircraft were built up to 1959, other variants being the MiG-19S with slab tailplanes and a revised powerplant, the MiG-19PF (later MiG-19SF) with *Izumrud* radar and 3300-kg (7,277-lb) RD-9BF turbojets, and the MiG-19PM with 'Scan Odd' radar and four AA-1 'Alkali' beam-riding AAMs.

Specification: Mikoyan-Gurevich MiG-19S 'Farmer' single-seat fighter and fighter-bomber
Span: 9.20 m (30 ft 2.25 in)
Length: 12.60 m (41 ft 4 in)
Powerplant: 2×Tumanskii RD-9B, 3250 kg (7,165 lb) st each
Armament: 1×37-mm and 2×23-mm cannon, plus provision for up to 500 kg (1,102 lb) of disposable stores carried on 2×underwing hardpoints
Max T/O weight: (MiG-19SF) 9100 kg (24,250 lb)q
Max speed: (MiG-19SF) Mach 1.36 at 36,090 ft
Operational range: 852 miles

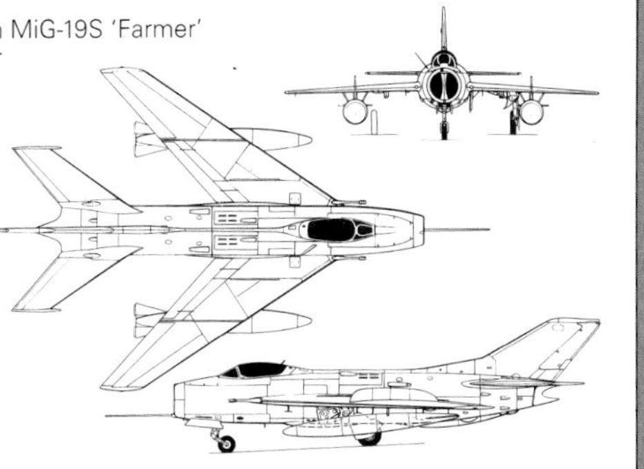

Yakovlev Yak-25 'Flashlight'

Resulting from a December 1951 requirement, the Yak-25 was the Yakovlev bureau's major programme of the 1950s and 1960s. The design was scaled up from the Yak-50 fighter prototype with twin underwing engines rather than a single fuselage-mounted engine to leave the nose clear for the 'Scan Three' radar. The untapered wing was swept at 45°, and the landing gear comprised a tandem arrangement of single-wheel nose unit and twin-wheel main unit under the fuselage, used in conjunction with retractable wingtip stabilizers. The first prototype flew in 1953, and between 1954 and 1958 about 1,000 production aircraft were built. The prototypes and early production aircraft were followed by two 2200-kg (4,850-lb) Mikulin AM-5 turbojets, but in later aircraft these were replaced by RD-9s. The type was also the starting point for an important series of derivatives. The data are speculative.

Specification: Yakovlev Yak-25 'Flashlight' two-seat all-weather and night interceptor
Span: 11.00 m (36 ft 1 in)
Length: 15.665 m (51 ft 4.75 in)
Powerplant: 2×Tumanskii RD-9, 2600 kg (5,732 lb) st each
Armament: 2×37-mm cannon
Max T/O weight: 14000 kg (30,864 lb)
Max speed: 677 mph at 16,405 ft
Operational range: 1,864 miles

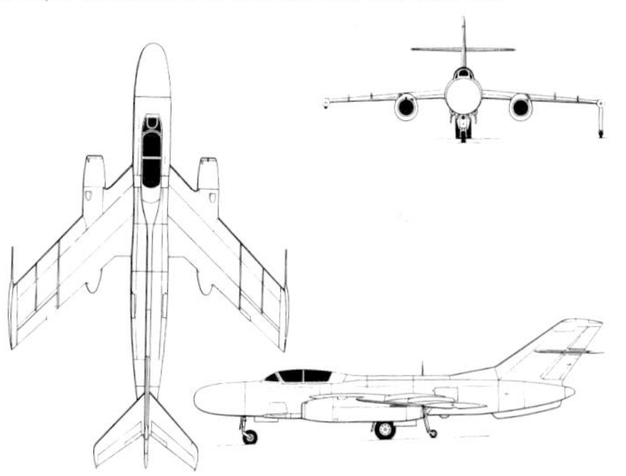

Sukhoi Su-7 'Fitter'

The Su-7 uses the configuration found inferior in the Ye-2 in the programme leading to the MiG-21, namely a conventional wing with 62° leading-edge sweep and, in definitive models, slab tailplanes. The S-2 prototype first flew in 1955, and the resulting Su-7 fighter with the 9000-kg (19,841-lb) thrust AL-7F turbojet was built only in very small numbers before the Su-7B marked the type's transformation into a ground-attack fighter of now legendary strength and accuracy of weapon-delivery. Later variants include the Su-7BKL optimised for soft-field operations with a larger nosewheel tyre and skids outboard of the main wheels, the Su-7BM with the AL-7F-1 engine, and the Su-7BMK with improved avionics, two more hardpoints and a KM-1 zero/zero ejector seat. There are also Su-7U, -7UM, -7UKM and -7UMK tandem-seat trainers equivalent to the single-seat models.

Specification: Sukhoi Su-7BMK 'Fitter-A' single-seat ground-attack fighter
Span: 8.93 m (29 ft 3.5 in)
Length: 16.60 m (54 ft 5.5 in) excluding probe
Powerplant: 1×Lyul'ka AL-7F-1, 9810 kg (21,827 lb) st
Armament: 2×30-mm cannon, plus provision for up to 4000 kg (8,818 lb) of disposable stores carried on 2×underfuselage and 4×underwing hardpoints
Max T/O weight: 14800 kg (32,628 lb)
Max speed: Mach 1.6 at 36,090 ft
Operational range: 400 miles

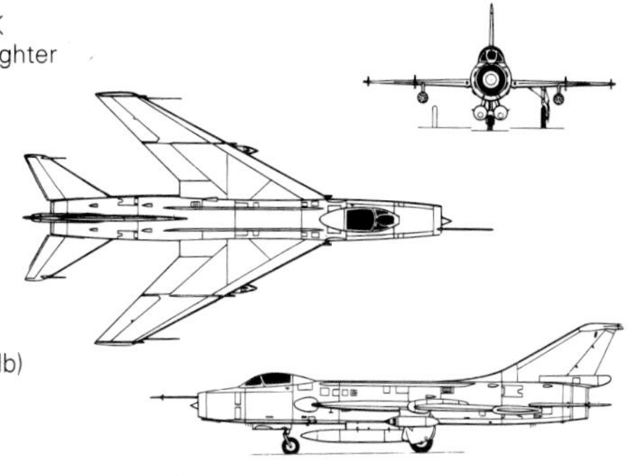

Mikoyan-Gurevich MiG-21 'Fishbed'

Produced in larger numbers than any other post-World War II warplane, the MiG-21 resulted from a 1953 requirement for a high-performance ground-controlled interceptor. Experimental aircraft were used to evaluate two configurations, the Ye-5/Ye-5A with a mid-set delta wing (swept at 57° on the leading edge), and slab tailplanes proving better and paving the way for the Ye-6 true prototype that first flew in late 1957 as precursor of the initial-production MiG-21 with the 5100-kg (11,243-lb) thrust R-11. Later variants were the upengined MiG-21F with a broader fin, the MiG-21PF with the 5950-kg (13,117-lb) thrust R-11F2S and the R1L search and tracking radar, the MiG-21PFS with blown flaps and R2L radar, the export MiG-21FL with unblown flaps, and the MiG-21PFM with the 6200-kg (13,668-lb) R-11F2S-300 and a side-opening rather than forward-hingeing canopy.

Specification: Mikoyan-Gurevich MiG-21F 'Fishbed-C' single-seat interceptor and ground-attack fighter
Span: 7.15 m (23 ft 5.5 in)
Length: 13.46 m (44 ft 2 in) without probe
Powerplant: 1×Tumanskii R-11F, 5750 kg (12,676 lb) st
Armament: 1×30-mm cannon, plus provision for 2×AA-2 'Atoll' AAMs or 2×16-tube rocket-launchers on 2×underwing hardpoints
Max T/O weight: 8630 kg (19,026 lb)
Max speed: Mach 2 at 36,090 ft
Operational range: 273 miles

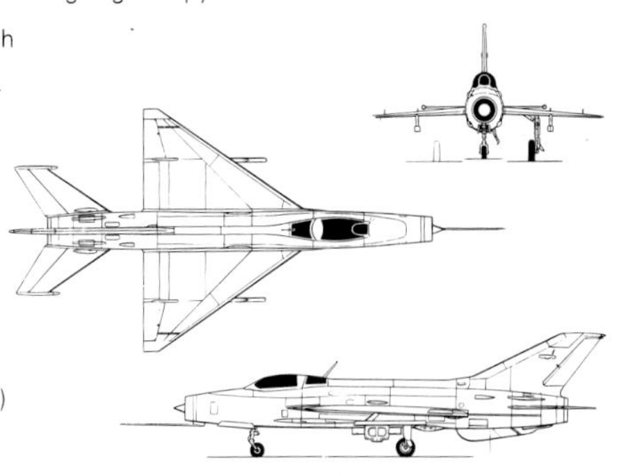

Mikoyan-Gurevich MiG-9 'Fargo'

Aeroplane F was planned in 1944 with two 1250-kg (2,756-lb) thrust Lyul'ka VRD-3 turbojets mounted laterally in the lower portion of the forward fuselage to exhaust under the wing trailing edges. Delays with the Soviet engine followed, and the design was recast with two 800-kg (1,764-lb) thrust BMW 003A turbojets. On 24 April 1946 this I-300 became the first Soviet jet-powered aeroplane to fly. About 1,000 MiG-9 production aircraft followed from 1947 with the Soviet copy of the BMW 003A engine, together with 80 MiG-9UTI tandem trainers developed with the designation I-301T. Variants were the MiG-9FF with RD-20F engines, the MiG-9PB with underwing slipper tanks, the MiG-9B with a revised nose to avoid engine ingestion of gun gas, and the MiG-9FR with 1000-kg (2,205-lb) thrust RD-21 engines, a pressurised cockpit, an ejector seat and revised armament.

Yakovlev Yak-9

The most successful and numerous Soviet fighter of World War II, the Yak-9 was taken out of production in August 1945 after 16,769 aircraft including more than 3,900 examples of the second-generation Yak-9U and its derivatives had been built. Several wartime variants remained in service, notably the long-range Yak-9D, the Yak-9DD escort fighter with drop tanks, the anti-tank Yak-9DK with a 45-mm nose cannon, the Yak-9P with three 20-mm fuselage cannon and the VK-107A engine, the Yak-9PVO night interceptor, the Yak-9R reconnaissance aeroplane, the Yak-9T-37 and Yak-9T-45 with 37- and 45-mm anti-tank nose cannon respectively, the upgraded Yak-9U with the VK-107A engine and an all-metal structure, the Yak-9UF reconnaissance aeroplane, and the Yak-9UT trainer. Modifications were made after the war, the most common being the addition of a radio compass.

Specification: Yakovlev Yak-9U single-seat fighter
Span: 9.77 m (32 ft 0.65 in)
Length: 8.55 m (28 ft 0.6 in)
Powerplant: 1×Klimov VK-107A, 1230 kW (1,650 hp)
Armament: 1×20-mm cannon and 1×12.7-mm (0.5-in) machine-gun
Normal T/O weight: 3098 kg (6,830 lb)
Max speed: 434 mph at 16,405 ft
Operational range: 540 miles

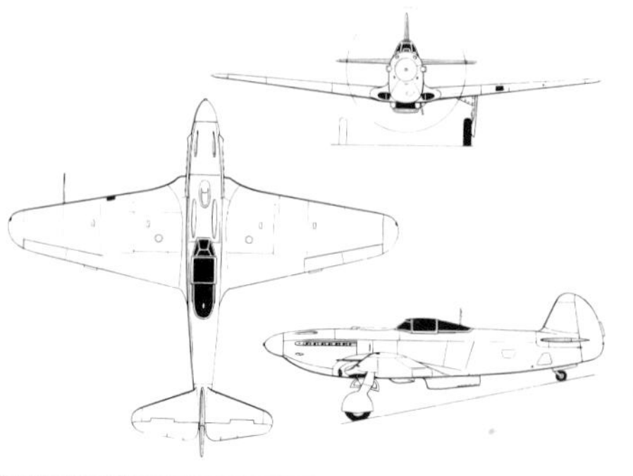

Lavochkin La-9 and La-11

Though descended directly from the La-7, the La-9 entered development in 1944 with a stressed-skin dural rather than plywood fuselage, square-cut wings, a revised tail unit, a wider and frameless canopy, and an improved engine installation. The La-130 prototype flew in June 1946 and production was authorized in November of the same year. Production of about 1,000 included some La-9UTI tandem trainers, and experimental variants were the La-138 with two underwing ramjets and the La-RD with two underwing pulsejets. The final evolution of this line was the La-11, a long-range escort whose development was started in 1946. The La-140 prototype flew in May 1947, and was followed by production aircraft with three NS-23 cannon and wingtip-mounted drop tanks for a speed of 419 mph and a range of 1,584 miles. There was also an La-11UTI trainer.

Specification: Lavochkin La-9 single-seat fighter
Span: 9.80 m (32 ft 1.75 in)
Length: 8.63 m (28 ft 3.75 in)
Powerplant: 1×Shvetsov ASh-82FN, 1379 kW (1,850 hp)
Armament: 3 or 4×20-mm cannon (early aircraft) or 23-mm cannon (later aircraft)
Normal T/O weight: 3676 kg (8,104 lb)
Max speed: 429 mph at 20,505 ft
Operational range: 1,078 miles

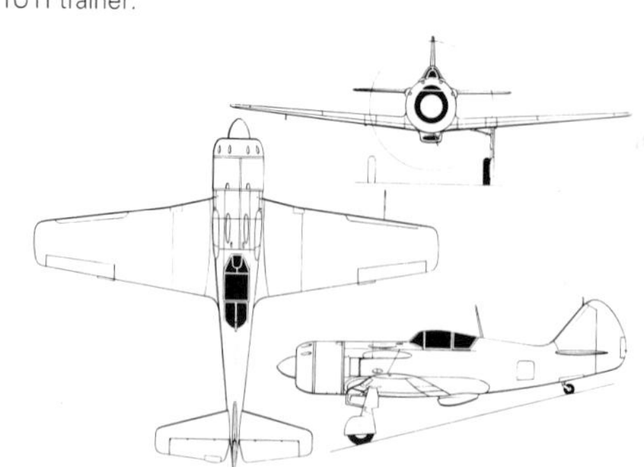

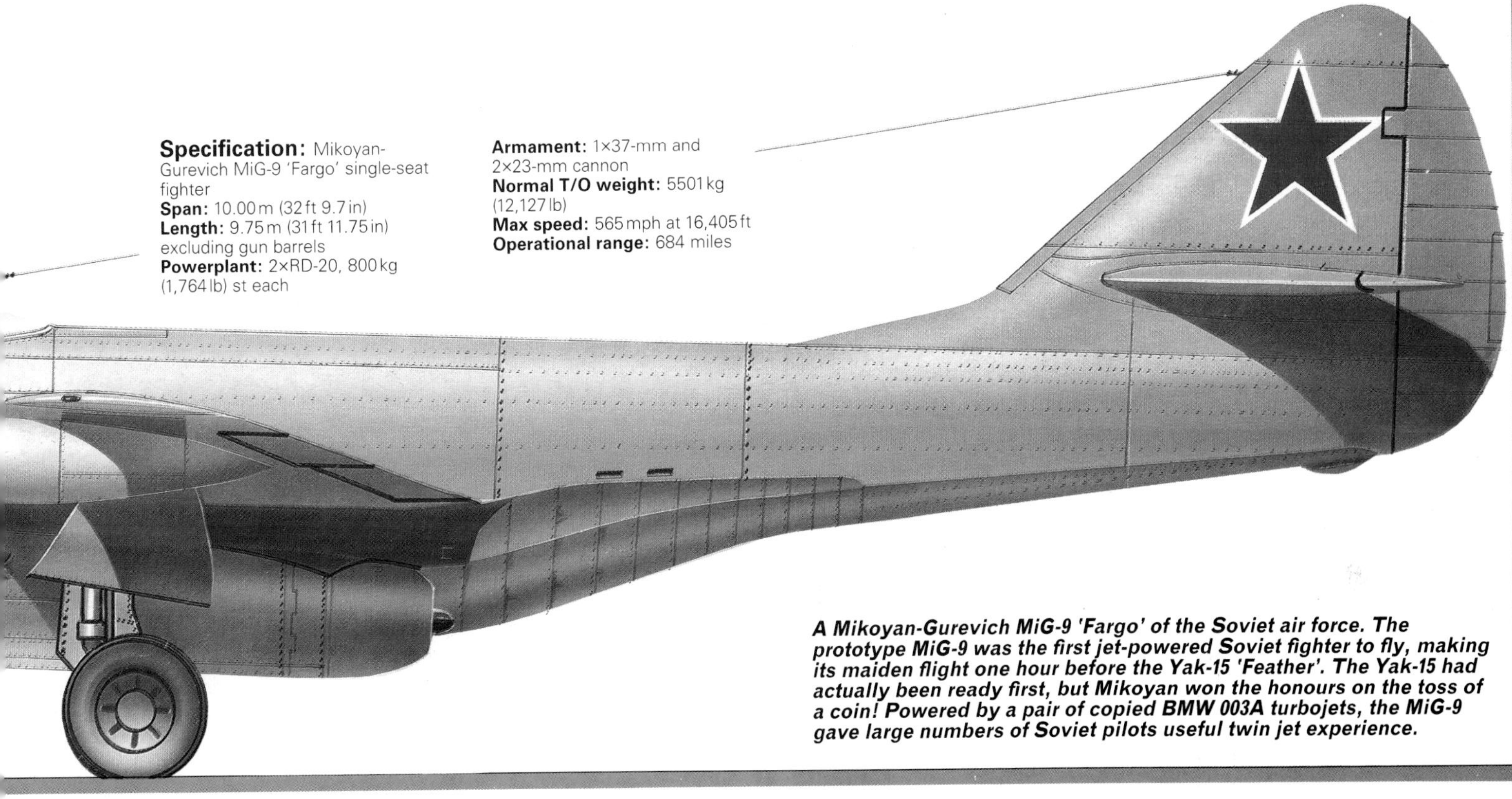

Specification: Mikoyan-Gurevich MiG-9 'Fargo' single-seat fighter
Span: 10.00 m (32 ft 9.7 in)
Length: 9.75 m (31 ft 11.75 in) excluding gun barrels
Powerplant: 2×RD-20, 800 kg (1,764 lb) st each
Armament: 1×37-mm and 2×23-mm cannon
Normal T/O weight: 5501 kg (12,127 lb)
Max speed: 565 mph at 16,405 ft
Operational range: 684 miles

A Mikoyan-Gurevich MiG-9 'Fargo' of the Soviet air force. The prototype MiG-9 was the first jet-powered Soviet fighter to fly, making its maiden flight one hour before the Yak-15 'Feather'. The Yak-15 had actually been ready first, but Mikoyan won the honours on the toss of a coin! Powered by a pair of copied BMW 003A turbojets, the MiG-9 gave large numbers of Soviet pilots useful twin jet experience.

Yakovlev Yak-15 'Feather'

This was the USSR's first turbojet-powered aeroplane, and was a derivative of the piston-engined Yak-3 lightweight fighter retaining the flying surfaces, landing gear and central/rear fuselage (with the metal skinning of the Yak-3U thickened on the underside to cope with hot exhaust gases), in combination with a new and deep forward fuselage accommodating an RD-10 (Soviet version of the Jumo 004B) in an angled installation to exhaust under the cockpit. Design and construction were undertaken very swiftly, and though taxiing trials were undertaken from October 1945 the prototype first flew just after the MiG-9 on 24 April 1946. Production amounted to perhaps 280 aircraft. The type was important in introducing jet power, but the low power of the engine meant that a full fuel load could seldom be carried. There was also a single Yak-21 tandem-seat trainer.

Specification: Yakovlev Yak-15 'Feather' single-seat fighter
Span: 9.20 m (30 ft 2.25 in)
Length: 8.78 m (28 ft 9.6 in)
Powerplant: 1×RD-10, 900 kg (1,984 lb) st
Armament: 2×23-mm cannon
Normal T/O weight: 2635 kg (5,809 lb)
Max speed: 488 mph at 16,405 ft
Operational range: 217 miles

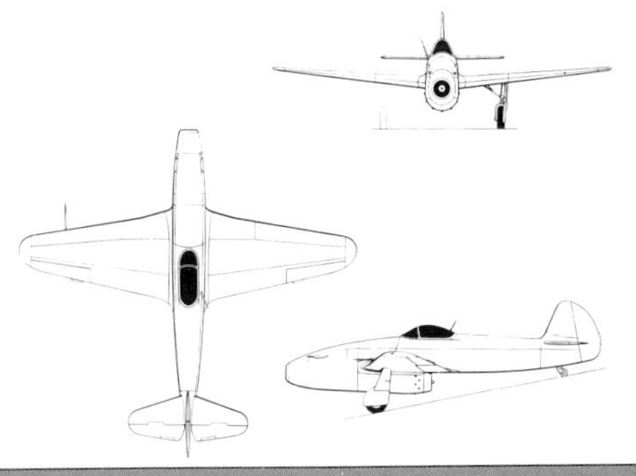

Yakovlev Yak-17 'Feather'

Experience with the Yak-15 suggested that relatively modest changes in this mixed-structure type would offer significant advantages. This resulted in the Yak-17 whose primary distinguishing features were tricycle landing gear to counter the increased forward area of the nosewheel unit's semi-external retracted accommodation, and a taller all-metal vertical tail. Other modifications were a revised engine installation with a larger inlet duct, structural strengthening and provision for wingtip drop tanks. The prototype flew in early 1947, and revealed such improvements that orders for the Yak-15 were switched to the newer type, of which some 430 were built by late 1948. As important as the basic fighter was the Yak-17UTI tandem-seat trainer, whose capabilities did much to persuade pilots that turbojet-powered aircraft were not to be feared.

Specification: Yakovlev Yak-17 'Feather' single-seat fighter
Span: 9.20 m (30 ft 2.25 in)
Length: 8.78 m (28 ft 9.6 in)
Powerplant: 1×RD-10A, 1000 kg (2,205 lb) st
Armament: 2×23-mm cannon
Normal T/O weight: 3323 kg (7,326 lb)
Max speed: 467 mph at 19,685 ft
Operational range: 466 miles

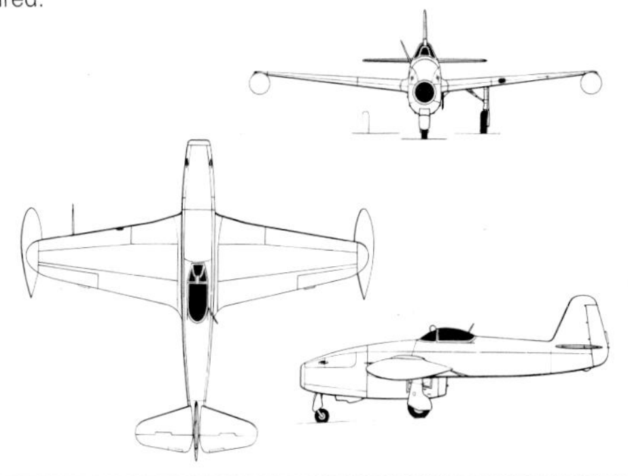

Sukhoi Su-9 'Fishpot'

Based on the T-3 series of tailed delta experimental aircraft, the T-40 was designed in 1957 as a production-capable prototype for an interceptor powered by the AL-7F afterburning turbojet aspirated through a circular nose inlet whose centrebody accommodated the antenna for the R1L search and tracking radar, matched to a quartet of AA-1 'Alkali' beam-riding AAMs carried as a pair under the leading edge of each 57° swept wing. As with the Su-7, two hardpoints under the fuselage were reserved for the use of drop tanks. The T-40 had flown by October 1958, and the Su-7 was in service by mid-1959. A T-431 unarmed variant was used to set a number of world altitude and closed-circuit speed records, and there was also an Su-9U tandem trainer version. Total Su-9 and Su-9U production was at least 1,000.

Specification: Sukhoi Su-9 'Fishpot' single-seat interceptor
Span: 8.43 m (27 ft 7.9 in)
Length: about 16.50 m (54 ft 2 in)
Powerplant: 1×Lyul'ka AL-7F, 9000 kg (19,841 lb) st
Armament: 4×AA-1 'Alkali' AAMs carried on 4×underwing hardpoints
Normal T/O weight: about 12000 kg (26,455 lb)
Max speed: Mach 1.8 at 36,090 ft
Operational range: 580 miles

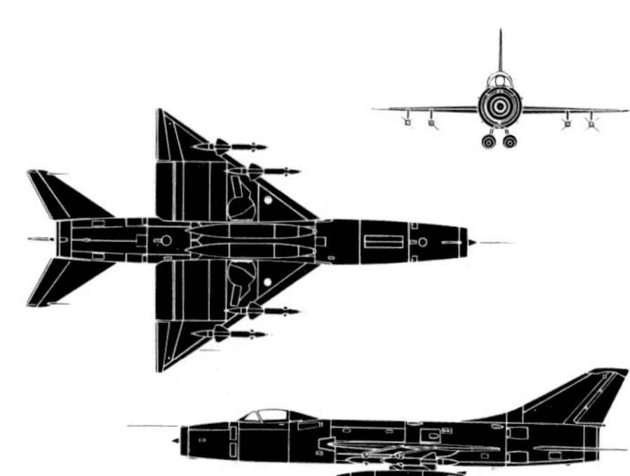

Yakovlev Yak-23 'Flora'

After experience with its first stressed-skin aeroplane, the interim and uninspired Yak-19 with 'straight-through' design for its afterburning RD-10F turbojet, the Yakovlev bureau moved to an altogether more satisfactory concept, the Yak-23 that reintroduced the 'stepped' engine installation with the nozzle under the centre/rear fuselage. More power was available in the form of the RD-500, the Soviet version of the Rolls-Royce Derwent V, and the prototype made its first flight probably in June 1947. Considerable production was planned but, despite the fact that it could outclimb the MiG-15, the Yak-23 was taken out of production after only 310 had been built: the main operators appear to have been Warsaw Pact air arms, which found the type impressive. There was also a single Yak-23UTI tandem-seat trainer with a taller tail.

Specification: Yakovlev Yak-23 'Flora' single-seat fighter and fighter-bomber
Span: 8.37 m (28 ft 7.75 in)
Length: about 8.16 m (26 ft 9.25 in)
Powerplant: 1×RD-500, 1590 kg (3,505 lb) st
Armament: 2×23-mm cannon, plus provision for 60-kg (132-lb) bombs under the wingtips
Normal T/O weight: 3384 kg (7,460 lb)
Max speed: 606 mph at altitude
Operational range: 469 miles

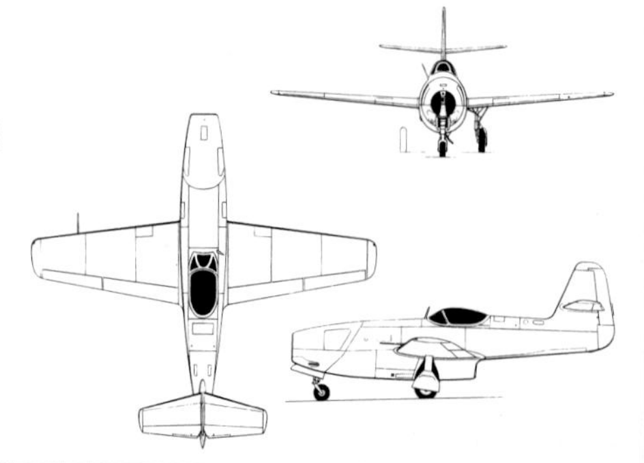

Mikoyan-Gurevich MiG-15 'Fagot'

One of history's classic warplanes, the MiG-15 spearheaded the communist air effort in the Korean War (1950-53), and though defeated by the F-86 Sabre came as a most unwelcome shock to Western air analysts. The type pioneered a wing swept 35° at quarter-chord and a massive swept vertical tail that allowed a short fuselage (and thus an efficient jetpipe length) while giving the tail-mounted control surfaces adequate moment arms. Designed as Aeroplane S, the type first flew in December 1947 as the I-310 with the RD-45 Soviet copy of the Rolls-Royce Nene. At least 5,000 single-seaters plus several thousand MiG-15UTI tandem trainers were built. There were several variants, the more important being the improved MiG-15bis with 2700-kg (5,952-lb) thrust Klimov VK-1, the MiG-15bisP with *Izumrud* radar, the MiG-15bisS escort with underwing slipper tanks, and the MiG-15bisR with two reconnaissance cameras.

Specification: Mikoyan-Gurevich MiG-15 'Fagot' single-seat fighter
Span: 10.08 m (33 ft 1 in)
Length: 10.04 m (32 ft 11.25 in)
Powerplant: 1×RD-45F, 2270 kg (5,004 lb) st
Armament: 1×37-mm and 2×23-mm cannon
Max T/O weight: 4806 kg (10,595 lb)
Max speed: 640 mph at 9,845 ft
Operational range: 882 miles

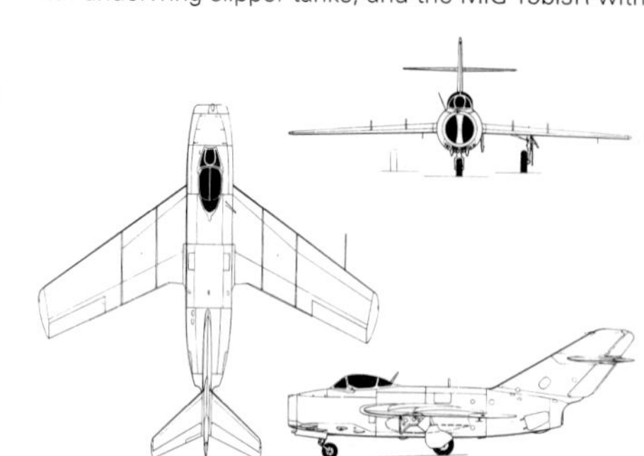

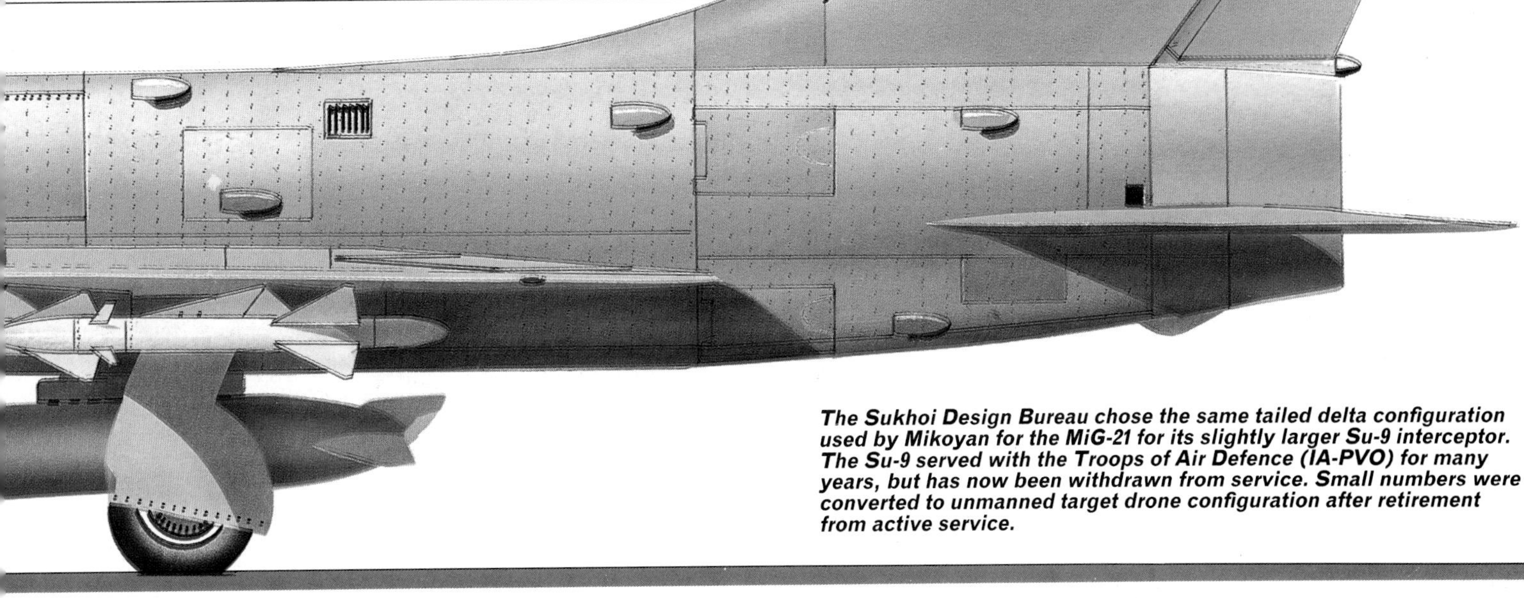

The Sukhoi Design Bureau chose the same tailed delta configuration used by Mikoyan for the MiG-21 for its slightly larger Su-9 interceptor. The Su-9 served with the Troops of Air Defence (IA-PVO) for many years, but has now been withdrawn from service. Small numbers were converted to unmanned target drone configuration after retirement from active service.

Lavochkin La-15 'Fantail'

After a number of straight- and swept-wing prototypes with a pod-and-boom fuselage thought desirable to keep the jetpipe of the RD-10 (Jumo 004 derivative) turbojet as short as possible, the Lavochkin bureau moved forward to a straight-through design in the La-174D prototype with leading-edge sweep of 37° 20'. The La-174D first flew in August 1948 on a Rolls-Royce Nene turbojet, and performance was so good that despite the earlier decision to mass produce the inferior Mikoyan-Gurevich MiG-15 the type was ordered into production as the La-15 with the Soviet RD-500 version of the Rolls-Royce Derwent V. It is thought that 500 were built, the type serving as a cannon-armed frontal fighter of great popularity. There were also 500 of the La-15UTI fighter trainer version developed as the La-180 with tandem cockpits, reduced fuel and a single 12.7-mm (0.5-in) machine-gun.

Specification: Lavochkin La-15 'Fantail' single-seat fighter and ground-attack aeroplane
Span: 8.83 m (28 ft 11.6 in)
Length: 9.56 m (31 ft 4.4 in)
Powerplant: 1×RD-500, 1590 kg (3,505 lb) st
Armament: 3×23-mm cannon
Normal T/O weight: 3708 kg (8,175 lb)
Max speed: 638 mph at 9,845 ft
Operational range: 727 miles

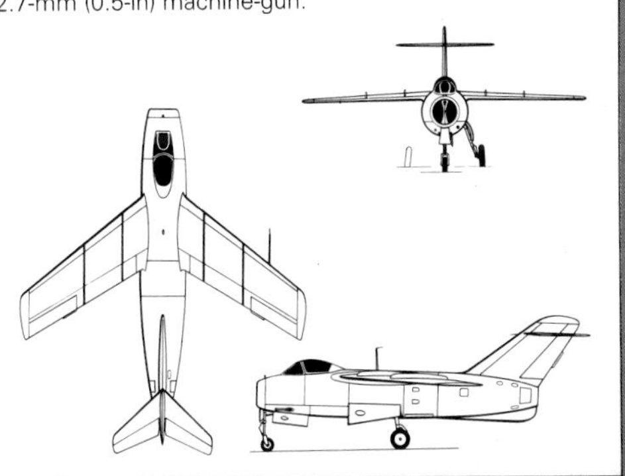

Mikoyan-Gurevich MiG-17 'Fresco'

Developed as the Aeroplane SI (S Improved) and flown in January 1950 as the I-330 prototype, this was in essence the MiG-15 with most of its failings remedied by the use of a new wing of 45° leading-edge sweep out to mid-span and thence 42° to the tip, a longer rear fuselage, a larger vertical tail, a more swept tailplane and a non-afterburning VK-1 turbojet. Production of the MiG-17 series totalled about 6,000, and the other main variants were the MiG-17P interceptor with *Izumrud* radar, the MiG-17F with the afterburning VK-1F engine delivering 3380-kg (7,451-lb) thrust, the MiG-17PF with radar, and the MiG-17PFU with four AA-1 'Alkali' beam-riding AAMs but no cannon. About 3,000 more aircraft were built in China (at least 2,000 J-4 and J-5 series aircraft) and Poland (1,000 LIM-5 series aircraft).

Specification: Mikoyan-Gurevich MiG-17 'Fresco' single-seat fighter and fighter-bomber
Span: 9.63 m (31 ft 7 in)
Length: 11.26 m (36 ft 11.3 in)
Powerplant: 1×Klimov VK-1A, 2700 kg (5,952 lb) st
Armament: 1×37-mm and 2 or 3×23-mm cannon, plus provision for 250 kg (551 lb) of disposable stores carried on 2×underwing hardpoints
Max T/O weight: 5932 kg (13,078 lb)
Max speed: 692 mph at 9,945 ft
Operational range: 1,336 miles

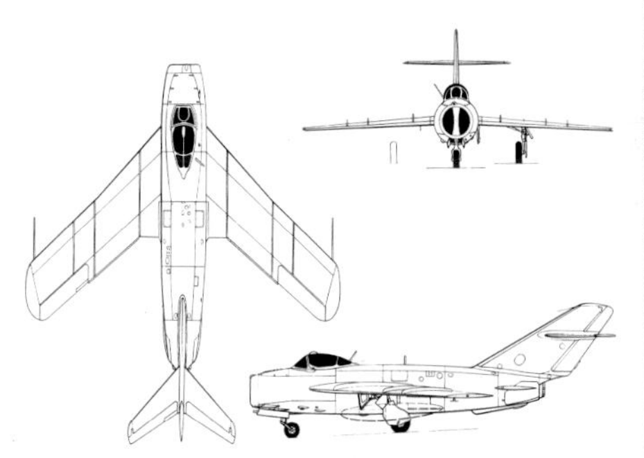

Mikoyan-Gurevich MiG-31 'Foxhound'

The MiG-31 was developed from the MiG-25MP for the long-range all-weather interception role at medium altitudes, and has an advanced radar that provides a genuine 'look-down/shoot-down' capability in conjunction with the new generation of Soviet AAMs including the radar-homing AA-9. Apart from the primary sensor and weapon suite, the MiG-31 differs from the MiG-25 in having a lengthened two-seat fuseage, an uprated version of the R-31 turbojet in an arragement that uses revised inlets and nozzles, and leading-edge root extensions. The net effect is an altogether more capable aeroplane in the operational sense, though in outright terms the performance is reduced from a Mach 3.2 dash speed to a 'mere' Mach 2.4 capability at high altitude. The type reached IOC in 1985, and production continues to provide defence against penetration bombers and cruise missiles.

Specification: Mikoyan-Gurevich MiG-31 'Foxhound' two-seat interceptor
Span: 14.00 m (45 ft 11.2 in)
Length: 25.00 m (82 ft 0.25 in)
Powerplant: 2×Tumanskii R-31F, 14000 kg (30,864 lb) st each
Armament: provision for up to 8×AAMs carried on 4×tangential underfuselage and 4×underwing hardpoints
Max T/O weight: 41150 kg (90,719 lb)
Max speed: Mach 2.4 at high altitude
Operational range: 1,865 miles

Yakovlev Yak-28 'Firebar'

The Yak-28 was developed from the Yak-25 interceptor as a multi-role combat aeroplane, and by comparison with its predecessor features more sharply swept flying surfaces and twin wheels on each of the tandem main landing gear units whose rear unit was shifted rearward to permit the installation of a lower-fuselage weapon bay. First flown in 1960, the Yak-28 was used in the strike bomber, reconnaissance and electronic escort roles in variants with the NATO reporting name 'Brewer', in the training role with the NATO name 'Maestro' and in the all-weather fighter role as the Yak-28P with 'Skip Spin' radar in a solid nose. The initial 'Firebar' fighter version was 21.70 m (71 ft 2.33 in) long, but from 1967 production aircraft introduced a longer nose and inlets for reduced trans-sonic drag.

Specification: Yakovlev Yak-28P 'Firebar' two-seat all-weather fighter
Span: 12.95 m (42 ft 6 in)
Length: 23.00 m (75 ft 5.5 in)
Powerplant: 2×Tumanskii R-11, 6200 kg (13,668 lb) st each
Armament: 4×AAMs carried on 4×underwing hardpoints
Max T/O weight: 20000 kg (44,092 lb)
Max speed: Mach 1.1 at 36,090 ft
Operational range: 1,120 miles

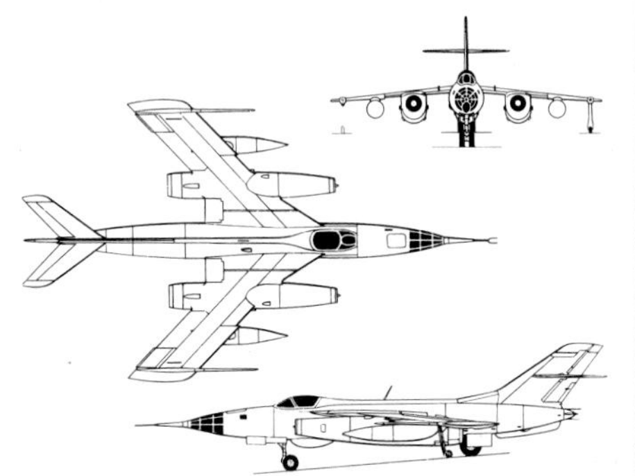

Mikoyan-Gurevich MiG-21 'Fishbed'

The first-generation MiG-21s were fighters with only the most modest dual-role capability This began to change with the MiG-21PFMA 'Fishbed-J', which was based on the MiG-21PFM 'Fishbed-F' with the 6200-kg (13,668-lb) thrust R-11-300, an enlarged dorsal fairing for additional avionics, more powerful 'Jay Bird' radar and four rather than two underwing hardpoints. Later variants of the MiG-21PFMA were the MiG-21R/RF 'Fishbed-H' reconnaissance platforms, the MiG-21MF 'Fishbed-J' with greater power, the 'Fishbed-K' with a larger dorsal fairing and detachable ECM pods mounted at the wingtips. Then came the third-generation MiG-21bis in two variants: the 'Fishbed-L' with a re-engineered airframe and greater fuel capacity, and the 'Fishbed-N' with the 7500-kg (16,535-lb) thrust R-25, improved avionics and provision for weapons such as the AA-8 'Aphid' AAM.

Specification: Mikoyan-Gurevich MiG-21MF 'Fishbed-J' single-seat dual-role fighter
Span: 7.15 m (23 ft 5.5 in)
Length: 15.76 m (51 ft 8.5 in) including probe
Powerplant: 1×Tumanskii R-13-300, 6600 kg (14,550 lb) st
Armament: 1×23-mm twin-barrel cannon, plus provision for 1500 kg (3,307 lb) of disposable stores carried on 4×underwing hardpoints
Max T/O weight: 9400 kg (20,723 lb)
Max speed: Mach 2.1 at 36,090 ft
Operational range: 683 miles without external stores

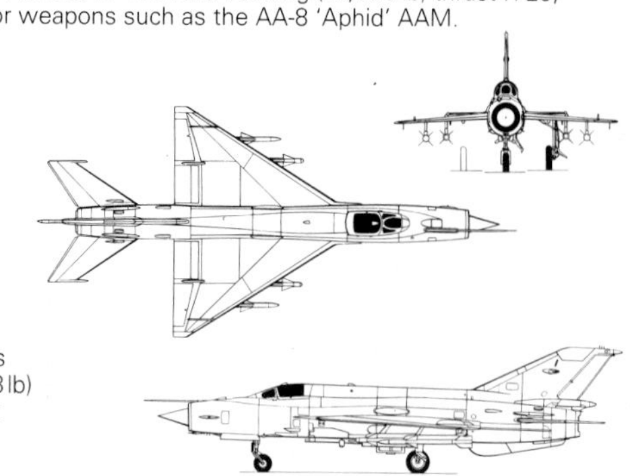

ong-range interception is the main role for the 'Foxhound', employing large pulse-Doppler radar to guide the long-range AA-9 'Amos' adar-guided missile, similar in specification to the Phoenix carried by he Tomcat. For closer work the MiG-31 carries the AA-8 'Aphid' heat-eeker, but more AA-9s can be carried instead. 'Foxhounds' are eployed in the Arkhangelsk area and in the Far East around Sakhalin sland.

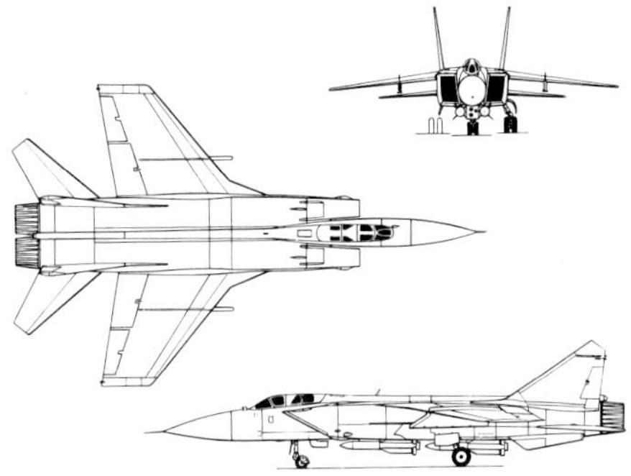

P. Oliver

Sukhoi Su-17, 20 and 22 'Fitter'

The Su-17 series is a development of the Su-7 with variable-geometry outer wing panels for mproved field and cruise performance with greater loads. The Su-17G 'Fitter-B' prototype irst flew in 1966, and large-scale production followed with the Lyul'ka AL-7 and Tumanskii R-29 afterburning turbojets in Su-17, Su-20 and Su-22 variants that are best identified by their NATO reporting names. The 'Fitter-C' has the AL-21F-3, the 'Fitter-D' has more-advanced avionics (including a head-up display and a laser rangefinder and marked-target seeker), the 'Fitter-E' is a two-seat trainer with angled-down nose, the 'Fitter-F' is the export C' with the Tumanskii engine, the 'Fitter-G' is the trainer version of the 'E', the 'Fitter-H' has a drooped nose and extra hardpoints, the 'Fitter-J' is the export 'H', and the 'Fitter-K' has extra ECM capability.

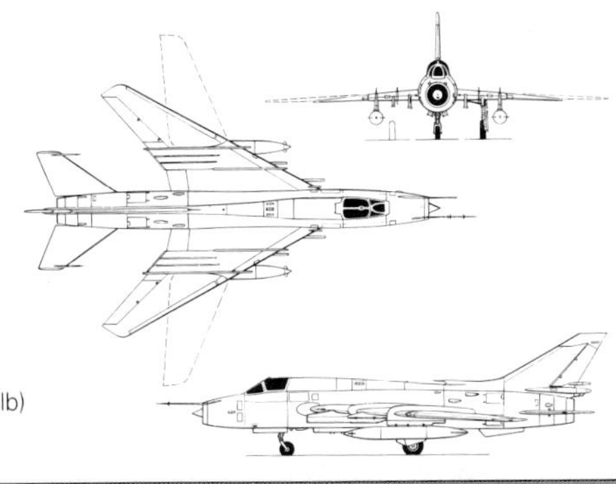

Specification: Sukhoi Su-20 'Fitter-K' variable-geometry single-seat ground-attack fighter
Span: 14.00 m (45 ft 11.2 in) spread and 10.60 m (34 ft 9.5 in) swept
Length: 19.20 m (63 ft 0 in)
Powerplant: 1×Lyul'ka AL-21F-3, 11200 kg (24,691 lb) st
Armament: 2×30-mm cannon, plus provision for up to 4000 kg (8,818 lb) of disposable stores carried on 4×underfuselage and 4×underwing hardpoints
Max T/O weight: 19500 kg (42,990 lb)
Max speed: Mach 2.2 at 36,090 ft
Operational range: 622 miles

Mikoyan-Gurevich MiG-23 'Flogger'

Planned from the late 1950s as successor to the MiG-21, the MiG-23 was developed via different evaluation aircraft to emerge in 1966 as the Ye-231 prototype with variable-geometry wings. A substantial number of MiG-23S/MS 'Flogger-A' pre-production aircraft used a Lyul'ka turbojet, but the type was then refined and fitted with the R-27 for service from 1971 as the MiG-23M 'Flogger-B', followed by the MiG-23MF with R-29 engine and full-capability 'High Lark' radar. Other variants are the 'Flogger-E' export version of the MiG-23M with downgraded electronics including 'Jay Bird' radar, the MiG-23BN 'Flogger-F' hybrid with the nose of the MiG-27 attacker, the 'Flogger-G' dedicated air-combat model with lighter radar, the 'Flogger-H' derivative of the 'Flogger-F', the aerodynamically improved 'Flogger-K', and two 'Flogger-C' trainers (MiG-23U and MiG-23UM).

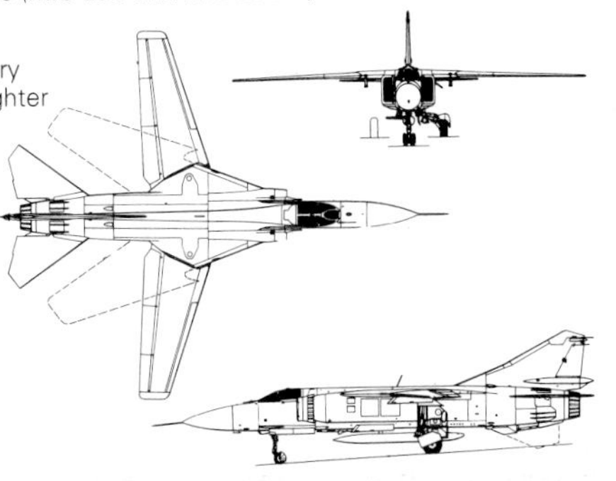

Specification: Mikoyan-Gurevich MiG-23MF 'Flogger-B' variable-geometry single-seat air-combat and multi-role fighter
Span: 14.25 m (46 ft 9 in) spread and 8.17 m (26 ft 9.5 in) swept
Length: 18.15 m (59 ft 6.5 in) including probe
Powerplant: 1×Tumanskii R-29, 11500 kg (25,353 lb) st
Armament: 1×23-mm twin-barrel cannon, plus provision for 3000 kg (6,614 lb) of disposable stores carried on 5×external hardpoints
Max T/O weight: 18900 kg (41,667 lb)
Max speed: Mach 2.3 at high altitude
Operational range: 1,180 miles

Sukhoi Su-27 'Flanker'

A larger aeroplane than the MiG-29 and more directly comparable with the McDonnell Douglas F-15 in the dedicated air-superiority role, the Su-27 was developed in the 1970s and first seen in Western satellite reconnaissance images during 1980. The Su-27 and MiG-29 have a similar configuration that suggests the use, in a modern parallel with the situation of the MiG-21 and Su-9/11 types, of a design concept from the USSR's central aerodynamic research centre. The pre-production 'Flanker-A' had rounded wingtips while the 'Flanker-B' that began to enter service in 1986 has relocated vertical surfaces and tips with missile-launch rails. A modern weapon fit is complemented by advanced avionics including a long-range radar of the pulse-Doppler variety for excellent 'look-down/shoot-down' capability.

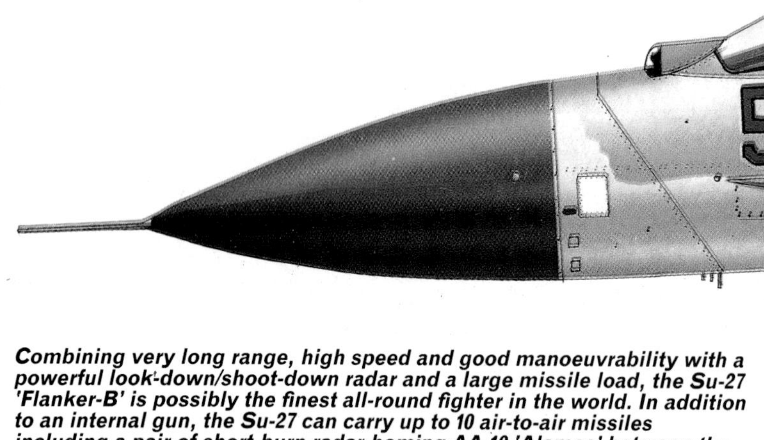

Combining very long range, high speed and good manoeuvrability with a powerful look-down/shoot-down radar and a large missile load, the Su-27 'Flanker-B' is possibly the finest all-round fighter in the world. In addition to an internal gun, the Su-27 can carry up to 10 air-to-air missiles including a pair of short-burn radar-homing AA-10 'Alamos' between the engine nacelles, two long-range radar-homing AA-10s under the engines, two infra-red AA-10s under the wings and four short-range AA-8s or AA-11s on the outer wings and wingtips.

Tupolev Tu-28P 'Fiddler'

Designed for long-range patrols of the USSR's vast northern and eastern reaches, the Tu-28 is of typical Tupolev design and is now an obsolescent type that remains the world's largest pure interceptor. The original Tu-102 prototype was planned as precursor of a multi-role fighter/reconnaissance type, but was then supplanted by the Tu-128 interceptor that entered limited service with the service designation Tu-28P, called 'Fiddler-A' by NATO. The definitive 'Fiddler-B' version entered production in 1966 and service in 1968: it has four-wheel bogies on the main landing gear units, these retracting rearwards into substantial 'bullets' appended to the wing trailing edges. The 'Fiddler' carries the powerful 'Big Nose' search and continuous-wave illumination radar for use with the AA-5 'Ash' long-range AAMs carried only by the Tu-28.

Specification: Tupolev Tu-28P 'Fiddler-B' two-seat long-range interceptor
Span: 18.10 m (59 ft 11.75 in)
Length: 27.20 m (89 ft 3 in)
Powerplant: 2×Lyul'ka AL-21F-3, 11000 kg (24,250 lb) st each
Armament: 4×AA-5 'Ash' AAMs carried on 4×underwing hardpoints
Max T/O weight: 45000 kg (99,206 lb)
Max speed: Mach 1.75 at 36,090 ft
Operational range: 3,100 miles

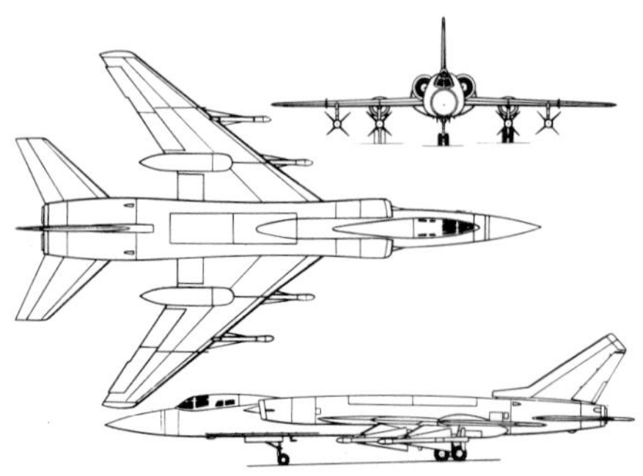

Sukhoi Su-11 'Fishpot'

In the early 1950s the USSR's main aerodynamic research centre worked on an optimum layout for supersonic fighters, and concluded that the tailed delta offered the best blend of characteristics. This resulted in the MiG-21 and the larger Su-9, the latter sized to the Lyul'ka AL-7 afterburning turbojet. The Su-9 was replaced in production during 1967 by the similar Su-11 with the AL-7F-1 engine fed via external fuel pipes along the upper fuselage. The Su-11 also introduced a new sensor and weapon fit, the Su-9's R1L 'High Fix' radar and four AA-1 'Alkali' beam-riding missiles being replaced by the Uragan 5B 'Skip Spin' radar and two AA-3 'Anab' missiles (usually one with semi-active radar and the other with infra-red homing). Underfuselage drop tanks were usually carried, and the Su-9/Su-11 force was phased out of service in the early 1980s.

Specification: Sukhoi Su-11 'Fishpot' single-seat interceptor
Span: 8.43 m (27 ft 8 in)
Length: 18.29 m (60 ft 0 in) including probe
Powerplant: 1×Lyul'ka AL-7F-1, 9600 kg (21,164 lb) st
Armament: 2×AAMs on 2×underwing hardpoints
Max T/O weight: 13600 kg (29,982 lb)
Max speed: Mach 2 at 36,090 ft
Operational range: 700 miles

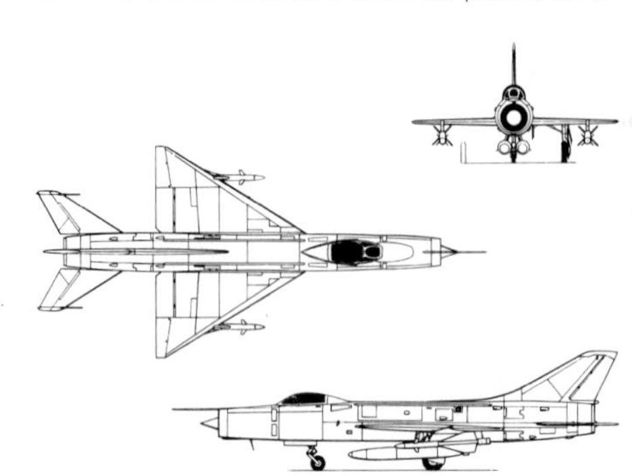

Specification: Sukhoi Su-27 'Flanker-B' single-seater air-superiority fighter
Span: 14.70 m (48 ft 2.75 in)
Length: 21.60 m (70 ft 10.4 in)
Powerplant: 2×Tumanskii R-32, 13600 kg (29,982 lb) st each
Armament: 1×23- or 30-mm rotary-barrel cannon, plus provision for up to 6000 kg (13,228 lb) of disposable stores carried on 10×external hardpoints
Max T/O weight: 28800 kg (63,492 lb)
Max speed: Mach 2.35 at high altitude
Operational range: 1,864 miles

Sukhoi Su-15/Su-21 'Flagon'

The Su-15 was designed to a 1959 requirement for a high-performance interceptor and flew in about 1965. The basic layout of the Su-9/11 was retained, but to ease the difficulties of accommodating a powerful nose radar the design bureau opted for lateral inlets for two AL-21F engines rather than the earlier types' nose inlet for a single engine. Entering service in 1969, the Su-15 'Flagon-A' had a pure delta wing. Later service variants were the Su-15U 'Flagon-C' tandem-cockpit trainer modelled on the 'D', the Su-15MF 'Flagon-D' with compound-sweep wings and AL-21F-3 engines, the Su-21 'Flagon-E' with twin nosewheels and 'Improved Skip Spin' or 'Twin Scan' radar in place of the original 'Skip Spin', the Su-21 'Flagon-F' definitive single-seater with an ogival rather than conical radome, and the Su-21U 'Flagon-G' two-seat trainer based on the 'Flagon-F'.

Specification: Sukhoi Su-21 'Flagon-F' single-seat interceptor
Span: 10.50 m (34 ft 5.4 in)
Length: 22.00 m (72 ft 2.1 in)
Powerplant: 2×Lyul'ka AL-21F-3, 11200 kg (24,691 lb) st each
Armament: possibly 1×23-mm twin-barrel cannon, plus provision for 1500 kg (3,307 lb) of disposable stores carried on 2×underfuselage and 4×underwing hardpoints
Max T/O weight: 20000 kg (44,092 lb)
Max speed: Mach 2.5 at 36,090 ft
Operational range: 900 miles

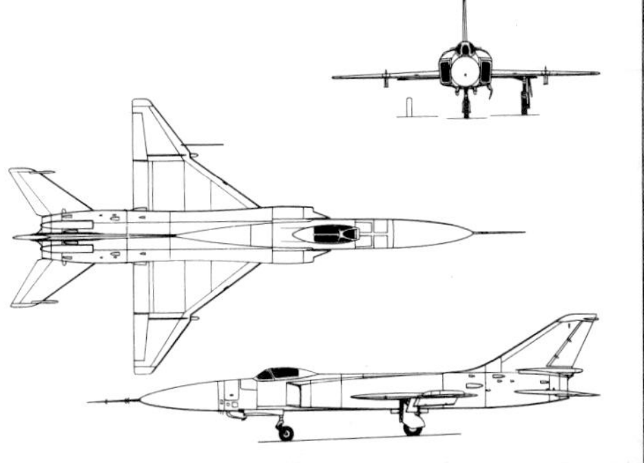

Mikoyan-Gurevich MiG-25 'Foxbat'

The MiG-25 was planned specifically to counter the USAF's North American B-70 Valkyrie high-level Mach 3 bomber, which was later cancelled. The MiG-25 was optimised for straight-line performance at high altitude, and uses a relatively unsophisticated structure (with a high proportion of steel), a powerful valve-technology radar, and engines with variable inlets and nozzles. The 'Foxbat-A' began to enter service in 1970. Later variants are the MiG-25R 'Foxbat-B' radar and visual reconnaissance platform, the MiG-25U 'Foxbat-C' two-seat conversion trainer, the MiG-25R 'Foxbat-D' radar and Elint reconnaissance platform, the MiG-25MP 'Foxbat-E' conversion of the 'A' with 14000-kg (30,864-lb) thrust R-31F engines and a radar/missile fit suitable for the 'look-down/shoot-down' role, and the 'Foxbat-F' defence-suppression model with AS-11 radiation-homing missiles.

Specification: Mikoyan-Gurevich MiG-25 'Foxbat-A' two-seat interceptor
Span: 13.95 m (45 ft 9 in)
Length: 23.82 m (78 ft 1.75 in)
Powerplant: 2×Tumanskii R-31, 12300 kg (27,116 kg) st each
Armament: 4×AAMs carried on 4×underwing hardpoints
Max T/O weight: 37425 kg (82,507 lb)
Max speed: Mach 3.2 at high altitude
Operational range: 1,400 miles

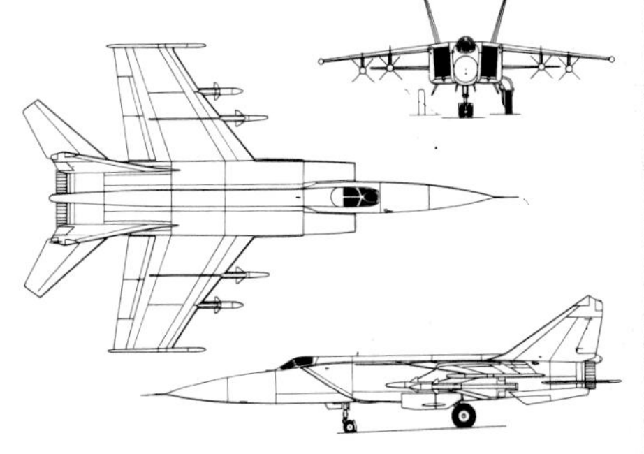

Mikoyan-Gurevich MiG-27 'Flogger'

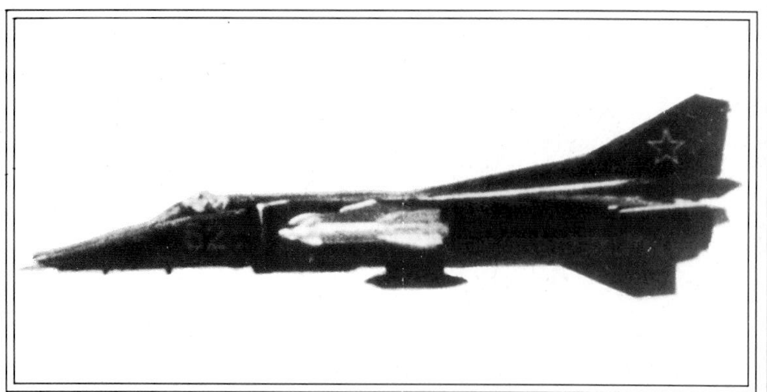

Developed from the MiG-23 as a dedicated ground-attack type, the MiG-27 has fixed rather than variable inlets, a two-position rather than variable nozzle, landing gear with wider and larger tyres for soft-field operations, revised armament and avionics, and a new 'ducknose' forward fuselage. This last lacks the radar of the MiG-23 but has a laser rangefinder and marked-target seeker plus armour protection for the pilot, who is seated in a higher cockpit optimised for the ground-attack role. The inbuilt weapon is a six-barrel rotary cannon rather than the MiG-23's two-barrel weapon, and extra hardpoints permit the carriage of more stores of greater diversity. The type first flew in about 1970, and current variants are the initial 'Flogger-D' and the 'Flogger-J' with revised avionics plus provision for two pods with 23-mm cannon angled for oblique downward fire.

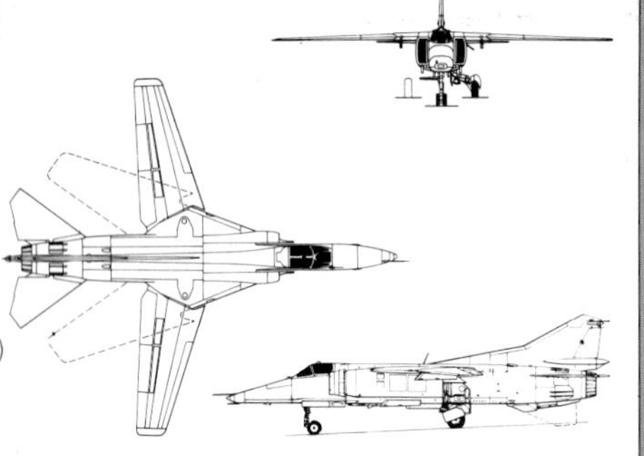

Specification: Mikoyan-Gurevich MiG-27 'Flogger-D' variable-geometry single-seat ground-attack fighter
Span: 14.25 m (46 ft 9 in) spread and 8.17 m (26 ft 9.6 in) swept
Length: 16.00 m (52 ft 5.9 in)
Powerplant: 1×Tumanskii R-29-300, 11500 kg (25,353 lb) st
Armament: 1×23-mm rotary-barrel cannon, plus provision for 4000 kg (8,818 lb) of disposable stores carried on 7×external hardpoints
Max T/O weight: 20100 kg (44,313 lb)
Max speed: Mach 1.7 at high altitude
Operational range: 480 miles with typical offensive load

Yakovlev Yak-38 'Forger'

First thought in the West to be designated Yak-36 (in fact the 'Freehand' VTOL research type), the Yak-38 is a STOVL aeroplane with modest combat capability. As important as its combat role, however, is the experience it has given the Soviet navy in the operation of fixed-wing carrier aircraft. The type first flew in 1971 and entered service in 1976 as the single-seat 'Forger-A' and two-seat 'Forger-B'. Unlike Western STOVL types, which have one vectoring turbofan for thrust and/or direct lift, the Yak-38 uses a mixed system with a single turbojet exhausting via two vectoring nozzles aft of the wing, and two direct-lift turbojets located vertically in the fuselage forward of the wing. Western analysts at first thought the type capable only of VTOL operations, photographic evidence of STOVL capability leading to an upward revision of payload estimates.

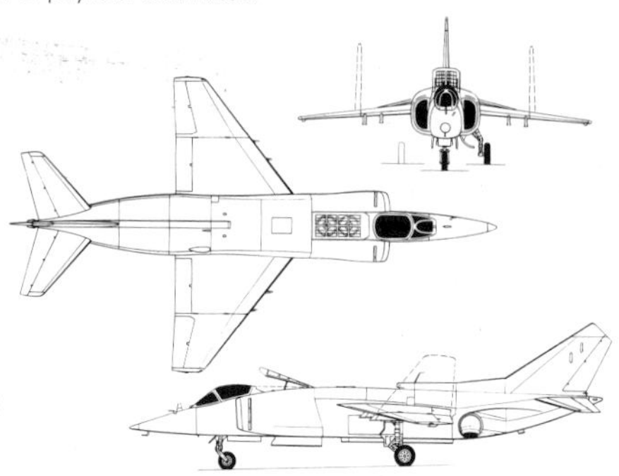

Specification: Yakovlev Yak-38 'Forger-A' single-seat carrierborne STOVL combat aeroplane
Span: 7.32 m (24 ft 0.2 in)
Length: 15.50 m (50 ft 10.3 in)
Powerplant: 1×Lyul'ka AL-21F, 8160 kg (17,989 lb) st, and two Koliesov ZM, 3750 kg (7,870 lb) st each
Armament: provision for up to 3600 kg (7,937 lb) of disposable stores carried on 4×underwing hardpoints
Max T/O weight: 13000 kg (28,660 lb)
Max speed: 700 mph at sea level
Operational range: 460 miles

Sukhoi Su-25 'Frogfoot'

The Su-25 is the USSR's counterpart to the Fairchild A-10A, but is an altogether smaller aeroplane resembling the Northrop A-9 beaten by the A-10 in the USAF's A-X competition. The Soviet project was defined and designed in the early and mid-1970s, and the Su-25 began to enter service in 1982, initially proving itself in Afghanistan before large-scale service deployment followed in 1983. The type features unusual split wingtip flaps/speedbrakes and a split rudder. The specialist avionics include a head-up display plus a laser rangefinder and marked-target seeker. The internal cannon is far less potent than the A-10A's extraordinary GAU-8/A, though of the same nominal calibre, while of the 10 hardpoints the inner pair are plumbed for drop tanks and the outer pair for AA-2/AA-8 self-defence AAMs.

Specification: Sukhoi Su-25 'Frogfoot' single-seat close-support aeroplane
Span: 15.50 m (50 ft 10 in)
Length: 14.50 m (47 ft 7 in)
Powerplant: 2×Tumanskii R-13-300, 5100 kg (11,244 lb) st each
Armament: 1×30-mm rotary-barrel cannon, plus provision for up to 4500 kg (9,921 lb) of disposable stores carried on 10×underwing hardpoints
Max T/O weight: 19200 kg (42,329 lb)
Max speed: 547 mph at optimum altitude
Operational range: 684 miles

Mikoyan-Gurevich MiG-29 'Fulcrum'

When it began to enter service in the mid-1980s, the MiG-29 was immediately appreciated as an excellent air-superiority fighter similar in layout to the McDonnell Douglas F-15 but in size to that company's F/A-18. The type features blended aerodynamics for high agility, but is not a 'fly-by-wire' type. The pilot has a helmet-mounted sight and head-up display, and other sensors include the NO-93 coherent pulse-Doppler radar and an infra-red search/tracker unit (with collimated laser rangefinder) for a genuine 'look-down/shoot-down' capability with the USSR's latest missiles. There appear to have been two pre-production (or one pre-production and one initial service) variants before the present 'Fulcrum-A' was revealed in 1988 with upward-firing chaff/flare launchers in lengthened dorsal fins. There is also a MiG-29U 'Fulcrum-B' two-seat trainer.

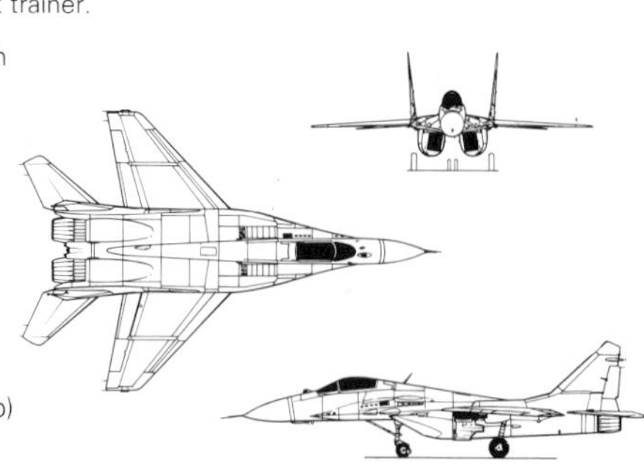

Specification: Mikoyan-Gurevich MiG-29 'Fulcrum-A' single-seat air-superiority and attack fighter
Span: 11.36 m (37 ft 7.25 in)
Length: 17.32 m (56 ft 8.25 in) including probe
Powerplant: 2×Tumanskii R-33D, 8300 kg (18,298 lb) st each
Armament: 1×30-mm twin-barrel cannon, plus provision for disposable stores carried on 6×underwing hardpoints
Max T/O weight: 18000 kg (39,683 lb)
Max speed: Mach 2.3+ at high altitude
Operational range: 1,430 miles

Avro Canada CF-105 Arrow

The Arrow was designed from 1953 as replacement for the CF-100, with supersonic performance and a far superior combination of electronics and weapons. Despite the technical problems associated with this ambitious project, construction of five Arrow Mk 1 prototypes began in 1954, and the first of these flew in March 1958 with two Pratt & Whitney J75 afterburning turbojets. This was only an interim engine, for the engine under development for the production fighter was the Orenda Iroquois of up to 12701-kg (28,000-lb) thrust. Considerable progress had been made with the Astra I/Sparrow II radar fire-control system/weapon combination when that was cancelled in September 1958, Canadair then switching to the Hughes MX1179/Genie nuclear-tipped rocket combination. In February 1959 the whole Arrow project was cancelled just as the first Iroquois-engined Arrow Mk 2 was about to fly.

Specification: Avro Canada CF-105 Arrow Mk 1 two-seat long-range all-weather fighter prototype
Span: 15.24 m (50 ft 0 in)
Length: 23.72 m (77 ft 9.75 in)
Powerplant: 2×Pratt & Whitney J75-P-5, 10699 kg (23,500 lb) st each
Armament: provision for up to 8×Sparrow II air-to-air missiles carried in the lower-fuselage weapons bay
Max T/O weight: 31144 kg (68,600 lb)
Max speed: Mach 2.3 at 36,000 ft
Operational range: not stated

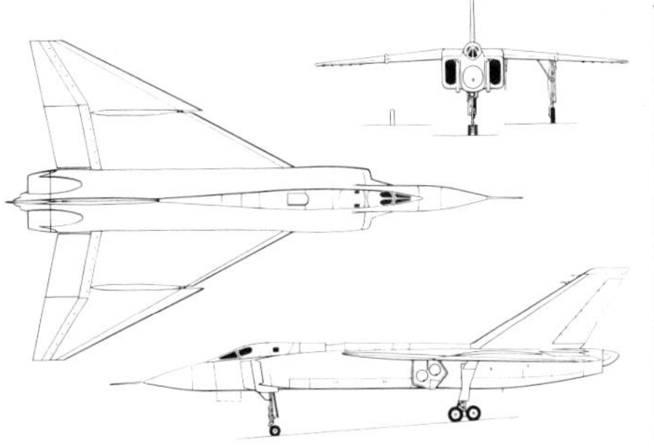

McDonnell Douglas F-4F Phantom II

The F-4F version of the F-4E was selected as successor to the F-104G in the air-defence role and the first of 175 aircraft began to enter service with Jagdgeschwader 71 and 74 at Wittmundhafen and Neuburg in 1973 and 1974 respectively: the Wings are allocated to the 2nd and 4th Allied Tactical Air Forces respectively. The aircraft also have an attack commitment, and in the 'Peace Rhine' programme that was completed in 1983 they were upgraded to carry the AGM-65 Maverick ASM and a wider range of AAMs. Between 1990 and 1992 the air-defence aircraft are to be further upgraded in air-defence capability with APG-65 radar, new IFF, an inertial navigation system with a ring-laser gyro, an improved cockpit and capability for AIM-120A AMRAAM missiles. Current taskings are 74 to interception and 80 to attack, the latter being the task of Jagdbombergeschwader 35 and 36 at Pferdsfeld and Hopsten respectively.

Specification: McDonnell Douglas F-4F Phantom II two-seat air-defence and attack fighter
Span: 11.77 m (38 ft 7.5 in)
Length: 19.20 m (63 ft 0 in)
Powerplant: 2×General Electric J79-GE-17A, 8119 kg (17,900 lb) st each
Armament: 1×20-mm rotary-barrel cannon plus provision for up to 7257 kg (16,000 lb) of disposable stores carried on 4×underfuselage missile stations, 1×underfuselage and 4×underwing hardpoints
Max T/O weight: 28030 kg (61,795 lb)
Max speed: Mach 2.17 at 36,000 ft
Operational range: 1,424 miles

Canadair CF-104 Starfighter

To replace its Sabre Mk 6s in Western Europe, Canada in 1959 decided to join several European nations in operating the F-104G multi-role version of the Lockheed Starfighter. Canadian production was entrusted to Canadair, whose CL-90 model was built for Canada as the CF-104 and the CL-201 model for some European partners as the F-104G. The Canadian single- and two-seat aircraft were originally designated CF-111 and CF-113 (later CF-104 and CF-104D) respectively, and were all powered by a Canadian-built engine: the 200 CF-104s were produced entirely in Canada, while the 38 CF-104Ds were built by Lockheed as 22 CF-104D Mk 1s and 16 CF-104D Mk 2s, the latter with improved equipment. The first CF-104 flew in May 1961 and, after entering service in 1962 with an eventual total of 12 European-based squadrons and one Canadian-based conversion unit, the type remained operational into the mid-1980s.

Specification: Canadair (Lockheed) CF-104 Starfighter single-seat strike and reconnaissance fighter
Span: 6.39 m (20 ft 11 in)
Length: 17.75 m (58 ft 3 in)
Powerplant: 1×Orenda-built General Electric J79-OEL-7, 7167 kg (15,800 lb) st
Armament: 1×20-mm M61A1 six-barrel cannon plus provision for up to 1955 kg (4,310 lb) of disposable stores on 1×underfuselage, 4×underwing and 2×wingtip hardpoints
Max T/O weight: 12156 kg (26,800 lb)
Max speed: Mach 2 at 35,000 ft
Operational range: 1,382 miles

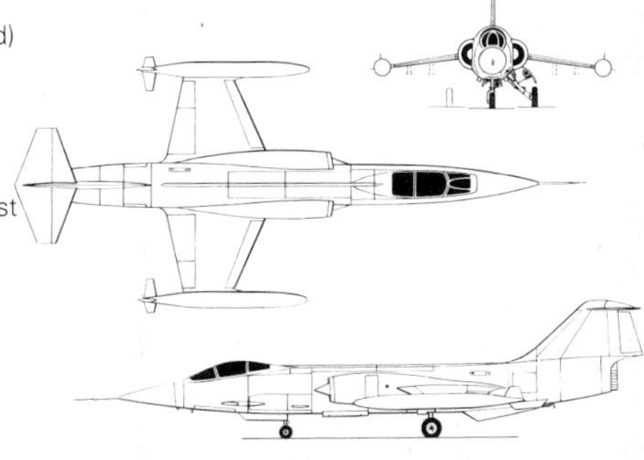

Dassault-Breguet Atlantic

To replace its Gannet AS.Mk 4 anti-submarine aircraft the Bundesmarine ordered from Breguet 20 examples of the Atlantic twin-turboprop maritime patroller. The aircraft were allocated to Marinefliegergeschwader 3, which moved from Schleswig to Nordholz in 1965 to re-equip with this French aeroplane. Some 19 Atlantics remain in service with two squadrons now at Kiel-Holtenau, the 14 still dedicated to the maritime task having been updated by Dornier with new Texas Instruments search radar, Loral electronic support measures, and improved navigation systems. The other five aircraft have been converted into dedicated Elint platforms for use along the borders of the Warsaw Pact nations in the Baltic region. Further updating of the Atlantic maritime patrollers has been foregone in favour of the purchase of a new type, the Lockheed P-7 advanced derivative of the P-3 Orion.

Specification: Dassault-Breguet Atlantic 12-seat maritime patrol and anti-submarine aeroplane
Span: 36.30 m (119 ft 1 in)
Length: 31.75 m (104 ft 2.5 in)
Powerplant: 2×Rolls-Royce Tyne RTy.20 Mk 21, 4638 kW (6,220 ehp) each
Armament: provision for up to 3500 kg (7,716 lb) of disposable stores carried internally and on 2×underwing hardpoints
Max T/O weight: 43500 kg (95,900 lb)
Max speed: 368 mph at sea level
Operational range: 4,950 miles

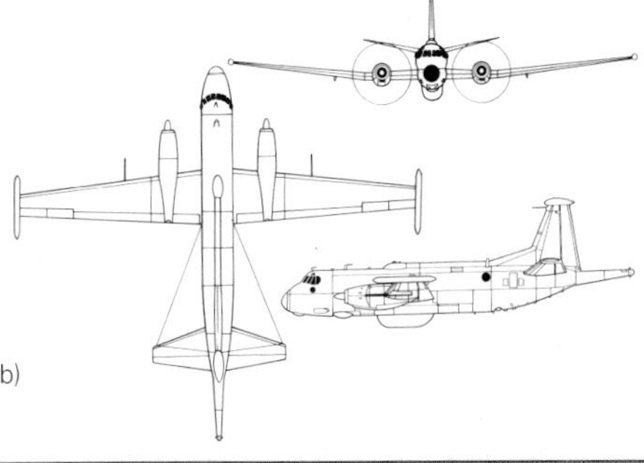

Chapter 3

NAVAL AIRCRAFT

Fairey Swordfish

Developed from the private-venture TSR.1 and first flown in April 1934, the Swordfish was a fabric-covered biplane with wheel or float landing gear, and acquired a legendary reputation in World War II. The type was contracted for production in April 1935 and began to enter service as the Swordfish Mk I (989 built) in July 1936. Some 13 Swordfish squadrons were operational at the beginning of World War II, and the type served right through that conflict. Later variants were the Swordfish Mk II (1,080 built) of 1943 with the Pegasus IIIM3 or 559-kW (750-hp) Pegasus 30 and strengthened lower wings for eight 60-lb (27-kg) rockets, the Swordfish Mk III (320 built) also of 1943 carrying ASV Mk X radar with its antenna under the forward fuselage, and the Swordfish Mk IV conversion of the Mk II with an enclosed cockpit for Canadian service.

Specification: Fairey Swordfish Mk I three-seat carrierborne and land-based torpedo-bomber and reconnaissance aeroplane
Span: 13.87 m (45 ft 6 in)
Length: 10.87 m (35 ft 8 in)
Powerplant: 1×Bristol Pegasus IIIM3, 514.5 kW (690 hp)
Armament: 2×0.303-in (7.7-mm) machine-guns, plus provision for 1×18-in (457-mm) torpedo, or 1×1,500-lb (680-kg) mine or 1,500 lb (680 kg) of bombs carried externally
Normal T/O weight: 3502 kg (7,720 lb)
Max speed: 139 mph at 4,750 ft
Operational range: 1,030 miles

Gloster Sea Gladiator

The Gladiator was the UK's last biplane fighter, and was celebrated beyond the measure of the numbers actually produced. The type first flew in 1934 and was a development of the Gauntlet with greater power and cantilever main landing gear legs, as well as features of contemporary monoplane fighters such as trailing-edge flaps and an enclosed cockpit. The type was ordered for the RAF as the Gladiator Mk I and entered service in January 1937. A naval version was ordered for the Fleet Air Arm as the Sea Gladiator. Beginning to enter service in February 1939, this differed from the land-based model in having the more powe ful engine of the Gladiator Mk II and naval items such as catapult points, an arrester hook and a dinghy under a small fairing. 60 Sea Gladiators were built, and another 38 were converted to Interim Sea Gladiator standard from RAF aircraft.

Specification: Gloster Sea Gladiator single-seat carrierborne and land-based fighter
Span: 9.83 m (32 ft 3 in)
Length: 8.36 m (27 ft 5 in)
Powerplant: 1×Bristol Mercury VIIIA or VIIIAS, 626 kW (840 hp)
Armament: 4×0.303-in (7.7-mm) machine-guns
Normal T/O weight: 1652 kg (5,420 lb)
Max speed: 245 mph at 14,500 ft
Operational range: 425 miles

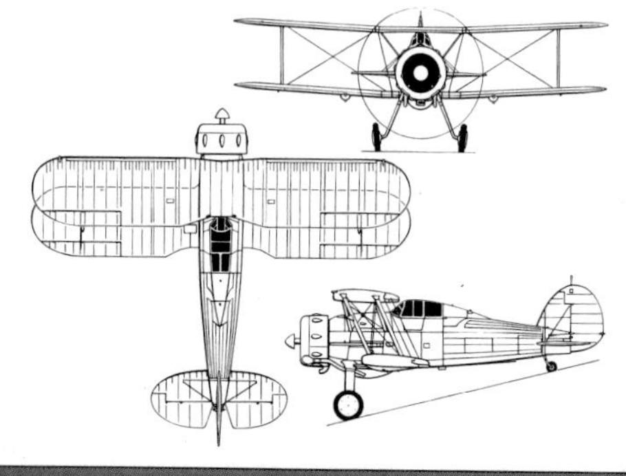

Fairey Albacore

The Albacore was intended as successor to the Swordfish, but was in fact outlived by the evergreen 'Stringbag'. The Albacore was in essence a 'cleaned up' Swordfish with features such as considerably more power, enclosed crew accommodation and hydraulically operated flaps. The landplane prototype was first flown in December 1938, and testing of this and a second unsuccessful floatplane prototype was followed by construction of an initial 98 Albacores from 1939. Production of the land-based variant eventually reached 798, and the type began to enter service in March 1940. Initial deployment was at shore bases in the minelaying and anti-shipping patrol roles, but carrier operations followed from 1941 in the torpedo-bomber, convoy escort and anti-submarine roles. The type was phased out of service during 1944.

Specification: Fairey Albacore three-seat carrierborne and shore-based torpedo-bomber and multi-role aeroplane
Span: 15.24 m (50 ft 0 in)
Length: 12.13 m (39 ft 9.5 in)
Powerplant: 1×Bristol Taurus II or XII, 794 or 842.5 kW (1,065 or 1,130 hp)
Armament: 3×0.303-in) (7.7-mm) machine-guns, plus provision for 1×18-in (457-mm) torpedo carried under the fuselage, or 4×500-lb (227-kg) bombs or 6×250-lb (113-kg) bombs carried under the wings
Max T/O weight: 5715 kg (12,600 lb)
Max speed: 161 mph at 4,000 ft
Operational range: 820 miles

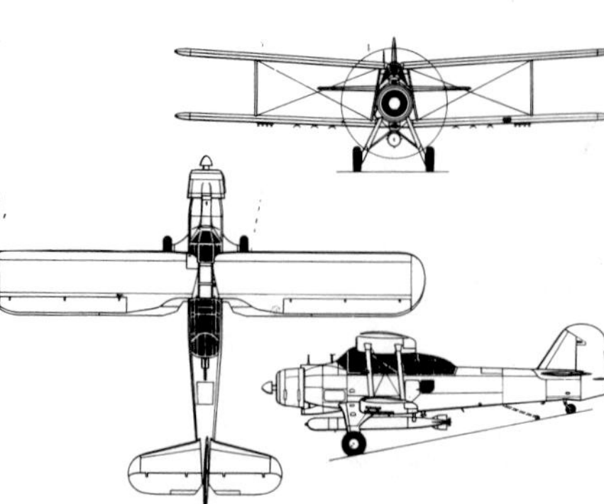

The Fairey Swordfish – lovingly known as the 'Stringbag' by its Fleet Air Arm crews – was in use throughout World War II. This Swordfish from 816 Squadron bears 'D-Day' striped markings and has eight rocket projectiles mounted under its wings.

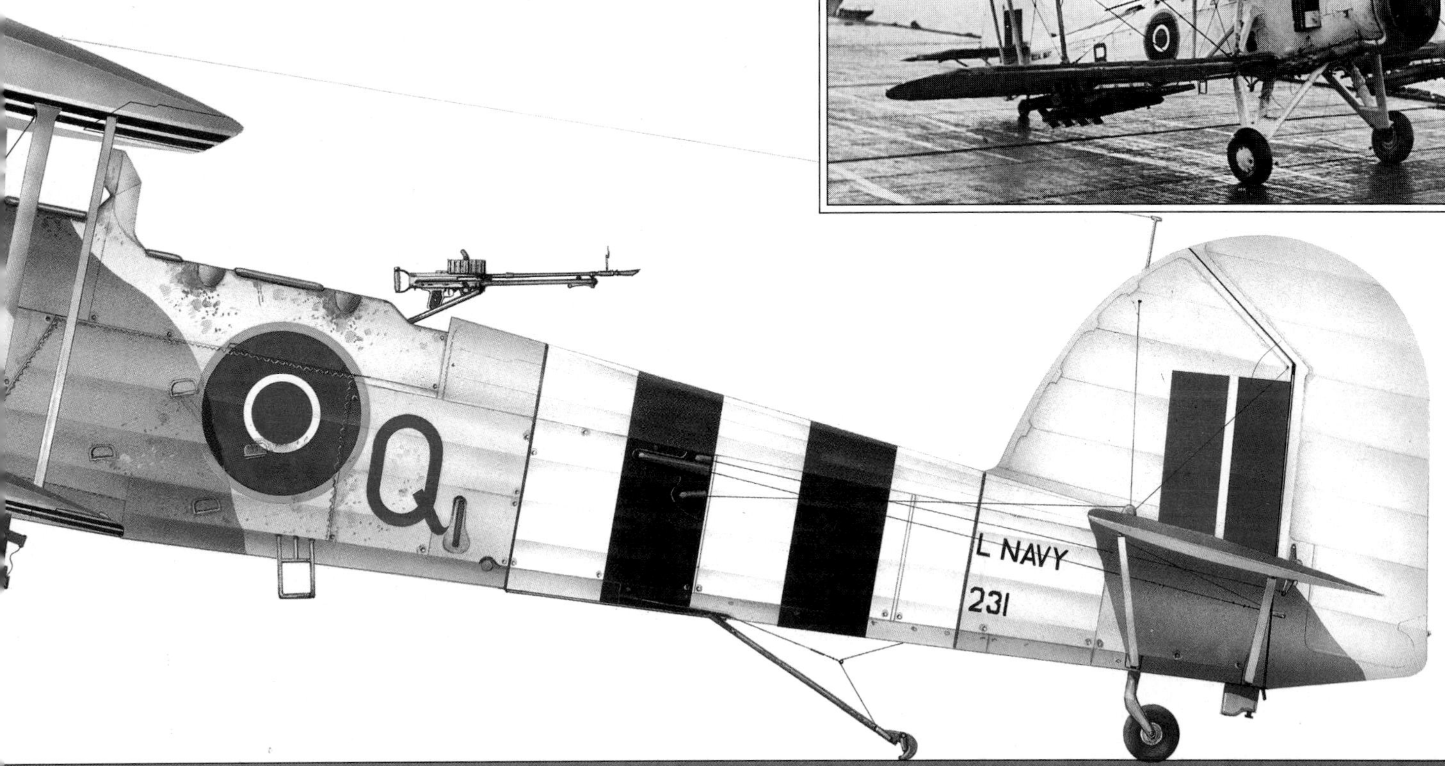

Blackburn Skua

The Skua was the Royal Navy's first operational combat monoplane, and had features such as an all-metal structure, retractable landing gear, flaps, a variable-pitch propeller and an enclosed (but highly angular) cockpit hood. The Skua Mk I prototype made its maiden flight in February 1937 on the 626kW (840hp) afforded by a Bristol Mercury IX radial. The need for a naval dive-bomber and fighter to supersede the Hawker Nimrod biplane was so acute that the type had been ordered into production 'straight off the drawing board' to the extent of 190 Skua Mk II aircraft with detail modifications and a different engine. The Skua Mk II began to enter service in late 1938. The type is credited with the first British destruction of a German aircraft in World War II and the sinking of the German cruiser *Konigsberg*, but from 1941 was relegated to target-towing and other secondary duties.

Specification: Blackburn Skua Mk II two-seat carrierborne and land-based fighter and dive-bomber
Span: 14.07m (46ft 2in)
Length: 10.84m (35ft 7in)
Powerplant: 1×Bristol Perseus XII, 663.5kW (890hp)
Armament: 5×0.303-in (7.7-mm) machine-guns, plus provision for 1×500-lb (227-kg) bomb carried externally
Max T/O weight: 3732kg (8,228lb)
Max speed: 229 mph at 6,500 ft
Operational range: 435 miles

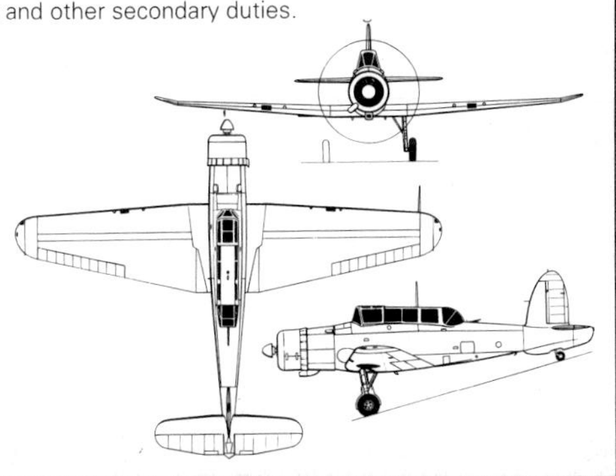

Blackburn Roc

The Roc was closely related to the Skua in configuration and structure but, like the Defiant land-based fighter, relied for armament on a four-gun turret located just to the rear of the pilot. The turret was nicely faired into the contours of the upper fuselage, the rear fairing being designed to lower automatically when the guns were trained aft. The type was designed for alternative use on fixed floats, and the prototype first flew in December 1938. Production was entrusted to Boulton Paul, the designer and builder of the turret, and 136 Rocs were built. These began to enter service in April 1939, but early operations confirmed the type's unsuitability as a first-line fighter, and from 1940 most Rocs were relegated to secondary tasks such as AA artillery co-operation and target-towing.

Specification: Blackburn Roc two-seat land-based naval fighter
Span: 14.02m (46ft 0in)
Length: 10.84m (35ft 7in)
Powerplant: 1×Bristol Perseus XII, 663.5kW (890hp)
Armament: 4×0.303-in (7.7-mm) machine-guns, plus provision for 1×(250-lb) (113-kg) bomb carried externally
Max T/O weight: 3606kg (7,950lb)
Max speed: 196 mph at 6,500 ft
Operational range: 810 miles

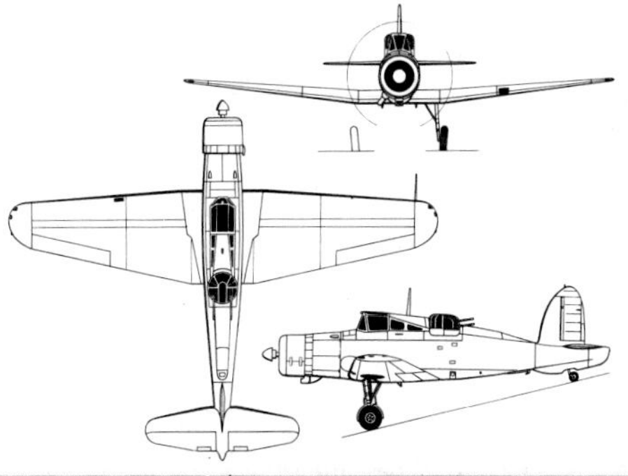

Grumman Martlet/Wildcat

After being recast from the XF4F-1 biplane into the XF4F-2 during 1936, this monoplane became the Allies' most important naval fighter of the early war years. The prototype first flew in September 1937, and great development in power and armament followed before the initial F4F-3 entered service in 1940. The type was used by the Royal Navy as the fixed- and folding-wing Martlet (later Wildcat) Mk I and Martlet Mk II, of which 100 and 90 respectively were received, the latter with two extra guns. The 60 similar Martlet Mk IIIs had catapult spools. The type was successively improved in variants such as the F4F-4 (200 Wildcat Mk IVs with two more wing guns) and similar General Motors FM-1 with manually-folding wings (312 Wildcat Mk Vs) and the FM-2 with more power, a revised nose and taller vertical tail (370 Wildcat Mk VIs).

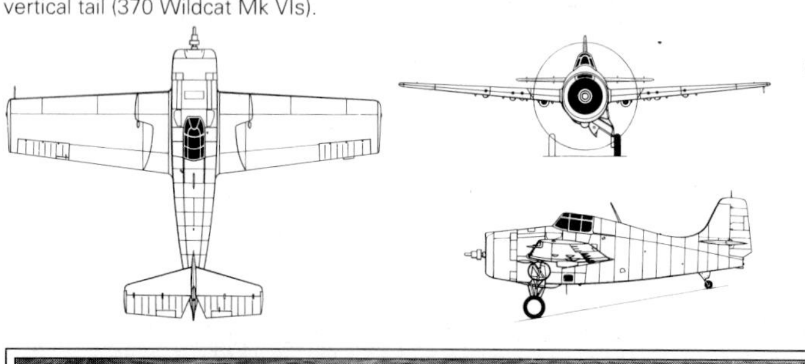

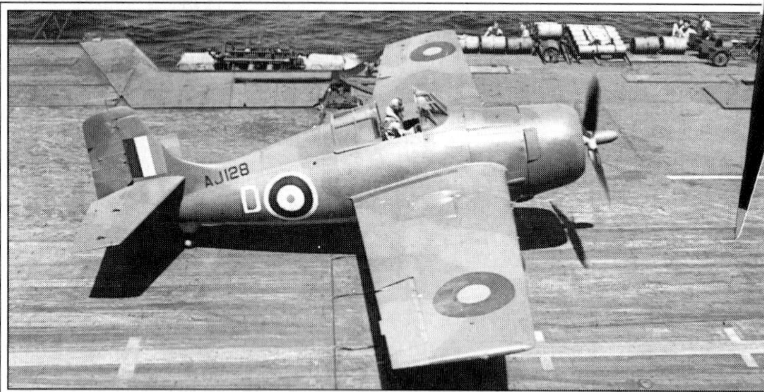

Specification: Grumman Wildcat Mk IV single-seat carrierborne fighter
Span: 11.58m (38ft 0in)
Length: 8.76m (28ft 9in)
Powerplant: 1×Pratt & Whitney R-1830-86 Twin Wasp, 895kW (1,200hp)
Armament: 6×0.5-in (12.7-mm) machine-guns plus 2×45-kg (100-lb) bombs
Max T/O weight: 3607kg (7,952lb)
Max speed: 318 mph at 19,400 ft
Operational range: 770 miles

Fairey Fulmar

The Fulmar was the Royal Navy's first eight-gun monoplane fighter, but was considerably hampered in its primary aerial combat role by the fact that it was a comparatively slow all-metal two-seater of generally uninspired low-wing layout with tailwheel landing gear whose main units only were retractable. Developed from the P.4/34 prototype which it closely resembled, the Fulmar prototype flew in January 1940 and the type was placed into immediate production. Deliveries of 250 Fulmar Mk Is began in June of the same year, production switching in the middle of the following year to the improved Fulmar Mk II with the 969-kW (1,300-hp) Merlin XXX and provision for tropical operations. Mk II production totalled 350, and some of these were completed as night fighters. The type remained in service up to 1945.

Specification: Fairey Fulmar Mk I two-seat carrierborne and land-based fighter and reconnaissance aeroplane
Span: 14.13m (46ft 4.5in)
Length: 12.27m (40ft 3in)
Powerplant: 1×Rolls-Royce Merlin VIII, 805kW (1,080hp)
Armament: 8×0.303-in (7.7-mm) fixed machine-guns, and (optional) one 0.303-in (7.7-mm) machine-gun in the rear cockpit
Normal T/O weight: 4445kg (9,800lb)
Max speed: 280 mph at optimum altitude
Operational range: 800 miles

Hawker Sea Hurricane

To bolster the Royal Navy's fighter strength it was decided in 1940 to convert the Hurricane to a naval fighter. After trials with a prototype carrying catapult spools and an arrester hook, some 50 Sea Hurricane Mk IAs were converted from Hurricane Mk Is as 'one-shot' fighters for use by catapult-equipped merchantmen that lacked landing-on capability, followed by 300 carrier-capable Sea Hurricane Mk IBs (converted from Merlin III-powered Hurricane Mk Is and Hurricane Mk IIAs) and Sea Hurricane IICs with the four-cannon wing of the Hurricane Mk IIC. Next came the Sea Hurricane Mk IIC with the Merlin XX engine. The final version was the new-build Sea Hurricane Mk XIIA, a Canadian navalised version of the locally built Hurricane Mk XII with the American-built Packard Merlin XXIX.

Specification: Hawker Sea Hurricane Mk IIC single-seat carrierborne fighter
Span: 12.19m (40ft 0in)
Length: 9.83m (32ft 3in)
Powerplant: 1×Rolls-Royce Merlin XX, 1089kW (1,460hp)
Armament: 4×20-mm cannon
Normal T/O weight: 3674kg (8,100lb)
Max speed: 342 mph at 22,000 ft
Operational range: 460 miles

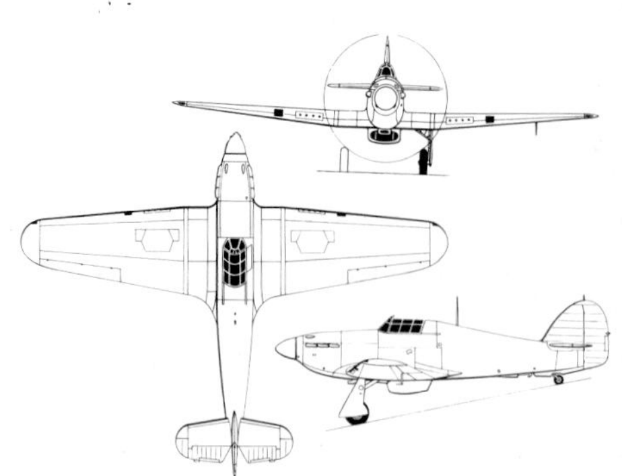

The '07' codes show this to be a Martlet II of No. 888 Squadron (note the squadron badge on the fin flash), part of the shore-based detachment at La Senia in December 1942 and January 1943. Flying from HMS Formidable, the squadron was involved in several operations, providing air cover for the landings on Madagascar in May 1942, and on Sicily and at Salerno in July and September 1943. The squadron also took part in Operation Torch as part of the North African invasion forces in late 1942, shooting down two enemy aircraft.

Supermarine Seafire

After the success of the Sea Hurricane in the fleet role, the Royal Navy decided that a navalised Spitfire offered the best method of obtaining a high-performance carrierborne fighter without undue delay, and after successful trials with a converted Spitfire Mk VB some 166 Spitfire Mk VBs were converted as Seafire Mk IBs with Merlin 45 or 46 engines. The first Seafires built as such were 372 Seafires Mk IICs produced in F, (L)F and FR variants but basically similar to the Seafire Mk IB apart from their catapult spools and universal wings for different armament options. The Seafire Mk III was produced to the extent of 1,270 aircraft in the same three variants and all but 50 (L)F.Mk IIIC aircraft, had folding wings. The Griffon-engined variants were the 786 Mks XV, XVII, 45, 46 and 47, but these all entered service after World War II.

Specification: Supermarine Seafire (L)F. Mk III single-seat carrierborne and land-based fighter and fighter-bomber
Span: 11.22 m (36 ft 10 in)
Length: 9.11 m (29 ft 11 in)
Powerplant: 1×Rolls-Royce Merlin 55M or 32, 1180 or 1227 kW (1,583 or 1,645 hp)
Armament: 2×20-mm cannon and 4×0.303-in (7.7-mm) machine-guns, plus provision for 1×500-lb (227-kg) bomb, or two 250-lb (113-kg) bombs or 8×60-lb (27-kg) rockets carried externally
Max T/O weight: 3900 kg (8,600 lb)
Max speed: 341 mph at 6,000 ft
Operational range: 465 miles

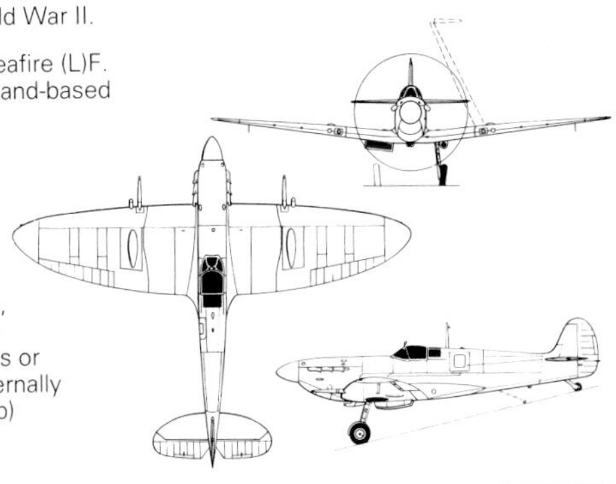

Fairey Firefly

Designed to succeed the Fulmar, the Firefly adhered to much the same basic design concept but was an altogether superior aeroplane in terms of performance and firepower, and also possessed better handling characteristics in the air and on a carrier deck. The first prototype flew in December 1941, and deliveries to the Royal Navy began in March 1943 for operational capability in October of the same year. Production amounted to 937 Firefly F.Mk Is, FR.Mk I fighter-reconnaissance aircraft and FR.Mk IA conversions of F.Mk Is to FR.Mk I standard with ASH radar. There followed 37 Firefly NF.Mk II night-fighters with a longer nose and AI Mk X radar, this total being boosted by conversions of F.Mk Is to NF.Mk I standard with radar and shrouded exhausts. Other variants were produced after the war in the type's 13-year operational career.

Specification: Fairey Firefly F.Mk I two-seat carrierborne and land-based fighter
Span: 13.56 m (44 ft 6 in)
Length: 11.46 m (37 ft 7.25 in)
Powerplant: 1×Rolls-Royce Griffon IIB or XII, 1290 or 1484 kW (1,730 or 1,990 hp)
Armament: 4×20-mm cannon, plus provision for 8×60-lb (27-kg) rockets or 2×1,000-lb (454-kg) bombs carried under the wings
Normal T/O weight: 6360 kg (14,020 lb)
Max speed: 316 mph at 14,000 ft
Operational range: 1,070 miles

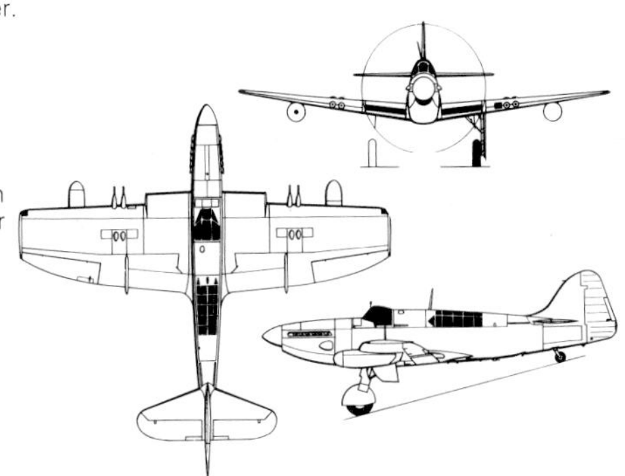

Douglas SBD Dauntless

The SBD was the US Navy's most important carrierborne bomber of the war against Japan, and was essentially a refinement of the Northrop BT-1 of 1935. The Dauntless prototype was the SBT-2, but the company was then bought by Douglas and the first production version of this sturdy monoplane was designated SBD-1, with deliveries of 57 to the US Marine Corps following in late 1940. The SBD-2 (87 built) had greater armament and fuel for the US Navy. Later models were the SBD-3 with heavier fixed armament and self-sealing tanks (780 built), the SBD-4 with a modified electrical system (780), the SBD-5 with greater power (3,025), the up-engined SBD-6 (451), the A-24 USAAF version of the SBD-3 (168), the A-24A USAAF version of the SBD-4 (170) and the Dauntless Mk I Fleet Air Arm version of the SBD-5 (9).

Specification: Douglas SBD-5 Dauntless two-seat carrier- and shore-based scout and dive-bomber.
Span: 12.65 m (41 ft 6.25 in)
Length: 10.06 m (33 ft 0 in)
Powerplant: 1×Wright R-1820-66 Cyclone 9, 1007 kW (1,350 hp)
Armament: 2×0.5-in (12.7-mm) and 2×0.3-in (7.62-mm) machine-guns plus up to 1021-kg (2,250-lb) of bombs carried externally
Max T/O weight: 4855 kg (10,700 lb)
Max speed: 245 mph at 15,800 ft
Operational range: 1,100 miles

Brewster F2A Buffalo

Developed from June 1936, the F2A was the US Navy's first monoplane fighter when it entered service in June 1939. The aircraft was conceptually akin to the SBA scout bomber, though smaller and providing accommodation only for a pilot. The initial F2A-1 variant had the 701-kW (940-hp) R-1820-34 radial engine, and was judged generally inadequate for carrierborne service: all but 11 were passed on to Finland early in 1940, these 43 F2A-1s being replaced by a similar number of F2A-2s with the 895-kW (1,200-hp) R-1820-40 engine and detail improvements. The main production model was the F2A-3 with armour and other operational features that degraded performance considerably. Some 303 more aircraft were built as land-based fighters for Belgium (40), the Dutch East Indies (92) and the UK (170 Buffalo Mk Is).

Specification: Brewster F2A-3 single-seat carrier- and land-based fighter
Span: 10.67 m (35 ft 0 in)
Length: 8.02 m (26 ft 4 in)
Powerplant: 1×Wright R-1820-40 Cyclone 895 kW (1,200 hp)
Armament: 4×0.5-in (12.7-mm) machine-guns
Max T/O weight: 3247 kg (7,159 lb)
Max speed: 321 mph at 16,500 ft
Operational range: 965 miles

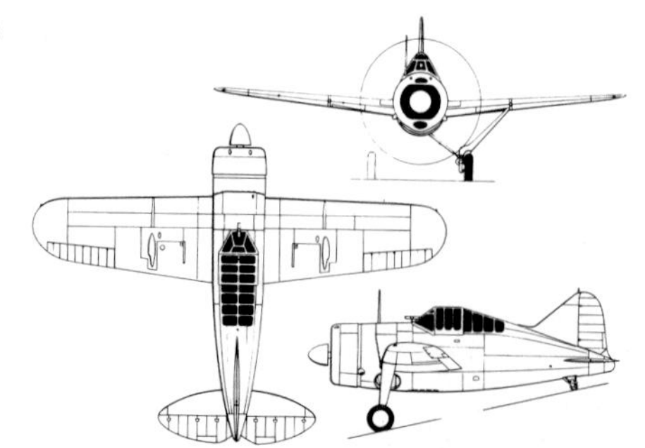

Curtiss SO3C Seamew

The SO3C was designed to a 1937 requirement for a scout monoplane to replace the SOC Seagull biplane on the US Navy's battleships and cruisers. The XSO3C-1 prototype first flew in October 1939 in landplane and floatplane layouts. Serious problems of control and stability were remedied by the adoption of a larger tail and upturned wingtips, and production SO3C-1s began to appear in July 1942 with the V-770-6 engine. The SO3C-2 variant was known to the British as the Sewmew Mk I and had carrier capability plus provision for an underfuselage bombload. The SO3C-1s were generally converted into radio-controlled targets, and only 39 examples of the lightened SO3C-3 with the V-770-8 engine were produced before production ended in January 1944 after 794 aircraft had been built. All Seamews were withdrawn in that year, the plans for other variants being cancelled.

Specification: Curtiss SO3C-2 Seamew two-seat ship- and shore-based scout and observation aeroplane
Span: 11.58 m (38 ft 0 in)
Length: 10.59 m (34 ft 9 in)
Powerplant: 1×Ranger V-770-6, 447 kW (600 hp)
Armament: 2×0.3-in (7.62-mm) machine-guns plus 1×227-kg (500-lb) bomb and 2×147-kg (325-lb) depth charges carried externally
Max T/O weight: 3175 kg (7,000 lb)
Max speed: 172 mph at 8,100 ft
Operational range: 940 miles

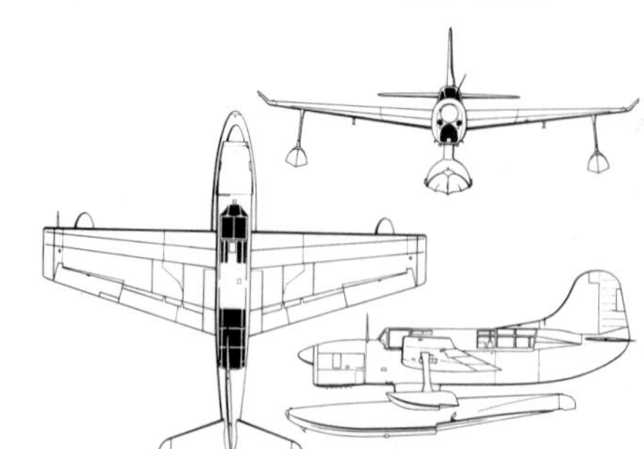

Curtiss SBC Helldiver

The SBC was the last combat biplane produced in the USA, but began life as the XF12C parasol-wing monoplane fighters with retractable landing gear. Complex evolution through scout (XF4C) and scout-bombing (XSBC) roles followed, together with redesign as the XSBC-2 biplane, before the type entered service in July 1937 as the SBC-3 dive-bomber scout with the R-1535-94 engine. The 83 SBC-3s were followed by 224 examples of the SBC-4 with greater bombload and a more powerful engine. Of the SBC-4s 50 were transferred to France, and just five went to the Royal Air Force as Cleveland Mk Is. The Helldiver was declared obsolete just after the attack on Pearl Harbor.

Specification: Curtiss SBC-4 Helldiver two-seat carrierborne scout bomber
Span: 10.36 m (34 ft 0 in)
Length: 8.63 m (28 ft 4 in)
Powerplant: 1×Wright R-1820-34 Cyclone 9, 708 kW (950 hp)
Armament: 1×0.5-in (12.7-mm) and 1×0.3-in (7.62-mm) machine-guns plus 1×227- or 454-kg (500- or 1,000-lb) bomb carried externally
Max T/O weight: 3462 kg (7,632 lb)
Max speed: 237 mph at 15,200 ft
Operational range: 590 miles

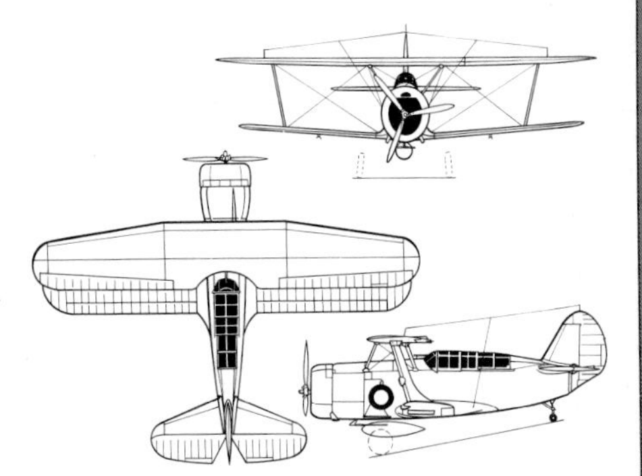

Curtiss SB2C Helldiver

The SB2C was the last Curtiss combat aeroplane for the US Navy, and the company's first monoplane bomber. The SB2C was designed to replace the SBC Helldiver, and had much the same portliness as the earlier design though with a large monoplane wing and landing gear that retracted into the wings rather than the fuselage. The type began to enter service in December 1942, and production amounted to 7,200 aircraft whose main variants were the SB2C-1 and upgunned SB2C-1C, the SB2C-3 with greater power, the SB2C-4 with underwing rockets or bombs, the SB2C-5 with larger fuel capacity, the SBF series built in Canada by Fairchild, the SBW series built by Canadian Car and Foundry, the A-25A land-based SB2C-1 model, and the Helldiver Mk I equivalent of the SB2C-1 for the Fleet Air Arm.

Specification: Curtiss SB2C-4 Helldiver two-seat carrierborne scout bomber
Span: 15.16 m (49 ft 9 in)
Length: 11.17 m (36 ft 8 in)
Powerplant: 1×Wright R-2600-20 Cyclone 14, 1417 kW (1,900 hp)
Armament: 2×20-mm cannon and 2×0.3-in (7.62-mm) machine-guns plus 454 kg (1,000 lb) of bombs carried internally and either 8×rockets or 454 kg (1,000 lb) of bombs carried under the wings
Max T/O weight: 7537 kg (16,616 lb)
Max speed: 295 mph at 16,700 ft
Operational range: 1,235 miles

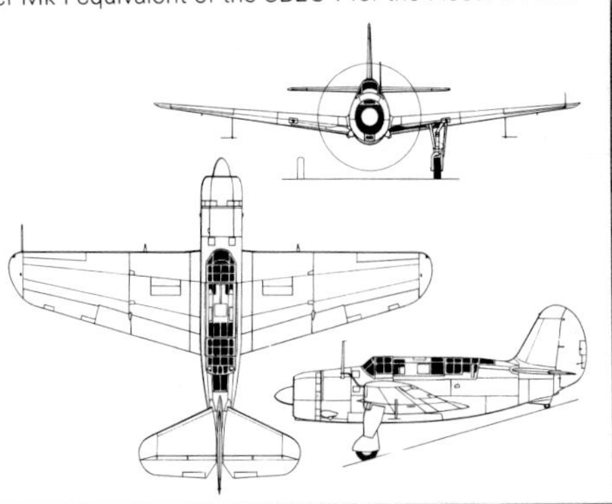

Grumman F6F Hellcat

The F6F was an evolutionary development of the F4F with greater size, power, weight and capabilities, and after its debut in August 1943 rapidly became the US Navy's most important carrierborne fighter of World War II, being credited with 5,156 kills against Japanese aircraft, 75 per cent of all US Navy victories. Prototypes were ordered in June 1941 with normal and supercharged R-2800 engines as the XF6F-1 and SF6F-2, design changes leading to redesignation as the XF6F-3 and XF6F-4 before a first flight in June 1942. The major variants were the F6F-3, the F6F-3N and -3E with night-fighting radar, the F6F-5 improved F6F-3 with fighter-bomber capability, the F6F-5N night-fighter, and the F6F-5P reconnaissance model. The type was known to the Fleet Air Arm as the Hellcat, and production totalled 12,275.

Specification: Grumman F6F-5 Hellcat single-seat carrierborne fighter and fighter-bomber
Span: 13.05 m (42 ft 10 in)
Length: 10.23 m (33 ft 7 in)
Powerplant: 1×Pratt & Whitney R-2800-10W Double Wasp, 1491 kW (2,000 hp)
Armament: 6×0.5-in (12.7-mm) machine-guns or 2×20-mm cannon and 4×0.5-in machine-guns, plus 6×rockets or 907 kg (2,000 lb) of bombs carried externally
Max T/O weight: 6991 kg (15,413 lb)
Max speed: 380 mph at 23,400 ft
Operational range: 945 miles

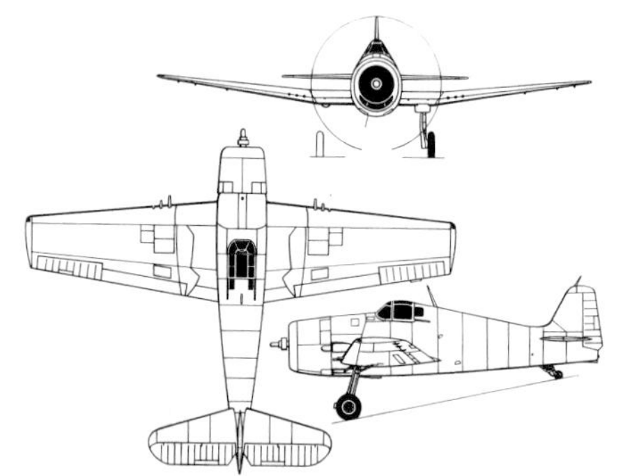

Curtiss SC Seahawk

The Seahawk was the last of the US Navy's scouting aircraft designed for operation from capital ships as well as aircraft carriers and land bases, and was a trim low-wing monoplane with the looks of a fighter. The type resulted from a mid-1942 requirement and the XSC-1 prototype first flew in February 1944, seven months after the production SC-1 had been ordered. The structure was as simple as possible to ease production, and there was provision for a stretcher to be carried in the rear fuselage. All SC-1s were delivered as landplanes with neat tailwheel landing gear, the Edo installation of a single main float and two smaller stabilising floats being fitted as and when required. The SC-2 had more power and other improvements, but only 10 were produced to complement the 566 SC-1s delivered.

Specification: Curtiss SC-1 Seahawk single-seat ship- or land-based scout and anti-submarine patrol aeroplane
Span: 12.50 m (41 ft 0 in)
Length: 11.09 m (36 ft 4.5 in)
Powerplant: 1×Wright R-1820-62 Cyclone 9, 1007 kW (1,350 hp)
Armament: 2×0.5-in (12.7-mm) machine-guns plus up to 295 kg (650 lb) of bombs carried externally
Max T/O weight: 4082 kg (9,000 lb)
Max speed: 313 mph at 28,600 ft
Operational range: 625 miles

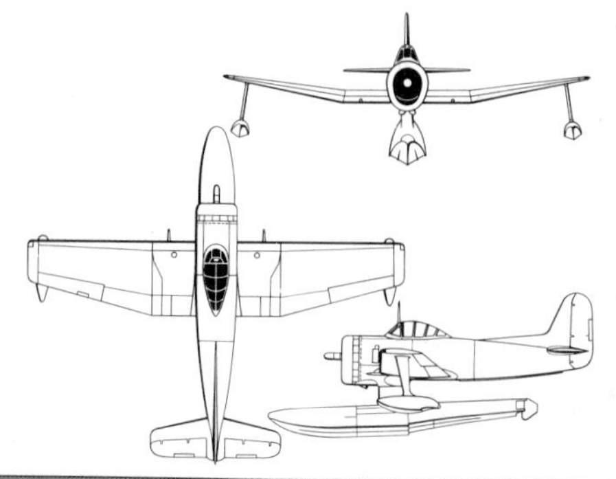

Curtiss SOC Seagull

First flown in April 1934, the SOC Seagull was the last Curtiss biplane operated by the US Navy. A delightful aircraft, it served for many years, even after the monoplane SO3C Seamew had been withdrawn from service. Mostly operating as a pure floatplane, the SOC was easily and quickly reconfigured with a tailwheel undercarriage for land-based training purposes. Its primary role was scout/observation, being catapulted from US Navy warships and then being hoisted back aboard after a water landing. It also made a good dive bomber for light attacks, and during the attack on Pearl Harbor two SOCs scored an unofficial victory over a Mitsubishi A6M. 262 Seagulls were built, including the SOC-1 and -3 floatplanes, SOC-2 landplanes and the SOC-4 (3 built) for the US Coast Guard.

Specification: Curtiss SOC 1 two-seat ship- and shore-based scout/observation platform
Span: 10.97 m (36 ft 0 in)
Length: 8.08 m (26 ft 6 in)
Powerplant: 1×1 Pratt & Whitney R-1340-18 Wasp, 447-kW (600-hp)
Armament: 2×0.30-in (7.62-mm) machine-guns plus up to 295 kg (650 lb) of bombs
Max T/O weight: 2466 kg (5,437 lb)
Max speed: 266 km/h (165 mph)
Operational range: 1086 km (675 miles)

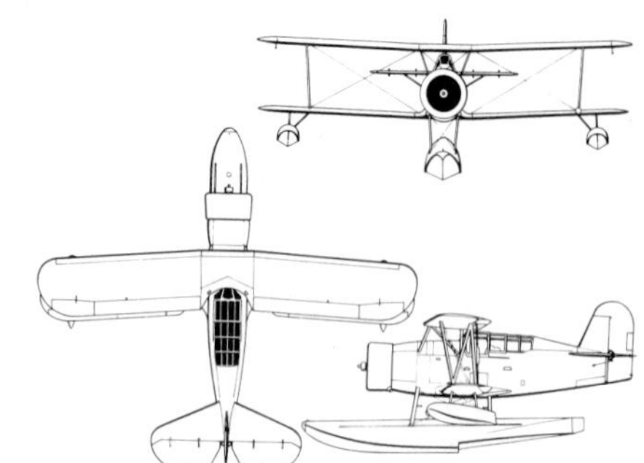

Douglas TBD Devastator

For service on its modern aircraft carriers that started in 1934 with the USS *Ranger*, the US Navy required a new torpedo-bomber and ordered prototypes from Great Lakes (the XTBG-1 biplane) and Douglas (the XTBD-1 monoplane). The latter first flew in April 1935, and was ordered into production as the US Navy's first production monoplane. This TBD-1 had folding wings and semi-retractable landing gear whose half-exposed mainwheels provided a measure of safety in a forced landing. Compared with the prototype the production model had 75-kW (100-hp) more power, a revised cowling and a raised canopy over the pilot. Production amounted to only 130 aircraft, and the sole Devastator squadron present at the Battle of Midway (June 1942) suffered such a mauling that the type was pulled out of front-line service.

Specification: Douglas TBD-1 Devastator three-seat carrierborne torpedo-bomber
Span: 15.24 m (50 ft 0 in)
Length: 10.67 m (35 ft 0 in)
Powerplant: 1×Pratt & Whitney R-1830-64 Twin Wasp, 671 kW (900 hp)
Armament: 1×0.5-in (12.7-mm) and 1×0.3-in (7.62-mm) machine-guns plus 1×454-kg (1,000-lb) torpedo under the fuselage
Max T/O weight: 4624 kg (10,194 lb)
Max speed: 206 mph at 8,000 ft
Operational range: 716 miles

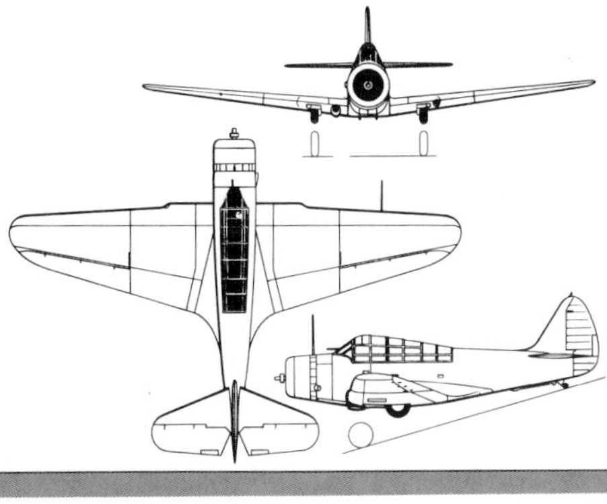

Grumman F4F Wildcat

The XF4F-1 of 1935 was designed as biplane insurance against failure of the Brewster XF2A monoplane, but then recast in 1936 as the XF4F-2 monoplane to become the Allies' most important naval fighter of the early war years. Grumman's typical portly fuselage and fuselage-attached retractable landing gear were retained, and the prototype first flew in September 1937 in competition with the XF2A. Considerable development in power and armament followed before the initial F4F-3 entered service in 1940. The type was successively improved in variants such as the F4F-4 and similar General Motors' FM-1 with manually-folding wings, the FM-2 with more power, and the F4F-7 unarmed reconnaissance aeroplane. The type was known to the British as the Martlet and then as the Wildcat, and production totalled 7,344.

Specification: Grumman F4F-4 Wildcat single-seat carrierborne fighter
Span: 11.58 m (38 ft 0 in)
Length: 8.76 m (28 ft 9 in)
Powerplant: 1×Pratt & Whitney R-1830-86 Twin Wasp, 895 kW (1,200 hp)
Armament: 6×0.5-in (12.7-mm) machine-guns plus 2×45-kg (100-lb) bombs
Max T/O weight: 3607 kg (7,952 lb)
Max speed: 318 mph at 19,400 ft
Operational range: 770 miles

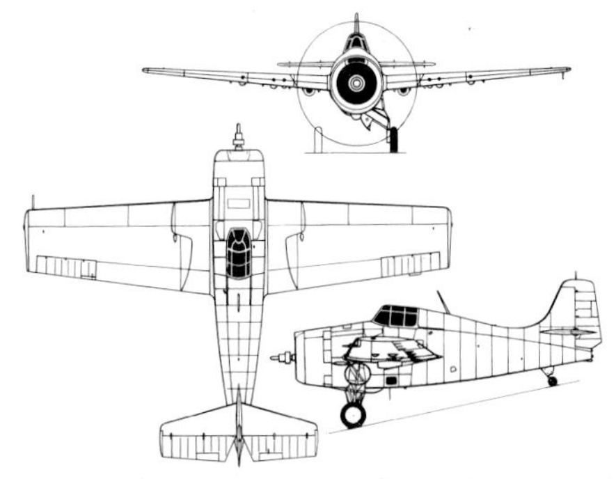

Grumman TBF Avenger

Despite a first mission in June 1942 from which only one of six aircraft returned, the TBF rapidly became the US Navy's most important torpedo bomber of World War II. The type was designed in 1940 to succeed the Devastator with greater performance and offensive/defensive power. Total production amounted to 9,839 aircraft in few variants. The TBF-1 had a 1268-kW (1,700-hp) R-2600-8 radial and was complemented by the General Motors-built TBM-1; versions with two additional wing guns were built as the TBF-1C and TBM-1C. The most important model was the General Motors-built TBM-3 with greater power, and like the TBF/TGBM-1 series this was built in variants indicated by letter suffixes. The British initially designated the type Tarpon, but then fixed on the name Avenger. The series remained in service into the 1950s.

Specification: Grumman (General Motors) TBM-3E three-seat carrierborne torpedo bomber
Span: 16.51 m (54 ft 2 in)
Length: 12.48 m (40 ft 11.5 in)
Powerplant: 1×Wright R-2600-20 Cyclone 14, 1417 kW (1,900 hp)
Armament: 3×0.5-in (12.7-mm) and 1×0.3-in (7.62-in) machine-guns plus up to 907 kg (2,000 lb) of bombs or 1×torpedo carried internally
Max T/O weight: 8117 kg (17,895 lb)
Max speed: 276 mph at 26,500 ft
Operational range: 1,010 miles

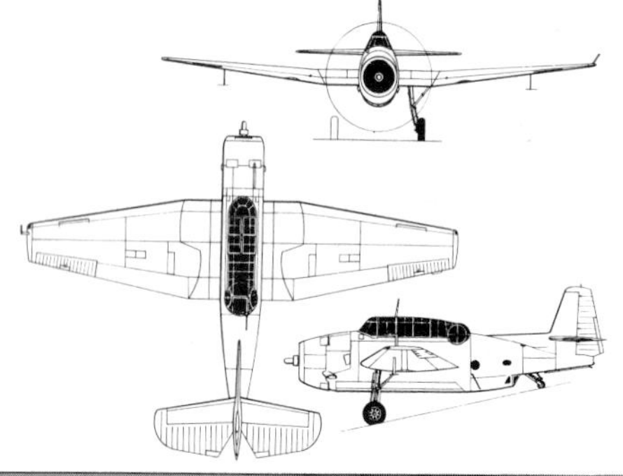

Vought F4U Corsair

Without doubt the best carrierborne fighter of World War II, the F4U remained in production longer than any other US fighter of the period, is credited with an 11:1 ratio of kills/losses against the Japanese, and excelled in performance and payload. The XF4U-1 prototype flew in May 1940, and after considerable development the F4U-1 began to enter service in October 1943, initially for shore-based Marine units. The F4U was also built by Brewster and Goodyear as the F3A and FG, and variants were the -1 with machine-gun armament, the -1A with fixed wings, the -1B for the British as the Corsair, the -1C with wing-mounted cannon, the -1D with rocket/bomb provision, and the -1P for reconnaissance. The F4U-2 was a night-fighter conversion, and the F4U-4 had greater power. Development and production continued after the war for a total of 12,571 aircraft.

Specification: Vought F4U-4 Corsair single-seat carrier- and shore-based fighter and fighter-bomber
Span: 12.48 m (40 ft 11.75 in)
Length: 10.26 m (33 ft 8 in)
Powerplant: 1×Pratt & Whitney R-2800-18W Double Wasp, 1566 kW (2,100 hp)
Armament: 4×20-mm cannon or 6×0.5-in (12.7-mm) machine-guns plus provision for 2×454-kg (1,000-lb) bombs or 8×127-mm (5-in) rockets
Max T/O weight: 6654 kg (14,670 lb)
Max speed: 446 mph at 26,200 ft
Operational range: 1,005 miles

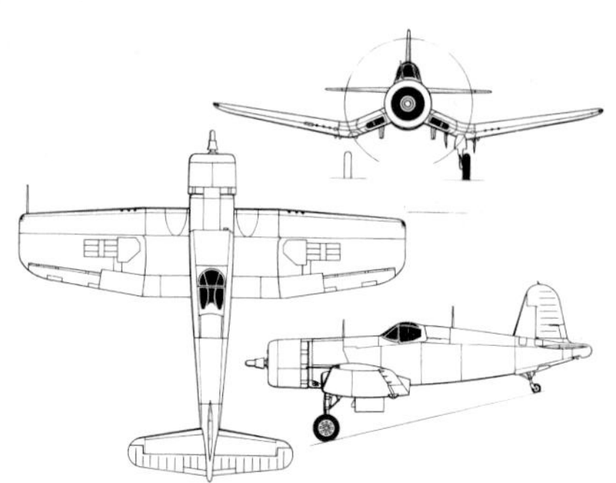

Vought OS2U Kingfisher

The OS2U was produced to the same specification as the SO3C, but was an altogether more successful aeroplane, and the best US Navy observation and scout type of World War II. The OS2U could be used on tailwheel landing gear, but was more usually seen as a waterplane with a central main float and two smaller stabilising floats. The prototype flew in July 1938, and the basically similar OS2U-1 with the 336-kW (450-hp) R-985-48 began to enter service in August 1940. After 54 OS2U-1s the line switched to the OS2U-2 (158 built) with the R-985-50, and then to the OS2U-3 (1,006) with additional fuel tankage and a measure of armour protection for the pilot and observer; the OS2U was known to the British as the Kingisher Mk I. An additional 300 aircraft were built by the Naval Aircraft Factory with the designation OSN-1.

Specification: Vought OS2U-3 Kingisher two-seat ship- and shore-based observation and scout aeroplane
Span: 10.94 m (35 ft 11 in)
Length: 10.25 m (33 ft 7.25 in)
Powerplant: 1×Pratt & Whitney R-985-AN-2 Wasp Junior, 336 kW (450 hp)
Armament: 2×0.3-in (7.62-mm) machine-guns plus provision for 295 kg (650 lb) of bombs carried externally
Max T/O weight: 2722 kg (6,000 lb)
Max speed: 164 mph at 5,500 ft
Operational range: 1,155 miles

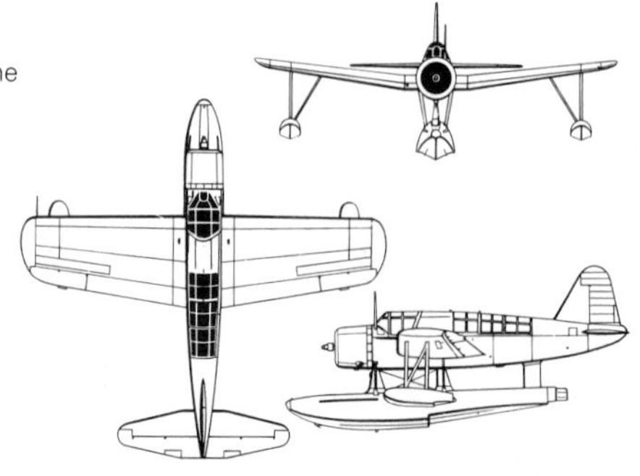

Vought SB2U Vindicator

The SB2U was the US Navy's first all-metal low-wing monoplane scout bomber with retractable landing gear, and as such introduced the pattern followed right through to the end of World II. The first XSB2U-1 flew in January 1936 and the production SB2U with the 615-kW (825-hp) R-1535-96 engine began to enter service in December 1937. These 54 aircraft were followed by 58 SB2U-2s with equipment changes, and by 57 examples of the SB2U-3 with a revised engine, greater fuel capacity, and improved defensive capability in the form of armour and 0.5-in (12.7-mm) machine-guns in place of the earlier versions' 0.3-in (7.62-mm) weapons. The French took 39 V-156F versions of the SB2U-1, and the British received 50 Chesapeake Mk Is. The type saw limited action but was replaced in 1942.

Specification: Vought SB2U-3 Vindicator two-seat carrierborne scout and dive-bomber
Span: 12.80 m (42 ft 0 in)
Length: 10.36 m (34 ft 0 in)
Powerplant: 1×Pratt & Whitney R-1535-02 Twin Wasp Junior, 615 kW (825 hp)
Armament: 2×0.5-in (12.7-mm) machine-guns plus 454 kg (1,000 lb) of bombs carried externally
Max T/O weight: 4732 kg (9,421 lb)
Max speed: 243 mph at 9,000 ft
Operational range: 1,120 miles

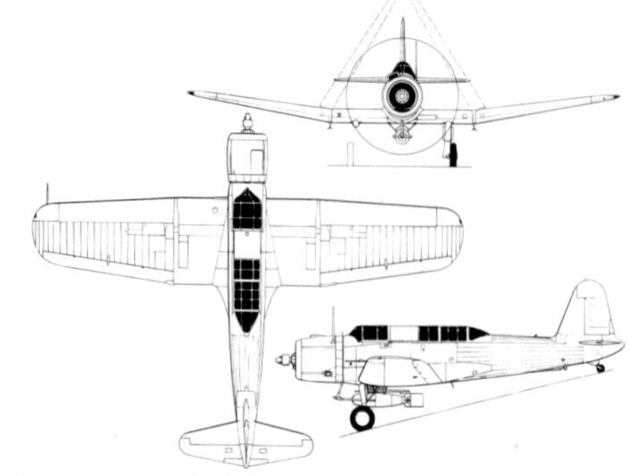

Fouga CM.175 Zéphyr

The Zéphyr (gentle breeze) is essentially a navalised version of the CM.170 Magister with an arrester hook and, after first flying in July 1956 with the name Esquif (skiff), entered service in 1959. Like the Magister, the type is notable for its long canopy with the instructor at the same height as the pupil, and for its V-shaped butterfly tail whose two control surfaces move collectively up and down for pitch control and collectively left and right for directional control. Production of the Zéphyr amounted to only 30 aircraft, and of these 23 remain. At any one time 12 are in service with Escadrille de Servitude 59S at Hyères in the deck landing role, aircraft being cycled into and out of storage to equalise flying hours. No Zéphyrs were produced for export.

Specification: Fouga CM.175 Zéphyr two-seat land-based basic and deck-landing trainer
Span: 12.15 m (39 ft 10 in) over tiptanks
Length: 10.06 m (36 ft 4 in)
Powerplant: 2×Turboméca Marbore IIA, 400 kg (882 lb) st each
Armament: none
Max T/O weight: 3200 kg (7,055 lb)
Max speed: 403 mph at optimum altitude
Operational range: 735 miles

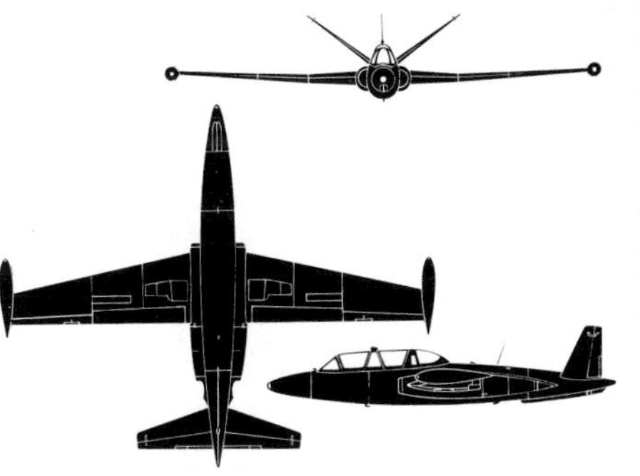

Dassault Etendard IVM

The Etendard (standard) was conceived as a French response to the competition won by the Fiat G91 light attack fighter. The type was developed in several forms, the first to fly in July 1956 being the Etendard II with two small turbojets. Dassault had been working in parallel on a version with a single larger turbojet, and this Etendard IV first took to the air just one day later. This formed the basis of the Etendard IVM carrierborne attack fighter that flew in May 1958 and entered service in 1961. Production totalled 69 for Flottilles 11F and 17F embarked on the *Clemenceau* and *Foch* as well as one shore-based training squadron, Escadrille de Servitude 59S. The type is distinguishable by its small Aida 7 ranging radar and folding refuelling probe, and some 23 aircraft survive in the advanced training role.

Specification: Dassault Etendard IVM single-seat carrierborne attack fighter
Span: 9.60 m (31 ft 5.75 in)
Length: 14.40 m (47 ft 3 in)
Powerplant: 1×SNECMA Atar 8B, 4400 kg (9,700 lb) st
Armament: 2×30-mm cannon plus provision for up to 1360 kg (2,998 lb) of disposable stores carried on 4×underwing pylons
Max T/O weight: 10275 kg (22,652 lb)
Max speed: 683 mph at sea level
Operational range: 1,056 miles

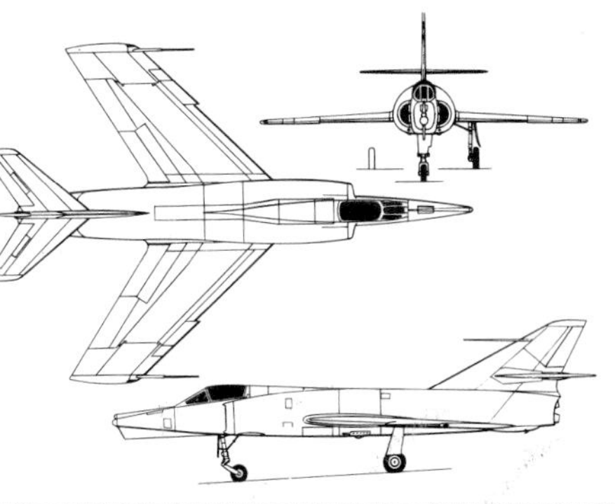

Dassault Etendard IVP

The Etendard IVM attack fighter was partnered in French carrierborne service by the Etendard IVP reconnaissance model with a fixed nose probe and no inbuilt cannon armament to allow the ventral installation of two Omera cameras that supplement the three similar cameras fitted in the nose. The type was built to the extent of 21 aircraft for Flottille 16F that served on either of the French carriers as required. The aeroplane is still in service to the extent of 9 aircraft, four surplus Etendard IVM attack fighters having been converted to Etendard IVM(P) standard to supplement the Etendard IVPs in this secondary 'buddy' refuelling task with a Douglas-designed refuelling pod in the ventral position. The type will remain in service until replaced by a reconnaissance version of the Rafale-M in the mid-1990s.

Specification: Dassault Etendard IVP single-seat carrierborne attack fighter
Span: 9.60 m (31 ft 5.75 in)
Length: 14.40 m (47 ft 3 in)
Powerplant: 1×SNECMA Atar 8B, 4400 kg (9,700 lb) st
Armament: none
Max T/O weight: 10275 kg (22,652 lb)
Max speed: 683 mph at sea level
Operational range: 1,056 miles

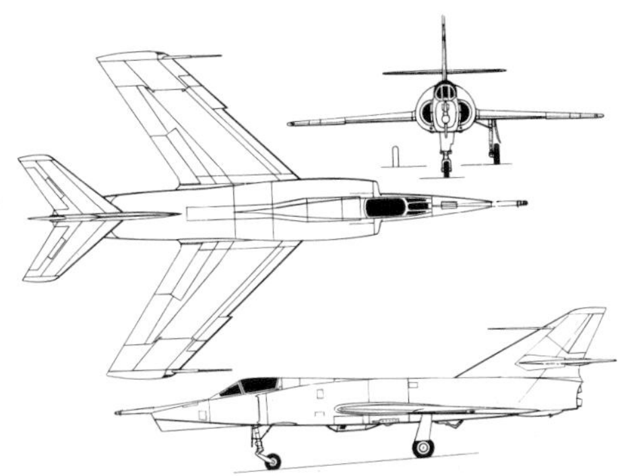

Dassault-Breguet Rafale-M

This new-generation warplane was first flown in July 1986 in the form of the Rafale-A demonstrator. The Rafale (squall) has a large measure of composite construction in its canard layout with a compound-sweep main wing and all-moving canard foreplanes, relaxed stability and a digital fly-by-wire control system, and a cockpit with a pilot's reclining seat, wide-angle HUD and provision for several advanced sensor displays. Service versions will be smaller and lighter, and are to be powered by two 7500-kg (16,534-lb) thrust SNECMA M88 afterburning turbofans. To meet the Aéronavale's ACM requirement for a Crusader and Etendard IVP successor, the Rafale-M navalised version is under development: 80 production aircraft are planned. The Rafale-A has undertaken carrier approach/landing tests successfully, and few problems are anticipated in producing the carrier-compatible version.

Specification: Dassault-Breguet Rafale-A single-seat fighter demonstrator aeroplane
Span: 11.20 m (36 ft 9 in)
Length: 15.80 m (51 ft 10 in)
Powerplant: 2×General Electric F404-GE-400, 7257 kg (16,000 lb) st each
Armament: 1×30-mm cannon plus provision for disposable stores on 12×hardpoints
Max T/O weight: 14000 kg (30,865 lb)
Max speed: Mach 2 at high altitude
Operational range: not revealed

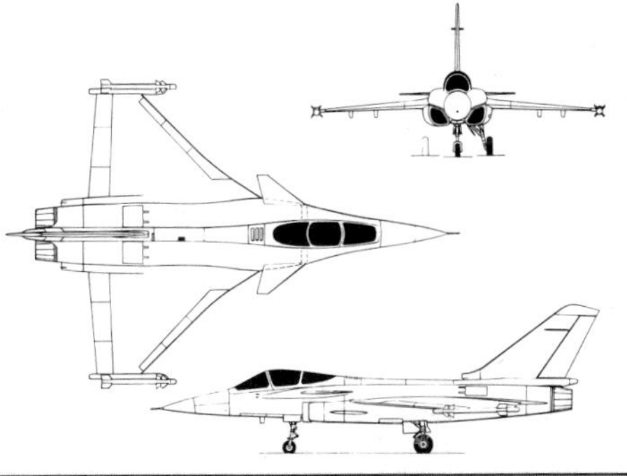

Vought F-8E(FN) Crusader

Specification: Vought F-8E(FN) single-seat carrierborne interceptor fighter
Span: 10.72 m (35 ft 2 in)
Length: 16.61 m (54 ft 6 in)
Powerplant: 1×Pratt & Whitney J57-P-20A, 8165 kg (18,000 lb) st
Armament: 4×20-mm cannon plus provision for 2268 kg (5,000 lb) of disposable stores on 2×fuselage side and 2×underwing hardpoints
Max T/O weight: 15422 kg (34,000 lb)
Max speed: Mach 1.7 at 40,000 ft
Operational range: 1,000 miles

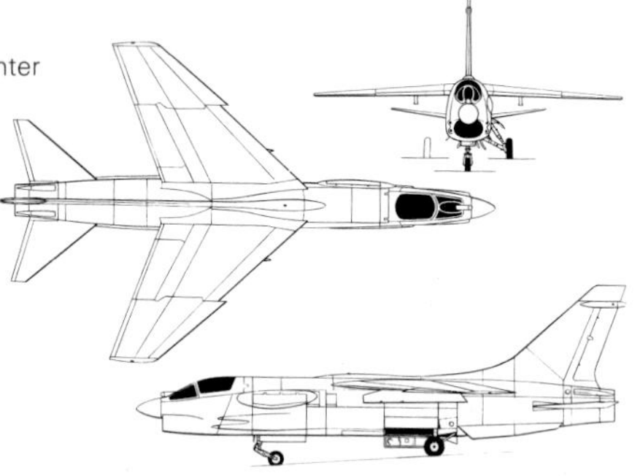

In the early 1960s the French navy found itself without a high-performance interceptor for use by its carrierborne air wings, and opted for an F-8E(FN) version of an American aeroplane, the Vought Crusader with its variable-incidence wing to provide a high angle of attack while maintaining the fuselage as level as possible for carrier operations. The F-8E introduced an upgraded engine and high-power radar, and the French version was first flown in February 1964 and delivered from January 1965 with features such as blown flaps and other high-lift improvements to reduce stalling and approach speeds to the values dictated by France's comparatively small aircraft-carriers. Some 42 aircraft were delivered, and of these 24 are operated by Flottille 12F. The type is at best obsolescent, but must remain in service until the advent of the Rafale-M in the mid-1990s.

Grumman F6F-5 Hellcat

The F6F-5 was the major production version of the Hellcat, and differed from the F6F-3 initial service model primarily in the R-2800-10W radial, modifications to the cowling and windscreen, additional armour protection, and revised armament. This last included provision for the two inboard machine-guns to be replaced by 20-mm cannon, and bombs under the centre section or rockets under the wings. The type began to appear in mid-1944, and in 1950 the Aéronavale began to acquire such aircraft for its part in the operations against the communists in Indo-China, where Flottilles 1F, 11F and 12F served aboard the *Arromanches*, and Flottille 12F aboard the *La Fayette*. Shortly after the end of France's rule in Indo-China during 1954 the Hellcats were retired as the type was already being replaced by the F4U-7.

Specification: Grumman F6F-5 Hellcat single-seat carrierborne fighter and fighter-bomber
Span: 13.05 m (42 ft 10 in)
Length: 10.20 m (33 ft 7 in)
Powerplant: 1×Pratt & Whitney R-2800-10W Double Wasp, 1640 kW (2,200 hp)
Armament: 6×12.7-mm (0.5-in) machine-guns plus provision for up to 907 kg (2,000 lb) of bombs or 6×127-mm (5-in) rockets carried under the wings
Max T/O weight: 6443 kg (14,250 lb)
Max speed: 376 mph at 23,200 ft
Operational range: 1,090 miles

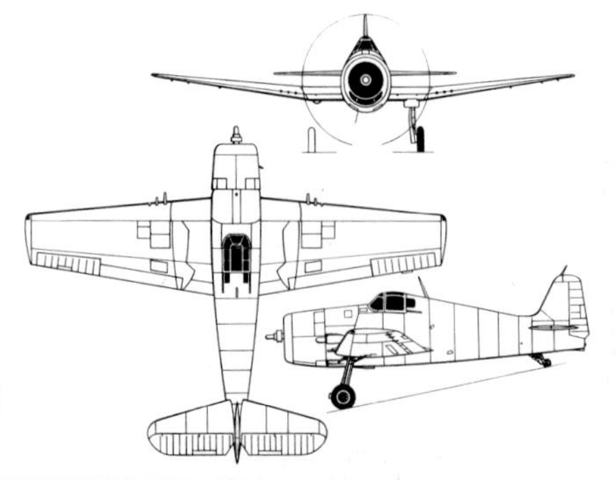

Douglas SBD-5 Dauntless

In the second half of 1943 the Free French air force was supplied with the A-24B land-based version of the Dauntless dive-bomber, but it was late 1944 before the Aéronavale began to receive its 32 SBD-5 aircraft for Flottilles 3B and 4B (later 3FB and 4FB). These two units supported the Allied advance in south-western France up to April 1945, and at the end of the war all surviving aircraft were concentrated in the hands of 4F aboard the escort carrier *Dixmude*, and of a training unit. The aircraft were used against the communists in Indo-China during 1947 and 1948, being replaced in the latter year by the aircraft of a revived 3F aboard the *Arromanches*. The aircraft were retired in 1949.

Specification: Douglas SBD-5 Dauntless two-seat carrierborne dive-bomber
Span: 12.66 m (41 ft 6.375 in)
Length: 10.09 m (33 ft 1.25 in)
Powerplant: 1×Wright R-1820-60 Cyclone, 895 kW (1,200 hp)
Armament: 2×12.7-mm (0.5-in) and 2×7.62-mm (0.3-in) machine-guns plus provision for 1021 kg (2,250 lb) of bombs carried on 1×underfuselage and 2×underwing hardpoints
Max T/O weight: 4853 kg (10,700 lb)
Max speed: 255 mph at 14,000 ft
Operational range: 1,115 miles

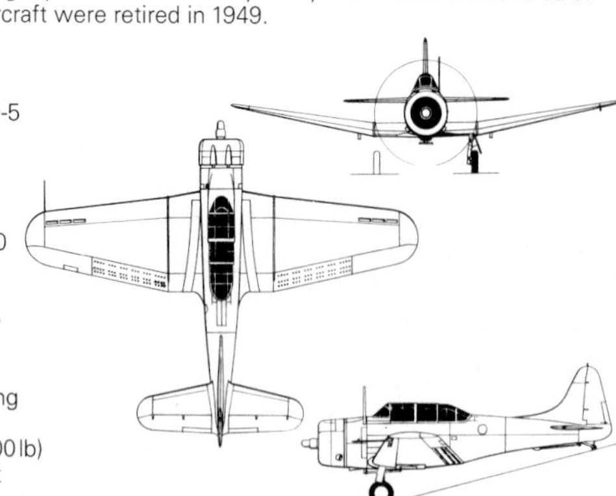

A Vought F-8E(FN) Crusader of Flottille 12F wears the new overall grey scheme only recently adopted by the surviving Aéronavale Crusaders. This aircraft carries R550 Magic IR-homing AAMs. The Crusader will eventually give way to Rafales, but in the interim F/A-18 Hornets may be leased.

Supermarine Seafire

Just before the end of World War II the UK transferred to France the escort carrier *Biter*, and this was followed after the war by the light carrier *Colossus*. Renamed respectively *Dixmude* and *Arromanches*, these carriers allowed the re-emergence of the Aéronavale as a carrierborne force, and to equip the carriers the British supplied a number of Seafires. First came 48 examples of the Seafire F.Mk III, folding-wing version of the Seafire F.Mk IIC (naval equivalent of the Spitfire F.Mk VC) with the 1182-kW (1,585-hp) Rolls-Royce Merlin 55M, and then 15 examples of the Seafire F.Mk XV, a much-improved model equivalent to the Spitfire F.Mk XII with a revised vertical tail and other improvements including the considerably more powerful Griffon inline. France was to receive another 45 Seafire F.Mk XVs, but it is uncertain how many more were in fact delivered.

Specification: Supermarine Seafire F.Mk XV single-seat carrierborne fighter and fighter-bomber
Span: 11.23 m (36 ft 10 in)
Length: 9.20 m (30 ft 2.5 in)
Powerplant: 1×Rolls-Royce Griffon VI, 1379 kW (1,850 hp)
Armament: 2×20-mm cannon and four 7.7-mm (0.303-in) machine-guns, plus provision for up to 227 kg (500 lb) of bombs carried externally
Max T/O weight: 3629 kg (8,000 lb)
Max speed: 392 mph at 36,000 ft
Operational range: 430 miles

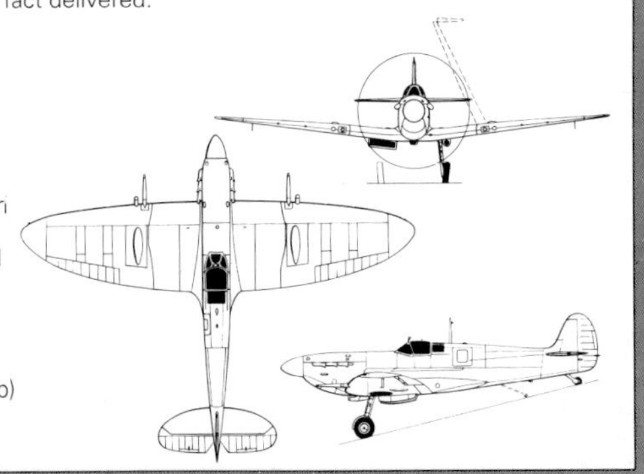

Curtiss SB2C-5 Helldiver

This was the last Curtiss-built variant of the Helldiver, and featured additional fuel by comparison with the SB2C-4, which was a development of the SB2C-3 with provision for underwing bombs or rockets. The SB2C-3 was in itself a development of the original SB2C-1 with the 1417-kW (1,900-hp) R-2600-20 radial driving a four- rather than three-blade propeller. Helldivers were needed for the support of French forces in Indo-China, and the aircraft were collected from the USA in 1950 by the carrier *Dixmude*. The Helldiver subsequently served with Flottilles 3F and 9F aboard the *Arromanches*, 9F aboard the *La Fayette*, and 3F aboard the *Bois Belleau*. In this theatre the Helldivers proved useful, but only in areas where the communists could be pinned some distance from their potent anti-aircraft artillery defences.

Specification: Curtiss SB2C-5 Helldiver two-seat carrierborne dive-bomber and close support aeroplane
Span: 15.15 m (49 ft 8.625 in)
Length: 11.17 m (36 ft 8 in)
Powerplant: 1×Wright R-2600-20 Cyclone, 1417 kW (1,900 hp)
Armament: 2×20-mm cannon and 2×7.62-mm (0.3-in) machine-guns plus provision for up to 454 kg (1,000 lb) of bombs carried internally and up to 454 kg (1,000 lb) of bombs or 8×127-mm (5-in) rockets carried under the wings
Max T/O weight: 7220 kg (15,918 lb)
Max speed: 260 mph at 16,100 ft
Operational range: 1,805 miles

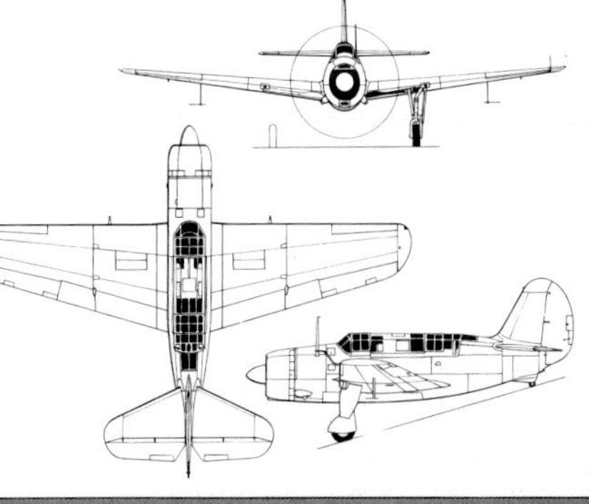

Dassault Super Etendard

As its name implies, the Super Etendard is a development of the Etendard IV. It first flew in October 1974 and features a more powerful engine, a revised airframe for operation at higher weights and speeds, more modern weapons and a revised electronic suite including an inertial navigation system and Agave lightweight multi-mode radar for optimum launch conditions with the Exocet anti-ship missile. Production aircraft were delivered from 1977, and the 71 aircraft serve with Flottilles 11F, 14F and 17F. Some 50 of the aircraft are being modified to carry and launch the ASMP stand-off nuclear missile, and due for retrofit from 1991 is an upgraded nav/attack system including a higher-performance inertial navigation system, improved cockpit instrumentation and displays, and the new Anemone multi-function radar. The Super Etendard is also operated by Argentina and Iraq.

Specification: Dassault-Breguet Super Etendard single-seat carrierborne strike and attack aeroplane
Span: 9.60m (31ft 5.75in)
Length: 14.31m (46ft 11.5in)
Powerplant: 1×SNECMA Atar 8K-50, 5000kg (11,023lb) st
Armament: 2×30-mm cannon plus provision for up to 2100kg (4,630lb) of disposable stores carried on 1×underfuselage and 4×underwing hardpoints
Max T/O weight: 12000kg (26,455lb)
Max speed: 733mph at sea level
Operational range: 1,056 miles

Grumman TBM-3 Avenger

The version of the TBF Avenger torpedo-bomber built by the Eastern Aircraft Division of General Motors was designated TBM, and the main production version of this aeroplane was the TBM-3 with the R-2600-20 radial and a fixed 12.7-mm (0.5-in) machine-gun in each wing. The final variant of this model was the TBM-3E with a lighter yet stronger airframe, a lengthened fuselage and centimetric search radar with its antenna in a radome under the starboard wing. Post-war conversion produced aircraft for the anti-submarine role, a team comprising one TBM-3W-2 (with APS-20 radar in a ventral radome) as the hunter and one TBM-3S-2 as the killer. Such aircraft were received by France in the 1950s, serving with Flottilles and Escadrilles 2S, 3S, 4F, 6F, 9F, 10S and 15S at shore bases as well as on the carriers *Arromanches, Bois Belleau* and *La Fayette*.

Specification: Grumman TBM-3S/W (TBM-3E) three-seat carrierborne or land-based anti-submarine hunter/killer aeroplane
Span: 16.51m (54ft 2in)
Length: 12.48m (40ft 11.5in)
Powerplant: 1×Wright R-2600-20 Cyclone, 1417 kW (1,900 hp)
Armament: 3×12.7-mm (0.5-in) and 1×7.62-mm (0.3-in) machine-guns plus provision for up to 907kg (2,000lb) of disposable weapons carried internally
Max T/O weight: 8117kg (17,895lb)
Max speed: 276mph at 16,500ft
Operational range: 1,010 miles

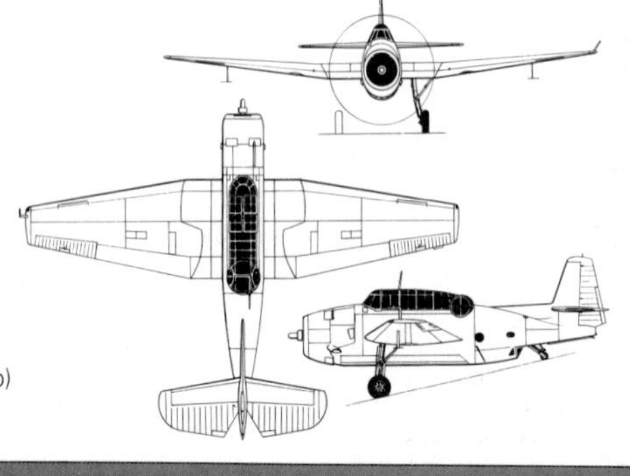

Vought F4U-7 Corsair

After World War II the Corsair production line was reopened to produce the F4U-5 with metal-skinned wings, and from this was developed the F4U-6 close-support variant incorporating four 20-mm cannon in the wings, 25 pieces of armour (including 21 for the undersurfaces) and the R-2800-83WA Twin Wasp rated for optimum performance at low altitude. This entered service as the AU-1, and from it was developed the last Corsair production variant, the F4U-7 required by the Aéronavale in the all-altitude role. This model was essentially the AU-1 with the R-2800-18W radial of the F4U-4, and after the first flight of the type in July 1952 production totalled 94 aircraft built in 1952 (79) and 1953 (15). The F4U-7 was widely used in the Indo-China war, and remained in French service up to 1962 with units that included Flottilles 12F, 14F and 17F.

Specification: Vought F4U-7 Corsair single-seat carrierborne fighter-bomber
Span: 12.50m (41ft 0in)
Length: 10.53m (34ft 6.5in)
Powerplant: 1×Pratt & Whitney R-2800-18W, 1827 kW (2,450 hp)
Armament: 4×20-mm cannon plus provision for up to 1814kg (4,000lb) of disposable stores carried under the wings
Max T/O weight: 6090kg (13,426lb)
Max speed: 450mph at 26,000ft
Operational range: not revealed

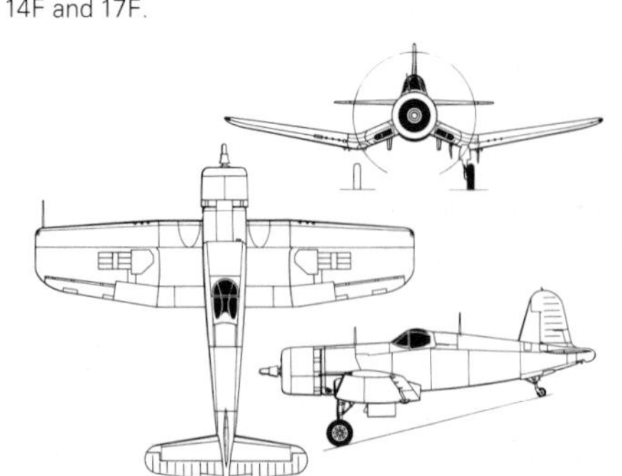

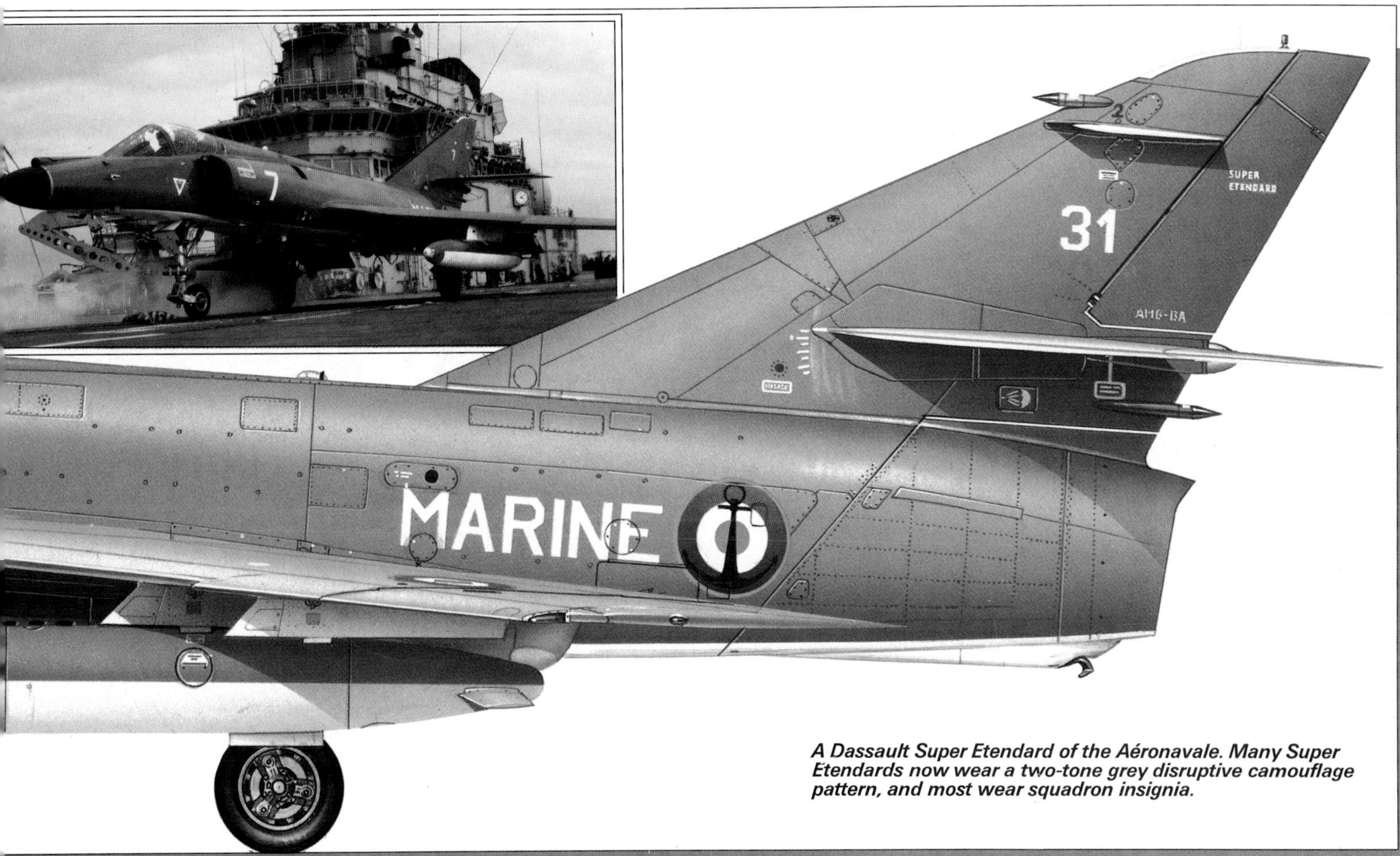

A Dassault Super Etendard of the Aéronavale. Many Super Etendards now wear a two-tone grey disruptive camouflage pattern, and most wear squadron insignia.

Sud-Est S.E.202 Aquilon

To meet a French naval requirement SNCASE secured a licence to produce the de Havilland Sea Venom in a special Mk 52 variant as the Aquilon with an Italian licence-built engine, strengthened structure and provision for ejector seats. The S.E.20 Aquilon prototype flew in October 1952, and was followed by four pre-production and 20 production aircraft with fixed seats (under an upward-opening hood) and Vampire-type landing gear suitable for operation only from shore bases. The S.E.201 prototype then paved the way for two carrier-capable variants with revised landing gear, the S.E.202 with twin ejector seats under a rear-sliding hood (25 built) and the single-seat S.E.203 with US radar in a dielectric nosecone (40 built) for use in conjunction with Nord 5103 air-to-air missiles. The last model was the S.E.204 trainer, of which 19 were built.

Specification: SNCASE S.E.202 Aquilon two-seat carrierborne fighter and fighter-bomber
Span: 13.07 m (42 ft 10.5 in)
Length: 11.13 m (36 ft 6 in)
Powerplant: 1×Fiat-built de Havilland Ghost 48 Mk 1, 2200 kg (4,850 lb) st
Armament: 4×20-mm cannon plus provision for up to 8×27-kg (60-lb) rockets carried under the wings
Max T/O weight: 7600 kg (16,755 lb)
Max speed: 581 mph at 9,845 ft
Operational range: 965 miles

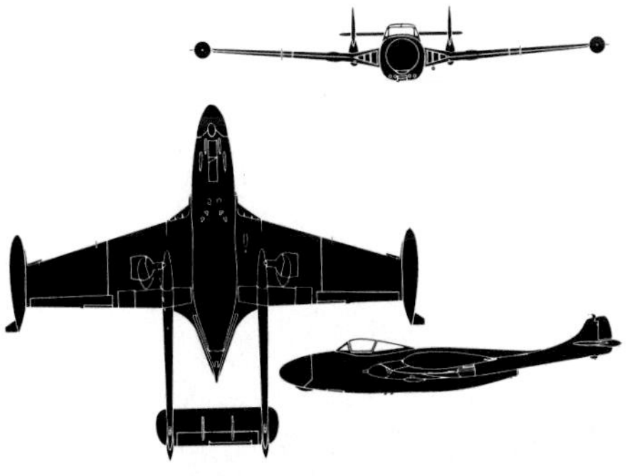

Breguet Br.1050 Alizé

In 1948 Breguet began work on its Br.960 Vultur single-seat carrierborne attack aeroplane with a hybrid powerplant comprising one Armstrong Siddeley Mamba turboprop in the nose for cruise supplemented for take-off and combat by one Rolls-Royce Nene in the tail. This first flew in 1951 and, proving abortive in its planned role, was developed into the three-seat Alizé (tradewind) anti-submarine type with a retractable radar radome replacing the turbojet; the other main sensors are sonobuoys, which are accommodated in the landing gear fairings. The Alizé first flew in March 1955, and 75 production aircraft followed. Some 30 remain in service, the 21 first-line machines of Flottilles 4F and 6F having been upgraded with Iguane radar, Doppler navigation and improved armament. Other machines were supplied to India, which also maintains the type in service.

Specification: Breguet Br.1050 Alizé three-seat carrierborne anti-submarine aeroplane
Span: 15.60 m (52 ft 2 in)
Length: 13.86 m (45 ft 6 in)
Powerplant: 1×Rolls-Royce Dart RDa.21, 1473 kW (1,975 shp)
Armament: 1×torpedo or 3×depth charges in the weapon bay plus provision for a varied assortment of missiles, rockets, bombs and depth charges carried on the underwing hardpoints
Max T/O weight: 8250 kg (18,190 lb)
Max speed: 295 mph at optimum altitude
Operational endurance: 5 hours 12 minutes

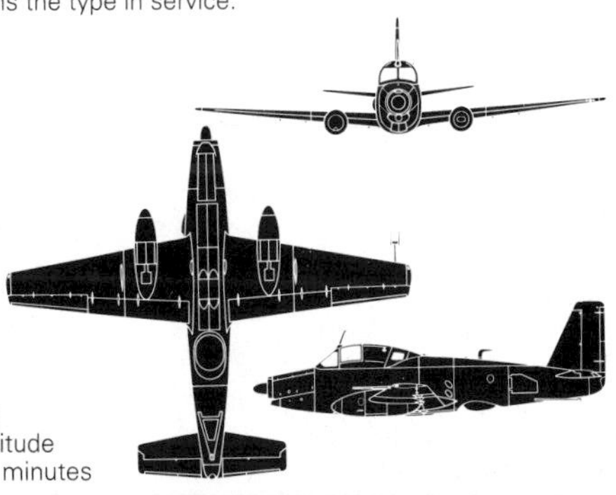

Douglas AD Skyraider

One of the most important carrierborne aircraft ever developed, and one of the few such machines that successfully achieved the transition to large scale land-based use, the Skyraider was designed as the XBT2D to a World War II specification for a single-seat dive/torpedo-bomber. The prototype flew in March 1945, and between 1945 and 1957 some 3,180 Skyraiders were built. The design was planned as a large airframe with a potent radial engine, and the decision to hang weapons externally on 15 hardpoints provided for great flexibility in a multitude of variants developed as single- and multi-seaters up to the AD-7 for roles as diverse as attack, forward air control, defence suppression and electronic warfare. The Skyraider was redesignated A-1 in 1962, and retired in 1968.

Specification: Douglas AD-7 Skyraider single-seat carrierborne attack bomber
Span: 15.25 m (50 ft 0.25 in)
Length: 11.84 m (38 ft 10 in)
Powerplant: 1×Wright R-3350-26WB Cyclone 18, 2013 kW (2,700 hp)
Armament: 4×20-mm cannon plus provision for 3629 kg (8,000 lb) of disposable stores carried externally
Max T/O weight: 11340 kg (25,000 lb)
Max speed: 343 mph at 20,000 ft
Operational range: 1,300 miles

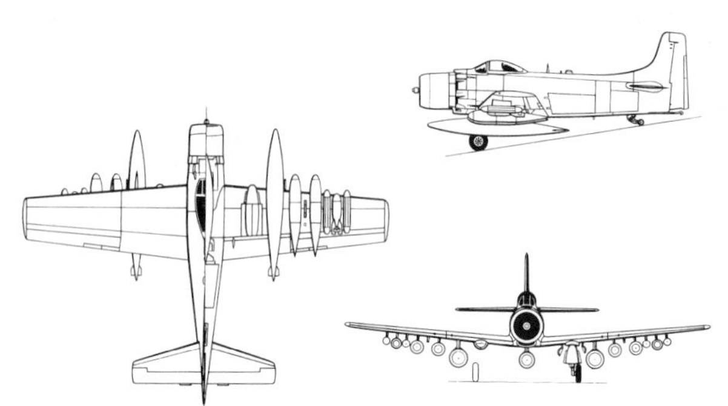

Martin AM Mauler

The Mauler was conceived in 1943 as a powerful single-seater that could undertake the dive-bombing and torpedo-bombing roles previously entrusted to separate multi-seat aircraft. The XBTM-1 prototype was a large low-wing aeroplane and first flew in August 1944 with a 2237 kW (3,000 hp) Pratt & Whitney XR-4360 radial, four 20-mm cannon and 15 hardpoints under the wings and fuselage. Some 750 BTM-1s were ordered, the designation being altered to AM-1 in 1946. The Mauler began to enter service in March 1948, but production was curtailed at the 149th production machine. The Mauler had prodigious load-carrying capability, but enjoyed only a short first-line career before passing to reserve units in the early 1950s when overtaken by the AD-1. The AM-1Q was an ECM variant.

Specification: Martin AM-1 Mauler single-seat carrierborne attack aeroplane
Span: 15.24 m (50 ft 0 in)
Length: 12.55 m (41 ft 2 in)
Powerplant: 1×Pratt & Whitney R-3350-4 Cyclone 18, 2218 kW (2,975 hp)
Armament: 4×20-mm cannon, plus provision for 4854 kg (10,700 lb) of disposable stores carried externally
Max T/O weight: 10608 kg (23,386 lb)
Max speed: 367 mph at 11,600 ft
Operational range: 1,800 miles

Grumman AF Guardian

The Guardian began life as the XTB3F-1, designed in 1944 as successor to the TBF torpedo-bomber. The design followed the TBF's basic concept but in place of defensive armament had a tail-mounted turbojet for high escape speed. The prototype flew in December 1945, and trials confirmed the uselessness of the jet. It was then decided to recast the design in the anti-submarine role with pairs of aircraft operating as a team: the four-man AF-2W in the 'hunter' role and the armed AF-2S in the 'killer' role. The AF-2W had ventral long- range search radar and the AF-2S underwing short-range acquisition radar. Deliveries of 156 AF-2Ws and 190 AF-2Ss were made between 1950 and 1953, the latter years also seeing the delivery of the improved AF-3 model in the form of 16 AF-3Ws and 25 AF-3Ss.

Specification: Grumman AF-2S Guardian three-seat carrierborne anti-submarine attack aeroplane
Span: 18.49 m (60 ft 8 in)
Length: 13.21 m (43 ft 4 in)
Powerplant: 1×Pratt & Whitney R-2800-48W Double Wasp, 1789 kW (2,400 hp)
Armament: 1×907 kg (2,000 lb) torpedo, or 2×907 kg (2,000 lb) bombs or two 726 kg (1,600 lb) depth charges carried internally
Max T/O weight: 11567 kg (25,500 lb)
Max speed: 317 mph at 16,000 ft
Operational range: 1,500 miles

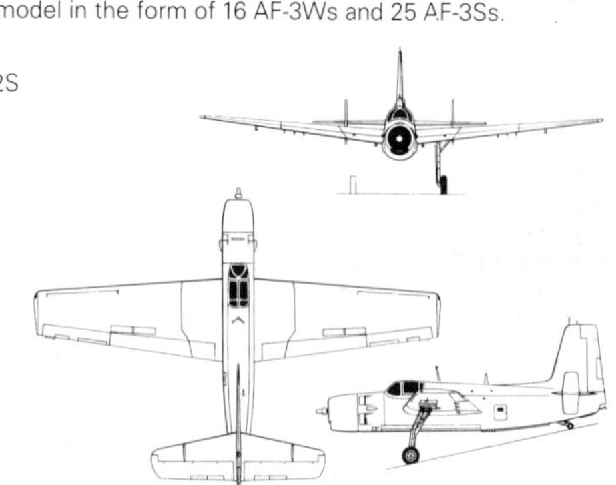

The AD Skyraider (A-1 after 1962) was the principal attack aircraft throughout the 1950s, serving with distinction in Korea. Later in South East Asia it played a prominent part in the US ground-attack capability. This aircraft is seen wearing the bright colours of the 'CAG' (air wing commander) aboard Ticonderoga during the combat cruise of 1966-67.

Ryan FR Fireball

Given the exigencies of carrierborne operations and the unreliability of early turbojets, the US Navy was keen to gain its first experience with jet propulsion via a hybrid type, the FR Fireball, that combined a standard piston-engined airframe with a booster turbojet in the tail. The design was conceived in 1942, and the first of three XFR-1 prototypes flew in June 1944. A total of 700 FR-1s was ordered, but the wholesale cancellation of contracts after VJ-Day reduced the figure to 66. Delivery began in January 1945 and ended in November of the same year. The Fireball played its part in developing the navy's experience with jet engines and operations, but was clearly an interim type and remained in service for only a very short time.

Specification: Ryan FR-1 Fireball single-seat carrierborne fighter
Span: 12.19 m (40 ft 0 in)
Length: 9.86 m (32 ft 4 in)
Powerplant: 1×Wright R-1820-72W Cyclone 9, 1007 kW (1,350 hp), and 1×General Electric J31, 726 kg (1,600 lb) st
Armament: 4×12.7-mm (0.5-in) machine-guns
Max T/O weight: 5285 kg (11,652 lb)
Max speed: 404 mph at 17,800 ft
Operational range: 1,620 miles

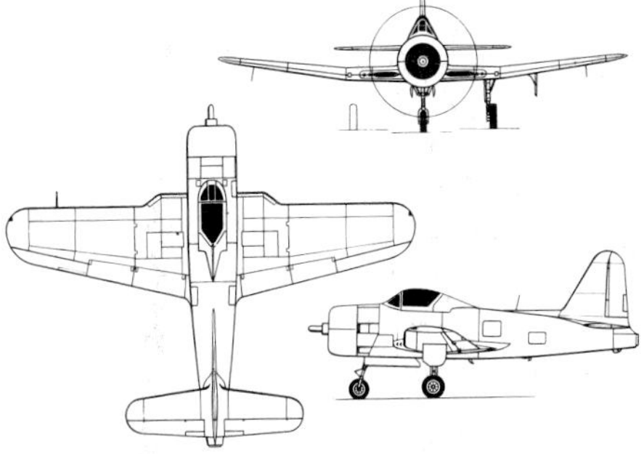

Vought F4U Corsair

The Corsair variant in production at the time of VJ-Day in 1945 was the F4U- 4, which was by any standards a devastating fighter-bomber. Production and development continued after World War II, and the first post-war variant was the F4U-5, essentially the F4U-4 revised with four 20-mm cannon and the 1715- kW (2,300-hp) R-2800-32W with two-stage supercharging. This model was procured in 1947 and 1948 to the extent of 223 F4U-5s, 315 radar-equipped F4U-5N night-fighters and 30 F4U-5P reconnaissance aircraft. The XF4U-6 has the single-stage R-2800-83W, additional armour and greater load-carrying capability: its production version was the low-level AU-1 for the US Marine Corps, which received 110 aircraft. The final Corsair variant was the F4U-7 based on the AU-1 with the R-2800-18W engine: all 90 were supplied to the French.

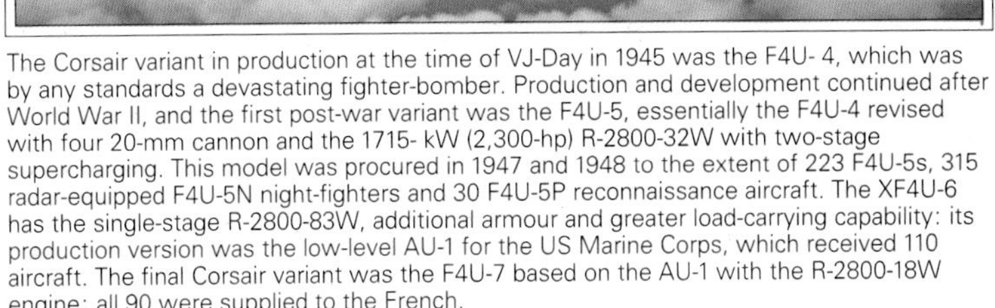

Specification: Vought AU-1 Corsair single-seat carrierborne fighter-bomber
Span: 12.50 m (41 ft 0 in)
Length: 10.39 m (34 ft 1 in)
Powerplant: 1×Pratt & Whitney R-2800-83W Double Wasp, 1715 kW (2,300 hp)
Armament: 4×20-mm cannon, plus provision for 4×454-kg (1,000-lb) bombs or rockets carried under the wings
Max T/O weight: 8799 kg (19,398 lb)
Max speed: 238 mph at 9,500 ft
Operational range: 484 miles

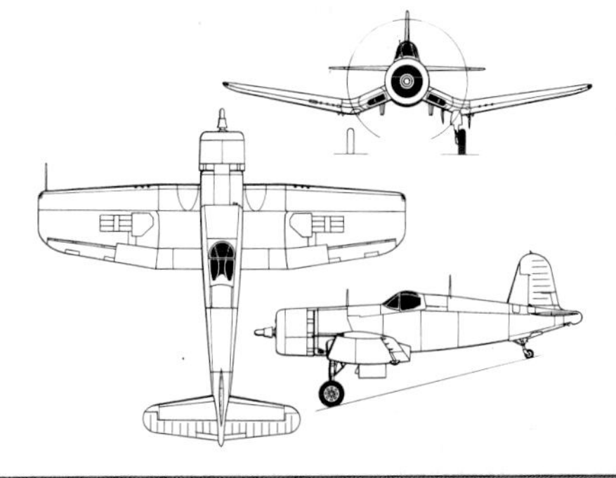

Grumman F9F Panther

The Panther was Grumman's first jet fighter, and was planned from 1945 as a night-fighter with four 1118-kg (1,500-lb) thrust Westinghouse J30s buried in the wings. The design was finally refined to that of a day fighter with a 2268kg (5,000lb) thrust Pratt & Whitney J42 (Rolls-Royce Nene) or 2089kg (4,600lb) thrust Allison J33 mounted in the fuselage. The XF9F-2 flew in November 1947, and paved the way for the J42-powered F9F-2 and J33-powered F9F-3. Evaluation proved the superiority of the former, of which 497 were built for service from May 1949. The J33-powered F9F-4 did not appear, and the final model was the F9F-5 (655 built) with a fuselage stretch of 0.61 m (2 ft), a taller fin and revised engine; the F9F-5P was a reconnaissance variant. The Panther was then overtaken by its swept-wing derivative, the F9F Cougar.

Specification: Grumman F9F-5 Panther single-seat carrierborne fighter
Span: 11.58m (38ft 0in)
Length: 11.84m (38ft 10in)
Powerplant: 1×Pratt & Whitney J48-P-6A, 2835kg (6,250lb) st
Armament: 4×20-mm cannon, plus 907kg (2,000lb) of bombs or rockets carried under the wings
Max T/O weight: 8492kg (18,721lb)
Max speed: 579mph at 5,000ft
Operational range: 1,300 miles

The first jet product from the famous Grumman 'Iron Works' was the F9F Panther, a worthy successor to the Hellcat and Bearcat which preceded it. The aircraft went to war in Korea, where it flew ground attack missions and scored the odd kill. It was used by both Navy and Marines, seen here in the colours of the latter's VMF-311. Marine aircraft usually operated from land bases but occasionally deployed to Navy ships for carrier operations. The later Cougar introduced swept swings and an uprated engine to become an enduring and tough attack aircraft.

Grumman F8F Bearcat

The F8F was designed to a 1943 requirement for an interceptor fighter able to operate from the smallest carriers as complement to the F6F Hellcat fighter- bomber. The same R-2800 engine was used in combination with a smaller and lighter airframe that ensured sparkling performance in speed and climb. The XF8F-1 prototype flew in August 1944 and orders were placed with Grumman for 2,023 F8F-1s and with General Motors for 1,876 F8M-1s. Service entry began in May 1945, but the Bearcat did not see action in World War II. After Japan's surrender orders were reduced to 765 F8F-1s, 100 F8F-1Bs each with four 20-mm cannon and 36 F8F-1N night-fighters. The last variant was the 1948 F8F-2 with taller fin: 293 F8F-2s were joined by 12 F8F-2N night-fighters and 60 F8F-2P reconnaissance aircraft. The type was retired in 1952.

Specification: Grumman F8F-1 Bearcat single-seat carrierborne interceptor fighter
Span: 10.92m (36ft 10in)
Length: 8.61m (28ft 3in)
Powerplant: 1×Pratt & Whitney R-2800-34W Double Wasp, 1566kW (2,100hp)
Armament: 4×12.7-mm (0.5-in) machine-guns, plus provision for 2×454-kg (1,000-lb) bombs carried under the wings
Max T/O weight: 5873kg (12,947lb)
Max speed: 421mph at 19,700ft
Operational range: 1,105 miles

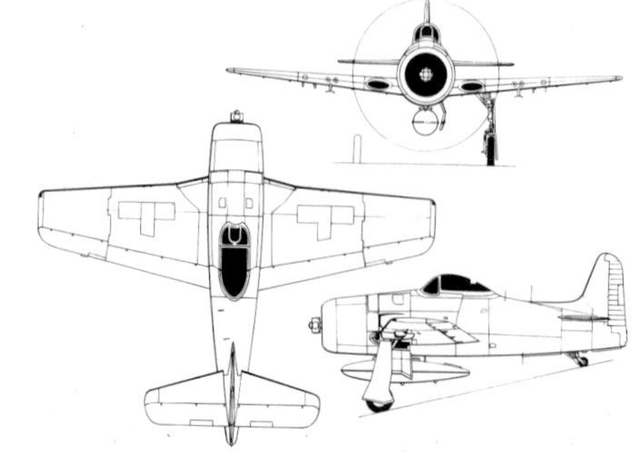

McDonnell FH Phantom

The Phantom was McDonnell's first aeroplane for the US Navy, and resulted from a 1943 request for this small company to undertake the design of a jet- powered carrierborne fighter. The company's initial concept had six small engines in the wing roots, but this was revised to two large engines before the XFD-1 prototype was ordered. This flew in January 1945 with 528kg (1,165lb) thrust Westinghouse 19XB-2B engines, and an order was placed for 100 (later reduced to 60) production aircraft designated FD-1, later changed to FH-1. Deliveries were made between July 1947 and May 1948, but as the FH-1 was avowedly an interim type, its service career was short. The XFD-1 has the distinction of having made the first all-American jet landing on an aircraft-carrier, on 21 July 1946.

Specification: McDonnell FH-1 Phantom single-seater carrierborne fighter
Span: 12.42m (40ft 9in)
Length: 11.81m (38ft 9in)
Powerplant: 2×Westinghouse J30-WE-20, 726kg (1,600lb) st each
Armament: 4×12.7-mm (0.5-in) machine-guns
Max T/O weight: 5459kg (12,035lb)
Max speed: 479mph at sea level
Operational range: 980 miles

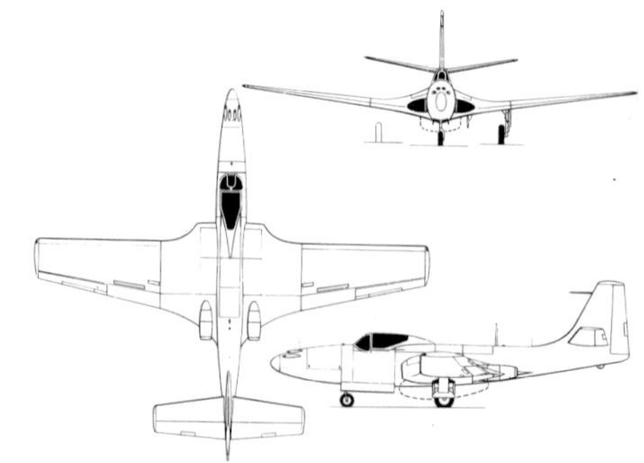

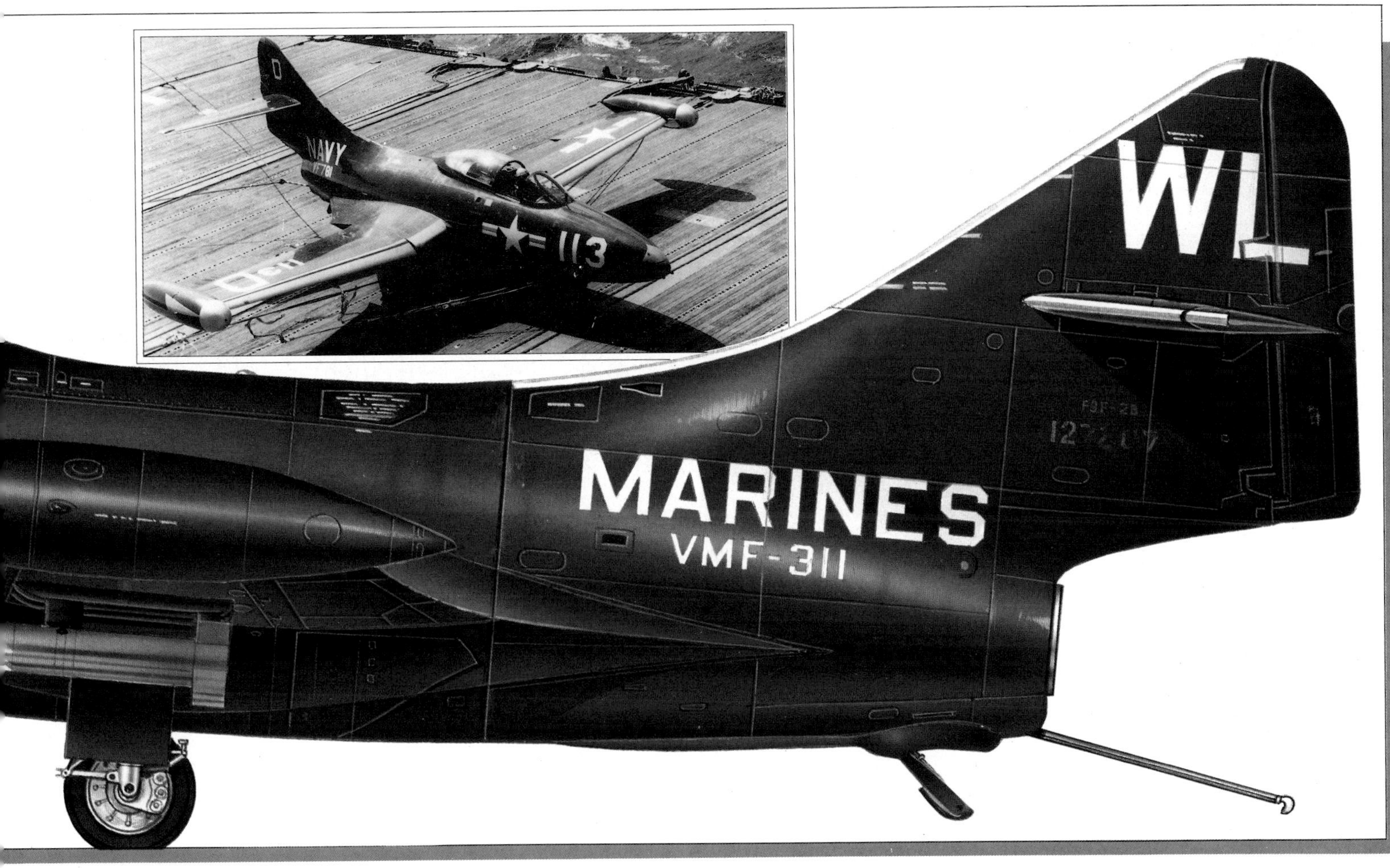

McDonnell F2H Banshee

As the FD-1 was entering production, McDonnell was told to press on towards a larger machine capable of undertaking the fighter-bomber role. The XF2D-1 prototype bore a marked similarity to the FD series though it was larger and heavier, and the powerplant comprised a pair of 1361-kg (3,000-lb) thrust J34-WE-22 turbojets. The prototype was redesignated XF2H-1 soon after completion, and first flew in January 1947. Delivery of 56 F2H-1s began in March 1949, and was followed by that of 364 F2H-2s with a longer fuselage and greater fuel capacity for the uprated powerplant, 14 F2H-2N radar-equipped night-fighters and 58 F2H-2Ps with reconnaissance cameras. The final variants were radar-fitted all-weather fighters: the 250 F2H-3s had an even longer fuselage for more fuel, and the 150 F2H-4s had 1633-kg (3,600-lb) thrust -38 engines.

Specification: McDonnell F2H-2 Banshee single-seat carrierborne fighter- bomber
Span: 13.67 m (44 ft 10 in)
Length: 12.24 m (40 ft 2 in)
Powerplant: 2×Westinghouse J34-WE-34, 1474 kg (3,250 lb) st each
Armament: 4×l0-mm cannon, plus provision for 2×227-kg (500-lb) bombs carried under the wings
Max T/O weight: 10121 kg (22,312 lb)
Max speed: 532 mph at 10,000 ft
Operational range: 1,475 miles

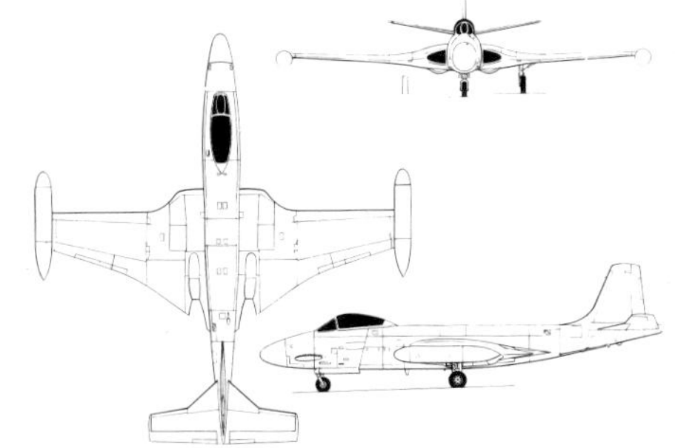

North American FJ Fury

The first naval fighter from North American was the FJ-1 Fury, an unswept design with straight-through engine layout. The XFJ-1 first flew in November 1946, and three prototypes were followed by just 30 FJ-1 production aircraft with a maximum speed of 547 mph at 9,000 ft. The FJ-1 paved the way for the USAF's F-86 Sabre swept-wing fighter, and this led to the swept-wing naval FJ-2, which was similar to the F-86E apart from navalisation and four-cannon armament. Three prototypes were followed by 200 production aircraft for the US Marine Corps, all with the 2722-kg (6,000-lb) thrust General Electric J47- GE-2 engine. The 538 FJ-3s were similar apart from their 3470-kg (7,650-lb) thrust J65-W-2 or -4 engines. The final version was the FJ-4, of which 374 were built with a different engine, more fuel, a recontoured fuselage and thinner flying surfaces.

Specification: North American FJ-4 Fury single-seat carrierborne fighter
Span: 11.91 m (39 ft 1 in)
Length: 11.07 m (36 ft 4 in)
Powerplant: 1×Wright J65-W-16A, 3493 kg (7,700 lb) st
Armament: 4×20-mm cannon, plus provision for 1361 kg (3,000 lb) of bombs, or five ASM-N-7 Bullpup ASMs, or four AAM-N-7 Sidewinder AAMs under the wings
Max T/O weight: 10750 kg (23,700 lb)
Max speed: 680 mph at sea level
Operational range: 2,020 miles

Douglas F3D Skyknight

The Skyknight was the US Navy's first jet-powered all-weather fighter, and resulted from a 1946 specification. The prototype featured side-by-side accommodation and two engines buried in the fuselage sides under the wings, and first flew in March 1948. The radar-equipped F3D-1 (28 built) was powered by two 1361-kg (3,000-lb) thrust J34-WE-22s and began to enter service in February 1951. The following the F3D-2 (237 built) was used operationally only by the US Marine Corps, and though originally powered by two 2087-kg (4,600-lb) thrust J46-WE-3 engines was re-engined when this engine was discontinued. Skyknights destroyed more communist aircraft than any other navy or marine aircraft in the Korean War, and several variants were tested in small numbers. The swept-wing F3D-3 was abandoned, and in 1962 the declining numbers of Skyknights were redesignated in the F-10 series.

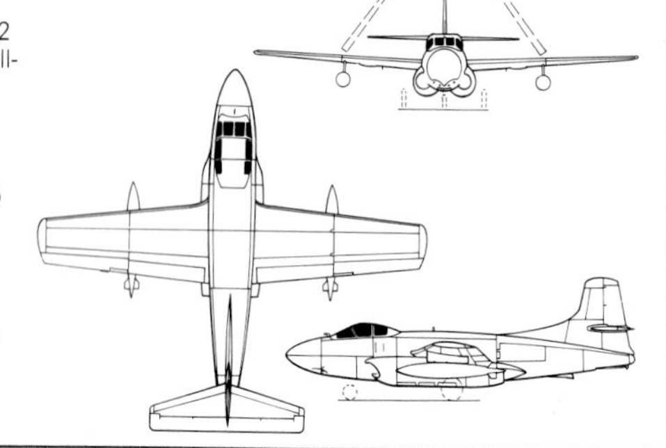

Specification: Douglas F3D-2 Skyknight two-seat carrierborne all-weather fighter
Span: 15.24 m (50 ft 0 in)
Length: 13.87 m (45 ft 5 in)
Powerplant: 2×Westinghouse J34-WE-36/36A, 1524 kg (3,400 lb) st each
Armament: 4×20-mm cannon
Max T/O weight: 12556 kg (27,681 lb)
Max speed: 565 mph at 20,000 ft
Operational range: 1,540 miles

Vought F6U Pirate

One of several jet-powered fighters ordered by the US Navy in the closing stages of World War II, the F6U was a conventional design with tricycle landing gear and a single 1361-kg (3,000-lb) J34-WE-22 engine located in the rear fuselage and aspirated via small inlets in the wing roots. Three XF6U-1 prototypes were ordered in 1944, the first of them flying in October 1946. Only 30 production aircraft were delivered from August 1949, these having considerably more power than the prototypes, together with a longer fuselage and greater wing area. The engine used in the production aircraft was fitted with a Solar afterburner. The only variant was a single F6U-1P reconnaissance aeroplane.

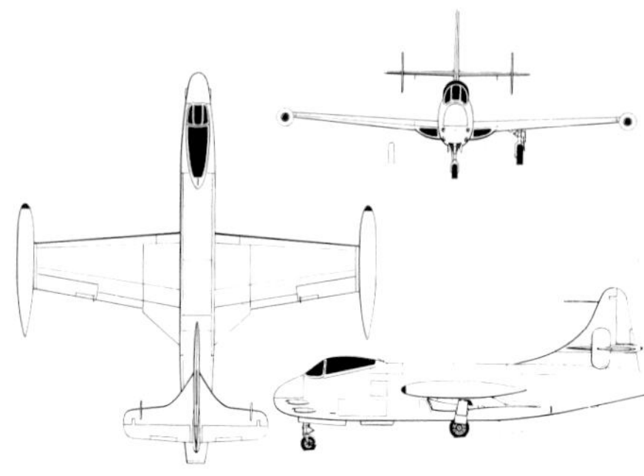

Specification: Vought F6U-1 Pirate single-seat carrierborne fighter
Span: 10.01 m (32 ft 10 in)
Length: 11.46 m (37 ft 7 in)
Powerplant: 1×Westinghouse J34-WE-30, 1916 kg (4,225 lb) st
Armament: 4×20-mm cannon
Max T/O weight: 5702 kg (12,571 lb)
Max speed: 564 mph at 20,000 ft
Operational range: 730 miles

Lockheed P2V Neptune

Initial design for the Neptune began in 1941. Only slow progress was made up to 1944, when the US Navy perceived a severe shortfall in land-based anti- submarine capability and ordered prototypes and production examples of a fully optimised patrol and anti-submarine aircraft with great range and potent offensive/defensive armament. The XP2V-1 flew in May 1945 and the P2V-1 began to enter service in March 1947. The Neptune remained in US production (838 aircraft) up to 1962, and was the US Navy's most important land-based anti-submarine aeroplane of the 1950s in variants such as the upengined P2V-2, the further upengined and upgunned P2V-3, the P2V-4 with extra fuel and yet more power, the P2V-5 with larger tiptanks, revised electronics and auxiliary turbojets, the updated P2V-6 and the definitive P2V-7 without gun armament.

Specification: Lockheed P2V-7 Neptune seven-crew land-based patrol and anti-submarine aeroplane
Span: 31.65 m (103 ft 10 in)
Length: 27.84 m (91 ft 4 in)
Powerplant: 2×Wright R-3350-32W Cyclone 18, 2610 kW (3,500 hp) each), and 2×Westinghouse J34-WE-34, 1542 kg (3,400 lb) st each
Armament: 3629 kg (8,000 lb) of bombs, torpedoes and depth charges carried internally
Max T/O weight: 34247 kg (75,500 lb)
Max speed: 345 mph at 10,000 ft
Operational range: 2,200 miles

Grumman TBM-3 Avenger

Of 9,836 Avengers from all sources, no fewer than 4,664 were TBM-3s built by the Eastern Aircraft Division of General Motors with an additional 149 kW (200 hp) by comparison with the basic TBM-1. The TBM-3 was built in several variants, and the TBM-3E torpedo-bomber with underwing submarine-detection radar became the most important post-World War II model of the Avenger. Further development produced the TBM-3W with the dorsal turret removed to allow the creation of an 'office' for the display and crew associated with the APS-20 search radar carried in a large ventral radome; the TBM-3W-2 was a variant with improved electronics. The TBM-3W variants remained in service up to 1954, generally operating as the 'hunter' element in teams with TBM-3S and TBM-3S-2 submarine 'killer' aircraft.

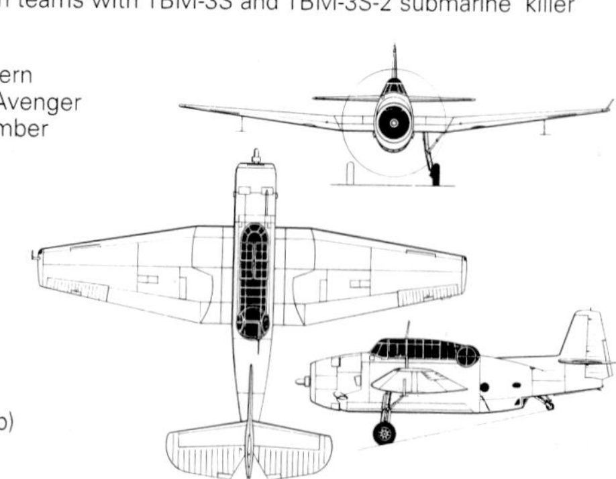

Specification: Grumman/Eastern Aircraft (General Motors) TBM-3E Avenger three-seat carrierborne torpedo-bomber and anti-submarine aeroplane
Span: 16.51 m (54 ft 2 in)
Length: 12.48 m (40 ft 11.5 in)
Powerplant: 1×Wright R-2600-20 Cyclone 14, 1417 kW (1,900 hp)
Armament: 3×12.7-mm (0.5-in) and 1×7.62-mm (0.3-in) machine-guns, plus provision for 907 kg (2,000 lb) of bombs or 1×torpedo carried internally
Max T/O weight: 8117 kg (17,895 lb)
Max speed: 276 mph at 15,000 ft
Operational range: 1,010 miles

Grumman F11F (F-11) Tiger

The design that began life as an effort to maximise the performance of the straight-wing F9F-2 finally emerged as the almost completely new Tiger with a thinner wing, landing gear mounted in the area-ruled fuselage, a low-set tailplane, and lateral inlets for the Wright J65 afterburning turbojet. Grumman's new design was ordered in 1953 as the F9F-8, though this was later changed to F9F-9 when an F9F-8 variant of the Cougar appeared. The YF9F-9 first flew in July 1954 with a non-afterburning J65-W-7, but by January 1955 the second prototype was flying with an afterburning engine and in April of the same year the designation F11F was adopted. Service deliveries began in March 1957, and the 199 F11F-1s were produced in two forms: 42 short-nose aircraft and 157 long-nose machines fitted for (but seldom with) radar. The type was redesignated F-11A in 1962.

Specification: Grumman F11F-1 (F-11A) Tiger single-seat carrierborne and land-based fighter
Span: 9.64 m (31 ft 7.5 in)
Length: 14.31 m (46 ft 11.25 in)
Powerplant: 1×Wright J65-W-18, 4990 kg (11,000 lb) st
Armament: 4×20-mm cannon, plus provision for up to 4×Sidewinder 1A/C AAMs carried under the wings
Max T/O weight: 10052 kg (22,160 lb)
Max speed: 750 mph at sea level
Operational range: 1,270 miles

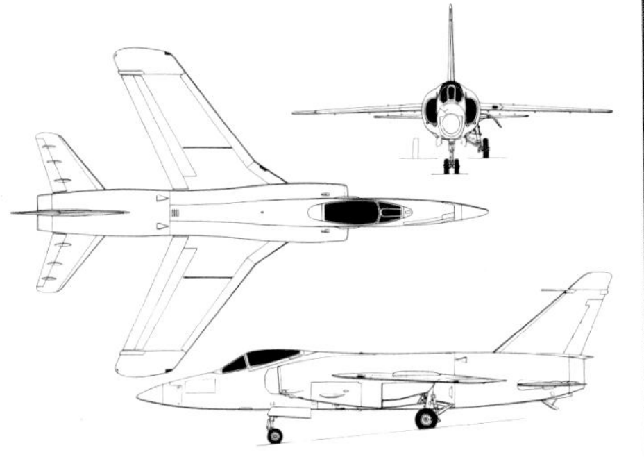

Grumman WF (E-1) Tracer

For carrier onboard delivery Grumman produced the TF-1 Trader version of the S2F with a new fuselage accommodating, in addition to the crew, nine passengers or freight; in 1962 this became the C-1A. Production amounted to 87 aircraft including a small number of the TF-1Q (EC-1A) version for electronic countermeasures. Another S2F derivative was the WF-2 Tracer, a carrier-capable airborne early warning type generally known as the 'Willy Fudd' and in 1962 redesignated as the E-1B. A converted TF-1 modified as the aerodynamic prototype flew in March 1957 with the massive dish-shaped radome for the APS-82 surveillance radar supported at its rear by the central portion of a revised empennage with endplate vertical surfaces. Production amounted to 88 aircraft, and these began to enter service in February 1958.

Specification: Grumman WF-2 Tracer (E-1B) four-seat carrierborne airborne early warning aeroplane
Span: 21.23 m (69 ft 8 in)
Length: 13.82 m (45 ft 4 in)
Powerplant: 2×Wright R-1820-82WA Cyclone 9, 1137 kW (1,525 hp) each
Armament: none
Max T/O weight: 12247 kg (27,000 lb)
Patrol speed: 120-160 mph at optimum altitude
Operational range: 1,000+ miles

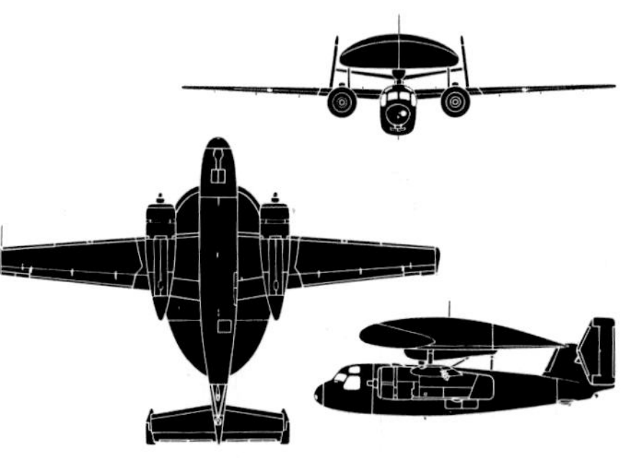

MD F4H (F-4) Phantom II

One of the most important warplanes of all time, the F4H was planned from 1953 as the AH-1 attack fighter but in 1955 recast as the F4H fleet-defence fighter with radar and a missile armament. This required a two-man crew and paired J79 engines with variable inlets, and the advanced nature of the design is attested by the fact that 23 F4H-1 test aircraft were ordered. The first XF4H-1 flew in May 1958, and trials confirmed the need for blown flaps, dihedralled outer wing panels, and anhedralled tailplane halves. The first 24 service aircraft were F4H-1Fs with J79-GE-2 engines, and were followed by 649 F4H-1s (F-4Bs) with more power, APQ-72 radar, an infra-red detector and many weapon options, 46 F4H-1P (RF-4B) reconnaissance aircraft, and 512 F-4Js with APG-59 radar, larger wheels, more fuel, a slotted tailplane and slats on the outer wing panels.

Specification: McDonnell Douglas F4H-1 (F-4B) Phantom II two-seat carrierborne and land-based fleet defence and multi-role fighter
Span: 11.70 m (38 ft 4.75 in)
Length: 17.77 m (58 ft 3.75 in)
Powerplant: 2×General Electric J79-GE-8, 7711 kg (17,000 lb) st each
Armament: provision for 6×Sparrow III AAMs or 4×Sparrow III and 4×Sidewinder AAMs, or up to 7258 kg (16,000 lb) of disposable stores carried on 5×external hardpoints
Max T/O weight: 24767 kg (54,600 lb)
Max speed: Mach 2.27 at optimum altitude
Operational range: 800 miles

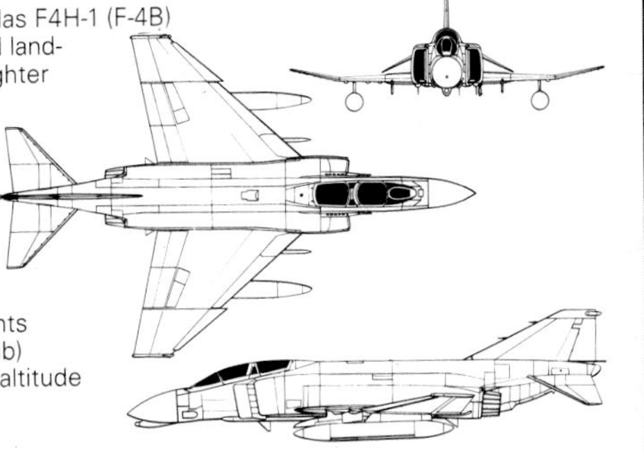

North American A3J (A-5) Vigilante

The A3J was planned from 1955 as a phenomenally advanced all-weather strike aircraft, and amongst the features it pioneered were inlets and nozzles with automatic scheduling, a 'slab' vertical tail, differential 'slab' tailplane halves, blown flaps, a linear bay between the two engines accommodating two fuel tanks and one nuclear weapon for rearward ejection, and the REINS integrated nav/attack system with radar and inertial inputs. The first of two YA3J-1 prototypes flew in August 1958, and these were followed by 56 A3J-1s (A-5As) with J79-GE-2, -4 or -8 engines, and by six A3J-2s (A-5Bs) with full-span leading-edge droop blowing for an extra 6804 kg (15,000 lb) of fuel in a humped fuselage. The US Navy had given up its strategic nuclear role, so the A-5Bs and 53 A-5As were converted to the same standard as 55 A3J-3P (RA-5C) long-range photo and electronic reconnaissance aircraft.

Specification: North American A3J-3P (RA-5C) Vigilante two-seat carrierborne and land-based multi-sensor reconnaissance aeroplane
Span: 16.15 m (53 ft 0 in)
Length: 23.32 m (76 ft 6 in)
Powerplant: 2×General Electric J79-GE-10, 8101 kg (17,860 lb) st each
Armament: none
Max T/O weight: 36288 kg (80,000 lb)
Max speed: Mach 2.1 at 40,000 ft
Operational range: 3,000 miles

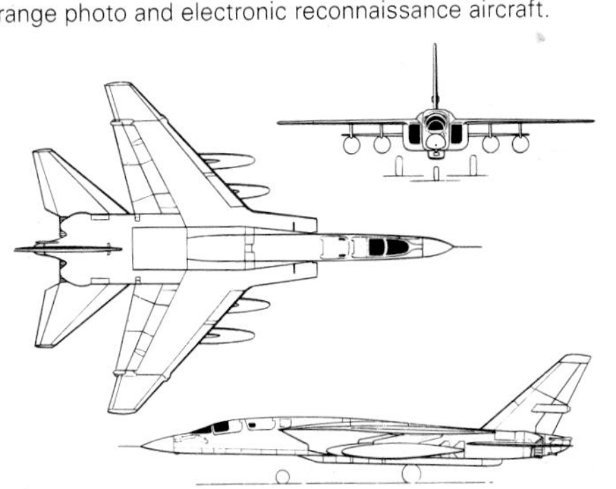

Douglas F4D (F-6) Skyray

One of several fighters based on German World War II research into tailless aircraft, the Skyray was schemed as a carrierborne interceptor optimised for rate of climb. Developed in the late 1940s as a low-aspect-ratio flying wing of modest sweep, rather than a true delta, the Skyray first flew as the XF4D-1 in January 1951 with a 2268-kg (5,000-lb) Allison J35-A-17 engine rather than the planned Westinghouse J40, which was suffering from development problems and then cancelled. It was decided in March 1953 to use the J57 in the Skyray, and this combination was first flown in June 1954, allowing service deliveries of the F4D-1 to begin in 1956 after some flight problems had been cured. Production totalled 420 F4D-1 aircraft, redesignated F-6A in 1962. The only Skyray variant was the F4D-2 with the J57-P-14 engine, but these four aircraft were redesignated F5D-1 before flying.

Specification: Douglas F4D-1 (F-6A) Skyray single-seat carrierborne interceptor and fighter-bomber
Span: 10.21 m (33 ft 6 in)
Length: 13.93 m (45 ft 8.25 in)
Powerplant: 1×Pratt & Whitney J57-P-2 or -8B, 4400- or 4763-kg (9,700- or 10,500-lb) st
Armament: 4×20-mm cannon, plus provision for up to 1814 kg (4,000 lb) of disposable stores carried on 6×external hardpoints

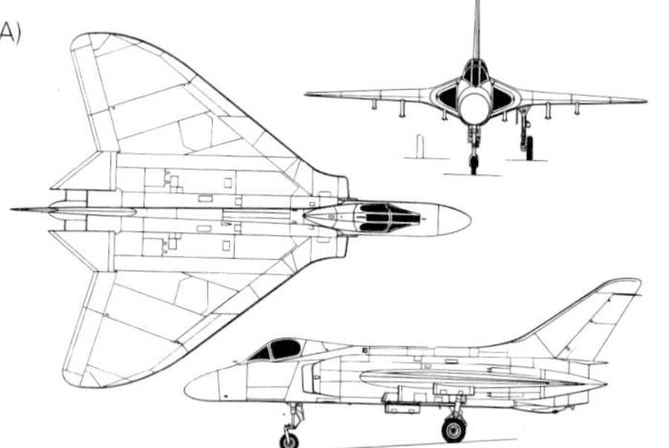

North American AJ (A-2) Savage

The Savage reflects the ambivalent approach to jet power immediately after World War II, this nuclear bomber being planned round a single tail-mounted turbojet and two wing-mounted piston engines. The Savage was otherwise conventional, and the first of three XAJ-1s flew in July 1948. There followed 40 examples of the AJ-1 with two 1789-kW (2,400-hp) R-2800-44Ws and one 1814-kg (4,000-lb) J33-A-19. Several difficulties curtailed the type's career, but further production was ordered as 70 AJ-2 bombers (engine changes, more fuel, taller tail and other modifications) plus 30 AJ-2P reconnaissance aircraft (revised nose). From 1959 most survivors were converted as tankers with a hose-and-reel unit replacing the turbojet, and in 1962 the AJ was designated in the A-2 series. The A2J with two 3803-kW (5,100-shp) Allison T40 turboprops did not progress past two prototypes.

Specification: North American AJ-2 Savage three-seat carrierborne and land-based strike bomber
Span: 22.91 m (75 ft 2 in) over tiptanks
Length: 19.23 m (63 ft 1 in)
Powerplant: 2×Pratt & Whitney R-2800-48, 1864 kW (2,500 hp) each, and 1×Allison J33-A-10, 2087 kg (4,600 lb) st
Armament: provision for up to 4536 kg (10,000 lb) of disposable stores carried internally
Max T/O weight: 23978 kg (52,862 lb)
Max speed: 471 mph at optimum altitude
Operational range: 2,200 miles

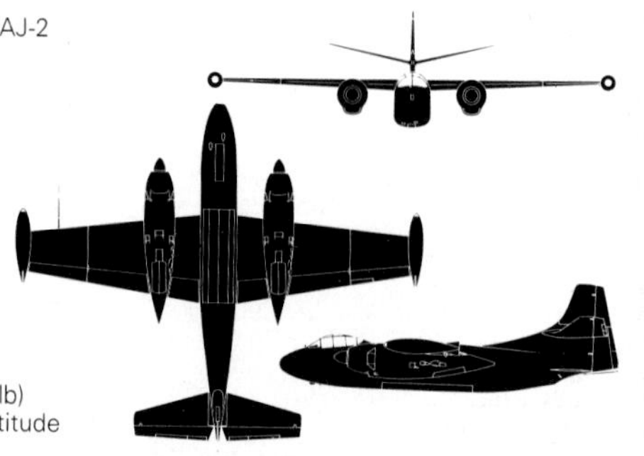

Vought F7U Cutlass

Drawing on the same type of research data as the F4D Skyray, the fast-climbing F7U interceptor was evolved in 1946 as a 38° swept flying wing with twin vertical surfaces and powered elevons. Three XF7U-1 prototypes were ordered, the first flying in September 1948 with J34-WE-32 turbojets, and these were followed by 14 F7U-1s. The 88 planned F7U-2s were cancelled because of difficulties with their J34-WE-42 engine, and experience with the F7U-1 led to extensive redesign of the F7U-3 with altered nose and fins to improve flight characteristics. Some 192 of this version were complemented by 98 F7U-3Ms (including 48 aircraft ordered as F7U-3s) with four Sparrow I beam-riding AAMs and by 12 F7U-3P armed reconnaissance aircraft carrying camera equipment.

Specification: Vought F7U-3 single-seat carrierborne interceptor fighter
Span: 11.79 m (38 ft 8 in)
Length: 13.49 m (44 ft 3 in)
Powerplant: 2×Westinghouse J46-WE-8A, 2087 kg (4,600 lb) st each
Armament: 4×20-mm cannon plus provision (F7U-3M) for 4×Sparrow I AAMs carried under the wings
Max T/O weight: 14353 kg (31,642 lb)
Max speed: 680 mph at 10,000 ft
Operational range: 660 miles

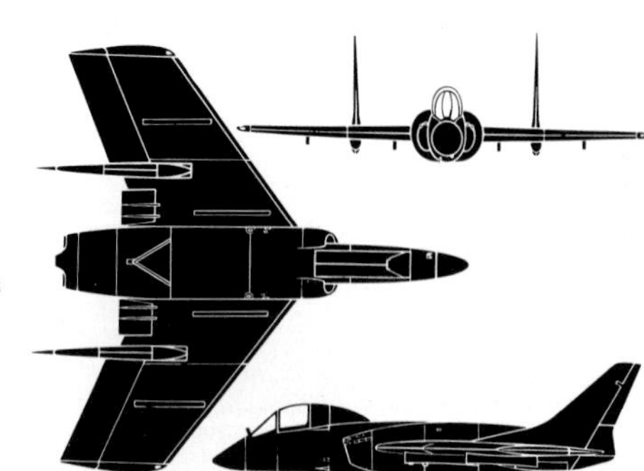

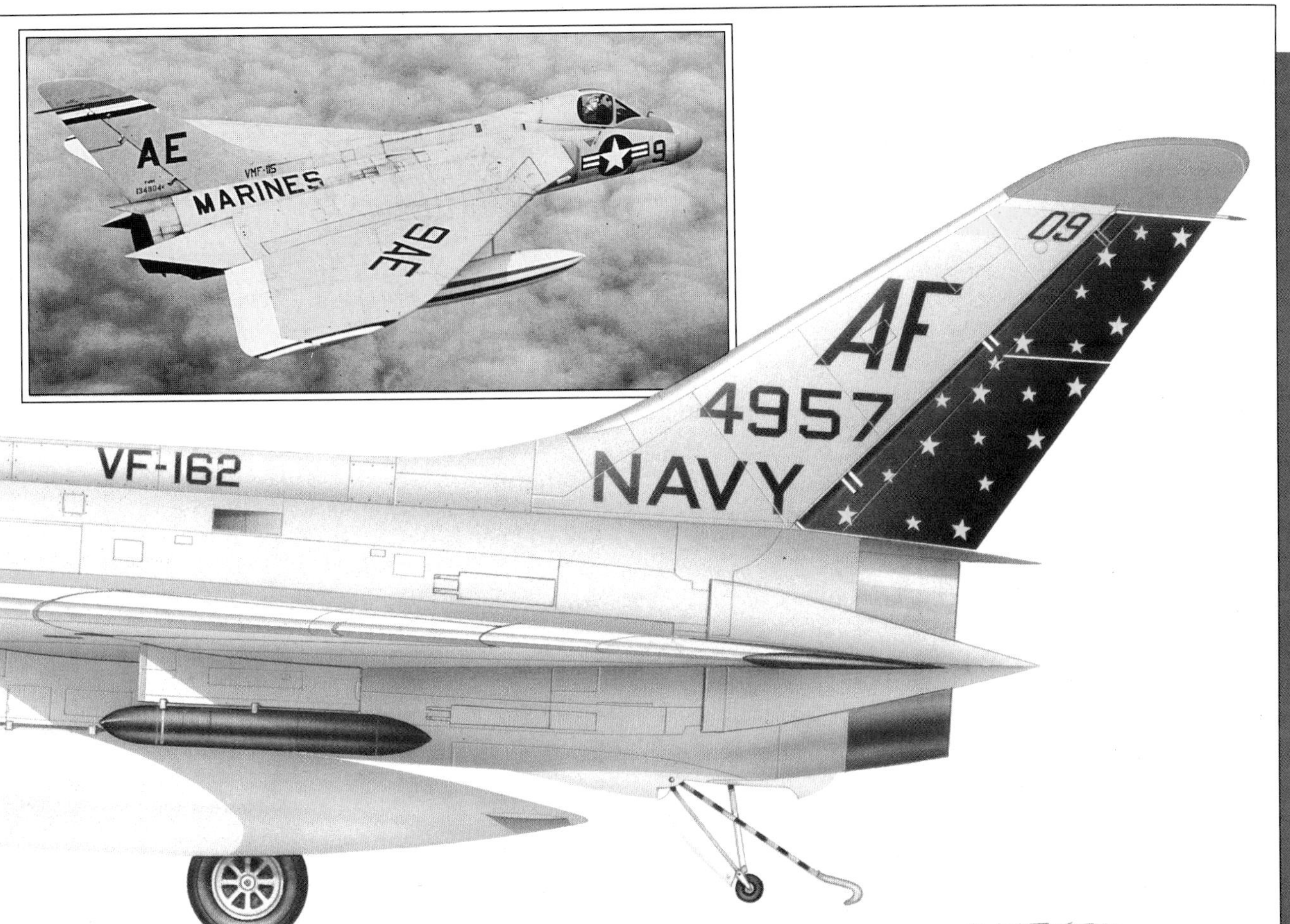

'he Douglas Skyray commonly known as the 'ord') featured cintillating climb erformance for its day, nd served with both the Aarines ashore and the Navy afloat in a pure nterceptor role. This ircraft flew with VF-162, whose star markings were o be seen adorning Crusaders during the Vietnam war.

McDonnell F3H (F-3) Demon

Developed from 1949 as a naval fighter in no significant respect inferior to its land-based counterparts, the F3H was designed with swept flying surfaces, an advanced airframe and the Westinghouse J40 afterburning turbojet, but the failure of this engine bedevilled the whole F3H programme. The Demon was McDonnell's first single-engined fighter and the XF3H-1, which made its maiden flight in August 1951, was powered by a 3266-kg (7,200-lb) XJ40-WE-6, destined to be replaced by the more-powerful J40-WE-24. This engine did not materialise and the 56 F3H-1Hs were drastically underpowered with the 3266-kg J40-WE-22. The following F3H-2, of which 239 were produced, had an Allison engine that was also used in two limited all-weather variants with APG-51 radar: 80 F3H-2Ms with four Sparrow III AAMs, and 144 F3H-2Ns with four Sidewinder AAMs.

Specification: McDonnell F3H-2 (F-3B) Demon single-seat carrierborne fighter and fighter-bomber
Span: 10.77 m (35 ft 4 in)
Length: 17.96 m (58 ft 11 in)
Powerplant: 1×Allison J71-A-2 or -2E, 6464 or 6691 kg (14,250 or 14,750 lb) st
Armament: 4×20-mm cannon, plus provision for up to 2994 kg (6,600 lb) of disposable stores carried on 4×external hardpoints
Max T/O weight: 15376 kg (33,000 lb)
Max speed: 647 mph at 30,900 ft
Operational range: 1,370 miles

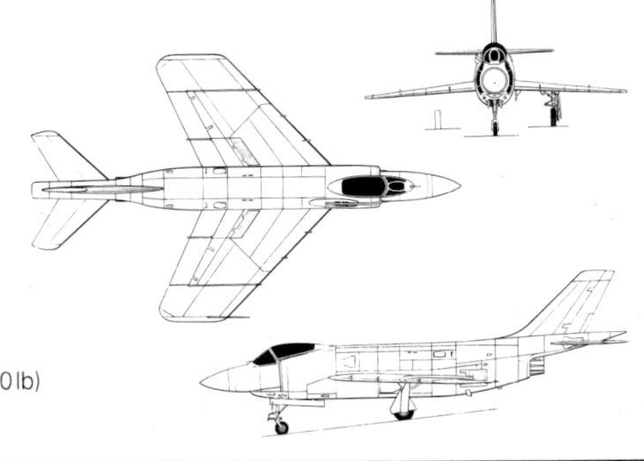

Grumman F9F-6/8 (F-9) Cougar

In 1951 the US Navy accepted Grumman's proposal for a swept-wing version of the F9F Panther, and this first flew in September 1951 as the XF6F-6 with a 3289-kg (7,250-lb) J48-P-8 and a new 35° swept wing carrying larger flaps, fences, leading-edge slats and spoilers in place of ailerons. Service deliveries of 706 F9F-6s began in November 1952, and this total included 60 F9F-6P reconnaissance aircraft. The 168 F9F-7s were identical to the F9F-6s apart from their Allison J33-A-16A turbojets. Then came 712 F8F-8s with the wing redesigned for an effective 15 per cent increase in chord, a recontoured cockpit canopy and a 20.3-cm (8-in) increase in fuselage length to provide additional fuel volume; the F9F-8 total included F8F-9B attack version with missile armament, and 110 F9F-8P reconnaissance aircraft. There were also 399 F9F-8T tandem-seat trainers.

Specification: Grumman F9F-6 (F-9F) Cougar single-seat carrierborne and land-based fighter and fighter-bomber
Span: 11.10 m (36 ft 5 in)
Length: 12.67 m (41 ft 7 in)
Powerplant: 1×Pratt & Whitney J48-P-8, 3289 kg (7,250 lb) st
Armament: 4×20-mm cannon, plus provision for 2×454-kg (1,000-lb) bombs carried under the wings
Max T/O weight: 9072 kg (20,000 lb)
Max speed: 690 mph at sea level
Operational range: 1,000 miles

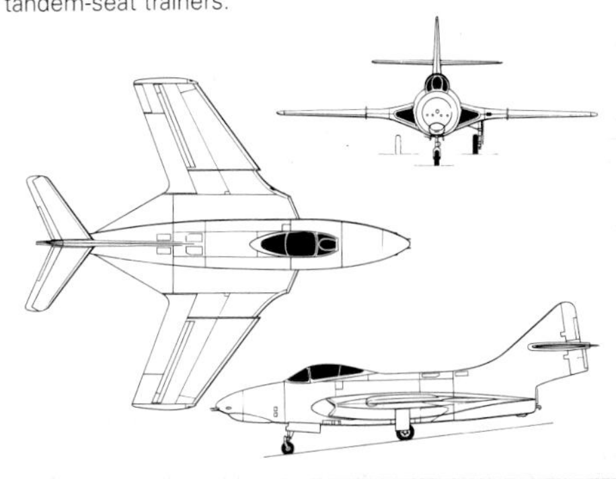

Vought F8U (F-8) Crusader

Generally superior to the F-100, its land-based but slightly earlier counterpart with the same engine, the F8U was the US Navy's first genuinely supersonic fighter. A high angle of wing incidence without a nose-high attitude during carrier operations was provided by a variable-incidence wing mechanism, and the first of two XF8U-1s flew in March 1955 with a 6713-kg (14,800-lb) J57-P-11 afterburning turbojet. Production followed steadily of 308 F8U-1s, 130 F8U-1Es with limited all-weather capability, 144 F8U-1P reconnaissance aircraft (53 later being upgraded to RF-8Gs with airframe strengthening), 187 F8U-2s with more power and reduced span, 152 F8U-2N limited all-weather fighters with two more Sidewinder AAMs in place of the F8U-1E's pack of 32 rockets, and 286 F8U-2NE (F-8E) multi-role fighters with APQ-94 radar and two underwing hardpoints.

Specification: Vought F8U-2NE (F-8E) Crusader single-seat carrierborne and land-based fighter and fighter-bomber
Span: 10.72 m (35 ft 2 in)
Length: 16.61 m (54 ft 6 in)
Powerplant: 1×Pratt & Whitney J57-P-20A, 8165 kg (18,000 lb) st
Armament: 4×20-mm cannon, plus provision for 4×Sidewinder AAMs or 2268 kg (5,000 lb) of disposable stores carried on 2×underwing hardpoints
Max T/O weight: 15422 kg (34,000 lb)
Max speed: Mach 1.7 at 40,000 ft
Operational range: 1,100 miles

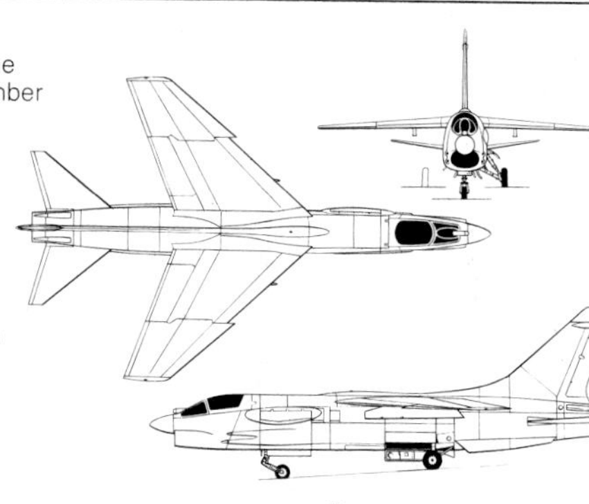

The superb Crusader was a popular and consummate fighter. Blessed with good agility and a powerful engine, it was easily supersonic and could outperform most of its land-based rivals. It earned the title 'Last of the Gunfighters' thanks to the retention of cannon at a time when the Phantom was becoming a missiles-only fighter. In Vietnam it returned a healthy kill-loss ratio over the MiGs.

Douglas A3D (A-3) Skywarrior

The Skywarrior was designed to give the US Navy a carrierborne strategic nuclear strike capability. Initial planning began in 1947, and Douglas completed project design in 1949 for a moderately swept bomber with underwing podded Westinghouse J40 turbojets and an internal bay for 5443 kg (12,000 lb) of nuclear or conventional weapons. The resulting XA3D-1 flew in October 1952 with XJ40-WE-3 engines, whose subsequent failure led to use of the 4400-kg (9,700-lb) J57-P-6 engine. Deliveries of 50 A3D-1s began in 1956, and later aircraft were 164 A3D-2s with greater power and inflight-refuelling capability, 30 A3D-2P photographic reconnaissance and 24 A3D-2Q electronic reconnaissance aircraft, and 12 A3D-2T radar/navigation trainers. From 1962 the aircraft were redesignated in the A-3 series, and developed for alternative roles with special mission equipment.

Specification: Douglas A3D-2 Skywarrior three-seat carrierborne and land-based strike and attack bomber
Span: 22.10 m (72 ft 6 in)
Length: 23.27 m (76 ft 4 in)
Powerplant: 2×Pratt & Whitney J57-P-10, 5625 kg (12,400 lb) st each
Armament: 2×20-mm cannon in a radar-controlled rear barbette, plus provision for up to 5443 kg (12,000 lb) of bombs and other stores carried internally
Max T/O weight: 37195 kg (82,000 lb)
Max speed: 610 mph at 10,000 ft
Operational range: 1,050 miles

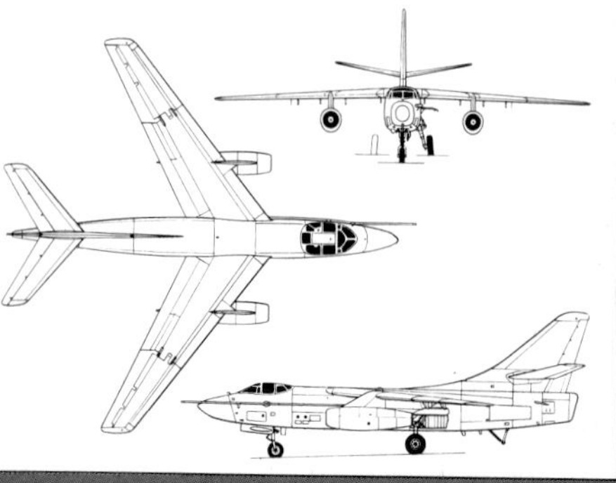

Grumman S2F (S-2) Tracker

Reflecting the increased importance of submarines and the capabilities of the sensor/weapon combination available to detect and attack them, the S2F was developed in the early 1950s as an aeroplane carrying both sensors and weapons, and as such a successor to the types operated in two-aircraft teams by the US Navy in the late 1940s. The high-wing S2F had a fuselage weapon bay, radar and a magnetic anomaly detector in the rear fuselage, and sonobuoys in the nacelles. The XS2F-1 flew in December 1952, and was followed by 740 S2F-1s including a number of S2F-1Ss with the Jezebel/Julie echo-location system. Next came 77 S2F-2s with a larger weapon bay for homing torpedoes, 100 S2F-3s with an improved forward fuselage, and 252 S2F-3Ss with the Jezebel/Julie combination; the S2F-1S1 was the S2F-1S with Jezebel/Julie. In 1962 the Tracker was redesignated in the S-2 series.

Specification: Grumman S2F-3S (S-2E) four-seat carrierborne and land-based anti-submarine aeroplane
Span: 22.12 m (72 ft 7 in)
Length: 13.26 m (43 ft 6 in)
Powerplant: 2×Wright R-1820-82WA Cyclone 9, 1137 kW (1,525 hp) each
Armament: provision for up to 2182 kg (4,180 lb) of disposable stores carried internally and on 6×external hardpoints
Max T/O weight: 12187 kg (26,867 lb)
Max speed: 253 mph at 5,000 ft
Operational range: 1,150 miles

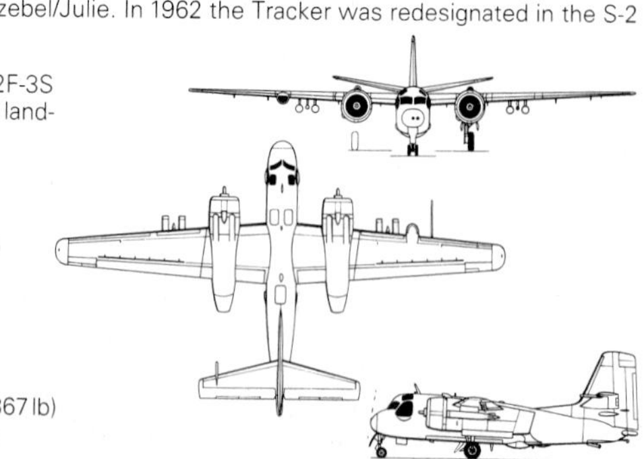

North American FJ-2/4 (F-1) Fury

The straight-wing FJ-1 naval fighter paved the way for the swept-wing F-86 Sabre, whose F-86E version led to the FJ-2. The XFJ-2 was a navalised F-86E with four 20-mm cannon in place of six 12.7-mm (0.5-in) machine-guns, and first flew in December 1951. The 200 FJ-2s had folding wings and the 2722-kg (6,000-lb) General Electric J47-GE-2 turbojet. Next came the FJ-3, an FJ-2 variant with a 3470-kg (7,650-lb) J65-W-4 engine and, in later models, fuel-filled extended leading edges and six underwing hardpoints: in 1962 survivors of these 458 aircraft were redesignated F-1C, and the FJ-3Ms (80 built) with Sidewinder AAMs became MF-1Cs. The FJ-4 (F-1E) had thinner flying surfaces and 50 per cent more internal fuel in a revised fuselage. These 150 aircraft were complemented by 222 close-support FJ-4Bs (AF-1Es) with six hardpoints and nuclear capability.

Specification: North American FJ-4 (F-1E) Fury single-seat carrierborne and land-based fighter and fighter-bomber
Span: 11.91 m (39 ft 1 in)
Length: 11.07 m (36 ft 4 in)
Powerplant: 1×Wright J65-W-16A, 2722 kg (6,000 lb) st
Armament: 4×20-mm cannon, plus provision for 4×Sidewinder AAMs or up to 1361 kg (3,000 lb) of disposable stores on 4×external hardpoints
Max T/O weight: 10750 kg (23,700 lb)
Max speed: 680 mph at sea level
Operational range: 2,020 miles

Douglas A4D (A-4) Skyhawk

One of the most versatile aircraft ever developed, the A4D was planned as an AD Skyraider successor, and through meticulous basic and detail planning the designers came up with a machine meeting all the US Navy's requirements at just half of the stipulated 13608-kg (30,000-lb) maximum weight. The XA4D-1 flew in August 1954 with the Wright J65 turbojet and was followed by 165 A4D-1s with the 3493-kg (7,700-lb) J65-W-4, 542 improved A4D-2s with the 3493-kg J65-W-16A engine and inflight-refuelling capability, 658 limited all-weather A4D-2Ns with Escapac ejector seats, 500 re-engineered A4D-4s (A-4Es) with a different engine for lower fuel consumption and greater load-carrying capability, and as the last version of the 1960s, 352 A-4Fs with extra avionics in a dorsal 'hump'. There were also TA-4E and TA-4F two-seat trainers, while the A-4M and A-4N entered service in the 1970s.

Specification: Douglas A4D-4 (A-4E) Skyhawk single-seat carrierborne and land-based light attack bomber
Span: 8.38 m (27 ft 6 in)
Length: 13.07 m (42 ft 10.75 in)
Powerplant: 1×Pratt & Whitney J52-P-6A, 3856 kg (8,500 lb) st
Armament: 2×20-mm cannon, plus provision for up to 3720 kg (8,200 lb) of disposable stores carried on 5×external hardpoints
Max T/O weight: 11113 kg (24,500 lb)
Max speed: 675 mph at sea level
Operational range: 700 miles

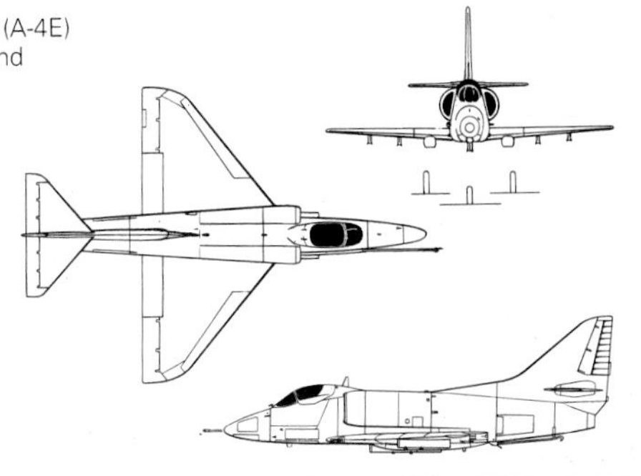

de Havilland Sea Devon

The D.H.104 Dove was developed late in World War II for use as a post-war feederliner, and first flew in September 1945. Initial production was of the Dove Mk 1 airliner and Dove Mk 2 executive transport, the planned Dove Mk 3 high-altitude survey type being cancelled. Then came the Dove Mk 4 for military operators in the communications role. The RAF led the way with orders for a total of 41 Devon C.Mk 1s, and the Fleet Air Arm procured an essentially similar version with the designation Sea Devon C.Mk 20. These 13 aircraft were delivered from 1955, and three remain in service to the present in the communications and liaison roles. In the mid-1960s these Devon versions were improved to Dove Mk 8 civil standard with a heightened flightdeck roof and Gipsy Queen 70 Mk 3 engines in place of the original 246-kW (330-hp) Gipsy Queen 71 engines.

Specification: de Havilland Sea Devon C.Mk 20 two-crew communications aeroplane
Span: 17.37 m (57 ft 0 in)
Length: 11.96 m (39 ft 3 in)
Powerplant: 2 x de Havilland Gipsy Queen 70 Mk 3, 298 kW (400 hp) each
Payload: up to 11 passengers
Max T/O weight: 3856 kg (8,500 lb)
Max speed: 210 mph at 8,000 ft
Operational range: 1,000 miles with a 771-kg (1,700-lb) payload

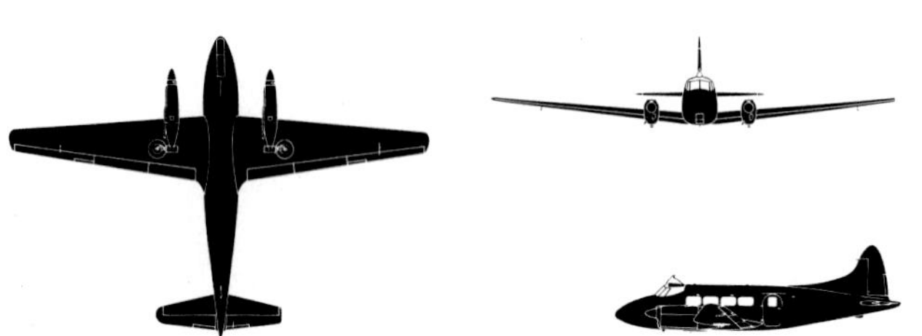

de Havilland Tiger Moth

First flown in October 1931 as the D.H.60T Moth Trainer, this important lightplane and trainer of the 1930s became the D.H.82 Tiger Moth with the adoption of a dihedralled lower wing. In military service this variant was the Tiger Moth Mk I. From 1934 this was supplemented by the D.H.82A with a smooth plywood rather than ridged stringer/fabric rear decking, and this entered service as the Tiger Moth Mk II. This latter became the most significant British basic trainer of World War II and the period immediately after it. Another important variant, especially for the training of naval AA gunners, was the radio-controlled D.H.82B, whose service designation was Queen Bee: this wheel- or float-equipped type could be flown by a pilot in the front cockpit, but in live firing exercises was used with radio-control equipment in the rear cockpit.

Specification: de Havilland Tiger Moth Mk II two-seat basic training aeroplane
Span: 8.94 m (29 ft 4 in)
Length: 7.29 m (23 ft 11 in)
Powerplant: 1 x de Havilland Gipsy Major 1, 97 kW (130 hp)
Armament: none
Max T/O weight: 828 kg (1,825 lb)
Max speed: 104 mph at sea level
Operational range: 300 miles

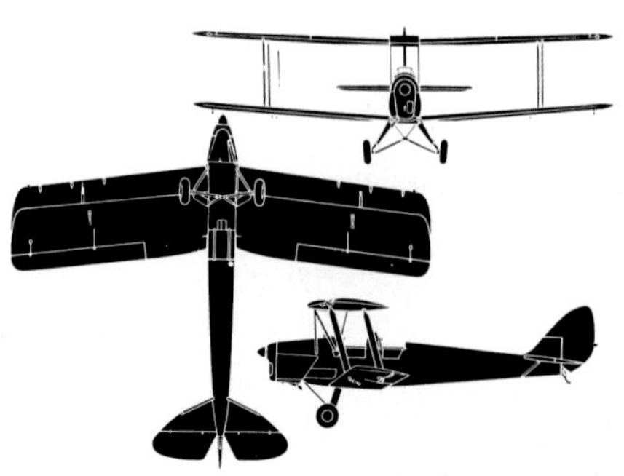

Fairey Firefly

The Firefly was one of the Fleet Air Arm's most important first-line aircraft in World War II and the period up to the mid-1950s, and this importance was reflected in the number of second-line derivatives. After the war surplus Firefly F.Mk I fighters with the Griffon XII engine were converted as Firefly T.Mk 1 unarmed and Firefly T.Mk 2 armed trainers, and also as Firefly T.Mk 3 ASW trainers and Firefly TT.Mk 1 target tugs. Introduction of the Griffon 74 engine resulted in the Firefly Mk 4 and improved Firefly Mk 5, and second-line variants were the Firefly TT.Mk 4 target tug and Firefly T.Mk 5 trainer. The Firefly Mk 7 had the Griffon 59 for ASW work, and its trainer equivalent was the Firefly T.Mk 7. Particularly important as targets in the Royal Navy's SAM programme were Firefly U.Mk 8 and U.Mk 9 target drone conversions of Firefly Mk 7 and Mk 4/5 aircraft respectively.

Specification: Fairey Firefly T.Mk 7 three-seat anti-submarine warfare training aeroplane
Span: 13.56 m (44 ft 6 in)
Length: 11.66 m (38 ft 3 in)
Powerplant: 1 x Rolls-Royce Griffon 59, 1465 kW (1,965 hp)
Armament: none
Max T/O weight: 6255 kg (13,790 lb)
Max speed: 300 mph at 10,750 ft
Operational range: 860 miles

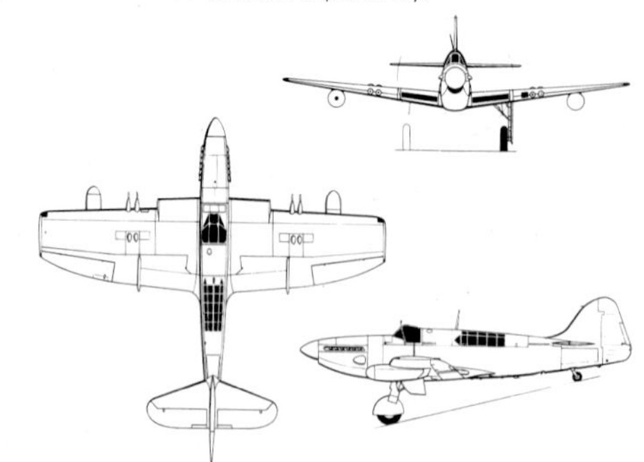

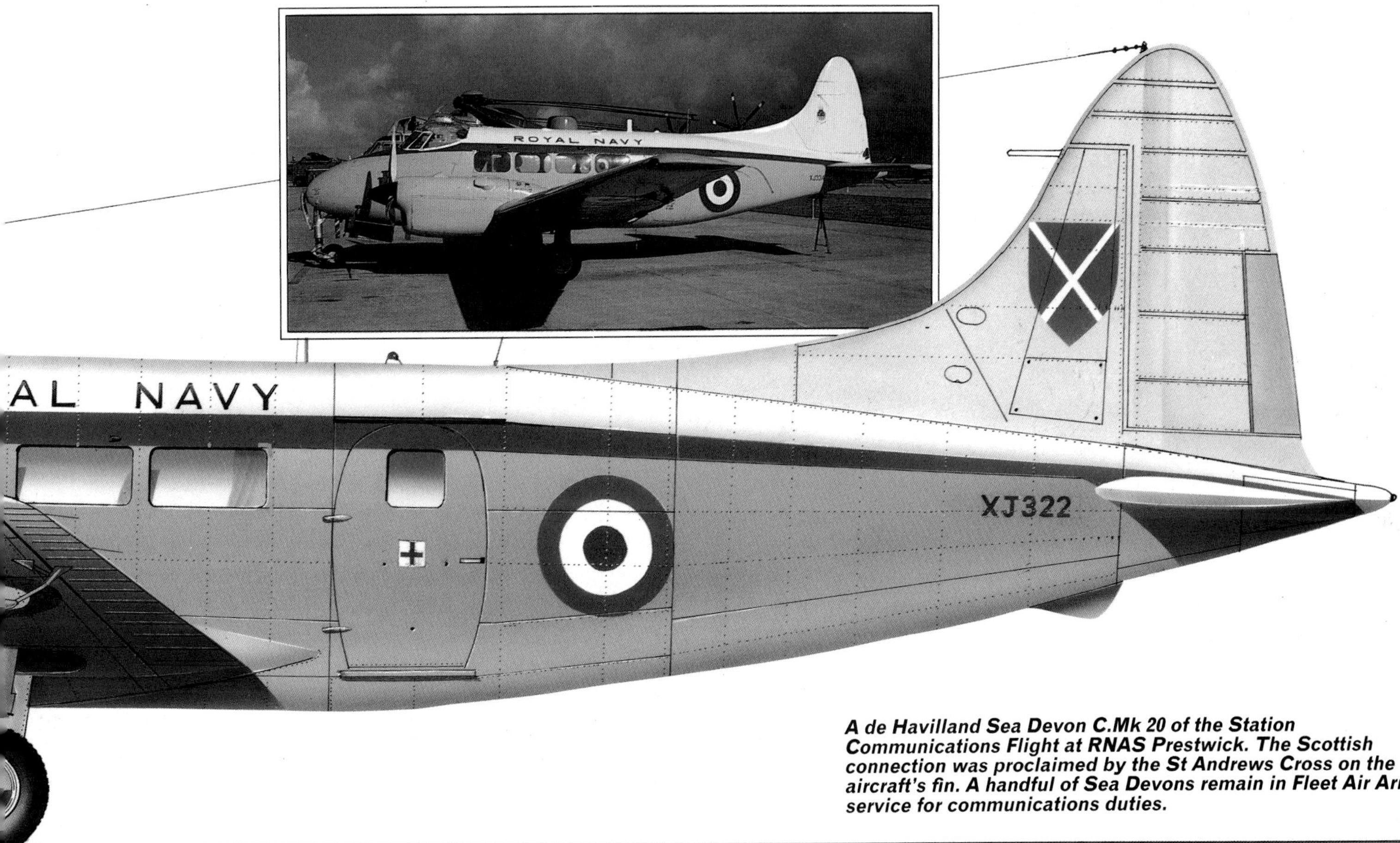

A de Havilland Sea Devon C.Mk 20 of the Station Communications Flight at RNAS Prestwick. The Scottish connection was proclaimed by the St Andrews Cross on the aircraft's fin. A handful of Sea Devons remain in Fleet Air Arm service for communications duties.

de Havilland Dominie

Built to the extent of 186 aircraft by de Havilland at Hatfield and, from 1942, 336 by Brush Coachworks at Loughborough, the Dominie was the D.H.89B service version of the Dragon Rapide local-service airliner. Nothing but the prototype came of the D.H.89M armed reconnaissance model for Coastal Command, but with the outbreak of World War II all civil D.H.89s and improved D.H.89As were impressed. Their success led to production of the Dominie version, which was ordered to provide Dominie Mk 1 navigation and radio trainers plus Dominie Mk 2 communications aircraft for both the Fleet Air Arm and the RAF. After the war many of these military aircraft were released to the civil market as a means of restoring air services, though as late as the 1960s the Fleet Air Arm still had three Dominies on charge.

Specification: de Havilland Dominie Mk 2 one-crew communications aeroplane
Span: 14.63 m (48 ft 0 in)
Length: 10.36 m (34 ft 6 in)
Powerplant: 2 x de Havilland Gipsy Queen Mk 3, 149 kW (200 hp) each
Payload: nine passengers
Max T/O weight: 2495 kg (5,500 lb)
Max speed: 157 mph at 1,000 ft
Operational range: 570 miles

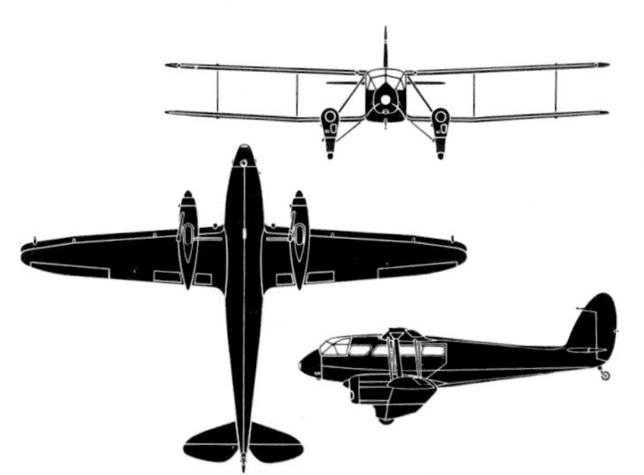

de Havilland Mosquito

The Mosquito is best remembered for its RAF service. However the type was also used in limited numbers by the Fleet Air Arm, beginning with the Mosquito T.Mk 3 dual-control trainer with Merlin 21, 23 or 25 engines and provision for drop tanks. This paved the way for the Sea Mosquito TF.Mk 33 (later TR.Mk 33) carrierborne torpedo and reconnaissance variant. The type first flew in March 1944 as a conversion of the Mosquito FB.Mk VI, and the 50 production aircraft had American ASH radar, folding wings, an arrester hook, revised landing gear, four-blade propellers and provision for RATO units. Other post-war variants were the Sea Mosquito TR.Mk 37 conversion of the TR.Mk 33 with British ASV.Mk XIII radar, and General Aircraft's Sea Mosquito TT.Mk 39 target tug conversion of the Mosquito B.Mk XVI with its fuselage lengthened to 13.21 m (43 ft 4 in).

Specification: de Havilland Sea Mosquito FR.Mk 33 two-seat carrierborne torpedo-bomber and reconnaissance aeroplane
Span: 16.51 m (54 ft 2 in)
Length: 12.88 m (42 ft 3 in)
Powerplant: 2 x Rolls-Royce Merlin 25, 1223 kW (1,640 hp) each
Armament: 4 x 20-mm cannon, plus provision for 454 kg (1,000 lb) of bombs carried internally or 907 kg (2,000 lb) of mines or 1 x 457-mm (18-in) torpedo carried under the fuselage, and up to 8 x 27-kg (60-lb) rockets carried under the wings
Max T/O weight: 10206 kg (22,500 lb)
Max speed: 385 mph at 13,500 ft
Operational range: 1,260 miles

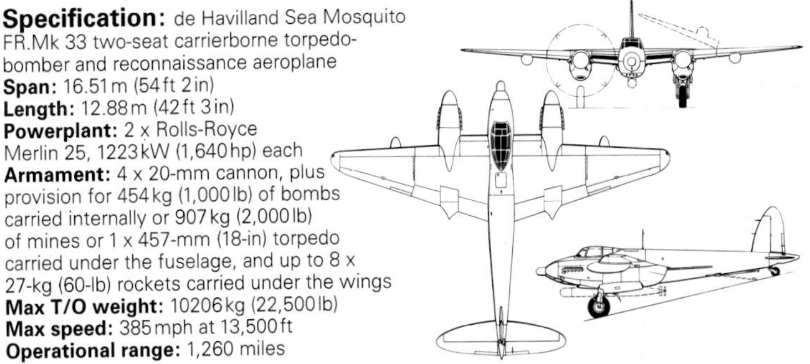

Gloster Meteor TT.Mk 20

The Fleet Air Arm's Gloster Meteor TT.Mk 20 was a conversion of the Meteor NF.Mk 11 two-seat night-fighter for the target tug role. The programme was entrusted to Armstrong Whitworth, which had been responsible for the development of the NF.Mk 11 and later night-fighter variants. Unlike the similar Meteor NF.Mk 14 with its single-piece blown Perspex canopy, the Meteor NF.Mk 11 had a framed canopy that was retained in the TT.Mk 20 conversion, which introduced a windmill winch above the starboard wing inboard of the engine nacelle for deployment and control of the towed target. The aircraft were used also by the RAF and some other NATO countries, and the programme between December 1957 and February 1965 involved only aircraft built at Baginton by Armstrong Whitworth.

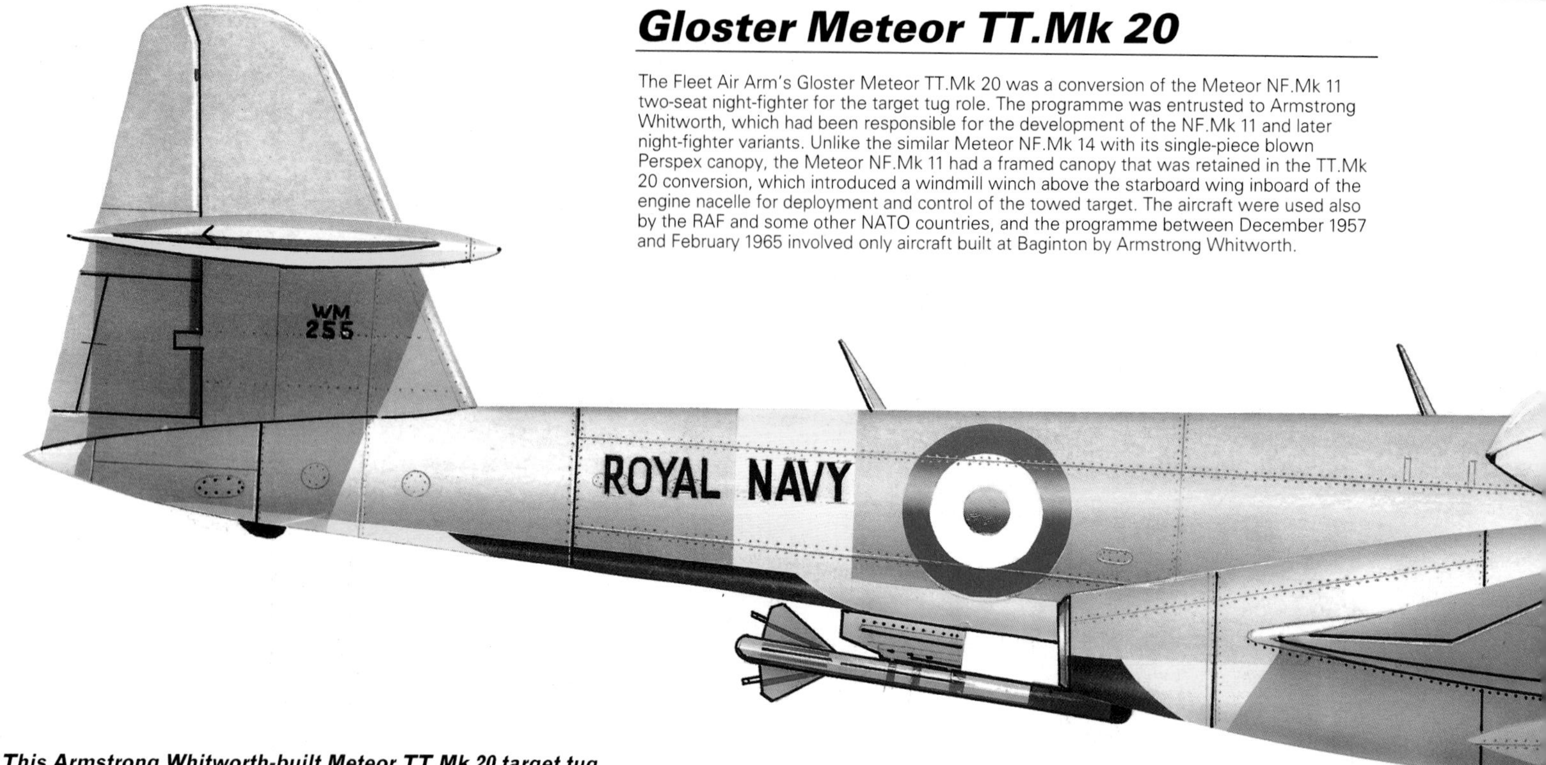

This Armstrong Whitworth-built Meteor TT.Mk 20 target tug wears the markings of the Royal Navy Fleet Requirements Unit, and carries a Rushton winch above the starboard wing root. Some later TT.Mk 20s wore fluorescent lime green and black stripes. The final Meteor TT.Mk 20s were retired in the early 1970s, and were replaced by Canberra TT.Mk 18s.

Bristol Beaufighter

Though designed for the RAF and most widely used by that service, the Beaufighter was also used in limited numbers by fleet requirements units of the Fleet Air Arm, mainly in the Mediterranean theatre. The three variants generally used in this role were the Beaufighter Mks I, II and VI. The Beaufighter Mk I was the original variant with 1185-kW (1,590-hp) Hercules XI radials and, in its maritime version, a chart table and additional radio equipment. The Beaufighter Mk II had 954-kW (1,280-hp) Rolls-Royce Merlin XX inlines and a dihedralled tailplane. And the Beaufighter Mk VI was modelled on the Mk I but with more powerful Hercules VI or XVI radials, a single 7.7-mm (0.303-in) dorsal machine-gun for a small measure of rearward defence, and provision for two 113-kg (250-lb) bombs under the wings.

Specification: Bristol Beaufighter Mk VIC two/three-seat anti-ship and general-purpose fighter
Span: 17.63 m (57 ft 10 in)
Length: 12.60 m (41 ft 4 in)
Powerplant: 2 x Bristol Hercules VI or XVI, 1194 kW (1,600 hp) each
Armament: 4 x 20-mm cannon and 1 x 7.7-mm (0.303-in) machine-gun, plus provision for 1 x 748- or 965-kg (1,650- or 2,127-lb) torpedo carried under the fuselage and 2 x 113-kg (250-lb) bombs or 8 x 27-kg (60-lb) rockets carried under the wings
Max T/O weight: 9526 kg (21,000 lb)
Max speed: 333 mph at 15,600 ft
Operational range: 1,500 miles

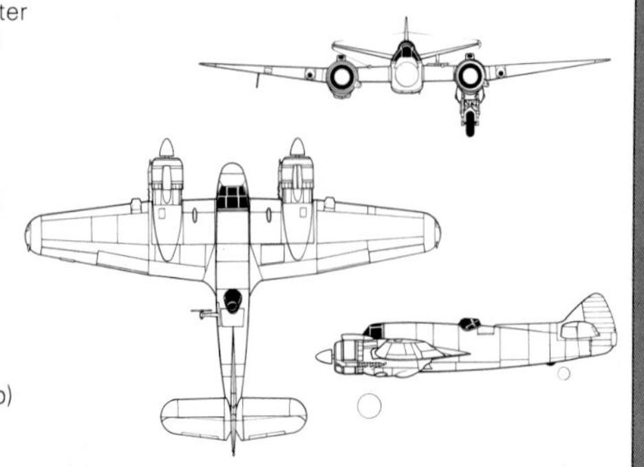

Hunting (Percival) Sea Prince

As first flown in 1948, the Prince was designed as a feederliner with a high wing to provide passengers with excellent fields of vision from the large side windows. The Prince clearly possessed potential as a communications type for the military, and this Pembroke variant flew in November 1952 with increased span, a strengthened cabin floor and beefed-up main landing gear with twin wheels on the main units. The variant was based on the Prince III and was ordered for the RAF as the Pembroke C.Mk 1, but the Fleet Air Arm preferred the civil Prince II as the basis of its initial Sea Prince C.Mk 1, a communications variant of which four were procured; the Sea Prince C.Mk 2 was an improved variant with greater payload. The main FAA model, however, was the Sea Prince T.Mk 1 'flying classroom': this was based on the upengined Prince III, and each had provision for three trainees.

Specification: Hunting (Percival) Sea Prince T.Mk 1 two/three-crew navigation and anti-submarine training aeroplane
Span: 17.07 m (56 ft 0 in)
Length: 14.12 m (46 ft 4 in)
Powerplant: 2 x Alvis Leonides 25, 410 kW (550 hp) each
Armament: none
Max T/O weight: 5375 kg (11,850 lb)
Max speed: 223 mph at 2,000 ft
Operational range: 400 miles

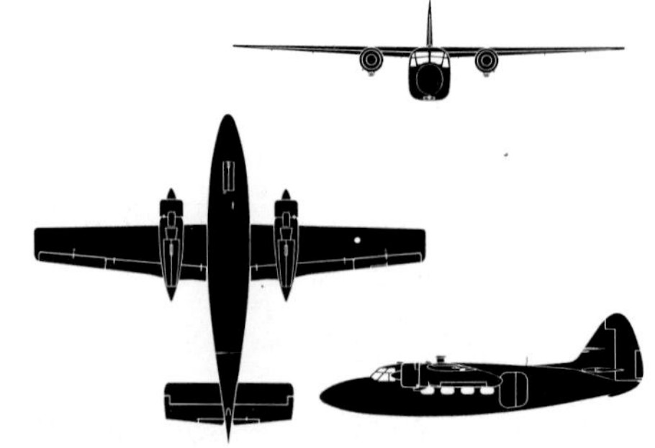

Specification: Gloster Armstrong Whitworth) Meteor TT.Mk 20 two-seat target tug aeroplane
Span: 13.11 m (43 ft 0 in)
Length: 14.78 m (48 ft 6 in)
Powerplant: 2 x Rolls-Royce Derwent 8, 1633 kg (3,600 lb) st each
Armament: none
Max T/O weight: about 9979 kg (22,000 lb)
Max speed: 575 mph at 10,000 ft
Operational range: 920 miles

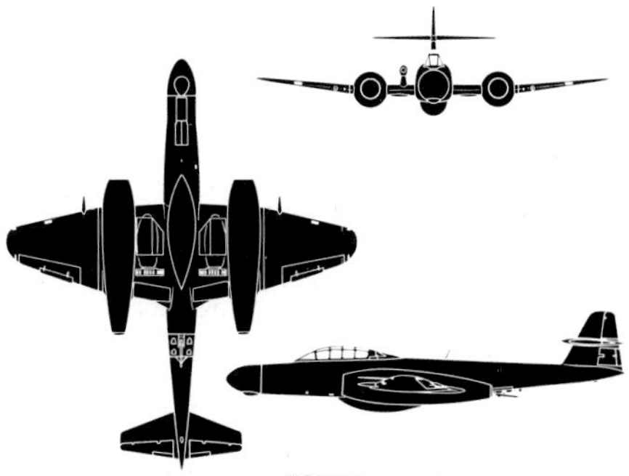

Boulton Paul Sea Balliol

Designed as a three-seat advanced trainer with an Armstrong Siddeley Mamba turboprop, the Balliol first flew in May 1947 with a 611-kW (820-hp) Bristol Mercury radial and entered RAF service as the two-seat Balliol T.Mk 2 with a 928-kW (1,245-hp) Merlin 35 inline. A navalized version was ordered for the Fleet Air Arm as the Sea Balliol T.Mk 21, and the 30 aircraft of this type had all been delivered by December 1954. The variant was designed for deck-landing capability and differed from the basic Balliol in having a smaller-diameter propeller for greater deck clearance, strengthened landing gear, naval equipment and an arrester hook. The aircraft served with No. 781 Squadron at RNAS Lee-on-Solent, and also with No. 1843 Squadron of the Royal Naval Volunteer Reserve at Abbotsinch near Glasgow.

Specification: Boulton Paul Sea Balliol T.Mk 21 two-seat advanced training aeroplane
Span: 11.99 m (30 ft 4 in)
Length: 10.71 m (35 ft 1.5 in)
Powerplant: 1 x Rolls-Royce Merlin 35, 928 kW (1,245 hp)
Armament: generally none, but provision for 1 x 7.7-mm (0.303-in) machine-gun and 4 x 27-kg (60-lb) rockets carried under the wings
Max T/O weight: about 3815 kg (8,410 lb)
Max speed: 285 mph at 9,000 ft
Operational range: 660 miles

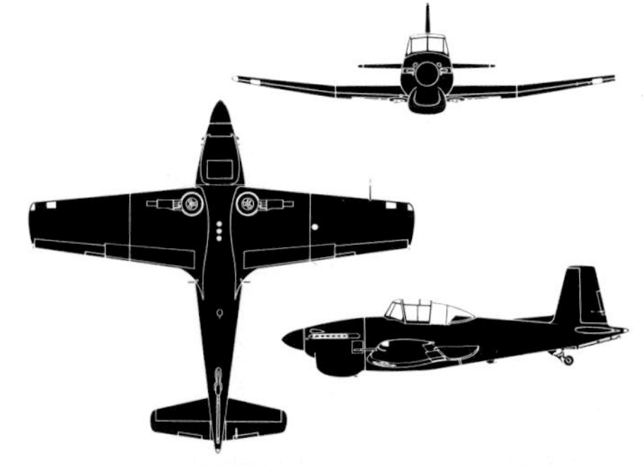

Short Sturgeon

The Sturgeon was designed as a torpedo-bomber/reconnaissance aeroplane for the large aircraft-carrier under construction late in World War II. The torpedo-bomber requirement was soon cancelled, and the Sturgeon ceased to have a front-line application when the carriers' construction was abandoned. The Sturgeon was then developed as a high-speed target tug, though the first two aircraft were Sturgeon S.Mk 1 gunnery trainers. The first of these flew in June 1946, while the third prototype led to orders for 23 Sturgeon TT.Mk 2 target tugs with contra-rotating propellers. Five of these were later modified to Sturgeon TT.Mk 3 standard with all carrier equipment removed. In an effort to produce a viable operational variant the last airframe was developed as the Short S.B.3 anti-submarine model with nose radar and Mamba turboprops, but this was inferior to the Fairey Gannet.

Specification: Short Sturgeon TT.Mk 2 two/three-seat high-speed target tug aeroplane
Span: 18.23 m (59 ft 11 in)
Length: 14.91 m (48 ft 11 in)
Powerplant: 2 x Rolls-Royce Merlin 140, 1238 kW (1,660 hp) each
Armament: none
Max T/O weight: 10136 kg (22,350 lb)
Max speed: 366 mph at medium altitude
Operational range: not revealed

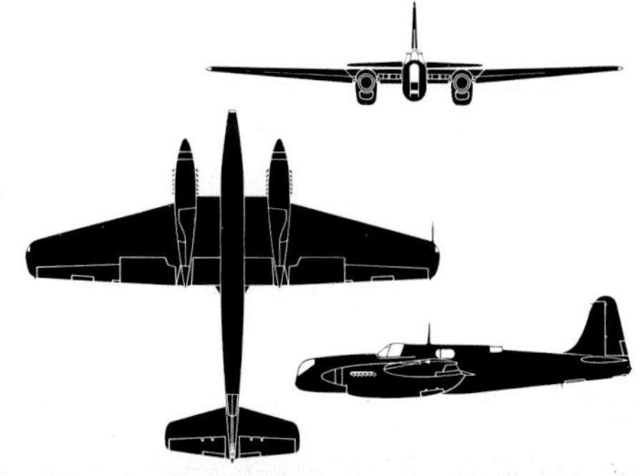

English Electric Canberra

The Canberra was one of the most important British warplanes of the 1950s and 1960s, and continues to perform in the electronic role to the present. The majority of British Canberras was used by the RAF, and it was only in small numbers and variants that this twin-jet type served with the Fleet Air Arm. In numerical order the variants were the Canberra U.Mk 10 remotely controlled target drone of which 24 were converted by Shorts from B.Mk 2 airframes, the Canberra D.Mk 14 remotely controlled target drone of which six were converted by Shorts from B.Mk 2s with the powered controls of the PR.Mk 9, the Canberra TT.Mk 18 target tug of which several were converted from B.Mk 2s with twin Rushton winches under the wings, and the Canberra T.Mk 22 specialist radar trainer of which seven were converted from PR.Mk 7s with the 'Blue Parrot' radar/radome from the Blackburn Buccaneer strike and attack aeroplane.

Specification: British Aerospace (English Electric) Canberra U.Mk 10 remotely controlled target drone aeroplane
Span: 19.48m (63ft 11in)
Length: 19.96m (65ft 6in)
Powerplant: 2 x Rolls-Royce Avon Mk 101, 2948kg (6,500lb) st each
Armament: none
Max T/O weight: 25515kg (56,250lb)
Max speed: 580mph at 40,000ft
Operational range: not revealed

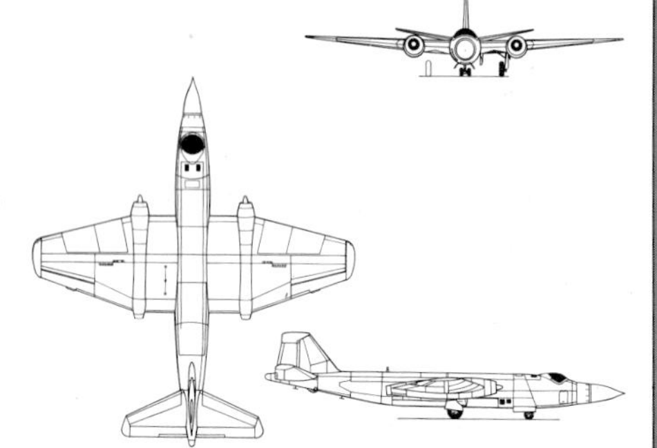

de Havilland Sea Heron

The Heron first flew in May 1950 as an enlarged version of the Dove with a four- rather than twin-engined powerplant and a larger airframe for the carriage of up to 17 passengers. The Heron Series 1 had fixed tricycle landing gear, but all Heron Series 2 aircraft have retractable gear and it is this variant that entered military service. The Queen's Flight of the RAF operated four of the type in the form of one Heron CC.Mk 3 and three Heron CC.Mk 4s. The Fleet Air Arm currently operates four Sea Heron C.Mk 1s and one Heron CC.Mk 4. The first are from an initial batch of five ex-civil Heron Series 2 aircraft (three Series 2s and two Series 2Bs) initially designated Sea Heron C.Mk 20 for the use of No. 781 Squadron at RNAS Lee-on-Solent. The single CC.Mk 4 is an ex-Queen's Flight machine.

Specification: de Havilland Sea Heron C.Mk 20 two-crew communications aeroplane
Span: 21.79m (71ft 6in)
Length: 14.78m (48ft 6in)
Powerplant: 4 x de Havilland Gipsy Queen 30 Mk 2, 186kW (250hp) each
Payload: up to 14 passengers
Max T/O weight: 6123kg (13,500lb)
Max speed: 183mph at 8,000ft
Operational range: 1,555 miles

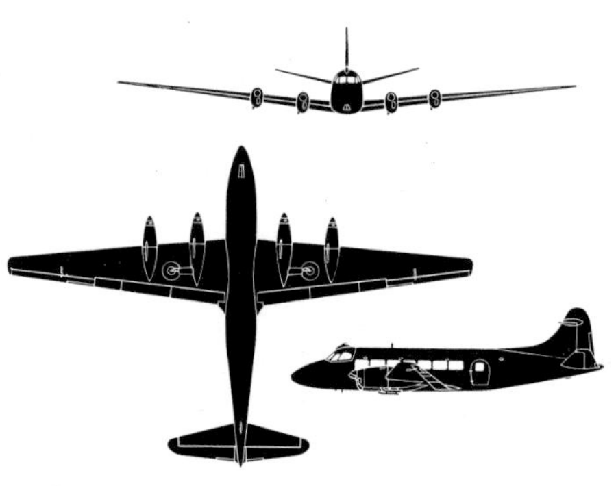

Hawker Hunter GA.Mk 11

The final British variant of the classic Hunter was the Fleet Air Arm's Hunter GA.Mk 11, which was developed as a ground-attack trainer. This was essentially a version of the RAF's Hunter FGA.Mk 9 with the Avon Mk 113 turbojet, an arrester hook and TACAN navigation equipment, but lacked the FGA.Mk 9's four fuselage-mounted 20-mm Aden cannon. Whereas the FGA.Mk 9 had been based on the Hunter F.Mk 6, the GA.Mk 11 was a conversion of the Hunter F.Mk 4, itself a development of the F.Mk 1 with greater power and underwing hardpoints for disposable stores and/or two drop tanks. Some 12 still remain in service, and a similar version was the Hunter PR.Mk 11, a reconnaissance trainer equivalent to the RAF's Hunter FR.Mk 10 with the Avon Mk 122 turbojet. Hunter GA.Mk 11 and PR.Mk 11 conversions totalled 40.

Specification: Hawker Hunter GA.Mk 11 single-seat ground-attack training aeroplane
Span: 10.26m (33ft 8in)
Length: 13.97m (45ft 10in)
Powerplant: 1 x Rolls-Royce Avon RA.21 Mk 113, 3651kg (8,050lb) st
Armament: a variety of bombs or rockets carried on 4 x underwing hardpoints
Max T/O weight: 9616kg (21,200lb)
Max speed: 702mph at sea level
Operational range: about 1,600 miles

British Aerospace Jetstream

Designed as an executive transport, the Jetstream proved the financial undoing of Handley Page though not before the RAF had ordered 26 Jetstream T.Mk 1 trainers with 720-kW (965-shp) Turbomeca Astazou XVI turboprops. These were completed by Scottish Aviation, but were then placed in store. Sixteen of them later became Jetstream T.Mk 2 observer trainers for the Fleet Air Arm with MEL E.190 nose radar operated in the weather and mapping modes. A further four aircraft were then procured as Jetstream T.Mk 3s: these are based on the thoroughly updated Jetstream 31 civil version with more power for much increased payload. The Jetstream T.Mk 3s have Racal ASR.360 multi-mode radar with its antenna in a ventral blister, as well as Doppler and TANS navigation equipment. All 20 aircraft are operated by No. 750 Squadron at RNAS Culdrose.

Specification: British Aerospace Jetstream T.Mk 3 two-crew radar observer training aeroplane
Span: 15.85m (52ft 0in)
Length: 14.37m (47ft 1.7in)
Powerplant: 2 x Garrett TPE331-10UF, 701kW (940 shp) each
Payload: radar trainees
Max T/O weight: 6900kg (15,212lb)
Max speed: 303mph at 15,000ft
Operational range: about 1,225 miles

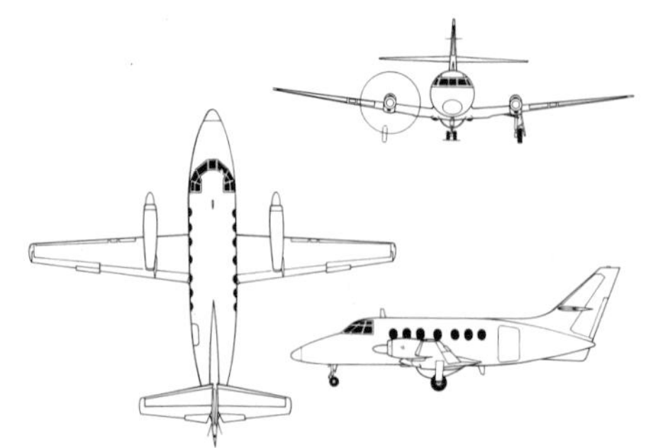

Vestland Sea King

om the S-61 Westland developed the structurally similar Sea King with a fully integrated ission package for the anti-submarine role. The first prototype flew in September 1967, d the first of 56 Sea King HAS.Mk 1s appeared in May 1967, doubling as 28-troop ansports. Later variants were the uprated Sea King HAS.Mk 2, the Sea King HAS.Mk 5 th 1238-kW (1,660-shp) Gnome H.1400-1s, Sea Searcher radar, sonobuoys, LAPADS oustic data-processing and a longer cabin, and the Sea King HAS.Mk 6 with uprated nome H.1400-1T engines driving advanced composite-structure main and tail rotors via a ronger transmission, improved radar and acoustic systems, and provision for attacks on ips with the Sea Eagle missile. All HAS.Mk 2s have been upgraded to HAS.Mk 5 standard d all older helicopters still in service are to have composite-structure rotor blades.

pecification: Westland Sea ng HAS.Mk 1 four-crew anti-submarine, AR and transport helicopter
ain rotor diameter: 18.90 m 2 ft 0 in)
ength overall, rotors turning: 2.15 m (72 ft 8 in)
owerplant: 2×1119-kW (1,500- p) Rolls-Royce (Bristol Siddeley) nome H.1400, flat-rated at 932 kW 250 shp) each
rmament: up to 4×torpedoes or depth charges
ax T/O weight: 9707 kg (21,400 lb)
ax speed: 130 mph at sea level
perational range: 691 miles

Westland Lynx

The Lynx was the only British helicopter included in the Franco-British helicopter agreement of April 1968, and is a high-performance type offering great agility in its basic military and naval variants. The prototype flew in March 1971, and models for the Royal Navy with fixed tricycle landing gear started with the Lynx HAS.Mk 2 that first flew in prototype form during May 1972. Production helicopters with radar, MAD and weapons for the anti-submarine and anti-ship roles followed from February 1976. Later models are the Lynx HAS.Mk 3 with 835-kW (1,120-shp) Gem 41-1 turboshafts, and the latest Lynx HAS.Mk 8 with Gem 42-1 engines, the new Racal Control Tactical system, and radar (either Sea Spray Mk 3 or Super Searcher) relocated to a chin position to allow the installation of the Passive Identification Device (an advanced infra-red imager).

Specification: Westland Lynx HAS.Mk 2 four-crew shipborne anti-submarine helicopter
Main rotor diameter: 12.802 m (42 ft 0 in)
Length overall, rotors turning: 15.163 m (49 ft 9 in)
Powerplant: 2×671-kW (900-shp) Rolls-Royce Gem 2, flat-rated at 559 kW (750 shp)
Armament: 2×torpedoes or 2×depth charges, or 4×Sea Skua anti-ship missiles
Max T/O weight: 4763 kg (10,500 lb)
Max speed: 144 mph at sea level
Operational range: 368 miles

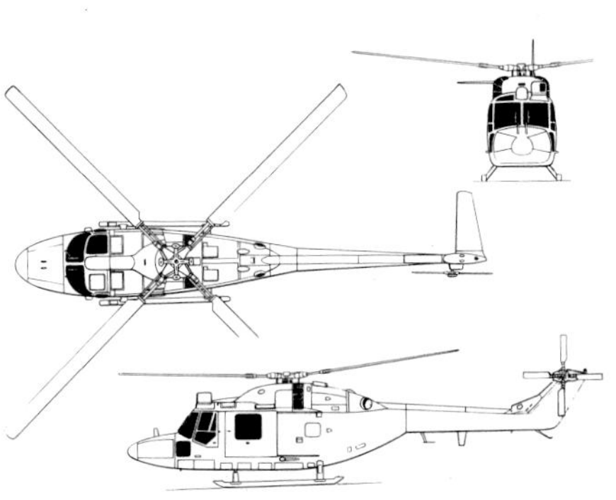

Vestland Sea King HC.Mk 4

om the Sea King Westland developed the Commando tactical transport version retaining e boat hull of the Sea King but using a non-folding main rotor and fixed tailwheel landing ear without sponsons in place of the retractable landing gear with main units folding into de sponsons. The type first flew in September 1973, and was soon qualified with a wide ssortment of armament in the defence-suppression role. Commando Mks 1 and 2 elicopters were sold to various Middle Eastern countries, and the Royal Navy took a ersion of the Commando Mk 2 as the Sea King HC.Mk 4 for use in the Royal Marine ssault transport role. The type first flew in September 1979, and 33 are currently operated th a secondary SAR tasking.

pecification: Westland Sea ng HC.Mk 4 three-crew assault ansport and SAR helicopter
ain rotor diameter: 18.90 m (62 ft 0 in)
ngth overall, rotors turning: 2.15 m (72 ft 8 in)
owerplant: 2×Rolls-Royce ristol Siddeley) Gnome H.1400-1, 38 kW (1,660 shp) each
ayload: up to 27 troops, or 22 kg (6,000 lb) of freight carried ternally or 3401 kg (7,500 lb) of eight carried externally
ax T/O weight: 5700 kg (12,566 lb)
ax speed: 129 mph at sea level
perational range: 765 miles

Westland Sea King AEW.Mk 2A

In 1978 the Fleet Air Arm lost its fixed-wing AEW capability, and this proved a distinct tactical disadvantage in the 1982 Falklands War. Given the Royal Navy's limitation to VTOL aircraft, the only solution was an AEW helicopter, and in an 11-week programme the Sea King AEW.Mk 2A was developed with Thorn-EMI Searchwater radar. Two Sea King HAS.Mk 2s were modified with this radar, Jubilee Guardsman IFF and MIR-2 'Orange Crop' ESM. The type was too late for the Falklands War, but is now standard on the UK's three carriers. The radar and IFF antennae are located on an exterior platform under a pressurised fabric dome, and this platform is carried on an arm cantilevered from a hydraulically operated fitting on the port side of the fuselage: the antenna assembly is rotated back when the helicopter is transiting, but turned down when the radar is to be used. Some 10 such helicopters are planned.

Specification: Westland Sea King AEW.Mk 2A four-crew carrierborne airborne early warning helicopter
Main rotor diameter: 18.90 m (62 ft 0 in)
Length overall, rotors turning: 22.15 m (72 ft 8 in)
Powerplant: 2×Rolls-Royce (Bristol Siddeley) Gnome H.1400-1, 1238 kW (1,660 shp) each
Armament: none
Max T/O weight: 9525 kg (21,000 lb)
Max speed: 104 mph at medium altitude
Operational endurance: 4 hours at unspecified radius

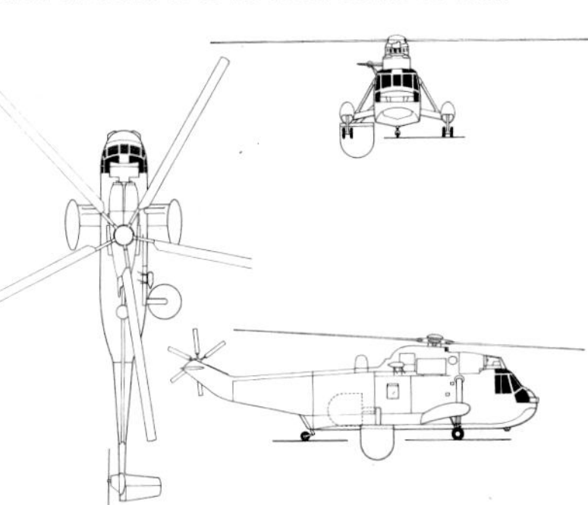

Douglas Skyraider AEW.Mk 1

Specification: Douglas Skyraider AEW.Mk 1 three-seat carrierborne airborne early warning aeroplane
Span: 15.25m (50ft 0.25in)
Length: 11.73m (38ft 6in)
Powerplant: 1×Wright R-3350-26WA Cyclone 18, 2013kW (2,700hp)
Armament: none
Max T/O weight: 10886kg (24,000lb)
Max speed: 305 mph at medium altitude
Operational range: 1,100 miles

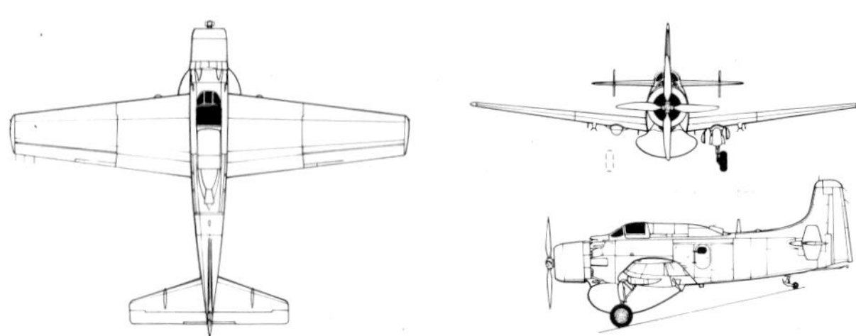

When the US Navy was planning development of its first carrierborne AEW aeroplane after World War II the Skyraider attacker offered the right payload/range combination plus a fuselage voluminous enough for the necessary additions of electronics and mission crew. The concept was pioneered in the XAD-1W: the APS-20 radar was located with its antenna in an undernose radome, and a compartment for the two operators was created by extending the fairing aft of the pilot. Production amounted to 31 AD-3Ws, 168 generally similar AD-4Ws with an autopilot, and 218 much improved AD-5Ws. From November 1951 50 examples of the AD-4W (20 new and 30 ex-navy) were transferred to the Royal Navy with the designation Skyraider AEW.Mk 1. The first unit was 778 Training Squadron, followed in July 1952 by 849 Squadron, which maintained an HQ and four sea-going operational flights up to November 1960.

Fairey Firefly

The Firefly was designed to a 1940 reconnaissance/fighter specification and was one of the more important British carrierborne aircraft late in World War II. The type had considerable development potential, and specifically post-war variants with the two-stage Griffon engine driving a four-blade propeller, radiators in the wing leading edges and two leading-edge pods (one containing fuel and the other radar) included 160 Firefly FR.Mk 4s with the 1566-kW (2,100-hp) Griffon 74, 352 Firefly Mk 5s for the specialised fighter/reconnaissance (FR), night-fighter (NF) and anti-submarine (AS) roles, 133 Firefly AS.Mk 6s with British rather than US mission equipment, and 151 Firefly AS.Mk 7 three-seaters that reverted to a chin radiator and the original wing. Many aircraft were also converted as trainers (T.Mks 5 and 7), target-tugs (TT.Mks 4, 5 and 6) and remote-control targets (U.Mks 8 and 9).

Specification: Fairey Firefly AS.Mk 5 two-seat carrierborne anti-submarine reconnaissance and attack aeroplane
Span: 12.55m (41ft 2in)
Length: 8.51m (37ft 11in)
Powerplant: 1×Rolls-Royce Griffon 74, 1678kW (2,250hp)
Armament: 4×20-mm cannon, plus provision for 16×27-kg (60-lb) rockets or 2×454-kg (1,000-lb) bombs carried under the wings
Max T/O weight: 7301kg (16,096lb)
Max speed: 386 mph at 14,000ft
Operational range: 1,300 miles

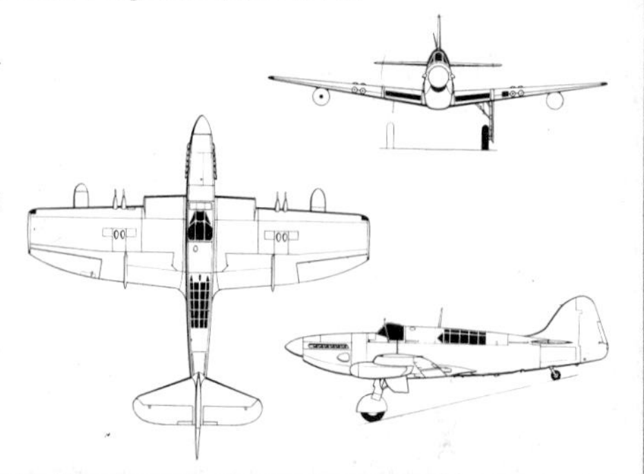

Grumman Avenger AS.Mk 4

The TBF/TBM Avenger was designed in World War II as a torpedo bomber, and up to 1946 variants in service with the Royal Navy were the Avenger Mk I (TBF-1B), Avenger Mk II (TBM-1C) and Avenger Mk III (TBM-3). In 1953, however, the service once again received some Avengers to fill the gap before the advent of its Gannet ASW aircraft. These 100 aircraft were of the TBM-3E and TBM-3S variants, and served with three regular (and between 1955 and 1957 three reserve) squadrons with the British designation Avenger AS.Mk 4. The TBM-3S was an anti-submarine attack conversion of the TBM-3E, itself an electronically upgraded and structurally strengthened version of the TBM-3, the main variant of the Avenger built by the Eastern Aircraft Division of General Motors. This lacked the heavy dorsal turret but was fitted with APS-4 search radar in a pod under the starboard wing.

Specification: Grumman Avenger AS.Mk 4 three-seat carrierborne anti-submarine aeroplane
Span: 16.51m (54ft 2in)
Length: 12.48m (40ft 11.5in)
Powerplant: 1×Wright R-2600-20 Cyclone 14, 1417kW (1,900hp)
Armament: 3×12.7-mm (0.5-in) and 1×7.62-mm (0.3-in) machine-guns, plus up to 907kg (2,000lb) of disposable stores carried internally and under the wings
Max T/O weight: 8117kg (17,895lb)
Max speed: 276 mph at 16,500ft
Operational range: 1,920 miles

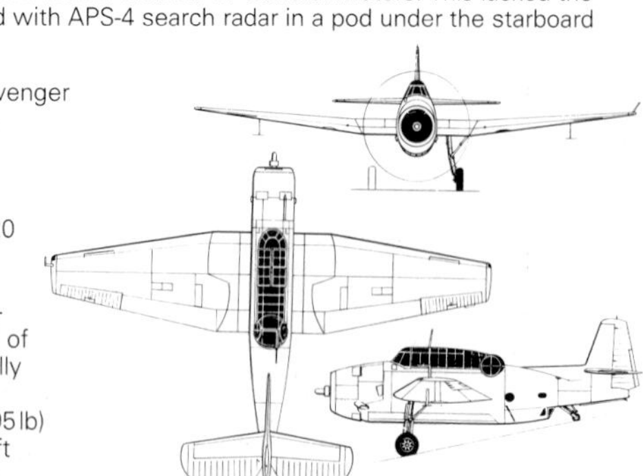

is Douglas Skyraider AEW.Mk 1 wears the markings A Flight, No. 849 Squadron, deployed on HMS Eagle ring the abortive Suez operations of 1956. No. 849 uadron formed as an Airborne Early Warning uadron in July 1952, from No. 778 Squadron, which d formed in October 1951. 50 Skyraider AEW.Mk 1s, uivalent to the US Navy AD-4W, were delivered, 20 them new aircraft, the rest refurbished ex-US Navy chines. When they finally retired in December 1960, Skyraiders of No. 849 Squadron were the FAA's t piston engined front-line aircraft.

Westland **Whirlwind** (piston-engined)

Vhirlwind was the name given to Westland's licence-built version of the Sikorsky S-55, and he first British-built machine flew in November 1952. As production was established, the Royal Navy created its first operational helicopter squadrons with 25 US-supplied machines: 10 Whirlwind HAR.Mk 21s with the 447-kW (600-hp) Pratt & Whitney R-1340-40 radial and 15 Vhirlwind HAS.Mk 22s with the 522-kW (700-hp) Wright R-1300-3 radial. Initial British-built naval helicopters were 10 Whirlwind HAR.Mk 1s with R-1340 engines and 20 Whirlwind HAR.Mk 3s with R-1300 engines. Later piston-engined models for the Royal Navy were three Whirlwind HAR.Mk 5s with the 582-kW (780-kW) Alvis Leonides Major Mk 155 or 755 radial, and 120 similarly engined Whirlwind HAS.Mk 7 anti-submarine helicopters with radar and dunking sonar, or weapons such as a torpedo or depth charges.

Specification: Westland Whirlwind HAS.Mk 7 four-seat anti-submarine helicopter
Main rotor diameter: 16.15 m (53 ft 0 in)
Length overall, rotors turning: 18.94 m (62 ft 1.5 in)
Powerplant: 1×582-kW (780-hp) Alvis Leonides Major Mk 755, derated to 559 kW (750 hp)
Armament: 1×torpedo or 2×depth charges
Max T/O weight: 3629 kg (8,000 lb)6
Max speed: 106 mph at sea level
Operational range: 335 miles

Short Seamew

This ungainly machine resulted from a 1951 requirement for a simple anti-submarine aeroplane able to operate from small carriers even in bad weather. The prototype first flew in August 1953, and was a mid-wing monoplane with fixed tailwheel landing gear, a large cockpit set well forward over the nose, and search radar with its antenna in an undernose radome, the latter two features being made possible by the small size of the single turboprop engine. The type proved to have some tricky handling problems, which development alleviated but never fully eradicated. Though 41 aircraft were ordered (including Seamew Mk 2s for the RAF), only 19 Seamew AS.Mk 1s were completed. Of these only seven had been accepted before the programme was cancelled as part of the 1957 defence cuts.

Specification: Short Seamew AS.Mk 1 two-seat carrierborne anti-submarine aeroplane
Span: 16.76 m (55 ft 0 in)
Length: 12.50 m (41 ft 0 in)
Powerplant: 1×Rolls-Royce (Armstrong Siddeley/Bristol Siddeley) Mamba ASM.6, 1186 kW (1,590 shp)
Armament: up to 836 kg (1,844 lb) of stores including 4×depth charges carried internally and 6×rockets carried under the wings
Max T/O weight: 6804 kg (15,000 lb)
Max speed: 235 mph at medium altitude
Operational range: 750 miles

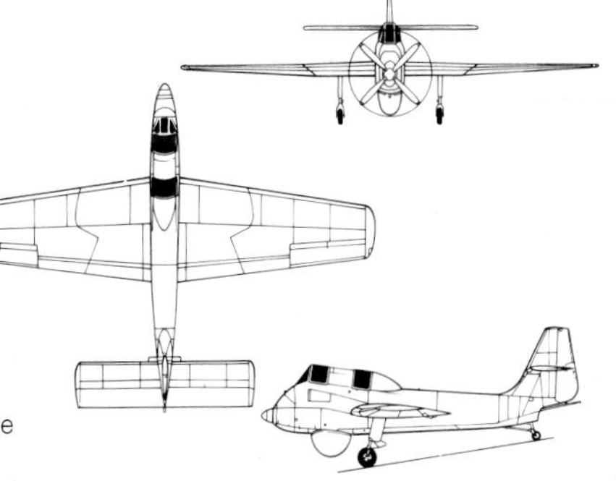

Westland ***Wessex*** *(singled-engined)*

Just as it produced the Whirlwind from the S-55, Westland developed the Wessex from the S-58 but in this instance immediately adapted the design for turbine power. A US-built helicopter was re-engined with the Gazelle NGa.11 turboshaft as a demonstrator and first flew in May 1957, being followed by the real prototype in June 1958. The first customer for the new type was the Royal Navy, which saw the Wessex as a helicopter able to combine the hunter and killer components of the anti-submarine role in a single airframe. The first of 130 Wessex HAS.Mk 1s entered service in July 1961 with the Gazelle Mk 161, and in its alternative role as a transport could carry 16 troops or 1814 kg (4,000 lb) of freight. Some 57 of these were later converted as Wessex HAS.Mk 3s with the 1193-kW (1,600-shp) Gazelle Mk 165, radar and automatic search and attack capability.

Specification: Westland Wessex HAS.Mk 1 one/three-crew anti-submarine helicopter
Main rotor diameter: 17.07 m (56 ft 0 in)
Length overall, rotors turning: 20.04 m (65 ft 9 in)
Powerplant: 1×Napier Gazelle NGa.13 Mk 161, 1081 kW (1,450 shp)
Armament: 2×torpedoes, or 4×AS.11 air-to-surface missiles
Max T/O weight: 5715 kg (12,600 lb)
Max speed: 132 mph at sea level
Operational range: 390 miles

Fairey Gannet

The Gannet resulted from a 1945 requirement, and emerged as a large machine whose most distinctive features were the massive internal weapon bay and the powerplant. The latter comprised two Mamba turboprops located side-by-side and arranged so that each of the engines drove one of the contra-rotating propellers, improving reliability and allowing long-range cruise on a single engine. The first Gannet flew in September 1949, but there then followed delay as the Royal Navy dithered about accommodation and the location of the search radar. The type entered service in 1955, and variants were the AS.Mk 1 with the 2200-kW (2,950-ehp) Double Mamba 100 (181 built), T.Mk 2 dual-control trainer (38 built), AEW.Mk 3 early warner (44 built), AS.Mk 4 improved anti-submarine model (75 built), T.Mk 5 improved trainer (eight built) and AS.Mks 6 and 7 conversions of the AS.Mk 4 with upgraded electronic equipment.

Specification: Fairey Gannet AS.Mk 4 three-seat carrierborne anti-submarine aeroplane
Span: 16.56 m (54 ft 4 in)
Length: 13.11 m (43 ft 0 in)
Powerplant: 1×Rolls-Royce (Armstrong Siddeley/Bristol Siddeley) Double Mamba Mk 101, 2263 kW (3,035 ehp)
Armament: 2×torpedoes or up to 907 kg (2,000 lb) of bombs carried internally, plus provision for up to 16×127-mm (5-in) or 24 76-mm (3-in) rockets carried under the wings
Max T/O weight: 10209 kg (22,506 lb)
Max speed: 300 mph at medium altitude
Operational range: not revealed

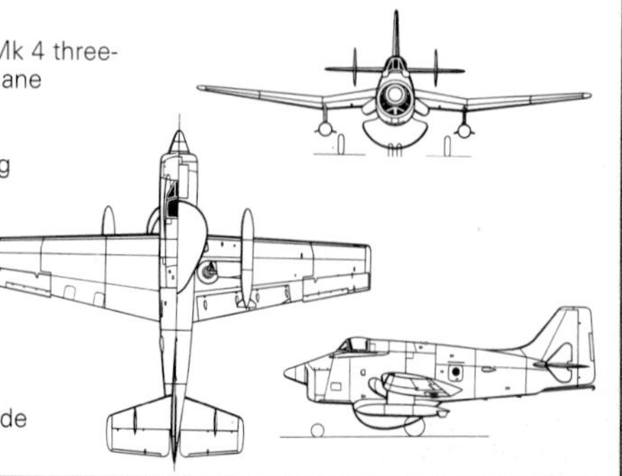

Westland Wasp

The Wasp is the navy's equivalent of the army's Scout, both types being offshoots of the Saunders-Roe P.531 that first flew in 1958. In 1959 Saro was bought by Westland, which continued development of this promising basic type. In appearance the Wasp differs from the Scout primarily in having quadricycle rather than twin-skid landing gear, and also possesses a folding main rotor amd tail section to reduce shipboard stowage problems. The Royal Navy ordered the type originally as the Sea Scout HAS.Mk 1, but the name was then changed to Wasp, and 98 production helicopters began to enter service from 1963. In addition to its general-purpose task aboard destroyers and. frigates, the type was also operated in the armed role against submarines and light surface vessels with torpedo or missile armament. Some eight are still used in the communications task. A few were also built for export.

Specification: Westland Wasp HAS.Mk 1 one/two-crew general-purpose light helicopter
Main rotor diameter: 9.83 m (32 ft 3 in)
Length overall, rotors turning: 12.29 m (40 ft 4 in)
Powerplant: 1×783-kW (1,050-shp) Rolls-Royce (Bristol Siddeley/Blackburn-Turboméca) Nimbus Mk 103 or Mk 104, flat-rated at 529 kW (710 shp)
Payload: up to four passengers or freight
Max T/O weight: 2404 kg (5,300 lb)
Max speed: 120 mph at sea level
Operational range: 303 miles

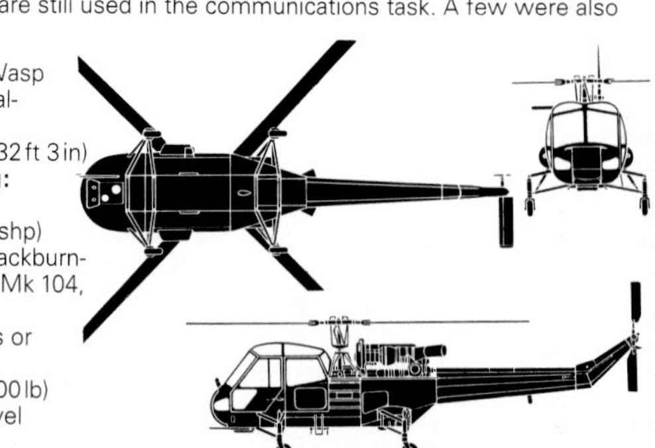

'Humphrey' was the Westland Wessex HAS.Mk 3 embarked on HMS Antrim during the Falklands war. This aircraft rescued SAS recce teams from South Georgia, attacked the submarine Santa Fe with depth charges, and landed the Royal Marines who recaptured South Georgia.

Westland **Wessex** (twin-engined)

The RAF fully appreciated the capabilities of the Gazelle-powered Wessex, but wanted the eliability advantages of a twin-engined powerplant. Westland therefore developed a variant with coupled Gnome turboshafts, allowing either engine to keep the helicopter airborne in he event of the other failing. This variant first flew in January 1962, and deliveries of the Wessex HC.Mk 2 began in February 1964. A basically similar model was then adopted for the Royal Marines as the Wessex HU.Mk 5 ship/shore-based commando assault transport helicopter. About 100 such machines were delivered, and these could be fitted with machine-gun, rocket or missile armament when used in the alternative support role. The standard accommodation was three fixed and 13 removable seats, the latter being replacable by seven litters for the casevac role.

Specification: Westland Wessex HU.Mk 5 one/three-crew assault transport helicopter
Main rotor diameter: 17.07 m (56 ft 0 in)
Length overall, rotors turning: 20.04 m (65 ft 9 in)
Powerplant: 2×1007-kW (1,350-shp) Rolls-Royce (Bristol Siddeley) Gnome Mk 110/111, combined rating 1156 kW (1,550 shp)
Payload: 16 troops or 1814 kg (4,000 lb) of freight
Max T/O weight: 6169 kg (13,600 lb)
Max speed: 133 mph at sea level
Operational range: 334 miles

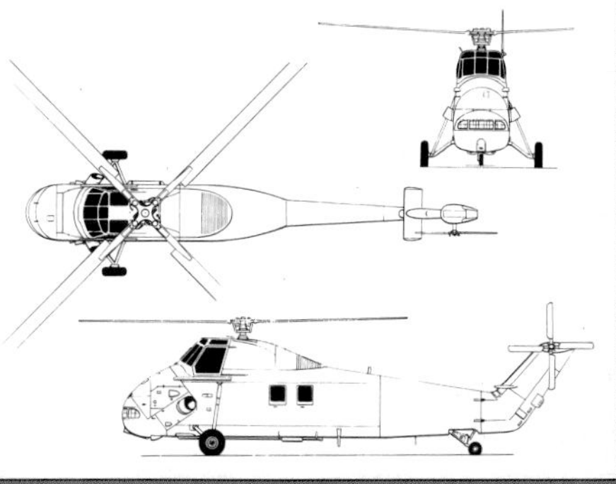

Westland **Whirlwind** (turbine-engined)

The Whirlwind was patently limited by the comparatively low power, high weight and considerable nose-mounted bulk of its radial engine, either of two US types in the Series 1 machines or the Alvis Leonides Major in Series 2 helicopters. For the civil market Westland developed the Series 3 version with turboshaft power in the form of the General Electric T58, built under licence in the UK as the Bristol Siddeley Gnome H.1000. Prototypes with the US and British engines flew respectively in February and September 1959: to ease installation without extensive redesign Westland retained the engine position, gearbox and transmission of the original piston-engined variants. The only turbine-engined version for the Royal Navy was the Whirlwind HAR.Mk 9, which began to enter service in 1966 for the SAR and ice patrol roles: these were not new-build helicopters but conversions of HAS.Mk 7s.

Specification: Westland Whirlwind HAS.Mk 9 three/four-crew SAR and ice patrol helicopter
Main rotor diameter: 16.15 m (53 ft 0 in)
Length overall, rotors turning: 18.94 m (62 ft 1.5 in)
Powerplant: 1×Rolls-Royce (Bristol Siddeley) Gnome H.1000, 783 kW (1,050 shp)
Payload: up to seven passengers or freight
Max T/O weight: 3629 kg (8,000 lb)
Max speed: 106 mph at sea level
Operational range: 300 miles

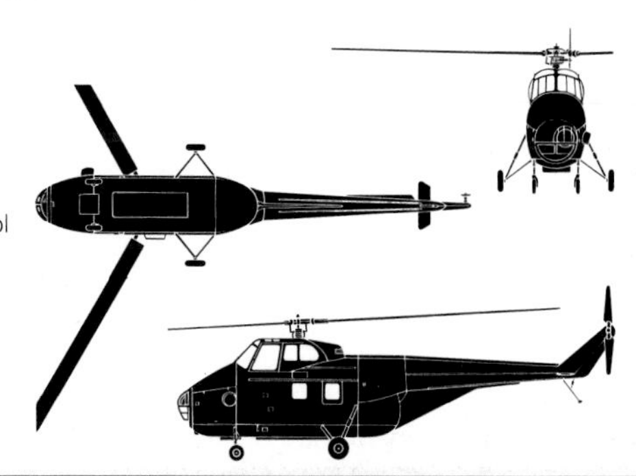

Westland Wyvern

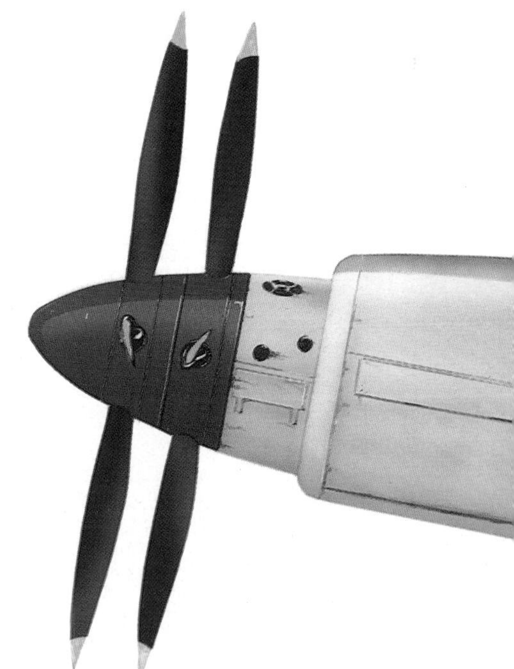

Specification: Westland Wyvern S.Mk 4 single-seat carrierborne attack aeroplane
Span: 13.41 m (44 ft 0 in)
Length: 12.88 m (42 ft 3 in)
Powerplant: 1×Armstrong Siddeley Python ASP.3, 3065 kW (4,110 shp)
Armament: 4×20-mm cannon, plus provision for 1×508-mm (20-in) torpedo, or bombs, or mines or, depth charges carried under the fuselage, and 16×267-kg (60-lb) rockets carried under the wings
Max T/O weight: 11113 kg (24,500 lb)
Max speed: 440 mph at optimum altitude
Operational range: 900 miles

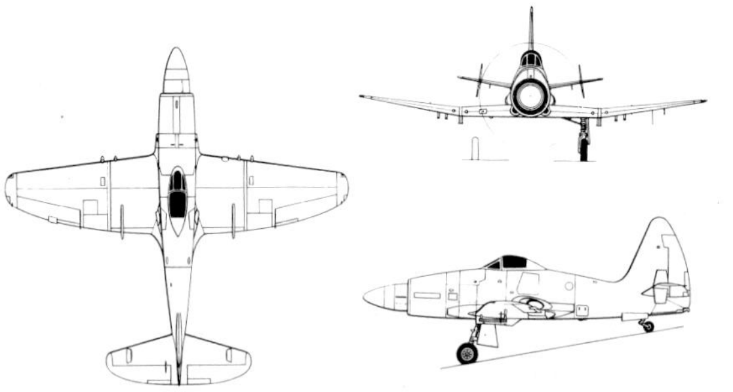

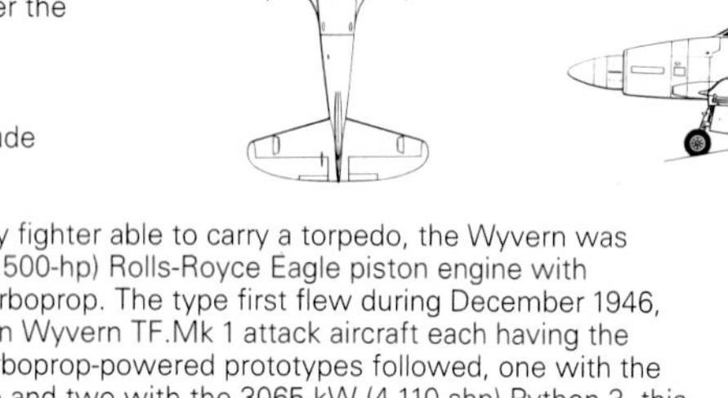

Planned to a 1944 requirement for a day fighter able to carry a torpedo, the Wyvern was initially schemed round the 2610-kW (3,500-hp) Rolls-Royce Eagle piston engine with provision for subsequent switch to a turboprop. The type first flew during December 1946, the six prototypes and 10 pre-production Wyvern TF.Mk 1 attack aircraft each having the 2006-kW (2,690-hp) Eagle 22. Three turboprop-powered prototypes followed, one with the 3005-kW (4,030-shp) Rolls-Royce Clyde and two with the 3065-kW (4,110-shp) Python 3, this latter being chosen for the pre-production batch of 13 Wyvern TF.Mk 2s, one Wyvern T.Mk 3 two-seat trainer and seven Wyvern TF.Mk 4s with cut-back cowling and auxiliary fins. There followed 87 full-production TF.Mk 4s whose designation was then changed to Wyvern S.Mk 4 as the type entered service in May 1953.

Fairey Firefly F and FR series

The Firefly was designed to meet a 1940 requirement for a two-seat cannon-armed carrierborne reconnaissance fighter, and the first prototype was flown in December 1941 with a 1290-kW (1,730-hp) Griffon IIB inline engine. The Firefly Mk I production version had the 1484-kW (1,990-hp) Griffon XII, and was produced as the F.Mk I fighter (459 built) and FR.Mk I reconnaissance fighter with ASH search radar (236 built). F.Mk Is modified to FR.Mk I standard became F.Mk IAs, and FR.Mk Is modified as night-fighter with AI.Mk X radar pod-mounted under the radiator became NF.Mk Is. Introduction of the two-stage Griffon 74 engine with wing root radiators in a reduced-span wing resulted in the Firefly FR.Mk 4, of which 160 were built. The 352 Firefly Mk 5s were similar apart from their folding wings, and included FR.Mk 5 and NF.Mk 5 variants.

Specification: Fairey Firefly FR.Mk 4 two-seat carrierborne reconnaissance fighter
Span: 12.55 m (41 ft 2 in)
Length: 11.56 m (37 ft 11 in)
Powerplant: 1×Rolls-Royce Griffon 74, 1674 kW (2,245 hp)
Armament: 4×20-mm cannon, plus provision for 2×454-kg (1,000-lb) bombs or 16×27-kg (60-lb) rockets carried under the wings
Max T/O weight: 7301 kg (16,096 lb)
Max speed: 386 mph at optimum altitude
Operational range: 760 miles

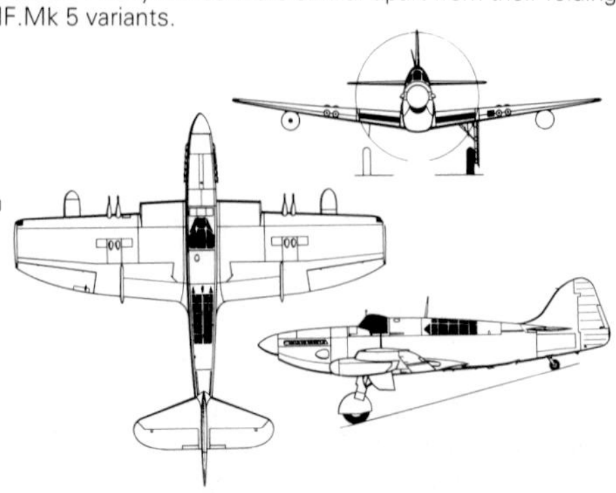

Blackburn Firebrand

The massive Firebrand was planned in response to a 1939 carrierborne fighter requirement and first flew in February 1942. The three prototypes and nine Firebrand F.Mk I production aircraft were powered by the 1719-kW (2,305-hp) Napier Sabre III inline. The type's load-carrying capability suggested an alternative role, and with their wing centre sections widened in span by 0.46 m (18 in) the 12 Firebrand TF.Mk IIs could carry a 839-kg (1,850-lb) between the wheel bays. The Sabre was needed more urgently for the Hawker Typhoon, and the design was then revised for the 1790-kW (2,400-hp) Centaurus VII radial, resulting in 27 Firebrand TF.Mk IIIs. These suffered from directional instability, and the 102 Firebrand TF.Mk 4s had a larger vertical tail. The final variants were 68 Firebrand TF.Mk 5s and TF.Mk 5As, the latter having a horn-balanced rudder and ailerons.

Specification: Blackburn Firebrand TF.Mk 5 single-seat carrierborne torpedo fighter
Span: 15.63 m (51 ft 3.5 in)
Length: 11.81 m (38 ft 9 in)
Powerplant: 1×Bristol Centaurus IX, 1879 kW (2,520 hp)
Armament: 4×20-mm cannon, plus provision for 1×torpedo carried under the fuselage or 16 27-kg (60-lb) rockets carried under the wings
Max T/O weight: 7938 kg (17,500 lb)
Max speed: 340 mph at 13,000 ft
Operational range: 740 miles

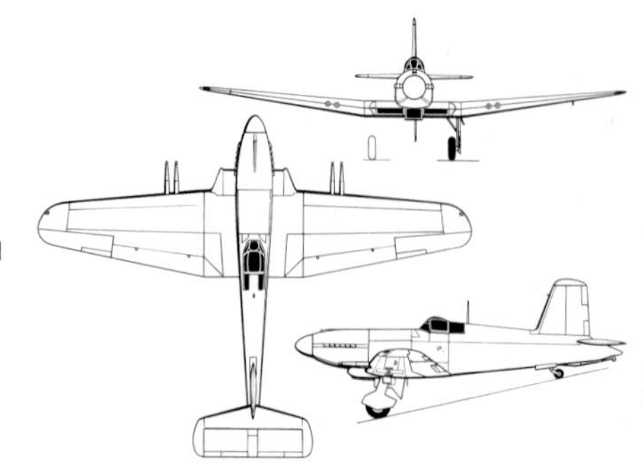

is Westland Wyvern S.Mk 4 wears the arkings of No. 830 Squadron, while the black d yellow 'invasion stripes' indicate that it was e of the aircraft deployed on HMS Eagle ring 1956 for Operation Musketeer, the Anglo ench invasion of Egypt. The Wyverns saw tensive service during the Suez operations, d at least one was lost to enemy groundfire.

Supermarine Seafire

With its Seafire version of the Spitfire the Fleet Air Arm finally secured a carrierborne fighter of performance comparable with that of contemporary land-based fighters. The Seafire's performance meant that development and production were continued until after World War II. The ultimate wartime models were the Seafire F.Mk 15 and F.Mk 17, the latter differing only in having a cut-down rear fuselage and a bubble canopy. The basic Seafire Mk III airframe was married to the broad-chord tail of the Spitfire Mk XII and fitted with a Griffon VI driving a four-blade propeller. Production was 390 and 232 respectively. Post-war developments were the Seafire F.Mk 45 (five-blade propeller or six-blade contra-prop), F.Mk 46 (bubble canopy) and F.Mk 47 (hydraulic folding wings) corresponding to the Spitfire F.Mk 21, F.Mk 22 and F.Mk 24 respectively: production was 50, 24 and 150.

Specification: Supermarine Seafire F.Mk 15 single-seat carrierborne fighter-bomber
Span: 11.23 m (36 ft 10 in)
Length: 9.21 m (30 ft 2.5 in)
Powerplant: 1×Rolls-Royce Griffon VI, 1379 kW (1,850 hp)
Armament: 2×20-mm cannon and 4×7.7-mm (0.303-in) machine-guns, plus provision for 1×227-kg (500-lb) or 2×113-kg (250-lb) bombs
Max T/O weight: 3629 kg (8,000 lb)
Max speed: 383 mph at 13,500 ft
Operational range: 640 miles

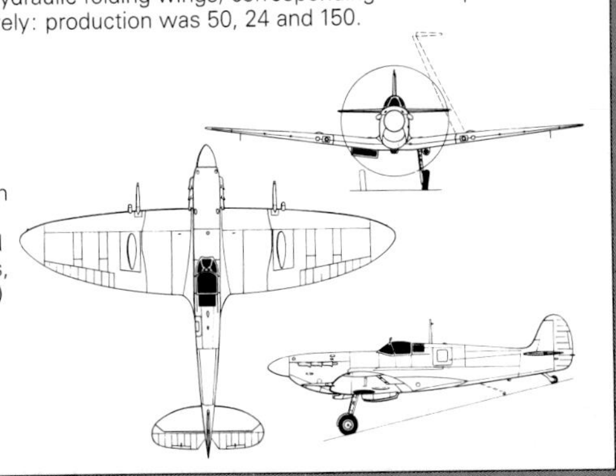

de Havilland D.H.103 Sea Hornet

The Hornet was a long-range single-seat fighter developed as a private venture by de Havilland, and in essence was a scaled-down Mosquito with more-powerful engines. The type first flew in July 1944, and 204 Hornet F.Mk 1, F.Mk 3 and FR.Mk 4 aircraft were delivered to the RAF, the first just too late to see service in World War II. The type clearly had potential as a naval fighter, and the first navalised Hornet flew in April 1945. Production variants, which began to enter service from 1946, were the Sea Hornet F.Mk 20 (77 built) with folding wings, arrester gear and naval equipment, and the two-seat Sea Hornet NF.Mk 21 night-fighter (78 built) with ASH radar in a revised nose, flame-damping exhausts, and a separate cockpit aft of the wing for the radar operator/navigator.

Specification: de Havilland Sea Hornet F.Mk 20 single-seat carrierborne fighter and fighter-bomber
Span: 13.72 m (45 ft 0 in)
Length: 11.18 m (36 ft 8 in)
Powerplant: 2×Rolls-Royce Merlin Mk 130/131, 1516 kW (2,030 hp) each
Armament: 4×20-mm cannon, plus provision for 2×454-kg (1,000-lb) bombs or 8×27-kg (60-lb) rockets carried under the wings
Max T/O weight: 8278 kg (18,250 lb)
Max speed: 467 mph at 22,000 ft
Operational range: 1,500 miles with drop tanks

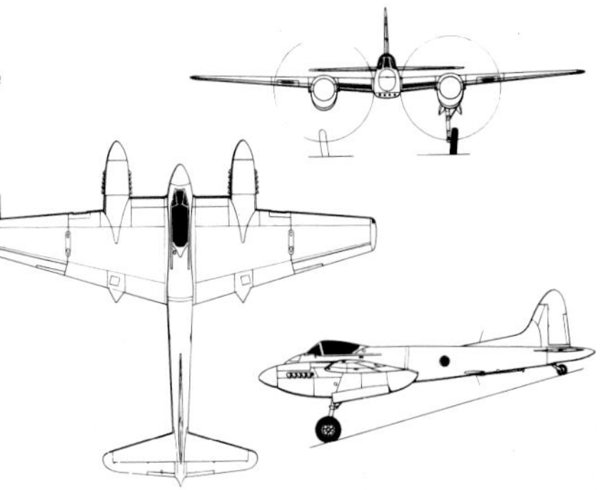

Supermarine Scimitar

Hawker Sea Fury

Arguably the finest piston-engined naval fighter ever built, the Sea Fury was a logical development of the Fury land-based fighter evolved to meet a 1942 requirement but then produced, after World War II, only for export. In the naval version the fuselage was tailored as slimly as possible round the powerful radial, and the outer wing panels of the Tempest fighter were butted together on the fuselage centreline. The first navalised prototype flew in February 1945 and the Sea Fury began to enter service in 1947. Production for the Royal Navy totalled 615: 50 Sea Fury F.Mk 10 fighters with cannon armament, 505 Sea Fury FB.Mk 11 fighter-bombers with a longer arrester hook plus provision for underwing stores and RATO gear, and 60 Sea Fury T.Mk 20 two-seat trainers. A Sea Fury is credited with the destruction of one Mikoyan-Gurevich MiG-15 jet fighter in the Korean War.

Specification: Hawker Sea Fury FB.Mk 11 single-seat carrierborne and land-based fighter and fighter-bomber
Span: 11.69 m (38 ft 4.75 in)
Length: 10.56 m (34 ft 8 in)
Powerplant: 1×Bristol Centaurus 18, 1901 kW (2,550 hp)
Armament: 4×20-mm cannon, plus provision for 2×454-kg (1,000-lb) bombs or 12×27-kg (60-lb) rockets carried under the wings
Max T/O weight: 5670 kg (12,500 lb)
Max speed: 460 mph at 18,000 ft
Operational range: 760 miles

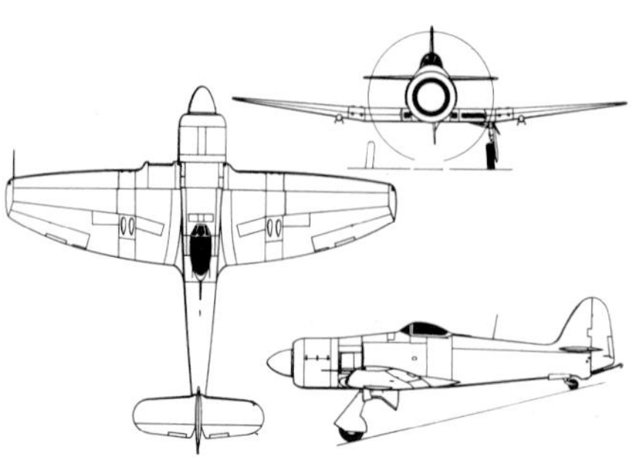

de Havilland D.H.112 Sea Venom

Despite its higher company designator, the D.H.112 was in concept a less-advanced design than the D.H.110, and resulted from a requirement for an interim Vampire replacement using the Ghost turbojet. The resultant Venom first flew in September 1949, and amongst its features were modest leading-edge sweep and wingtip tanks. Just as it had done with the Vampire, de Havilland developed a two-seater as a private venture, and this formed the basis for the Sea Venom FAW.Mk 20 (54 built including prototypes) that first flew in February 1951 and featured the Ghost Mk 103 engine, AI Mk 10 radar, naval equipment, arrester hook and folding wings. Next came 167 Sea Venom FAW.Mk 21s with American APS-57 radar, Ghost Mk 104 engine, redesigned tail, powered ailerons and modified canopy. Production ended with 39 Sea Venom FAW.Mk 22s with more power and provision for AAMs.

Specification: de Havilland Sea Venom FAW.Mk 22 two-seat carrierborne night-fighter
Span: 13.08 m (42 ft 11 in)
Length: 11.15 m (36 ft 7 in)
Powerplant: 1×de Havilland (Bristol Siddeley) Ghost Mk 105, 2404 kg (5,300 lb) st
Armament: 4×20-mm cannon, plus provision for 2×Firestreak AAMs
Max T/O weight: 7167 kg (15,800 lb)
Max speed: 575 mph at sea level
Operational range: 705 miles

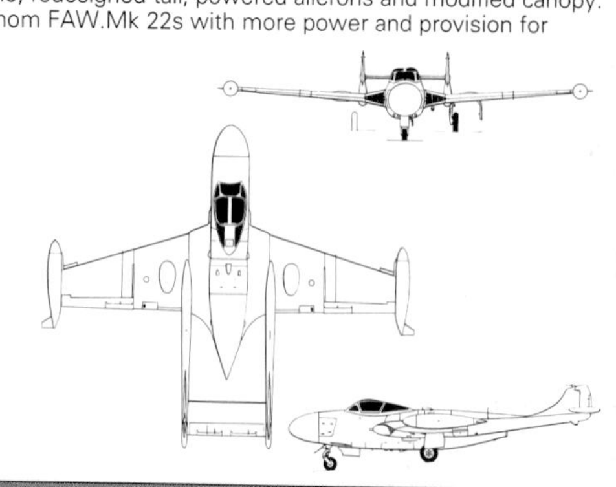

ecification: Supermarine
mitar F.Mk 1 single-seat carrierborne
erceptor and strike fighter
an: 11.33 m (37 ft 2 in)
ngth: 16.87 m (55 ft 4 in)
werplant: 2×Rolls-Royce Avon Mk 202,
)3 kg (11,250 lb st each
mament: 4×30-mm cannon, plus
vision for disosable stores such as
×unguided rockets, 4×Sidewinder
Ms, 4×Bullpup ASMs, bombs or
actical nuclear weapon on
underwing hardpoints
ax T/O weight: 18144 kg (40,000 lb
ax speed: 710 mph at optimum altitude
erational range: 600 miles

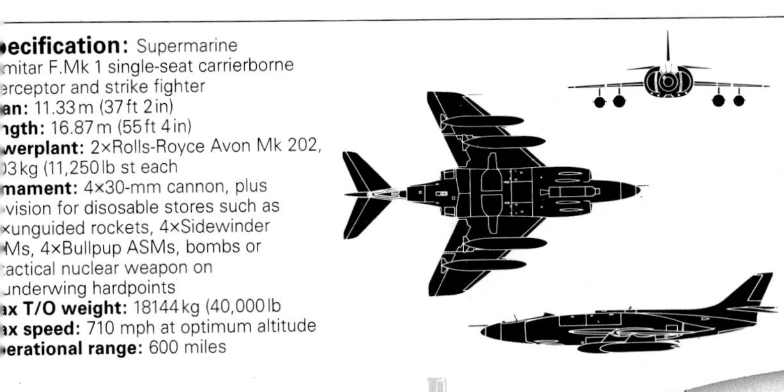

The Scimitar was the first all-swept aeroplane produced for the Fleet Air Arm, and was planned in the late 1940s as an interceptor and strike fighter of transonic performance. Particular features of the design were dogtoothed wing leading edges, blown trailing-edge flaps (each of the side-by-side turbojets providing compressor bleed air for the flap on that side of the aeroplane) and an anhedralled tailplane. The Type 508 prototype with straight wings and a butterfly tail first flew in August 1951, and was followed by the swept-wing Type 525 prototype in April 1954 and by the definitive Type 544 (dogtoothed wings, blown flaps, area-ruled fuselage and a slab tailplane) in January 1956. Service deliveries of the Scimitar F.Mk 1 began in January 1957, these 76 production aircraft having provision for a camera nose or buddy refuelling pack. The type was phased out in 1965.

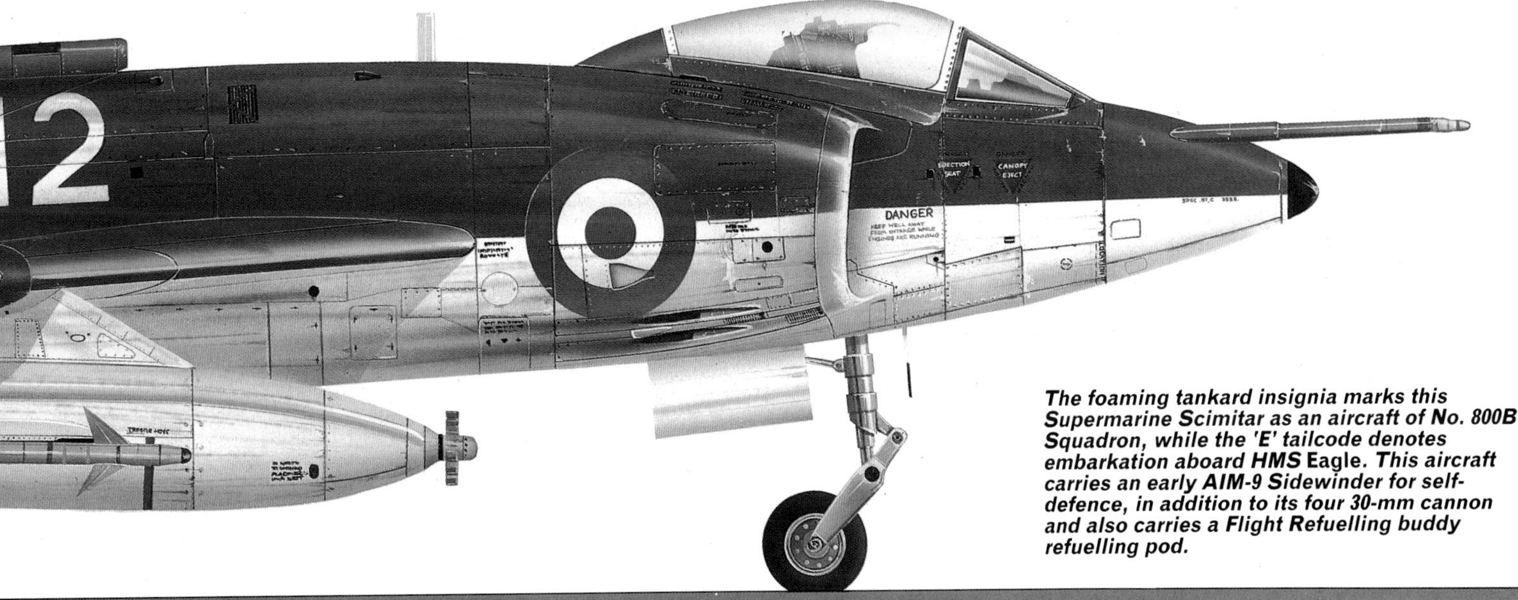

The foaming tankard insignia marks this Supermarine Scimitar as an aircraft of No. 800B Squadron, while the 'E' tailcode denotes embarkation aboard HMS Eagle. This aircraft carries an early AIM-9 Sidewinder for self-defence, in addition to its four 30-mm cannon and also carries a Flight Refuelling buddy refuelling pod.

Supermarine Attacker

The Attacker was planned to a 1944 RAF requirement and in its basic form married the laminar-flown wing of the Spiteful to a fuselage portly enough to accommodate a Nene centrifugal-flow turbojet. The type first flew in July 1946, but soon lost the interest of the RAF. Naval enthusiasm was growing, however, and in June 1947 there flew a semi-navalised version with long-stroke main units on the tailwheel type landing gear, wing spoilers and an arrester hook. Further development was slow, and it was August 1951 before deliveries of the Attacker F.Mk 1 began to 800 Squadron. Sixty-one examples of the F.Mk 1 and comparable Attacker FB.Mk 1 with provision for underwing armament were followed by 84 Attacker FB.Mk 2s with a stiffer cockpit canopy, more effective ailerons and other improvements. Some 36 land-based equivalents were built for the Pakistan air force.

Specification: Supermarine Attacker FB.Mk 2 single-seat carrierborne fighter-bomber
Span: 11.25 m (36 ft 11 in)
Length: 11.43 m (37 ft 6 in)
Powerplant: 1×Rolls-Royce Nene 3, 2313 kg (5,100 lb) st
Armament: 4×20-mm cannon, plus provision for 2×454-kg (1,000-lb) bombs or 8×27-kg (60-lb) rockets carried under the wings
Max T/O weight: 5216 kg (11,500 lb)
Max speed: 590 mph at optimum altitude
Operational range: 590 miles

Hawker/Armstrong Whitworth Sea Hawk

Developed as a naval interceptor from the experimental Hawker P.1040, the Sea Hawk was conventional in design and construction, but unusual in that its single turbojet exhausted via bifurcated nozzles in the wing trailing edges, allowing a large fuel tank to be accommodated in the rear fuselage. The P.1040 prototype flew in September 1948, the first Sea Hawk F.Mk 1 following in November 1951 for a service entry date of March 1953 with the 2268-kg (5,000-lb) thrust Nene Mk 101. F.Mk 1 production totalled 95, all aircraft from the 36th being produced by Armstrong Whitworth. There followed 40 Sea Hawk F.Mk 2s with powered ailerons but the same four-cannon armament, 116 Sea Hawk FB.Mk 3s with provision for two underwing bombs, and 90 Sea Hawk FGA.Mk 4s with four underwing hardpoints. Many Mk 3 and Mk 4 aircraft were later upgraded to Mk 5 and Mk 6 standard with more power.

Specification: Hawker (Armstrong Whitworth) Sea Hawk FGA.Mk 6 single-seat carrierborne and land-based fighter/ground-attack aeroplane
Span: 11.89 m (39 ft 0 in)
Length: 12.08 m (39 ft 8 in)
Powerplant: 1×Rolls-Royce Nene Mk 103, 2449 kg (5,400 lb) st
Armament: 4×20-mm cannon, plus provision for 4×227-kg (500-lb) bombs or rockets carried under the wings
Max T/O weight: 7348 kg (16,200 lb)
Max speed: 599 mph at sea level
Operational range: 740 miles

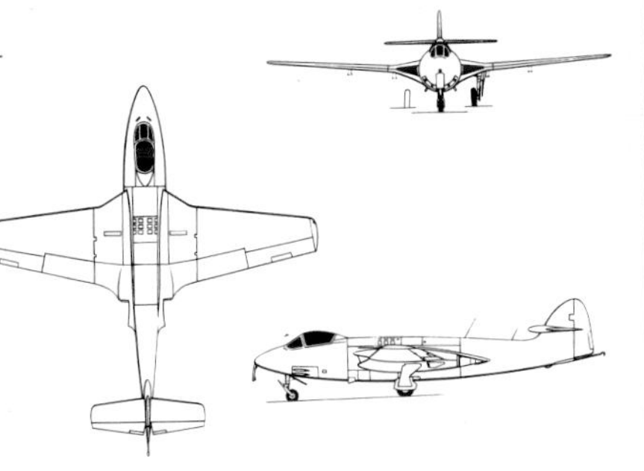

de Havilland D.H.110 Sea Vixen

The Sea Vixen resulted from Air Ministry and Admiralty requirements issued in 1946 for an advanced night-fighter, and de Havilland responded with the potentially world-beating D.H.110 that first flew in September 1951 as an extremely attractive all-metal machine of typical de Havilland twin-boom jet design with swept wings, the tailplane located between the tops of the swept vertical surfaces, powered controls, the pilot seated under a fighter-type canopy offset to the left, and the radar operator in the fuselage offset to the right. An unfortunate accident in 1952 led to official dithering, and it was no fewer than six years later before the first of 91 Sea Vixen FAW.Mk 1s began to enter naval service. The 57 Sea Vixen FAW.Mk 2s had more fuel and an all-aspect engagement capability with improved missiles and radar. Many FAW.Mk 1s were upgraded to this standard.

Specification: de Havilland Sea Vixen FAW.Mk 2 two-seat carrierborne all-weather fighter
Span: 15.24 m (50 ft 0 in)
Length: 16.94 m (55 ft 7 in)
Powerplant: 2×Rolls-Royce Avon Mk 208, 5102 kg (11,250 lb) st each
Armament: 4×Red Top AAMs and (never used) 2×flip-out boxes for 28×51-mm (2-in) unguided rockets, plus provision for 2×454-kg (1,000-lb) bombs or 2×Bullpup ASMs carried externally
Max T/O weight: 16783 kg (37,000 lb)
Max speed: 640 mph at 20,000 ft
Operational range: 800 miles

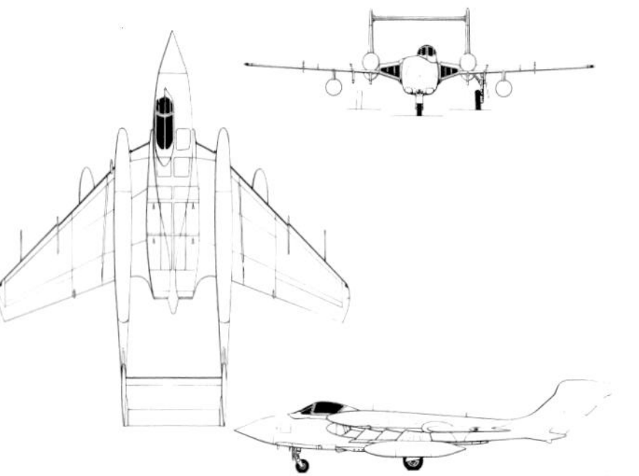

Blackburn B-103 Buccaneer

The Buccaneer was planned as a carrierborne strike aeroplane with an advanced nav/attack system and transonic performance at sea level. This ambitious machine first flew in April 1958 and began to enter service in July 1962 as the Buccaneer S.Mk 1 with Gyron Junior Mk 101 turbojets in an airframe of area-ruled design with 'super-circulation' boundary-layer control on the flying surfaces, a split tail cone serving as an airbrake and a slab tailplane mounted at the top of the vertical tail. The moderate weapons load was carried on the rotating door of the internal bomb bay. From 1965 the S.Mk 1 was superseded by the Buccaneer S.Mk 2 with slightly greater span, four underwing hardpoints for a total load of 7258 kg (16,000 lb), and 5105-kg (11,255-lb) thrust Rolls-Royce RB168 Spey turbofans for greater range and an all-round improvement in performance.

Specification: Blackburn (Hawker Siddeley) Buccaneer S.Mk 1 two-seat carrierborne and land-based strike and attack aeroplane
Span: 12.90 m (42 ft 4 in)
Length: 19.33 m (63 ft 5 in)
Powerplant: 2×Bristol Siddeley (de Havilland) Gyron Junior Mk 101, 3221 kg (7,100 lb) st each
Armament: 1814 kg (4,000 lb) of disposable stores carried internally
Max T/O weight: 20866 kg (46,000 lb)
Max speed: 645 mph at sea level
Operational range: about 1,000 miles

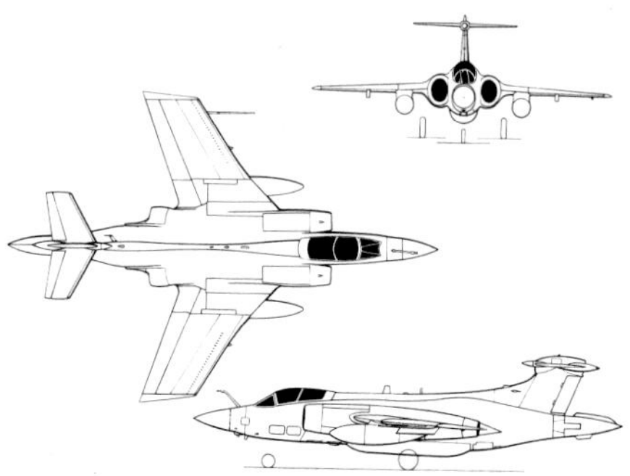

McDonnell Douglas Phantom II

First flown in May 1958 and delivered for service from February 1960, the Phantom II secured its first export order in 1964, when the Royal Navy contracted for two YF-4K prototypes and then 50 F-4K production aircraft based on the US Navy's F-4J but with Spey turbofans rather than General Electric J79 turbojets, 20 per cent larger inlets, reduced tailplane anhedral, a longer nosewheel leg, AWG-10 radar in a folding radome, Martin-Baker ejector seats and other items of British equipment. The first YF-4K flew in June 1966, and the F-4Ks were delivered from April 1968 with the British designation Phantom FG.Mk 1. Three Phantom squadrons were formed, but only one went to sea on the carrier HMS *Ark Royal* between 1970 and 1978, when the aircraft were transferred to the RAF with the phasing out of the navy's fixed-wing carrier strength.

Specification: McDonnell Douglas Phantom FG.Mk 1 two-seat carrierborne and land-based multi-role fighter
Span: 11.71 m (38 ft 5 in)
Length: 17.55 m (57 ft 7 in)
Powerplant: 2×Rolls-Royce Spey Mk 202, 9306 kg (20,515 lb) st each
Armament: 1×podded 20-mm multi-barrel cannon, plus provision for up to 7257 kg (16,000 lb) of disposable stores carried on 5×external hardpoints
Max T/O weight: 26309 kg (58,000 lb)
Max speed: 1,386 mph at 40,000 ft
Operational range: about 1,000 miles

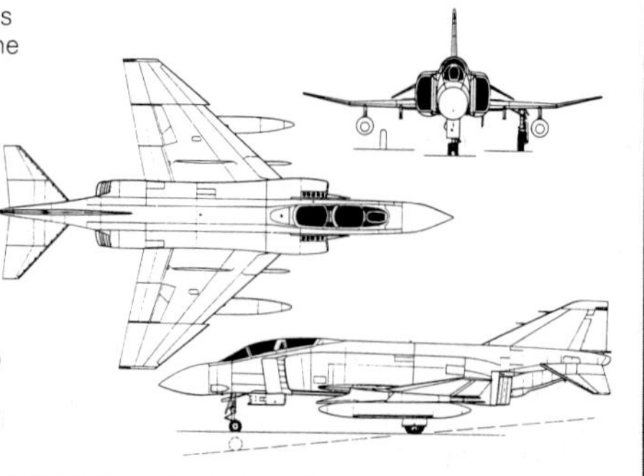

British Aerospace Sea Harrier

Development of the Sea Harrier from the Harrier close-support aeroplane began in 1975 to provide the three 'Invincible' class carriers with fixed-wing multi-role air strength in the fighter, reconnaissance and strike/attack roles. The Sea Harrier has a revised structure less susceptible to salt-water corrosion, naval equipment and a totally new forward fuselage that seats the pilot higher (under an air-combat bubble canopy in a revised cockpit with displays for the new nav/attack system) and accommodates the Blue Fox multi-role radar. The Sea Harrier FRS.Mk 1 began to enter service in 1981 and proved itself in the Falklands War of 1982.

Specification: British Aerospace Sea Harrier FRS.Mk 1 single-seat carrierborne fighter, reconnaissance and strike/attack aeroplane
Span: 7.70 m (25 ft 3 in)
Length: 14.50 m (47 ft 7 in)
Powerplant: 1×Rolls-Royce Pegasus 11 Mk 104, 9752 kg (21,500 lb) st
Armament: 2×30-mm cannon, plus provision for up to 2268+ kg (5,000+ lb) of disposable stores carried on 5×external hardpoints
Max T/O weight: 11880 kg (26,190 lb)
Max speed: 735 mph at sea level
Operational range: 920 miles

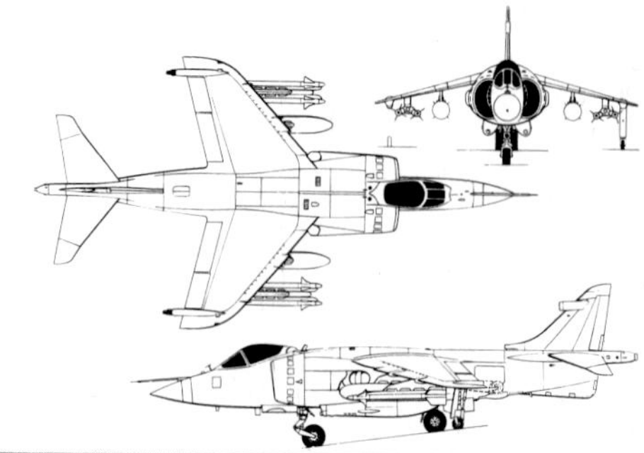

Vertol (Piasecki) HUP-2 Retriever

The twin-rotor helicopter was planned to a US requirement for a carrierborne SAR, planeguard and transport helicopter. The original model was the HUP-1 with a 391-kW (525-hp) Continental R-975 radial, endplate vertical surfaces at the tips of the tailplane located on the sides of the rear rotor pylon, and provision for five passengers or three litters in addition to the two-man crew. The HUP-2 was a generally improved model with more power, and was distinguishable from the HUP-1 by its lack of any tailplane/fin assembly. The type featured a hatch offset to starboard in the cabin floor through which a 181-kg (400-lb) rescue hoist could operate. Some 15 of the 165 HUP-2s were delivered to the Aéronavale, remaining in service into the 1960s as the service's standard planeguard and light vertical replenishment helicopter.

Specification: Vertol (Piasecki) HUP-2 two-crew SAR, planeguard and light transport helicopter
Rotor diameter, each: 10.67 m (35 ft 0 in)
Length, fuselage: 9.75 m (32 ft 0 in)
Powerplant: 1×Continental R-975-46, 410 kW (550 hp)
Payload: three passengers or freight
Max T/O weight: 2608 kg (5,750 lb)
Max speed: 108 mph at sea level
Operational range: 340 miles

Lockheed P2V (P-2) Neptune

Though design of the Neptune began before the USA's entry into World War II, this advanced project was shelved for more easily realised types until 1944, and it was May 1945 before the prototype first flew. The type then proved a real winner with enormous growth potential, and was also built extensively for other countries as well as for the US Navy. The Aéronavale was the largest export customer for the Neptune, receiving 31 P2V-6s in 1953 for Flottilles 23F, 24F and 25F, and then 34 P2V-7s for the same three flottilles as well as Escadrilles 9S and 12S. The P2V-6 (later P-2F) had 2423-kW (3,250-hp) R-3350-30WA radials and, in addition to six 20-mm cannon, equipment for the minelaying and photo-reconnaissance roles. The P2V-7 (P-2H) had underwing turbojet boosters, a MAD 'sting' in the tail and other revisions. Some Aéronavale aircraft survived into the 1980s.

Specification: Lockheed P2V-7 9/10-seat maritime patrol and anti-submarine aeroplane
Span: 31.65 m (103 ft 10 in)
Length: 27.94 m (91 ft 8 in)
Powerplant: 2×Wright R-3350-32W, 2610 kW (3,500 hp) each, and 2×Westinghouse J34-WE-36, 1542 kg (3,500 lb) st each
Armament: provision for 3629 kg (8,000 lb) of disposable stores carried internally
Max T/O weight: 36240 kg (79,895 lb)
Max speed: 403 mph at 14,000 ft
Operational range: 3,685 miles

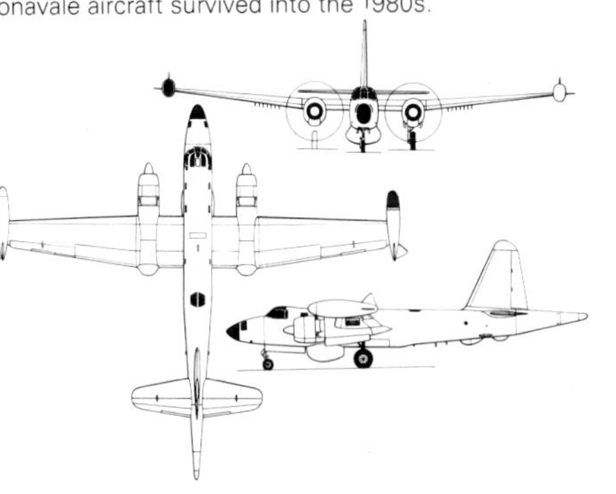

Westland Lynx

The Lynx was the sole British type involved in the 1967 Franco-British agreement on the co-production of three helicopters, and is now used by the French navy in two forms as the anti-submarine helicopter of smaller warships. In common with other naval Lynxes the French Lynx Mk 2 baseline model has tricycle landing gear, and its electronic fit includes ORB 31W search radar and a choice of Crouzet MAD (in a rigid mount on the nose) or dunking sonar (Thomson DUAV 4 or Alcatel HS 12). Some 24 Lynx Mk 2s are in service, and these are complemented by 14 Lynx Mk 4s, the French equivalent of the Royal Navy's Lynx HAS.Mk 3 with 835-kW (1,120-shp) Gem 41-1 turboshafts and other refinements including more-advanced electronics. Its greater installed power means that the Mk 4 is often used in the secondary SAR role.

Specification: Westland Lynx Mk 2(FN) four-seat utility and anti-submarine helicopter
Main rotor diameter: 12.80 m (42 ft 0 in)
Length overall, rotors turning: 15.16 m (49 ft 9 in)
Powerplant: 2×Rolls-Royce Gem 2, 671 kW (900 shp) each
Armament: a wide assortment of disposable stores carried on the fuselage sides including 2×torpedoes or depth bombs, or 4×AS.12 air-to-surface missiles
Max T/O weight: 4536 kg (10,000 lb)
Max speed: 144 mph at optimum altitude
Operational range: 368 miles

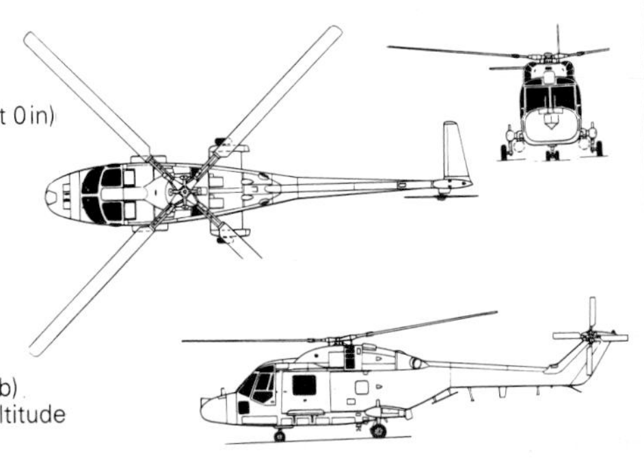

Aérospatiale SA 321 Super Frelon

The SA 3210 Super Frelon was developed from the smaller SA 3200 Frelon with the aid of Sikorsky in the design of the rotors. The first prototype was powered by three 985-kW (1,320-shp) Turmo IIIC2 turboshafts and flew on 7 December 1982 in form representative of the tactical troop transport model. The naval model is the amphibious SA 321G used by the French navy's Flottille 32F (17 airframes) as a land-based heavy anti-submarine helicopter to 'sanitise' the approaches to its main nuclear base at Brest. The helicopter is fitted with stabilising floats, and its sensor suite includes Sylphe panoramic search radar, and HS.12 or Bendix ASQ-13 dunking sonar plus Crouzet DHAX-3 MAD in the anti-submarine role, with an alternative of ORB 31 (Heracles I) or ORB 32 (Heracles II) designation radar matched to AM.39 Exocet missiles in the anti-ship role.

Specification: Aérospatiale SA 321G Super Frelon medium anti-submarine and anti-ship helicopter
Main rotor diameter: 18.90 m (62 ft 0 in)
Length overall, rotors turning: 23.03 m (75 ft 6.7 in)
Powerplant: 3×Turboméca Turmo IIIC6, 170 kW (1,570 shp) each
Armament: 2×AM.39 Exocet anti-ship missiles, or 4×Mk 46 or L4 torpedoes, or 8×250-kg (551-lb) mines, or Mk 49, Mk 52 or Mk 54 depth charges
Max T/O weight: 13000 kg (28,660 lb)
Cruising speed: 154 mph at sea level
Operational range: 506 miles

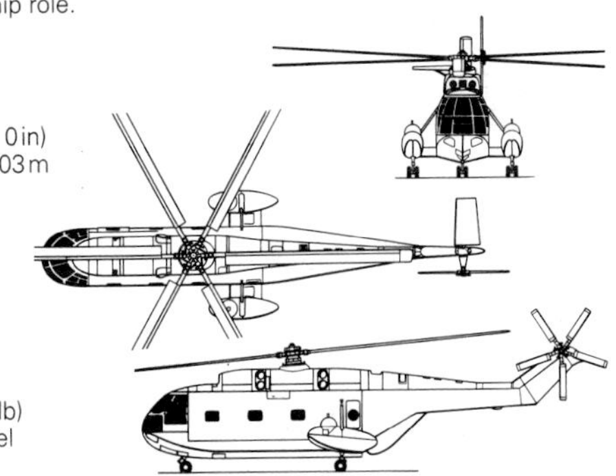

Avro Lancaster

Specification: Avro Lancaster GR.Mk 3 seven-seat general reconnaissance aeroplane
Span: 31.09 m (102 ft 0 in)
Length: 21.18 m (69 ft 6 in)
Powerplant: 4×Rolls-Royce Merlin 24, 1238 kW (1,640 hp) each
Armament: 6×7.7-mm (0.303-in) machine-guns plus provision for up to 8165 kg (18,000 lb) of disposable stores carried internally
Max T/O weight: 29484 kg (65,000 lb)
Max speed: 250 mph at sea level
Operational range: 2,530 miles

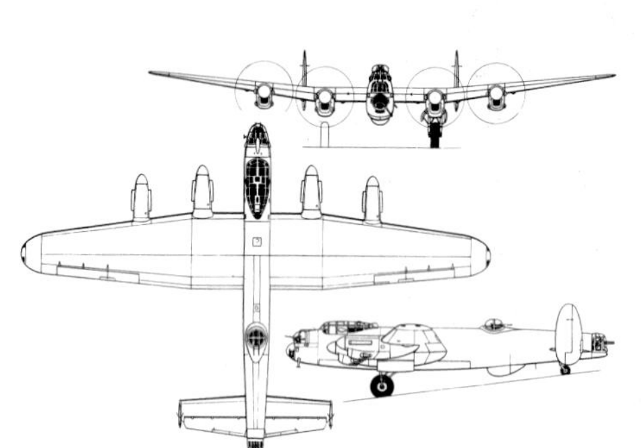

An Avro Lancaster of Flottille 25F, based at Lartique, Algeria, during 1953. The Lancaster served mainly with Aéronavale units in North Africa, the last units being Escadrille de Servitude 9 and Flottille 24F, which were based in the New Hebrides and which finally relinquished their Lancasters in 1964, by which time most wore an overall white colour scheme.

Loire 130M

The Loire 130 was designed as a light general-purpose flying boat stressed for catapult launches from major warships, and first flew in November 1934. The type was developed in two forms, namely the 130M for French metropolitan service and the strengthened 130C for colonial service. It was the end of 1938 before production boats began to reach the Aéronavale, and in addition to France's main warships, several overseas naval bases received examples of the type for coastal reconnaissance. Some 150 of the type were produced, about 30 of them under the auspices of the Vichy regime, and shore-based examples remained in limited service at French overseas bases up to 1949, when Escadrille 8S was stood down in Indo-China. In its later days the type served as a shore-based liaison and coastal escort flying boat.

Specification: Loire 130M three-crew general-purpose flying boat
Span: 16.00 m (52 ft 6 in)
Length: 11.30 m (37 ft 1 in)
Powerplant: 1×Hispano-Suiza 12Xbrs-1, 537 kW (720 hp)
Armament: 2×7.5-mm (0.295-in) machine-guns plus provision for up to 150 kg (330 lb) of disposable stores carried on the fuselage sides
Max T/O weight: 3396 kg (7,487 lb)
Max speed: 140 mph at 9,185 ft
Operational range: 684 miles

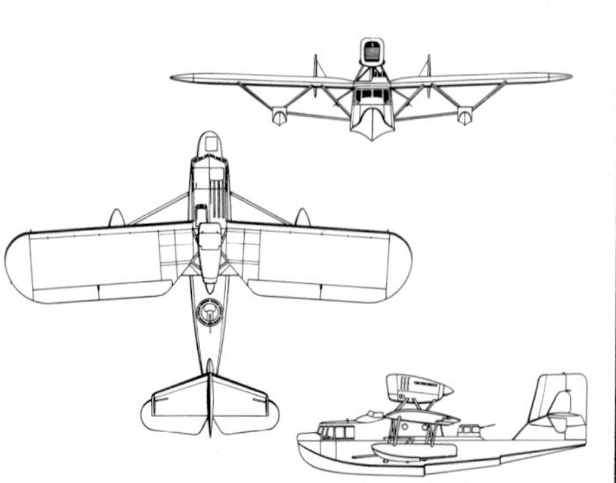

Consolidated PBY Catalina

Free French forces based in the UK and North Africa carried the torch of French military aviation through the years of World War II, and as the tide of war flowed in the Allies' favour these French air units expanded in numbers and capabilities with the receipt of new British and US aircraft. Amongst the latter were examples of the PBY-5A amphibian. This served in the war and immediate post-war years as a maritime reconnaissance type pending the delivery of more modern types. The PBY-5A was thus an important first-line asset to the Aéronavale until the late 1950s, and also played a significant SAR and communications role into the 1960s. Another task was the spotting of uncleared minefields dating from World War II, together with mines that had broken free of their moorings and so constituted a free-floating hazard.

Specification: Consolidated PBY-5A eight-seat maritime patrol and SAR amphibian
Span: 31.70 m (104 ft 0 in)
Length: 19.47 m (63 ft 10 in)
Powerplant: 2×Pratt & Whitney R-1830-92 Twin Wasp, 895 kW (1,200 hp) each
Armament: 2×12.7-mm (0.5-in) and 3×7.62-mm (0.3-in) machine-guns plus provision for up to 1814 kg (4,000 lb) of disposable stores carried under the wings
Max T/O weight: 16067 kg (35,420 lb)
Max speed: 175 mph at optimum altitude
Operational range: 2,350 miles with full warload

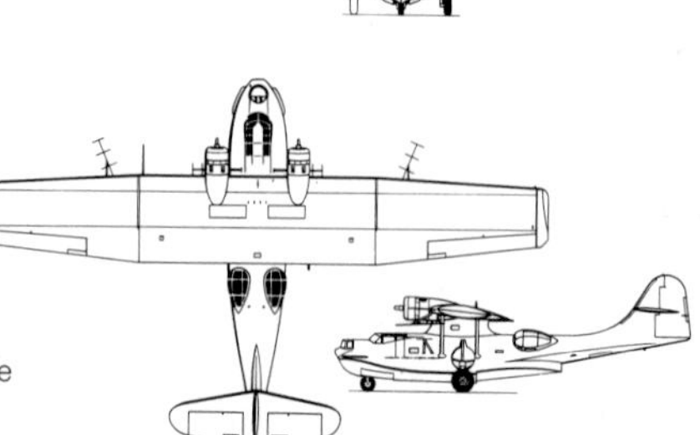

Under a Western Union agreement of 1948 the UK supplied the re-emergent Aéronavale with 54 Lancasters revised for air/sea rescue and maritime reconnaissance. The aircraft were 32 Mk I and 22 Mk VII bombers with their dorsal turrets removed, additional fuel tankage fitted in the bomb bay, provision made for the addition of search radar, and lugs attached for the carriage of an air-dropped lifeboat. Deliveries were made from January 1952, and most aircraft were deployed to naval air stations in North Africa. The aircraft were essentially similar to the Lancaster ASR.Mk 3 standard with the Lifeboat Airborne Mk IIA. The Lancasters were gradually shifted from the rescue to the reconnaissance role, and by the time that only Escadrille 9S was left as an operator unit its aircraft were similar in standard to the Lancaster GR.Mk 3 with specialist maritime reconnaissance equipment.

CAMS (Dornier) Do 24

Between 1940 and 1944 the French aircraft-manufacturing industry was used by the Germans to bolster their own production capability, and amongst the types produced in France was the Dornier Do 24 parasol-winged flying boat. Between 1942 and 1944 the Chantiers Aero-Maritimes de la Seine (CAMS) produced about 50 complete examples as well as a number of incomplete airframes of the Do 24T-1, a transport and air/sea rescue variant of the Do 24N with a German rather than American engine. Between the liberation of 1944 and 1953 the Aéronautique Navale operated those aircraft that had not been flown off by the Germans, together with another 22 completed after the German evacuation, in the air/sea rescue task and also for the spotting of wartime mines floating in French coastal waters.

Specification: CAMS (Dornier) Do 24T-1 six-seat air/sea rescue flying boat
Span: 27.00 m (88 ft 7 in)
Length: 22.00 m (72 ft 4 in)
Powerplant: 3×BMW-Bramo 323R-2 Fafnir, 746 kW (1,000 hp) each
Armament: generally none, though provision was retained for 1×20-mm cannon and 2×7.92-mm (0.312-in) machine-guns
Max T/O weight: 16207 kg (35,715 lb)
Max speed: 211 mph at 9,845 ft
Operational range: 2,920 miles

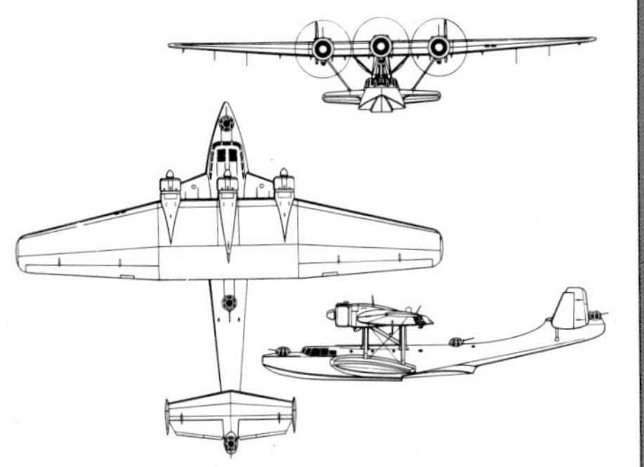

Lockheed Harpoon

By comparison with the PV-1 Ventura, the PV-2 Harpoon that began to enter service in 1944 had wings of increased span and larger fuel capacity, a redesigned tail with larger vertical surfaces, and improved armament. Production of 535 Harpoons was completed (500 PV-2s including several PV-2C trainer conversions plus 35 PV-2Ds with heavier nose armament), and after World War II large numbers were transferred to the naval air arms of friendly countries. In 1944 the Free French had received a small quantity of PV-1s, and these were replaced after World War II by Bloch M.B.175 bombers. However, the re-formed Aéronavale later received a comparatively small number of PV-2s to equip Escadrilles 11S and 12S. The aircraft remained in service into the late 1950s, when they were passed on to Portugal.

Specification: Lockheed PV-2 Harpoon four/five-seat patrol bomber
Span: 22.86 m (75 ft 0 in)
Length: 15.51 m (51 ft 1 in)
Powerplant: 2×Pratt & Whitney R-2800-31 Double Wasp, 1491 kW (2,000 hp) each
Armament: 9×7.62-mm (0.3-in) machine-guns plus provision for up to 1814 kg (4,000 lb) of disposable stores carried internally and 907 kg (2,000 lb) of bombs carried under the wings
Max T/O weight: 16330 kg (36,000 lb)
Max speed: 282 mph at 13,700 ft
Operational range: 2,930 miles

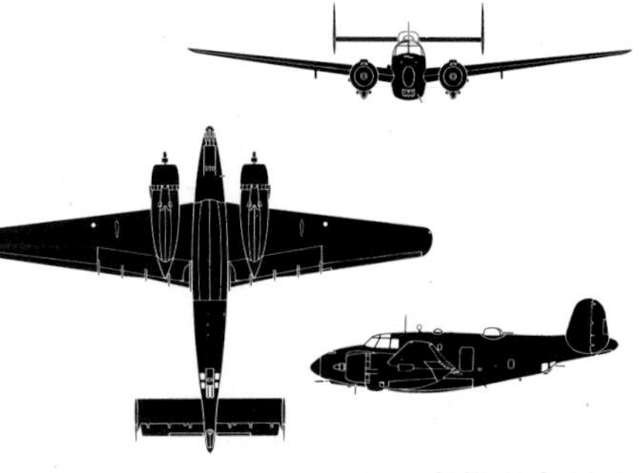

Martin P5M Marlin

The Marlin evolved from the PBM Mariner of World War II, and first flew in May 1948 as an advanced patrol flying boat with radar-directed nose and tail turrets plus a power-operated dorsal turret. The type was ordered into production as the P5M-1 without the dorsal turret, with the nose turret replaced by the radome/antenna for the APS-80 search radar, and with more-powerful engines in nacelles that also accommodated the disposable weapon load. The P5M-2 introduced a T-tail, APS-44 search radar, MAD with its sensor in a 'sting' behind the fin/tailplane junction, more power and a revised fuselage. In 1959 10 of this version were delivered to the Aéronavale, in whose service they were allocated to Flottille 27F for long-range anti-submarine patrols until replaced in the late 1960s by Breguet Atlantics.

Specification: Martin P5M-2 Marlin 11-seat medium-range maritime patrol and anti-submarine flying boat
Span: 36.02 m (118 ft 2 in)
Length: 30.66 m (100 ft 7 in)
Powerplant: 2×Wright R-3350-32QA Turbo Compound, 2573 kW (3,450 hp) each
Armament: provision for 3629 kg (8,000 lb) of disposable stores carried internally plus 8×454-kg (1,000-lb) bombs or mines carried under the wings
Max T/O weight: 38555 kg (85,000 lb)
Max speed: 251 mph at sea level
Operational range: 2,050 miles

Grumman JRF Goose

First flown in 1937, the Goose proved a remarkably successful aeroplane that appealed to civil and military operators alike for its amphibious capability, capacious fuselage and modest fuel requirements. The version taken by the US Navy was designated JRF, and this was developed in variants up to the JRF-5 with cameras for photo-survey, and the JRF-6B Lend-Lease model intended for air/sea rescue and navigation training. A number of these essentially similar models were delivered to France after World War II for use in the coastal reconnaissance and air/sea rescue roles, proving invaluable as the French authorities redrew their coastal charts to take account of World War II wrecks and other features. The main operator of the type in Aéronavale service was Escadrille 8S, which used the type into the mid-1960s.

Specification: Grumman JRF-5 Goose two-crew utility and coastal reconnaissance amphibian
Span: 14.95 m (49 ft 0 in)
Length: 11.73 m (38 ft 6 in)
Powerplant: 2×Pratt & Whitney R-985-AN-6 Wasp Junior, 336 kW (450 hp) each
Payload: seven passengers or freight
Max T/O weight: 3629 kg (8,000 lb)
Max speed: 201 mph at 5,000 ft
Operational range: 640 miles

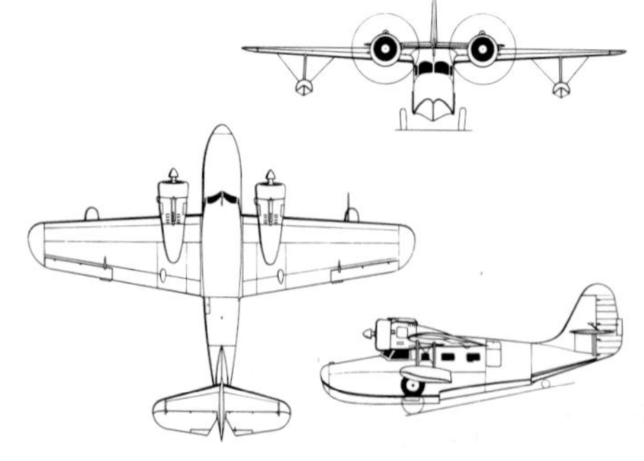

Morane-Saulnier M.S.470 Vanneau

The Vanneau (plover) was developed in Vichy France as an advanced trainer with tandem seating for the pupil and instructor, but first flew in December 1944, after the liberation of France, in M.S.470 prototype form with the 515-kW (690-hp) Hispano-Suiza 12X inline. The type was ordered for the Armée de l'Air as the M.S.472 Vanneau II with the 522-kW (700-hp) Gnome-Rhone 14M radial. The equivalent version for the Aéronavale was the M.S.474 Vanneau IV, of which 70 were delivered from December 1946. The Vanneau IV was basically similar to the Vanneau II in all essential details, but had specialised naval equipment and, to permit the training of pilots in carrier landings, an arrester hook. The Vanneau IV remained in Aéronavale service into the late 1960s.

Specification: Morane-Saulnier M.S.474 Vanneau IV two-seat advanced flying trainer
Span: 10.65 m (34 ft 11.25 in)
Length: 8.61 m (28 ft 3 in)
Powerplant: 1×Gnome-Rhone 14M-9, 522 kW (700 hp)
Armament: 2×7.5-mm (0.295-in) machine-guns plus provision for light bombs carried under the wings
Max T/O weight: 2400 kg (5,291 lb)
Max speed: 290 mph at optimum altitude
Operational range: 950 miles

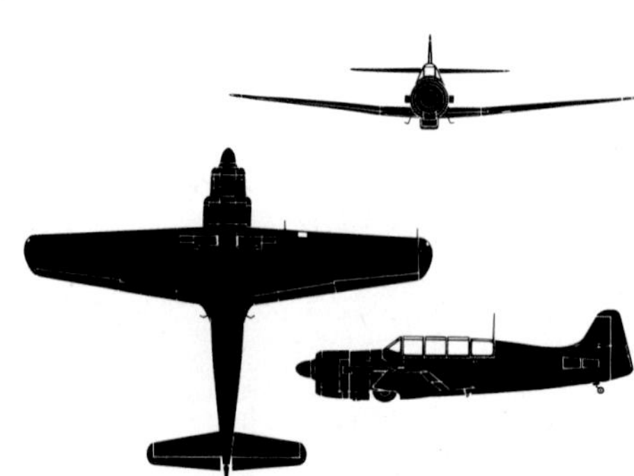

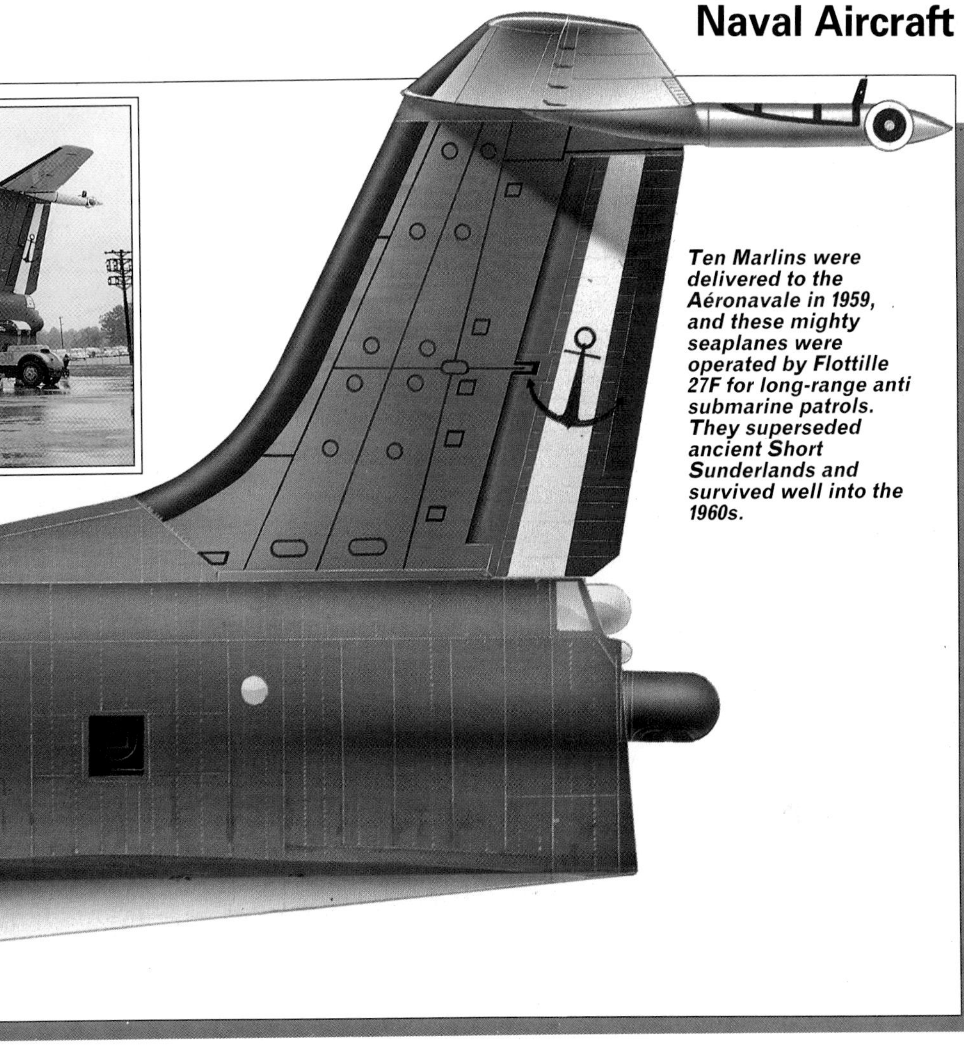

Ten Marlins were delivered to the Aéronavale in 1959, and these mighty seaplanes were operated by Flottille 27F for long-range anti submarine patrols. They superseded ancient Short Sunderlands and survived well into the 1960s.

Consolidated PB4Y/P4Y Privateer

After it had used a version of the B-24 Liberator bomber as the PB4Y-1 in the long-range patrol bomber role, the US Navy called for the development of a Liberator derivative optimised for the role, and this resulted in the PB4Y-2 Privateer that first flew in September 1943. This retained the wing and landing gear of the B-24D but had unturbocharged engines in revised nacelles for the low-altitude role, a single tall fin/rudder assembly, and a lengthened fuselage with twin dorsal rather than single dorsal and ventral turrets. Production amounted to 736 aircraft and in the later 1940s a number of these machines, by then redesignated P4Y-2, were supplied to the Aéronavale for service as land-based anti-submarine patrollers. The aircraft operated until the early 1960s with Flottille 8F.

Specification: Consolidated PB4Y-2/Convair P4Y-2 Privateer 10/11-seat long-range maritime patrol bomber
Span: 33.53 m (110 ft 0 in)
Length: 22.73 m (74 ft 7 in)
Powerplant: 4×Pratt & Whitney R-1830-94 Twin Wasp, 1007 kW (1,350 hp) each
Armament: 12×12.7-mm (0.5-in) machine-guns plus provision for 8×726-kg (1,600-lb) bombs carried internally
Max T/O weight: 29484 kg (65,000 lb)
Max speed: 237 mph at 13,700 ft
Operational range: 2,800 miles

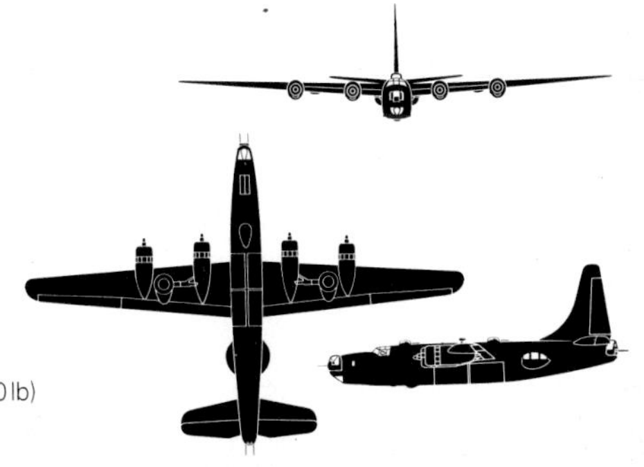

Short Sunderland

In 1951 Shorts of Belfast reconditioned 19 ex-RAF Sunderland Mk V flying boats for the Aéronautique Navale, which had found itself short of a long-range maritime patrol flying boat at a time when there were beginning to emerge in the West fears about the growth of a powerful Soviet submarine threat. The Sunderlands were allocated mostly to Flottille 7FE operating from Dakar in Senegal, this location at the western edge of Africa allowing radar and visual patrols deep into the central and south Atlantic, through which plied much of the West's trade in food and raw materials from South America and South Africa. The Sunderland was withdrawn from French service in the late 1950s, the last three machines being retired in 1960. One of these boats was returned to the UK in March 1961 for preservation.

Specification: Short Sunderland MR.Mk 5 10/13-seat maritime patrol and anti-submarine flying boat
Span: 34.39 m (112 ft 9.5 in)
Length: 26.01 m (85 ft 4 in)
Powerplant: 4×Pratt & Whitney R-1830-90B Twin Wasp, 895 kW (1,200 hp) each
Armament: 2×12.7-mm (0.5-in) and eight or 12×7.7-mm (0.303-in) machine-guns plus provision for 2250 kg (4,960 lb) of disposable stores carried internally
Max T/O weight: 27216 kg (60,000 lb)
Max speed: 213 mph at optimum altitude
Operational range: 2,900 miles

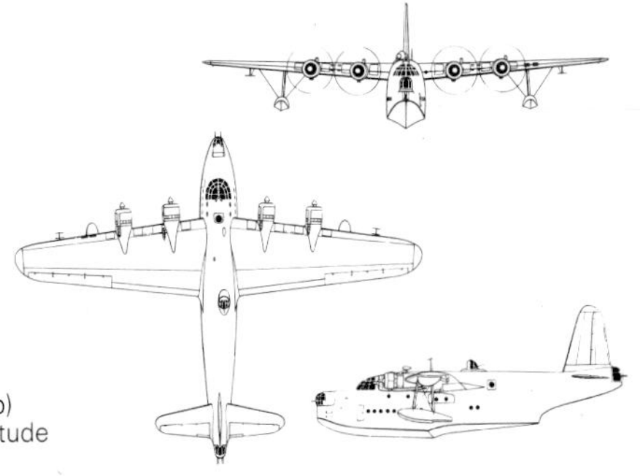

British Aerospace **Sea Harrier**

The Sea Harrier was evolved from the Harrier from 1975 to provide the three 'Invincible' class carriers with a STOVL fighter, strike/attack and reconnaissance capability. The Sea Harrier has aluminium rather than magnesium alloy components for protection against salt-water corrosion, but is otherwise very similar to the Harrier except for its taller fin, naval equipment and a totally new forward fuselage. This accommodates the Blue Fox multi-role radar and a cockpit optimised for air combat rather than close support: the pilot is seated higher under a bubble canopy, and the cockpit features displays for the new nav/attack system. The Sea Harrier FRS.Mk 1 began to enter service in 1981 and proved itself in the Falklands War of 1982. A mid-life update is currently under way to produce the more capable Sea Harrier FRS.Mk 2 with Blue Vixen radar and AMRAAM medium-range missiles.

Dassault-Breguet **Br.1050 Alizé**

Based on the abortive Br.960 Vultur naval strike aeroplane with a hybrid turboprop/turbojet powerplant, the Alizé (trade wind) was developed as a carrierborne anti-submarine type with a more powerful turboprop so that the rear-fuselage turbojet could be replaced by DRAA 2A search radar with its antenna in a retractable 'dustbin' radome; sonobuoys are accommodated in the wing fairings for the main units of the tricycle landing gear. The first example flew in October 1956, and service deliveries began in May 1959. Some 12 aircraft were delivered to the Indian navy, and these remained to basic standard with DRAA 2B radar, but the surviving French aircraft have been updated with Thomson-CSF Iguane search radar, internal ECM equipment and improved acoustic data-processing equipment.

Specification: Dassault-Breguet Br.1040 Alizé three-seat carrierborne anti-submarine aeroplane
Span: 15.60 m (51 ft 2 in)
Length: 13.86 m (45 ft 6 in)
Powerplant: 1×Rolls-Royce Dart RDa.7 Mk 21, 1473 kW (1,975 shp)
Armament: 1×500-kg (1,102-lb) torpedo or 3×160-kg (353-lb) depth charges carried internally, plus provision for up to 2×175-kg (386-lb) depth charges under the inner wings and 6×127-mm (5-in) rockets or 2×AS.12 ASMS under the outer wings
Max T/O weight: 8200 kg (18,078 lb)
Max speed: 323 mph at 9,845 ft
Operational range: 1,553 miles

Dassault-Breguet **Super Etendard**

In the late 1960s Dassault persuaded the French Navy to abandon the planned SEPECAT Jaguar M in favour of an updated version of the Etendard (banner) attack fighter. Thus emerged the Super Etendard, which first flew in October 1974 and began to enter service in June 1978. By comparison with its predecessor, the Super Etendard has 11% more thrust, improved high-lift devices for unimpaired carrier operations at higher weights, a beefed-up structure and a revised nav/attack system including the Agave multi-mode radar (replacing the Aida ranging radar) in a larger nose, an inertial navigation system and podded countermeasures. The type carries the formidable AM.39 Exocet anti-ship missile (used operationally by Argentine and Iraqi Super Etendards), and some French aircraft are configured for the ASMP nuclear stand-off missile.

Specification: Dassault-Breguet Super Etendard single-seat carrierborne and land-based strike fighter
Span: 9.60 m (31 ft 6 in)
Length: 14.31 m (46 ft 11.5 in)
Powerplant: 1 x SNECMA Atar 08K-50, 5000 kg (11,023 lb) st
Armament: 2×30-mm cannon, plus provision for up to 2100 kg (4,630 lb) of disposable stores carried on 5×external hardpoints
Max T/O weight: 12000 kg (26,455 lb)k
Max speed: 745 mph at sea level
Operational range: 805 miles

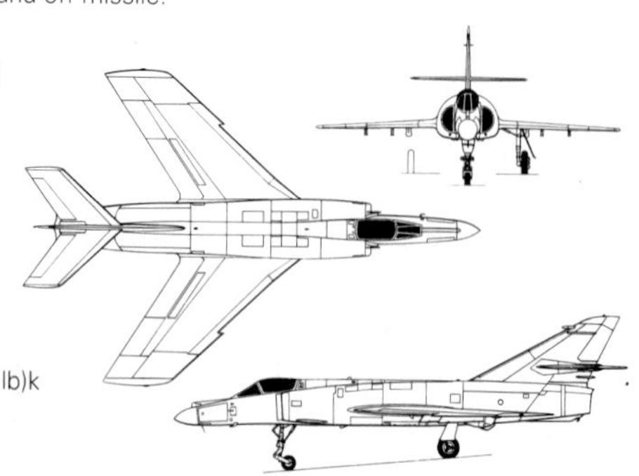

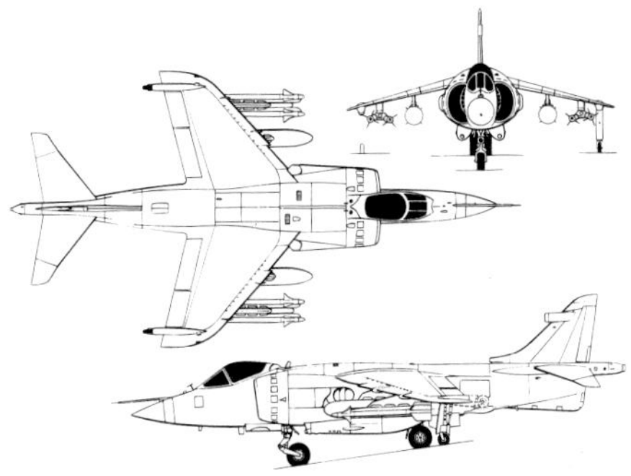

Specification: British Aerospace Sea Harrier FRS.Mk 1 single-seat carrierborne STOVL fighter, reconnaissance and strike/attack aeroplane
Span: 7.70 m (25 ft 3 in)
Length: 14.50 m (47 ft 7 in)
Powerplant: 1×Rolls-Royce Pegasus 11 Mk 104, 9752 kg (21,500 lb) st
Armament: 2×30-mm cannon, plus provision for up to 2268+ kg (5,000+ lb) of disposable stores carried on 5×external hardpoints
Max T/O weight: 11880 kg (26,190 lb)
Max speed: 735 mph at sea level
Operational range: 920 miles

Britain's Sea Harrier shot to fame during the Falklands war when it completely outfought the Argentine navy and air force. At the heart of the aircraft's success is a useful radar and excellent agility during close-in air-to-air fighting. The current FRS.Mk 1 version will be supplanted by the FRS.Mk 2, this being a more formidable opponent with look-down/shoot-down radar allied to AMRAAM missiles.

Grumman A-6 Intruder

First flown in April 1960 for service from 1963 as the US Navy's most important carrierborne all-weather strike and attack aeroplane, the Intruder remains in production to the present, with emphasis now placed on the type's electronics and a stronger wing. Though firmly subsonic, the Intruder retains its importance through a devastating combination of high warload and excellent electronics, allowing blind first-pass attacks against point targets after a long approach under any weather conditions. Core of the navigation system is the APQ-146/148 multi-mode radar plus ASN-92 inertial navigation system, while attack in the current A-6E version is aided by the FLIR- and laser-carrying Target Recognition and Attack Multi-sensor package. There is also the KA-6D buddy-refuelling version.

Specification: Grumman A-6E Intruder two-seat carrierborne all-weather strike and attack aeroplane
Span: 16.15 m (53 ft 0 in)
Length: 16.69 m (54 ft 9 in)
Powerplant: 2×Pratt & Whitney J52-P-8B, 4218 kg (9,300 lb) st each
Armament: provision for up to 8165 kg (18,000 lb) of disposable stores carried on 5×external hardpoints
Max T/O weight: 27397 kg (60,400 lb)
Max speed: 644 mph at sea level
Operational range: 1,011 miles with maximum payload

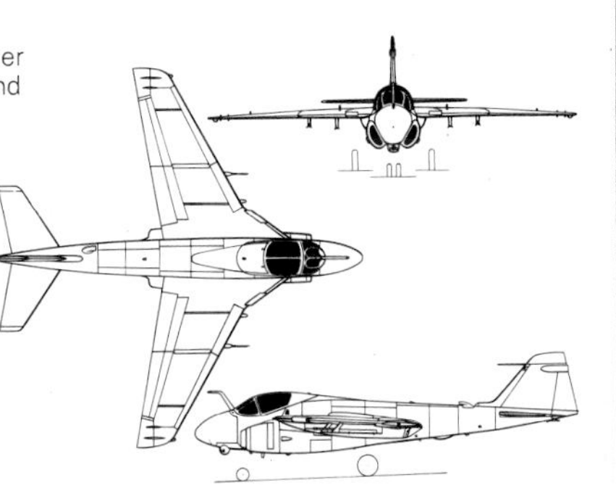

Grumman EA-6 Prowler

Experience with the EA-6A strike support variant of the A-6 Intruder was instrumental in spurring development of the EA-6B dedicated stand-off electronic warfare aeroplane for the US Navy. Evolved from the A-6A with a strengthened airframe and a 1.37-m (4.5-ft) fuselage stretch to allow the insertion of additional cockpit volume for the two specialist system operators, the EA-6B first flew in May 1968. Service deliveries began in January 1971 and the programme continues. The core of the EW system is the ALQ-99 tactical jamming system with its receivers in a fintop pod, a central analytical computer in the fuselage, and five external jammer pods. Each windmill-powered unit has two noise jammers, and successive operational standards are Expanded Capability, Improved Capability, Improved Capability 2, Defensive Electronic Countermeasures and Advanced Capability.

Specification: Grumman EA-6B four-seat carrierborne and land-based electronic warfare aeroplane
Span: 16.15 m (53 ft 0 in)
Length: 18.24 m (59 ft 10 in)
Powerplant: 2×Pratt & Whitney J52-P-408, 5080 kg (11,200 lb) st each
Armament: none
Max T/O weight: 29483 kg (65,000 lb)
Max speed: 623 mph at sea level
Operational range: about 1,145 miles

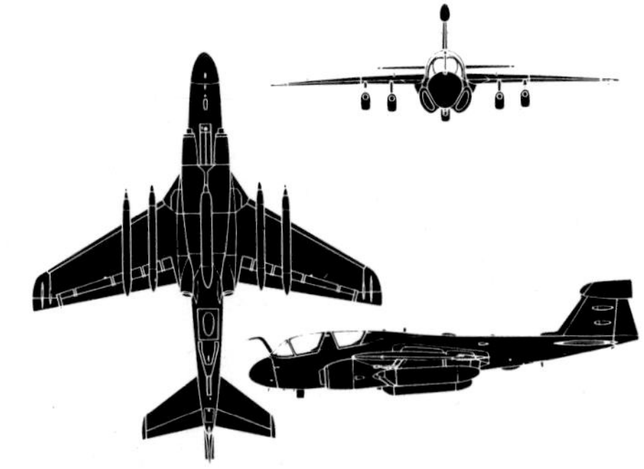

Grumman F-14 Tomcat

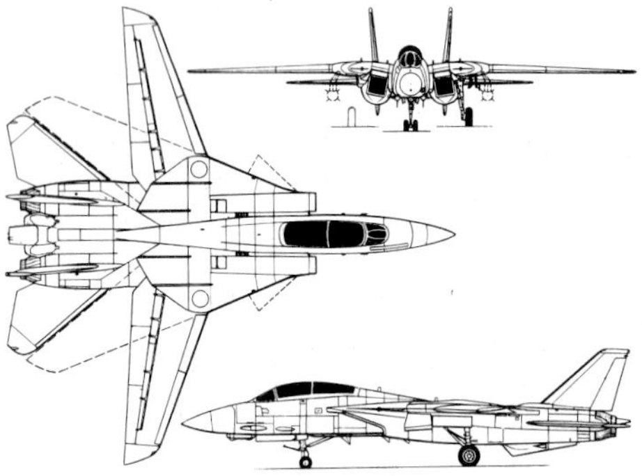

The F-14 was designed from 1968 as a fleet-defence fighter incorporating the engines, swing-wing technology and the immensely capable AWG-9/AIM-54 radar fire-control system/AAM combination developed for the abortive General Dynamics F-111B naval fighter. The prototype flew in December 1970 and the type began to enter service as the F-14A in October 1972. Development and production continue, the current F-14A Plus having more reliable 13154-kg (29,000-lb) thrust General Electric F110 turbofans, and the imminent F-14D having these engines and a radically improved digital electronic suite including the APG-71 radar, ALR-67 threat-warning and recognition system, ALQ-165 airborne self-protection jammer, JTIDS secure data-link, and an IR search-and-track sensor. Other features are the AIM-120 and improved AIM-54C AAMs, plus NACES ejector seats.

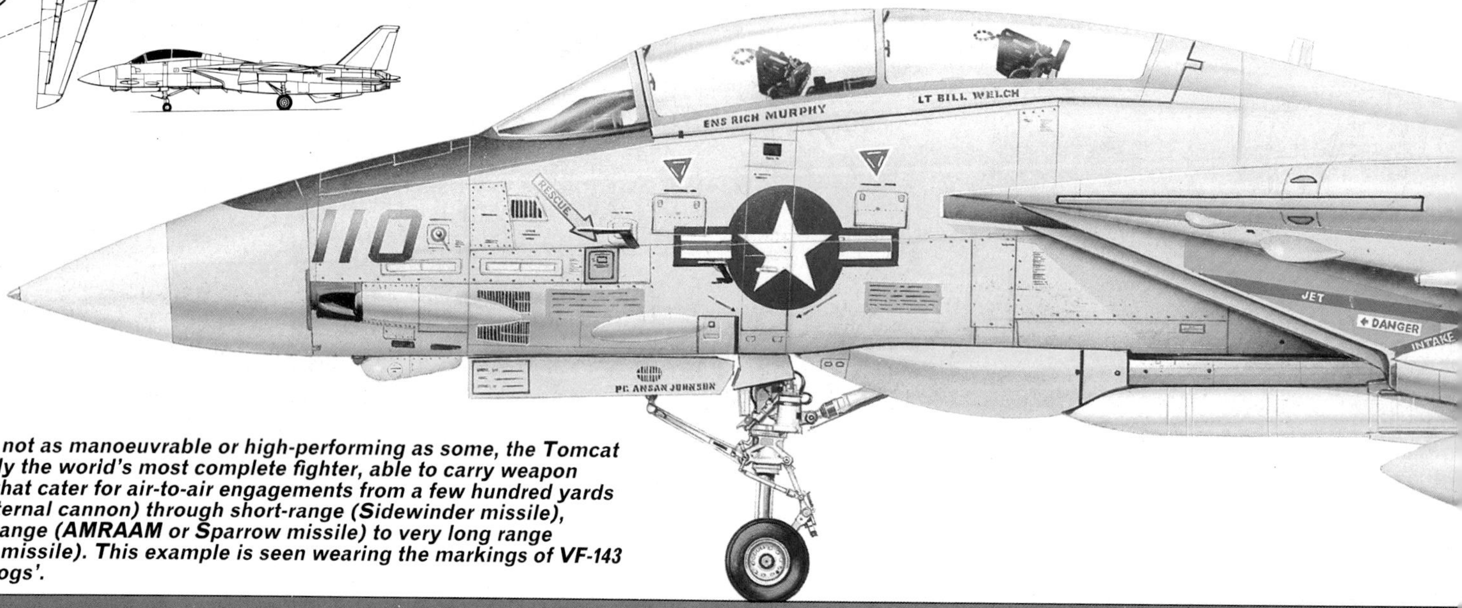

Although not as manoeuvrable or high-performing as some, the Tomcat is certainly the world's most complete fighter, able to carry weapon systems that cater for air-to-air engagements from a few hundred yards range (internal cannon) through short-range (Sidewinder missile), medium range (AMRAAM or Sparrow missile) to very long range (Phoenix missile). This example is seen wearing the markings of VF-143 'Pukin' Dogs'.

Grumman E-2 Hawkeye

Though carried in only small numbers by US carriers, the E-2 is a vital component of the embarked carrier air wing, providing unparalleled early-warning and control capability in defence of the carrier battle group through its powerful combination of surveillance radar (with its antenna in an overfuselage rotodome) and Litton L-504 digital computer. The initial E-2A version flew in October 1960 and entered service in January 1964 with APS-96 radar, being followed by the E-2B with APS-120 radar and by the current E-2C with APS-125 radar (replaced by APS-138/139 with APS-145 to follow) and ALR-73 passive detection system. The APS-125 has sophisticated electronic counter-countermeasures and can detect aircraft at 370-km (230-mile) range, tracking a maximum of 250 of them while controlling 30 or more interceptions.

Specification: Grumman E-2C Hawkeye five-seat carrierborne and land-based early warning and control aeroplane
Span: 24.56 m (80 ft 7 in)
Length: 17.54 m (57 ft 6.75 in)
Powerplant: 2×Allison T56-A-425, 3663 kW (4,910 shp) each
Armament: none
Max T/O weight: 23503 kg (51,817 lb)
Max speed: 374 mph at optimum altitude
Operational range: 400 miles with 4 hours on station

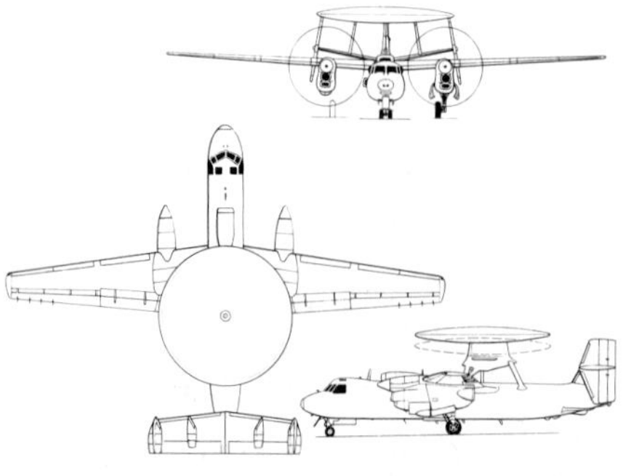

Lockheed S-3 Viking

The S-3 is a truly remarkable aeroplane, the designers having managed to package into a comparatively small carrier-capable airframe a sizeable weapon load, the electronic capability of the P-3 Orion land-based maritime patrol aeroplane, and the fuel to give considerable range to this twin-turbofan design. The type first flew in January 1973, and amongst the mission electronics of the baseline S-3A are APS-116 radar, ALR-87 ESM, ASQ-81 MAD, 60 sonobuoys for the OL-82 processing system, and a FLIR sensor. Many examples are being upgraded to S-3B standard with better acoustic and radar processing, expanded ESM capability, a sonobuoy reference system and provision for two Harpoon anti-ship missiles, and it is possible that others will be modified to ES-3A electronic reconnaissance configuration.

Specification: Lockheed S-3A Viking four-seat carrierborne anti-submarine aeroplane
Span: 20.93 m (68 ft 8 in)
Length: 16.26 m (53 ft 4 in)
Powerplant: 2×General Electric TF34-GE-2, 4207 kg (9,275 lb) st each
Armament: provision for up to 3175 kg (7,000 lb) of disposable stores carried internally and on 2×external hardpoints
Max T/O weight: 23832 kg (52,540 lb)
Max speed: 518 mph at optimum altitude
Operational range: more than 2,300 miles

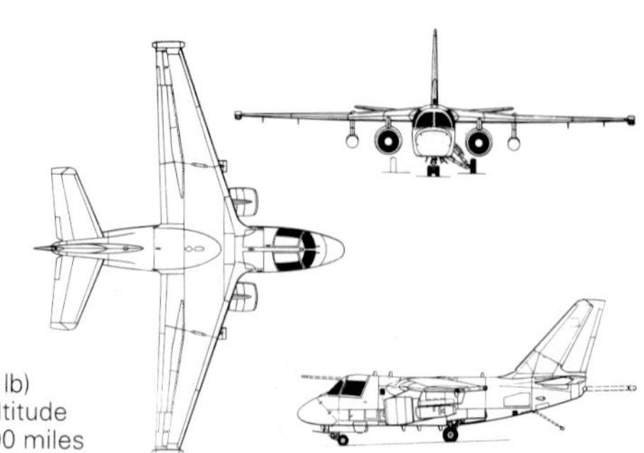

Specification: Grumman F-14A Tomcat two-seat carrierborne and land-based variable-geometry fleet-defence fighter
Span: 19.54 m (64 ft 1.5 in) spread and 11.65 m (38 ft 2.5 in) swept
Length: 19.10 m (62 ft 8 in)
Powerplant: 2×Pratt & Whitney TF30-P-412A, 9480 kg (20,900 lb) st each
Armament: 1×20-mm rotary-barrel cannon, plus (typically) 4×AIM-54 Phoenix, 2×AIM-7 Sparrow and 4×AIM-9 Sidewinder AAMs on 4×underfuselage and 2×underwing hardpoints, or 6577 kg (14,500 lb) of disposable stores carried externally
Max T/O weight: 33724 kg (74,348 lb)
Max speed: Mach 2.34 at high altitude
Operational range: about 2,000 miles

McDonnell Douglas *A-4 Skyhawk*

First flown in June 1954 and entering service in October 1956 as the A4D-1 replacement for the Skyraider series of carrierborne attack aircraft, the Skyhawk soon built up as great a reputation as its predecessor, and in 1962 was redesignated as the A-4. From the A-4F variant with the 4218-kg (9,300-lb) thrust J52-P-8A the Skyhawk has been fitted with a distinct dorsal hump for the additional electronics that have proved necessary with the increasing sophistication of modern warfare, and the most important carrierborne version is the A-4M Skyhawk II operated by the US Marine Corps. This has considerably more power than its predecessors, and its internal modifications include the Hughes ASB-19 Angle/Rate Bombing System, ALR-45 radar-warning and ALR-50 SAM-warning systems, ALE-39 chaff/flare dispenser and a Marconi head-up display. There is also an OA-4M two-seat forward air control variant.

Specification: McDonnell Douglas A-4M Skyhawk II single-seat carrierborne and land-based light attack aeroplane
Span: 8.38 m (27 ft 6 in)
Length: 12.29 m (40 ft 4 in) excluding probe
Powerplant: 1×Pratt & Whitney J52-P-408, 5080 kg (11,200 lb) st
Armament: 2×20-mm cannon, plus provision for up to 4153 kg (9,155 lb) of disposable stores carried on 5×external hardpoints
Max T/O weight: 12437 kg (27,420 lb)
Max speed: 685 mph at sea level
Operational range: about 920 miles

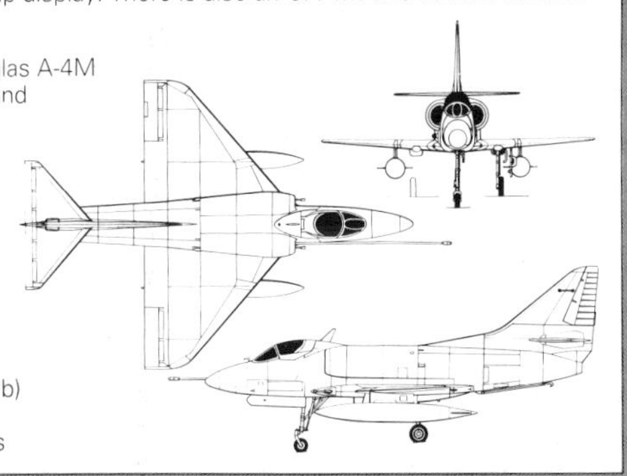

McDonnell Douglas *F/A-18 Hornet*

Evolved from the Northrop YF-17 competitor to the F-16 Fighting Falcon, the F/A-18 was planned as successor to the F-4 Phantom II and A-7 Corsair II in the fighter and attack roles respectively through use of an exceptional electronic suite centred on the APG-65 multi-mode radar and an advanced cockpit with HOTAS controls plus one head-up and three head-down displays. The machine developed by McDonnell Douglas with Northrop support is considerably larger than the YF-17, and is optimized for controllability and weapon load rather than outright performance. The first example flew in November 1978, and the F/A-18A began to enter service in 1983. Other variants are the F/A-18B two-seater, the upgraded F/A-18C single-seater with missiles such as the AGM-65 and AIM-120, the F/A-18D two-seater, and the RF-18D reconnaissance variant, with development continuing.

Specification: McDonnell Douglas F/A-18C Hornet single-seat carrierborne and land-based fighter and attack aeroplane
Span: 11.43 m (37 ft 6 in) over missile rails
Length: 17.07 m (56 ft 0 in)
Powerplant: 2×General Electric F404-GE-400, 7258 kg (16,000 lb) st each
Armament: 1×20-mm rotary-barrel cannon, plus provision for up to 8165 kg (18,000 lb) of disposable stores carried on 9×external hardpoints
Max T/O weight: 22328 kg (49,224 lb)
Max speed: Mach 1.8+ at high altitude
Operational range: 920+ miles

MD/BAe AV-8B Harrier II

Developed mainly in the USA for the US Marine Corps, the Harrier II is a very considerable evolutionary step from the original AV-8A (Harrier) with a larger wing (of supercritical section and graphite/epoxy composite construction with additional hardpoints, larger flaps, drooping ailerons, leading-edge root extensions), enhanced underfuselage lift-improvement devices, strengthened landing gear, larger inlets and a revised forward fuselage for better fields of vision. The type first flew in November 1981 and immediately displayed considerably greater load-carrying capability than the AV-8A. Service deliveries began in October 1983. The Harrier II has the Hughes Angle/Rate Bombing System and other capable electronics, while the forthcoming Harrier II Plus will have APG-65 radar and night-vision equipment. The TAV-8B is a two-seater.

Specification: McDonnell Douglas/British Aerospace AV-8B Harrier II single-seat carrierborne and land-based STOVL multi-role combat aeroplane
Span: 9.25 m (30 ft 4 in)
Length: 14.12 m (46 ft 4 in)
Powerplant: 1×Rolls-Royce F402-RR-406 (Pegasus 11-21), 9979 kg (22,000 lb) st
Armament: 1×25-mm rotary-barrel cannon, plus provision for up to 7711 kg (17,000 lb) of disposable stores carried on 7×external hardpoints
Max T/O weight: 13494 kg (29,750 lb)
Max speed: 673 mph at sea level
Operational range: 345 miles with typical warload

Vought F-8 Crusader

The F8U (from 1962 F-8) was the US Navy's first supersonic fighter, its most distinctive feature being the variable-incidence wing designed to provide a high angle of incidence without a nose-high attitude during carrier operations. The first XF8U-1 flew in March 1955 with a 6713-kg (14,800-lb) J57-P-11 turbojet, and production followed steadily of the F8U-1, the F8U-1E with limited all-weather capability, the F8U-1P reconnaissance aircraft, the F8U-2 with more power and reduced span, the F8U-2N limited all-weather fighter with two more Sidewinder AAMs in place of the F8U-1E's pack of 32 rockets, and the F8U-2NE (F-8E) multi-role fighter with APQ-94 radar and two underwing hardpoints. The only current carrier aircraft are the French F-8E(FN)s with blown flaps and other high-lift improvements, plus modifications to allow the carriage of French weapons.

Specification: Vought F-8E(FN) Crusader single-seat carrierborne fighter and fighter-bomber
Span: 10.87 m (35 ft 8 in)
Length: 16.61 m (54 ft 6 in)
Powerplant: 1×Pratt & Whitney J57-P-20A, 8165 kg (18,000 lb) st
Armament: 4×20-mm cannon, plus provision for 4×Sidewinder or 2×R530 AAMs carried on the fuselage sides, or 2268 kg (5,000 lb) of disposable stores carried on 2×external hardpoints
Max T/O weight: 15422 kg (34,000 lb)
Max speed: Mach 1.7 at 40,000 ft
Operational range: 1,100 miles

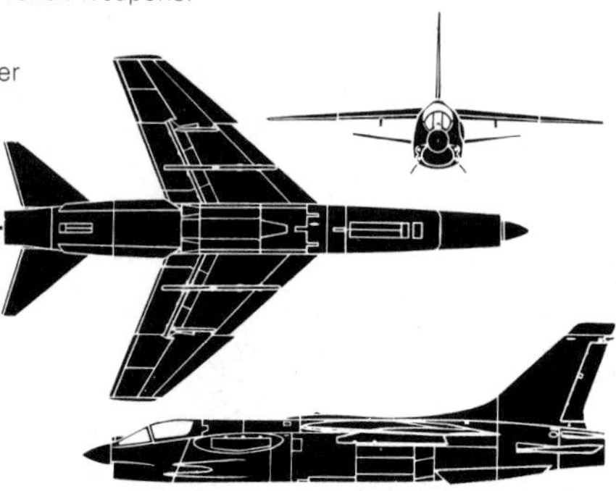

Vought A-7 Corsair II

Though based aerodynamically on the F-8, the A-7 is a more conventional aeroplane without the F-8's unique pivoting variable-incidence wing. The type was planned in 1964 as a heavier replacement for the A-4, and first flew in September 1965, entering service in October 1966 as the A-7A with the 5148-kg (11,350-lb) thrust TF30-P-6 turbofan. The following A-7B and A-7C retained the same basic engine, but in the still-serving A-7E the switch was made to a licence-built Rolls-Royce Spey, pioneered in the USAF's A-7D version. The A-7E has an advanced nav/attack system using APQ-126 multi-mode radar, an AVQ-7 head-up display, an inertial navigation system and a projected-map display, and can carry an extensive range of external sensors, designators and defensive electronics to complement its useful internal fit.

Specification: Vought A-7E Corsair II single-seat carrierborne and land-based medium attack aeroplane
Span: 11.80 m (38 ft 9 in)
Length: 14.06 m (46 ft 1.5 in)
Powerplant: 1 x Allison TF31-A-2, 6804 kg (15,000 lb) st
Armament: 1×20-mm rotary-barrel cannon, plus provision for up to 6804 kg (15,000 lb) of disposable stores carried on 8×external hardpoints
Max T/O weight: 19050 kg (42,000 lb)
Max speed: 690 mph at sea level
Operational range: 2,280 miles

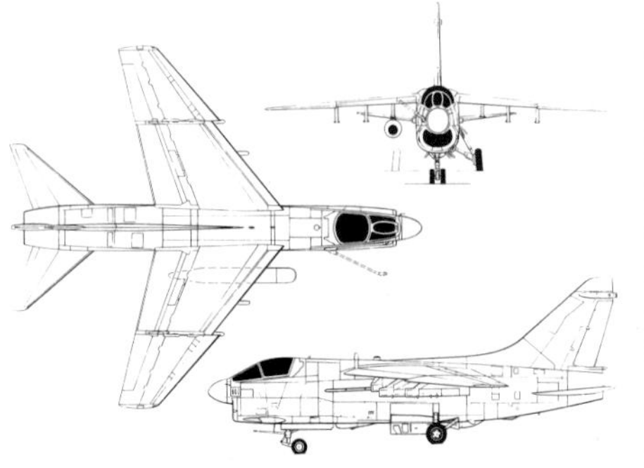

Yakovlev Yak-38 'Forger'

Originally thought in the West to be designated Yak-36, the Yak-38 is a subsonic STOVL aeroplane with modest combat capability, but more importantly has allowed the Soviet navy to gain experience of fixed-wing carrier air operations. The type is believed first to have flown in 1971 before entering service in 1976 as the single-seat 'Forger-A' and two-seat 'Forger-B'. Unlike the Harrier and its relatives, which have a single vectored-thrust turbofan for thrust and/or direct lift, the Yak-38 uses a hybrid propulsion system with a single non-afterburning turbojet exhausting via two vectoring nozzles aft of the wing, and two direct-lift turbojets accommodated vertically forward of the wing. Western analysts initially thought the type suitable only for VTOL operations, evidence of STOVL capability leading to a sharp upward revision of payload estimates.

Specification: Yakovlev Yak-38 'Forger-A' single-seat carrierborne STOVL combat aeroplane
Span: 7.32 m (24 ft 0.2 in)
Length: 15.50 m (50 ft 10.3 in)
Powerplant: 1×Lyul'ka AL-21F, 8160 kg (17,989 lb) st, and two Koliesov ZM, 3750 kg (7,870 lb) st each
Armament: provision for up to 3600 kg (7,937 lb) of disposable stores carried on 4×external hardpoints
Max T/O weight: 13000 kg (28,660 lb)
Max speed: 700 mph at sea level
Operational range: 460 miles

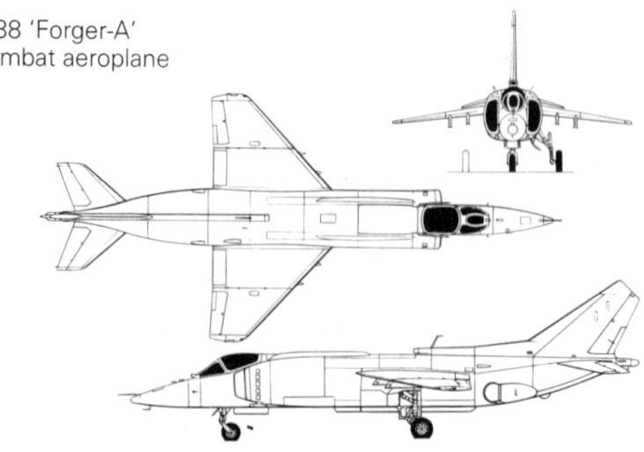

de Havilland Canada CSF Tracker

n the period after World War II the Royal Canadian Navy used as its standard anti-submarine aeroplane the Grumman Avenger, but in 1954 decided to replace this elderly single-engined type with a derivative of its US Navy successor, the twin-engined S2F-1 Tracker. For speed of delivery the RCN would have preferred to order directly from the US manufacturer, but to compensate the Canadian aero industry for large losses resulting from cancellations after the Korean War, the contract for 25 (later 99) aircraft was placed with de Havilland Canada. The aircraft differed from their American counterparts only in details of equipment, and the first flew in May 1956. Initial aircraft were to CSF-1 standard, though the 44th and later machines were to CSF-2 standard. Deliveries began in October 1956 for service with No. 880 Squadron on HMCS *Bonaventure* from 1957 and with Nos 32 and 33 Squadrons from shore bases.

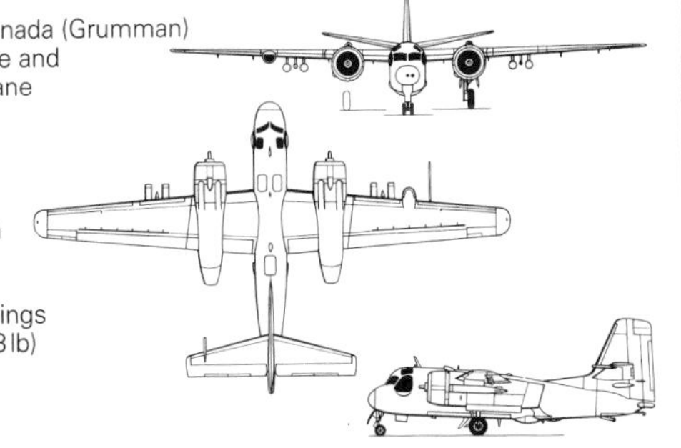

Specification: de Havilland Canada (Grumman) CSF-2 Tracker four-seat carrierborne and shore-based anti-submarine aeroplane
Span: 21.23 m (69 ft 8 in)
Length: 12.88 m (42 ft 3 in)
Powerplant: 2×Canadian Pratt & Whitney Aircraft-built Wright R-1820-82, 1137 kW (1,525 hp) each
Armament: 6×Mk 43 torpedoes carried two in the lower-fuselage weapons bay and four under the wings
Max T/O weight: 10984 kg (24,193 lb)
Max speed: 287 mph at optimum altitude
Operational range: 900 miles

Canadair CL-28 Argus

Looking to replace its Lancaster Mk 10MR maritime patrol and anti-submarine aircraft, the Royal Canadian Air Force decided in 1952 to procure a development of the turboprop-powered Bristol Britannia airliner. The resultant CL-28 used the wings, empennage and landing gear of the Britannia married to a new, unpressurised fuselage and four Wright Turbo-Compound piston engines; additionally, advanced electronics were specified for the six-man mission crew. The prototype flew in March 1957 and entered service as the first of 13 CP-107 Argus Mk 1s in May of the same year. There followed 20 Argus Mk 2s with improved equipment, and these aircraft served with Nos 404 and 405 Squadrons at Greenwood on Nova Scotia, and with No. 415 Squadron at Summerside on Prince Edward Island until replaced by Auroras from 1980.

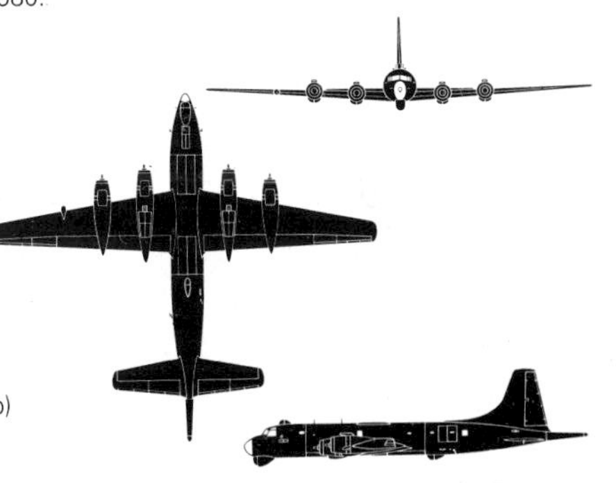

Specification: Canadair CL-28-2 Argus Mk 2 15-seat maritime reconnaissance and anti-submarine aeroplane
Span: 43.38 m (142 ft 3.5 in)
Length: 39.09 m (128 ft 3 in)
Powerplant: 4×Wright R-3370 TC981 EA-1, 2759 kW (3,700 hp) each
Armament: provision for up to 3632 kg (8,000 lb) of disposable stores carried in the lower-fuselage weapons bay
Max T/O weight: 67192 kg (148,000 lb)
Max speed: 315 mph at 10,000 ft
Operational range: 4,000 miles

Fairey Gannet

To provide a dedicated anti-submarine counterpart to the Sea Hawk strike fighters in naval service, West Germany ordered 16 examples of the Gannet carrierborne aeroplane in only marginally modified form for shore-based use: the great attractions of the type were ready availability and a twin-turboprop powerplant, which allowed twin-engined take-off but thereafter long-range cruise/extended loiter on a single engine. The aircraft were 15 Gannet AS.Mk 4 operational aircraft and one Gannet T.Mk 5 trainer built in 1958 and diverted from a cancelled Royal Navy order. The Gannets' operating unit was Marinefliegergeschwader 3, which followed the lead set by MFG 1 and 2 in being formed in the UK during 1958, though in this instance at RNAS Eglinton in Northern Ireland before moving to Schleswig. From 1965 the Gannets were replaced by Breguet Atlantics, and in 1967 and 1968 the Gannets were withdrawn.

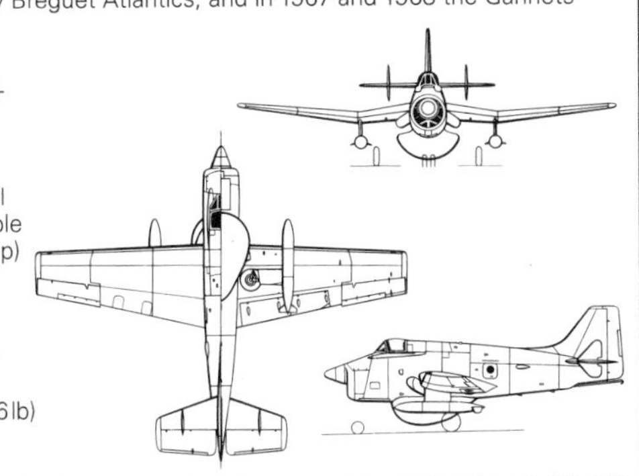

Specification: Fairey Gannet AS.Mk 4 three-seat land-based anti-submarine aeroplane
Span: 16.50 m (54 ft 4 in)
Length: 13.10 m (43 ft 0 in)
Powerplant: 1×Rolls-Royce (Bristol Siddeley/Armstrong Siddeley) Double Mamba Mk 101, 2263 kW (3,035 shp)
Armament: provision for up to 2×torpedoes or 907 kg (2,000 lb) of other disposable stores carried internally and 24×76.2-mm (3-in) or 16×127-mm (5-in)
Max T/O weight: 10635 kg (23,446 lb)
Max speed: 299 mph at sea level
Operational range: 662 miles

Sikorsky CH-124 Sea King

To provide its destroyers and larger frigates with a heavy anti-submarine helicopter, the Royal Canadian Navy (now CAF – Maritime Group) ordered a derivative of the SH-3A Sea King with the designation CHSS-2, later altered to CH-124. The total requirement was 41 such helicopters, and while the first four were delivered by Sikorsky from May 1963, the last 37 were assembled by United Aircraft of Canada from Sikorsky-supplied components. The initial operator was No. 406 Squadron, the operational conversion unit for the type at CAF Shearwater, and this unit still retains two CH-124U helicopters without sonar. The other 32 helicopters are the sonar-fitted CH-124As flown by Nos 423 and 443 Squadrons at Shearwater, with two helicopters on each of the four 'Iroquois' class destroyers and one helicopter on each of six 'St Laurent' and two 'Annapolis' class frigates. The Sea Kings are probably to be replaced by EH.101s.

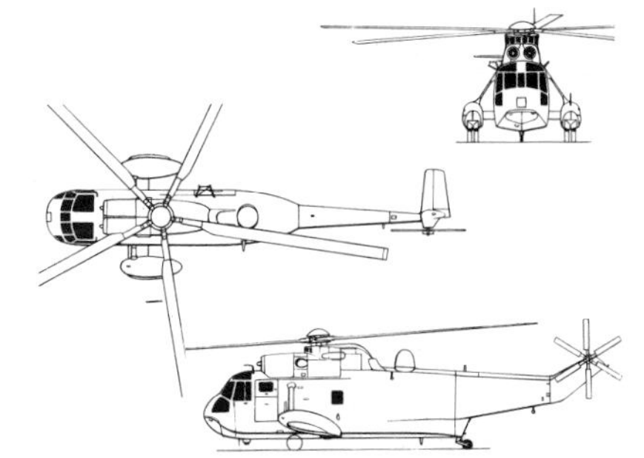

Specification: Sikorsky CH-124A Sea King four-seat shore- and ship-based anti-submarine helicopter
Main rotor diameter: 18.90 m (62 ft 0 in)
Length, fuselage: 16.69 m (54 ft 9 in)
Powerplant: 2×General Electric T58-GE-8B, 932 kW (1,250 shp) each
Armament: provision for up to 381 kg (840 lb) of disposable stores on 2×fuselage lateral hardpoints
Max T/O weight: 9299 kg (20,500 lb)
Max speed: 153 mph at sea level
Operational range: 625 miles

Chapter 4

ATTACK AIRCRAFT

PZL P.11

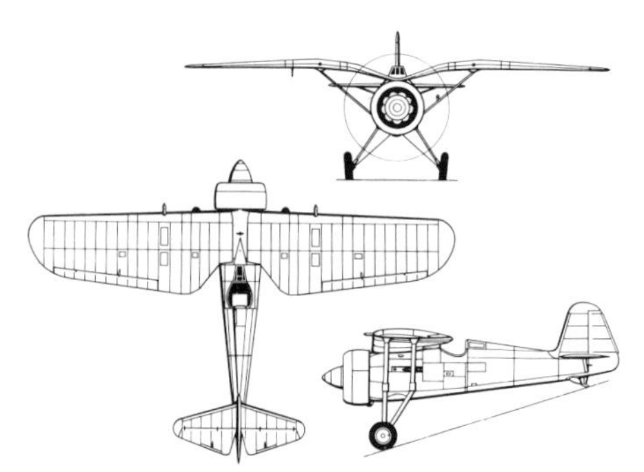

This PZL P.11 wears the startled-owl insignia of No. 113 Squadron, IV Dyon, 1st Air Regiment, based at Warsaw, and is finished in the pre-war, factory-applied dark green colour scheme. These sturdy fighters equipped 12 Polish fighter squadrons at the outbreak of war, but proved no match for the Messerschmitt Bf 109s of the Luftwaffe. The similar P.24 was exported to Greece and Bulgaria, and was licence-built in Turkey and Romania.

PZL P.7

The P.7 was the first production version of the fighter series that began with the inline-engined P.1 prototype of 1929. The series was distinguishable by its braced gull wing, which was characterised by main panels that tapered in chord and thickness outboard of the thin and down-sloped inner panels that gave the pilot good fields of vision. In 1931 PZL flew two P.6 and two P.7 prototypes with the Bristol Jupiter radial: the P.7/II was ordered as the P.7a with a licence-built Jupiter engine, and 150 aircraft were built. These entered service from 1933 to make Poland the first country in the world to field a force of all-metal monoplane fighters. In September 1939 about 100 were still in service with three squadrons, and of the Polish campaign's survivors half were flown to Romania and the other half captured by the Germans. Both Germany and Romania used these aircraft for training.

Specification: PZL P.7a single-seat fighter
Span: 10.30 m (33 ft 9.5 in)
Length: 7.15 m (23 ft 5.5 in)
Powerplant: 1×Skoda-built Bristol Jupiter VII, 362 kW (485 hp)
Armament: 2×7.7-mm (0.303-in) machine-guns
Max T/O weight: 1410 kg (3,109 lb)
Max speed: 199 mph at 13,125 ft
Operational range: 348 miles

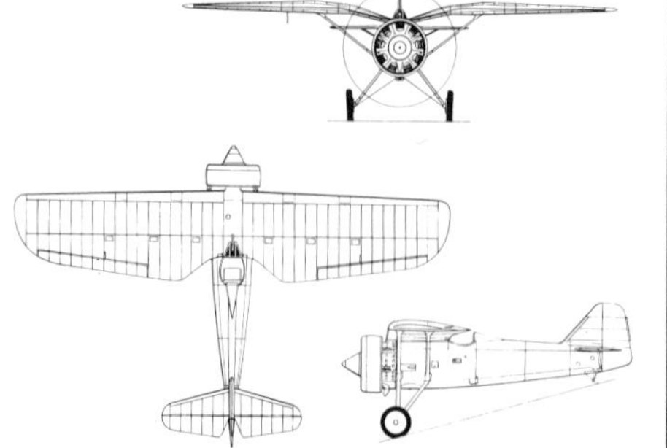

Plage & Laskiewicz (Lublin) R.XIII

The origins of the R.XIII can be traced back to the R.X developed to meet a 1927 Polish requirement for a two-seat observation and liaison aeroplane. The R.X was unsuccessful but paved the way for 15 R.XIV trainers, of which the last was completed as a reconnaissance type. From this was developed the improved R.XIII, which flew in prototype form during August 1931 at the beginning of a programme that saw the construction of 273 aircraft in variants that included the R.XIIIB initial model, the R.XIIIbis twin-float seaplane, the improved R.XIIIC, the R.XIIID with Townend-ringed engine, the R.XIIIter/hydro floatplane, and the upengined R.XIIIF and R.XIIIG/hydro floatplane. Most surviving aircraft were lost to ground fire ('friendly' as well as German) in the September 1939 campaign, 17 aircraft that escaped to Romania being impressed for training and liaison.

Specification: Plage & Laskiewicz (Lublin) R.XIIID two-seat reconnaissance and liaison aeroplane
Span: 13.20 m (43 ft 3.75 in)
Length: 8.48 m (29 ft 9.25 in)
Powerplant: 1×Skoda-built Wright Whirlwind J-5, 164 kW (220 hp)
Armament: 1×7.7-mm (0.303-in) machine-gun
Max T/O weight: 1330 kg (2,932 lb)
Max speed: 121 mph at sea level
Operational range: 373 miles

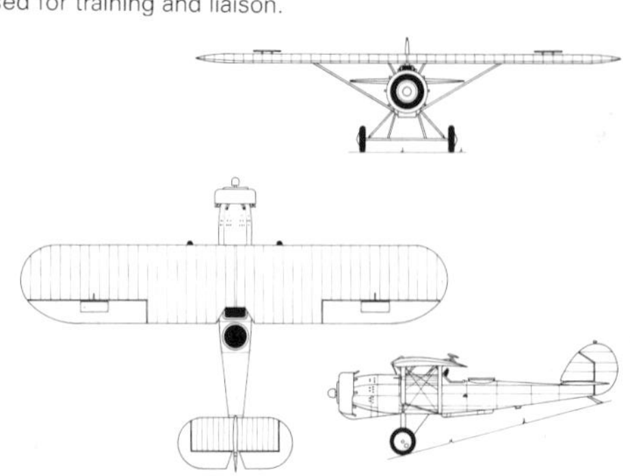

The P.7a's radial engine reduced the pilot's fields of vision by comparison with those of the P.1, and PZL proposed to mitigate this defect by the use of the narrower-diameter Mercury radial. The P.11/I prototype flew with a Jupiter IXASb in August 1931, but the P.11/II had the Mercury IVA and Gnome-Rhone 9K Mistral. The P.11/III was the prototype for the P.11a, of which 30 were ordered with the Skoda-built 385-kW (517-hp) Mercury IVS2. The variant was in fact preceded by 50 P.11b fighters ordered by Romania with the IAR-built 391-kW (525-hp) Mistral. The definitive variant was the P.11c, of which 175 were built with a lowered engine and a raised pilot's seat. IAR built 80 similar but Mistral-engined P.11f aircraft for Romania. After the fall of Poland the Germans used captured P.11s as trainers, and the type remained operational with Romania until the mid-war years.

Specification: PZL P.11c single-seat fighter and fighter-bomber
Span: 10.72 m (35 ft 2 in)
Length: 7.55 m (24 ft 9.25 in)
Powerplant: 1×PZL-built Bristol Mercury VIS2, 481 kW (645 hp)
Armament: 2×7.7-mm (0.303-in) machine-guns plus provision for up to 50 kg (110 lb) of light bombs carried under the wings
Max T/O weight: 1630 kg (3,594 lb)
Max speed: 242 mph at 18,045 ft
Operational range: 435 miles

Aero and Avia (Bloch) MB.200

The same basic designation was retained for the version of the Bloch MB.200 medium bomber, a French design, built under licence in Czechoslovakia by Aero and Avia to the extent of 124 aircraft. The type had first flown in 1933, and some 208 examples were built for the French air force. The Czech aircraft were similar to the French machines in all essential respects but particular items of equipment and their lower-rated engines (licence-built Gnome-Rhone 14K radials), which reduced maximum speed. After the German takeover of Czechoslovakia in 1939 the aircraft were used by the Luftwaffe for crew training as well as a number of trials purposes, and many of these obsolescent Czech aircraft were later passed on to Germany's allies and satellites including Bulgaria (12 aircraft), Croatia (an unknown number) and Romania (25 aircraft).

Specification: Aero and Avia MB.200 medium four-seat bomber
Span: 22.45 m (73 ft 8 in)
Length: 16.00 m (52 ft 6 in)
Powerplant: 2×Walter K-14 (licence-built Gnome-Rhone 14K Mistral Major), 633 kW (840 hp) each
Armament: 3×7.7-mm (0.303-in) machine-guns plus provision for up to 1200 kg (2,746 lb) of bombs carried internally
Max T/O weight: 7480 kg (16,490 lb)
Max speed: 152 mph at 14,110 ft
Operational range: 620 miles

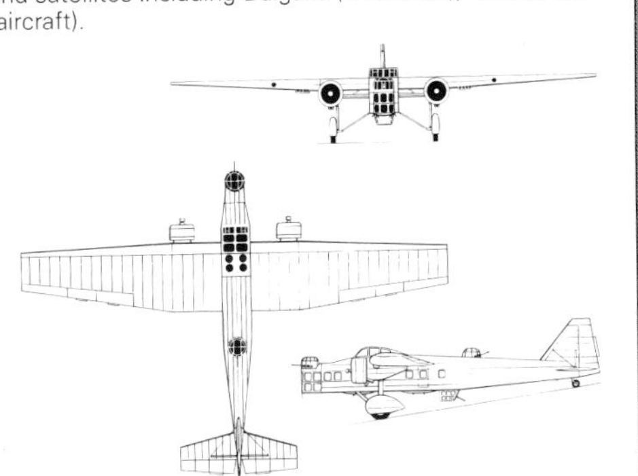

PZL P.24

The P.24 was essentially a revision of the P.11 to accept the Gnome-Rhone 14K as Polish-built Bristol engines could not be exported, and this had hampered sales of the P.7. The P.24/I prototype flew in May 1933, and the following P.24/II and III prototypes plus six P.24 pre-production aircraft offered heavier armament, greater structural strength and different engines for more power. Polish and licensed production totalled some 300 aircraft including the P.24A with the Gnome-Rhone 14Kfs and an armament of two 20-mm cannon and two machine-guns, the P-24B with modified spats, the P.24C with four machine-guns, the P-24E with the Gnome-Rhone 14KIIc32 or 14KMc36, and the P-24F and similar P.24G with a redesigned cowling. These variants were taken by Bulgaria, Greece, Romania and Turkey, while Poland was to have taken the P.24H with the Gnome-Rhone 14N-25.

Specification: PZL P.24F single-seat fighter
Span: 10.70 m (35 ft 1.25 in)
Length: 7.60 m (24 ft 11.25 in)
Powerplant: 1×Gnome-Rhone 14N-07 Mistral Major, 723 kW (970 hp)
Armament: 2×20-mm cannon and 2×7.7-mm (0.303-in) machine-guns
Max T/O weight: 2000 kg (4,409 lb)
Max speed: 267 mph at 14,765 ft
Operational range: 435 miles

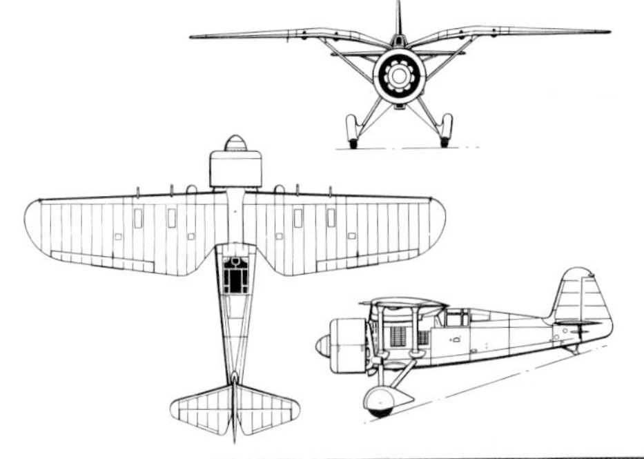

Avia B.534

Specification: Avia B.534-IV single-seat fighter and fighter-bomber
Span: 9.40 m (30 ft 10 in)
Length: 8.20 m (26 ft 10.75 in)
Powerplant: 1×Hispano-Suiza HS 12Ydrs, 634 kW (850 hp)
Armament: 4×7.7-mm (0.303-in) machine-guns plus provision for up to 6×20-kg (44-lb) bombs carried under the wings
Max T/O weight: 2120 kg (4,674 lb)
Max speed: 245 mph at 14,425 ft
Operational range: 360 miles

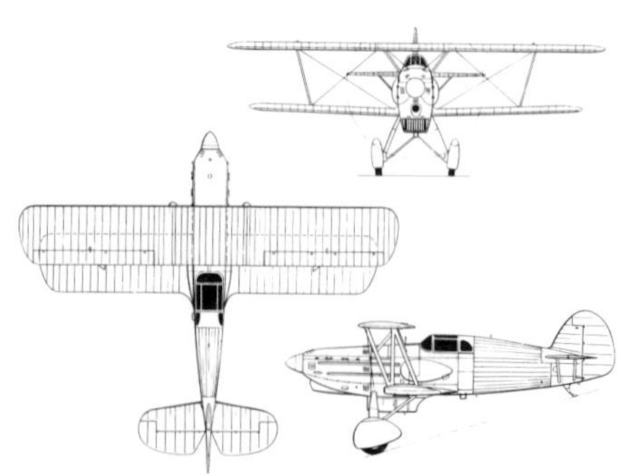

The B.534 was Czechoslovakia's most important fighter of the mid-1930s. The type was a development of the B.34/2 with more refined lines and greater power. The B.534/1 prototype flew in August 1933 and the B.534/2 introduced an enclosed cockpit, this latter forming the basis of the B.534-I initial production model. Some 46 were built with two machine-guns in the fuselage and two more on the lower wings, and an open cockpit. There followed 100 examples of the B.534-II with all guns grouped into the fuselage plus underwing bomb racks. Then came 66 (including 20 export) B.534-IIIs with faired mainwheels, 253 B.534-IVs with an aft-sliding cockpit canopy and 35 Bk.534s modelled on the B.534-II but with an engine-mounted 20-mm cannon. There were also many experimental developments, and the aircraft survived in service with the Germans and their allies until well into World War II.

Aero A.100 and A.101

From its A.30 two-seat light bomber and reconnaissance aeroplane the company developed the A.430 prototype. This was extensively developed as the A.100 with better performance than the A.30. In 1933 the type won a Czech air force competition for an A.30 reconnaissance replacement and was ordered into production, some 44 aircraft being built up to 1935. There also appeared a bomber version, the A.101 with a 597-kW (800-hp) Praga-built Isotta Fraschini Asso 1000 engine, a larger rear cockpit, an enlarged rudder and slightly increased overall dimensions including a span of 17.00 m (55 ft 9.25 in). Production totalled 29, and a subvariant was the Ab.101, a stop-gap bomber produced from 1936 with a prone bomber's position, internal bomb stowage and, with a 559-kW (750-hp) Hispano-Suiza 12Ydrs inline, performance inferior to that of the A.101; some 64 aircraft were built. Slovakia used some of the type in World War II.

Specification: Aero A.100 two-seat long-range reconnaissance aeroplane with secondary bombing capability
Span: 14.70 m (48 ft 2.75 in)
Length: 10.60 m (34 ft 9.25 in)
Powerplant: 1×Avia Vr-36, 485 kW (650 hp)
Armament: 4×7.7-mm (0.303-in) machine-guns plus provision for up to 600 kg (1,322 lb) of bombs
Max T/O weight: 3220 kg (7,099 lb)
Max speed: 168 mph
Operational range: 590 miles

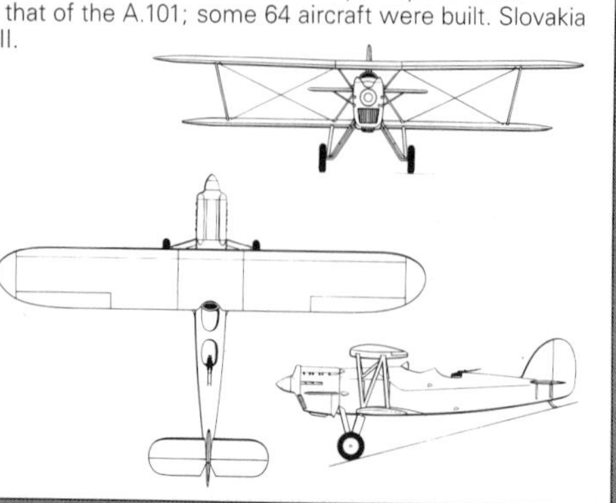

Letov S 328

The S 328 was developed from the S 228, ordered by the Estonian air force as a variant of the S 128 developed for but not accepted by the Czech air force. The spur for the S 328's development was a possible Finnish order. The S 328F prototype flew in 1932, but the Finnish order did not materialise and it was 1934 before Czechoslovakia finally ordered the S 328 as a reconnaissance aeroplane with secondary bombing capability. Production totalled 470 of all marks, which included the S 328N night-fighter with four fixed and two trainable machine-guns (13), S 328V twin-float seaplane with target-towing capability (4), S 428 with the 485-kW (650-hp) Avia Vr-36 radial (1) and S 538 with the 596.5-kW (800-hp) Gnome-Rhone Mistral Major (6). S 328s were used in comparatively large numbers by Bulgaria, Germany and Slovakia for anti-partisan operations during World War II, and the USSR employed examples captured from the Slovaks.

Specification: Letov S 328 two-seat reconnaissance/ observation and bomber aeroplane
Span: 13.71 m (44 ft 11.75 in)
Length: 10.36 m (33 ft 11.75 in)
Powerplant: 1×Walter-built Bristol Pegasus IIM2, 474 kW (635 hp)
Armament: 4×7.92-mm (0.312-in) machine-guns plus provision for 500 kg (1,102 lb) of bombs carried externally
Max T/O weight: 2640 kg (5,820 lb)
Max speed: 174 mph at sea level
Operational range: 435 miles

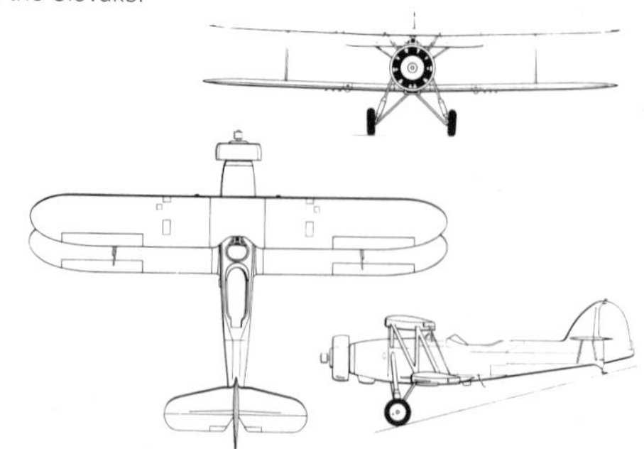

n Avia B.543-I of the 31st Squadron, First Air Regiment, Czechoslovak 'r force, based at Uzhorod, just before the General Mobilisation of 1938, hen squadron insignia was crudely overpainted. The Avia 'bird' badge carried on the tailfin. On the dissolution of the Czech Republic, many f these aircraft were taken on charge by the Luftwaffe, and used as ghters initially and then as fighter trainers. 72 were later sold to ulgaria. A handful formed the nucleus of the German puppet Slovak air rce, who used them operationally in Russia. Some took part in the lovak national uprising in September 1944, as part of the insurgent air rce.

PZL P.23 Karas

The Karas (crucian carp) was a development of the P.13 transport design of 1931, extensively revised with a Pegasus radial as an army co-operation aeroplane. P.23/I to III prototypes were built with a lowered engine, the accommodation revised and the internal bomb stowage altered to underwing racks. The first flew in August 1934, and 40 Karas As with the 433-kW (580-hp) Pegasus II were ordered. These were delivered from June 1936, but problems with the Pegasus II relegated the type to training. The operational model was thus the Karas B, of which 210 were built for service with 14 squadrons. The type was then developed via the P.42 prototype (with endplate vertical surfaces and the Pegasus VIIA) into the P 43 for Bulgaria, which ordered 12 P 43A and 42 P 43B aircraft with the Gnome-Rhone 14K and 14N radials respectively. Most Polish P 23s were destroyed in September 1939.

Specification: PZL P.23 Karas B three-seat light bomber, reconnaissance and army co-operation aeroplane
Span: 13.95 m (45 ft 9.25 in)
Length: 9.70 m (31 ft 9.75 in)
Powerplant: 1×PZL-built Bristol Pegasus VIII, 507 kW (680 hp)
Armament: 3×7.7-mm (0.303-in) machine-guns plus provision for up to 700 kg (1,543 lb) of bombs carried on underwing racks
Max T/O weight: 3525 kg (7,771 lb)
Max speed: 199 mph at 11,975 ft
Operational range: 783 miles

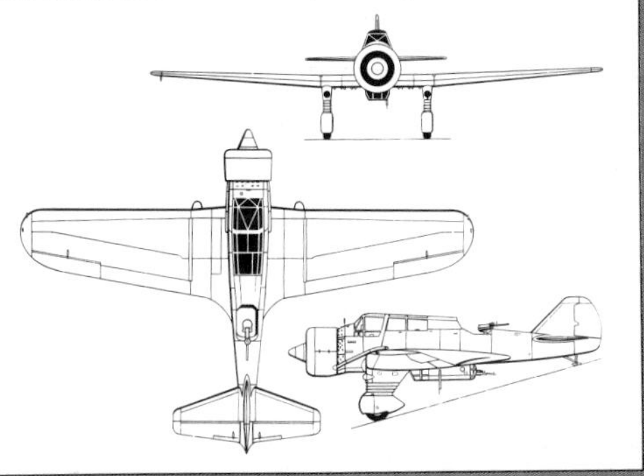

PZL P.37 Los

The Los (elk) was the Polish air force's most important bomber at the beginning of World War II, and indeed the only thoroughly modern Polish warplane. The P.37/I to III prototypes flew from June 1936 with Bristol Pegasus and Gnome-Rhone 14N radials, the former being selected for the Los A initial production model, of which 10 were produced with a single vertical tail before the advent of 20 Los Abis bombers with endplate twin surfaces. In the 60 Los B bombers the Pegasus XIIs were replaced by Pegasus XXs. Uncompleted export variants were the P.37C for Bulgaria and Yugoslavia with the Gnome-Rhone 14N-07, and the P.37D for Romania and Turkey with the Gnome-Rhone 14N-20. Surviving aircraft were flown to Romania at the end of the Polish campaign, and were kept in second-line service up to the 1950s. The P.49 Mis (teddy bear) was planned with greater power and armament.

Specification: PZL P.37 Los B four-seat medium bomber
Span: 17.95 m (58 ft 10.75 in)
Length: 12.92 m (42 ft 4.75 in)
Powerplant: 2×PZL-built Bristol Pegasus XX, 690 kW (920 hp) each
Armament: 3×7.7-mm (0.303-in) machine-guns plus provision for 2580 kg (5,688 lb) of bombs carried internally
Max T/O weight: 8900 kg (19,621 lb)
Max speed: 277 mph at 11,155 ft
Operational range: 932 miles with a 2200-kg (4,850-lb) bombload

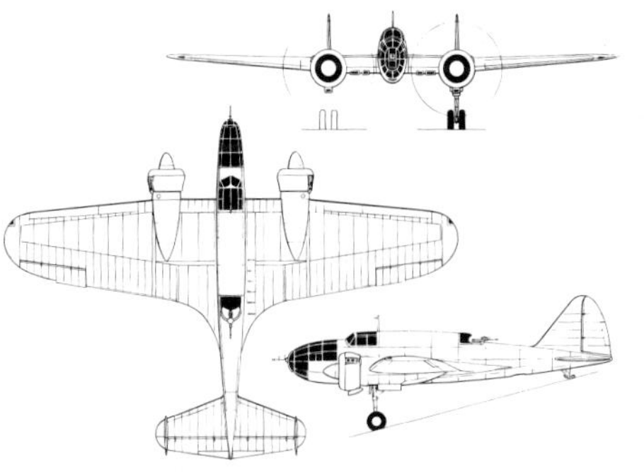

Consolidated Liberator

Specification: Consolidated Liberator GR.Mk VI eight-seat long-range general reconnaissance and anti-submarine aeroplane
Span: 33.53 m (110 ft 0 in)
Length: 20.47 m (67 ft 2 in)
Powerplant: 4×Pratt & Whitney R-1830-43 or -65, 895 kW (1,200 hp) each
Armament: 9×12.7-mm (0.5-in) machine-guns plus provision for 5806 kg (12,800 lb) of bombs (generally much less) carried internally
Max T/O weight: 28123 kg (62,000 lb)
Max speed: 270 mph at 20,000 ft
Operational range: 2,290 miles

The Liberator was designed as a bomber, but its efficient wing and thus its considerable range suggested many alternative roles including deep-ocean general reconnaissance with radar and specialist armament in the hands of a force that eventually totalled 12 Coastal Command squadrons. The UK's first operational variant of the series was the Liberator Mk I equivalent to the B-24A, and this entered Coastal Command service in June 1941 with a ventral gun tray. These 20 aircraft were followed by some of the 139 Mk IIs (B-24Cs) with dorsal and tail turrets, by many of the 260 Mk IIIs (B-24Ds) and similar Mk IVs (B-24Es), and by about half of the 112 Mk Vs (B-24Gs). The most important versions, however, were the GR.Mks VI and VIII modelled on the B-24J with a nose turret. Some 1,668 Mk VI and VIII aircraft were delivered for bomber and maritime use.

Avro Anson

The Anson was a coastal reconnaissance development of the Type 652 light transport with square rather than oval cabin windows, a manually operated Armstrong Whitworth dorsal turret, military equipment and Cheetah VI radials in place of the civil model's Cheetah Vs. The type first flew in March 1935, and entered production as the Anson Mk I with larger cabin windows and a wider tailplane; the intended Cheetah IX radial was not available for production aircraft until 1936, in the March of which year the Anson entered service as the RAF's first monoplane with retractable landing gear. Some 6,704 Mk Is were built, and these were the mainstay of Coastal Command until replaced by Lockheed Hudsons from mid-1940. The Anson served with no fewer than 21 squadrons including seven air/sea rescue units, and was not finally replaced until 1942.

Specification: Avro Anson Mk I three-seat coastal reconnaissance aeroplane
Span: 17.22 m (56 ft 6 in)
Length: 12.87 m (42 ft 3 in)
Powerplant: 2×Armstrong Siddeley Cheetah IX or XIX, 250 or 295 kW (335 or 395 hp) respectively each
Armament: 2×7.7-mm (0.303-in) machine-guns plus provision for up to 163 kg (360 lb) of bombs carried under the wings
Max T/O weight: 3629 kg (8,000 lb)
Max speed: 188 mph at 7,000 ft
Operational range: 660 miles

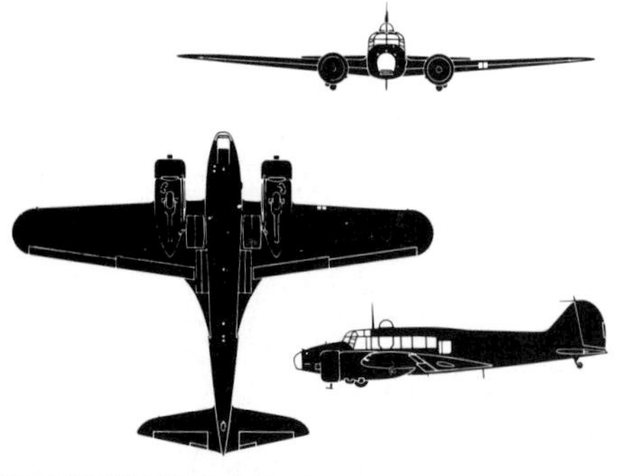

Short Sunderland

The UK's finest flying-boat of World War II, the Sunderland was one of the greatest such aircraft of all time. The type was a military version of the 'C' class Empire type, and when it made its maiden flight in October 1937 it was the first British 'boat with a power-operated defensive turret. The type equipped a maximum of 28 squadrons in a service career that spanned the period from the summer of 1938 to retirement in May 1959. Production totalled 739 including 90 Sunderland Mk Is with 753-kW (1,010-hp) Bristol Pegasus XXIIs and five or seven machine-guns, 43 Sunderland Mk IIs with 794-kW (1,065-hp) Pegasus XVIIIs and a twin-gun dorsal turret instead of the two beam guns, 456 Sunderland Mk IIIs with ASV.Mk III or, in Sunderland Mk IIIA variant, ASV.Mk IIIA radar, and 150 Sunderland Mk Vs with different engines and ASV.Mk VIC radar with antennae in radomes under the wingtips.

Specification: Short Sunderland Mk V 10-seat general-reconnaissance and anti-submarine flying-boat
Span: 34.36 m (112 ft 9.5 in)
Length: 26.01 m (85 ft 4 in)
Powerplant: 4×Pratt & Whitney R-1830 Twin Wasp, 895 kW (1,200 hp) each
Armament: 2×12.7-mm (0.5-in) and 10×7.7-mm (0.303-in) machine-guns plus provision for up to 2250 kg (4,960 lb) of bombs carried internally
Max T/O weight: 29482 kg (65,000 lb)
Max speed: 213 mph at 5,000 ft
Operational range: 2,980 miles

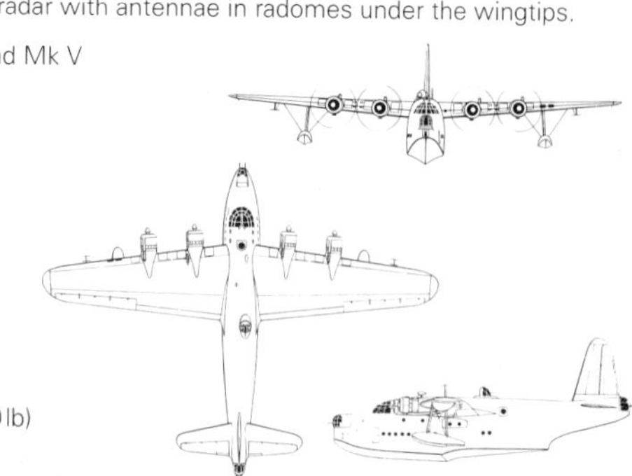

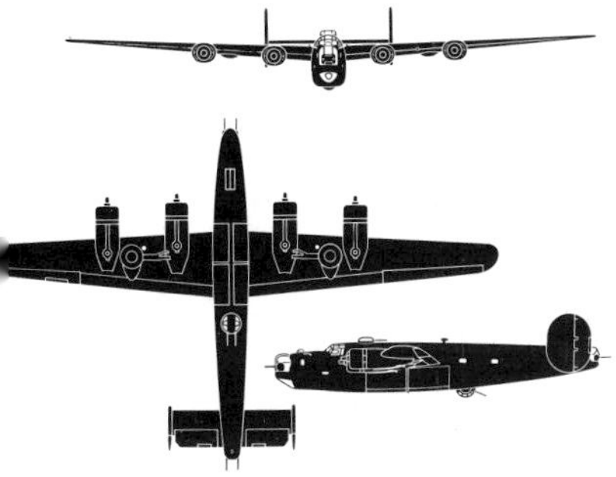

A Consolidated B-24J Liberator GR.Mk VII of Coastal Command proudly wears the white and grey-green camouflage common to British maritime patrol aircraft during the latter half of the war. Heavily armed and possessing long range, the Liberators helped the Allies to take and maintain control of the vital sea-lanes.

Lockheed Hudson and Ventura

The Hudson was developed from the Model 14 Super Electra civil transport to meet a British requirement for a general-reconnaissance aeroplane, and first flew in December 1938. The type proved an invaluable replacement for the Anson in 17 Coastal Command squadrons, and eventually some 2,000 were delivered in variants up to the Hudson Mk VI. By 1944 most first-line Hudson squadrons had re-equipped with more-modern aircraft including the Ventura, as the similarly militarised version of the Model 18 Lodestar civil transport was known. This was again produced to a requirement of the British, who took 640 aircraft. The Coastal Command variants were the Ventura GR.Mks I and V, the latter being the designation for Lend-Lease PV-1 Harpoons, and these served with only two Coastal Command home-based squadrons mainly for meteorological purposes rather than anti-submarine warfare.

Specification: Lockheed Ventura GR.Mk V four/five-seat general-reconnaissance aeroplane
Span: 19.96 m (65 ft 6 in)
Length: 15.77 m (51 ft 9 in)
Powerplant: 2×Pratt & Whitney R-2800-31 Double Wasp, 1491 kW (2,000 hp) each
Armament: 4×12.7-mm (0.5-in) and 2×7.7-mm (0.303-in) machine-guns plus provision for bombs or torpedoes
Max T/O weight: 14097 kg (31,077 lb)
Max speed: 296 mph at sea level
Operational range: 1,660 miles

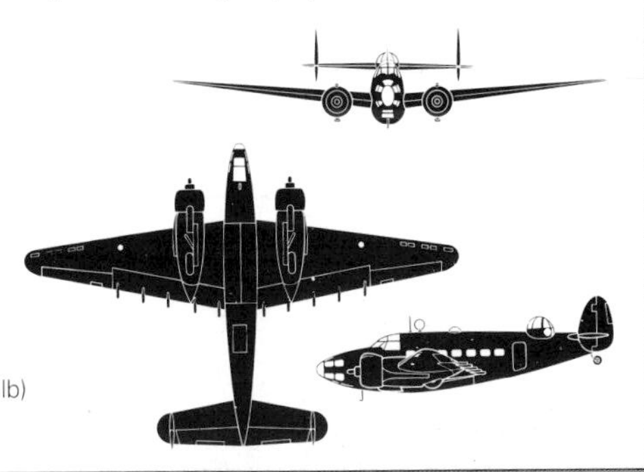

Blackburn Botha

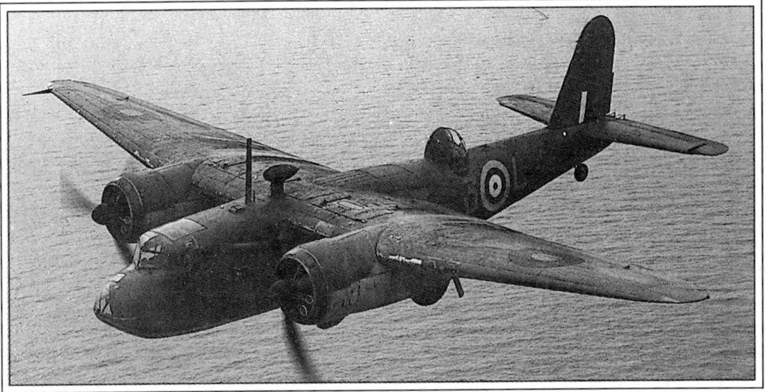

The Botha was schemed as a torpedo-bomber and general reconnaissance aeroplane and, ordered 'off the drawing board' in 1936, it entered service in the period of the RAF's greatest expansion just before the outbreak of World War II. The first of two prototypes flew in December 1938, the first Botha Mk I production aeroplane following in July 1939. Some 580 aircraft were built, and the first operational unit was No.608 Squadron of the Auxiliary Air Force, which began to receive its aircraft in May 1940. Operational use confirmed that the Botha was drastically underpowered as well as possessing other shortcomings, and the only other Coastal Command unit equipped with the type was No.502 Squadron. The type was withdrawn from first-line service in November 1940, thereafter serving into 1944 as a trainer in a variety of specialist schools.

Specification: Blackburn Botha Mk I four-seat torpedo-bomber and general reconnaissance aeroplane
Span: 17.98 m (59 ft 0 in)
Length: 15.56 m (51 ft 0.5 in)
Powerplant: 2×Bristol Perseus X or XA, 676 or 693 kW (880 or 930 hp) respectively each
Armament: 3×7.7-mm (0.303-in) machine-guns plus provision for 1×Mk XII or Mk XIV torpedo or up to 907 kg (2,000 lb) of bombs carried internally
Max T/O weight: 8369 kg (18,450 lb)
Max speed: 253 mph at 15,000 ft
Operational range: 1,270 miles

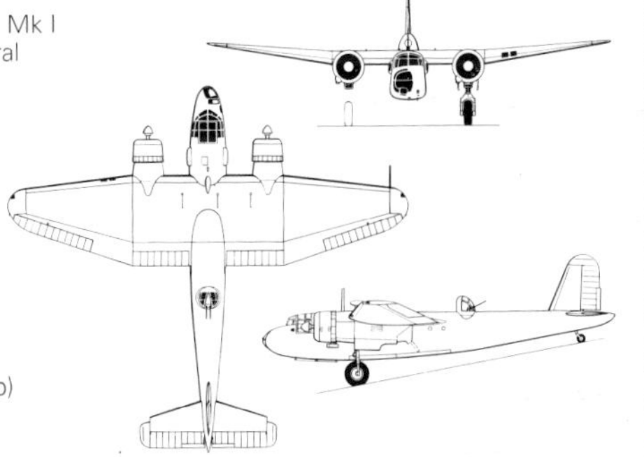

Vickers Warwick

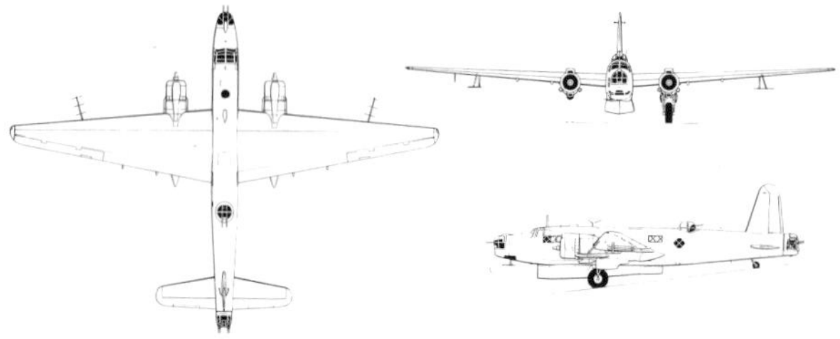

Vickers Warwick GR.Mk V of No. 179 Sqn. This maritime patrol dedicated squadron operated out of RAF St Eval during late 1944. Warwicks of No. 179 Sqn spent countless hours patrolling the Western approaches of the Atlantic and the Bay of Biscay in search of the German U-boat menace.

The Warwick was designed as successor to the Wellington bomber. The prototype flew in August 1939 with Rolls-Royce Vulture inlines, changed to Bristol Centaurus radials in the second prototype. Shortages of the Centaurus meant that the production version used 1379-kW (1,850-hp) Pratt & Whitney R-2800 radials, and performance was so inadequate for a bomber that the type was deployed from the summer of 1943 as four subvariants of the Warwick ASR.Mk I carrying an air-dropped lifeboat. The 275 aircraft equipped an eventual total of nine home, five Mediterranean and one Far East air/sea rescue squadrons that also used the 132 Warwick GR.Mk IIs with 1864-kW (2,500-hp) Centaurus VI. The only version that was used for the general-reconnaissance role was thus the Warwick GR.Mk V, of which 210 were built with a Leigh light and undernose radar for post-war service with three squadrons.

Armstrong Whitworth Whitley

The Whitley was one of Bomber Command's most important aircraft in the period leading up to World War II, but so pressing were the needs of Coastal Command for a long-range maritime reconnaissance aircraft that No.58 Squadron and its standard bombers were transferred to Coastal Command in September 1939. Other Whitley Mk Vs were used to replace Avro Ansons from the autumn of 1940, but by the end of 1941 Coastal Command began to receive the Whitley GR.Mk VII, a dedicated general reconnaissance type with ASV.Mk II surface-search radar and specialist weapons. Production of this variant totalled 146 aircraft, and these equipped Nos 58, 77, 502 and 612 Squadrons. Such an aeroplane of No.502 scored Coastal Command's first radar-aided 'kill' of a U-boat in November 1941. By July 1943 the Whitley GR.Mk VI had been supplanted by more advanced aircraft.

Specification: Armstrong Whitworth Whitley GR.Mk VII five-seat general reconnaissance aeroplane
Span: 25.60 m (84 ft 0 in)
Length: 21.11 m (69 ft 3 in)
Powerplant: 2×Rolls-Royce Merlin X, 854 kW (1,150 hp) each
Armament: 5×7.7-mm (0.303-in) machine-guns plus provision for up to 3175 kg (7,000 lb) of bombs (generally much less) carried internally
Max T/O weight: 15400 kg (33,390 lb)
Max speed: 215 mph at 16,400 ft
Operational range: 2,300 miles

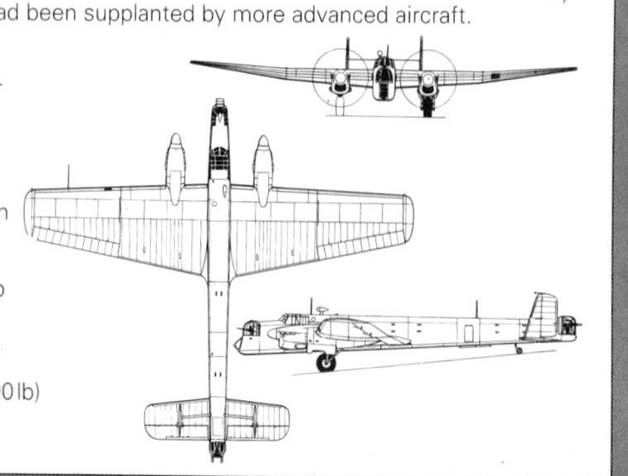

Bristol Beaufort

This was Coastal Command's most important torpedo-bomber between 1940 and 1940, and first flew in October 1938 as a moderately close relative of the Blenheim light bomber. Production of the Beaufort Mk I totalled 965, initially with the 753-kW (1,010-hp) Taurus II radials but later with 843-kW (1,130-hp) Taurus VIs, revised and additional armament and, in some aircraft, surface-search radar. The next variant was the Beaufort Mk IIs (including 12 turretless trainers) with the 843-kW (1,130-hp) Taurus VI, XII and XVI, but only 164 of these aircraft were produced before the line reverted to the Mk I up to the end of production in 1944. The Beaufort entered generally undistinguished service in January 1940, and was retired in 1944 after service with six Coastal Command squadrons for home service, as well as with four Middle Eastern squadrons.

Specification: Bristol Beaufort Mk II four-seat torpedo-bomber
Span: 17.62 m (57 ft 10 in)
Length: 13.49 m (44 ft 3 in)
Powerplant: 2×Bristol Taurus VI, XII or XVI, 843 kW (1,130 hp) each
Armament: 6 or 9×7.7-mm (0.303-in) machine-guns plus provision for 1×728-kg (1,605-lb) torpedo carried semi-internally or up to 680 kg (1,500 lb) of bombs carried internally
Max T/O weight: 9630 kg (21,230 lb)
Max speed: 265 mph at 6,000 ft
Operational range: 1,600 miles

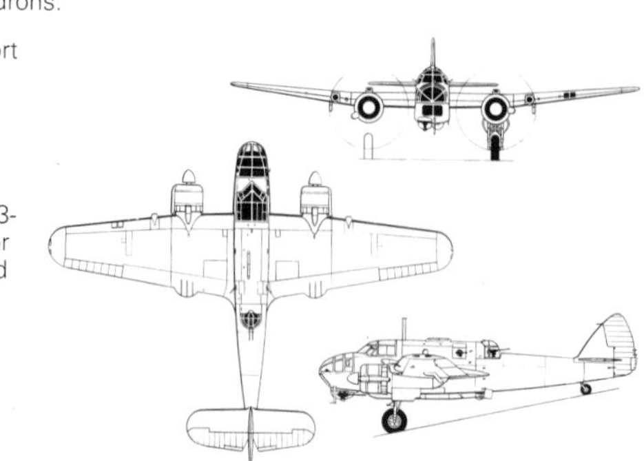

pecification: Vickers
Varwick GR.Mk V six-seat general
econnaissance aeroplane
pan: 29.47 m (96 ft 8.5 in)
ength: 21.49 m (70 ft 6 in)
owerplant: 2×Bristol Centaurus
'II, 1879 kW (2,520 hp) each
rmament: 7×12.7-mm (0.5-in)
nachine-guns plus provision for
07 kg (2,000 lb) of bombs carried
nternally
Aax T/O weight: 22680 kg
50,000 lb)
Aax speed: 290 mph at 2,000 ft
)perational range: 3,050 miles

Saro Lerwick

The Lerwick was the second monoplane flying-boat ordered for the RAF, and was an all-metal type of advanced concept designed as the medium-range counterpart of the long-range Short Sunderland. The first of three prototypes flew in 1938, and full production amounted to only 18 aircraft which were delivered between 1939 and May 1941. The type served only with No.4 Operational Training Unit and No.209 Squadron, the latter flying the Lerwick between December 1939 and May 1941 as a replacement for the Short Singapore Mk III. But the Lerwick was itself replaced after only a short career by the altogether more effective Catalina. There was little wrong with the Lerwick's outright performance and good armament, but as an aeroplane the type had handling deficiencies including lateral instability and tricky stalling. In 1942 the type was declared obsolete after several accidents.

Specification: Saro Lerwick six-seat general-reconnaissance flying-boat
Span: 24.63 m (80 ft 10 in)
Length: 19.39 m (63 ft 7.5 in)
Powerplant: 2×Bristol Hercules II, 1120 kW (1,375 hp) each
Armament: 7×7.7-mm (0.303-in) machine-guns plus provision for up to 907 kg (2,000 lb) of bombs carried under the wings
Max T/O weight: 15060 kg (33,200 lb)
Max speed: 216 mph at 4,000 ft
Operational range: not known

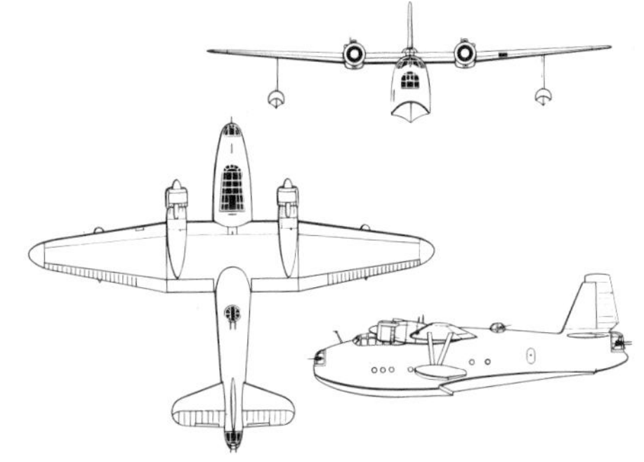

Bristol Beaufighter

The Beaufighter was developed as a long-range fighter and first flew in July 1939. The type came to prominence as a night-fighter, but was more important as an anti-shipping fighter. The first such variant was the Beaufighter Mk IC, of which 397 were built for service from March 1941 with 1186-kW (1,590-hp) Hercules VIs. Next came the torpedo-carrying Mk VIC with 1193-kW (1,600-hp) Hercules VIs, and these 693 aircraft were bolstered by 60 Mk VI (ITF)s with eight underwing rockets in place of the six wing machine-guns. These were followed by the definitive TF.Mk X based on the Mk VIC but with more power and AI.Mk VII rather than Mk VI radar in a thimble nose. The 60 Mk VI (ITF)s were thus converted, and 2,205 were built. The last 163 aircraft were torpedo-less Mk XICs. The Beaufighter served with 14 Coastal Command squadrons, and extensively with overseas squadrons.

Specification: Bristol Beaufighter TF.Mk X two/three-seat anti-shipping strike fighter
Span: 17.63 m (57 ft 10 in)
Length: 12.70 m (41 ft 8 in)
Powerplant: 2×Bristol Hercules XVII, 1320 kW (1,770 hp) each
Armament: 4×20-mm cannon and 1×7.7-mm (0.303-in) machine-gun plus provision for 1×748- or 965-kg (1,650- or 2,127-lb) torpedo plus 2×113-kg (250-lb) bombs or 8×41-kg (90-lb) rockets carried under the wings
Max T/O weight: 11521 kg (25,400 lb)
Max speed: 303 mph at 13,000 ft
Operational range: 1,470 miles

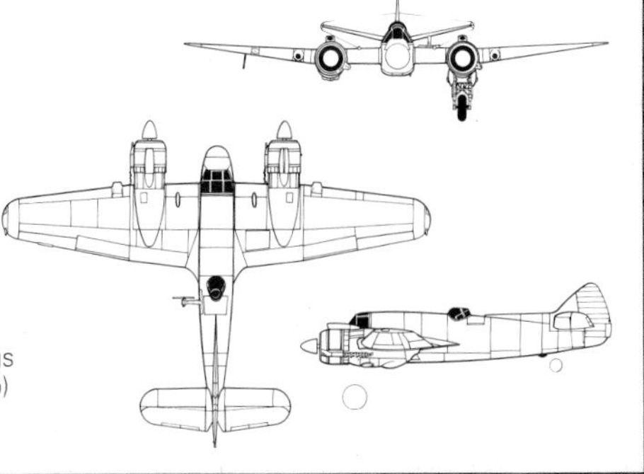

Consolidated Catalina

The success of the PBY in US service prompted the British into an evaluation of the type. In 1939 the PBY-5 variant was ordered as the Catalina Mk I, and this started to enter service in 1941. The type was just as effective in British service, and large-scale orders (including Lend-Lease deliveries) followed for service with Coastal Command. The 91 Mk Is were followed by 223 improved Catalina Mk IBs, seven Catalina Mk IIs (PBY-5s built by the Naval Aircraft Factory), 36 Catalina Mk IIAs transferred from the Royal Canadian Air Force, 11 Catalina Mk III amphibians, 97 Catalina Mk IVAs in the general reconnaissance role, and 190 Catalina Mk IVB Canadian-built PB2B-2 'boats used mainly in the air/sea rescue role. The Catalina was used by 24 RAF squadrons, nine of them home-based Coastal Command units.

Specification: Consolidated Catalina Mk IB eight/nine-seat general reconnaissance flying-boat
Span: 31.70 m (104 ft 0 in)
Length: 19.86 m (65 ft 1.75 in)
Powerplant: 2×Pratt & Whitney R-1830-S1C3-G Twin Wasp, 895 kW (1,200 hp) each
Armament: 6×7.7-mm (0.303-in) machine-guns plus provision for up to 907 kg (2,000 lb) of bombs carried under the wings
Max T/O weight: 12283 kg (27,080 lb)
Max speed: 190 mph at 10,500 ft
Operational range: 4,000 miles

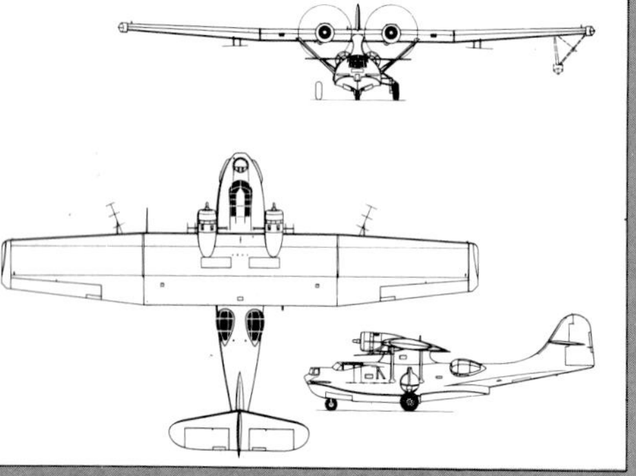

Vickers Wellington

In the spring of 1942 the ubiquitous Wellington began to appear in Coastal Command service in the form of the Wellington GR.Mk VIII, a development of the Wellington Mk IC with ASV.Mk II radar: subvariants of the 394 aircraft were the day torpedo and level bomber, and the night attack version with a Leigh light. There followed 180 ASV.Mk II or III-equipped Wellington GR.Mk XI day aircraft based on the Wellington Mk X with 1249-kW (1,675-hp) Hercules VI or XVI radials, 58 Wellington GR.Mk XII nocturnal anti-submarine aircraft with ASV.Mk III radar and a Leigh light, 844 Wellington GR.Mk XIII day torpedo-bombers with ASV.Mk II and 1294-kW (1,735-hp) Hercules XVIIs, and 841 Wellington GR.Mk XIV nocturnal version of the Mk XIII with ASV.Mk III and a Leigh light. A total of 14 Coastal Command squadrons flew the Wellington, which remained in service until the end of the war.

Specification: Vickers Wellington GR.Mk VIII six/seven-seat torpedo-bomber and general reconnaissance aeroplane
Span: 26.26 m (86 ft 2 in)
Length: 19.68 m (64 ft 7 in)
Powerplant: 2×Bristol Pegasus XVIII, 783 kW (1,050 hp) each
Armament: 6×7.7-mm (0.303-in) machine-guns plus provision for 2×191-kg (420-lb) depth charges or 2×torpedoes carried internally
Max T/O weight: 13080 kg (30,000 lb)
Max speed: 235 mph at 15,500 ft
Operational range: 2,550 miles

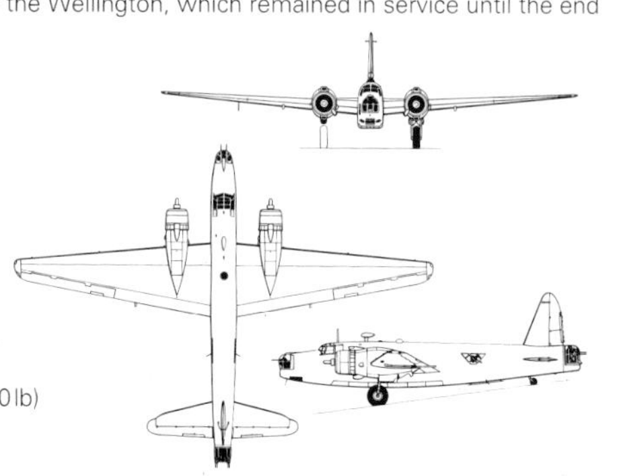

Boeing Fortress

The UK was an early recipient of the B-17 bomber, the USA wishing amongst other things to see how it performed in combat. A total of 20 B-17Cs was delivered from spring 1941, and after a poor time of it as bombers the survivors of these Fortress Mk Is were allocated in October 1942 to Coastal Command's Nos 206 and 220 Squadrons. From mid-1942 the Fortress Mk Is were replaced by 45 examples of the Fortress Mk IIA (B-17E) with improved armament and 19 examples of the Fortress Mk II (B-17F) with operational improvements and further improved armament. These aircraft served with Nos 59, 86, 206 and 220 Squadrons on operations designed to close the mid-Atlantic 'gap' where convoys received only limited air cover from Liberators and now these long-range Fortresses. The Fortress Mks II and IIA also served with four meteorological squadrons.

Specification: Boeing Fortress Mk II 10-seat long-range general reconnaissance aeroplane
Span: 31.63 m (103 ft 9.5 in)
Length: 22.78 m (74 ft 9 in)
Powerplant: 4×Wright R-1820-97, 895 kW (1,200 hp) each
Armament: 1×7.62-mm (0.3-in) and 12×12.7-mm (0.5-in) machine-guns plus provision for up to 7983 kg (17,600 lb) of bombs (generally very much less) carried internally
Max T/O weight: 32660 kg (72,000 lb)
Max speed: 325 mph at 25,000 ft
Operational range: 4,420 miles

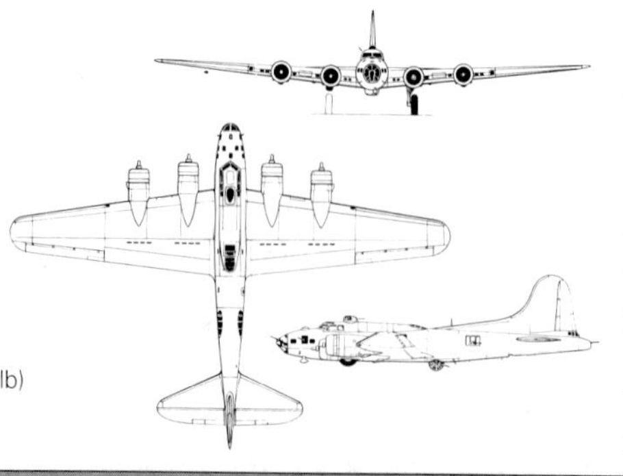

de Havilland Mosquito

After the success of the Mosquito NF.Mk II in the night intruder role it was decided to produce a specialist fighter-bomber version, and this emerged as the Mosquito FB.Mk VI prototype for a first flight in February 1943. The standard armament of four cannon and four machine-guns was complemented in Series 1 aircraft by two internal and two external 113-kg (250-lb) bombs, increased in Series 2 aircraft to four 227-kg (500-lb) bombs. Early aircraft had 1089-kW (1,460-hp) Merlin 21 or 23 engines, while aircraft from later in the 2,718-machine production run had Merlin 25s. The type entered Fighter and Coastal Command service respectively in May 1943 and February 1944, and equipped seven Coastal Command squadrons. From October 1943 there were also 25 Mosquito FB.Mk XVIIIs for Coastal Command with a 57-mm gun in place of the cannon, and provision for underwing rockets.

Specification: de Havilland Mosquito FB.Mk VI Series 2 two-seat fighter-bomber and anti-shipping strike fighter
Span: 16.51 m (54 ft 2 in)
Length: 12.34 m (40 ft 6 in)
Powerplant: 2×Rolls-Royce Merlin 25, 1219 kW (1,650 hp) each
Armament: 4×20-mm cannon and 4×7.7-mm (0.303-in) machine-guns plus provision for 2×227-kg (500-lb) bombs carried internally and 2×227-kg (500-lb) bombs or 8×27-kg (60-lb) rockets carried under the wings
Max T/O weight: 10096 kg (22,258 lb)
Max speed: 380 mph at 13,000 ft
Operational range: 1,885 miles

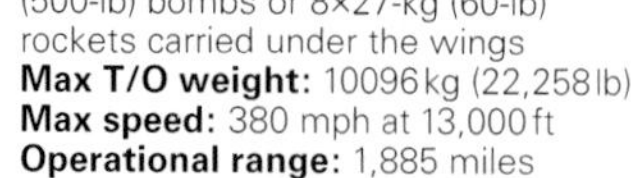

Lockheed Ventura

To supplant and then replace the Hudson the Royal Australian Air Force opted for the logical successor, the Ventura from the same company with greater power, a heavier warload and usefully improved all-round performance. In May 1943 the service received the first of 20 Ventura Mk IIA aircraft, Lend-Lease machines built as USAAF B-34 Lexingtons. The aircraft were allocated mostly to Nos 4 and 11 Communications Units in a neat regression to the Ventura's origins as the Model 18 Lodestar transport. A more belligerent role was entrusted to the 55 PV-1s diverted from US Navy procurement. These were used mainly in New Guinea by No.13 Squadron until replaced by Beauforts from the Australian production line. The Ventura and PV-1s remained in service into 1947, and were then stored or broken down for components, the last aircraft being sold in 1953.

Specification: Lockheed PV-1 Ventura four/five-seat maritime patrol bomber
Span: 19.96 m (65 ft 6 in)
Length: 15.77 m (51 ft 9 in)
Powerplant: 2×Pratt & Whitney R-2800-31, 1491 kW (2,000 hp) each
Armament: 4×12.7-mm (0.5-in) and 2×7.7-mm (0.303-in) machine-guns plus provision for up to 1361 kg (3,000 lb) of bombs or torpedoes carried internally and 907 kg (2,000 lb) of bombs carried under the wings
Max T/O weight: 14097 kg (31,077 lb)
Max speed: 322 mph at 13,800 ft
Operational range: 1,660 miles

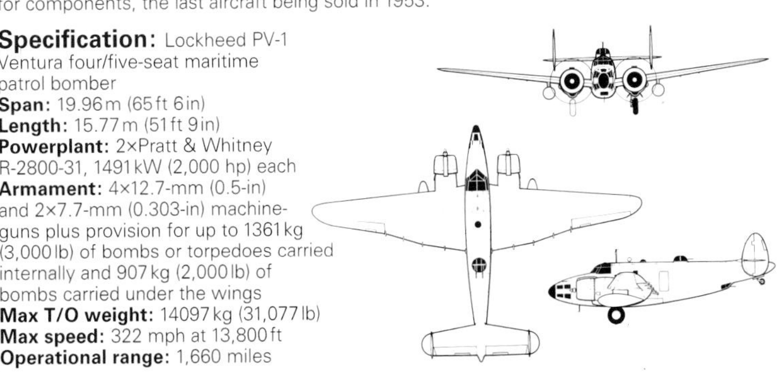

de Havilland Australia Mosquito

Although other variants of the Mosquito were used by Australian bomber and photo-reconnaissance units serving mainly with the RAF, the Mosquito variant associated particularly with the Royal Australian Air Force is the Mosquito FB.Mk 40 produced at DHA's new factory at Bankstown near Sydney. Local knowledge of the type started with the reassembly of a Mosquito Mk II shipped out in June 1942, but the FB.Mk 40 was essentially the Australian version of the FB.Mk VI fighter-bomber. The first such aeroplane flew only in July 1943 because of the difficulties in obtaining special parts from the UK, and service deliveries were then slowed by gluing problems. The first 100 aircraft had Packard Merlin 31 engines, subsequent machines using the Merlin 33. Wartime production amounted to 178 aircraft, post-war deliveries adding another 34 aircraft by 1948.

Specification: de Havilland Australia Mosquito FB.Mk 40 two-seat fighter bomber
Span: 16.51 m (54 ft 2 in)
Length: 12.34 m (40 ft 6 in)
Powerplant: 2×Packard Merlin 33, 1219 kW (1,635 hp) each
Armament: 4×20-mm cannon and 4×7.7-mm (0.303-in) machine-guns plus provision for 907 kg (2,000 lb) of bombs carried internally or externally, or 454 kg (1,000 lb) of bombs carried internally and 8×27-kg (60-lb) rockets carried under the wings
Max T/O weight: 10096 kg (22,058 lb)
Max speed: 380 mph at 13,000 ft
Operational range: 1,885 miles

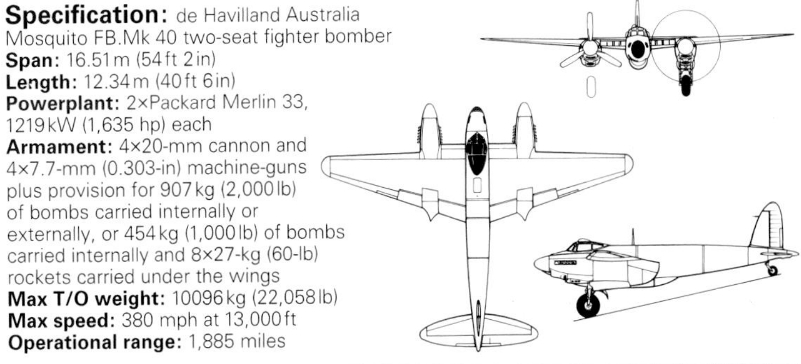

CAC CA-4 Woomera

The Woomera (an Aboriginal word for spear-thrower) was designed to succeed the Bristol Beaufort in the torpedo bomber role, and first flew in September 1941 with twin-wheel main landing gear units, accommodation for small bombs in the engine nacelles, and remotely controlled barbettes, each with two 7.7-mm (0.303-in) machine-guns, in the rear of each nacelle for rearward defence. The CA-4 prototype revealed a number of problems, but an order was placed for 20 CA-11 production aircraft with a wider-chord centre section, increased dihedral on the outer wing panels, a larger tail unit and more extensive canopy glazing. The first CA-11 was flown in July 1944, but with a second aeroplane almost complete the project was cancelled in favour of increased procurement of readily available American medium bombers.

Specification: Commonwealth Aircraft Corporation CA-11 Woomera three-seat bomber and reconnaissance aeroplane
Span: 18.05 m (59 ft 2.5 in)
Length: 12.06 m (39 ft 7 in)
Powerplant: 2×Pratt & Whitney R-1830-S3C3-G, 895 kW (1,200 hp) each
Armament: 2×20-mm cannon and 7×7.7-mm (0.303-in) machine-guns plus provision for 2×533-mm (21-in) torpedoes or up to 1452 kg (3,200 lb) of bombs carried internally and externally
Max T/O weight: 10380 kg (22,885 lb)
Max speed: 282 mph at optimum altitude
Operational range: 2,225 miles

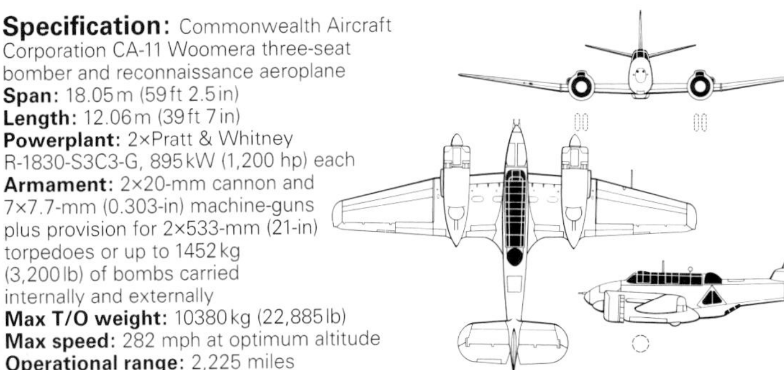

CAC CA-15

This was the most advanced aeroplane developed in Australia in World War II, and was a response to a 1942 requirement for a high-performance fighter with exceptional range. The type was conceived as a low-wing monoplane resembling the North American Mustang but powered by a 1491-kW (2,000-hp) Pratt & Whitney R-2800-10W radial engine with an additional 224 kW (300 hp) available for combat through use of a water injection system. With the design well advanced it was learned that R-2800 engines might not be available, and the aeroplane was recast with the Rolls-Royce Griffon inline. This seriously delayed the programme, and it was March 1946 before the CA-15 prototype first flew. Extensive trials were undertaken, but with licensed Mustangs in production and jet fighters about to be procured the type was not seriously considered for service.

Specification: Commonwealth Aircraft Corporation CA-15 single-seat fighter and fighter-bomber
Span: 10.95 m (36 ft 0 in)
Length: 11.04 m (36 ft 2.5 in)
Powerplant: 1×Rolls-Royce Griffon 61, 1719 kW (2,305 hp)
Armament: 6×12.7-mm (0.5-in) machine-guns plus provision for 2×454-kg (1,000-lb) bombs or 10×rockets carried under the wings
Max T/O weight: 5597 kg (12,340 lb)
Max speed: 448 mph at 26,400 ft
Operational range: 2,540 miles

CAC CA-1 Wirraway

The Wirraway (an Aboriginal word for challenge) was the Australian licence-built NA-33 version of the North American NA-16 general-purpose and training monoplane with a strengthened wing and tail plus provision for heavier armament. The first of 40 CA-1s flew in March 1939, and up to the end of production in 1946 755 aircraft were built. Later variants were the CA-3 (60 aircraft), CA-5 (32), CA-7 (100), CA-8 (20), CA-9 (188) and CA-16 (135) each with detail modifications. Two variants that failed to materialise were the CA-10 bomber and CA-10A dive-bomber. The type was used mostly for training, but in the period up to mid-1943 the lack of more advanced aircraft meant that the Wirraway was also used for first-line duties by Nos 4, 5, 12, 22, 23, 24 and 245 Squadrons for convoy escort in the waters off northern Australia, and for army co-operation and tactical reconnaissance in the New Guinea campaign.

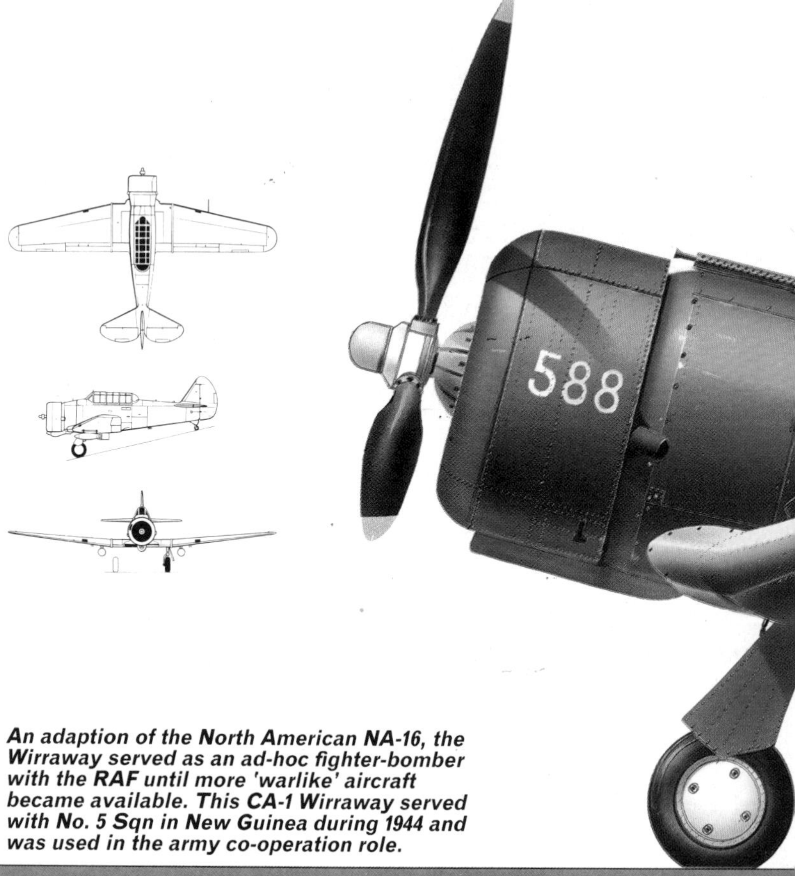

An adaption of the North American NA-16, the Wirraway served as an ad-hoc fighter-bomber with the RAF until more 'warlike' aircraft became available. This CA-1 Wirraway served with No. 5 Sqn in New Guinea during 1944 and was used in the army co-operation role.

Consolidated Catalina

In common with several other Allied nations, Australia relied on the Catalina as its main maritime patrol bomber. The type was originally ordered in 1940 to the extent of just 18 aircraft, the Americans specifying that the aircraft should not become Australian property until they reached Hawaii on a long transpacific delivery route in the hands of Qantas pilots. The Catalina was operated by Nos 11, 20, 42 and 43 Squadrons from bases in Queensland for a wide assortment of operational roles, and the Royal Australian Air Force eventually received 169 aircraft mainly of the Catalina Mks I and VI corresponding to the PBY-5 and Canadian Boeing PB2N-2 variants, the latter with the revised tail of the NAF PBN-1 Nomad. The type was phased out of service shortly after the end of World War II, and by late 1946 the RAAF's last Catalina unit had been disbanded.

Specification: Consolidated Catalina Mk I seven/nine-seat maritime patrol and bomber flying-boat
Span: 31.70 m (104 ft 0 in)
Length: 19.45 m (63 ft 10 in)
Powerplant: 2×Pratt & Whitney R-1830-82, 895 kW (1,200 hp) each
Armament: 2×12.7-mm (0.5-in) and 2×7.7-mm (0.303-in) machine-guns plus provision for 2×533-mm (21-in) torpedoes or 4×454-kg (1,000-lb) bombs carried under the wings
Max T/O weight: 15145 kg (33,389 lb)
Max speed: 200 mph at 5,700 ft
Operational range: 1,895 miles

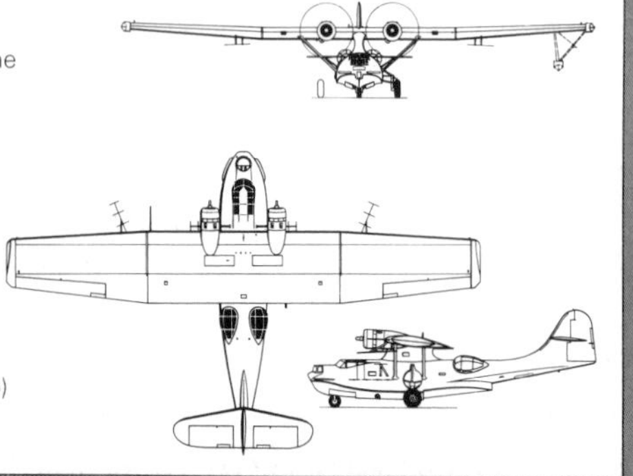

Lockheed Hudson

The Royal Australian Air Force decided to buy the Hudson shortly after the RAF had ordered the type, and kicked off with a 1938 contract for 50 Hudson Mk Is similar to the British Hudson Mk IVs, and these were delivered from February 1940. The next Australian variant was again similar to the British Hudson Mk IV but in this instance designated Hudson Mk II: these 50 aircraft were supplemented by 96 Hudson Mk IIIAs diverted from British Lend-Lease supplies, and by 52 Hudson Mk IVAs built as USAAF A-28s. The aircraft were allocated to Nos 1, 2, 6, 7, 8, 13, 14, 23, 24, 25 and 32 Squadrons as well as to Nos 1, 3, 4 and 6 Communications Units, No. 1 OTO and a few lesser units. The type remained in RAAF service until 1949, but was phased out of first-line service as a bomber in autumn 1943 and as a maritime patroller in spring 1944.

Specification: Lockheed Hudson Mk I four-seat light bomber and maritime patrol aeroplane
Span: 19.96 m (65 ft 6 in)
Length: 13.51 m (44 ft 4 in)
Powerplant: 2×Pratt & Whitney R-1830-SC3G, 783 kW (1,050 hp) each
Armament: 3 or 5×7.7-mm (0.303-in) machine-guns plus provision for up to 726 kg (1,600 lb) of bombs carried internally
Max T/O weight: 10142 kg (22,360 lb)
Max speed: 284 mph at 15,000 ft
Operational range: 2,160 miles

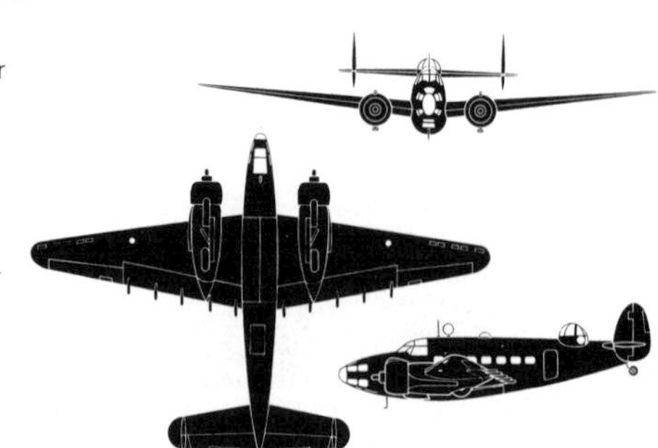

Specification: Commonwealth Aircraft Corporation CA-1 Wirraway two-seat trainer and general-purpose aeroplane
Span: 13.11 m (43 ft 0 in)
Length: 8.48 m (27 ft 10 in)
Powerplant: 1×CAC-built Pratt & Whitney R-1340-S1H1-G, 447 kW (600 hp)
Armament: 3×7.7-mm (0.303-in) machine-guns plus provision for up to 454 kg (1,000 lb) of bombs carried under the wings
Max T/O weight: 2991 kg (6,595 lb)
Max speed: 220 mph at 5,000 ft
Operational range: 720 miles

DAP (Bristol) Beaufort

The Beaufort was ordered for licensed production in July 1939 to provide the Royal Australian Air Force with a modern torpedo-bomber. New factories were created at Fishermen's Bend near Melbourne and at Mascot near Sydney to assemble aircraft from subassemblies built at three other factories from components produced by a host of smaller companies. The first Australian Beaufort flew in August 1941, and production totalled 700 aircraft. The first model was the Beaufort Mk V with 895-kW (1,200-hp) R-1830-S3C4-G radials, and these 90 aircraft were followed by 30 Beaufort Mk VAs with a larger fin, 40 Beaufort Mk VIs with Curtiss propellers, 60 Beaufort Mk VIIs with Hamilton Standard propellers and a larger fin, and 520 Beaufort Mk VIIIs with a Bristol dorsal turret. Some 46 of this last variant were later modified as Beaufort Mk IX transports

Specification: Department of Aircraft Production (Bristol) Beaufort Mk VIII four-seat torpedo-bomber and reconnaissance aeroplane
Span: 17.62 m (57 ft 10 in)
Length: 13.49 m (44 ft 3 in)
Powerplant: 2×CAC-built Pratt & Whitney R-1830-S3C4-G, 895 kW (1,200 hp) each
Armament: 4×7.7-mm (0.303-in) machine-guns or 2×12.7-mm (0.5-in) and 2×7.7-mm machine-guns plus provision for 1×533-mm (21-in) torpedo carried semi-internally or 680 kg (1,500 lb) of bombs carried internally and externally
Max T/O weight: 10206 kg (22,500 lb)
Max speed: 268 mph at 14,500 ft
Operational range: 1,450 miles

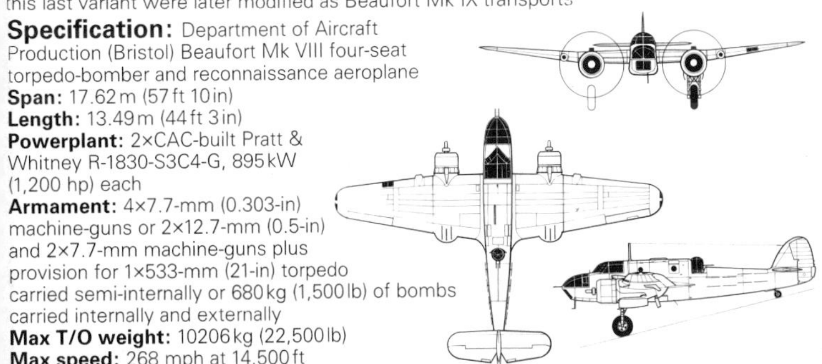

Consolidated Liberator

The Liberator's high aspect ratio wing conferred excellent range, and this was a potent incentive to the type's use in the Pacific theatre, where Japanese targets could often be attacked only at long range after overwater flights. The Royal Australian Air Force's first aircraft of this type were 12 Liberator IIIs broadly equivalent to the USAAF's B-24D with a glazed but turretless nose. Far more important for the bombing and maritime patrol roles, however, were the 275 examples received of the Liberator Mk VI, essentially the Lend-Lease version of the definitive B-24J with R-1830-65 rather than R-1830-43 radials, an autopilot and a nose turret. The type served with four RAAF bomber squadrons in the Pacific theatre, and some aircraft were modified to a standard comparable with the RAF's Liberator GR.Mk VIII for maritime patrol.

Specification: Consolidated Liberator Mk VI eight/twelve-seat heavy bomber
Span: 33.53 m (110 ft 0 in)
Length: 20.47 m (67 ft 2 in)
Powerplant: 4×Pratt & Whitney R-1830-65, 895 kW (1,200 hp) each
Armament: 10×12.7-mm (0.5-in) machine-guns plus provision for up to 3992 kg (8,800 lb) of bombs carried internally
Max T/O weight: 29484 kg (65,000 lb)
Max speed: 300 mph at 30,000 ft
Operational range: 2,100 miles

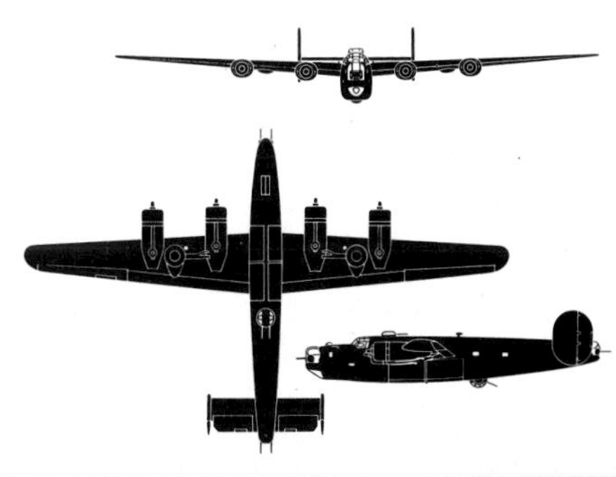

CAC CA-12 Boomerang

Specification:
Commonwealth Aircraft Corporation CA-13 Boomerang Mk II single-seat fighter and army co-operation aeroplane
Span: 10.97 m (36 ft 0 in)
Length: 7.77 m (25 ft 6 in)
Powerplant: 1×Pratt & Whitney R-1830-S3C4-G, 895 kW (1,200 hp)
Armament: 2×20-mm cannon and 4×7.7-mm (0.303-in) machine-guns plus provision for 4×9-kg (20-lb) smoke bombs carried under the wings
Max T/O weight: 3742 kg (8,249 lb)
Max speed: 305 mph at 15,500 ft
Operational range: 1,600 miles

In December 1941 its lack of a modern fighter was a profound problem for the RAAF, but an interim solution was found by combining the flying surfaces and landing gear of the Wirraway with a new fuselage and more powerful engine to produce a fast-climbing fighter. The prototype flew in May 1942, and the first 105 Boomerang Mk Is were completed by June 1943. There followed 95 examples of the CA-13 with minor improvements, and these entered service with the name Boomerang Mk II. The CA-14 with a turbocharger did not get past the prototype stage, so the last production series, also designated Boomerang Mk II by the RAAF but produced as the CA-19, was built up to February 1945 with slight improvements and, in some cases, a reconnaissance camera. These 49 aircraft completed a run of 250 aircraft that were used as fighters and then as army co-operation aircraft by Nos 4, 5, 83, 84 and 85 Squadrons.

Curtiss Kittyhawk

In common with New Zealand, Australia made very extensive use of the Kittyhawk series in the hands of Nos 75, 76, 77, 78, 80, 82, 84 and 86 Squadrons for the ground-attack role against the Japanese. The aircraft were supplied under the terms of the Lend-Lease Act, and began with diversion of 163 examples of the Kittyhawk Mk IA that were to have gone to the UK. The Mk IA was the export version of the P-40E with six heavy machine-guns and the 857-kW (1,150-hp) Allison V-1710-39 engine. Next came 210 examples of the Kittyhawk Mk III, the designation used for P-40K and P-40M aircraft with the 988- and 895-kW (1,325- and 1,200-hp) V-1710-73 and -81 engines respectively. Finally there were 468 examples of the Kittyhawk IV, the designation used for P-40N aircraft with a lightweight structure, four or later six wing guns and a variety of 895-kW (1,200-hp) V-1710 inline engines.

Specification: Curtiss Kittyhawk Mk IV single-seat fighter and fighter-bomber
Span: 11.38 m (37 ft 4 in)
Length: 10.16 m (33 ft 4 in)
Powerplant: 1×Allison V-1710-89, -99 or -115, 895 kW (1,200 hp)
Armament: 6×12.7-mm (0.5-in) machine-guns plus provision for one 227-kg (500-lb) bomb carried under the fuselage
Max T/O weight: 5171 kg (11,400 lb)
Max speed: 350 mph at 16,500 ft
Operational range: 310 miles

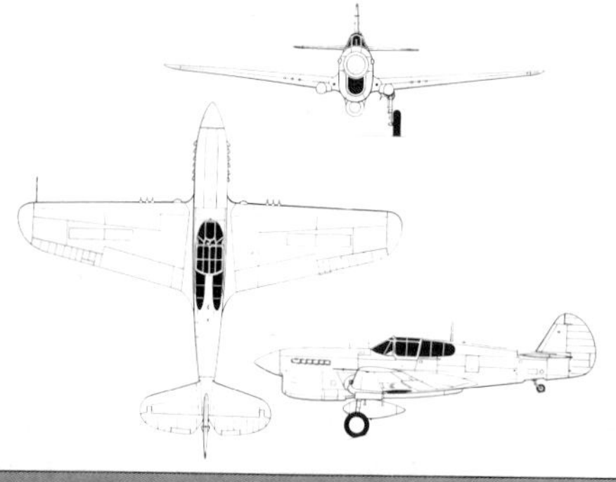

DAP (Bristol) Beaufighter

The war fought by the Australians against the Japanese placed great emphasis on elimination of the enemy's coastal supply network. This task was first entrusted to Beauforts, but the superior capabilities of the Beaufighter resulted in the allocation of 76 Beaufighter Mk ICs for the RAAF: these entered service in mid-1942. With Beaufort production running down, the Australians decided in January 1943 to produce their own aircraft, initial thoughts being for the Beaufighter Mk VIC with Hercules 26 radials to be built as the Beaufighter Mk VII, or with variants of the Wright GR-2600-A5B as the Beaufighter Mks VIII and IX. But Hercules supplies were guaranteed, however, and Australia produced 364 examples (out of a planned 500) of the TF.Mk X as the Beaufighter TF.Mk 21 with heavy machine-guns in the wings and a Sperry autopilot. The first such aeroplane flew in May 1944.

Specification: Department of Aircraft Production (Bristol) Beaufighter TF.Mk 21 two/three-seat anti-ship strike fighter
Span: 17.63 m (57 ft 10 in)
Length: 12.70 m (41 ft 8 in)
Powerplant: 2×Bristol Hercules XVIII, 1320 kW (1,770 hp) each
Armament: 4×20-mm cannon, 6×12.7-mm (0.5-in) and 1×7.7-mm (0.303-in) machine-guns plus provision for torpedoes or bombs and rockets
Max T/O weight: 11521 kg (25,400 lb)
Max speed: 303 mph at 13,000 ft
Operational range: 1,470 miles

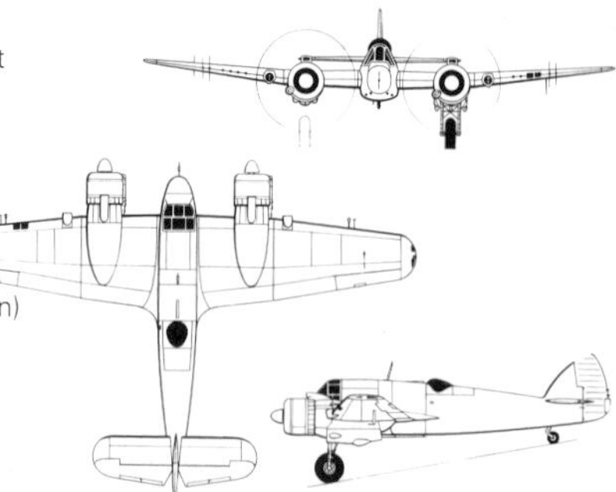

Used in the army co-operation role, this Commonwealth Aircraft CA-12 Boomerang was operated by No. 5 Sqn during the New Guinea campaign. With Japan's overwhelming success during 1941-2 Australia was caught off guard, and desperately needed a credible fighter to replace its obsolescent Brewster Buffaloes. With incredible speed a new fuselage was added to the Wirraway wing to create the CA-12 Boomerang, a stopgap fighter with excellent climbing capabilities. The Boomerang acquitted itself well against Japanese opposition until replaced by more advanced fighters.

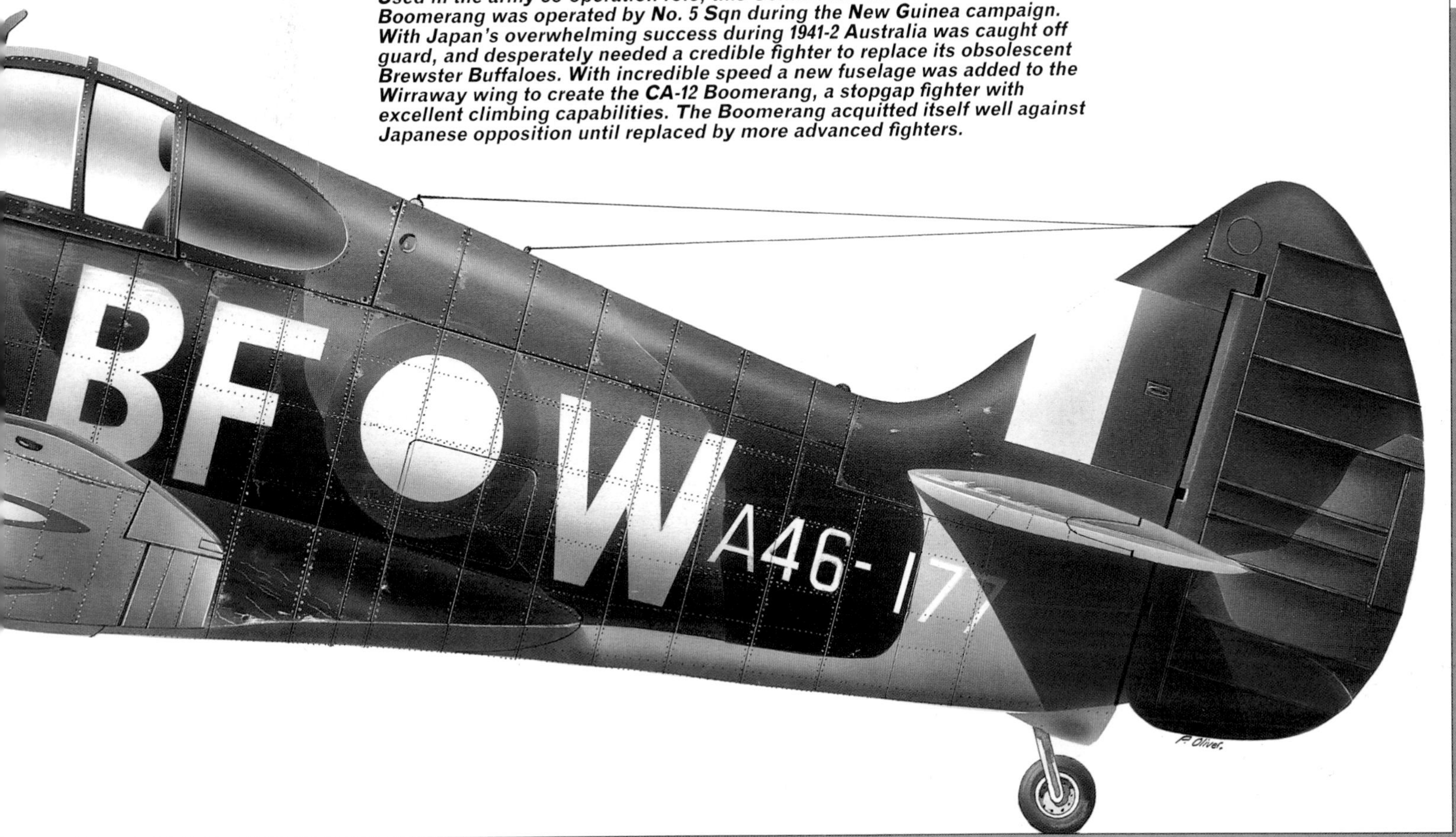

Supermarine Spitfire

Nos 452 and 457 Squadrons were the RAAF's first Spitfire units, but both these squadrons formed in the UK during the first half of 1941. In 1942 these units were recreated in Australia to form, with the RAF's No.54 Squadron, No.1 Fighter Wing for the protection of northern Australia with Spitfire F.Mk VCs, of which a total of 245 was received. These aircraft were later replaced by 410 examples of the Spitfire F.Mk VIII, the tropicalised version of the Mk VII but without a pressurised cockpit as the type was intended for low- and medium-altitude operations. With more aircraft available the Spitfire force was expanded: the defence of Australia was entrusted to Nos 54, 548 and 549 Squadrons, while operations in New Guinea and the Solomons were allocated to Nos 79, 452 and 457 Squadrons of the 1st Tactical Air Force. A few Spitfire F.Mk XIVs were being received at the end of the war.

Specification: Supermarine Spitfire LF.Mk VIII single-seat fighter and fighter-bomber
Span: 9.80 m (32 ft 2 in)
Length: 9.54 m (31 ft 3.5 in)
Powerplant: 1×Rolls-Royce Merlin 66, 1178 kW (1,580 hp)
Armament: 2×20-mm cannon and 4×7.7-mm (0.303-in) machine-guns plus provision for 1×227-kg (500-lb) bomb carried under the fuselage and 2×113-kg (250-lb) bombs carried under the wings
Max T/O weight: 3629 kg (8,000 lb)
Max speed: 404 mph at optimum altitude
Operational range: 660 miles

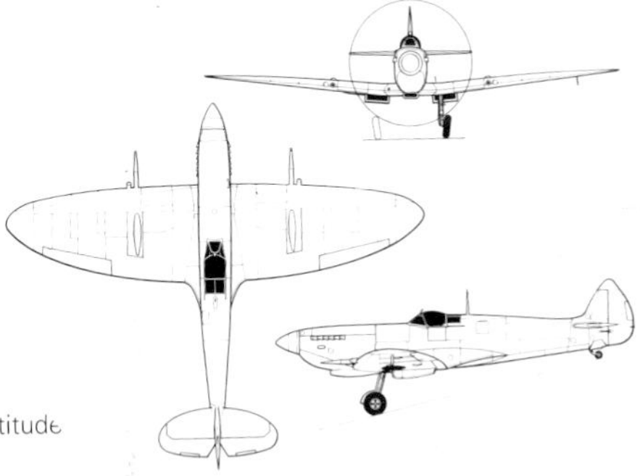

Vultee Vengeance

Designed as a private venture with the export market primarily in mind, the V-72 was conceived as a dedicated dive-bomber and ordered initially by the British after their experience with the Junkers Ju 87 early in World War II. The first aeroplane flew in July 1941 and deliveries of an initial 457 (out of an order for 700) with the 1193-kW (1,600-hp) R-2600-19 radial began about 12 months later; some 32 of these Vengeance Mk Is were passed on to the Royal Australian Air Force. Of the 1,931 Vengeances built a total of 342 found their way to the RAAF, the balance of 310 aircraft being Vengeance Mk IVs equivalent to the USAAF's A-35B model with heavy rather than rifle-calibre machine-guns, more power and a number of detail improvements. These aircraft were little used in their intended role, most being converted as target-towing machines.

Specification: Vultee Vengeance Mk IV two-seat dive-bomber and target-tug
Span: 14.63 m (48 ft 0 in)
Length: 12.11 m (39 ft 9 in)
Powerplant: 1×Wright R-2600-13, 1268 kW (1,700 hp)
Armament: 7×12.7-mm (0.5-in) machine-guns plus provision for up to 907 kg (2,000 lb) of bombs carried internally
Max T/O weight: 7439 kg (16,400 lb)
Max speed: 279 mph at 13,500 ft
Operational range: 2,300 miles

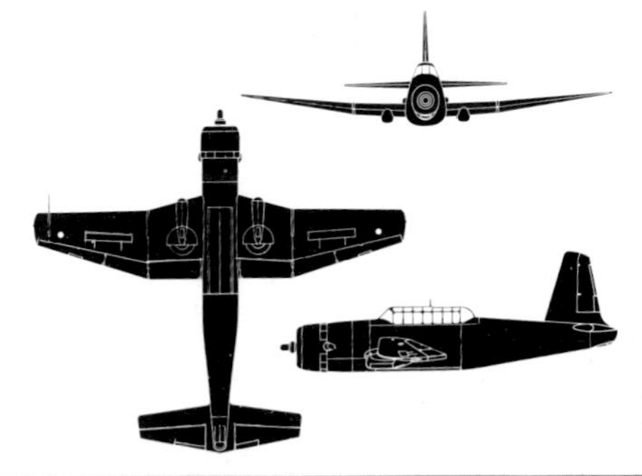

Messerschmitt Me 262 Schwalbe

The world's first turbojet-powered aeroplane to enter operational service in summer 1944, the Schwalbe (swallow) began life as early as 1938 when the company was asked to create a fighter using two BMW or Junkers turbojets. The first prototype flew in April 1941 with a piston engine, the first jet flight following in July 1942 with Junkers 109-004 engines. Pre-production Me 262A-0s followed, but Hitler authorised production only in November 1943, and then on the proviso that the type be used as the Sturmvogel (stormbird) high-speed bomber. Total production amounted to just over 1,100 aircraft, the service variant being the Me 262A-1 variant with different armaments in the fighter and fighter-bomber roles, and the Me 262B two-seaters in the training and night-fighter roles. Projects were the rocket-boosted Me 262C, and the rocket-armed Me 262D/E bomber interceptors.

Red and blue 'Defence of the Reich' bands and a leaping greyhound nose badge identify this aircraft as an Me 262A-1a of 9.Staffel/ Jagdgeschwader 7, based at Parchim. The Me 262 was incredibly sleek and streamlined, its swept wing giving it excellent high speed handling characteristics. By the time it entered service the war was already lost, and chronic shortages of pilots and fuel lessened the contribution it might have made.

Heinkel He 178

The He 178 has the distinction of being the first aeroplane in the world to have flown purely on turbojet power, this feat being accomplished on 27 August 1939. In 1936 Heinkel employed the jet pioneer Hans Joachim Pabst von Ohain, whose first HeS 1 hydrogen-fuelled demonstration engine was bench-running by September 1937. The more powerful, but also more controllable, petrol-fuelled HeW 3 was running by March 1938 and delivering some 500-kg (1,102-lb) thrust. The HeW 3 was flight-trialled under an He 118, and it was then decided to produce the He 178 prototype round the improved HeW 3b, whose large diameter dictated the high cockpit location and shoulder mounting of the wooden wing to maintain a straight-through air/gas flow. Development flying was undertaken with the more powerful HeS 6, and the He 178 was then placed in a museum where it was destroyed during a 1943 air raid.

Specification: Heinkel He 178 single-seat turbojet engine prototype
Span: 7.20 m (23 ft 3.5 in)
Length: 7.48 m (24 ft 6.5 in)
Powerplant: 1×Heinkel HeS 3b, 500 kg (1,102 lb) st
Armament: none
Normal T/O weight: 1998 kg (4,396 lb)
Max speed: about 435 mph at sea level
Operational range: not known

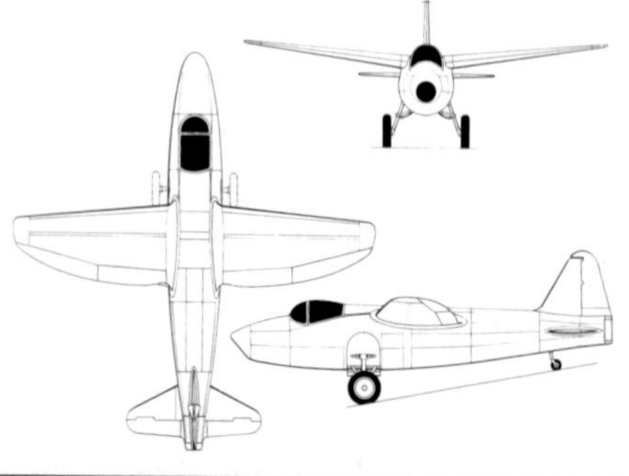

Heinkel He 280

The He 280 was a consequence of the He 178 programme, being based on an airframe designed from the start for development into a fighter. From late 1939 Heinkel had been working on two turbojets, the HeS 30 (109-006) whose design arrived with Max Mueller from Junkers, and the von Ohain-designed HeS 8 (109-001). The first He 280 prototype was ready before either of the engine types, and initial flight trials were made in ballasted glider form. The first powered flight followed in April 1941 with two HeS 8s, and trials were later undertaken with BMW and Junkers engines after the promising HeS 30 was unreasonably cancelled. In 1943 political factors swayed the Nazi administration towards the longer-ranged and more heavily armed Me 262, and the survivors of nine prototypes were used for research tasks.

Specification: Heinkel He 280 V5 single-seat research aeroplane with fighter potential
Span: 12.20 m (40 ft 0 in)
Length: 10.40 m (34 ft 1.5 in)
Powerplant: 2×Heinkel HeS 8A (109-001A), 750 kg (1,653 lb) st each
Armament: 3×20-mm cannon
Normal T/O weight: 4310 kg (9,482 lb)
Max speed: 559 mph at 19,685 ft
Operational range: 404 miles

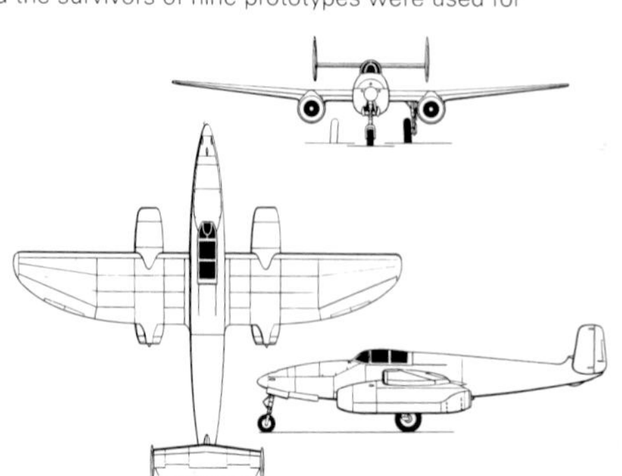

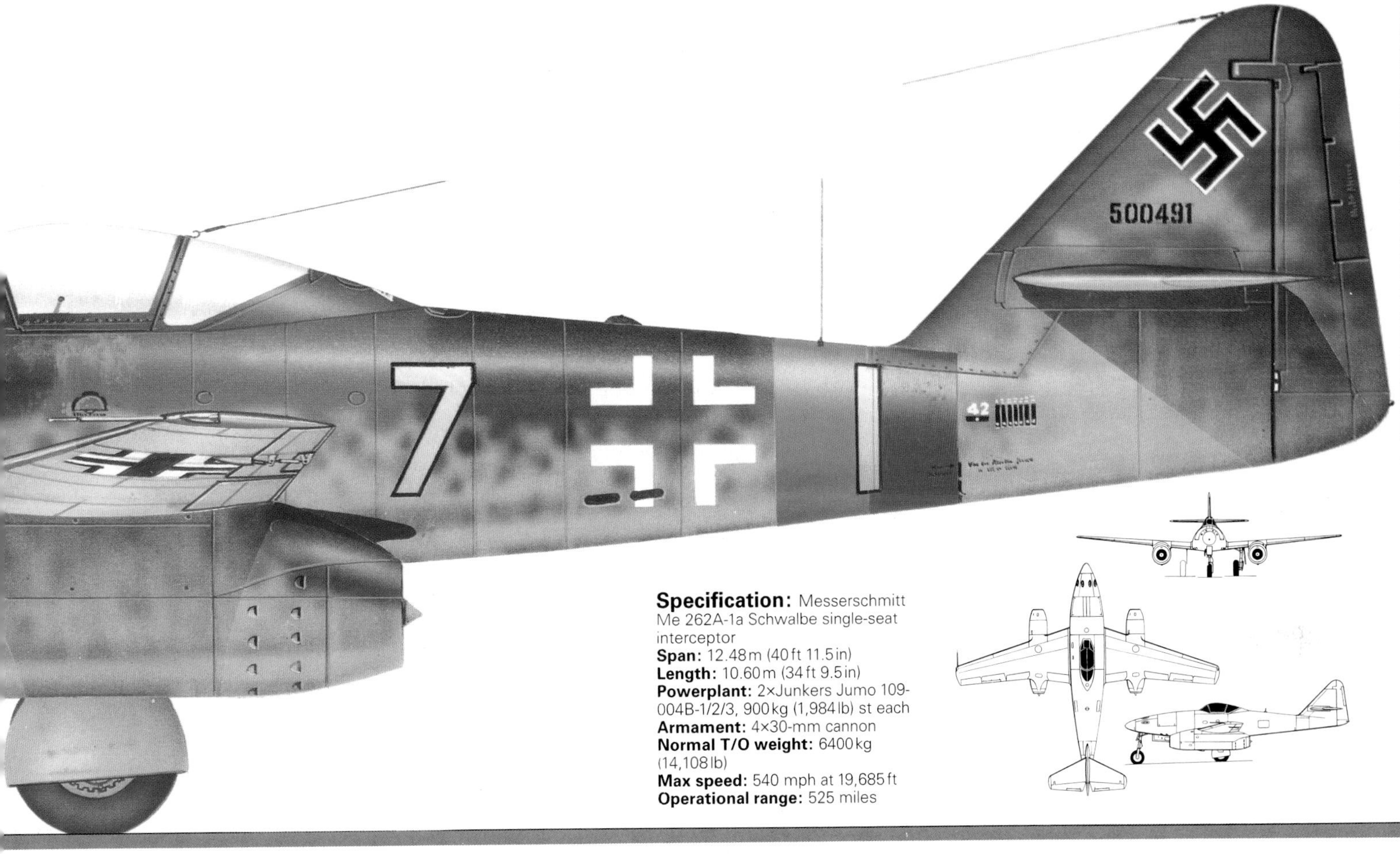

Specification: Messerschmitt Me 262A-1a Schwalbe single-seat interceptor
Span: 12.48 m (40 ft 11.5 in)
Length: 10.60 m (34 ft 9.5 in)
Powerplant: 2×Junkers Jumo 109-004B-1/2/3, 900 kg (1,984 lb) st each
Armament: 4×30-mm cannon
Normal T/O weight: 6400 kg (14,108 lb)
Max speed: 540 mph at 19,685 ft
Operational range: 525 miles

Gloster E.28/39

Known only by the designation of the official specification that led to its development, the E.28/39 was the UK's counterpart to Germany's He 178 as the vehicle that proved the practicality of turbojet-powered flight. The spur for the E.28/39 requirement was the successful development of the Whittle W.1 turbojet, and the requirement called for a fighter-type aeroplane with tricycle landing gear and provision for armament. The resultant E.28/39 was a workmanlike all-metal low-wing design with straight-through air/gas flow for the centrifugal-flow turbojet, which also required a portly fuselage.A number of hops were followed by the first real flight on 15 May 1941 with a 390-kg (860-lb) thrust W.1. Improved engines were later fitted, and the second prototype is preserved as a museum exhibit.

Specification: Gloster E.28/39 single-seat turbojet engine prototype
Span: 8.84 m (29 ft 0 in)
Length: 7.72 m (25 ft 3.75 in)
Powerplant: 1×Power Jets (Whittle) W.2/500, 798 kg (1,760 lb) st
Armament: fitted for, but not with, 4×0.303-in (7.7-mm) machine-guns
Max T/O weight: 1700 kg (3,748 lb)
Max speed: 466 mph at 10,000 ft
Operational range: not revealed

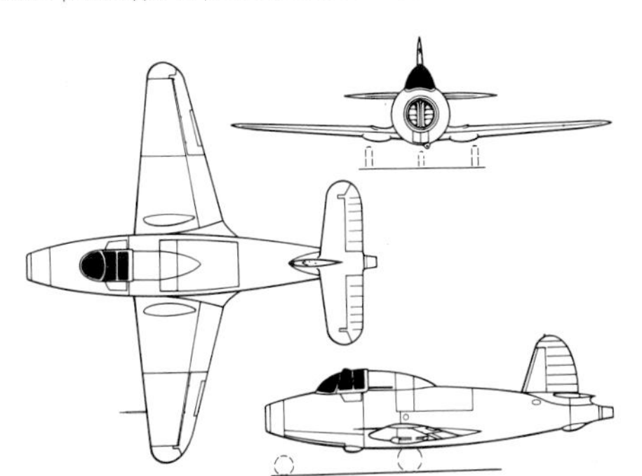

Messerschmitt Me 163 Komet

The most radical aeroplane to enter operational service in World War II, the Komet (comet) was planned as a point interceptor with phenomenal climb performance (30,000 ft in about 2.5 minutes) assured by liquid-fuelled rocket propulsion, tailless layout and take-off from a jettisonable trolley. There was considerable service and political disagreement about the programme, and though the first 12 prototypes flew in August 1941, the first Luftwaffe test group was not formed until late 1944. The initial 10 Me 163As were training gliders, and were followed by about 370 Me 163B powered aircraft and Me 163S training gliders. Limited operations were undertaken, but suffered from the volatility of the residual fuel, which tended to explode as aircraft landed on their skids. Improved models were planned as the Me 163C/D and Me 263.

Specification: Messerschmitt Me 163B-1a Komet single-seat point interceptor
Span: 9.33 m (30 ft 7.25 in)
Length: 5.85 m (19 ft 2.3 in)
Powerplant: 1×Walter HWK 509A-2, 1700 kg (3,748 lb) st
Armament: 2×30-mm cannon
Max T/O weight: 4300 kg (9,480 lb)
Max speed: 596 mph at 9,845 ft
Operational range: 50 miles

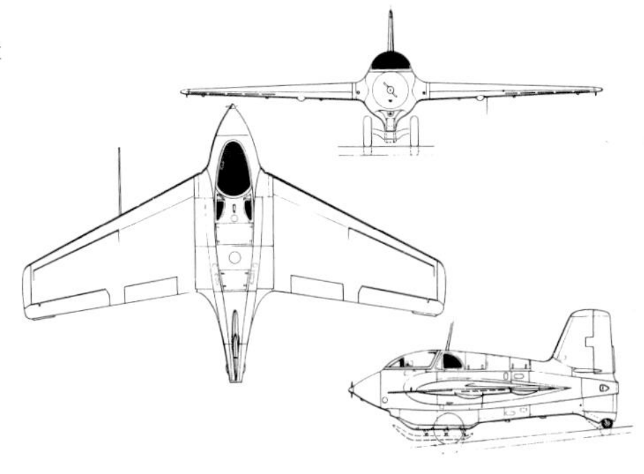

Arado Ar 234 Blitz

The Blitz (lightning) was the world's first jet bomber, and stemmed from a 1940 German requirement for a reconnaissance aeroplane powered by two turbojets of the types under development by BMW and Junkers. The high wing and narrow fuselage precluded the use of conventional landing gear, so the Ar 234 was designed to take-off from a three-wheel trolley and land on skids. The first of 18 prototypes flew in June 1943, and trials compared the use of two Junkers 109-004B or four BMW 109-003A turbojets. It was then decided to fit tricycle landing gear in a widened fuselage, and this paved the way for the Ar 232B, of which 230 were built in B-0/B-1 reconnaissance and B-2 bomber models. The four-engine production model was the Ar 234C, but here 12 prototypes were followed by only 14 production aircraft of the C-1 reconnaissance and C-3 bomber/ground-attack versions.

Bell P-59 Airacomet

The P-59 was the first US jet-powered aeroplane, and was designed in response to a requirement for a fighter using two 635-kg (1,400-lb) thrust General Electric 1-A turbojets. The airframe was completely conventional, an all-metal structure with a mid-set wing and tricycle landing gear, and the engines were located in short nacelles under the wing roots. Three XP-59A prototypes were ordered in September 1941, and the first of these flew in October 1942. Performance was considerably below that demanded, and the type was also a poor gun platform. Some 13 YP-59A pre-production aircraft followed with 748-kg (1,650-lb) thrust I-16 (later J31) engines: these were no better than the XP-59As, and the 100-aircraft production order was reduced to just 20 P-59As and 30 P-59Bs with more fuel. The aircraft were used only for evaluation and training purposes.

Specification: Bell P-59A Airacomet single-seat fighter and fighter-bomber
Span: 13.69 m (45 ft 6 in)
Length: 11.84 m (38 ft 10 in)
Powerplant: 2×General Electric J31-GE-5, 907 kg (2,000 lb) st each
Armament: 1×37-mm cannon and 3×o.5-in (12.7-mm) machine-guns, plus provision for 8×60-lb (27-kg) rockets or 2×1,000-lb (454-kg) bombs carried under the wings
Max T/O weight: 3871 kg (12,700 lb)
Max speed: 413 mph at 30,000 ft
Operational range: 240 miles

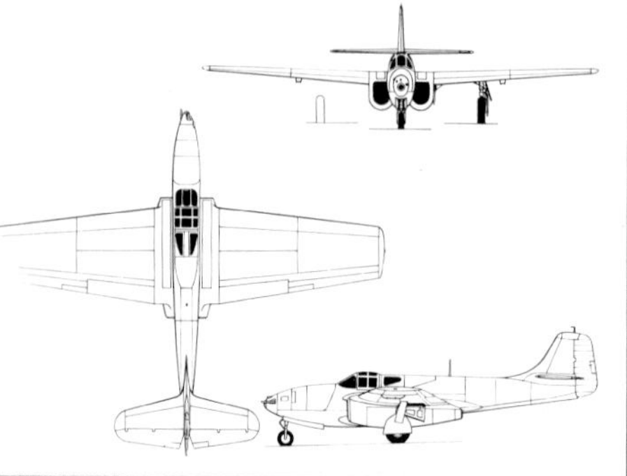

Gloster Meteor

The Meteor was the Allies' only jet fighter to enter service in World War II. The design capitalized on Gloster's experience with the E.28/39, but wing-mounted nacelles were chosen because of the large diameter of the fighter's two centrifugal-flow turbojets. The first Meteor flew in March 1943, and while the prototypes were flown with an assortment of Halford, Metrovick and Whittle engines, the 771-kg (1,700-lb) st Rolls-Royce Welland I was selected for the production Meteor F.Mk I. The first production Meteor was supplied to the USA in exchange for a Bell P-59 Airacomet, and only 16 of the 20 Meteor F.Mk Is entered service from July 1944, making their debut against German V-1 flying bombs launched against southern England. The improved Meteor F.Mk III began to enter service at the beginning of 1945, the first 15 of the 280 built being powered by Welland turbojets.

Specification: Gloster Meteor F.Mk III single-seat fighter
Span: 13.11 m (43 ft 0 in)
Length: 12.57 m (41 ft 3 in)
Powerplant: 2×Rolls-Royce Derwent I, 907 kg (2,000 lb) st each
Armament: 4×20-mm cannon
Max T/O weight: 6033 kg (13,300 lb)
Max speed: 493 mph at 30,000 ft
Operational range: 1,340 miles

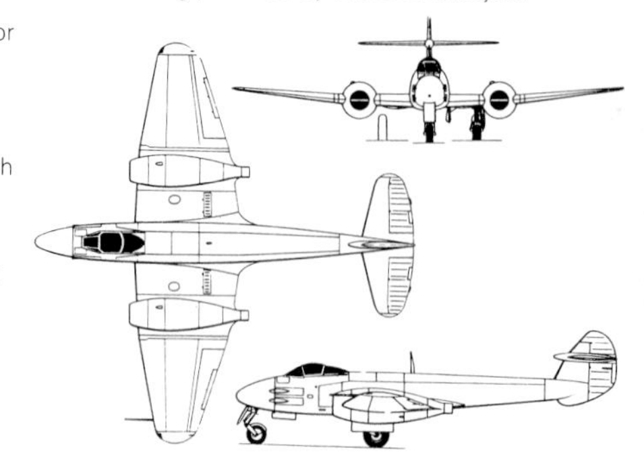

Specification: Arado Ar 234B-2 Blitz single-seat reconnaissance bomber
Span: 14.41 m (47 ft 3.25 in)
Length: 12.64 m (41 ft 5.25 in)
Powerplant: 2×Junkers Jumo 109-004B-1, 900 kg (1,984 lb) st each
Armament: 2×20-mm rear-firing cannon, plus provision for up to 1500 kg (3,307 lb) of bombs carried externally
Max T/O weight: 9800 kg (21,605 lb)
Max speed: 457 mph at 19,685 ft
Operational range: 1,013 miles

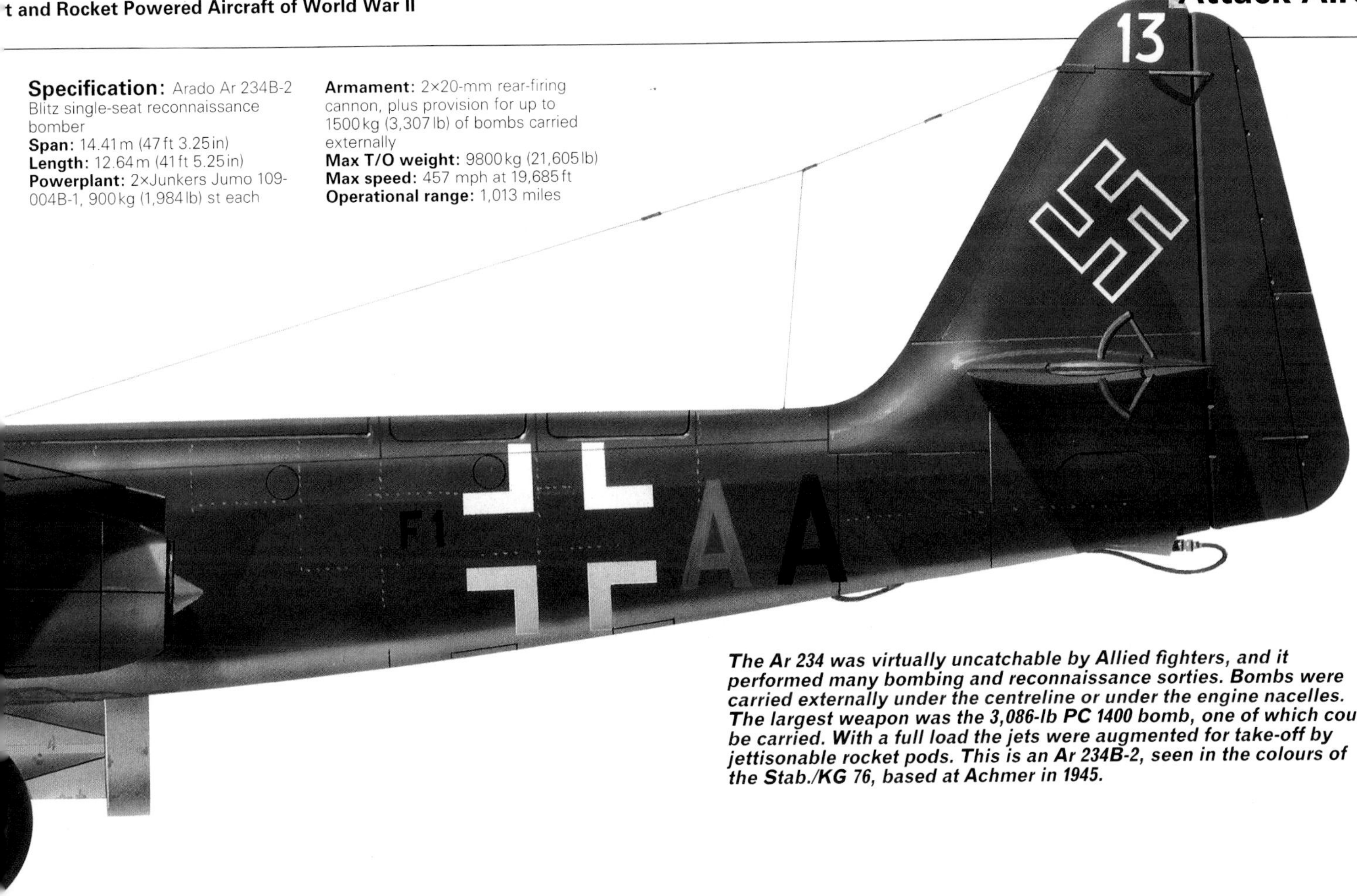

The Ar 234 was virtually uncatchable by Allied fighters, and it performed many bombing and reconnaissance sorties. Bombs were carried externally under the centreline or under the engine nacelles. The largest weapon was the 3,086-lb PC 1400 bomb, one of which could be carried. With a full load the jets were augmented for take-off by jettisonable rocket pods. This is an Ar 234B-2, seen in the colours of the Stab./KG 76, based at Achmer in 1945.

de Havilland Vampire

Though developed to the E.6/41 specification for a fighter-type experimental aeroplane, the Vampire displayed such promise in flight trials that it was evolved into the UK's first single-turbojet fighter, and this was just too late for service in World War II. In layout the Vampire was based on a wooden fuselage with unswept metal wings and twin booms supporting a broad-span tailplane surmounted by twin vertical surfaces. The aeroplane was supported on tricycle landing gear, and the twin-boom arrangement was chosen for greatest possible efficiency with the modest 1225-kg (2,700-lb) thrust of the early Goblin I aspirated through wing-root inlets. The first of three Spider Crab (later Vampire) prototypes flew in September 1943, and the first of 172 Vampire F.Mk 1s began to enter service in April 1946.

Specification: de Havilland Vampire F.Mk 1 single-seat fighter
Span: 12.19 m (40 ft 0 in)
Length: 9.37 m (30 ft 9 in)
Powerplant: 1×de Havilland Goblin II, 2311 kg (3,100 lb) st
Armament: 4×20-mm cannon
Max T/O weight: 4754 kg (10,480 lb)
Max speed: 531 mph at 7,500 ft
Operational range: 730 miles

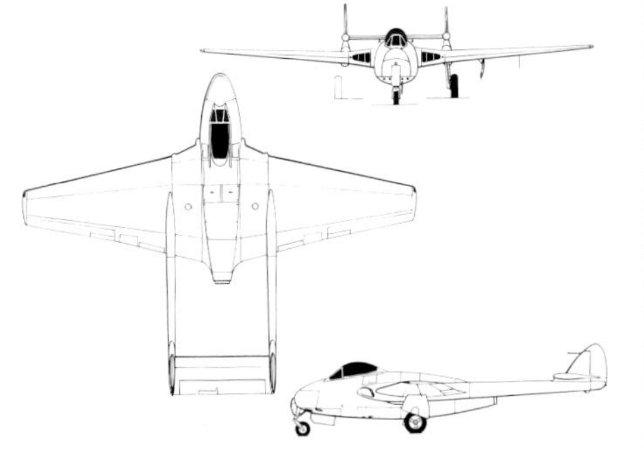

Lockheed P-80 Shooting Star

The first turbojet-powered aeroplane accepted for USAAF combat service, the Shooting Star was a remarkable type whose development potential has kept its derivatives in service up to the present. The type's origins lay with Bell's P-59B proposal with a single I-16 aspirated by wing-root inlets. Bell was too busy to undertake development and the project was allocated to Lockheed, which recast the concept as an extremely clean low-wing monoplane with a de Havilland Goblin turbojet. The XP-80 prototype was completed in only 143 days, first flying in January 1944. American licence-production of the Goblin was thought too time-consuming, so the design was revised with the I-40 (J33) engine as the XP-80A, which first flew in June 1944 and prompted orders for 13 YP-80As and 5,000 P-80As! Only two reached a combat zone, and orders were cut back to 917 after the war.

Specification: Lockheed P-80A Shooting Star single-seat fighter and fighter-bomber
Span: 11.85 m (38 ft 10.5 in)
Length: 10.52 m (34 ft 6 in)
Powerplant: 1×General Electric J33-GE-9 or -11, 1746 kg (3,850 lb) st
Armament: 6×12.7-mm (0.5-in) machine-guns, plus provision for 10×5-in (127-mm) rockets or two 1,000- or 500-lb (454- or 227-kg) bombs carried under the wings
Max T/O weight: 6350 kg (14,000 lb)
Max speed: 558 mph at sea level
Operational range: 625 miles

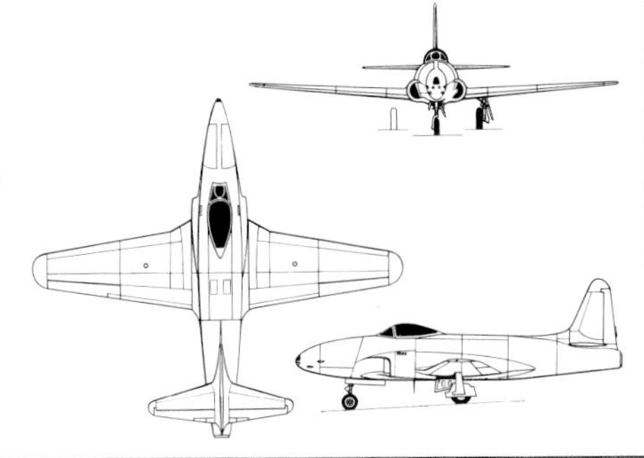

Junkers Ju 287

The Ju 287 was developed as part of a 1944 Luftwaffe scheme to replace all piston-engine bombers except the Ju 88, with turbojet-powered aircraft. From June 1943 Junkers had already formulated the concept that began to mature as the Ju 287 with a swept-forward wing to maintain controllability at high speeds and allow the spars to pass behind the bomb bay. Prototype development was ordered in March 1944, and the first step was the low-speed Ju 287 V1 with a swept-forward wing married to an He 177 fuselage, a Ju 388 tail unit and fixed landing gear using Ju 352 main wheels and Consolidated B-24 nose wheels! The aeroplane first flew in August 1944, displaying both good and bad handling characteristics, but further development was overtaken by Germany's defeat and the two prototypes fell into Soviet hands. The V2 had the definitive fuselage and retractable landing gear.

Specification: Junkers Ju 287 V1 bomber concept-evaluation prototype
Span: 20.11 m (65 ft 11.25 in)
Length: 18.30 m (60 ft 0.5 in)
Powerplant: 4×Junkers Jumo 109-004B-1, 900 kg (1,984 lb) st each
Armament: none
Max T/O weight: 20000 kg (44,092 lb)
Max speed: 347 mph at 19,685 ft
Operational range: 932 miles

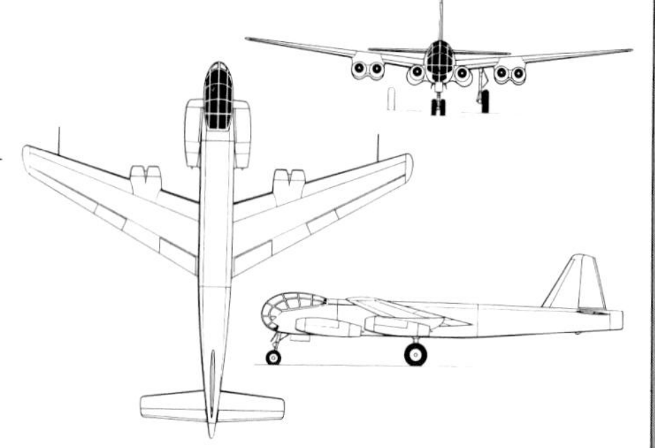

Heinkel He 162 Volksjäger

The Volksjäger (people's fighter), otherwise known as the Salamander or Spatz (sparrow), was planned, designed and flown in just 10 weeks during 1944 as a high-performance defensive fighter making minimal demands on strategic materials and skilled manpower. The first of many prototypes flew in December 1944 as a shoulder-wing monoplane of largely wooden construction but fitted with tricycle landing gear and a tailplane with endplate vertical surfaces so that the single turbojet could be mounted in an easy-maintenance position above the fuselage. A number of handling deficiencies were countered by the enlargement of the vertical tail surfaces, anhedralling the wingtips and moving forward the centre of gravity in the He 162A production model, of which about 250 were completed. The first He 162 unit became operational in the last days of the war but the type did not enter combat.

Specification: Heinkel He 162A-2 Volksjäger single-seat interceptor
Span: 7.20 m (23 ft 7.5 in)
Length: 9.05 m (29 ft 8.3 in)
Powerplant: 1×BMW 109-003E-1/2, 800 kg (1,764 lb) st
Armament: 2×20-mm cannon
Max T/O weight: 2700 kg (5,953 lb)
Max speed: 562 mph at 19,685 ft
Operational range: 621 miles

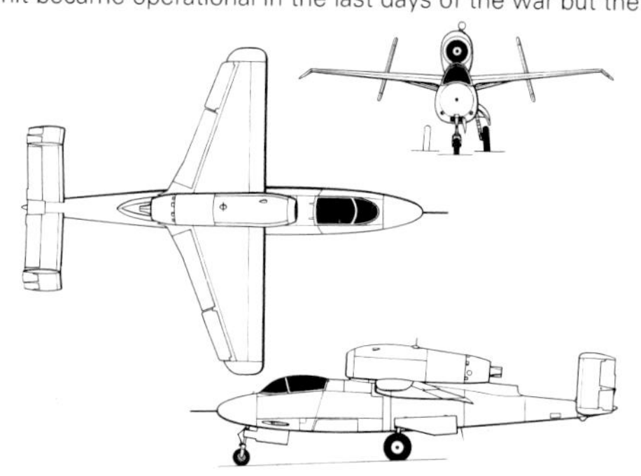

Bachem Ba 349 Natter

Planned in 1944 as an exceptionally fast-climbing interceptor for the protection of German industry and communications against the attentions of US bombers, the Natter (viper) was a semi-expendable rocket-powered interceptor of high performance but low cost through the use of a simple airframe that could be mass-produced in small woodworking factories. The type was planned round the concept of vertical launch, attack of the bomber stream with rockets, and then the separation of the fuselage at the cockpit to allow the pilot and rear fuselage (plus rocket) to descend separately for re-use. Gliding tests began in October 1944, and unmanned powered launches in December. The only manned test killed the pilot, and the programme was then overtaken by Germany's defeat with about 20 Ba 349A production aircraft completed but unflown.

Specification: Bachem Ba 349A Natter single-seat point interceptor prototype
Span: 3.60 m (11 ft 9.75 in)
Length: 6.10 m (20 ft 0 in)
Powerplant: 4×Schmidding 109-533 jettisonable booster rockets, 1200 kg (2,646 lb) st each, and 1×Walter HWK 109-509A-2 sustainer rocket, 1700 kg (3,748 lb) st
Armament: 24×73-mm (2.87-in) Hs 217 Fohn or 33×55-mm (2.17-in) R4M unguided rockets
Max T/O weight: 2200 kg (4,850 lb)
Max speed: 497 mph at low altitude
Operational range: 25 miles

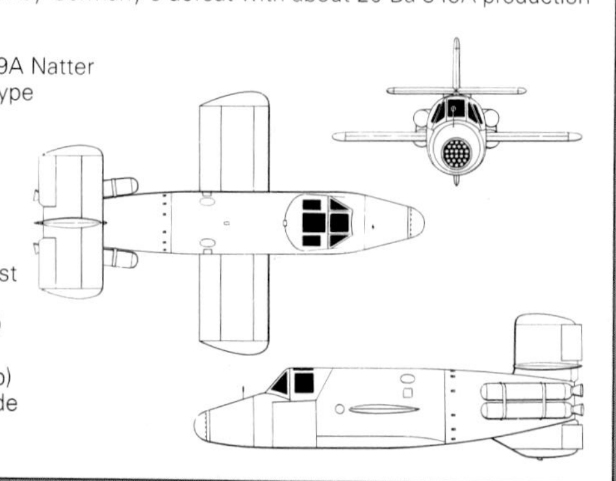

Henschel Hs 132

Given the successes of their dive-bombers in the opening campaigns of World War II, it is hardly surprising that technologically minded Germans were soon envisaging the possibility of a turbojet-powered dive-bomber, a type that appealed increasingly towards the end of the war as a high-performance type that could attack with pinpoint accuracy the Allies' overwhelming superiority in armour. The result was the Hs 132, which had conceptual and structural similarities with the He 162 but, given its operational role, was stressed to 12 *g* rather than the fighter's 8 *g* for high-speed pullouts: it was fitted with a prone pilot position for the same reason. Construction of three prototypes was begun in March 1945, and only the prototype for the Hs 132A had been completed but not flown when the factory was overrun by the Soviets.

Specification: Henschel Hs 132A single-seat dive-bomber
Span: 7.20 m (23 ft 7.5 in)
Length: 8.90 m (29 ft 2.5 in)
Powerplant: 1×BMW 109-003E-2, 800 kg (1,764 lb) st
Armament: 2×20-mm cannon, plus provision for 1×500-kg (1,102-lb) bomb carried semi-externally
Normal T/O weight: 3400 kg (7,497 lb)
Max speed: 485 mph at 19,685 ft
Operational range: 422 miles

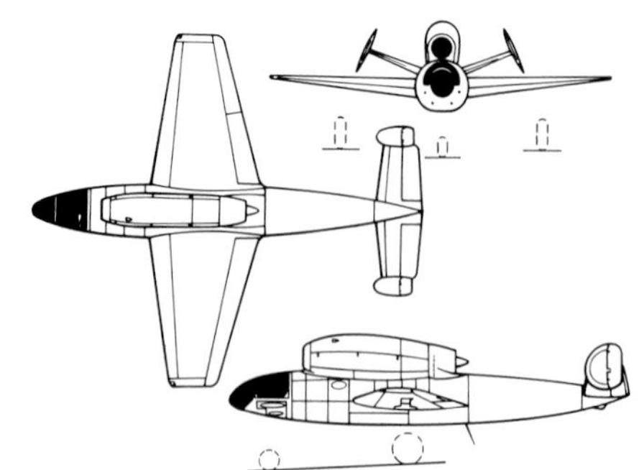

Hawker Siddeley Harrier

No. 1 Squadron became the world's first operational front-line VTOL fighter unit when it converted to the revolutionary Harrier during June 1969. The Harrier's unique vectored-thrust Pegasus turbofan gives it an unequalled ability to operate from semi-prepared dispersed sites, deploying 'into the field' away from vulnerable airfields. Three squadrons in RAF Germany received the Harrier, although one of these disbanded due to the aircraft shortages caused by a high accident rate. Harriers are frequently deployed away 'out of area', and were used in action in the Falkland War. The GR.Mk 3 with its small payload and primitive avionics, will soon be replaced by the new Anglo-American BAe McDonnell-Douglas AV-8B, which will be known as the Harrier GR.Mk 5 in RAF service.

Specification: Hawker Siddeley Harrier GR.Mk 3 single-seat ground attack fighter
Span: 7.69 m (25 ft 3 in)
Length: 14.12 m (46 ft 4 in)
Powerplant: Rolls-Royce Pegasus 103 vectored thrust turbofan, 21,500 lb st
Armament: 2×30-mm Aden cannon, plus up to 8,000 lb of bombs, rockets etc underwing and on centreline
Maximum speed: 703 mph
Operational range: 400 miles

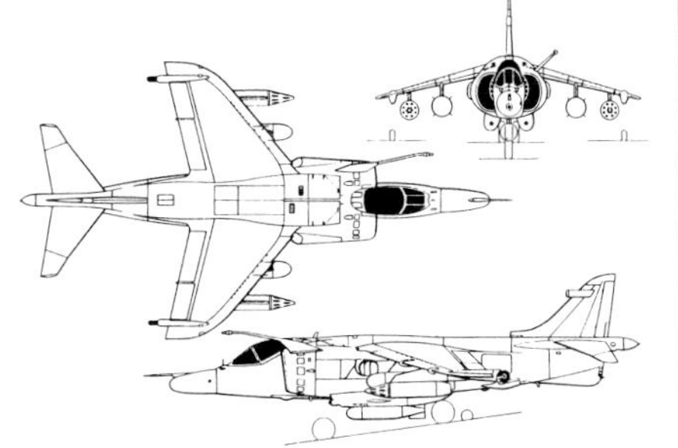

McDonnell Douglas Phantom

The first of the RAF's Spey-engined Phantoms entered service with No. 43 Squadron in September 1969 in the air defence role. Later deliveries went to strike-fighter and tactical reconnaissance units, in the UK and Germany. When SEPECAT Jaguar entered service these aircraft became available to replace air defence Lightnings in six UK- and Germany-based squadrons. Ex-RN Phantoms equipped a further unit when the Royal Navy's last carrier, HMS *Ark Royal*, was retired. After the Falklands War, one unit moved to RAF Stanley and then to Mount Pleasant. A shortage of fighter aircraft led to the purchase of 15 refurbished ex-US Navy F-4Js, allowing No. 74 Squadron to reform. The RAF's Phantom force is now being replaced by Tornado F.Mk 3s, but four squadrons will be retained.

Specification: Phantom FGR.Mk 2 two-seat air defence fighter
Span: 11.69 m (38 ft 4.75 in)
Length: 17.95 m (58 ft 11 in)
Powerplant: 2×Roll-Royce Spey 204 (20,515 lb st with reheat)
Armament: 1×20-mm SUU-23 Vulcan cannon (optional) on centreline; 4×BAe Sky Flash AAms under belly, plus 4×AIM-9L Sidewinder cannon
Maximum speed: Mach 2.1
Operational range: 750 miles

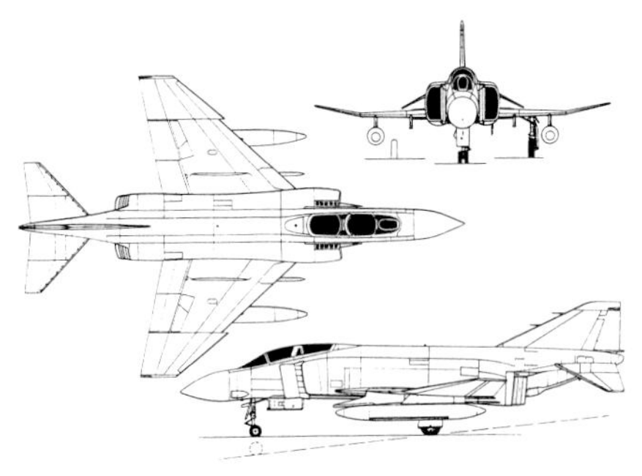

SEPECAT Jaguar

Originally intended as an advanced trainer to replace the Folland Gnat, the RAF decided at the last moment to procure its Jaguars as operational low-level strike fighters, equipped with advanced navigation and attack avionics. The first aircraft were delivered during 1973 and the first squadron, No. 54, formed in March 1974. The Jaguar replaced the Phantom in the strike, attack and reconnaissance roles, and eventually equipped eight units. The German-based Jaguar strike squadrons converted to the Tornado IDS between 1983 and 1986. No. 11 Squadron, the RAF Germany Jaguar recce unit, will convert to Tornados in 1989, but the three squadrons based at RAF Coltishall form part of NATO's strategic reserve, and will retain the aircraft well into the 1990s.

Specification: SEPECAT Jaguar GR.Mk 1 single-seat strike fighters
Span: 8.68 m (28 ft 6 in)
Length: 15.51 m (50 ft 11 in)
Powerplant: 2×Rolls-Royce Turboméca RT172 Adour 102, 5,320 lb st (8,040 lb st with reheat) each
Armament: 2×30-mm Aden cannon plus up to 10,500 lb of bombs
Maximum speed: Mach 1.1 at sea level; Mach 1.6 at 30,000 ft
Operational range: 875 miles

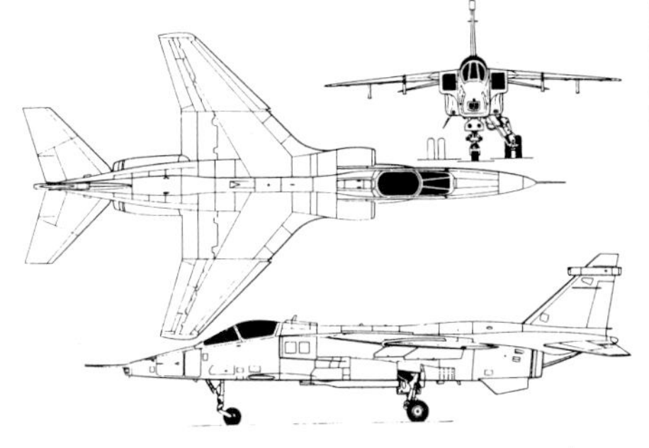

Panavia Tornado *(Air Defence Variant)*

After evaluating the Grumman F-14 Tomcat, the McDonnell Douglas F-15 Eagle and the French ACF, the RAF decided to procure an optimised version of its Tornado tactical strike aircraft to fulfil its requirement for a long-range interceptor to guard the UK Air Defence Region. The prototype Tornado ADV flew on, and soon proved that the aircraft was more than a bomber wearing a different hat, demonstrating impressive acceleration, speed and agility. Equipped with an advanced AI-24 Foxhunter radar and armed with a mix of BAe Skyflash and AIM-9 Sidewinder AAMs, the Tornado is an extremely effective interceptor, ideally suited for operations in the UK environment. The first operational squadron, No. 29, was declared operational on 1 November 1987.

Specification: Panavia Tornado F.Mk 3 two-seat, long-range interceptor
Span: 13.90 m (45 ft 7½ in) spread, 8.59 m (28 ft 2½ in) swept
Length: 18.07 m (59 ft 3¾ in)
Powerplant: 2×Turbo Union RB199-34R Mk 104 turbofans, 10,600 lb st (18,600 lb st with reheat) each
Armament: 1×27-mm Mauser cannon, 4×BAe Sky Flash missiles, 4×AIM-9L
Maximum speed: Mach 2.2
Operational range: 1,151 miles

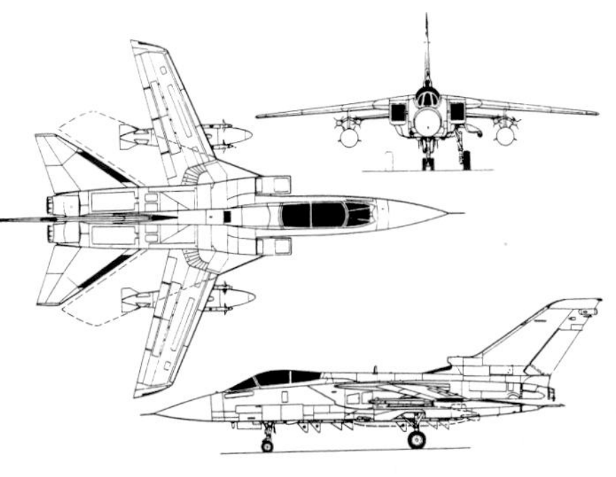

Gloster Meteor (day fighter)

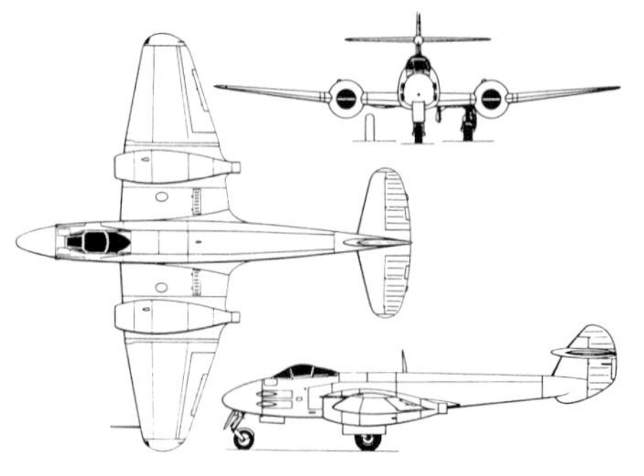

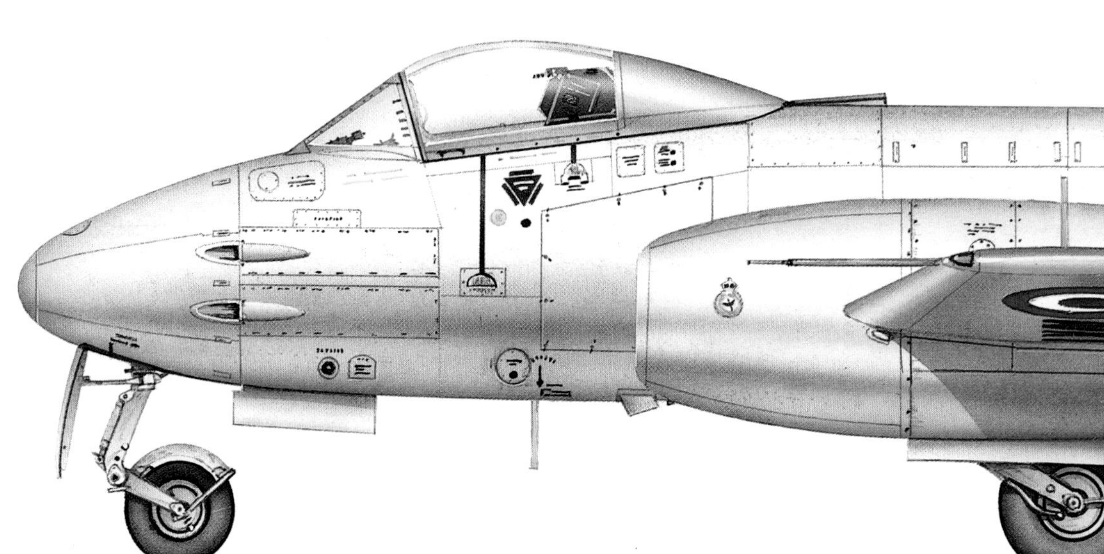

The Meteor F.Mk 8 formed the backbone of RAF Fighter Command between 1950 and 1955, equipping 19 regular and 10 auxiliary squadrons. This aircraft 'belonged' to the CO of North Weald-based No. 601 'County of London' Squadron, Royal Auxiliary Air Force.

De Havilland Vampire

The Vampire's unique twin-boom layout was chosen to keep the jet pipe as short and efficient as possible. Although the prototype first flew in September 1943, the aircraft did not enter service until after the war. It saw limited service with Fighter Command and the Royal Auxiliary Air Force, but was used more widely by squadrons based overseas until replaced by de Havilland Venoms. The later Vampire marks served as hacks, advanced trainers and target tugs after retirement from front-line units. The NF.Mk 10, a two-seat, radar-equipped night fighter, originally designed for export, saw limited RAF service. The Vampire T.Mk 11 was the RAF's standard advanced trainer from 1952 until the introduction of the Gnat in the early 1960s.

Specification: de Havilland Vampire FB.Mk 9 single-seat fighter bomber
Span: 12.19 m (40 ft)
Length: 9.37 m (30 ft 9 in)
Powerplant: de Havilland Goblin, 3,350 lb st
Armament: 4×20-mm cannon in nose, plus bombs or rockets underwing
Maximum speed: 540 mph at 20,000 ft
Operational range: 730 miles

Armstrong Whitworth Meteor

Until 1951, the wartime Mosquito was the RAF's standard night fighter, and a radar-equipped jet night fighter was obviously needed. Gloster were busy producing Meteor day fighters, so Armstrong Whitworth took on the design and production of a Meteor night fighter. The prototype was converted from a Meteor T.Mk 7, the two-seat trainer variant, and first flew on 31 May 1950. The first Meteor night fighter, the NF.Mk 11, entered service in January 1951, and was followed by the NF.Mk 12, 13 and 14. From 1956 the Meteor was replaced by the Javelin in the night fighter role, the final unit, No. 60 Squadron at RAF Tengah, Singapore, converting in August 1961. Converted Meteor night fighters remained in service for target towing and training duties until 1968.

Specification: Armstrong Whitworth Meteor NF.Mk 11 two-seat night fighter
Span: 13.10 m (43 ft)
Length: 14.78 m (48 ft 6 in)
Powerplant: 2×Rolls-Royce Derwent 8, 3,600 lb st each
Armament: 4×20-mm cannon in wings
Maximum speed: 579 mph at 10,000 ft
Operational range: 920 miles

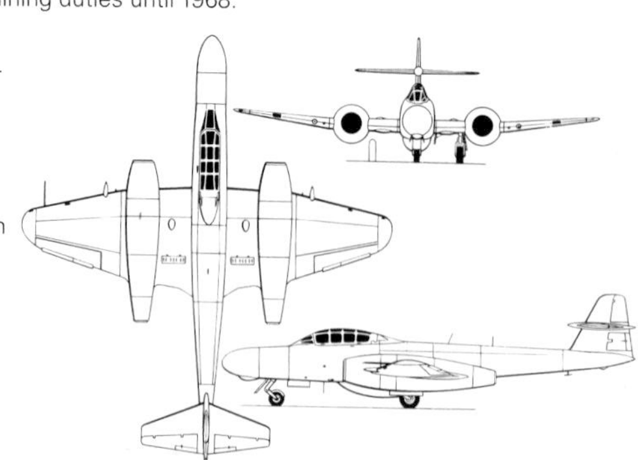

pecification: Gloster Meteor Mk 8 single-seat day fighter
pan: 11.32m (37ft 2in)
ength: 13.58m (44ft 7in)
owerplant: 2×Rolls-Royce erwent 8; 3,600lbst each
rmament: 4×20mm cannon in ose, rockets or fuel tanks nderwing
aximum speed: 590mph at sea vel
perational range: 980 miles

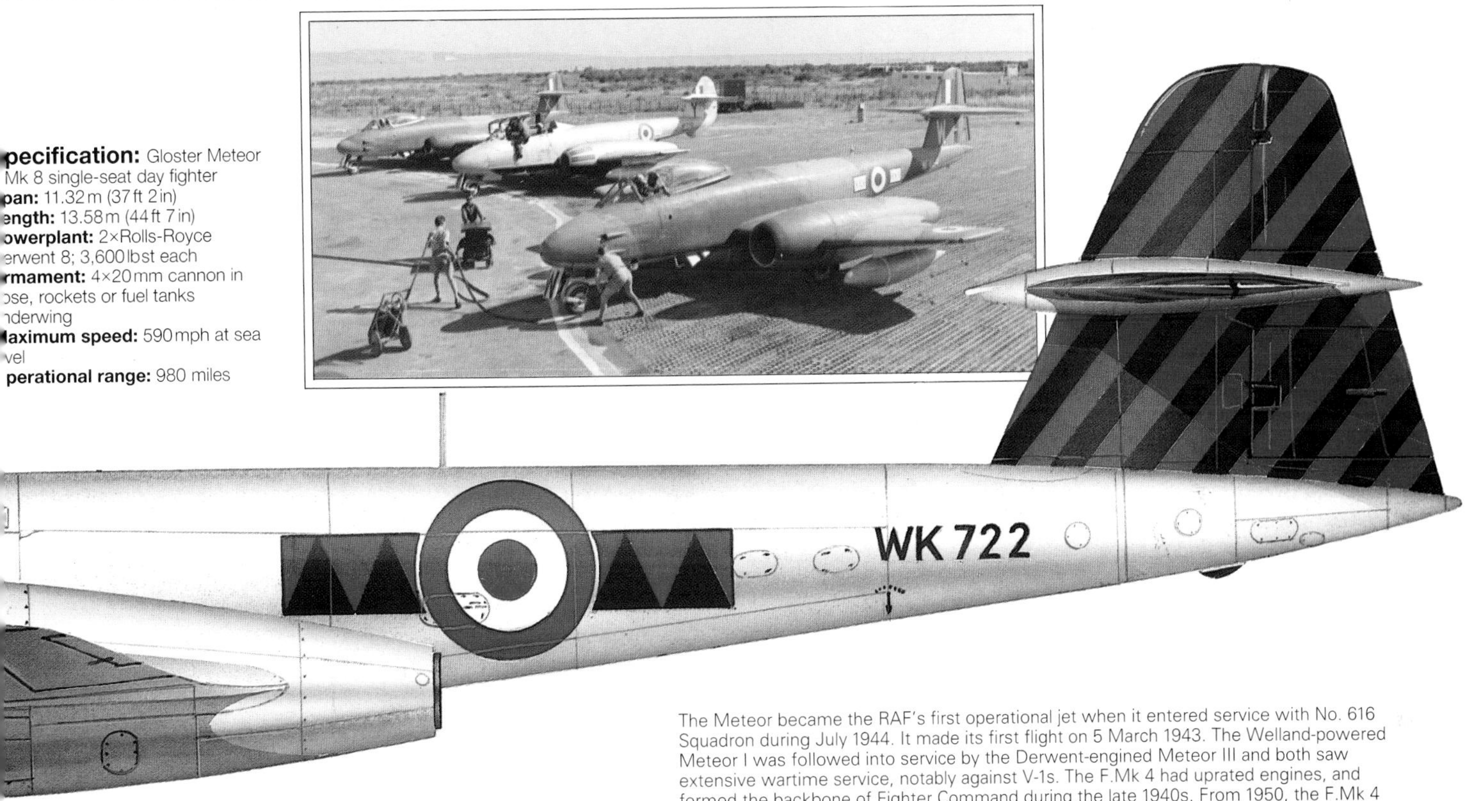

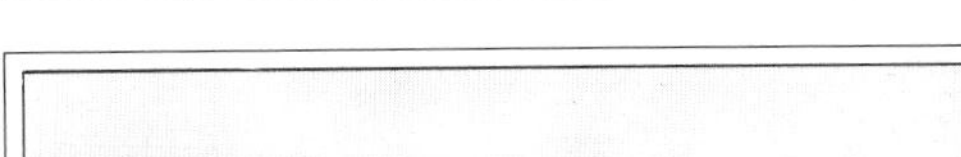

The Meteor became the RAF's first operational jet when it entered service with No. 616 Squadron during July 1944. It made its first flight on 5 March 1943. The Welland-powered Meteor I was followed into service by the Derwent-engined Meteor III and both saw extensive wartime service, notably against V-1s. The F.Mk 4 had uprated engines, and formed the backbone of Fighter Command during the late 1940s. From 1950, the F.Mk 4 was replaced by the much improved F.Mk 8, which had uprated engines and a lengthened fuselage which gave greater fuel capacity and much improved high-speed handling. A new tail unit was fitted and an ejector seat was standard equipment. The last front-line squadron disbanded in April 1957, but Meteors continued in use as hacks and target tugs until 198?.

De Havilland Venom *(fighter bomber)*

The Venom was designed as a replacement for the Vampire, using the same basic design, but with a thinner section, moderately swept wing and a more powerful Ghost engine in place of the Vampire's Goblin. The Venom FB.Mk 1 entered service with No. 11 Squadron during August 1952. The FB. Mk 1 was replaced by the FB.Mk 4, with powered ailerons and large rudders, and which entered service in 1955. The Venom never served with home-based squadrons, but equipped nine German-based squadrons between 1952 and 1957, three squadrons in the Far East, and seven in the Middle East. The aircraft was used in action at Suez, during the Oman rebellion, and during the long war in Malaya. The last Venom FB.Mk 4s were retired from No. 28 Squadron, at Kai Tak, Hong Kong, during July 1962.

Specification: de Havilland Venom FB.Mk 4 single-seat fighter bomber
Span: 12.69m (41ft 8in)
Length: 9.70m (31ft 10in)
Powerplant: de Havilland Ghost 103, 4,850lbst
Armament: 4×20-mm cannon in nose, plus 2,000lb of bombs or rockets underwing
Maximum speed: 640mph at sea level
Operational range: 500 miles

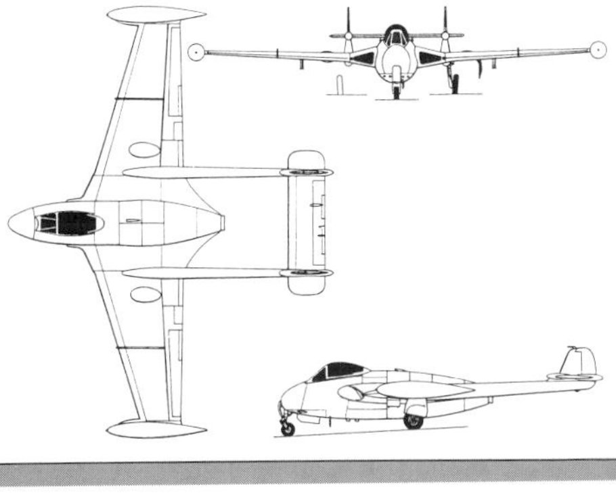

North American Sabre

The North American Sabre, star of the air war in Korea, was acquired by the RAF to equip front-line squadrons in Germany pending the arrival of Britain's own swept-wing fighters, the Swift and the Hunter. The first of some 430 Sabres for the RAF was delivered to Abingdon on 8 December 1952 and Nos 3, 67 and 71 Squadrons converted to the aircraft between March and May 1953, forming the Wildenrath Sabre wing. The Sabre eventually equipped 10 squadrons in Germany and two home-based Fighter Command units, giving the RAF its first modern, transonic fighter. The Sabres delivered to the Royal Air Force were Canadair-built F-86Es, designated Sabre F.Mk 4 by the RAF and RCAF. The last Sabres were retired during June 1956, replaced by Hawker Hunters.

Specification: Canadair Sabre F.Mk 4 single-seat day fighter
Span: 11.28m (37ft 1in)
Length: 11.43m (37ft 6in)
Powerplant: General Electric J-47 GE-13, 5,200lbst
Armament: 6×0.5-in machine-guns in nose
Maximum speed: 670mph
Operational range: 520 miles

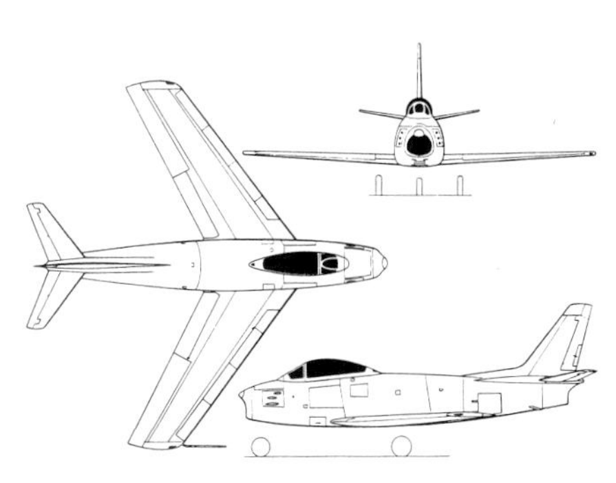

Hawker Hunter

The Hunter, which first flew on 20 July 1941, remains in use with a handful of RAF units, albeit in various support roles. This long-lived fighter was designed to replace the Gloster Meteor, and went on to replace the Venom and the Sabre with squadrons based overseas. The introduction of the Hunter revolutionised Fighter Command, with its quick-change cannon pack allowing speedy turnaround. On retirement from Fighter Command the Hunter was widely used in the ground attack role, and saw active service in Indonesia and the Gulf. The last Hunter squadrons, Nos 45 and 58, were used to provide a pool of single-seat ground attack pilots for the Jaguar force, disbanding in 1976. They remained in service with the Tactical Weapons Unit at Brawdy until replaced by BAe Hawks in 1982.

The Hunter had a brief career as a front-line interceptor, serving with 18 fighter squadrons in the UK and 13 in Germany until replaced by the Lightning in the early 1960s. This F.Mk 6 wears the markings of No. 65 Squadron, based at RAF Duxford.

De Havilland Venom *(night fighters)*

The Venom night fighter was developed from the Venom fighter bomber, with a second seat for the radar navigator in a widened forward fuselage and with a lengthened bulbous nose housing an AI radar scanner. The 180 night-fighting Venoms built served with seven RAF squadrons and superseded Vampires and Meteors. The Venom NF.Mk 2 entered service in 1953 with No. 23 Squadron, with the NF.Mk 3, with improved radar, power-operated rudders and a frameless canopy, following in June 1955 with No. 141 Squadron. The last Venom NF.Mk 3s were with drawn from RAF Fighter Command in 1958, replaced by Gloster Javelins. Although service aircraft carried four 20-mm cannon in the nose, some aircraft were used for Firestreak missile trials.

Specification: de Havilland Venom NF.Mk 3 two-seat night fighter
Span: 12.69 m (41 ft 8 in)
Length: 11.17 m (36 ft 8 in)
Powerplant: de Havilland Ghost 104, 4.950 lb st
Armament: 4×20-mm cannon in nose
Maximum speed: 630 mph
Operational range: 1,000 miles

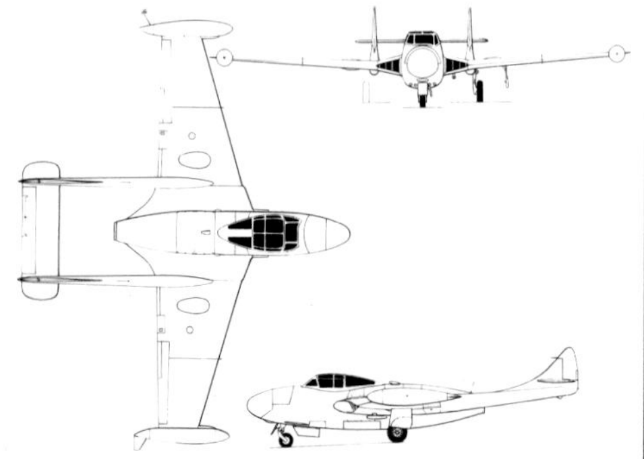

Supermarine Swift

The Supermarine Swift was the first British swept-wing jet fighter to enter service, but it encountered such severe problems that its career as a day fighter lasted only 15 months, and it equipped only one squadron. The first production Swift F.Mk 1s were delivered to No. 56 Squadron in February 1954, and were followed by examples of the F.Mk 2, F.Mk 3 and F.Mk 4. Each mark introduced minor improvements, such as a four-gun armament, reheat and an all-flying tail. The basic problems were not solved, and No. 56 converted back to the Meteor in May 1955. The later FR.Mk 5 enjoyed a successful career as a fighter reconnaissance aircraft in RAF Germany until 1961. A handful of F.Mk 7s were used by the Guided Weapon Development Squadron at RAF Valley for missile trials.

Specification: Supermarine Swift F.Mk 1 single-seat day fighter
Span: 9.85 m (32 ft 4 in)
Length: 13.55 m (41 ft 5½ in)
Powerplant: Rolls-Royce Avon RA7, 7,500 lb st
Armament: 2×30-mm Aden cannon in nose
Maximum speed: 685 mph
Operational range: 480 miles

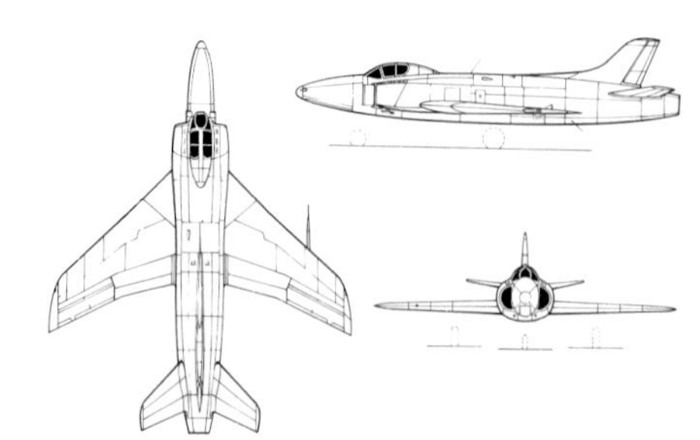

ecification: Hawker Hunter
Ik 6 single-seat day fighter
an: 10.26m (33ft 8in)
ngth: 13.98m (45ft 10½in)
werplant: Rolls-Royce Avon
), 10,000lb st
nament: 4×30-mm cannon in
se; rockets, fuel tanks or bombs
derwing
ximum speed: 715mph
erational range: 1,840 miles
n underwing tanks

Gloster Javelin

Following competitive trials with the de Havilland D.H.110 (which later became the Sea Vixen), the Javelin was selected to replace the Meteor and Venom night fighters in service with the all-weather fighter squadrons of the RAF. The prototype made its maiden flight on 26 November 1951, but the type broke much new ground, and it was not until February 1956 that No. 46 Squadron received its first aircraft. Successive variants introduced new engines, new radar, and the FAW.Mk 7 Firestreak missiles. By the 1960s the Javelin offered few advantages over the single-seat Lightning, however, and the aircraft were retired from Fighter Command service in 1964, from RAF Germany in 1966 and in the Far East in April 1968, when the type was declared obsolete.

Specification: Gloster Javelin FAW.Mk 9 two-seat all-weather interceptor
Span: 15.84m (52ft)
Length: 17.29m (56ft 9in)
Powerplant: 2×Bristol Siddeley Sapphire 6, 8,300lb st
Armament: 2×30-mm Aden cannon in nose; four Firestreak AAMs on underwing pylons
Maximum speed: 620mph
Operational range: 930 miles

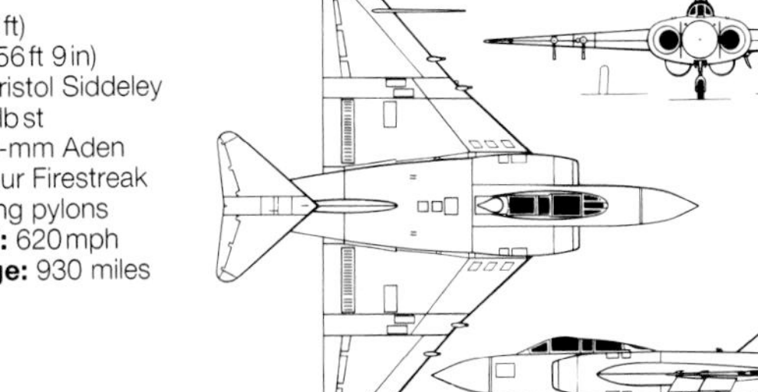

English Electric Lightning

The first of two Sapphire-engined prototype P-1As flew on 4 August 1954 and the much improved P-1B, later named Lightning, on 4 April 1957, and it soon became the first British aircraft to exceed Mach 2. From the start it was obviously a pilot's aeroplane, with superb handling and a breathtaking performance. Ten UK-based squadrons eventually received this fast-climbing, missile-armed, radar-equipped, all-weather interceptor, which marked a huge improvement over the subsonic Hunters and Javelins that it replaced. Four units moved abroad, two to RAF Germany, one to Cyprus, and one to Singapore. Most of the Force converted to Phantoms during the mid-1970s, but the Binbrook wing lingered on, Nos 5 and 11 Squadrons converting to the Tornado F.Mk 3 during 1987 and 1988.

Specification: English Electric Lightning F.Mk 2A single-seat interceptor fighter
Span: 10.61m (34ft 10in)
Length: 16.84m (55ft 3in)
Powerplant: 2×Rolls-Royce Avon 301
Armament: 2×30-mm Aden cannon in upper nose; 2 more in belly; 2×Firestreak AAMs on fuselage pylons
Maximum speed: Mach 2.27
Operational range: 373 miles

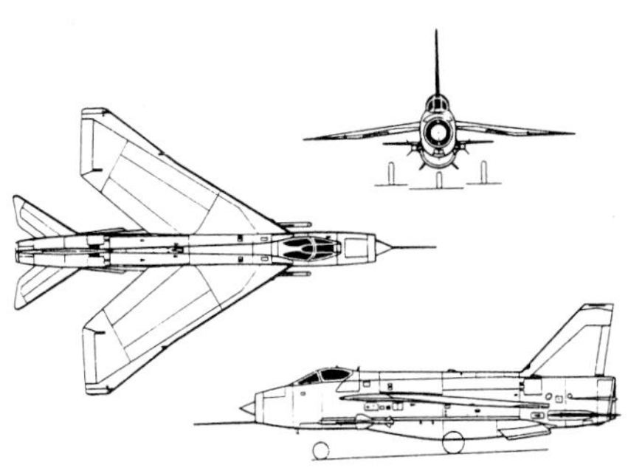

Dassault Super Mystère

From the Mystère IV Dassault evolved the supersonic Mystère IVB with an afterburning Atar 101G turbojet. This was France's first supersonic aeroplane, and flew in December 1953 with advanced features such as integral tankage, flush antennae and a radar gunsight. The prototype was followed by two pre-production and only 16 production aircraft, for the type had been overtaken by the radically improved Super Mystère that first flew in March 1955 with features derived from those of the North American F-100 Super Sabre: thin 'dogtoothed' wings swept at 45° and a flattened nose section. The Super Mystère B-1 was powered by a Rolls-Royce Avon RA.7R, but the 180 production Super Mystère B-2s reverted to a French turbojet. The only variant was a single Super Mystère B-4 with an Atar 9 engine for very high rate of climb.

The Super Mystère B2 represented the end of an era for the Armée de l'Air, being the last day fighter in service before the radar-equipped Mirage III was taken on charge. It served with three Escadres, EC 5, 10 and 12, the latter flying the type until 1977. Towards the end of its career it was employed as a general-purpose fighter bomber.

Sud-Est S.E.535 Mistral

The 1936 nationalization of the French aero industry grouped Lioré et Olivier, Romano and SPCA into the SNCASE group, and in 1941 this absorbed the SNCA du Midi. In 1948 SNCASE secured a licence to build the de Havilland Vampire FB.Mk 5 with the 1361-kg (3,000-lb) thrust de Havilland Goblin 2 turbojet, and the first of these flew in January 1950. SNCASE had meanwhile been developing the Vampire FB.Mk 51 variant with a 2268-kg (5,000-lb) thrust Rolls-Royce Nene built in France by Hispano-Suiza. This flew in December 1950, and 183 of these variants were delivered. SNCASE also developed its own Mistral variant as the S.E.532 (fixed seat) and S.E.535 (ejector seat) with larger air inlets contributing to a significant increase in performance. The Mistral first flew in April 1951, and production totalled 250.

Specification: SNCASE S.E.535 Mistral single-seat fighter and fighter-bomber
Span: 11.58 m (38 ft 0 in)
Length: 9.37 m (30 ft 9 in)
Powerplant: 1×Hispano-Suiza HS 104 (Rolls-Royce Nene Mk 104), 2268 kg (5,000 lb) st
Armament: 4×20-mm cannon, and provision for two 227- or 454-kg (500- or 1,000-lb) bombs or 8×27-kg (60-lb) rockets carried under the wings
Max T/O weight: 5740 kg (12,654 lb)
Max speed: 575 mph at sea level
Operational range: about 1,170 miles

Sud-Est S.E.202 Aquilon

To meet a French naval requirement SNCASE secured a licence to produce the de Havilland Sea Venom in a special Mk 52 variant as the Aquilon with an Italian-built turbojet, strengthened structure and provision for ejector seats. The S.E.20 Aquilon prototype flew in October 1952, and was followed by four pre-production and 20 production aircraft with fixed seats (under an upward-opening hood) and Vampire type landing gear suitable for operation only from shore bases. The S.E.201 prototype then paved the way for two carrier-capable variants with revised landing gear, the S.E.202 with twin ejector seats under a rear-sliding hood (25 built) and the single-seat S.E.203 with US radar in a dielectric nosecone (40 built) for use in conjunction with Nord 5103 air-to-air missiles. The last model was the S.E.204 trainer, of which 19 were built.

Specification: SNCASE S.E.202 Aquilon carrierborne two-seat fighter and fighter-bomber
Span: 13.07 m (42 ft 10.5 in)
Length: 11.13 m (36 ft 6 in)
Powerplant: 1×Fiat-built de Havilland Ghost 48 Mk 1, 2200 kg (4,850 lb) st
Armament: 4×20-mm cannon, plus provision for 8×27-kg (60-lb) rockets carried under the wings
Max T/O weight: 7600 kg (16,755 lb)
Max speed: 581 mph at 9,845 ft
Operational range: 965 miles

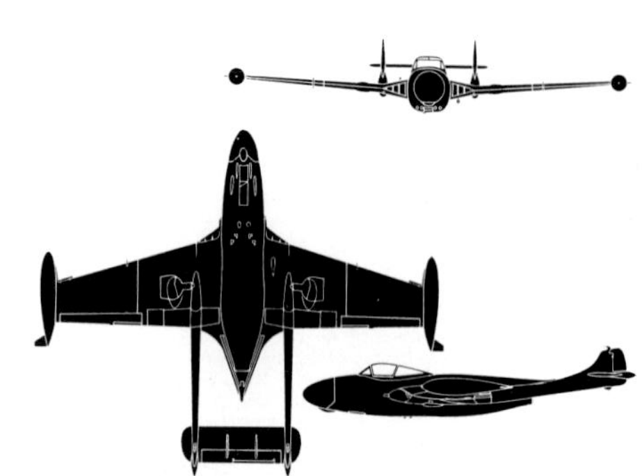

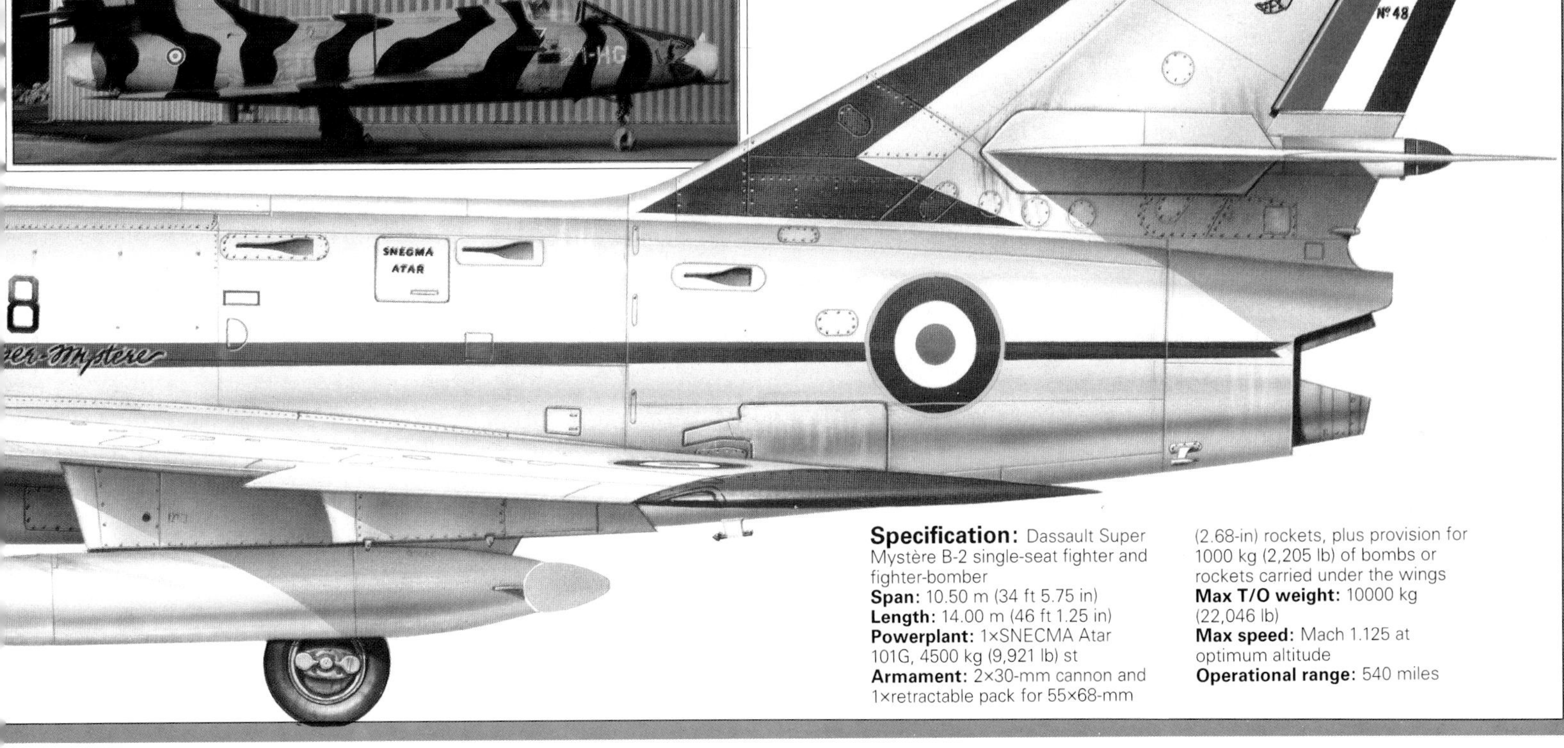

Specification: Dassault Super Mystère B-2 single-seat fighter and fighter-bomber
Span: 10.50 m (34 ft 5.75 in)
Length: 14.00 m (46 ft 1.25 in)
Powerplant: 1×SNECMA Atar 101G, 4500 kg (9,921 lb) st
Armament: 2×30-mm cannon and 1×retractable pack for 55×68-mm (2.68-in) rockets, plus provision for 1000 kg (2,205 lb) of bombs or rockets carried under the wings
Max T/O weight: 10000 kg (22,046 lb)
Max speed: Mach 1.125 at optimum altitude
Operational range: 540 miles

Sud-Ouest S.0.4050 Vautour

In the 1936 nationalization of the French aero industry Blériot-Aéronautique and the Société des Avions Marcel Bloch were grouped as the SNCASO, which in 1941 absorbed the SNCA d'Ouest. In 1951 the SNCASO flew its S.O.4000 twin-jet experimental bomber, and so promising were the trials that the type was rapidly developed as the S.O.4050 multi-role combat aeroplane: Vautour IIA cannon/bomb-armed single-seat attacker, Vautour IIB two-seat bomber with provision for a load of 4500kg (9,921lb) carried internally and externally, and Vautour IIN two-seat all-weather fighter. Trials were held with Armstrong Siddeley Sapphire and Rolls-Royce Avon turbojets, but the Atar 101 was chosen for production aircraft, which began to enter service in early 1956. Orders for the three variants totalled 300, 40 and 140 respectively, but production reached only 30, 40 and 70.

Specification: SNCASO S.O.4050 Vautour IIN two-seat all-weather interceptor and night-fighter
Span: 14.20m (49ft 6.5in)
Length: 15.84m (51ft 11.75in)
Powerplant: 2×SNECMA Atar 101E-3, 3500kg (7,716lb) st each
Armament: 4×30-mm cannon and 2×Matra 104A retractable packs each with 116×68-mm (2.68-in) rockets, plus provision for 4×Nord 5103 or Matra R511 air-to-air missiles, or 4×Matra M116E launchers each with 19×68-mm (2.68-in) rockets carried under the wings
Max speed: 684 mph at sea level
Operational range: 2,485 miles

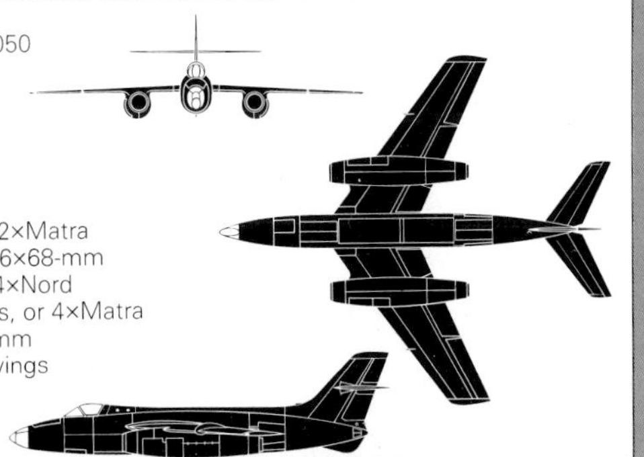

Dassault M.D.450 Ouragan

After World War II Bloch changed his name to Dassault and established the Société des Avions Marcel Dassault, whose first product was the M.D.450 light fighter to a requirement demanding four-cannon armament and a Hispano-built Nene turbojet. The design was simple yet highly effective, and the first Ouragan flew in February 1949. A pre-production batch of 12 aircraft was followed by 350 aircraft for the French air force, 194 Toofani aircraft for the Indian air force with the 2350-kg (5,181-lb) thrust HS 105A, and 12 aircraft for the Israeli air force supplemented by at least another 42 (and possibly 65 or more) from French stocks: both the Indian and Israeli aircraft were used in combat, while several French machines were trialled with features such as a braking parachute, lateral air inlets and twin-wheel main landing gear units.

Specification: Dassault M.D.450 Ouragan single-seat fighter and fighter-bomber
Span: 13.16m (43ft 2in) over tiptanks
Length: 10.74m (35ft 2.75in)
Powerplant: 1×Hispano-Suiza HS 104B (Rolls-Royce Nene Mk 104B), 2270kg (5,004lb) st
Armament: 4×20-mm cannon, plus provision for 2×454-kg (1,000-lb) bombs or 16×105-mm (4.13-in) rockets carried under the wings
Max speed: 584 mph at sea level
Operational range: 560 miles

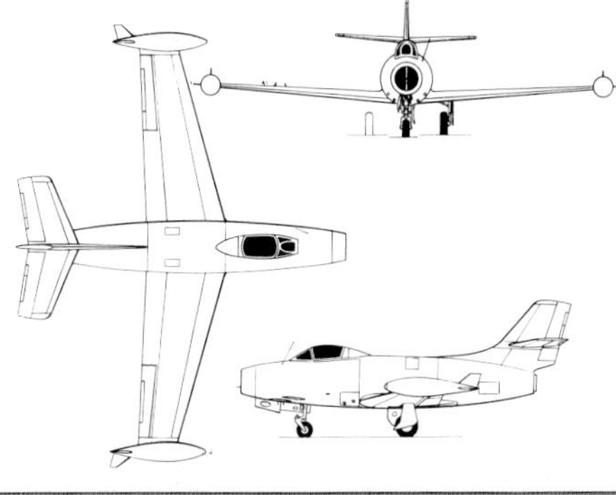

Dassault-Breguet Mirage F.1

Specification: Dassault-Breguet Mirage F.1C single-seat interceptor and multi-role fighter
Span: 8.40 m (27 ft 6.75 in)
Length: 15.00 m (49 ft 2.5 in)
Powerplant: 1×SNECMA Atar 9K-50, 7200 kg (15,873 lb) st
Armament: 2×30-mm cannon, plus provision for up to 4000 kg (8,818 lb) of disposable stores carried on 7×external hardpoints
Max T/O weight: 16200 kg (35,714 lb)
Max speed: Mach 2.2 at 39,370 ft
Operational range: 560 miles

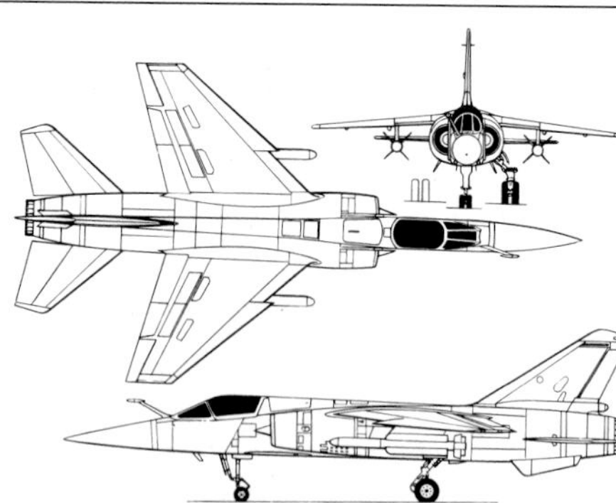

In response to an official requirement for a Mirage III successor, Dassault designed the 20-tonne Mirage F.2 powered by a TF306 turbofan. This flew in June 1966, but Dassault had already seen the advantages of a smaller machine and started development of the similarly configured Mirage F.1 that flew in December 1966. Official enthusiasm swung to the cheaper F.1 with its Cyrano IV radar, high-capacity integral tankage, considerable weapon load, and good performance/agility combination. Deliveries began in 1973, and since then the F.1 has secured an enviable sales record in variants such as the F.1A clear-weather ground-attack aeroplane, F.1B two-seat trainer, F.1C interceptor and its F.1C-200 long-range version with inflight-refuelling capability, F.1CR-200 reconnaissance model with inflight-refuelling capability, and F.1E multi-role export model.

Dassault Mystère

A firm believer in evolutionary development, Dassault moved forward by fitting the Ouragan's fuselage with 30° swept wings to create the M.D.452 Mystère I (HS 104 engine), Mystère IIA (HS 250 engine), similarly engined Mystère IIB and pre-production Mystère IIC (Atar 101 engine). The Mystère I flew in February 1951, and from 1954 180 production Mystère IICs were built. These were followed by the M.D.454 Mystère IVA, of which 421 were built after the flight of the first in September 1952. The Mystère IVA bore only an external resemblance to its predecessor, and had a different engine, oval-section fuselage, powered controls, and thinner yet stronger wings swept at 41° and covered with tapered skins. Deliveries included 67 to India and 50 to Israel, and several advanced developments paved the way for later fighters.

Specification: Dassault M.D.454 Mystère IVA single-seat fighter and fighter-bomber
Span: 11.10 m (36 ft 5.75 in)
Length: 12.90 m (42 ft 2 in)
Powerplant: 1×Hispano-Suiza HS 250A (Rolls-Royce Nene) or HS 350 Verdon, 2850 or 3500 kg (6,280 or 7,716 lb) st respectively
Armament: 2×30-mm cannon, plus provision for 1000 kg (2,205 lb) of bombs or rockets carried under the wings
Max T/O weight: 9500 kg (20,944 lb)
Max speed: 696 mph at sea level
Operational range: 820 miles

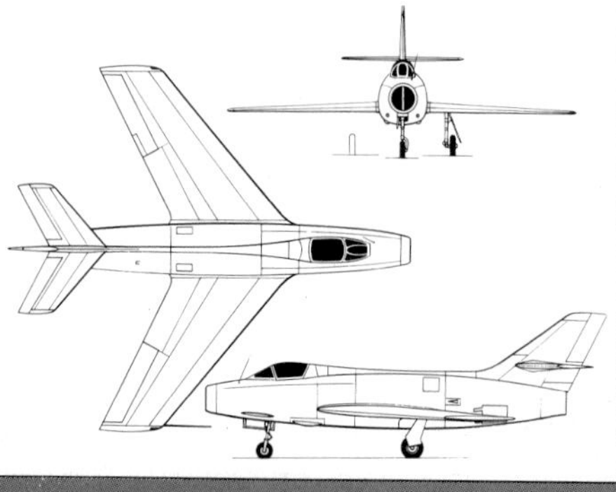

Dassault Etendard

In the early 1950s NATO issued a requirement for a light fighter, and among the responses was Dassault's Etendard VI powered by a 2200-kg (4,850-lb) Bristol Orpheus turbojet. The company had already begun work on a variant for France and, powered by two 1100-kg (2,425-lb) thrust Turboméca Gabizo turbojets, this Etendard II flew in July 1956. Neither variant progressed past the prototype stage (three aircraft each), but Dassault felt that with more power the design had considerable promise. The result was the Etendard IV with approximately double the power of the earlier variants. The prototype flew in July 1956 (eight months before the Etendard VI), and was then developed as the Etendard IVM attack fighter for the French navy. The first Etendard IVM flew in May 1958, and the 69 production examples were joined in service by 21 Etendard IVP photo-reconnaissance aircraft.

Specification: Dassault Etendard IVM carrierborne single-seat attack fighter
Span: 9.60 m (31 ft 5.75 in)
Length: 14.40 m (47 ft 3 in)
Powerplant: 1×SNECMA Atar 8B, 4400 kg (9,700 lb) st
Armament: 2×30-mm cannon, plus provision for up to 1360 kg (2,998 lb) of disposable stores carried on 4×underwing hardpoints
Max T/O weight: 10200 kg (22,487 lb)
Max speed: 683 mph at sea level
Operational range: 1,056 miles

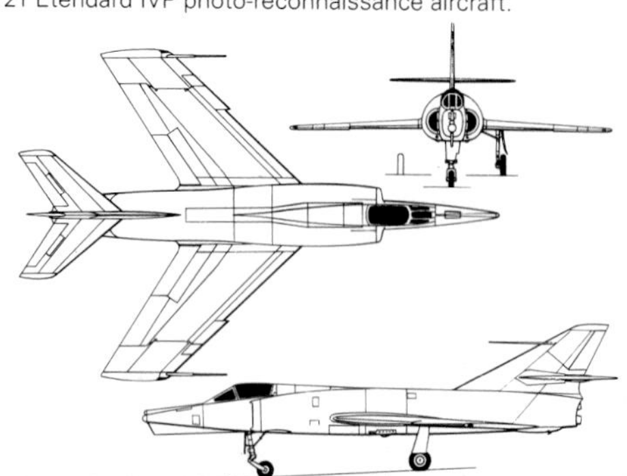

eplacing the Super Mystère B2 and Vautour IIN in French rvice, the Mirage F.1 is a potent radar-equipped interceptor. 'ssile armament is used for medium range work, and DEFA -mm cannon are carried for short-range encounters. rcraft currently carry the MATRA 550 Magic missile on the ngtip rails and the Super 530 radar-homing missile. This : 12 aircraft is seen carrying the earlier MATRA 530 on the 'ng pylons.

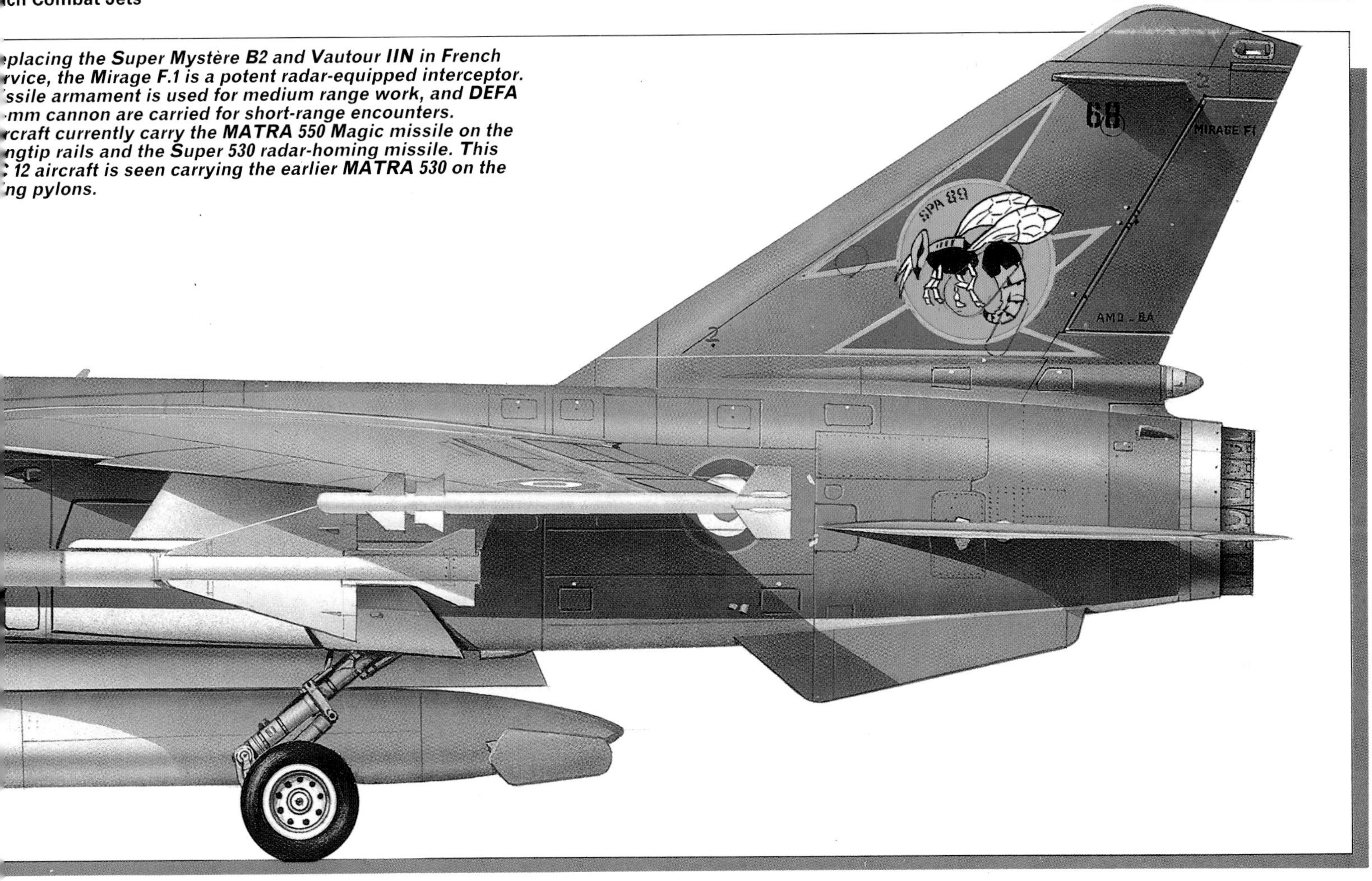

Dassault Mirage IIIC

Vith the Mirage series Dassault adopted a wholly new configuration, the 60° tailless delta esigned to promote climb and altitude performance in an interceptor. Flown in June 1955, ie M.D.550 Mirage I had two 1000-kg (2,205-lb) thrust Dassault-built Armstrong Siddeley iper turbojets and a booster rocket for Mach 1.3 performance, while the unbuilt Mirage II vould have had two Turboméca Gabizo turbojets. As with the Etendard, Dassault opted for nore power and thereby produced the Mirage III with an afterburning Atar 101G-2 turbojet nd jettisonable rocket pack. This flew in November 1956 and later reached Mach 1.9, and vas developed into the Mach 2.2 Mirage IIIA with a redesigned and thinner wing. This led to ne Mirage IIIC production fighter and the Mirage IIIB two-seat trainer, successful aircraft nat paved the way for a highly successful family.

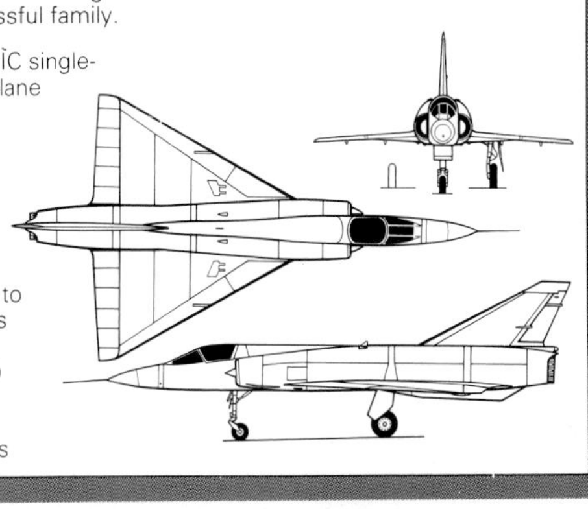

Specification: Dassault Mirage IIIC single-eat interceptor and light attack aeroplane
pan: 8.22 m (26 ft 11.75 in)
ength: 15.50 m (50 ft 10.25 in)
owerplant: 1×SNECMA Atar 9B nd 1×optional SEPR 844, 6000 kg 3,228 lb) and 1675 kg (3,693 lb) st espectively
rmament: 2×30-mm cannon without rocket), plus provision for up to 360 kg (2,998 lb) of disposable stores arried on 3×external hardpoints
Max T/O weight: 8935 kg (19,698 lb)
Max speed: Mach 2.2 mph at ptimum altitude
perational range: about 1,000 miles

Dassault Mirage IIIE

From the Mirage IIIC Dassault developed the Mirage IIIE interdiction and strike aeroplane with a longer fuselage, more fuel, Cyrano II rather than Ibis radar matched to a new fire-control system, Marconi Doppler navigation, and five hardpoints for a greater disposable load. The first Mirage IIIE flew in April 1961, and more than 1,250 of its type were built. The Mirage IIIE was used by France in the strike role, while export versions were used as multi-role fighters. Variants included the Mirage IIIO (and two-seat Mirage IIID) for Australia, the Mirage IIIR reconnaissance sub-family, and the Mirage IIIS for Switzerland with Hughes TARAN radar matched to Falcon AAMs. Many of the Z-suffixed South African aircraft have the higher-rated Atar 9K-50, an engine offered in retrofit packages that can add modern electronics, a 'fly-by-wire' control system and canard foreplanes.

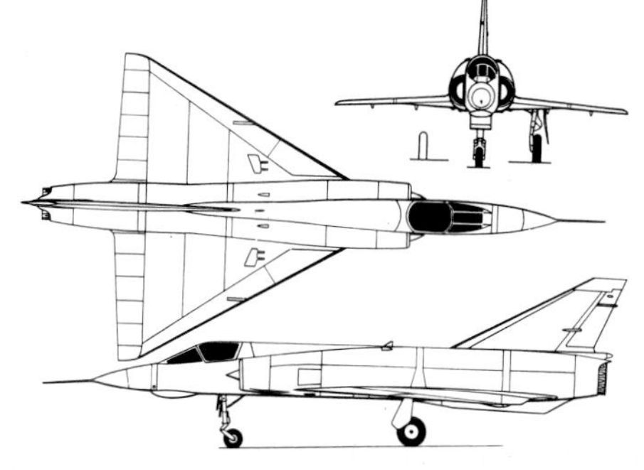

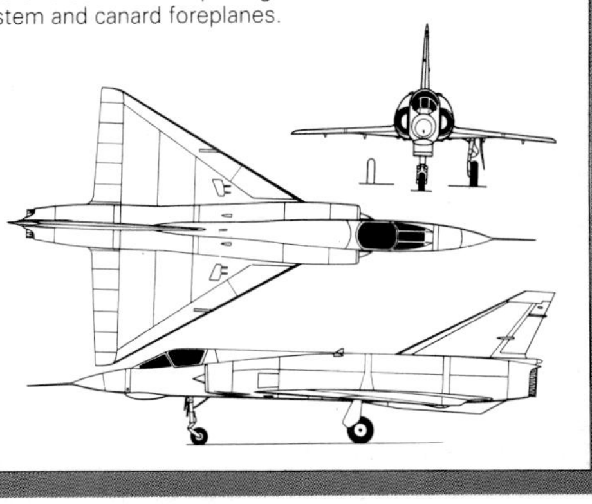

Specification: Dassault Mirage IIIE single-seat strike, interdiction and multi-role fighter
Span: 8.22 m (26 ft 11.75 in)
Length: 15.03 m (49 ft 3.5 in)
Powerplant: 1×SNECMA Atar 9C, 6200 kg (13,670 lb) st
Armament: 2×30-mm cannon, plus provision for up to 4000 kg (8,818 lb) of disposable stores carried on 5×external hardpoints
Max T/O weight: 13700 kg (30,200 lb)
Max speed: Mach 2.2 at 39,370 ft
Operational range: about 1,000 miles

Dassault Mirage IV

To meet the requirements of France's strategic nuclear force, in 1956 Dassault was asked to create a supersonic bomber able to reach a high percentage of strategic targets in Europe with the 60-kiloton AN-22 free-fall nuclear bomb. The company responded with a derivative of a twin-engined night-fighter project, and in 1957 this was enlarged to accommodate two Pratt & Whitney J75 turbojets. Further refinement led to the Atar-engined Mirage IV that flew in June 1959, the necessary payload/range requirement being met by the adoption of Boeing C-135F tankers to support the bombers. Delivery of 62 Mirage IVAs was made between 1964 and 1968. Some 12 were modified as reconnaissance aircraft, and in the mid-1980s 18 more were modified to Mirage IVP standard with the 150-kiloton ASMP stand-off nuclear missile and Thomson-CSF Arcana radar and low-level penetration system.

Specification: Dassault Mirage IVA two-seat strategic bomber
Span: 11.85 m (38 ft 10.5 in)
Length: 23.50 m (77 ft 1 in)
Powerplant: 2×SNECMA Atar 9K-50, 7000 kg (15,432 lb) st each
Armament: 1×AN-22 free-fall nuclear bomb semi-recessed under the fuselage, or provision for 16×450 kg (992 lb) bombs or 4×AS.37 Martel air-to-surface missiles carried on 4 hardpoints
Max T/O weight: 33475 kg (73,799 lb)
Max speed: Mach 2.2 at 40,060 ft
Operational range: 1,540 miles

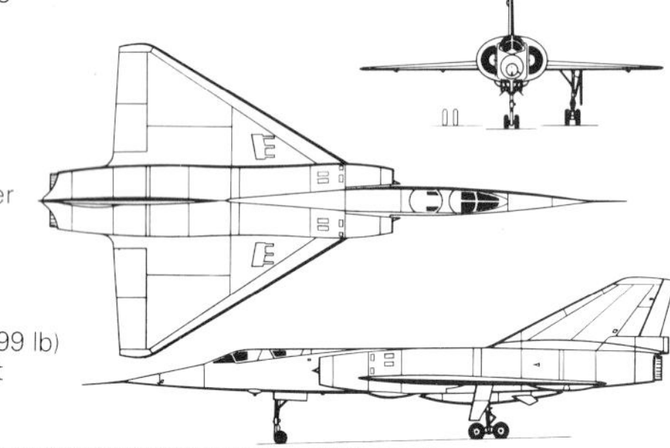

Dassault Mirage 5

In 1965 Israel suggested to Dassault a clear-weather version of the Mirage III with the weighty electronics of the latter omitted to provide additional fuel volume and weight-carrying capability. Thus was born the Mirage 5 that first flew in May 1967. The variant is distinguishable from the Mirage III by its additional hardpoints and slimmer nose carrying optional Aida ranging radar. The basic model is the Mirage 5A (called 5F in France), and othe variants are the Mirage 5D two-seater, Mirage 5R reconnaissance platform and updated Mirage 5-50 multi-role version with the 7200-kg (15,873-lb) thrust Atar 9K-50, greater weights and performance, and electronic sophistication greater than that of the Mirage III through the adoption of Thomson-CSF Agave or Cyrano IVM multi-role radar matched to weapons such as the AM.39 Exocet anti-ship missile.

Specification: Dassault Mirage 5A single-seat ground-attack and interceptor fighter
Span: 8.22 m (26 ft 11.75 in)
Length: 15.55 m (51 ft 0.25 in)
Powerplant: 1×SNECMA Atar 9C, 6200 kg (13,670 lb) st
Armament: 2×30-mm cannon, plus provision for up to 4200 kg (9,259 lb) of disposable stores carried on 7×external hardpoints
Max T/O weight: 13700 kg (30,200 lb)
Max speed: Mach 2.2 at 39,370 ft
Operational range: about 1,000 miles

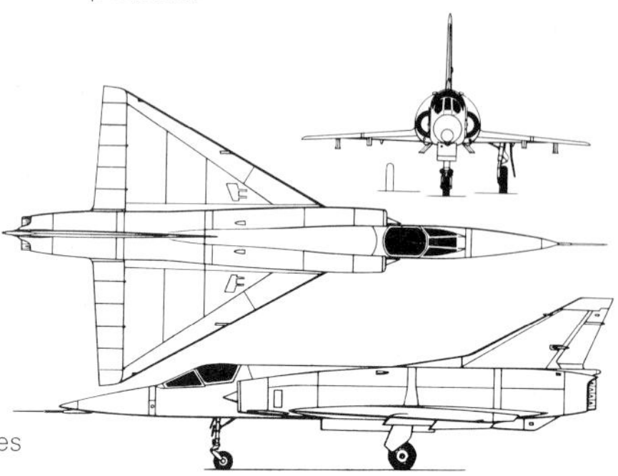

Dassault Super Etendard

In the late 1960s Dassault persuaded the French authorities that an updated Etendard would make a better replacement for the Etendard than the currently envisaged Jaguar-M proposed by SEPECAT. Thus was created the Super Etendard with a redesigned structure for operation at higher speeds and weights, a revised powerplant (essentially that of the Mirage F.1 with the afterburner removed), Agave multi-function radar for use with weapons such as the AM.39 Exocet anti-ship missile, a new inertial navigation system, and a larger and more diverse weapon load. The concept was pioneered in a rebuilt Etendard IVM that flew as the prototype in October 1974, allowing deliveries of production Super Etendards from 1977. The type has been used in combat by Argentina, France and Iraq, and French aircraft have been modified to carry the 150-kiloton ASMP stand-off nuclear missile.

Specification: Dassault-Breguet Super Etendard carrierborne single-seat strike and attack fighter
Span: 9.60 m (31 ft 6 in)
Length: 14.31 m (46 ft 11.5 in)
Powerplant: 1×SNECMA Atar 8K-50, 5000 kg (11,023 lb) st
Armament: 2×30-mm cannon, and provision for up to 2100 kg (4,630 lb) of disposable stores carried on 5×external hardpoints
Max T/O weight: 12000 kg (26,455 lb)
Max speed: Mach 1 at 36,090 ft
Operational range: 1,056 miles

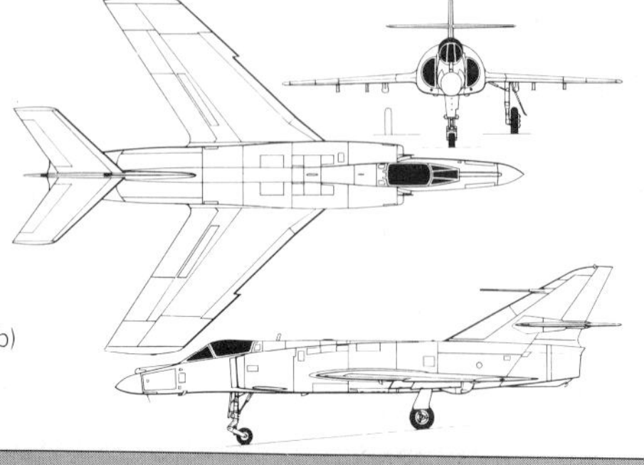

Dassault Mirage 2000

Though resembling the Mirage III, the Mirage 2000 is a completely different aeroplane that overcomes most of the delta's limitations by use of a 'fly-by-wire' control system and a virtually variable-camber wing (full-span leading-edge slats and trailing-edge elevons). Designed to supersede the Mirage III and complement the Mirage F.1, the Mirage 2000 first flew in March 1978 and began to enter service in 1983 with increasingly capable radars for a varied warload. Since then the type has proliferated in French service and secured considerable export success. Current variants are the Mirage 2000B two-seat trainer, Mirage 2000C interceptor, Mirage 2000N low-level nuclear penetration fighter with Antilope radar and the ASMP stand-off missile, the Mirage 2000-5 non-nuclear export version of the Mirage 2000N, and the Mirage 2000R reconnaissance platform.

Specification: Dassault-Breguet Mirage 2000C single-seat interceptor and air-superiority fighter with attack capability
Span: 9.00 m (29 ft 6 in)
Length: 14.35 m (47 ft 1 in)
Powerplant: 1×SNECMA M53-P2, 9700 kg (21,385 lb) st
Armament: 2×30-mm cannon, plus provision for up to 6300 kg (13,889 lb) of disposable stores carried on 9×external hardpoints
Max T/O weight: 17000 kg (37,478 lb)
Max speed: Mach 2.35 at 39,370 ft
Operational range: 870 miles

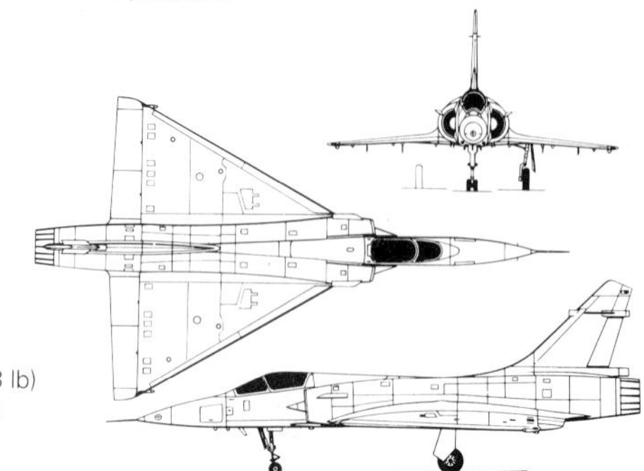

awker Siddeley Harrier GR.Mk 3

e Harrier is truly a truly decisive type, marking as it does the appearance of the first OVL combat aeroplane, in this instance using a single turbofan with a quartet of vectoring zzles for balanced distribution of the thrust. The Harrier resulted from the P.1127 ototype that first flew in October 1960, and was developed into the Kestrel evaluation that uipped a joint British, American and West German squadron from 1965. Plans then called the development of the Mach 2 P.1154, but this was cancelled in favour of the transonic t cheaper Harrier GR.Mk 1 with the 8618-kg (19,000-lb) Pegasus Mk 101, later upgraded to arrier GR.Mk 1A standard with the 9072-kg (20,000-lb) thrust Pegasus Mk 102. The GR.Mk began to enter service in 1969, and 92 surviving aircraft were upgraded to GR.Mk 3s with ore power and a revised nose for a laser ranger and marked-target seeker.

pecification: Hawker Siddeley arrier GR.Mk 3 single-seat STOVL ose-support and reconnaissance roplane
an: 7.70 m (25 ft 3 in)
ngth: 14.38 m (47 ft 2 in)
owerplant: 1×Rolls-Royce (Bristol ddeley) Pegasus Mk 103, 9752 kg 1,500 lb) st
rmament: 2×30-mm cannon, us provision for up to 3629 kg ,000 lb) of disposable stores arried on 7×hardpoints
ax T/O weight: 11431+kg (25,200+lb)
ax speed: 737+mph at low altitude
perational range: 520 miles

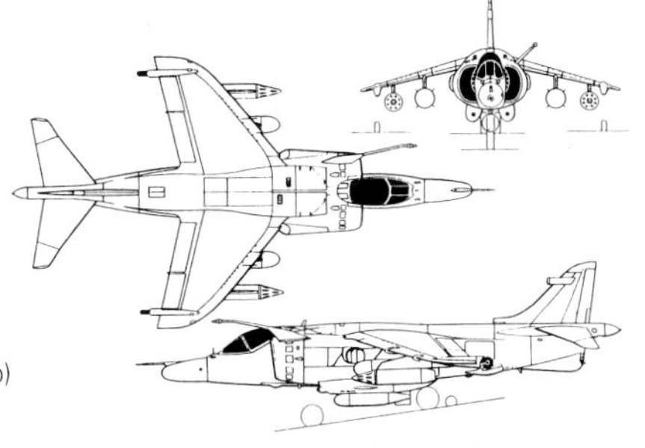

McDonnell Phantom FGR.Mk 2

When, in the mid-1960s the UK ordered the McDonnell F-4 Phantom for the Royal Navy and RAF, it was decided for political reasons that the type should be re-engined with Spey turbofans in place of the original General Electric J79 turbojets. This delayed the programme, led to higher unit costs and demanded the establishment of a separate logistic supply line, but failed to produce the anticipated improvements in range. The version for the RAF was the Phantom FGR.Mk 2, known to the Americans as the F-4M and first flown in February 1967. FGR.Mk 2 production totalled 120, deliveries being completed in October 1969: the variant has the AWG-12 radar fire-control system, Sky Flash AAM capability, a Ferranti inertial navigation system, a flush-fitting EMI reconnaissance package and, as a retrofit, a radar-warning receiver at the top of the fin. Two squadrons serve with RAF Germany at Wildenrath.

Specification: McDonnell Douglas Phantom FGR.Mk 2 two-seat all-weather fighter, ground-attack and tactical reconnaissance aeroplane
Span: 11.77 m (38 ft 4.75 in)
Length: 17.55 m (58 ft 11 in)
Powerplant: 2×Rolls-Royce Spey Mk 202, 9306 kg (20,350 lb) st each
Armament: 4×Sky Flash or Sparrow AAMs and 4×AIM-9 Sidewinder AAMs, or provision for up to 7258 kg (16,000 lb) of disposable stores on 5×hardpoints
Max T/O weight: 26309 kg (58,000 lb)
Max speed: Mach 2.1 at 40,000 ft
Operational range: 300 miles

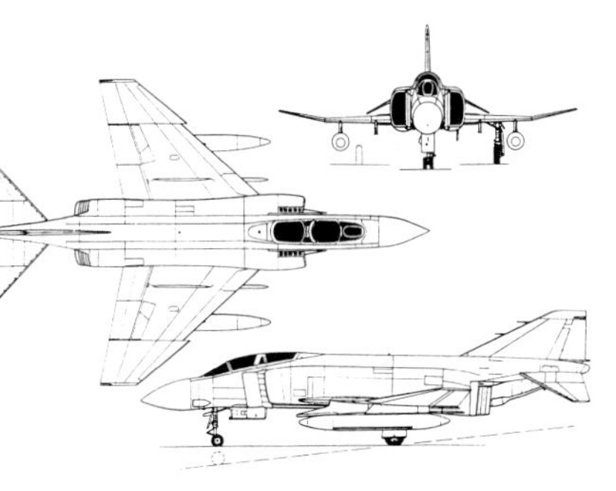

SEPECAT Jaguar GR.Mk 1

he Jaguar resulted from a pooling of separate British and French efforts of the early 1960s owards a supersonic trainer with limited combat capability. The Jaguar is similar to the rench Breguet Br.121 in its high-wing layout allowing considerable underwing store-carrying eight, and first flew in September 1968. Under British pressure the type then matured with o good a weapons-carriage capability and so capable a nav/attack system (without radar but elying instead on a high-quality inertial navigation system, central computer, laser ranger nd marked-target seeker, and HUD) that training became very much the subsidiary role. he two British versions are the Jaguar GR.Mk 1 with 3315-kg (7,305-lb) thrust Adour Mk 02 turbofans (upgraded from 1978 with Adour Mk 104 engines) and the Jaguar T.Mk 2 onversion trainer with a lengthened fuselage for the second cockpit.

Specification: SEPECAT Jaguar GR.Mk 1 ingle-seat all-weather attack, close-upport and reconnaissance aeroplane
Span: 8.69 m (28 ft 6 in)
Length: 16.83 m (55 ft 2.5 in) ncluding probe
Powerplant: 2×Rolls-Royce/ urbomeca Adour Mk 104, 3647 kg (8,040 lb) st each
Armament: 2×30-mm cannon, plus provision for up o 4763 kg (10,500 lb) of disposable stores carried on 5×hardpoints
Max T/O weight: 15700 kg (34,610 lb)
Max speed: Mach 1.6 at 36,000 ft
Operational range: 668 miles

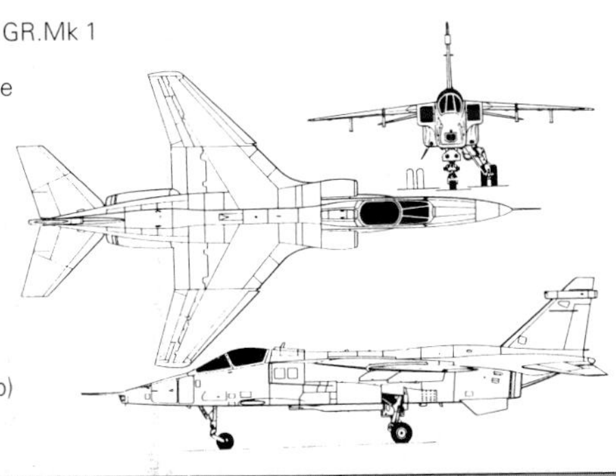

Harrier GR.Mk 5 and GR.Mk 7

The Harrier II is largely a US development of the Harrier with several major improvements. Among these are a wing (plus fuselage and tail unit sections) made of graphite epoxy composite, a bigger supercritical-section wing fitted with larger flaps, drooping ailerons and leading-edge root extensions, extra hardpoints, enhanced lift improvement devices, and a redesigned forward fuselage to provide the pilot with better fields of vision. The type flew in YAV-8B prototype form in November 1978, and service deliveries began in 1983. The British version is the Harrier GR.Mk 5, largely equivalent to the Americans' AV-8B but assembled in the UK and featuring a Martin-Baker ejector seat, a Zeus ECM system, a FIN1075 inertial navigation system, a moving map display, and provision for different weapons. There is also to be a Harrier GR.Mk 7 night-attack version with a thermal imaging attack system.

Specification: McDonnell Douglas/British Aerospace Harrier GR.Mk 5 single-seat close-support aeroplane
Span: 9.25 m (30 ft 4 in)
Length: 14.12 m (46 ft 4 in)
Powerplant: 1×Rolls-Royce Pegasus 11-21 Mk 105, 9979 kg (22,000 lb) st
Armament: 2×25-mm cannon, plus provision for up to 7711 kg (17,000 lb) of disposable stores carried on 9×hardpoints
Max T/O weight: 14061 kg (31,000 lb)
Max speed: 673 mph at sea level
Operational range: 325 miles with 2722-kg (6,000-lb) warload

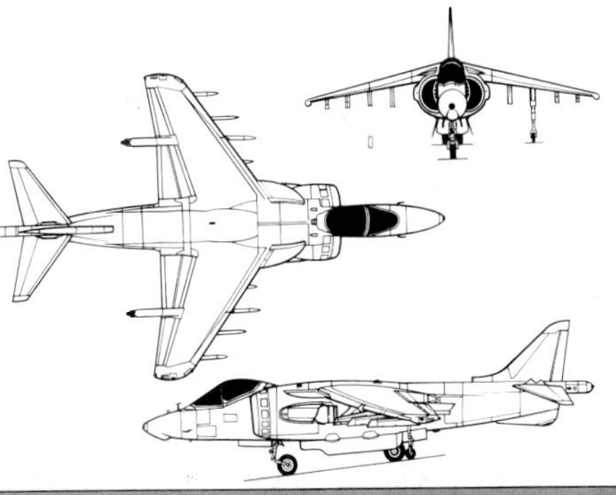

de Havilland **Venom FB.Mk 1/4**

The Venom was a logical extension of the Vampire's design philosophy using the more powerful Ghost turbojet and wings with very slight leading-edge sweep for improved performance, especially in climb. The D.H.112 prototype first flew in September 1949, and the type was developed in three forms as a two-seat night-fighter, as a two-seat naval all-weather and strike fighter, and as a single-seat fighter-bomber. The Venom FB.Mk 1 single-seater entered service in 1952, and 379 aircraft equipped squadrons in Germany and the Middle East. In 1955 there appeared the Venom FB.Mk 4 with power-operated ailerons, redesigned tail surfaces and an ejector seat: the type was used in combat during the 1956 Suez campaign and the 1957 Omani rebellion. Production amounted to 150 aircraft, and the FB.Mk 4 survived in Far Eastern service until supplanted by the Hunter FGA.Mk 9 during 1962.

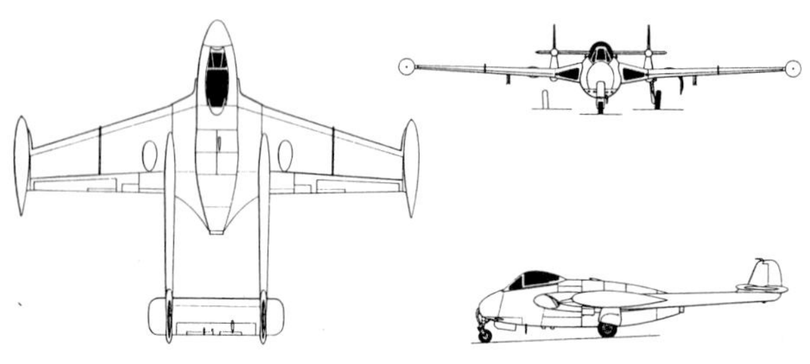

Bristol Beaufighter TF.Mk X

The only version of the classic Beaufighter to see first-line service after World War II was the last variant for Coastal Command, the Beaufighter TF.Mk X anti-ship strike fighter which served with one home and several Far Eastern squadrons. The 2,205 TF.Mk Xs succeeded the Mk VIC and interim Mk XIC from 1943 and were notable for their great power, the shipping search radar with its antenna in a 'thimble' radome on the nose, and the provision for torpedo, rocket and bomb (or mixed) armament. The last aircraft was delivered in September 1945, and the type was retired from first-line service in 1950 with the arrival of the Brigand in the Far East. Between 1948 and 1950 some 35 TF.Mk Xs were converted as TT.Mk 10 target-tugs, the last of these being retired only in 1960.

Specification: Bristol Beaufighter TF.Mk X two-seat torpedo bomber and anti-ship strike fighter
Span: 17.63 m (57 ft 10 in)
Length: 12.70 m (41 ft 8 in)
Powerplant: 2×Bristol Hercules XVII, 1320 kW (1,770 hp) each
Armament: 4×20-mm cannon, 1×7.7-mm (0.303-in) machine-gun, 1×728- or 954-kg (1,605- or 2,127-lb) torpedo under the fuselage, and 2×454-kg (1,000-lb) bombs or 8×27-kg (60-lb) rockets under the wings
Normal T/O weight: 11521 kg (25,400 lb)
Max speed: 303 mph at 1,300 ft
Operational range: 1,540 miles

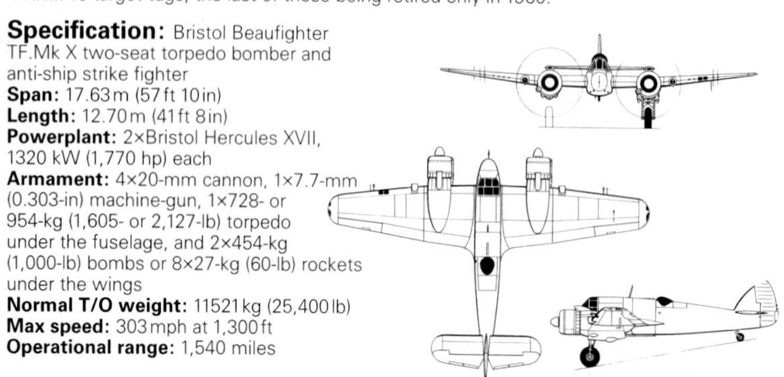

Hawker Tempest F.Mk 2

Just too late for service in World War II, the Tempest Mk II (post-war F.Mk 2) was one of the finest piston-engined fighters ever built. The type was a close relative of the earlier Tempest Mks V and VI, but whereas these were powered by the massive Napier Sabre H-configured engine with a chin radiator, the F.Mk 2 had the superb Centaurus air-cooled radial for better performance and superior handling. The first Mk II had flown in June 1943, but production of the initial 500 machines ordered was slowed by a switch from Gloster to Bristol as manufacturer. The first production machine flew in October 1944, and the type began to enter service in November 1945. More than 1,000 aircraft were cancelled, just 472 being built by Bristol (50) and Hawker (422). The F.Mk 2 was flown by 10 squadrons (two in the UK, three in Germany, four in India and one in the Far East) before the type was withdrawn in 1951.

Specification: Hawker Tempest F.Mk 2 single-seat fighter and fighter-bomber
Span: 12.50 m (41 ft 0 in)
Length: 10.49 m (34 ft 5 in)
Powerplant: 1×Bristol Centaurus, 1883 kW (2,526 hp)
Armament: 4×20-mm cannon, plus provision for up to 907 kg (2,000 lb) of bombs or 8×27-kg (60-lb) rockets carried under the wings
Max T/O weight: 6010 kg (13,250 lb)
Max speed: 440 mph at 15,000 ft
Operational range: 820 miles

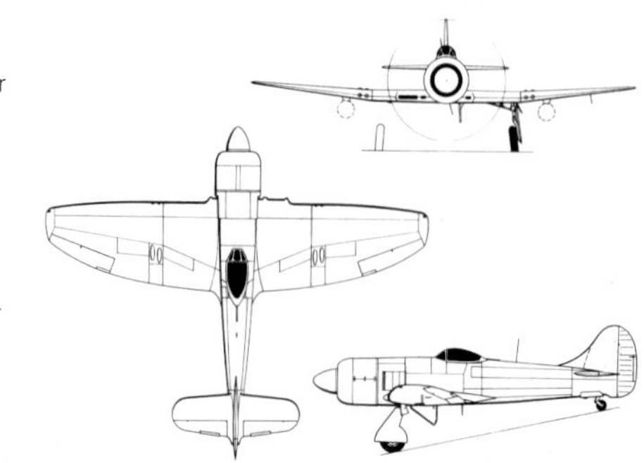

Specification: de Havilland Venom FB.Mk 1 single-seat fighter-bomber
Span: 12.70 m (41 ft 8 in)
Length: 9.70 m (31 ft 10 in)
Powerplant: 1×de Havilland Ghost Mk 103, 2200 kg (4,850 lb) st
Armament: 4×20-mm cannon, plus provision for up to 907 kg (2,000 lb) of bombs and 8×27-kg (60-lb) rockets carried under the wings
Normal T/O weight: 6985 kg (15,400 lb)
Max speed: 640 mph at high altitude
Operational range: not revealed

This Venom is one of No. 6 Squadron's FB.Mk 4s, depicted wearing the black and yellow stripes applied to British, French and Israeli aircraft taking part in the 1956 Suez campaign against Egypt. During the conflict the Venoms flew from Cyprus on ground attack missions, using their internal 20-mm cannon and eight unguided rockets on the pylons mounted under the engine intakes.

de Havilland *Mosquito FB.Mk VI*

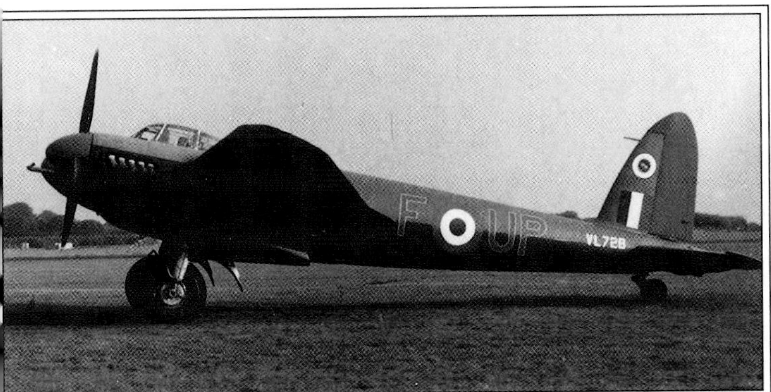

The legendary Mosquito was one of the decisive aircraft of World War II, and was produced in large numbers and in many variants optimised for the bomber, reconnaissance, night-fighter and fighter-bomber roles. The most numerous version (2,584 built) was the Mosquito FB.Mk VI fighter-bomber, and this survived into limited post-war employment. The type was developed in two forms, namely the FB.Mk VI Series 1 with 1080-kW (1,460-hp) Merlin 21s or 23s and internal accommodation for two 113-kg (250-lb) bombs aft of the four cannon breeches, and the FB.Mk VI Series 2 with 1219-kW (1,635-hp) Merlin 25s and provision for two 227-kg (500-lb) bombs or eight 27-kg (60-lb) rockets in place of the drop tanks carried by Series 1 aircraft. Post-war FB.Mk VI units mainly formed six squadrons of the British Air Forces of Occupation in Germany and two in Iraq.

Specification: de Havilland Mosquito FB.Mk VI Series 2 two-seat fighter-bomber
Span: 16.51 m (54 ft 2 in)
Length: 12.34 m (40 ft 6 in)
Powerplant: 2×Rolls-Royce Merlin 25, 1219 kW (1,635 hp) each
Armament: 4×20-mm cannon, plus provision for 2×113-kg (250-lb) bombs carried internally, and 2×227-kg (500-lb) bombs or 8×27-kg (60-lb) rockets carried under the wings
Max T/O weight: 10115 kg (22,300 lb)
Max speed: 380 mph at 13,000 ft
Operational range: 1,705 miles

Bristol Brigand B.Mk 1

The Brigand was planned as a three-seat torpedo bomber with Hercules VIII radials to replace the Beaufighter, but when the Buckingham (planned as a Blenheim replacement) was selected in this role the Brigand was developed for overseas squadrons as a light bomber with a fuselage of smaller section, no power-operated turret, and the flying surfaces plus more-powerful engines of the Buckingham. The Type 164 prototype flew in December 1944 with Centaurus VII radials, and the Brigand B.Mk 1 began to enter service in 1949, finally equipping two Near Eastern and two Far Eastern squadrons. The type was used extensively in the Malayan Emergency between 1950 and 1954, and the 143 production aircraft included 16 Brigand Met.Mk 3 weather reconnaissance aircraft as well as nine Brigand T.Mk 4 night-fighter radar trainers; some B.Mk 1s were converted to a similar Brigand T.Mk 5 standard.

Specification: Bristol Brigand B.Mk 1 three-seat light ground-attack bomber
Span: 22.05 m (72 ft 4 in)
Length: 14.15 m (46 ft 5 in)
Powerplant: 2×Bristol Centaurus 57, 2095 kW (2,810 hp) each
Armament: 4×20-mm cannon, plus provision for up to 907 kg (2,000 lb) of bombs under the fuselage or 16×rockets under the wings
Max T/O weight: 17690 kg (39,000 lb)
Max speed: 358 mph at 16,000 ft
Operational range: 1,980 miles

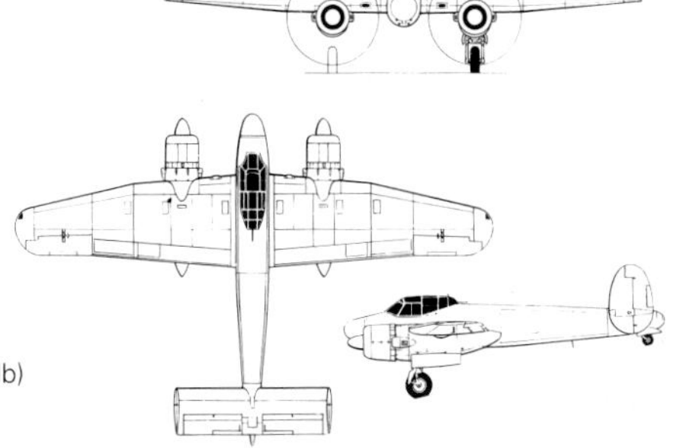

English Electric **Canberra B(I) series**

Conversions of the Canberra B.Mk 6 British-based light bombers for Near and Far Eastern service with three squadrons were the Canberra B.Mk 15 and similar B.Mk 16, the latter differing only in radar. Both types could carry 2722 kg (6,000 lb) of nuclear or conventional bombs internally, and for the ground-attack role had underwing capability for 74 rockets or two AS.30 air-to-surface missiles. More versatile still was the intruder pioneered in the 22 Canberra B(I).Mk 6 conversions of B.Mk 6s with an underfuselage gun pack and provision for underwing bombs or AS.30 missiles, and brought to a peak in the 73 Canberra B(I).Mk 8s. This latter type first flew in June 1954, and while having the same armament provision as the B(I).Mk 6 had a revised forward fuselage with the pilot offset to port under a fighter-type canopy. The type served with five squadrons in West Germany.

de Havilland **Vampire FB.Mk 5/9**

After experience with the F.Mk 1 and F.Mk 3 variants of its Vampire fighter, de Havilland moved forward to a pure fighter-bomber version, the Vampire FB.Mk 5 that began to supplement the F.Mk 3 in 1949. The FB.Mk 5 was based on the F.Mk 3 with its lowered tailplane between vertical surfaces of the classic de Havilland shape, but had a completely restressed wing with square-cut tips reducing span by 0.61 m (2 ft 0 in), long-stroke landing gear units, and provision for underwing weapons. Production for the RAF amounted to 931 aircraft, plus another 317 produced to Vampire FB.Mk 9 standard. This latter was intended for deployment in 'hot-and-high' areas, and thus had an uprated powerplant, the 1520-kg (3,350-lb) thrust Goblin DGn.3 turbojet, and an air-conditioning system with its refrigeration unit in one of the wings.

Specification: de Havilland Vampire FB.Mk 5 single-seat fighter-bomber
Span: 11.58 m (38 ft 0 in)
Length: 9.37 m (30 ft 9 in)
Powerplant: 1×de Havilland Goblin DGn.2, 1406 kg (3,100 lb) st
Armament: 4×20-mm cannon, plus provision for up to 907 kg (2,000 lb) of bombs or 8×27-kg (60-lb) rockets carried under the wings
Max T/O weight: 5607 kg (12,360 lb)
Max speed: 535 mph at 30,000 ft
Operational range: 1,170 miles

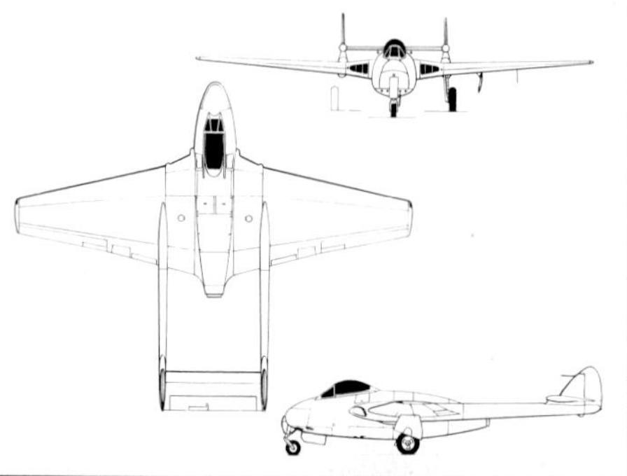

Gloster Meteor F.Mk 8

The Meteor F.Mk 8 bridged the British fighter gap before the advent of the Hunter in 1954, and though developed from the F.Mk 4 it differed from its predecessor in significant features such as a longer fuselage with greater internal fuel capacity, a revised vertical tail of more angular shape, more-powerful Derwent turbojets, and a bubble canopy over an ejector seat. The results were an improvement in handling characteristics and a welcome boost to performance. Late-production aircraft had larger inlets, spring-tab ailerons and a modified canopy. The first F.Mk 8 flew in October 1948, and production of 1,090 aircraft in the UK was completed by April 1954. This consisted of 19 regular plus 10 auxiliary squadrons, plus a number for export; 480 more aircraft were built in Europe. The type was generally kitted out as an interceptor, but could be configured as a useful fighter-bomber.

Specification: Gloster Meteor F.Mk 8 single-seat fighter and fighter-bomber
Span: 11.33 m (37 ft 2 in)
Length: 13.59 m (44 ft 7 in)
Powerplant: 2×Rolls-Royce Derwent 8, 1633 kg (3,600 lb) each
Armament: 4×20-mm cannon, plus provision for 2×907 kg (21000 lb) bombs or 8×27-kg (60-lb) rockets carried under the wings
Max T/O weight: 8664 kg (19,100 lb)
Max speed: 590 mph at sea level
Operational range: 980 miles

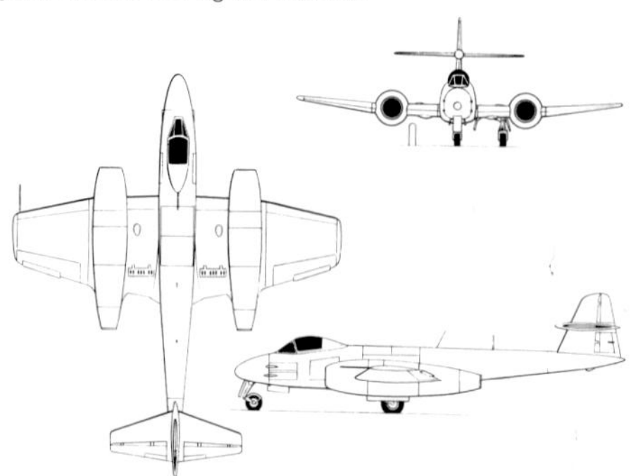

pecification: English Electric
anberra B(I).Mk 8 two-seat light
omber, night intruder and target
arking aeroplane
pan: 19.49m (63ft 11.5in)
ength: 19.96m (65ft 6in)
owerplant: 2×Rolls-Royce Avon
k 109, 3402kg (7,500lb) st each
rmament: 4×20-mm cannon,
us provision for 1361kg (3,000lb)
disposable stores carried
ternally and 907kg (2,000lb) of
ombs, missiles or rockets carried
n 2×underwing hardpoints
ax T/O weight: 24925kg
4,950lb)
ax speed: 541mph at 40,000ft
perational range: 805 miles

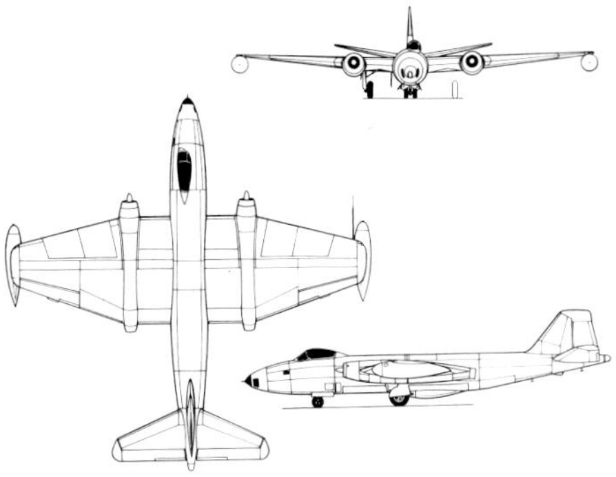

The Canberra B(I).Mk 8 was the most potent of the variants, built with a fighter-style cockpit for the interdictor mission. Bombs could be carried internally and externally, the aircraft also having provision for an underbelly cannon pack. This machine is in the distinctive markings of No. 16 Squadron, which flew the B(I).Mk 8 from Laarbruch between 1958 and 1972 on tactical nuclear strike duties.

Hawker Hunter FGA.Mk 9

The obsolescence of the de Havilland Venom fighter-bomber then in service with Middle Eastern units led the RAF to organise a 1958 competition for a replacement. After serious consideration of the Folland Gnat, the decision finally went to a development of the Hunter F.Mk 6, which was ordered in a large-scale conversion programme as the Hunter FGA.Mk 9 with tropical equipment, a braking parachute and four underwing hardpoints for drop tanks and/or ground-attack weapons. Deliveries of 109 aircraft began in 1959, and so impressive were the type's capabilities that the FGA.Mk 9 was issued to home units (four squadrons) from 1960 and units in the Near and Far East as well as East Africa (six squadrons) from 1961. Many other surplus fighters were converted to a similar standard for export. The model began to be phased out of first-line service in 1970.

Specification: Hawker Hunter FGA.Mk 9 single-seat fighter and ground-attack aeroplane
Span: 10.26m (33ft 8in)
Length: 13.98m (45ft 10.5in)
Powerplant: 1×Rolls-Royce Avon Mk 207, 4604kg (10,150lb) st
Armament: 4×20-mm cannon, plus provision for up to 907kg (2,000lb) of bombs, rockets or other stores carried on 4×underwing hardpoints
Max T/O weight: 10886kg (24,000lb)
Max speed: 710mph at sea level
Operational range: 440 miles

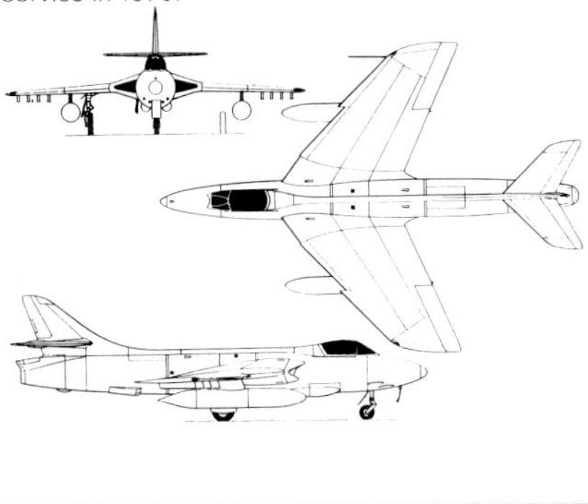

Hawker P.1211

In February 1955 the Air Ministry issued specification F.155T for a Mach 2 fighter able to reach 60,000ft in six minutes. Hawker responded with its P.1103 proposal, and from this developed from 1956 the P.1116 and P.1121 twin- and single-seat strike derivatives. The P.1121 had a de Havilland Gyron (later Olympus) turbojet aspirated via an underfuselage inlet, an area-ruled fuselage and wings swept at 40.6° on the leading edges. It was planned that production aircraft would be powered by either the Olympus or the Rolls-Royce Conway turbofan, and analysis suggests that the P.1121 would have possessed performance comparable with that of the F-4 Phantom. But in 1957 the British government lost interest in development of manned combat aircraft, and in 1958 the project was abandoned with the prototype's fuselage and wings largely complete.

Specification: Hawker P.1221 single-seat multi-role air-superiority and strike fighter
Span: 11.28m (37ft 0in)
Length: 20.27m (66ft 6in)
Powerplant: 1×Bristol Siddeley Olympus BOl.2R, 13154kg (29,000lb) st
Armament: cannon, plus 2×AAMs and 50×51-mm (2-in) rockets in 2×retractable packs, or 907+kg (2,000+lb) of disposable stores
Normal T/O weight: 19731kg (43,500lb)
Max speed: Mach 2.25 at 36,000ft
Operational range: 1,200 miles

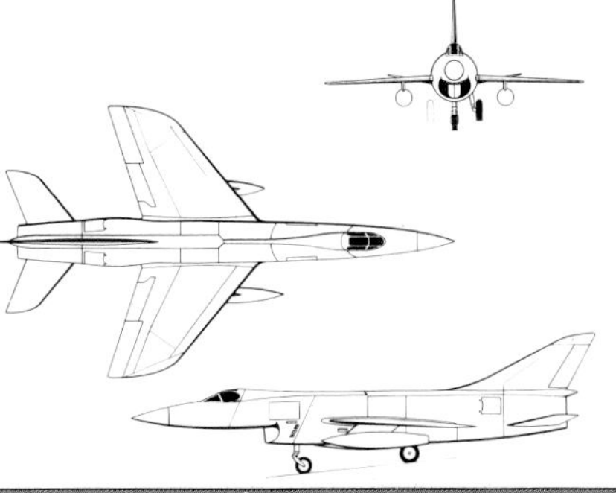

BAe Canberra T.Mk 17

The English Electric Canberra remained in production from 1949 until the early 1960s. This aircraft, originally a B.Mk 2 bomber, was refurbished by BAC and converted to T.Mk 17 configuration for use in the electronic countermeasures training role with the joint RAF/RN No. 360 Squadron, initially based at RAF Cottesmore but later moving to RAF Wyton. Twelve T.Mk 17s remain in service today, of 24 converted.

Antonov An-12

Developed in the mid-1950s as a military freighter derivative of the An-10 airliner, the An-12 'Cub-A' is still in widespread service in its primary role. The type is obsolescent, however, and the Soviets have converted a number for electronic warfare in several variants. The Soviet designations remain unknown, so use of the NATO reporting names remains the only effective manner of differentiating these variants. The two ECM models are the 'Cub-C' and 'Cub-D'. The former is a dedicated ECM platform with an ogival tailcone in place of the normal cannon turret, and with several tonnes of ECM gear including palletised jammers (operating in up to 10 wavebands) and chaff dispensers. The latter is used for Elint as well as ECM, and has a large fairing for electronic equipment extending aft from each main landing gear blister, as well as active jammers and decoys.

Specification: Antonov An-12 'Cub-D' five/six-crew Elint and ECM aeroplane
Span: 38.00 m (124 ft 8.1 in)
Length: 33.10 m (108 ft 7.25 in)
Powerplant: 4×Ivchyenko AI-20K, 2983 kW (4,000 ehp) each
Armament: 2×23-mm cannon in tail turret
Payload: several tonnes of Elint and ECM equipment plus its specialist operating crew
Max T/O weight: up to 61000 kg (134,480 lb)
Max speed: 482 mph at optimum altitude
Operational range: 3,542 miles with maximum fuel

BAe (Avro/Hawker Siddeley) HS 748

The Avro 748 twin-turboprop airliner first flew in June 1960, and was later produced in a freighter version with a large port-side door. This latter variant found a number of military buyers including Australia, where the Royal Australian Air Force currently operates 10 of the type. These are mostly employed for navigation training, but two have been adapted in Australia as specialist trainers for ECM operators, with the cabin modified for trainee consoles supplied with electromagnetic data from exterior antennae in low-drag installations. India also operates some 50 or more licence-built HS 748s, and though the plan to develop an indigenous AEW platform on the aerodynamic basis of the HS 748 appears to have stalled, it is also possible that some of the HS 748s have been modified for an electronic warfare role, if only in training.

Specification: BAe (Avro/Hawker Siddeley) HS 748 two/three-crew ECM training aeroplane
Span: 31.23 m (102 ft 5.5 in)
Length: 20.42 m (67 ft 0 in)
Powerplant: 2×Rolls-Royce Dart RDa.7 Mk 536-2, 1700 kW (2,280 ehp) each
Payload: ECM equipment plus instructors and trainees
Max T/O weight: 23133 kg (51,000 lb)
Max speed: 280 mph at optimum altitude
Operational range: 1,475 miles

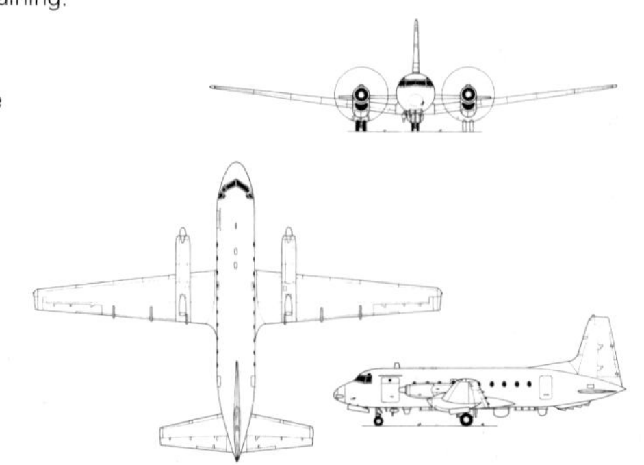

The venerable Canberra first flew as far back as May 1949, but in common with several other bombers of a comparable vintage is still in valuable service as an electronic aircraft. In the case of this British light bomber the variant is the Canberra T.Mk 17, which serves at RAF Wyton with No.360 (Joint Services) Squadron as an ECM trainer. Some 24 conversions were made from B.Mk 2 standard with V-bomber jammers in the modified and enlarged nose (with four forward-facing blister fairings round its circumference) and a chaff-dispensing system in the rear portion of the bomb bay with two lateral outlets in its lower sides. Warning of an 'attack' is provided by a radar-warning receiver system with its antennae in the nose and tail. The location of electronic equipment in the erstwhile bomb bay is indicated by the row of cooling-air inlets let into the underside of what were the bomb bay doors.

Specification: BAe (English Electric/BAC) Canberra T.Mk 17 two-seat ECM training aeroplane
Span: 19.51 m (64 ft 0 in) excluding tiptanks
Length: 20.90 m (68 ft 6 in)
Powerplant: 2×Rolls-Royce Avon Mk 101, 2948 kg (6,500 lb) st each
Payload: ECM equipment
Max T/O weight: 20865 kg (46,000 lb)
Max speed: 570 mph at medium altitude
Operational range: 2,660 miles

assault-Breguet Falcon 10 and 200

hough developed primarily as a 'bizjet', the Falcon series has found a number of military plications including electronic warfare. The first of these EW variants was the Falcon MER, a multi-role type with a pair of 1465-kg (3,230-kg) thrust Garrett TFE731-2 turbofans: e French have three fitted with four underwing hardpoints that can carry ESM and radar-arning receivers for use with podded ECM and/or chaff-dispenser systems. The larger lcon 20 has spawned the Falcon 200 variant with three-spool engines, additional fuel nkage and other improvements, and this has in turn been developed into two specialist ardian maritime versions. Of these the Gardian 2 is the export version with lower levels of stalled equipment but with its four underwing hardpoints able to accommodate much the me type of ECM equipment as the Falcon 10MER.

pecification: Dassault-Breguet ardian 2 six-seat ECM aeroplane
pan: 16.30 m (53 ft 6 in)
ngth: 17.15 m (56 ft 3 in)
werplant: 2×Garrett ATF3-6A-3C, 68 kg (5,440 lb) st each
mament: provision for an sortment of weapons on underwing hardpoints
yload: provision for ECM uipment plus a specialist erating crew
ax T/O weight: 15200 kg 3,510 lb)
ax speed: 541 mph at 30,000 ft
erational range: 2,790 miles

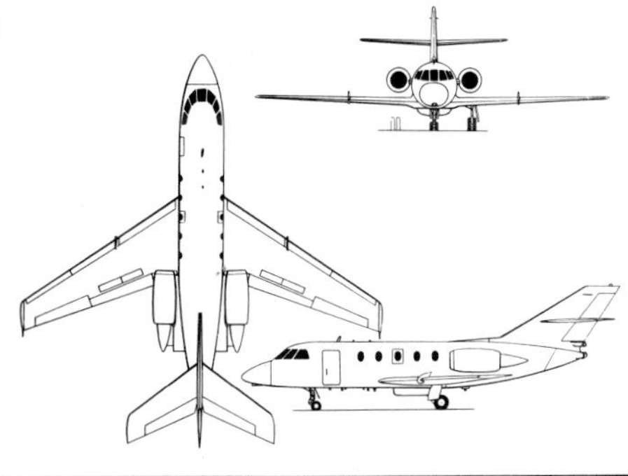

Douglas EA-3 Skywarrior

The Skywarrior remains the world's heaviest carrierborne aeroplane, and was developed as a naval strike bomber. In parallel with the A2D-2 (later A-3B) bomber, Douglas produced an A3D-2Q (later EA-3B) ECM variant. The model first flew in December 1958, and of 25 such aircraft some 18 remain in US Navy service. The type has a pressurised compartment in what was the bomb bay, and this houses the primary ECM equipment, which includes the ALR-40 surveillance system and ALR-63 frequency-measuring system. The type also possesses forward- and side-looking radars. Combined tanker/ECM aircraft are designated EKA-3B, with the ECM (including the ALQ-76 noise jammer) and refuelling equipment in the forward and rear portions of the bomb bay respectively, and the ERA-3B is an EA-3B 'aggressor' subvariant with special ECM gear for use in the testing of US Navy electronic counter-countermeasures equipment.

Specification: Douglas EA-3B Skywarrior three-crew carrierborne ECM aeroplane
Span: 22.10 m (72 ft 6 in)
Length: 23.27 m (76 ft 4 in)
Powerplant: 2×Pratt & Whitney J57-P-10, 4763 kg (10,500 lb) st each
Payload: ECM equipment plus its four-man specialist operating crew
Max T/O weight: 37195 kg (82,000 lb)
Max speed: 610 mph at 10,000 ft
Operational range: 2,900 miles

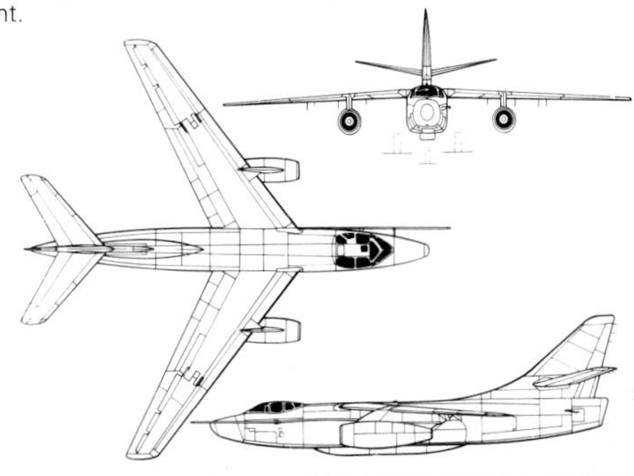

EF-111A Raven

The Raven is the land-based counterpart of the Prowler with the ECM system packaged in the weapons bay of a converted F-111A strike and interdiction aeroplane. The package has been revised to ALQ-99E form with greater automation, and can thus be operated by a single officer rather than the Prowler's three, the receivers in the highly distinctive fintop fairing passing radar data to the computer system and its powerful jammers. The type also features the ALQ-137 ECM system, ALR-62 threat-warning system, ALR-23 radar countermeasures receiver and ALE-28 chaff dispenser; the underwing hardpoints can also carry ECM pods. The first of 42 conversions began to enter service late in 1981, and work continuing to improve the ALQ-99E system with counterparts to the Prowler's electronic advances.

Specification: General Dynamics/Grumman EF-111A Raven two-seat ECM aeroplane
Span: 19.20 m (63 ft 0 in) spread and 9.74 m (31 ft 11.4 in) swept
Length: 23.16 m (76 ft 0 in)
Powerplant: 2×Pratt & Whitney TF30-P-3, 8391 kg (18,500 lb) st each
Armament: provision for 2×AGM-88 HARM anti-radar missiles carried under the wings may be retrofitted
Payload: ECM equipment
Max T/O weight: 40346 kg (88,948 lb)
Max speed: Mach 2.14 at high altitude
Operational range: 1,434 miles

Grumman EA-6B Prowler

The EA-6B is a dedicated ECM platform designed to support US Navy strike and attack aircraft penetrating enemy airspace. Such a type had been presaged by the US Marines' EA-6A version of the A-6A Intruder, and development of the EA-6B began in the late 1960s using the A-6A airframe stretched to provide four- rather than two-seat accommodation. Three specialist officers run the ALQ-99 ECM system, which has receivers in the fintop fairing to feed hostile radar data to a computer system that records, analyses and identifies them. Radars can then be jammed using the five self-powered pods carried externally: each pod has two jammers and covers one of seven frequency bands. The type entered service in 1971, and has been steadily updated. Some 90 aircraft are in service, and production continues of aircraft to the ICAP-2 standard, with the ADCAP standard to follow in 1992.

Specification: Grumman EA-6B Prowler four-seat carrierborne ECM aeroplane
Span: 16.15 m (53 ft 0 in)
Length: 18.24 m (59 ft 10 in)
Powerplant: 2×Pratt & Whitney J52-P-408, 5080 kg (11,200 lb) st each
Armament: provision for 2×AGM-88 HARM anti-radar missiles carried under the wings
Payload: ECM equipment and its three specialist operators
Max T/O weight: 29483 kg (65,000 lb)
Max speed: 623 mph at sea level
Operational range: 1,099 miles

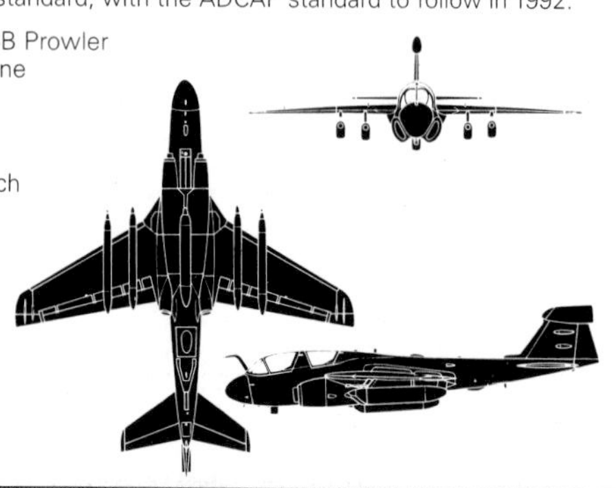

Kawasaki C-1

The C-1 was produced as a turbofan replacement for the piston-engined C-46 Commando in the tactical transport role, and first flew in November 1970 as a typical example of the modern 'hunch-backed' airlifter. Production totalled 31 including prototypes, and of these one has been converted for the ECM training role with the designation C-1Kai. This has the TRDI/Mitsubishi X/JALQ-5 ECM system located in the hold, and its primary external features are the bulbous radomes on nose and under the tail plus a number of other blister radomes on and under the fuselage. Trials were completed by the Japan Air Self-Defence Force's Air Proving Wing in 1986, and this singleton aeroplane is now in service with the Electronic Warfare Training Unit. The Japanese have not revealed if there are plans to convert other C-1s to this standard.

Specification: Kawasaki C-1Kai three/four-crew ECM training aeroplane
Span: 30.60 m (100 ft 4.7 in)
Length: slightly more than 29.00 m (95 ft 1.7 in)
Powerplant: 2×Mitsubishi-built Pratt & Whitney JT8D-M-9, 6577 kg (14,500 lb) st each
Payload: ECM equipment plus instructors and trainees
Max T/O weight: up to 45000 kg (99,208 lb)
Max speed: 501 mph at 25,000 ft
Operational range: 808 miles

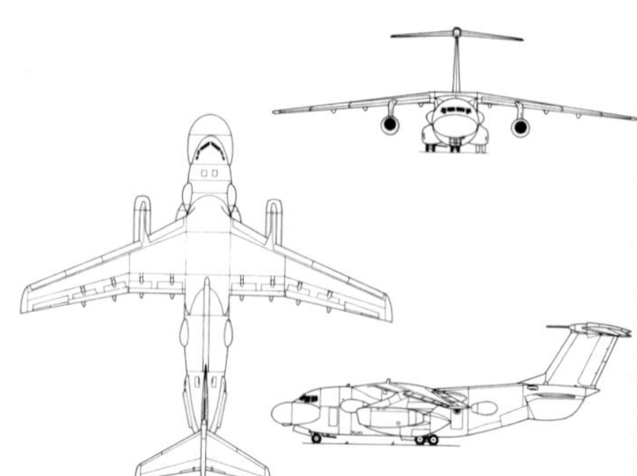

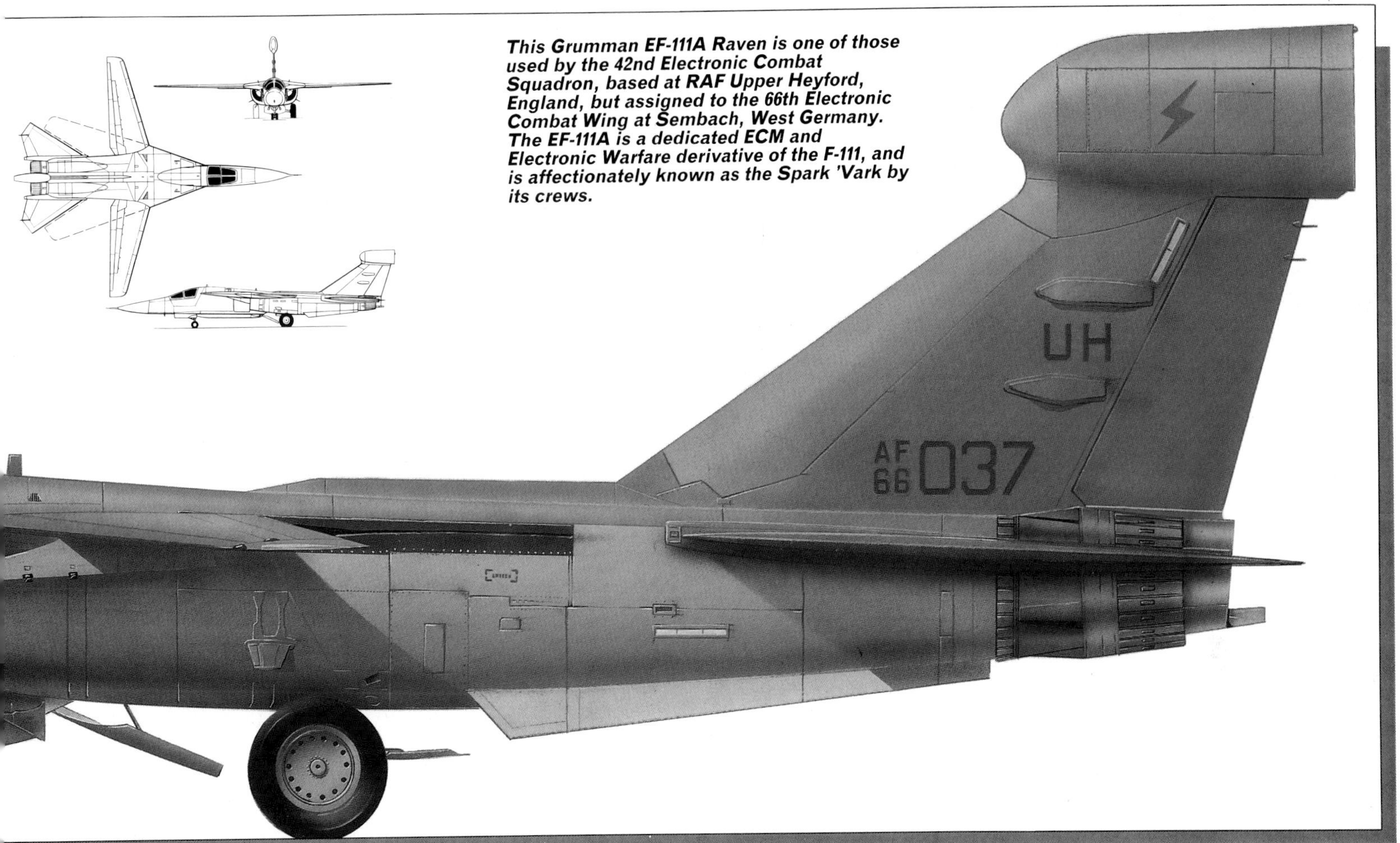

This Grumman EF-111A Raven is one of those used by the 42nd Electronic Combat Squadron, based at RAF Upper Heyford, England, but assigned to the 66th Electronic Combat Wing at Sembach, West Germany. The EF-111A is a dedicated ECM and Electronic Warfare derivative of the F-111, and is affectionately known as the Spark 'Vark by its crews.

Lockheed EC-130H Hercules

The hold volume and the payload of the Hercules made the type attractive for conversion to the electronic warfare role at an early date in its service career, and after two Sigint variants the first ECM Hercules was the EC-130E, converted under the 'Coronet Solo II' battlefield electronic surveillance and ECM programme with an internal mission station, a large dorsal fillet and two large axe-blade antennae under the wings. There are two subvariants of the EC-130E, of which eight serve with one ANG squadron in the USA. The other ECM version is the EC-130H, of which seven are in service with one USAFE squadron in the battlefield communications jamming role after modification from transport standard under the 'Compass Call II' programme.

Specification: Lockheed EC-130E Hercules multi-seat electronic surveillance and ECM aeroplane
Span: 40.41 m (132 ft 7 in)
Length: 29.79 m (97 ft 9 in)
Powerplant: 4×Allison T56-A-7, 3020 kW (4,050 ehp) each
Payload: 20412 kg (45,000 lb) of electronic surveillance and ECM equipment plus its multi-man specialist operating crew
Max T/O weight: up to 70308 kg (155,000 lb)
Max speed: 380 mph at 30,000 ft
Operational range: 4,700 miles

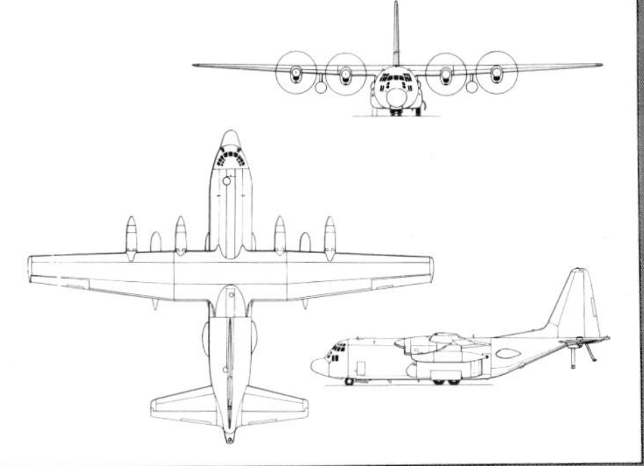

MBB (HFB.320) Hansa Jet

The Hansa Jet was planned in the 1960s as a 'bizjet' with the unusual feature of a forward-swept wing that permitted the structural wing box to pass through the rear fuselage and so provide a large and unobstructed cabin. The first machine flew in April 1964, and the type proved a commercial failure with only 45 built. The type was also adopted by the Luftwaffe as a VIP transport. However, another seven are based at Lechfeld for ECM operator training. These aircraft were modified by MBB for their specialist role, and are most notable for the thimble radome on the nose, the teardrop radome under the belly, a small radome under the rudder, and a number of under- and over-fuselage blade antennae. The aircraft have proved very successful in the ECM role, and are to be retained for the foreseeable future.

Specification: MBB (HFB.320) Hansa Jet multi-seat ECM training aeroplane
Span: 14.49 m (47 ft 6.5 in)
Length: 16.61 m (54 ft 6 in) excluding thimble radome
Powerplant: 2×General Electric CJ601-9, 1406 kg (3,100 lb) st each
Payload: ECM equipment plus instructors and trainees
Max T/O weight: 9200 kg (20,283 lb)
Max speed: 513 mph at optimum altitude
Operational range: 1,473 miles

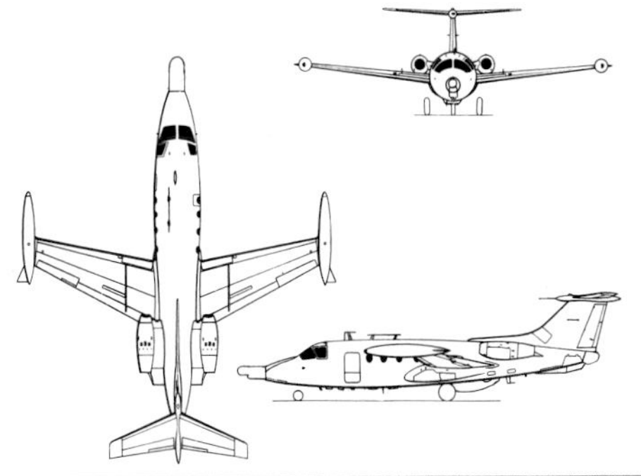

NAMC YS-11

The YS-11 first flew in August 1962 as a twin-turboprop airliner, and of the total production of 182 aircraft some 23 were delivered to the Japanese armed forces. During the 1970s three or four of these transports were withdrawn for conversion as ECM trainers, re-entering service with the designation YS-11E. One of these aircraft, or possibly another basic transport, was withdrawn in 1982 for conversion to the Elint and jamming roles, the primary system in this case being the ALR-1 receiving and analysis set complemented by active jammers. All four YS-11Es are operated by the Japan Air Self-Defence Force, and are notable for their three large and three small radomes above and below the fuselage, plus a selection of small blisters and blades. In the 1990s a new ECM variant of the YS-11 is to be developed with American turboprops and a completely new ECM system.

Specification: NAMC YS-11E two/three-crew ECM aeroplane
Span: 32.00m (104ft 11.8in)
Length: 26.30m (86ft 3.4in)
Powerplant: 2×Rolls-Royce Dart Mk 542-10K, 2282kW (3,060ehp) each
Payload: ECM equipment plus its specialist operators
Max T/O weight: 24500kg (54,013lb)
Max speed: 291mph at 15,000 ft
Operational range: 1,998 miles

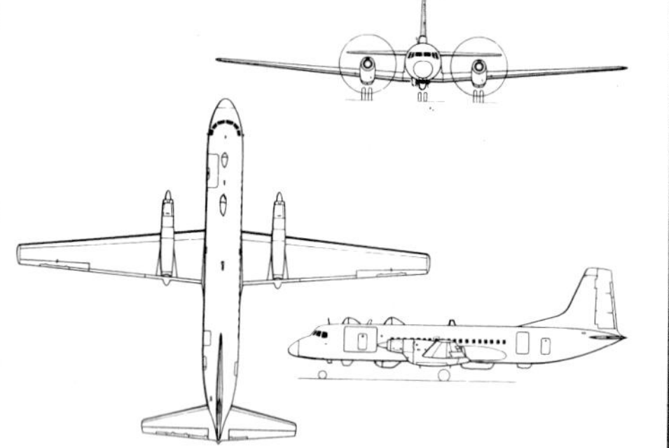

Piaggio PD-808

The PD-808 was first flown in August 1965 after development by Piaggio and Douglas, which would have produced aircraft for the North American market had the type's sales warranted such a move. The PD-808 was designed as a utility transport, and secured only small production orders of which the largest came from the Italian air force for a total of 21 aircraft. The third and final variant for the service was the PD-808ECM, otherwise known as the PD-808GE, whose six examples are operated by the 71° Gruppo Guerra Elettronica of the 14° Stormo from Pratica di Mare in central Italy for the ECM role. The aircraft are flown in camouflage, and no details have been released of the electronic suite carried by the machines. Italy is to buy the ECR version of the Panavia Tornado, but it is unclear what effect this will have on continued PD-808ECM service.

Specification: Piaggio PD-808ECM two-crew ECM aeroplane
Span: 13.20m (43ft 3.7in) including tiptanks
Length: 12.85m (42ft 2in)
Powerplant: 2×Piaggio-built Rolls-Royce Viper Mk 526, 1524kg (3,360lb) st each
Payload: ECM equipment plus its three specialist operators
Max T/O weight: 8165kg (18,001lb)
Max speed: 529mph at 19,685 ft
Operational range: 1,322 miles

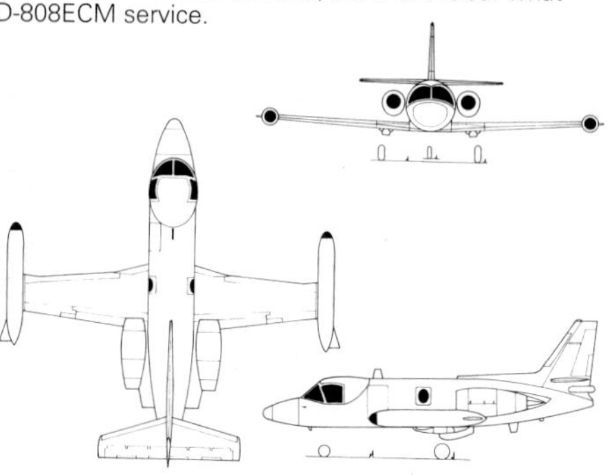

Tupolev Tu-16

Despite the fact that it first flew in 1952, the Tu-16 'Badger' remains in service as a bomber, but comparatively large numbers have been modified for electronic warfare roles, in which the type's high performance and considerable load-carrying capability have been found very useful. The 'Badger-D, -F, -K and -L' are Elint platforms, while dedicated ECM types are the 'Badger-H' and 'Badger-J'. Of these two ECM platforms the former is intended for the escort and stand-off roles with its bomb bay revised for broadband receiver/analysis and jammer gear; the type has teardrop radomes fore and aft of this bay, has a large ventral hatch and can release a mass of chaff, flares and decoys from a ventral tube and other ejectors. The latter is a variant of the 'Badger-H' with improved receiver/analysis electronics as well as spot/barrage jammers in a ventral canoe fairing that replaces the dispenser of the 'Badger-H'.

Specification: Tupolev Tu-16 'Badger-H' five/six-seat escort and/or stand-off ECM aeroplane
Span: 32.93m (108ft 0.5in)
Length: 34.80m (114ft 2in)
Powerplant: 2×Mikulin AM-3M, 9500kg (20,944lb) st each
Armament: 7×23-mm cannon in fixed nose installation and dorsal, ventral and tail turrets
Payload: ECM equipment and dispensers for about 9000kg (19,841lb) of chaff, flares and decoys, plus their specialist operating crew
Max T/O weight: up to 75800kg (167,108lb)
Max speed: 615mph at 19,685 ft
Operational range: 3,604 miles

Yakovlev Yak-28

The Yak-28 entered service in steadily improved 'Brewer-A, -B and -C' supersonic bomber variants, and though these types are obsolete in their original roles the combination of a payload bay and supersonic performance commended the Yak-28's development as an electronic escort aeroplane for support of Frontal Aviation strike packages. The 'Brewer-E' was introduced in the late 1960s, and is probably a conversion of the 'Brewer-D' reconnaissance model with the officer in the marginally glazed nose compartment responsible for operation of the type's electronic systems, which include receivers and jammers (of both the spot and barrage types) located in the erstwhile bomb bay with the jammer pack protruding slightly below the belly. It is thought that the type's underwing pods, originally considered to be rocket launchers, may be dispensers for fired payloads (chaff, decoys etc).

Specification: Yakovlev Yak-28 'Brewer-E' two-seat escort ECM aeroplane
Span: 12.95m (42ft 6in)
Length: 22.30m (73ft 2in)
Powerplant: 2×Tumanskii R-11F, 6200kg (13,370lb) st each
Payload: ECM equipment and (possibly) dispensers
Max T/O weight: up to 19000kg (41,887lb)
Max speed: Mach 1.11 at 32,810 ft
Operational range: about 1,000 miles

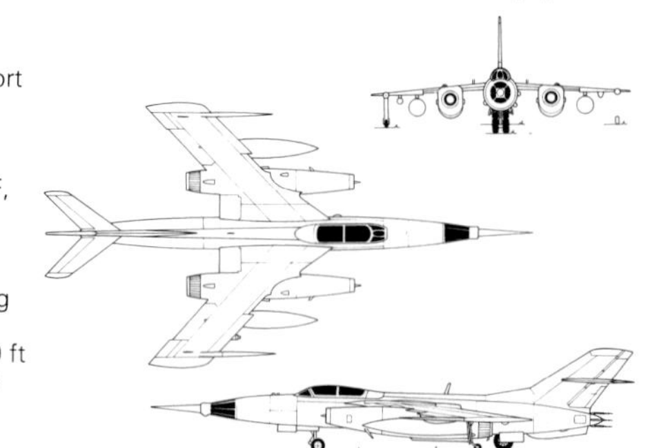

SEPECAT Jaguar

Designed as an Anglo-French supersonic operational trainer and close-support/attack aeroplane, the Jaguar matured as so capable a machine that it is only little used in the training role. The type first flew in September 1968, and has been produced in five variants including the combat-capable Jaguar T.Mk 2 (Jaguar B) and Jaguar E two-seaters. The French Jaguar A has relatively simple avionics and 3315-kg (7,305-lb) thrust Adour Mk 102 turbofans, but can carry the 15-kiloton AN 52 free-fall nuclear bomb or, when fitted with a designator pod, AS.30L laser-guided missiles. The basically similar British Jaguar GR.Mk 1 (Jaguar S) has considerably more advanced avionics. The Jaguar International has more-powerful Adour Mk 804 or Mk 811 engines, two overwing hardpoints for AAMs, and provision for the nose radar needed for weapons such as anti-ship missiles.

Specification: SEPECAT Jaguar GR.Mk 1 single-seat attack and close-support fighter
Span: 8.69 m (28 ft 6 in)
Length: 16.83 m (55 ft 2.5 in) including probe
Powerplant: 2×Rolls-Royce/Turbomeca Adour Mk 104, 3647 kg (8,040 lb) st each
Armament: 2×30-mm cannon, plus provision for up to 4763 kg (10,500 lb) of stores carried on 5×external hardpoints
Max T/O weight: 15700 kg (34,610 lb)
Max speed: Mach 1.6 at 36,000 ft
Operational range: 668 miles

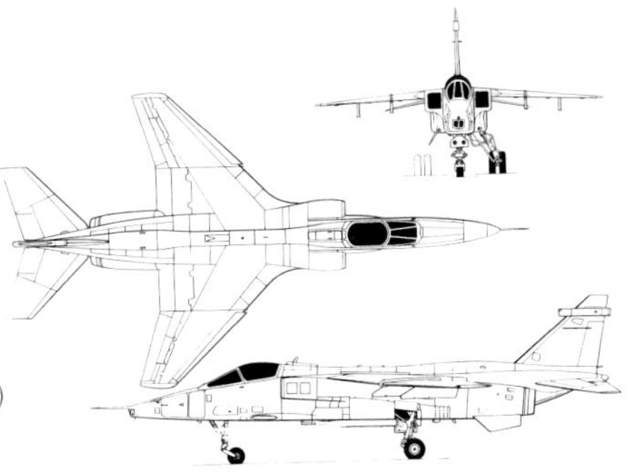

Su-17, Su-20, Su-22 'Fitter'

Developed from the Su-7 and first flown in 1966, the Su-17 and its Su-20 and Su-22 derivatives have variable-geometry outer wing panels for better field performance and greater range with a larger warload. The family includes the 'Fitter-C' with the 7000-kg (15,432-lb) thrust AL-21F-1 and then AL-21F-3 plus more advanced avionics, the nuclear-capable 'Fitter-D' with a longer nose and improved avionics (including terrain-avoidance radar and laser ranger/marked-target seeker), the 'Fitter-E' two-seat conversion trainer with a lengthened and drooped nose, the 'Fitter-F' export 'Fitter-C' with a Tumanskii R-29 and inferior avionics, the 'Fitter-G' laser-fitted 'Fitter-E', the 'Fitter-H' version of the 'Fitter-C/D' with a drooped nose and two more hardpoints, the 'Fitter-J' Tumanskii-powered export 'Fitter-H', and the 'Fitter-K' based on the 'Fitter-H' with improved ECM.

Specification: Sukhoi Su-20 'Fitter-K' single-seat ground-attack fighter
Span: 14.00 m (45 ft 11.2 in) spread and 10.60 m (34 ft 9.5 in) swept
Length: 19.20 m (63 ft 0 in)
Powerplant: 1 x Lyul'ka AL-21F-3, 11200 kg (24,691 lb) st
Armament: 2×30-mm cannon, plus provision for up to 4000 kg (8,818 lb) of stores carried on 8×external hardpoints
Max T/O weight: 19500 kg (42,990 lb)
Max speed: Mach 2.2 at 36,090 ft
Operational range: 622 miles

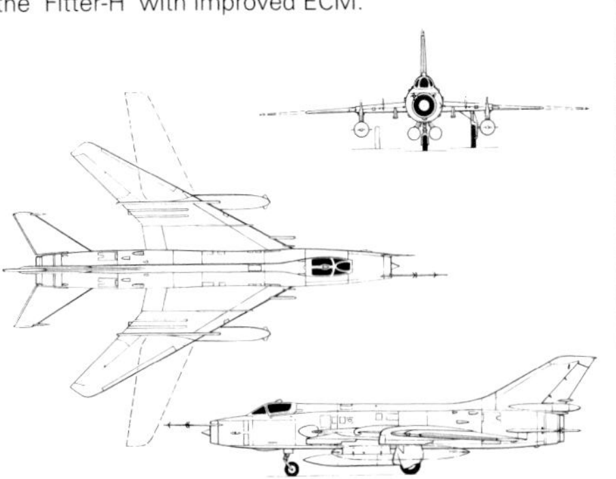

Tupolev Tu-26 'Backfire'

The 'Backfire' was developed from the Tu-22 'Blinder' with variable-geometry outer wing panels and the aft-mounted podded turbojets replaced by a more conventional internal arrangement of two turbofans aspirated via variable-geometry inlets. The type flew as the Tu-136 prototype in 1969, and then came a small number of Tu-22M 'Backfire-As' (possibly Tu-22 conversions) from 1973. It is likely that this variant suffered from excessive drag as a result of the trailing-edge pods for its retracted main landing gear units, so the Tu-26 'Backfire-B' was developed during the mid-1970s with inward-retracting main units and a completely re-engineered airframe for higher performance. The only other variant is the 1983 'Backfire-C' with ramp inlets and possibly new engines for high dash performance.

Specification: Tupolev Tu-26 'Backfire-B' four-seat strategic medium bomber and maritime reconnaissance aeroplane
Span: 34.45 m (113 ft 0 in) spread and 26.21 m (86 ft 0 in) swept
Length: 42.00 m (137 ft 10 in)
Powerplant: 2×Kuznetsov NK-144, 20000 kg (44,092 lb) st each
Armament: 2×23-mm cannon in a remote-control tail barbette, plus provision for up to 12000 kg (26,455 lb) of stores carried internally and on 4×external hardpoints
Max T/O weight: 122500 kg (270,062 lb)
Max speed: Mach 2 at high altitude
Operational range: 6,800 miles

Tupolev Tu-160? 'Blackjack'

Still largely unknown in the West in all but its basic format, the 'Blackjack' has many design similarities to the USAF's B-1B, and like the American bomber was clearly designed as a 'swing-wing' penetration bomber in the strategic role with a primary armament of at least eight AS-15 'Kent' air-launched cruise missiles. The Soviet bomber is some 20 per cent larger than the Rockwell machine and has two internal bomb bays: it can undoubtedly carry a substantial load of free-fall nuclear or conventional weapons. If the Western estimate of weapon load quoted below is accurate, the 'Blackjack' should have greater range than commonly estimated, but in all probability the weapon load is considerably larger than the quoted figure. First flown in 1982, the 'Blackjack' should enter service in late 1988 or early 1989.

Specification: Tupolev Tu-160? 'Blackjack' four-seat strategic heavy bomber
Span: 52.50 m (172 ft 2.9 in) spread and 33.75 m (110 ft 8.75 in) swept
Length: 50.65 m (166 ft 2 in)
Powerplant: 4×afterburning turbofans, 23000 kg (50,705 lb) st each
Armament: provision for up to 16500 kg (36,376 lb) of stores carried internally and on underglove hardpoints
Max T/O weight: 270000 kg (595,238 lb)
Max speed: Mach 2.1 at high altitude
Operational range: 9,070 miles

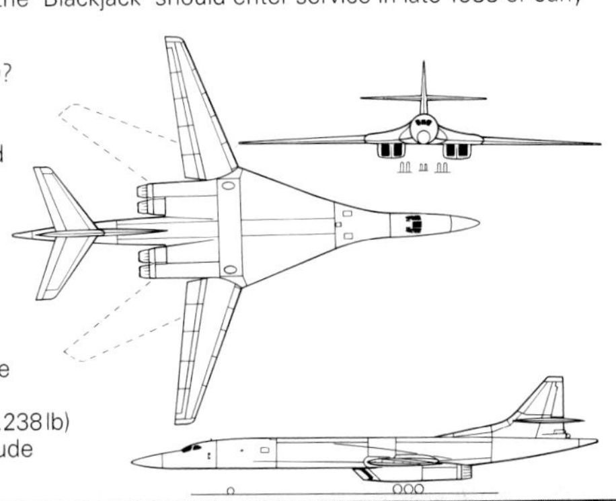

Panavia Tornado IDS

First flown in April 1974 for service in 1980, the Tornado IDS is a remarkable achievement in the interdiction role. The capable avionics offer blind but highly accurate first-pass weapon delivery after automatically controlled low-level ingress at unexcelled speed. The complete package provides great warload, good range and superb field performance in an aeroplane notable for its compact dimensions, 'swing wings' with full-span leading-edge slats and double-slotted trailing-edge flaps, and economical turbofans fitted with thrust reversers. The Tornado can carry a diverse assortment of weapons within its large offensive load, and this is to be improved yet further by the type's mid-life update in the early 1990s with digital electronics for better navigation, target acquisition and range with still-lower attack altitudes.

Boeing B-52 Stratofortress

Variants of the Stratofortress still in service are the B-52G and B-52H, the former with a tail barbette (carrying four machine-guns) and turbojet propulsion, and the latter with a single 20-mm multi-barrel cannon and eight 7711-kg (17,000-lb) thrust each Pratt & Whitney TF33-P-3 turbofans for a range of 10,000 miles. In numerical terms the variants are the Strategic Air Command's most important missile-carrying asset, both models carrying Phase VI ECM and Phase I offensive avionics systems, including the ALQ-151 Electro-optical Viewing System. Both variants carry 12 AGM-86B air-launched cruise missiles under the wings, while the B-52H has provision for an internal rotary launcher with another eight missiles. Alternatively, both models can carry heavy loads of conventional weapons or be used in the maritime surveillance and support roles with anti-ship missiles.

Specification: Boeing B-52G Stratofortress six-seat strategic heavy bomber
Span: 56.39 m (185 ft 0 in)
Length: 48.03 m (157 ft 7 in)
Powerplant: 8 x Pratt & Whitney J57-P-43W, 5080 kg (11,200 lb) st each
Armament: 4×12.7-mm (0.5-in) machine guns in a remote-control tail barbette, plus provision for 12 air-launched cruise missiles carried externally or up to 22680 kg (50,000 lb) of bombs or other stores carried internally and externally
Max T/O weight: 221357+ kg (488,000+ lb)
Max speed: 595 mph at optimum altitude
Operational range: 7,500+ miles

BAe (Blackburn) Buccaneer

First flown in April 1958 as the Blackburn B-103 (NA.39) carrierborne strike aeroplane with 3221-kg (7,100-lb) de Havilland Gyron Junior turbojets for high subsonic performance at very low altitude, the Buccaneer S.Mk 1 was soon overtaken by the S.Mk 2 variant with Spey turbofans for greater range on a given fuel load. The run-down of the UK's carrier force then allowed the Buccaneer to be switched to the RAF, which lacked a low-level strike aeroplane after the cancellation of the TSR.2 and problems with the proposed purchase of F-111s. The type still serves in the strike and maritime attack roles, its elderly avionics being the poorest feature of the Buccaneer. The three current variants are the S.Mk 2A and S.Mk 2B respectively without and with Martel capability, and the S.Mk 50 used by South Africa as a potential launch platform for its newly revealed nuclear capability.

Specification: BAe (Blackburn) Buccaneer S.Mk 2B two-seat strike and attack aeroplane
Span: 13.41 m (44 ft 0 in)
Length: 19.32 m (63 ft 5 in)
Powerplant: 2×Rolls-Royce Spey RB.168-1A Mk 101, 5035 kg (11,100 lb) st each
Armament: provision for up to 7257 kg (16,000 lb) of stores carried on the rotary bomb-bay door and on 4×external hardpoints
Max T/O weight: 28123 kg (68,000 lb)
Max speed: 645 mph at sea level
Operational range: 2,300 miles

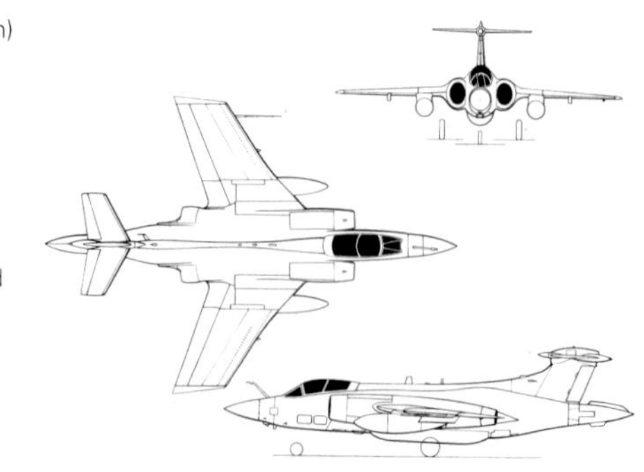

Specification: Panavia Tornado IDS wo-seat strike and interdictor aeroplane
pan: 13.91 m (45 ft 7.5 in) spread nd 8.60 m (28 ft 2.5 in) swept
ength: 16.72 m (54 ft 10.25 in)
owerplant: 2×Turbo-Union RB.199-34R Ak 103, 7620 kg (16,800 lb) st each
rmament: 2×27-mm cannon, plus provision or up to 9000 kg (19,840 lb) of stores carried n 7×external hardpoints
Max T/O weight: 27215 kg (60,000 lb)
Max speed: Mach 2.2+ at high altitude
Operational range: 1,725 miles

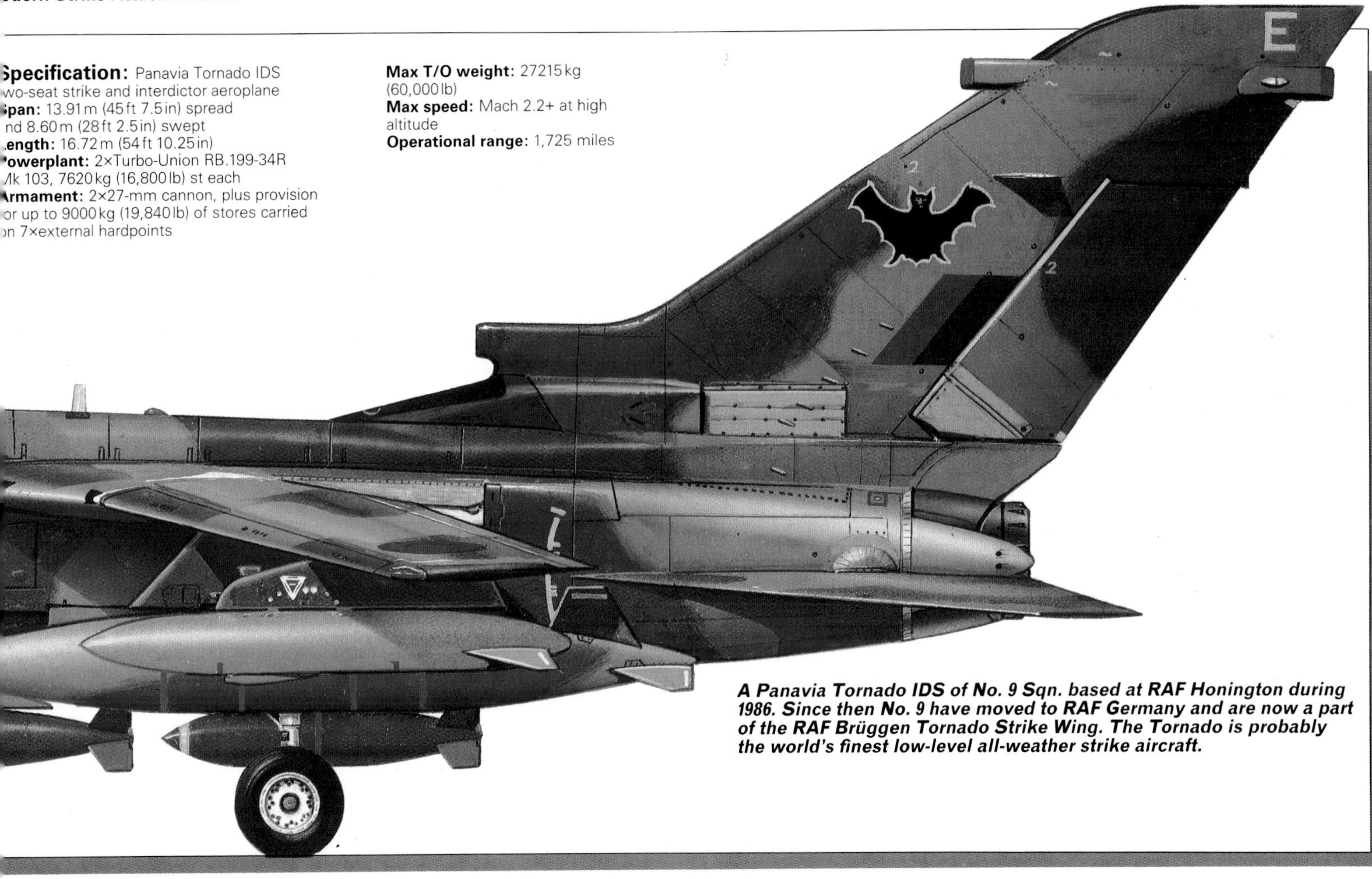

A Panavia Tornado IDS of No. 9 Sqn. based at RAF Honington during 1986. Since then No. 9 have moved to RAF Germany and are now a part of the RAF Brüggen Tornado Strike Wing. The Tornado is probably the world's finest low-level all-weather strike aircraft.

Dassault-Breguet Mirage IVP

Obsolete in its original role as a high-level bomber with the 60-kiloton AN 22 free-fall nuclear weapon, the Mirage IV has been recast for low-altitude penetration in the theatre role with the 150-kiloton Aérospatiale ASMP missile. The carrier for this missile is designated Mirage IVP, of which 18 have been produced by conversion from Mirage IV standard. Entering service in May 1986 and designed to remain in service up to 1996, the Mirage IVP has a strengthened structure and completely revised avionics, the latter including a low-level penetration system based on dual inertial navigation systems (replacing the original Doppler type) and Thomson-CSF Arcana pulse-Doppler radar. The type also has an improved electronic warfare suite including jammers and chaff dispensers on the outer pair of underwing hardpoints.

Specification: Dassault-Breguet Mirage IVP two-seat theatre/strategic bomber
Span: 11.85 m (38 ft 10.5 in)
Length: 23.50 m (77 ft 1 in)
Powerplant: 2×SNECMA Atar 9K-50, 7000 kg (15,432 lb) st each
Armament: 1×ASMP nuclear missile
Max T/O weight: 33475 kg (73,799 lb)
Max speed: Mach 2.2 at 40,060 ft
Operational range: 1,540 miles

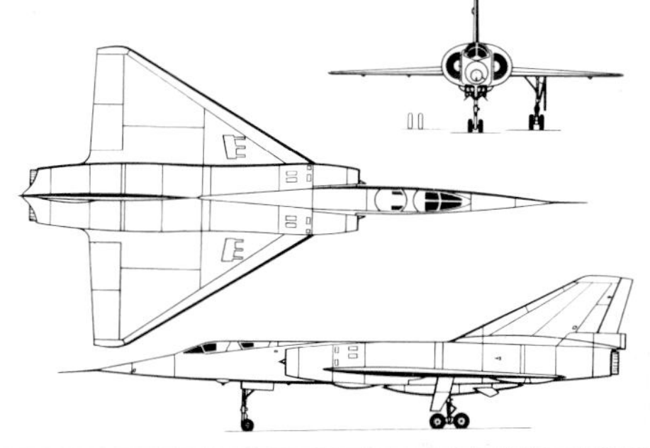

D-B Mirage 2000N

Designed to complement the Mirage F.1, the Mirage 2000 first flew in March 1978 and began to enter service in 1983 with increasingly capable radar, a 'fly-by-wire' control system and 'variable-camber' wings. Since then the type has proliferated in French service and secured considerable export success in its single- and tandem-seat variants with conventional weapons. France is also buying 70 Mirage 2000N strike and up to 32 Mirage 2000N-1 attack fighters. Both have a strengthened airframe for low-level operations, ESD Antilope V terrain-following/ground-mapping radar, twin Uliss 52 inertial platforms and colour cockpit displays, but while the Mirage 2000N has the ASMP stand-off nuclear missile, the Mirage 2000N-1 is optimised for conventional weapons. The Mirage 2000S is the export version of the Mirage 2000N-1, but no orders for this variant have been announced.

Specification: Dassault-Breguet Mirage 2000N two-seat strike and attack fighter
Span: 9.00 m (29 ft 6 in)
Length: 14.55 m (47 ft 8.8 in)
Powerplant: 1×SNECMA M53-P2, 9700 kg (21,385 lb) st
Armament: 2×30-mm cannon, plus provision for up to 6300 kg (13,889 lb) of stores carried on 9×external hardpoints
Max T/O weight: 17000 kg (37,478 lb)
Max speed: Mach 2.35 at 39,370 ft
Operational range: 870 miles

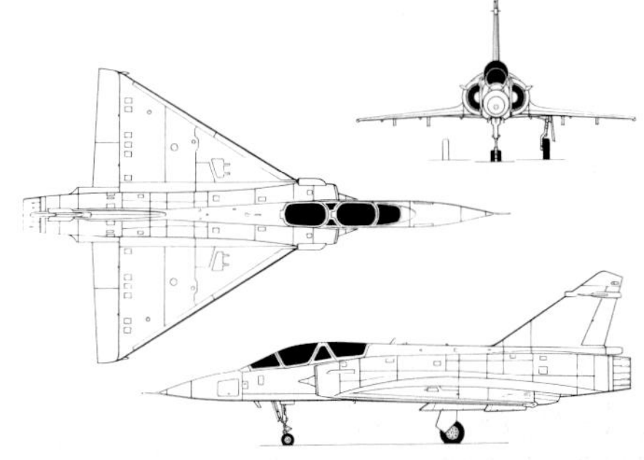

Sukhoi Su-24 'Fencer'

The Su-24 is the USSR's counterpart of the F-111 and a truly formidable long-range interdictor. The type is nuclear capable, and can also be used to carry a substantial load of conventional weapons for delivery with great accuracy as a result of an advanced avionic system that includes a pulse-Doppler multi-mode main radar, twin terrain-following radars, Doppler navigation and an inertial navigation system. The 'swing-wing' Su-24 first flew in 1969, and current variants are the baseline 'Fencer-A' with 10000-kg (22,046-lb) thrust AL-21F-1s, the 'Fencer-B' with a braking parachute, the upgraded 'Fencer-C' with a radar-warning system and possibly mid-course missile update capability, the 'Fencer-D' with a retractable inflight-refuelling probe and possibly new radar, the 'Fencer-E' electronic warfare version, and the 'Fencer-F' reconnaissance model.

General Dynamics F-111

First flown in December 1964, the F-111 was the world's first operational 'swing-wing' aeroplane, and despite a number of problems with the structure, avionics and engine installation, the type has matured as a quite exceptional all-weather, low-level interdiction and strike platform in six production versions. Most F-111As have been relegated to secondary duties or for rebuilding as EF-111A electronic warfare aircraft, so the main versions are now the FB-111A bomber with longer wings and up to six nuclear weapons, the Australian F-111C version of the F-111A with the FB-111A's wings, the F-111D improvement of the F-111A with greater power and Mk 2 avionics, the F-111E with modified inlets, and the F-111F definitive tactical variant with the 'Pave Tack' target-acquisition/designation pod used with laser-guided weapons.

Specification: General Dynamics F-111F two-seat strike and interdictor aeroplane
Span: 19.20 m (63 ft 0 in) spread and 9.74 m (31 ft 11.4 in) swept
Length: 22.40 m (73 ft 6 in)
Powerplant: 2×Pratt & Whitney TF30-P-100, 11385 kg (25,100 lb) st each
Armament: 1×optional 20-mm multi-barrel cannon, plus provision for up to 14288 kg (31,500 lb) of stores carried internally and on 6×external hardpoints
Max T/O weight: 45360 kg (100,000 lb)
Max speed: Mach 2.5 at high altitude
Operational range: 2,925+ miles

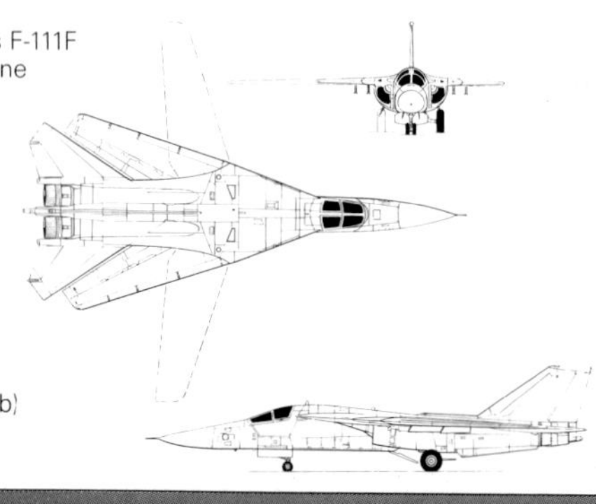

Mikoyan-Gurevich MiG-27 'Flogger'

The MiG-27 is the dedicated attack variant of the MiG-23 'swing-wing' fighter with simplified propulsion (downrated engine with fixed inlets and two-position nozzle), modified arrangement of seven rather than five hardpoints, revised landing gear for forward-airfield operations, and a 'ducknose' forward fuselage lacking radar but fitted with armour and offering the pilot superior fields of vision in the attack role. The two MiG-27 variants are the 'Flogger-D' with terrain-avoidance radar, a laser ranger/marked-target seeker and downward-firing gunpods, and the 'Flogger-J' with leading-edge root extensions and a revised sensor fit; the Indian version of the latter is the MiG-27M Bahadur. Hybrid variants are the MiG-23 'Flogger-F' and 'Flogger-H' that combine the MiG-23's airframe and powerplant with the MiG-27's nose and sensors, revised in the 'Flogger-H'.

Specification: Mikoyan-Gurevich MiG-27 'Flogger-D' single-seat ground-attack aeroplane
Span: 14.25 m (46 ft 9 in) spread and 8.17 m (26 ft 9.7 in) swept
Length: 16.00 m (52 ft 5.9 in)
Powerplant: 1×Tumanskii R-29-300, 11500 kg (25,352 lb) st
Armament: 1×23-mm multi-barrel cannon, plus provision for up to 4000 kg (8,818 lb) of stores carried on 7×external hardpoints
Max T/O weight: 20100 kg (44,313 lb)
Max speed: Mach 1.7 at high altitude
Operational range: 480 miles

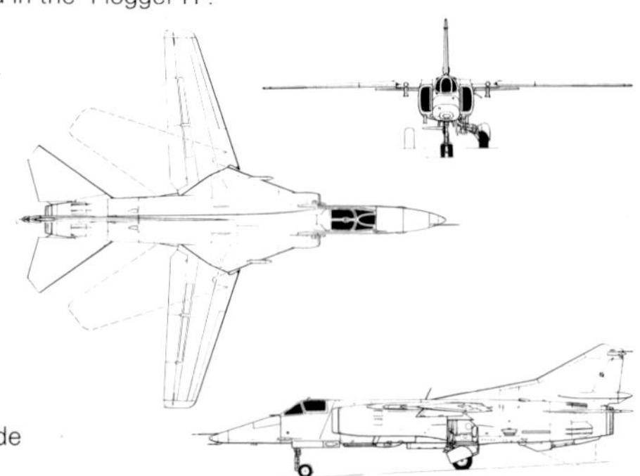

pecification: Sukhoi Su-24
encer-C' two-seat strike and
terdictor aeroplane
pan: 17.50 m (57 ft 5 in) spread
id 10.50 m (34 ft 5.5 in) swept
ength: 21.29 m (69 ft 10 in)
cluding probe
owerplant: 2×Lyul'ka AL-21F-3,
200 kg (24,691 lb) st each
rmament: 1×30-mm multi-barrel
nnon and (possibly) 1×30-mm
nnon, plus provision for up to
000 kg (24,250 lb) of stores
rried on 8×external hardpoints
ax T/O weight: 41000 kg
0,388 lb)
ax speed: Mach 2.18 at 36,090 ft
perational range: 1,610 miles

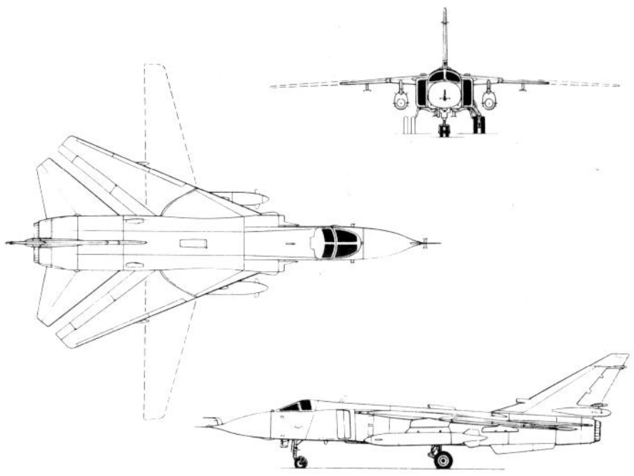

This Sukhoi Su-24 'Fencer-C' belongs to a bomber regiment based on the Kola peninsula. It carries the Sukhoi Design Bureau badge on the nose, but no unit markings are carried. Large underwing fuel tanks extend the aircraft's already impressive radius of action.

Northrop B-2

Very little has been revealed about the B-2 'stealth' bomber, which is due to fly in late 1988 as successor to the B-1B in the low-level strategic bomber role. The B-2 is a flying wing making maximum use of advanced design, structural and propulsion technologies to reduce the type's acoustic, infra-red, radar and visual signatures to a minimum as a means of facilitating deep penetration of enemy airspace. The design is optimised for subsonic flight performance with non-afterburning turbofans, and the use of radar-absorbent materials in the structure is complemented by an advanced electronic countermeasures system intended to operate mainly in the passive mode. Production of 132 is planned, and a service date of 1992 is anticipated. The type will carry several types of weapon, including the new Convair Advanced Cruise Missile.

Specification: Northrop B-2
four-seat strategic heavy bomber
Span: about 52.4 m (172 ft 0 in)
Length: about 21.0 m (69 ft 0 in)
Powerplant: 4×General Electric F118, between 11340 and 13608 kg (25,000 and 30,000 lb) st each
Armament: not revealed
Max T/O weight: about 170100 kg (375,000 lb)
Max speed: high subsonic at low altitude
Operational range: not revealed

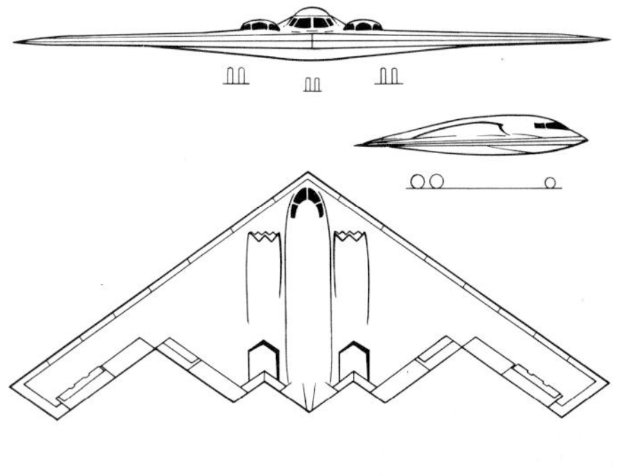

Rockwell B-1B

The B-1 began life during 1969 in response to a requirement for a supersonic B-52 replacement, and flew in December 1974 as the B-1A 'swing-wing' type able to deliver ordnance over long ranges at high altitude with a dash speed of Mach 2.2+. In 1977 the programme was seen as obsolete and cancelled, but revived in 1981 as the basis of a modestly supersonic low-level bomber with a much increased payload including air-launched cruise missiles. Much was achieved in reducing an already low radar signature by the incorporation of absorbent materials and S-shaped ducts with streamwise baffles in the fixed-geometry inlets. The first true B-1B flew in September 1984 and the type began to enter service in 1985. It is currently the USAF's most important strategic bomber despite the fact that there are still problems with the ALQ-161 defensive ECM system.

Specification: Rockwell B-1B
four-seat strategic heavy bomber
Span: 41.67 m (136 ft 8.5 in) spread and 23.84 m (78 ft 2.5 in) swept
Length: 44.81 m (147 ft 0 in)
Powerplant: 4×General Electric F101-GE-102, 13608 kg (30,000 lb) st each
Armament: provision for up to about 36288 kg (80,000 lb) of stores carried in 3×internal bays and 8×underfuselage hardpoints
Max T/O weight: 216365 kg (477,000 lb)
Max speed: Mach 1.25 at high altitude
Operational range: about 7,455 miles

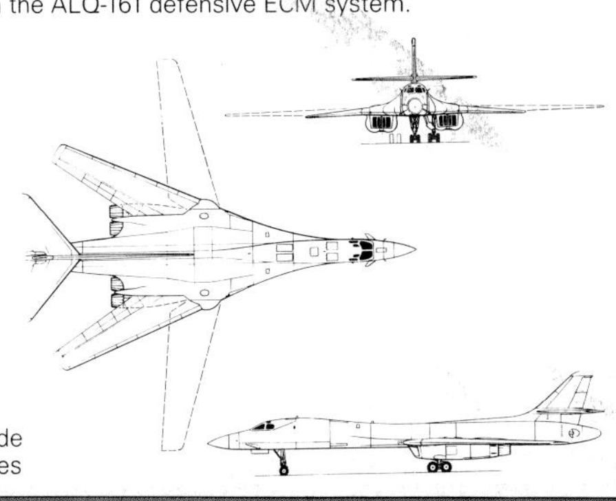

Chapter 5

RECONNAISSANCE AIRCRAFT

Lockheed U-2

Specification: Lockheed U-2C single-seat high-altitude strategic reconnaissance aeroplane
Span: 24.43 m (80 ft 2 in)
Length: 15.24 m (50 ft 0 in)
Powerplant: 1×Pratt & Whitney J75-P-13B, 7711 kg (17,000 lb) st
Armament: none
Max T/O weight: 10225 kg (22,452 lb)
Cruising speed: 465 mph at 65,000 ft
Operating altitude: 70,000+ ft
Operational range: 2,880 miles

The early U-2s were some of the trickiest aircraft to fly. At the top end of their performance the stalling speed and never-exceed speed converged alarmingly, while their central undercarriage and long wing made them tricky to land. This is a U-2A seen in the CIA's black colour scheme (with white canopy hood), wearing a civil registration for maintenance work while back in the US.

Designed to make high-altitude reconnaissance flights over the USSR, the U-2 is a technically remarkable type that was in its time controversial, especially when Gary Powers was downed in a U-2 over the USSR during 1960. Work began on the U-2 during 1954, resulting in what is essentially a powered sailplane of marginal flying qualities. The type entered service in 1956, and operational variants included the 48 U-2As and U-2Bs with the 5080-kg (11,200-lb) J57-P-37A and more powerful J75-P-13 respectively, the U-2C Elint platforms converted from U-2Bs, and the completely redesigned U-2R produced to the extent of 25 aircraft to produce a better airframe/powerplant match with span increased to 31.39 m (103 ft) and weight to 18144+ kg (40,000+ lb), plus wing pods for extra Sigint and/or optical reconnaissance gear. The U-2R paved the way for the current TR-1A tactical type.

Avro Lincoln

Designed as successor to the Lancaster as the UK's mainstay heavy bomber, the Lincoln B.Mk 1 was just too late for service in World War II, but was built to the extent of 528 aircraft for post-war service, when it was operated by 24 squadrons. The type adhered to the Lancaster's design formula, but had higher aspect ratio wings, more power and heavier defensive firepower. Though little publicized at the time or later, the Lincoln was also used for strategic intelligence-gathering purposes by three squadrons of No.90 Group. In these aircraft additional mission crew were carried, and the ventral radome for the H2S bombing radar's antenna was enlarged and modified in shape to accommodate some of the antennae associated with the modified type's Sigint (signals intelligence) role, probing the outer defences of the USSR's western and southern reaches.

Specification: Avro Lincoln multi-seat strategic reconnaissance aeroplane (data for B.Mk 1)
Span: 89.47 m (120 ft 0 in)
Length: 23.86 m (78 ft 3.5 in)
Powerplant: 4×Rolls-Royce Merlin 85, 1305 kW (1,750 hp) each
Armament: 7×12.7-mm (0.5-in) machine-guns in twin-gun nose, dorsal and tail turrets, and single ventral position
Normal T/O weight: 34020 kg (75,000 lb)
Max speed: 295 mph at 15,000 ft
Operational range: 2,930 miles

B-29/RB-50 Stratofortress

The reconnaissance version of the B-29 Superfortress was the F-13A: 117 B-29s and B-29As were modified for the Photint role with K-18 and K-22 cameras plus fuel tanks in the bomb bay, becoming operational in December 1944. In 1945 the type was redesignated FB-29A and in 1948 RB-29A, cameras then giving way to electronics for the Sigint role. Similar conversion of two YB-29Js with Wright R-3350-CA-2 engines produced FB-29Js (later RB-29Js). The Pratt & Whitney-engined version of the B-29 was eventually designated B-50, and reconnaissance versions were 44 RB-50Bs with four camera stations and two 2650-litre (700-US gal) underwing tanks: 43 of these were later upgraded to 14 RB-50Es with revised cameras, 14 RB-50Fs with SHORAN radar and 15 RB-50Gs with five Sigint radomes and a 16-man crew.

Specification: Boeing RB-29 multi-seat strategic reconnaissance aeroplane (data for B-50B)
Span: 43.05 m (141 ft 3 in)
Length: 30.18 m (99 ft 0 in)
Powerplant: 4×Pratt & Whitney R-4360, 2610 kW (3,500 hp) each
Armament: 1×20-mm cannon and 12×12.7-mm (0.5-in) machine-guns in four-gun forward dorsal barbette, twin-gun aft dorsal, fore and aft ventral barbettes, and twin-gun/single-cannon tail turret
Max T/O weight: 77112 kg (170,000 lb)
Max speed: 385 mph at 25,000 ft
Operational range: 4,650 miles

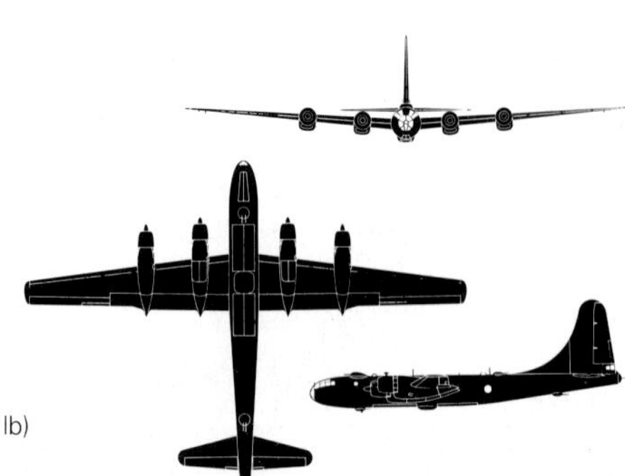

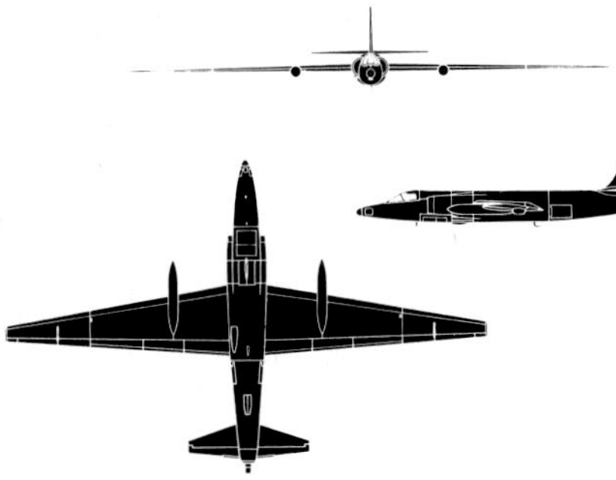

Boeing Washington

Washington B.Mk 1 was the designation allocated by the RAF to 88 B-29 and B-29A Stratofortresses de-cocooned and handed over to the British in 1950 to supplement the Avro Lincoln pending deliveries of the first jet-powered V-bombers. Several of these Washingtons were modified in a fashion similar to the RB-29A for the Sigint role to supplement and then supplant the Lincoln, and it is known that four served with No.192 Squadron. All Washington bombers were returned to the USA during 1954, but the modified aircraft of No.90 Group remained in British service up to 1958. The aircraft were normally employed in the Baltic region, but were also seen on detachment to other areas around the USSR's perimeter. Their most important success was the first Western recording of the 'Scan Odd' air-interception radar carried by the Mikoyan-Gurevich MiG-19 fighter.

Specification: Boeing Washington
multi-seat strategic reconnaissance aeroplane (data for B.Mk 1)
Span: 43.05m (141ft 3in)
Length: 30.18m (99ft 0in)
Powerplant: 4×Wright R-3350 Cyclone 18, 1640kW (2,200hp) each
Armament: 10×12.7-mm (0.5-in) machine-guns in twin-gun fore and aft dorsal, and fore and aft ventral barbettes, and twin-gun tail turret
Max T/O weight: 63504kg (140,000lb)
Max speed: 350 mph at 35,000ft
Operational range: 4,100 miles

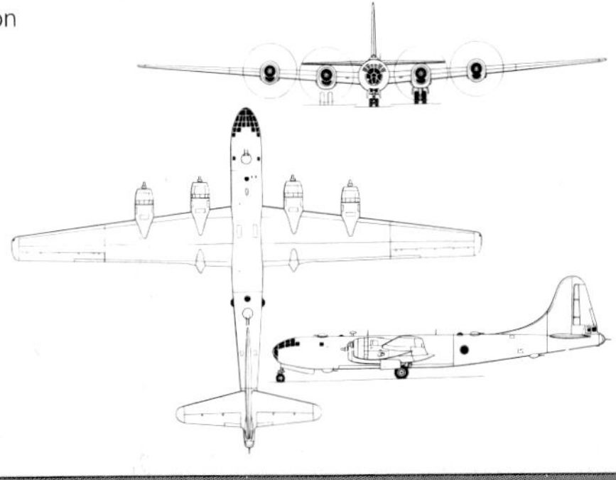

Convair RB-36 Peacemaker

The massive B-36 was the USAAF's mainstay strategic heavy bomber in the late 1940s and early 1950s, and a logical candidate for development into strategic reconnaissance variants. First of these was the RB-36B, as 39 B-36Bs were designated after temporary conversion with a camera installation. The first definitive model was the RB-36D with four underwing turbojets to boost the performance provided by the six pusher piston engines, and fitted with an array of 14 cameras in two of the four bomb bays, plus Sigint gear elsewhere in the airframe. The crew was 22 instead of the usual 15, and 22 B-36As were modified to comparable RB-36E standard. The 24 RB-36Fs were similar but had more-powerful piston engines and additional fuel. The final variant was the RB-36H, of which 73 were built with an improved flightdeck and a number of equipment modifications.

Specification: Convair RB-36D Peacemaker
22-seat strategic reconnaissance aeroplane (data for B-36D)
Span: 70.10m (230ft 0in)
Length: 49.40m (162ft 1in)
Powerplant: 6×Pratt & Whitney R-4360-41 Wasp Major, 2610kW (3,500hp) each, and 4×General Electric J47-GE-19, 2359kg (5,200lb) st each
Armament: 16×20-mm cannon in 6×twin-cannon fuselage barbettes and twin-cannon nose and tail turrets
Max T/O weight: 162162kg (357,500lb)
Max speed: 439 mph at 32,120ft
Operational range: 7,500 miles

de Havilland Comet R.Mk 2

The Comet R.Mk 2 was successor to the Washington, and though a development of the Comet C.Mk 2 transport is notable for introducing to British service an overtly reconnaissance designation to RAF Signals Command, whose No.192 Squadron (later renumbered No.51 Squadron) operated the variant between 1958 and 1974. There were seven Comet R.Mk 2s used at various times for Sigint work, the most notable external features being a small radome under the forward fuselage, a larger radome under the rear fuselage, and wire antennae above the fuselage. The type operated around Eastern European frontiers, but also went as far afield as Cyprus, Turkey and Iran to probe the USSR's southern perimeter defences, especially the ground-based surveillance and SAM-control radars of these regions.

Specification: de Havilland Comet R.Mk 2 multi-seat strategic reconnaissance aeroplane (data for C.Mk 2)
Span: 35.05 m (115 ft 0 in)
Length: 29.26 m (96 ft 0 in)
Powerplant: 4×Rolls-Royce Avon Mk 117/118, 3334 kg (7,350 lb) st each
Armament: none
Max T/O weight: 54432 kg (120,000 lb)
Max cruising speed: 480 mph at 40,000 ft
Operational range: 2,500 miles

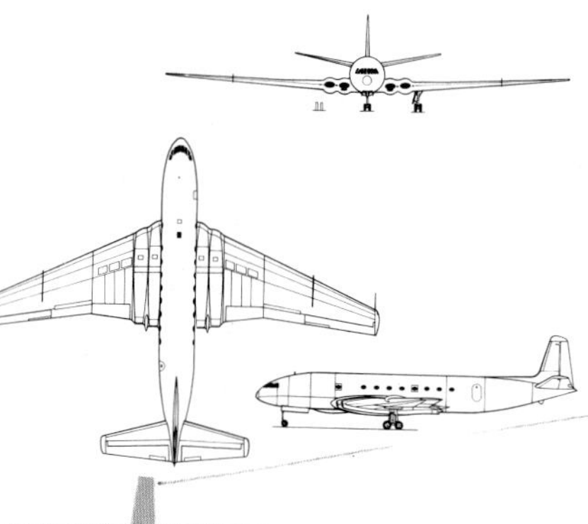

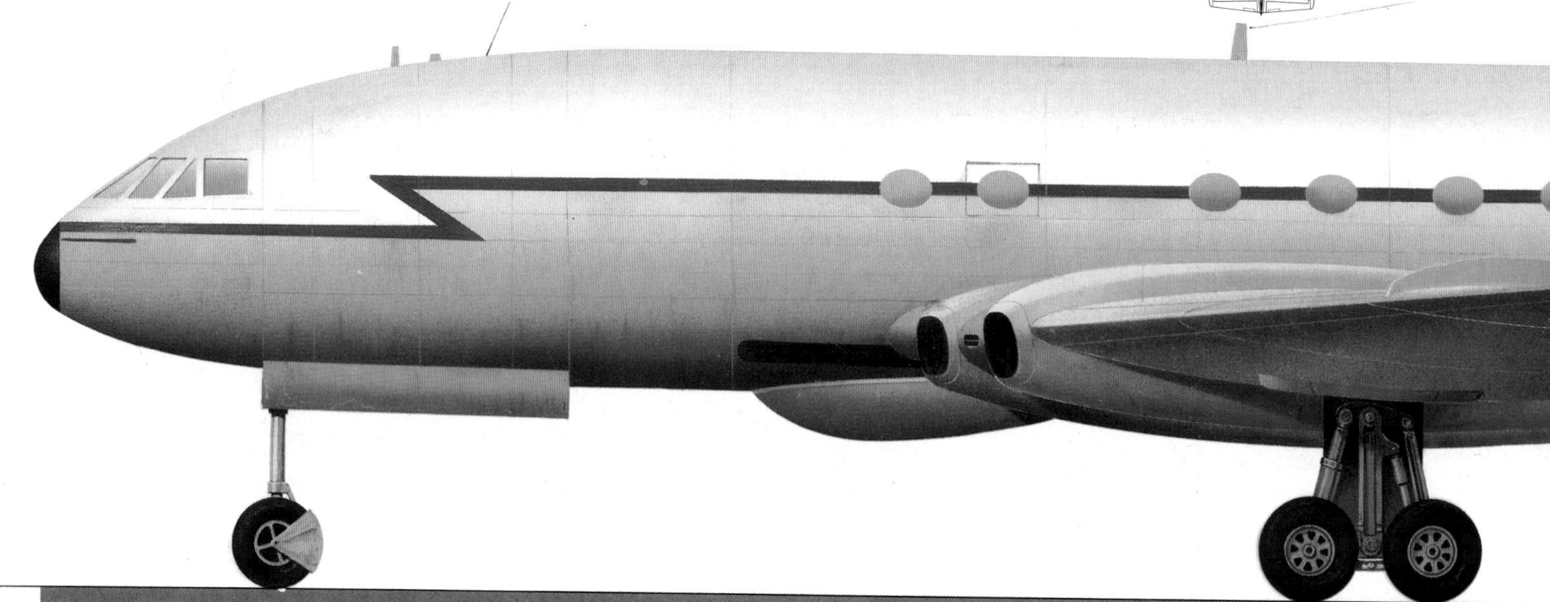

Martin P4M Mercator

Designed as a patrol bomber with two piston engines supplemented by two turbojets located in the rear of the main nacelles, the P4M fell to the P2V for large-scale production in its designed role, but was ordered to the extent of 19 P4M-1Q Sigint aircraft for two US Navy squadrons, VQ-1 operating in the Pacific theatre and VQ-2 in the Atlantic theatre. The type served with the utmost distinction between 1950 and 1960, not infrequently being required to use its defensive armament as sorties were pressed close to Soviet and Chinese shores. The type was partnered from 1958 by the EA-3 version of the carrierborne but shorter-ranged Douglas Skywarrior, and was distinguishable by two underfuselage radomes (one small and one large farther to the rear) plus a number of less noticeable antennae.

Specification: Martin P4M-1Q Mercator 16-seat strategic reconnaissance aeroplane (data for P4M-1)
Span: 34.75 m (114 ft 0 in)
Length: 25.60 m (84 ft 0 in)
Powerplant: 2×Pratt & Whitney R-4360-4 Wasp Major, 2218 kW (2,975 hp) each, and two Allison J33-A-23, 2087 kg (4,600 lb) st each
Armament: 4×20-mm cannon and 4×12.7-mm (0.5-in) machine-guns
Max T/O weight: 40088 kg (88,378 lb)
Max speed: 415 mph at 20,100 ft
Operational range: 2,840 miles

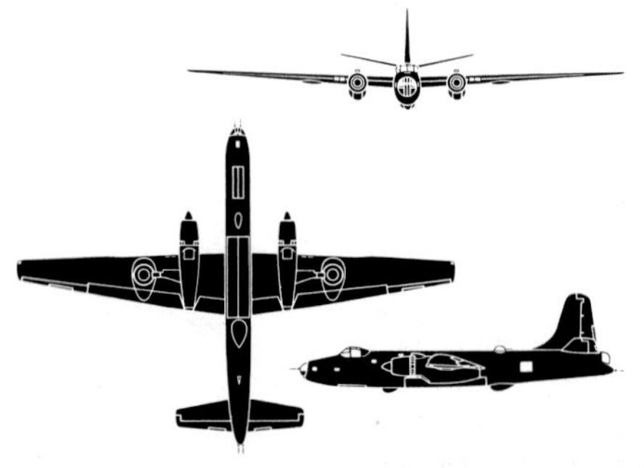

Consolidated PB4Y Privateer

The designation PB4Y-1 was used for the version of the B-24D Liberator used by the US Navy from 1942 as long-range maritime patrollers. Some 64 of these were modified for photo-reconnaissance with the designation PB4Y-1P, and these survived with two squadrons into the early 1950s, being redesignated P4Y-1P in 1952. A Liberator variant better suited to naval needs was developed in 1943 as the PB4Y-2 with a longer fuselage, single vertical tail surfaces and different nacelles for the unturbocharged engines. A specialist photo-reconnaissance version was produced by converting PB4Y-2B anti-shipping aircraft, these PB4Y-2S aircraft being redesignated P4Y-1S in 1952. The type retained full defensive armament capability, but was festooned on the fuselage with radomes covering the antennae of the Sigint equipment.

Specification: Consolidated PB4Y-2S Privateer multi-seat strategic reconnaissance aeroplane (data for PB4Y-2)
Span: 33.53 m (110 ft 0 in)
Length: 22.73 m (74 ft 7 in)
Powerplant: 4×Pratt & Whitney R-1830-94 Twin Wasp, 1007 kW (1,350 hp) each
Armament: 12×12.7-mm (0.5-in) machine-guns in twin-gun nose, two dorsal and tail turrets, and twin-gun waist positions
Max T/O weight: 29484 kg (65,000 lb)
Max speed: 237 mph at 13,750 ft
Operational range: 2,800 miles

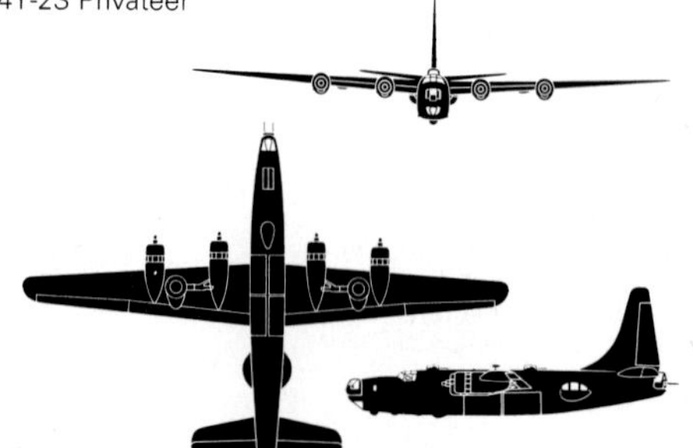

The RAF was heavily involved in signals intelligence work following the end of the war, the main effort centring around No. 192 Sqn, later renumbered No. 51. Canberras were widely used, as were Comet R.Mk 2s, which were distinguishable from transport versions by the additional antennas and large belly fairings. No. 51's Comets were active in Europe and the Mediterranean.

Vickers Varsity

The Varsity T.Mk 1 was developed from the Viking and Valetta as a long-range crew trainer in succession to the Vickers Wellington T.Mk 10, and began to enter service in 1951. The type's good payload/range performance and voluminous cabin combined with its unobtrusiveness to commend development of a Sigint variant, often seen in the guise of navaid calibration aircraft, for use by Signals Command's No.51 Squadron in areas such as West Germany, where it could operate along their air corridors linking Berlin with West Germany to detect and record the various Soviet radars, both airborne and ground-based, in the area. The Varsity was also used by the Swedish air force in a similar role. Apparently only one aeroplane was modified, this featuring underfuselage radomes and a number of projecting rod antennae above the fuselage.

Specification: Vickers Varsity multi-seat strategic reconnaissance aeroplane (data for T.Mk 1)
Span: 29.16 m (95 ft 8 in)
Length: 20.57 m (67 ft 6 in)
Powerplant: 2×Bristol Hercules 264, 1454 kW (1,950 hp) each
Armament: none
Normal T/O weight: 17010 kg (37,500 lb)
Max speed: 288 mph at 10,000 ft
Operational range: 2,648 miles

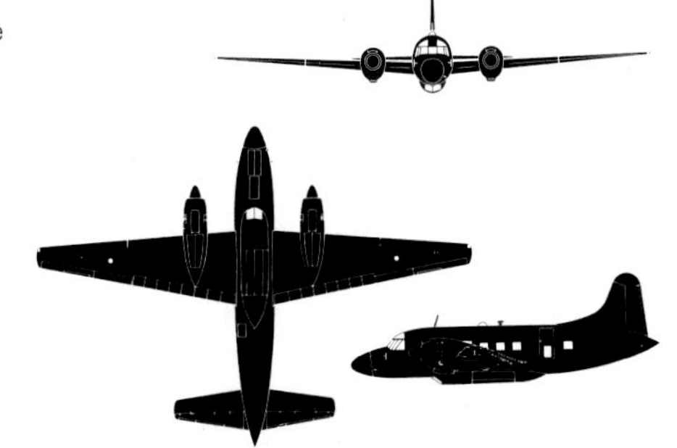

Lockheed P2V/RB-69 Neptune

The range and payload of the P2V (from 1962 P-2) Neptune land-based patrol bomber made it a natural choice for conversion to other roles, including the electronic warfare and reconnaissance roles. The P2V-6 (P-2F) was a multi-role model of which 67 were built from 1952: the type's enlarged bomb bay could accommodate an optical reconnaissance pack. The USAF operated the RB-69A (naval P2V-7U), these seven machines being used for the combined Photint and Sigint roles, a portside SLAR later being added. The designation OP-2E applied to several P-2Es fitted with a General Dynamics sensor package for area surveillance in Vietnam, and some of these were transferred to the USAF as AP-2Es. Finally there were a few AP-2H conversions of the P-2H with the E-System TRIM (Trails & Roads Interdiction, Multi-sensor) reconnaissance and interdiction package for use in Vietnam.

Specification: Lockheed RB-69A multi-seat strategic reconnaissance aeroplane (data for P2V-7)
Span: 31.65 m (103 ft 10 in)
Length: 27.84 m (91 ft 4 in)
Powerplant: 2×Wright R-3350-32W Cyclone 18, 2610 kW (3,500 hp) each, and 2×Westinghouse J34-WE-34, 1542 kg (3,400 lb) st each
Armament: none
Max T/O weight: 34247 kg (75,500 lb)
Max speed: 345 mph at 10,000 ft
Operational range: 2,200 miles

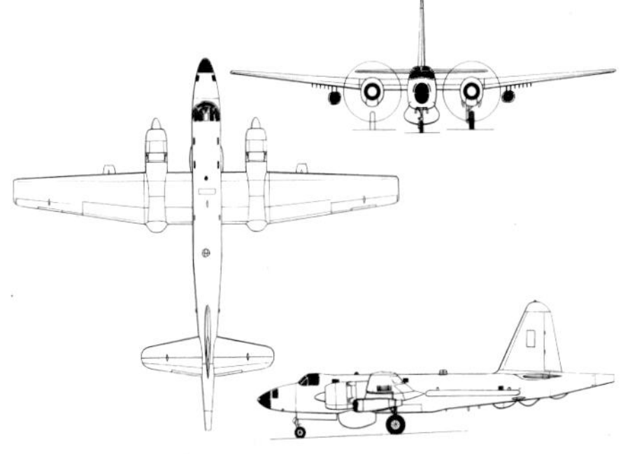

Boeing RB-47 Stratojet

The reconnaissance version of the B-47 strategic medium bomber was the RB-47, and this appeared in several versions. First were 24 RB-47B conversions from B-47B standard with an eight-camera pack in the bomb bay as crew trainers for the RB-47E, of which 240 were built with the camera kit, a lengthened nose and an inbuilt JATO pack. The last two reconnaissance models of the Stratojet were based on the RB-47E. The 32 RB-47Hs were intended for electronic reconnaissance: three additional crew members were accommodated in a revised bomb bay, and radomes were added at the nose, on the wings and under the rear fuselage for the ALD-4 Sigint system. In addition, three RB-47Es were converted to a similar ERB-47H standard for special missions with a crew of five. The 15 RB-47Ks were intended for alternative reconnaissance and weather reconnaissance roles at high and low altitude.

Specification: Boeing RB-47E multi-seat strategic reconnaissance aeroplane (data for B-47E-II)
Span: 35.36 m (116 ft 0 in)
Length: 33.48 m (109 ft 10 in)
Powerplant: 6×General Electric J47-GE-25/25A, 2722 kg (6,000 lb) st each
Armament: 2×20-mm cannon in a remote-control tail barbette
Max T/O weight: 93759 kg (203,600 lb)
Max speed: 606 mph at 16,300 ft
Operational range: 4,000 miles

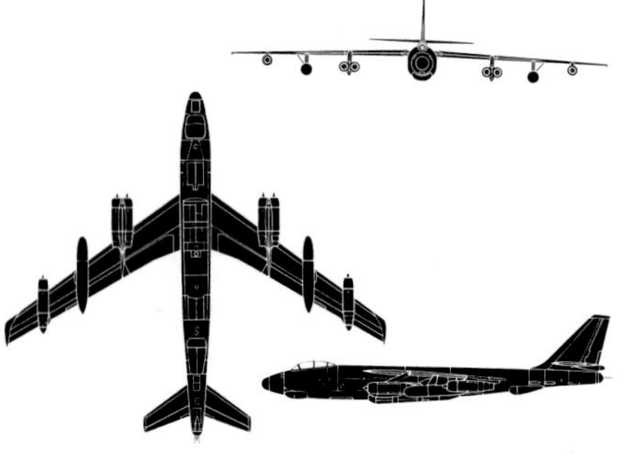

Lockheed EC-121

The C-69 transport of World War II was the L-049 Constellation airliner modified for military use, and development led to a whole series of Constellation transports, of which the L-749 and later variants were ordered for USAF as the C-121. The type was extensively developed for AEW in a number of RC-121 and EC-121 variants with Sigint capability, but the most important models configured for the Sigint role were the five EC-121S and about 23 EC-121T aircraft modified from C-121C and from the older EC-121D, EC-121H and EC-121J standards. The US Navy also used the Constellation under a number of designations, the airborne early warning version being the WV Warning Star: at least five of these were modified as WV-2Q (from 1962 EC-121M) ECM and reconnaissance aircraft.

Specification: Lockheed RC-121D Constellation 27-seat airborne early warning and strategic reconnaissance aeroplane
Span: 38.46 m (126 ft 2 in)
Length: 35.41 m (116 ft 2 in)
Powerplant: 4×Wright R-3350-34/91 Cyclone 18, 2423 kW (3,250 hp)
Armament: none
Max T/O weight: 65137 kg (143,600 lb)
Max speed: 321 mph at 20,000 ft
Operational range: 4,600 miles

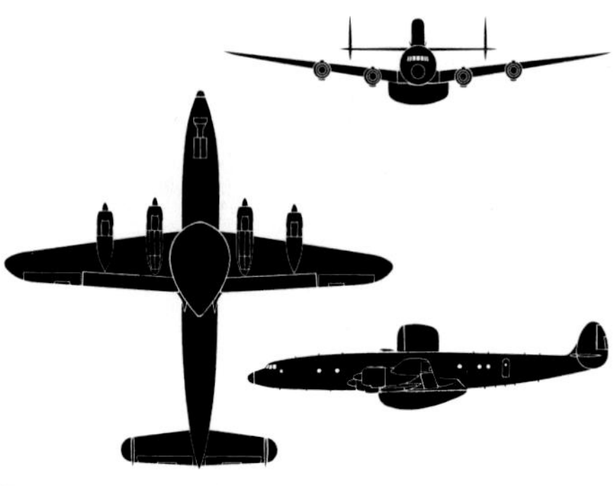

EE Canberra B.Mk 2/B.Mk 6

In the Canberra the RAF had a small bomber whose performance and internal payload offered admirable capabilities for conversion to the reconnaissance role. There were many conventional reconnaissance version in the PR series, but strategic work was entrusted to three Signals Command squadrons flying Canberra B.Mk 2, B.Mk 2 (mod), B.Mk 6BS, B.Mk 6RC and B.Mk 6 (mod) aircraft. These were tasked mainly with Sigint around the perimeters of Soviet airspace, and as the technology and targets evolved went through various phases of modification with lengthened noses (carrying hemispherical or pointed radomes), tailcones modified with various types of antennae, and warty excrescences above the fuselage. The various Canberra marks were generally withdrawn from the Sigint role in 1976 when this was assumed by the BAe Nimrod R.Mk 1

Specification: English Electric Canberra B.Mk 2 three-seat strategic reconnaissance aeroplane (data for B.Mk 2 bomber)
Span: 19.49 m (63 ft 11.5 in)
Length: 19.96 m (65 ft 6 in)
Powerplant: 2×Rolls-Royce Avon Mk 101, 2948 kg (6,500 lb) st each
Armament: none
Max T/O weight: 20866 kg (46,000 lb)
Max speed: 570 mph at 40,000 ft
Operational range: 2,660 miles

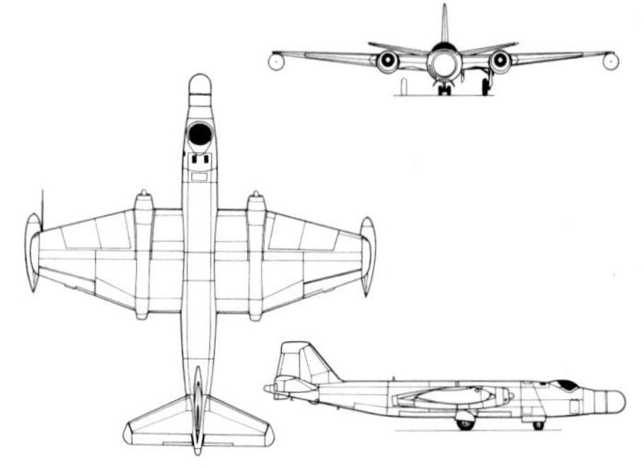

Martin RB-57D/F

US version of the Canberra, the B-57 began to enter service in 1954 and was soon developed into a Photint version, the RB-57A of which 67 were built with a camera pack aft of the bomb bay; the improved B-57B and B-57C had RB-57B and RB-57C equivalents. Considerably more important was the RB-57D high-altitude platform with J57 engines in place of the less-powerful Wright J65s, considerably increased span and Photint and Sigint gear; 20 were built in four single- and two-seat subvariants with and without inflight-refuelling capability. Structural problems beset the type in 1963, and this spurred the development of the extraordinary RB-57F spanning 37.19 m (122 ft) and powered by two TF33 turbofans and two underwing J60 turbojets. Production from surplus airframes amounted to 21, and the variant could climb to nearly 95,000 ft.

Specification: Martin RB-57D one/two-seat strategic reconnaissance aeroplane
Span: 32.31 m (106 ft 0 in)
Length: 19.96 m (65 ft 6 in)
Powerplant: 2×Pratt & Whitney J57-P-37A, 4763 kg (10,500 lb) st each
Armament: none
Max T/O weight: not revealed
Max speed: 632 mph at 40,000 ft
Service ceiling: 70,000 ft
Operational range: not revealed

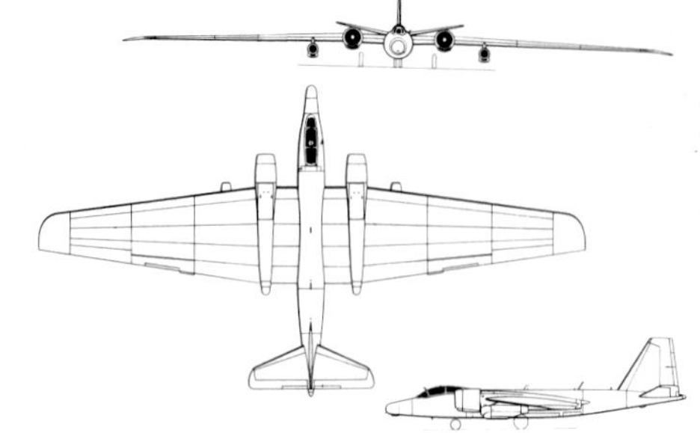

Westland Sea King AEW.Mk. 2A

n 1978 the Fleet Air Arm lost its fixed-wing AEW capability, and this proved a distinct actical disadvantage in the 1982 Falklands War. Given the Royal Navy's limitation to VTOL ircraft, the only solution was an AEW helicopter, and in an 11-week programme the Sea King AEW.Mk 2A was developed with Thorn-EMI Searchwater radar. Two Sea King HAS.Mk 's were modified with this radar, Jubilee Guardsman IFF and MIR-2 'Orange Crop' ESM. The type was too late for the Falklands War, but is now standard on the UK's three carriers. The radar and IFF antennae are located on an exterior platform under a pressurised fabric dome, and this platform is carried on an arm cantilevered from a hydraulically operated itting on the port side of the fuselage: the antenna assembly is rotated to face backward when the helicopter is transiting, but turned to face downward when the radar is to be used.

Specification: Westland Sea King AEW.Mk 2A four-seat carrierborne airborne early warning helicopter
Main rotor diameter: 18.90 m (62 ft 0 in)
Overall length, rotors turning: 22.15 m (72 ft 8 in)
Powerplant: 2×Rolls-Royce Gnome H.1400-1, 1238 kW (1,660 shp) each
Armament: none
Max T/O weight: 9525 kg (21,000 lb)
Max speed: 104 mph at medium altitude
Operational endurance: 4 hours at unspecified radius

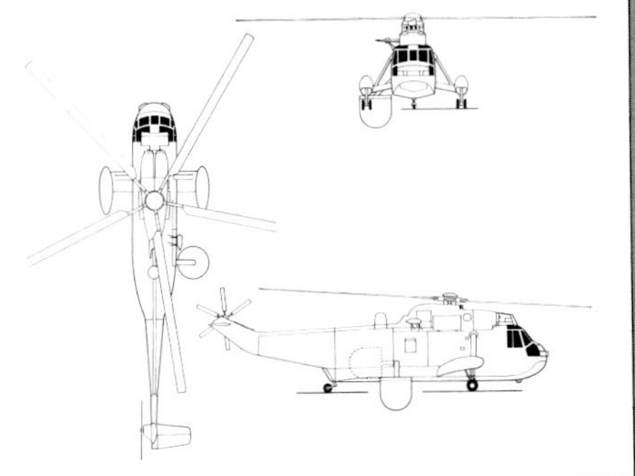

Antonov An-74 'Madcap'

The 'Madcap' may be considered the Soviet counterpart to the Americans' E-2 with the exception that it is land- rather than ship-based. The type is a development of the An-74 freighter with its rotodome mounted on top of the much-modified vertical tail. As the freighter is a version of the An-72 optimised for STOL operations in arctic conditions, it may be surmised that the 'Madcap' is optimised for operations in the USSR's hostile and comparatively ill-provided northern and eastern reaches. The type has interchangeable wheel or ski landing gear, and the use of upper surface blowing in conjunction with an extensive array of high-lift devices offers excellent STOL performance under the most adverse of conditions. The type was under final development in the late 1980s, and comparatively large-scale production may be expected in the 1990s.

Specification: Antonov An-74 'Madcap' multi-seat land-based airborne early warning and control system aeroplane
Span: 31.89 m (104 ft 7.5 in)
Length: 28.07 m (92 ft 1.1 in)
Powerplant: 2×Lotarev D-36, 6500 kg (14,330 lb) st each
Armament: none
Max T/O weight: 34500 kg (76,069 lb)
Max speed: 438 mph at optimum altitude
Operational range: 2,920 miles

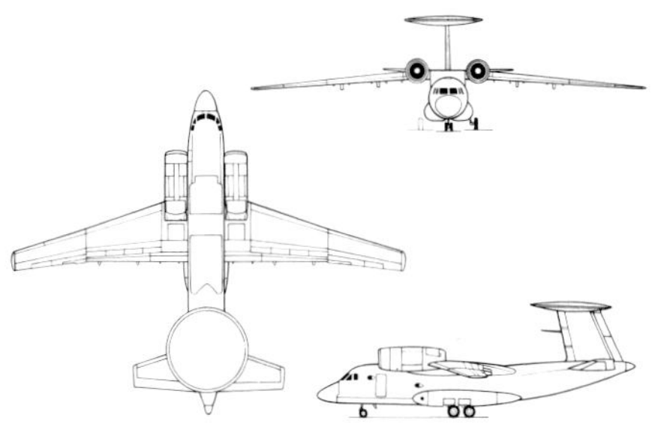

Pilatus B-N AEW Defender

After developing an Islander variant to carry the Ferranti ASTOR (Airborne STand-Off Radar) in a bulged nose as part of a British army/air force development programme for an aerial battlefield support radar, the company decided to exploit this experience with variants of the turbine-powered BN-2T airframe. The most interesting of these is the AEW Defender, in which a huge nose bulge accommodates the antenna of the Thorn-EMI Skymaster lightweight pulse-Doppler radar. This is a multi-mode equipment capable of automatic acquisition and tracking of multiple land and sea targets, and the radar can also be integrated with an IFF system, air-to-air and air-to-surface data-links, and a navigation system. The company has also proposed an upgraded AEW/MR Defender and a border patrol version with long-range air-to-surface surveillance radar capable of synthetic-aperture mapping.

Specification: Pilatus Britten-Norman AEW Defender two/three-seat land-based airborne early warning aeroplane
Span: 14.94 m (49 ft 0 in)
Length: 12.65 m (41 ft 6 in)
Powerplant: 2×298-kW (400-shp) Allison 250-B17C, flat-rated to 239 kW (320 shp) each
Armament: none
Max T/O weight: 3175 kg (7,000 lb)
Max speed: 196 mph at 10,000 ft
Operational endurance: 4 hours at 185-km (115-mile) radius

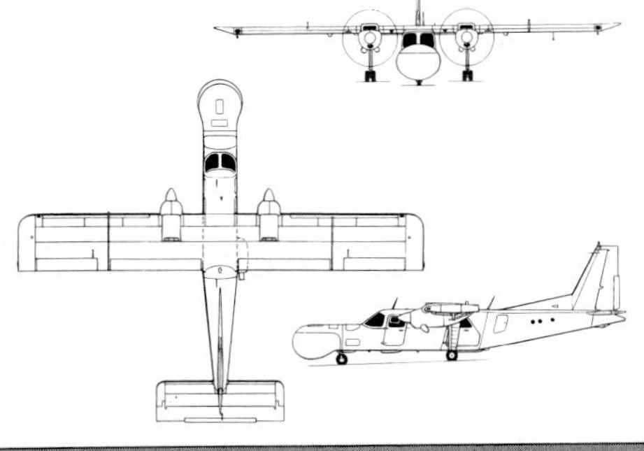

Lockheed Orion AEW & C

Many air forces would like to procure AEW aircraft but lack the financial resources to buy advanced aircraft such as the Sentry. Into this gap Lockheed has stepped, offering to convert Orions obsolescent in the MR role with an AEW suite similar to that of the E-2 but combined with a bigger tactical compartment allowing the installation of more display consoles for a larger mission crew. Such a conversion offers good tactical characteristics, and also provides existing Orion operators with considerable purchase, spares, maintenance and training savings. In its fully fledged form the Orion AEW & C would have APS-138 radar with its antenna in a new over-fuselage rotodome, but the only existing customer is the US Customs Service whose Blue Sentinel version has lower-standard APS-125 radar for patrols off Florida in the task of intercepting drug smugglers.

Specification: Lockheed Orion AEW & C multi-seat land-based airborne early warning and control system aeroplane
Span: 30.38 m (99 ft 8 in)
Length: 35.61 m (116 ft 10 in)
Powerplant: 4×Allison T56-A-14, 3661 kW (4,910 ehp) each
Armament: none
Max T/O weight: 57833 kg (127,500 lb)
Max cruising speed: 230 mph at 30,000 ft
Operational endurance: 14 hours at unspecified radius

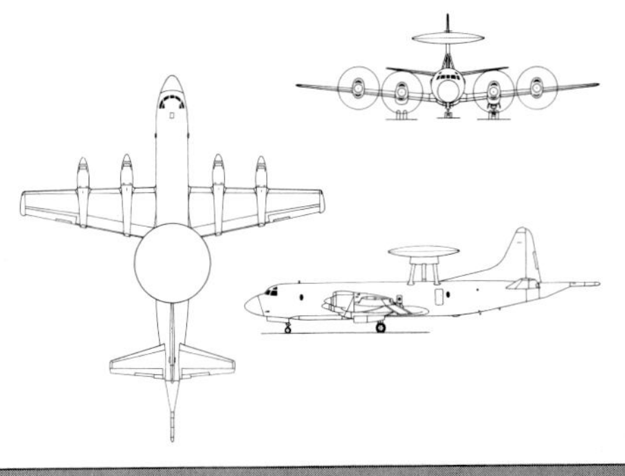

Boeing E-3 Sentry

This is the West's most important 'force multiplier' platform, and was designed for the surveillance of all air activity within a radius of 370 km (230 miles) and for the control of all friendly aircraft. The type began to enter service in 1977, and is essentially the airframe of the Model 707-300 airliner carrying APY-1 radar and APX-103 IFF with their antennae in a 9.14-m (30-ft) diameter rotodome above the fuselage. The tactical compartment has nine situation display consoles and two auxiliary units, with data handled by an IBM 4 Pi CC-1 computer. Early aircraft are being upgraded to E-3B standard with the CC-2 computer, radar modified to give a limited over-water capability, Joint Tactical Information Distribution System, and 'Have Quick' communications, while later machines are becoming E-3Cs with these features plus five extra display consoles and Sidewinder AAM capability.

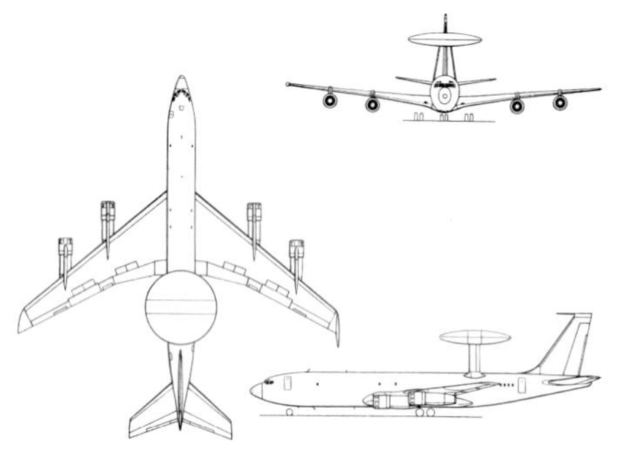

Lockheed WV-2 and EC-121

Serving with US Navy and Air Force as the R7V and C-121, the L-1049 Super Constellation transport clearly possessed the payload/range for development as the USA's first long-range AEW aeroplane. The navy took the lead with the experimental PO-1W based on the L-749 Constellation but carrying above- and under-fuselage radomes for height- and bearing-finding radars, 140 other antennae, and a mission crew of five plus a relief crew. This first flew in June 1949. Production amounted to 222 navy WV-2s (later EC-121K) with tip tanks, of which one was modified as a WV-2E (EC-121L) with a rotodome, 10 air force RC-121C (TC-121C) trainers without tip tanks, and 73 air force RC-121Ds (EC-121Ds) with full operational equipment and tip tanks. Many were later upgraded for other tasks, and 42 EC-121Hs became EC-121Hs with equipment for data transfer to the SAGE ground radar/command network.

Specification: Lockheed RC-121D Warning Star 20-seat land-based airborne early warning aeroplane
Span: 37.62 m (123 ft 5 in)
Length: 35.41 m (116 ft 2 in)
Powerplant: 4×Wright R-3350-34/42 Turbo Compound, 2535 kW (3,400 hp) each
Armament: none
Max T/O weight: 65136 kg (143,600 lb)
Max speed: 321 mph at 20,000 ft
Operational range: 4,600 miles

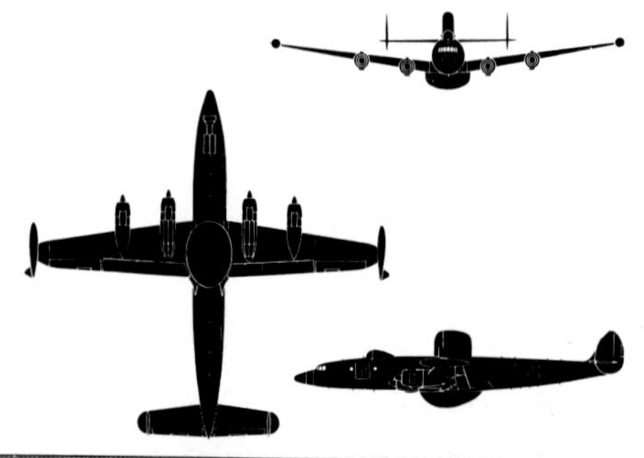

Douglas AD Skyraider

At the time the US Navy was considering development of its first post-World War II carrierborne AEW aircraft, the Skyraider offered the right combination of payload/range plus a fuselage voluminous enough to accept the necessary additions. The concept was pioneered in the single XAD-1W: the APS-20 radar was located with its antenna in an under-nose radome, and a compartment for the two operators was created by extending the fairing aft of the pilot. Production amounted to 31 AD-3Ws with the 2013-kW (2,700-hp) R-3350-26W radial, 168 AD-4Ws (including 50 transferred to the UK as Skyraider AEW.Mk 1s) with an autopilot, and 218 AD-5Ws (later EA-1Es) with the same engine as the AD-4W but a longer and wider fuselage allowing the carriage of two flightcrew as well as the mission crew of two under a larger rear canopy made of metal rather than the earlier variants' opaque plastics material.

Specification: Douglas AD-5W Skyraider four-seat carrierborne airborne early warning aeroplane
Span: 15.47 m (50 ft 9 in)
Length: 12.22 m (40 ft 1 in)
Powerplant: 1×Wright R-3350-26WA Cyclone 18, 2013 kW (2,700 hp)
Armament: none
Max T/O weight: 11340 kg (25,000 lb)
Max speed: 260 mph at medium altitude
Operational range: 1,294 miles

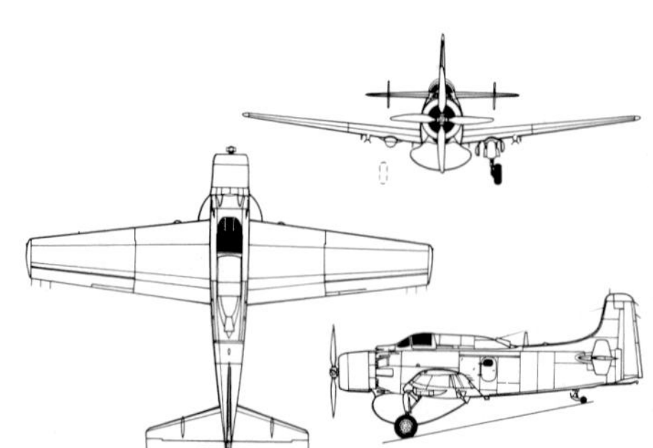

ecification: Boeing E-3A
try 17-seat land-based airborne
y warning and control system
oplane
an: 44.42 m (145 ft 9 in)
gth: 46.61 m (152 ft 11 in)
verplant: 4×Pratt &
itney TF33-P-100/100A,
6 kg (21,000 lb) st each
Armament: none
Max T/O weight: 147240 kg (325,000 lb)
Max speed: 530 mph at 30,000 ft
Operational endurance: 6 hours at 1609-km (1,000-mile) radius

NATO operates a multinational squadron of Boeing E-3 Sentries. These are based at Geilenkirchen in West Germany, but for political reasons they carry the national insignia of the Duchy of Luxembourg, which has no air force. The British Royal Air Force and the French Armée de l'Air have also procured the E-3.

rumman WF-2 Tracer

hough the AEW versions of the Skyraider proved successful in service, the US Navy was ll too aware of the limitations imposed on the type by its cramped accommodation and ingle engine. So after the twin-engined S2F Tracker anti-submarine aeroplane had been laced in service the navy ordered an AEW version that immediately became known as the Willy Fudd' after its WF-2 designation. The type carried the antenna for its APS-82 urveillance radar in a vast teardrop-shaped radome above the fuselage and supported at the ail by a new empennage with endplate vertical surfaces complementing the truncated entral surface. The first Tracer flew in March 1957, and total production amounted to 88 ircraft for use by two large squadrons serving one each with the Atlantic and Pacific Fleets. The type was redesignated E-1B in 1962 and then supplanted by the E-2.

Specification: Grumman
VF-2 Tracer four-seat carrierborne
irborne early warning aeroplane
Span: 21.23 m (69 ft 8 in)
ength: 13.82 m (45 ft 4 in)
owerplant: 2×Wright R-1820-
32WA Cyclone 9, 1137 kW (1,525
p) each
Armament: none
Max T/O weight: 12247 kg
27,000 lb)
Patrol speed: 120-160 mph at
optimum altitude
Operational range: 1,000+ miles

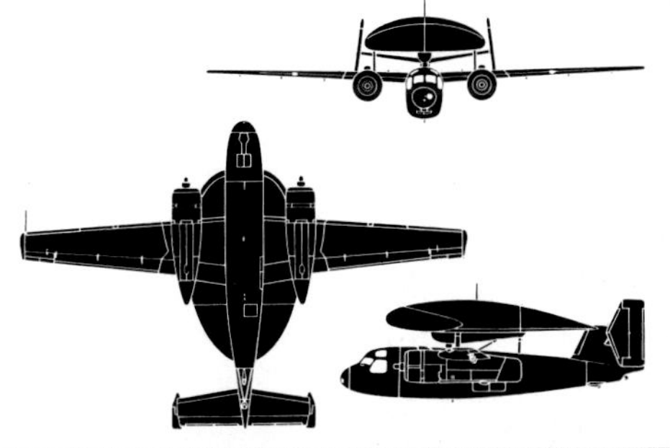

Fairey Gannet AEW.Mk 3

Though the Douglas Skyraider AEW.Mk 1 served the Fleet Air Arm well during the early part of the 1950s, it was appreciated that the type's single engine was a serious constraint on reliability. It was thus decided in the middle of the decade to develop an AEW version of the Gannet anti-submarine aeroplane that had first flown in September 1949 with a powerful coupled-turboshaft powerplant driving contra-rotating propellers. The type was developed with a new and more capacious fuselage, with internal accommodation for the two AEW operators, as well as longer-stroke landing gear to provide clearance for the under-fuselage radome used with the APS-20 radar removed from Skyraiders. The first example flew in August 1958, production was completed in December 1962 and the 44 aircraft served with the Fleet Air Arm up to 1978.

Specification: Fairey Gannet AEW.Mk 3 three-seat carrierborne airborne early warning aeroplane
Span: 16.56 m (54 ft 4 in)
Length: 13.41 m (44 ft 0 in)
Powerplant: 1×Rolls-Royce (Armstrong Siddeley/Bristol Siddeley) Double Mamba Mk 102, 2890 kW (3,875 ehp)
Armament: none
Max T/O weight: about 11340 kg (25,000 lb)
Max speed: 250 mph at medium altitude
Operational range: 700 miles

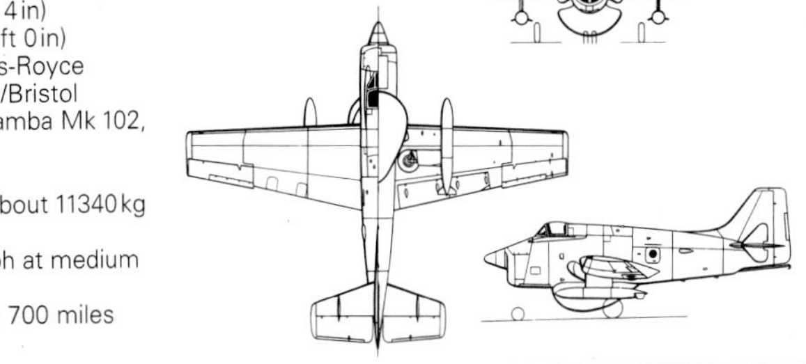

Ilyushin Il-76 'Mainstay'

One of the main tactical limitations imposed on the Tu-126 by its derivation from the Tu-114 is the radar interference of its four pairs of massive contra-rotating propellers. This failing has been obviated in the USSR's next AEW platform, the four-turbofan 'Mainstay' that began to enter service in the late 1980s again with an over-fuselage rotodome. The proper designation for this type remains unknown, but it is an altogether more capable aeroplane based on the airframe of the Il-76 logistic freighter. It carries a radar capable of effective use over land and water, and able to detect and track targets as small and difficult as low-flying cruise missiles: these factors make the 'Mainstay' a more versatile and useful type than the Tu-126. Details are scarce, but it is expected that production will soon provide five aircraft per year against an anticipated total of 50.

Grumman E-2 Hawkeye

The Hawkeye was the US Navy's first purpose-designed AEW type, and featured a layout of the type pioneered in the Tracer but in this instance improved with a pair of reliable turboprops. The first Hawkeye flew in October 1960, and the E-2A began to enter service in 1964 with the APS-96 radar with its antenna in a large rotodome above the rear fuselage. In 1969 there appeared the E-2B with an L-304 digital computer and the APS-120 radar with limited over-land capability. In 1973 the E-2C began to enter service with APS-125 radar able to detect and track 250 sea and air targets out to a range of 370km (230 miles), and allowing the crew to control 30+ interceptions. In the latest aircraft the APS-125 radar gives way to the much enhanced APS-138 or APS-139, the latter able to deal with slow or even stationary targets. All aircraft are to be retrofitted with the latest APS-145 radar.

Specification: Grumman E-2C Hawkeye five-seat carrierborne and land-based airborne early warning and control system aeroplane
Span: 24.56m (80ft 7in)
Length: 17.54m (57ft 6.75in)
Powerplant: 2×Allison T56-A-425, 3663kW (4,910ehp) each
Armament: none
Max T/O weight: 23503kg (51,817lb)
Max speed: 374mph at optimum altitude
Operational endurance: 4 hours at 320-km (200-mile) radius

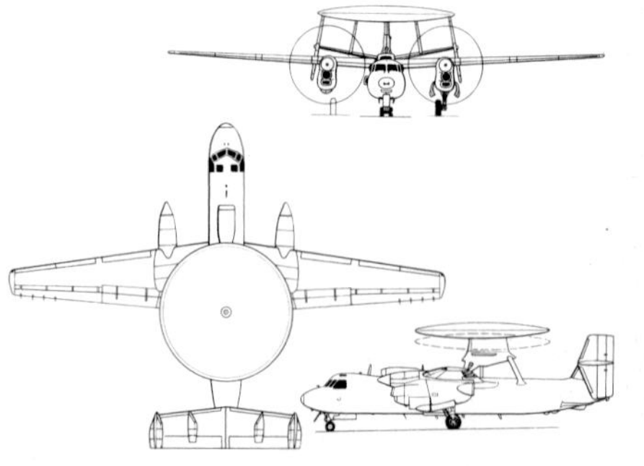

Tupolev Tu-126 'Moss'

The USSR was slow to enter the AEW field, and when it did the platform selected for the task was the Tu-114 airliner, a civil development of the Tu-95 bomber and multi-role aeroplane. Some 30 airframes were available for development as AEW aircraft, the Soviets planning a conversion analogous to that in which the E-3 was developed from the Model 707: an over-fuselage rotodome, a mass of other antennae and dielectric panels, and the cabin modified to contain the specialist mission crew. The type first flew in 1967 and began to enter service in 1971, and the primary role of the 12 converted aircraft appears to be support of Soviet interceptor forces, which can be vectored into targets most economically by a type such as the Tu-126. The USA has been constantly dismissive of the Tu-126's radar capability, but this may well be far superior to most Western estimates.

Specification: Tupolev Tu-126 'Moss' multi-seat land-based airborne early warning and control system aeroplane
Span: 51.20m (167ft 11.7in)
Length: 55.20m (181ft 1.2in)
Powerplant: 4×Kuznetsov NK-12MV, 11033kW (14,795ehp) each
Armament: none
Max T/O weight: about 170000kg (374,786lb)
Max speed: 528mph at high altitude
Operational range: 7,798 miles

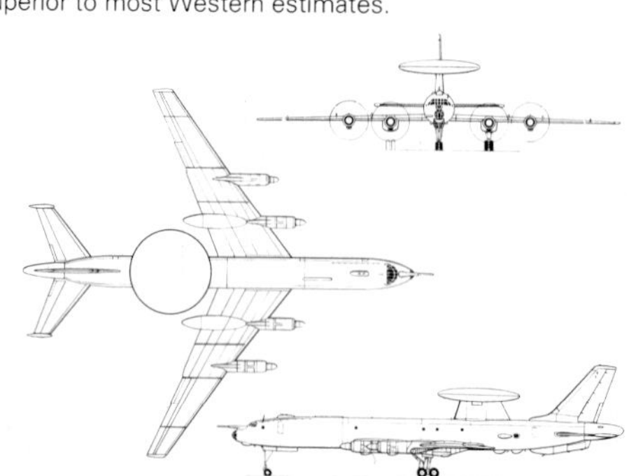

Specification: Ilyushin Il-76 'Mainstay' multi-seat land-based airborne early warning and control system aeroplane
Span: 50.50 m (165 ft 8.2 in)
Length: 46.59 m (152 ft 10.25 in)
Powerplant: 4×Soloviev D-30KP, 12000 kg (26,455 lb) st each
Armament: none
Max T/O weight: about 170000 kg (374,786 lb)
Max speed: about 500 mph at 36,090 ft
Operational range: not known

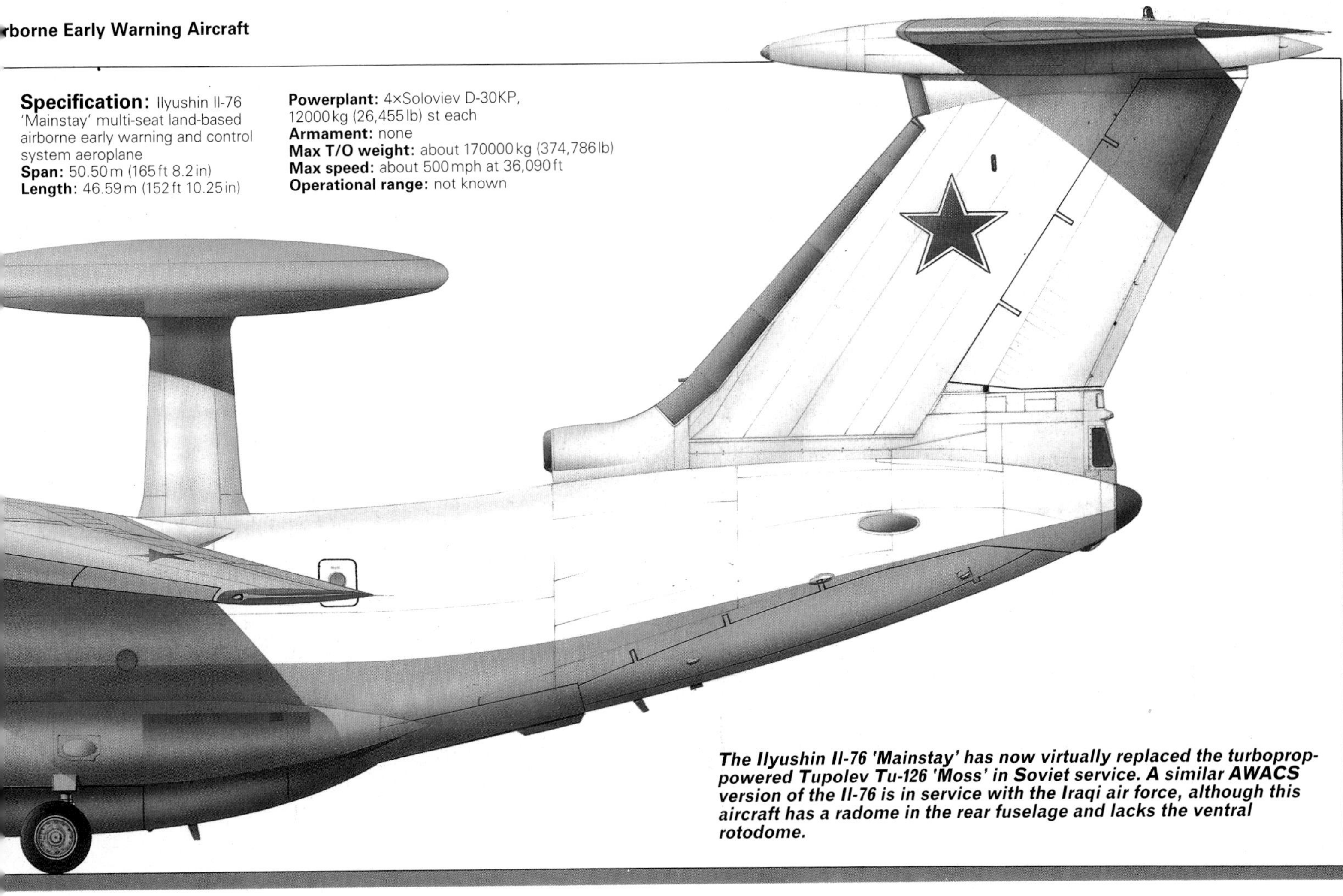

The Ilyushin Il-76 'Mainstay' has now virtually replaced the turboprop-powered Tupolev Tu-126 'Moss' in Soviet service. A similar AWACS version of the Il-76 is in service with the Iraqi air force, although this aircraft has a radome in the rear fuselage and lacks the ventral rotodome.

BAe Shackleton AEW.Mk 2

The Shackleton is the last piston-engined aeroplane in RAF first-line service, and given the failure of the Nimrod AEW.Mk 3 this direct descendant of the Lancaster is soldiering on until it can be replaced by the Sentry in the early 1990s. The AEW version was developed in the early 1970s, some 12 surplus MR.Mk 2s being converted between 1971 and 1974: APS-20 radar removed from Douglas Skyraiders and Fairey Gannets was updated to APS-20F(I) standard and installed with its antenna in an under-nose radome, while other equipment included 'Orange Harvest' broadband ESM and APX-7 IFF equipment. The tactical crew comprises three AEW operators, an avionics operator, an AEW controller and a tactical co-ordinator. The six surviving aircraft serve with No.8 Squadron at RAF Lossiemouth.

Specification: British Aerospace Shackleton AEW.Mk 2 10-seat land-based airborne early warning aeroplane
Span: 36.58 m (120 ft 0 in)
Length: 26.62 m (87 ft 4 in)
Powerplant: 4×Rolls-Royce Griffon 57A, 1831 kW (2,455 hp) each
Armament: none
Max T/O weight: 44452 kg (98,000 lb)
Max speed: 273 mph at medium altitude
Operational range: 3,050 miles

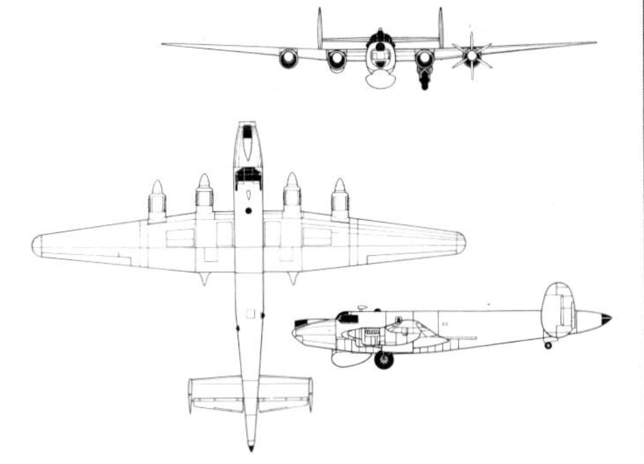

BAe Nimrod AEW.Mk 3

Development of the Nimrod AEW.Mk 3 was launched in 1977 in face of the RAF's urgent need to replace its obsolete Shackleton AEW.Mk 2s. It was decided to use the airframes of surplus Nimrod MR.Mk 1s for the programme, but instead of adopting the US practice of an over-fuselage rotodome, the British designers opted for nose and tail antennae. These would each sweep a 180° sector to provide 360° coverage for the Marconi pulse-Doppler radar. The first AEW.Mk 3 flew in July 1980, but the programme was already in severe difficulties because of radar problems (inadequate signal/noise ratio) and customer changes to the requirement, which was successively increased to the extent that computing power was overwhelmed and so much fuel had to be reserved as an avionic system heat sink that mission endurance was seriously eroded. The programme was cancelled in 1986.

Specification: British Aerospace Nimrod AEW.Mk 3 land-based multi-seat airborne warning and control system prototype
Span: 35.08 m (115 ft 1 in)
Length: 41.97 m (137 ft 8 in)
Powerplant: 4×Rolls-Royce Spey Mk 251, 5507 kg (12,140 lb) st each
Armament: none
Max T/O weight: about 85185 kg (187,800 lb)
Max speed: 575 mph at optimum altitude
Operational endurance: 10+ hours at unspecified mission radius

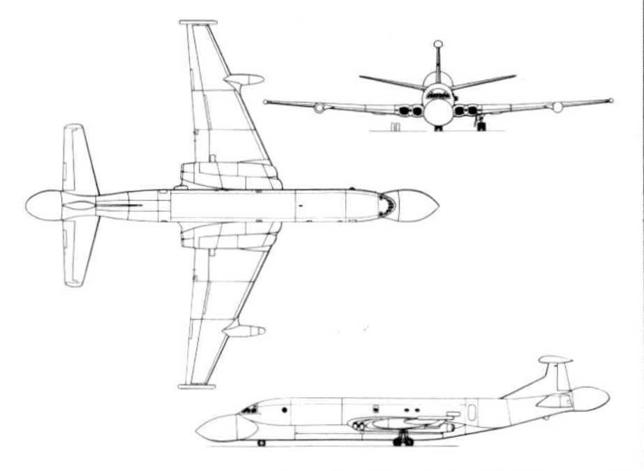

British Aerospace Nimrod

The Nimrod is perhaps the world's most competent aerial sub-hunter, with a full array of sensors for tracking the quietest of submarines. It is also superb at tracking and attacking surface targets. This MR.Mk 2P has twin Sidewinders fitted on the wing pylon, these being carried during the Falklands war for self-defence or attacks against Argentine transport aircraft.

Designed as replacement for the piston-engined Shackleton and based on the Comet 4C airliner, the turbofan-powered Nimrod flew in prototype form during May 1967. It has been developed into one of the world's premier patrol and anti-submarine aircraft, with high transit speed and extended loiter endurance at low level. The current Nimrod MR.Mk 2 has a first-rate electronics suite based on radar, MAD, ESM and a singularly advanced acoustic data-processing system for dropped sonobuoys, while the large unpressurised lower lobe of the fuselage serves as a weapons bay for nuclear or conventional depth bombs, advanced torpedoes or mines, while underwing hardpoints can support defensive air-to-air or offensive anti-ship missiles. There are also three Nimrod R.Mk 1 Elint aircraft with highly classified electronics.

Specification: British Aerospace Nimrod MR.Mk 2 12-seat maritime patrol and anti-submarine aircraft
Span: 35.00 m (114 ft 10 in) without wingtip ESM pods
Length: 38.63 m (126 ft 9 in)
Powerplant: 4×Rolls-Royce Spey 250, 5507 kg (12,140 lb) st each
Armament: up to 6124 kg (13,500 lb) of disposable stores
Max speed: 575 mph at optimum altitude
Operational endurance: 12 hours

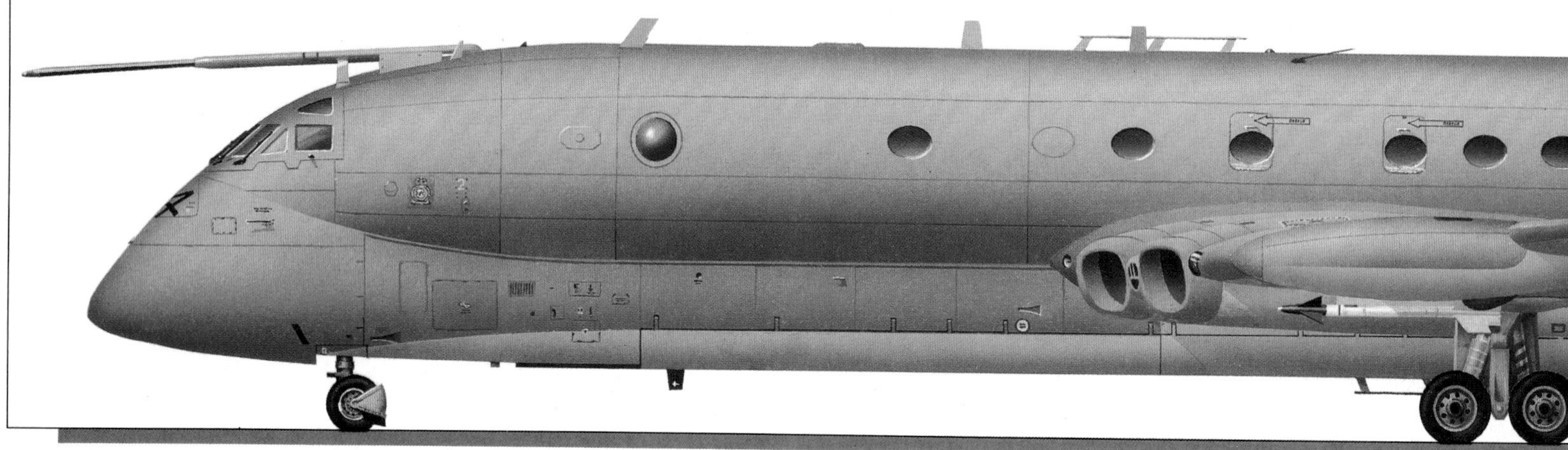

Beriev Be-12 Tchaika 'Mail'

One of the few amphibians still in front-line military service, the Be-12 traces its origins back to the LL-143 prototype of 1945 via the Be-6 piston-engined machine that remained in service to 1967. A gull-wing configuration was selected to keep the turboprop blades well clear of the water, and the type first flew in about 1960. Like its predecessor, the Be-12 was designed for maritime patrol and anti-submarine work, the tail gun turret and retractable ventral radome of the Be-6 being replaced by a MAD 'sting' and thimble nose radome respectively. The Be-12 has set a number of world class records with large payloads, but details of this machine remain sparse. Since the early 1970s the Be-12 has served increasingly as a search-and-rescue machine.

Specification: Beriev Be-12 Tchaika 'Mail' multi-seat maritime reconnaissance and anti-submarine amphibian
Span: 29.71 m (97 ft 5.7 in)
Length: 30.95 m (101 ft 6.5 in)
Powerplant: 2×Ivchyenko AI-20D, 3124 kW (4,190 shp) each
Armament: up to 5000 kg (11,023 lb) of stores carried under the wings and in fuselage bays
Max speed: 378 mph at optimum altitude
Operational range: 2,485 miles

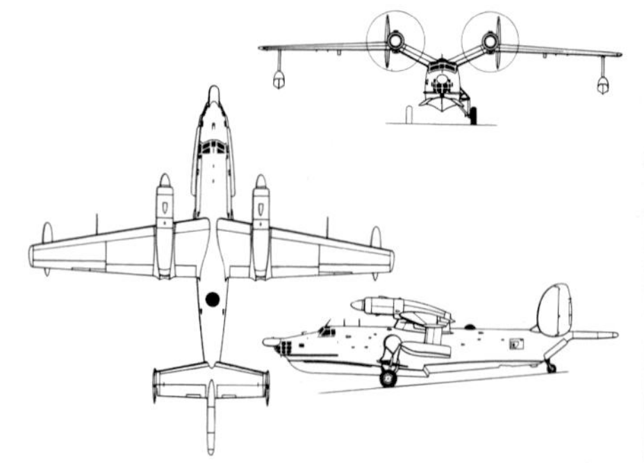

Dassault-Breguet Atlantic 1

Developed as the Br.1150 to meet a 1958 NATO requirement for a long-range maritime patrol aircraft, the Atlantic (now Atlantic 1) was judged best of 27 design submissions from 11 countries. The prototype flew in October 1961, and production aircraft were delivered to France, Italy, the Netherlands and West Germany, some French aircraft being transferred subsequently to Pakistan. Possessing excellent range and loiter, the Atlantic is a mid-wing monoplane of high aspect ratio with twin-turboprop powerplant. The design is based on a double-bubble fuselage, the pressurised upper lobe for the crew and comparatively modest electronics (radar, MAD, ESM and acoustic systems) and the unpressurised lower lobe for the large weapons bay, whose load is supplemented by four underwing hardpoints.

Specification: Dassault-Breguet Atlantic 1 12/24-seat maritime patrol and anti-submarine aircraft
Span: 36.30 m (119 ft 1 in)
Length: 31.75 m (104 ft 2 in)
Powerplant: 2×Rolls-Royce Tyne RTy.20 Mk 21, 4553 kW (6,106 shp) each
Armament: up to 3500 kg (7,716 lb) of disposable stores
Max speed: 409 mph at high altitude
Operational range: 5,590 miles

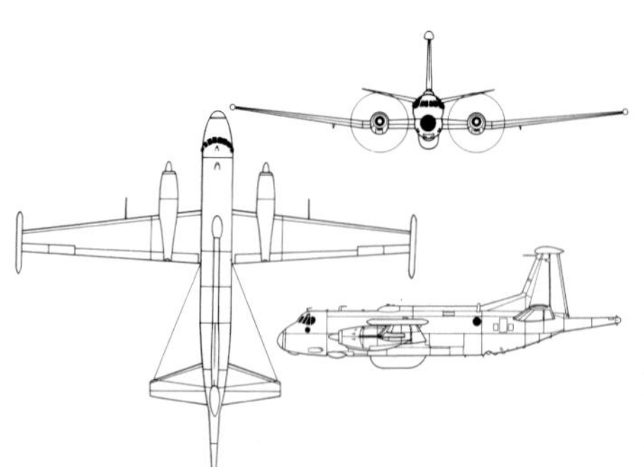

Dassault-Breguet Atlantique 2

The Atlantique 2 is a much-updated version of the Atlantic 1 for the French navy, with a longer-life airframe possessing superior resistance to corrosion. The electronic suite has been completely revised to more advanced standards with Thomson-CSF Iguane search radar, SAT Tango FLIR, Crouzet Mk 3 MAD, Thomson-CSF ARAR 13 ESM system and Thomson-CSF Sadang acoustic data-processing system for the aeroplane's air-dropped active/passive sonobuoys. A high-accuracy navigation system is fitted. The first prototype flew in May 1981, with the original Atlantic consortium being recreated in 1984 to resume production of this significantly enhanced variant of the first version. Deliveries of 42 aircraft are due to begin in 1989.

Specification: Dassault-Breguet Atlantique 2 12/24-seat maritime patrol and anti-submarine aircraft
Span: 37.42 m (122 ft 9.25 in) over top pods
Length: 33.63 m (110 ft 4 in)
Powerplant: 2×Rolls-Royce Tyne RTy.20 Mk 21, 4638 kW (6,220 shp) each
Armament: up to 3500 kg (7,716 lb) of disposable stores
Max speed: 400 mph at optimum altitude
Operational range: 5,640 miles, or a patrol endurance of 5 hours at 1,150-mile radius

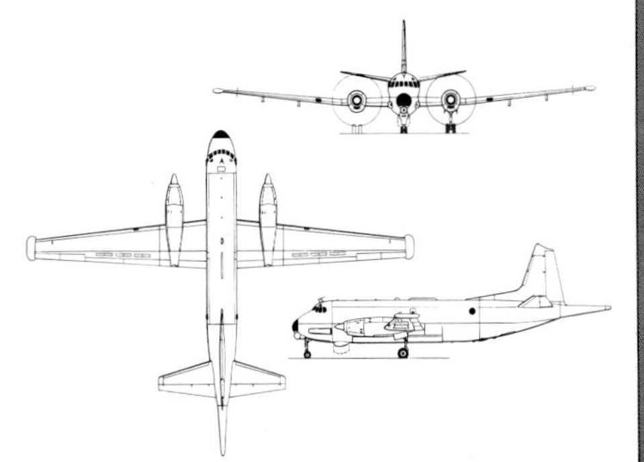

EMBRAER EMB-111

The EMB-111 is the land-based maritime patrol derivative of the EMB-110, the highly successful civil/military general-purpose transport developed by the Brazilian company EMBRAER. Compared with the transport version, the EMB-111 has wingtip fuel tanks for greater range/endurance with uprated engines, an inertial navigation system, nose-mounted SPAR-1 search radar able to detect small targets at a range of 96 km (60 miles) in a disturbed sea, a wing-mounted searchlight, and underwing hardpoints for 127 mm (5 in) rockets or sonobuoy dispensers. Secondary roles include emergency trooping and freighting. The EMB-111 is designed for offshore rather than oceanic tasks, and is operated by Brazil and Chile.

Specification: EMBRAER EMB-111 5-seat offshore patrol aircraft
Span: 15.96 m (52 ft 4.5 in)
Length: 14.83 m (48 ft 7.9 in)
Powerplant: 2×Pratt & Whitney Canada PT6A-34, 559 kW (750 hp) each
Armament: 8×127 mm (5 in) or 28×70 mm (2.75 in) rockets
Max speed: 251 mph at 10,000 ft
Operational range: 1,695 miles

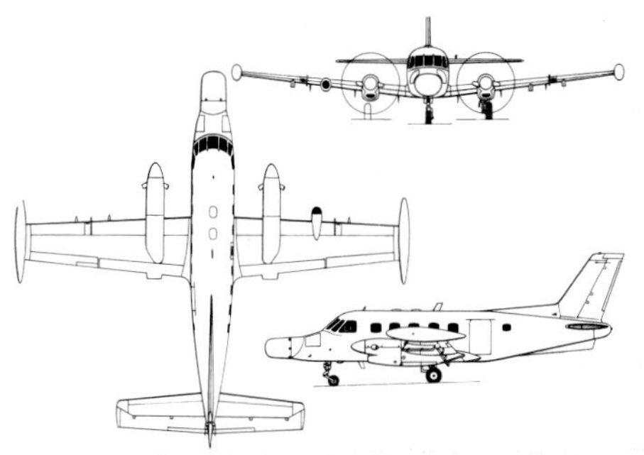

Lockheed P-3 Orion

The P-3 was developed from the Electra four-turboprop airliner as a land-based long-range oceanic patroller to replace the P-2 Neptune. The prototype flew in August 1958, and P-3s began to enter service in 1962. Since that time the Orion has been extensively built, widely deployed and exported, upgraded modestly in engine power and completely revised with more modern electronics. The current variant in front-line service with US Navy squadrons is the P-3C Update III with APS-115 search radar, ASQ-81 MAD, ALQ-77 ESM, forward-looking infrared, low-light-level TV, and an acoustic system using the IBM Proteus processor for the complement of 84 air-launched sonobuoys. The proposed P-3D Update IV variant with GE27 turboprops may be supplanted by the LRAACA requirement based on a Boeing airliner.

Fokker F27 Maritime

The Maritime is a dedicated maritime patrol derivative of Fokker's best-selling F27 Friendship airliner. The airframe differences are small, being concerned mostly with increased fuel capacity and a measure of corrosion resistance, but internally the fuselage has been reconfigured for its specialist role with a mission crew of six in the tactical cabin. The main sensor is a Litton search radar, and an advanced navigation system is fitted. The Maritime is designed largely for civil and resources-protection roles. For the offensive anti-submarine role Fokker has developed an F27MPA Maritime Enforcer with a Marconi-integrated tactical system (central system with radar, ESM and acoustic inputs) and provision for 3930kg (8,664lb) of weapons on two underfuselage and six underwing hardpoints.

Specification: Fokker F27 Maritime 9-seat maritime patrol aircraft
Span: 29.00m (95ft 2in)
Length: 23.56m (77ft 3.5in)
Powerplant: 2×Rolls-Royce Dart RDa.7 Mk 537-7R, 1730kW (2,320shp) each
Armament: none
Max speed: 289mph at 20,015ft
Operational range: 3,107 miles

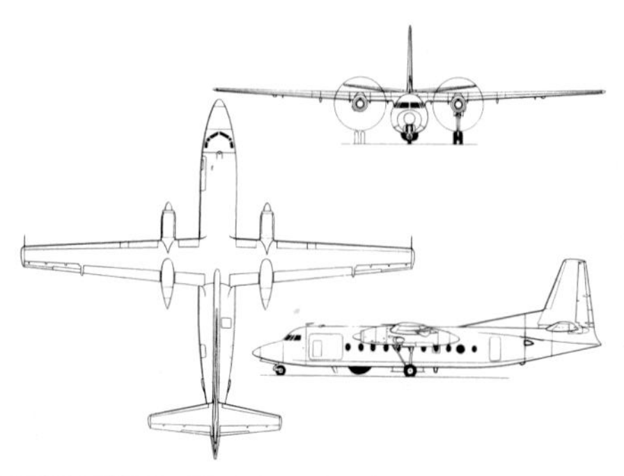

Grumman S-2 Tracker

A venerable carrierborne anti-submarine aircraft still in extensive service mainly as a land-based maritime patrol and anti-submarine aircraft, the Tracker first flew in December 1952. Variants still in widest service are the S-2E and S-2G: the former was the definitive anti-submarine version with radar, MAD and an acoustic data-processing system for active/passive sonobuoys, and the latter was the S-2E with upgraded electronics. Great interest is being shown by current operators in the S-2(T) Turbo-Tracker concept, an updated version of the S-2E with two 1227kW (1,645shp) Garrett TPE331-15AW turboprops for improved performance at a maximum take-off weight of 12683kg (27,962lb). The type is being projected as conversion of older aircraft, and features much-improved ASW capability.

Specification: Grumman S-2E Tracker 4-seat maritime patrol and anti-submarine aircraft
Span: 22.12m (72ft 7in)
Length: 13.26m (43ft 6in)
Powerplant: 2×Wright R-1820-82WA, 1138kW (1,525hp) each
Armament: Torpedoes, bombs or depth charges in the lower-fuselage bay, and bombs, rockets or air-to-surface missiles on the four underwing hardpoints
Max speed: 265mph at sea level
Operational range: 1,300 miles

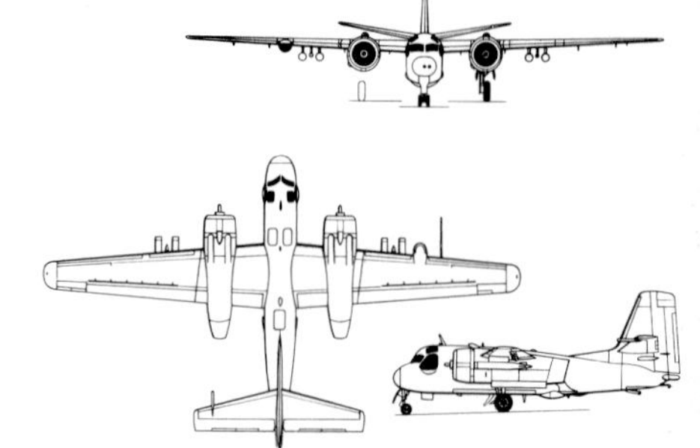

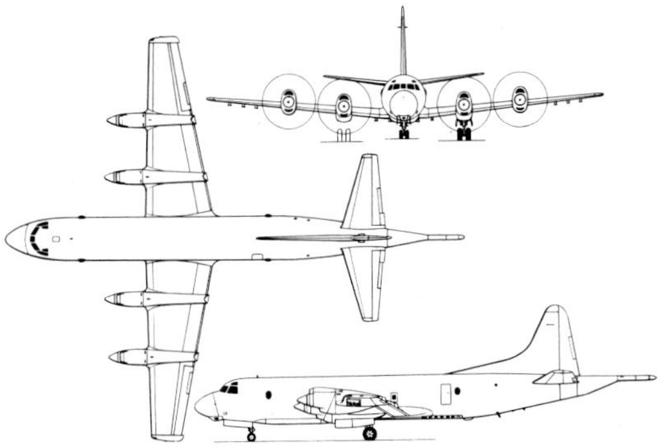

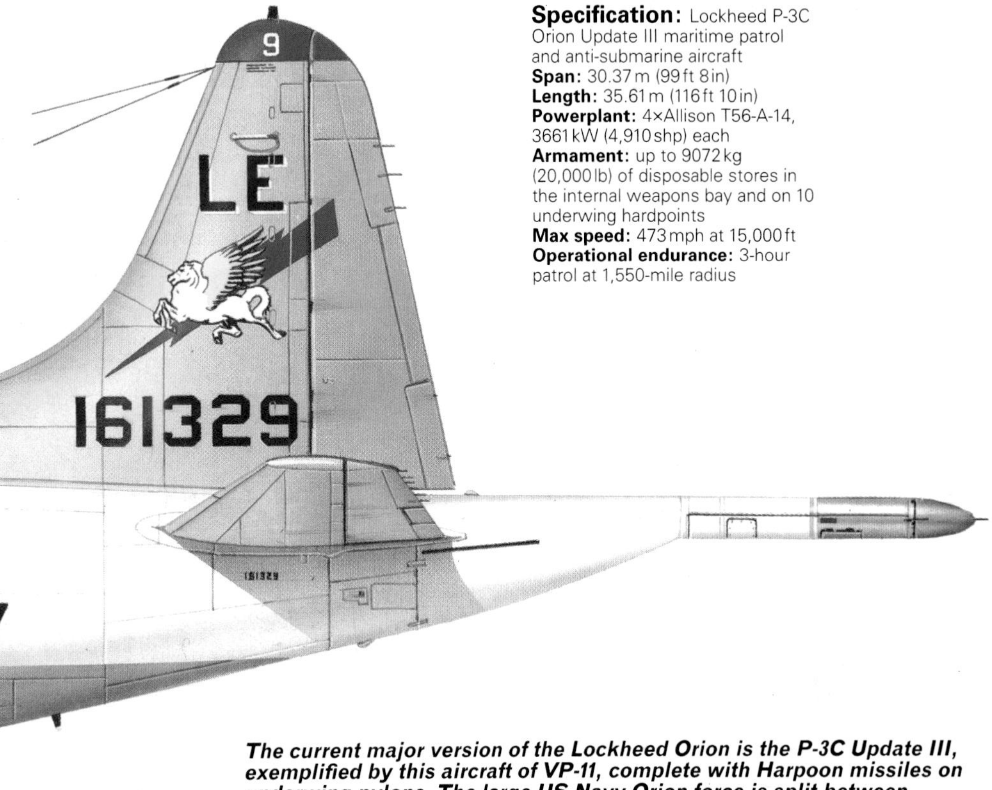

Specification: Lockheed P-3C Orion Update III maritime patrol and anti-submarine aircraft
Span: 30.37 m (99 ft 8 in)
Length: 35.61 m (116 ft 10 in)
Powerplant: 4×Allison T56-A-14, 3661 kW (4,910 shp) each
Armament: up to 9072 kg (20,000 lb) of disposable stores in the internal weapons bay and on 10 underwing hardpoints
Max speed: 473 mph at 15,000 ft
Operational endurance: 3-hour patrol at 1,550-mile radius

The current major version of the Lockheed Orion is the P-3C Update III, exemplified by this aircraft of VP-11, complete with Harpoon missiles on underwing pylons. The large US Navy Orion force is split between Atlantic and Pacific fleets, although aircraft deploy to various bases around the world to maintain submarine patrols internationally. The fleet is no longer this colourful, having removed all of the squadron insignia and most of the other markings from the aircraft.

Tupolev Tu-142 'Bear-F'

First flown in 1954, the mighty Tu-95 'Bear' was produced in some numbers as a bomber and general purpose maritime aircraft. An extensive redesign with lengthened fuselage and more highly cambered wings resulted in the Tu-142, the first major version of which was the 'Bear-F'. First entering service in 1970, this is a dedicated long-range anti-submarine warfare platform which has so far been recorded in five major stages of development. The current standard is 'Bear-F Mod 4' which has a refuelling probe, MAD sting projecting from the fin top, underbelly search radar, nose radome for ECM and numerous small antennae. 60 'Bear-Fs' are in service with the Soviet Union, while five fly with India.

Specification: Tupolev Tu-142 'Bear-F' long-range anti-submarine aircraft
Span: 51.11 m (167 ft 8 in)
Length: 49.5 m (162 ft 5 in)
Powerplant: 4×Kuznetsov 12MV turboprops of 11033 kW (14,795 ehp) each
Armament: two 23-mm cannon in tail turret; two weapon bays for nuclear depth charges, torpedoes and sonobuoys
Max T/O weight: 188000 kg (414,470 lb)
Max speed: 925 km/h (575 mph)
Operational range: 16570 km (10,300 miles)

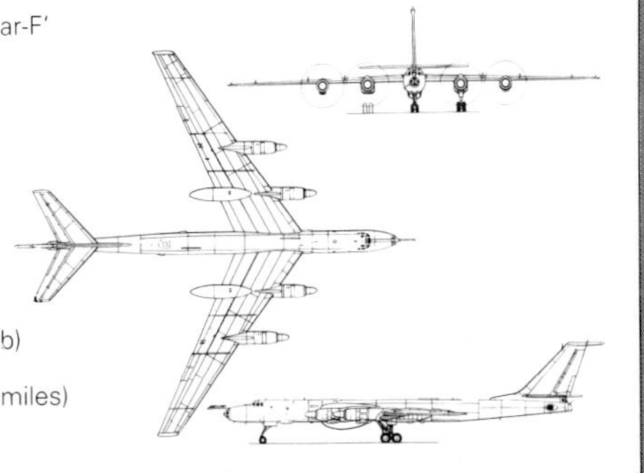

Ilyushin Il-38 'May-A'

Mainstay of the USSR's oceanic patrol and anti-submarine capability, the Il-38 resembles its US counterpart (P-3 Orion) in being derived from a four-turboprop airliner, in this instance the Il-18. The Il-38 has its wing set farther forward than on the Il-18, suggesting that the forward fuselage accommodates weighty mission equipment, probably a rugged electronic processor derived from existing land-based equipment. The type first flew in 1967 and entered service in 1970, and its equipment includes radar, MAD, sonobuoys and ESM, all thought to be inferior to Western equipments. In 1984 a 'May-B' variant was revealed, but as this has a second large radome under the erstwhile weapon bay it is probably designed for mid-course guidance update for long-range missiles.

Specification: Ilyushin Il-38 'May-A' 13-seat maritime patrol and anti-submarine aircraft
Span: 37.40 m (122 ft 8.5 in)
Length: 39.60 m (129 ft 10 in)
Powerplant: 4×Ivchyenko AI-20M, 3169 kW (4,250 shp) each
Armament: conventional or nuclear depth charges, torpedoes and possibly anti-ship missiles
Max speed: 401 mph at optimum altitude
Operational range: 4,500 miles

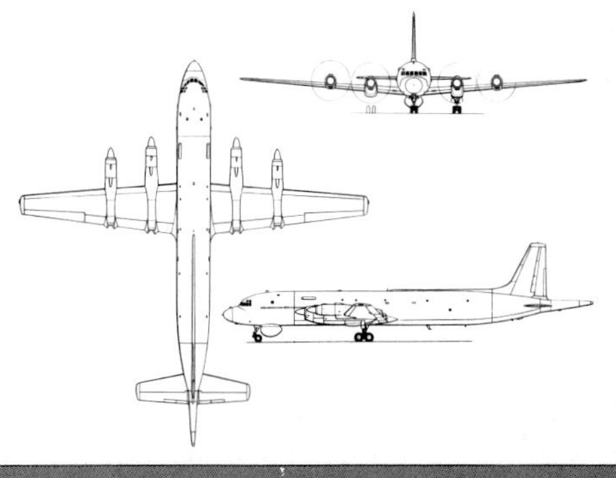

Kawasaki (Lockheed) P-2J Neptune

The Lockheed P-2 was developed at the end of World War II as a land-based maritime patroller incorporating all the lessons of that war, and has enjoyed an extremely lengthy career. The ultimate development in the USA was the P-2H, but this was further enhanced in Japan as the P-2J with a longer fuselage, additional power in the form of two podded turbojets under the wings, and largely Japanese electronics. The first prototype flew in July 1966 and the type began to enter service in October 1969 with mission equipment such as search radar, MAD, ESM and sonobuoys feeding data to an on-board data-processing system. Ironically, the P-2J was developed to avoid the cost of buying the P-3, but in the second half of the 1980s the Orion is finally replacing the P-2J in Japanese service.

Specification: Kawasaki (Lockheed) P-2J Neptune 10-seat maritime patrol and anti-submarine aircraft
Span: 29.78 m (97 ft 8.5 in) without tiptanks
Length: 29.23 m (95 ft 10.75 in)
Powerplant: 2×Ishikawajima-Harima T64-IHI-10E turboprops, 2282 kW (3,060 shp) each, and 2×Ishikawajima-Harima J3-IHI-7D turbojets
Armament: depth charges, torpedoes or mines in an internal bay
Max speed: 249 mph at optimum altitude
Operational range: 2,765 miles

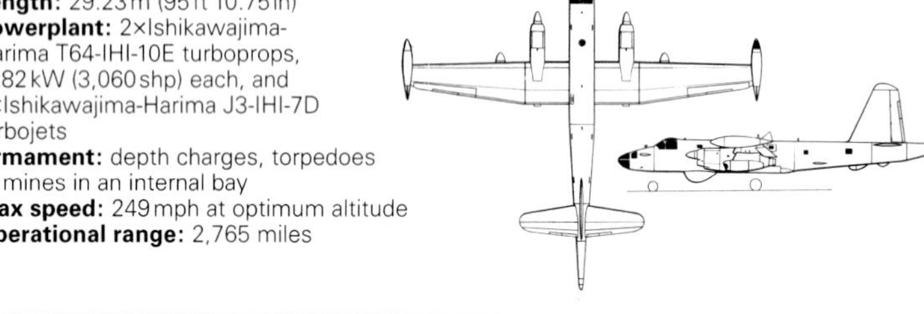

Lockheed CP-140 Aurora

This was designed specifically to meet the requirements of the Canadian Armed Forces for an aircaft for an anti-submarine and multi-role maritime patrol (including SAR, pollution monitoring, resources surveying, ice reconnaissance and Arctic surveillance) to replace the venerable Canadair CP-107 Argus. Selected in July 1976, the Aurora combines the airframe of the Lockheed P-3 Orion land-based patroller with the electronic package (based in the AYK-14 digital computer) of the same company's S-3 carrierborne anti-submarine aeroplane. The Aurora is generally deemed to have a tactical compartment layout superior to the P-3, and for its civil tasks can be fitted with a special sensor and electronics package in the lower-fuselage weapons bay.

Specification: Lockheed CP-140 Aurora 11-seat multi-role maritime patrol and anti-submarine aircraft
Span: 30.37 m (99 ft 8 in)
Length: 35.61 m (116 ft 10 in)
Powerplant: 4×Allison T56-A-14LFE, 3661 kW (4,910 shp) each
Armament: up to 2247 kg (5,350 lb) of depth charges, mines or torpedoes in the weapon bay, and a substantial load of similar weapons on 10 underwing hardpoints
Max speed: 455 mph at optimum altitude
Operational endurance: 8.2 hours at 1,150-mile radius

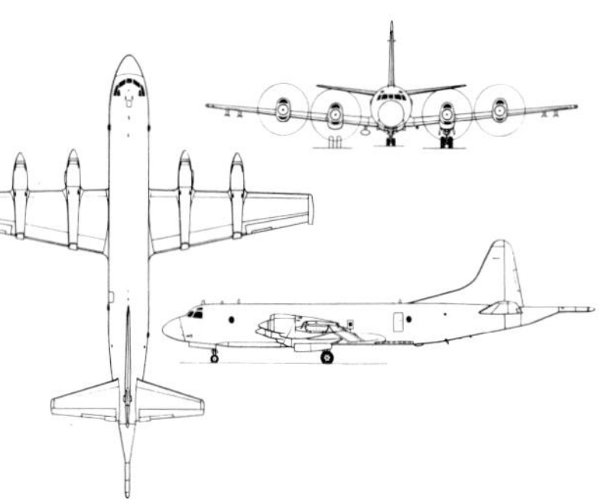

Lockheed S-3 Viking

The S-3A Viking is the US Navy's carrierborne counterpart of the P-3, and represents an extraordinary effort in packing maximum mission capability into minimum airframe. The prototype flew in January 1972, with the type entering service in February 1974. The portly fuselage with high-set wings supporting two podded turbofans is optimised for volume rather than outright performance, and in addition to APS-116 radar the Viking carries ESM, MAD and acoustic systems, the last for use with the complement of 60 sonobuoys carried in the rear fuselage. The electronics suite is highly automated to reduce the mission crew requirement to just two men, and the latest S-3B version features more capable electronics as well as provision for AGM-84 Harpoon anti-ship missiles.

Specification: Lockheed S-3A Viking carrierborne 4-seat maritime patrol and anti-submarine aircraft
Span: 20.93 m (68 ft 8 in)
Length: 16.26 m (53 ft 4 in)
Powerplant: 2×General Electric TF34-GE-2, 4207 kg (9,275 lb) st each
Armament: up to 3175 kg (7,000 lb) of disposable stores in a split internal bay and on two underwing hardpoints
Max speed: 518 mph at optimum altitude
Operational range: more than 2,300 miles

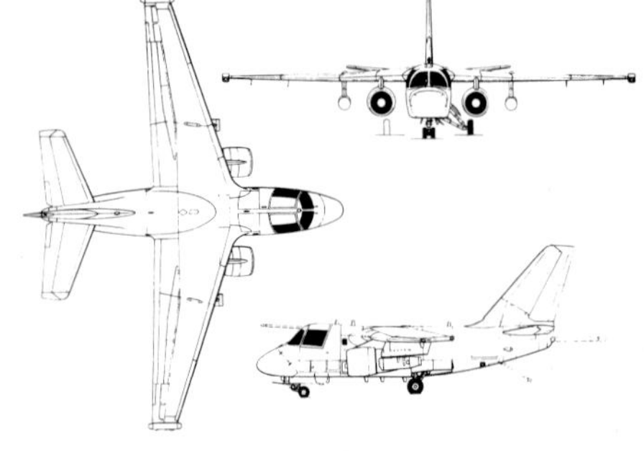

Shin Meiwa PS-1

Given its sea-locked island nature, Japan has quite naturally turned to flying boats for its maritime patrol purposes, and the latest in this sequence has been the PS-1, whose development began in 1960 as an adapatable machine with STOL capabilities so that the type could operate from rough seas: this capability is provided by a boundary-layer control system powered by a 932 kW (1,250 shp) General Electric T58 turboshaft. The prototype flew in October 1967, and a small number of production aircraft began to enter service in 1973. The PS-1 carries a typical anti-submarine electronic suite, though the fact that the type is a flying boat means that dunking sonar is used in preference to a sonobuoy system for acoustic detection. There is also a US-1 SAR amphibian version.

Specification: Shin Meiwa PS-1 10-seat maritime patrol and anti-submarine flying boat
Span: 33.14 m (108 ft 8.75 in)
Length: 33.50 m (109 ft 11 in)
Powerplant: 4×Ishikawajima-Harima T64-IHI-10, 2285 kW (3,064 shp) each
Armament: depth charges, bombs, torpedoes and rockets can be carried in an internal bay, two underwing pods and two wingtip hardpoints
Max speed: 340 mph at 5,000 ft
Operational range: 1,350 miles

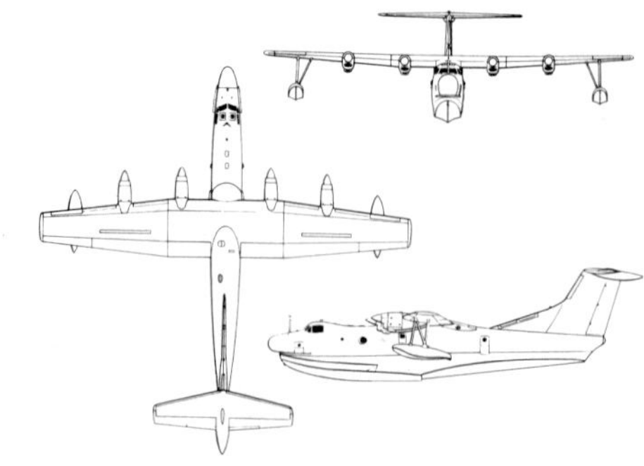

Handley Page Victor SR.Mk 2

'hough the Valiant was a highly useful aeroplane, the RAF appreciated from the beginning f its career that the Valiant was essentially an interim type. This applied as much to the econnaissance as the bomber variants, and as a result great hope was pinned on the Victor SR.Mk 2, the reconnaissance version of the last of the 'V' bomber marks. First flown in rototype form during February 1965, this was based on the B.Mk 2 bomber but had dditional tankage for 40 per cent greater range, a service ceiling of nearly 70,000 ft, and specialist optical and radar equipment for the surveillance of 1942380 km^2 (750,000 sq miles) in six hours. From autumn 1965 the type entered service with No.543 Squadron, which used all nine SR.Mk 2 conversions (including one that retained 'Blue Steel' capability) n the maritime reconnaissance role.

Specification: Handley Page Victor SR.Mk 2 five-seat long-range reconnaissance aeroplane
Span: 36.58 m (120 ft 0 in)
Length: 35.03 m (114 ft 11 in)
Powerplant: 4×Rolls-Royce Conway RCo.17 Mk 201, 8959 kg (19,750 lb) st each
Armament: none
Max T/O weight: about 105688 kg (233,000 lb)
Max speed: 640 mph at 40,000 ft
Operational range: 6,440 miles

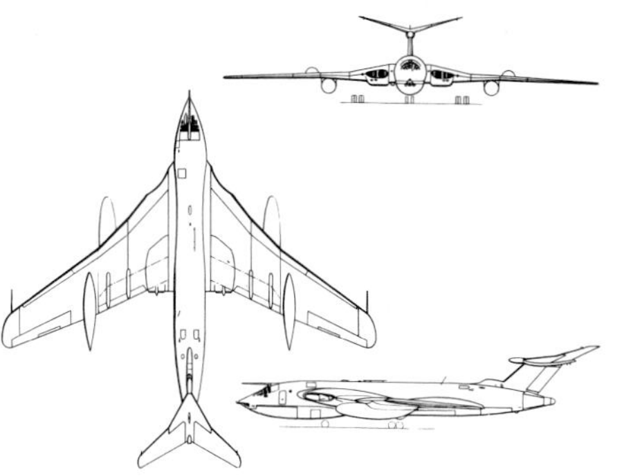

Avro Vulcan SR.Mk 2A

By the early 1970s the UK's strategic reconnaissance force was decidedly obsolescent at a time when the USSR and other potential enemies were making great strides in the deployment of major weapon systems. The well established SAM meant that overflights were no longer possible except by specialist aircraft capable of extremely high altitude, so optical reconnaissance was complemented or indeed supplanted by electronic reconnaissance of various types. The UK's chosen platform in this role was the Vulcan B.Mk 2, which had the payload and internal volume to make possible a major reconnaissance role. At least four B.Mk 2As were modified as Vulcan SR.Mk 2As in 1973, and these were operational with No.27 Squadron from 1974 to 1982. The aircraft served in the maritime reconnaissance role with additional fuel in bomb bay tanks, and with radar, optical and other equipment that remains classified.

Specification: British Aerospace (Avro) Vulcan SR.Mk 2A five-seat strategic maritime reconnaissance aeroplane
Span: 33.83 m (111 ft 0 in)
Length: 30.51 m (100 ft 1 in) excluding probe
Powerplant: 4×Rolls-Royce (Bristol Siddeley) Olympus Mk 301, 9072 kg (20,000 lb) st each
Armament: none
Max T/O weight: possibly 113400 kg (250,000 lb)
Max speed: 645 mph at high altitude
Operational range: 4,600+ miles

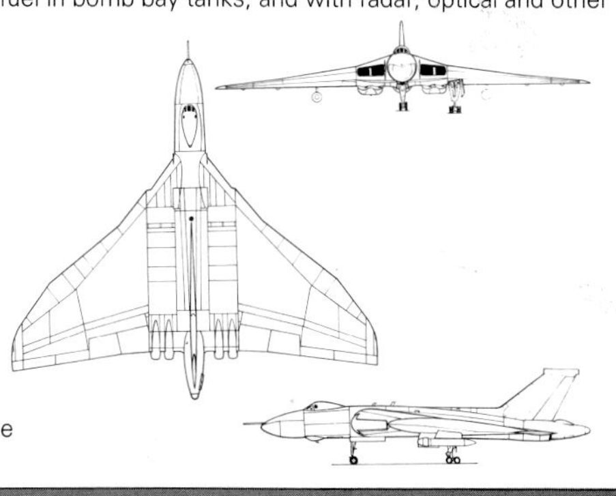

SEPECAT Jaguar GR.Mk 1

An Anglo-French collaborative project stemming aerodynamically from the Breguet Br.121 design, the Jaguar was planned as a supersonic trainer with attack capability, but in British service matured largely as the Jaguar GR.Mk 1, an exceptional tactical strike aeroplane that accounted for most of the UK's 200-aircraft order. The prototype flew in September 1968, and the type has displayed admirable low-level ride characteristics combined with the accuracy of navigation deriving from use of a FIN1064 inertial navigation system and an advanced projected map display. This commended the type as a dual-role strike and day/night tactical reconnaissance platform, the latter in the hands of two squadrons using a BAe centreline pod containing four F.95 cameras (two high oblique and two low oblique) plus an IR linescanner with navigation data automatically recorded on the reconnaissance film.

Specification: SEPECAT Jaguar GR.Mk 1 single-seat tactical reconnaissance aeroplane
Span: 8.69 m (28 ft 6 in)
Length: 15.52 m (50 ft 11 in)
Powerplant: 2×Rolls-Royce/Turbomeca Adour Mk 104, 3647 kg (8,040 lb) st each
Armament: 2×30-mm cannon, plus provision for 3402 kg (7,500 lb) of disposable stores carried on 4×underwing hardpoints
Max T/O weight: 15700 kg (34,610 lb)
Max speed: 1,056 mph at 36,000 ft
Operational range: 670 miles

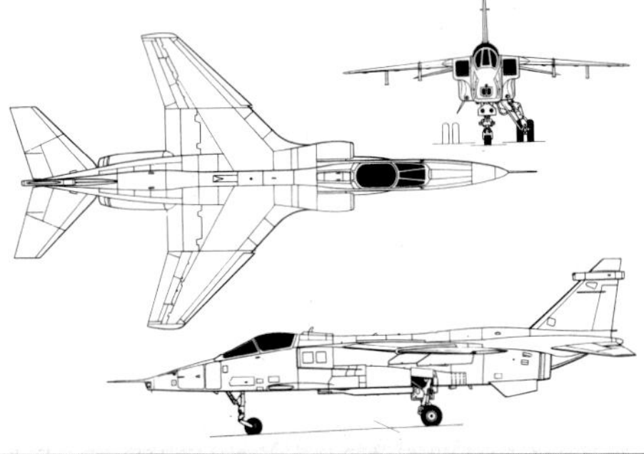

British Aerospace Harrier GR.Mk 3

From the time it was accepted as the basis of a combat type, the revolutionary Harrier STOVL aeroplane was developed as a dual-role close support and tactical reconnaissance platform. In the latter role the type's ability to operate very close to the front is a decided advantage, allowing speedy out and return missions. The Harrier types that have served with front-line RAF squadrons are the GR.Mk 1 with 8618-kg (19,000-lb) thrust Pegasus Mk 101, the GR.Mk 1A with 9299-kg (20,500-lb) thrust Pegasus Mk 102 turbofan plus laser ranger and marked target seeker, and the GR.Mk 3 with uprated Pegasus Mk 103. All have had a oblique nose camera facing to port behind a nose transparency, and for the dedicated reconnaissance role can carry a centreline pod containing one F.135 forward camera and four F.95 cameras (two high oblique and two low oblique).

Specification: British Aerospace Harrier GR.Mk 3 single-seat tactical reconnaissance aeroplane
Span: 7.70 m (25 ft 3 in)
Length: 14.27 m (46 ft 10 in)
Powerplant: 1×Rolls-Royce Pegasus Mk 103, 9752 kg (21,500 lb) st
Armament: 2×30-mm cannon, plus provision for up to 2404 kg (5,300 lb) of disposable stores on 4×underwing hardpoints
Max T/O weight: 11431+ kg (25,200+ lb)
Max speed: 737+ mph at low altitude
Operational range: 830 miles

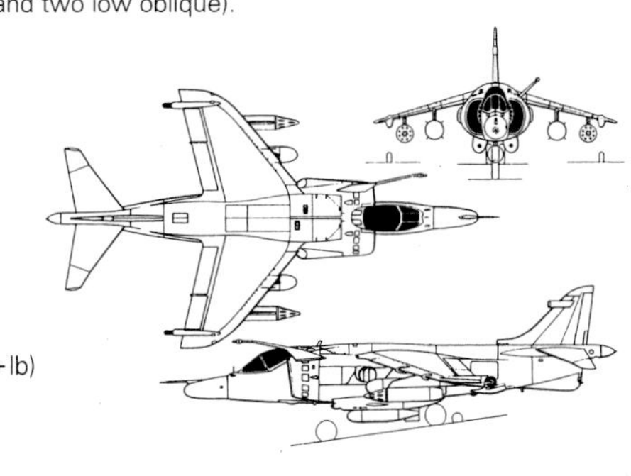

Supermarine Swift FR.Mk 5

After the failure of the Swift in its intended interceptor role, it was decided to concentrate development on a version that would capitalise on the Swift's excellent speed performance. This emerged as a reconnaissance fighter version, the Swift FR.Mk 5, to replace the Meteor FR.Mk 9. The type first flew in production form during May 1955, began to enter service with two squadrons of the 2nd Tactical Air Force in West Germany early in 1956 and remained in service up to 1962, when it was replaced by the Hunter FR.Mk 10. Compared with the Swift's fighter versions, the FR.Mk 5 had a revised and lengthened nose with three F.95 cameras (one in the extreme nose and two just ahead of the inlets for oblique photography), a clear-view canopy, 'sawtooth' outer wing panels of increased chord, a variable-incidence tailplane, an afterburning engine and provision for a ventral drop tank. Production totalled 62.

Specification: Supermarine Swift FR.Mk 5 single-seat photographic reconnaissance fighter
Span: 9.86 m (32 ft 4 in)
Length: 12.88 m (42 ft 3 in)
Powerplant: 1×Rolls-Royce Avon Mk 114, 4286 kg (9,450 lb) st
Armament: 2×30-mm cannon, plus provision for bombs or rockets carried under the wings
Max T/O weight: 9707 kg (21,400 lb)
Max speed: 685 mph at sea level
Operational range: 480 miles

Though it had a brief and inglorious career as a day fighter, the Swift enjoyed more success as a reconnaissance aircraft, serving in RAF Germany from 1956 until 1961. This FR.Mk5 of No.IV Squadron still carries the arrow insignia of No. 79 Squadron, which was renumbered during January 1961.

Mosquito PR.Mk 16/34

The multi-role Mosquito became the UK's most important reconnaissance aeroplane in World War II, and the ultimate developments were classic machines. The PR.Mk XVI was the reconnaissance version of the B.Mk XVI high-altitude bomber with a pressurised cabin and Merlin 70-series engines. The first PR.Mk XVI was a B.Mk XVI conversion and flew at the end of 1943: production amounted to 432, and a subvariant (five aircraft) was the PR.Mk 32 with extended-span wings and Merlin 113 engines. The last production version was the PR.Mk 34, which became the mainstay of post-war reconnaissance squadrons. The type first flew in December 1944, and the 50 such aircraft had drop tanks, a bomb-bay tank, and five cameras (four vertical and one oblique); some were modified as PR.Mk 34As with Merlin 114A engines. A few B.Mk 35s were also converted to PR.Mk 35s for special reconnaissance.

Specification: de Havilland Mosquito PR.Mk 34 two-seat long-range photographic reconnaissance aeroplane
Span: 16.51 m (54 ft 2 in)
Length: 12.65 m (41 ft 6 in)
Powerplant: 2×Rolls-Royce Merlin 114, 1260 kW (1,690 hp) each
Armament: none
Max T/O weight: 11566 kg (25,500 lb)
Max speed: 425 mph at 30,500 ft
Operational range: 3,500 miles

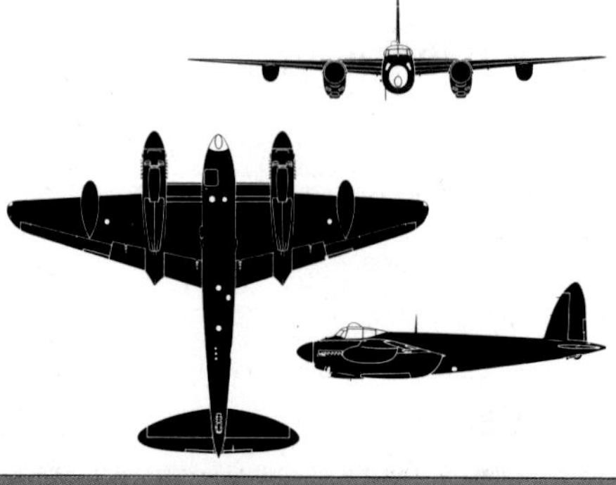

Supermarine Spitfire PR.Mk 19

The shorter-range counterpart to the Mosquito in the photographic reconnaissance role during World War II, the Spitfire went through a number of marks of which the last was the PR.Mk XIX (post-war PR.Mk 19) developed as replacement for the PR.Mk XI. The type was a hybrid combining the fuselage of the F.Mk XIV fighter, Mk VC wings modified for greater fuel capacity, and the 'universal' camera installation of one port-facing oblique F.24, two fanned vertical F.52, and two fanned vertical F.8 or F.24 cameras. The type began to enter service in May 1944, and while the prototype and first 20 aircraft were unpressurised and fitted with Griffon 65 engines, the rest of the 225-aircraft run had pressurisation, Griffon 66 engines and wings further modified to increase fuel capacity. A PR.Mk 19 flew the RAF's last operational Spitfire mission in April 1954.

Specification: Supermarine Spitfire PR.Mk 19 single-seat photographic reconnaissance aeroplane
Span: 11.27 m (36 ft 10 in)
Length: 9.96 m (32 ft 8 in)
Powerplant: 1×Rolls-Royce Griffon Mk 66, 1528.5 kW (2,050 hp)
Armament: none
Max T/O weight: 4740 kg (10,450 lb)
Max speed: 446 mph at 20,000 ft
Operational range: 1,550 miles

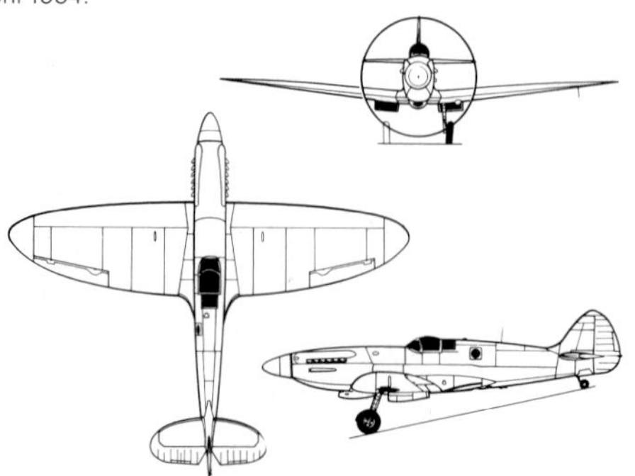

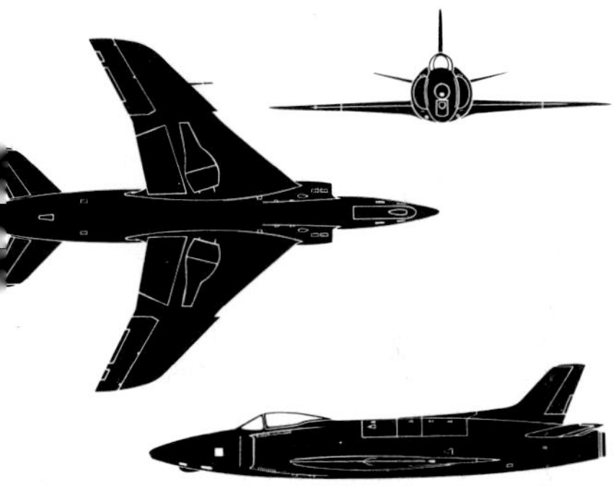

Avro Lancaster PR.Mk 1

Given the large numbers of Lancasters in service at the end of World War II it is hardly surprising that not inconsiderable numbers surplus to Bomber Command requirements should be converted for other tasks. The most numerous modified types were the air/sea rescue Lancaster ASR.Mk 3 and the maritime reconnaissance Lancaster GR.Mk 3 (later MR.Mk 3). But within Bomber Command some B.Mk Is were modified as Lancaster PR.Mk 1 photographic reconnaissance and survey aircraft, mainly for No.82 Squadron. These aircraft had their turrets removed and their openings faired over, and were extensively equipped with photographic equipment. No.82 Squadron photo-mapped large parts of East, Central and West Africa between 1946 and October 1952, and a PR.Mk 1 was Bomber Command's last Lancaster when retired in October 1956. Canada had a similar Lancaster 10-PR version.

Specification: Avro Lancaster PR.Mk 1 multi-seat photographic reconnaissance, and survey aeroplane
Span: 31.09m (102ft 0in)
Length: 21.18m (69ft 6in)
Powerplant: 4×Rolls-Royce Merlin 24, 1223 kW (1,640 hp) each
Armament: none
Max T/O weight: about 26309kg (58,000lb)
Max speed: about 285mph at 15,000ft
Operational range: about 2,500 miles

Gloster Meteor FR.Mk 9

In the five years after World War II the RAF's main reconnaissance aeroplane was the Supermarine Spitfire in three versions optimised for armed fighter reconnaissance (one variant) and unarmed strategic reconnaissance (two variants). It was clear from a date soon after the war, however, that a derivative of the Meteor would offer greater performance in the fighter reconnaissance role, and this led to the development of the Meteor FR.Mk 9. This was based on the Meteor F.Mk 8 but had a revised nose accommodating a universal mounting for a camera operated remotely by the pilot for oblique photography straight ahead or to either side through transparent panels. The prototype flew in March 1950, and 126 FR.Mk 9 production aircraft served from July of the same year mainly with four squadrons of the 2nd Tactical Air Force in Germany and one squadron of the Middle East Air Force.

Specification: Gloster Meteor FR.Mk 9 single-seat photographic reconnaissance fighter
Span: 11.33m (37ft 2in)
Length: 13.26m (43ft 6in)
Powerplant: 2×Rolls-Royce Derwent 8, 1588kg (3,500lb) st each
Armament: 4×20-mm cannon
Normal T/O weight: 7103kg (15,660lb)
Max speed: 595mph at 10,000ft
Operational range: 690 miles

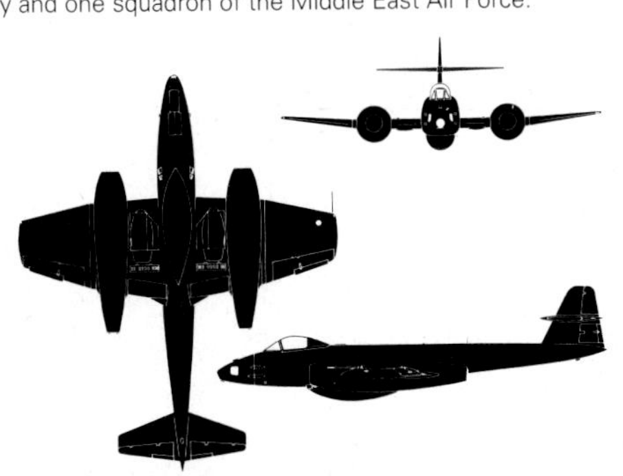

English Electric Canberra PR.Mk 9

Though the altitude performance of the Canberra PR.Mk 7 was good, it was not adequate to remove the type from threat of fighter interception, and to remedy this failing there appeared the Canberra PR.Mk 9. As first flown in July 1955 this was based on the PR.Mk 7 but with 5103kg (11,250lb) thrust Avon Mk 206 turbojets and wider-span wings that were also of increased chord inboard of the engine nacelles. The prototype was a converted PR.Mk 7, but the 23 production aircraft from Shorts introduced the offset fighter-type cockpit of the B(I).Mk 8. The first such aeroplane flew in July 1958, and the type later equipped two squadrons, one in the UK and the other in Cyprus. The force was disbanded in 1983, but five aircraft have been rebuilt for advanced reconnaissance and Elint work based, with all other surviving Canberras, at RAF Wyton in Cambridgeshire.

Specification: English Electric Canberra PR.Mk 9 two-seat high-altitude long-range photographic reconnaissance aeroplane
Span: 20.68m (67ft 10in)
Length: 20.32m (66ft 8in)
Powerplant: 2×Rolls-Royce Avon Mk 206, 5103kg (11,250lb) st each
Armament: none
Max T/O weight: about 25514kg (56,250lb)
Max speed: about 650mph at medium altitude
Operational range: 3,650+ miles

Gloster Meteor PR.Mk 10

At the same time that the Meteor FR.Mk 9 was being developed as replacement for the Spitfire FR.Mk 18 in the tactical role, the Meteor PR.Mk 10 was being evolved to succeed the Spitfire PR.Mk 11 and PR.Mk 19 in the strategic role. This reverted to the long-span wing of the early Meteor fighters to improve high-altitude capability, and also reverted to the more shapely tail unit of the earlier aircraft. All armament was removed and a ventral fuel tank was added, while in addition to a camera installation in the nose the type featured other cameras farther aft for vertical photography. The first Meteor PR.Mk 10 flew in March 1950 and the type began to enter service from February 1951, the last of 58 aircraft being delivered in April 1952. The PR.Mk 10 served with one Middle Eastern and one Far Eastern squadron up to July 1961.

Specification: Gloster Meteor PR.Mk 10 singe-seat medium-range photographic reconnaissance aeroplane
Span: 13.11m (43ft 0in)
Length: 13.49m (44ft 3in)
Powerplant: 2×Rolls-Royce Derwent 8, 1588kg (3,500lb) st each
Armament: none
Max T/O weight: 6954kg (15,330lb)
Max speed: 575mph at 10,000ft
Operational range: 1,400 miles

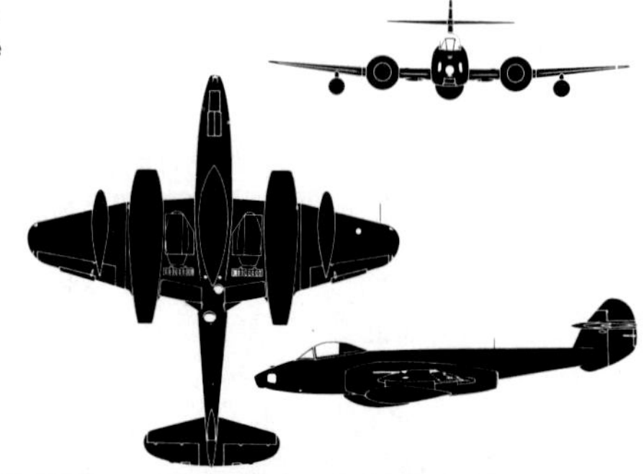

English Electric Canberra PR.Mk 3/7

Just as the reconnaissance Meteors were evolved to replace the Spitfire variants of World War II, the Canberra bomber was developed to succeed the Mosquito PR.Mk 34 and PR.Mk 35 as a reconnaissance platform. The resulting Canberra PR.Mk 3 was based on the B.Mk 2 bomber, and first flew in March 1950. The lengthened fuselage had greater fuel capacity, and also held one 15.2-cm (6-in) F.49 vertical camera plus six 914-mm (36-in) F.52 or four 508-mm (20-in) F.52 cameras. The first of 35 production aircraft entered service in 1952, and the type eventually equipped one home and two West Germany-based squadrons. In October an equivalent version based on the B.Mk 6 bomber first flew with more power and additional fuel for greater range, and production of this Meteor PR.Mk 7 totalled 74 for service with three home and two German squadrons, plus single squadrons in Malta, Cyprus and the Far East.

Specification: English Electric Canberra PR.Mk 7 two-seat long-range photographic reconnaissance aeroplane
Span: 19.49m (63ft 11.5in)
Length: 20.32m (66ft 8in)
Powerplant: 2×Rolls-Royce Avon Mk 109, 3402kg (7,500lb) st each
Armament: none
Max T/O weight: 24948kg (55,000lb)
Max speed: 580mph at 40,000ft
Operational range: 4,340 miles

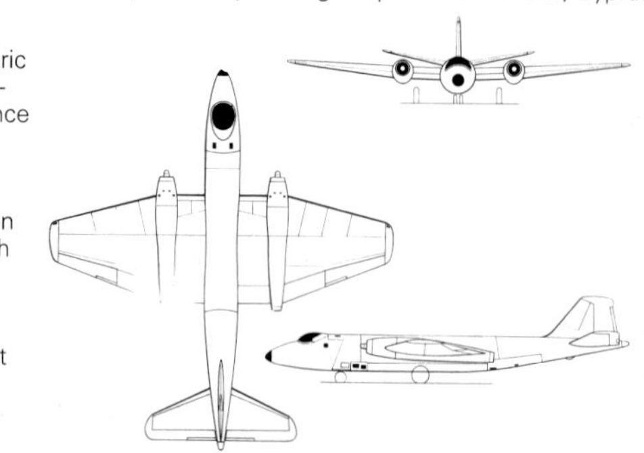

A Canberra PR.Mk 9 of the RAF's No.1 Photographic Reconnaissance Unit, based at RAF Wyton. The unit's five aircraft are virtually the last RAF reconnaissance machines using conventional optical cameras and 'wet film' technology, the Harriers having given up the recce role, and the Tornados being equipped with infra-red linescan. This aircraft carries an unidentified ventral bulge, possibly a radome for a synthetic aperture radar, and has picked up a zap from an indigenous Belizean airline.

Vickers Valiant B(PR).Mk 1

The 1954 entry into service of the Valiant B.Mk 1 as the first of the RAF's nuclear-armed strategic 'V' bombers soon prompted the notion that the type should form the basis of a strategic reconnaissance version, and ultimately there were two such models. The first was the Valiant B(PR)K.Mk 1: 14 of this variant were built for the multi-role bomber, photographic reconnaissance and inflight-refuelling tanker roles, all being delivered between August 1955 and March 1956. The second was the Valiant B(PR).Mk 1: 11 of this variant were built for long-range photographic reconnaissance, all being delivered between March and July 1956 for use mainly by No.543 Squadron. In common with other Valiants, these two models were grounded in October 1964 and subsequently scrapped because of fatigue problems with the wing primary structure.

Specification: Vickers Valiant B(PR).Mk 1 long-range photographic reconnaissance aeroplane
Span: 34.85 m (114 ft 4 in)
Length: 33.00 m (108 ft 3 in)
Powerplant: 4×Rolls-Royce Avon Mk 201, 4536 kg (10,000 lb) st each
Armament: none
Max T/O weight: about 63504 kg (140,000 lb)
Max speed: 567 mph at 30,000 ft
Operational range: 4,500 miles

Hawker Hunter FR.Mk 10

The Hunter FR.Mk 10 was the reconnaissance fighter counterpart of the Hunter FGA.Mk 9, and was developed as successor to the Supermarine Swift FR.Mk 5 in the 2nd Tactical Air Force in Germany and for the Meteor FR.Mk 9 in the Far East Air Force, though in the event the type equipped only two squadrons in West Germany and one flight in Aden. The airframe was based on that of the Hunter F.Mk 6 fighter, and was very similar to that of the FGA.Mk 9 (braking parachute, large drop tanks and additional oxygen for long ferry flights) apart from its internal equipment, which included one forward-facing and two oblique cameras in the nose in addition to the standard cannon armament. The first FR.Mk 10 flew in November 1958, and like the other 33 aircraft of this variant was converted from a surplus Hunter F.Mk 6. Another 17 aircraft were modified to similar standards for four export customers.

Specification: Hawker Hunter FR.Mk 10 single-seat photographic reconnaissance fighter
Span: 10.26 m (33 ft 8 in)
Length: 14.05 m (46 ft 1 in)
Powerplant: 1×Rolls-Royce Avon Mk 207, 4604 kg (10,150 lb) st
Armament: 4×20-mm cannon
Max T/O weight: 12066 kg (26,600 lb)
Max speed: 710 mph at sea level
Operational range: 1,840 miles

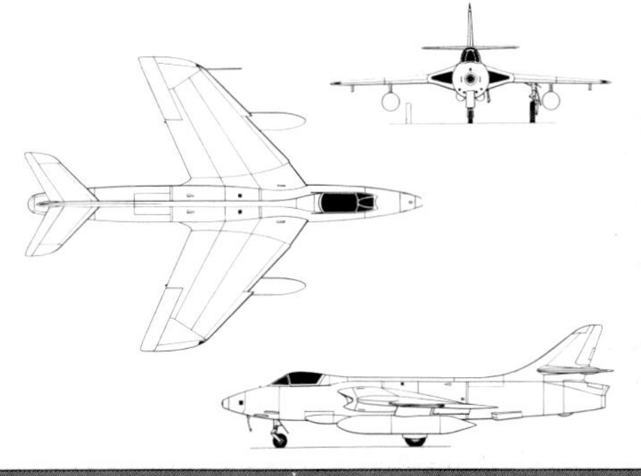

Lockheed SR-71A 'Blackbird

Making its operational debut in 1966, the Lockheed SR-71A continued the clandestine reconnaissance effort previously undertaken by the similar Lockheed A-12. Its design is optimised for flight in excess of Mach 3 speed and 85,000 ft altitude, its engines operating almost as ramjets at high speed. Sensors are carried in interchangeable nose cones and in the areas along the side of the fuselage, and can be optical, infra-red or electronic in nature. Currently about 12 are in service, although this will drop to six, serving with the 9th Strategic Reconnaissance Wing at Beale AFB, California. These are used on direct overflights of lightly defended nations, and peripheral missions around the Soviet Union. Two are permanently based at RAF Mildenhall in Suffolk.

From any angle the SR-71A is a strange aircraft, its shape dictated by the aerodynamics of Mach 3 flight. The giant J58 engines are aspirated by a complex intake system consisting of a moveable inlet spike which travels forward and aft to optimise the airflow. Auxiliary intake and bleed doors also serve to regulate the airflow. Sensors are carried in the nose cone and along the sides of the fuselage.

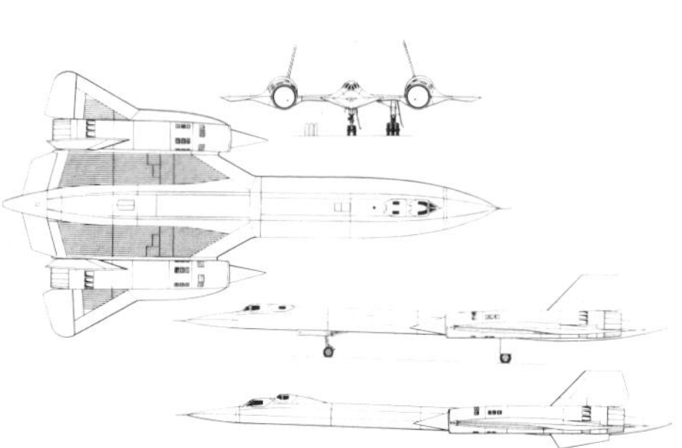

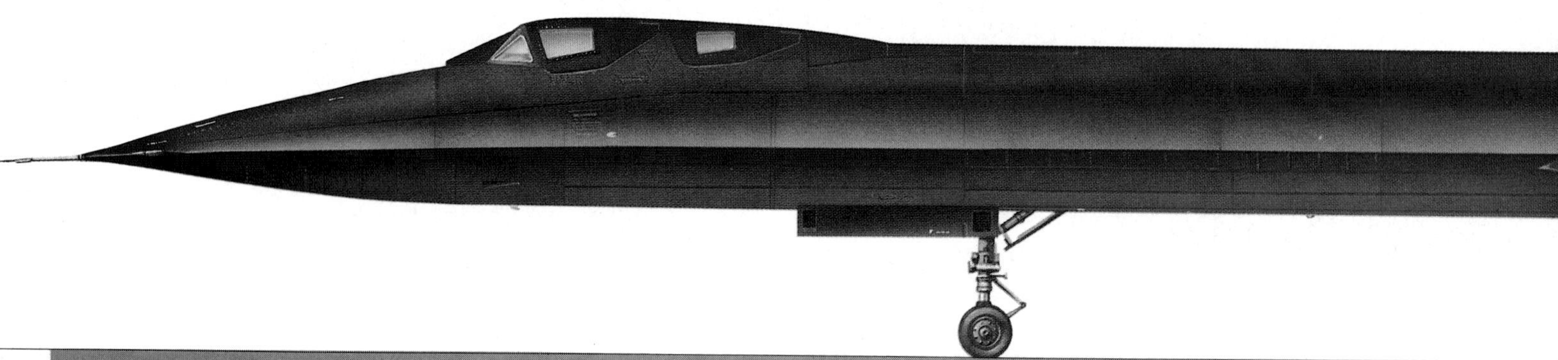

Lockheed U-2R/TR-1

The U-2R was a complete redesign of the earlier U-2 versions, incorporating greater sensor payload carried over a greater range. It saw much service over China, Vietnam and the Middle East, and is still in use today with the 9th Strategic Reconnaissance Wing. The TR-1A is a similar aircraft tailored for high altitude radar reconnaissance, principally in Europe where it is based at RAF Alconbury with the 17th Reconnaissance Wing. Sensors in both variants are carried in the nose, rear fuselage, behind the cockpit and in the detachable wing 'super pods'. The outsize wings are designed to give high altitude capability at subsonic speeds, and allows the TR-1A very long endurance. It is thus an excellent platform for communications intelligence (Comint).

Specification

Lockheed TR-1A single-seat high altitude radar reconnaissance aircraft
Span: 31.39 m (103 ft 0 in)
Length: 19.12 m (62 ft 9 in)
Height: 4.87 m (16 ft 0 in)
Wing area: 92.9 m^2 (1,000 sq ft)
Take-off weight: 18733 kg (41,300 lb)
Maximum speed: 430 mph
Ceiling: 80,000 ft
Range: 6,250 miles
Sensors: electronic, optical and radar

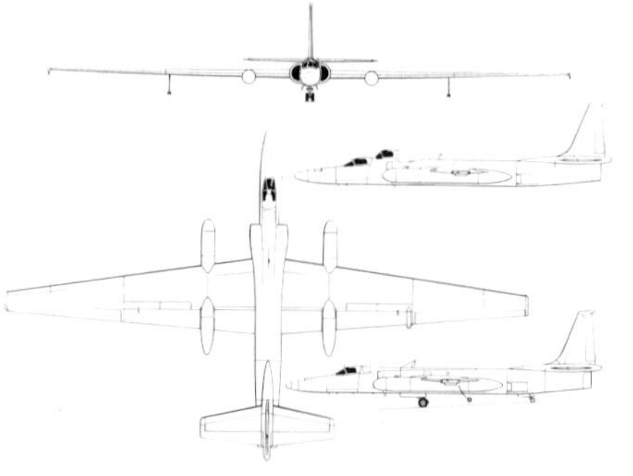

Boeing RC-135

The US Air Force's primary signals intelligence (Sigint) gatherer is the Boeing RC-135, a vastly modified version of the well-known C-135 tanker/transport. Most of the aircraft are employed on general Sigint duties with the 55th Strategic Reconnaissance Wing, operating around the world on electronic surveillance missions. These are the RC-135U, RC-135V and RC-135W, the latter two variants readily identified by a 'thimble' nose and cheek fairings hiding sensitive recording antennae. In Alaska the RC-135S and RC-135X aircraft of the 6th Strategic Wing are specialist missile-watchers, monitoring and recording Soviet tests of ICBMs. Internally all the RC-135s are packed with electronic equipment and crew stations for equipment operators.

Specification

Boeing RC-135V Sigint platform; four flight crew approx 19 operators
Span: 39.87 m (130 ft 10 in)
Length: 42.82 m (140 ft 6 in)
Height: 12.69 m (41 ft 8 in)
Wing area: 226 m^2 (2,433 sq ft)
Take-off weight: (299,000 lb)
Maximum speed: 600 mph
Ceiling: 40,600 ft
Range: 5,655 miles
Sensors: electronic, radar, jamming capability

Specification
Lockheed SR-71A two-seat high altitude strategic reconnaissance platform
Span: 16.94 m (55 ft 7 in)
Length: 32.74 m (107 ft 5 in)
Height: 5.63 m (18 ft 6 in)
Wing area: 167.22 m² (1,800 sq ft)
Take-off weight: 77110 kg (170,000 lb)
Maximum speed: above Mach 3
Ceiling: above 85,000 ft
Range: approx 3,000 miles
Sensors: electronic, optical, infra-red and radar

Lockheed EC-130E

With its capacious internal volume, heavy load-carrying capability and good endurance, the Lockheed C-130 Hercules transport has been a natural choice for conversion to the electronic reconnaissance role. Several versions have been seen in the past, and two are in service currently. The most radically altered are the EC-130E 'Volant Solo II' aircraft of the 193rd Special Operations Squadron, Pennsylvania Air National Guard, which have a huge dorsal fillet and large 'axe-head' antennae under the wings for the collection of hostile signals. These aircraft saw active service during the invasion of Grenada. The other variant is an inconspicuous version used for electronic reconnaissance along the air corridor to Berlin across East Germany.

Specification
Lockheed EC-130E 'Volant Solo II' battlefield electronic surveillance aircraft
Span: 40.41 m (132 ft 7 in)
Length: 29.79 m (97 ft 9 in)
Height: 11.65 m (38 ft 3 in)
Wing area: 162.15 m² (1,745.5 sq ft)
Take-off weight: 70306 kg (155,000 lb)
Maximum speed: 380 mph
Ceiling: 33,000 ft
Range: 4,700 miles
Sensors: electronic for recording radar and communications traffic

Douglas EA-3B Skywarrior

Serving alongside the EP-3E in US Navy service with VQ-1 and VQ-2, the EA-3B is an electronic reconnaissance version of the A-3 Skywarrior bomber. In addition to three flight crew, four systems operators are carried to work the extensive electronic suite, antennae for much of which are located in a large 'canoe' fairing under the belly. In addition to missions from shore bases, the EA-3B is carrier-compatible and deploys regularly with on-line ships to provide Sigint: being carrier-capable allows it greater flexibility in areas of operation. It has been in service since the late 1950s and is due for replacement, the most likely type being the Lockheed ES-3A Viking. The two squadrons operate about a dozen aircraft between them.

Specification
Douglas EA-3B Skywarrior naval Sigint platform; three flight crew plus four operators
Span: 22.09 m (72 ft 6 in)
Length: 23.26 m (76 ft 4 in)
Height: 6.94 m 22 ft 9½ in)
Wing area: 75.43 m² (812 sq ft)
Take-off weight: 33112 kg (73,000 lb)
Maximum speed: 610 mph
Ceiling: 41,000 ft
Range: 2,900 miles
Sensors: electronic for recording radar and communications traffic

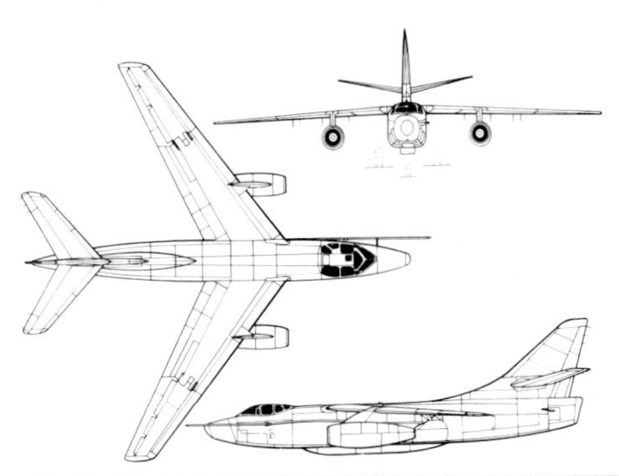

Ilyushin Il-20 'Coot-A'

This strange aircraft is usually intercepted over European waters, particularly around the United Kingdom and in the Baltic Sea. Believed to be conversions of Il-18 airliners, the 'Coot-As' number only a handful, but their capabilities are thought to be very sophisticated, probably on a par with the American EP-3E and RC-135. The pod under the fuselage is likely to contain a SLAR for radar imagery and accurate mapping purposes, whereas that on the side of the fuselage has windows for either infra-red or optical sensors. Elsewhere a plethora of aerials collect electronic data. The two large aerials on top are thought to be for satellite communications, allowing the Il-20 to pass vital information to ground commanders in near real-time.

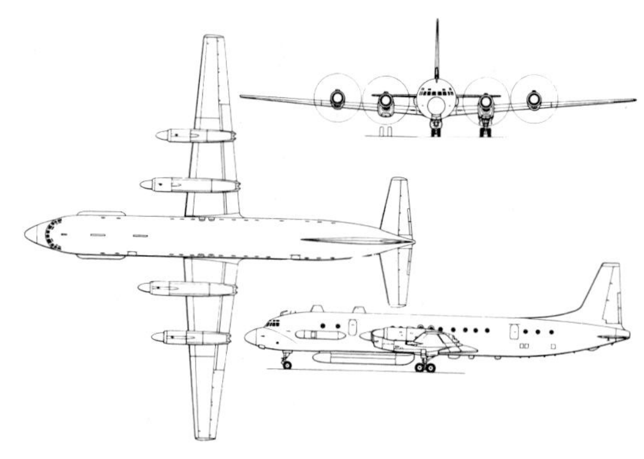

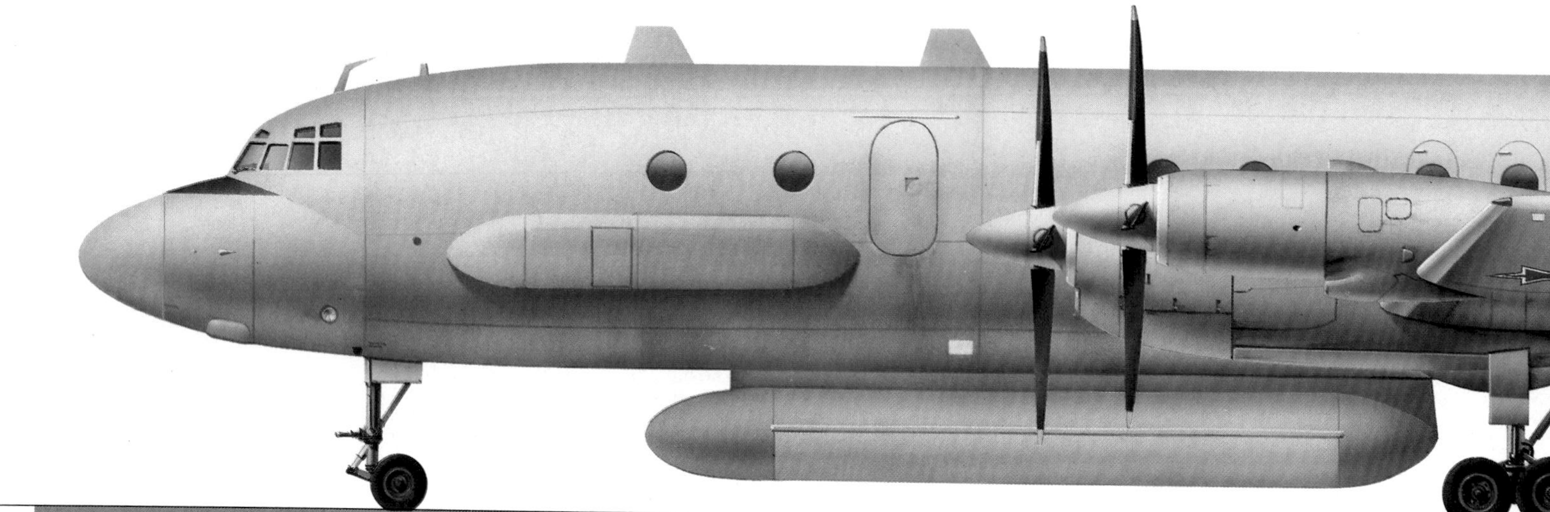

Lockheed EP-3E Orion

Based on the P-3 maritime patrol airframe, the EP-3E is used solely for electronic reconnaissance, readily identified by the various antenna fairings along the spine and belly. Most of these recorders are used against hostile shipping, the EP-3E being able to produce a 'fingerprint' of the radars carried by any ship, so helping to identify it. Many of the antennae are dedicated to radiation intelligence (Rint) gathering, which gathers signals from radars that are switched on but not transmitting. Twelve EP-3Es are currently in service, split equally between the Pacific Fleet (squadron VQ-1) and Atlantic Fleet (VQ-2). Like the RC-135, the EP-3E carries active jammers to provoke electronic activity and to protect itself.

Specification

Lockheed EP-3E Orion naval Elint platform; three flight crew plus operators
Span: 30.37 m (99 ft 8 in)
Length: 35.61 m (116 ft 10 in)
Height: 10.27 m (33 ft 8½ in)
Wing area: 120.77 m² (1,300 sq ft)
Take-off weight: 64410 kg (142,000 lb)
Maximum speed: 437 mph
Ceiling: 28,000 ft
Range: 5,060 miles
Sensors: electronic for recording radar and communications traffic

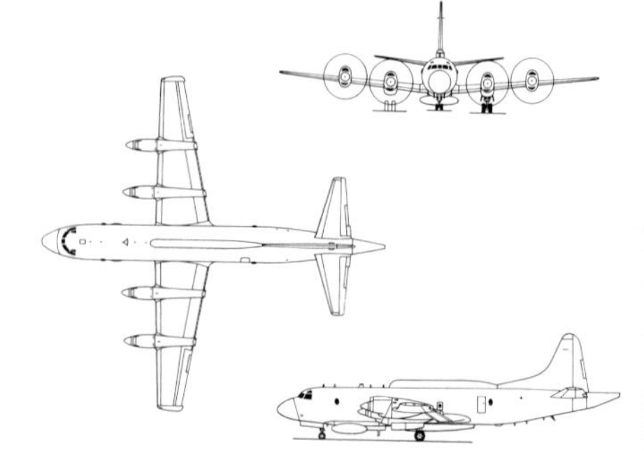

Antonov An-12

Similar to the American Lockheed Hercules, the Antonov An-12 'Cub' has for many years been the standard Soviet tactical transport, and like its Western counterpart has provided the necessary capacity and endurance for conversion to the Sigint role. Seen in many forms, the 'Cub-B' is the main electronic intelligence version, commonly encountered over the Baltic. Two underfuselage blisters are a constant feature, although antennae detail has altered over the years. In the past these aircraft have been intercepted wearing spurious markings of Aeroflot and the Egyptian air force. Other versions of the 'Cub' are used for electronic countermeasures and for trials work, the latter testing equipment for signals intelligence gathering.

Specification

Antonov An-12 'Cub-B' transport converted for electronic reconnaissance
Span: 37.99 m (124 ft 8 in)
Length: 33.10 m (108 ft 7¼ in)
Height: 10.52 m (34 ft 6½ in)
Wing area: 121.69 m² (1,310 sq ft)
Take-off weight: 60998 kg (134,480 lb)
Maximum speed: 482 mph
Ceiling: 33,500 ft
Range: 3,540 miles
Sensors: cabin packed with electronic recording gear

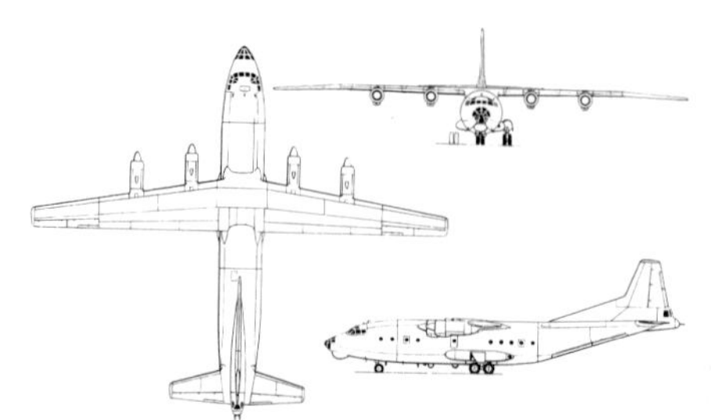

Specification
Ilyushin Il-20 'Coot-A' advanced Sigint platform
Span: 37.42 m (122 ft 9¼ in)
Length: 35.89 m (117 ft 9 in)
Height: 10.15 m (33 ft 4 in)
Wing area: 140 m² (1,507 sq ft)
Take-off weight: 64000 kg (141,100 lb)
Maximum speed: 419 mph
Ceiling: 32,800 ft
Range: 4,040 miles
Sensors: electronic for Comint/Elint/Rint, infra-red/optical, SLAR

A large signals intelligence (Sigint) gathering campaign is maintained by the Soviet Union, undertaken by aircraft of both the air force (V-VS) and navy (AV-MF). Although the 'Bears', 'Cubs' and 'Badgers' are the most commonly intercepted types, it is the Ilyushin Il-20 'Coot-A' that is the most important in European airspace, where its comprehensive sensor suite is used against the latest in Western defences.

Tupolev Tu-95 'Bear'

The most visible form of Soviet strategic reconnaissance are the ultra-long range 'Bears' which regularly shadow Western fleets and probe air defence systems. Packed with much electronic reconnaissance equipment, the 'Bear' is principally involved in cataloguing Western naval forces and in gathering information from Western communications and radars. Many versions are involved in this, including the bomber/missile carriers, which have enough electronic equipment also to undertake the reconnaissance mission. Dedicated reconnaissance aircraft are the 'Bear-C', 'Bear-D' and 'Bear-E'. The 'C' is totally dedicated to Sigint gathering, while the 'D' undertakes mid-course guidance duties for ship-launched missiles. The 'E' carries a battery of cameras.

Specification
Tupolev Tu-95 'Bear-C' long-range maritime surveillance/Sigint platform
Span: 51.09 m (167 ft 7¾ in)
Length: 49.49 m (162 ft 4¾ in)
Height: 12.12 m (39 ft 9¼ in)
Wing area: 297.00 m² (3.197 sq ft)
Take-off: approx 187786 kg (414,000 lb)
Maximum speed: 541 mph
Ceiling: 41,010 ft
Range: 8,000 miles
Sensors: full suite of electronic recording and jamming gear

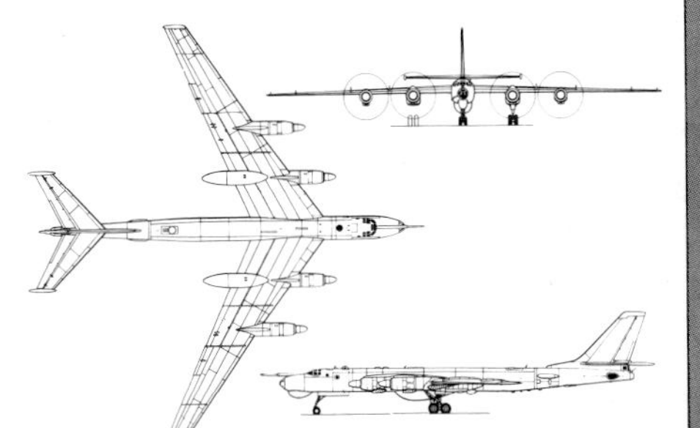

Tupolev Tu-16 'Badger'

The remarkable 'Badger' first flew in 1952 and still serves the Soviet air force and naval air arm in huge quantities. Many of the aircraft are currently involved in electronic warfare, either as jamming platforms or reconnaissance aircraft. These are also often seen around Western ships and air defence regions, and are quickly intercepted and escorted by scrambled fighters. Sigint forms the major reconnaissance discipline, with the 'Badger-D', 'F' and 'K' configured for the role. The 'Badger-E' also undertakes some Sigint gathering, allied to a battery of cameras in the vacant weapons bay. The 'E' model is usually operated in concert with a 'D' or 'F'. Reconnaissance 'Badgers' were seen in the early 1970s wearing Egyptian air force markings, although they were Soviet machines.

Specification
Tupolev Tu-16 'Badger-F' bomber converted for general Sigint duties
Span: 37.93 m (108 ft 0½ in)
Length: 36.25 m (118 ft 11¼ in)
Height: 14.00 m (45 ft 11¼ in)
Wing area: 164.64 m² (1,772.3 sq ft)
Take-off weight: 75000 kg (165,350 lb)
Maximum speed: 616 mph
Ceiling: 40,350 ft
Range: 3,910 miles
Sensors: electronic sensors mainly in weapons bay

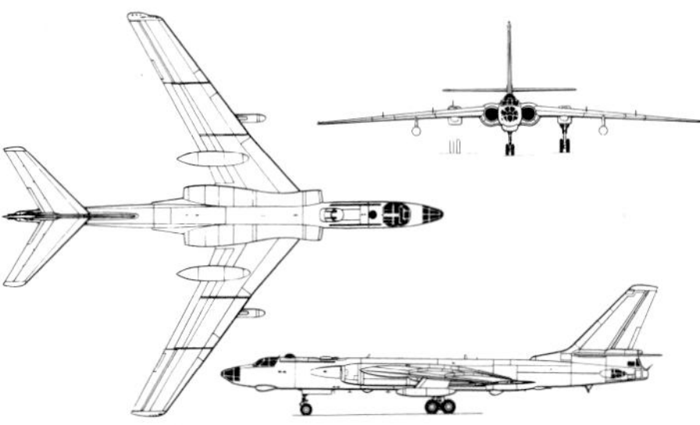

MiG-25R 'Foxbat'

The phenomenal performance of the MiG-25 interceptor led to the type being adopted for the strategic reconnaissance role. In fact, the MiG-25R recon version has a better speed performance than the fighter, although it cannot sustain this for as long as the SR-71. Two versions are in service, one ('Foxbat-B') carrying a fan of cameras for photographic reconnaissance with a small side-looking airborne radar (SLAR) for radar imagery. The more strategically-orientated 'Foxbat-D' carries a much larger SLAR and no cameras, although electronic reconnaissance equipment is thought to be fitted. These aircraft occasionally make high-speed runs along the East German border, and they have been spotted on radar during the 1970s overflying Israel and Iran.

Specification

Mikoyan-Gurevich MiG-25R 'Foxbat-B' single-seat high altitude reconnaissance aircraft
Span: 13.41 m (44 ft 0 in)
Length: 63.64 m (63 ft 7¾ in)
Height: 6.10 m (20 ft 0¼ in)
Wing area: approx 53.88 m^2 (580 sq ft)
Take-off weight: 33400 kg (73,635 lb)
Maximum speed: Mach 3.2
Ceiling: 88,580 ft
Range: 1,120 miles
Sensors: five cameras, small SLAR, some Sigint equipment

Sud Aviation Caravelle

Many European nations maintain a small Sigint gathering effort of their own, and Sweden is no exception. Two ex-SAS airliner Caravelles are in service for the task, modified with 'thimble' radomes and 'canoe' fairings hiding electronic reconnaissance antennae. Serving with F13M at Malmslatt, the pair continue the task originally performed by a BAC Canberra and a Vickers Varsity. With the military designation Tp-85, the two Caravelles usually fly over the Baltic Sea, eavesdropping on Soviet and Warsaw Pact military advances. Due to Sweden's technological achievements and its experience in the strategic reconnaissance role, it is safe to assume that the Caravelles carry a wide range of sophisticated equipment for most regimes of signals intelligence.

Specification

Sud Aviation Caravelle III converted airliner for Sigint duties
Span: 32.35 m (112 ft 6½ in)
Length: 37.00 m (105 ft 0 in)
Height: 8.71 m (28 ft 7¼ in)
Wing area: 46.70 m^2 (1,579.12 sq ft)
Take-off weight: 46000 kg (101,413 lb)
Maximum speed: 497 mph
Ceiling: approx 35,000 ft
Range: 1,450 miles
Sensors: electronic for recording WarPac signals.

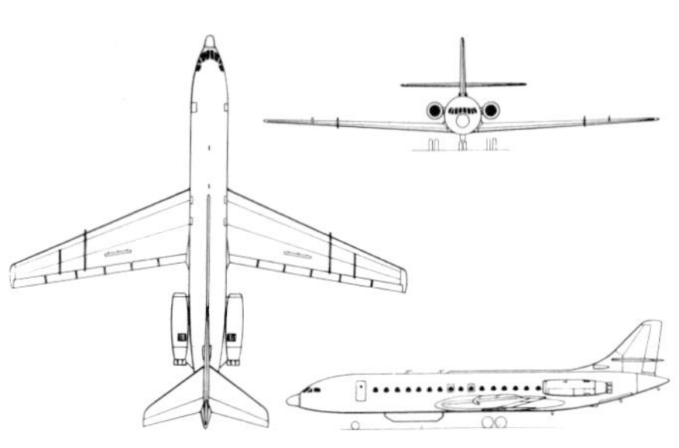

Dassault-Breguet Atlantic

West Germany has chosen the Atlantic to form the basis for a Sigint-gathering aircraft, and five were modified under the 'Peace Peek' programme to perform the task. Four of these aircraft are still in service, flying with the 2nd Staffel of Marinefliegergeschwader 3 from Nordholz, distinguished from their maritime patrol cousins by the underfuselage fairing and two large HF probes projecting forward from the underside of the wing. These aircraft are used mainly over Baltic waters, spying on WarPac nations from the safety of international airspace. The French have also used Atlantics for Sigint flights, operating regular maritime patrol aircraft in the role over northern Chad to monitor Libyan military signals traffic.

Specification

Dassault-Breguet Atlantic Elint/Rint platform with flight crew of four
Span: 36.29 m (119 ft 1 in)
Length: 31.74 m (104 ft 2 in)
Height: 11.32 m (37 ft 2 in)
Wing area: 120.33 m^2 (1,295.3 sq ft)
Take-off weight: 43499 kg (95,900 lb)
Maximum speed: 409 mph
Ceiling: 32,000 ft
Range: 4,950 miles
Sensors: electronic for naval monitoring

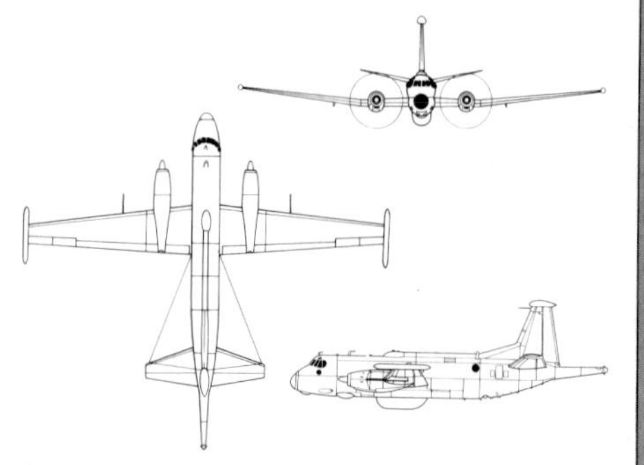

BAe Nimrod R.Mk 1

The United Kingdom has always been the 'third force' in strategic reconnaissance, operating a large fleet of Sigint aircraft. Currently it flies a trio of specially-modified Nimrods, identified by the bulged wing fairings and hemispherical tail fairing, which hide conical spiral antennae for receiving and locating hostile radar signals. A large 'farm' of antennae suggests the Nimrods are fully equipped for other tasks such as Rint and Comint. The weapons bay of the maritime Nimrod variants has been replaced by more equipment, including a SLAR (side-looking airborne radar). One of the the aircraft was given a refuelling boom for Falkland operations. All three fly with No. 51 Squadron, from RAF Wyton, employed not only around the periphery of WarPac nations but also in the Mediterranean.

Specification

British Aerospace Nimrod R.Mk 1 dedicated Comint/Elint/Rint gathering aircraft
Span: 35.07 m (115 ft 1 in)
Length: 36.49 m (119 ft 9 in)
Height: 9.08 m (29 ft 9½ in)
Wing area: 197.04 m^2 (2,121 sq ft)
Take-off weight: 87089 kg (192,000 lb)
Maximum speed: 575 mph
Ceiling: 42,000 ft
Range: 5,755 miles
Sensors: electronic and radar; full defensive electronics

Lockheed EC-130 Hercules

Another of the mantles worn by the incredibly versatile Hercules is tactical ECM using the EC-130 variant of the basic airlifter. The USAFE operator of this important type is the 17th Air Force's 66th Electronic Combat Wing based at Sembach in West Germany, and this unit is tasked with battlefield surveillance and co-operation with the EF-111As of the 42nd Electronic Combat Squadron in supporting deep strikes into enemy territory. The main model is the EC-130H 'Compass Call II' jammer version with rear fuselage side blisters and two large antennae under the tail. This is used for jamming enemy Command, Control and Communications (C^3) networks over the battlefield. Three special C-130E aircraft undertake electronic warfare duties from Rhein-Main.

Specification: Lockheed EC-130H multi-crew battlefield surveillance and electronic warfare aeroplane
Span: 40.41 m (132 ft 7 in)
Length: 29.79 m (97 ft 9 in)
Powerplant: 4×Allison T56-A-7, 3020 kW (4,050 ehp) each
Armament: none
Max T/O weight: up to 70308 kg (155,000 lb)
Max speed: 380 mph at 30,000 ft
Operational range: 4,700 miles

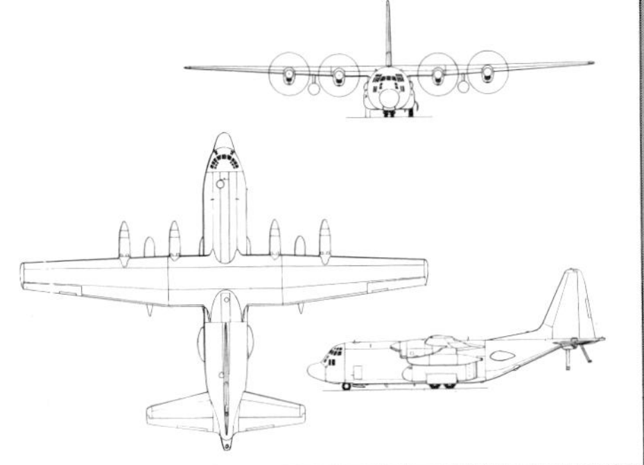

McDonnell Douglas RF-4C Phantom II

The RF-4C is still the US Air Force's primary tactical reconnaissance platform despite the fact that the type first flew in prototype and production forms during August 1963 and May 1964. The type is generally equivalent to the US Marine Corps' RF-4B and is based on the airframe of the F-4C with APQ-99 forward-looking/mapping radar and APQ-102 side-looking radar complemented by an AAS-18A infra-red linescanning unit and a combination of KS-72 or KS-77 oblique plus KA-55 high-altitude and KA-56 low-altitude panoramic cameras. The USAF still deploys more than 325 of this important reconnaissance type, and though most of these are in the USA some 20 are on the strength of the 26th Tactical Reconnaissance Wing of the USAFE's 17th Air Force, based at Zweibrücken in West Germany.

Specification: McDonnell Douglas RF-4C Phantom II two-seat tactical reconnaissance aeroplane
Span: 11.77 m (38 ft 7.5 in)
Length: 19.18 m (62 ft 11 in)
Powerplant: 2×General Electric J79-GE-15, 7711 kg (17,000 lb) st each
Armament: none
Max T/O weight: 26309 kg (58,000 lb)
Max speed: Mach 2.17 at 36,000 ft
Operational range: not revealed

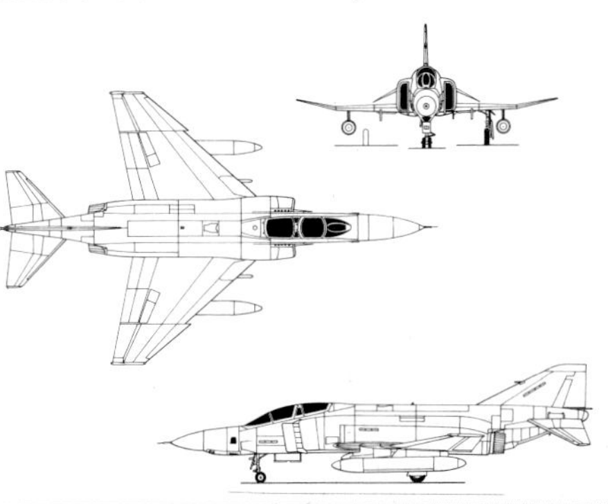

Aeritalia G91R

The G91R was designed to a NATO requirement of the early 1950s for a light attack fighter, but was adopted in its new-production forms only by Italy and West Germany. Italy still deploys some 45 such aircraft of the G91R/1A and B variants, the latter with a reinforced structure and landing gear: these are operated by the 14° and 103° Gruppi at Treviso-San Angelo for light attack and reconnaissance. The Aeronautica Militare Italiana uses larger numbers of the G91T, the two-seat version of the basic design, for conversion as well as advanced and weapon training. The specific variant is the G91T/1 with an armament of two 12.7-mm (0.5-in) machine-guns plus disposable stores on two underwing hardpoints. These 71 aircraft are operated mainly by the 201° and 204° Gruppi of the Scuola Volo Basico Avanzato Aviogetti at Amendola.

Specification: Aeritalia G91R/1B single-seat light attack and reconnaissance aeroplane
Span: 8.56 m (28 ft 1 in)
Length: 10.30 m (33 ft 9.25 in)
Powerplant: 1×Fiat-built Rolls-Royce (Bristol) Orpheus Mk 803, 2268 kg (5,000 lb) st
Armament: 4×12.7-mm (0.5-in) machine-guns plus provision for up to 680 kg (1,500 lb) of disposable stores carried on 4×underwing hardpoints
Max T/O weight: 5500 kg (12,125 lb)
Max speed: 674 mph at 4,920 ft
Operational range: 398 miles

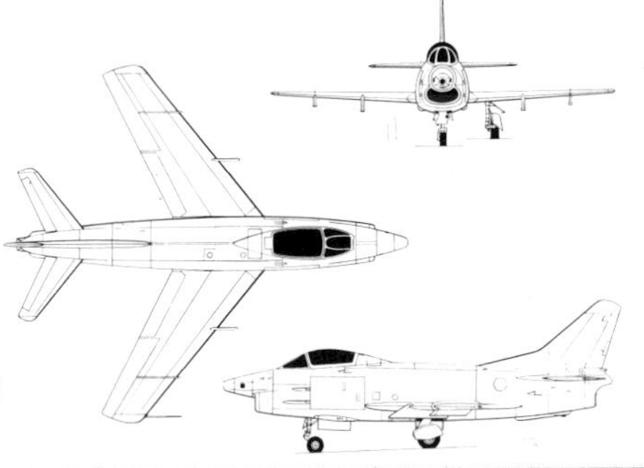

Aeritalia G91Y

Soon after the introduction of its G91R, Fiat (now Aeritalia) appreciated that the basic airframe was sound but modestly underpowered. The result was the G91Y developed from the G91T but re-engined with two J85 turbojets for 63 per cent more power for a mere 18 per cent increase in empty weight. This increased combat survivability, boosted performance, enhanced payload/range, and permitted the incorporation of a zero/zero ejector seat in a pressurised and fully air-conditioned cockpit. The type first flew in December 1966 and production totalled 67 aircraft, and some 38 of these are still in service in the light attack and reconnaissance roles, mainly with the 13° Gruppo at Brindisi and the 101° Gruppo at Cervia-San Giorgio. The G91Ys are to be replaced by the new AMX attack aircraft once the last G91Rs have been supplanted by the Italo-Brazilian aeroplane.

Specification: Aeritalia G91Y single-seat light attack and reconnaissance aeroplane
Span: 9.01 m (29 ft 6.5 in)
Length: 11.67 m (38 ft 3.5 in)
Powerplant: 2×General Electric J85-GE-13A, 1850 kg (4,080 lb) st each
Armament: 2×30-mm cannon plus provision for up to 1814 kg (4,000 lb) of disposable stores on 4×underwing hardpoints
Max T/O weight: 8700 kg (19,180 lb)
Max speed: 708 mph at sea level
Operational range: 480 miles with a heavy warload

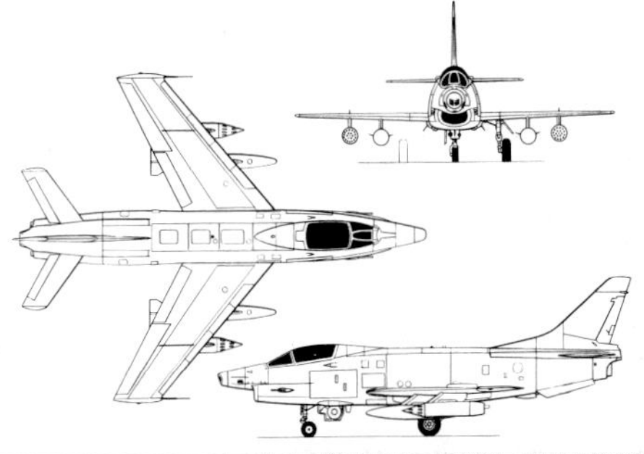

Chapter 6
TRAINERS

Bucker Bu 131 Jungmann

Specification: Bucker Bu 131B two-seat primary trainer
Span: 7.40 m (24 ft 3.25 in)
Length: 6.60 m (21 ft 8 in)
Powerplant: 1×Hirth HM 504A-2, 78 kW (105 hp)
Armament: none
Max T/O weight: 680 kg (1,499 lb)
Max speed: 114 mph at sea level
Operational range: 404 miles

The Jungmann was designed by a Swede, Anders Andersson, and was the German company's first production aeroplane. The prototype flew in April 1934 with a 60-kW (80-hp) Hirth HM 60R inline, and proved immensely successful. The type became Germany's most important primary trainer of World War II, and fairly large numbers were exported or built under licence. The Bu 131B was an improved model with the HM 504A-2 engine, and like the Bu 131A this was not infrequently used for night harassment over the Eastern Front with light bombs. Production figures have not survived, but some indication of scale is provided by the fact that Hungary took 100 and Romania 150, while Switzerland built 75. Some 1,254+ were built in Japan by Watanabe and Kyushu as the army's Kokusai Ki-86A (1,037) and the navy's K9W1 (217+). Many still survive, and production was boosted by the post-war C.4 from Czechoslovakia.

Bucker Bu 133 Jungmeister

The success of the Jungmann led Bucker to open a second factory where a single-seat derivative could be produced in parallel with the original two-seater. The single-seater was the Jungmeister (young champion) advanced trainer, essentially a scaled-down Jungmann. The initial Bu 133A had the 101-kW (135-hp) Hirth HM 6 inline but better performance than the higher-powered Bu 131. Quantity production was undertaken for the Luftwaffe, though precise details are lacking. The Bu 133B export version was produced to the extent of some 100 aircraft by Dornier in Switzerland and CASA in Spain with the 119-kW (160-hp) Hirth HM 506 inline. The definitive version, however, was the Bu 133C with a radial engine: this had excellent agility and performance, and was used as a fighter lead-in trainer as well as for advanced flying training. This model too was built in Switzerland and Spain.

Specification: Bucker Bu 133C Jungmeister single-seat advanced flying and fighter lead-in trainer
Span: 6.60 m (21 ft 7.75 in)
Length: 6.00 m (19 ft 8.25 in)
Powerplant: 1×Siemens Sh 14A-4, 119 kW (160 hp)
Armament: none
Max T/O weight: 585 kg (1,290 lb)
Max speed: 137 mph at sea level
Operational range: 311 miles

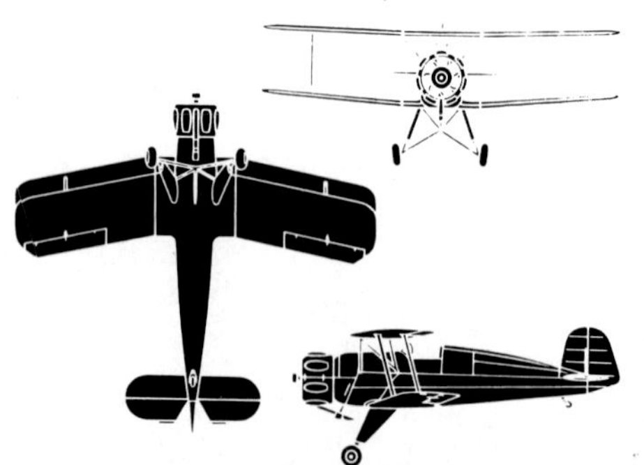

Bucker Bu 181 Bestmann

The Bu 181 low-wing monoplane trainer was a development of the Bu 180 Student with enclosed side-by-side accommodation for the crew of two and typical mixed construction (ply/fabric-covered wooden flying surfaces, aluminium alloy-covered steel-tube forward fuselage and wooden monocoque rear fuselage) with fixed tailwheel landing gear. The production version for the Luftwaffe was the Bu 181A, of which several thousand were built in Germany. More production was undertaken in Holland (708) and Sweden (125 Sk 25s) during and just after the war, while post-war production was launched in Czechoslovakia and, under Czech licence, Egypt. The final war-time development was the Bu 181D with a number of detail improvements over the Bu 181A. In addition to its designed role, the Bu 181 was used as a communications aeroplane and, in small numbers, as a tug for light training gliders.

Specification: Bucker Bu 181A two-seat primary trainer
Span: 10.60 m (34 ft 9.25 in)
Length: 7.85 m (25 ft 9 in)
Powerplant: 1×Hirth HM 504, 78 kW (105 hp)
Armament: none
Max T/O weight: 750 kg (1,653 lb)
Max speed: 134 mph at sea level
Operational range: 497 miles

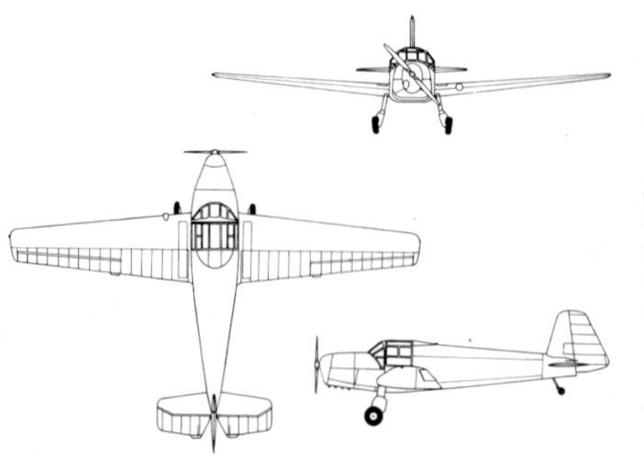

A Bucker Jungmann of I/ZG 26 'Horst Wessel', based at Yvrenche near Abbeville in France during 1940 while being used as a 'hack' by this Bf 110-equipped Gruppe. It proved to be an excellent trainer, with superior handling characteristics to its allied counterparts, the Tiger Moth and Stearman. Production continued after the war, and Spain has only just retired its last Jungmanns, a testament to its sound design.

Caproni Ca 100

The appearance of the Ca 100 confirms the type's derivation at only very short remove from the de Havilland D.H.60 Moth. The type had several detail differences including an extension of the lower wing to give it noticeably greater span than the upper wing, and about 700 aircraft were built from 1929. The type was bought by civil as well as military operators, and was flown with an assortment of engines including the original Gipsy, 63-kW (85-hp) Fiat A.50, 67-kW (90-hp) Blackburn Cirrus Minor, 86-kW (115-hp) Isotta Fraschini Asso 80R, and 108-kW (145-hp) Colombo S.63. Built by Macchi, the Ca 100 Idro was a twin-float seaplane trainer, and there was also a bomber trainer with a 97-kW (130-hp) radial engine and provision for a quartet of light bombs. The type was built under licence in Bulgaria as the KN-1, and also in Peru.

Specification: Caproni Ca 100
two-seat primary trainer
Span: 10.00 m (32 ft 10 in)
Length: 7.30 m (23 ft 1.25 in)
Powerplant: 1×de Havilland Gipsy, 63 kW (85 hp)
Armament: none
Max T/O weight: 680 kg (1,499 lb)
Max speed: 102 mph at sea level
Operational range: 435 miles

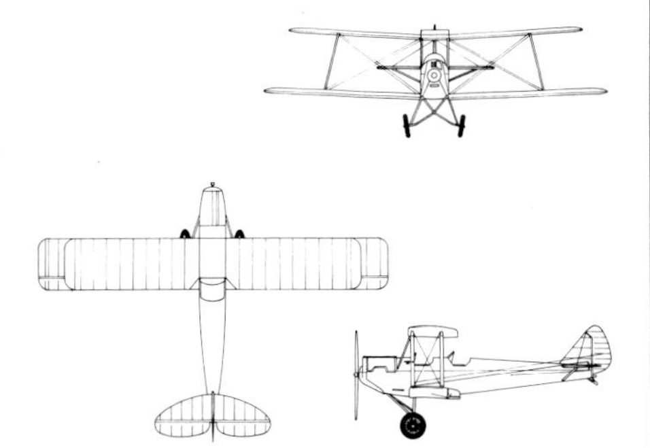

Gotha Go 145

Because of the impact of the bombers it had produced in World War I Gotha was closed by the terms of the Treaty of Versailles. In 1933 the company resumed aircraft manufacture, and its first product was the Go 145 trainer. This first flew in February 1934 with a fabric-covered all-wood airframe, and was ordered into immediate production as a Luftwaffe basic trainer with the designation Go 145A. Slightly under 10,000 aircraft were built, BFW and Focke-Wulf), and such was the utility of the type that in World War II large numbers were used by the *Storkampfstaffeln* (later *Nachtschlachtgruppen)* to harass the Soviet forces. The type was also built in Spain as the CASA 1115-L, and in Turkey. German variants were the Go 145B with an enclosed cockpit and landing gear spats, and the Go 145C gunnery trainer with a pivoted 7.92-mm (0.312-mm) machine-gun in the rear cockpit.

Specification: Gotha Go 145A
two-seat basic trainer
Span: 9.00 m (29 ft 6.25 in)
Length: 8.70 m (28 ft 6.5 in)
Powerplant: 1×Argus As 10C, 179 kW (240 hp)
Armament: none
Max T/O weight: 1380 kg (3,043 lb)
Max speed: 132 mph at sea level
Operational range: 391 miles

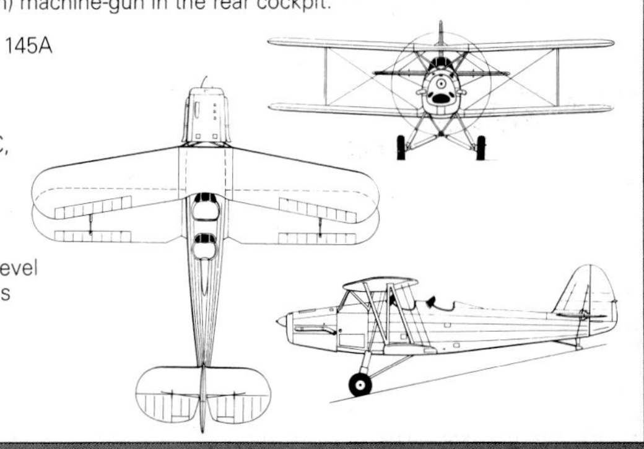

Heinkel He 51

Specification: Heinkel He 51B-1 single-seat fighter and fighter trainer
Span: 11.00 m (36 ft 1 in)
Length: 8.40 m (27 ft 6.75 in)
Powerplant: 1×BMW VI 7,3Z, 559 kW (750 hp)
Armament: 2×7.92-mm (0.312-in) machine-guns
Max T/O weight: 1895 kg (4,178 lb)
Max speed: 205 mph at sea level
Operational range: 354 miles

Focke-Wulf Fw 56 Stosser

The Stosser (hawk) was the first Focke-Wulf design undertaken by Kurt Tank, and resulted for a German requirement for an advanced trainer with the As 10C engine. The resultant Fw 56a prototype that flew in November 1933 was a parasol-winged aeroplane of mixed construction with cantilever main landing gear units: two more prototypes followed. In the summer of 1935 the Stosser was selected in preference to the Arado Ar 76 and Heinkel He 74, so three Fw 56A-0 pre-production and about 900 Fw 56A-1 production aircraft followed up to 1940. These were extensively used as advanced trainers in fighter schools, though after trials that helped to validate the concept of dive-bombing the type was also used in dive-bomber schools. Austria ordered the type before its annexation by Germany, and 12 Stossers were also delivered to Hungary.

Specification: Focke-Wulf Fw 56A-1 Stosser single-seat advanced trainer and fighter trainer
Span: 10.50 m (34 ft 5.5 in)
Length: 7.70 m (25 ft 3 in)
Powerplant: 1×Argus As 10C, 179 kW (240 hp)
Armament: 1 or 2×7.92-mm (0.312-in) machine-guns plus provision for 3×10-kg (22-lb) bombs carried externally
Max T/O weight: 995 kg (2,194 lb)
Max speed: 173 mph at sea level
Operational range: 249 miles

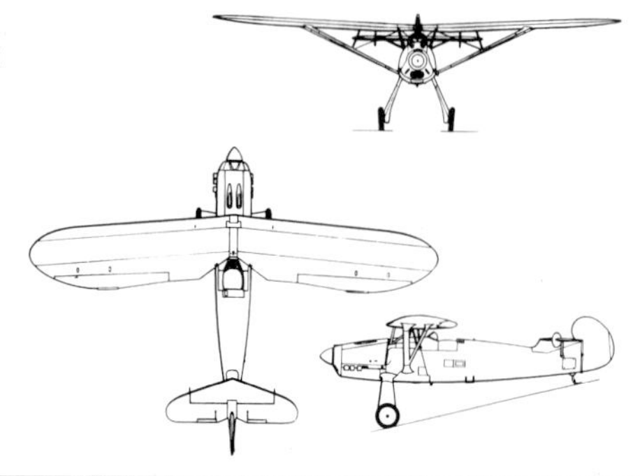

Focke-Wulf Fw 44 Stieglitz

The Stieglitz (goldfinch) was the company's second most prolific design after the Fw 190 fighter, and the Fw 44A prototype first flew in the summer of 1932 with an Sh 14A radial. In its basic form the type had severe handling problems, and these were eradicated by the newly arrived Kurt Tank in an intensive development programme that turned the Stieglitz into a superb aerobatic machine. In addition to export orders from Bolivia, Chile, China, Czechoslovakia, Finland, Romania, Switzerland and Turkey, the Fw 44 was built under licence in Argentina, Austria, Brazil, Bulgaria and Sweden. The major operator, however, was the Luftwaffe with the Fw 44B using the 109-kW (135-hp) Argus As 8 inline, followed by the Fw 44C that reverted to the Sh 14A. Variants of the Fw 44C with detail improvements were the Fw 44D, F and J.

Specification: Focke-Wulf Fw 44C Stieglitz two-seat basic trainer and liaison aeroplane
Span: 9.00 m (29 ft 6.25 in)
Length: 7.30 m (23 ft 11.5 in)
Powerplant: 1×Siemens Sh 14A, 112 kW (150 hp)
Armament: none
Max T/O weight: 900 kg (1,984 lb)
Max speed: 115 mph at sea level
Operational range: 419 miles

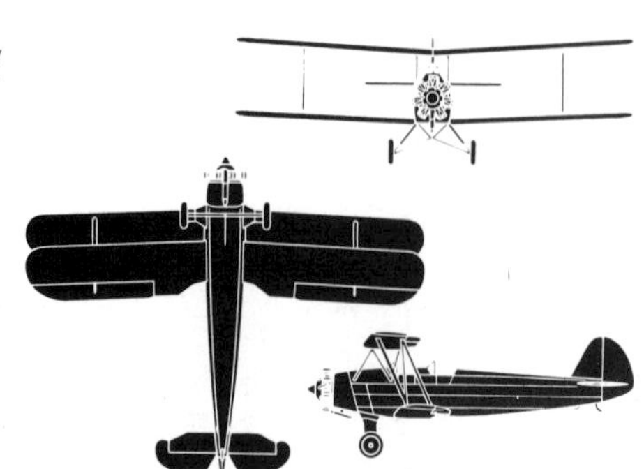

A Heinkel He 51 of II/JG 132 'Richthofen', based at Döberitz. This particular aircraft was the personal mount of the Gruppe commandant, and wears his chevrons on the fuselage and centre section. Introduced as a fighter during the 1930s, the He 51 was soon outclassed by more modern types and was relegated to second-line roles, mainly advanced training, for which it is best known.

From the He 49 fighter prototype Heinkel developed the He 51 that first flew in May 1933 in He 51A-0 pre-production form. The nine He 51A-0s were followed by 150 He 51A-1 production aircraft, of which one was converted to an He 51A-2 floatplane. Subsequent variants were the He 51B-1 with a jettisonable ventral tank (450 including 46 He 51B-2 floatplanes), and the He 51C ground-attack fighter (79 C-1 and 21 C-2 variants with improved radio). With the advent of the Messerschmitt Bf 109 monoplane fighter these worthy but unexceptional examples of the biplane fighter were relegated initially to the ground-attack role, but finally to the advanced flying training and fighter lead-in roles. The type survived in this role up to 1943, though the elimination of the type from the Luftwaffe's inventory had started in 1942.

Heinkel He 46

The He 46 was first flown in 1931 as a response to a German requirement for a tactical reconnaissance and army co-operation aeroplane. This prototype was an unequal-span biplane, but complaints about the poor downward fields of vision resulted in the type's revision with a parasol wing. This and a second prototype were powered by Bristol Jupiter radials, later changed for the SAM 22B adopted for production aircraft, which began with the He 46C. Production totalled 481, and later variants were seven unarmed He 46D reconnaissance aircraft, 43 He 46Es generally flown without their NACA ring cowls, and 14 He 46F observer trainers with 418-kW (560-hp) Armstrong Siddeley Panther radials. The type was replaced by the Henschel Hs 126 from 1938, but thereafter played an important part in the training role into the middle years of the war.

Specification: Heinkel He 46C-1 two-seat tactical reconnaissance and army co-operation aeroplane, later trainer
Span: 14.00 m (45 ft 11.25 in)
Length: 9.50 m (31 ft 2 in)
Powerplant: 1×Bramo 322B (SAM 22B), 485 kW (650 hp)
Armament: 1×7.92-mm (0.312-in) machine-gun plus provision for up to 200 kg (440 lb) of bombs carried externally
Max T/O weight: 2300 kg (5,071 lb)
Max speed: 161 mph at 2,625 ft
Operational range: 615 miles

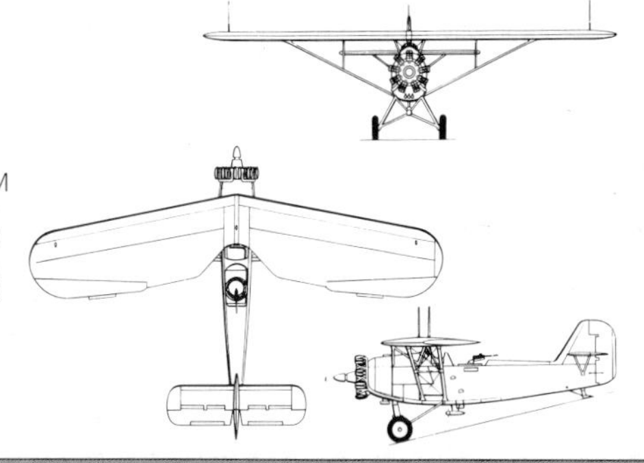

Heinkel He 72 Kadett

The Kadett (cadet) was a thoroughly conventional fabric-covered biplane trainer and liaison aeroplane of its period, and first flew in 1933 with the As 8B engine and nicely spatted main landing gear units. The type entered official service first with the training schools of the National Socialist Flying Corps, and then with the Luftwaffe. Comparatively large numbers were built, the production variants being the He 72A with the 104-kW (140-hp) Argus As 8B or later the 112-kW (150-hp) As 8R inlines, the He 72B major variant with a radial engine, and the He 72BW twin-float seaplane. Some 30 civil aircraft were built with the designation He 72B-2 Edelkadett (honour cadet), and there was a single He 172 with a NAC-cowled engine. Some aircraft were supplied to Slovakia during World War II, and these were even used as tactical reconnaissance machines during 1945.

Specification: Heinkel He 72B two-seat primary trainer
Span: 9.00 m (29 ft 6.25 in)
Length: 7.50 m (24 ft 7.25 in)
Powerplant: 1×Siemens Sh 14A, 119 kW (160 hp)
Armament: none
Max T/O weight: 865 kg (1,907 lb)
Max speed: 115 mph at sea level
Operational range: 295 miles

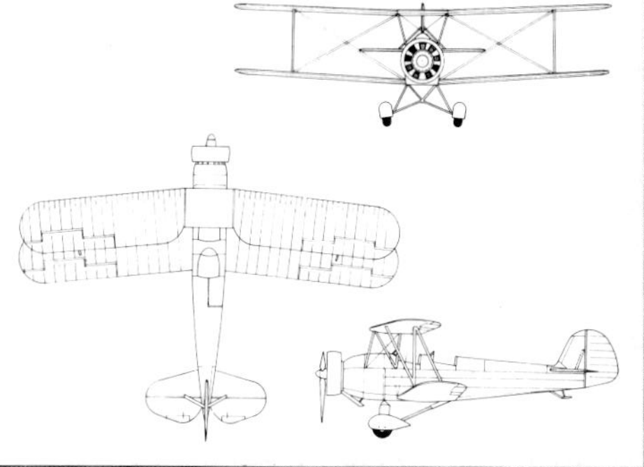

Boeing (Stearman) PT-17

Specification: Boeing (Stearman) PT-17 two-seat primary trainer
Span: 9.80 m (32 ft 2 in)
Length: 7.54 m (24 ft 9 in)
Powerplant: 1×Continental R-670-5, 164 kW (220 hp)
Armament: none
Max T/O weight: 1195 kg (2,635 lb)
Max speed: 135 mph at sea level
Operational range: 500 miles

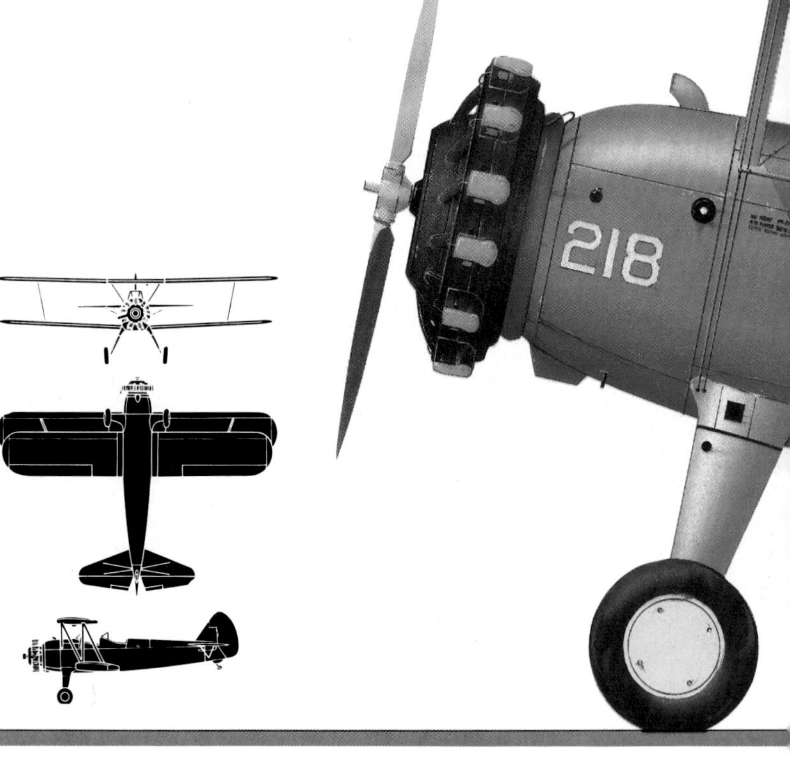

The Kaydet series stems from the X70 trainer produced in 1934. The type was ordered for the USAAC as the PT-13, these 32 aircraft being powered by a 160-kW (215-hp) Lycoming R-680-5 radial. Then came 92 PT-13As with the 164-kW (220-hp) R-680-7, 220 PT-13Bs with the 209-kW (280-hp) R-680-11s of which six became blind-flying PT-13Cs, and 895 PT-13Ds with R-680-1 engines. A change to the R-670 engine produced the PT-17, of which 2,942 were built including 136 blind-flying PT-17As. The PT-18 was the same basic airframe with the Jacobs R-755-7, and these 150 aircraft included six blind-flying PT-18As. Similar aircraft were ordered for the US Navy: the X70 with the Wright R-790-8 became the NS-1, and these 61 were followed by 250 N2S-1s with the R-670-14, 125 N2S-2s with the R-680-8, 1,875 N2S-3s with the R-670-4, 577 N2S-4s with the R-670-4/5, and 1,430 N2S-5s with the R-680-17. Canada used the Kaydet as the PT-27.

Naval Aircraft Factory N3N

Designed for the US Navy in 1934, and outwardly similar to the service's current Consolidated NY-2 and -3, the N3N featured an all-metal primary structure covered with fabric except along the fuselage sides, which featured removable alloy panels. The XN3N-1 prototype flew in August 1935 with a 164-kW (220-hp) Wright J-5 radial, an engine that was out of production but stocked in considerable numbers. The prototype was evaluated as a landplane and floatplane, resulting in an order for 179 N3N-1s. Single XN3N-2 and XN3N-3 prototypes were used to evaluate the 179-kW (240-hp) R-760 engine that was then used in the last 20 N3N-1s and retrofitted in the earlier aircraft. There followed 816 N3N-3s with a revised tail and modified landing gear, and the N3Ns were amongst the Navy's most important wheel- and float-equipped primary trainers throughout World War II.

Specification: Naval Aircraft Factory N3N-3 primary trainer
Span: 10.36 m (34 ft 0 in)
Length: 7.77 m (25 ft 6 in)
Powerplant: 1×Wright R-760-2 Whirlwind 7, 175 kW (235 hp)
Armament: none
Max T/O weight: 1266 kg (2,792 lb)
Max speed: 126 mph at sea level
Operational range: 470 miles

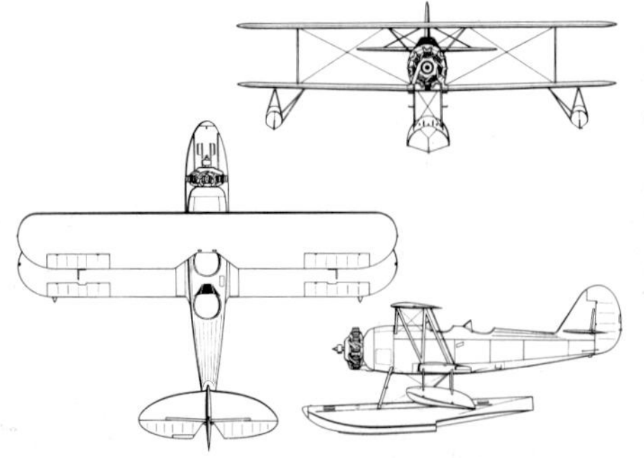

North American BT-9

In 1935 North American flew its NA-16 private-venture trainer, and after evaluation by the USAAC the type was adopted as a basic trainer with the designation BT-9, and these 42 aircraft were powered by the 298-kW (400-hp) R-975-7 radial; the US Navy took a similar type as the NJ-1, and these 40 aircraft had the 373-kW (500-hp) Pratt & Whitney R-1340 radial. The 40 BT-9As that followed introduced a fixed forward gun (with gun camera) and a trainable gun in the rear cockpit. Only small changes were made in the 117 BT-9Bs and 67 BT-9Ds. The basic type was then improved with the flying surfaces of the BC-1A and a metal-covered fuselage to produce the BT-14, of which 251 were built with the 336-kW (450-hp) Pratt & Whitney R-985-25 radial. Some 27 were later converted to BT-14A standard with the 298-kW (400-hp) R-985-11 engine. Canada operated the BT-14 as the Yale Mk I.

Specification: North American BT-9B two-seat basic trainer
Span: 12.80 m (42 ft 0 in)
Length: 8.41 m (27 ft 7 in)
Powerplant: 1×Wright R-975-7, 298 kW (400 hp)
Armament: 2×7.62-mm (0.3-in) machine-guns
Max T/O weight: 2028 kg (4,471 lb)
Max speed: 170 mph at sea level
Operational range: 882 miles

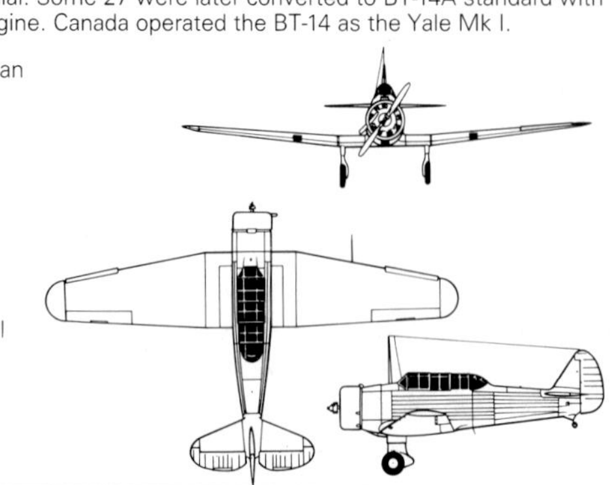

The Stearman Kaydet was the standard US Army basic trainer of World War II, fulfilling the same vital training role as the RAF's Tiger Moths. After the war, many Stearmans passed into private hands, and some were used as agricultural crop dusters. Today, the Stearman is a highly sought-after vintage aircraft, much prized for its superb handling and open cockpit biplane configuration.

North American *AT-6 and SNJ-5*

Basically the BT-9 with a refined airframe, retractable landing gear and more power, the BC-1 was ordered in 1937 to the extent of 41 aircraft with the R-1340-45 radial. Blunt wing tips and a straight-edged rudder characterised the BC-1A, of which 92 were ordered and the last six delivered as AT-6s after a change in designation policy during 1940. AT-6 orders covered an extra 85 aircraft, and production then switched to 1,429 AT-6As with the R-1340-49 engine and modified fuel tankage. The full production flood now saw 400 AT-6B gunnery trainers with the R-1340-AN-1, 2,970 AT-6Cs with a high proportion of non-strategic materials, 3,713 AT-6Ds with the original structure and 24-volt electrics, and 25 AT-6Fs with a strengthened airframe. US Navy variants equivalent to the BC-1, AT-6, AT-6A, AT-6C, AT-6D and AT-6F were the SNJ-1 to -6 respectively, of which 4,765 were delivered. The type was used by the British as the Harvard.

Specification: North American SNJ-5 Texan two-seat basic and advanced trainer
Span: 12.81 m (42 ft 0.25 in)
Length: 8.99 m (29 ft 6 in)
Powerplant: 1×Pratt & Whitney R-1340-AN-1 Wasp, 410 kW (550 hp)
Armament: 2 or 3×7.62-mm (0.3-in) machine-guns
Max T/O weight: 2404 kg (5,300 lb)
Max speed: 205 mph at 5,000 ft
Operational range: 750 miles

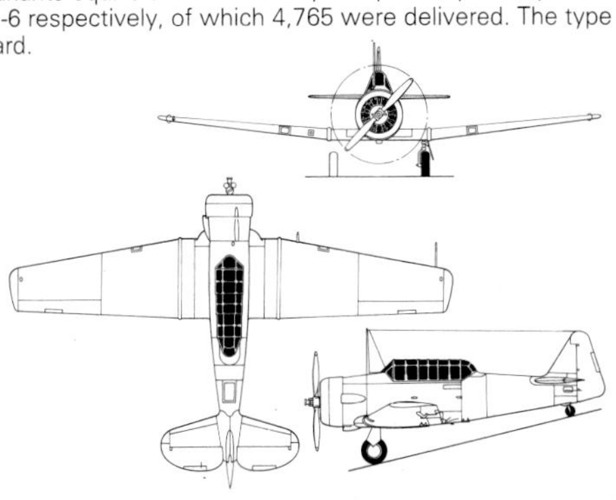

Waco PT-14

In 1937 Waco introduced its Model UPF-7 as an open-cockpit biplane with a 164-kW (220-hp) Continental W-670-K radial engine and seating for two or three. The type was intended for training and sport use, and as such designed with an exceptionally sturdy airframe. This commended the type to the USAAC as a primary trainer, and a single example was evaluated during 1939 with the designation XPT-14. There followed 13 YPT-14 service trials aircraft, which were later redesignated PT-14; a single civil Model UPF-7 was impressed with the designation PT-14A. However, another 600 aircraft of the same basic type were ordered with three engine types for the Civilian Pilot Training Program that undertook pilot training at educational institutions to provide a pool of trained pilots in the event of war. Another 31 similar aircraft were bought by the Civil Aeronautics Authority for its own flying unit.

Specification: Waco PT-14 two-seat primary trainer
Span: 9.14 m (30 ft 0 in)
Length: 7.16 m (23 ft 5 in)
Powerplant: 1×Continental R-670-3, 164 kW (220 hp)
Armament: none
Max T/O weight: 1202 kg (2,650 lb)
Max speed: 138 mph at sea level
Operational range: not recorded

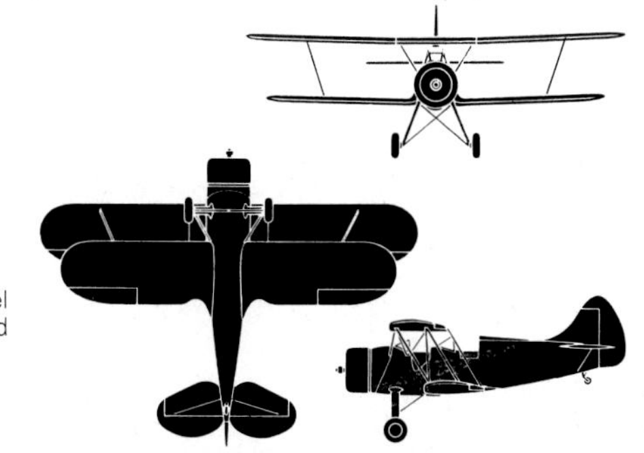

Vultee BT-13 and SNV

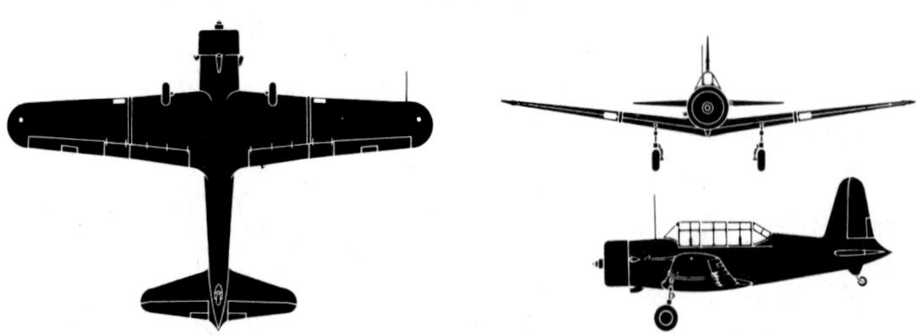

The aircraft of this important basic training family far outnumbered all other basic trainers in a production career that lasted from 1940 to 1944. Following 1939 tests with the BC-3 variant with retractable landing gear and a 447-kW (600-hp) Pratt & Whitney R-1320-45 radial, the army opted for the lower-powered Model 54 with fixed landing gear. The initial contract called for 300 aircraft, and these BT-13s were followed by orders for no fewer than 6,407 BT-13As and 1,125 BT-13Bs with a 24- rather than 12-volt electrical system. Demand far outstripped engine supplies, however, and in 1941 the USAAF ordered the BT-15 variant with the 336-kW (450-hp) Wright R-975-11 radial, and production of this model totalled 1,693. US Navy procurement began with 1,350 SNV-1s equivalent to the BT-13A, and was completed by 650 SNV-2s equivalent to the BT-13B. The aircraft were retired soon after the war.

Cessna AT-8 and AT-17

The Model T-50 was developed as a five-seat light transport, and in World War II some 3,437 were produced for the US forces as the UC-78 Bobcat (3,370 for the USAAF) and JRC-1 (68 for the US Navy). The type was also developed for the Royal Canadian Air Force as a trainer for pilots transitioning to multi-engined aircraft. This Crane Mk I was produced to the extent of 640 aircraft, and in 1940 the USAAC procured 33 similar AT-8s with the same 220-kW (295-hp) Lycoming R-680-9 radials. USAAC expansion prompted the 1941 decision to buy considerably larger numbers, though these differently engined aircraft comprised 450 AT-17s with wooden propellers, 223 AT-17As with metal propellers and a lighter maximum weight, 466 AT-17Bs with different equipment, and 60 AT-17Cs with different radio. Of these 1,199 aircraft, 550 were delivered to Canada with the name Crane Mk IA.

Specification: Cessna AT-17 four-seat advanced and multi-engined conversion trainer
Span: 12.80 m (41 ft 11 in)
Length: 10.00 m (32 ft 9 in)
Powerplant: 2×Jacobs R-775-9, 183 kW (245 hp) each
Armament: none
Max T/O weight: 22586 kg (5,700 lb)
Max speed: 195 mph at sea level
Operational range: 750 miles

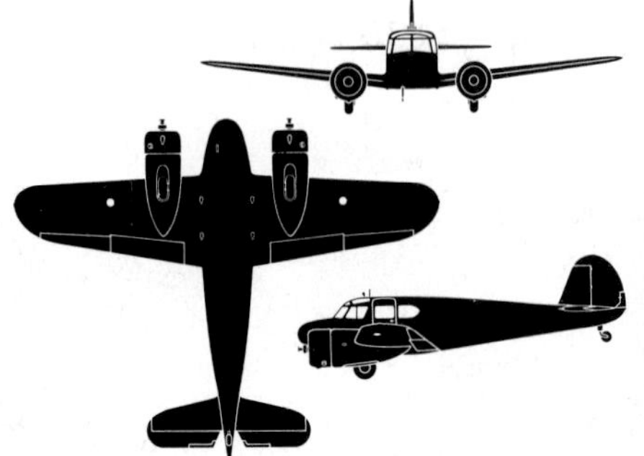

Curtiss-Wright SNC Falcon

This relatively simple aeroplane was developed within the context of the US Navy's enormous increase in pilot training during 1940, and was in essence an advanced combat trainer evolved from the CW-19 light fighter and trainer project with features such as retractable landing gear from the CW-21 Demon export fighter bought by the air forces of China and of the Netherlands East Indies. The CW-22 prototype resembled the CW-21 with a longer, two-seat fuselage but considerably lower power in the form of the 313-kW (420-hp) Wright R-975 Whirlwind radial. Some 136 CW-22s were exported, and the US Navy version was the CW-22N that entered service as the SNC-1. The initial order for 150 aircraft was later bolstered by five impressed aircraft and two other orders for a total of 305 aircraft, of which the last batch featured a higher cockpit canopy.

Specification: Curtiss SNC-1 Falcon two-seat advanced combat trainer
Span: 10.66 m (35 ft 0 in)
Length: 8.22 m (27 ft 0 in)
Powerplant: 1×Wright R-975-28 Whirlwind, 336 kW (450 hp)
Armament: 2×7.62-mm (0.3-in) machine-guns
Max T/O weight: 1718 kg (3,788 lb)
Max speed: 198 mph at sea level
Operational range: 780 miles

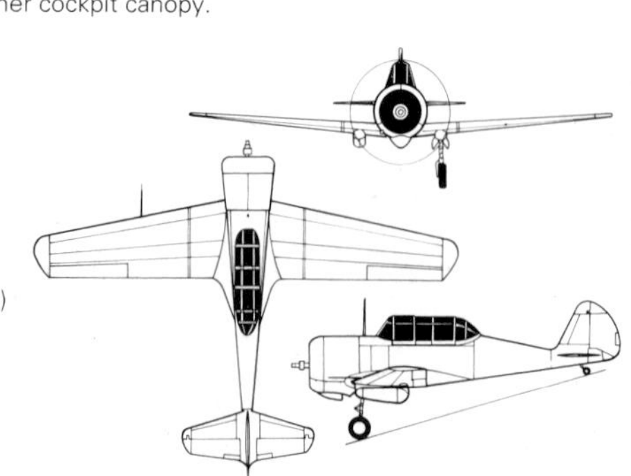

A Vultee BT-13 Valiant trainer of the US Army Air Corps. The BT-13 was designed as a private venture and was selected for Army use in September 1939. The BT-13 was the most numerous USAAF trainer of the war.

Specification: Vultee BT-13A Valiant two-seat basic trainer
Span: 12.80 m (42 ft 0 in)
Length: 8.79 m (28 ft 10 in)
Powerplant: 1×Pratt & Whitney R-984-AN-1, 336 kW (450 hp)
Armament: none
Max T/O weight: 2039 kg (4,496 lb)
Max speed: 180 mph at sea level
Operational range: 725 miles

Fairchild PT-19 series

n apparent contradiction of the USAAC's preference for biplane primary trainers, the PT-19 series was built in very large numbers. The aeroplane was developed as the M-62, and was ordered in 1940 as the PT-19 with open cockpits and the 130.5-kW (175-hp) Ranger L-440-1 nline. These 270 aircraft proved to be only the beginning of a veritable flood, for next came 3,703 PT-19As with minor improvements and the 149-kW (200-hp) L-440-3 engine, and 917 PT-19B blind-flying trainers with a hooded front cockpit. With airframe construction outstripping Ranger supplies, the 869 PT-23s switched to the Continental R-670 radial; the PT-23A was the blind-flying equivalent of which 261 were built. For Canadian operation Fairchild developed the Ranger-engined PT-26 with a long glasshouse canopy over the two cockpits, and 1,727 of this type were built in PT-26, PT-26A and PT-26B variants named Cornell in Canada.

Specification: Fairchild PT-23A two-seat primary trainer
Span: 10.97 m (36 ft 0 in)
Length: 7.90 m (25 ft 11 in)
Powerplant: 1×Continental R-670-4, -5 or -11, 164 kW (240 hp)
Armament: none
Max T/O weight: 1111 kg (2,450 lb)
Max speed: 128 mph at sea level
Operational range: 330 miles

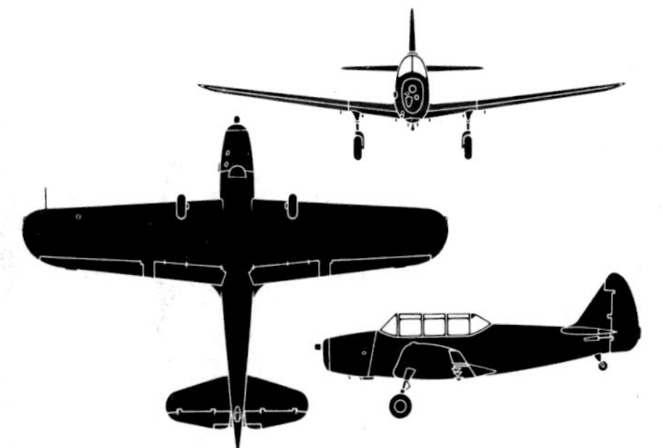

Ryan PT-20 and NR series

With Stearman and Vultee, Ryan was one of three companies selected in 1940 to produce primary trainers for the USAAC's great expansion of the period, and its initial type was the PT-16 modelled on the civil S-T with wheel spats/leg fairings, a wire-braced low-set monoplane wing, and the 93-kW (125-hp) Menasco L-365-1 inline. The 16 prototype and trials aircraft were followed by 40 improved PT-20s. Adoption of the 94-kW (132-hp) Kinner R-440-3 radial led to the PT-21, of which 10 were produced; re-engining of older aircraft with the R-440-1 produced the PT-16A and PT-20A. Next came the PT-22 Recruit with the 119-kW (160-hp) Kinner R-540-1 radial, and the 1,023 army aircraft were complemented by 100 naval equivalents designated NR. The designations PT-22A and PT-22B were applied respectively to 25 aircraft taken over from a Dutch order in 1942, and to 250 PT-22s retrofitted with the R-540-3 radial.

Specification: Ryan PT-16 two-seat primary trainer
Span: 9.14 m (30 ft 0 in)
Length: 6.55 m (21 ft 6 in)
Powerplant: 1×Menasco L-365-1, 93 kW (125 hp)
Armament: none
Max T/O weight: 726 kg (1,600 lb)
Max speed: 128 mph at sea level
Operational range: 350 miles

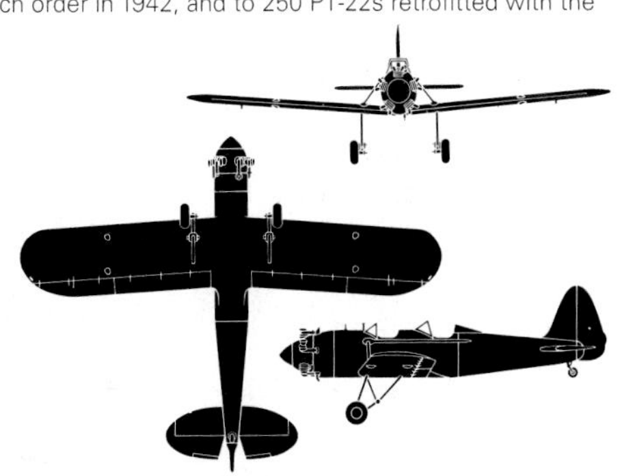

Republic AT-12

From its P-35 single-seat fighter Republic (latterly Seversky) developed the Model 2PA Guardsman two-seat escort fighter and fighter-bomber with the same type of rearward semi-retracting main landing gear units and the glazed rear portion of the cockpit expanded rearward to accommodate the second crewman. There was no US market for such an aeroplane, so the company looked for export sales. Two were sold to the USSR as 2PA-L/As, 20 2PA-B3s went to Japan with the local designation A8V1, and 52 2PA-204Ls were ordered by Sweden to supplement her J 9 fighters (P-35s sold with the company designation EP-1-06s). Early in World War II the US administration embargoed the delivery of the 2PA-204Ls to Sweden, and these were taken into the USAAC inventory as AT-12 advanced fighter trainers with the designation AT-12. The aircraft saw limited use in this role during the first part of World War II.

Specification: Republic (Seversky) AT-12 two-seat advanced fighter trainer
Span: 12.50 m (41 ft 0 in)
Length: 8.43 m (27 ft 8 in)
Powerplant: 1×Pratt & Whitney R-1830-45, 783 kW (1,050 hp)
Armament: 4 or 7×7.62-mm (0.3-in) machine-guns plus provision for up to 227 kg (500 lb) of bombs carried under the wings
Max T/O weight: 2918 kg (6,433 lb)
Max speed: 285 mph at 10,000 ft
Operational range: 1,200 miles

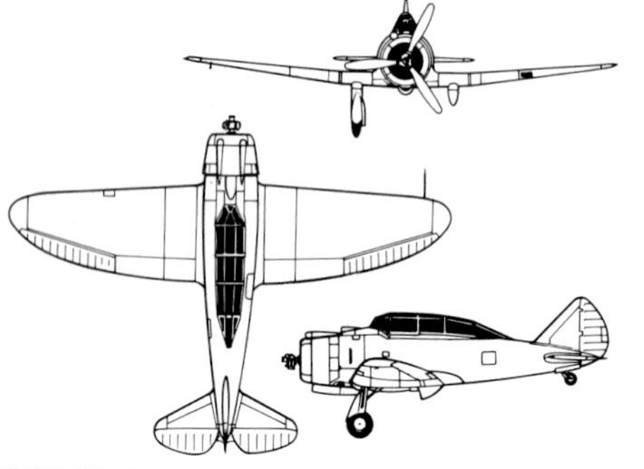

Beech AT-7 Kansan

Though the US forces used purchase-built and impressed Model 18s as light transports under the overall designations C-45 (1,401 USAAF aircraft) and JRB (377 US Navy aircraft), the same basic airframe was used in considerably larger numbers as a trainer. The USAAF's first such version was the AT-7 navigation trainer with positions for three pupils: there were 577 AT-7As with 336-kW (450-hp) R-985-25 radials, six AT-7A floatplanes, nine winterised AT-7Bs and 549 AT-7Cs with R-985-AN-3 engines. The AT-11 was a bombing and gunnery trainer with R-985-AN-1 engines, a dorsal gun position, and a revised nose with bomb-aimer's and gunner's positions: production from 1941 totalled 1,582. The US Navy procured 1,364 aircraft of basically similar types, the 320 SNB-1s approximating to the AT-11, the 509 SNB-2s being basically similar to the AT-7 and the 376 SNB-2Cs being modelled on the AT-7C.

Specification: Beech AT-11 Kansan six/seven-seat bombing and gunnery trainer
Span: 14.50 m (47 ft 8 in)
Length: 10.41 m (34 ft 2 in)
Powerplant: 2×Pratt & Whitney R-985-AN-1, 336 kW (450 hp) each
Armament: 2×7.62-mm (0.3-in) machine-guns plus provision for 10×45-kg (100-lb) bombs carried externally
Max T/O weight: 3959 kg (8,727 lb)
Max speed: 215 mph at sea level
Operational range: 850 miles

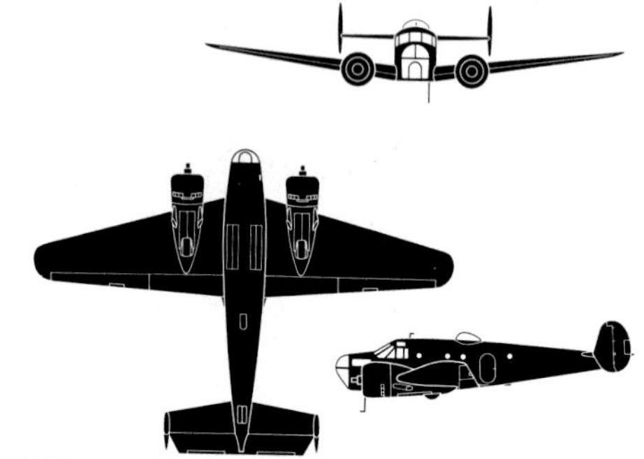

Fairchild AT-21 Gunner

The increasing importance and complexity of multi-engined aircraft fitted with power-operated turrets compelled the development for the USAAF of a specialist trainer, and such a machine appeared in the form of the all-plywood XAT-13 medium bomber crew trainer with two 447-kW (600-hp) R-1340-AN-1 radials, a ball-mounted nose gun, a turret-mounted dorsal gun, a small bomb bay and, in addition to an instructor, stations for a pilot, bomb-aimer, navigator, gunner and radio operator. The XAT-14 second prototype switched to 388-kW (520-hp) Ranger V-770-6 inlines, and this formed the basis of the AT-21 production type, which was optimised for gunnery training with a two-gun turret but no bomb bay. Production totalled 175 aircraft, and as trainer versions of front-line aircraft became available the AT-21s were relegated to alternative tasks such as target-towing.

Specification: Fairchild AT-21 Gunner five-seat gunnery trainer
Span: 16.05 m (52 ft 8 in)
Length: 11.28 m (37 ft 0 in)
Powerplant: 2×Ranger V-770-11 or -15, 388 kW (520 hp) each
Armament: 3×7.62-mm (0.3-in) machine-guns
Max T/O weight: 5670 kg (12,500 lb)
Max speed: 195 mph at 12,000 ft
Operational range: 870 miles

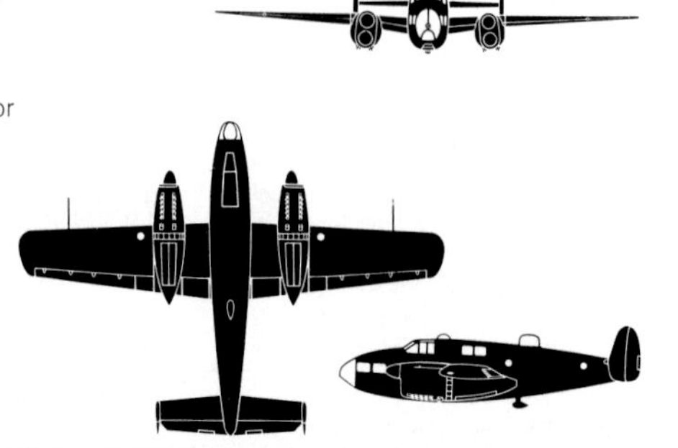

Timm N2T Tutor

Under the trade name Aeromold, the Timm Aircraft Corporation developed a special form of construction using bonded plywood. To validate the new structural medium and ultimately to provide a commercial outlet, the company produced its private-venture PT-160K cantilever low-wing trainer with tandem accommodation in open cockpits and fixed tailwheel landing gear whose main units looked very spartan with their unfaired tubular metal legs. This prototype was developed into the PT-175K for the civil market, and 262 of a modified variant with the Continental R-670 radial engine were ordered by the US Navy with the designation N2T-1, the aircraft being delivered in three batches during the course of 1943.

Specification: Timm N2T Tutor two-seat primary trainer
Span: 10.97 m (36 ft 0 in)
Length: 7.57 m (25 ft 10 in)
Powerplant: 1×Continental R-670-4, 164 kW (220 hp)
Armament: none
Max T/O weight: 1236 kg (2,725 lb)
Max speed: 144 mph at sea level
Operational range: not recorded

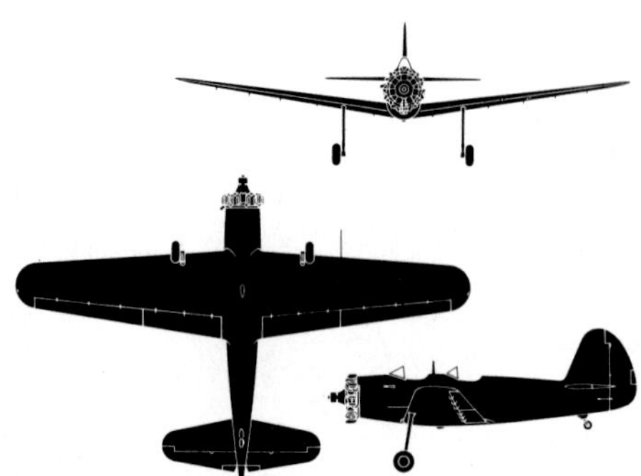

Hunting Percival P.56 Provost

The P.56 was designed as a lead-in to the de Havilland Vampire, and as such was successor to the Prentice (lead-in to the Harvard) in the basic training role. The aeroplane was an all-metal stressed-skin monoplane with fixed tailwheel landing gear and side-by-side seating, and first flew in prototype form during February 1950 with an Armstrong Siddeley Cheetah 18 radial. Trials against the Handley Page H.P.R.2 confirmed the overall superiority of the Percival design, which was adopted for service as the Provost T.Mk 1 with the Leonides radial of the type pioneered in the third prototype. Production amounted to 387 up to April 1956, and the Provost thus has the distinction of having been the last piston-engined trainer accepted for RAF service. Its major attributes were viceless aerobatic qualities and good power-to-weight ratio.

Specification: Hunting Percival Provost T.Mk 1 two-seat basic training monoplane
Span: 10.72 m (35 ft 2 in)
Length: 8.74 m (28 ft 8 in)
Powerplant: 1×Alvis Leonides 126, 410 kW (550 hp)
Normal T/O weight: 1996 kg (4,400 lb)
Cruising speed: 162 mph at 5,000 ft
Operational range: 648 miles

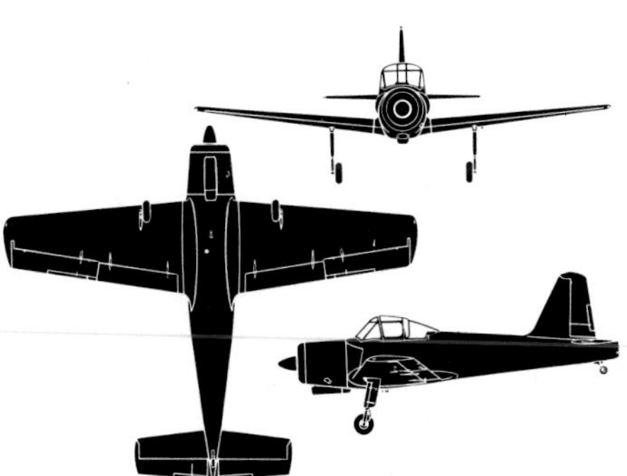

Boulton Paul P.108 Balliol

The origins of the P.108 lay with an Air Ministry requirement for a three-seat turboprop-powered advanced trainer to replace the North American Harvard, and this all-metal stressed-skin monoplane first flew in May 1947 with a 611-kW (820-hp) Bristol Mercury 30 as temporary engine; the side-by-side cockpit enclosure was heavily framed, and the tailwheel landing gear had retractable main units. The second prototype was the world's first single-turboprop aeroplane when it flew with an Armstrong Siddeley Mamba. But official interest in a turboprop-powered three-seater was waning and the P.108 was revised as the two-seat Balliol T.Mk 2 with a Merlin 35 piston engine. Four prototypes were followed by 17 pre-production aircraft and just 162 production aircraft as official interest veered towards a turbojet-powered advanced trainer.

Specification: Boulton Paul Balliol T.Mk 2 two-seat advanced training monoplane
Span: 11.99 m (39 ft 4 in)
Length: 10.71 m (35 ft 1.5 in)
Powerplant: 1×Rolls-Royce Merlin 35, 928 kW (1,245 hp)
Armament: 1×7.7-mm (0.303-in) machine-gun, plus provision for up to 4×27-kg (60-lb) rockets carried under the wings
Normal T/O weight: 3815 kg (8,410 lb)
Max speed: 288 mph at 9,000 ft
Operational range: 660 miles

Hunting P.84 Jet Provost

With the establishment of the Provost/Vampire trainer sequence, the RAF soon gave thought to a jet basic trainer that would remove the need for pupils to transition between piston- and jet-engined trainers. This had been foreseen by Hunting Percival, which offered a type based on the flying surfaces of the Provost married to a new fuselage accommodating a turbojet and tricycle landing gear. The Jet Provost T.Mk 1 was ordered in 1953, the first of 10 flying in June 1954 with a 794-kg (1,750-lb) Viper ASV.5. There followed 201 Jet Provost T.Mk 3s with the Viper Mk 102, tiptanks and lightweight ejector seats, 185 Jet Provost T.Mk 4s with the 1134-kg (2,500-lb) Viper Mk 202, and 110 Jet Provost T.Mk 5s with a pressurized cockpit and greater load-carrying capability. Retrofits with improved equipment have produced the Jet Provost T.Mk 3A and T.Mk 5A.

Specification: Hunting Percival Jet Provost T.Mk 5 two-seat basic training monoplane
Span: 10.77 m (35 ft 4 in)
Length: 10.36 m (34 ft 0 in)
Powerplant: 1×Rolls-Royce (Bristol Siddeley/Armstrong Siddeley) Viper Mk 202, 1134 kg (2,500 lb) st
Armament: provision for 2×7.62-mm (0.3-in) machine-guns, plus a wide assortment of disposable stores carried externally
Max T/O weight: 4173 kg (9,200 lb)
Max speed: 440 mph at 25,000 ft
Operational range: 900 miles

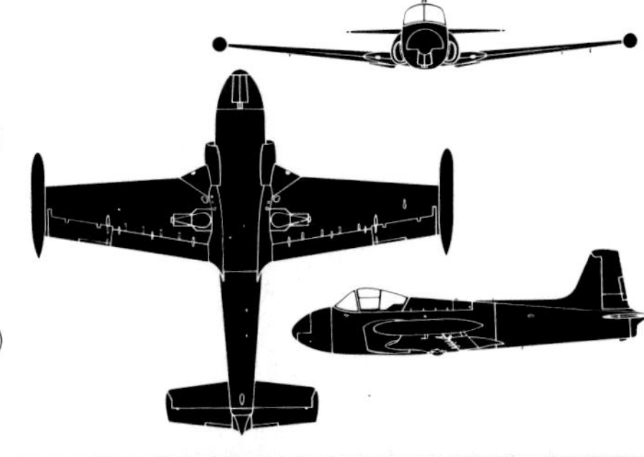

Folland Fo 141 Gnat

After developing the Fo 139 Midge with a 744-kg (1,640-lb) Viper turbojet as a high-performance fighter reversing the trend towards ever-larger and ever-costlier fighting aircraft, Teddy Petter evolved the Gnat as a more capable machine that first flew in July 1955 and secured limited export sales as well as an Indian licence-production agreement for the Ajeet variant. The RAF evaluated six Gnats in its development flying programme, and saw the potential of the type as a lively advanced trainer with a stronger airframe, a lengthened fuselage, revised inlets, a larger wing and tail unit, increased internal fuel, flaps and outboard ailerons. An initial order was placed for 14 pre-production Gnat T.Mk 1s. The first of these flew in August 1959, and later orders covered 30, 20 and finally 38 more aircraft before production ceased in 1965.

Specification: Folland Gnat T.Mk 1 two-seat advanced training monoplane
Span: 7.32 m (24 ft 0 in)
Length: 9.65 m (31 ft 9 in)
Powerplant: 1×Rolls-Royce (Bristol Siddeley) Orpheus Mk 101, 1920 kg (4,230 lb) st
Armament: provision for 454 kg (1,000 lb) of disposable stores carried on 4×underwing hardpoints
Max T/O weight: 4240 kg (9,350 lb)
Max speed: 636 mph at optimum altitude
Operational range: 1,180 miles

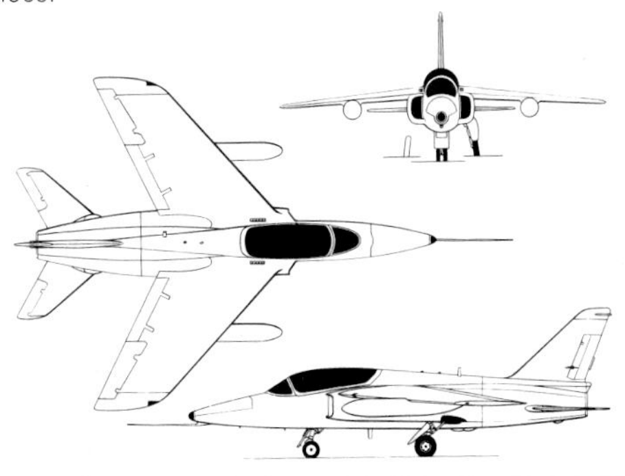

D.H.82 Tiger Moth

Developed from the D.H.60M Gipsy Moth, of which 124 were used by the RAF, the Tiger Moth was one of the world's best known trainers and remained in service with the RAF from 1932 to as late as 1951. The Tiger Moth was a comparatively straightforward development of the D.H.60M with staggered and slightly swept wings (the latter to aid a parachute-equipped pilot to escape from the front seat) and an 89.5-kW (120-hp) Gipsy III inverted engine to improve forward fields of vision. The prototype flew in October 1931 and was followed by the Tiger Moth Mk I (34 built) and the D.H.82A Tiger Moth Mk II with the Gipsy Major and a number of detail modifications such as a smooth plywood-covered rear decking in place of fabric-covered stringers and an optional blind-flying hood for the rear cockpit. Production exceeded 4,200 for the RAF, plus another 2,949 for the Commonwealth Air Training Plan.

Specification: de Havilland D.H.82A Tiger Moth Mk II elementary training biplane
Span: 8.94 m (29 ft 4 in)
Length: 7.29 m (23 ft 11 in)
Powerplant: 1×de Havilland Gipsy Major, 97 kW (130 hp)
Normal T/O weight: 803 kg (1,770 lb)
Cruising speed: 93 mph at 1,000 ft
Operational range: 302 miles

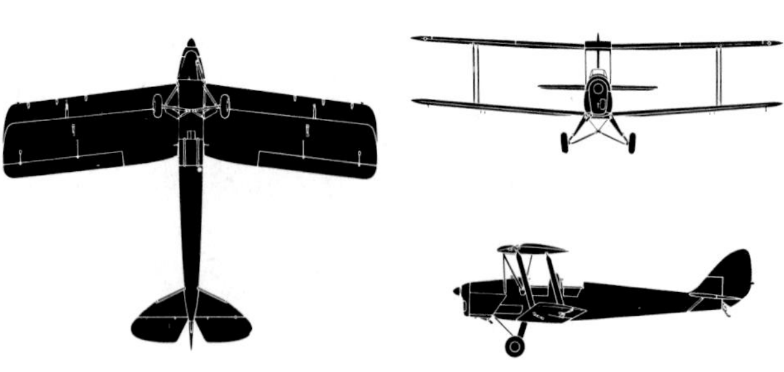

Avro Type 504N

Sometimes known as the Lynx-Avro, the Type 504N was planned as replacement for the Type 504K of 'Great War' vintage, and as such was the first trainer adopted by the RAF after World War I. Use of the Lynx radial was pioneered in two converted Type 504Ks before the two Type 504N prototypes flew, and production aircraft began to appear in 1927 with standard Type 504 features such as twin fuel tanks under the upper wing, oleo-pneumatic main landing gear units, tapered ailerons, and a rounding out of the contours of the wooden fuselage with fabric covering over stringers. Later production aircraft had a fabric-covered steel-tube fuselage and rectangular Frise ailerons. Production totalled 570 up to 1933 and, fitted with a blind-flying hood, a turn indicator and reduced dihedral, the type helped to pioneer instrument flying training. Many ex-RAF Type 504Ns passed into civil service, often with Mongoose radials.

Specification: Avro Type 504N two-seat elementary training biplane
Span: 10.97 m (36 ft 0 in)
Length: 8.69 m (28 ft 6 in)
Powerplant: 1×Armstrong Siddeley Lynx IV or IVC, 119/134 or 160 kW (160/180 or 215 hp) respectively
Normal T/O weight: 1016 kg (2,240 lb)
Cruising speed: 85 mph at 2,000 ft
Operational range: 250 miles

Avro Type 621 Tutor

The Tutor was selected in 1932 as successor to the Type 504N, the basic capability of this Avro design having been proved by 22 Armstrong Siddeley Mongoose-powered Avro Trainers that had been in service since 1930. The Tutor was of fabric-covered all-metal construction and, by comparison with the Trainer, had a different engine with a drag-reducing Townend ring (omitted from some early aircraft), low-pressure tyres and revised vertical tail surfaces. Production up to 1936 totalled 394 aircraft including 14 Type 646 Sea Tutors with twin floats and a maximum weight of 1265 kg (2,788 lb). Another variant was the 1247-kg (2,750-lb) Type 626 Prefect, a navigation trainer of which seven were delivered in 1935. The Tutor served with most flying training schools, and was also used as a communications aeroplane by the RAF and Auxiliary Air Force.

Specification: Avro Tutor two-seat elementary training biplane
Span: 10.36 m (34 ft 0 in)
Length: 8.08 m (26 ft 6 in)
Powerplant: 1×Armstrong Siddeley Lynx IVC, 160/179 kW (215/240 hp)
Normal T/O weight: 1115 kg (2,458 lb)
Cruising speed: 105 mph at 1,000 ft
Operational range: 250 miles

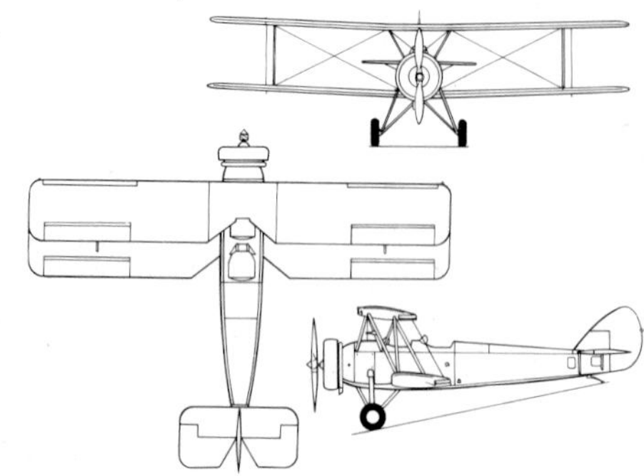

From well before World War II until after it, the Tiger Moth was the ubiquitous basic trainer with the RAF and Commonwealth air forces, training a vast amount of pilots to fuel the war effort. The pupil's rear canopy could be fitted with a hood for basic night flying training, with communication between the cockpits effected by a tube. This aircraft is seen in the post-war colours of the University of London Air Squadron, based at Fairoaks.

Miles M.14 Magister

Introduced in September 1937 as the RAF's first monoplane trainer, the Magister was unusual in being of wooden construction (plywood covering over a timber frame) to ease production and, despite having fixed tailwheel landing gear, was fitted with trailing-edge flaps to produce a very modest landing speed and to accustom new pilots to a feature that was standard on all new RAF aircraft. Many elements of the Magister's design can be traced back to the Miles civil aircraft of the early 1930s, so the Magister was a low-risk proposition. The type was fully aerobatic, could be fitted with a rear-seat blind-flying hood, and from 1938 was fitted with a larger-area rudder for better spin recovery. Production amounted to 1,293 essentially identical Mk I to Mk III aircraft, and during World War II most of these were stripped of their wheel spats.

Specification: Miles Magister Mk I two-seat elementary training monoplane
Span: 10.31 m (33 ft 10 in)
Length: 7.51 m (24 ft 7.5 in)
Powerplant: 1×de Havilland Gipsy Major 1, 97 kW (130 hp)
Armament: 8×11.3-kg (25-lb) bombs carried under the wings
Normal T/O weight: 862 kg (1,900 lb)
Cruising speed: 123 mph at 1,000 ft
Operational range: 367 miles

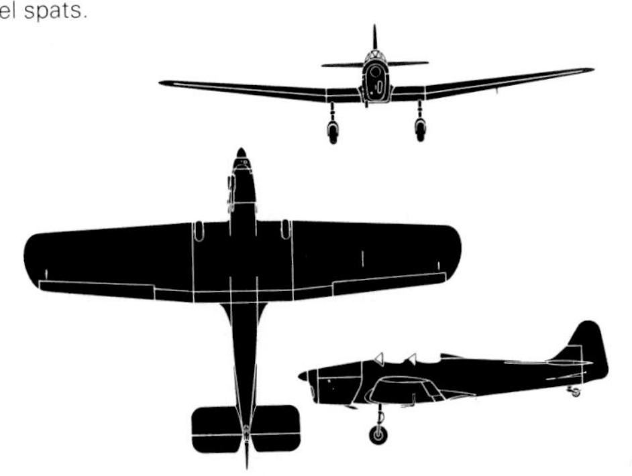

North American Harvard

One of the most important machines of its type ever developed, the NA-16 was planned as a high-performance advanced trainer and served with many air forces. The RAF gave the name Harvard to the type, which began to enter service in December 1938 and remained operational into the late 1950s. The Harvard Mk I (400 equivalents to the USAAC's BC-1) had round wingtips and a fabric-covered steel-tube rear fuselage. Next came the Harvard Mk II (1,173 equivalents to the AT-6) with blunt wingtips, triangular vertical tail, and a light alloy semi-monocoque rear fuselage, the Harvard Mk IIA (726 equivalents to the AT-6C) with a plywood rear fuselage, the Harvard Mk IIB (2,485 equivalents to the AT-6A) built in Canada, and the Harvard Mk III (351 equivalents to the AT-6D).

Specification: North American Harvard Mk IIB two-seat advanced training monoplane
Span: 12.80 m (42 ft 0.25 in)
Length: 8.84 m (29 ft 0 in)
Powerplant: 1×Pratt & Whitney R-1340-49 Wasp, 410 kW (550 hp)
Max T/O weight: 2381 kg (5,550 lb)
Cruising speed: 170 mph at 5,000 ft
Operational range: 750 miles

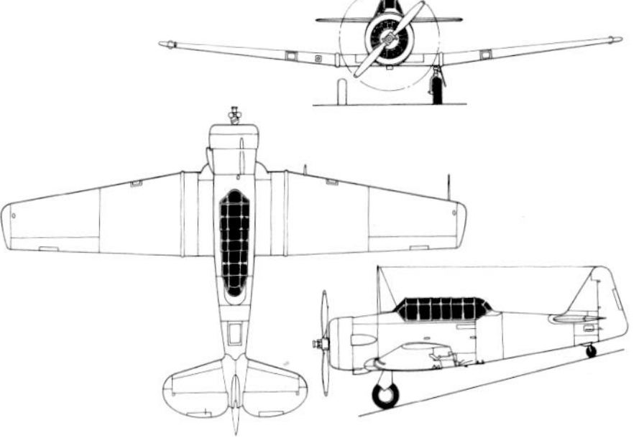

D.H.115 Vampire T.Mk 11

Like the Meteor Trainer, the Vampire Trainer started as a private venture. It was based on the all-metal stressed-skin airframe of the D.H.113 Vampire night-fighter, with the side-by-side cockpit revised for instructor and pupil with dual controls, and first flew in November 1950. Official interest was immediate, and when the Vampire T.Mk 11 began to enter service with the Royal Navy and RAF in 1952 it was the first turbojet-powered type on which pupils of those services could gain their wings. The RAF received 534 T.Mk 11s, and one of these made the type's last operational flight in November 1967. Improvements during the T.Mk 11's production run were a moulded rather than framed cockpit canopy, curved dorsal fin extensions and ejector seats, and these features were retrofitted on earlier aircraft.

Specification: de Havilland Vampire T.Mk 11 two-seat advanced training monoplane
Span: 11.58m (38ft 0in)
Length: 10.49m (34ft 5in)
Powerplant: 1×de Havilland Goblin 35, 1588kg (3,500lb) st
Armament: 2×20-mm cannon plus provision for 8×11- or 27-kg (25- or 60-lb) rockets and 2×227-kg (500-lb) bombs
Max T/O weight: 5806kg (12,800lb)
Max speed: 549 mph at 20,000ft
Operational range: 787 miles

M.9, M.19 and M.27 Master

The M.9 Master was evolved from the private-venture Kestrel as an advanced trainer offering flight characteristics comparable with those of the RAF's new monoplane fighters. The Kestrel had reached 295 mph on its 555.5-kW (745-hp) Rolls-Royce Kestrel XVI, but the Master prototype that first flew in 1938 had much inferior performance, including a maximum speed down 70 mph on that of the Kestrel, with the 533-kW (715-hp) Kestrel XXX. Production of the basically similar Master Mk I reached 900 (including 25 emergency-use Master Fighters with six machine-guns) before the M.19 Master Mk II appeared with the 649-kW (870-hp) Bristol Mercury XX radial for a maximum speed of 242 mph. Some 1,799 Mk IIs were built, and the last variant was the M.27 Master Mk III with the Wasp Junior radial. Production of 603 aircraft was followed in 1942 by that of the Martinet target-tug based on the Master.

Specification: Miles Master Mk III two-seat advanced training monoplane
Span: 10.85m (35ft 7in)
Length: 9.195m (30ft 2in)
Powerplant: 1×Pratt & Whitney Wasp Junior, 615kW (825hp)
Armament: provision for 1×7.7-mm (0.303-in) machine-gun plus practice bombs
Normal T/O weight: 2527kg (5,570lb)
Max speed: 232 mph at 7,200ft
Operational range: 320 miles

Percival P.40 Prentice

The P.40 was designed as a basic trainer, and served as the RAF's main type in this field between 1948 and 1953. An all-metal low-wing monoplane with fixed tailwheel landing gear, the prototype flew in March 1946 and marked a radical departure from its predecessors, the Tiger Moth and Magister, in having a higher power-to-weight ratio, an enclosed cockpit for all-weather operation, flaps and radio. The roomy cockpit was planned for one instructor and two pupils, but was generally used by the instructor and just one pupil seated side-by-side. Early flight trials showed inadequacy of rudder control so production Prentice T.Mk 1s had a bigger rudder, a large cut-out in the elevators and, on later aircraft, upturned wingtips. Twenty pre-production aircraft were complemented in service by 370 full-production machines.

Specification: Percival Prentice T.Mk 1 two/three-seat basic training monoplane
Span: 14.02m (46ft 0in)
Length: 9.525m (31ft 3in)
Powerplant: 1×de Havilland Gipsy Queen 32, 187kW (251hp)
Normal T/O weight: 1905kg (4,200lb)
Cruising speed: 136 mph at sea level
Operational range: 396 miles

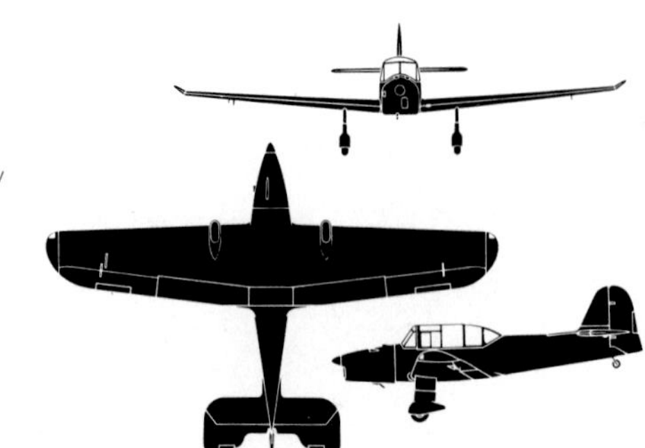

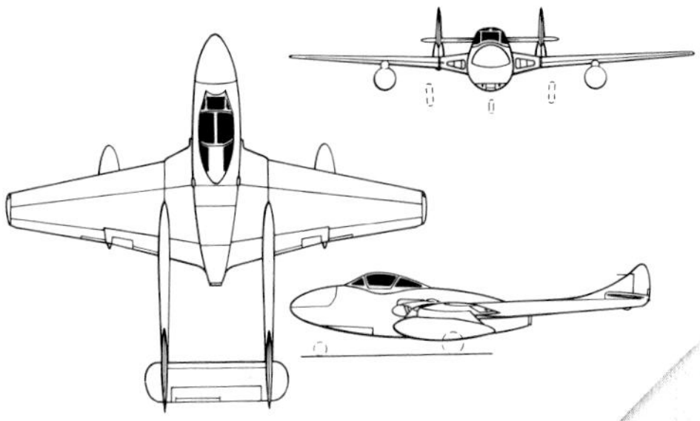

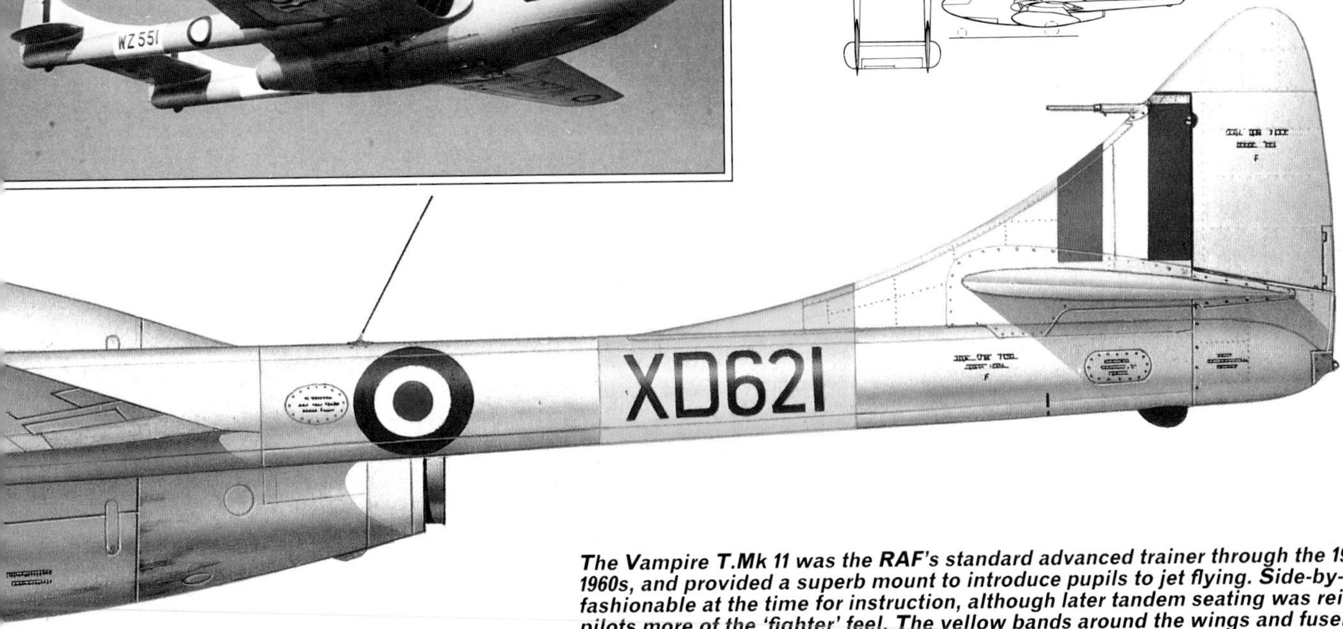

The Vampire T.Mk 11 was the RAF's standard advanced trainer through the 1950s and early 1960s, and provided a superb mount to introduce pupils to jet flying. Side-by-side seating was fashionable at the time for instruction, although later tandem seating was reintroduced to give pilots more of the 'fighter' feel. The yellow bands around the wings and fuselage booms were the standard RAF trainer markings for the day, illustrated by this example from the Central Flying School.

Gloster G.43 Meteor T.Mk 7

The RAF's first operational turbojet-powered trainer was a tandem-seat derivative of the Meteor fighter, the Meteor T.Mk 7 was developed as the private-venture Meteor Trainer and first flew in March 1948 with Derwent 5 engines for performance superior to that of the Meteor F.Mk 4 fighter. The trainer differed structurally from the basic fighter series only in having its fuselage lengthened by 0.762 m (30 in) for the insertion of the second cockpit, but carried no armament and had provision for three drop tanks as a means of extending endurance. The first Meteor T.Mk 7 for the RAF flew in October 1948, and up to July 1954 production amounted to more than 500. Later aircraft had Derwent 8 engines and the tail unit of the Meteor F.Mk 8, and the aircraft were generally used for conversion and continuation training.

Specification: Gloster Meteor T.Mk 7 two-seat advanced training monoplane
Span: 11.33 m (37 ft 2 in)
Length: 13.26 m (43 ft 6 in)
Powerplant: 2×Rolls-Royce Derwent 5, 1633 kg (3,600 lb) st each
Normal T/O weight: 7983 kg (17,600 lb)
Max speed: 585 mph at optimum altitude
Operational range: 450 miles without droptanks

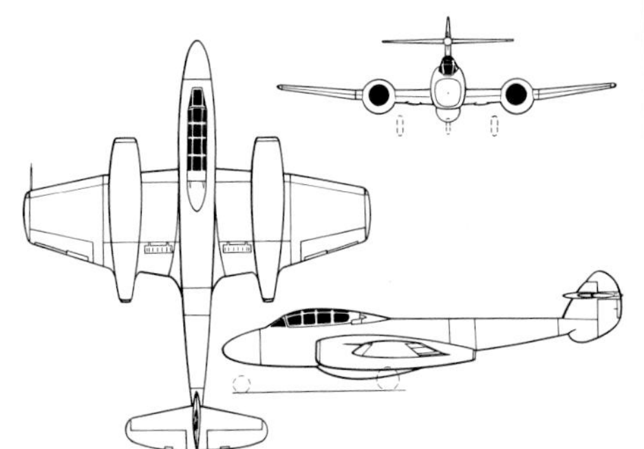

DHC-1 Chipmunk

Developed in Canada as a successor to the Tiger Moth, the Chipmunk was flown in May 1946 as an extremely neat and attractive low-wing monoplane of all-metal stressed-skin construction with fixed tailwheel landing gear and tandem accommodation for the two crew under a 'greenhouse' canopy. Production of 217 Chipmunks was undertaken in the parent country, and in 1948 the RAF decided to adopt the type as the Chipmunk T.Mk 10 with features such as blind-flying instruments, radio and a variable-pitch propeller. Deliveries to the RAF began from the British lines in 1950 and ended in October 1953 with the 735th aeroplane, production continuing to 1956 to satisfy export orders. In RAF service the Chipmunk generally took over from the Prentice, and small numbers survive with units such as Air Experience Flights.

Specification: de Havilland Canada Chipmunk T.Mk 10 two-seat elementary training monoplane
Span: 10.45 m (34 ft 4 in)
Length: 7.75 m (25 ft 4 in)
Powerplant: 1×de Havilland Gipsy Major 1C, 108 kW (145 hp)
Normal T/O weight: 907 kg (2,000 lb)
Cruising speed: 119 mph at sea level
Operational range: 300 miles

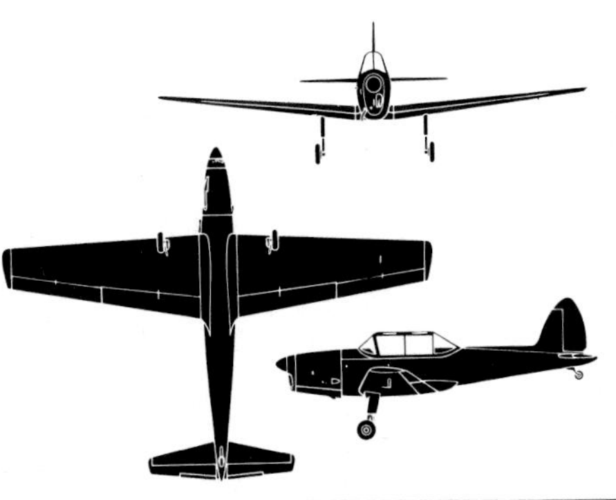

British Aerospace Bulldog

Beagle was successor to the Auster firm, and in April 1967 flew the first example of the B.121 Pup two-seater with which it hoped to secure a firm niche in world lightplane manufacture. The type was a delight, and offered in variants with power between 75 and 119kW (100 and 160hp). In May 1969 the company flew its military derivative, the B.125 Bulldog. This was taken over by Scottish Aviation (now the Scottish Division of British Aerospace) when Beagle collapsed in 1970, and eventually some 340 military trainers of this basic type were produced in Series 100 and improved Series 120 variants. The Bulldog T.Mk 1s of the RAF are of the Series 120 variety. Scottish Aviation also flew one example of the Series 200, a derivative of the Series 120 with retractable landing gear, but this did not enter production.

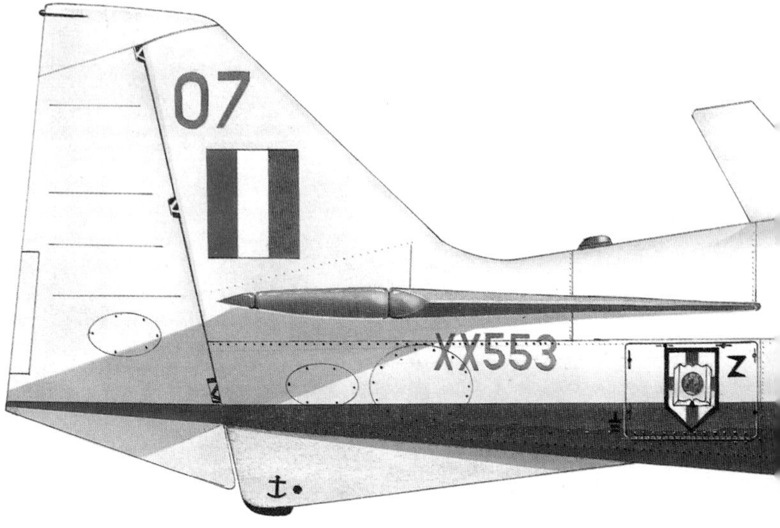

Specification: British Aerospace Bulldog T.Mk 1 two/three-seat primary training monoplane
Span: 10.06m (33ft 0in)
Length: 7.09m (23ft 3in)
Powerplant: 1×Avco Lycoming IO-360-A1B6, 149kW (200hp)
Armament: normally none, but provision is made for up to 290kg (640lb) of disposable stores on 4×underwing hardpoints
Max T/O weight: 1066kg (2,350lb)
Max speed: 150mph at sea level
Operational range: 621 miles

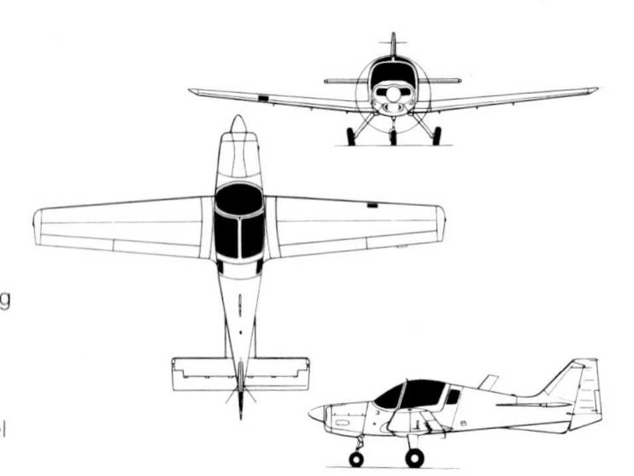

Aérospatiale Epsilon

The Epsilon was developed as the TB-30 to meet a French air force requirement for a light trainer to weed out unsuitable candidates before the beginning of basic training on the jet-powered Magister. The design was refined over a period of several years with an all-metal airframe possessing a life of not less than 10,000 hours in the exacting flying training role, a jet-type cockpit, and avionics for the full range of flying training including IFR flight and aerobatics. First flown in December 1978 for delivery from 1982 after construction at Socata, a subsidiary of the parent company, the basic version has no armament provision. The export model received by Togo has four hardpoints. An Epsilon is also being used as test-bed for the Turbomeca TP319 turboprop, opening the possibility that the Epsilon could be marketed or retrofitted with such an engine.

Specification: Aérospatiale Epsilon two-seat primary training monoplane
Span: 7.90m (25ft 11in)
Length: 7.60m (24ft 11.25in)
Powerplant: 1×Avco Lycoming AEIO-540-K, 224kW (300hp)
Armament: provision for up to 300kg (661lb) of disposable stores on 4×underwing hardpoints
Max T/O weight: 1190kg (2,623lb)
Max speed: 221mph at sea level
Operational range: 808 miles

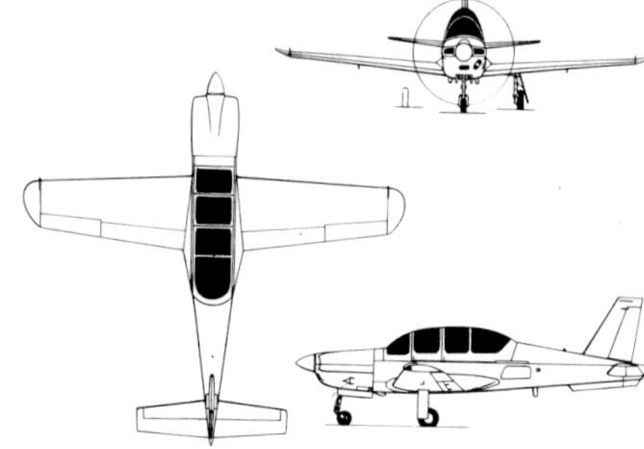

Beech T-34 Mentor

The Mentor was first flown in December 1948 as a derivative of the Bonanza with tandem seats and a conventional tail. In 1950 the USAF evaluated three YT-34s and chose this Beech aeroplane for production as the T-34A primary trainer with a 168-kW (225-hp) Continental O-470-13 piston engine: production totalled 450, another 423 similar T-34Bs going to the US Navy. In 1973 the US Navy decided that its future training requirement could best be met by the Mentor, albeit with turboprop powerplant. This was evaluated from September 1973 as the YT-34C with a torque-limited PT6A-25, and led to production of 353 T-34Cs, with structural strengthening for a 16,000-hour life, between 1977 and 1990. Beech also developed an uprated T-34C-1 version with four hardpoints for 544kg (1,200lb) of stores and an unarmed Turbine Mentor 34C, both securing export sales.

Specification: Beech T-34C Mentor two-seat primary training monoplane
Span: 10.16m (33ft 4in)
Length: 8.75m (28ft 8.5in)
Powerplant: 1×533-kW (715-shp) Pratt & Whitney Canada PT6A-25, torque- limited to 298kW (400 shp)
Armament: none
Max T/O weight: 1950kg (4,300lb)
Max speed: 246mph at 17,000ft
Operational range: 814 miles

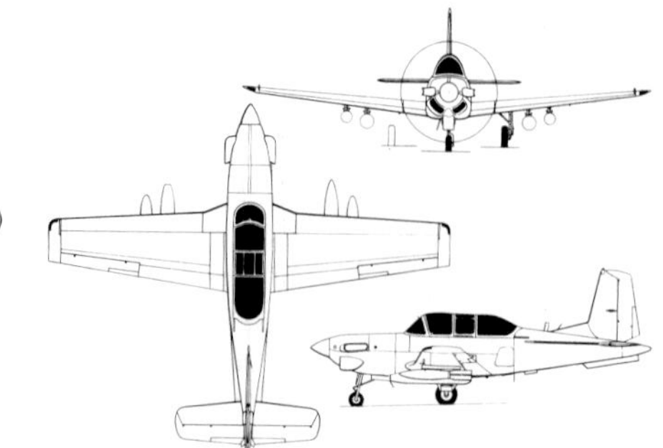

The Scottish Aviation Bulldog replaced the Chipmunk with the RAF's 17 University Air Squadrons, and a handful are also used for the basic flying training of Royal Navy pilots. The aircraft is rugged enough to withstand the rigours of the basic military training role and is a pleasant aerobatic mount. Derived from the Beagle Pup, the Bulldog achieved some export success, being exported to Sweden, Jordan, Hong Kong, Malaysia, Botswana, Kenya, Nigeria, Ghana, and the Lebanon.

ENAER T-35 Pillan

Though known by the name of its Chilean manufacturer and by its Chilean air force designation, the Pillan was in fact developed in the USA by Piper on the basis of the PA-28 Dakota and PA-321 Saratoga lightplanes to a Chilean requirement that emphasised development of the country's nascent aero industry as much as the training and counter-insurgency capabilities of the resulting aeroplane. The first two Piper-built prototypes flew in 1981, followed in 1982 by the first Chilean-built example. Production started in 1985, and current variants are the T-35A primary and T-35B instrument trainers for Chile, the T-34C for Spain, the T-35D for Panama and the T-35S aerobatic single-seater. Further development of the turboprop-powered T-35TX Aucan with an Allison 250-B17D was discontinued in 1987 despite earlier plans to begin production in 1988.

Specification: ENAER T-35A Pillan two-seat basic training monoplane
Span: 8.81 m (28 ft 11 in)
Length: 7.97 m (26 ft 1.75 in)
Powerplant: 1×Avco Lycoming AEIO-540-H1K5, 224 kW (300 hp)
Armament: provision for up to 227 kg (500 lb) of disposable stores on 2×underwing hardpoints
Max T/O weight: 1315 kg (2,900 lb)
Max speed: 193 mph at sea level
Operational range: 789 miles

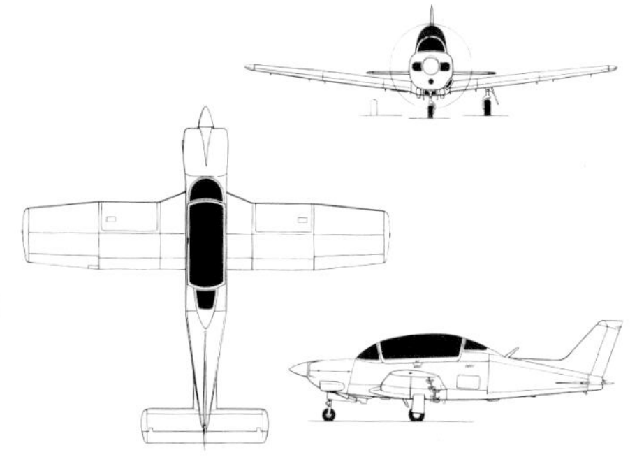

Fuji KM-2B and T-3

In 1952 Japan was permitted to resume aircraft production, and in the following year Fuji was established as successor to the Nakajima company of World War II fame. The new company's first venture was the Beech 45 Mentor built under licence, and from this the company evolved a four/five-seat utility type used by the military as the LM, and by civil operators as the KM. In 1962 Fuji introduced the KM-2 side-by-side trainer version, and in September 1974 the wheel came full circle when there appeared the first KM-2B military trainer with tandem seating like that of the T-34A: this was adopted as the KM-2B and T-3 respectively by the Japanese Maritime and Air Self-Defence Forces. Fuji then moved to turboprop power in the form of the 317-kW (425-shp) Allison 250-B17, and the JMSDF has ordered this latest model as the KM-2B Kai, the first examples being delivered in 1988.

Specification: Fuji KM-2B two-seat primary training monoplane
Span: 10.01 m (32 ft 10 in)
Length: 8.03 m (26 ft 4.25 in)
Powerplant: 1×Avco Lycoming IGSO-480-A1F6, 254 kW (340 hp)
Armament: none
Max T/O weight: 1542 kg (3,400 lb)
Max speed: 228 mph at 8,000 ft
Operational range: 600 miles

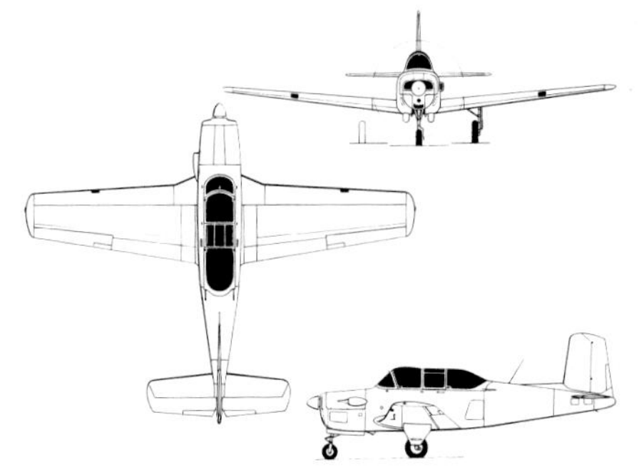

Pilatus PC-9

Developed from 1983 as contender in the British competition to find a successor to the Jet Provost, the PC-9 is a straightforward development of the PC-7 with greater power, a four- rather than three-blade propeller, slightly reduced span, a ventral airbrake, larger ailerons, a longer dorsal fin, and a redesigned cockpit offering more-advanced avionics, a higher position for the instructor in the rear seat, and Martin-Baker Mk 11 zero/zero ejector seats for the two crew members. The first PC-9 flew in May 1984 and revealed much improved performance over the PC-7, especially in low-level factors such as speed, rate of climb and time to height. The PC-9 was losing finalist to the EMBRAER Tucano in the RAF competition, but has gone on to notch up a number of useful sales to a current five overseas customers, including Australia which is building the PC-9/A under licence.

Specification: Pilatus PC-9 two-seat multi-role training monoplane
Span: 10.12 m (33 ft 2.4 in)
Length: 10.18 m (33 ft 4.8 in)
Powerplant: 1×857-kW (1,150-shp) Pratt & Whitney Canada PT6A-62, flat-rated to 708 kW (950 shp)
Armament: provision for up to 1040 kg (2,293 lb) of disposable stores carried on 6×underwing hardpoints
Max T/O weight: 3200 kg (7,055 lb)
Max speed: 345 mph at 20,000 ft
Operational range: 955 miles

EMBRAER EMB-312 Tucano

In recent years Brazil has emerged as a major aircraft manufacturer, and one of its most successful offerings has been the EMB-312 Tucano (toucan). Work began in 1978 to a Brazilian air force requirement for a high-performance basic trainer with armament capability, and the first example flew in August 1980 as an attractive low-wing monoplane with a single-piece canopy over twin ejector seats, the rear unit raised to afford the instructor an unobstructed forward view. The type was ordered into production for Brazil as the T-27, and a comparative spate of export orders has followed. The most important of these is for the British Tucano T.Mk 1 (over 120 aircraft), a variant built by Shorts with a number of modifications including an 820-kW (1,100-shp) Garrett TPE331 turboprop. Other major operators are Egypt (80 aircraft) and Iraq (100 aircraft), while Brazil has 168 in service or on order.

Specification: EMBRAER EMB-312 Tucano two-seat basic training monoplane
Span: 11.14 m (36 ft 6.5 in)
Length: 9.86 m (32 ft 4.25 in)
Powerplant: 1×559-kW (750-shp) Pratt & Whitney Canada PT6A-25C, flat-rated to 436 kW (585 hp)
Armament: provision for 1000 kg (2,205 lb) of disposable stores carried on 4×underwing hardpoints
Max T/O weight: 3175 kg (7,000 lb)
Max speed: 254 mph at 13,500 ft
Operational range: 1,190 miles

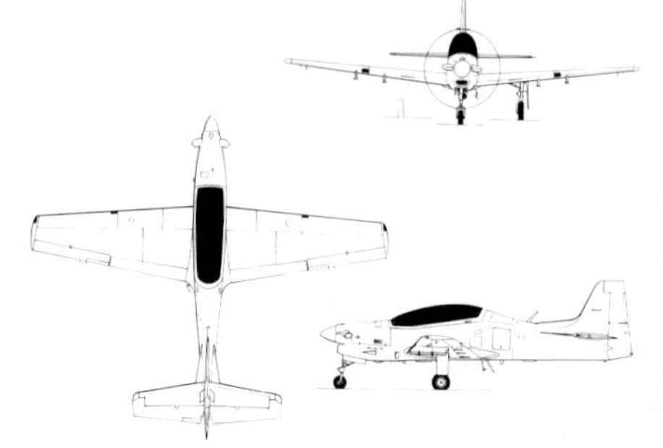

Hindustan Aeronautics Ltd HPT-32

Featuring fully aerobatic capability, the HPT-32 is an unexceptional trainer of typical low-wing configuration and light alloy construction. The type was planned as a multi-role successor to the HT-2 with side-by-side rather than the earlier aeroplane's tandem seating, and first flew in January 1977. Subsequent development was very protracted, and deliveries began only in 1985 against an Indian air force order for 50. There is room in the cockpit for third and fourth seats, allowing the type to be used in the liaison role, and the HPT-32 can also be used for glider or target towing. In June 1984 the manufacturer flew the first example of the HTT-34 variant with an Allison 250-B-17D turboprop, and the Indian air force may take 90 of this model. Plans for a version with retractable landing gear appear to have been dropped indefinitely.

Specification: HAL HPT-32 two/three-seat basic training monoplane
Span: 9.50 m (31 ft 2 in)
Length: 7.72 m (25 ft 3.9 in)
Powerplant: 1×Avco Lycoming AEIO-540 D4B5, 194 kW (260 hp)
Armament: provision for up to 255 kg (562 lb) of disposable stores carried on 4×underwing hardpoints
Max T/O weight: 1250 kg (2,756 lb)
Max speed: 157 mph at 10,000 ft
Operational range: 463 miles

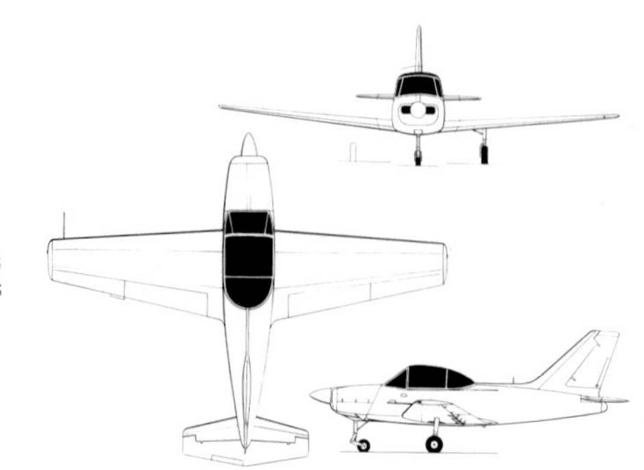

The Pilatus PC-9 has been called the 'aircraft the RAF really wanted', and it was certainly a strong contender in the competition for an RAF Jet Provost replacement, before being rejected on political and economic grounds. Burma, Saudi Arabia, Australia, Iraq and Angola have placed orders for this superb trainer, however.

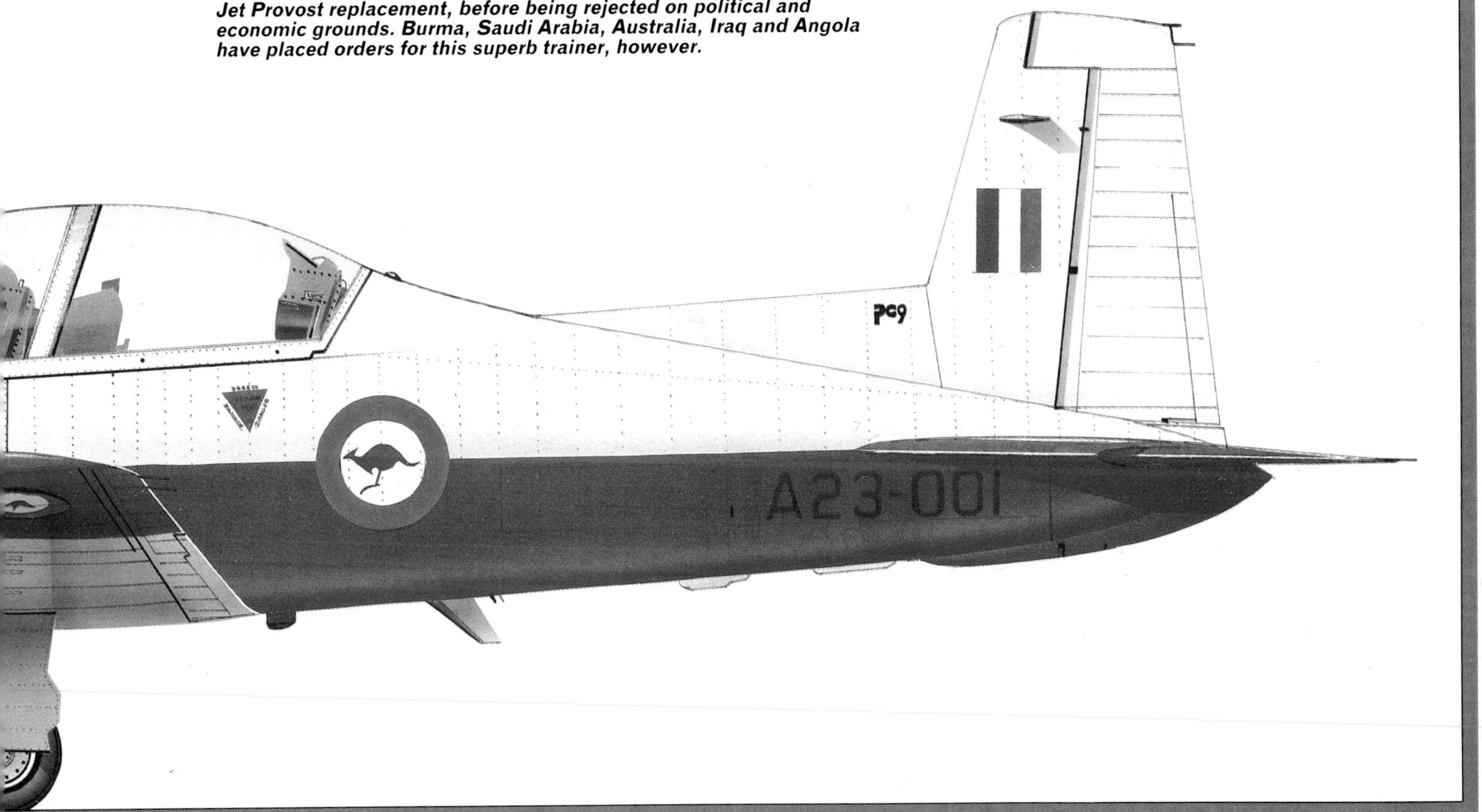

Neiva T-25 Universal

The Universal was designed from the early 1960s to meet a Brazilian air force requirement for a North American T-6 replacement with full aerobatic and light armament capabilities. The result was an attractive low-wing monoplane of light alloy construction with side-by-side seats and retractable tricycle landing gear. The N621 prototype flew in April 1966, and in 1968 the type was ordered for the Brazilian air force with the designation T-25. Deliveries of 150 aircraft took place between 1971 and 1975, another 28 Brazilian and 10 Chilean aircraft following later in the decade. It was planned that the T-25 should be complemented by an improved T-25B (N622 Universal II) with greater attack capability bestowed by a 298-kW (400-hp) IO-720 engine and six underwing hardpoints, but this was overtaken by the Tucano.

Specification: Neiva T-25 Universal two/three-seat basic training monoplane
Span: 11.00 m (36 ft 1 in)
Length: 8.60 m (28 ft 2.5 in)
Powerplant: 1×Avco Lycoming IO-540-K1D5, 224 kW (300 hp)
Armament: provision for light armament on 2×underwing hardpoints
Max T/O weight: 1700 kg (3,747 lb)
Max speed: 186 mph at sea level
Operational range: 621 miles

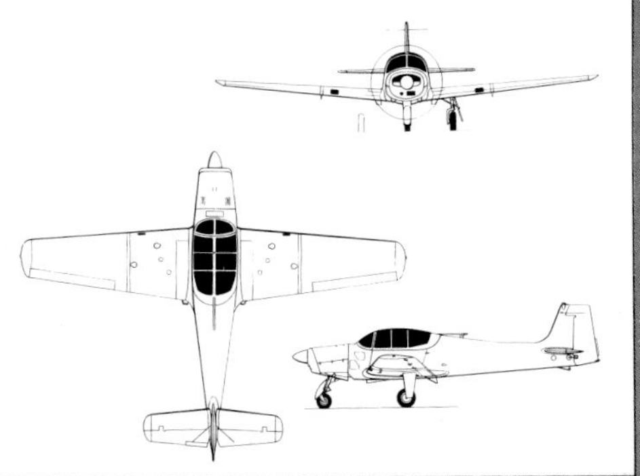

Pilatus PC-7 Turbo-Trainer

Given its experience in converting the piston-engined PC-6 Porter into the turboprop-powered PC-6 Turbo-Porter, Pilatus saw considerable promise in a turbine-powered version of its P-3 trainer. Initially known as the P-3B and then PC-7, this first flew in April 1966. Oddly enough there were no orders for several years, and the first production aeroplane flew only in August 1978, orders then increasing to a useful extent for a current total of 14 military operators. The two crew are seated in tandem under a rearward sliding and jettisonable canopy, and new-production aircraft are offered with the option of Martin-Baker Mk 15 lightweight ejector seats, which can be retrofitted on older aircraft. The type can also be fitted with external hardpoints for the carriage of a significant load in the weapons training and/or light attack roles.

Specification: Pilatus PC-7 Turbo-Trainer two-seat multi-role training monoplane
Span: 10.40 m (34 ft 1.5 in)
Length: 9.78 m (32 ft 0.75 in)
Powerplant: 1×485-kW (650-shp) Pratt & Whitney Canada PT6A-25A, flat-rated to 410 kW (550 shp)
Armament: provision for up to 1040 kg (2,293 lb) of disposable stores carried on 6×underwing hardpoints
Max T/O weight: 2770 kg (6,107 lb)
Max speed: 256 mph at 20,000 ft
Operational range: 1,634 miles

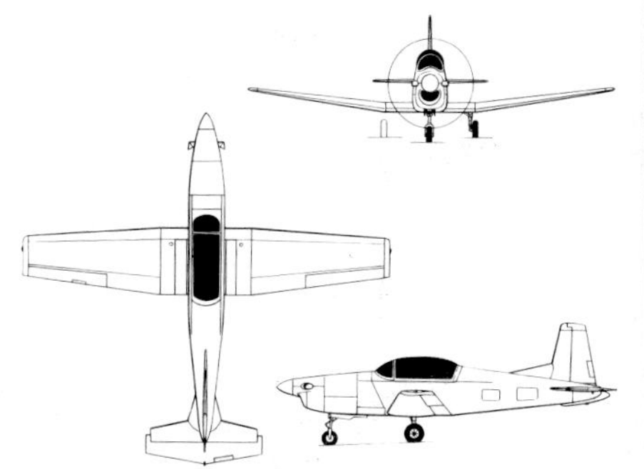

SIAI-Marchetti SF.260

Designed by Stelio Frati and developed to prototype form by Aviamilano, the F.250 first flew in July 1964 and was then entrusted to SIAI-Marchetti for production as the more powerful SF.260. The type is a neat low-wing monoplane of light alloy construction with retractable landing gear, and remains in production in three forms. The basic trainer is the SF.260M with a 194-kW (260-hp) O-540 piston engine, and this paved the way for an armed derivative, the SF.260W Warrior, suitable for the weapons training and counter-insurgency roles with underwing armament. The latest version is the armament-capable SF.260TP with turboprop power in the form of a 261-kW (350-shp) Allison 250-B17C. This last version is 7.40 m (24 ft 3.25 in) long and offers all-round advantages in performance as well as the handling advantages of turbine power.

Specification: SIAI-Marchetti SF.260W Warrior two-seat basic flying and weapon training monoplane
Span: 8.35 m (27 ft 4.7 in) over tiptanks
Length: 7.10 m (23 ft 3.5 in)
Powerplant: 1×Avco Lycoming O-540-E4A5, 194 kW (260 hp)
Armament: provision for up to 300 kg (661 lb) of disposable stores carried on 4×underwing hardpoints
Max T/O weight: 1300 kg (2,866 lb)
Max speed: 190 mph at sea level
Operational range: 1,066 miles

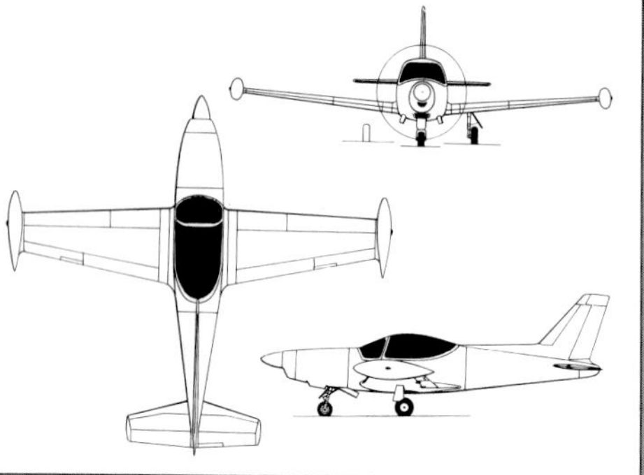

Valmet L-70 Vinka

Intended to supersede the Saab 91 in the basic training role, the Leko-70 was designed from 1970 as a low-wing monoplane with fixed tricycle landing gear and side-by-side seating under a large rearward-sliding canopy. Soon after the prototype flew in July 1975 the name was altered to L-70 Miltrainer, and 30 of these were ordered by the Finnish air force with the name Vinka: deliveries were made between 1980 and 1982. Valmet has also produced a turboprop version known as the L-80TP in its intermediate stage with four seats, retractable landing gear and slightly enlarged dimensions, and finally as the L-90TP Redigo. This has been flown with the 313-kW (420-hp) Allison 250-B17D and 358-kW (480-shp) Turbomeca TM319, the former being planned for the 10 aircraft wanted by the Finnish air force. The L-90TP has provision for 800 kg (1,764 lb) of disposable stores on six underwing hardpoints.

Specification: Valmet L-70 Vinka two-seat basic training monoplane
Span: 9.63 m (31 ft 7.1 in)
Length: 7.50 m (24 ft 7.3 in)
Powerplant: 1×Avco Lycoming AEIO-360-A1B6, 149 kW (200 hp)
Armament: provision for up to 300 kg (661 lb) of disposable stores carried on 4×underwing hardpoints
Normal T/O weight: 1040 kg (2,293 lb)
Max speed: 146 mph at sea level
Operational range: 590 miles

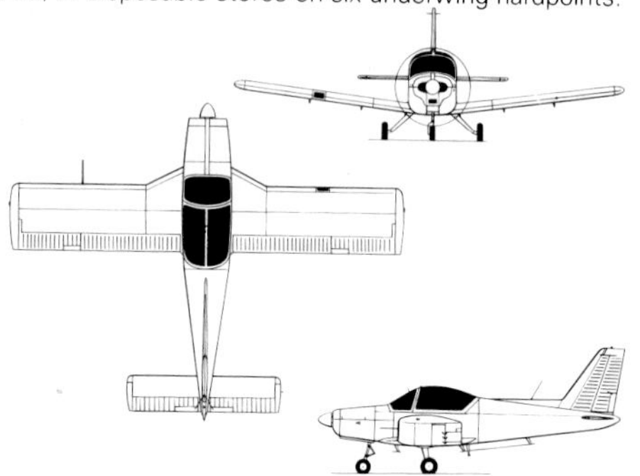

Yakovlev Yak-52

Using many features of the Yak-18, the Yak-50 aerobatic monoplane was introduced in 1976 and proved enormously successful in the World Aerobatic Championships of the same year. From the Yak-50 was evolved the Yak-52 primary trainer that is basically similar to the Yak-50 apart from its tandem two-seat accommodation and different semi-retractable landing gear, modified from the Yak-50's tailwheel type to a tricycle arrangement with the nosewheel unit retracting rearward and the main units forward. After development in the USSR, the type was handed over to IAv Bacau in Romania for production: deliveries began in 1979, and by 1986 well over 500 examples had been delivered to Warsaw Pact air forces. There is also a Yak-53 aerobatic trainer, this being based on the Yak-52 but reverting to the single-seat configuration of the Yak-50.

Specification: Yakovlev Yak-52 two-seat primary training monoplane
Span: 9.30 m (30 ft 6.25 in)
Length: 7.745 m (25 ft 5 in)
Powerplant: 1×Vedeneyev M-14P, 268 kW (360 hp)
Armament: none
Max T/O weight: 1290 kg (2,844 lb)
Max speed: 186 mph at 1,640 ft
Operational range: 341 miles

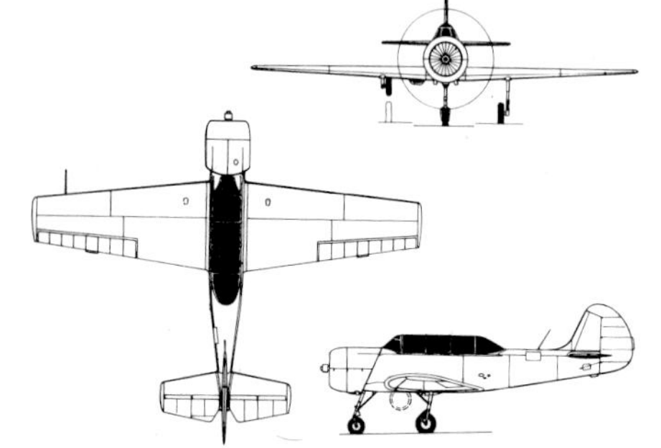

Zlin 42 and 142

Designed as a two-seat light touring aeroplane with full training capability, the Zlin 42 was planned in the mid-1960s as a type of unusual appearance because of its slightly forward-swept wings. Otherwise the aeroplane was a conventional low-wing monoplane primarily of light alloy construction with fixed tricycle landing gear. The crew of two was seated side-by-side in a well-glazed cockpit with side doors, and the first example flew in October 1967 with the 134-kW (180-hp) Avia M137A piston engine. A four-seat version that first flew in December 1968 with the 157-kW (210-hp) M337 engine was designated Zlin 43, and the same powerplant was used in the improved Zlin 42M. This in turn paved the way for the Zlin 142 that first flew in December 1978 as a multi-purpose and aerobatic trainer with better levels of instrumentation and an optional IFR capability.

Specification: Zlin 142 two-seat touring and training monoplane
Span: 9.16 m (30 ft 0.6 in)
Length: 7.33 m (24 ft 0.6 in)
Powerplant: 1×Walter M337K, 157 kW (210 hp)
Armament: none
Normal T/O weight: 970 kg (2,138 lb)
Max speed: 144 mph at 1,640 ft
Operational range: 326 miles

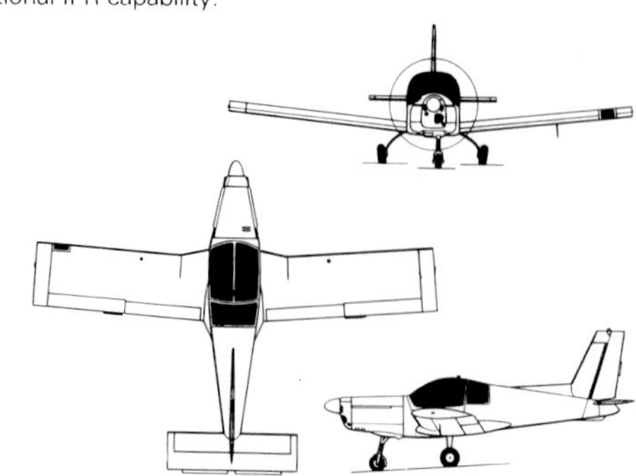

Mitsubishi T-2

The last of 94 T-2s was delivered to the Japanese Air Self-Defense Force (the sole customer) in March 1988, completing the equipment of 4 Kokudan (4th Air Wing) at Matsushima. T-2s provide the last 140 hours of Japanese pilot training after earlier instruction on piston-engined Fuji T-3s and jet-powered Fuji T-1s and Lockheed T-33s. As well as Nos 21 and 22 Hikotai (squadrons), 4 Wing includes the *Blue Impulse* national aerobatic team, which re-equipped with T-2s in 1982. T-2 training involves weapon instruction on the armed (20-mm Vulcan cannon) T-2 *Zenki*, or T-2A model – the remainder being unarmed T-2 *Koki* variants. Two early production T-2s (not included in the total of 94) were converted to single-seat attack prototypes of the Mitsubishi F-1.

Specification: Mitsubishi T-2A two-seat weapons trainer
Span: 7.88 m (25 ft 10.25 in)
Length: 17.68 m (58 ft 7 in)
Powerplant: 2×Rolls-Royce/Turboméca Adour Mk 801A, 3207 kg (7,070 lb) st each
Armament: 1×20-mm rotary cannon, 2×AAMs and an unrevealed weight of disposable stores
Max speed: Mach 1.6 at 36,000 ft
Range: not revealed

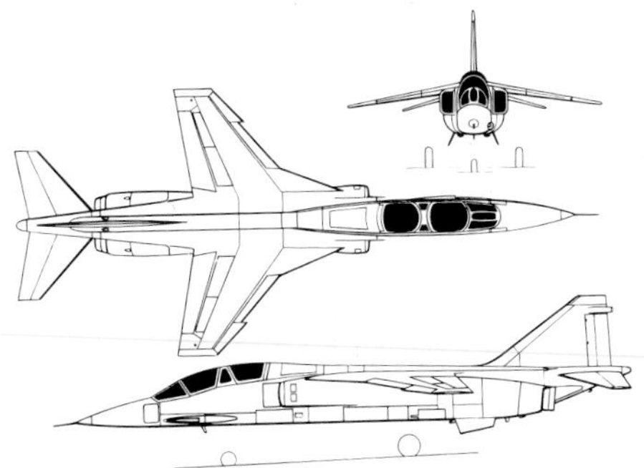

Northrop T-38A Talon

The advanced stage of the USAF pilot training course comprises 105 hours on the T-38A as a prelude to operational training, in which the same aircraft also plays a significant part. Beginning in 1961, USAF Air Training Command received 1,187 examples of the world's first purpose-designed supersonic trainer, although the syllabus calls for only a minute fraction of the time to be flown in excess of Mach 1.0. Some 890 T-38s remain in current service (17 went to the US navy, 34 to NASA, 12 to Portugal and 30 to Turkey), of which 115 were converted to AT-38B armament trainers, with underwing pylons, for Tactical Air Command's 479th TTW at Holloman AFB under the Fighter Lead-In Trainer programme. Students from many NATO countries are trained by USAF T-37/T-38 schools.

Specification: Northrop T-38A Talon two-seat advanced and weapons trainer
Span: 7.70 m (25 ft 3 in)
Length: 14.13 m (46 ft 4.5 in)
Powerplant: 2×General Electric J85-GE-5A, 1746 kg (3,850 lb) st each
Armament: rockets and practice bombs
Max speed: Mach 1.23+ at 36,000 ft
Range: 1,100 miles

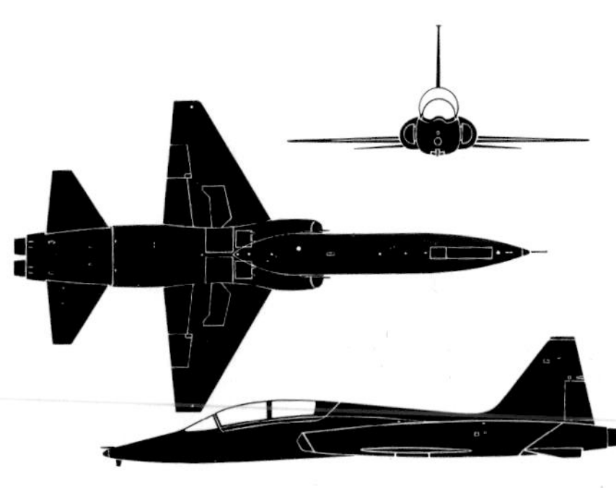

SIAI-Marchetti S.211

Conceived as a low-cost, economic-to-operate trainer, the S.211 first flew in 1981. Extensive use is made of composite materials (61 per cent of external surfaces) to reduce weight, although the optional weapons load on the four underwing hardpoints is modest. Marketing the S.211 without the benefit of a home air force order, SIAI-Marchetti succeeded in selling 30 to Singapore, all but the first six of which are being assembled locally by Singapore Aircraft Industries for No. 131 Squadron at Paya Lebar. Four more were delivered to Haiti in 1985, although they were offered for sale two years later, two of them still in their crates. Development is proceeding with an undisclosed partner of a 'stretched' version of the design.

Specification: SIAI-Marchetti S.211 two-seat basic trainer
Span: 8.43 m (27 ft 8 in)
Length: 9.31 m (30 ft 6.5 in)
Powerplant: 1×Pratt & Whitney Canada JT15D-4C 1134 kg (2,500 lb) st
Armament: up to 660 kg (1,455 lb) of disposable stores
Max speed: 414 mph at 25,000 ft
Endurance: 4 hours 20 minutes

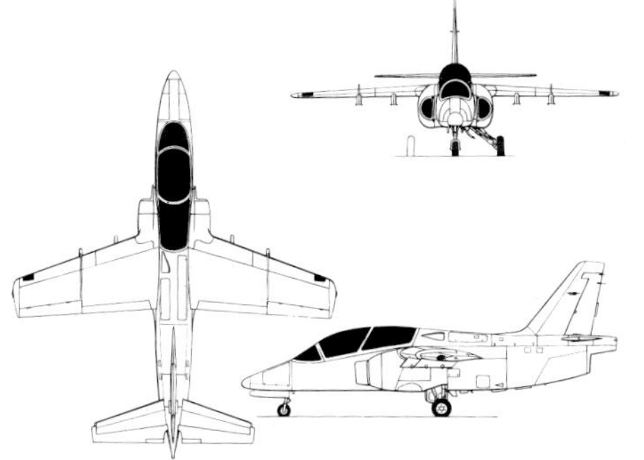

SOKO G-4 Super Galeb

Intended to replace the G-2 Galeb and Lockheed T-33 basic/advanced trainer in Yugoslav service, the G-4 differs substantially from its namesake, though retaining its reliable yet uneconomic turbojet. Flown for the first time in 1978, the Super Galeb entered service in 1982, flying initially with the basic school at Mostar and, from 1985, the weapon-training unit at Pula. Student pilots progress to the aircraft after primary instruction on UTVA-75s. Armament capability for emergency defensive service was an integral part of the G-4 specification, and production is expected to total some 200. Despite low production costs, the Super Galeb has been unable to secure an export order, although small-scale deliveries are possible to left-leaning third-world countries.

Specification: SOKO G-4 Super Galeb two-seat trainer and attack aircraft
Span: 9.88 m (32 ft 5 in)
Length: 11.86 m (38 ft 11 in)
Powerplant: 1×Rolls-Royce Viper Mk 632, 1814 kg (4,000 lb) st
Armament: up to 1950 kg (4,299 lb) of stores including a ventral twin 23-mm cannon pack
Max speed: 565 mph at 19,685 ft
Endurance: 4 hours 20 minutes

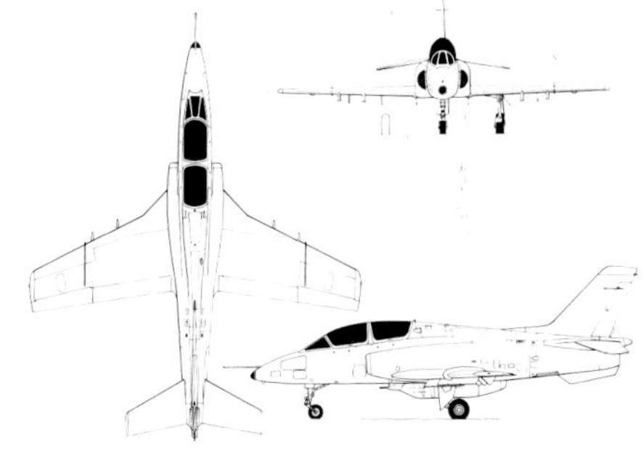

BAe Hawk T.Mk 1A

Specification: BAe Hawk T.Mk 1A two-seat advanced trainer, light attack and air-defence aircraft
Span: 9.39 m (30 ft 9.75 in)
Length: 11.86 m (38 ft 11 in)
Powerplant: 1×Rolls-Royce/ Turboméca Adour Mk 151, 2422 kg (5,340 lb) st
Armament: 1×30-mm cannon, 2×AIM-9 Sidewinder AAMs and up to 3084 kg (6,800 lb) of disposable stores
Max speed: 630 mph at low altitude
Endurance: about 4 hours 30 minutes

Designed to meet an RAF specification for an advanced instructional aircraft and weapons trainer, the Hawk has been adapted for the dedicated attack role and is even due to provide aircraft carrier training for US Navy pilots. Following from the Jet Provost (or Tucano) course, RAF students fly Hawks for 60 hours of advanced training, then 54 hours of weapons practice. The RAF has converted 88 of its Hawk T.Mk 1s to Mk 1A standard (including those of the *Red Arrows* national aerobatic team) to carry two Sidewinder missiles for emergency air defence duties. Other operators comprise Abu Dhabi (16 aircraft), Dubai (8), Finland (50), Indonesia (20), Kenya (12), Kuwait (12), Saudi Arabia (30), Switzerland (20), US Navy (300 McDonnell Douglas T-45 Goshawks) and Zimbabwe (8).

Aero L-39 Albatros

Czechoslovakia has become established as the provider of basic jet trainers to the communist bloc, with the exception only of Poland. The L-39 flew in 1968 as a successor to the widely used L-29 Delfin and began training its first student pilots in 1974. Production now exceeds 2,000 and is continuing at some 200 per year. At least 16 countries operate the aircraft. The basic L-39C has two underwing weapon pylons, but the L-39ZO and L-39ZA have four, the latter mounting an under-fuselage GSh-23 23-mm cannon and also being used for tactical reconnaissance. Armed L-39s of the Libyan air force have seen combat in Chad. Development is under way of an improved L-39MS model with increased power and an improved avionics suite.

Specification: Aero L-39C Albatros two-seat trainer and light attack aircraft
Span: 9.46 m (31 ft 0.5 in)
Length: 12.13 m (39 ft 9.5 in)
Powerplant: 1×Walter Titan, 1720 kg (3,972 lb) st
Armament: up to 500 kg (1,102 lb) or in the L-39Z 1100 kg (2,425 lb) of disposable stores
Max speed: 466 mph at optimum altitude
Endurance: 2 hours 30 minutes

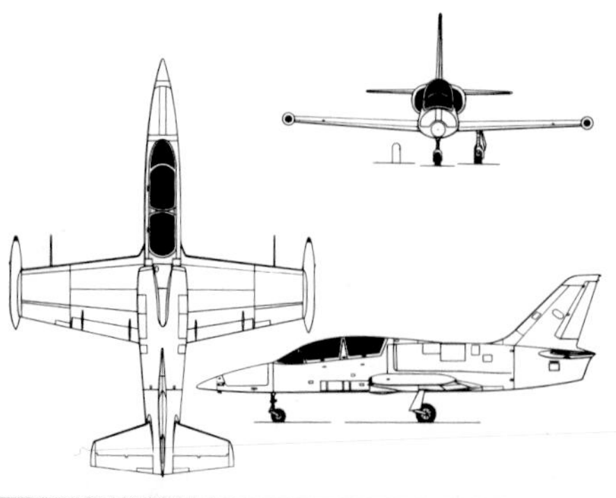

Aermacchi MB-326

Many of the MB-326s built in the home country of Italy, as well as Australia (97 Commonwealth CA.30s), Brazil (182 EMBRAER AT-26 Xavantes) and South Africa, remain in service as basic trainers or COIN (counter insurgency) aircraft. The Italian air force, however, has largely consigned the survivors of its fleet of 137 to communications duties, although a target drone conversion is planned. Originally unarmed, the aircraft received wing pylons in its later forms, being used by Argentina (navy), Dubai, Ghana, Paraguay, Togo, Tunisia, Zaire and Zambia. Atlas of South Africa built the majority of the SAAF's 151 MB-326M Impala Mk Is, and followed-up with 100 single-seat MB-326K Impala Mk IIs which have seen extensive combat in Namibia and Angola. Production totalled 761.

Specification: Aermacchi MB-326 GB two-seat basic trainer and attack aircraft
Span: 10.85 m (35 ft 7 in)
Length: 10.64 m (34 ft 11 in)
Powerplant: 1×Rolls-Royce Viper Mk 540, 1547 kg (3,410 lb) st
Armament: up to 1814 kg (4,000 lb) of disposable stores
Max speed: 539 mph at 30,000 ft
Range: 1,150 miles

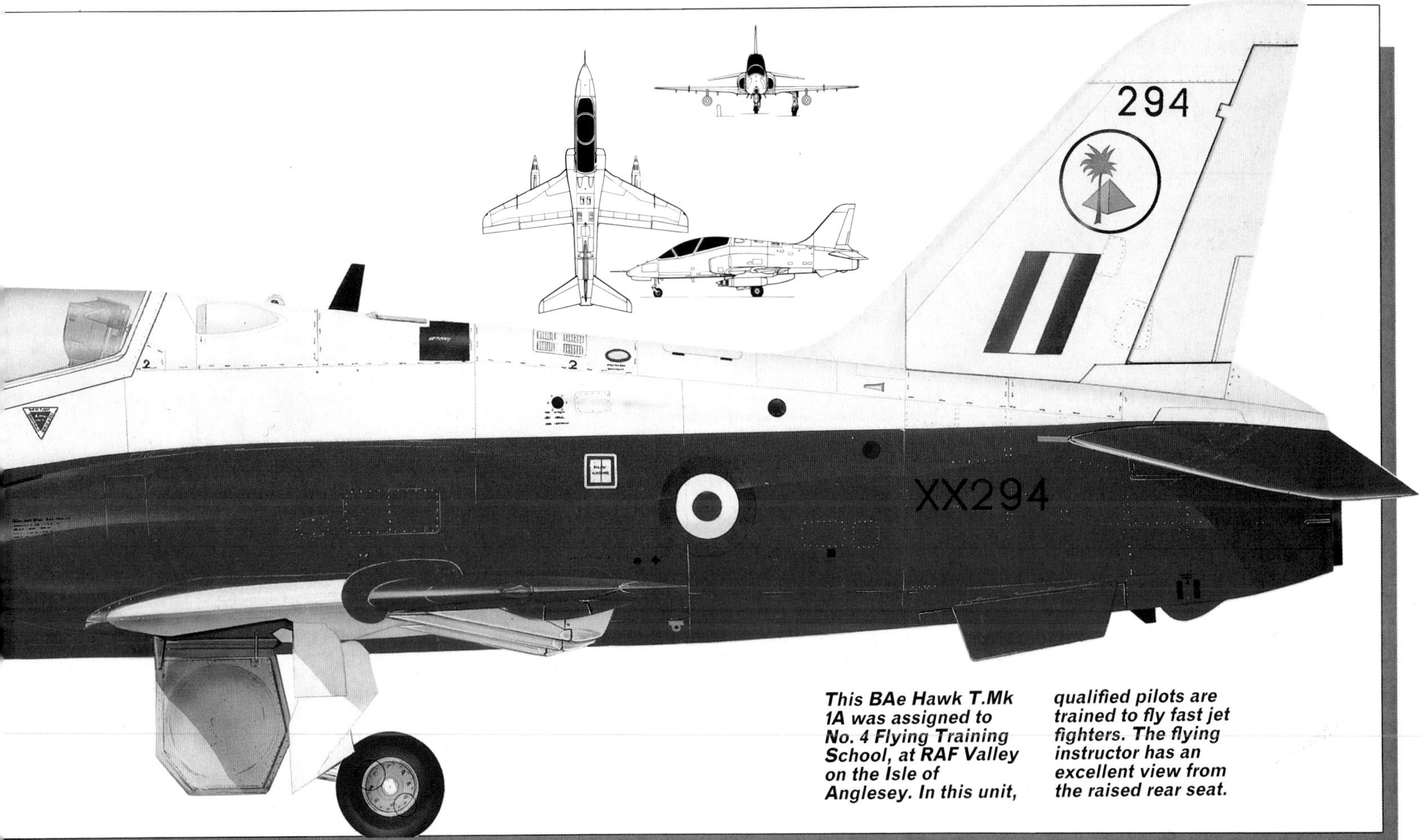

This BAe Hawk T.Mk 1A was assigned to No. 4 Flying Training School, at RAF Valley on the Isle of Anglesey. In this unit, qualified pilots are trained to fly fast jet fighters. The flying instructor has an excellent view from the raised rear seat.

Aermacchi MB-339

This successor to the MB-326 retains the Viper turbojet, but features the raised rear seat now considered essential to provide the instructor with a good forward view – particularly during weapon practice. Italy has received 101 MB-339s for basic and advanced training between the SF-260 and G.91T stages of the pilot syllabus (MB-339A); navaids calibration (MB-339RM); and the *Frecce Tricolori* aerobatic team (MB-339PAN). The final 50 were delivered with light armament provision for emergency wartime use (including anti-helicopter missions) and others are being similarly modified. Some of the 10 Argentine navy MB-339s were used in combat during the Falklands war, and others are operated by Dubai (5), Malaysia (13), Nigeria (12) and Peru (16).

Specification: Aermacchi MB-339A two-seat trainer and light attack aircraft
Span: 10.86 m (35 ft 7.5 in)
Length: 10.97 m (36 ft 0 in)
Powerplant: 1×Rolls-Royce Viper Mk 632, 1814 kg (4,000 lb) st
Armament: up to 1814 kg (4,000 lb) of disposable stores
Max speed: 558 mph at sea level
Endurance: 2 hours 50 minutes

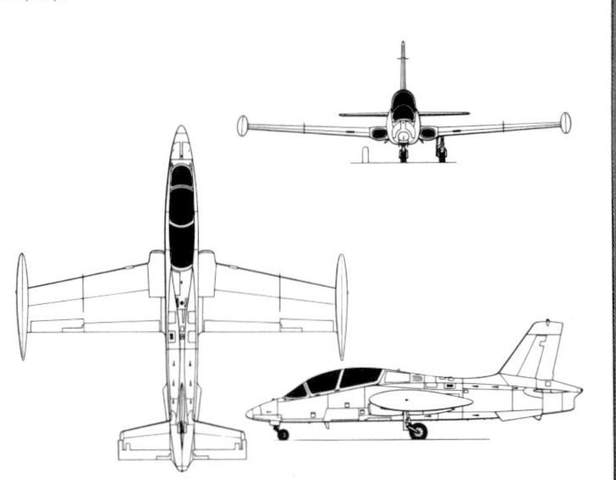

CASA C-101 Aviojet

Designed and built to a Spanish air force specification, the Aviojet equips one squadron (Escuadrón 793) of the Air Academy at San Javier to provide basic jet training for prospective pilots. Further examples of the 88 C-101EBs delivered between 1980 and 1985 are used by Escuadrones 411 and 412 at Matacán to provide refresher training to officers on ground tours. Progressive increases in power have been provided for the armed export models, comprising the C-101BB trainer and a light attack variant designated C-101CC. The former has been bought by Chile (as the T-36 Halcón) and Honduras; whilst the latter has also been adopted by Chile (A-36 Halcón) as well as Jordan. No purchases have yet been reported for the C-101DD enhanced trainer with more sophisticated avionics.

Specification: CASA C-101CC Aviojet two-seat basic trainer and COIN aircraft
Span: 10.60 m (34 ft 9.33 in)
Length: 12.50 m (41 ft 0 in)
Powerplant: 1×Garrett TFE731-5-1J, 2132 kg (4,700 lb) st
Armament: 1×20-mm cannon or 2×12.7-mm (0.5-in) machine-guns, and up to 2250 kg (4,960 lb) of disposable stores
Max speed: 478 mph at 25,000 ft
Endurance: 7 hours

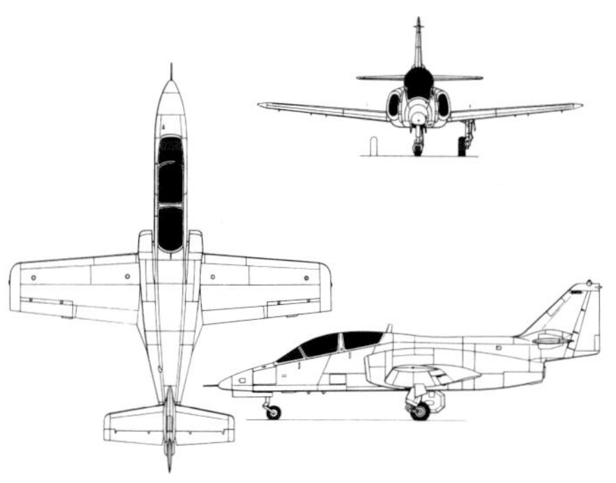

Dassault Alpha Jet E

Comparable in many respects to Britain's Hawk, this Franco-German product is used solely as a front-line close-support aircraft by the Luftwaffe, although in Armée de l'Air service it provides 91 hours of basic training and 54 hours of weapons instruction after the Epsilon or Magister stage. France received 176 Alpha Jet Es, including those of the *Patrouille de France* aerobatic team, and West Germany built 175 'A' models for three fighter-bomber wings and a weapons training unit permanently deployed to Portugal. Other operators are Belgium (33), Egypt (30), Ivory Coast (7), Morocco (24), Nigeria (24), Qatar (6) and Togo (6). The attack/trainer Alpha Jet 2, which has a laser-ranger in the nose has been bought by Egypt (15) and Cameroun (6).

Cessna T-37

Well over 30 years after entering service, the 'Tweet' remains the USAF's basic jet trainer, giving students 95 hours of flying between the Cessna T-41 and Northrop T-38 components of their course. Deliveries totalled 534 T-37As and 400 T-37Bs with improved avionics. A further 66 T-37Bs were built to foreign order, as were 269 armed T-37Cs delivered to numerous US allies (later augmented by some surplus T-37A/Bs). At least 122 aircraft released from training duties were converted to OA-37B forward air control platforms and others were detached to SAC bomber and tanker bases to give co-pilots extra flying time. In Europe, operators include the *Asas de Portugal* aerobatic team. A further 577 specifically attack-configured A-37B Dragonflies were built.

Specification: Cessna T-37B two-seat basic trainer and (T-37C) COIN aircraft
Span: 10.29 m (33 ft 9.25 in)
Length: 8.92 m (29 ft 3 in)
Powerplant: 2×Teledyne J69, 465 kg (1,025 lb) st each
Armament: up to 227 kg (500 lb) of disposable stores
Max speed: 425 mph at 16,000 ft
Range: 831 miles

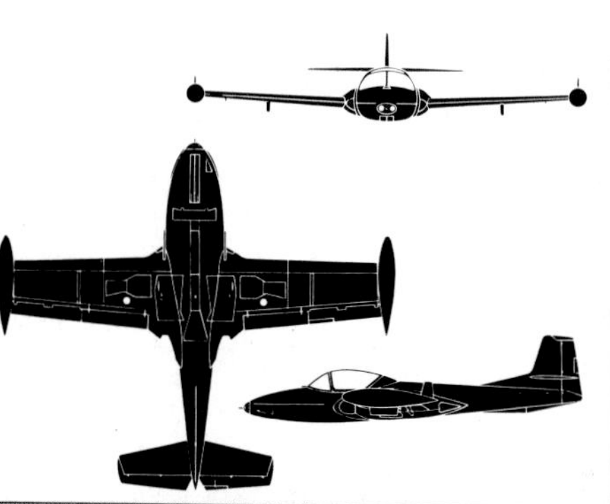

FMA IA.63 Pampa

Similar to the Alpha Jet – although powered by only a single engine – the Pampa reflects the design assistance provided by Dornier; in particular the supercritical wing which provides high aerodynamic efficiency. The Pampa first flew in October 1984 as the designated successor to ageing Morane-Saulnier Paris basic/advanced trainers of the Argentine air force. The initial production order is for 67, the first of which were delivered to the Escuela de Aviacion Militar (Military Aviation School) at Cordoba in March 1988. Later aircraft, perhaps including a follow-on batch of 36, are destined for light attack duties in front-line units, the first of which will be IV Grupo de Caza at El Plumerillo, where two Paris squadrons are currently based.

Specification: FMA IA.63 Pampa two-seat trainer and light attack aircraft
Span: 9.69 m (31 ft 9.25 in)
Length: 10.90 m (35 ft 9.25 in)
Powerplant: 1×Garrett TFE731-2-2N, 1588 kg (3,500 lb) st
Armament: up to 3200 kg (7,054 lb) of disposable stores
Max speed: 510 mph at 29,525 ft
Endurance: 2 hours 28 minutes

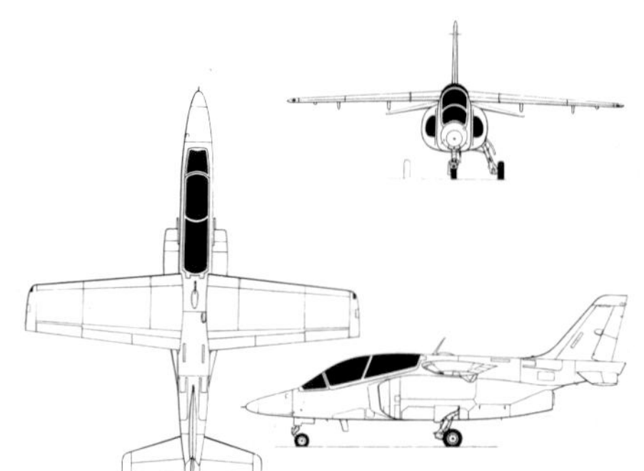

Specification: Dassault-Breguet/Dornier Alpha Jet two-seat advanced trainer and attack aircraft
Span: 9.11 m (29 ft 10.75 in)
Length: 12.29 m (40 ft 3.75 in)
Powerplant: 2×SNECMA/Turboméca Larzac 04, 1350 kg (2,976 lb) st each
Armament: 1×27- or 30-mm cannon and up to 2500 kg (5,511 lb) of disposable stores
Max speed: 624 mph at 9,845 ft
Endurance: 3 hours 30 minutes

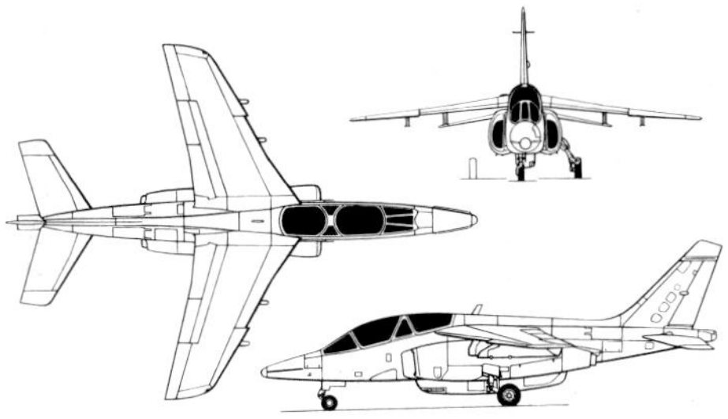

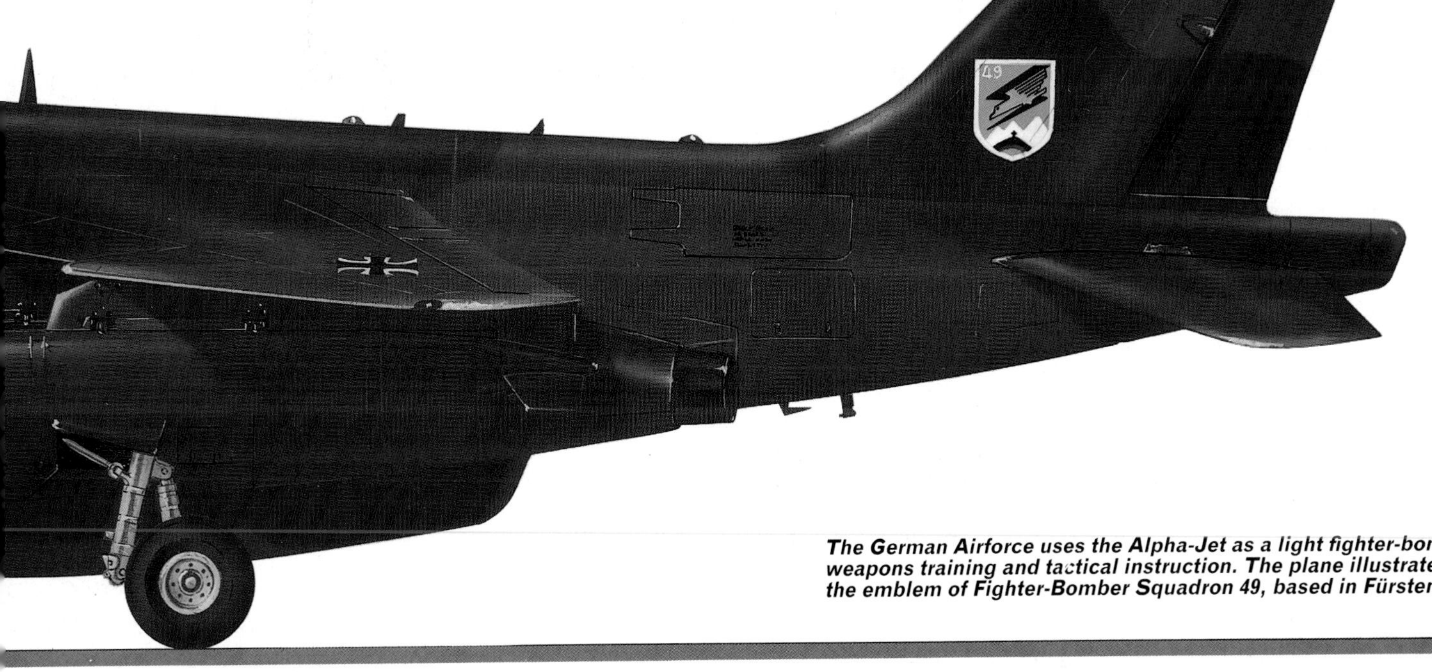

The German Airforce uses the Alpha-Jet as a light fighter-bomber for weapons training and tactical instruction. The plane illustrated here has the emblem of Fighter-Bomber Squadron 49, based in Fürstenfeldbruck.

HAL HJT-16 Kiran II

Delayed for a decade through development problems – despite being merely an upgraded version of an existing aircraft – the Kiran II first flew in July 1976 and began deliveries in April 1984. Orders total 57 (but may increase to 100) as a follow-on to 190 Mk Is, including 72 gun-armed Mk IAs. The Kiran II introduces four underwing hardpoints and an Orpheus to replace its predecessor's lower-powered Viper. Used in the armament training role, it is based at the Air Force Academy out-station at Bidar to provide students with six months of training after they have followed the HPT-32 and Kiran I syllabus. They then progress to Hunters or MiG-21s. Six Kiran IIs are to be supplied to the Indian navy for training future Sea Harrier pilots.

Specification: HAL HJT-16 Kiran II two-seat trainer and light attack aircraft
Span: 10.70 m (35 ft 1.25 in)
Length: 10.60 m (34 ft 9.5 in)
Powerplant: 1×Rolls-Royce Orpheus Mk 701, 1905 kg (4,200 lb) st
Armament: 2×7.62-mm (0.3-in) machine-guns and up to 1000 kg (2,205 lb) of disposable stores
Max speed: 418 mph at optimum altitude
Operational range: 457 miles

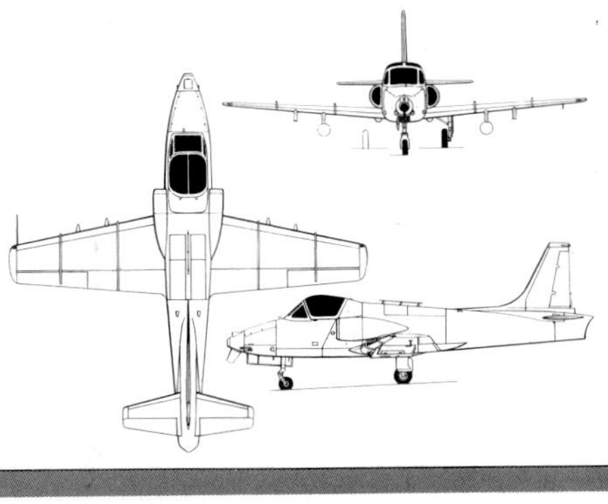

Kawasaki T-4

The first of four XT-4 prototypes conducted its maiden flight in July 1985, and preparations are now being made to deliver the first of an anticipated 200 T-4s to the Japanese Air Self-Defense Force to replace the Fuji T-1 basic jet trainers of 13 Air Training Wing at Ashiya as well as the Lockheed T-33s of Hamamatsu-based 1 ATW in the first part of the advanced syllabus. Kawasaki's Ka-850 design forms the basis of the T-4, although Fuji and Mitsubishi each have a 30 per cent share of the design and manufacturing programme. In addition, Ishikawajima-Harima produced the turbofan engine specifically for the T-4. Light armament for weapons training is included in the T-4's specification, although Japanese neutrality makes it unlikely that export orders will be sought.

Specification: Kawasaki T-4 two-seat basic/advanced flying and weapons trainer
Span: 9.90 m (32 ft 5.75 in)
Length: 13.00 m (42 ft 8 in)
Powerplant: 2×Ishikawajima-Harima F3-IHI-30, 1665 kg (3,671 lb) st each
Armament: up to 907 kg (2,000 lb) of disposable stores
Max speed: 593 mph at optimum altitude
Range: 806 miles

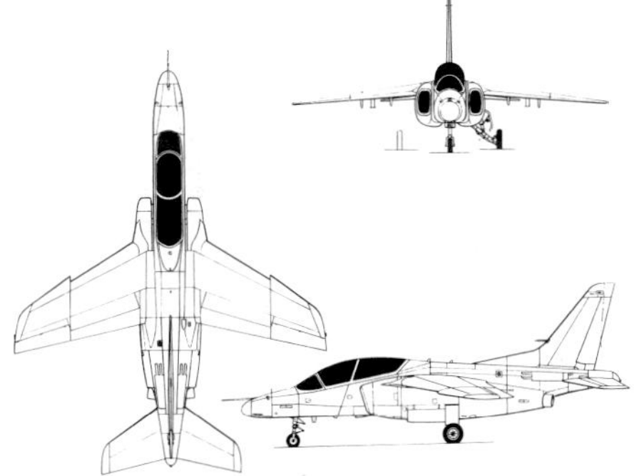

Chapter 7

LIGHT AIRCRAFT

de Havilland D.H.60

First flown in February 1925, the Moth was a milestone in aviation history and brought de Havilland to the fore as an aircraft manufacturer. The type was designed as a reliable two-seater of low cost but adequate performance. The type was widely used for classic long-distance flights, and was produced in several variants. The first 425 aircraft were powered by an ADC Cirrus inline. Then came 685 D.H.60G Gipsy Moths with the Gipsy I, II or III inline. These were followed by 748 D.H.60M Metal Moths with a steel-tube rather than wooden fuselage structure. Further development produced the wooden-fuselage D.H.60G III Moth with the inverted Gipsy III: production totalled 134, aircraft from the 48th onward being Moth Majors with the uprated Gipsy Major inline. The final development was the D.H.60T Moth Trainer, of which 64 were built for military service with dual controls.

Specification: de Havilland D.H.60G Gipsy Moth two-seat touring aeroplane
Span: 9.14 m (30 ft 0 in)
Length: 7.29 m (23 ft 11 in)
Powerplant: 1×de Havilland Gipsy I, 75 kW (100 hp)
Max T/O weight: 748 kg (1,650 lb)
Max speed: 102 mph at optimum altitude
Operational range: 320 miles

The characteristic unswept, untapered wings, long, externally mounted exhaust pipe and non-inverted Gipsy engine identify this aircraft as an example of the enchanting D.H.60G Gipsy Moth. It wears a convincing-looking period colour scheme, albeit with a 1960s British civil registration. The machine had previously spent most of its life in Switzerland from the early 1930s until its homecoming in 1965. 'Bravo Lima' remains airworthy to this day, owned by Tony Haig-Thomas, and based at Southend.

Avro Avian

Though not so famous as the Moth, the Avian was also important and was the type on which several celebrated flights were made. The Type 581 first flew in 1926 with a 56-kW (75-hp) Armstrong Siddeley Genet radial. The aeroplane entered production as the Type 594, variants being two Avian Mk Is with the 63-kW (85-hp) Cirrus II, nine Avian Mk IIs with improved landing gear, 33 Avian Mk IIIs with revised struts, 58 Avian Mk IIIAs with the 71-kW (95-hp) Cirrus III, and 90 Avian Mk IVs with modified ailerons and engines up to the 78-kW (105-hp) Cirrus Hermes I. These had been of wooden construction, but in the Type 616 Avian Mk IVM a steel-tube fuselage was introduced. British production of this variant was supplemented by Canadian and US construction for a total of 190. There were also 14 Type 616 Sports Avians, two long-distance variants, and two Type 625 Avian Monoplanes.

Specification: Avro Type 594 Avian Mk IIIA two-seat touring aeroplane
Span: 8.53 m (28 ft 0 in)
Length: 7.39 m (24 ft 3 in)
Powerplant: 1×ADC Cirrus III, 71 kW (95 hp)
Max T/O weight: 651 kg (1,435 lb)
Max speed: 102 mph at optimum altitude
Operational range: 400 miles

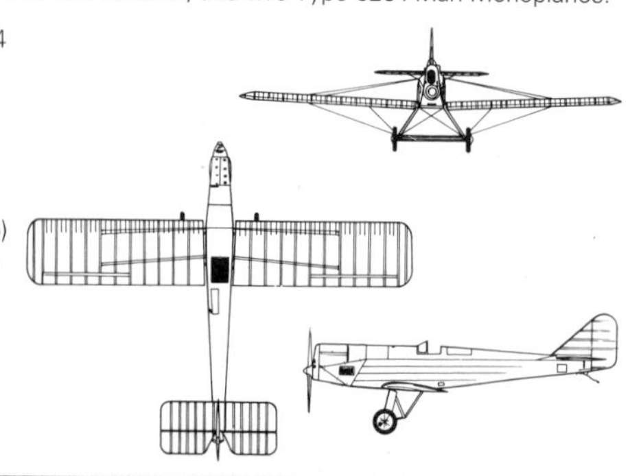

British Aircraft Swallow

First flown in Germany during 1927, the all-wooden Klemm L.25 tandem two-seater soon acquired an excellent reputation for reliability as a result of its sturdy wooden construction and Salmson radial. After he had imported 27 such aircraft to the UK, Major E. F. Stephen formed British Klemm for the licence production of the type as the Swallow. This was essentially similar to the German original apart from local strengthening to comply with British requirements, and was offered with a choice of the Salmson AD.9 or slightly more powerful Pobjoy Cataract III radial. The first was delivered in November 1933 with the Salmson, and this powered five others of the 28 production aircraft. In 1935 the company changed its name to British Aircraft Manufacturing and built 107 improved Swallow 2s, 60 with an uprated Pobjoy and the others with the similarly rated Blackburn Cirrus Minor I.

Specification: British Aircraft Swallow 2 two-seat sporting aeroplane
Span: 13.02 m (42 ft 8.5 in)
Length: 8.00 m (26 ft 3 in)
Powerplant: 1×Pobjoy Cataract III, 67 kW (90 hp)
Max T/O weight: 680 kg (1,500 lb)
Max speed: 112 mph at optimum altitude
Operational range: 420 miles

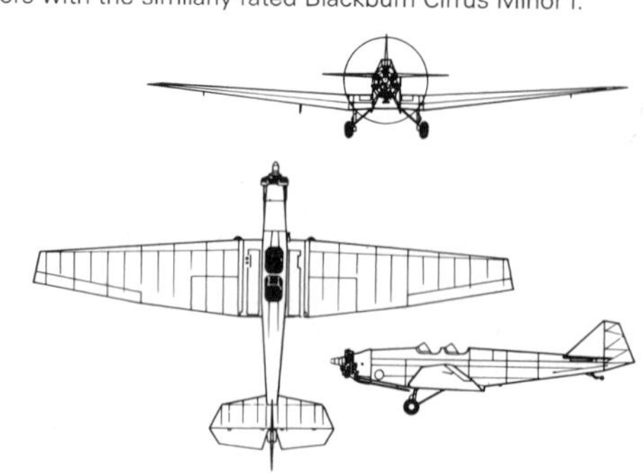

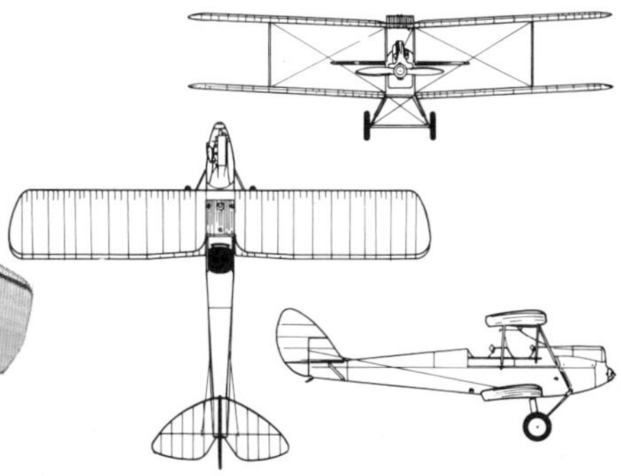

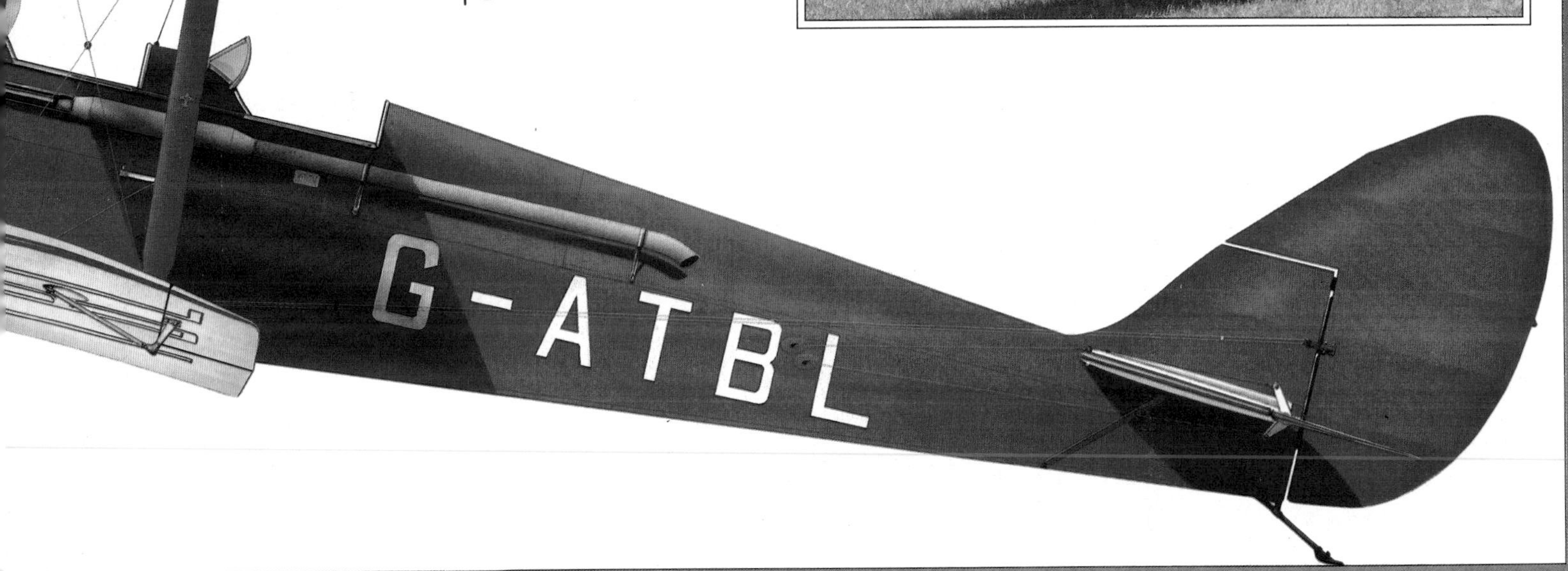

de Havilland D.H.80 *Puss Moth*

The success of the Gipsy Moth opened the possibility of private owners flying sufficiently far afield that overnight baggage would be useful, and to cater for this new market de Havilland developed the D.H.80 two/three-seat cabin tourer with useful baggage volume; it was also the first aeroplane to have the low-drag installation of an inverted Gipsy III. The D.H.80 first flew in September 1929, but was not put into production as the company felt that its wooden primary structure should be revised to metal for a longer structural life and thus better sales. Such a D.H.80A therefore flew in March 1930 as an attractive braced high-wing monoplane with a fabric-covered steel-tube fuselage and folding fabric-covered wooden wings. The type was used for a number of notable long-distance flights, and production totalled 259 in the UK together with 25 assembled in Canada.

Specification: de Havilland D.H.80A Puss Moth two/three-seat touring aeroplane
Span: 11.20 m (36 ft 9 in)
Length: 7.62 m (25 ft 0 in)
Powerplant: 1×de Havilland Gipsy III, 89 kW (120 hp) or de Havilland Gipsy Major, 97 kW (130 hp)
Max T/O weight: 862 kg (1,900 lb)
Max speed: 130 mph at optimum altitude
Operational range: 450 miles

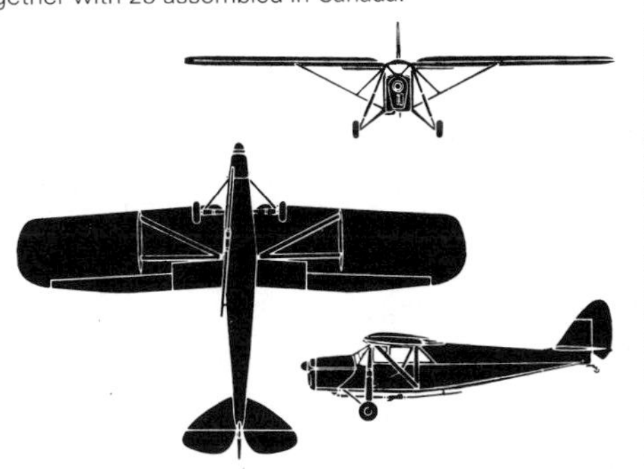

de Havilland D.H.82 *Tiger Moth*

One of the greatest training and sport aircraft ever developed, the Tiger Moth first flew in October 1931 as combination of the D.H.60M's metal-tube fuselage with an inverted Gipsy III engine and the upper-wing centre section moved forward to allow easy egress by the front-seater. The upper wings were swept back to maintain the centre of gravity position, and this layout has always been one of the Tiger Moth's most distinctive features. The first eight aircraft were designated D.H.60T Tiger Moth, but then the introduction of dihedral on the lower wings to improve ground clearance resulted in the designation D.H.82, and 134 of this variant were built with the 89-kW (120-hp) Gipsy III. In the upengined D.H.82A variant, of which 8,706 were built including large numbers of military trainers, the rear decking was of smooth plywood rather than the previous corrugated stringer/fabric finish.

Specification: de Havilland D.H.82A Tiger Moth two-seat training aeroplane
Span: 8.94 m (29 ft 4 in)
Length: 7.29 m (23 ft 11 in)
Powerplant: 1×de Havilland Gipsy Major I, 97 kW (130 hp), or de Havilland Gipsy Major IC, 108 kW (145 hp)
Max T/O weight: 828 kg (1,825 lb)
Max speed: 104 mph at optimum altitude
Operational range: 300 miles

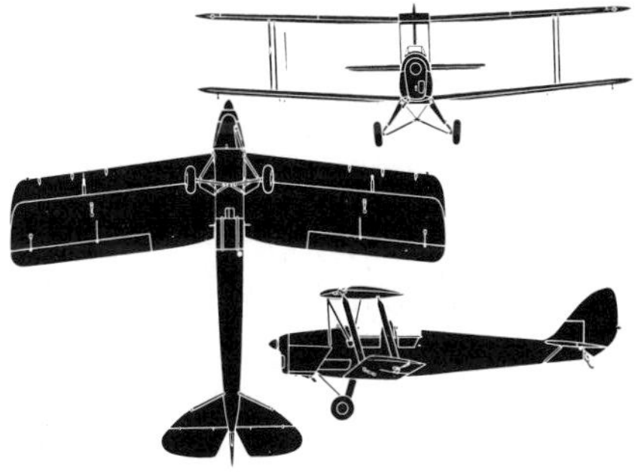

Comper C.L.A.7 Swift

First flown in May 1930 with a 30-kW (40-hp) ABC Scorpion radial, the Swift was, for its time, a small and elegant monoplane of wooden construction with plywood and fabric covering. The high wing was braced by V-struts to the bottom of the deep fuselage aft of the shallow main landing gear units with their small faired wheels. The pilot was located in an open cockpit aft of the wing trailing edge and had good fields of vision. Production aircraft followed, the first seven with the 37-kW (50-hp) Salmson AD.9 and the rest of the 41-machine production run with the Pobjoy R, which was also retrofitted to most of the earlier aircraft. There were also three racers, two with the 89-kW (120-hp) de Havilland Gipsy III and the last with the 97-kW (130-hp) Gipsy Major.

Specification: Comper C.L.A.7 Swift single-seat sporting aeroplane
Span: 7.32 m (24 ft 0 in)
Length: 5.40 m (17 ft 8.5 in)
Powerplant: 1×Pobjoy R, 56 kW (75 hp)
Max T/O weight: 447 kg (985 lb)
Max speed: 140 mph at optimum altitude
Operational range: 380 miles

Blackburn B-2

After its success with the side-by-side two-seat Bluebird, Blackburn turned to a derivative of the Bluebird IV with an all-metal semi-monocoque fuselage and fabric-covered metal wings. The prototype first flew in December 1931 with an 89-kW (120-hp) de Havilland Gipsy III inline. The company found, however, that there was little demand for a side-by-side trainer and orders were slow to materialise. The type was trialled with four other engines, and the Cirrus Hermes IVA became standard on production aircraft, which Blackburn built largely for its two flying training school subsidiaries at Hanworth in Middlesex and Brough in Yorkshire. Total production was 42 aircraft, the last three ordered by the Air Ministry for the Elementary and Reserve Flying Training School at Brough. Only two B-2s survived World War II in flyable condition.

Specification: Blackburn B-2 two-seat basic training aeroplane
Span: 9.19 m (30 ft 2 in)
Length: 7.39 m (24 ft 3 in)
Powerplant: 1×Blackburn Cirrus Hermes IVA, 89 kW (120 hp)
Max T/O weight: 839 kg (1,850 lb)
Max speed: 112 mph at optimum altitude
Operational range: 320 miles

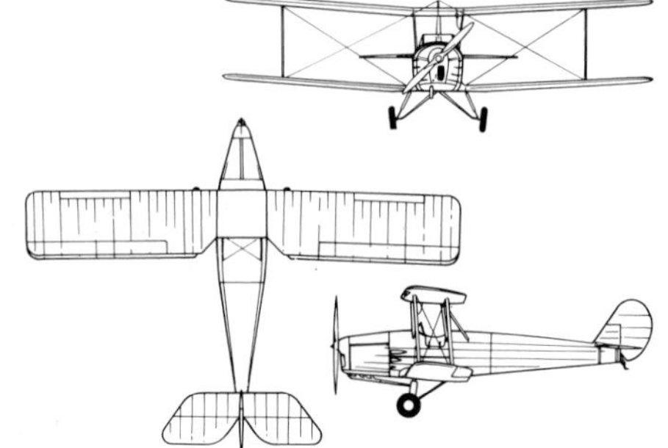

de Havilland D.H.83 Fox Moth

The Fox Moth was first flown in January 1932 as a light family tourer and air taxi, a new fuselage being used with the wings of the Tiger Moth and the tail unit of the Gipsy Moth/Puss Moth. Enclosed accommodation was provided for four passengers on the centre of gravity, and the pilot was located in an open cockpit behind and above this cabin. The operating economics of the Fox Moth were such that many were used for light passenger and freight transport, especially in bush regions, and this tendency was promoted by the Fox Moth's ability to accept alternative ski or float landing gear. Production of the basic version totalled 101 in the UK (97), Australia and Canada, the last developing the post-war D.H.83C version (52 built) with an enclosed cockpit, a larger door to facilitate the loading of freight, and a 108-kW (145-hp) Gipsy Major IC engine.

Specification: de Havilland D.H.83 Fox Moth single-pilot touring and light transport aeroplane
Span: 9.41 m (30 ft 10.75 in)
Length: 7.85 m (25 ft 9 in)
Powerplant: 1×de Havilland Gipsy Major, 97 kW (130 hp)
Payload: four passengers or 272 kg (600 lb) of freight
Max T/O weight: 939 kg (2,070 lb)
Max speed: 123 mph at optimum altitude
Operational range: 415 miles

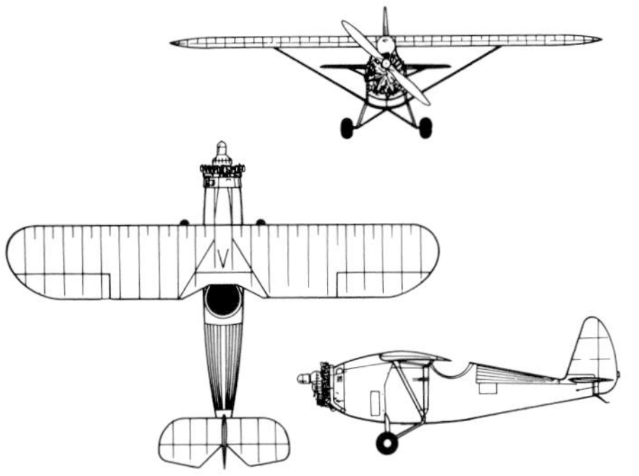

This Pobjoy-engined Comper CLA.7 Swift wears an Indian civil registration. The Comper Aircraft Company was formed in 1929 to produce the single-seat monoplane. The Swift was ugly, but a delight to fly, and one made a record-breaking flight to Australia in October/November 1931. A few of the 40 or so Swifts built remain airworthy today.

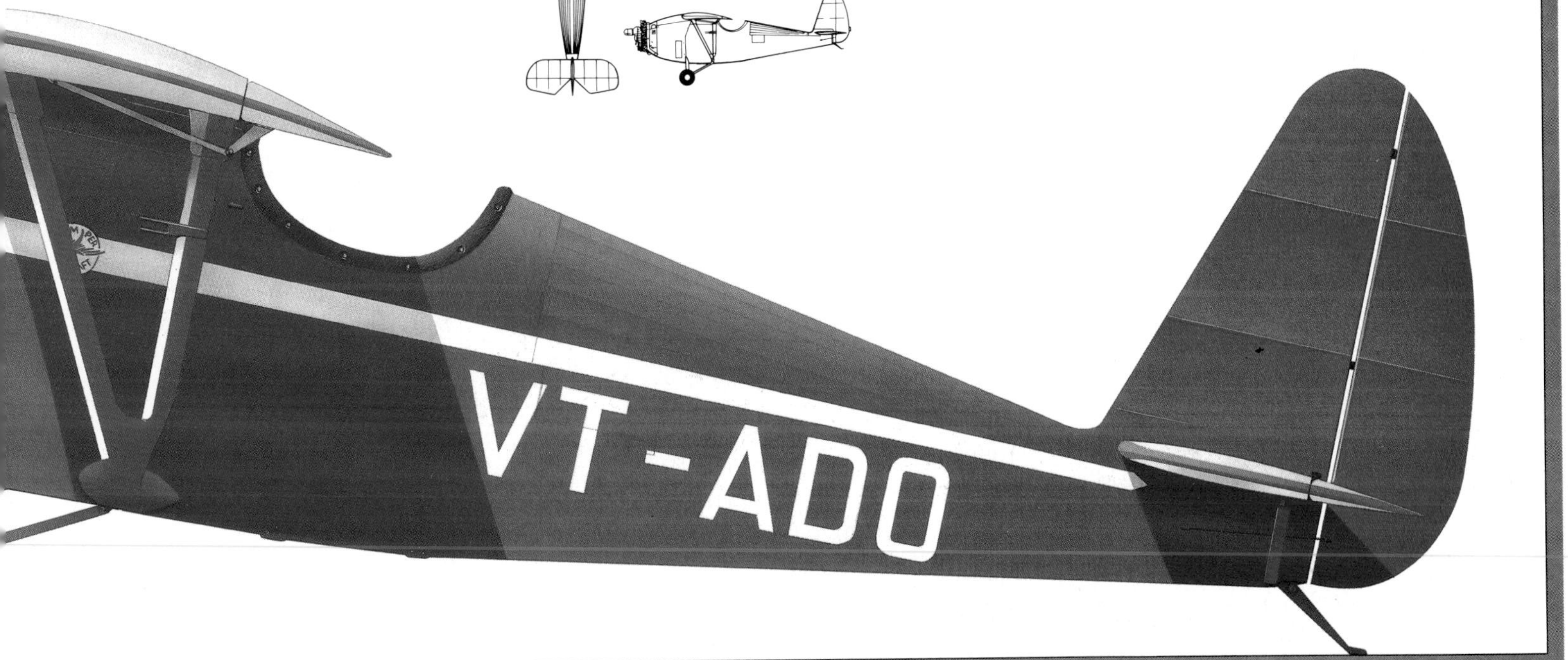

Percival Gull

The Gull low-wing monoplane remains a classic amongst interwar lightplanes, notable for its clean contours and wooden construction with elegantly spatted main landing gear units. The series began with the D.1 Gull that first flew in 1932. The success of this aeroplane as a racer led to orders for 24 D.2 Parnall-built production aircraft generally called Gull Fours and fitted with a variety of engines. Percival then moved into manufacture for 19 examples of the refined D.3 Gull Six with a Gipsy Six inline and, in all but one aeroplane, an enclosed cockpit. A four-seat derivative was the K.1 Vega Gull with the Gipsy Six, dual controls and flaps: production totalled 90. The ultimate expression of the Gull concept was the Mew Gull single-seat racer, produced in initial E.1 and then completely redesigned E.2 forms to the extent of one and four aircraft respectively.

Specification: Percival K.1 Vega Gull four-seat touring aeroplane
Span: 12.04 m (39 ft 6 in)
Length: 7.77 m (25 ft 6 in)
Powerplant: 1×de Havilland Gipsy Six Series II, 153 kW (205 hp)
Max T/O weight: 1474 kg (3,250 lb)
Max speed: 174 mph at optimum altitude
Operational range: 660 miles

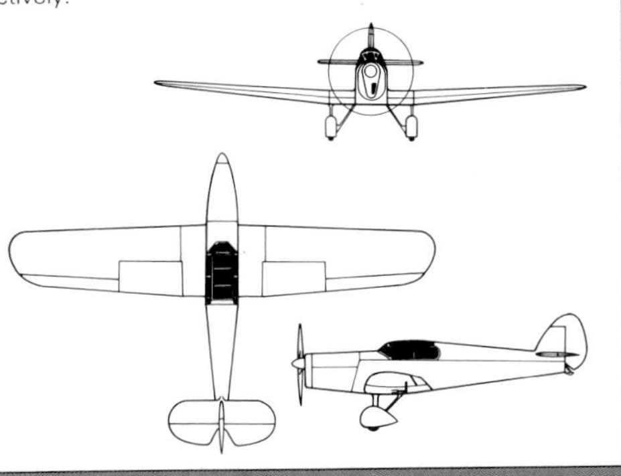

Miles M.2 Hawk

F.G.Miles was a firm advocate of the monoplane layout, and his M.2 Hawk was designed to provide a low-cost trainer and tourer of wooden construction with neatly faired main landing gear units and cantilever monoplane wings that folded aft to reduce hangar requirements. The type first flew in March 1933 with the 71-kW (95-hp) ADC Cirrus IIIA inline, and there followed 47 generally similar M.2 production aircraft. One-off variants were the enclosed three-seat M.2A with the Gipsy III, enclosed single-seat M.2B with the Cirrus Hermes IV and open two-seat M.2C with the Gipsy III. The six M.3Ds were open three-seaters with the Cirrus IIIA. Further development produced the Hawk Major (76 aircraft in M.2F, M.2H and other models up to the M.2T) and Hawk Speed Six single-seat racer (three aircraft with an enclosed cockpit).

Specification: Miles M.2 Hawk two-seat training and touring aeroplane
Span: 10.06 m (33 ft 0 in)
Length: 7.32 m (24 ft 0 in)
Powerplant: 1×ADC Cirrus IIIA, 71 kW (95 hp)
Max T/O weight: 816 kg (1,800 lb)
Max speed: 115 mph at optimum altitude
Operational range: 450 miles

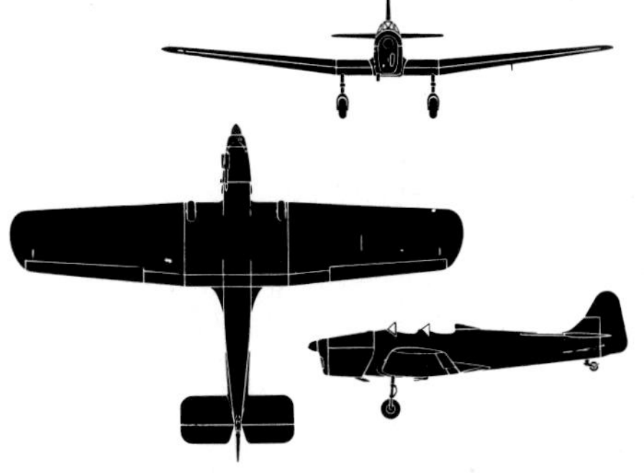

de Havilland D.H.85 Leopard Moth

The Leopard Moth was a development of the braced high-wing monoplane tourer concept pioneered in the Puss Moth but with a primary structure of wood for a useful reduction of weight and with improvements such as a fuselage widened sufficiently for the side-by-side accommodation of two passengers. The type first flew in May 1933, and soon began to attract attention because of its successes in several important air races; the D.H.85 was also used for a number of notable long-distance flights. Production of 131 aircraft ended in 1937, and many of those in the UK were impressed as communications aircraft during World War II. A few returned to the civil register after the war, and their number was swelled by the construction during 1963 of a last example from spare parts. The type was also used as an executive transport and as an air taxi.

Specification: de Havilland D.H.85 Leopard Moth two/three-seat touring aeroplane
Span: 11.43 m (37 ft 6 in)
Length: 7.47 m (24 ft 6 in)
Powerplant: 1×de Havilland Gipsy Major, 97 kW (130 hp)
Max T/O weight: 1009 kg (2,225 lb)
Max speed: 141.5 mph at optimum altitude
Operational range: 715 miles

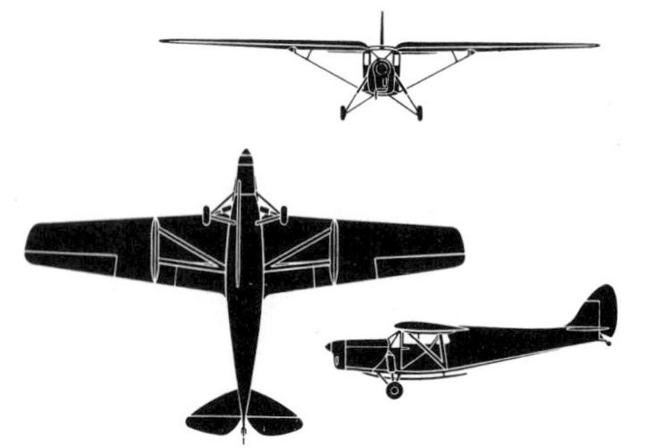

de Havilland D.H.87 Hornet Moth

The Hornet Moth was designed as a side-by-side trainer with what was for the time the luxury of an enclosed cabin, but the provision of baggage space also made possible the type's use as a tourer. In configuration the Hornet Moth could be regarded as a biplane development of strutted high-wing types such as the D.H.80 Puss Moth and D.H.85 Leopard Moth, and first flew during May 1934. The wings needed some development, and in its initial D.H.87A form with tapered wings the Hornet Moth was too tricky an aeroplane for novice pilots. The D.H.87B introduced rectangular wings and proved more tractable. Total production amounted to 195 aircraft. A few examples were fitted with twin floats, and a useful number survived service as communication aircraft in World War II to re-emerge on the civil register.

Specification: de Havilland D.H.87B Hornet Moth training and touring aeroplane
Span: 9.73 m (31 ft 11 in)
Length: 7.61 m (24 ft 11.5 in)
Powerplant: 1×de Havilland Gipsy Major, 97 kW (130 hp)
Max T/O weight: 885 kg (1,950 lb)
Max speed: 124 mph at optimum altitude
Operational range: 620 miles

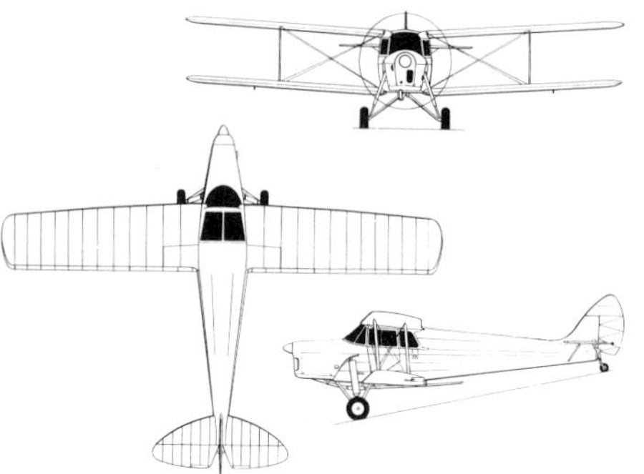

Miles M.3 Falcon

The Falcon was based on the M.2 Hawk Major low-wing monoplane with fixed tailwheel landing gear and retained that type's excellent handling, but as first flown in October 1934 was enlarged to provide enclosed side-by-side seating for two passengers behind the pilot. The production type of 1935 introduced a forward-sloping windscreen and accommodation for four, and production amounted to 18 M.3A Falcon Majors, 11 M.3B Falcon Sixes with the 149-kW (200-hp) de Havilland Gipsy six inline, and six M.3C and M.3F Falcon Sixes for the Royal Aircraft Establishment. A futher development was the M.4A Merlin, enlarged for five-seat accommodation in the air taxi role, and four examples were built with the Gipsy Six engine, a span of 11.28 m (37 ft 0 in) and a maximum speed of 155 mph after take-off at a gross weight of 1361 kg (3,000 lb).

Specification: Miles M.3A Falcon four-seat touring aeroplane
Span: 10.69 m (35 ft 0 in)
Length: 7.62 m (25 ft 0 in)
Powerplant: 1×de Havilland Gipsy Major, 97 kW (130 hp)
Max T/O weight: 998 kg (2,200 lb)
Max speed: 145 mph at optimum altitude
Operational range: 615 miles

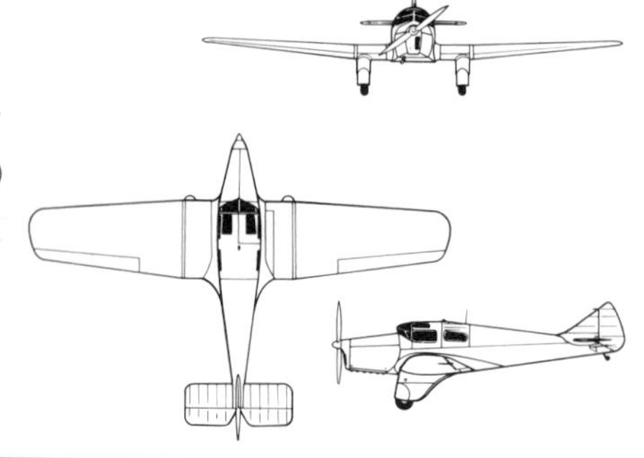

de Havilland D.H.94 Moth Minor

The Moth Minor first flew in June 1937, de Havilland's intention being to produce a viceless and fully aerobatic basic trainer of modern concept but of lower cost than the company's successors to the Moth. In layout the Moth Minor was a low-wing monoplane with fixed tailwheel landing gear and tandem open cockpits located over the centre of gravity so that the type could be flown solo from either cockpit. Production began in September 1938 in basic trainer or alternative coupé tourer forms, both featuring wheel brakes, an airbrake and folding wings for reduced hangar requirements. Total production amounted to 115 aircraft, including 42 in Australia after the production line had been shipped out in 1939. British construction totalled 63 trainers and 10 coupé tourers. Many Moth Minors were impressed during World War II, only 12 returning to the civil register after the war.

Specification: de Havilland D.H.94 Moth Minor two-seat training or touring aeroplane
Span: 11.15 m (36 ft 7 in)
Length: 7.44 m (24 ft 5 in)
Powerplant: 1×de Havilland Gipsy Minor, 60 kW (80 hp)
Max T/O weight: 703 kg (1,550 lb)
Max speed: 118 mph at optimum altitude
Operational range: 300 miles

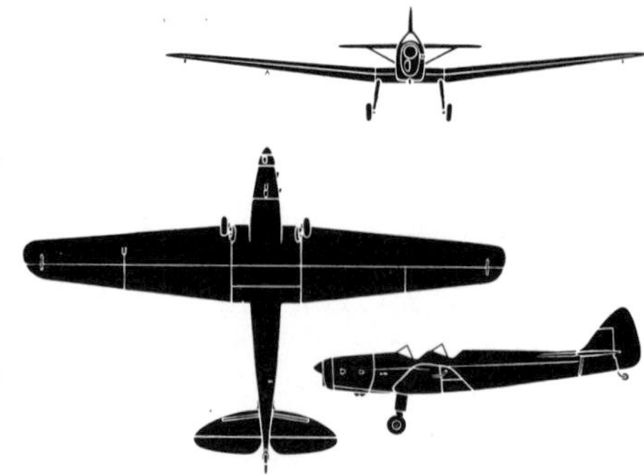

Nash Petrel

In 1978 Alan Nash bought Procter Aircraft Associates, and in 1980 renamed it Nash Aircraft. A low-wing monoplane with fixed tricycle landing gear, the Petrel is based on the Procter Kittiwake I of the 1970s, but the basic design has been considerably refined for its planned glider-towing role, and is fitted with a larger wing. The airframe is all-metal, and a notable feature of the design is the large bubble canopy that provides the two side-by-side occupants with excellent fields of vision. The first Petrel flew in November 1980, and certification flying revealed a number of features that could profitably be improved. As a consequence the Petrel now has Frise-type ailerons operated by pushrods rather than cables, and this considerably enhances lateral control while lowering stick forces. Small numbers have been built for glider-towing with a secondary sport application.

Specification: Nash Petrel two-seat light glider-towing and sport monoplane
Span: 8.94 m (29 ft 4 in)
Length: 6.22 m (20 ft 5 in)
Powerplant: 1×Avco Lycoming O-320-D2A, 119 kW (160 hp)
Max T/O weight: 762 kg (1,680 lb)
Max speed: 130 mph at sea level
Range: not known

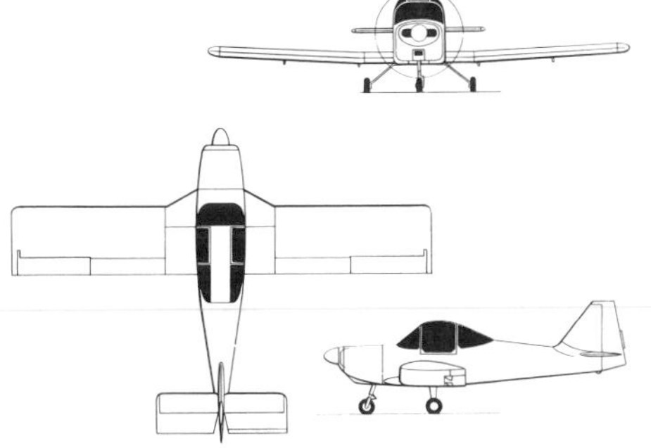

Slingsby T.67 Firefly

The T.67 is essentially the Fournier RF-6B, a French type built under British licence, and is an elementary trainer with aerobatic capability. The original T.67A retains the all-wooden construction of the RF-6B, but later models are of glass-reinforced plastics construction and come in a variety of forms. The T.67B has an 86-kW (113-hp) O-235-N2A engine while the T.67C and T.67D are powered by the 119-kW (120-hp) Avco Lycoming O-320-D2A driving fixed-pitch and constant-speed propellers respectively. Slingsby also offers the T.67M variant optimised for military customers with a fuel-injected AEIO-360-D1B engine, constant-speed propeller and no provision for the two 68-litre (15-Imp gal) root tanks of the other variants. The T.67M-200 has a 149-kW (200-hp) AEIO-360-A1E and a variable-pitch propeller.

Specification: Slingsby T.67B Firefly two-seat light training monoplane
Span: 10.59 m (34 ft 9 in)
Length: 7.26 m (23 ft 10 in)
Powerplant: 1×Avco Lycoming O-235-N2A, 86 kW (120 hp)
Max T/O weight: 907 kg (2,000 lb)
Cruising speed: 127 mph at 8,000 ft
Range: 356 miles

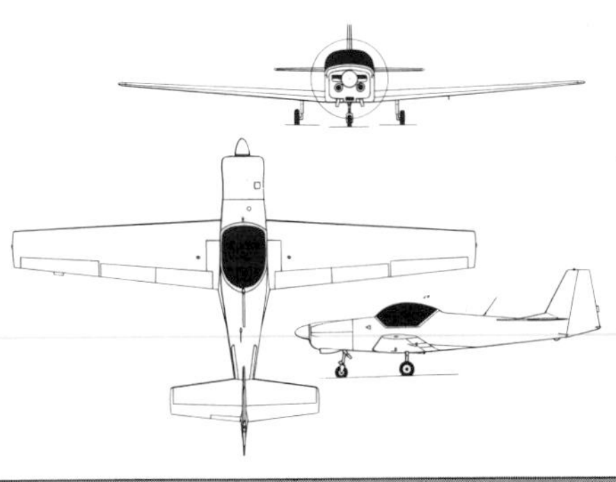

Norman NAC-1 Freelance

First flown in September 1984 after design by one of the originators of the successful Islander light transport (and the generally similar BN-3 Nymph), the Freelance is in appearance a conventional braced high-wing monoplane with fixed tricycle landing gear. However, the type has folding wings to reduce hangar requirements (folding and unfolding requiring a mere 2 minutes each), and though designed primarily for the touring role it can also be fitted for the utility role with an optional glider/banner-towing hook. With the optional 175-kW (235-hp) Avco Lycoming O-540-J engine the Freelance can be used in a military role with stores carried on underwing hardpoints, this type taking-off at the same maximum weight with a slightly lighter useful load of 444 kg (980 lb) carried at a maximum speed of 153 mph, or at a cruising speed of 145 mph over a range of 710 miles.

Specification: Norman NAC-1 Freelance four-seat light general-purpose monoplane
Span: 12.11 m (45 ft 2.5 in)
Length: 7.20 m (23 ft 7.75 in)
Powerplant: 1×Avco Lycoming O-360-A3A, 175 kW (235 hp)
Max T/O weight: 1224 kg (2,700 lb)
Max speed: 143 mph at sea level
Operational range: 1,216 miles

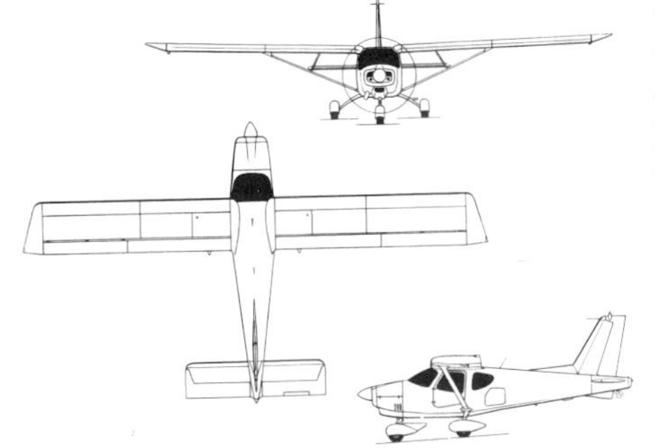

ARV Aviation Super2

Designed as a two-seat club trainer offering good performance at highly affordable price, the Super2 has proved successful as an aeroplane but is currently troubled by the financial instability of its manufacturer after a serviceability problem associated with the engine. The type is a notably compact side-by-side two-seater, uses a high proportion of superplastically formed aluminium alloy pressings, and in configuration is a monoplane with braced and slightly forward-swept wings plus fixed tricycle landing gear. The Super2 prototype first flew in March 1985, and its combination of low cost and excellent handling characteristics led to useful initial sales. The type's only problem has centred on the all-new two-stroke three-cylinder engine from a company whose light engines are intended for use mainly in microlight aircraft.

Specification: ARV Aviation Super2 two-seat light primary training monoplane
Span: 8.69 m (28 ft 6 in)
Length: 5.49 m (18 ft 0 in)
Powerplant: 1×Hewland Engineering AE.75, 57 kW (77 hp)
Max T/O weight: 474 kg (1,045 lb)
Cruising speed: 107 mph at 2,000 ft
Range: 311 miles

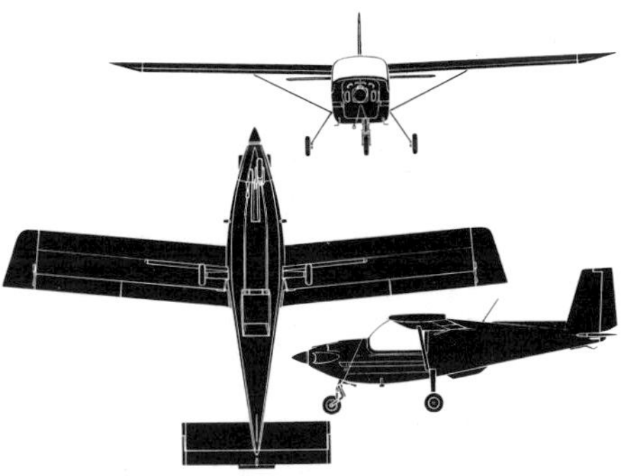

Beagle B.121 Pup

It was with the B.121 that Beagle sought to regain the position enjoyed by the UK before World War II as a major lightplane manufacturer. The aeroplane was a highly attractive low-wing monoplane of all-metal construction fitted with fixed tricycle landing gear, and first flew in April 1967 as a two-seater with a 75-kW (100-hp) Rolls-Royce (Continental) O-200-A engine. This prototype was followed by two four-seat production versions with a larger rudder and more power: the Pup Series 2 had the O-320 engine and was more generally known as the Pup 150, and the Pup Series 3 had the 119-kW (160-hp) Avco Lycoming O-360-A engine and was more generally known as the Pup 160. The company put more effort into sales than production and after-sales support, however, and collapsed in January 1970 with 276 aircraft sold but only 152 aircraft flown.

Specification: Beagle B.121 Pup Series 2 four-seat light touring and sport monoplane
Span: 9.45 m (31 ft 0 in)
Length: 7.06 m (23 ft 2 in)
Powerplant: 1xAvco Lycoming O-320-A2B, 112 kW (150 hp)
Max T/O weight: 873 kg (1,925 lb)
Max speed: 138 mph at sea level
Range: 633 miles

Auster series

The company that became Auster was established in 1938 as the British branch of the USA's Taylorcraft Aviation Company, and began work with a version of the Taylorcraft Model A designated Auster Plus C or, with more power, Plus D. Wartime construction was concerned with AOP types, but late in the war Auster began to think of post-war commercial sales and opted for a more economical version of the military Auster Mk V. This evolved into the three-seat J-1 Autocrat and the more powerful J-1B Aiglet. More than 400 J-1s were built, and the same basic design formula was followed in the 190 J-5 Autocar four-seaters, the 87 J-5 Aiglet Trainer four-seaters, and small numbers of the D-series of two/three-seat tourers and trainers produced in D.4, D.5 and D.6 variants with engines of several types and ratings.

Specification: Auster J-5B Autocar four-seat light touring monoplane
Span: 10.97 m (36 ft 0 in)
Length: 7.11 m (23 ft 4 in)
Powerplant: 1×de Håvilland Gipsy Major 1, 112 kW (130 hp)
Max T/O weight: 1089 kg (2,400 lb)
Max speed: 117 mph at sea level
Range: 260 miles

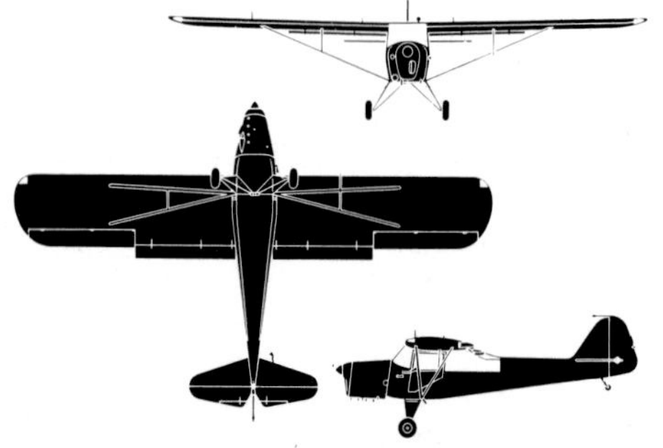

DHC-1 Chipmunk

The first aeroplane designed by de Havilland's Canadian subsidiary, the DHC-1 flew in May 1946 as a trainer to succeed the D.H.82 Tiger Moth. Large-scale production followed in Canada and in the UK mainly for military operators up to 1956, though a comparatively small number were produced for civil operators. As British-built Chipmunk T.Mk 10 trainers became surplus to requirements several passed into civil hands with the designations Chipmunk Mk 22 (re-engined with the Gipsy Major 10), Chipmunk Mk 22A (additional fuel capacity) and Chipmunk Mk 23 (crop-spraying modifications). These aircraft were complemented by 28 other machines produced specifically for the civil market as Chipmunk Mk 21s with the Gipsy Major 10 engine. There was also a Chipmunk 'Masefield Variant', a single conversion by Bristol Aircraft with a blown canopy, wheel spats, greater fuel capacity and luggage accommodation in the wings.

Specification: de Havilland Canada DHC-1 Chipmunk Mk 20 two-seat training monoplane
Span: 10.45 m (34 ft 4 in)
Length: 7.75 m (25 ft 5 in)
Powerplant: 1×de Havilland Gipsy Major 10, 108 kW (145 hp)
Max T/O weight: 953 kg (2,100 lb)
Max speed: 145 mph at sea level
Range: 485 miles

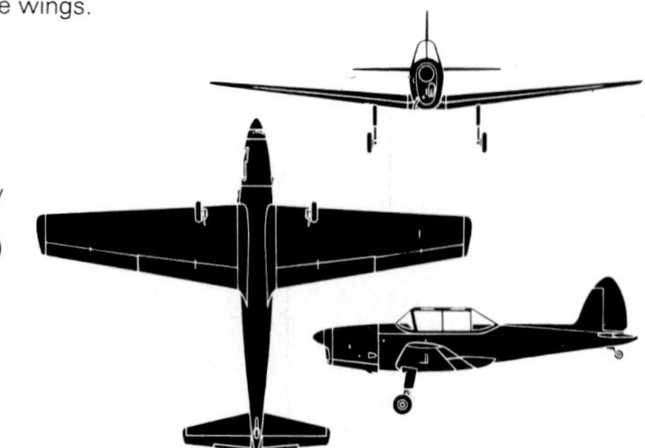

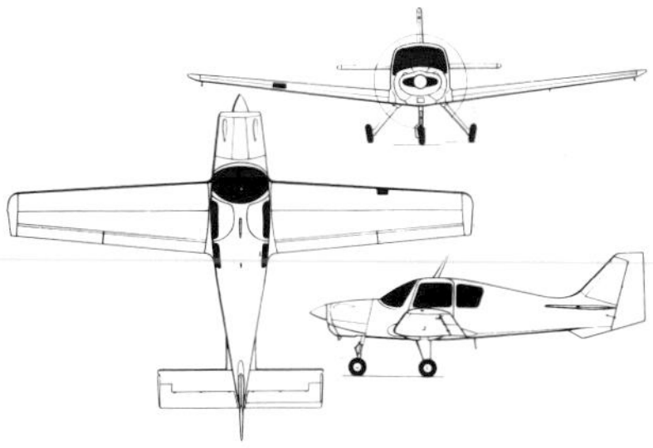

Designed as a trainer able to break into the American/French-dominated light aircraft market, the Pup was an attractive and challenging aircraft. G-AXPN is an example of the Series 2 Pup, which featured a 150-hp Lycoming engine and capacity for a third person on an optional seat in the rear of the cabin. This model first flew in 1968.

Thruxton Jackaroo

is was a fairly simple development of the de Havilland D.H.82A Tiger Moth to provide nclosed four-seat accommodation. Proposed by the Wiltshire School of Flying in 1956, the onversion was not approved by the parent company but nonetheless was undertaken at ruxton airfield by Jackaroo Aircraft Ltd. The modification involved a widening of the selage from 0.61 m (24 in) to 0.94 m (37 in) to provide two pairs of side-by-side seats in ace of the original two seats, together with an aft-sliding, flat-topped Perspex canopy ection that bridged the gap between the windscreen and a glazed aft section that tapered to a revised rear decking. The first conversion flew in March 1957, and was followed in the eriod up to 1959 by another 25 (24 by Jackaroo and one by Rollason), of which only 19 ere sold. Three were used for crop-spraying, and most of the others for training.

pecification: Thruxton ckaroo four-seat light training and uring biplane
pan: 9.25 m (30 ft 4.25 in)
ength: 7.62 m (25 ft 0 in)
owerplant: 1×de Havilland Gipsy ajor 1C, 108 kW (145 hp)
ax T/O weight: 989 kg (2,180 lb)
ax speed: 90 mph at sea level
ange: 275 miles

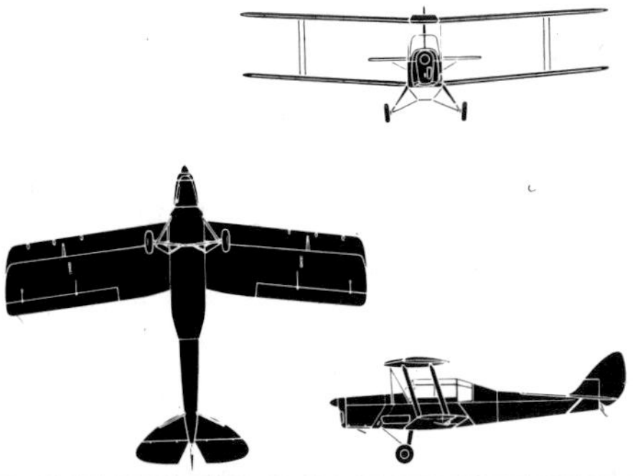

Tipsy Nipper

Designed by a Belgian, E.O.Tips, and first built in Belgium by Avions Fairey, the T.66 Tipsy Nipper is a diminutive semi-aerobatic monoplane with shoulder-mounted wings. The flying surfaces were of fabric-covered wooden construction, and the fuselage and vertical tail were of fabric-covered steel-tube construction, and fixed tricycle landing gear was fitted. The T.66 Mk 1 first flew in December 1957 with a 30-kW (40-hp) Polmann KFM 40.3500 flat-four engine, and was also produced in T.66 Mk 2 form with another flat-four engine, the 33.5-kW (45-hp) Stark Stamo 1400A. Between 1960 and 1967 14 Mk 2s were imported to the UK, and 32 Nipper Mk 3 and Mk 3A aircraft were then built for Nipper Aircraft Ltd by Slingsby with 1500- and 1600-cc (91.5- and 97.6-cu in) Rollason Ardem Mk X engines respectively. After production had been ended by a fire that destroyed the factory in 1968, plans and components were supplied for homebuilders as the Mk 3B powered by the 41-kW (55-hp) Ardem Mk XI engine.

Specification: Nipper Aircraft Tipsy Nipper Mk 3 single-seat light sport monoplane
Span: 6.00 m (19 ft 8 in)
Length: 4.50 m (14 ft 9 in)
Powerplant: 1×Rollason Ardem Mk X, 33.5 kW (45 hp)
Max T/O weight: 329 kg (725 lb)
Max speed: 90 mph at sea level
Range: 200 miles

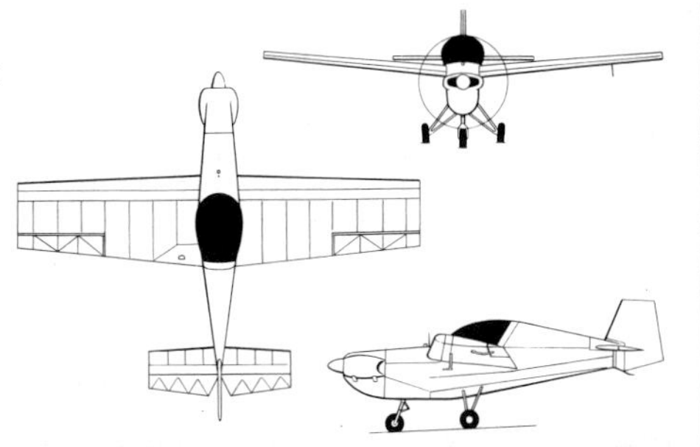

Trago Mills/Orca SAH-1

Intended to meet much the same need as the ARV Super2 but at slightly higher performance levels, the SAH-1 was designed from October 1977 and first flown in August 1983 after design by Sidney A.Holloway as a comparatively simple side-by-side two-seater for light touring and sporting use, the latter including full aerobatic capability. The type is of conventional low-wing layout and light alloy construction (with portions of the wing and tailplane skinning stabilised by PVC foam), and has fixed tricycle landing gear. The SAH-1 was envisaged from the start as a very reliable type of low cost but requiring little maintenance and offering attractive operating economics. The aeroplane has proved docile yet tractable in the air, but production plans have been severely hampered by financial problems. It is hoped to start production by Orca, newly formed for the purpose, by the early 1990s.

Beagle A.61 Terrier/A.113 Husky

When its AOP.Mk 9 observation aeroplane began to enter service in the late 1950s, Auster bought back 100 or more examples of its earlier AOP.Mks 6 and 7 aircraft for sale on the civil market after they had been remanufactured with a larger vertical tail. Powered by a 108-kW (145-hp) de Havilland Gipsy Major 10, the two variants were the Auster 6A glider-tug and utility type, and the Auster 6B three-seat tourer. The Auster 6B later became the A.61 Terrier 1, and was joined by 41 Terrier 2s with a larger tailplane and a single Terrier 3 with the 119-kW (160-hp) Avco Lycoming O-320-B engine. Introduced in May 1963, the Husky was a utility version of the Auster D.5/180, and 14 production aircraft were built with the O-360-A engine; a similar type was built in Portugal by OGMA with the original D.5/180 designation and used mainly for agricultural purposes.

Specification: Beagle A.113 Husky three-seat light general-purpose monoplane
Span: 10.97 m (36 ft 0 in)
Length: 7.06 m (23 ft 2 in)
Powerplant: 1×Avco Lycoming O-360-A2A, 134 kW (180 hp)
Max T/O weight: 1089 kg (2,400 lb)
Max speed: 125 mph at sea level
Range: 580 miles

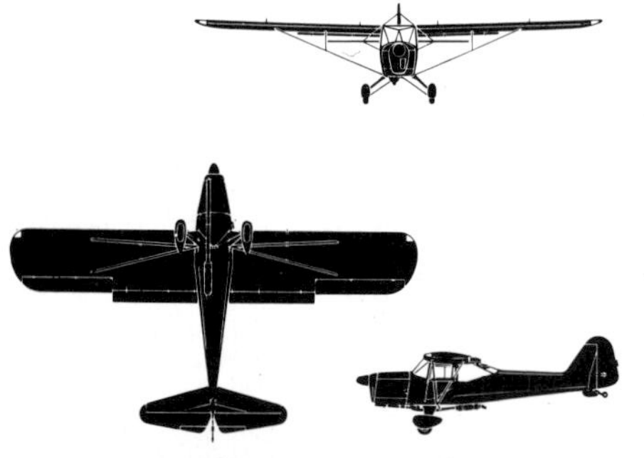

Beagle A.109 /Airedale

As is suggested by its alphanumeric designator, this four-seat type was designed by Auster before its transformation into Beagle Aircraft. Though the aeroplane sported the fixed tricycle landing gear and the swept fin and rudder assembly that were so modish in light aircraft of this type during the late 1950s and early 1960s, it was otherwise of typical Auster concept with great structural strength. It also possessed typical Auster limitations such as fabric covering, a large external exhaust system, an over-elaborate strut arrangement, and excessive structural weight. The Airedale first flew in April 1961, and when production ceased in August 1964 only 43 sales had been made to 36 British and seven export customers: most potential buyers were attracted by all-metal types such as the aerodynamically more refined Cessna 172 and 175.

Specification: Beagle A.109 Airedale four-seat light touring monoplane
Span: 11.07 m (36 ft 4 in)
Length: 8.03 m (26 ft 4 in)
Powerplant: 1×Avco Lycoming O-360-A1A, 134 kW (180 hp)
Max T/O weight: 1202 kg (2,650 lb)
Max speed: 148 mph at sea level
Range: 650 miles

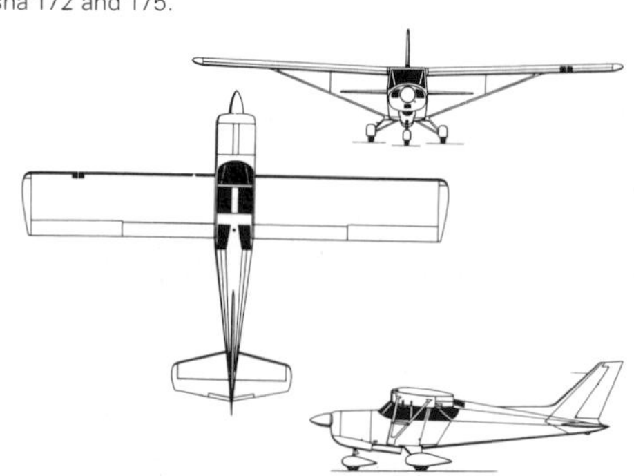

*Wearing a smart blue and white scheme, **G-SAHI** is the prototype **SAH-1**, the latest British attempt to break into the light civil training aircraft market. Despite its name (Orca being the latin for 'whale'), the **SAH-1** is a diminutive, graceful aircraft with pleasing lines. First flown during 1983, the **SAH-1** has proved docile and reliable, but unfortunately financial problems have been a restricting influence in its development. The way ahead now looks secure, however, and production deliveries should begin during 1990.*

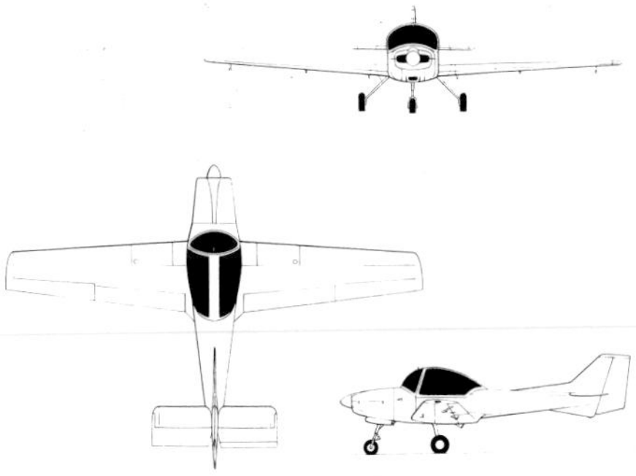

Specification: Trago Mills/Orca SAH-1 two-seat light touring and sport monoplane
Span: 9.36 m (30 ft 8.4 in)
Length: 6.66 m (21 ft 10.25 in)
Powerplant: 1×Avco Lycoming O-235-N2A, 87 kW (116 hp)
Max T/O weight: 794 kg (1,750 lb)
Max speed: 140 mph at sea level
Operational range: 714 miles

Rollason D.62 Condor

\fter starting as a sales and service organisation, Rollason moved into lightplane onstruction with a licence to produce Druine aircraft, initially the single-seat D.31 Turbulent vith versions of the Ardem flat-four engines rated at between 25 and 30 kW (34 and 40 hp). n the early 1960s Rollason began construction of the side-by-side two-seat D.62 Condor. he prototype was powered by a 56-kW (75-hp) Continental A75 engine, but production ircraft were two D.62As with the 75-kW (100-hp) Rolls-Royce (Continental) O-200-A, 42 nproved D.62Bs with the same engine, and four D.62C glider-tugs with the 97-kW (130-hp) olls-Royce (Continental) O-240-A engine. The D-62B was 0.102 m (4 in) shorter than the).62A, all but the first four aircraft were fitted with trailing-edge flaps, and some aircraft had lipped wings with endplate surfaces.

pecification: Rollason D.62B ondor two-seat light sport onoplane
pan: 8.38 m (27 ft 6 in)
ength: 6.96 m (22 ft 10 in)
owerplant: 1×Rolls-Royce Continental) O-200-A, 75 kW 00 hp)
ax T/O weight: 669 kg (1,475 lb)
ax speed: 100 mph at sea level
ange: 385 miles

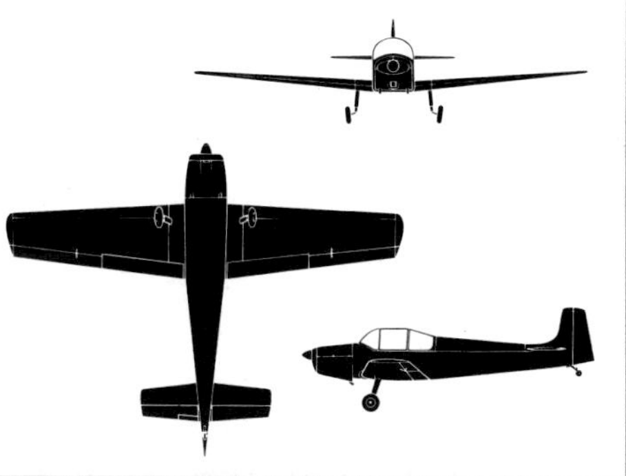

Britten-Norman BN-3 Nymph

First flown in May 1969, the Nymph was planned as a low-cost general-purpose lightplane specifically for the export market, and featured optional folding wings to reduce hangar requirements. The idea was for batches of aircraft to be supplied as kits of precision-made components for easy assembly by any adequate aircraft repair and maintenance organisation in the ordering country: this reduced shipping costs and avoided most customs duties, so improving the chances of the type's penetration into the Middle Eastern and Third World markets. The initial model was to have been joined by uprated variants with a 97-kW (130-hp) Rolls-Royce (Continental) O-240 or a 119-kW (160-hp) Avco Lycoming O-320 engine, but the demands of BN-2 Islander production and the company's financial problems of the early 1970s led to the abandonment of the plan.

Specification: Britten-Norman BN-3 Nymph four-seat light general-purpose monoplane
Span: 11.98 m (39 ft 3.9 in)
Length: 7.20 m (23 ft 7.7 in)
Powerplant: 1×Avco Lycoming O-235-C1B, 86 kW (115 hp)
Max T/O weight: 1065 kg (2,350 lb)
Max speed: 117 mph at sea level
Operational range: 600 miles

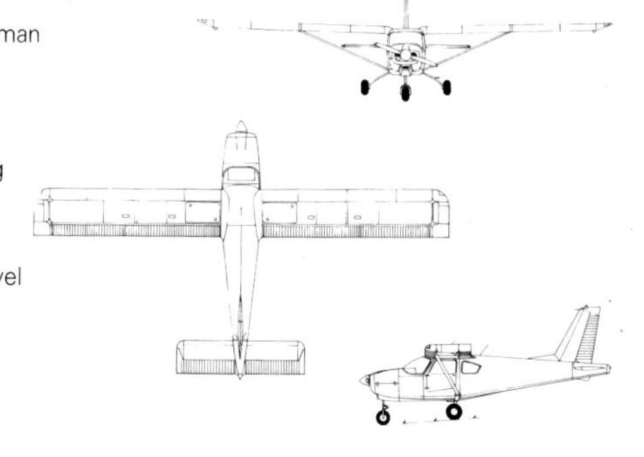

SAN (Jodel) D.140

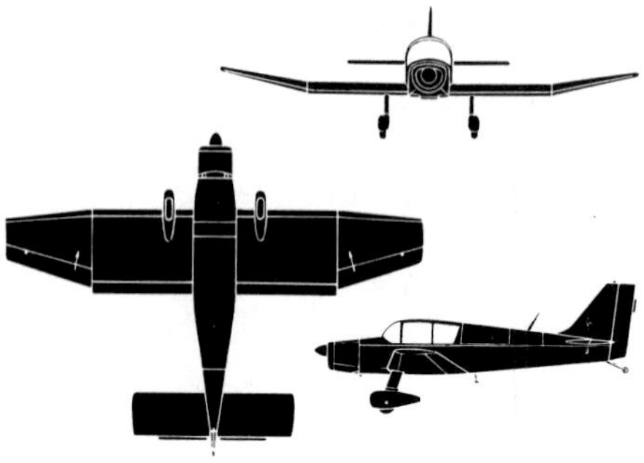

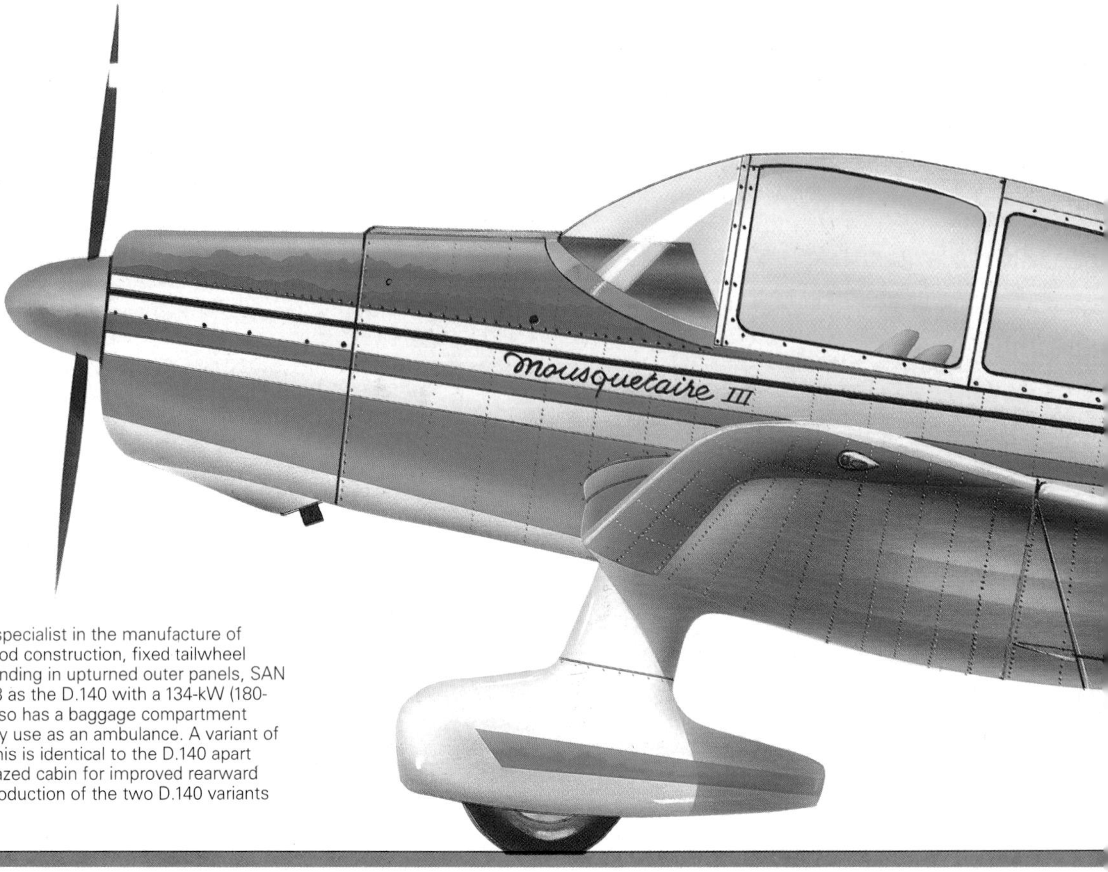

Like Robin, the Société Aéronautique Normande was a specialist in the manufacture of Jodel designs. From the basic Jodel concept with all-wood construction, fixed tailwheel landing gear and the highly characteristic low-set wing ending in upturned outer panels, SAN evolved a four/five-seat model that first flew in July 1958 as the D.140 with a 134-kW (180-hp) O-360 engine. Behind the cabin the Mousquetaire also has a baggage compartment large enough to accommodate a stretcher for emergency use as an ambulance. A variant of the Mousquetaire is the D.140R Abeille glider tug, and this is identical to the D.140 apart from its glider-towing fitment and a more extensively glazed cabin for improved rearward fields of vision. In 1969 SAN went into liquidation and production of the two D.140 variants was shifted to Avions Pierre Robin.

Nord 1203/II Norécrin II

After the French liberation of 1944 Nord continued its production of the Bf 108 monoplane as the Nord 1000 and 1100. Using the same basic configuration, the company then developed the Nord 1200 with fixed tricycle landing gear, whose prototype flew in December 1945 with a 75-kW (100-hp) Mathis G4R engine. There were several military and civil variants, the main versions to enter civil service being the three-seat Nord 1201 Norécrin I with the 104-kW (140-hp) Renault 4Pei engine, the four-seat Nord 1203/II Norécrin II with the 101-kW (135-hp) Regnier 4L00, the Nord 1203/III Norécrin III with modified landing gear, the Nord 1203/IV Norécrin IV with the 127-kW (170-hp) Regnier 4L02, the Nord 1203/VI Norécrin VI with the 108-kW (145-hp) Regnier 4L14, and the final Nord 1204 and Nord 1204/II models of 1959 with the 93- and 108-kW (125- and 145-hp) Continental C125 and C145 engines respectively.

Specification: Nord 1203/II Norécrin II four-seat touring lightplane
Span: 10.22 m (33 ft 6.25 in)
Length: 7.21 m (23 ft 8 in)
Powerplant: 1×Regnier 4L00, 101 kW (135 hp)
Max T/O weight: 1050 kg (2,315 lb)
Max speed: 137 mph at sea level
Operational range: 559 miles

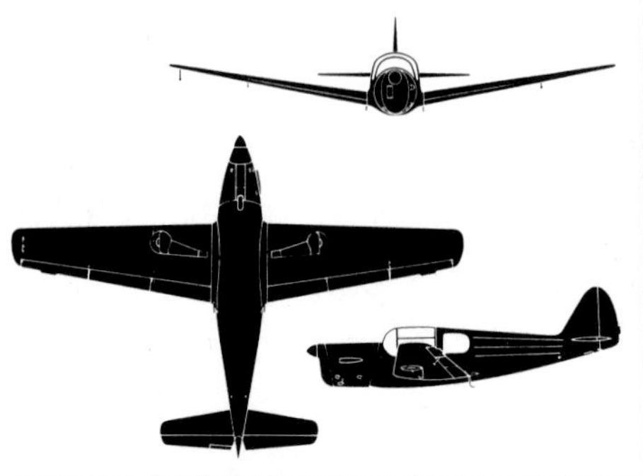

SIPA (CAB/Gardan) GY.20 & GY.201

First flown in February 1949 after development by Yves Gardan, the Minicab is a trim cabin monoplane of low-wing configuration with fixed tailwheel landing gear whose cantilever main units are neatly but optionally spatted to reduce drag as well as improve an already attractive appearance. Production was entrusted to the Constructions Aéronautiques du Bearn, which delivered the first aircraft in 1952, and support for this light type subsequently passed to SIPA (the Société Industrielle Pour l'Aéronautique). There were two production variants of the Minicab, the GY.20 and GY.201, these differing from each other only in details of equipment and other small features. Small numbers of both variants are still flying.

Specification: SIPA (CAB/Gardan) GY.20 Minicab two-seat sport and touring lightplane
Span: 7.59 m (24 ft 11 in)
Length: 5.45 m (17 ft 10.5 in)
Powerplant: 1×Continental A65-8, 48.5 kW (65 hp)
Max T/O weight: 485 kg (1,069 lb)
Max speed: 124 mph at sea level
Operational range: 466 miles

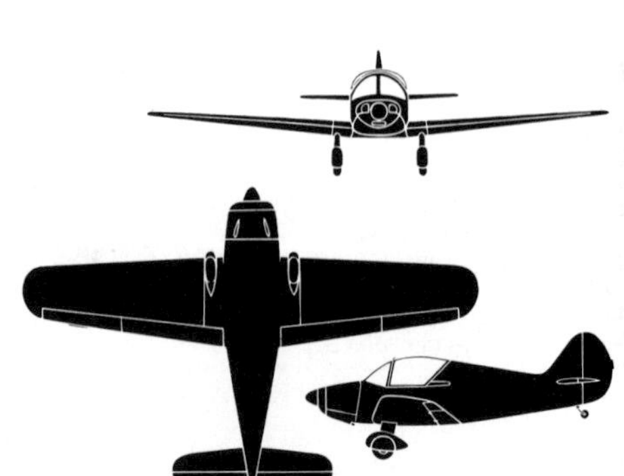

pecification: SAN (Jodel) .140 Mousquetaire four/five-seat port and touring lightplane
pan: 10.27 m (33 ft 8.25 in)
ength: 7.82 m (25 ft 8 in)
owerplant: 1×Avco Lycoming -360-A2A, 134 kW (180 hp)
lax T/O weight: 1200 kg ,646 lb)
lax speed: 158 mph at sea level
perational range: 870 miles

A French civil-registered Jodel D.140C, Mousquetaire III. The Jodel D.140 family uses the same all-wood construction and fixed tailwheel landing gear as the smaller Jodels, and has the same characteristic upturned wingtips.

Jodel DR.100 series

he DR.100 was developed jointly by Pierre Robin and the original designer of the Jodel eries, Jean Delemontez, as a high-performance three-seater with the 71-kW (95-hp) ontinental C90 engine. The aeroplane entered production in 1958, and after 10 had been uilt the type was redesignated D.1050 Ambassadeur during 1961. Production of the R.1050 and its improved DR.1051 variant totalled 148. Subsequent versions were the R.1050/M Sicile and DR.1050 Sicile Record each with the 70-kW (150-hp) Rolls-Royce Continental) O-200-A, of which 114 and 58 were built respectively. The final type was the R.1052 Excellence, a 1963 development of the DR.1050 with either the O-200-A or the 8-kW (105-hp) Potez 4 E-20 engine. These types were produced in similar forms by Avions ierre Robin and also by the Société Aéronautique Normande.

pecification: SAN/Robin Jodel) DR.1050 Sicile Record two/ hree-seat sport and touring ghtplane
pan: 8.71 m (28 ft 7.25 in)
ength: 6.35 m (20 ft 10 in)
owerplant: 1×Rolls-Royce Continental) O-200-A, 75 kW 00 hp)
lax T/O weight: 780 kg (1,720 lb)
lax speed: 133 mph at sea level
perational range: 775 miles

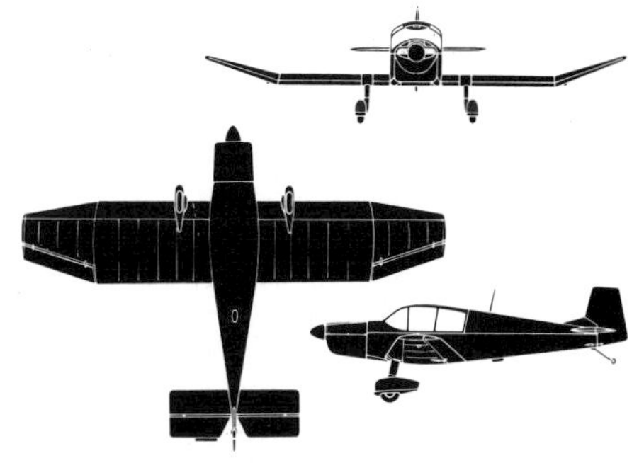

Wassmer WA-40 series

The Société des Etablissements Benjamin Wassmer cut its teeth on licensed production of Jodel aircraft, and its first own-design type was the WA-40 Super IV that first flew in June 1959 as a mixed-construction four/five-seat tourer with the 134-kW (180-hp) O-360-A1A: some 180 aircraft were produced in three variants (the Directeur basic model, the Commandant du Bord de luxe model and the President IFR model) with different equipment standards. In 1965 the company introduced a variant with fixed landing gear, and this WA-41 Baladou also had a different engine and simplified systems for lower purchase cost. The final development of this initial series was the WA 4/21 Prestige with the 175-kW (235-hp) IO-540 engine, a variable-pitch propeller and refinements such as an autopilot, blind-flying instrumentation and electrically operated flaps. The Cerva CE-43 Guepard is an all-metal derivative.

Specification: Wassmer WA-41 Baladou four/five-seat touring lightplane
Span: 10.00 m (32 ft 9.4 in)
Length: 8.09 m (26 ft 6.5 in)
Powerplant: 1×Avco Lycoming O-360-A2A, 134 kW (180 hp)
Max T/O weight: 1200 kg (2,646 lb)
Max speed: 158 mph at sea level
Operational range: 1,056 miles

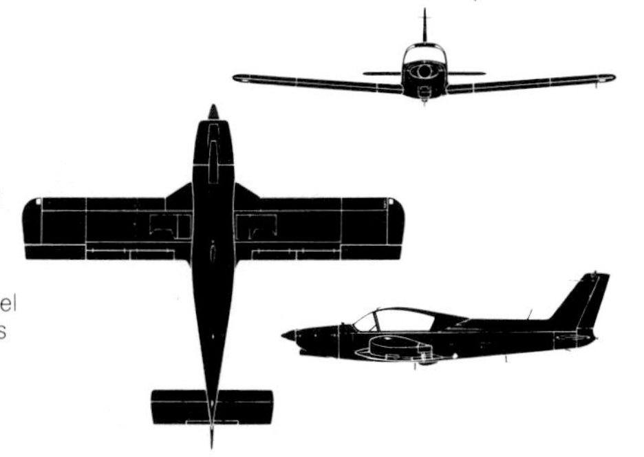

Avions Pierre Robin **DR.400 series**

Specification: Avions Pierre Robin DR.400/180 Regent four-seat sport and touring lightplane
Span: 8.72 m (28 ft 7.25 in)
Length: 6.96 m (22 ft 10 in)
Powerplant: 1×Avco Lycoming O-360-A, 134 kW (180 hp)
Max T/O weight: 1100 kg (2,425 lb)
Max speed: 173 mph at sea level
Operational range: 900 miles

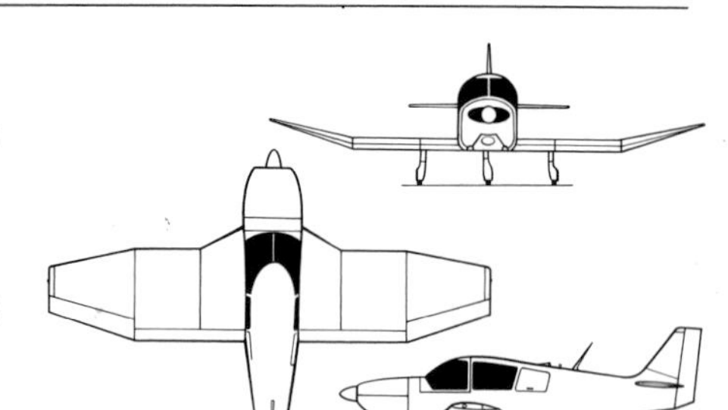

This Robin DR.400/212 carries a French civil registration. Avions Pierre Robin have produced a range of lightplanes loosely based on the Jodel design, and the four-seat DR.400 is probably the best known and most popular.

SOCATA Rallye

The Rallye series began life with the Morane-Saulnier M.S.880, an all-metal low-wing monoplane with retractable landing gear. It first flew in June 1959 and was then produced in a number of variants. In 1965 the company became a subsidiary of Sud-Aviation, which in 1966 created its SOCATA lightplane subsidiary that is now a part of Aérospatiale. In 1979 the SOCATA product line was redesignated, and the Rallye series was renamed. Thus the Rallye 110ST two-seat trainer with the 82-kW (110-hp) O-235-L2A engine became the Galopin, the Rallye 180T glider tug with the 134-kW (180-hp) O-360-A3A became the Galerien, and the Rallye 235GT high-performance STOL four-seater with the O-540 became the Gabier with options of tricycle or tailwheel landing gear. These major models were complemented by other variants with Franklin or Rolls-Royce/Continental engines.

Specification: SOCATA Gabier four-seat touring lightplane
Span: 9.75 m (31 ft 11.75 in)
Length: 7.25 m (23 ft 9.5 in)
Powerplant: 1×Avco Lycoming O-540-B4B5, 175 kW (235 hp)
Max T/O weight: 1200 kg (2,646 lb)
Max speed: 171 mph at sea level
Operational range: 677 miles

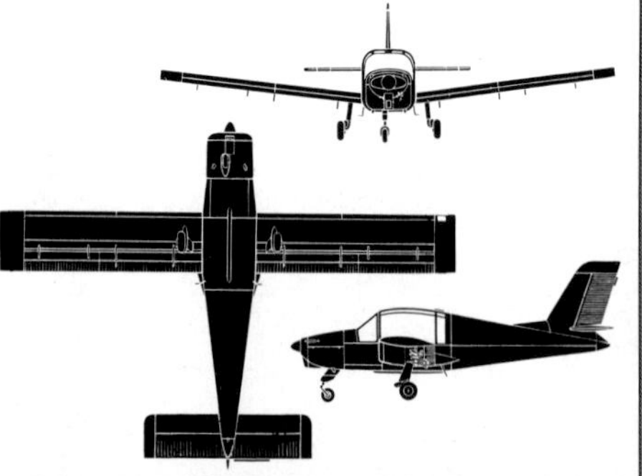

SOCATA (Gardan) **GY.80 Horizon**

One of SOCATA's first products was the GY.80 Horizon under licence from Yves Gardan, the well-known French designer of lightplanes. The type first flew in July 1960 and is of all-metal construction with standard low-wing monoplane configuration and full-span Fowler-type flaps and Frise-type ailerons. The tricycle landing gear is somewhat unusual in that all three units retract to the rear and leave their wheels partially exposed: this increases drag but offers a measure of protection to the aeroplane's undersurfaces in the event of a wheels-up landing. The first 75 aircraft have the 119-kW (160-hp) O-320-D engine driving a fixed-pitch two-blade wooden propeller, later aircraft having more power and a constant-speed three-blade propeller. Production of 260 aircraft lasted to 1969.

Specification: SOCATA (Gardan) GY.80 Horizon four-seat sport and touring lightplane
Span: 9.70 m (31 ft 9.75 in)
Length: 6.64 m (21 ft 9.5 in)
Powerplant: 1×Avco Lycoming O-360-A, 134 kW (180 hp)
Max T/O weight: 1150 kg (2,535 lb)
Max speed: 155 mph at sea level
Operational range: 777 miles

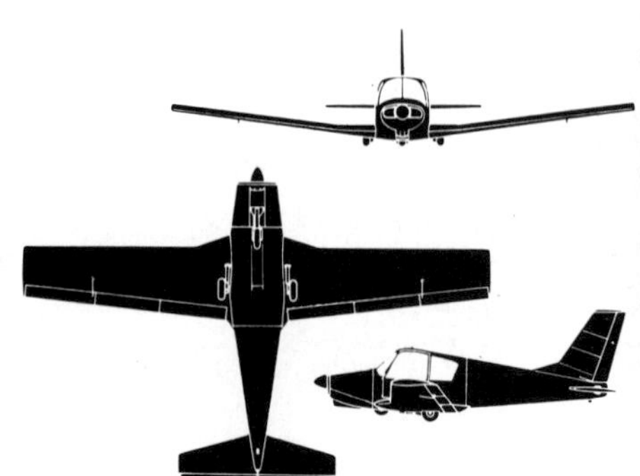

Formed in 1957 as Centre-Est Aéronautique and becoming Avions Pierre Robin in 1969, this company has produced several lightplanes based on Jodel basic designs. From the fabric-covered wooden DR.300 series with fixed tricycle landing gear the company evolved the DR.400, introduced in May 1972 with features such as a forward-sliding canopy and lower cabin sides for improved fields of vision. The series has generally featured Avco Lycoming engines of a horsepower indicated by the designation suffix, and the original 1972 types include the DR.400/2+2 for two adults and two children, the three/four-seat DR.400/125 Petit Prince, the four-seat DR.400/140 Major, the DR.400/160 Chevalier, the DR.400/180 Regent and the DR.400/180R Remorquer glider tug. Later additions have been the DR.400/100 Cadet, the DR.400/120 Dauphin 80 and a DR.400/180 variant with the 158-kW (212-hp) Porsche PFM.3200 engine.

Wassmer WA-50 series

Wassmer started development of an all-plastics lightplane in 1962 with the object of producing a comparatively cheap but durable and easily maintained type for the private owner. The WA-50 prototype flew in March 1966 as a four-seater powered by the 112-kW (150-hp) O-320 engine. Production began in the form of the WA-51 Pacific with fixed tricycle landing gear and the 112-kW (150-hp) O-320-E2A engine, though a companion model was produced as the WA-52 Europa with the 119-kW (160-hp) IO-320-B1A driving a variable-pitch propeller. As these two initial models went out of production in 1973 the company introduced the WA-54 Atlantic with the 134-kW (180-hp) O-360-A engine, more baggage volume, revisions to the landing gear, and other modifications. Wassmer went into liquidation in 1977, and by that time sales of the WA-50 series totalled 190 aircraft.

Specification: Wassmer WA-54 Atlantic four-seat touring lightplane
Span: 9.40 m (30 ft 10 in)
Length: 7.50 m (24 ft 7.25 in)
Powerplant: 1×Avco Lycoming O-360-A, 134 kW (180 hp)
Max T/O weight: 1130 kg (2,491 lb)
Max speed: 174 mph at sea level
Operational range: 839 miles

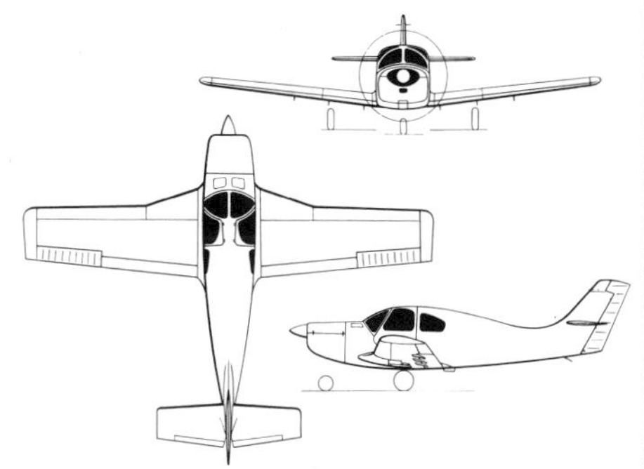

Avions Pierre Robin HR.100 series

The HR.100 first flew in April 1969, and is in essence a development of the DR.253 Régent with metal construction. The first production variant was the HR.100/180 with the 134-kW (180-hp) Avco Lycoming O-360, but this was soon replaced by the HR.100/200 with a 149-kW (200-hp) IO-360. The HR.100/320/4+2 upengined variant for two children as well as four adults failed to progress past the prototype stage, so the next model was the HR.100/210 with a 157-kW (210-hp) engine. At this stage retractable landing gear and Continental engines entered the picture to produce the HR.100/285 with the 239-kW (285-hp) Tiara: this model entered production with the Tiara 6-285B version of the engine. This basic model was also produced in the HR.100/250TR version with the 186-kW (250-hp) Avco Lycoming IO-540 engine.

Specification: Avions Pierre Robin HR.100/285 four-seat sport and touring lightplane
Span: 9.08 m (29 ft 9.5 in)
Length: 7.59 m (24 ft 10.75 in)
Powerplant: 1×Teledyne Continental Tiara 6-285B, 239 kW (285 hp)
Max T/O weight: 1400 kg (3,086 lb)
Max speed: 202 mph at sea level
Operational range: 1,323 miles

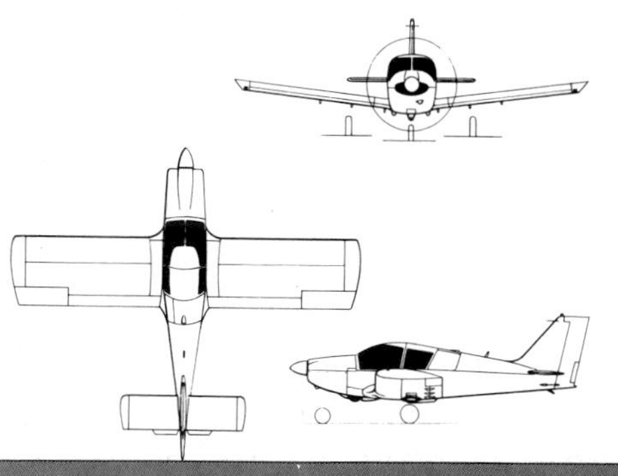

SOCATA ST.10 Diplomate

From the all-metal GY.80 Horizon SOCATA developed an improved model that first flew in November 1967 with a lengthened fuselage, a redesigned cabin, a modified tail unit, a more powerful engine and revised landing gear. This last adopted main units that retracted inwards into the undersurfaces of the wings, while the nosewheel unit retracted to leave about one-quarter of the wheel exposed. Initially designated Super Horizon 2000 and then Provence, the type eventually became the ST.10 Diplomate by the time production deliveries began at the end of 1969. Despite the fact that it offered a usefully higher level of performance than the Horizon, the type failed to attract any real sales enthusiasm and SOCATA ended production in 1975 after delivery of only 56 examples.

Specification: SOCATA ST.10 Diplomate four-seat sport and touring lightplane
Span: 9.70 m (31 ft 9.75 in)
Length: 7.26 m (23 ft 9.75 in)
Powerplant: 1×Avco Lycoming IO-360-C1B, 149 kW (200 hp)
Max T/O weight: 1220 kg (2,690 lb)
Max speed: 174 mph at sea level
Operational range: 860 miles

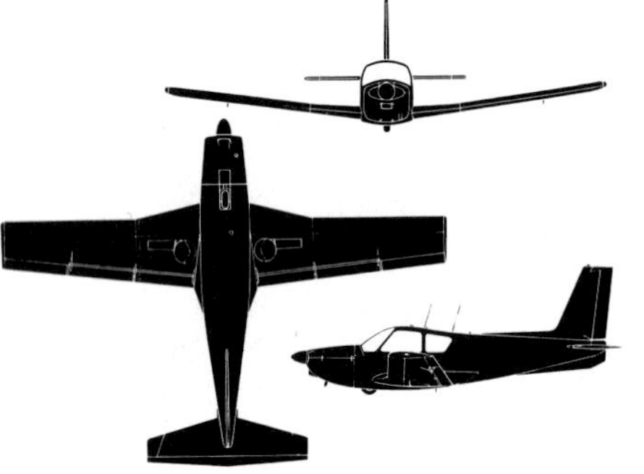

Robin HR.200 series

The HR.200 was produced in response to a French flying school and club requirement for a two-seat trainer with modest touring capability, and first flew in prototype form during July 1971 as a low-wing monoplane of all-metal construction with fixed but elegantly spatted tricycle landing gear and a large clear-view canopy with a forward-sliding front section. Like other Robin types the HR.200 was produced in variants with Avco Lycoming engines of different ratings. The basic models were the HR.200/100 Club with the 81-kW (108-hp) O-235-H2C, the HR.200/120 with the 93-kW (125-hp) O-235-J2A, the HR.200/140 with the O-320-E and the HR.200/160 with the IO-320-D. Later two low-cost versions were produced as the HR.200/100S based on the HR.200/100 but with simpler equipment and no wheel spats, and the HR.200/120B with the 88-kW (118-hp) O-235-L2A.

Specification: Avions Pierre Robin HR.200/160 two-seat training and sport lightplane
Span: 8.33 m (27 ft 4 in)
Length: 6.64 m (21 ft 9.5 in)
Powerplant: 1×Avco Lycoming IO-320-D, 119 kW (160 hp)
Max T/O weight: 800 kg (1,763 lb)
Max speed: 161 mph at sea level
Operational range: 581 miles

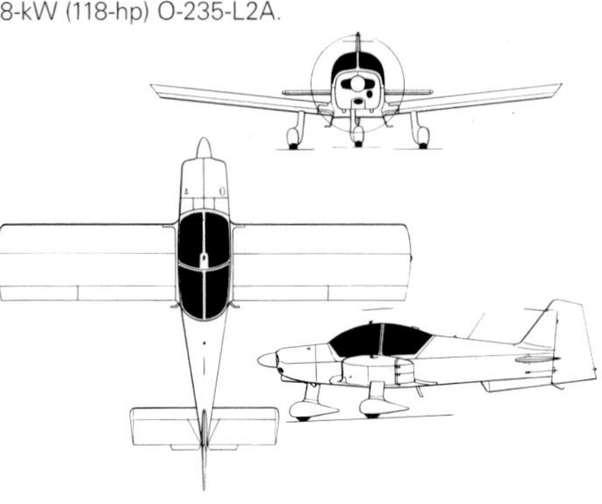

SOCATA TB.9, 10/11 & TB.20

This series was originated in 1975 as a supplement to the Rallye family with fixed landing gear and lower performance but greater accommodation. The series began with the TB.10 that first flew in February 1977 with a 119-kW (160-hp) O-320-D2A engine. The type was later named Tobago, but with the development of a higher-powered model the original type became the four-seat TB.9 Tampico so that the designation TB.10 Tobago could be accorded to the newer four/five-seat model with the 134-kW (180-hp) O-360-A1AD. The third member of the family flew in November 1980 as the TB.20 Trinidad with more power and, more importantly, retractable tricycle landing gear. The latest variant was introduced in 1983 as the TB.11 aerobatic version of the Tobago with an inverted flight engine/fuel system for the training of professional pilots.

Specification: SOCATA TB.20 Trinidad four/five-seat touring lightplane
Span: 9.76 m (32 ft 0.25 in)
Length: 7.71 m (25 ft 3.5 in)
Powerplant: 1×Avco Lycoming IO-540-C4D5D, 186 kW (250 hp)
Max T/O weight: 1335 kg (2,943 lb)
Max speed: 193 mph at sea level
Operational range: 1,109 miles

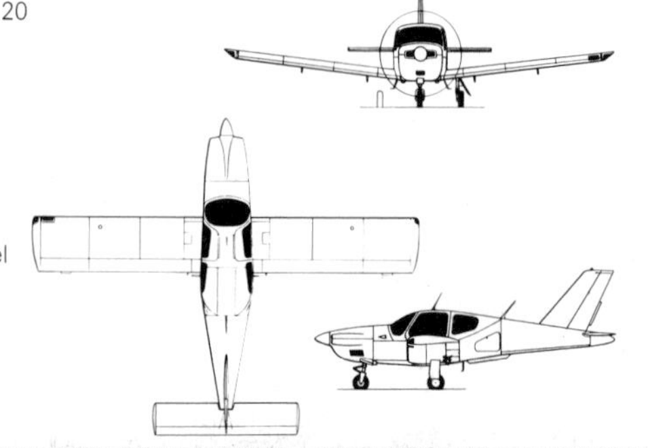

Avions Pierre Robin ATL

Robin began work on its Avion Tres Léger (very light aeroplane) in 1981 with the intention of producing a lightplane that would be cheap both to buy and to operate. The concept matured with a pod-and-boom fuselage whose wide side-by-side cockpit section tapers into a slim rear section terminating in a V-tail, fixed tricycle landing gear and a specially developed 35-kW (47-hp) Ateliers JPX air-cooled engine. Construction is mixed, the wings being of wood with fabric covering and the fuselage being a glassfibre/honeycomb/epoxy unit. The first example flew in June 1983, and testing led to certification to FAR Pt 23 standards. The far-sighted French government has ordered the type for government-sponsored training schools, and production is also being undertaken for private operators. The definitive version is the ATL Club with a more powerful engine and a number of operationally desirable refinements.

Specification: Avions Pierre Robin ATL Club two-seat sport lightplane
Span: 10.25 m (33 ft 7.5 in)
Length: 6.70 m (21 ft 11.8 in)
Powerplant: 1×Ateliers JPX 4T-60A, 44.7 kW (60 hp)
Max T/O weight: 580 kg (1,279 lb)
Max speed: 112 mph at sea level
Operational range: 714 miles

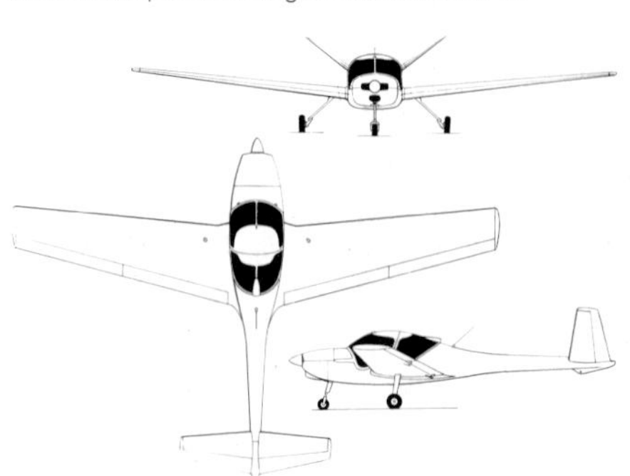

Robin DR.400 series

Formed in 1957, Centre Est Aeronautique became Avions Pierre Robin in 1969, and is the major producer of Jodel designs. Jodel's first design with tricycle landing gear was produced from 1967 as the Robin DR.253 Regent, and this was followed by derivatives such as the DR.315 Cadet, DR.330, DR.340 Major, DR.360 Chevalier and DR.380 Prince with different engines. In 1972 Robin introduced the DR.400 series based on the DR.300 type but with a forward-sliding canopy and lowered cabin sidewalls. The series includes the DR.400/125 Petit Prince, DR.400/140 Earl, DR.400/180 Regent, DR.400/160 Knight, DR.400/160 Major 80, DR.400/180R Remorqueur, DR.400/2+2 and DR.400/120 Dauphin 80. The Remorqueur is a glider tug, and the others are three/four-seaters with engine power indicated by the figure after the oblique stroke.

Specification: Robin DR.400/180 Regent four-seat cabin monoplane
Span: 8.72 m (28 ft 7.25 in)
Length: 6.96 m (22 ft 10 in)
Powerplant: 1×Avco Lycoming O-360-A, 134 kW (180 hp)
Max T/O weight: 1,100 kg (2,425 lb)
Cruising speed: 166 mph at optimum altitude
Range: 900 miles

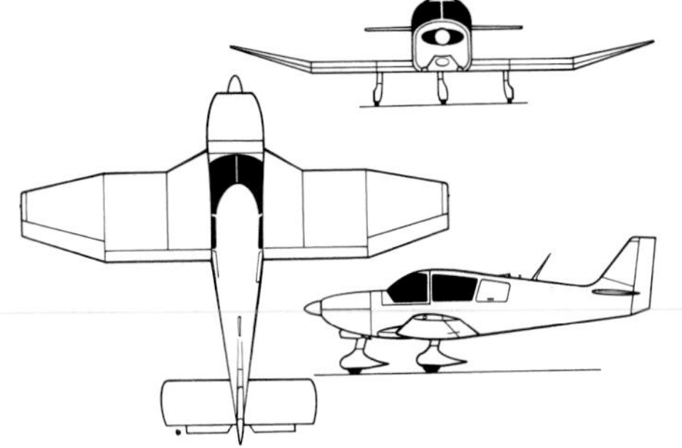

Robin HR.200 and R.2000

The HR.200 was produced in response to a perceived requirement for a light all-metal two-seater suitable for flying clubs and training schools. The prototype flew in July 1971 and the type entered production as the HR.200/100 Club with an 81-kW (108-hp) Avco Lycoming O-235-H2C engine. The only other variant with this engine was the HR.200/120, and development continued with the more powerful O-320 engine in the HR.200/140 and HR.200/160. Lower-cost models with fewer 'frills' were the HR.200/100S and the HR.200/120B. The R.2000 series was introduced in 1976 to replace the HR.200. This aerobatic type retains the fuselage but has larger flying surfaces. Variants are the R.2160 (known as the Akrobin and then Alpha Sport), the lower-powered R.2100A trainer and its successor, the R.2112 Alpha.

Specification: Robin R.2160 Alpha Sport two-seat cabin monoplane
Span: 8.33 m (27 ft 4 in)
Length: 7.10 m (23 ft 3.5 in)
Powerplant: 1×Avco Lycoming O-320-D, 119 kW (160 hp)
Max T/O weight: 800 kg (1,764 lb)
Cruising speed: 160 mph at sea level
Range: 494 miles

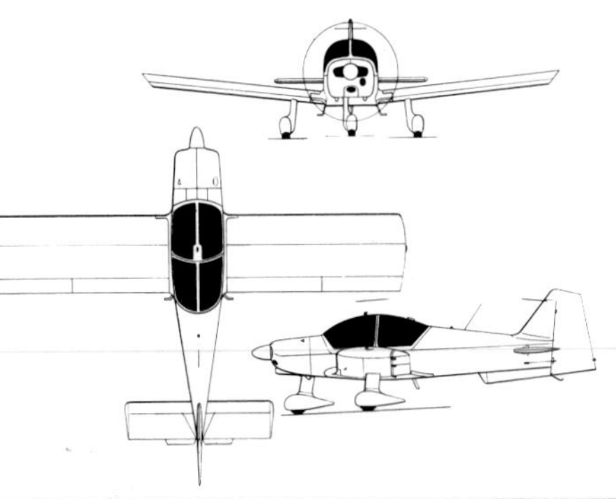

Slingsby T.67 Firefly

The T.67 is essentially the British licence-built version of a French aeroplane, the Fournier RF-6B, and is an elementary trainer with aerobatic capability. The original T.67A retains the all-wooden construction of the RF-6B, but later models are of glass-reinforced plastics construction and come in a variety of forms. The T.67B has an 86-kW (113-hp) O-235 engine while the T.67C and T.67D are powered by the 119-kW (160-hp) Avco Lycoming O-320 driving fixed-pitch and constant-speed propellers respectively. Slingsby also offers the T.67M variant optimized for military customers with a fuel-injected AEIO-360 engine, constant-speed propeller and no provision for the two 68-litre (15-Imp gal) root tanks of the other variants. The T.67M-200 has a 149-kW (200-hp) AEIO-360 engine and a variable-pitch propeller.

Specification: Slingsby T.67B Firefly two-seat training aeroplane
Span: 10.59 m (34 ft 9 in)
Length: 7.26 m (23 ft 10 in)
Powerplant: 1×Avco Lycoming O-235-N2A, 86 kW (120 hp)
Max T/O weight: 907 kg (2,000 lb)
Cruising speed: 127 mph at 8,000 ft
Range: 356 miles

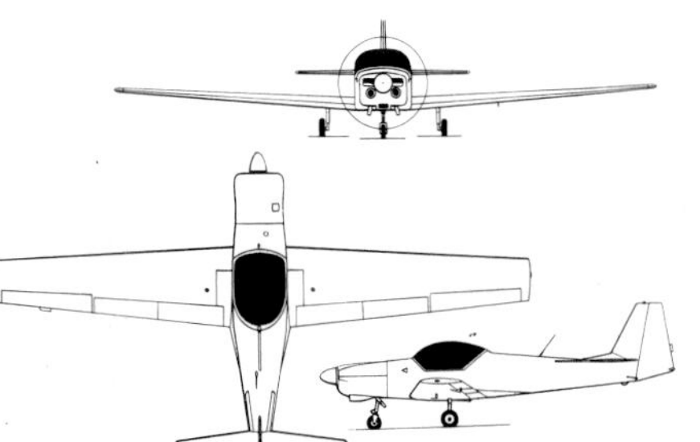

SOCATA Rallye series

The Rallye series began life in June 1959 with the first flight of the Morane-Saulnier MS.880A Rallye-Club, which was certificated in 1961 and remains the source of the series still in production. Morane-Saulnier became a Sud-Aviation subsidiary in 1965, and this nationalised concern hived off light aircraft production to newly created SOCATA in 1966. The original MS.880A was followed by the uprated MS.880B and more powerful MS.885 Super Rallye. Further development produced the 75-kW (100-hp) Rallye 100T tourer, Rallye 100S two-seat sport aeroplane, 82-kW (110-hp) Rallye 110ST Galopin, 93-kW (125-hp) Rallye 125, 112-kW (150-hp) Rallye 150GT, 116-kW (160-hp) Rallye 160ST Garnament, 134-kW (180-hp) Rallye 180T Galerian glider tug and 180GT Gaillard tourer, 164-kW (220-hp) Rallye 220GT and 175-kW (240-hp) Rallye 235GT Gabier.

Specification: SOCATA Rallye 235GT Gabier four-seat cabin monoplane
Span: 9.74 m (31 ft 11.5 in)
Length: 7.25 m (23 ft 9.5 in)
Powerplant: 1×Avco Lycoming O-540-B4B5, 175 kW (240 hp)
Max T/O weight: 1,200 kg (2,646 lb)
Cruising speed: 152 mph at optimum altitude
Range: 677 miles

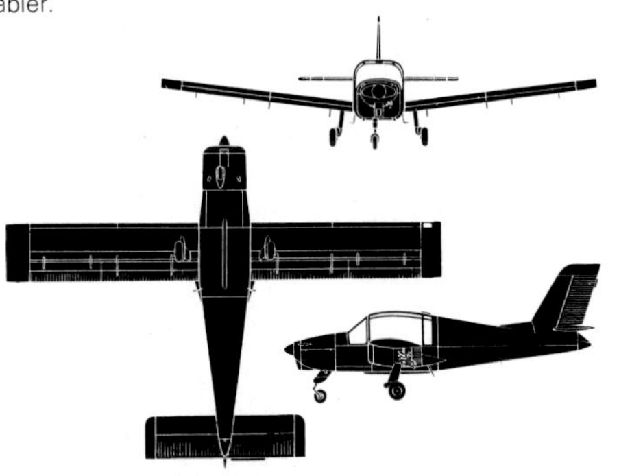

Cessna 150 and 152

Specification: Cessna 150 two-seat cabin monoplane
Span: 9.97 m (32 ft 8.5 in)
Length: 7.29 m (23 ft 11 in)
Powerplant: 1×Teledyne Continental O-200-A, 75 kW (100 hp)
Max T/O weight: 726 kg (1,500 lb)
Cruising speed: 122 mph at 7,000 ft
Range: 835 miles

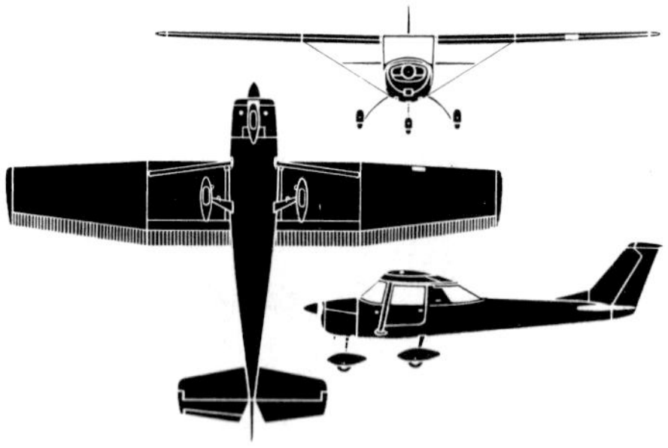

ARV Aviation Super 2

Designed as a two-seat club trainer, offering good performance at an affordable price, the Super 2 has proved successful as an aeroplane but is currently troubled by the financial instability of its manufacturer after an engine-associated problem. The type is a notably compact side-by-side two-seater, uses a high proportion of superplastically formed aluminium alloy pressings, and possesses fixed tricycle landing gear and a high-set braced wing with distinctive forward sweep. The Super 2 prototype was first flown on 11 March 1985, and immediately displayed excellent handling, leading to useful initial sales. The type's only problem has centred on the all-new two-stroke three-cylinder engine from a company noted for its light engines for use in microlight aircraft.

Specification: ARV Aviation Super 2 two-seat primary training aeroplane
Span: 8.69 m (28 ft 6 in)
Length: 5.49 m (18 ft 0 in)
Powerplant: 1×Hewland Engineering liquid-cooled engine, 57 kW (77 hp)
Max T/O weight: 474 kg (1,045 lb)
Cruising speed: 107 mph at 2,000 ft
Range: 311 miles

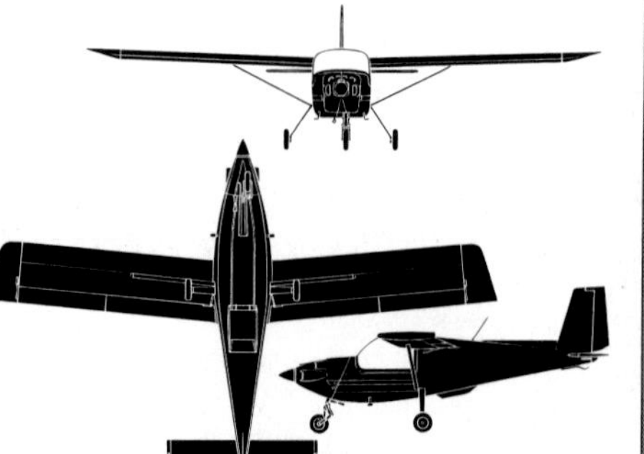

Beagle B.121 Pup series

Beagle was the successor to Auster, and designed the Pup in the hope of regaining a British niche in the light aircraft world. This was not to be, but the Pup remains a good example of its type, and is still very popular. The Pup 100 aerobatic two-seater flew in October 1967 with a 75-kW (100-hp) Rolls-Royce/Continental O-200-A engine, though after only three such aircraft a 112-kW (150-hp) engine was installed to produce the two/four-seat Pup 150, which was first flown in October 1967. The first Pup 150 was later re-engined with a 119-kW (160-hp) Lycoming O-360-A and flew as the Pup 160 in September 1968, followed in April 1969 by the first Pup 200 with a 149-kW (200-hp). Continental engine. Beagle went into receivership in December 1969, and total deliveries of Pups amounted to 152 aircraft with a large number of orders outstanding.

Specification: Beagle B.121 Pup 150 two/four-seat cabin monoplane
Span: 9.45 m (31 ft 0 in)
Length: 7.06 m (23 ft 2 in)
Powerplant: 1×Avco Lycoming O-320-A2B, 112 kW (150 hp)
Max T/O weight: 873 kg (1,925 lb)
Cruising speed: 131 mph at 7,500 ft
Range: 633 miles

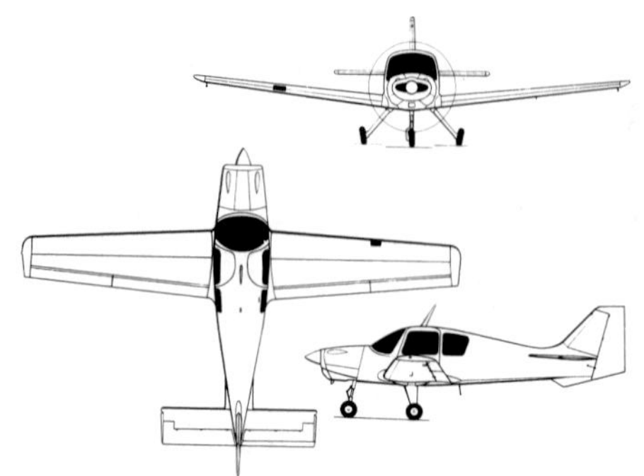

-DFTS is a French-built Reims Cessna FA.152 Aerobat. This high inged monoplane is probably the world's most popular private lot training and touring aircraft. Viceless handling and asonable performance have contributed to its phenomenal ccess. Large numbers are in service throughout the globe.

The Cessna 150 is one of the world's most popular aircraft, and has been built in large numbers in France as well as the USA. The type was designed to provide a 'no-frills' two-seater, and first flew in September 1957 as the aeroplane with which Cessna re-entered the two-seat light aviation market after a seven-year lapse. The Model 150 is of standard Cessna layout and construction, with a high-set braced wing and fixed tricycle landing gear of cantilever type, but has been modernised over the years with features such as a swept fin and cut-down rear fuselage. Models include the Standard, Commuter, Commuter II and Aerobat (stressed to −3*g* and +6*g*). In 1977 the Model 150 was replaced by the Model 152: this is similar in all respects but power, which is provided by an 82-kW (110-hp) Lycoming O-235.

Beech 23 Musketeer series

The Model 23 was developed to compete with various low-cost Cessna and Piper designs after the Bonanza's switch up-market to the luxury range. The first Musketeer flew in October 1961, and was developed into a complete family of touring and aerobatic fixed-gear aircraft with 112/149-kW (150/200-hp) engines. In 1969 the type was revised with retractable landing gear as the Super R, but in 1971 a marketing ploy resulted in a new series of names: the basic four-seat Sundowner C23 with a 134-kW (180-hp) and fixed gear, the two-seat Sport B19 trainer with a 112-kW (150-hp) engine and fixed gear, and the four/six-seat Sierra A24 with a 149-kW (200-hp) engine and retractable gear. A wide range of options was offered, and the series was finally renamed Sundowner 180, Sport 150 and Sierra 200 respectively.

Specification: Beech Sierra 200 four/six-seat cabin monoplane
Span: 9.98 m (32 ft 9 in)
Length: 7.85 m (25 ft 9 in)
Powerplant: 1×Avco Lycoming O-360-A1B6, 149 kW (200 hp)
Max T/O weight: 1,247 kg (2,750 lb)
Cruising speed: 158 mph at optimum altitude
Range: 790 miles

Beech 77 Skipper

The Skipper was designed expressly for use in Beech Aero Center training schools, and first flew in February 1976 with a low-set tailplane. The machine was conceived round the concept of low manufacturing and maintenance costs, excellent handling characteristics, a high-visibility cockpit, and the use of torque tubes in place of pulleys and wires for activation of the control surfaces and flaps. Development was slow, and this allowed Piper to secure an edge in commercial sales with the rapid development and production of its rival Tomahawk. The only major modification before production aircraft began to come off the line in April 1979 was the adoption of a T-tail.

Specification: Beech 77 Skipper two-seat primary training aeroplane
Span: 9.14 m (30 ft 0 in)
Length: 7.32 m (24 ft 0 in)
Powerplant: 1×Avco Lycoming O-235-L2C, 86 kW (115 hp)
Max T/O weight: 760 kg (1,675 lb)
Cruising speed: 121 mph at 4,500 ft
Range: 475 miles

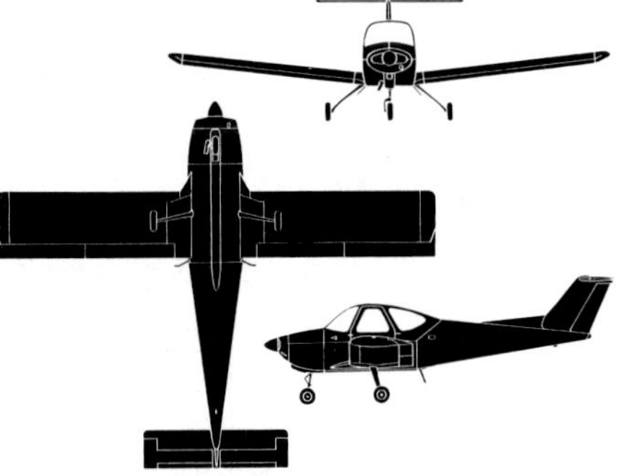

Piper PA-38 Tomahawk

The PA-38 was designed by Piper in the light of answers supplied by some 10,000 flying instructors approached by the company. The Tomahawk is thus an aerobatic two-seater that bears a conceptual likeness to the Beech Skipper it beat into production: a low-wing monoplane with fixed tricycle landing gear, a T-tail and 360° vision cockpit enclosure. The type was announced in October 1977 as a side-by-side two-seat ab initio trainer, and achieved certification as the PA-38-112 Tomahawk in December 1977 before entering service with Piper's large establishment of flying schools as well as other customers. In 1982 the company introduced the improved Tomahawk II.

Specification: Piper PA-38-112 Tomahawk II two-seat trainer and utility cabin monoplane
Span: 10.36 m (34 ft 0 in)
Length: 7.04 m (23 ft 1.5 in)
Powerplant: 1×Avco Lycoming O-235-L2C, 84 kW (112 hp)
Max T/O weight: 757 kg (1,670 lb)
Cruising speed: 126 mph at sea level
Range: 539 miles

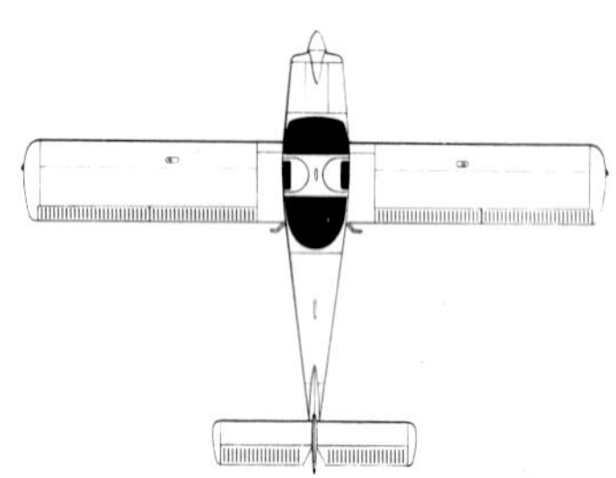

Cessna 172 series

The series that began with the Cessna 170 in 1948 has been the world's best-selling aircraft family, with sales standing at well over 30,000. The Model 170 has tailwheel landing gear and was replaced in 1955 by the Model 172 with tricycle landing gear. In 1958 there appeared the Model 175 with a number of refinements, and in 1959 the manufacturer introduced de luxe versions of the Models 172 and 175 as the Skyhawk and Skylark. The Model 175/Skylark was dropped in 1963, and Cessna introduced the Skyhawk II with a swept fin and cut-down rear fuselage. Running in parallel was the Model 182 Skylane series with greater power, and further development of the Models 172 and 182 has concentrated on additional power and refinement, though there are also Cutlass RG and Skylane RG versions with retractable landing gear.

Specification: Cessna R172E four-seat cabin monoplane
Span: 10.92 m (35 ft 10 in)
Length: 8.20 m (26 ft 11 in)
Powerplant: 1×Teledyne Continental IO-360-D, 157 kW (210 hp)
Max T/O weight: 1,156 kg (2,550 lb)
Cruising speed: 105 mph at 10,000 ft
Range: 1,010 miles

Fuji FA-200 Aero Subaru

After building the Beech Mentor under licence, Fuji embarked on the design of a new four-seat light aeroplane in 1964, and the prototype FA-200 flew in August 1965. The type was certificated as a four-seater in 1966 and entered production as the FA-200-160 with the 119-kW (160-hp) Avco Lycoming O-320-D2A, subsequent certification encompassing the type's use as a three-seater in the utility role and as a two-seater in the aerobatic role. In 1968 the FA-200-180 was certificated with the standard combination of this IO-360-B1B engine and constant-speed propeller. With this combination replaced by a similarly rated O-360-A5AD and a fixed-pitch propeller, the type becomes the FA-200-190AO. The only variant was a single FA-203S STOL prototype with boundary-layer control, leading-edge slats and trailing-edge 'flaperons'.

Specification: Fuji FA-200-180 Aero Subaru four-seat cabin monoplane
Span: 9.42 m (30 ft 11 in)
Length: 8.17 m (26 ft 9.5 in)
Powerplant: 1×Avco Lycoming IO-360-B1B, 134 kW (180 hp)
Max T/O weight: 1,150 kg (2,535 lb)
Cruising speed: 104 mph at 5,000 ft
Range: 835 miles

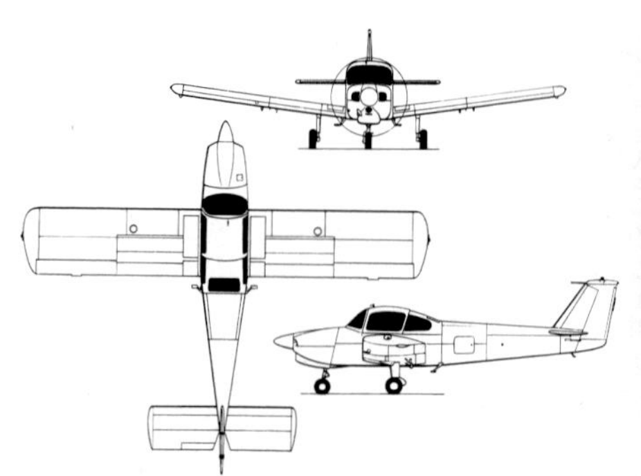

A Piper PA-38 Tomahawk of the Booker based British Airways Flying Club. The club's Tomahawks have been given registrations the last three letters of which read YOU, TOO, CAN, and FLY. The Tomahawks success has been blunted by largely unfounded worries over its spin worthiness, and by criticism of its stodgy handling characteristics.

Grumman AA-5 Cheetah/Tiger

Design work on the AA-5 Traveler was begun in 1970 by American Aviation, which wished to introduce an enlarged version of its AA-1 Yankee to provide four- rather than two-seat accommodation. The prototype flew in August 1970, and the type was certificated in November 1971. In 1972 Grumman bought American Aviation as Grumman American, and in 1974 an improved standard was introduced with a new fin, larger rear windows and greater baggage capacity, and in 1976 there appeared the AA-5A (larger tailplane and more propeller ground clearance) as well as a de luxe version, the Cheetah. A parallel series was pioneered in 1974 with the AA-5B, powered by a 134-kW (180-hp) Avco Lycoming O-360-A4K, and the de luxe version of the AA-5B is the Tiger. In 1978 American Jet Industries bought Grumman American as Gulfstream American.

Specification: Gulfstream American AA-5A four-seat cabin monoplane
Span: 9.60 m (31 ft 6 in)
Length: 6.71 m (22 ft 0 in)
Powerplant: 1×Avco Lycoming O-320-E2G, 112 kW (150 hp)
Max T/O weight: 998 kg (2,200 lb)
Cruising speed: 136 mph at 8,500 ft
Range: 647 miles

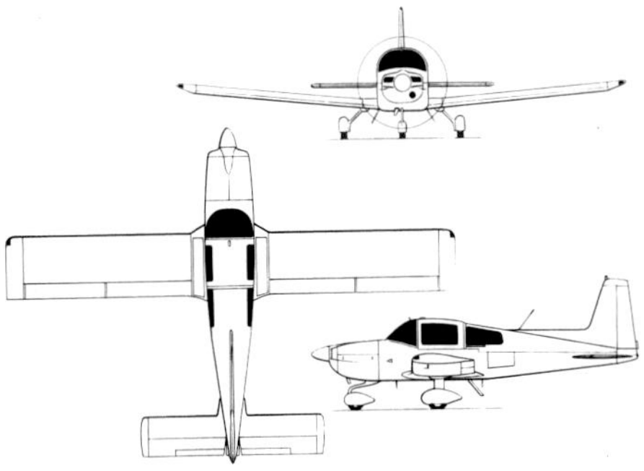

Piper PA-28 Cherokee series

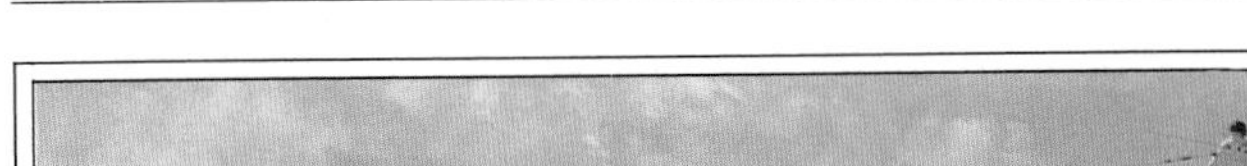

The PA-28 was developed as a replacement for the PA-22 Tri-Pacer. The prototype flew in January 1960, and production began in 1961 with 112- or 119-kW (150- or 160-hp) O-320 engines as the PA-28-160. Later variants have been the PA-28-180 (later Cherokee Challenger and Cherokee Archer), PA-28-235 (Cherokee Charger and Cherokee Pathfinder) and PA-28-140 (Cherokee Flite Liner trainer and Cherokee Cruiser 2 Plus 2 de luxe model). The PA-28-180R Cherokee Arrow of 1967 introduced retractable gear, and the PA-28-200R Cherokee Arrow has more power. In 1974 the PA-28-151 Cherokee Warrior introduced a larger wing. The Cruiser and Pathfinder were phased out in 1977 in favour of an Archer development as the PA-28-236 Dakota and turbocharged as the PA-28-201T Turbo Dakota, complemented by the PA-28-161 Warrior II, PA-28-181 Archer II and PA-28RT-201T Turbo Arrow IV.

Specification: Piper PA28RT-201T Turbo Arrow IV four-seat cabin monoplane
Span: 10.80 m (35 ft 5 in)
Length: 8.33 m (27 ft 3.75 in)
Powerplant: 1×Teledyne Continental TSIO-360-FB, 149 kW (200 hp)
Max T/O weight: 1,315 kg (2,900 lb)
Cruising speed: 205 mph at optimum altitude
Range: 1,035 miles

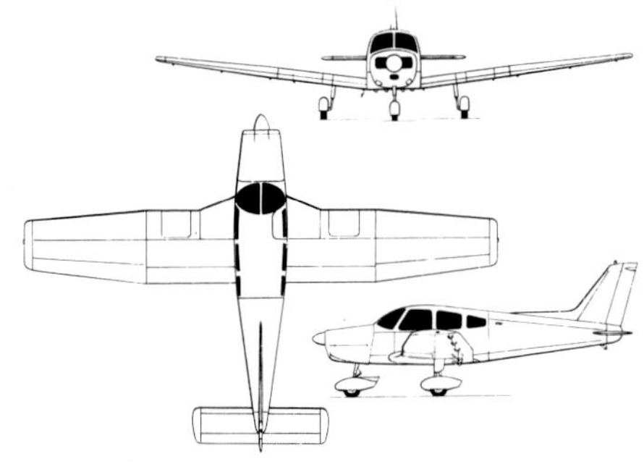

Piper PA-23 Aztec

In the late 1950s sales of the somewhat dated Apache were beginning to decline steadily, so in 1959 the company introduced the updated PA-23-250 Aztec with a swept vertical tail to revive the series' flagging fortunes. The five-seat Aztec A had O-540-A1D5 engines, the six-seat Aztec B introduced a longer and more capacious nose, the Aztec C had revised landing gear and IO-540-C4B5 engines, the Aztec D featured further refinement, the Aztec E had a yet longer nose and an optional autopilot, and the Aztec F had reduced control forces, interconnected flaps and tailplane, and several other modifications. Most of the later models were available in basic Custom, de luxe Sportsman, de-iced Professionals and Turbo forms, the last with engines carrying AiResearch turbochargers to allow them to maintain their rated power to an altitude of 20,000 ft.

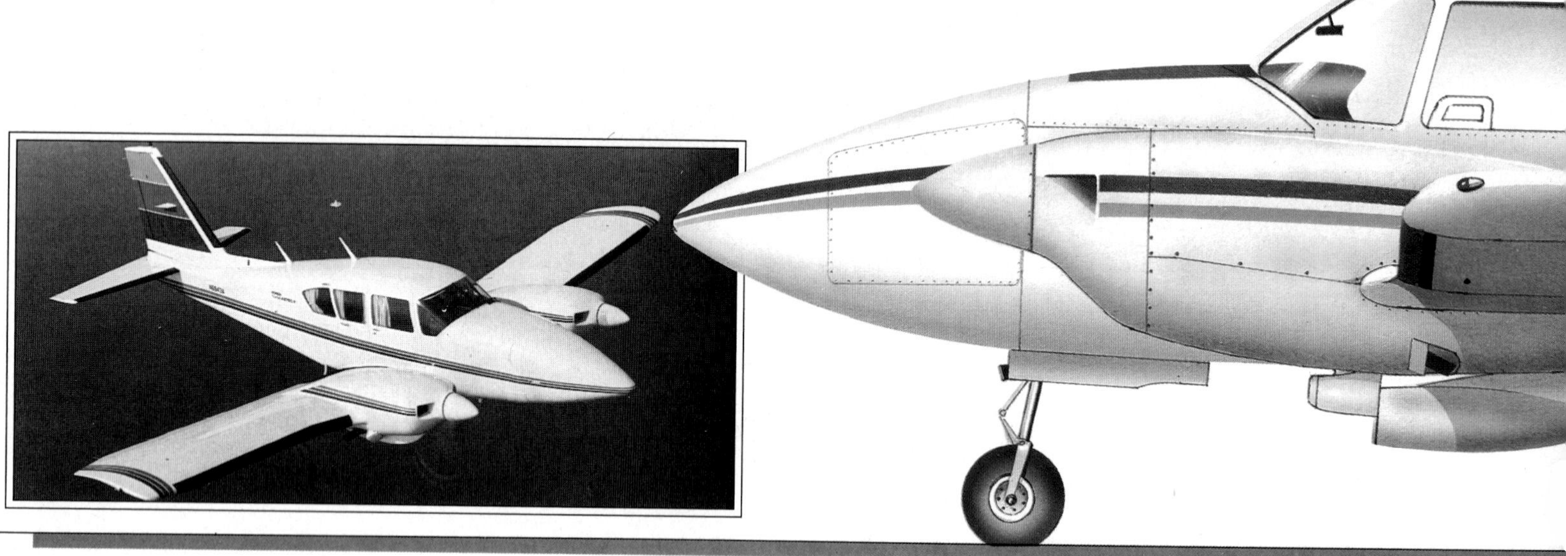

Beagle B.206

First flown in August 1961 as the B.206X, this was Beagle's first completely original design: an all-metal five-seater powered by a pair of 194-kW (260-hp) Continental engines and fitted with retractable tricycle landing gear. Beagle then revised the design as a seven-seater with geared Continental engines and span increased by 2.44 m (8 ft); this B.206Y first flew August 1962. The first production version was the B.206Z (20 Basset CC.Mk 1s for the RAF), and this was followed by three civil variants. These comprised 11 B.206 Series 1s, 47 B.206 Series 2s with supercharged engines, and three B.206 Series 3 10-seaters with a deeper rear fuselage and equipment for the flying and instrument training roles. Production of the B.206 ended in 1969 after the delivery of 85 aircraft, the civil total being bolstered as ex-military aircraft were released onto the commercial market.

Specification: Beagle B.206 Series 2 five/eight-seat cabin monoplane
Span: 13.96 m (45 ft 9.5 in)
Length: 10.26 m (33 ft 8 in)
Powerplant: 2×Rolls-Royce/Continental GTSIO-520-C, 254 kW (340 hp) each
Max T/O weight: 3401 kg (7,499 lb)
Cruising speed: 218 mph at 8,000 ft
Range: 1,600 miles

Gulfstream GA-7/Cougar

The GA-7/Cougar was planned as a twin-engined light four-seater for two main markets: flying schools that needed an economical trainer for their twin-engined conversion courses, and private pilots changing up from high-performance single-engined types. The prototype first flew in December 1974 with retractable tricycle landing gear and two O-320-D1D engines, and deliveries were made from 1978 just before Grumman American was bought by American Jet Industries, who renamed the company Gulfstream American. Production was ended in 1979, the two versions of the basic design at this time being the standard GA-7 and the de luxe Cougar. The latter has as standard: dual controls, a tinted windscreen, better lights, more capable communications equipment and improved instrumentation including turn and vertical speed indicators, and directional and horizon gyros.

Specification: Gulfstream American Cougar four-seat cabin monoplane
Span: 11.23 m (36 ft 10.25 in)
Length: 9.09 m (29 ft 10 in)
Powerplant: 2×Avco Lycoming O-320-D1D, 119 kW (160 hp) each
Max T/O weight: 1724 kg (3,800 lb)
Cruising speed: 131 mph at 8,500 ft
Range: 1,336 miles

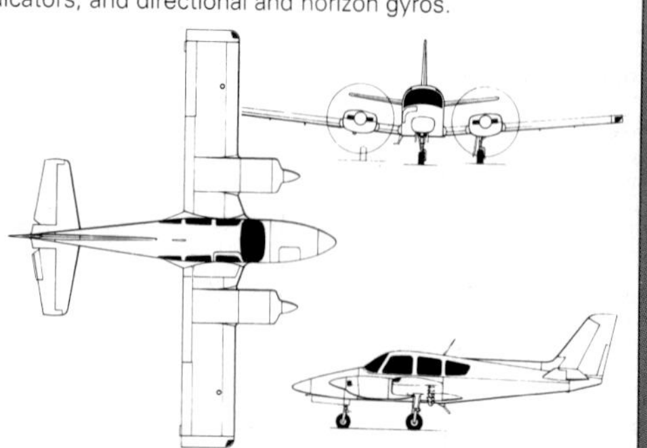

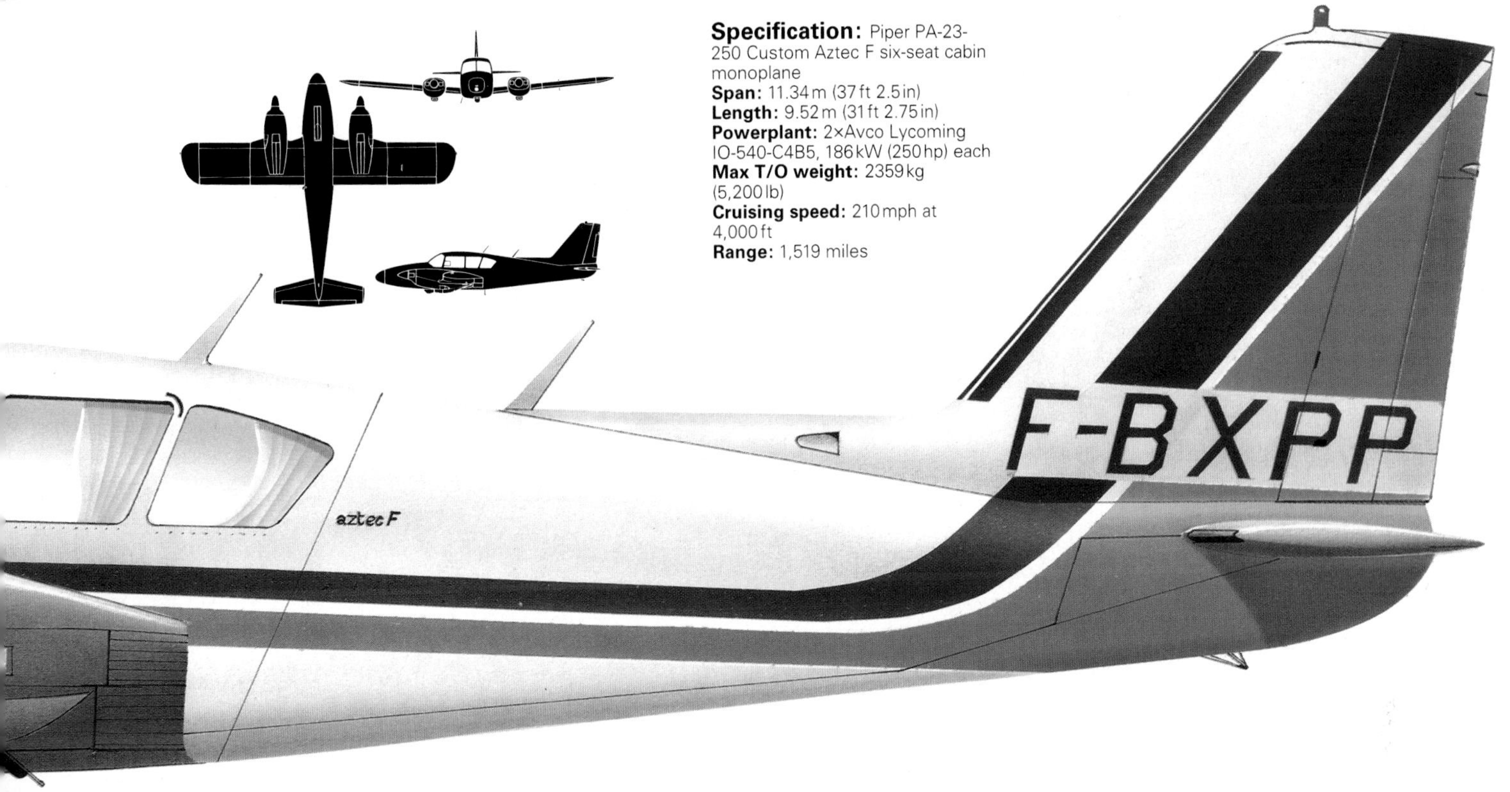

Specification: Piper PA-23-250 Custom Aztec F six-seat cabin monoplane
Span: 11.34 m (37 ft 2.5 in)
Length: 9.52 m (31 ft 2.75 in)
Powerplant: 2×Avco Lycoming IO-540-C4B5, 186 kW (250 hp) each
Max T/O weight: 2359 kg (5,200 lb)
Cruising speed: 210 mph at 4,000 ft
Range: 1,519 miles

For many years the Piper Aztec was the standard light twin. Available in ever more advanced versions, it provides speedy transport between small airfields able to carry six passengers and a sizeable baggage load. Many are in company service, often fitted with full navigation and communication suites.

Let L-200 Morava

The L-200 Morava from the Czech manufacturer Let was first flown in April 1957 as successor to the Aero 145, and like its predecessor secured useful export sales to the USSR in the liaison and air taxi roles. Keynotes of the design are: retractable tricycle landing gear, a low-set wing with tip tanks and underslung engines, a high cabin section protruding well above the shallow fuselage, and a tailplane with endplate vertical surfaces. Production amounted to more than 1,000 aircraft in variants such as the original L-200 with 119-kW (160-hp) Walter Minor 6-III engines, the L-200A with M337 engines driving electrically operated two-blade propellers, and the L-200D with a number of detail improvements (strengthened landing gear and improved hydraulics), plus the same engines driving hydraulically operated three-blade variable-pitch propellers.

Specification: Let L-200D Morava four/five-seat cabin monoplane
Span: 12.31 m (40 ft 4.5 in)
Length: 8.61 m (28 ft 3 in)
Powerplant: 2×Walter M337, 157 kW (210 hp) each
Max T/O weight: 1950 kg (4,299 lb)
Cruising speed: 159 mph at 8,200 ft
Range: 1,063 miles

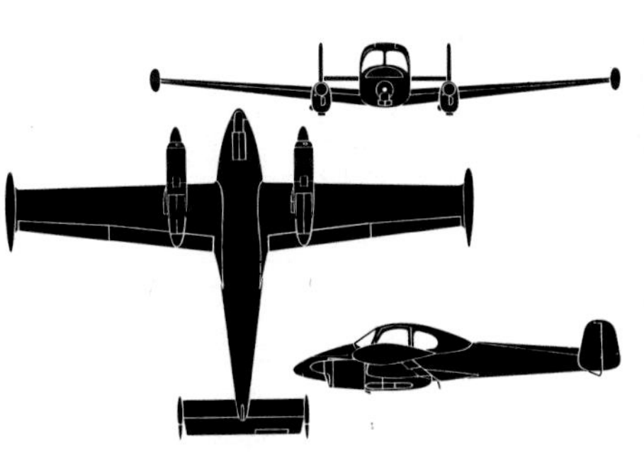

Cessna 336 & 337 Skymaster

First flown in February 1961, the Model 336 was an attempt to remove asymmetric engine-out problems in a twin-engine design by locating the two 157-kW (210-hp) IO-360-A engines in a pull/push arrangement at the front and rear of the central nacelle of this twin-boom aeroplane. Deliveries of this four/six-seater began in May 1963 but sales were modest because the type's fixed tricycle landing gear was 'old-fashioned'. Thus 195 Model 336s were followed by 2,134 examples of the Model 337 series with retractable landing gear and provision for a 136-kg (300-lb) underfuselage baggage container. The main variants were the Model 337, the Model 337 Turbo System Super Skymaster with TSIO-210-A turbocharged engines, and the Model T337 Skymaster with 168-kWQ (225-hp) TSIO-360 engines and cabin pressurization. Variants were also built in France by Reims as the F337.

Specification: Cessna Model 337 Skymaster six-seat cabin monoplane
Span: 11.63 m (38 ft 2 in)
Length: 9.07 m (29 ft 9 in)
Powerplant: 2×Continental IO-360-GB, 157 kW (210 hp) each
Max T/O weight: 2100 kg (4,630 lb)
Cruising speed: 196 mph at 5,500 ft
Range: 1,422 miles

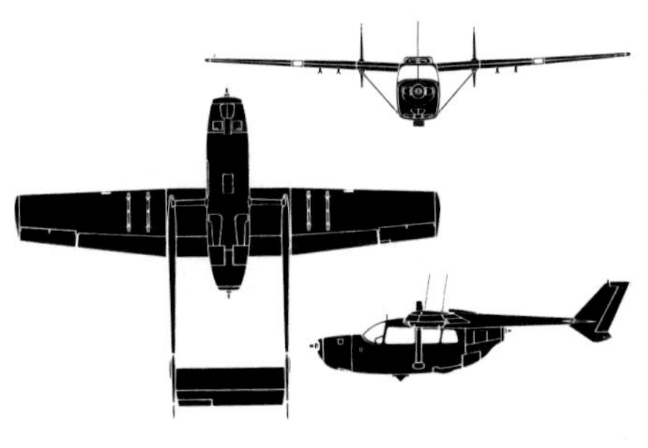

Partenavia P.68 Victor

This Italian light twin first flew in May 1970, and was immediately notable for its odd combination of sleek fuselage and fixed tricycle landing gear. Some 13 P.68A pre-production aircraft were followed in 1974 by the first examples of the P.68B production type with its fuselage lengthened by 15.2cm (6in) forward of the wing, and in 1979 by the first examples of the P.68C with several internal changes, a longer nose for weather radar, and more fuel. In 1980 Partenavia introduced the P.68C-TC with 157-kW (210-hp) TIO-360-C1A6D turbocharged engines. With Aeritalia, Partenavia then developed the higher-capacity AP.68 Turbo with retractable landing gear and 313-kW (420-shp) Allison 250-B17C turboprops, but the second prototype and AT.68TP-600 production versions reverted to fixed landing gear. The AT.68TP-600 carries 10 persons over a range of 1,015 miles at a speed of 253mph.

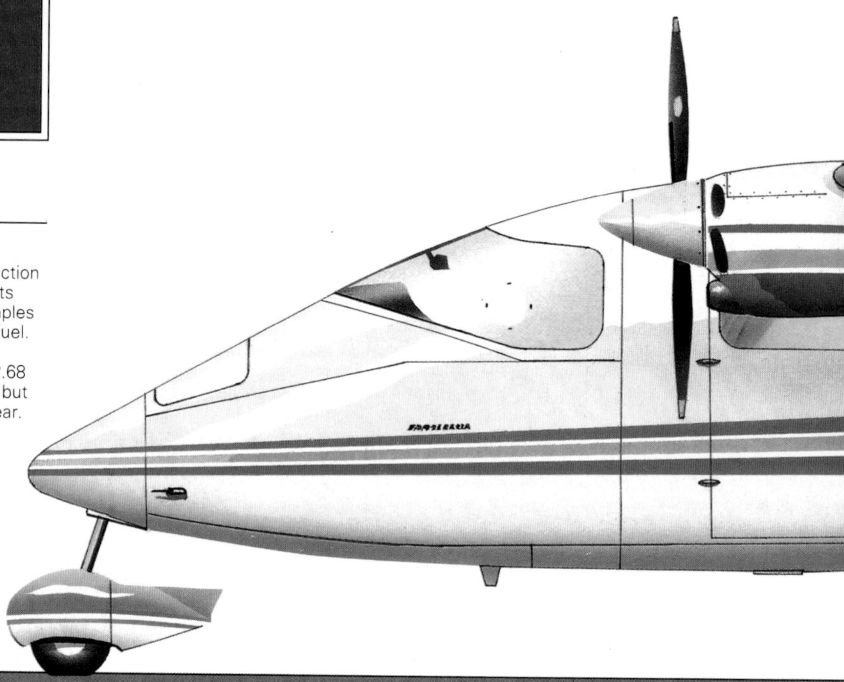

Piper PA-23 Apache

Known as the Twin-Stinson when it first flew in March 1952, Piper's first major step into the field of light twins was the PA-23 Apache, in its first production form a four seater with 112-kW (150-hp) Lycoming O-320 engines, tricycle landing gear and an unswept vertical tail. The Twin-Stinson had featured a tailplane set high on the rear fuselage and fitted with twin endplate vertical surfaces, but this had been replaced by a more conventional unit by the time production started early in 1954. Some 2,166 Apaches were built up to 1965, the 1,231 Apache 150s being complemented from 1958 by 816 Apache 160s with 119-kW (160-hp) O-320-B engines (four-seat Apache Fs and five-seat Apache Gs), and from 1962 by 119 Apache 235s (Apache Hs) with O-540-B1A5 engines, a swept tail and other features adopted from the first model of the later five-seat Aztec.

Specification: Piper PA-23-160 Apache G four/five-seat cabin monoplane
Span: 11.28m (37ft 0in)
Length: 8.27m (27ft 1.5in)
Powerplant: 2×Avco Lycoming O-320-B, 119kW (160hp) each
Max T/O weight: 1724kg (3,800lb)
Cruising speed: 173mph at 7,500ft
Range: 1,260 miles

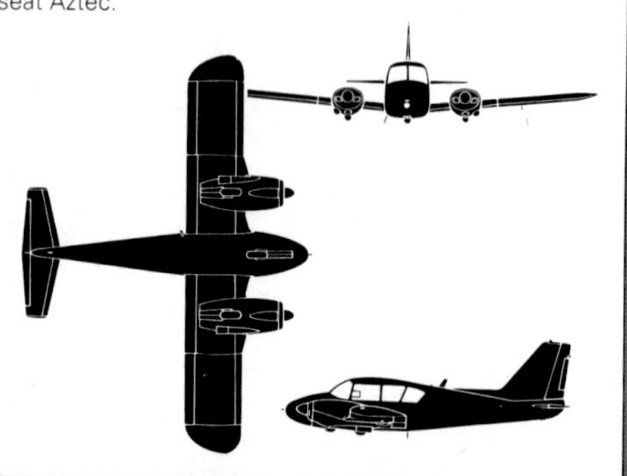

Beech Model 76 Duchess

Reports of a new twin from Beech circulated in 1974, but it was 1978 before the Model 76 Duchess was ready for delivery as a highly attractive low-wing monoplane with hydraulically retractable tricycle landing gear and a swept vertical tail surmounted by a straight tailplane. The type, designed as direct competition for the Cessna Model 310 and Piper PA-34 Seneca, is suitable for day or night VFR or IFR operations, is powered by counter-rotating engines and is available with a number of factory-installed options of interior equipment, avionics and finish to customer requirement. The type was developed with the training needs of the Beech Aero Centres in mind, and is thus notable for its good low-speed and uncomplicated single-engine handling characteristics. This factor helped to make the Duchess attractive to the pilot moving up to a light twin, and also to charter operators.

Specification: Beech Model 76 Duchess four-seat cabin monoplane
Span: 11.58m (38ft 0in)
Length: 8.86m (29ft 0.5in)
Powerplant: 2×Avco Lycoming O-360-A1G6D, 134kW (180hp) each
Max T/O weight: 1769kg (3,900lb)
Cruising speed: 174mph at 12,000ft
Range: 898 miles

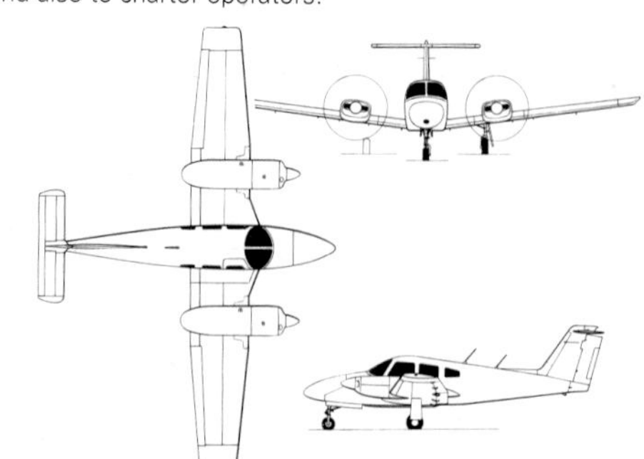

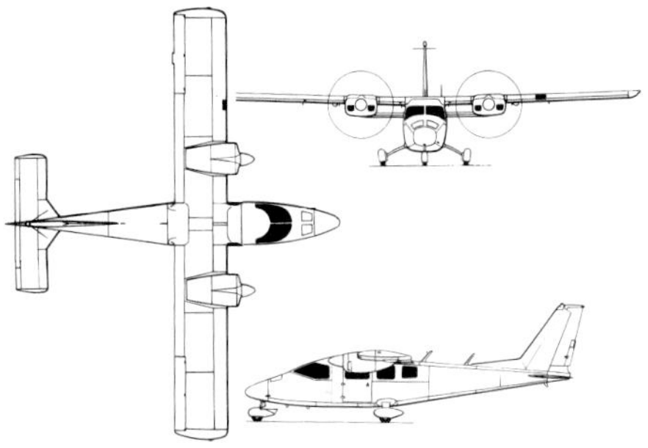

Specification: Partenavia P.68C Victor six/seven-seat cabin monoplane
Span: 12.00 m (39 ft 4.5 in)
Length: 9.55 m (31 ft 4 in)
Powerplant: 2×Avco Lycoming IO/-360-A1B6, 149 kW (200 hp) each
Max T/O weight: 1990 kg (4.387 lb)
Cruising speed: 191 mph at optimum altitude
Range: 1,313 miles

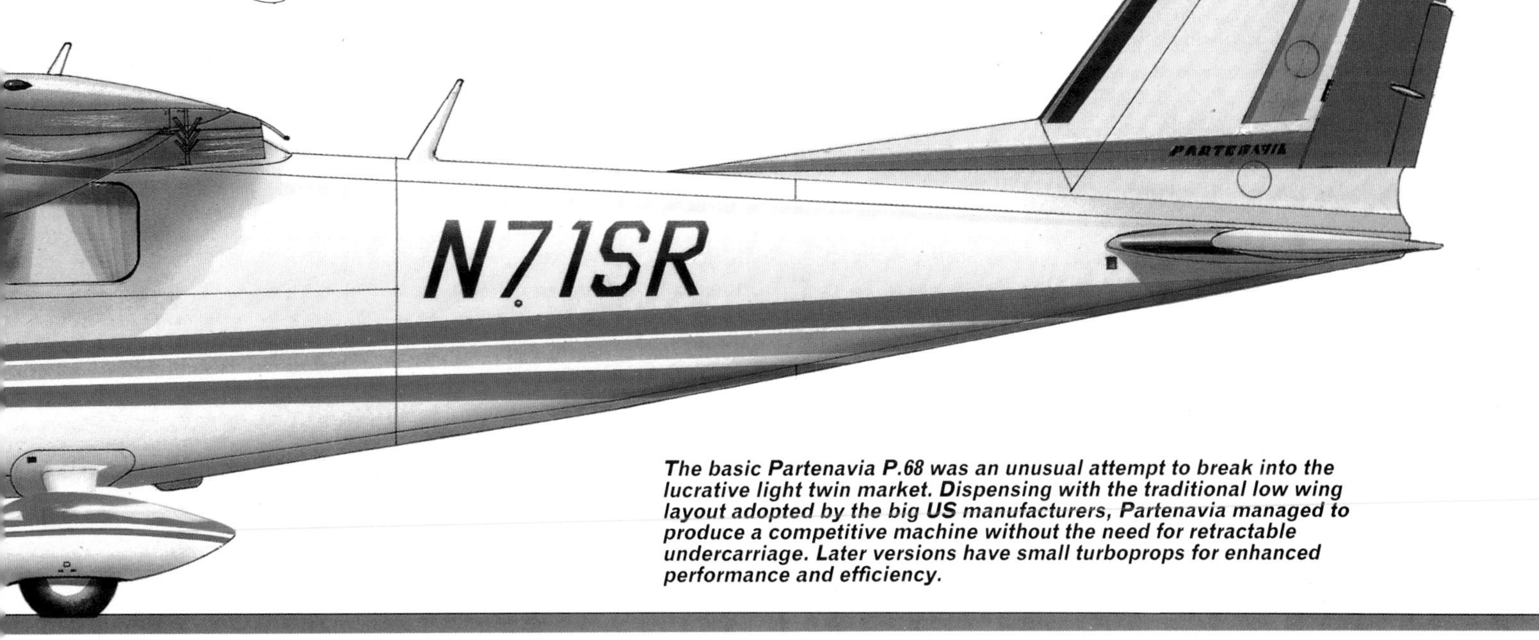

N71SR

PARTENAVIA

The basic Partenavia P.68 was an unusual attempt to break into the lucrative light twin market. Dispensing with the traditional low wing layout adopted by the big US manufacturers, Partenavia managed to produce a competitive machine without the need for retractable undercarriage. Later versions have small turboprops for enhanced performance and efficiency.

Beech 55, 58 & 58 Baron

)eveloped from the Model 95 Travel Air, the four/five-seat Model 95-55 Baron first flew in ebruary 1960 with 194-kW (260-hp) IO-470s, a swept vertical tail and improved IFR apability. Later came the five/six-seat B55 with 194-kW IO-470-Ls, the six-seat C55 with 13-kW (285-hp) IO-520-Cs, the improved D55 and the E55 with a number of cosmetic nodifications. In September 1967 the company began deliveries of the Model 56TC Baron, a ariant with turbocharged 283-kW (380-hp) TIO-541-E1B4Ws and optional air conditioning. he range was further extended by the Model 58 Baron, based on the E55 but with the uselage lengthened by 0.25 m (10 in) for more comfortable accommodation. Later variants re the Model 58P with a pressurized cabin and turbocharge 231-kW (310-hp) TSIO-520-Ls or 42-kW (325-hp) TSIO-520-WBs, and the unpressurized Model 58TC. French and US ompanies have also developed turboprop conversions in small numbers.

specification: Beech Model 355 Baron four/six-seat cabin nonoplane
pan: 11.53 m (37 ft 10 in)
ength: 8.53 m (28 ft 0 in)
owerplant: 2×Continental O-470-L, 194 kW (260 hp) each
Max T/O weight: 2313 kg (5,100 lb)
ruising speed: 216 mph at ,000 ft
ange: 1,141 miles

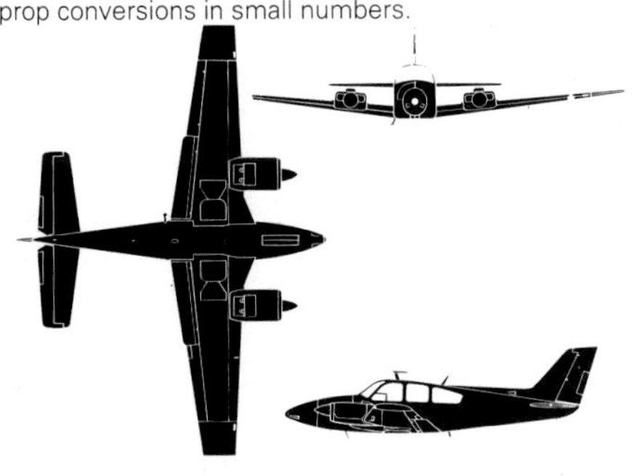

PA-30/PA-39 Twin Comanche

As indicated by its name, this successor to the Apache was based on the single-engined PA-24 Comanche, and featured a low-wing layout and retractable tricycle landing gear. The type first flew in November 1962, and deliveries began in 1963. In 1965 there appeared the improved four/six-seat PA-30B-160 with the same 119-kW (160-hp) IO-320-B engines, and Piper also produced a PA-30B Turbo Twin Comanche with Rayjay-turbocharged IO-320-C1A engines. The PA-30C Twin Comanche and Turbo Twin Comanche introduced a number of cosmetic and detail improvements. In 1970 the normally aspirated and turbocharged B and C versions were replaced respectively by the PA-39 Twin Comanche C/R and PA-39 Turbo Twin Comanche with counter-rotating propellers, both models being available in Standard, Custom and Sportsman variants. Production of all Comanche models ended in 1972 after the delivery of 2,142 aircraft.

Specification: Piper PA-30C Twin Comanche C four/six-seat cabin monoplane
Span: 10.97 m (36 ft 0 in)
Length: 7.67 m (25 ft 2 in)
Powerplant: 2×Avco Lycoming IO-320-B, 119 kW (160 hp) each
Max T/O weight: 1690 kg (3,725 lb)
Cruising speed: 198 mph at optimum altitude
Range: 1,200 miles

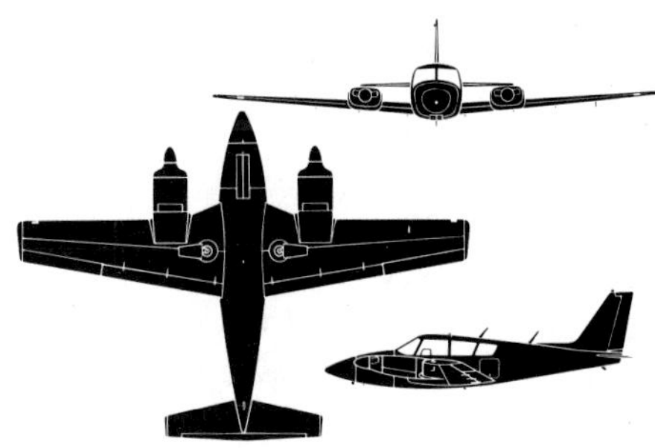

Piper PA-44 Seminole

In May 1976 Piper flew the prototype of the type announced in February 1978 as the new PA-44-180 Seminole low-cost cabin monoplane with accommodation for four in a low-wing airframe with a T-tail, retractable tricycle landing gear and 134-kW (180-hp) Avco Lycoming O-360-E1AD counter-rotating engines. In common with other Piper aircraft, however, this low-cost twin can be delivered to customer requirement with a number of factory-installed finish and equipment improvements to turn it into an increasingly expensive but sophisticated aeroplane. In April 1980 the basic Seminole was complemented by the PA-144-180T Turbo Seminole with turbocharged engines and an optional oxygen system for cruise at heights up to 20,000ft. Production of both types was completed in 1982 with the delivery of the 431st aeroplane.

Specification: Piper PA-44-180T Turbo Seminole four-seat cabin monoplane
Span: 11.77m (38ft 7.25in)
Length: 8.41m (27ft 7.25in)
Powerplant: 2×Avco Lycoming TO/LTO-360-E1AD, 134kW (180hp) each
Max T/O weight: 1780kg (3,925lb)
Cruising speed: 192mph at 10,000ft
Range: 943 miles

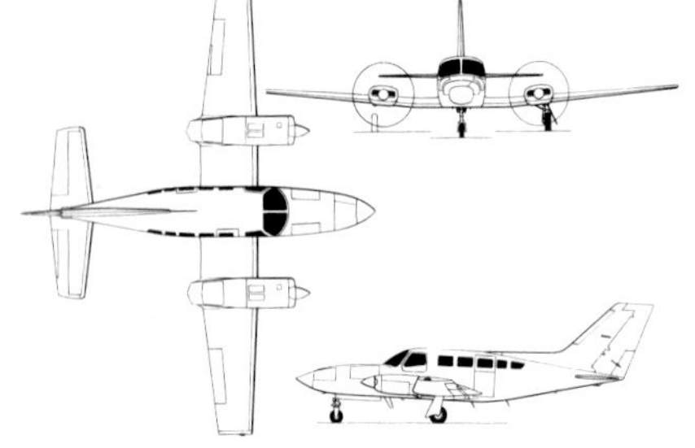

Cessna 310 series

Design of the five/six-seat Model 310 was launched in 1952 as a light twin with low-set wing, retractable landing gear, and all the fuel accommodated in two large wingtip tanks. The prototype flew in January 1953 at the beginning of a programme that lasted into the 1980s with the delivery of 5,241 civil aircraft in a number of forms with different engines and a host of factory-installed equipment, avionic and finish options. The Model 310 was powered by two 194-kW (260-hp) Continental IO-470 engines, later changed to IO-520 units, and the basic design was evolved through variants such as the Model 310D of 1960 with a swept vertical tail, and the Model 310P with many updated features and a ventral fin. The basic design was also developed in the mid-1960s as the de luxe air-conditioned Model 320 Skyknight (and then as the Turbo-System T310), with TSIO-520 turbocharged engines.

Specification: Cessna Model 310 five/six-seat cabin monoplane
Span: 11.25m (36ft 11in)
Length: 9.74m (31ft 11.5in)
Powerplant: 2×Continental IO-520-MB, 213kW (285hp) each
Max T/O weight: 2495kg (5,500lb)
Cruising speed: 160mph at 10,000ft
Range: 1,765 miles

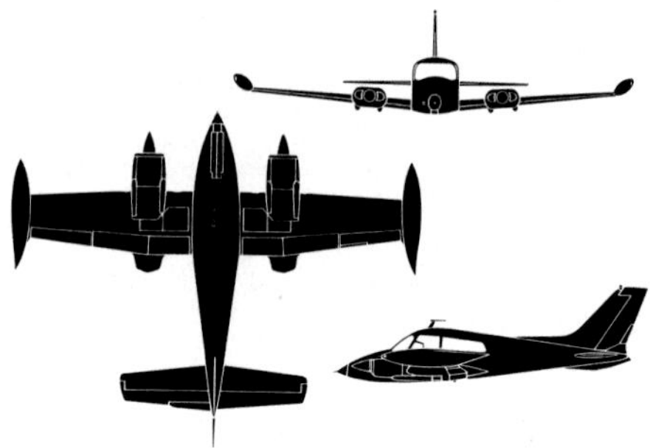

Cessna 401 & 402 series

Related to the heavier Model 411 that was dropped in 1968 after delivery of 301 examples, the Models 401 and 402 were first flown during August 1965 as prototypes, with less power and a reduced level of equipment by comparison with the Model 411. The six/eight-seat Model 401 was aimed at the executive market, and when production ended in 1973 slightly more than 400 had been built. Development was then concentrated on the versatile Model 402 with a redesigned interior to suit the type to the 9/10-seat commuter and light freight roles. In 1971 the type was named Utililiner, and a six/eight-seat Businessliner variant was introduced at the same time. There is also a longer-nose Model 402B and improved Model 402C, like the Model 402 available with different levels of factory-installed avionics. AJI has developed a Turbo Star conversion with 298-kW (400-shp) Allison 250-B17 turboprops.

Specification: Cessna Model 402C Businessliner six/eight-seat cabin monoplane
Span: 13.45m (44ft 1.5in)
Length: 11.09m (44ft 4.5in)
Powerplant: 2×Continental TSIO-520-VB, 242kW (325hp) each
Max T/O weight: 3107kg (6,850lb)
Cruising speed: 245mph at 20,000ft
Range: 1,132 miles

PA-31 Navajo Chieftain

Introduced in 1964 as Piper's then-largest aeroplane, the Navajo was schemed as an executive transport and air taxi. Deliveries began in 1967 of the basic version with 224-kW (300-hp) IO-540-K engines, and this was available in Standard, Commuter and Executive layouts. Also available at the same time was the PA-31T Turbo Navajo with 231-kW (310-hp) TIO-540-A engines, complemented from 1970 by the PA-31P Pressurized Navajo with 317-kW (425-hp) TIGO-541-E1A engines. Navajo production ended in 1972 as Piper introduced the PA-31-350 Navajo Chieftain (later Chieftain), with a 0.61-m (2-ft) longer fuselage and greater power; the PA-31-325 Turbo Navajo C/R was identical but for its lower-rated engines driving counter-rotating propellers. The 1983 PA-31P-350 Mojave combines the airframe of the Cheyenne II with the powerplant of the PA-31-350.

Specification: Piper PA-31-350 Chieftain six/eight-seat cabin monoplane
Span: 12.40m (40ft 8in)
Length: 10.55m (34ft 7.5in)
Powerplant: 2×Avco Lycoming TIO/LTIO-540-J2BD, 261kW (350hp) each
Max T/O weight: 3175kg (7,000lb)
Cruising speed: 254mph at 20,000ft
Range: 1,094 miles

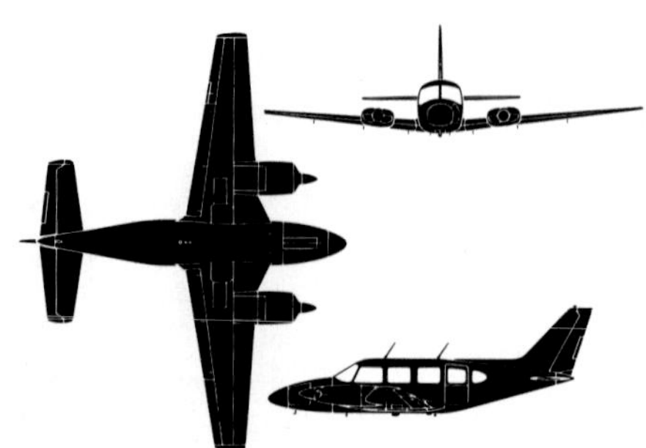

Pitts S-1 Special

Designed in 1943 and first flown in September 1944, the Pitts Special remains one of the world's best known aerobatic aircraft in factory- and home-built versions with ever more power in a structure of steel except for the wooden wings. Both fuselage and flying surfaces are covered with fabric, and the airframe is stressed structurally to +9 and −4.5*g*. The S-1 series of single-seaters includes the homebuilt S-1C with a 93-kW (125-hp) Lycoming O-290-D engine, the homebuilt S-1D with an engine of up to 134-kW (180-hp), the homebuilt S-1E with a symmetrical airfoil section, the factory- or kit-built S-1S with a 75- to 134-kW (100- to 180-hp) engine, and the factory- or kit-built S-1T in kit form with symmetrical-section wings moved slightly forward and the 149-kW (200-hp) AEIO-36-A1E engine.

Specification: Pitts S-1S
Special single-seat aerobatic biplane
Span: 5.29 m (17 ft 4 in)
Length: 4.71 m (15 ft 5.5 in)
Powerplant: typically 1×Avco Lycoming IO-360-B4A, 134 kW (180 hp)
Max T/O weight: 521 kg (1,150 lb)
Max speed: 176 mph at sea level
Range: 315 miles

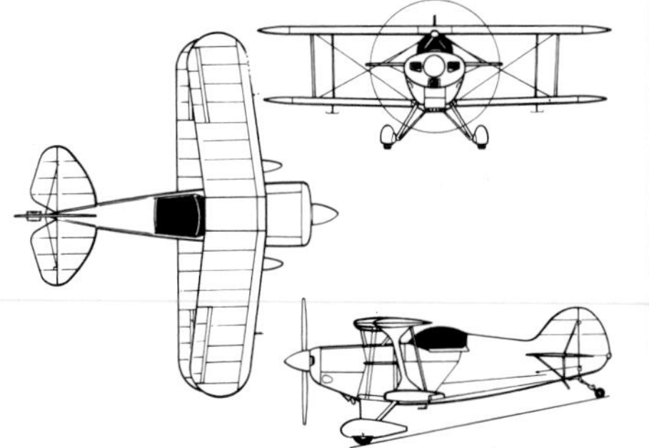

Pitts S-2 Special

In parallel with the S-1 single-seaters there has been the S-2 series of two-seaters, of which the first example was flown in 1967. The S-2 is basically an enlarged and up-engined version of the S-1, again stressed to +9 and −4.5*g*, the greater size and power providing enhanced aerobatic capability as well as better stability in rough air. Symmetrical ailerons are fitted, and these provide a higher roll rate at low airspeeds as well as the facility for vertical rolls. A symmetrical airfoil section is also used, and this gives the S-2 better inverted-flight and outside-loop capabilities than the S-1. Variants are the factory-built S-2A with the 149-kW (200-hp) IO-360-A1A engine, the factory-built S-2B with the 194-kW (260-hp) AEIO-540 and movement of the wings slightly forward, and the kit-built S-2E with engines of up to 149 kW (200-hp). There is also a factory- or kit-built S-2S single-seat version of the S-2A.

Specification: Pitts S-2S
Special single-seat aerobatic biplane
Span: 6.10 m (20 ft 0 in)
Length: 5.28 m (17 ft 4 in)
Powerplant: 1×Avco Lycoming AEIO-540-D4A5, 194 kW (260 hp)
Max T/O weight: 680 kg (1,500 lb)
Max speed: 187 mph at sea level
Range: not revealed

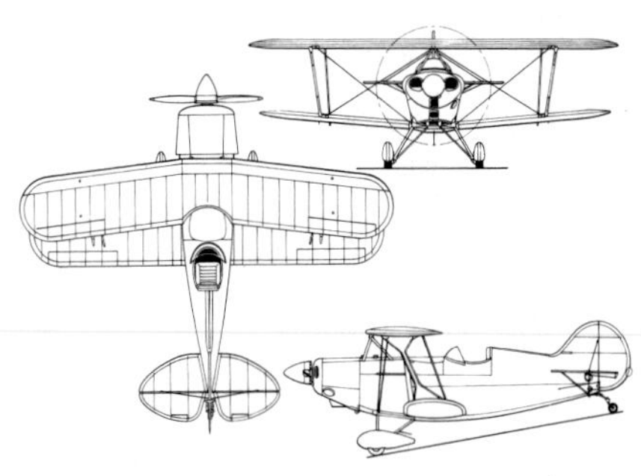

U.A. (Pitts) Special

Under this designation Ultimate Aerobatics of Ontario, Canada, is marketing completely or partially assembled kits for the modification of Pitts Special biplanes, allowing them to perform manoeuvres up to +8.5g/−8.5g. The main modification entailed in this programme is the replacement of the standard wing cellule with one of reduced span but greater structural strength, carrying wingtip endplates and fitted with additional bracing in the form of rear flying and landing wires. In combination with oversized ailerons on upper and lower wings, this modification produces a roll rate of 360° per second. The modification also includes knife-edge interplane struts, a low-profile canopy, a low-drag cowling and a lightweight but more powerful engine driving a two-blade Hoffmann propeller.

Specification: Ultimate Aerobatics (Pitts) S-1 Special single-seat aerobatic biplane
Span: 4.77 m (15 ft 8 in)
Length: 4.71 m (15 ft 5.5 in)
Powerplant: 1×Avco Lycoming O-360-A, 171.5 kW (230 hp)
Max T/O weight: 521 kg (1,150 lb)
Max speed: 176 mph at sea level
Range: 315 miles

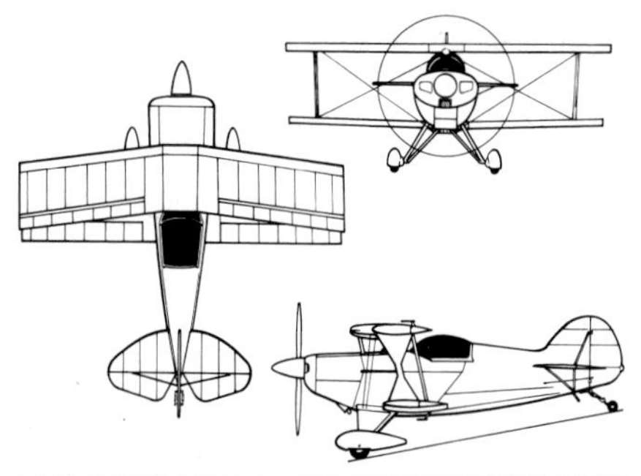

Zlin Z 526AFS Akrobat

The Z 526AFS was developed from the tandem-seat Z 526F Trener as a single-seat aerobatic type for championship-level competitions using the Aresti system of adjudication. Development began in the late 1960s and the first example flew in October 1970, and small-scale production was undertaken in the early 1970s. Like its parent the Akrobat is of all-metal construction, stressed to +7g/−4.5g, with a stressed-skin wing and a metal/fabric-covered steel-tube fuselage. In configuration the aeroplane is a low-wing monoplane with retractable tailwheel landing gear, and by comparison with the Trener the Akrobat is smaller in span and length, is lighter, has larger differentially-operating double ailerons instead of flaps, and has a semi-bubble canopy.

Specification: Zlin Z 526AFS
Akrobat single-seat aerobatic monoplane
Span: 8.84 m (29 ft 0 in)
Length: 7.81 m (25 ft 7.5 in)
Powerplant: 1×Avco Lycoming AIO-360-B1B, 149 kW (200 hp)
Max T/O weight: 740 kg (1,631 lb) for aerobatics
Max speed: 157 mph at sea level
Range: not revealed

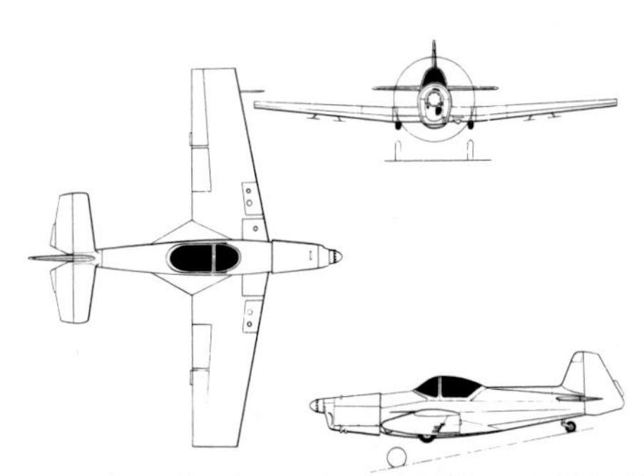

Extra 230

Designed by Walter Extra and produced by his Extra-Flugzeugbau in West Germany, the Extra 230 was planned for championship-level aerobatic competitions and first flew in July 1983. An Extra 230 took third place in the 1985 European aerobatic championships, with six other Extra 230s finishing in the first 25. The type is available as a complete aeroplane or in kit form, and is stressed structurally to +10g/–10g. The Dacron-covered wooden wing has 0° incidence and virtually no curvature except on the leading edge, the fuselage is fabricated of steel tube with aluminium and Dacron covering, and the landing gear is of the fixed tailwheel type. All the control surfaces have 52° of movement, and the long-span ailerons occupy about three-quarters of the thick trailing edge.

Christen Eagle

Christen Industries of California produces two essentially similar strut-braced aerobatic biplanes, the single-seat Eagle I and two-seat Eagle II which are each stressed to structural limits of +9g/-6g and possess a roll rate of 187° per second. The basic structure is of steel tube with wooden wing spars and ribs covered in light alloy sheet and fabric; the cantilever landing gear is of the fixed tailwheel type. Design began in 1974, and the first Eagle II flew in February 1977, followed by the Eagle I. Each type is available in the form of 26 parts-kits for home building in between 1,400 and 1,600 hours. While the Eagle II is an unlimited-class aerobatic aeroplane with training and cross-country capabilities, the Eagle I is a competition type with the larger 194-kW (260-hp) AEIO-540-E4B5 engine.

Specification: Christen Eagle II two-seat aerobatic biplane
Span: 6.07 m (19 ft 11 in)
Length: 5.64 m (18 ft 6 in)
Powerplant: 1×Avco Lycoming AEIO-360-A1D, 149 kW (200 hp)
Max T/O weight: 716 kg (1,578 lb)
Max speed: 184 mph at sea level
Range: 380 miles

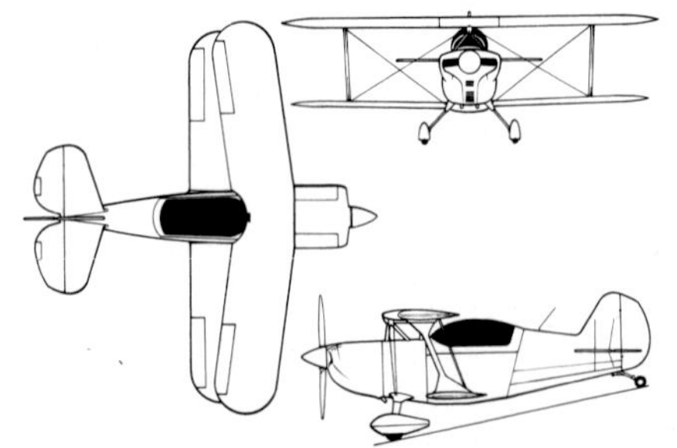

Ultimate Aircraft 10 Dash Albertan

Experience with its upgrade package for the Pitts Special has proved most useful in Ultimate's 10 Dash Albertan series of kit-assembly aerobatic biplanes, of which the first flew in October 1985. The baseline variant is the 10 Dash 100 with a steel-tube airframe and wooden wings, plus a 75- or 134-kW (100- or 180-hp) engine, but the two more important models are the 10 Dash 200 competition and 10 Dash 300 'state of the art' competition aircraft. The 10 Dash 200 has a 149-kW (200-hp) engine and a constant-speed composite propeller, while the 10 Dash 300 is stressed to +7 and –5g, has wings of 1.12 m (3 ft 8 in) greater span with full-span symmetrical ailerons, a longer fuselage, and more power plus a three-blade propeller. There are also two 20 Dash 300 twin-seat variants, the 20 Dash 300T aerobatic trainer and the 20 Dash 300E exhibition aeroplane.

Specification: Ultimate Aircraft 10 Dash 300 Albertan single-seat aerobatic biplane
Span: 5.95 m (19 ft 6 in)
Length: 6.40 m (21 ft 0 in)
Powerplant: 1×Avco Lycoming piston engine, 224 or 261 kW (300 or 350 hp)
Max T/O weight: 748 kg (1,650 lb)
Max speed: 250 mph at low altitude
Range: 600 miles

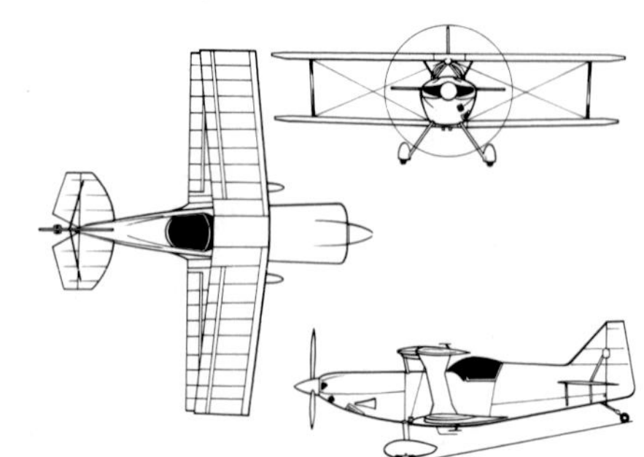

Specification: Extra 230 single-seat aerobatic monoplane
Span: 7.40 m (24 ft 3.5 in)
Length: 5.82 m (19 ft 1.75 in)
Powerplant: 1×Avco Lycoming AEIO-360-A1E, 149 kW (200 hp)
Max T/O weight: 560 kg (1,234 lb)
Max speed: 218 mph at sea level
Endurance: 2 hours 30 minutes

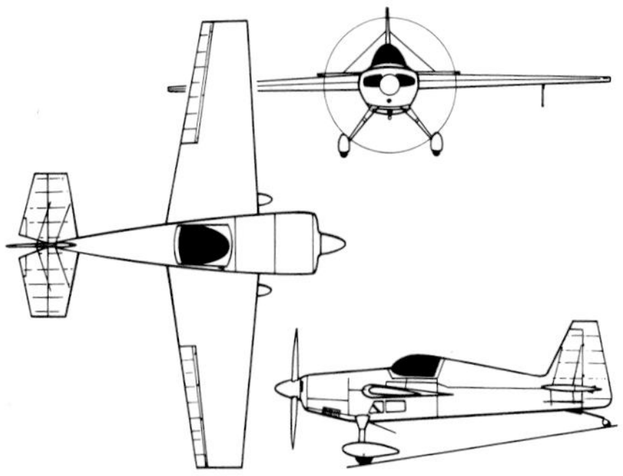

The Extra 230 was designed by Walter Extra as a refined and redesigned version of the Australian Laser Akro Model Z, which was itself derived from the US Stephens Akro. The Extra 230 has an entirely new 0° incidence wing with a Polish pine box spar covered with Dacron fabric. The Extra is probably the West's best aerobatic machine.

Aerobatics Akro Model Z

As its name implies, the Akro Model Z from Laser Aerobatics of Victoria, Australia, has its origins in the Stephens Akro though the two types are of different design in everything but general configuration and details such as the wing attachment, aileron layout and landing gear legs. The type was certificated in March 1982 and is available in plan form, though it is intended only for the experienced homebuilder. The airframe is based on an aluminium/fabric-covered steel tube fuselage and tail unit, plywood-covered wooden wings, and fixed tail wheel landing gear with cantilever main units made of aluminium. The wing is mid-set, lacking both incidence and dihedral, and the wide-span ailerons and rudder are horn-balanced. The pilot sits under a low-profile side-hinged canopy that is jettisonable in emergencies.

Specification: Laser Aerobatics Akro Model Z single-seat aerobatic monoplane
Span: 7.42 m (24 ft 4 in)
Length: 6.20 m (20 ft 4 in)
Powerplant: 1×Avco Lycoming IO-360, 149 kW (200 hp)
Max T/O weight: 553 kg (1,220 lb) for aerobatics
Max speed: 184 mph at sea level
Range: 345 miles

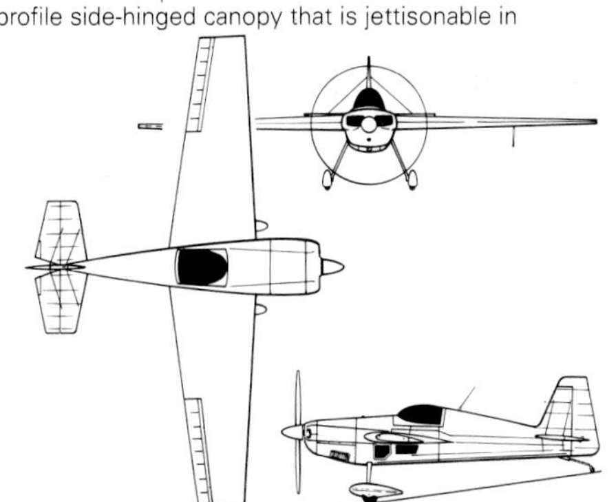

Mudry CAP 20

Developed in the late 1960s as a single-seat aerobatic equivalent to the two-seat all-wood CAP 10 but with a redesigned but still wooden structure for limits of +8g/−6g, the CAP 20 prototype first flew in July 1969 and was followed by eight aircraft with the 149-kW (200-hp) Avco Lycoming AIO-360-B1B engine before production switched to the CAP 20L with a number of revised features and a measure of structural lightening to make it more competitive. This version first flew in January 1976 as the CAP 20L-180 with 134-kW (180-hp) AEIO-360 engine, but is built as the CAP 20LS-200 with the 149-kW (200-hp) AIO-360-B1B engine and constant-speed propeller for a higher power-to-weight ratio and enhanced precision in the aerobatic arena. The roll rate is 130° per second.

Specification: Mudry CAP 20LS-200 single-seat aerobatic monoplane
Span: 7.57 m (24 ft 10 in)
Length: 6.46 m (21 ft 2.5 in)
Powerplant: 1×Avco Lycoming AIO-360-B1B, 149 kW (200 hp)
Max T/O weight: 650 kg (1,433 lb) for aerobatics
Max cruising speed: 165 mph at sea level
Endurance: 2 hours

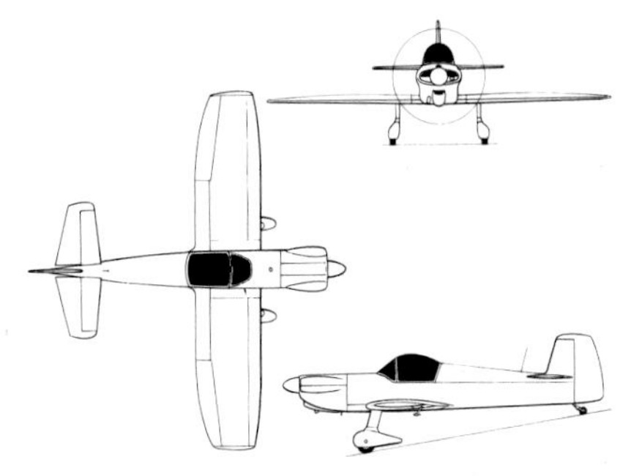

Sukhoi Su-26

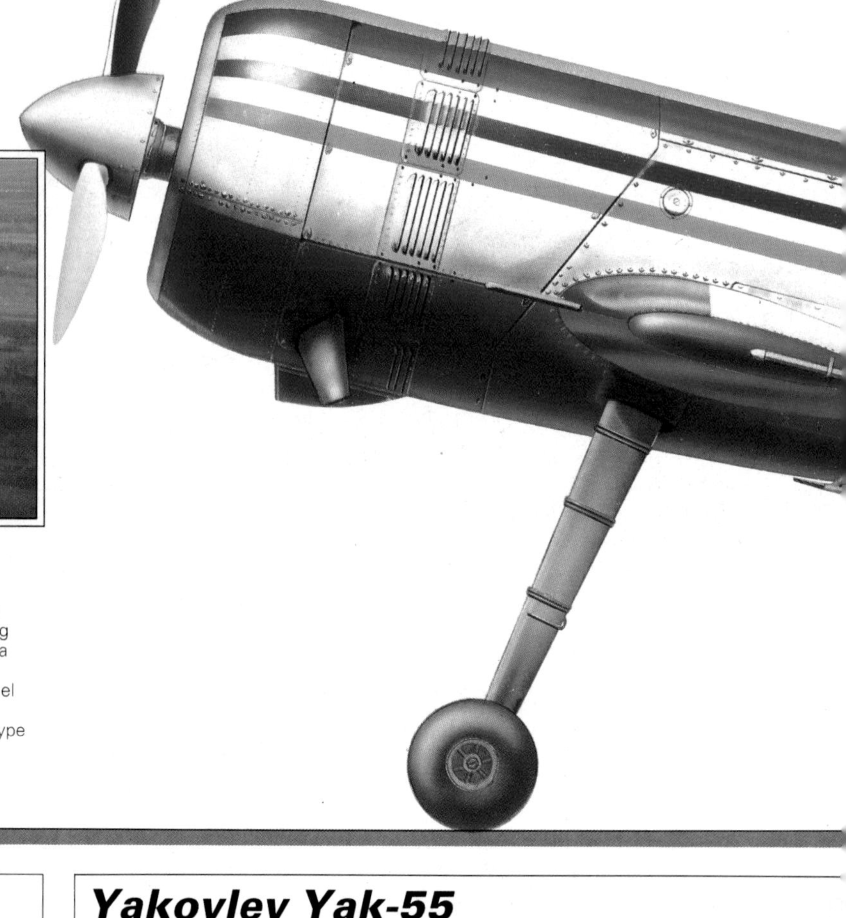

First flown in 1984 for use in that year's world aerobatic championships, the Su-26 was developed into the Su-26M for the 1986 event, when the type was flown by the winning Soviet men's and women's teams. The Su-26M has reduced fuselage side glazing and a sharp- rather than round-cornered rudder. The well-tried M-14P radial is used, and for structural limits of +11g/–9g the elegant airframe is based on a fuselage of stainless steel covered with aluminium sheet and glassfibre/epoxy panels; the flying surfaces have carbonfibre spars and glassfibre/epoxy skinning. Landing gear is of the fixed tailwheel type with cantilever main units of titanium alloy. The symmetrical-section wing has neither incidence nor dihedral, and the large ailerons provide a roll rate of more than 360° per second.

Yakovlev Yak-50

Designed for the 1976 world aerobatic championships, in which it took first and second places in the men's competition (and the first five places in the women's competition), in aerodynamic terms the Yak-50 is based on the fuselage of the well established Yak-18PS and the wings of the Yak-20 sport aeroplane, but with a strengthened structure (metal covering and a semi-monocoque fuselage) for manoeuvres to +9g/–6g, realigned control surfaces, and smaller size. The landing gear is of the retractable tailwheel type, and to provide a high power-to-weight ratio an M-14P radial with a variable-pitch two-blade (later three-blade) propeller is fitted. Modest production followed, and there are also a two-seat Yak-52 primary trainer with retractable tricycle gear, and a Yak-53 competition single-seater with retractable tricycle gear.

Specification: Yakovlev Yak-50 single-seat aerobatic monoplane
Span: 9.50 m (31 ft 2 in)
Length: 7.676 m (25 ft 2.25 in)
Powerplant: 1×Vedeneyev (Ivchyenko) M-14P, 268 kW (360 hp)
Max T/O weight: 900 kg (1,984 lb)
Max speed: 199 mph at sea level
Range: 307 miles

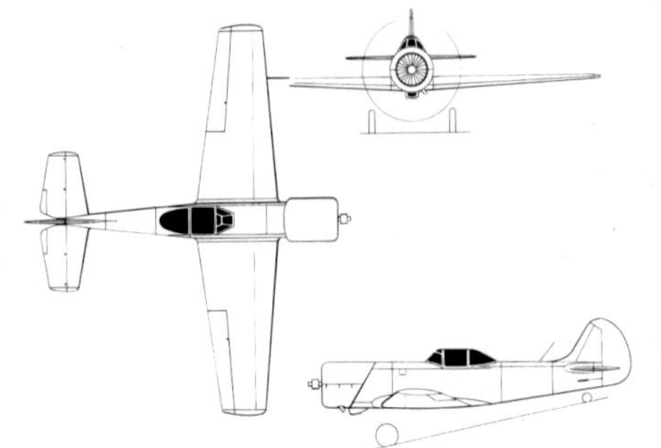

Yakovlev Yak-55

Flown with only indifferent results in the 1982 world aerobatic championships, the Yak-55 marks a departure in the bureau's aerobatic aircraft stemming from the basic Yak-18 series. Though still powered by the useful M-14P radial driving a two-blade propeller, the all-metal Yak-55 is smaller and lighter than its predecessors, and therefore has a higher power-to-weight ratio for superior performance. The type has fixed tailwheel landing gear with cantilever spring steel main legs and a steerable tailwheel, a thick-section mid-set wing without incidence or dihedral, horn-balanced control surfaces and a bubble canopy. The structure is stressed to +9g/–9g.

Specification: Yakovlev Yak-55 single-seat aerobatic monoplane
Span: 8.20 m (26 ft 10.75 in)
Length: 7.48 m (24 ft 6.5 in)
Powerplant: 1×Vedeneyev (Ivchyenko) M-14P, 268 kW (360 hp)
Max T/O weight: 840 kg (1,852 lb)
Max speed: 199 mph at sea level
Range: not revealed

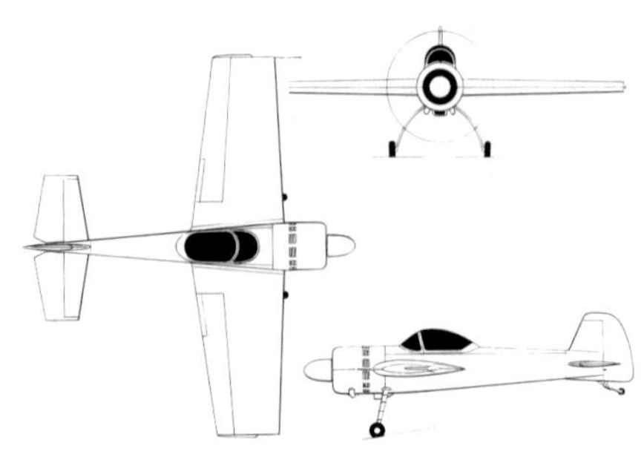

Specification: Sukhoi Su-26M single-seat aerobatic monoplane
Span: 7.80 m (25 ft 7 in)
Length: 6.90 m (22 ft 7.75 in)
Powerplant: 1×Vedeneyev (Ivchyenko) M-14P, 268 kW (360 hp)
Max T/O weight: 720 kg (1,587 lb) for aerobatics
Max speed: 217 mph at sea level
Range: 497 miles for ferrying

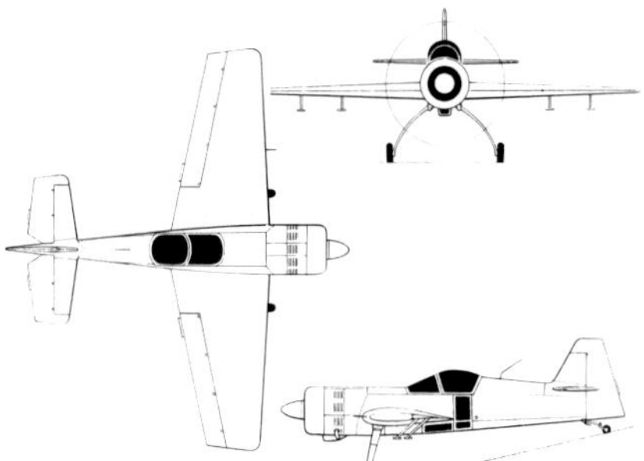

Sukhoi Su-26 of the Soviet national aerobatic team. The Su-26 and its viet pilots have proved to be a winning combination of international mpetitions. This compact competition aerobatic aircraft is powered by a)-hp Vedeneyev 9-cylinder radial engine, driving a three-bladed Hoffmann riable pitch propeller. This gives a huge power to weight ratio and in dition its advanced structure gives enormous strength.

Mudry CAP 21 and 230

n mid-1980 Mudry decided to switch production from the CAP 20 to the further improved CAP 21, and this latter flew in June of that year with the CAP 20's fuselage married to evised cantilever landing gear and a new wing boosting roll rate 0 to 180° per second. A ersion evolved by an Italian owner is the CAP 21-260 with a 194-kW (260-hp) engine and nodifications such as a revised main spar boosting the structural limits to +10g/–10g. Another variant, announced in January 1985 in the form of an order for four aircraft placed by ne Royal Moroccan air force, is the CAP 230 that first flew in October 1985. This is essentially the CAP 21 with a beefed-up airframe for structural limits of +10g/–10g and fitted with the flat-six engine of the Aérospatiale Epsilon trainer. The CAP 230 has also been ordered by the French air force in replacement for its CAP 20s.

Specification: Mudry CAP 230 single-seat aerobatic monoplane
Span: 8.08 m (26 ft 6 in)
Length: 6.75 m (22 ft 1.75 in)
Powerplant: 1×Avco Lycoming AEIO-540-L1, 224 kW (300 hp)
Max T/O weight: 720 kg (1,587 lb)
Max cruising speed: 198 mph at sea level
Range: 466 miles

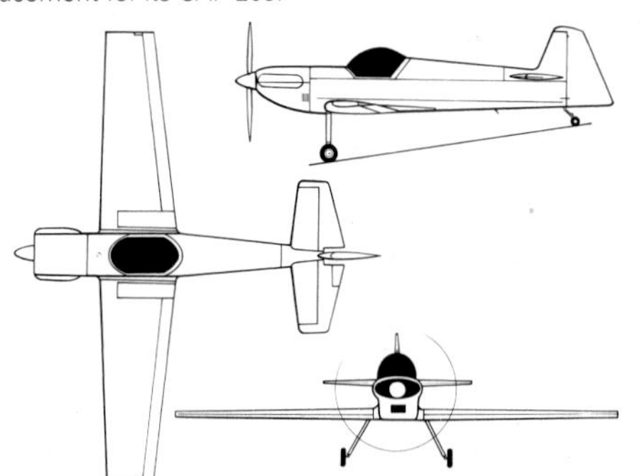

Zlin Z 50L

Designed from 1973 as a championship-level aerobatic aeroplane, the Z 50L was first flown in July 1975. After some success in the 1978 world aerobatic championships, the type proved itself in the 1978 championships in which it took first and third places in the men's competition and first place in the team competition. The Z 50L accommodates its pilot under a semi-bubble canopy over the rear portion of the wing, is stressed to +9g/–6g, and is of all-metal construction with a semi-monocoque fuselage, the fixed tailwheel landing gear having titanium cantilever main units. The low-set wing has mass-balanced ailerons running across virtually the full span, and the fabric-covered control surfaces on the empennage are aerodynamically balanced. There is also a Z 50LS version with a higher power-to-weight ratio for more sprightly handling.

Specification: Zlin Z 50L single-seat aerobatic monoplaneE
Span: 8.58 m (28 ft 1.75 in)
Length: 6.62 m (21 ft 8.75 in)
Powerplant: 1×Avco Lycoming AEIO-540-D4B5, 194 kW (260 hp)
Max T/O weight: 720 kg (1,587 lb) for aerobatics
Max speed: 180 mph at sea level
Range: 397 miles with optional tiptanks

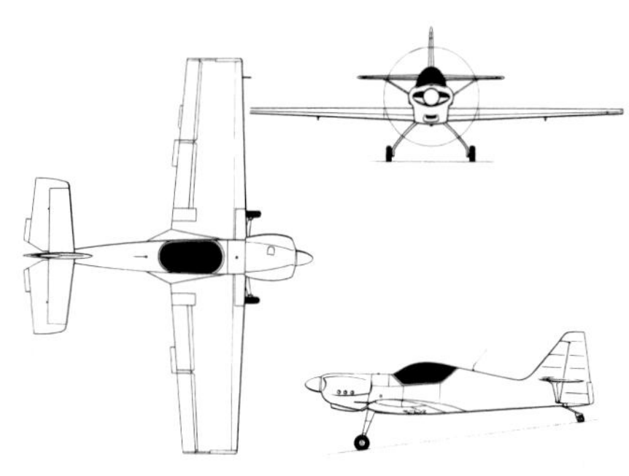

Chapter 8

HELICOPTERS

McDonnell Douglas AH-64A Apache

Formerly the Hughes Model 77, the AH-64 went on to be developed by McDonnell Douglas to meet US Army demands for a full day-night/adverse weather anti-armour ground support helicopter with high survivability potential. Prototype YAH-64s flew in 1975 and first production deliveries were made in January 1984; the programme calls for 675 aircraft to be completed by 1990. Equipment includes Hellfire anti-armour missiles, Bendix rocket control system, Martin TADS/PNVS, International laser rangefinder/designator, provision for Honeywell integrated helmet and display sighting, lightweight Doppler nav system, passive radar warning receiver and IR and radar jammers.

Specification: AH-64A Apache two-crew all-weather attack/ support helicopter
Powerplant: two 1265-kW (1,696-shp) General Electric T700-GE-701 turboshafts
Rotor diameter: 14.63 m (48 ft 0 in)
Length: (overall) 17.76 m (58 ft 3 in)
Max weight: 9525 kg (21,000 lb)
Max speed: 227 mph
Ceiling: 21,000 ft
Range: 482 km (300 miles)
Armament: MD 30-mm Chain Gun, plus up to 16 Hellfire anti-armour missiles or 76×7.0-cm (2.75-in) folding-fin air-ground rockets

Aérospatiale Gazelle

Originally the subject of joint Anglo-French development in the 1960s, the first SA.340 Gazelle utility helicopter was flown on 7 April 1967. It was followed by the AH.Mk 1 (SA.341B) for the British Army, the HT.Mk 2 (SA.341C) for the Royal Navy, the HT.Mk 3 and HCC.Mk 4 (SA.341D and E) for the RAF, and the SA.341F for the French army. Current military versions are the SA.342L1 with Astazou XIV turboshaft, and SA.342M, developed to an ALAT requirement, including SFIM PA85G autopilot, Crouzet self-contained navigation system, Decca 80 Doppler and provision for a variety of attack weapons including HOT wire-guided missiles in conjunction with various types of stabilised sights.

Specification: Gazelle (SA.342M) five-crew attack helicopter
Powerplant: one 640-kW (858-shp) Astazou XIVM turboshaft with shrouded anti-torque tail rotor
Rotor diameter: 10.50 m (34 ft 5½ in)
Length (overall) 11.97 m (39 ft 3½ in)
Height: 3.19 m (10 ft 5½ in)
Max weight: 2000 kg (4,410 lb)
Max speed: 174 mph
Ceiling: 13,450 ft
Armament: up to six HOT missiles, two 7.62-mm or one GIAT 20-mm guns, two AS.12 missiles or two pods of 68-mm unguided rockets

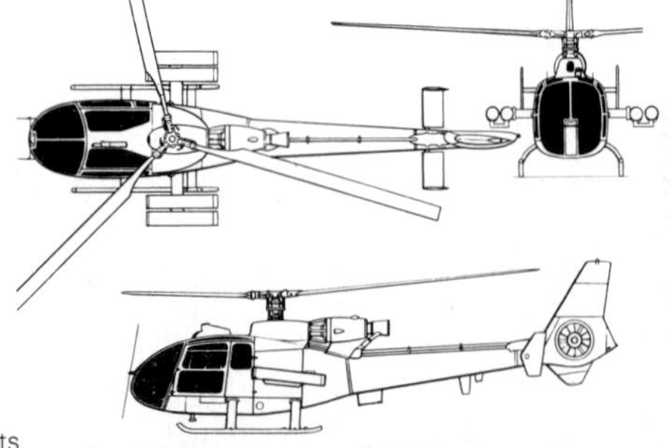

Agusta A 129 Mangusta

The 129 Mangusta (Mongoose) attack and anti-armour helicopter was developed to an Italian army requirement, possessing adverse weather/day-night capabilities. First flown on 15 September 1983, it was scheduled for service entry in 1987, initial funding for 66 examples being sanctioned. For typical anti-armour operation the A 129 would normally be armed with eight TOW missiles together with 7-cm (2.75-in) rockets for counter-fire suppression. An updated version (referred to currently as the *Tonal*) is under study to combine anti-armour, anti-helicopter and scout roles, and may feature a single RTM.322 turboshaft in place of the twin Rolls-Royce RR.1004 turboshafts in the A 129.

Specification: A 129 Mangusta two-crew anti-armour attack helicopter
Powerplant: two 683-kW (915-shp) Rolls-Royce Gem 1004D turboshafts
Rotor diameter: 11.9 m (39 ft 0½ in)
Fuselage length: 12.27 m (40 ft 3½ in)
Max weight: 3800 kg (8,377 lb)
Max speed: 196 mph
Range: 348 miles
Armament: provision to mount eight TOW missiles and four 7-cm (2.75-in) rocket launchers

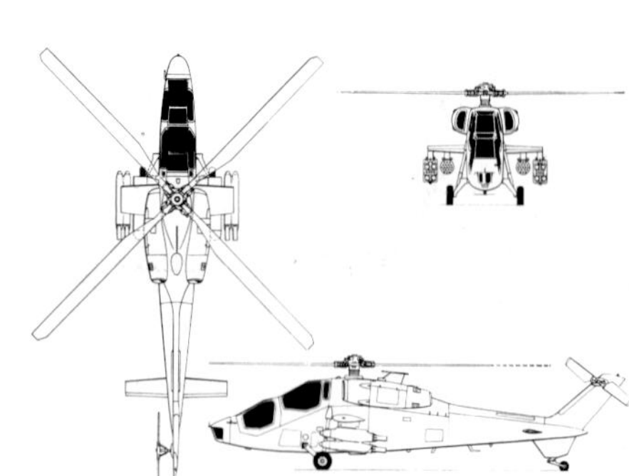

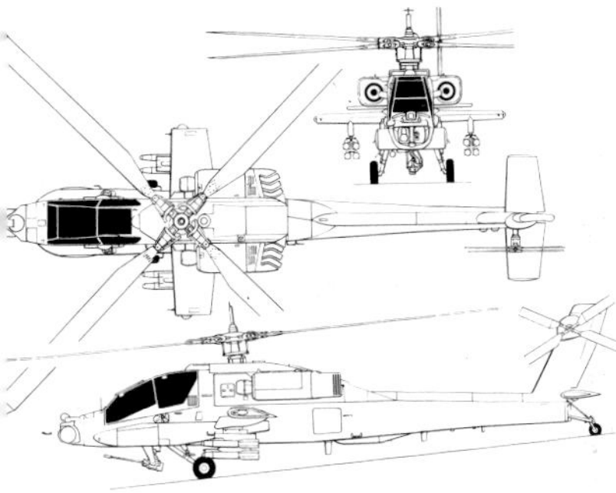

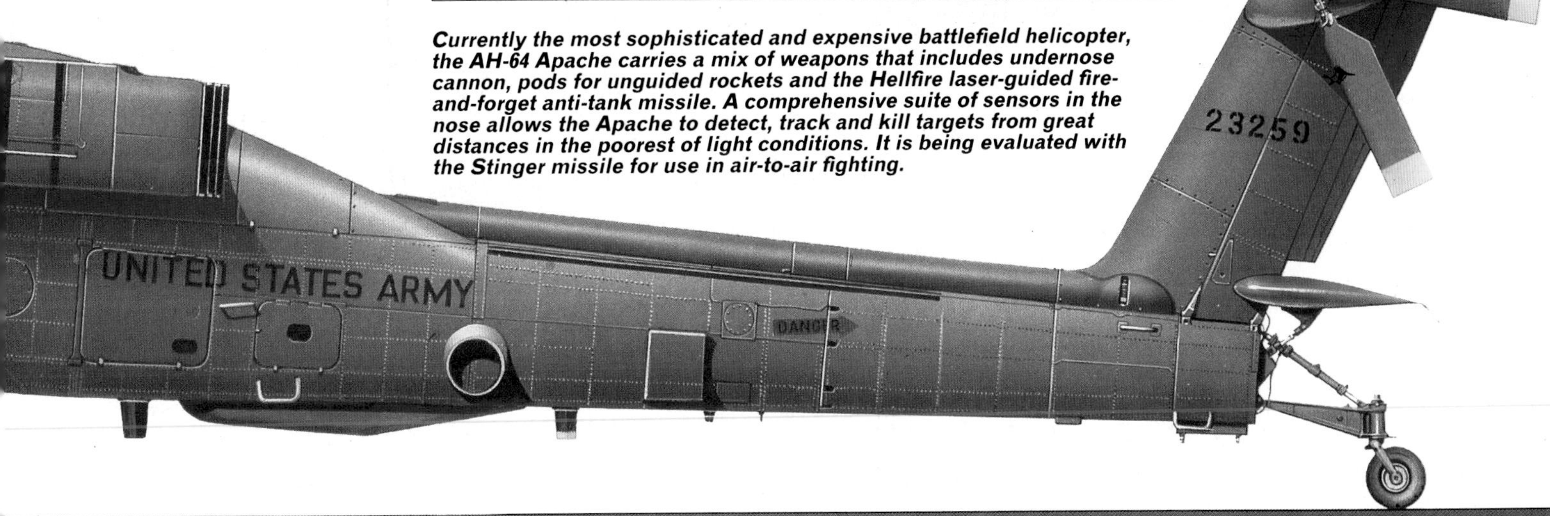

Currently the most sophisticated and expensive battlefield helicopter, the AH-64 Apache carries a mix of weapons that includes undernose cannon, pods for unguided rockets and the Hellfire laser-guided fire-and-forget anti-tank missile. A comprehensive suite of sensors in the nose allows the Apache to detect, track and kill targets from great distances in the poorest of light conditions. It is being evaluated with the Stinger missile for use in air-to-air fighting.

Bell UH-1 Iroquois

The Bell Helicopter Company won a US Army competition in 1955 to develop a light utility support helicopter, from which emerged the Model 204. Numerous variants appeared, of which the UH-1E assault support helicopter entered service in the early 1960s with the US Marine Corps. Other military variants were the UH-1D (Model 205) assault gunship, which joined US Army units in 1963, and the UH-1H that entered service in 1967. An all-weather capability was added in 1971 with the introduction of HELMS (helicopter multi-function system) – rotor blade radar that permitted flight in adverse weather. Minigun armament with radar interface was introduced at the same time.

Specification: UH-1H Iroquois two-crew/10-troop assault/utility helicopter
Powerplant: one 1044-kW (1,400-shp) Lycoming T53-L13 turboshaft
Rotor diameter: 14.63 m (48 ft 0 in)
Length: (overall) 17.4 m (57 ft 1 in)
Height: (overall) 4.42 m (14 ft 6 in)
Max weight: 4309 kg (9,500 lb)
Max speed: 127 mph
Ceiling: 12,600 ft
Range: 318 miles
Armament: provision to mount one forward-firing 7.62-mm Minigun and two others on pintle mounts in cabin doors

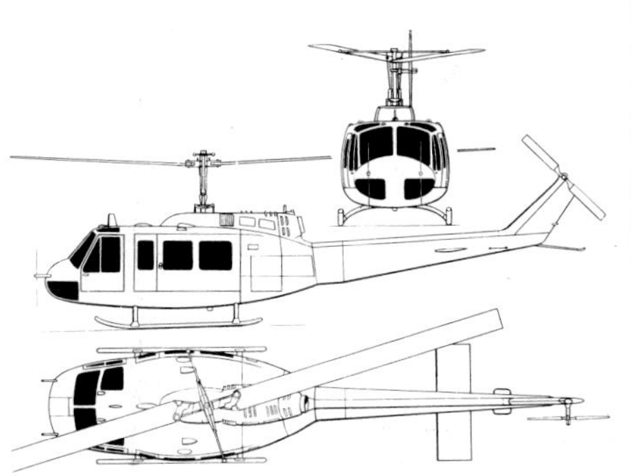

Bell AH-1F Cobra

Formerly carrying the interim designation "Modernised AH-1S", the latest in the Cobra attack helicopter range is the AH-1F, with laser rangefinder and tracker, ballistics computer, pilot's HUD, air data system, Doppler navigator, hot metal and plume IR suppressor and newly-developed composite rotor blades. A total of about 130 of these helicopters has been acquired by the US Forces, while future deliveries are to include laser augmented TOW (LAAT), stabilised sights and an automatic airborne laser tracker (ALT) system. All-weather operation will be achieved with a Hughes-developed FLIR-augmented Cobra TOW-sight, enabling the gunner to "see" in smoke and darkness.

Specification: AH-1F two-crew anti-armour attack helicopter
Powerplant: one 1342-kW (1,800-shp) Avco Lycoming T53-L-703 turboshaft
Rotor diameter: 14.63 m (48 ft 0 in)
Length: (overall) 16.18 m (53 ft 1 in)
Height: (overall) 4.09 m (13 ft 5 in)
Max weight: 4535 kg (10,000 lb)
Max speed: 195 mph
Ceiling: 12,200 ft
Range: 315 miles
Armament: 20- or 30-mm cannon in chin turret and M65 system with eight Hughes TOW missiles

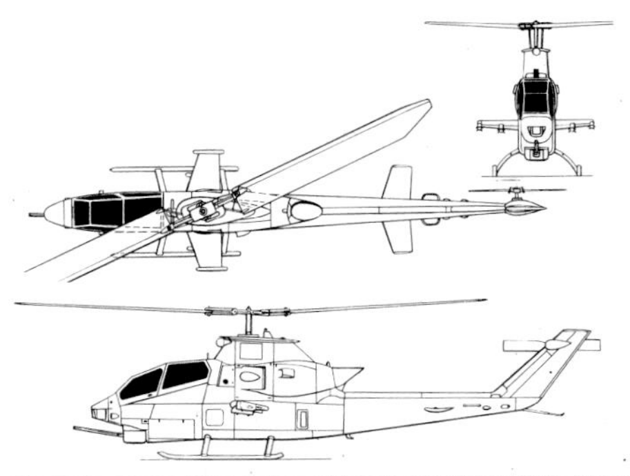

Mil Mi-24 ('Hind-D')

Early versions of the Mi-24 'Hind' served in large numbers from 1972 onwards in support of Soviet ground forces, the 'Hind-D' being first identified in 1976 and produced in very large numbers. This assault and anti-armour helicopter featured an entirely redesigned nose, the pilot and weapons operator being accommodated in tandem. Provision for mounting four UV-32-57 57-mm rocket pods under the wings was complemented by a turreted four-barrel 12.7-mm machine-gun. A developed version followed in 1981, the 'Hind-E', with added provision for four AT-2 'Swatter' anti-armour missiles, IR jammer and IR suppression exhaust mixers. The Mi-25 is the export variant.

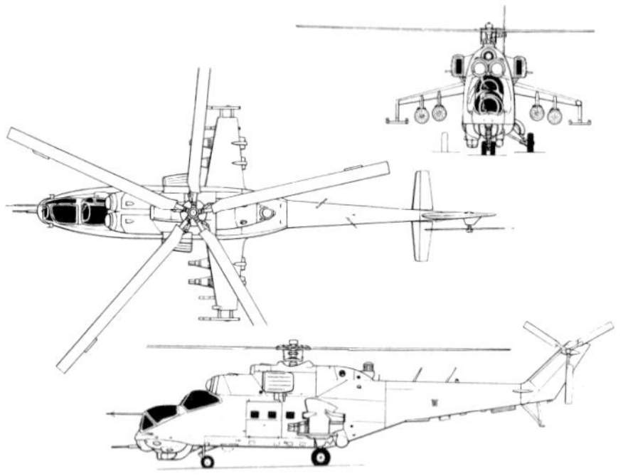

The export versions of the Mi-24 Hind-D attack helicopters, such as this example from Grupo Aero 3 of the Peruvian air force with impressive shark-teeth markings, are designated Mi-25. Peruvian Mi-25s were frequently engaged against Maoist guerrillas.

Bell AH-1W SuperCobra

In 1980 a modified AH-1T was test flown with two uprated T700-GE-700 turboshafts as part of a proposed programme to develop an attack helicopter for the US Marine Corps with much enhanced operational capability. From this was evolved the SuperCobra (originally termed the AH-1T+), deliveries of which started to the USMC in March 1986. Duties of this twin-turboshaft aircraft included troop-carrying helicopter escort and anti-armour multiple weapon fire support. Weapons include chin turret-mounted three-barrel M 197 20-mm gun and provision for four multiple 7-cm (2.75-in) rocket pods, two CBU-55B weapons, Minigun pods, TOW or Hellfire anti-armour missile installations.

Specification: AH-1W SuperCobra two-crew attack anti-armour helicopter
Powerplant: two 1212-kW (1,625-shp) General Electric T700-GE-401 turboshafts
Rotor diameter: 14.63 m (48 ft 0 in)
Length: (overall) 17.68 m (58 ft 0 in)
Height: (overall) 4.32 m (14 ft 2 in)
Max weight: 6900 kg (4,285 lb)
Max speed: 190 mph
Range: 250 miles
Armament: three-barrelled 20-mm gun in chin turret plus rocket pods, cluster weapons, Minigun, TOW or Hellfire anti-armour missiles

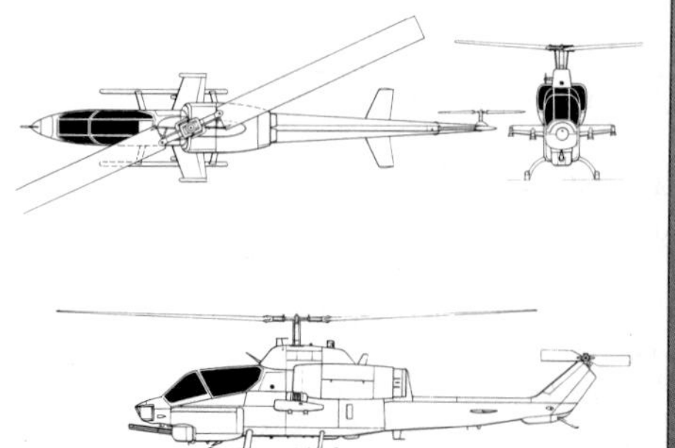

Kamov 'Hokum'

One of the Soviet Union's latest combat helicopters, 'Hokum' features the Kamov trademark, the superimposed, counter-rotating rotors that obviate the need for counter-torque tail rotor. The helicopter is believed to feature Isotov TV3-117-series turboshafts mounted at the roots of high-set stub wings which incorporate four store pylons. With high performance figures (estimated by the US DoD), the aircraft is clearly capable of air-to-air and air-to-ground combat and is assumed to carry IR suppressors. The two-man crew is thought to be accommodated side-by-side and armament is believed to include a large-calibre gun in addition to rocket packs. Service is believed to have started in 1987.

Specification: Kamov 'Hokum' two-crew combat helicopter
Powerplant: two Isotov TV30117-series turboshafts of approx 1660-kW (2,225-shp)
Rotor diameter: 18.2 m (59 ft 8 in)
Length: (overall) 16.00 m (52 ft 6 in)
Height: 5.4 m (17 ft 8 in)
Max weight: 5450 kg (12,000 lb)
Max speed: 217 mph
Combat radius: 144 miles
Armament: believed to include one large calibre machine-gun and up to four underwing rocket packs for AAMs or AGMs (anti-armour)
All figures estimated by US DoD

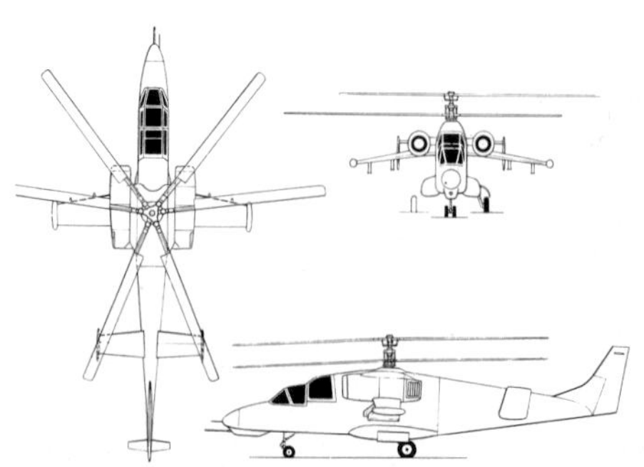

Specification: Mi-24 ('Hind-D') 2-crew/8-troop assault helicopter
Powerplant: two 1640-kW (2,200-shp) Isotov TV3-117 turboshafts
Rotor diameter: 16.76 m (55 ft 0 in)
Fuselage length: 16.9 m (55 ft 6 in)
Max weight: 10940 kg (24,100 lb)
Max speed: 200 mph
Combat radius: 140 miles
Armament: four barrel 12.7-mm machine-gun in nose, plus four 32×57-mm rocket launcher pods and four AT-2 'Swatter' IR-homing anti-armour missiles

MD 500-Series Defender

Formerly the Hughes 500M Defender, McDonnell Douglas continued development of this helicopter following manufacture acquisition in January 1984. Current versions include the 500MD Scout Defender with former universal weapon provisions, the MD/TOW Defender dedicated anti-tank helicopter with TOW missiles and stabilised telescopic sight, the MD/MMS-TOW version with mast-mounted sight, the MD/ASW anti-submarine helicopter with search radar, AN/ASQ-81 towed-MAD and two homing torpedoes, and 530MG all-weather attack helicopter. Defenders are produced under licence in the Republic of Korea.

Specification: 530MG Defender two-crew light attack helicopter
Powerplant: one 317-kW (425-ehp) Allison 250-series turboshaft
Rotor diameter: 8.05 m (26 ft 5 in)
Length: (overall) 9.78 m (32 ft 1 in)
Height: (MMS) 3.41 m (11 ft 2½ in)
Max weight: 1610 kg (3,550 lb)
Max speed: 150 mph
Ceiling: 4880 m (16,000 ft)
Range: 233 miles
Armament: provision for four Stinger AAMs, for TOW anti-armour missiles, four 12-tube rocket launchers, and/or one 7.62-mm MD Chain Gun or 0.50-cal (12.7-mm) machine-gun

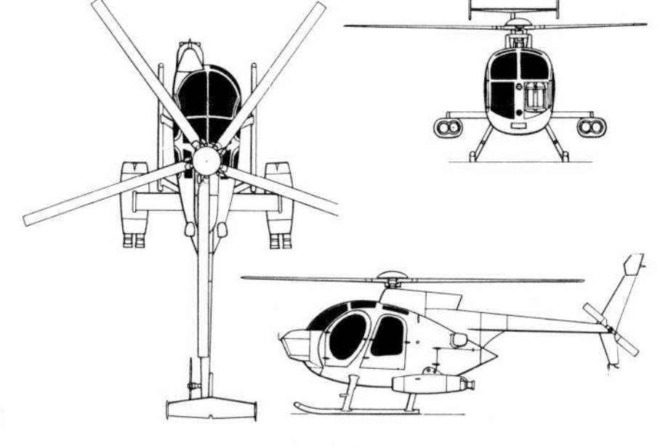

MBB BO 105

Stemming from a basic design of the early 1960s, the five-seat BO 105 light helicopter has enjoyed continuous development since, and by the mid-1980s well over 1,000 were in service in 36 countries. A military version, the BO 105M, was produced for the Federal German Army with strengthened transmission and rotor components, 100 being built to replace ageing Alouette IIs, and from this was derived the current BO 105 P (PAH-1), a light anti-armour version with outrigged store carriers for six Euromissile HOT missiles, a stabilised sight located above the second pilot's station and a Singer AN/ASN-128 Doppler navigation system. A night/all-weather derivative is the BO 105CB.

Specification: BO 105 five-seat all-weather attack light helicopter
Powerplant: two 313-kW (400-shp) Allison 250-C20B turboshafts
Rotor diameter: 9.84 m (32 ft 3½ in)
Length: (overall) 11.86 m (38 ft 11 in)
Height: 3.00 m (9 ft 10 in)
Max weight: 2500 kg (5,511 lb)
Max speed: 167 mph
Range: 408 miles
Armament: provision for up to six Euromissile HOT missiles or eight TOW anti-armour missiles with associated stabilised sight

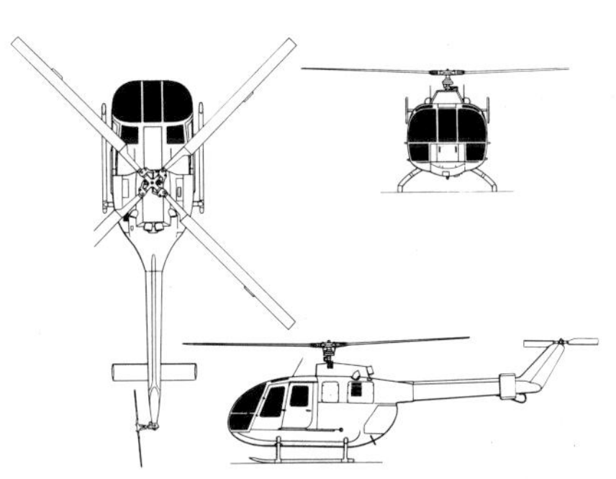

Mil Mi-8/Mi-17 ('Hip-H')

Developed from the Mi-8 general utility helicopter which first flew (as the 'Hip-A') in 1961, this widely-used aircraft has progressed through numerous versions, including the 'Hip-C' of which over 10,000 were produced, the 'Hip-E' and '-F' armed helicopters to the current Mi-17 ('Hip-H') assault aircraft. Production of the latter is continuing at the rate of about 700 per year. 'Hip-H' is fairly conventional by recent standards, being powered by a pair of turboshafts located above the cabin and geared together to drive a single five-blade rotor. Outrigged structures carry up to six store pylons and when used in the assault transport role carries about 20 fully-armed troops.

Specification: Mi-17 ('Hip-H')
20/24-seat assault transport helicopter
Powerplant: two 1420-kW (1,900-shp) Isotov TV3-117MT turboshafts
Rotor diameter: 21.29 m (69 ft 10 in)
Fuselage length: 18.31 m (60 ft 1 in)
Height: 5.65 m (18 ft 6½ in)
Max weight: 12260 kg (27,000 lb)
Max speed: 168 mph
Range: 290 miles
Armament: one 12.7-mm machine-gun in nose and up to six rocket packs and four AT-2 'Swatter' anti-armour missiles

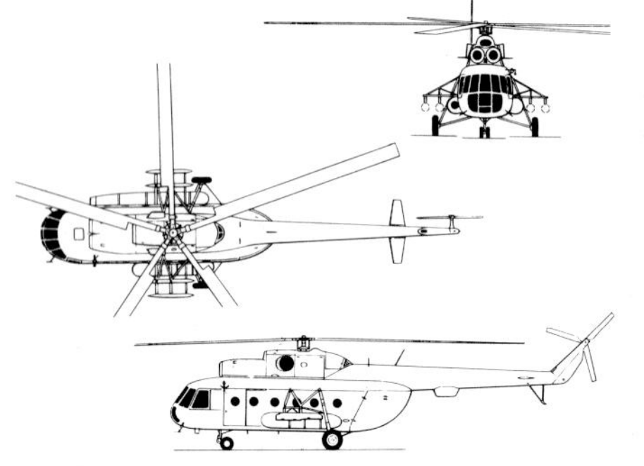

Mil Mi-24 ('Hind-F')

A recent derivative of the 'Hind-D/E' has been identified and designated 'Hind-F' on account of its enhanced target acquisition by means of an enlarged radar designator employed in conjunction with the tube-launched, folding-fin AT-6 'Spiral' anti-armour missiles carried on the stub-wing strongpoints. In addition the heavier twin-barrelled GSh-23L 23-mm cannon is mounted on the starboard side of the nose, almost certainly replacing the former four-barrel 12.7-mm rotary machine-gun in the central nose mounting. All IR jammer and suppression systems of the 'Hind-D/E' are assumed to be retained.

Specification: Mi-24 ('Hind-F')
dedicated anti-armour attack helicopter
Powerplant: two 1640-kW (2,200-shp) Isotov TV3-117 turboshafts
Rotor diameter: 16.76 m (55 ft 0 in)
Fuselage length: 16.9 m (55 ft 6 in)
Max weight: 11000 kg (24,420 lb)
Max speed: 200 mph
Combat radius: 140 miles
Armament: twin-barrel GSh-23L 23-mm cannon on side of nose, plus four AT-6 'Spiral' anti-armour missiles and 57-mm rocket launcher pods.

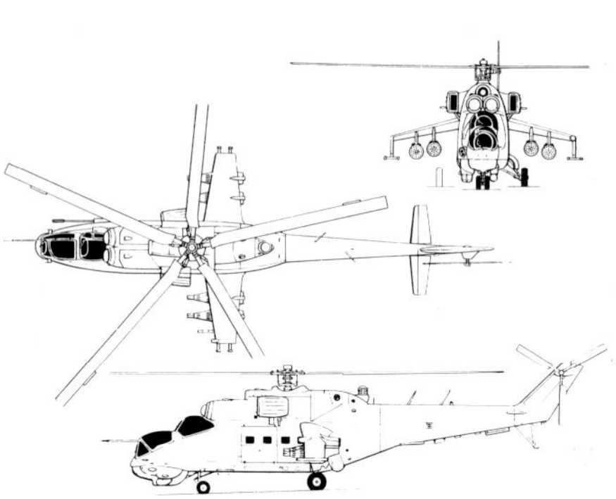

Mil Mi-28 ('Havoc')

Believed to have undergone trials in operational conditions in Afghanistan in 1985 and entered full service late in 1987 with attack helicopter regiments of the Soviet forces, 'Havoc' is said to be comparable in capability with the American AH-64 Apache, with full air-to-air and air-to-ground faculties. It appears to feature armoured protection in the vicinity of the two-seat tandem cockpits, and is armed with a single barbette-mounted gun, probably of 23-mm calibre. The twin turboshafts feature upward-deflected jet pipes. Laser-guided anti-armour missiles can be loaded under the stub wings, and IR suppressors and IR decoy dischargers are fitted.

Specification: Mi-28 ('Havoc')
two-crew attack helicopter
Powerplant: two 1865-kW (2,500-shp) Isotov TV3-117-related turboshafts
Rotor diameter: 17.0 m (55 ft 9 in)
Fuselage length: 17.4 m (57 ft 1 in)
Max speed: 186 mph
Combat radius: 150 miles
Armament: one nose barbette-mounted 23-mm cannon, plus two tube-launched air-to-air missiles and four laser-guided anti-armour missiles
All figures estimated by US DoD

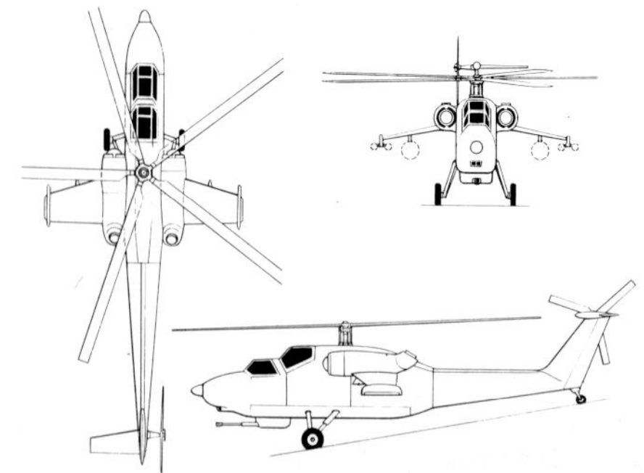

Westland Lynx

First flown on 21 March 1971, the Lynx did not appear in production form until 1976, the AH.Mk 1 being the British Army's general utility version and the HAS.Mk 2 the Royal Navy's anti-submarine helicopter. The Lynx Mk 3 is a dedicated anti-armour variant with adverse weather/day-night operating capability, with provision to mount Stinger self-defence missiles, Euromissile HOT, Hughes TOW and Rockwell Hellfire anti-armour missiles; gun armament can include a 20-mm cannon and pintle-mounted 7.62-mm machine-gun. The Lynx has been fairly widely exported, France, Argentina, Denmark, Germany, Brazil, the Netherlands, Nigeria and Qatar being among the recent customers.

Specification: Lynx Mk 3 two-crew anti-armour helicopter
Powerplant: two 832-kW (1,115-shp) Rolls-Royce Gem 60 turboshafts
Rotor diameter: 12.8 m (42 ft 0 in)
Length: 13.79 m (45 ft 3 in)
Max weight: 5896 kg (13,000 lb)
Max speed: 190 mph
Range: 385 miles
Armament: one 20-mm and one 7.62-mm machine-guns and provision to mount Stinger missiles, Euromissile HOT, Hughes TOW and Rockwell Hellfire anti-armour missiles

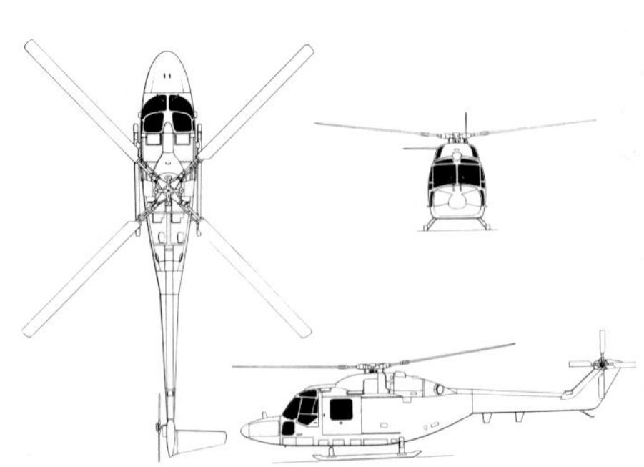

Sikorsky UH-60 Black Hawk

First flown in October 1974 to the US Army's Utility Tactical Transport Aircraft System competition for a UH-1 replacement, the UH-60 began to enter service in 1979 and has quickly matured as an excellent type. Costs have been too high to allow the advanced UH-60 to replace the UH-1 on a one-for-one basis, but substantial numbers are being procured for major 'tooth' formations. Though a number of special-role and naval variants have been suggested and produced, the sole tactical model is the UH-60A able to carry a full infantry squad or, by removal of eight seats, four litters in the medevac role. The UH-60A has a high degree of air-portability by partial disassembly, and the large sliding doors on each side make for rapid troop ingress/egress in the field.

Specification: Sikorsky UH-60A Black Hawk light assault transport helicopter
Rotor diameter: 16.36 m (53 ft 8 in)
Overall length, rotors turning: 19.76 m (64 ft 10 in)
Powerplant: 2×General Electric T700-GE-700, 1151 kW (1,560 shp) each
Payload: 14 troops or freight carried internally, or 3629 kg (8,000 lb) of freight carried externally
Max T/O weight: 9185 kg (20,250 lb)
Cruising speed: 167 mph at 4,000 ft
Operational range: 373 miles

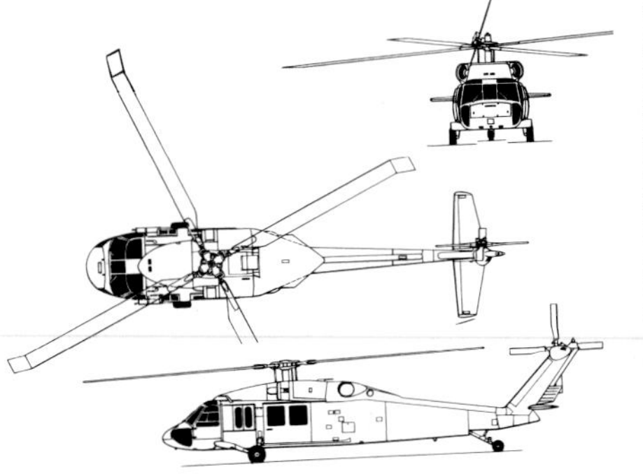

Westland Commando

In addition to building the Sikorsky S-61 under licence as the Sea King anti-submarine helicopter for the Royal Navy and export, Westland has produced a dedicated assault model as the Sea King HC.Mk 4 (British service) and Commando (export sales as the baseline Mk 1 and improved Mk 2). This resembles the Sea King in its overall configuration and dynamic system, but has non-retractable landing gear in place of the Sea King's gear with main units retracting into the stabilising sponsons. All specifically naval and anti-submarine gear has been removed from the Commando, which first flew in September 1973, and payload/range performance has been optimised together with a significant and versatile armament capability.

Specification: Westland Commando Mk 2 assault and medium tactical transport helicopter
Rotor diameter: 18.90 m (62 ft 0 in)
Overall length, rotors turning: 22.15 m (72 ft 8 in)
Powerplant: 2×Rolls-Royce Gnome H.1400-1, 1238 kW (1,660 shp) each
Payload: 28 troops or 2722 kg (6,000 lb) of freight carried internally, or 3402 kg (7,500 lb) of freight carried externally
Max T/O weight: 9526 kg (21,000 lb)
Cruising speed: 129 mph at sea level
Operational range: 276 miles

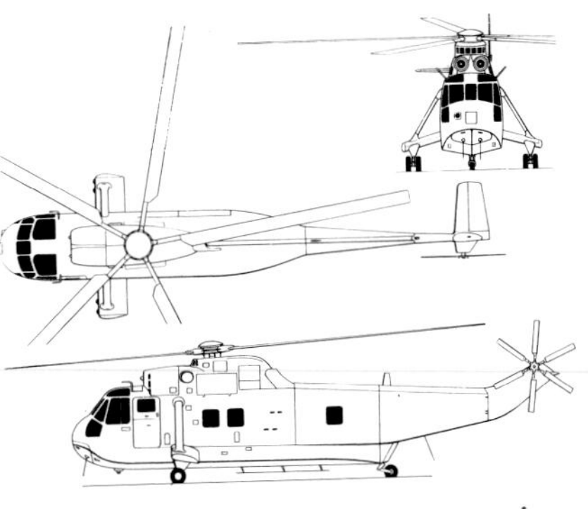

Westland Lynx

The Lynx was planned in parallel navy and army forms, the former with wheeled tricycle landing gear and the latter with twin skids, and first flew in March 1971. The Lynx, notable for its performance, agility and facility for constant upgrade in systems and role equipment, began to enter service as the Lynx AH.Mk 1 during 1977. This variant can be used as an eight-man transport or as an anti-tank type with up to eight TOW missiles, and is complemented by the Lynx AH.Mk 7 with 835 kW (1,120 shp) Gem 41-1 turboshafts for better hover and manoeuvre capability in the nap-of-the-earth anti-tank role, and by the imminent Lynx AH.Mk 9 with tricycle landing gear, Gem 42-1 engines and the new BERP rotor blades. The Mk 9 is an unarmed variant designed for the command post and transport roles.

Specification: Westland Lynx AH.Mk 1 anti-tank and light assault transport helicopter
Rotor diameter: 12.802 m (42 ft 0 in)
Overall length, rotors turning: 15.163 m (49 ft 9 in)
Powerplant: 2×Rolls-Royce Gem 2, 559 kW (750 shp) each
Payload: 10 troops or 907 kg (2,000 lb) of freight carried internally, or 1361 kg (3,000 lb) of freight carried externally
Max T/O weight: 4536 kg (10,000 lb)
Cruising speed: 161 mph at sea level
Operational range: 336 miles

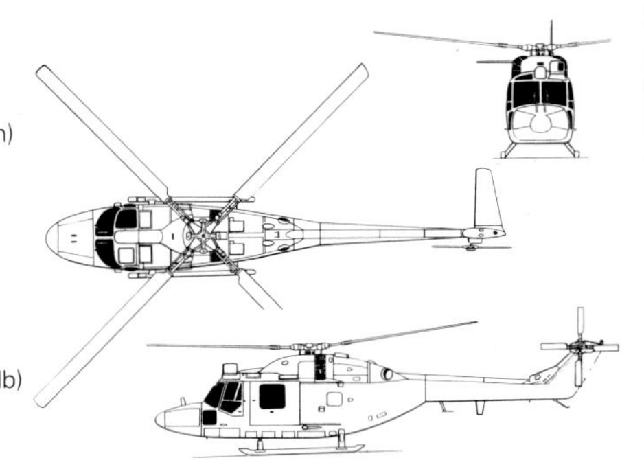

Westland Wessex

Westland has enjoyed a long association with Sikorsky, and the Wessex is essentially a licence-built S-58 with gas turbine rather than piston-engine power. The first prototype flew in June 1958, and the type was extensively built for the anti-submarine, utility and transport roles. The first models were powered by a single 1081 kW (1,450 shp) Napier Gazelle, though the Wessex HC.Mk 2 communications variant introduced coupled Gnome turboshafts for greater reliability and engine-out flight capability. The first dedicated trooping variant was the Wessex HU.Mk 5 based on the HC.Mk 2, and after an initial flight in May 1963 this model was built to the extent of about 100 helicopters, with provision for armament in the defence-suppression role.

Specification: Westland Wessex HU.Mk 5 light assault transport helicopter
Rotor diameter: 17.07 m (56 ft 0 in)
Overall length, rotors turning: 20.04 m (65 ft 9 in)
Powerplant: 2×Bristol Siddeley Gnome Mk 110/111, 1007 kW (1,350 shp) each
Payload: 16 troops or 1814 kg (4,000 lb) of freight carried internally or externally
Max T/O weight: 6124 kg (13,500 lb)
Cruising speed: 121 mph
Operational range: 390 miles

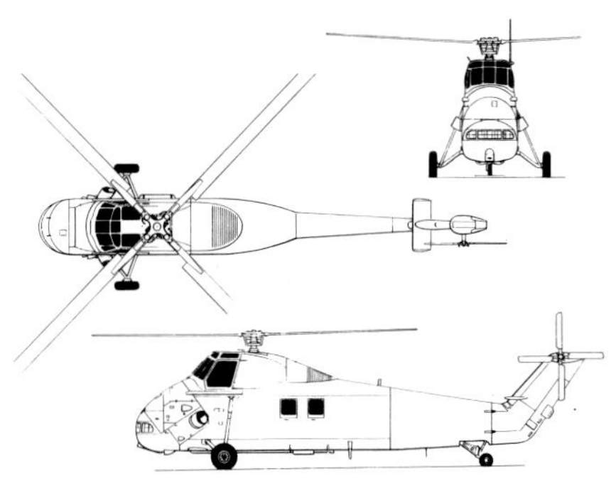

Aérospatiale SA 330 Puma

Specification: Aérospatiale SA 330L Puma medium tactical transport helicopter
Main rotor diameter: 15.00 m (49 ft 2.5 in)
Overall length, rotors turning: 18.15 m (59 ft 6.5 in)
Powerplant: 2×Turboméca Turmo IVC, 1175 kW (1,575 shp) each
Payload: 20 troops or 3000 kg (6,616 lb) of freight carried internally, or 3200 kg (7,055 lb) of freight carried externally
Max T/O weight: 7400 kg (16,315 lb)
Cruising speed: 160 mph at sea level
Operational range: 341 miles

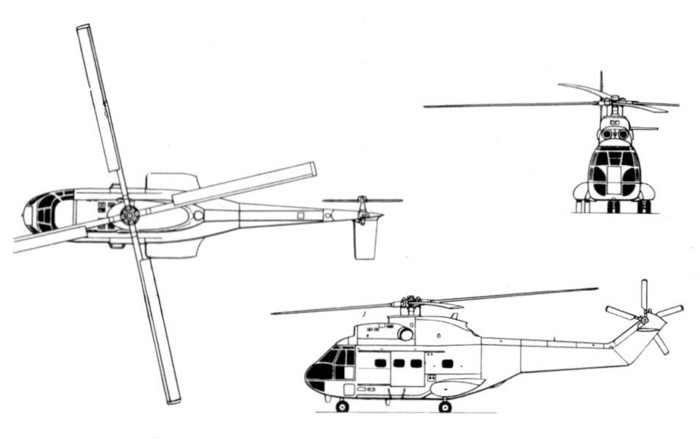

Aérospatiale SA 321 S Frelon

The SA 3210 Super Frelon was developed from the smaller SA 3200 Frelon with the aid of Sikorsky in the design of the rotors. The first prototype was powered by three 985 kW (1,320 shp) Turmo IIIC$_2$ turboshafts and flew on 7 December 1982 in form representative of the tactical troop transport model. This entered service as the SA 321H Super Frelon with revised powerplant, and can be differentiated from naval Super Frelons by its lack of stabilising floats or fuselage fairings. The Israeli SA 321K is based on the SA 321J civil model, but is generally similar to the SA 321H apart from its use of General Electric T58 turboshafts, and the SA 321L is an SA 321J military derivative for Libya, South Africa and China, which builds the type as the Harbin Z-8.

Specification: Aérospatiale SA 321H Super Frelon medium assault and tactical transport helicopter
Main rotor diameter: 18.90 m (62 ft 0 in)
Overall length, rotors turning: 23.03 m (75 ft 6.7 in)
Powerplant: 3×Turboméca Turmo IIIE$_6$, 1170 kW (1,570 shp) each
Payload: 30 troops or 5000 kg (11,023 lb) of freight carried internally or externally
Max T/O weight: 13000 kg (28,660 lb)
Cruising speed: 154 mph at sea level
Operational range: 506 miles

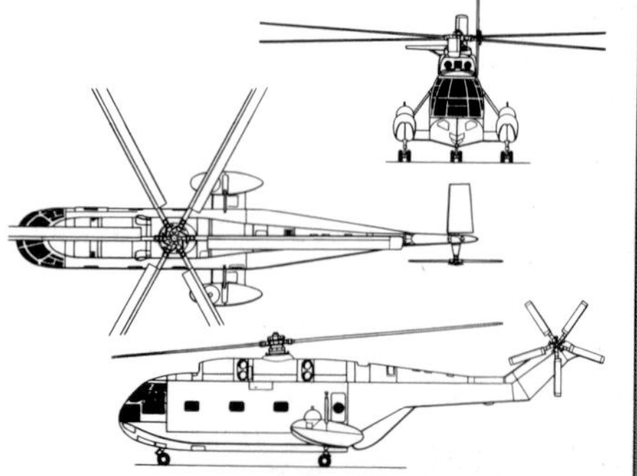

Bell UH-1 Iroquois or 'Huey'

Produced in larger numbers than any other Western helicopter and slated for a service life into the next century, the 'Huey' series was originated as the Model 204 in response to a US Army utility transport helicopter requirement and first flew in XH-40 form during October 1956. The type entered service in 1959 with the 574 kW (770 shp) T53-L-1A as the HU-1A, revised during 1962 to UH-1A. Subsequent Model 204 variants have power up to 1044 kW (1,400 shp) and can carry up to 10 passengers. The Model 205 was introduced in 1961 as the UH-1D with the 820 kW (1,100 shp) T53-L-11 and a larger cabin for 12 troops, the UH-1H having capacity for 14 troops on 1044 kW (1,400 shp). Further development of the Model 205 concept led to the Model 212 of 1969 with coupled turboshafts for service as the UH-1N.

Specification: Bell UH-1N Iroquois light utility tactical helicopter
Main rotor diameter: 14.69 m (48 ft 2.25 in)
Overall length, rotors turning: 17.46 m (57 ft 3.25 in)
Powerplant: 1×Pratt & Whitney Canada T400-CP-400, 1342 kW (1,800 shp) flat-rated to 962 kW (1,290 shp)
Payload: 14 troops or 1814 kg (4,000 lb) of freight carried internally or externally
Max T/O weight: 4762 kg (10,500 lb)
Cruising speed: 142 mph at sea level
Operational range: 248 miles

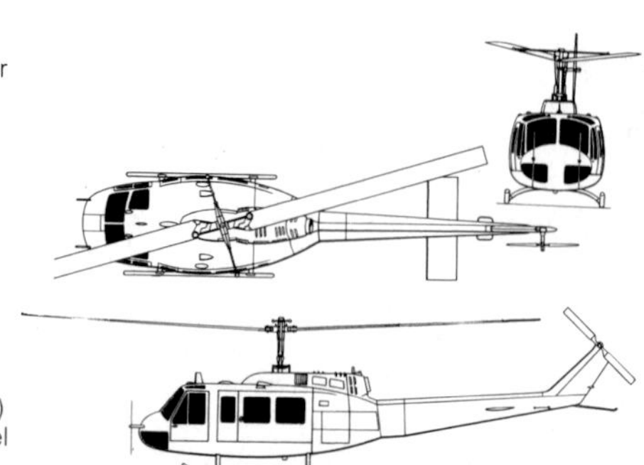

The Puma resulted from a French army requirement of the early 1960s for an all-weather day/night tactical transport helicopter, and flew in prototype form on 15 April 1965. The first production SA 330B was delivered in September 1968, by which time Westland was co-producing the type in the UK for the Royal Air Force. The SA 330B is powered by Turmo $IIIC_4$ turboshafts, as is the Puma HC.Mk 1 for the RAF; the SA 330C export model has Turmo IVCs. Improved models are the SA 330H for France and the SA 330L export model with rotor blades of composite construction plus inlet anti-icing and rotor blade de-icing. Further development has led to the AS 332B Super Puma with Makila turboshafts for greater performance and payload (21 troops). The current version is the AS 332M with a lengthened cabin for 25 troops. Licence production is undertaken in Indonesia and Romania.

This Puma HC.1 is from RAF 230 Squadron, based at Gütersloh. These helicopters operate in support of the British Army of the Rhine, and are backed-up by the Chinooks of 18 Squadron, also stationed there. In time of war they would be transferred from their peace-time positions to preselected bases.

Kamov Ka-27 'Helix'

Introduced to service in the early 1980s, the Ka-27 series has the NATO reporting name 'Helix' and can be regarded as the modern equivalent of the long-serving Ka-25 'Hormone' with the same arrangement of super-imposed co-axial, three-blade rotors turning in opposite directions to remove the torque problem that would otherwise require a longer tail carrying an anti-torque rotor. This eases the accommodation of the helicopter on board Soviet warships, and also simplifies the provision of a capacious fuselage. The Ka-27 is thus roomier and also more powerful than the Ka-25, allowing the development of the 'Helix-B' dedicated Naval Infantry assault version that had proved impossible in the 'Hormone' series. The 'Helix-A' anti-submarine variant has a secondary assault capability with a squad of Naval Infantry or a slung load of 5000 kg (11,023 lb).

Specification: Kamov Ka-27 'Helix-B' light assault transport helicopter
Rotor diameter: 15.90 m (52 ft 2 in)
Fuselage length: 11.30 m (37 ft 0.9 in)
Powerplant: 2×Isotov TV3-117V, 1660 kW (2,226 shp) each
Payload: 16 troops or 4000 kg (8,818 lb) of freight carried internally, or 5000 kg (11,023 lb) of freight carried externally
Max T/O weight: 12600 kg (27,778 lb)
Cruising speed: 138 mph
Operational range: 497 miles

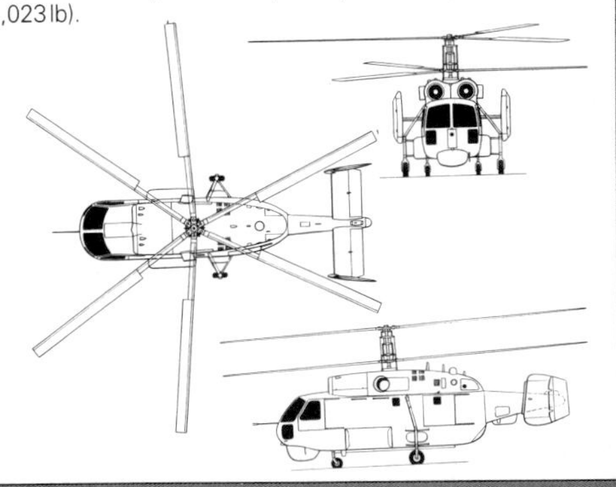

Boeing CH-46 Sea Knight

The Sea Knight was developed as the Vertol 107M to meet a US Marine Corps requirement for a twin-rotor helicopter suitable for the beach assault role from US Navy specialist ships lying offshore. The Sea Knight began to enter service in 1965 as the Boeing Vertol CH-46A with two 932 kW (1,250 shp) T58-GE-8B turboshafts and a payload of 25 troops or 1814 kg (4,000 lb) of freight accessed by a rear loading/unloading ramp. Later variants included the CH-46D with 1044 kW (1,400 shp) T58-GE-10s, revised rotors and capability for a slung load of 4536 kg (10,000 lb), and the similar UH-46D 'vertrep' and HH-46D SAR types. Surviving helicopters are being upgraded to the CH-46E standard with glassfibre rotor blades, crash-attenuating seats and a crash-resistant fuel system.

Specification: Boeing CH-46E Sea Knight light/medium assault transport helicopter
Rotor diameter: 15.54 m (52 ft 0 in) each
Overall length, rotors turning: 25.70 m (84 ft 4 in)
Powerplant: 2×General Electric T58-GE-16, 1394 kW (1,870 shp) each
Payload: 25 troops or 3175 kg (7,000 lb) of freight carried internally, or 4536 kg (10,000 lb) of freight carried externally
Max T/O weight: 10433 kg (23,000 lb)
Cruising speed: 165 mph at sea level
Operational range: 238 miles with a 2064 kg (4,550 lb) payload

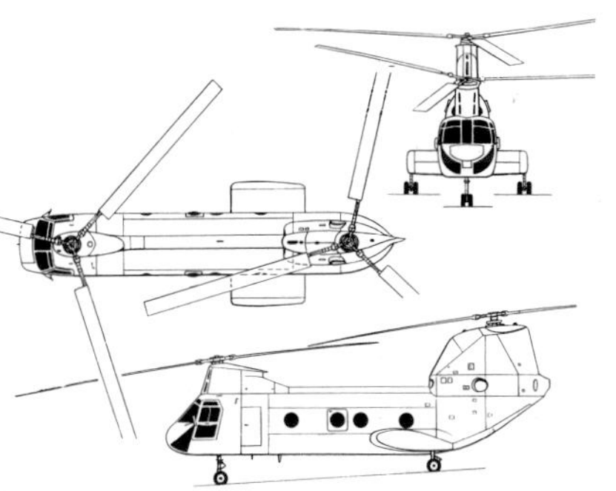

Boeing CH-47 Chinook

The Chinook shown here is one of 12 CH-47C Chinooks used by the Air Corps of the Spanish Army. The helicopters serve in Los Remedios, with the Batallon de Helicopteros de Transporte V.

Essentially a scaled-up version of the Model 107 with quadricycle rather than tricycle landing gear and far greater power, the Model 114 was developed to meet a US Army requirement for a medium transport helicopter. The YHC-1B prototype flew in September 1961, and CH-47A production helicopters began to enter service in 1962 with 1641 kW (2,200 shp) T55-L-5 turboshafts for a payload of 44 troops or a slung load of 7257 kg (16,000 lb). The CH-47B and CH-47C variants introduced additional power. A large-scale programme is now seeing surviving aircraft updated to CH-47D standard with yet more power and features such as composite rotor blades, crash-resistant systems, more advanced avionics and a three-point suspension system. Licence production is undertaken in Italy.

Mil Mi-6 'Hook'

First flown in September 1957, the Mi-6 was at the time the world's largest helicopter and is still a prodigious machine. The type is powered by two turboshafts located above the capacious cabin to drive the single five-blade main rotor and four-blade tail rotor. The conventional appearance of this single-rotor type disguises its considerble size, which would in itself be a great hindrance to tactical mobility. Stub wings help to offload the main rotor and so boost performance with the helicopter's considerable internal payload, which can include light weapons and vehicles as clamshell rear doors are provided. The original Mi-6 was succeeded by larger numbers of the Mi-6A with a number of operational improvements.

Specification: Mil Mi-6A 'Hook' heavy transport helicopter
Rotor diameter: 35.00 m (114 ft 10 in)
Overall length, rotors turning: 41.74 m (136 ft 11.5 in)
Powerplant: 2×Soloviev D-35V (TV-2BM), 4100 kW (5,500 shp) each
Payload: 65 troops or 12000 kg (26,455 lb) of freight carried internally, or 8000 kg (17,637 lb) of freight carried externally
Max T/O weight: 42500 kg (93,700 lb)
Cruising speed: 155 mph
Operational range: 385 miles with an 800 kg (17,637 lb) payload

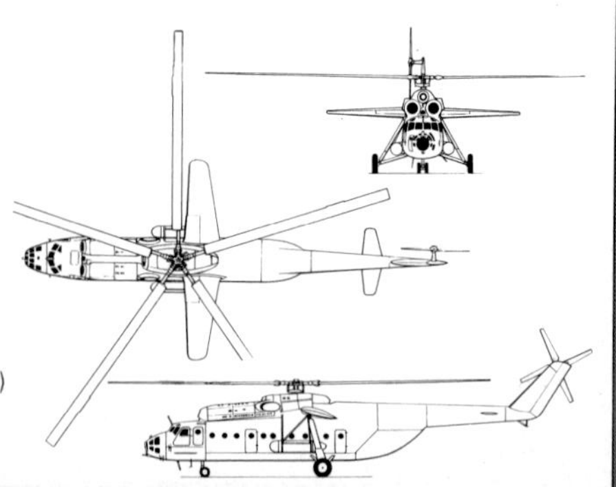

Mil Mi-8 and Mi-17 'Hip'

The machine known to NATO as the 'Hip' is by far the most important helicopter in the Soviet inventory, and serves in vast numbers for a variety of tactical tasks. The Mi-8 'Hip-A' prototype first flew in 1961 with a single Soloviev turboshaft and four-blade main rotor, this combination being replaced in the 'Hip-B' second prototype by two 1270 kW (1703 shp) TV2-117A and a five-blade main rotor. The 'Hip-C' began to enter service in the mid-1960s as a 32-man transport, and in addition to its considerable internal volume has external provision for a heavy load of rockets and/or anti-tank missiles. Further development of the battlefield 'Hip' led to the 'Hip-E' with greater armament capability, the 'Hip-F' export model and then to the Mil-17 'Hip-H' with the uprated powerplant of the Mi-14 'Haze' anti-submarine helicopter, itself a Mi-8 derivative.

Specification: Mil Mi-17 'Hip-H' medium assault transport helicopter
Rotor diameter: 21.29 m (69 ft 10.5 in)
Overall length, rotors turning: 25.352 m (83 ft 2 in)
Powerplant: 2×Isotov TV3-117MT, 1420 kW (1,905 shp) each
Payload: 32 troops or 4000 kg (8,818 lb) of freight carried internally, or 3000 kg (6,616 lb) of freight carried externally
Max T/O weight: 13000 kg (28,660 lb)
Cruising speed: 149 mph
Operational range: 307 miles

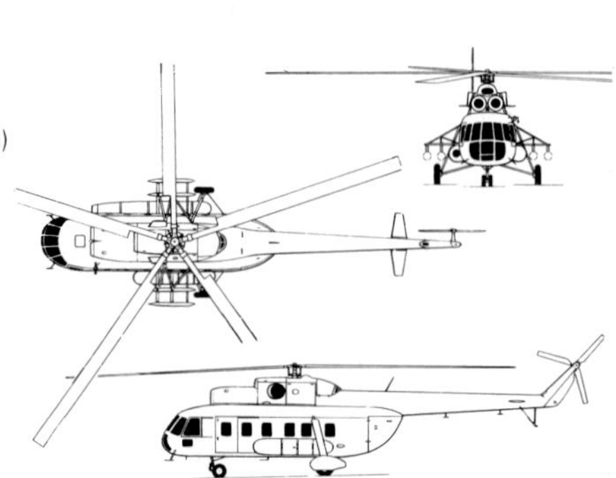

Specification: Boeing CH-47D Chinook medium transport helicopter
Rotor diameter: 18.29 m (60 ft 0 in) each
Overall length, rotors turning: 30.18 m (99 ft 0 in)
Powerplant: 2×Avco Lycoming T55-L-712, 3356 kW (4,500 shp) each
Payload: 44 troops or 8164 kg (18,000 lb) of freight carried internally, or 9389 kg (20,700 lb) of freight carried externally
Max T/O weight: 22680 kg (50,000 lb)
Cruising speed: 185 mph at sea level
Operational range: 115 miles with an 8164 kg (18,000 lb) load

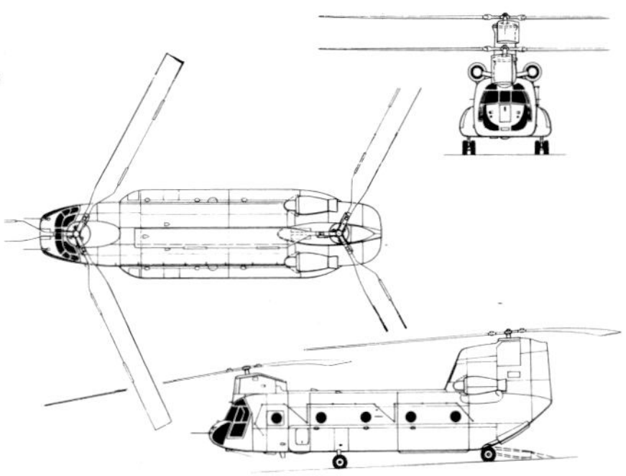

Mil Mi-26 'Halo'

The Mi-26 was designed in the early 1970s to provide a replacement for the Mi-6 and Mi-10 in the heavy-lift role, and the result is the world's heaviest helicopter. The design is typical of the mainstream of Mil single-rotor helicopter design but with an eight-blade main rotor, twin wheels on each of the tricycle landing gear units and a massive hold accessed by clamshell rear doors and an integral ramp. The prototype flew in 1979, and the type began to enter service in the early 1980s. The capabilities of the 'Halo' are attested by a number of impressive payload-to-height records, and the primary military role of the type is logistic support (including movement of vehicles and artillery) rather than battlefield operations.

Specification: Mil Mi-26 'Halo' heavy transport helicopter
Rotor diameter: 32.00 m (105 ft 9 in)
Overall length, rotors turning: 40.025 m (131 ft 3.8 in)
Powerplant: 2×Lotarev D-136, 8500 kW (11,400 shp) each
Payload: 20 troops or 20000 kg (44,092 lb) of freight carried internally or externally
Max T/O weight: 56000 kg (123,457 lb)
Cruising speed: 158 mph
Operational range: 497 miles

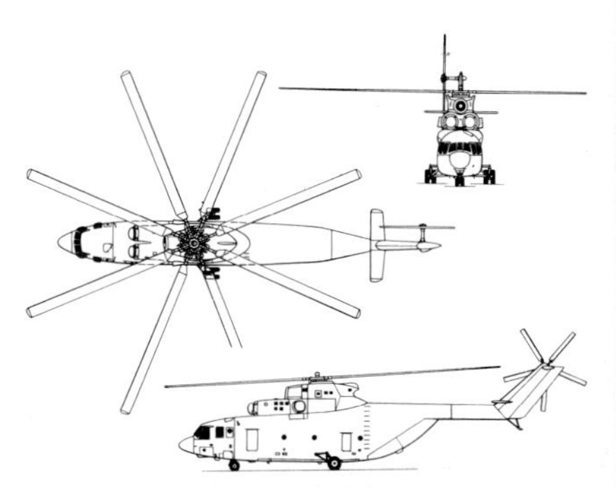

Sikorsky CH-53 Sea Stallion

The Sea Stallion was developed as the S-65 to meet a US Marine Corps requirement for an assault transport offering considerably higher payload and performance than the Sea Knight, but again with a rear ramp. The prototype flew in October 1964, and in 1966 deliveries began of the CH-53A with two 2125 kW (2,850 shp) T64-GE-6 turboshafts and provision for 37 troops or one 105-mm (4.13-in) howitzer. Further assault transport variants are the CH-53D with greater payload and performance, and the radically upgraded CH-53E Super Stallion with three 3266 kW (4,380 shp) T64-GE-416 engines driving a seven- rather than six-blade main rotor for the carriage of 55 troops or 16329 kg (36,000 lb) slung load.

Specification: Sikorsky CH-53D Sea Stallion heavy assault transport helicopter
Rotor diameter: 22.02 m (75 ft 3 in)
Overall length, rotors turning: 26.90 m (88 ft 3 in)
Powerplant: 2×General Electric T64-GE-413, 2927 kW (3,925 shp) each
Payload: (nominal) 37 troops or 3629 kg (8,000 lb) of freight carried internally
Max T/O weight: 19051 kg (42,000 lb)
Cruising speed: 173 mph
Operational range: 257 miles

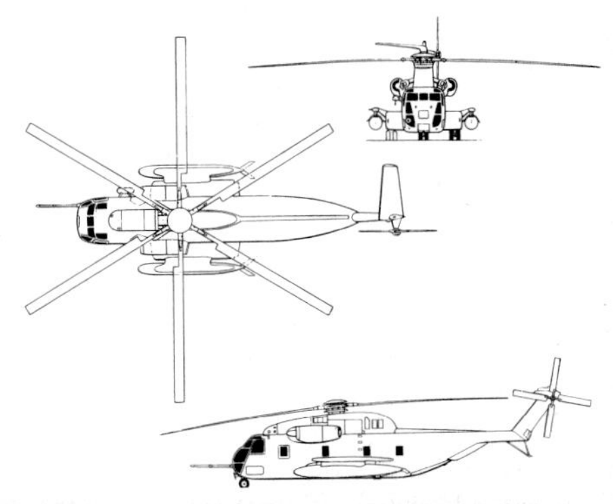

Sikorsky SH-60 Seahawk

The Seahawk is the naval counterpart of the US Army's UH-60 Black Hawk, and designed as a Light Airborne Multi-Purpose System Mk III helicopter for use by cruisers and destroyers in the anti-submarine and ship-targeting roles. The type first flew in December 1979 for service from 1983 as the SH-60B, and the main differences from the UH-60A are a revised powerplant and landing gear, a folding main rotor, naval equipment and weapons, and an electronic fit that includes APS-124 radar, ASQ-81(V)2 towed MAD, 125 sonobuoys, ALQ-124 ESM and ARQ-44 data-link. A variant designed for the close protection of carrier battle groups is the SH-60F 'CV helo' with a different electronic fit centred on the ASQ-13F dunking sonar. There are several export variants, and future developments include greater power and composite-structure main rotor blades.

Standard shipborne anti-submarine helicopter for the US Navy is the SH-60B Seahawk, intended for service from most larger surface vessels except aircraft carriers (which will receive the SH-60F version). Principal sensors are ESM, undernose radar, towed MAD 'bird' (on starboard side) and sonobuoys ejected from the port side. Torpedoes are the principal weapon. This aircraft wears the colours of the Pacific Fleet Replenishment Squadron, HSL-41.

Specification: Sikorsky SH-60B Seahawk four/five-seat multi-role naval helicopter
Main rotor diameter: 16.36 m (53 ft 8 in)
Overall length, rotors turning: 19.76 m (64 ft 10 in)
Powerplant: 2×General Electric T700-GE-401, 1260 kW (1,690 shp) each
Armament: 2×Mk 46 torpedoes or 2×AGM-84 Harpoon or AGM-119 Penguin anti-ship missiles
Max T/O weight: 9927 kg (21,884 lb)
Maximum speed: 145 mph at 5,000 ft
Operational range: not revealed

Aérospatiale Alouette III Astazou

The Alouette III was developed as an upgraded version of the SE 313B Alouette II with a more powerful dynamic system, including a 425-kW (570-shp) Turboméca Artouste IIIB turboshaft, a covered pod-and-boom fuselage and a larger cabin for greater payload and performance. The first example flew in February 1959 and production SA 316A helicopters were delivered from 1961, with the improved SA 316B following in 1968. Some of the type have been used in the naval utility role, but greater capabilities in this role are offered by the SA 319B Alouette III Astazou with more power for the carriage of a more capable sensor/ weapon fit including ORB 31 radar and four AS.11/AS.12 missiles (aimed with an APX-Bézu 260 stabilised sight) in the anti-ship role, or this radar plus Crouzet MAD and two Mk 46 torpedoes in the anti-submarine role.

Specification: Aérospatiale SA 319B Alouette III Astazou three/ seven-seat naval utility helicopter
Main rotor diameter: 11.02 m (36 ft 1.75 in)
Fuselage length, rotor folded: 10.03 m (32 ft 10.75 in)
Powerplant: 1×Turboméca Astazou XIV, 649 kW (750 shp) derated to 447 kW (600 shp)
Armament: 4×AS.11 or AS.12 air-to-surface missiles, or 2×Mk 46 torpedoes
Max T/O weight: 2250 kg (4,960 lb)
Cruising speed: 136 mph at sea level
Operational range: 375 miles

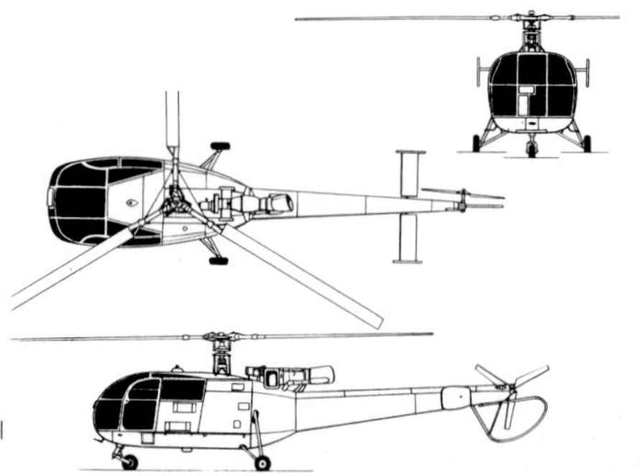

Aérospatiale SA 321 Super Frelon

The SA 3210 Super Frelon was developed from the smaller SA 3200 Frelon with the aid of Sikorsky in the design of the rotors. The first prototype was powered by three 985-kW (1,320-shp) Turmo IIIC turboshafts and flew on 7 December 1982 in form representative of the tactical troop transport model. The naval model is the SA 321G used by the French navy with a land-based heavy anti-submarine helicopter for guarding the approaches to its main nuclear base at Brest. The type is amphibious and fitted with stabilising floats, and its sensor suite includes Sylphe panoramic search radar, and HS.12 or Bendix ASQ-13 dunking sonar plus Crouzet DHAX-3 MAD in the anti-submarine role, with an alternative of ORB 31 (Héracles I) or ORB 32 (Héracles II) designation radar matched to AM.39 Exocet missiles in the anti-ship role.

Specification: Aérospatiale SA 321G Super Frelon medium anti-submarine and anti-ship helicopter
Main rotor diameter: 18.90 m (62 ft 0 in)
Fuselage length: 19.40 m (63 ft 7.75 in)
Powerplant: 3×Turboméca Turmo $IIIC_6$, 1170 kW (1,570 shp) each
Armament: 2×AM.39 Exocet anti-ship missiles, or 4×Mk 46 or L4 torpedoes, or 8×250-kg (551-lb) mines, or Mk 49, Mk 52 or Mk 54 depth charges
Max T/O weight: 13000 kg (28,660 lb)
Cruising speed: 154 mph at sea level
Operational range: 506 miles

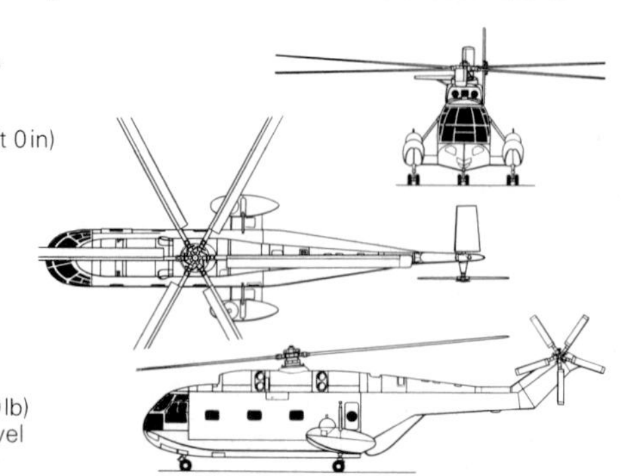

gusta-Bell AB.212ASW

vin-engined version of the Bell 205 (UH-1H), the Model 212 is built under licence in Italy as e AB.212 by Agusta, which has developed the AB.212ASW as a specialist anti-submarine d limited anti-ship variant for operation from larger ship's platforms and shore bases. The sic airframe has been strengthened for operation at higher weights, and a new sensor/ mament fit has been installed without detriment to the helicopter's ability to lift a 2268-kg 000-lb) slung load in the utility role. The primary sensors are SMA APS-705 search radar d Bendix ASQ-13B or ASQ-18 dunking sonar, the tactical plot being controlled via a /A-708B/ASW computer system. For the midcourse guidance of Otomat surface-unched anti-ship missiles a TG-2 data-link can be installed, and the helicopter can also be ted with the Marte system and associated Sea Killer anti-ship missiles.

pecification: Agusta-Bell .212ASW four-seat anti-bmarine and anti-ship helicopter
ain rotor diameter: 14.63m 3ft 0in)
verall length, rotors turning: .40m (57ft 1in)
werplant: 1×Pratt & Whitney nada PT6T-6 Turbo Twin Pac, 98kW (1,875shp)
mament: 2×Mk 46 or A244/S pedoes; or 2×AS.12 or Sea Killer k 2 or Sea Skua anti-ship missiles
ax T/O weight: 5070kg (11,177lb)
uising speed: 115 mph at sea level
erational range: 382 miles

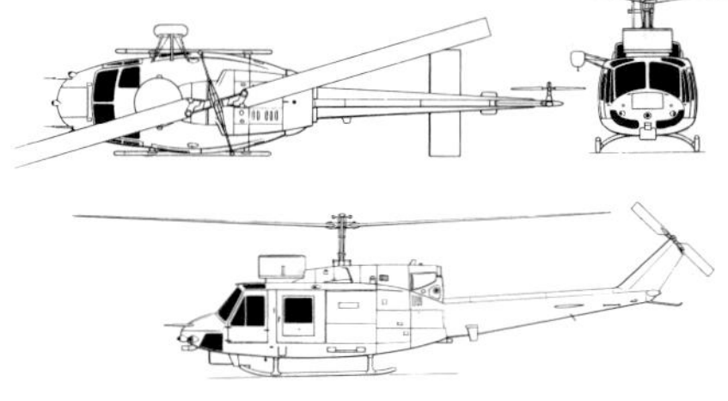

Boeing Vertol CH-46 Sea Knight

The Sea Knight is a US Marine Corps twin-rotor assault transport helicopter with side doors and a rear ramp, known to the manufacturer as the Model 107M, a development of the Model 107-II commercial helicopter. The initial military version, entering service in 1965, was the CH-46A with two 932-kW (1,250-shp) T58-GE-8B turboshafts and the ability to carry 25 troops or 1814kg (4,000lb) of freight over 185 km (115 miles), and the HH-46A was a naval rescue and vertical replenishment equivalent. There followed the CH/UH-46D types with T58-GE-10s, cambered rotor blades and the ability to carry a 4536-kg (10,000-lb) slung load, the CH-46E with 1394-kW (1,870-shp) T58-GE-16s, and the updated CH-46F. CH-46A equivalents are used by Canada as the CH-113A Labrador and CH-113B Voyageur, and Kawasaki in Japan currently produces KV-107/II and KV107/IIA variants in roles such as minesweeping and SAR.

Specification: Boeing Vertol CH-46D Sea Knight 3+25-seat assault transport helicopter
Rotor diameter, each: 15.54m (51ft 0in)
Overall length, rotors turning: 25.70m (84ft 4in)
Powerplant: 2×General Electric T58-GE-10, 1044kW (1,400shp) each
Armament: none
Max T/O weight: 10433kg (23,000lb)
Cruising speed: 165 mph at sea level
Operational range: 238 miles with 2064-kg (4,550-lb) payload

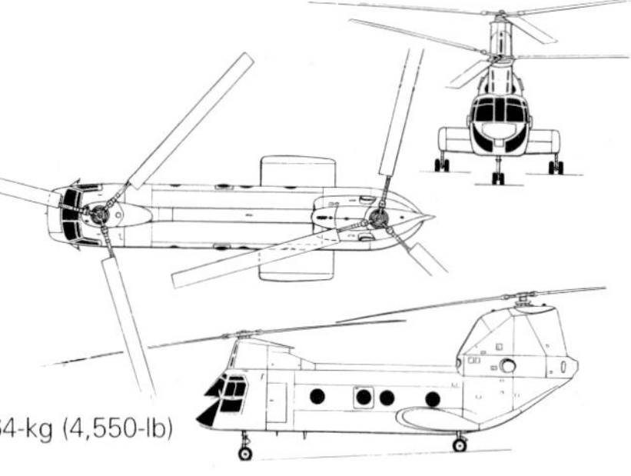

Westland Lynx

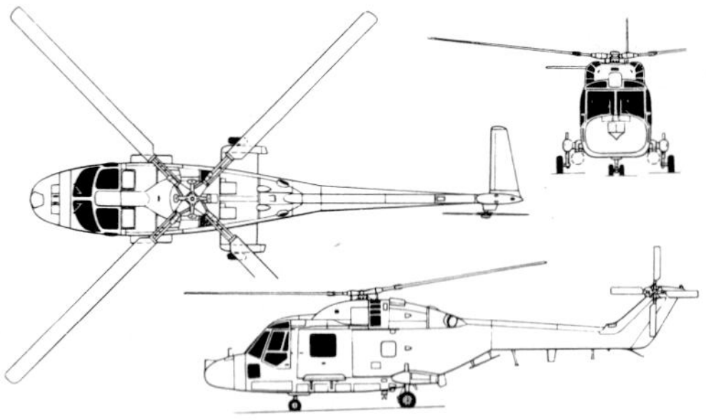

ESM, dunking sonar and search radar are the principal sensors fitted to the Westland Lynx anti-submarine helicopters of the Aéronautique Navale. For the anti-submarine role the Lynx carries torpedoes, while for anti-surface attack it employs AS.12 optically-guided missiles. They serve with 31, 34 and 35 Flotilles at Lanvéoc-Poulmic and 20 Escadrille de Servitude at St Raphaël.

Kamov Ka-25 'Hormone'

Introduced to service in 1965, the Ka-25 is of typical Kamov design with co-axial contra-rotating rotors to provide a compact overall layout for deployment on comparatively small ship platforms. The type was derived from the Ka-20 prototype revealed in 1961, this itself being a development of the concept previously pioneered in the Ka-15 and Ka-18. Production lasted up to 1975, and it is believed that some 460 Ka-25s were delivered in three versions identified only by their NATO reporting names. The 'Hormone-A' is the anti-submarine variant with 'Big Bulge' search radar, 'Tie Rod' optronic sensor, a box of sonobuoys and either dunking sonar or towed MAD. The 'Hormone-B' is the missile-support variant with a data-link for midcourse guidance update of long-range anti-ship missiles. And the 'Hormone-C' is the SAR/utility variant with a winch.

Specification: Kamov Ka-25 'Hormone-A' five-seat anti-submarine helicopter
Rotor diameter, each: 15.74 m (51 ft 8 in)
Fuselage length: 9.75 m (32 ft 10 in)
Powerplant: 2 x Glushenkov GTD-3BM, 671 kW (900 shp) each
Armament: 2×406- or 450-mm (15.98- or 17.72-in) torpedoes or depth charges (conventional or nuclear) carried internally, or one wire-guided torpedo carried in a semi-external housing
Max T/O weight: 7500 kg (16,534 lb)
Cruising speed: 120 mph at sea level
Operational range: 249 miles

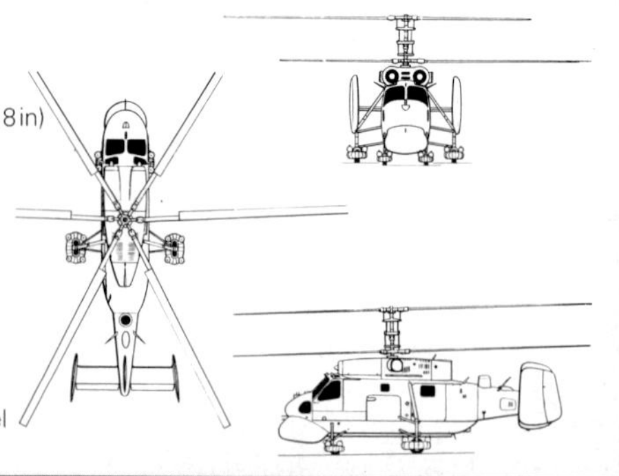

Kamov Ka-27 'Helix'

Introduced in the early 1980s as successor to the Ka-25, the Ka-27 adheres to the same basic design concept as its predecessor, but is slightly larger and considerably more powerful for greater payload and performance with an airframe that can nonetheless still fit into shipboard hangars designed for the Ka-25. There are again three basic variants, but these are somewhat different from the Ka-25 models. The 'Helix-A' is the anti-submarine variant but can carry a squad of Naval Infantry in the cabin or alternatively a 5000-kg (11,023-lb) slung load. The 'Helix-B' is a dedicated assault transport for a 16-man Naval Infantry squad. The 'Helix-C' is the utility model with provision for a winch and vertical replenishment equipment. Sensors in the 'Helix-A' include surveillance radar, dunking sonar, towed MAD and directional ESM.

Specification: Kamov Ka-27 'Helix-A' five-seat anti-submarine helicopter
Rotor diameter, each: 15.90 m (52 ft 2 in)
Fuselage length: 11.30 m (37 ft 1 in)
Powerplant: 2×Isotov TV3-117V, 1659 kW (2,225 shp) each
Armament: 2×torpedoes or depth charges (conventional or nuclear) carried internally
Max T/O weight: 12600 kg (27,778 lb)
Cruising speed: 143 mph at sea level
Operational range: 497 miles

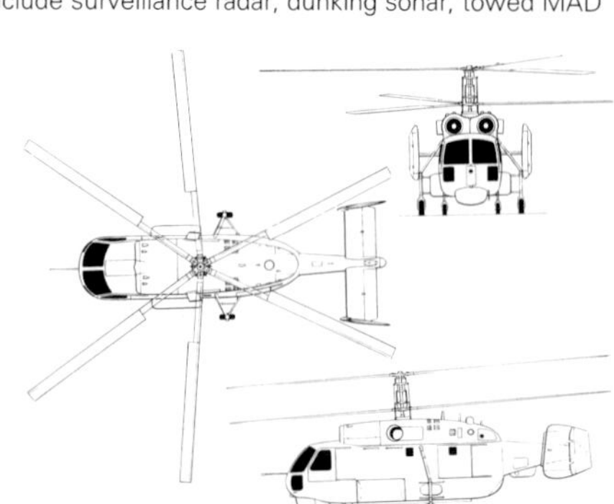

The Lynx is a compact helicopter of very high performance, and is available in battlefield and naval forms, the latter first flying in May 1972 and differing from its land-based counterpart in its folding tail, fixed tricycle landing gear and naval electronic fit. The British baseline version is the Lynx HAS.Mk 2 with Ferranti Seaspray radar, Texas Instruments ASQ-81(V) towed MAD and Racal MIR-2 Orange Crop ESM, the French Mk 2 version having ORB 31W radar, Crouzet MAD and Alcatel dunking sonar. The Lynx HAS.Mk 3 and French Mk 4 version have 835-kW (1,120-shp) Gem 41-1 turboshafts. There are various export variants with differing engines and electronic fits, and the latest British version is the HAS.Mk 8 with the Racal Control Data System, a thermal imaging Passive Identification Device and either Seapray Mk 3 or MEL Super Searcher radar. The export Super Lynx is similar to the HAS.Mk 8.

Specification: Westland Lynx HAS.Mk 2 four-seat anti-submarine and anti-ship helicopter
Main rotor diameter: 12.802 m (42 ft 0 in)
Fuselage length: 11.92 m (39 ft 1.3 in)
Powerplant: 2 x Rolls-Royce Gem 2, 671 kW (900 shp) each
Armament: 2×Mk 44, Mk 46 or Sting Ray torpedoes, or 2×depth charges, or 4×Sea Skua, Penguin or AS.12 anti-ship missiles
Max T/O weight: 4536 kg (10,000 lb)
Cruising speed: 144 mph at sea level
Operational range: 368 miles

Mil Mi-14 'Haze'

o complement the shipborne Kamov helicopters, the Mil design bureau was tasked in the arly 1970s with development of a heavy shore-based anti-submarine helicopter with a boat ull for amphibious capability. The resulting Mi-14 flew in 1973 as a development of the Mi-8 ulti-role transport helicopter featuring the more powerful dynamic system of the Mi-17 self a minimum-change Mi-8 development) and a revised boat hull with stabilising oonsons plus retractable landing gear. There are two basic variants of the Mi-14: the laze-A' anti-submarine model and the 'Haze-B' mine-countermeasures model. The 'Haze-A' as a full-length weapon bay in each chine of the planing bottom as well as sensors such as urveillance/search radar, dunking sonar, sonobuoys and towed MAD. The 'Haze-B' has only e main radar and specialist minesweeping gear of the towed variety.

pecification: Mil Mi-14 laze-A' five-seat anti-submarine elicopter
lain rotor diameter: 21.29 m 9 ft 10.2 in)
uselage length: 18.424 m (60 ft 4 in)
owerplant: 2×Isotov TV2-117, 640 kW (2,200 shp) each
rmament: torpedoes or depth harges (conventional or nuclear) rried internally
lax T/O weight: 14000 kg 0,864 lb)
ruising speed: 124 mph at sea level
perational range: 497 miles

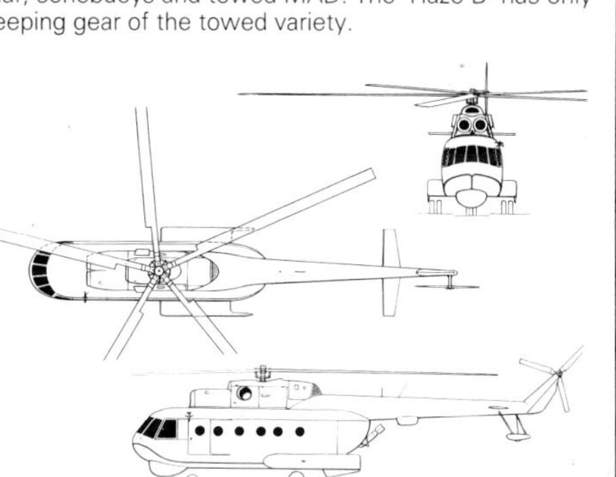

Sikorsky SH-3 Sea King

Built under licence in Italy by Agusta as the ASH-3 and in Japan by Mitsubishi as the HSS-2, the Sea King was developed in the late 1950s as a turboshaft-powered helicopter able to undertake the submarine hunting and killing role that had previously required a two-helicopter team. The first HSS-2 flew in March 1959 with a boat hull, comprehensive electronics and retractable landing gear whose main units lifted into the stabilising sponsons. The type entered service in September 1961 with 932-kW (1,250-shp) T58-GE-8Bs as the HSS-2, revised 13 months later to SH-3A. The SH-3D had more power, the SH-3G is a utility variant with removable equipment, and the SH-3H is a multi-role variant with Canadian Marconi LN-66 radar, Bendix ASQ-13B or ASQ-18 dunking sonar, sonobuoys, Texas Instruments ASQ-81(V) towed MAD and General Instrument ALR-66(V)1 radar-warning receiver.

Specification: Sikorsky SH-3H Sea King four-seat multi-role (anti-submarine, anti-ship and missile-detection) helicopter
Main rotor diameter: 18.90 m (62 ft 0 in)
Fuselage length: 16.69 m (54 ft 9 in)
Powerplant: 2×General Electric T58-GE-10, 1044 kW (1,400 shp) each
Armament: torpedoes, depth charges and anti-ship missiles carried externally
Max T/O weight: 9526 kg (21,000 lb)
Cruising speed: 136 mph at sea level
Operational range: 625 miles

Sikorsky CH-53 Sea Stallion

The CH-53 was designed as a day/night assault and logistic transport for the US Marine Corps, which required a ramp-accessed hold for small vehicles and artillery. The six-blade main rotor and transmission of the CH-54 Tarhe flying crane were used with a new powerplant and watertight hull stabilised by two lateral sponsons holding the retracted main landing gear units. The first prototype flew in October 1964 and in 1966 deliveries started of the CH-54A with two 2125-kW (2,850-shp) T64-GE-6 turboshafts, provision for 38 troops and, in most cases, provision for towing a minesweeping sled. Further developments have been the CH-53D with greater power and provision for more troops, and the CH-53E Super Stallion with a seven-blade main rotor of 24.08-m (79-ft) diameter and three 3266-kW (4,380-shp) T64-GE-416s for a load of 16329 kg (36,000 lb) in or under a lengthened fuselage.

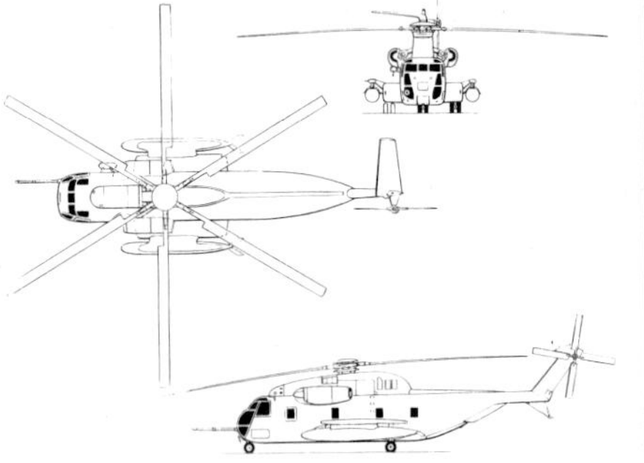

Specification: Sikorsky CH-53D Sea Stallion 3+55-seat assault and logistic helicopter
Main rotor diameter: 22.02 m (72 ft 3 in)
Overall length, rotors turning: 26.90 m (88 ft 3 in)
Powerplant: 2×General Electric T64-GE-413, 2927 kW (3,925 shp) each
Armament: none
Max T/O weight: 19051 kg (42,000 lb)
Cruising speed: 173 mph at sea level
Operational range: 257 miles

RH/MH-53 Sea Stallion/Dragon

The high power and load capability of the Sea Stallion commended the type as a minesweeping helicopter, and after trials with 15 RH-53A conversions from CH-53A standard with 2927-kW (3,925-shp) T64-GE-413 turboshafts the first RH-53D was flown in 1972 with two 3266-kW (4,380-shp) T64-GE-415s and additional fuel: the variant can operate the Mk 103 mechanical, Mk 104 acoustic, Mk 105 magnetic and Mk 106 magnetic/acoustic sweeps as well as the SPU-1 Magnetic Orange Pipe effective against shallow-water magnetic mines. Most impressive, though, is the three-engined MH-53E Sea Dragon equivalent of the CH-53E with yet more fuel and provision for inflight-refuelling. Developments planned for the variant are composite rather than light alloy rotor blades, IR suppressors for more powerful engines, night-vision equipment and other enhanced operational features.

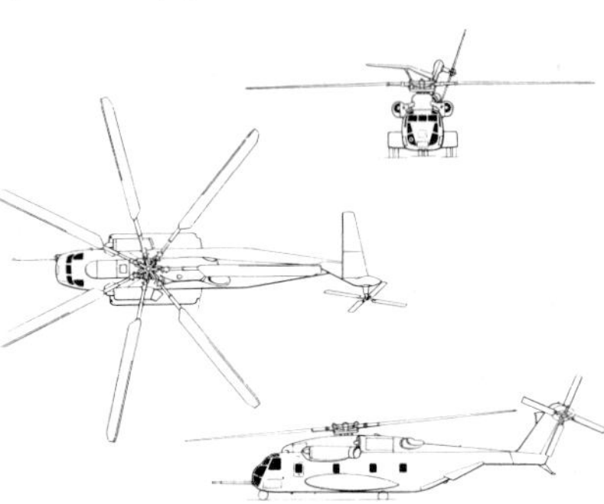

Specification: Sikorsky MH-53E Sea Dragon five-seat minesweeping helicopter
Main rotor diameter: 24.08 m (79 ft 0 in)
Overall length, rotors turning: 30.19 m (99 ft 0.5 in)
Powerplant: 3×General Electric T64-GE-416, 3266 kW (4,380 shp) each
Armament: none
Max T/O weight: 33339 kg (73,500 lb)
Cruising speed: 173 mph at sea level
Operational range: 1,290 miles

Westland Sea King

This is the British equivalent of the SH-3, essentially a licence-built airframe/engine combination plus more advanced British electronics. The first example flew in May 1969. Initial variants had Ekco AW391 radar and Plessey 195 dunking sonar, the Sea King HAS.Mk 1 and HAS.Mk 2 having Rolls-Royce Gnome H.1400 and H.1400-1 turboshafts respectively. The HAR.Mk 3 is an SAR variant, the HC.Mk 4 is an assault transport, and the current naval models are the Sea King AEW.Mk 2 with Searchwater early warning radar, and the Sea King HAS.Mk 5 with MEL Sea Searcher radar, Type 195 (or in export models Bendix ASQ-13) dunking sonar, sonobuoys, an advanced LAPADS (or in Indian helicopters GEC AQS-902) acoustic processing system, and Racal MIR-2 Orange Crop ESM. The forthcoming Sea King HAS.Mk 6 will have greater power, composite rotor blades and electronic/armament improvements including Sea Eagle anti-ship missiles.

Specification: Westland Sea King HAS.Mk 5 four-seat anti-submarine helicopter
Main rotor diameter: 18.90 m (62 ft 0 in)
Overall length, rotors turning: 22.15 m (72 ft 8 in)
Powerplant: 2×Rolls-Royce Gnome H.1400-1, 1238 kW (1,660 shp) each
Armament: 4×Mk 46 or Sting Ray torpedoes, or 4×depth charges
Max T/O weight: 9526 kg (21,000 lb)
Cruising speed: 129 mph at sea level
Operational range: 764 miles

Westland Sea King HC.Mk 4

The Sea King HC.Mk 4 is the Royal Marine commando assault transport version of the Commando tactical helicopter, itself derived from the Sea King for land use with revised non-retracting tailwheel landing gear and no sponsons. The Commando first flew in September 1973, the first Sea King HC.Mk 4 following in September 1979. The type is designed for the carriage of 27 troops in the amphibious assault role, and therefore retains the folding tail and main rotor blades of the standard Sea King anti-submarine helicopter. Alternative loads are 2722 kg (6,000 lb) of freight carried internally or 3400 kg (7,500 lb) of freight carried as a slung load, and there is provision for two door-mounted 7.62-mm (0.3-in) machine-guns in the defence-suppression role. Other weapons are possible but rarely fitted.

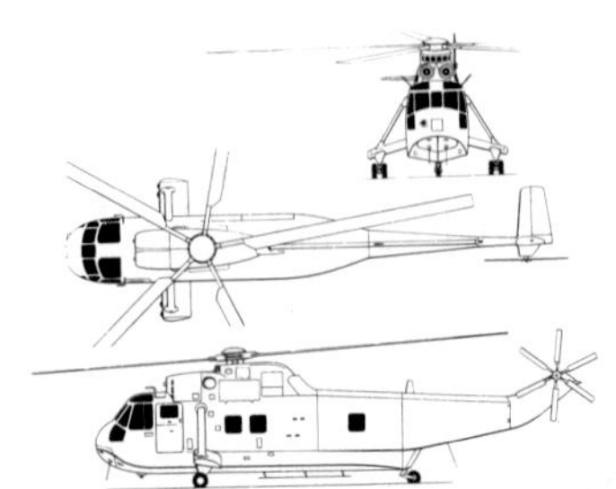

Specification: Westland Sea King HC.Mk 4 2/3+27-seat assault transport helicopter
Main rotor diameter: 18.90 m (62 ft 0 in)
Fuselage length: 17.01 m (55 ft 9.75 in)
Powerplant: 2×Rolls-Royce Gnome H.1400-1, 1238 kW (1,660 shp) each
Armament: 2×7.62-mm (0.3-in) machine-guns
Max T/O weight: 9526 kg (21,000 lb)
Cruising speed: 129 mph at sea level
Operational range: 276 miles

Aerospatiale Gazelle

'he Gazelle was designed as replacement for the Alouette II series of utility helicopters, and irst flew in April 1967. The type was covered in the 1968 Anglo-French co-production greement together with the Puma and Lynx, and as a result Westland was responsible for ne British order. Most of this went to the Army in the form of Gazelle AH.Mk 1, but small umbers went to the Royal Navy and RAF. The latter's variants are the Gazelle HT.Mk 3 and ;azelle HCC.Mk 4, which began to enter service from July 1973. The HT.Mk 3 is a training elicopter generally similar to the AH.Mk 1 but fitted with a stability augmentation system, vhile the HCC.Mk 4 is a communications type. Current strengths of these two types are 27 nd three respectively, the HT.Mk 3s serving mainly with No. 2 Flying Training School at RAF Shawbury and the HCC.Mk 4s plus some HT.Mk 3s with No. 32 Squadron at RAF Jortholt.

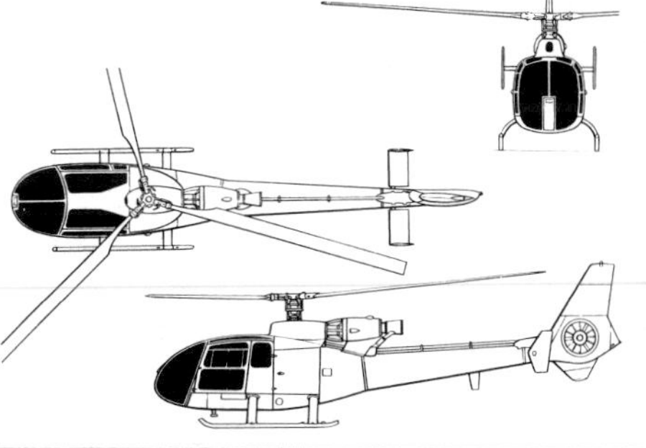

Specification: Aerospatiale ;azelle HT.Mk 3 five-seat utility and training helicopter
Main rotor diameter: 10.50 m 34 ft 5.5 in)
Fuselage length: 9.53 m (31 ft 3.2 in)
Powerplant: 1×Turbomeca Astazou IIIA, 440 kW (590 shp)
Armament: none
Max T/O weight: 1800 kg 3,968 lb)
Max speed: 164 mph at sea level
Operational range: 416 miles

Westland Wessex

With the Wessex, Westland moved directly to a turboshaft-powered version of an American baseline model, the Sikorsky S-58. The immediate spur for the type's development was the Royal Navy's desire for a helicopter able to combine the submarine hunter and killer roles in a single airframe, and an imported S-58 was re-engined with a Napier Gazelle turboshaft for a first flight in May 1957. The Navy's Wessex HAS.Mk 1 had a single 1081-kW (1,450-shp) Gazelle NGa.13 Mk 161, but the RAF wanted higher performance for its general-purpose version, and the resultant Wessex HC.Mk 2 had coupled Gnome turboshafts for performance combined with single-engined flight capability. The type could carry 16 troops or a 1814-kg (4,000-lb) slung load, andthe HC.Mk 2 began to enter service in February 1964. The two Wessex HC.Mk 4s are comparable VIP versions for The Queen's Flight.

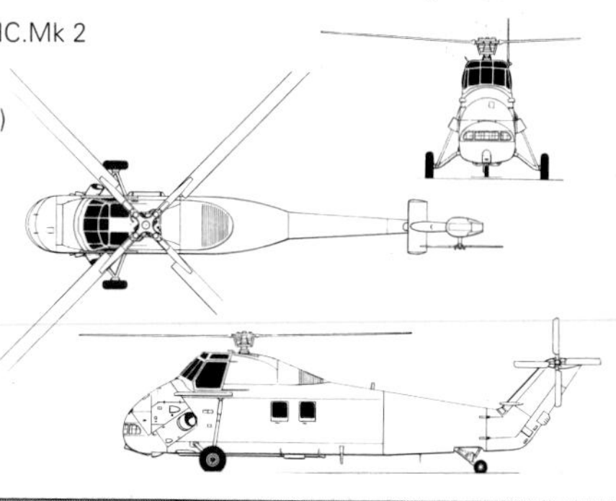

Specification: Westland Wessex HC.Mk 2 three-crew tactical transport and general-purpose helicopter
Main rotor diameter: 17.10 m (56 ft 0 in)
Length overall, rotors turning: 20.04 m (65 ft 9 in)
Powerplant: 2×Rolls-Royce (Bristol Siddeley) Gnome H.1000 Mk 110/111, 1007 kW (1,350 shp) each
Armament: provision for AS.11 anti-tank missiles and/or machine-guns
Max T/O weight: 6123 kg (13,500 lb)
Max speed: 132 mph at sea level
Operational range: 478 miles

Aerospatiale Puma

he Puma was designed to meet a French army requirement for an all-weather tactical elicopter, and though originally schemed with a single 1417-kW (1,900-shp) Turbomeca astan turboshaft the type appeared for its first flight in April 1965 with a pair of Turmo III urboshafts from the same manufacturer. In April 1968 the UK and France agreed to co-perate on three new helicopter programmes, one of them that for the Puma. Westland ecame responsible for the 40 examples of the SA 330E variant ordered for the RAF as uma HC.Mk 1 tactical transport with the ability to carry 16 soldiers or 2500 kg (5,512 lb) of eight. The first British-built Puma flew in July 1968, and the type began to enter service ate in 1972. A further eight helicopters were ordered to SA 330L standard with composite otor blades, Turmo IVC turboshafts and particle separators in the inlets.

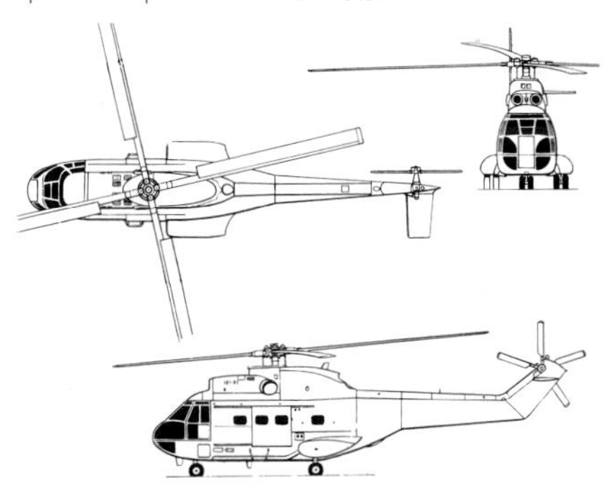

Specification: Aerospatiale uma HC.Mk 1 two-crew tactical ansport helicopter
Main rotor diameter: 15.00 m 49 ft 2.5 in)
uselage length: 14.06 m (46 ft .5 in)
Powerplant: 2×Turbomeca Turmo IC4, 984 kW (1,320 shp) each
Armament: provision for anti-tank nissiles, rockets, fixed cannon or ide-firing machine-guns
Max T/O weight: 6400 kg 14,110 lb)
Max speed: 174 mph at sea level
Operational range: 391 miles

Boeing Vertol Chinook

The Chinook is the Western world's most important medium/heavy-lift tactical helicopter, the twin-rotor design being chosen to provide adequate lifting power within modest overall dimensions and to allow use of a long fuselage with a rectangular-section hold accessed by a rear ramp/door. The type first flew in September 1961, and the variant used by the RAF is the Chinook HC.Mk 1, essentially a development of the Canadian Armed Forces' CH-147 but with T55-L-11E turboshafts and a triple hook system for the carriage of external loads up to 12701 kg (28,000 lb) in weight. The hold can accommodate 44 troops or 24 litters plus two attendants, and a hydraulic winch is standard for freight handling or rescue. The RAF ordered a total of 41, and the type began to enter service in 1981. Some 36 still serve with Nos. 7, 18 and 78 Squadrons plus No. 240 OCU.

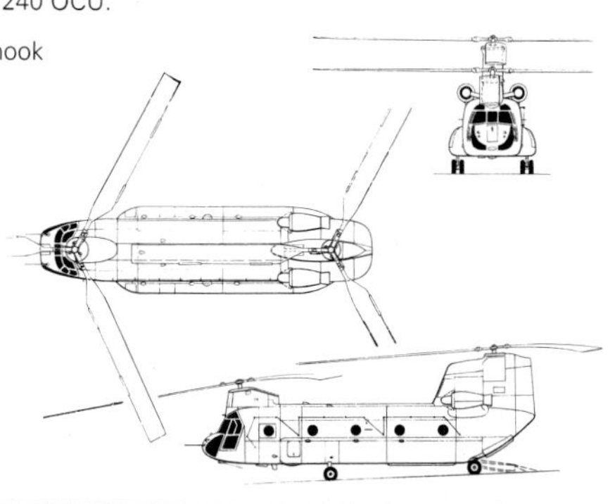

Specification: Boeing Vertol Chinook HC.Mk 1 three-crew medium tactical transport helicopter
Rotor diameter, each: 18.29 m (60 ft 0 in)
Fuselage length: 15.54 m (51 ft 0 in)
Powerplant: 2×Avco Lycoming T55-L-11E, 2796 kW (3,750 shp) each
Armament: generally none, though cannon and/or machine-guns can be installed
Max T/O weight: 22680 kg (50,000 lb)
Max speed: 178 mph at sea level
Operational range: 70 miles with a 10446-kg (23,030-lb) payload

Westland (Bristol) Belvedere

Specification: Westland (Bristol) Belvedere HC.Mk 1 two/three-crew tactical transport helicopter
Rotor diameter, each: 14.91m (48ft 11in)
Fuselage length: 16.56m (54ft 4in)
Powerplant: 2×Napier Gazelle NGa.2 Mk 101, 1230kW (1,650 shp) each
Armament: none
Max T/O weight: 9072kg (20,000lb)
Max speed: 138mph at sea level
Operational range: 445 miles

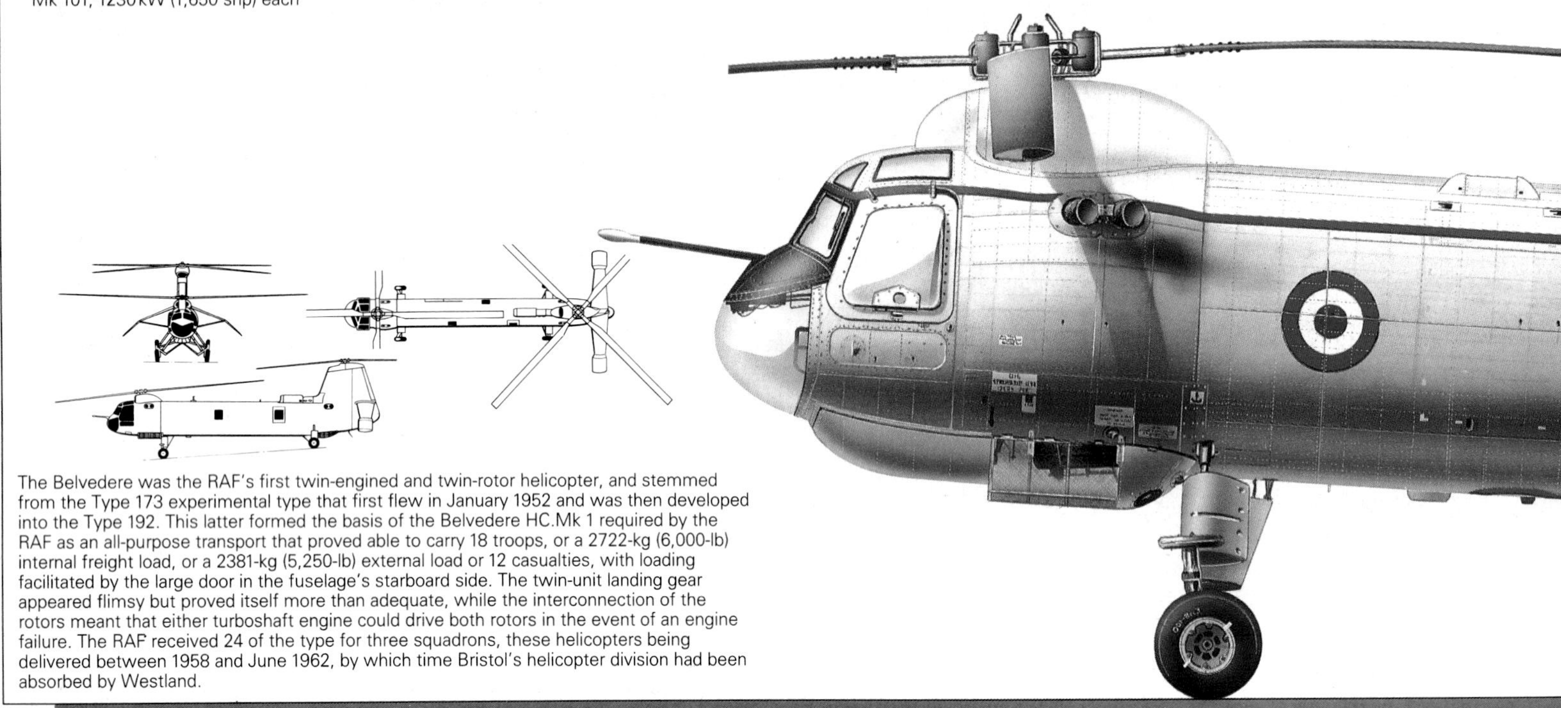

The Belvedere was the RAF's first twin-engined and twin-rotor helicopter, and stemmed from the Type 173 experimental type that first flew in January 1952 and was then developed into the Type 192. This latter formed the basis of the Belvedere HC.Mk 1 required by the RAF as an all-purpose transport that proved able to carry 18 troops, or a 2722-kg (6,000-lb) internal freight load, or a 2381-kg (5,250-lb) external load or 12 casualties, with loading facilitated by the large door in the fuselage's starboard side. The twin-unit landing gear appeared flimsy but proved itself more than adequate, while the interconnection of the rotors meant that either turboshaft engine could drive both rotors in the event of an engine failure. The RAF received 24 of the type for three squadrons, these helicopters being delivered between 1958 and June 1962, by which time Bristol's helicopter division had been absorbed by Westland.

Cierva Autogyro & Avro Rota

In October 1925 Juan de la Cierva brought his C.6A Autogyro to the UK for official trials, and these were sufficiently promising for the Air Ministry to order small numbers of development models produced by Avro under licence from the Cierva Autogyro Company. Trials with these models lasted into the early 1930s, and a batch of production aircraft then followed. The type was the C.30A, of which 12 were supplied to the RAF between August 1934 and May 1935 with the designation Rota Mk I. Two of these were used for trials purposes, and the other 10 by the School of Army Co-Operation at Old Sarum. The aircraft served with No. 1448 Flight in 1940 and were then joined by 13 similar aircraft impressed from civil operations in the radar calibration and general-purpose roles in the hands of No. 529 Squadron until its disbandment in October 1945.

Specification: Avro Rota Mk I single-seat utility Autogyro
Rotor diameter: 1.28m (37ft 0in)
Fuselage length: 6.01m (19ft 8.5in)
Powerplant: 1×Armstrong Siddeley Genet Major 1A, 104kW (140hp)
Armament: none
Max T/O weight: 816kg (1,800lb)
Max speed: 110mph at sea level
Operational range: 285 miles

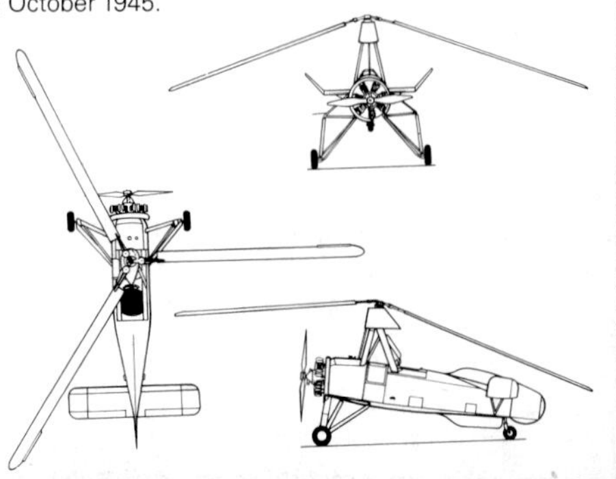

Sikorsky Hoverfly

The Hoverfly Mk I was the first helicopter used by the RAF, and was supplied from US production of the Sikorsky VS-316A (R-4). The type could be operated on wheels or floats, and was powered by a 134-kW (180-hp) Warner R-550 radial for a maximum speed of 82mph at a weight of 1150kg (2,535lb). Seven such helicopters were used in 1945, mainly for training, and the type was then supplanted by the more advanced Hoverfly Mk II, essentially equivalent to the R-6A (VS-316B) in US service. The type had the same rotor and transmission as the Hoverfly Mk I, but more powerful engine and a considerably improved pod-and-boom fuselage of lower drag. Some 26 were received in 1946 for RAF and Fleet Air Arm use, and the type was employed for training and as an artillery observation type in the hands of No. 657 Squadron.

Specification: Sikorsky Hoverfly Mk II two-seat utility helicopter
Main rotor diameter: 11.58m (38ft 0in)
Fuselage length: 10.39m (34ft 1in)
Powerplant: 1×Franklin O-405-9, 183kW (245hp)
Armament: none
Max T/O weight: 1175kg (2,590lb)
Max speed: 96mph at sea level
Endurance: 5 hours

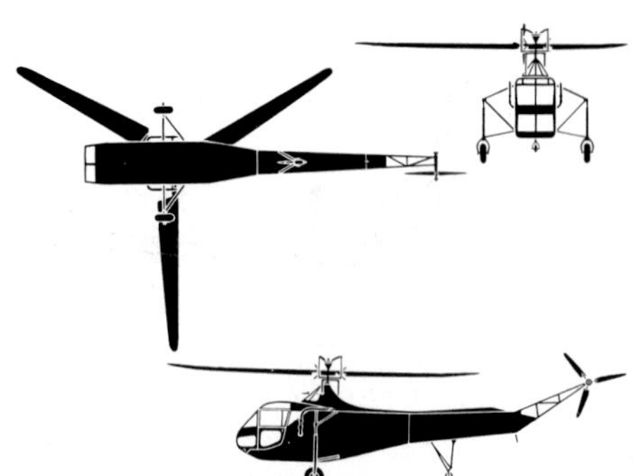

Westland Belvedere HC.Mk 1 of No. 26 Squadron wears e original transport command scheme applied to these rcraft. The Belvederes of No. 26 Squadron saw active rvice in Aden and Tanganyika and action in Brunei and rneo, where they wore a camouflage scheme.

Bell Sioux

The Bell Model 47 first flew in December 1945, and the type was the world's first helicopter to achieve civil certification in March 1946. The helicopter was then produced in large numbers and in many variants for civil and military operators, the latter including the British who took 300 examples built by Agusta (50) and, under secondary licence from Agusta as Bell's European licensee, Westland (250). Most of these were Sioux AH.Mk 1 general-purpose helicopters for the Army Air Corps, but the generally similar model for the RAF was the Sioux HT.Mk 2 trainer, of which 15 were built. This was essentially the Bell Model 47G-3B-4 variant, and was used as a trainer at the RAF Central Flying School's Helicopter Wing at RAF South Cerney and at RAF Tern Hill.

Specification: Westland (Agusta-Bell) Sioux HT.Mk 2 three-seat general-purpose and training helicopter
Main rotor diameter: 11.32 m (37 ft 1.5 in)
Overall length, rotors turning: 13.17 m (43 ft 2.5 in)
Powerplant: 1×Avco Lycoming TVO-435-A1A, 194 kW (260 hp)
Armament: none
Max T/O weight: 1338 kg (2,950 lb)
Max speed: 105 mph at sea level
Operational range: 315 miles

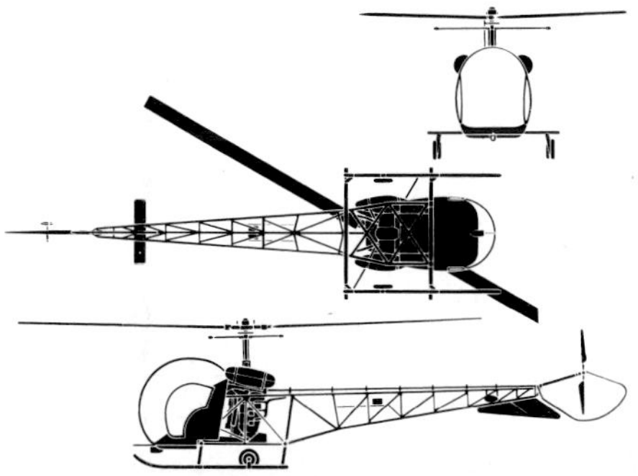

Saro (Saunders-Roe) Skeeter

In 1951 Saro bought Cierva and continued development of the W.14 Skeeter 1, which had first flown in October 1948 with a 79-kW (106-hp) Jameson FF-1 engine. The Skeeter 2 of 1949 had a 108-kW (145-hp) de Havilland Gipsy Major 10 engine, a larger-diameter main rotor and a boom of circular rather than triangular section. The Skeeter 3 used the Gipsy Major 8, later changed to the 134-kW (180-hp) Blackburn Bombardier 702 also used in the Skeeter 4. The Skeeter 5 was the first of these prototype helicopters free of ground resonance problems, and used the Gipsy Major 200 Mk 3, as did the Skeeter 6s that paved the way for service evaluation types delivered as three Skeeter AOP.Mk 10s and one Skeeter T.Mk 11 dual-control trainer. There followed 64 Skeeter AOP.Mk 12 production helicopters, of which the RAF used a few as Skeeter T.Mk 12 (or sometimes Skeeter T.Mk 13) trainers up to 1964.

Specification: Saro Skeeter T.Mk 12 two-seat training helicopter
Main rotor diameter: 9.75 m (32 ft 0 in)
Fuselage length: 8.08 m (26 ft 6 in)
Powerplant: 1×de Havilland Gipsy Major 200 Mk 30, 149 kW (200 hp)
Armament: none
Max T/O weight: 998 kg (2,200 lb)
Max speed: 101 mph at sea level
Operational range: 215 miles

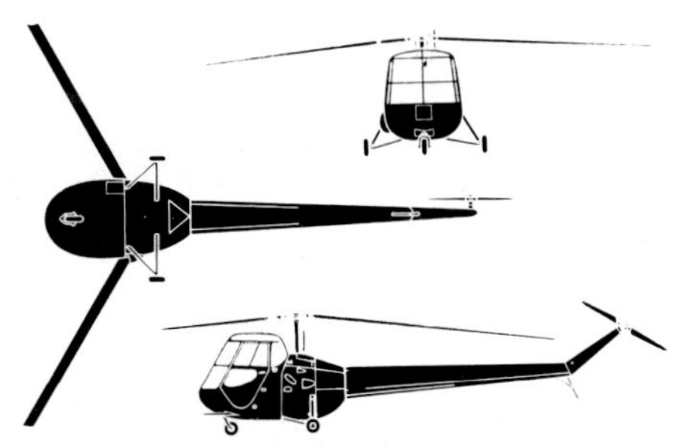

Westland Sea King

A search and rescue Westland Sea King HAR.Mk 3 of No. 222 Squadron wears the traditional yellow scheme. Recently such aircraft have sometimes worn low-visibility grey colours, which were first applied during the Falklands campaign.

Specification: Westland Sea King HAR.Mk 4 four-crew Search and Rescue helicopter
Main rotor diameter: 18.90 m (62 ft 0 in)
Fuselage length: 17.01 m (55 ft 9.75 in)
Powerplant: 2×Rolls-Royce Gnome H.1400-1, 1238 kW (1,660 shp) each
Armament: none
Max T/O weight: 9526 kg (21,000 lb)
Max speed: 143 mph at sea level
Operational range: 765 miles

Westland Dragonfly

The first British-built helicopter to enter RAF service, the Dragonfly was the licence-built version of the Sikorsky S-51. Like its US original, the Dragonfly was designed primarily for the civil market, but after an initial flight in October 1948 secured its best sales from the military. The first RAF versions were the Dragonfly HC.Mk 2 casualty-evacuation type with the Leonides 50 radial and composite rotor blades (three built with provision for the carriage of two litters on external panniers) and the Dragonfly HC.Mk 4 with all-metal rotor blades and a hydraulic servo-control mechanism for the main rotor (12 built, with similar pannier provision to the HC.Mk 2). Total production was 139, including 80 for the Royal Navy in the planeguard (HR.Mk 1) and SAR/utility (HC.Mk 3) roles, many of them later upgraded to HR.Mk 5 standard to complement nine new-build helicopters of this type.

Specification: Westland Dragonfly HC.Mk 4 four-seat utility and casualty evacuation helicopter
Main rotor diameter: 14.94 m (49 ft 0 in)
Fuselage length: 12.45 m (40 ft 10 in)
Powerplant: 1×Alvis Leonides 50, 410 kW (550 hp)
Armament: none
Normal T/O weight: 2495 kg (5,500 lb)
Max speed: 103 mph at sea level
Operational range: 300 miles

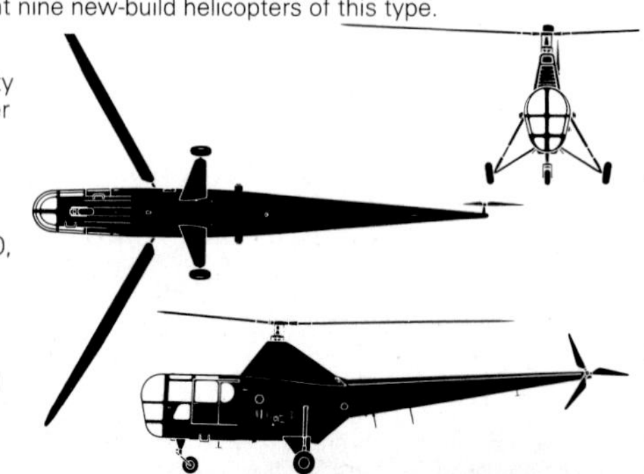

Bristol Sycamore

The Sycamore was the first British-designed helicopter to enter RAF service, and was developed from the Type 171 Mk I that initially flew in July 1947 with a 336-kW (450-hp) Pratt & Whitney R-985 radial. Production helicopters switched to the Alvis Leonides radial, and the initial RAF version was the Sycamore HR.Mk 12 anti-submarine reconnaissance and SAR type, the first of four being received in February 1952. Later models were two winch-equipped Sycamore HR.Mk 13 SAR helicopters for Fighter Command, and 85 Sycamore HR.Mk 14s with the pilot relocated to the right, additional cabin doors, taller landing gear units and other improvements. The type served with four home squadrons and another three overseas, making a considerable contribution to the development of early air-mobility tactics in operations against guerrillas in Cyprus and Malaya.

Specification: Bristol Sycamore HC.Mk 14 five-seat utility and SAR helicopter
Main rotor diameter: 14.81 m (48 ft 7 in)
Fuselage length: 14.07 m (46 ft 2 in)
Powerplant: 1×Alvis Leonides 73, 410 kW (550 hp)
Armament: none
Max T/O weight: 2540 kg (5,600 lb)
Max speed: 127 mph at sea level
Operational range: 268 miles

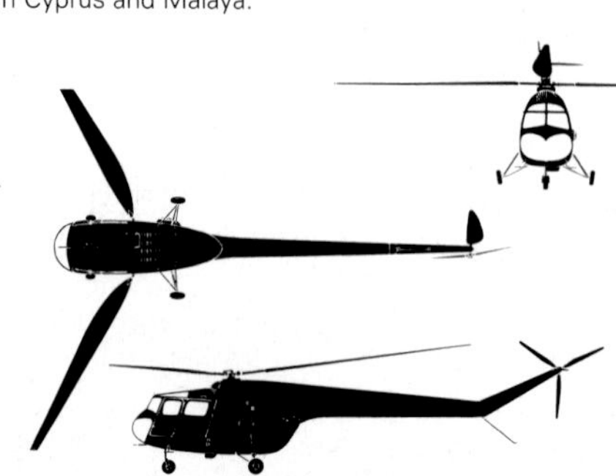

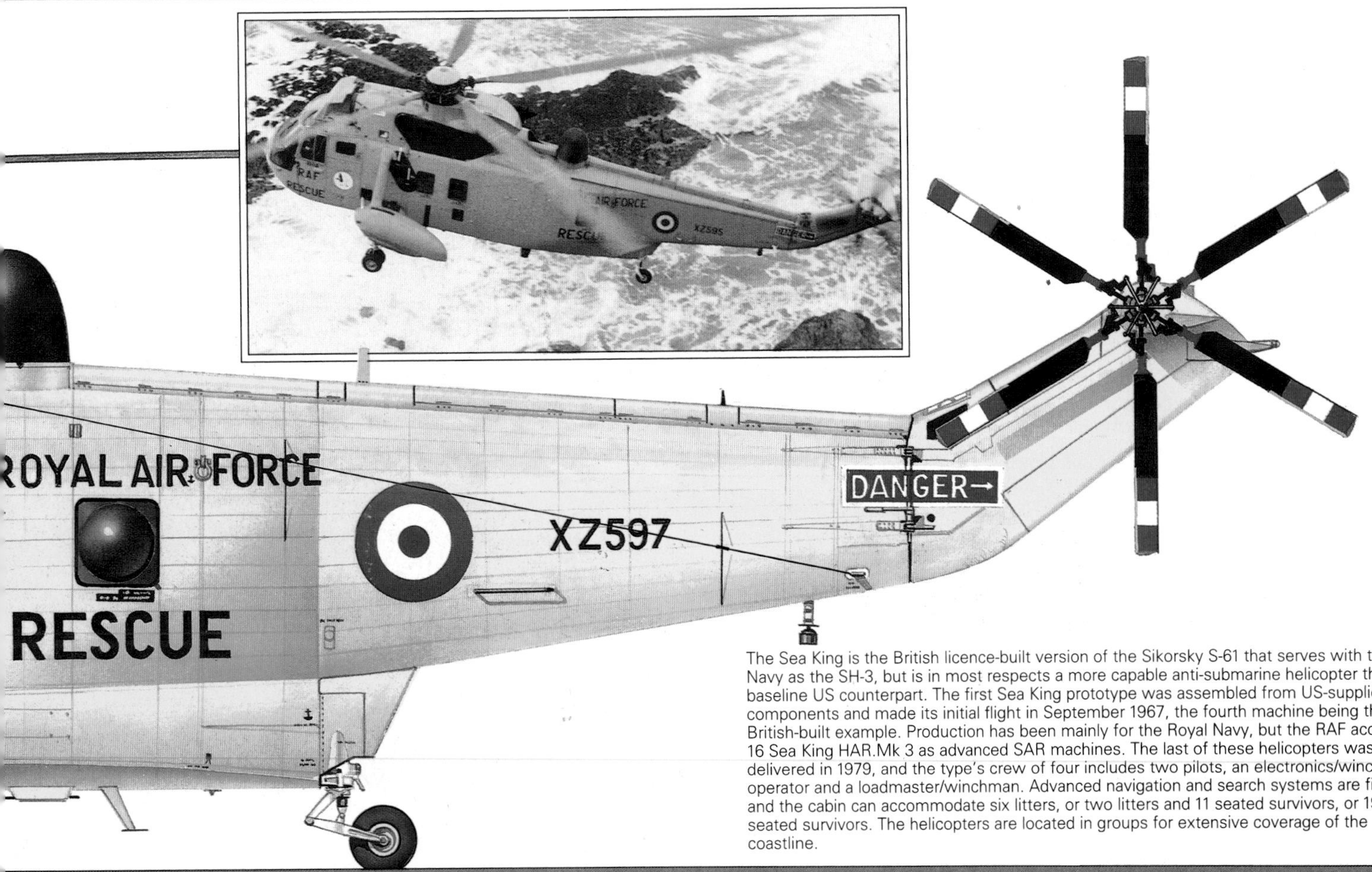

The Sea King is the British licence-built version of the Sikorsky S-61 that serves with the US Navy as the SH-3, but is in most respects a more capable anti-submarine helicopter than its baseline US counterpart. The first Sea King prototype was assembled from US-supplied components and made its initial flight in September 1967, the fourth machine being the first British-built example. Production has been mainly for the Royal Navy, but the RAF accepted 16 Sea King HAR.Mk 3 as advanced SAR machines. The last of these helicopters was delivered in 1979, and the type's crew of four includes two pilots, an electronics/winch operator and a loadmaster/winchman. Advanced navigation and search systems are fitted, and the cabin can accommodate six litters, or two litters and 11 seated survivors, or 19 seated survivors. The helicopters are located in groups for extensive coverage of the UK coastline.

Westland Whirlwind

The Whirlwind started life as the licence-built version of the Sikorsky S-55 and as such first flew in November 1952. It was then transformed by turboshaft power into a much more capable helicopter. The RAF's initial model was the Whirlwind HAR.Mk 2, of which about 60 were built for the SAR and communications roles with the 447-kW (600-hp) Pratt & Whitney R-1340-40 radial. Then came about 30 HAR.Mk 4s with the 'hot-and-high' R-1350-57 for Malayan operations, and two HCC.Mk 8s for The Queen's Flight with the 552-kW (740-hp) Alvis Leonides Major Mk 160 radial. Westland now added turboshaft power in the form of a licence-built General Electric T58, and the result for the RAF was the vastly improved HAR.Mk 10 able to lift eight troops: in addition to new helicopters, the RAF had older machines modified to this standard. The two HCC.Mk 12s were HAR.Mk 10 equivalents for The Queen's Flight.

Specification: Westland Whirlwind HAR.Mk 10 three-crew tactical transport and SAR helicopter
Main rotor diameter: 16.15 m (53 ft 0 in)
Fuselage length: 13.46 m (44 ft 2 in)
Powerplant: 1×Rolls-Royce (Bristol Siddeley) Gnome H.1000, 783 kW (1,050 shp)
Armament: 4×AS.11 anti-tank missiles or 2×7.62-mm (0.3-in) machine-guns
Normal T/O weight: 3629 kg (8,000 lb)
Max speed: 104 mph at sea level
Operational range: 300 miles

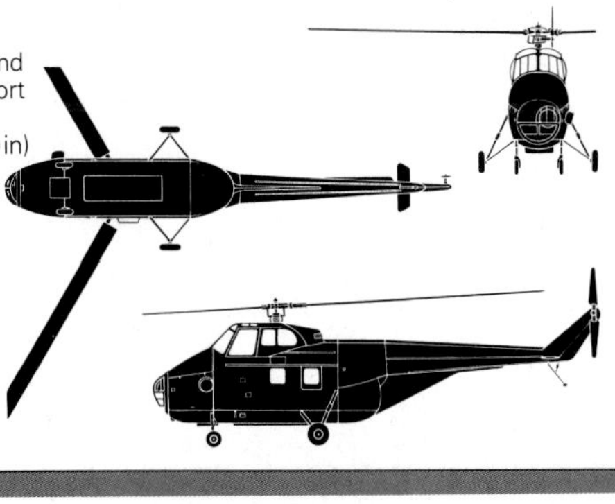

Westland (Fairey) Rotodyne

The Rotodyne is a story of what might have been, for this ambitious hybrid type was cancelled in 1962 after lack of government support. The type stemmed from the Gyrodyne helicopter that flew in 1947 with an Alvis Leonides radial driving the rotor and a tractor propeller at the tip of one stub wing. The following Jet Gyrodyne used a two- rather than three-blade rotor and tip-mounted pressure jets, in which kerosene was mixed and burned with air supplied from a fuselage-mounted compressor, for torqueless lift; pusher engines were provided at each wing tip. This paved the way for the Rotodyne ordered in 1953 as a potential 40-seat transport and was first flown in November 1957. Early flights were in helicopter mode, the first translation to wing-borne flight occurring in April 1958. In 1960 Fairey was bought by Westland, which proposed a Rotodyne Z for the RAF as a 75-man or vehicle transport.

Specification: Fairey Rotodyne three-crew hybrid helicopter/aeroplane transport prototype
Rotor diameter: 27.43 m (90 ft 0 in)
Span: 14.17 m (46 ft 6 in)
Fuselage length: 17.88 m (58 ft 8 in)
Powerplant: 2×Napier Eland NEl.3, 2237 kW (3,000 ehp) each
Armament: none
Max T/O weight: 17237 kg (38,000 lb)
Max speed: 185 mph at 5,000 ft
Operational range: 450 miles

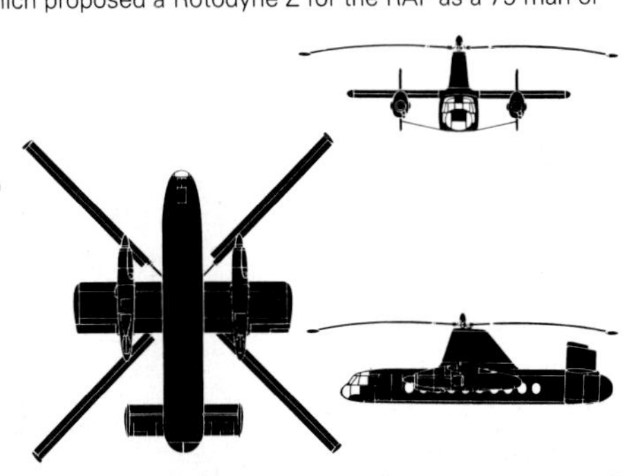

Mil Mi-14

The Mi-14 first flew in 1973 as an anti-submarine helicopter with the dynamic system of the Mi-17 (itself an uprated Mi-8) combined with boat hull and stabilising sponsons already proposed for several abortive naval developments of the Mi-8. This shore-based type is called 'Haze' by NATO, and its combination of amphibious capability, all-weather flight instrumentation, a large hold and twin-engined powerplant made the helicopter a natural choice for the SAR role. This variant has not been allocated a NATO suffix designation so far as is known, and is operated by Poland and the USSR. The model has search radar with its antenna in an undernose radome, other specialist sensors, and a rescue hoist mounted above the sliding door on the port side of the fuselage.

Aérospatiale SA 365/366

Though the Dauphin was initially placed in production as the SA 360C with a single Turboméca Astazou turboshaft and fixed landing gear, it began to come of age in the form of the SA 365 Dauphin 2 with retractable landing gear and twin Turboméca Arriel turboshafts for increased performance, payload and reliability in more exacting roles such as SAR, in which the prevalent variant is the SA 365F. This can be fitted with search radar (generally the Thomson-CSF ORB 32 Heracles II or Bendix RDR 1500), an autopilot, an advanced navigation system such as the Crouzet ONS 200A and, of course a side-mounted rescue hoist: in the case of the SA 365F this has 90m (295ft) of cable and is rated at 275kg (606lb). The US Coast Guard operates the SA 366G-1 version as the HH-65A Dolphin. This has 507-kW (680-shp) Avco Lycoming LTS101-750A-1 turboshafts and a Northrop Sea Hawk FLIR sensor.

Specification: Aérospatiale SA 365F Dauphin 2 three-crew SAR helicopter
Main rotor diameter: 11.93m (39ft 1.7in)
Length overall, rotors turning: 13.46m (44ft 2in)
Powerplant: 2×Turboméca Arriel 1M, 522kW (700shp) each
Payload: eight survivors, or four litters plus an attendant, or 1600kg (3,527lb) of freight
Max T/O weight: 4100kg (9,039lb)
Max speed: 184mph at sea level
Operational range: 547 miles

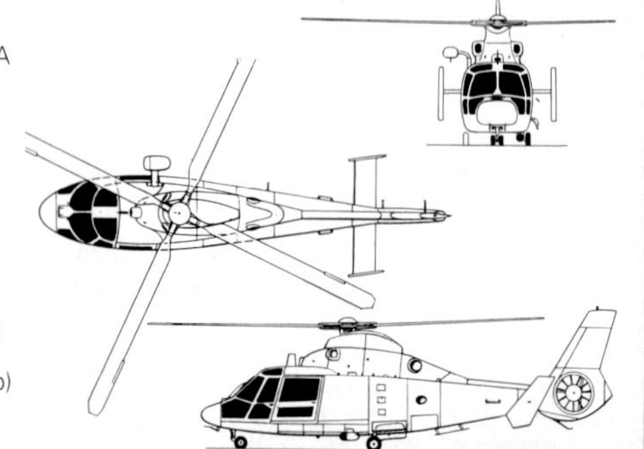

Aérospatiale SA 330 Puma

Though developed as a battlefield helicopter, the Puma has all the features required of an effective SAR helicopter, most notably an all-weather flight capability, a twin-engined powerplant for good payload and performance combined with reliability, and a capacious hold to accommodate a useful number of survivors. The type's suitability for the SAR role is also enhanced by all-weather survivability features such as the optional inlet de-icing and snow/ice shields. The rescue hoist has a rating of 275kg (606lb) and 90m (295ft) of cable, and SAR Pumas generally have an advanced navigation system and nose-mounted search radar (most frequently Bendix RDR 1400 or RCA Primus 40/50). The AS 332 Super Puma can also be used for the SAR role with similar equipment but also has the advantages accruing from the use of two 1327-kW (1,780-shp) Turboméca Makila 1A turboshafts.

Specification: Aérospatiale SA 330L Puma three/four-crew SAR helicopter
Main rotor diameter: 15.00m (49ft 2.6in)
Length overall, rotors turning: 18.15m (59ft 6.6in)
Powerplant: 2×Turboméca Turmo IVC, 1175kW (1,575shp) each
Payload: 16 survivors, or six litters and six seated survivors, or 3000kg (6,614lb) of freight
Max T/O weight: 7500kg (16,535lb)
Max speed: 163mph at sea level
Operational range: 342 miles

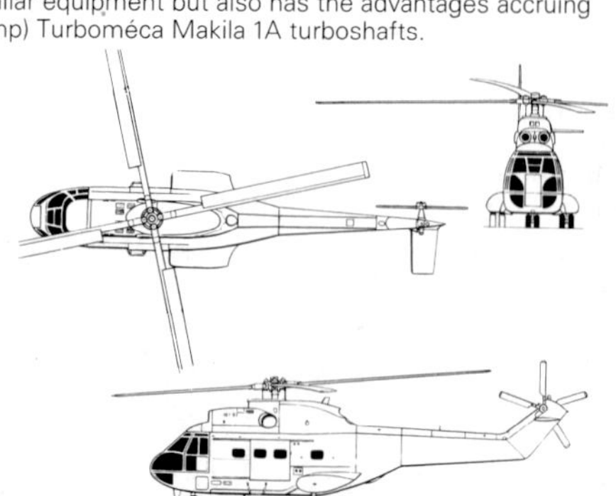

The Mil Mi-14, code-named 'Haze' by NATO's Air Standards Co-ordinating Committee, is the standard Soviet land-based ASW and SAR helicopter. It also serves with the Polish and East German navies.

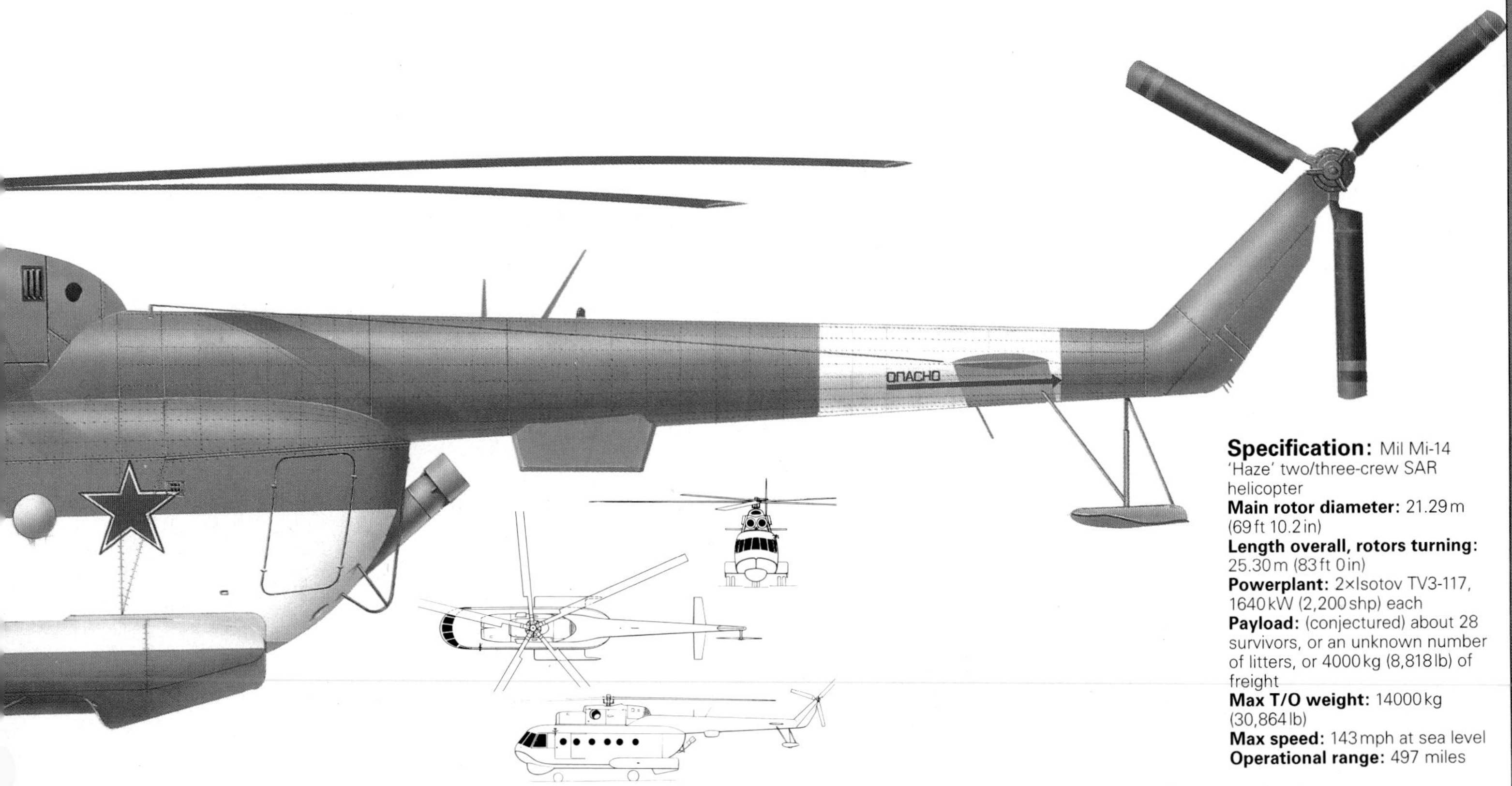

Specification: Mil Mi-14 'Haze' two/three-crew SAR helicopter
Main rotor diameter: 21.29 m (69 ft 10.2 in)
Length overall, rotors turning: 25.30 m (83 ft 0 in)
Powerplant: 2×Isotov TV3-117, 1640 kW (2,200 shp) each
Payload: (conjectured) about 28 survivors, or an unknown number of litters, or 4000 kg (8,818 lb) of freight
Max T/O weight: 14000 kg (30,864 lb)
Max speed: 143 mph at sea level
Operational range: 497 miles

Aérospatiale Super Frelon

The Super Frelon was designed as an all-weather type with the performance and reliability advantages of a three-engined powerplant. The variant operated by the French navy is the SA 321G, and though this is tasked primarily with protection of the approaches to the nuclear submarine base at Brest, it has a secondary SAR tasking. In this role the type's large cabin allows the accommodation of a considerable load of survivors, who can be detected with the aid of the helicopter's Sylphe search radar and then rescued with the standard 275-kg (606-lb) capacity winch located in the starboard door with 90 m (295 ft) of cable. The Super Frelon also has an air-opening rear ramp/door that facilitates the launching of bulky rescue items such as inflatable rafts. The Super Frelons operated by China and Libya also have an SAR tasking, while those of Israel and South Africa apparently do not.

Specification: Aérospatiale SA 321G Super Frelon three/four-crew SAR helicopter
Main rotor diameter: 18.90 m (62 ft 0 in)
Length overall, rotors turning: 23.03 m (75 ft 6.7 in)
Powerplant: 3×Turboméca Turmo IIIC6, 1156 kW (1,550 shp) each
Payload: 27 survivors, or 15 litters plus two attendants, or 5000 kg (11,023 lb) of freight
Max T/O weight: 13000 kg (28,660 lb)
Max speed: 171 mph at sea level
Operational range: 633 miles

Agusta-Bell AB.212

The Model 212 was developed by Bell from the Model 205 specifically to provide the Canadian Armed Forces with a medium-lift helicopter possessing a reliable coupled-turboshaft powerplant. The AB.212 is the variant built under licence in Italy for a number of roles, and is operated by the Italian air force in the dedicated SAR role; other air arms operate the AB.212ASW type for the armed anti-submarine/ship role with a secondary SAR tasking. In the SAR role the helicopter's high level of instrumentation is an important factor. Items include search radar with its antenna in a radome above the cockpit (AB.212ASW model), and the combination of advanced navigation systems and an automatic flight control system allow automatic navigation and automatic transition into hover at a designated spot. The rescue winch is located on the starboard side of the fuselage and is rated at 272 kg (600 lb).

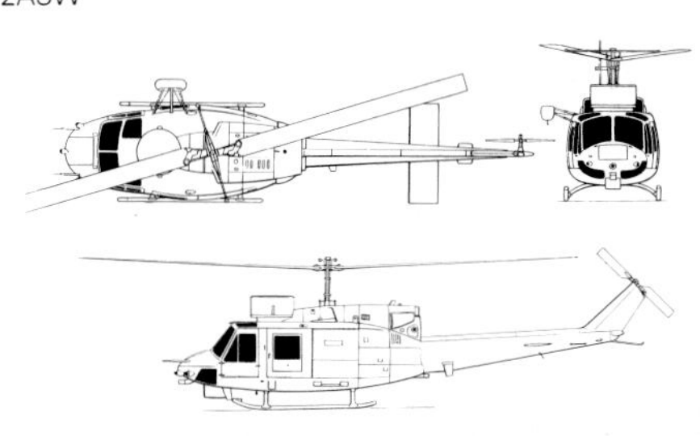

Specification: Agusta-Bell AB.212ASW two/three-seat SAR helicopter
Main rotor diameter: 14.63 m (48 ft 0 in)
Length overall, rotors turning: 17.40 m (57 ft 1 in)
Powerplant: 1×Pratt & Whitney Canada PT6T-6 Turbo Twin Pac, 1398 kW (1,875 shp)
Payload: seven survivors, or four litters plus an attendant, or 2268 kg (5,000 lb) of freight
Max T/O weight: 5070 kg (11,177 lb)
Max speed: 115 mph at sea level
Operational range: 382 miles

Sikorsky HH-53 Super Jolly

Specification: Sikorsky MH-53H Super Jolly three/four-crew combat SAR helicopter
Main rotor diameter: 22.02 m (72 ft 3 in)
Length overall, rotors turning: 26.90 m (88 ft 3 in)
Powerplant: 2×General Electric T64-GE-413, 2927 kW (3,925 shp) each
Armament: 2 or 3×7.62-mm (0.3-in) Miniguns
Payload: 38 survivors/troops, or 24 litters plus attendants, or 3629 kg (8,000 kg) of freight
Max T/O weight: 19051 kg (42,000 lb)
Max speed: 196 mph at sea level
Operational range: 257 miles

This Sikorsky MH-53J of the 21st Special Operations Squadron is based at RAF Woodbridge, Suffolk, as part of the 67th Aerospace Rescue and Recovery Wing. These powerful and well-equipped helicopters were converted from HH-53Cs, and have already proved their mettle in daring long-range rescue missions over the Atlantic.

The CH-53 Sea Stallion is one of the West's most important heavy-lift/assault helicopters and first flew in October 1964. From the baseline model have been developed several combat SAR and special forçes' helicopters, starting with the HH-53B combat SAR type with the same provisions as the HH-3E but using two 2297-kW (3,080-shp) T64-GE-3 turboshafts. Later versions are the HH-53C combat SAR type with terrain-following radar and night-vision equipment for all-weather operation with two 2927-kW (3,925-shp) T64-GE-7 turboshafts, the MH-53H combat SAR/special forces' type based on the HH-53C with an improved navigation system and an infra-red sensor, and the MH-53J special forces' insertion/extraction type based on the MH-53H with three Miniguns, a further improved navigation system and 454 kg (1,000 lb) of titanium armour protection.

Bell Model 205

This ultimate development of the 'Huey' series has been produced in many forms both in the original USA and under licence in Italy, Japan, Taiwan and West Germany. The Model 205, together with its UH-1D/H military versions, is used in a number of roles including short-range SAR. The type has only a single engine and lacks all-weather flight instrumentation/search capability, and is therefore limited to clear-weather operations. Nevertheless the Model 205 series has an admirable record for reliability, and is therefore in fairly widespread use for SAR with equipment such as a rescue hoist above the sliding door on the starboard side of the cabin. Such operators include Brazil, Canada, Chile, the Dominican Republic, Greece, Honduras, Mexico, New Zealand, Saudi Arabia, South Korea, Taiwan, Turkey and Venezuela.

Specification: Bell UH-1H Iroquois two/three-crew SAR helicopter
Main rotor diameter: 14.63 m (48 ft 0 in)
Length overall, rotors turning: 17.62 m (57 ft 9.7 in)
Powerplant: 1×Avco Lycoming T53-L-13, 1044 kW (1,400 shp)
Payload: 14 survivors, or six litters plus one attendant, or 1759 kg (3,880 lb) of freight
Max T/O weight: 4309 kg (9,500 lb)
Max speed: 127 mph at sea level
Operational range: 318 miles

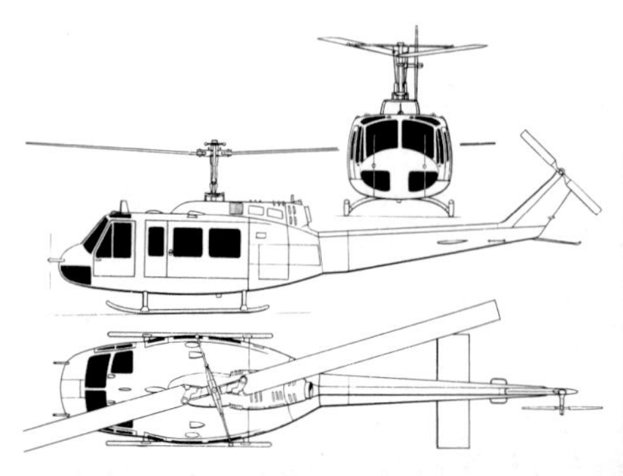

Bell UH-1N Iroquois

In both its military UH-1N and civil Model 212 Twin Two-Twelve variants, this is an important utility helicopter that is used by several nations as an SAR type. The helicopter was first flown in 1968 after development from the Model 205 with a twin-engined powerplant for greater reliability and payload: if either half of the coupled powerplant unit fails the other runs up to full power for continued flight capability. The type is configured for IFR flight and thus possesses a useful all-weather capability, but lacks the search radar of more-capable SAR helicopters. In the SAR role the helicopter is fitted with the standard US rescue hoist, which is rated at 272 kg (600 lb) and located above the sliding cabin door on the starboard side of the fuselage.

Specification: Bell UH-1N Iroquois two-crew SAR helicopter
Main rotor diameter: 14.69 m (48 ft 2.25 in)
Length, fuselage: 12.92 m (42 ft 4.75 in)
Powerplant: 1×Pratt & Whitney Canada T400-CP-400, 962 kW (1,290 shp)
Payload: 12 survivors, or 1534 kg (3,383 lb) of freight
Max T/O weight: 4762 kg (10,500 lb)
Max speed: 142 mph at sea level
Operational range: 248 miles

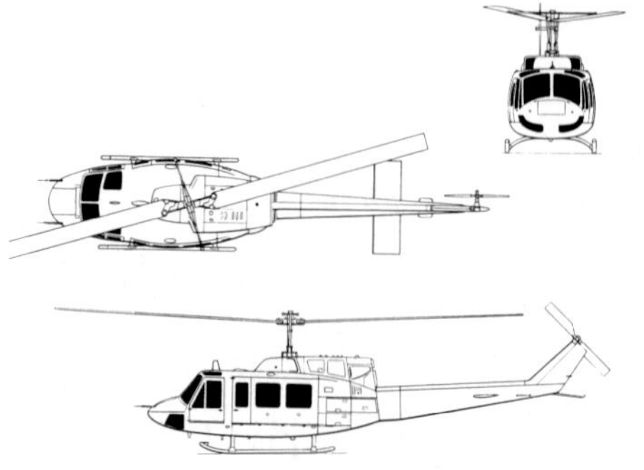

Kamov Ka-25

The Ka-25 was designed as a compact shipboard helicopter, and here Kamov's design hallmark, a pair of superimposed contra-rotating rotors, proved invaluable in combination with a capacious fuselage. The type first flew in about 1960 and proved very successful in terms of reliability and overall weight-lifting capability. Proper Soviet designations for the anti-submarine, missile-targeting and SAR/utility versions have not been revealed, so these are best known by A, B and C suffixes to the NATO reporting name 'Hormone'. The 'Hormone-C' operates in the utility and planeguard as well as SAR roles, and its equipment includes search radar with its antenna in an undernose radome, a searchlight, a loudspeaker, other items (in a ventral dome and forward projection of the ventral fin) and a rescue hoist located above the sliding door on the port side of the fuselage.

Specification: Kamov Ka-25 'Hormone-C' three-crew SAR helicopter
Rotor diameter, each: 15.74 m (51 ft 7.7 in)
Length, fuselage: 9.75 m (32 ft 0 in)
Powerplant: 2×Glushenkov GTD-3BM, 738 kW (990 shp) each
Payload: 12 survivors, or an unknown number of litters, or freight
Max T/O weight: 7500 kg (16,535 lb)
Max speed: 137 mph at sea level
Operational range: 404 miles

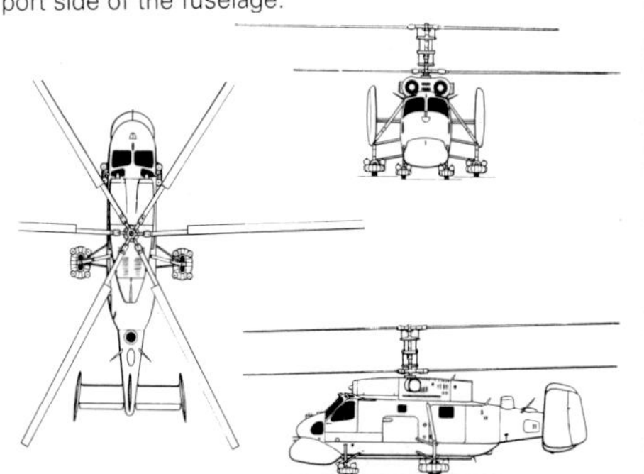

Kamov Ka-27

The Ka-27 has an identical configuration to the Ka-25 and first flew in about 1979. The rotors are only very slightly larger in diameter than those of the Ka-25, but the fuselage is longer and proportionally more capacious than that of the Ka-25. In combination with considerably more-powerful engines and improved rotor design this boosts payload very considerably, and this factor is reflected in the type's variants. Again the Soviet designations remain unknown, so the NATO reporting name 'Helix' is used with suffixes A for the anti-submarine model, B for the Naval Infantry assault transport, C for the civil Ka-32 model with a 5000-kg (11,023-lb) payload, and D for the SAR and utility model. This last has search radar with its antenna in a trim undernose radome, other role-optimised electronics and, above the sliding door on the port side of the cabin, a rescue hoist.

Specification: Kamov Ka-27 'Helix-C' three/four-crew SAR helicopter
Rotor diameter, each: 15.90 m (52 ft 2 in)
Length, fuselage: 11.30 m (37 ft 0.9 in)
Powerplant: 2×Isotov TV3-117V, 1659 kW (2,225 shp) each
Payload: 14 survivors, or an unknown number of litters, or 4000 kg (8,818 lb) of freight
Max T/O weight: 12600 kg (27,778 lb)
Max speed: 152 mph at sea level
Operational range: 800 miles

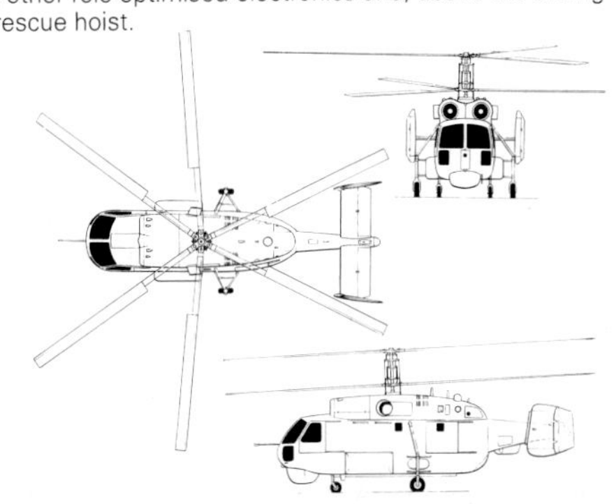

Sikorsky S-58 and Wessex

The S-58 was first flown in 1954 and entered widespread service as the HSS-1 for the US Navy and Marine Corps and the H-34 for the US Army and Air Force, all using variants of the Wright R-1820 radial rated at about 1137 kW (1,525 hp). Like the occasional civil model, some of these military variants were operated in the clear-weather SAR role with a rescue hoist on the starboard side of the fuselage above the cabin's large sliding door. Some helicopters were later modified to turbine power with the 1342-kW (1,800-shp) Pratt & Whitney PT6T Turbo Twin Pac to provide capability comparable with that of the British-developed Wessex in its later forms (HC.Mk 2 and HU.Mk 5) with its coupled Gnome turboshafts replacing the single Gazelle turboshaft of the HAS.Mks 1, 3 and 31. There were also civil models.

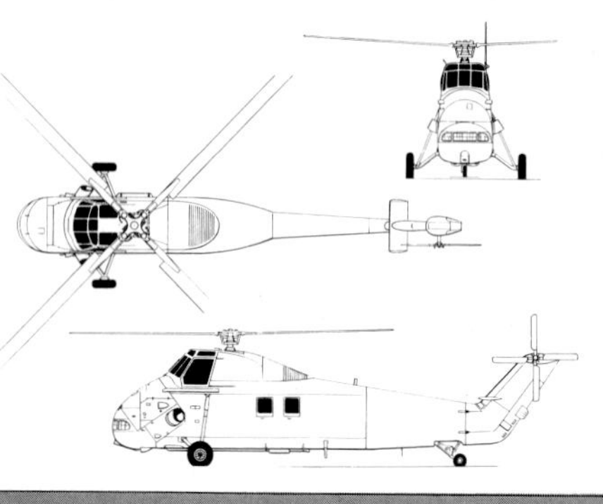

Specification: Westland Wessex Mk 60 two/three-crew SAR helicopter
Main rotor diameter: 17.07 m (56 ft 0 in)
Length overall, rotors turning: 20.04 m (65 ft 9 in)
Powerplant: 2×Rolls-Royce (Bristol Siddeley) Gnome Mk 110/111, 1007 kW (1,350 shp) each
Payload: 15 survivors, or eight litters and two seated survivors plus one attendant, or freight
Max T/O weight: 6169 kg (13,600 lb)
Max speed: 133 mph at sea level
Operational range: 334 miles

Sikorsky S-61 and Sea King

The S-61 was first flown in 1959 as a twin-turbine helicopter able to replace the S-58 by combining the submarine hunter and killer roles in a single airframe with all-weather avionics and a boat hull for amphibious capability. The type has an optional 272-kg (600-lb) capacity rescue hoist in its American SH-3 versions, and this capability is retained in export and licence-built versions, which include Italian and Japanese production by Agusta and Mitsubishi respectively. The most capable dedicated SAR version, however, is the Westland Sea King HAR.Mk 3 for the Royal Air Force. This has all-weather flight instrumentation, a stability-augmentation system, an advanced navigation system, MEL search radar and, of course, a rescue hoist.

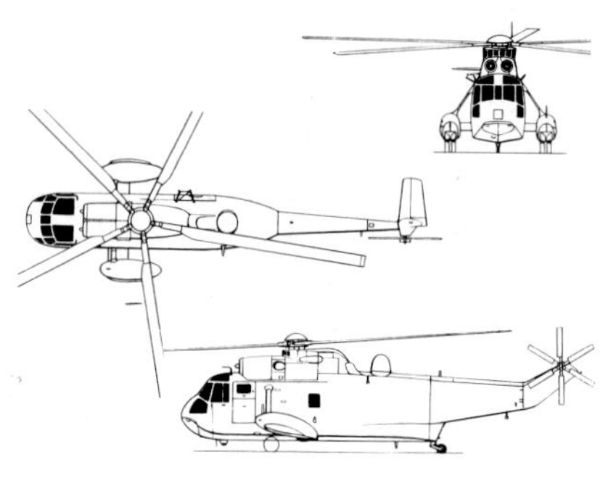

Specification: Westland Sea King HAR.Mk 3 four-crew SAR helicopter
Main rotor diameter: 18.90 m (62 ft 0 in)
Length overall, rotors turning: 22.15 m (72 ft 8 in)
Powerplant: 2×Rolls-Royce (Bristol Siddeley) Gnome H.1400-1, 1238 kW (1,660 shp) each
Payload: 19 survivors, or six litters, or two litters and 11 seated survivors, or 2722 kg (6,000 lb) of freight
Max T/O weight: 9525 kg (21,000 lb)
Max speed: 129 mph at sea level
Operational range: 765 miles

Sikorsky HH-3

The payload, range and performance of the Sea King commended the type for development in the combat SAR role, and a few SH-3As were converted for US Navy trials as HH-3As with more power and fuel, a high-speed hoist, armour and two 7.62-mm (0.3-in) Minigun turrets. The US Air Force took the concept to fruition with the HH-3E Jolly Green Giant. This has basically the same equipment as the HH-3A combined with the airframe of the CH-3E, itself developed as the S-61R with more power and a revised fuselage incorporating a hydraulically operated rear ramp/door. The type also has a retractable inflight-refuelling probe, self-sealing fuel tanks and specialist electronics including an advanced navigation system and sensors. The US Coast Guard operates the HH-3F Pelican model without armour, armament and self-sealing fuel tanks, and the similar Agusta ASH-3F is built in Italy.

Specification: Sikorsky HH-3E Jolly Green Giant three/four-crew combat SAR helicopter
Main rotor diameter: 18.90 m (62 ft 0 in)
Length overall, rotors turning: 22.25 m (73 ft 0 in)
Powerplant: 2×General Electric T58-GE-5, 1118 kW (1,500 shp) each
Armament: 2×7.62-mm (0.3-in) Miniguns
Payload: 25 survivors, or 15 litters plus two attendants, or 2268 kg (5,000 lb) of freight
Max T/O weight: 10002 kg (22,050 lb)
Max speed: 162 mph at sea level
Operational range: 465 miles

Sikorsky HH-60

From the UH-60 utility tactical helicopter that first flew in October 1974 have emerged several important combat SAR and derived special forces insertion/extraction helicopters. First of these is the HH-60A Night Hawk combat SAR type for the US Air Force based on the SH-60B Seahawk's dynamic system and rescue hoist together with radar, FLIR and an inertial navigation system. Other derivatives will be the HH-60H Rescue Hawk combat SAR type for the US Navy based on the SH-60F Seahawk, the HH-60J Seahawk SAR type for the US Marine Corps based on the HH-60H but without its combat features, and the MH-60K Black Hawk special forces type for the US Army and based on the latest UH-60M utility helicopter with a number of advanced features, special sensors and a 'glass' cockpit based on the Boeing package for the MH-47E version of its Chinook twin-rotor helicopter.

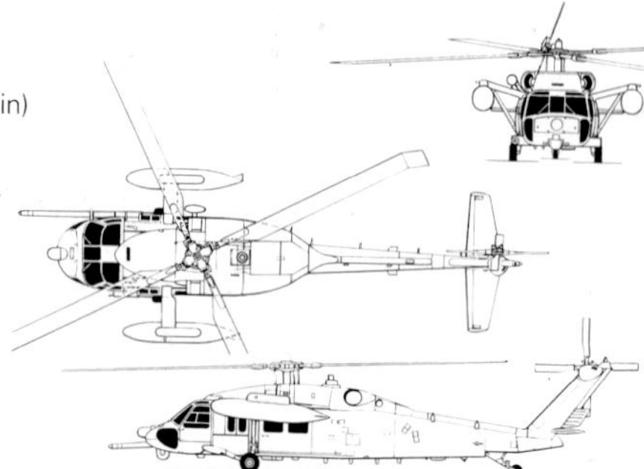

Specification: Sikorsky HH-60A Night Hawk three-crew combat SAR helicopter
Main rotor diameter: 16.36 m (53 ft 8 in)
Length overall, rotors turning: 19.76 m (64 ft 10 in)
Powerplant: 2×General Electric T700-GE-401, 1260 kW (1,690 shp) each
Armament: 2×7.62-mm (0.3-in) machine-guns
Payload: 12 survivors, or six litters, or four litters and three seated survivors, or 3629 kg (8,000 lb) of freight
Max T/O weight: 9979 kg (22,000 lb)
Max speed: 167 mph at sea level
Operational range: 720 miles

Kamov Ka-26

Though possessing the NATO reporting name 'Hoodlum', the Ka-26 is a civil helicopter with only the most limited of paramilitary applications. The type adheres to the well-proven Kamov design concept of two co-axial and contra-rotating three-blade rotors above an aeroplane-type fuselage with substantial tail surfaces, and first flew in 1965. The type was planned mainly for the agricultural role, but the payload volume behind the flightdeck and between the podded radial engines/main landing gear units can be fitted with payload pods other than the standard 900- or 1065-kg (1,984- or 2,348-lb) chemical hopper and associated duster or spraybars. This allows the type's use as a six-passenger transport, freighter with an open load platform, and flying crane, or in alternative roles such as firefighting, resources-exploitation support, and cable-laying.

Specification: Kamov Ka-26 light general-purpose helicopter
Rotor diameter, each: 13.00 m (42 ft 8 in)
Fuselage length: 7.75 m (25 ft 5 in)
Powerplant: 2×Vedeneyev M-14V-26, 242.5 kW (325 hp) each
Payload: pilot and co-pilot plus six passengers or 1065 kg (2,348 lb) of freight/chemicals, or a 1100-kg (2,425-lb) slung load
Max T/O weight: 3250 kg (7,165 lb)
Cruising speed: 93 mph at sea level
Operational range: 248 miles

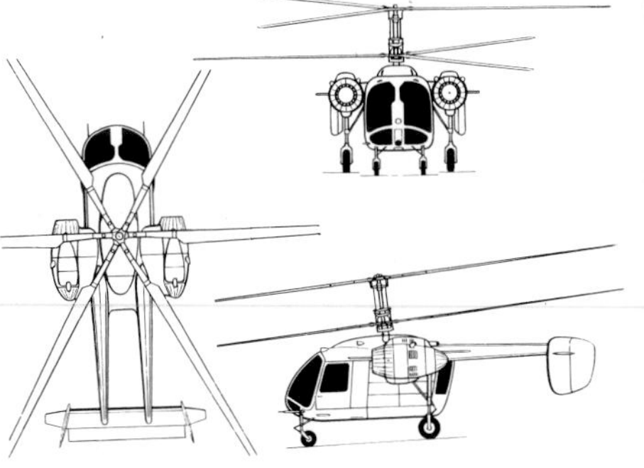

MBB/Kawasaki BK 117

In 1977 MBB and Kawasaki agreed to supersede the separate efforts towards their proposed BO 107 and KH-7 helicopters in favour of a collaborative BK 117 using the rotor head of the existing BO 105 and the transmission of the KH-7. Kawasaki is responsible for the fuselage, fuel, transmission and electrical systems. Two ground-test and two flight-test prototypes were built, the West German and Japanese examples of the latter flying in June and August 1979 respectively. The BK 117 is conventional in basic layout, but somewhat unusually for a civil helicopter has a cargo compartment (in the rear of the pod section) accessed by twin clamshell doors below the laterally mounted turboshafts. VFR and IFR certification has been granted, and the type's comparatively poor sales are attributable to a combination of modest payload and high capital cost.

Specification: MBB/Kawasaki BK 117 light multi-purpose helicopter
Main rotor diameter: 11.00 m (36 ft 1 in)
Overall length, rotors turning: 12.98 m (42 ft 7 in)
Powerplant: 2×Avco Lycoming LTS101-650B-1, 485 kW (650 shp) each
Payload: pilot and co-pilot plus 6-7 passengers and 1.34 m^3 (47.3 cu ft) of freight carried internally, or a slung load
Max T/O weight: 2850 kg (6,283 lb)
Cruising speed: 160 mph at sea level
Operational range: 338 miles with maximum internal payload

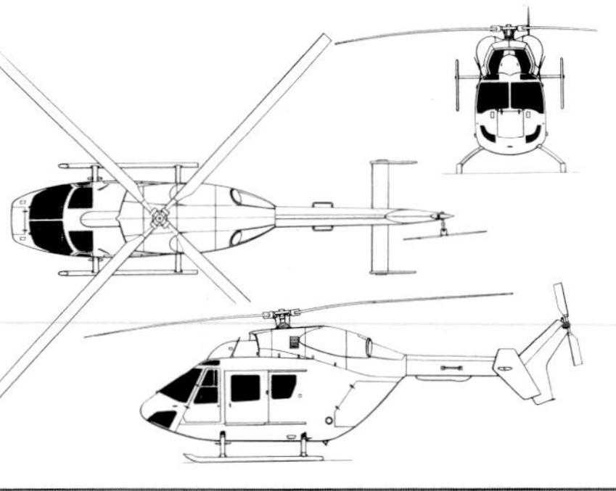

Mil Mi-34

Designed as replacement for the elderly Mi-1, the Mi-34 (NATO codename 'Hermit') was first revealed in 1987 as a conventional helicopter of light alloy pod-and-boom layout with skid landing gear and a T-tail. The semi-articulated four-blade main rotor has blades of glassfibre reinforced with carbonfibre, and the two-blade tail rotor is of the same construction. Unlike its Eastern bloc competitor, the PZL Swidnik SW-4 from Poland, the Soviet helicopter is powered by a piston engine. This is the same Vedeneyev radial as used in current Yakovlev fixed-wing trainers and the Kamov Ka-26 helicopter, a fact that eases the logistics and spares-holding problems of operators of these Soviet types. The first of two flying prototypes was completed in 1986, and Mil gained certification in 1988. If the type is placed in production, it will probably be at WSK-PZL Swidnik factory in Poland.

Specification: Mil Mi-34 two/four-seat light general-purpose and training helicopter
Main rotor diameter: 10.00 m (32 ft 9.75 in)
Fuselage length: 8.71 m (28 ft 7 in)
Powerplant: 1×Vedeneyev M-14V-26, 242 kW (325 hp) each
Payload: not revealed
Max T/O weight: 1250 kg (2,755 lb)
Max Cruising speed: 112 mph at low altitude
Operational range: 112 miles with 165-kg (364-lb) payload

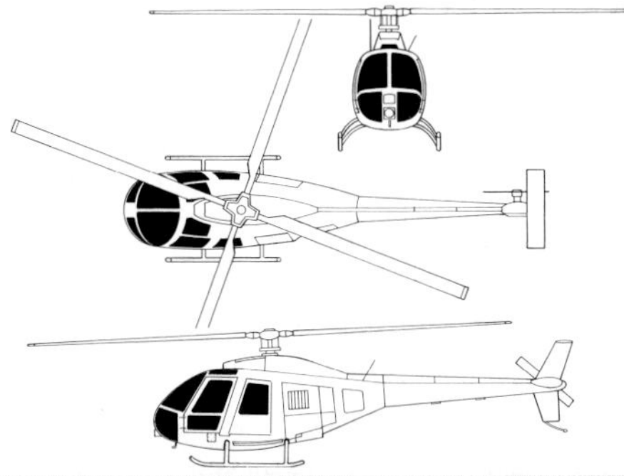

Sikorsky S-61

The S-61 is best known in its Sea King naval forms as built by Sikorsky and three licensees, but was also developed in two civil variants as the S-61L and S-61N. First of these to fly, in December 1960, was the 28-passenger S-61L retaining the rotor system of the military version powered by CT58 civil variants of the T58 turboshafts used by the Sea King. Intended for non-amphibious operation, the S-61L has fixed tailwheel landing gear, the basic watertight boat-shape hull being retained for emergency alightings. The S-61N was planned as an amphibious type and retains the Sea King's stabilizing side sponsons with retractable main wheel units. Power is provided again by 1007-kW (1,350-shp) CT58-140 turboshafts, and passenger accommodation is 26. The S-61N Mk II is an upgraded version, and in Italy Agusta is producing an AS-61N1 variant with 24 seats but greater range.

Specification: Sikorsky S-61N Mk II medium transport helicopter
Main rotor diameter: 18.90 m (62 ft 0 in)
Overall length, rotors turning: 22.20 m (72 ft 10 in)
Powerplant: 2×General Electric CT58-140-1/2, 1118 kW (1,500 shp) each
Payload: flightcrew of three plus 28 passengers or freight carried internally
Max T/O weight: 9299 kg (20,500 lb)
Cruising speed: 150 mph at optimum altitude
Operational range: 495 miles

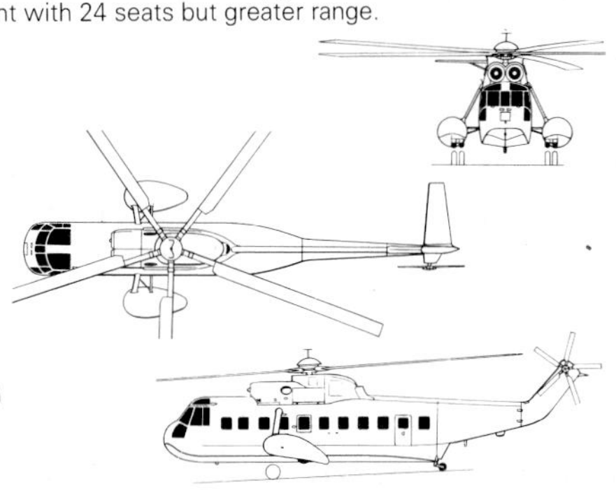

Sikorsky S-76 Spirit

Designed in the mid-1970s to increase Sikorsky's share of the corporate and civil helicopter market, the S-76 first flew in March 1977 and soon revealed excellent performance as a result of its careful streamlining combined with two 485-kW (650-shp) Allison 250-C30 turboshafts driving a rotor system derived from that of the S-70 (UH-60 Black Hawk) military helicopter. The basic type is certificated for flight in IFR conditions, and can be configured without difficulty for a number of applications as diverse as corporate transport and support of offshore resources exploitation. From 1982 deliveries have been of the S-76 Mk II variant with 40 improvements to the standard airframe, improved ventilation and dynamic systems, and uprated Allison turboshafts.

SA 360/SA 365 Dauphin

Designed as successor to the Alouette III, the SA 360 was planned as a larger partner to the Ecureuil and first flew in June 1972 with a 730-kW (980-shp) Astazou XVI turboshaft. Since that time the helicopter has been produced in single- and twin-engined civil and military variants. The main civil variants are the 10-seat SA 360C Dauphin with the 783-kW (1,050-shp) Turbomeca Astazou XVIIIA and either fixed tailwheel or skid landing gears, the SA 365C Dauphin 2 version of the SA 360C with two Arriel 1A turboshafts for greater flight safety, and the 14-seat SA 365N Dauphin 2 with about 90 per cent alteration of the components, use of composite materials in about 20 per cent of the structure, retractable tricycle landing gear, and two 530-kW (710-shp) Arriel 1C turboshafts for a cruising speed of 172 mph at sea level after take-off at a maximum of 3850 kg (8,488 lb).

Specification: Aérospatiale SA 365C Dauphin 2 general-purpose helicopter
Main rotor diameter: 11.68 m (38 ft 4 in)
Overall length, rotors turning: 11.97 m (39 ft 3.25 in)
Powerplant: 2×Turbomeca Arriel 1A, 492 kW (660 shp) each
Payload: pilot plus nine passengers or 1360 kg (2,998 lb) of freight carried internally, or a 1300-kg (2,866-lb) slung load
Max T/O weight: 3400 kg (7,496 lb)
Cruising speed: 158 mph at sea level
Operational range: 289 miles

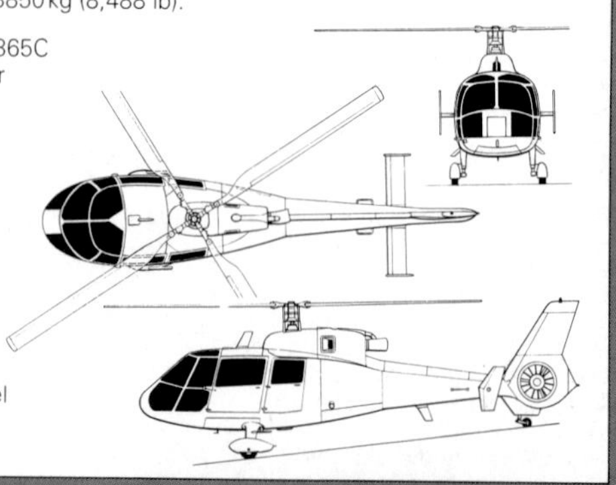

AS 350/AS 355 Ecureuil

Designed as successor to the Alouette II, the Ecureuil (squirrel) was designed for low maintenance and operating costs combined with modest vibration and noise levels. The first prototype flew in April 1974, and with the second machine validated the alternative Turbomeca Arriel and 459-kW (616-shp) Lycoming LTS101 turboshafts. The latter is used for the AS 350C and AS 350D Astar variants sold in the North American market, and the former for the AS 350B sold elsewhere. The AS 350 is also made in Brazil as the Helibras Esquilo. There is also a twin-engine version, the AS 355 sold in North America as the Twinstar and elsewhere as the Ecureuil 2 in AS 355E and improved AS 355F variants with beefed-up fuselage structure, different rotor blades, modified transmission and two 317-kW (425-shp) Allison 250-C20F turboshafts.

Specification: Aérospatiale AS 350B Ecureuil light general-purpose helicopter
Main rotor diameter: 10.69 m (35 ft 0.75 in)
Overall length, rotors turning: 12.99 m (42 ft 7.5 in)
Powerplant: 1×Turbomeca Arriel, 478 kW (641 shp)
Payload: pilot plus five passengers or freight carried internally, or a slung load
Max T/O weight: 2100 kg (4,630 lb)
Cruising speed: 144 mph
Operational range: 435 miles at sea level

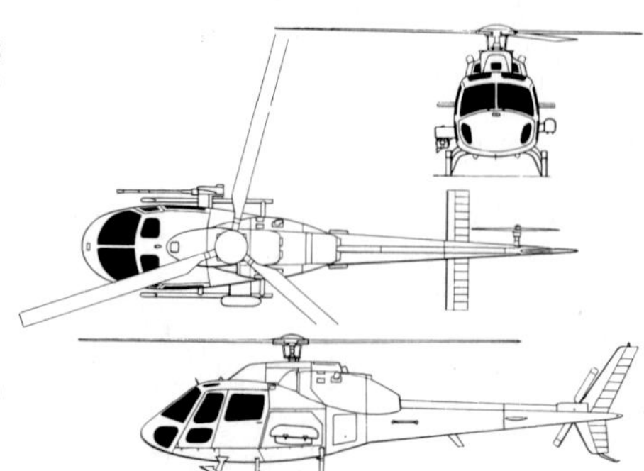

Specification: Sikorsky S-76 Mk II Spirit light/medium general-purpose and transport helicopter
Main rotor diameter: 13.41 m (44 ft 0 in)
Overall length, rotors turning: 16.00 m (52 ft 6 in)
Powerplant: 2×Allison 250-C30S, 508.5 kW (682 shp) each
Payload: pilot and co-pilot plus 12 passengers or freight carried internally, or a 1814-kg (4,000-lb) slung load
Max T/O weight: 4672 kg (10,300 lb)
Cruising speed: 178 mph at optimum altitude
Operational range: 465 miles with 12 passengers

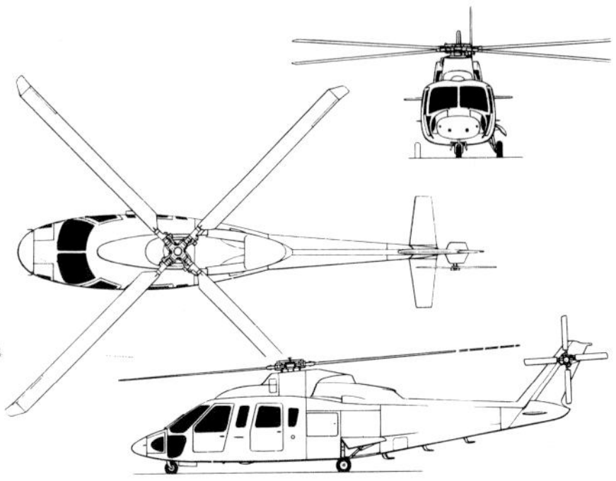

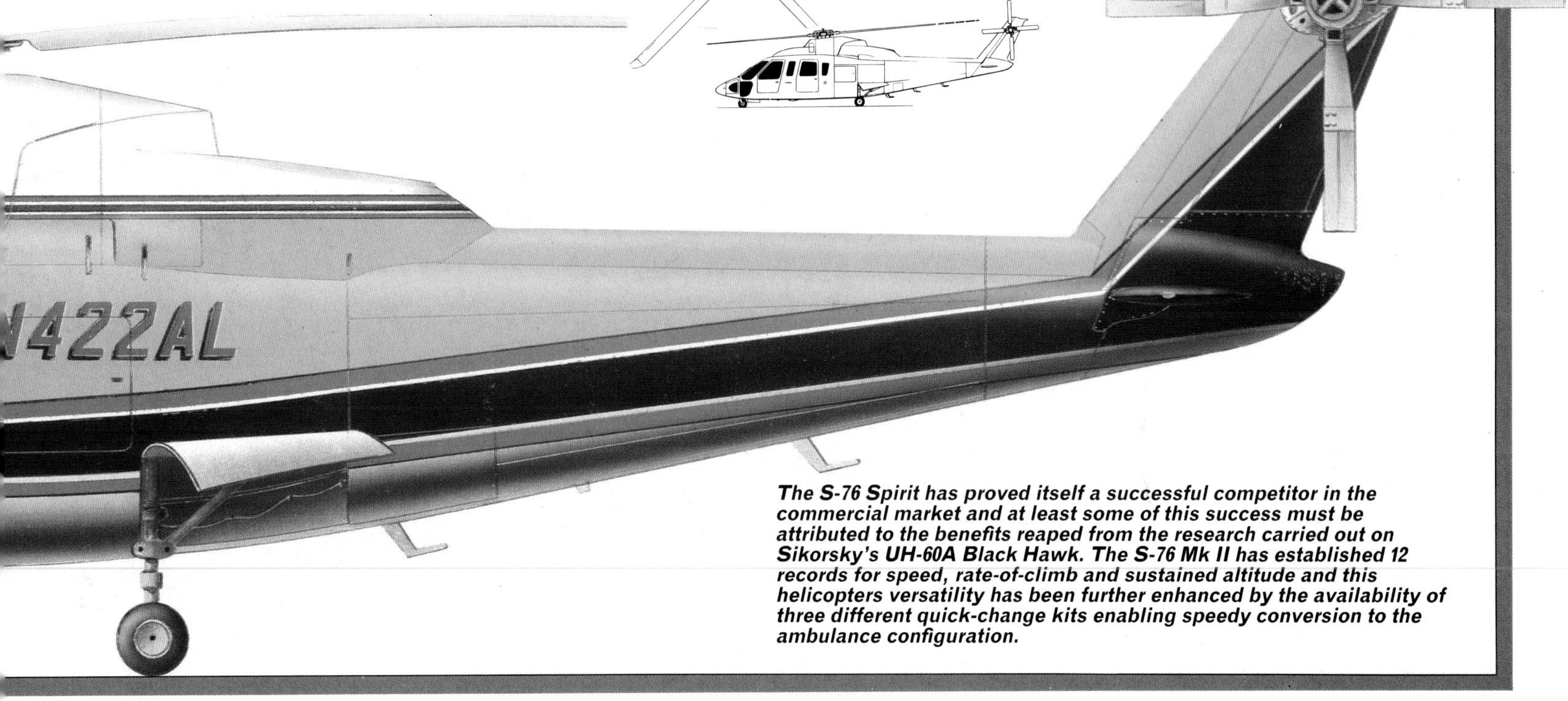

The S-76 Spirit has proved itself a successful competitor in the commercial market and at least some of this success must be attributed to the benefits reaped from the research carried out on Sikorsky's UH-60A Black Hawk. The S-76 Mk II has established 12 records for speed, rate-of-climb and sustained altitude and this helicopters versatility has been further enhanced by the availability of three different quick-change kits enabling speedy conversion to the ambulance configuration.

Aérospatiale AS 332 Super Puma

The Super Puma is a comparatively straightforward development of the SA 330 Puma with more power, revised air inlets, uprated transmission, a Starflex lightweight rotor head and thermally de-iced main rotor blades. The AS 331 prototype flew in September 1977, paving the way for the AS 332 with greater performance and payload plus reduced maintenance requirements, vibration and noise. Like other Aérospatiale helicopters, the Super Puma has been produced in parallel civil and military streams. The two main civil variants are the AS 332C with a cabin seating 17 persons, and the stretched AS 332L with the cabin lengthened by 0.76 m (29.9 in) to provide accommodation for another four persons. This variant has two extra cabin windows and greater fuel capacity. A variant for Bristow Helicopters is the Tiger designed for over-water operations with special equipment.

Specification: Aérospatiale AS 332L Super Puma medium general-purpose and transport helicopter
Main rotor diameter: 15.08 m (49 ft 5.5 in)
Overall length, rotors turning: 18.73 m (61 ft 5.5 in)
Powerplant: 2×Turbomeca Makila 1A, 1324 kW (1,725 shp) each
Payload: pilot and co-pilot plus 20-24 passengers or 2727 kg (6,012 lb) of freight carried internally, or a 4500-kg (9,921-lb) slung load
Max T/O weight: 8350 kg (18,410 lb)
Cruising speed: 173 mph at sea level
Operational range: 394 miles

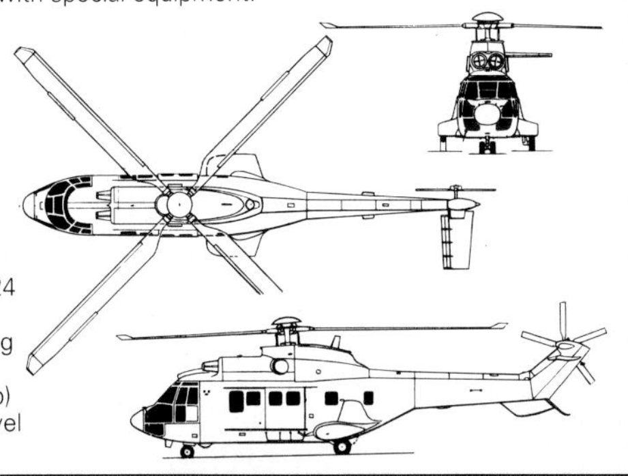

Agusta A 109

Developed as a high-speed utility helicopter for the civil market, the A 109 has fully retractable tricycle landing gear and sleek lines. As first projected in the late 1960s, the Hirundo (swallow) was to have been powered by a single 514-kW (690-shp) Turbomeca Astazou XII turboshaft but, with the improved marketability of a more reliable twin-turbine powerplant in mind, was then recast with two Allison turboshafts. The first prototype flew in August 1971, but protracted trials plus a number of problems delayed delivery of A 109A production helicopters into 1975. In September 1981 Agusta began delivery of the A 109A Mk II with uprated transmission, a new tail rotor to reduce vibration to a minimum, revised engine mountings again to reduce vibration and noise, and a number of other operating improvements.

Specification: Agusta A 109A Mk II light general-purpose helicopter
Main rotor diameter: 11.00 m (36 ft 1 in)
Overall length, rotors turning: 13.05 m (42 ft 9.75 in)
Powerplant: 2×Allison 250-C20B, 313 kW (420 shp) each
Payload: pilot and co-pilot plus six passengers or freight in the cabin, or a 907-kg (2,000-lb) slung load
Max T/O weight: 2600 kg (5,732 lb)
Cruising speed: 174 mph at sea level
Operational range: 363 miles

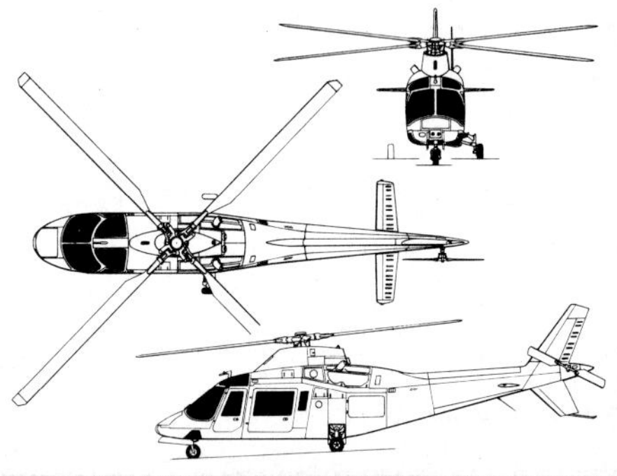

Mil Mi-8 and Mi-17

This Mil Mi-17 (called 'Hip-H' by NATO) was purchased by a Japanese civil operator. The Mil-17 uses the upgraded engines and transmission of the Mi-14 anti-submarine helicopter, and has its tail rotor on the left, rather than the right, as in the earlier Mi-8 (see 3-view, left). A large number of these adaptable helicopters is deployed worldwide.

Specification: Mil Mi-8 medium general-purpose helicopter
Main rotor diameter: 21.29m (69ft 10.2in)
Overall length, rotors turning: 25.24m (82ft 9.75in)
Powerplant: 2×Isotov TV2-117A, 1267kW (1,700 shp) each
Payload: pilot and co-pilot plus 28-32 passengers or 4000kg (8,818 lb) of freight carried internally, or a 3000-kg (6,614-lb) slung load
Max T/O weight: 12000kg (26,455lb)
Cruising speed: 140 mph at optimum altitude
Operational range: 311 miles with 28 passengers

Bell 206L LongRanger

Developed in the early 1970s, the LongRanger series was evolved as the Model 206L to meet a perceived capacity demand between the five-seat Model 206 JetRanger series and 15-seat Model 205A-1. It was planned round Bell's Noda-Matic cabin-suspension system (to reduce vibration levels) and an easily reconfigured 2.35-m^3 (83-cu ft) cabin for maximum flexibility of use. The Model 206L LongRanger is essentially the JetRanger II with a longer cabin and a larger-diameter main rotor driven by a 313-kW (420-shp) 250-C20B turboshaft. The Model 206L-1 LongRanger II introduces the 373-kW (500-shp) 250-C28B, and the Model 206L-3 LongRanger III has the further uprated 250-30P turboshaft, the two more powerful engine types allowing greater payload or higher performance.

Specification: Bell Model 206L-3 LongRanger III light general-purpose helicopter
Main rotor diameter: 11.28m (37ft 0in)
Overall length, rotors turning: 13.02m (42ft 8.5in)
Powerplant: 1×Allison 250-C30P, 485kW (650 shp)
Payload: pilot and co-pilot plus five passengers or freight in the cabin
Max T/O weight: 1882kg (4,150lb)
Cruising speed: 134 mph at 5,000ft
Operational range: 395 miles

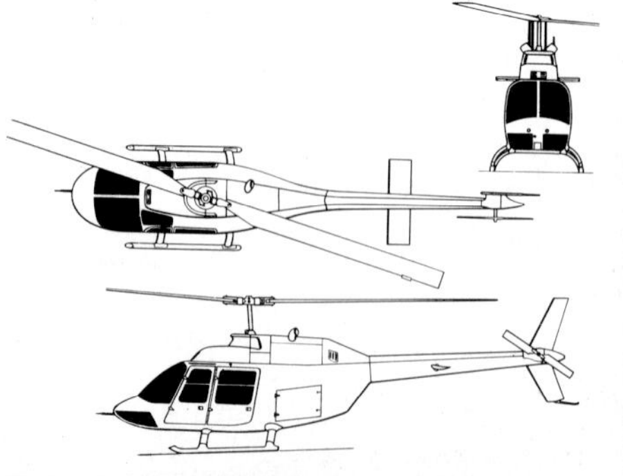

Bell 214ST

Developed from the UH-1H military helicopter via the Model 214 Huey Plus with structural strengthening, greater power and upgraded features, the Model 214ST (originally Stretched Twin and now Super Transport) is a commercial type based on the 16-seat Model 214A evolved for Iran in the utility role with a single 2185-kW (2,930-shp) Lycoming LTC4B-8D turboshaft. The primary modification required to produce the Model 214ST was a twin-turbine powerplant for greater reliability, especially in the type of over-water operations required by the resources-exploitation industries with two pilots and certification for IFR flight. The first Model 214ST flew in November 1977, and the type is available in 16-passenger standard or 18-passenger resources-exploitation layouts.

Specification: Bell Model 214ST medium general-purpose helicopter
Main rotor diameter: 15.85m (52ft 0in)
Overall length, rotors turning: 18.95m (62ft 2.25in)
Powerplant: 2×General Electric CT7-2A, 1212kW (1,625 shp) each
Payload: two pilots plus 16-18 passengers or 8.95m^3 (316 cu ft) of freight carried internally
Max T/O weight: 7938kg (17,500lb)
Cruising speed: 155 mph at 4,000ft
Operational range: 501 miles

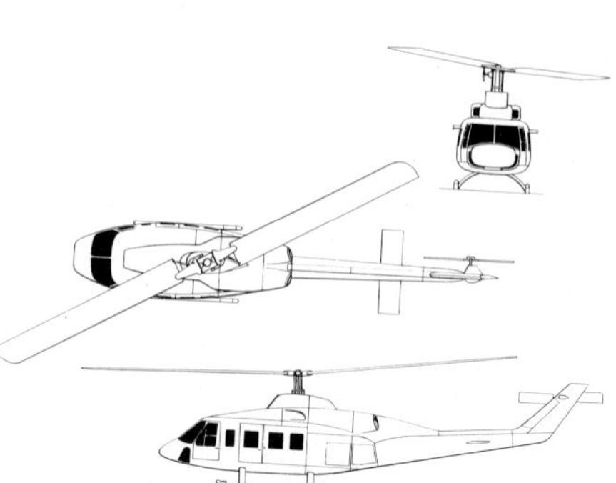

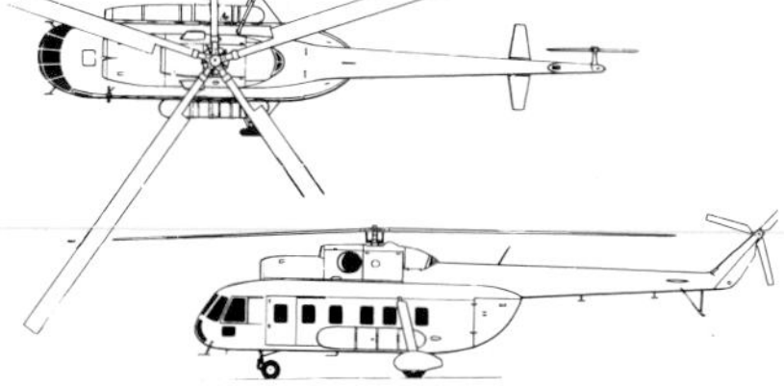

First flown in 1961 with a single 2013-kW (2,700-shp) Soloviev turboshaft plus four-blade main rotor, and currently known most widely as the 'Hip' series of military helicopters, the Mi-8 was developed in parallel military and civil versions. The definitive 'Hip-B' second prototype with twin-turbine powerplant plus five-blade main rotor was flown in September 1962. The civil version has rectangular rather than the military version's circular cabin windows, and the three variants are the Mi-8 with cabin accommodation for 28-32, the Mi-8T utility version with 24 tip-up seats and provision for internal or external freight, and the Mi-8 Salon with VIP accommodation for 11 passengers. The Mi-17 is essentially the Mi-8 with two 1417-kW (1,900-shp) Isotov TV3-117 turboshafts and uprated transmission for superior 'hot-and-high' performance.

Bell 222

Though designed very much in accordance with Bell's established principles, the Model 222 was the first twin-turbine commercial helicopter to be produced as such in the USA. The type was announced in 1974 and first flew in August 1976, subsequently receiving certification for VFR and then single- or twin-pilot IFR operations. Features include retractable tricycle landing gear, low-vibration Noda-Matic cabin suspension, glassfibre/stainless steel main rotor blades, and a no-lubrication elastomeric main rotor hub. The initial model is the Model 222A available in Executive and Offshore configurations, the latest variant being the Model 222B with single-pilot IFR qualification without a stability-augmentation system. This variant has 507-kW (680-shp) LTS101-750C-1 turboshafts driving a 12.8-m (42-ft) diameter main rotor for a 3810-kg (8,400-lb) maximum take-off weight.

Specification: Bell 222A light utility helicopter
Main rotor diameter: 12.12 m (39 ft 9 in)
Fuselage length: 10.98 m (36 ft 0.25 in)
Powerplant: 2×Avco Lycoming LTS101-650C-3, 462 kW (620 shp) each
Payload: pilot and co-pilot plus 6-8 passengers or freight carried internally, or a 1588-kg (3,500-lb) slung load
Max T/O weight: 3674 kg (8,100 lb)
Cruising speed: 153 mph at 4,000 ft
Operational range: 325 miles

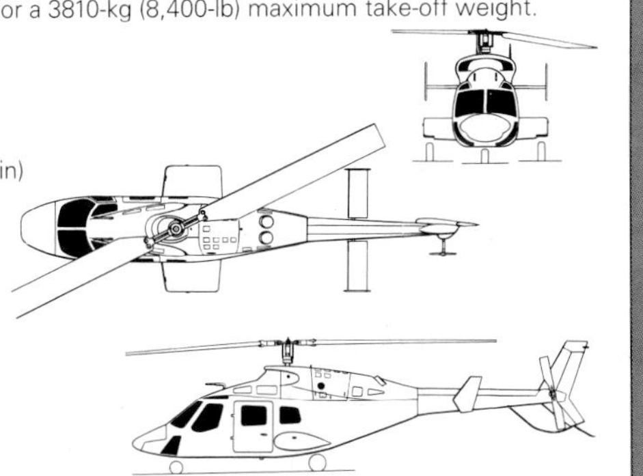

Boeing Model 234 Chinook

The largest-capacity commercial helicopter in service in the Western world, the Model 234 is the civil counterpart of Boeing's immensely successful twin-rotor Model 114 military helicopter, better known as the CH-47 Chinook. The type was announced in 1978 and uses the airframe of the CH-47C/D with new features such as wide-chord glassfibre rotor blades, revised fuselage side fairings, a longer nose with weather radar, and relocation further forward of the two front units of the quadricycle landing gear. The two versions planned were the long-range Model 234 LR and the utility Model 234 UT, the latter without side fairings and with two internal fuel tanks to allow operation with 24 passengers or a single-point slung load of 12701 kg (28,000 lb). To date, only the Model 234 LR has been placed in service.

Specification: Boeing Model 234 LR Commercial Chinook medium/heavy utility and transport helicopter
Rotor diameter, each: 18.29 m (60 ft 0 in)
Overall length, rotors turning: 30.18 m (99 ft 0 in)
Powerplant: 2×Avco Lycoming AL 5512, 3039 kW (4,075 shp) each
Payload: pilot and co-pilot plus 44 passengers or freight carried internally, or a 12701-kg (28,000 lb) slung load
Max T/O weight: 22226 kg (49,000 lb)
Cruising speed: 167 mph at 2,000 ft
Operational range: 661 miles

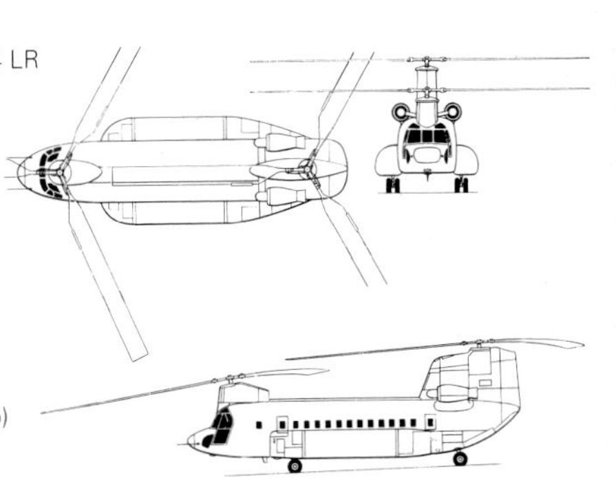

Chapter 9

EXPERIMENTAL AIRCRAFT

North American X-15

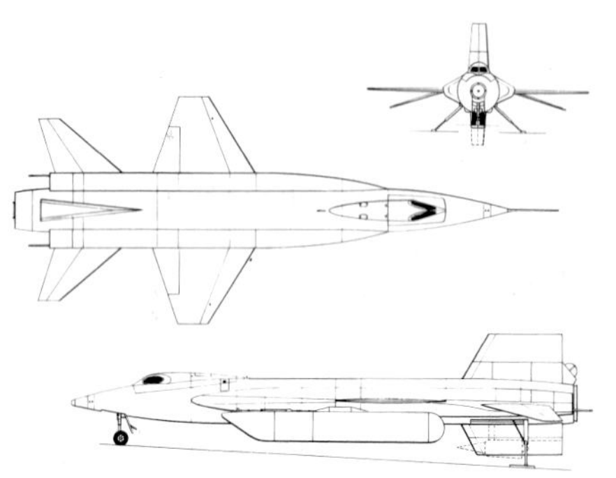

Specification: North American X-15A-2 single-seat hypersonic high-altitude research aeroplane
Span: 6.70 m (22 ft 0 in)
Length: 15.98 m (52 ft 5 in)
Powerplant: 1×Thiokol (Reaction Motors) XLR99-RM-2, 25855 kg (57,000 lb) st at 45,000 ft
Max T/O weight: 25461 kg (56,130 lb)
Max speed: 4,534 mph at high altitude
Operational range: 275 miles

Though the X-15 flew in powered mode as long ago as September 1959, it is not likely that any other aeroplane will ever surpass it for speed and altitude. The type was planned within the US programme to investigate heat, stability and control problems with re-entry vehicles and was thus a winged stainless-steel and titanium vehicle launched from a motherplane before igniting its rocket for climb to extreme altitude (354,200 ft being attained by the X-15A-2) and speed; reaction control jets were provided for control at these extreme altitudes, for which the pilot wore a spacesuit. Three X-15s were built, and completed 199 flights in their basic and advanced X-15A-2 forms, the latter having additional fuel in two jettisonable underfuselage tanks and a revised nose later coated with Emerson Electric T-500 ablative material. One X-15 and the X-15A-2 survived to the end of the programme in November 1968.

The second X-15 is seen after its rebuild to X-15A-2 configuration, with lengthened fuselage and strap-on external fuel tanks.

Bell X-1

The X-1 was designed for the investigation of supersonic flight, and three of the type were ordered. The airframe was based on a tapered bullet-shaped fuselage with unswept mid-set wings and an empennage with the straight tailplane set slightly up the fin. The X-1 had a bi-propellant rocket, but its first flights in January 1946 were glides after release from a B-29. The initial powered flight was achieved in December 1946, and in October 1947, with 'Chuck' Yeager at the controls, the type became the first to fly faster than sound. One machine was destroyed before making a powered flight, and the other two completed 156 flights. Second-generation improved X-1s were the single X-1A, X-1B and X-1D with pump- rather than pressure-driven fuel systems, and were used for high-altitude/high-speed research. The X-1E was the second X-1 fitted with thin wings, turbo-pumps and a knife-edge windscreen.

Specification: Bell X-1 single-seat supersonic research aeroplane
Span: 8.53 m (28 ft 0 in)
Length: 9.45 m (31 ft 0 in)
Powerplant: 1×Reaction Motors E6000-C4 (Thiokol XLR11), 2722 kg (6,000 lb) st
Max T/O weight: 6078 kg (13,400 lb)
Max speed: Mach 1.47 at high altitude
Powered endurance: 5 minutes at full power

Northrop X-4

The X-4 was planned for the investigation of the flight characteristics and stability of the tailless swept-wing configuration at subsonic speeds, and for this layout Northrop was the obvious choice. The X-4, whose diminutive size earned it the nickname 'Bantam', had retractable tricycle landing gear, a pilot's ejector seat under a manually operated canopy, wings swept at 41°33' on a short fuselage terminating in a swept fin/rudder assembly, and two turbojet engines buried in the wing roots. Two aircraft were built, the first flying in December 1948. The test programme was conducted under the auspices of NACA and included about 60 flights before the aircraft were retired in 1954. The programme yielded invaluable data about the pitch instability of swept-wing tailless aircraft as they approached the transonic region.

Specification: Northrop X-4 single-seat tailless subsonic research aeroplane
Span: 8.18 m (26 ft 10 in)
Length: 7.10 m (23 ft 3 in)
Powerplant: 2×Westinghouse J30-WE-9, 726 kg (1,600 lb) st each
Max T/O weight: 3547 kg (7,820 lb)
Max speed: Mach 0.89 at 30,000 ft
Operational range: 420 miles

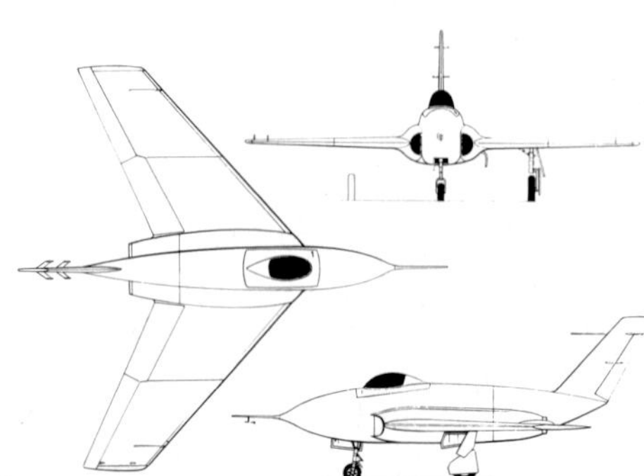

Bell X-5

'he X-5 was designed to investigate the aerodynamic consequences of altering a wing's weep in flight. The configuration was derived from that of the Messerschmitt P.1011, whose ground-adjustable swept wings Bell engineers studied closely in the USA after the 'elivery of a captured airframe. A pod-and-boom fuselage with swept tail surfaces was dopted, and the wings could be mechanically swept between a forward position of 20° to n aft position of 60°, and translated fore-and-aft to maintain the centre of gravity; there was lso a special fairing at each root to ensure that a smooth airflow was maintained at the eading and trailing edges. Two aircraft were built, and the first of these flew in June 1951.)ne aeroplane was lost in October 1953, and the other completed a valuable flight-test rogramme before being retired in late 1955.

Specification: Bell X-5 single-eat variable-geometry research eroplane
Span: 10.21 m (33 ft 6 in) spread nd 6.32 m (20 ft 9 in) swept
ength: 10.16 m (33 ft 4 in)
'owerplant: 1×Allison J35-A-17, '222 kg (4,900 lb) st
Max T/O weight: 4479 kg),875 lb)
Max speed: 705 mph at high ltitude
)perational range: 750 miles

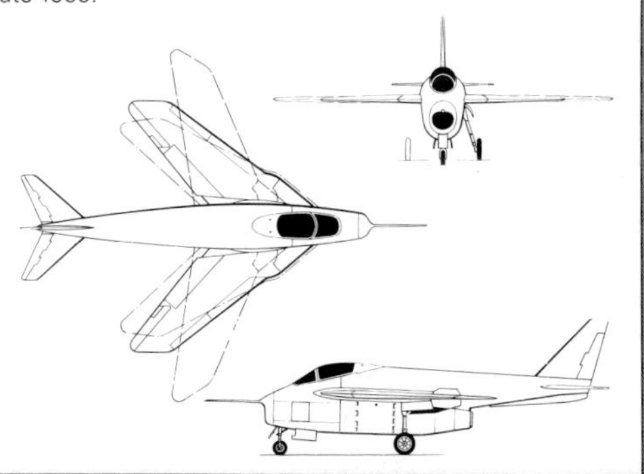

Douglas X-3

The X-3 was designed for the investigation of the efficiency of turbojet power and short-span double-wedge flying surfaces, and of thermodynamic heating at speeds up to Mach 3. This resulted in an extraordinary airframe with a very long fuselage and diminutive flying surfaces including 850 pressure, 150 temperature and 185 strain measurement points. Manufacture began in 1949, but because of difficulties with this early use of titanium it was October 1952 before the type first flew. Delays were also occasioned by the non-availability of the proposed 2994-kg (6,600-lb) thrust Westinghouse J46 turbojets, and the aeroplane was eventually flown with lower-rated but dimensionally similar J34s. This severely curtailed the flight performance, but valuable data was nonetheless recorded in the course of 20 flights for NACA before the aeroplane was retired in May 1956.

Specification: Douglas X-3 single-seat 'supersonic' research aeroplane
Span: 6.91 m (22 ft 8.25 in)
Length: 20.35 m (66 ft 9 in)
Powerplant: 2×Westinghouse J34-WE-17, 1905 kg (4,200 lb) st each
Max T/O weight: 10025 kg (22,100 lb)
Max speed: Mach 0.95 at high altitude
Operational range: 500 miles

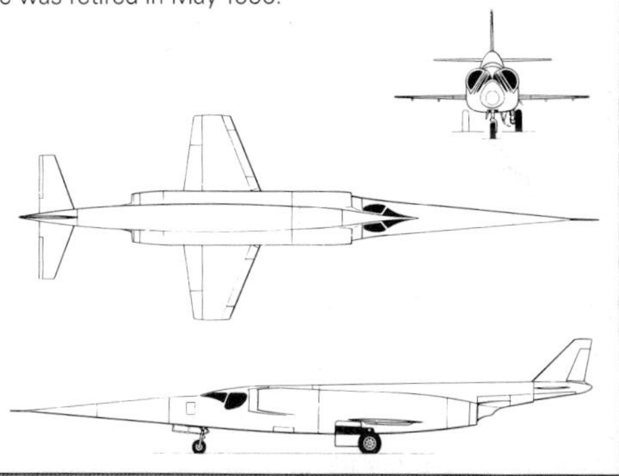

Grumman X-29A

The X-29A was developed to demonstrate the technological feasibility of a forward-swept wing, a planform with advantages such as reduced stalling speed, improved manoeuvrability and elimination of the spin tendency. With the advent of modern composite materials it became possible to create such a wing without the likelihood of aero-elastic deformation at high air speeds, and the X-29A uses such wings mounted towards the rear of a fuselage based on the forward section of the Northrop F-5's body and fitted with all-moving canard foreplanes in the close-coupled position on the sides of the inlets' trunks. The type first flew in December 1984 and completely validated the concept, and with the advent of the second aeroplane in the late 1980s the USA is exploring the flight envelope of this fascinating aeroplane at angles of attack that were up to this time impossibly high.

Specification: Grumman X-29A single-seat forward-swept wing research aeroplane
Span: 8.29 m (27 ft 2.4 in)
Length: 14.66 m (48 ft 1 in) excluding probe
Powerplant: 1×General Electric F404-GE-400, 7258 kg (16,000 lb) st
Max T/O weight: 7848 kg (17,303 lb)
Max speed: Mach 1.6 at high altitude
Operational range: not revealed

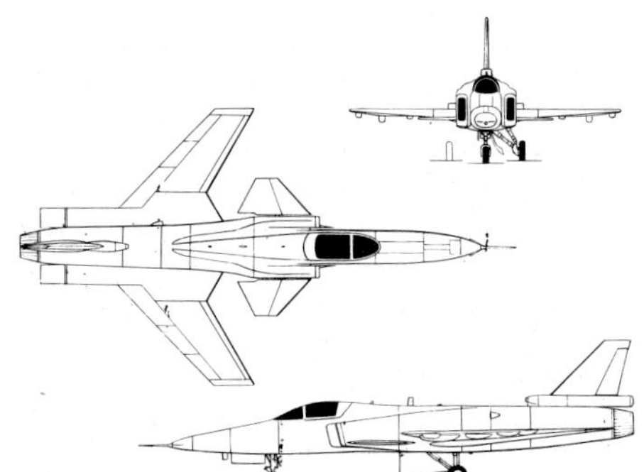

The first Grumman X-29A Forward Swept Wing Demonstrator has now been joined by a second prototype for exploration of high angle of attack handling. The first X-29A made its maiden flight on 14 December 1984, and has now made more than 200 flights.

Bell X-2

The X-2 was planned as successor to the X-1 series in the investigation of supersonic flight, and was fitted with swept flying surfaces, a throttlable rocket and mixed landing gear with a nosewheel and two skids. Two aircraft were built, the first making three glide flights before being lost in May 1954 when it was jettisoned after an explosion in the motherplane. The other machine made its first glide flight in August 1954 and its initial powered flight in November 1955, and in the course of exploring an extensive flight envelope attained an altitude of 126,200 ft in September 1956. The aeroplane was lost in a landing accident later in the same month after a flight in which a speed of just under Mach 3.2 had been recorded. The whole programme managed only 20 flights, but these were invaluable in the development of supersonic military aircraft.

Specification: Bell X-2 single-seat supersonic research aeroplane
Span: 9.83 m (32 ft 3 in)
Length: 13.84 m (45 ft 5 in)
Powerplant: 1×Curtiss-Wright XLR25-CW-1, 6804 kg (15,000 lb) st
Max T/O weight: 11299 kg (24,910 lb)
Max speed: Mach 3.196 at high altitude
Powered endurance: 10 minutes 55 seconds

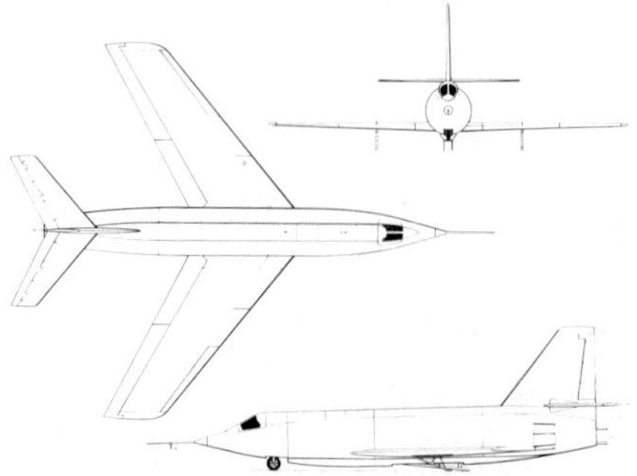

Ryan X-13 Vertijet

Ryan began investigation of a tail-sitting VTOL aeroplane in 1947, and after successful evaluation of two J33-powered test rigs, the company was contracted to build the X-13. The type had a large delta wing with small tip fins to complement the large central surface. It first flew in December 1955 as a conventional landplane with temporary fixed landing gear, but by 1956 had progressed to vertical take-offs and simulated landings by the engagement of the undernose hook on a horizontal nylon rope. VTOL control was effected by thrust deflection and thrust variation, while conventional surfaces were provided for wingborne flight. As part of a full test programme the aeroplane made its first full translational flight (from VTO to wingborne flight and back again to vertical landing) in April 1957. Both aircraft have been preserved.

Specification: Ryan X-13 Vertijet single-seat tail-sitting VTOL research aeroplane
Span: 6.40 m (21 ft 0 in)
Length: 7.14 m (23 ft 5 in)
Powerplant: 1×Rolls-Royce Avon RA.29 Mk 49, 4534 kg (10,000 lb) st
Max T/O weight: 3317 kg (7,313 lb)
Max speed: 483 mph at optimum altitude
Operational range: 192 miles

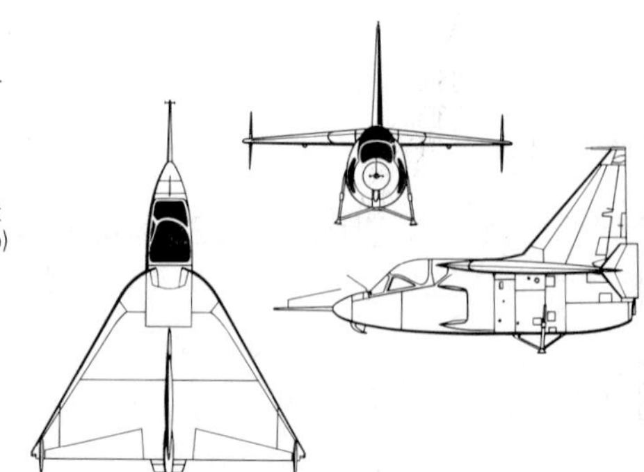

Bell X-14

The X-14 was conceived as a research tool for the evaluation of jet-deflection for VTOL applications. The type was intended only for low-speed trials, and therefore designed with an open cockpit and fixed tricycle landing gear. The Viper turbojets were located side-by-side in the nose, and simple deflectors on the centre of gravity were used to divert their exhausts 90° downward for VTO; the exhausts were then angled increasingly backward to provide a forward thrust component and thus allow translation into wingborne flight. Compressed-air nozzles at the wingtips and tail were used for control at zero and low speeds. The type first flew in February 1957 in the hovering mode, and completed its first transition to wingborne flight in May 1958. The Vipers were later replaced by 1216-kg (2,680-lb) thrust General Electric J85-GE-5s when the type was shifted from the USAF to NASA in 1969.

Specification: Bell X-14 single-seat thrust-vectoring VTOL research aeroplane
Span: 10.36m (34ft 0in)
Length: 7.62m (25ft 0in)
Powerplant: 2×Armstrong Siddeley ASV.8 Viper, 794kg (1,750lb) st each
Max T/O weight: 1936kg (4,269lb) with J85 turbojets
Max speed: 172 mph at low altitude with J85 turbojets
Operational range: 300 miles

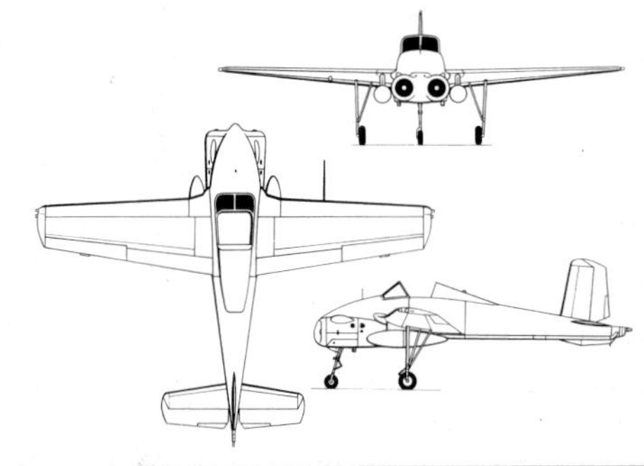

Hiller X-18

This was one of the real pioneers amongst full-size convertiplane prototypes, and was based on a large number of existing components including the fuselage of the Chase YC-122 transport and the engine/contra-rotating propeller assembly of the US Navy's 'tail-sitter' VTOL programme aircraft. The wing was designed to tilt through 90° between vertical for take-off and horizontal for wing-borne flight, while in hovering and translational flight, control of pitch was effected by a tail-mounted gas diverter using the efflux of a J34 turbojet in the rear fuselage. The development contract was let in February 1957, and the type first flew as a conventional aeroplane in November 1959. The X-18 explored the envelope at angles of attack up to +50°, and as such contributed significantly to the development of the Vought-Hiller-Ryan XC-142A convertiplane.

Specification: Hiller X-18 two/three-seat convertiplane research aeroplane
Propeller/rotor diameter, each: 4.88m (16ft 0in)
Span: 14.63m (48ft 0in)
Length: 19.20m (63ft 0in)
Powerplant: 2×Allison T40-A-14, 4362kW (5,850 ehp) each, and 1×Westinghouse J34, 1542kg (3,400lb) st
Max T/O weight: 14969kg (33,000lb)
Max speed: 250 mph at optimum altitude
Operational range: not revealed

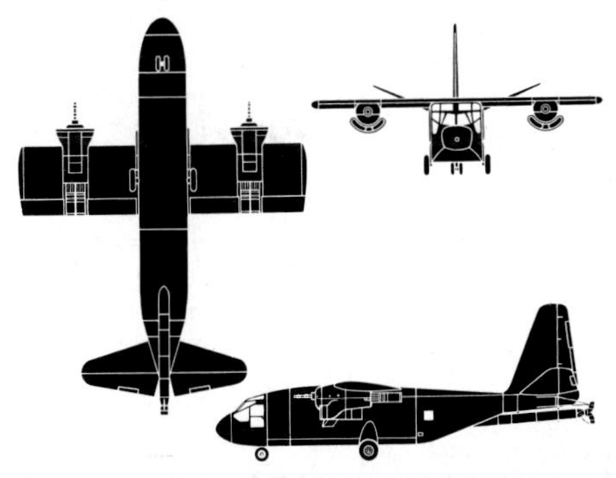

Curtiss-Wright X-19A

The X-100 first flew in March 1960 as part of the manufacturer's investigation of the 'radial lift force' effect, in which the propellers of a convertiplane continue to deliver lift even when swivelled to the forward position, thereby allowing the use of very small wings. The X-100's single 615-kW (825-shp) Avco Lycoming YT53-L-1 turboshaft drove two 3.05-m (10-ft) diameter propellers/rotors with the efflux exhausted through tail nozzles for low-speed pitch and yaw control. The success of the X-100 paved the way for the considerably more refined X-200, of which two were ordered by the USAF with the designation X-19A. This was configured as a four-propeller/rotor executive transport, and first flew in November 1963. The type proved to possess considerable potential, but the programme was cancelled after the loss of the first prototype and before full transitions had been tried.

Specification: Curtiss-Wright X-19A two-crew convertiplane transport prototype/research aeroplane
Propeller/rotor diameter, each: 3.96 m (13 ft 0 in)
Span: 5.94 m (19 ft 6 in) for front wing and 6.55 m (21 ft 6 in) for rear wing
Length: 12.83 m (42 ft 1 in)
Powerplant: 2×Avco Lycoming T55-L-5, 1640 kW (2,200 shp) each
Payload: six passengers or 454 kg (1,000 lb) of freight carried internally
Max T/O weight: 6196 kg (13,660 lb)
Max speed: 454 mph at optimum altitude
Operational range: 325 miles

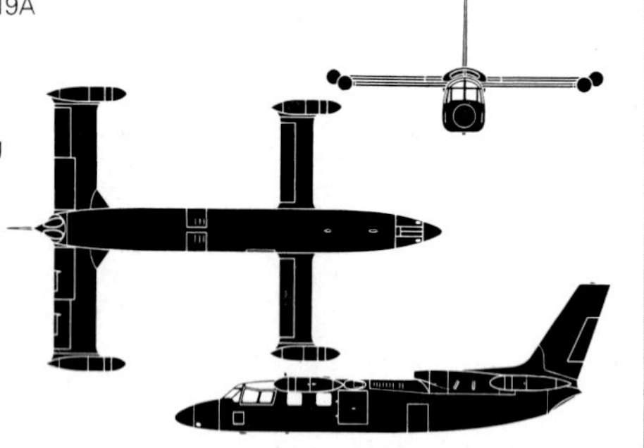

Northrop X-21A

The X-21A was planned as part of the US Air Force's programme to use control of the boundary layer of air flowing round a wing for the reduction of drag, and thus the enhancement of range, on large aircraft. The two X-21As were conversions of WB-66D weather research aircraft. The engines were shifted to pylon-mounted positions in the rear fuselage, and the new aluminium alloy/honeycomb wing had some 5177 m (16,986 ft) of suction slots cut into it. These slots varied in width from 0.0076 to 0.025 cm (0.003 to 0.01 in), and allowed air to be sucked into the wing by an AiResearch pump, compressed and then exhausted via two wing-mounted nozzles to provide additional thrust. The first aeroplane flew in April 1963, and though excellent results were achieved the programme was terminated because of the apparently insoluble problem of keeping clean the suction slots of any service type.

Specification: Northrop X-21A three-seat boundary-layer control research aeroplane
Span: 28.50 m (93 ft 6 in)
Length: 23.01 m (75 ft 6 in)
Powerplant: 2×General Electric J79-GE-13, 4264 kg (9,400 lb) each
Max T/O weight: 37649 kg (83,000 lb)
Max speed: 560 mph at high altitude
Operational range: 4,780 miles

Bell X-22A

This joint-service research aeroplane was sponsored by the US Navy to investigate the feasibility of an arrangement of four tilting ducts. The type was developed as the D2127 light transport and ordered in November 1964. The four engines were located in pairs on the leading edges of the aft wing, and control was effected by modulation of each duct's thrust through propeller pitch change, and by the elevon located in the slipstream of each duct. The first X-22A flew in March 1966 and proved a workable machine until its accidental loss in August of the same year. The second machine expanded the flight envelope, and proved successful especially when fitted in the spring of 1968 with the variable stability system designed by Cornell Aeronautical Laboratory. After evaluation by the US services the X-22A was handed over to Cornell as a research tool.

Specification: Bell X-22A two-crew convertiplane transport prototype/research aeroplane
Internal duct diameter: 2.13 m (7 ft 0 in)
Span: 7.01 m (23 ft 0 in) across front ducts and 11.96 m (39 ft 3 in) across rear ducts
Length: 12.04 m (39 ft 6 in)
Powerplant: 4×General Electric YT58-GE-8D, 932 kW (1,250 shp) each
Payload: passengers or 544 kg (1,200 lb) of freight carried internally
Max T/O weight: 7600 kg (16,755 lb)
Max speed: 255 mph at optimum altitude
Operational range: 445 miles

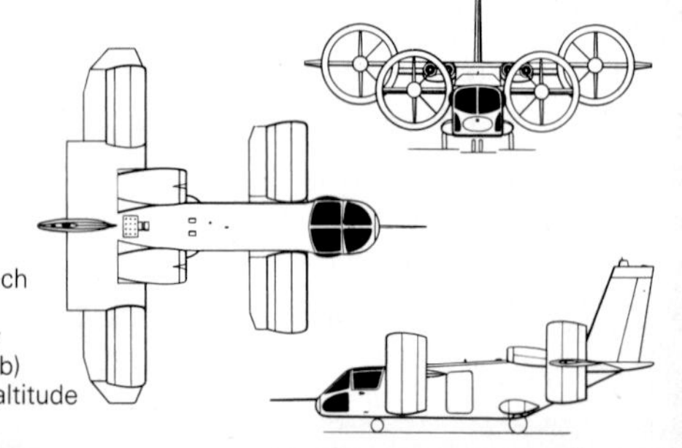

Martin Marietta X-24

The X-24 was produced to investigate the flight and manoeuvring capabilities of a lifting-body vehicle. The type was initially developed as the single X-24A, a machine of triangular basic planform with flattened under- and curved upper-surfaces terminating at the rear in triple fin/rudder assemblies whose outer units could be considered almost vertically upturned wings. Power was provided by a 3629-kg (8,000-lb) thrust XLR11 rocket. The type made its first rocket-powered flight in March 1970 after release from a B-52 motherplane, and made a total of 28 flights before it was extensively remodelled as the dart-shaped X-24B. In this form the aeroplane first flew in August 1973, making 10 glide and 26 powered flights before the programme ended in November 1975. The X-24 was invaluable in the research that has fully validated the concept of lifting-body vehicles.

Specification: Martin Marietta X-24B single-seat supersonic lifting-body vehicle research aeroplane
Span: 5.84 m (19 ft 2 in)
Length: 11.43 m (37 ft 6 in)
Powerplant: 1×Thiokol XLR11, 3629 kg (8,000 lb) st
Max T/O weight: 5896 kg (13,000 lb)
Max speed: Mach 1.76 at high altitude
Powered endurance: 15 minutes

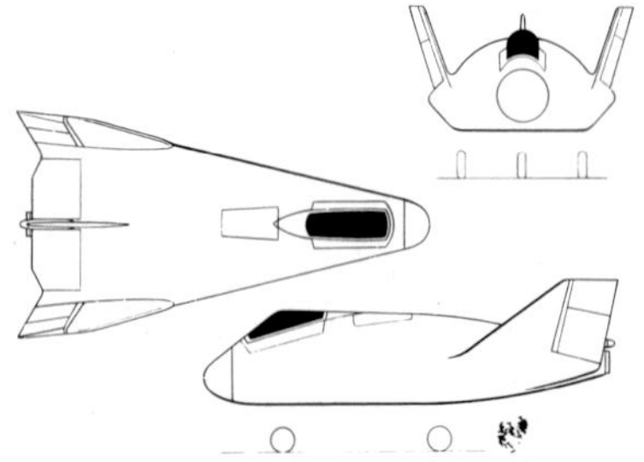

Vought-Hiller-Ryan XC-142A

This ambitious design was planned as a tactical transport using the technology pioneered in the X-18, retaining the same tilt-wing layout but in this instance with a four-engined powerplant and hover/translation pitch control provided by a small vertical-axis propeller at the extreme tail. The design was sponsored by the three primary US services, and first flew in September 1964 as a conventional aeroplane, the rectangular-section fuselage and tricycle landing gear (with its main units retracting into fuselage side blisters) indicating its proposed transport role. The five prototypes did much to validate the convertiplane concept in a number of tactical roles, but no production was ordered despite the promise of a growth project with 2535-kW (3,400-shp) T64-GE-S4A turboshafts for a maximum take-off weight of 21274 kg (46,900 lb).

Specification: Vought-Hiller-Ryan XC-142A two/three-crew convertiplane tactical transport prototype
Span: 20.57 m (67 ft 6 in)
Length: 17.71 m (58 ft 1.25 in)
Powerplant: 4×General Electric T64-GE-1, 2125 kW (2,850 shp) each
Payload: 32 troops or 3629 kg (8,000 lb) of freight carried internally for VTO; or 32 troops or 5443 kg (12,000 lb) of freight carried internally for STO
Max T/O weight: 16998 kg (37,474 lb)
Max speed: 430 mph at 20,000 ft
Operational range: 460 miles with VTO payload or 690 miles with STO payload

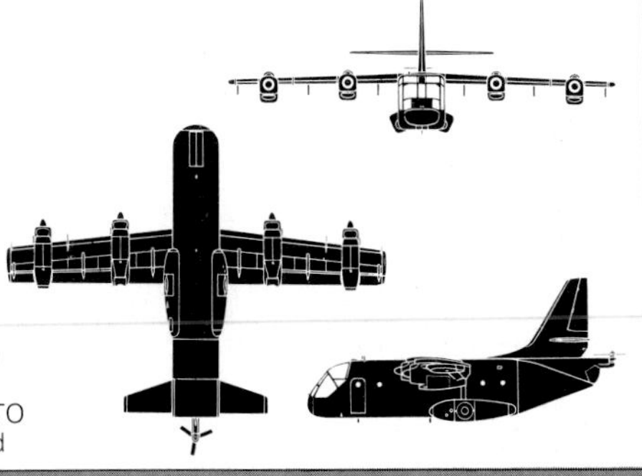

Bell X-22A

This joint-service research platform was sponsored by the US Navy to investigate the feasibility of an arrangement of four tilting ducts. The type was developed as the D2127 light transport and ordered in November 1964. The four engines were located in pairs on the leading edges of the aft wing, and control was effected by modulation of each duct's thrust through propeller pitch change, and by the elevon located in the slipstream of each duct. The first X-22A flew in March 1966 and proved a workable machine until its accidental loss in August of the same year. The second machine expanded the flight envelope, and proved successful especially when fitted in the spring of 1968 with the variable stability system designed by Cornell Aeronautical Laboratory. After evaluation by the US services, the X-22A was handed over to Cornell as a research tool.

Specification: Bell X-22A two-crew convertiplane transport prototype/research aeroplane
Internal duct diameter: 2.13 m (7 ft 0 in)
Span: 7.01 m (23 ft 0 in) across front ducts and 11.96 m (39 ft 3 in) across rear ducts
Length: 12.04 m (39 ft 6 in)
Powerplant: 4×General Electric YT58-GE-8D, 932 kW (1,250 shp) each
Payload: passengers or 544 kg (1,200 lb) of freight carried internally
Max T/O weight: 7600 kg (16,755 lb)
Max speed: 255 mph at optimum altitude
Operational range: 445 miles

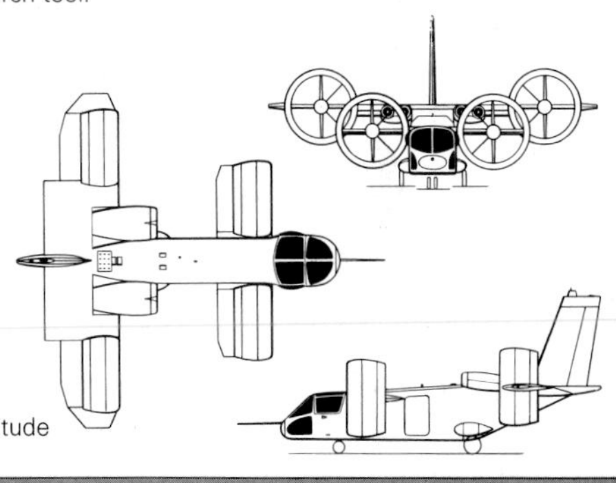

Nord 500

This aeroplane was produced as part of the French convertiplane programme, its specific remit being the investigation of the tilting-duct concept. Making its first tethered flight in July 1968, the Nord 500 had two five-blade fans enclosed in ducts at the tips of the stub wings that rotated with the ducts outboard of a short-span fixed section attached to the fuselage. An interconnected shaft arrangement transmitted power from the two fuselage-mounted engines, and each duct was provided with extensive trailing-edge control surfaces. Differential thrust and tilt were used for control and yaw control, with collective tilt for pitch control. The first prototype was used only for hover and transition trials, and the programme was cancelled before full flight trials could be attempted with an upgraded version powered by a 276-kW (370-shp) Allison 250-C20 turboshaft.

Specification: Nord 500 single-seat convertiplane research aeroplane
Internal duct diameter: 1.58 m (5 ft 2 in)
Span: 6.14 m (20 ft 1.5 in) over ducts
Length: 6.58 m (21 ft 7 in)
Powerplant: 2×Allison 250-C18, 236 kW (317 shp) each:
Max T/O weight: 1250 kg (2,756 lb)
Max speed: 217 mph at optimum altitude with fully developed ducts
Operational range: not revealed

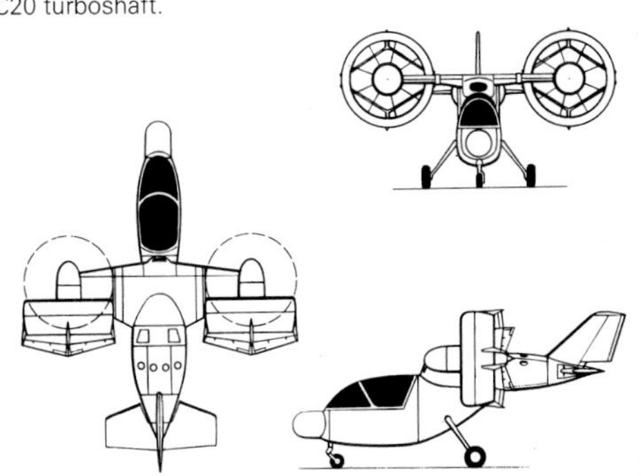

Bell XV-15

Developed as the Model 301, the XV-15 resulted from a joint US Army and NASA contract to develop a production-standard tilt-rotor convertiplane based on a conventional fuselage with retractable landing gear. The XV-15 had an empennage with twin vertical surfaces, and a cantilever wing tipped by the rotating nacelles each housing a turboshaft engine that drove a large propeller/rotor unit. The wings also incorporated flaps/ailerons and flaps, and an advanced feature was the stability and control augmentation system. Two examples were built, the first making an initial hovering flight in May 1977, and the second completing the type's first full translation in July 1979. Both aircraft contributed very significantly to the USA's tilt-rotor research programme, and thus paved the way for the V-22 Osprey.

Specification: Bell XV-15 two-seat tilt-rotor research aeroplane
Propeller/rotor diameter, each: 7.62 m (25 ft 0 in)
Span: 17.42 m (57 ft 2 in) with rotors turning
Length: 12.83 m (42 ft 1 in)
Powerplant: 2×Avco Lycoming LTC1K-4K, 1156 kW (1,550 shp) each
Max T/O weight: 5897 kg (13,000 lb)
Max speed: 346 mph at optimum altitude
Operational range: 500 miles

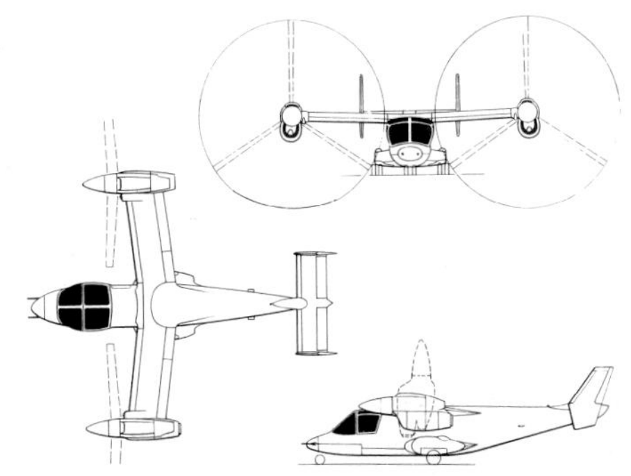

Bell/Boeing V-22 Osprey

After decades of experimentation, it seems that the first operational convertiplane will be the V-22. Working on the basis of the XV-15 prototype, Bell teamed with Boeing to offer a proposal to meet the Joint Services Advanced Vertical Lift Aircraft requirement. This was selected for prototype construction in April 1983, and the first machine flew in 1989. Several hundreds of the type may be built for the US forces, of whom the Marine Corps will hope to be the main operator of the type as the MV-22 assault transport for troops and/or freight in a hold accessed by a rear ramp/door; other versions are the USAF's CV-22A special operations and US Navy's HV-22A combat SAR variants. A key feature of the design is the mechanical cross-linking of the engines, which allows a single swivelling engine unit to drive both propellers/rotors in the event of an engine failure.

Bell XV-3

Developed as the Model 200, this was one of the USA's first convertiplanes, and was developed by Bell with the USAF Research and Development Command as a result of a 1951 contract from the USAF and US Army. Though perched on twin-skid landing gear, the XV-3 had the appearance of a conventional aeroplane apart from its use of a swivelling propeller/rotor unit at each wing tip. These were originally of the three-blade articulated type, though two-blade semi-rigid units were fitted in 1957; power was provided by a single piston engine buried in the fuselage. The first XV-3 first flew in August 1955 and made partial translations before being heavily damaged. The second aeroplane achieved the first full translation in December 1958, becoming the first convertiplane in the world to achieve this feat. The type completed more than 250 flights and 125 flying hours.

Specification: Bell XV-3 four-seat convertiplane research aeroplane
Propeller/rotor diameter, each: 10.06m (33ft 0in)
Span: 9.54m (31ft 3.5in)
Length: 9.23m (30ft 3.5in)
Powerplant: 1×Pratt & Whitney R-985-AN-3, 336kW (450 hp)
Max T/O weight: 2177kg (4,800lb)
Max speed: 181 mph at optimum altitude
Operational range: not revealed

Vertol VZ-2A

This was one of the USA's first convertiplanes, designed by Vertol to a 1956 contract from the US Army and US Navy. The Model 76 design was essentially a test rig to validate the convertiplane concept, and in addition to the tilting wing/propeller combination had two ducted fans located horizontally and vertically at the tail for control and stability augmentation in hovering, translational and low-speed flight. And as the wing tilted downward during translation to wing-borne flight the propellers/rotors' differential collective-pitch system was phased out as the ailerons began to become effective. The VZ-2A first flew in August 1957, and several hundreds of successful flights were undertaken before the aeroplane was passed to NASA with an upgraded transmission and features to improve the type's stability and control in the descent.

Specification: Vertol VZ-2A two-seat convertiplane research aeroplane
Propeller/rotor diameter, each: 2.90m (9ft 6in)
Span: 7.59m (24ft 11in)
Length: 8.05m (26ft 5in)
Powerplant: 1×Avco Lycoming YT53-L-1, 641kW (860shp)
Max T/O weight: not revealed
Max speed: not revealed
Operational range: not revealed

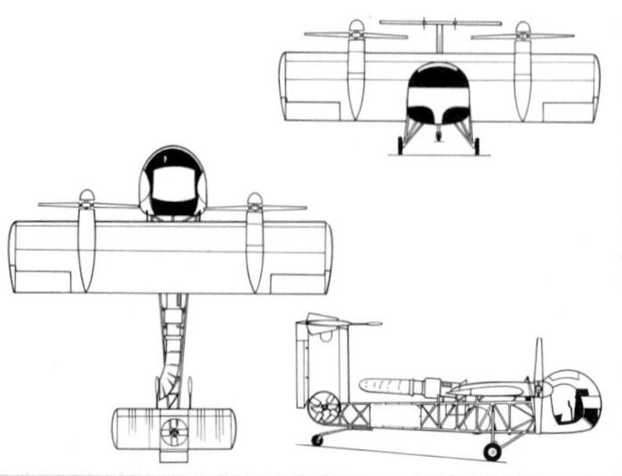

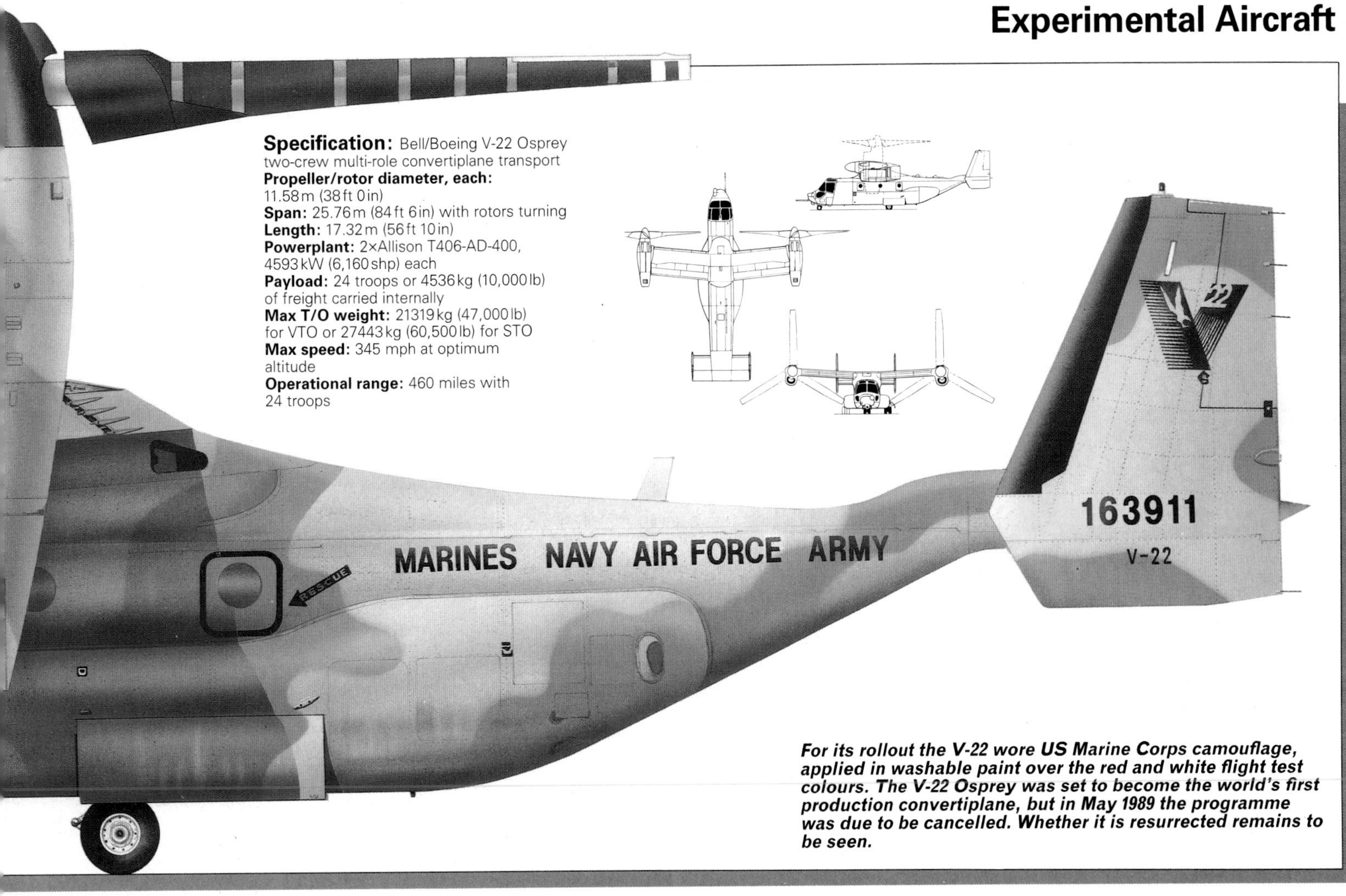

Specification: Bell/Boeing V-22 Osprey
two-crew multi-role convertiplane transport
Propeller/rotor diameter, each: 11.58 m (38 ft 0 in)
Span: 25.76 m (84 ft 6 in) with rotors turning
Length: 17.32 m (56 ft 10 in)
Powerplant: 2×Allison T406-AD-400, 4593 kW (6,160 shp) each
Payload: 24 troops or 4536 kg (10,000 lb) of freight carried internally
Max T/O weight: 21319 kg (47,000 lb) for VTO or 27443 kg (60,500 lb) for STO
Max speed: 345 mph at optimum altitude
Operational range: 460 miles with 24 troops

For its rollout the V-22 wore US Marine Corps camouflage, applied in washable paint over the red and white flight test colours. The V-22 Osprey was set to become the world's first production convertiplane, but in May 1989 the programme was due to be cancelled. Whether it is resurrected remains to be seen.

Doak VZ-4DA

The VZ-4DA was a simple research platform into the behaviour of ducted propellers for VTOL purposes, and the single Model 16 aeroplane was produced under US Army contract. The two ducted propellers were located at the tips of the wings, and could be turned through 90° between the horizontal and the vertical: each duct contained 14 glassfibre inlet vanes, a propeller with eight stainless steel blades, and nine stator blades behind the propeller. Both propellers were driven by a single turboshaft buried in the fuselage aft of the cockpit, and the turbine's exhaust was piped to the tail where it could be diverted by horizontal and vertical vanes of stainless steel to provide control in hovering and translational flight. The type first flew in February 1958, and proved a remarkably stable flying machine without any artificial aids.

Specification: Doak VZ-4DA
single-seat convertiplane research aeroplane
Span: 7.77 m (25 ft 6 in) over ducts
Length: 9.75 m (32 ft 0 in)
Powerplant: 1×Avco Lycoming YT53, 626 kW (840 shp)
Max T/O weight: 1452 kg (3,200 lb)
Max speed: 230 mph at sea level
Operational range: 230 miles

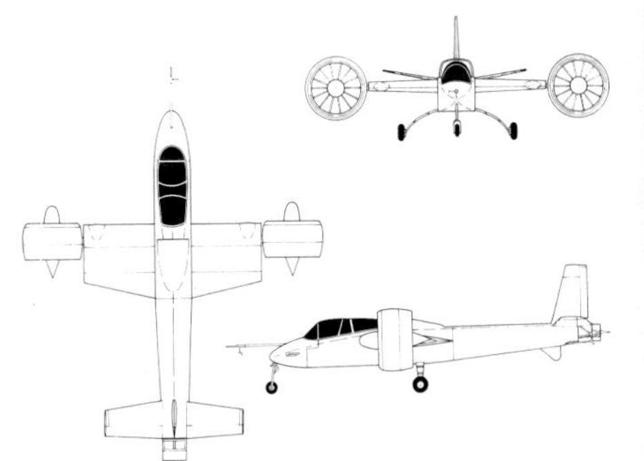

Dornier Do 29

Given its experience with STOL aircraft such as the Do 27 and Do 28, Dornier was a natural choice to work with the Deutsche Versuchsanstalt fur Luftfahrt in the development of an experimental V/STOL aeroplane type, and the result was the Do 29 built to the extent of three aircraft. The type was based on the airframe of the Do 27 but with two wing-mounted piston engines driving opposite-rotating Hartzell three-blade pusher propellers via a gear arrangement that allowed the propellers to be swivelled down as far as -90° for an increasing component of vertical lift. As was standard in such convertiplanes, the pilot was located well forward in the nose on an ejector seat. The first Do 29 flew in December 1958, and the three aircraft generated a mass of invaluable data, thereby proving very useful in the development of vectored thrust for V/STOL applications.

Specification: Dornier Do 29
single-seat convertiplane research aeroplane
Span: 13.20 m (43 ft 4 in)
Length: 9.50 m (31 ft 2 in)
Powerplant: 2×Avco Lycoming GO-480-B1A6, 201 kW (27 hp) each
Max T/O weight: 2500 kg (5,511 lb)
Max speed: 180 mph at optimum altitude
Operational range: not revealed

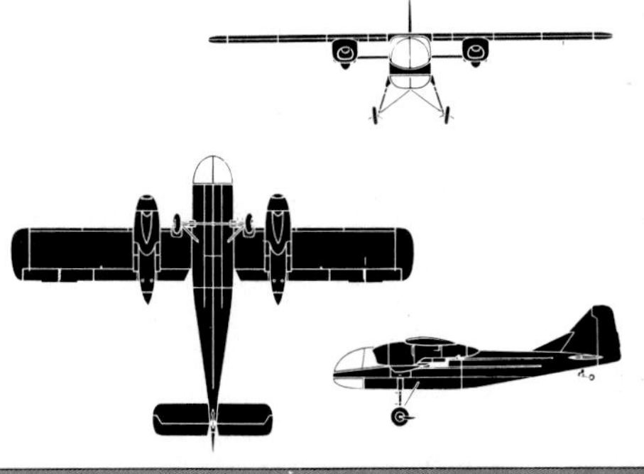

Canadair CL-84

Four examples of the CL-84 were built and conducted a successful flight test programme between 1965 and 1974, although plans for a production version came to nothing. The V-22 owes much to the pioneering work carried out by this Canadian machine.

Ryan VZ-3RY

Developed as the Model 76 Vertiplane, the VZ-3RY was a V/STOL aeroplane built for the US Army under the control of the Office of Naval Research. The type was very simple, with exceptionally stalky tricycle landing gear, an open cockpit, a shoulder-set wing with deep endplate surfaces and extensive double flaps extending behind and below the large-diameter propellers, spoilers instead of ailerons, a T-tail with variable-incidence tailplane, and at the tail a universally jointed jet efflux-deflection nozzle for control in the hover and translation. The VZ-3RY first flew in December 1958, and in trials proved capable of near-vertical take-off at 25 mph, hovering at zero ground speed, and transition to forward flight. The aeroplane was later handed over to NASA and played a significant part in the USA's extensive research in VTOL flight.

Specification: Ryan VZ-3RY single-seat V/STOL research aeroplane
Span: 7.14 m (23 ft 5 in)
Length: 8.43 m (27 ft 8 in)
Powerplant: 1×Avco Lycoming T53-L-1, 746 kW (1,000 shp)
Max T/O weight: about 1179 kg (2,600 lb)
Max speed: not revealed
Operational range: not revealed

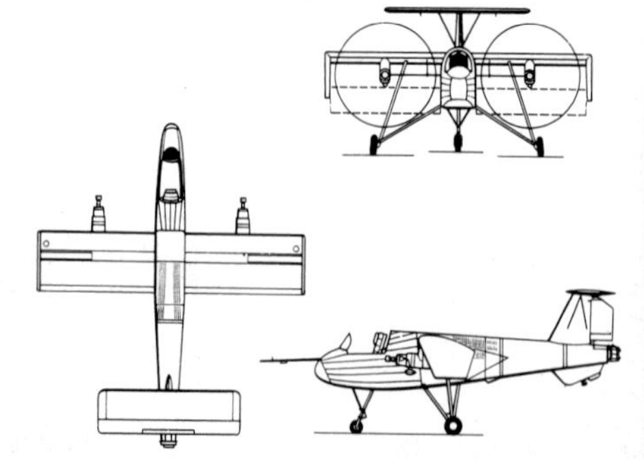

Hiller X-18

This was one of the real pioneers amongst full-size convertiplane prototypes, and was based on a large number of existing components including the fuselage of the Chase YC-122 transport and the engine/contra-rotating propeller assembly of the US Navy's 'tail-sitter' VTOL programme aircraft. The wing was designed to tilt through 90° between vertical for take-off and horizontal for wing-borne flight, while control of pitch was effected in hovering and translational flight by a tail-mounted gas diverter using the efflux of a J34 turbojet in the rear fuselage. The development contract was let in February 1957, and the type first flew as a conventional aeroplane in November 1959. The X-18 explored the envelope at angles of attack up to +50°, and as such contributed significantly to the development of the Vought-Hiller-Ryan XC-142A convertiplane.

Specification: Hiller X-18 two/three-seat convertiplane research aeroplane
Propeller/rotor diameter, each: 4.88 m (16 ft 0 in)
Span: 14.63 m (48 ft 0 in)
Length: 19.20 m (63 ft 0 in)
Powerplant: 2×Allison T40-A-14, 4362 kW (5,850 ehp) each, and 1×Westinghouse J34, 1542 kg (3,400 lb) st
Max T/O weight: 14969 kg (33,000 lb)
Max speed: 250 mph at optimum altitude
Operational range: not revealed

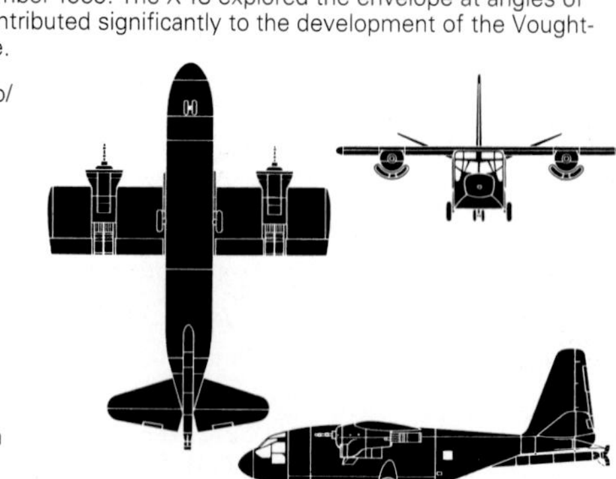

The CL-84 was an outstanding convertiplane research platform in which the whole wing pivoted to give the propellers/rotors a translation arc of +2° to +102°. In appearance the CL-84 was a conventional high-wing monoplane, and apart from the large diameter of the propellers/rotors the most unusual features were the short span of the wings and the contra-rotating horizontal propellers at the fuselage rear for pitch control and attitude stabilisation in the hover and translation. One CL-84 was built, first flying in May 1965 and being lost in September 1967. There followed three basically similar CL-84-1s with greater power and improved controls, and these fully confirmed the promise of the CL-84. Plans were made for upengined production versions in several passenger and/or freight configurations, but none of these came to fruition before the programme ended in 1974.

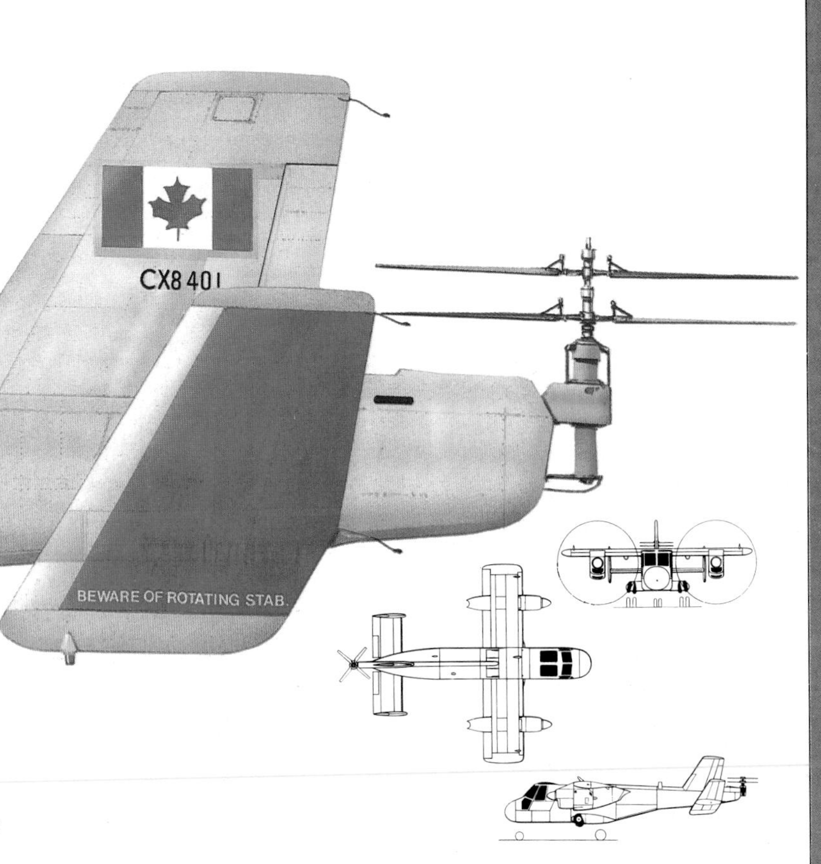

Specification: Canadair CL-84-1 two-seat multi-role convertiplane transport prototype
Propeller/rotor diameter, each: 4.30m (14ft 1.25in)
Span: 10.56m (34ft 8in)
Length: 16.34m (53ft 7.5in)
Powerplant: 2×Avco Lycoming T53, 1118kW (1,500shp) each
Payload: 1050kg (2,315lb) for VTO or 1912kg (4,215lb) for STO
Max T/O weight: 5715kg (12,600lb) for VTO or 6577kg (14,500lb) for STO
Max speed: 321 mph at optimum altitude
Operational range: 340 miles with maximum VTO payload

Kamov Ka-22 Vintokryl 'Hoop'

The first Soviet convertiplane was the Ka-22, known locally as the Vintokryl (screw wing), which made its first appearance at the annual Aviation Day display at Tushino in July 1961. The Ka 22 was powered by a pair of 5,622-hp Ivchenko TV-2 turboshafts, mounted on the wingtips and driving both conventional propellers for forward flight and four-bladed helicopter-type rotors for take-off, hovering and landing. The Ka-22 was assigned the reporting name 'Hoop' by NATO's Air Standards Co-ordinating Committee, but there is no evidence that it was ever intended to be anything but a research aircraft. During 1961 the aircraft established a number of FAI World Convertiplane Records, including a straight line speed of 192.39 knots and an altitude of 8,941 feet. These records still stand today, while the closed circuit speed record is still held by the British Fairey Rotodyne.

Specification: Kamov Ka-22 Vintokryl 'Hoop' 80-100 seat convertiplane research aircraft
Span: Approx 31m (103ft)
Rotor diameter: Approx 24m (79ft)
Powerplant: Two 5,622hp Ivchenko turboshaft engines
Max T/O weight: not revealed
Max speed: 192 knots
Operational range: not revealed

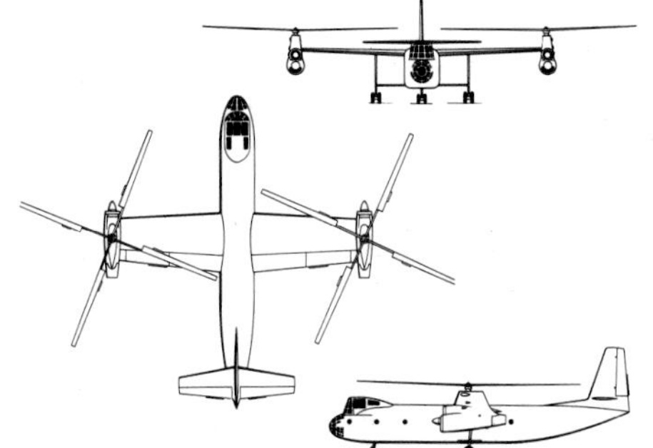

Curtiss-Wright X-19A

The X-100 first flew in March 1960 as part of the manufacturer's investigation of the 'radial lift force' effect, in which the propellers of a convertiplane continue to deliver lift even when swivelled to the forward position, thereby allowing the use of very small wings. The X-100's single 615-kW (825-shp) Avco Lycoming YT53-L-1 turboshaft drove two 3.05-m (10-ft) diameter propellers/rotors with the efflux exhausted through tail nozzles for low-speed pitch and yaw control. The success of the X-100 paved the way for the considerably more refined X-200, of which two were ordered by the USAF with the designation X-19A. This was configured as a four-propeller/rotor executive transport, and first flew in November 1963. The type proved to possess considerable potential, but the programme was cancelled after the loss of the first prototype and before full transitions had been tried.

Specification: Curtiss-Wright X-19A two-crew convertiplane transport prototype
Propeller/rotor diameter, each: 3.96m (13ft 0in)
Span: 5.94m (19ft 6in) for front wing and 6.55m (21ft 6in) for rear wing
Length: 12.83m (42ft 1in)
Powerplant: 2×Avco Lycoming T55-L-5, 1640kW (2,200shp) each
Payload: six passengers or 454kg (1,000lb) of freight carried internally
Max T/O weight: 6196kg (13,660lb)
Max speed: 454 mph at optimum altitude
Operational range: 325 miles

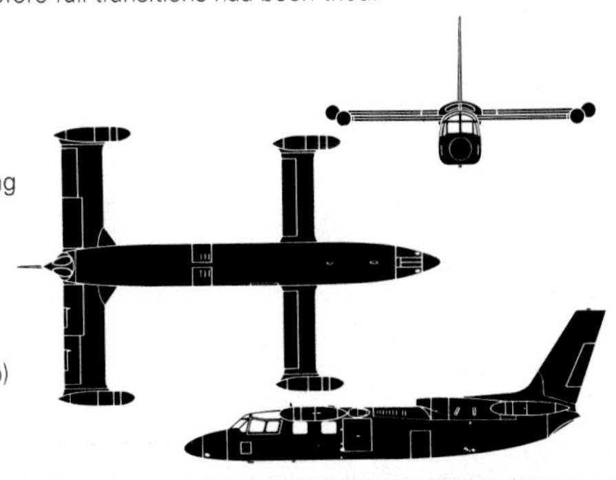

Hawker P.1127

This research type led directly to the world's first operational VTOL type, and is therefore of great historical importance. The type was planned round the four-poster lift arrangement of the Pegasus vectored-thrust turbofan, the diameter of this engine's fan dictating a portly fuselage accommodating the tandem main landing gear units (plus retractable wingtip stabilizer units). For obvious reasons the anhedralled wing had to be located above the four nozzles of the lift/propulsion system, and control in the hover was provided by reaction jets at the airframe extremities using air tapped from the engine. The type first flew in October 1960, and the two prototypes then undertook the complete testing of the hovering, translational and wingborne flight envelopes paving the way for the Kestrel evaluation and Harrier operational aircraft.

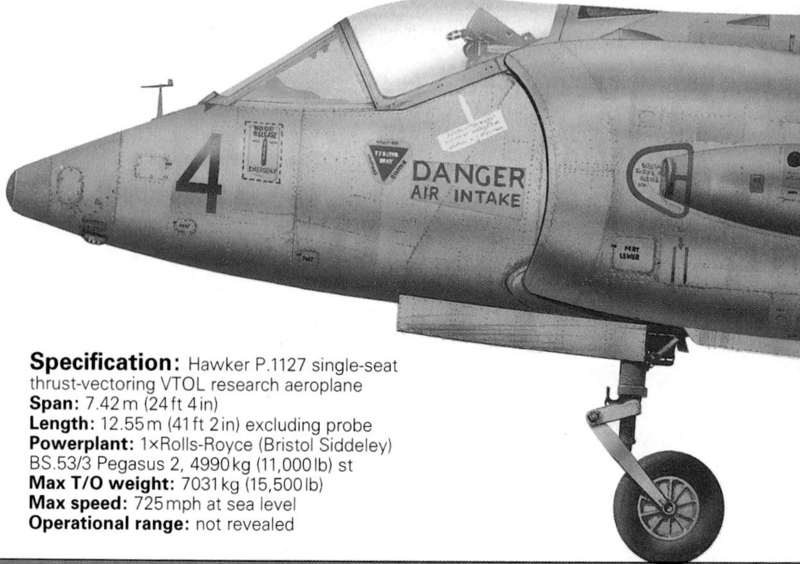

Specification: Hawker P.1127 single-seat thrust-vectoring VTOL research aeroplane
Span: 7.42 m (24 ft 4 in)
Length: 12.55 m (41 ft 2 in) excluding probe
Powerplant: 1×Rolls-Royce (Bristol Siddeley) BS.53/3 Pegasus 2, 4990 kg (11,000 lb) st
Max T/O weight: 7031 kg (15,500 lb)
Max speed: 725 mph at sea level
Operational range: not revealed

Lockheed XFV-1

Because of the nature of its operational role the US Navy has long been interested in the VTOL aeroplane, and in 1950 held a competition for a fighter of this type with conventional flight performance in no way significantly inferior to that of contemporary operational aircraft. One of the results was the XFV-1: the massive forward fuselage accommodated a turboprop driving a 4.88-m (16-ft) diameter Curtiss-Wright contra-rotating propeller unit, the pilot sat in a gimballed seat that allowed 45° of swivelling, and the long-chord wings were trailed by a cruciform empennage each of whose surfaces ended in a castoring tailwheel. For initial flight trials the aeroplane was fitted with stalky fixed landing gear of the conventional type, and flew in this form in March 1954. The programme was cancelled before vertical take-off had been attempted with the planned 5294-kW (7,100-ehp) T40-A-14 engine.

Specification: Lockheed XFV-1 single-seat tail-sitting VTOL experimental fighter prototype
Span: 9.40 m (30 ft 10.1 in) over tiptanks
Length: 11.23 m (36 ft 10.25 in)
Powerplant: 1×Allison YT40-A-6, 4362 kW (5,850 ehp)
Armament: (proposed) 4×20-mm cannon or 46×70-mm (2.75-in) rockets
Max T/O weight: 7358 kg (16,221 lb)
Max speed: about 500 mph at optimum altitude
Operational range: not revealed

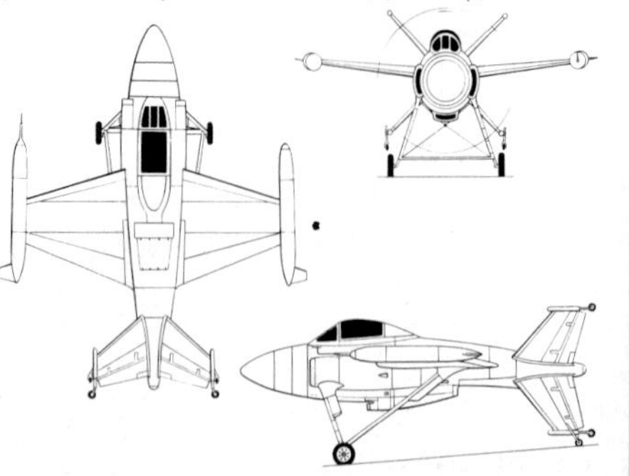

Convair XFY-1

The XFY-1 resulted from the same competition as the XFV-1 and, not unnaturally, bore a number of conceptual affinities to the Lockheed design including the same engine, the same type of contra-prop unit, a gimballed pilot's seat and small castors at the rear tips of the flying surfaces for VTOL operation. However, the Convair design was stubbier than the Lockheed offering, with large delta wings allied to massive upper and lower vertical surfaces that completed the aeroplane's cruciform of flight surfaces. Some 280 tethered flights were completed in an airship hangar before the type made its first free flight in August 1954, and the first translations into and from wingborne flight followed in November of the same year. The programme was cancelled in 1955 because of handling problems and the fact that there was no hope of producing such a fighter with flight performance equal to that of current jet-powered aircraft.

Specification: Convair XFY-1 single-seat tail-sitting VTOL experimental fighter prototype
Span: 8.43 m (27 ft 7.75 in)
Length: 10.66 m (22 ft 11 in)
Powerplant: 1×Allison YT40-A-6, 4362 kW (5,850 ehp)
Armament: (proposed) 4×20-mm cannon or 46×70-mm (2.75-in) rockets
Max T/O weight: 7371 kg (16,250 lb)
Max speed: 610 mph at 15,000 ft
Operational range: not revealed

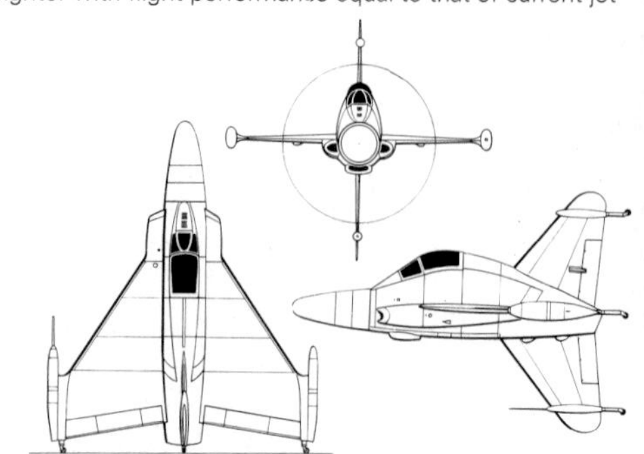

his is one of nine Hawker P.1127 Kestrels assigned to the 'est Raynham-based Tripartite Evaluation Squadron. The olourful markings reflect the nationalities of the articipating air arms: Britain's RAF, the USAF and US 'arine Corps, and the German Luftwaffe and Bundesmarine.

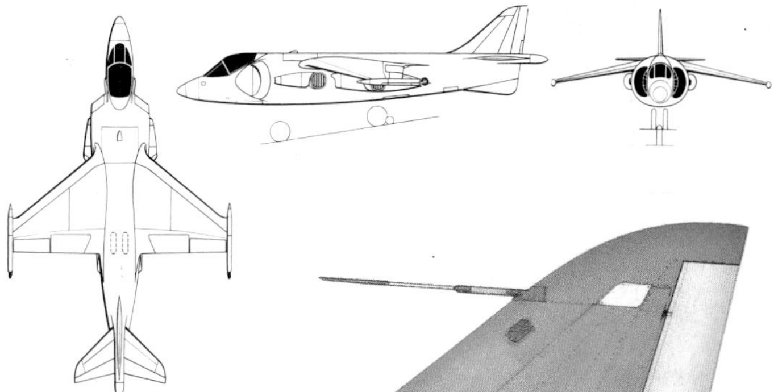

Ryan X-13 Vertijet

Ryan began investigation of a tail-sitting VTOL aeroplane in 1947, and after successful evaluation of two J33-powered test rigs the company was contracted to build the X-13. The type had a large delta wing with small tip fins to complement the large central surface. It first flew in December 1955 as a conventional landplane with temporary fixed landing gear, but by 1956 had progressed to vertical take-offs and simulated landings by the engagement of the undernose hook on a horizontal nylon rope. VTO control was effected by thrust deflection and thrust variation, while conventional surfaces were provided for wingborne flight. As part of a full test programme the aeroplane made its first full translational flight (from VTO to wingborne flight and back again to vertical landing) in April 1957. Both aircraft have been preserved.

Specification: Ryan X-13 Vertijet single-seat tail-sitting VTOL research aeroplane
Span: 6.40 m (21 ft 0 in)
Length: 7.14 m (23 ft 5 in)
Powerplant: 1×Rolls-Royce Avon RA.29 Mk 49, 4534 kg (10,000 lb) st
Max T/O weight: 3317 kg (7,313 lb)
Max speed: 483 mph at optimum altitude
Operational range: 192 miles

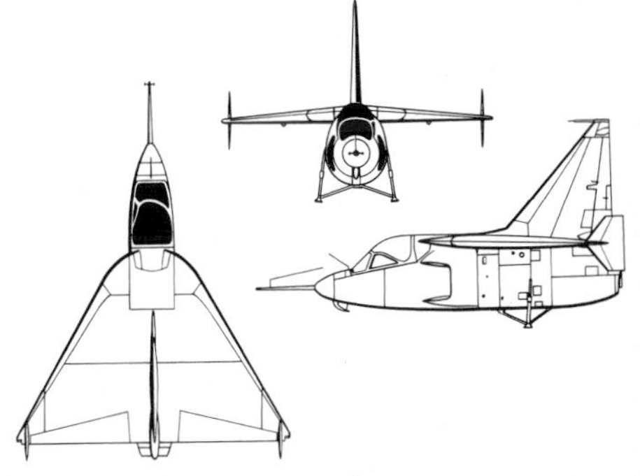

Dornier Do 31E

This ambitious design was developed to West German requirements as the prototype for a VTOL transport able to support VTOL combat aircraft in the field. The fuselage was left free for the accommodation of troops, supplies or freight by the location of the powerplant in four wing-mounted nacelles: the inner pair each accommodated two thrust-vectoring Pegasus turbofans, and the optional outboard pair each contained four RB.162 direct-lift turbojets. The Do 31 E1 first prototype flew with two Pegasus engines in February 1967, the Do 31 E3 second flight prototype following with all 10 engines. Full forward and backward translations were made from December 1967, and Dornier also proposed a Do 231 100-seat passenger or similar freight derivative for production with 12 5942-kg (13,100-lb) thrust RB.202 lift engines and two 10886-kg (24,000-lb) thrust RB.220 propulsion engines.

Specification: Dornier Do 31 E3 two-crew thrust-vectoring/direct-lift VTOL transport prototype
Span: 18.06 m (59 ft 3 in)
Length: 20.88 m (68 ft 8 in)
Powerplant: 2×Rolls-Royce Pegasus 5-2, 7031 kg (15,000 lb) st each, and 8×Rolls-Royce RB.162-4D, 1996 kg (4,400 lb) st each
Payload: 34 troops or 4990 kg (11,001 lb) of freight
Max T/O weight: 27442 kg (60,500 lb)
Cruising speed: 400 mph at 20,000 ft
Operational range: not revealed

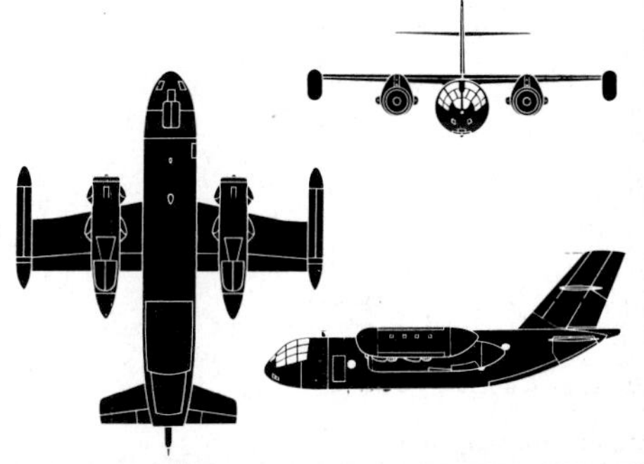

VFW-Fokker VAK-191B

This was developed as the prototype for a subsonic attack/reconnaissance fighter to succeed the Fiat G.91 series. The project was initially an Italo-German venture, but in 1968 Aeritalia withdrew and the former Focke-Wulf company continued alone. The design was basically conventional but featured tandem main landing gear units under the fuselage (with retractable outrigger units near the wingtips), and a lift/propulsion system comprising two RB.162 lift turbojets in the forward fuselage plus one RB.193 vectored-thrust lift/thrust turbofan farther aft in the fuselage. The first of three prototypes flew in September 1971, and before the programme was terminated in the mid-1970s satisfactory exploration had been made of the complete translational envelope (including the shut-down and relight of the lift engines in flight) and most of the flight envelope.

Specification: VFW-Fokker VAK-191B single-seat thrust-vectoring/direct-lift VTOL attack/reconnaissance fighter prototype
Span: 6.16 m (20 ft 2.5 in)
Length: 16.335 m (53 ft 7 in)
Powerplant: 2×Rolls-Royce RB.162-81, 2530 kg (5,577 lb) st each), and 1×Rolls-Royce/MTU RB.193-12, 4603 kg (10,150 lb) st
Max T/O weight: 9000 kg (19,841 lb)
Max speed: 345 mph at optimum altitude
Operational range: not revealed

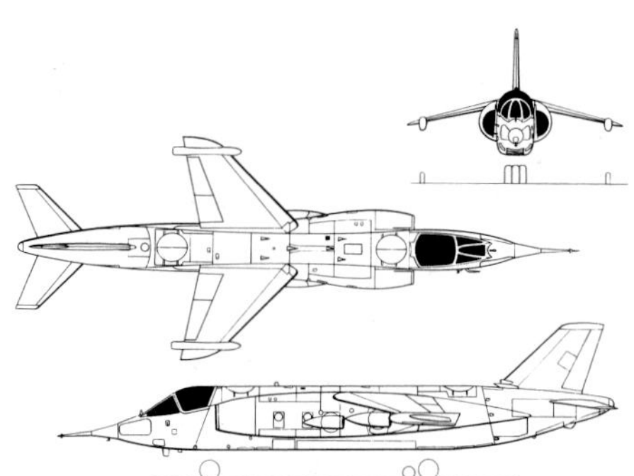

The VFW-Fokker VAK-191B was a German attempt to produce a VTOL strike fighter as a Fiat G-91 replacement, but the programme was eventually cancelled after only three prototypes had flown.

Bell X-14

The X-14 was conceived as a tool for the evaluation of the jet-deflection type of VTOL. The type was intended only for low-speed trials, and therefore designed with an open cockpit and fixed tricycle landing gear. The two Viper turbojets were located side-by-side in the extreme nose, and simple thrust deflectors on the centre of gravity were used to divert the exhausts 90° downward for VTO; the exhausts were then angled increasingly backward to provide a forward component and thus allow the aeroplane to translate into wingborne flight. Compressed-air nozzles were provided at the wingtips and tail for control at zero and low speeds. The type first flew in February 1957 in the hovering mode, and completed its first transition to wingborne flight in May 1958. The Vipers were later replaced by 1216-kg (2,680-lb) thrust General Electric J85-GE-5s when the type was shifted from the USAF to NASA in 1969.

Specification: Bell X-14 single-seat thrust-vectoring VTOL research aeroplane
Span: 10.36 m (34 ft 0 in)
Length: 7.62 m (25 ft 0 in)
Powerplant: 2×Armstrong Siddeley ASV.8 Viper, 794 kg (1,750 lb) st each
Max T/O weight: 1936 kg (4,269 lb) with J85 turbojets
Max speed: 172 mph at low altitude with J85 turbojets
Operational range: 300 miles

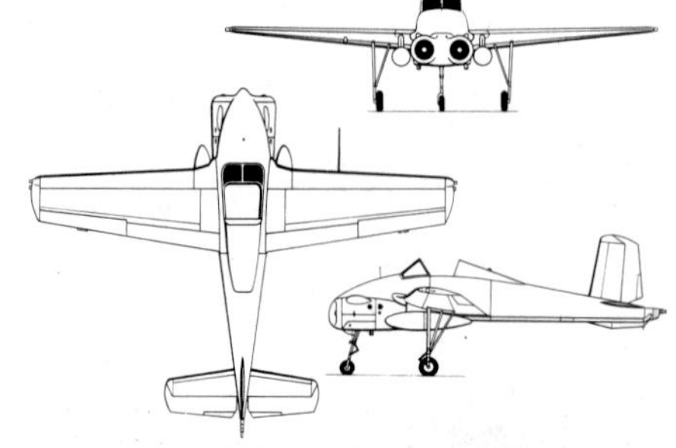

Short SC.1

This was the first fixed-wing VTOL aeroplane built in the UK, and was produced as a flight platform for the newly developed RB.108 lift turbojet. The aeroplane was an ungainly type with a low-set delta wing and fixed tricycle landing gear, and the powerplant arrangement comprised a single engine in the rear of the fuselage for forward thrust and four fuselage-mounted engines, the latter located in transverse pairs with a slight degree of fore-and-aft movement for braking, direct-lift and forward thrust components. The first prototype flew on 2 April 1957 with just the single tail engine, and was joined from August 1958 by the five-engined second prototype. The vectored-thrust powerplant of the P.1127 made the SC.1's VTOL system obsolete, but an exhaustive trials programme was completed before the aircraft were finally retired.

Specification: Short SC.1 single-seat direct-lift VTOL research aeroplane
Span: 7.16 m (23 ft 6 in)
Length: 9.11 m (29 ft 10 in)
Powerplant: 5×Rolls-Royce RB.108, 966 kg (2,130 lb) st each
Max T/O weight: 3651 kg (8,050 lb) for VTO
Max speed: 246 mph at sea level
Operational range: 150 miles

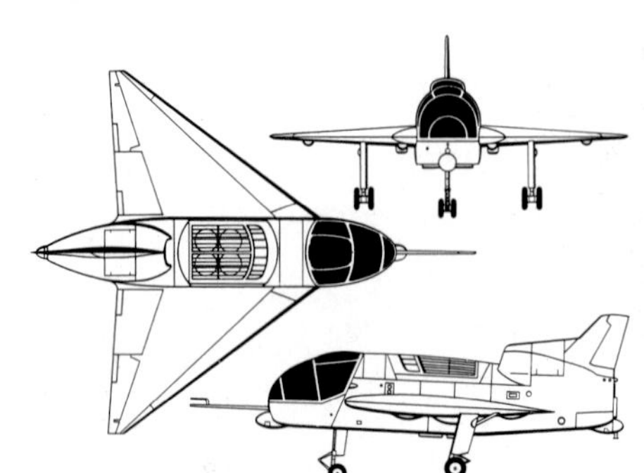

SNECMA C.450-01 Coléoptère

his was an ambitious, almost visionary, ttempt to develop the technology for a ompact combat aeroplane with very high erformance. In 1952 this French ompany acquired the rights to the nnular-wing concept pioneered by von 'borowski and launched a programme hat progressed through the C.400 Atar 'olant series of remotely controlled and iloted research platforms in which the eroplane rose vertically on the thrust of :s turbojet and was then accelerated to a peed at which the wing generated ufficient lift for translation to forward light. Then came the Coléoptère with its nnular wing. This first flew in May 1959 sing pneumatic deflection of the jet xhaust for control in vertical flight. The ingle prototype crashed in July of the ame year after a short but generally uccessful test programme that was then erminated.

;pecification: SNECMA :.450-01 Coléoptère single-seat ail-sitting VTOL research aeroplane
Ving diameter: 3.20 m (10 ft 6 in)
.ength: 8.022 m (26 ft 3.5 in)
'owerplant: 1×SNECMA Atar 01E.V, 3700 kg (8,157 lb) st
Max T/O weight: about 3000 kg ;,614 lb)
Max speed: not revealed
)perational range: not revealed

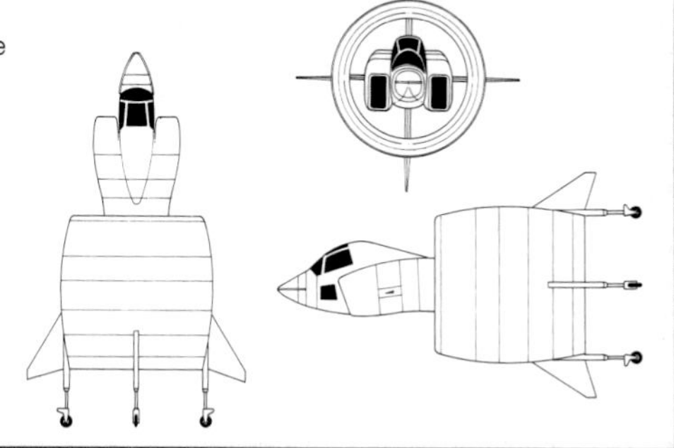

Lockheed VZ-10 (XV-4A)

This interesting design originated from a US Army Transportation Research Command contract for two VZ-10 experimental aircraft using the augmented-jet ejector lift principle, in which VTO was made possible by diverting the exhaust of both turbojets downward through ejector ducts through 20 rows of multiple nozzles into two ejector chambers in which free air was drawn, heated and exhausted with the main effluxes to boost direct lift by more than 40 per cent. Once VTO had been achieved, one and then both engines were switched to forward thrust so that the aeroplane translated to wingborne flight. The first flight was made in July 1962, and after one machine had crashed in July 1964 the other was converted as the XV-4B Hummingbird II with four engines for direct jet-lift research. This aeroplane crashed in 1969 and the programme was ended.

Specification: Lockheed XV-4A Hummingbird two-seat ejector-lift VTOL research aeroplane
Span: 7.82 m (25 ft 8 in)
Length: 9.96 m (32 ft 8 in)
Powerplant: 2×Pratt & Whitney JT12A-3LH, 1361 kg (3,000 lb) st each
Max T/O weight: 3266 kg (7,200 lb)
Max speed: 518 mph at 10,000 ft
Operational range: 335 miles after VTO

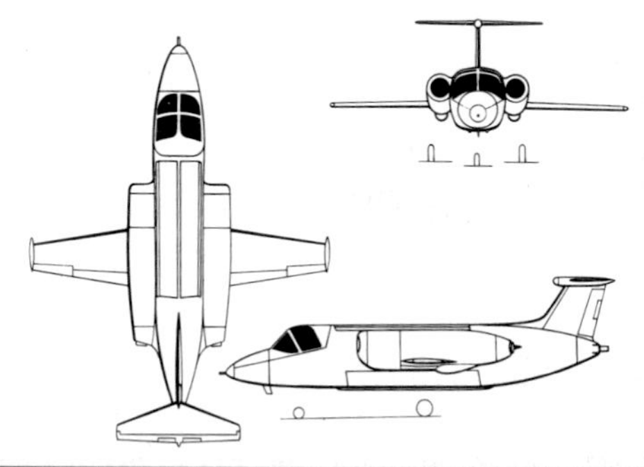

Chapter 10

TRANSPORTERS

Douglas C-47 and Dakota

The C-47, called Dakota by the RAF, was the military derivative of the DC-3 and was produced in far larger numbers (and variants) than the airliner. Civil aircraft impressed by the military were designated C-48, C-49, C-50, C-51, C-68 and US Navy/Marine Corps R4D-2, while military production was of the C-47 Skytrain utility and C-53 Skytrooper personnel transports. The C-47/Dakota series was widely used for paratrooping and glider-towing. Some 953 examples of the militarized DC-3 with a freight door and strengthened floor were built as C-47s (plus 53 Dakota Mk Is and 106 R4D-1s), and these were followed by 4,931 C-47As (plus 962 Dakota Mk IIIs and 238 R4D-5s) with revised electrics, 3,421 C-47Bs (plus 896 Dakota Mk IVs and 188 R4D-6s) with better altitude performance, 370 C-53s (plus 30 R4D-3/4s) and 17 C-117 personnel transport version of the C-47B.

Specification: Douglas C-47 Skytrain medium-range transport
Span: 28.90 m (95 ft 0 in)
Length: 19.63 m (64 ft 5.5 in)
Powerplant: 2×Pratt & Whitney R-1830-92, 895 kW (1,200 hp) each
Payload: three flightcrew plus 28 passengers, or 18 litters and attendants, or 4536 kg (10,000 lb) of freight
Normal T/O weight: 11805 kg (26,000 lb)
Cruising speed: 185 mph at optimum altitude
Operational range: 1,500 miles

Officially known to the USAF as the Skytrain, the C-47 was perhaps better known by its RAF/RCAF name, Dakota. This aircraft served with the 81st Troop Carrier Squadron of the Membury-based 36th Troop Carrier Group.

Arado Ar 232

The Ar 232 was an innovatory transport design with a pod-and-boom fuselage to allow the incorporation in the former of a hydraulically operated rear door for the loading/unloading of bulky freight. Another unusual feature was the retractable tricycle landing gear, whose units could be 'broken' on the ground to allow the fuselage to rest firmly on a central row of 11 pairs of independently sprung idler wheels. The Ar 232 V1 first flew early in 1941 and, like the following V2, was powered by a pair of 1193-kW (1,600-hp) BMW 801MA radials. The Ar 232 V3 had only 10 idlers and a 1.7-m (66.9-in) increase in span to permit the use of four radials. There followed a pre-production batch of about 19 generally similar Ar 232B-0 transports, and these were used operationally on the Eastern Front. One had ski landing gear and another had Gnome-Rhone 14M radials.

Specification: Arado Ar 232B-0 short-range transport
Span: 33.50 m (109 ft 10.75 in)
Length: 23.52 m (77 ft 2 in)
Powerplant: 4×BMW-Bramo 323R-2 Fafnir, 895 kW (1,200 hp) each
Armament: 1×20-mm cannon, 2 or 3×13-mm (0.51-in) machine-guns and provision for up to 8×7.92-mm (0.312-in) machine-guns
Payload: four/five flightcrew plus passengers or 4580 kg (10,097 lb) of freight
Max T/O weight: 20000 kg (44,092 lb)
Cruising speed: 180 mph at 6,560 ft
Operational range: 658 miles

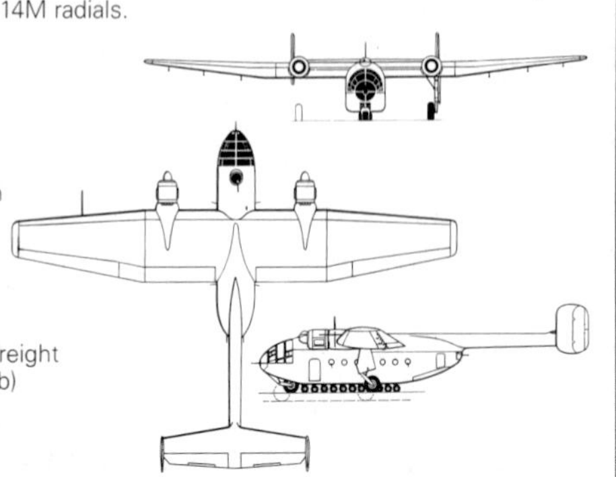

A.W.38 Whitley

The Whitley twin-engined bomber first flew in March 1936 and was a mainstay of RAF Bomber Command up to the end of 1941. With the advent of more modern twin- and four-engined bombers carrying larger payloads at higher speeds over great ranges, the Whitley was relegated to secondary tasks such as transport and airborne forces' use. The Whitley's narrow fuselage militated against extensive transport use, but BOAC used 15 Whitley Mk V Freighter conversions on the route between Gibraltar and Malta during late 1942. From 1940 Whitley Mk IIs (and then examples of all variants but the Mk VII) were converted as paratroop trainers with a drop hatch in the fuselage bottom, and from 1941 the Whitley Mk V was adapted as a glider tug with the tow attachment initially replacing the rear turret and then being attached to a yoke below the turret.

Specification: Armstrong Whitworth A.W.38 Whitley Mk V Freighter long-range transport
Span: 25.60 m (85 ft 0 in)
Length: 21.49 m (70 ft 6 in)
Powerplant: 2×Rolls-Royce Merlin X, 854 kW (1,145 hp) each
Payload: three/four flightcrew plus a small volume of freight
Max T/O weight: 12792 kg (28,200 lb)
Cruising speed: 185 mph at optimum altitude
Operational range: 2,000 miles

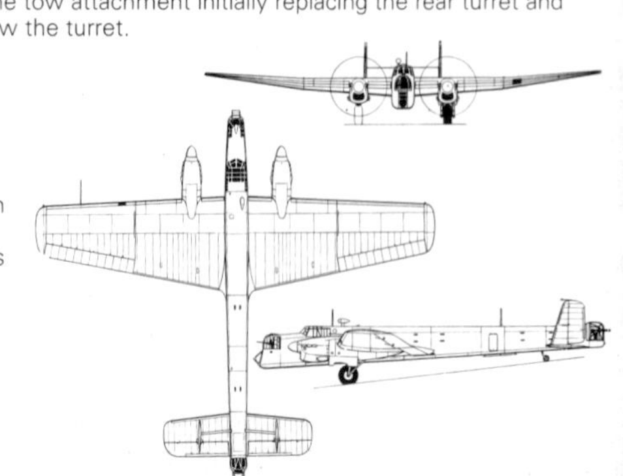

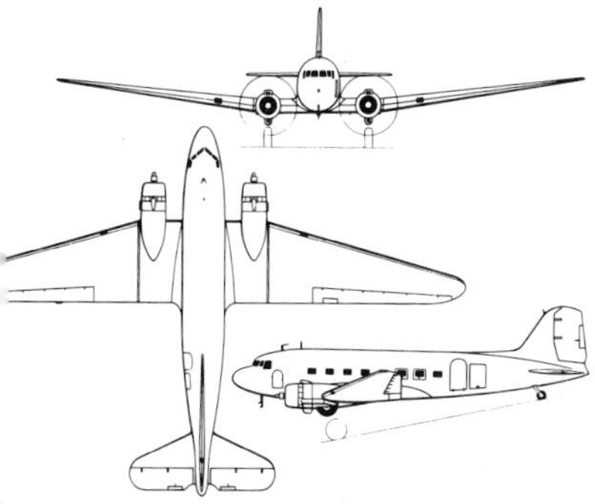

A.W.41 Albemarle

'lanned as the Taurus-powered Bristol Type 155 medium bomber and then completed by rmstrong Whitworth as the A.W.41 reconnaissance bomber with a wood/steel structure nd Hercules radials, the Albemarle first flew in March 1940 and soon showed itself, ecause of its considerable structure weight, to have inadequate performance for its lanned role. Thus only 200 Albemarle Mk I bombers were built, most of these soon being evised for use by airborne forces: 80 became glider tugs and 78 were converted as aratroop transports. These were the Albemarle's only two operational roles, and later 'ariants were the Mk II (99 special transports and one glider tug), the Mk V (49 glider tugs) nd the Mk VI (133 special transports and 117 glider tugs). The differences between marks vere mainly of internal layout and armament.

pecification: Armstrong Vhitworth A.W.41 Albemarle Mk II aratroop transport and glider tug
pan: 23.47 m (77 ft 0 in)
ength: 18.26 m (59 ft 11 in)
owerplant: 2×Bristol Hercules XI, 186 kW (1,590 hp) each
rmament: 2×7.7-mm (0.303-in) nachine-guns
ayload: four flightcrew plus paratroops r one Airspeed Horsa glider
lax T/O weight: 10251 kg 22,600 lb) as a glider tug or 16556 kg 36,500 lb) as a special transport
ruising speed: 170 mph at optimum altitude
perational range: 1,300 miles

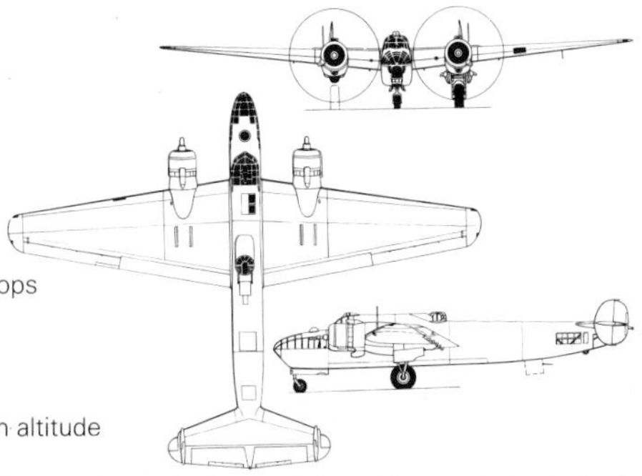

Avro York

Designed to provide the RAF with a long-range transport at minimum design effort, the York was conceived in 1942 on the basis of the wing, landing gear and powerplant of the Avro Lancaster heavy bomber married to a completely new fuselage and tail unit. The shoulder-mounted wing provided excellent fields of vision from the 19 circular windows along each side of the capacious fuselage. The first prototype flew in July 1942 with twin endplate tail surfaces, but from the third prototype all Yorks had triple vertical tail surfaces. The second prototype was later fitted with Bristol Hercules radial engines to become the sole York C.Mk II, while the 253 York C.Mk Is had Merlin inlines. Wartime production was very slow, the aircraft being used as VIP transports until an increased production flow after the war allowed freight and passenger use.

Specification: Avro York C.Mk I long-range transport
Span: 31.09 m (102 ft 0 in)
Length: 23.92 m (78 ft 6 in)
Powerplant: 4×Rolls-Royce Merlin 24 or 502, 1208 kW (1,620 hp) each
Payload: five flightcrew plus 24 passengers or 4536 kg (10,000 lb) of freight
Max T/O weight: 30845 kg (68,000 lb)
Cruising speed: 223 mph at 10,000 ft
Operational range: 2,700 miles

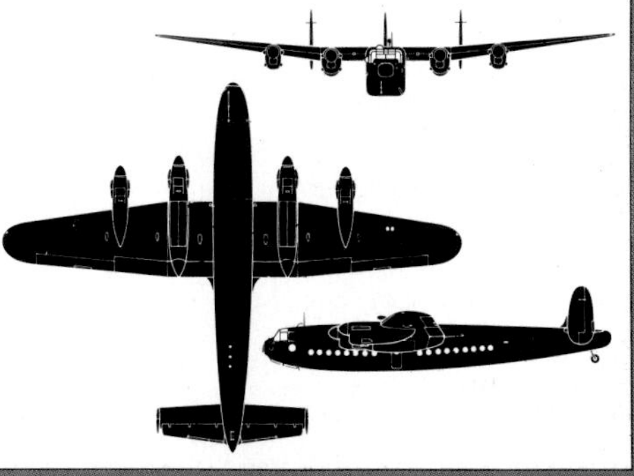

Junkers Ju 52/3m

Specification: Junkers Ju 52/3m g7e medium-range transport
Span: 29.20 m (95 ft 10 in)
Length: 18.90 m (62 ft 0 in)
Powerplant: 3×BMW 132T-2, 619 kW (830 hp) each
Payload: three flightcrew plus 18 passengers, or 13 litters and attendants, or freight
Normal T/O weight: 11030 kg (24,320 lb)
Cruising speed: 160 mph at optimum altitude
Operational range: 930 miles

Rivalling the C-47/Dakota for fame, the Ju 52/3m was Germany's transport workhorse throughout World War II, about 4,850 of all Ju 52 variants being built. The Ju 52/3m was conceived and first built as a civil transport, and initially adopted by the Luftwaffe as the Ju 52/3m g3e dual-role bomber and transport with 541-kW (750-hp) BMW 132A-3 radials and a 'dustbin' ventral turret, and the improved g4e. Next came the transport series proper in the form of the Ju 52/3m g5e with 619-kW (830-hp) BMW 132T-2 engines, no 'dustbin' and interchangeable wheel/ski/float landing gear, the g6e with improved radio equipment, the g7e with an autopilot and larger loading hatch, the g8e improved version of the g6e, the g9 with BMW 132Zs and glider-towing capability, the g11e with BMW 132Ls, and the g14e wi armour protection and revised armament.

Bristol Type 130 Bombay

The Bombay was designed to a 1931 requirement for dual-role troop-carrier and bomber intended mainly for the Indian and Middle Eastern areas, and featured a high wing plus a substantial fixed landing gear arrangement. The first Type 130 flew in June 1935 with spatted wheels and Pegasus X radial engines driving fixed-pitch propellers. After evaluation against the Armstrong Whitworth A.W.23 (forerunner of the Whitley bomber) and Handley Page 51 (forerunner of the Harrow bomber), the Bristol design was selected, and 50 Bombay Mk I aircraft were eventually built by Short and Harland in Northern Ireland. Deliveries were made in 1939, and most aircraft were used in the Middle East. Some bombing raids were flown, but the type was used mainly for troop and occasionally freight transport.

Specification: Bristol Type 130 Bombay Mk I medium/long-range transport
Span: 29.18 m (95 ft 9 in)
Length: 21.11 m (69 ft 3 in)
Powerplant: 2×Bristol Pegasus XXII, 753 kW (1,010 hp) each
Armament: 2×7.7-mm (0.303-in) machine-guns, plus provision for up to 907 kg (2,000 lb) of bombs carried externally
Payload: flightcrew plus 24 passengers or freight
Max T/O weight: 9072 kg (20,000 lb)
Cruising speed: 160 mph at optimum altitude
Operational range: 2,230 miles

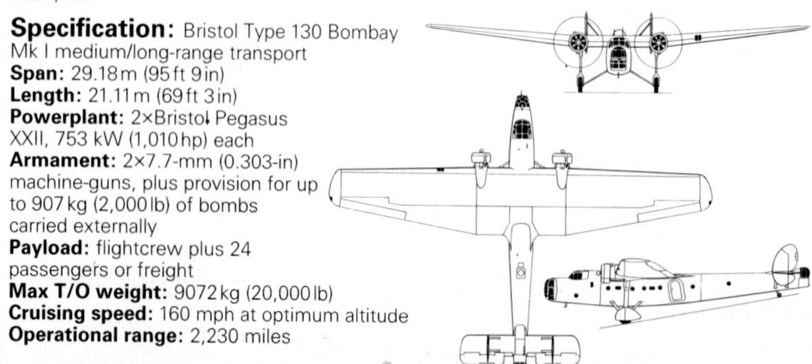

Consolidated C-87

The B-24 bomber's long range and roomy fuselage were features that prompted the type's development as a transport. In 1942 a dedicated transport was evolved from the B-24D bomber as the C-87: this variant lacked turrets and possessed a row of windows along each side of the fuselage. Production amounted to 280 including 24 for the RAF as Liberator C.Mk VIIs. The only variant was the C-87A, of which six were produced as VIP transports with 10 night berths and R-1830-45 radial engines. In US Navy service the C-87 and C-87A were designated RY-2 and RY-1, of which three and five were operated. The C-109 was a conversion of the B-24E with tanks for 10978 litres (2,900 US gal) of ferry fuel. The single-finned PB4Y Privateer patrol bomber version also spawned a transport version in the RY-3 (46 built) and Liberator C.Mk IX (27 for the RAF).

Specification: Consolidated C-87 long-range transport
Span: 33.53 m (110 ft 0 in)
Length: 20.22 m (66 ft 4 in)
Powerplant: 4×Pratt & Whitney R-1830-43, 895 kW (1,200 hp) each
Payload: five flightcrew plus 25 passengers or 3992 kg (8,800 lb) of freight
Normal T/O weight: 25674 kg (56,600 lb)
Cruising speed: 200 mph at optimum altitude
Operational range: 2,900 miles

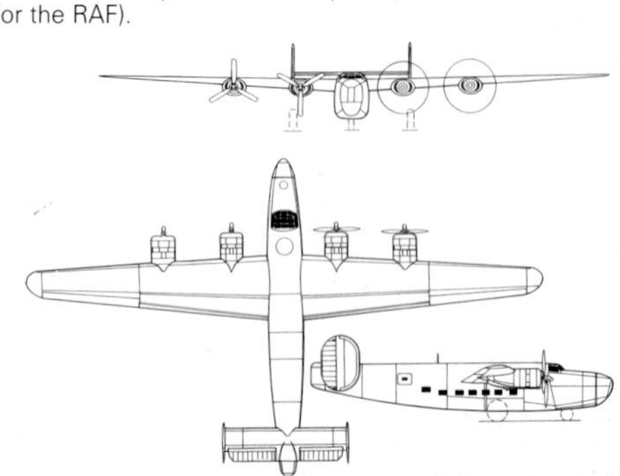

This 'Tante Ju' wears the markings of 2 Staffel, KGzbV 1. The unit was heavily involved in Operation Merkur, the invasion of Crete, in which 170 of the 493 Ju 52s committed were lost, along with one in four of the paratroops dropped. The box-like, corrugated fuselage of the Ju 52 gave it enormous strength, and this ruggedness allowed the aircraft to sustain major damage and still limp home.

Curtiss C-46 Commando

The C-46 was most extensively used in the Pacific theatre, and was the military version of the Curtiss-Wright CW-20 airliner planned in the pre-war period as a larger and longer-ranged competitor to the Douglas DC-3. The CW-20's capacious fuselage attracted military interest, and an initial order was placed for 25 C-46s with 1491-kW (2,000-hp) R-2800-43 radials and a gross weight of 22986 kg (50,675 lb). There followed 1,491 C-46As with more power and a large freight door accessing a strengthened floor, 1,410 C-46Ds with a revised nose and double freight doors, 17 C-46Es with a stepped windscreen and single door, 234 C-46Fs with double doors and blunt wingtips, and 160 examples of the US Marine Corps' R5C-1 equivalent to the C-46A. The C-46B, C and G were development models, and C-55 was the designation under which the CW-20 was evaluated.

Specification: Curtiss C-46A Commando medium-range transport
Span: 32.94 m (108 ft 1 in)
Length: 23.26 m (76 ft 4 in)
Powerplant: 2×Pratt & Whitney R-2800-51, 1491 kW (2,000 hp) each
Payload: four flightcrew plus 50 passengers, or 33 litters and four attendants, or 4536 kg (10,000 lb) of freight
Normal T/O weight: 25402 kg (56,000 lb)
Cruising speed: 183 mph at optimum altitude
Operational range: 1,200 miles

Douglas C-54 Skymaster

The C-54 was the military version of the DC-4A designed for transcontinental airline operations, and began to enter service with the USAAF's Air Transport Command late in 1942 as a long-range transport spanning the Atlantic, Pacific and Indian Oceans. The type was unpressurized but had features such as tricycle landing gear and large flaps. The first 24 C-54s were commandeered DC-4As, and these basically civil aircraft were followed by 207 convertible passenger/freight C-54As with a strengthened floor and a freight door, 220 C-54Bs with a gross weight of 33113 kg (73,000 lb), one C-54C VIP transport, 350 C-54Ds based on the C-54B but with R-2000-11 radials, 75 long-range C-54Es, and 76 C-54Gs with high-density seating and R-2000-9 engines. The US Navy received 211 R5D-1/4 aircraft similar to the C-54/A/D/G, and the RAF had 23 Skymaster Mk Is to C-54D standard.

Specification: Douglas C-54A Skymaster long-range transport
Span: 35.81 m (117 ft 6 in)
Length: 28.60 m (93 ft 10 in)
Powerplant: 4×Pratt & Whitney R-2000-7, 962 kW (1,290 hp) each
Payload: six flightcrew plus 50 passengers or 6441 kg (14,200 lb) of freight
Max T/O weight: 28123 kg (62,000 lb)
Cruising speed: 207 mph at 10,000 ft
Operational range: 3,900 miles

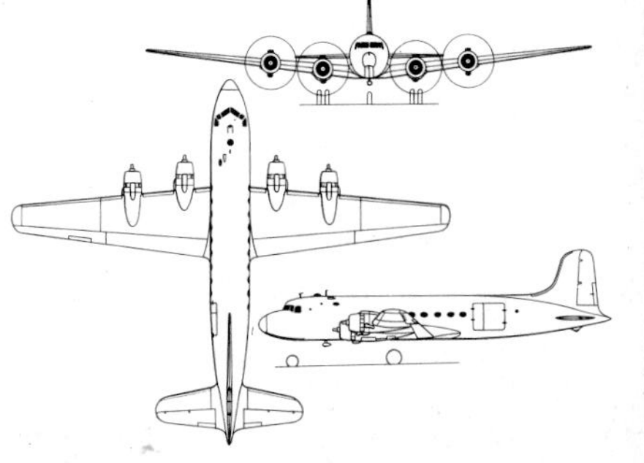

Lisunov Li-2

In 1936 the USSR signed a licence agreement with Douglas aircraft for Soviet production of the DC-3 airliner. Boris Lisunov spent more than 3 years in California assessing the production and in-service support of the airliner and then returned to the USSR to supervise the Soviet production line for the initial PS-84 variant. This had 1,293 engineering modifications to suit Soviet production practices, and a completely different powerplant in the form of two Shvetsov ASh-62IR radials offering inferior performance to the DC-3 with either of its two US engine types. The PS-84 entered Aeroflot service in 1940, and in its definitive and redesignated Li-2 form was produced as the Li-2P passenger, Li-2G civil and Li-2T military freight, Li-2D paratroop, Li-2R survey, Li-2PG convertible, Li-2DB long-range and Li-2V turbocharged aircraft. Production amounted to about 2,930 aircraft.

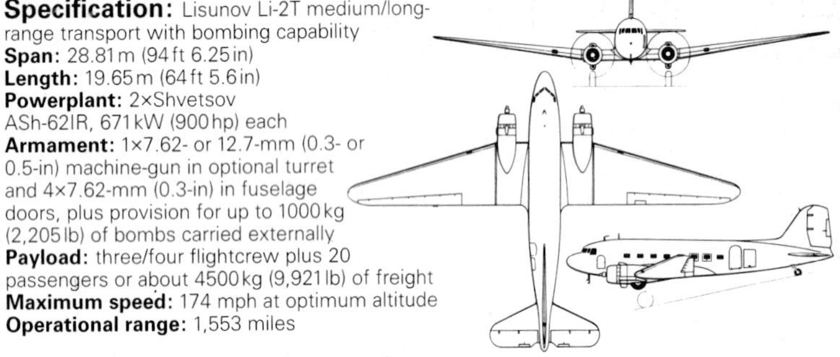

Specification: Lisunov Li-2T medium/long-range transport with bombing capability
Span: 28.81 m (94 ft 6.25 in)
Length: 19.65 m (64 ft 5.6 in)
Powerplant: 2×Shvetsov ASh-62IR, 671 kW (900 hp) each
Armament: 1×7.62- or 12.7-mm (0.3- or 0.5-in) machine-gun in optional turret and 4×7.62-mm (0.3-in) in fuselage doors, plus provision for up to 1000 kg (2,205 lb) of bombs carried externally
Payload: three/four flightcrew plus 20 passengers or about 4500 kg (9,921 lb) of freight
Maximum speed: 174 mph at optimum altitude
Operational range: 1,553 miles

Messerschmitt Me 323

In March 1940 Messerschmitt flew the first example of its huge Me 321 transport glider towed by three Bf 110 heavy fighters or the extraordinary Heinkel He 111Z. The difficulty of towing this beast led to proposals for a powered version, which emerged for a first flight in April 1942 with multi-wheel landing gear and four 850-kW (1,140-hp) Gnome-Rhône 14N48/49 radials. This Me 323 V1 was followed by a V2 prototype with six engines, paving the way for the Me 323D series with a number of propeller and armament fits. The next series was the Me 323E with more power (in later versions six Jumo 211F engines) and steadily more capable defensive armament including two wing turrets. Losses were so heavy that the Me 323E-2/WT escort was developed with 11 20-mm cannon and four 13-mm (0.51-in) machine-guns in a fit that included four wing turrets. Total production was 211.

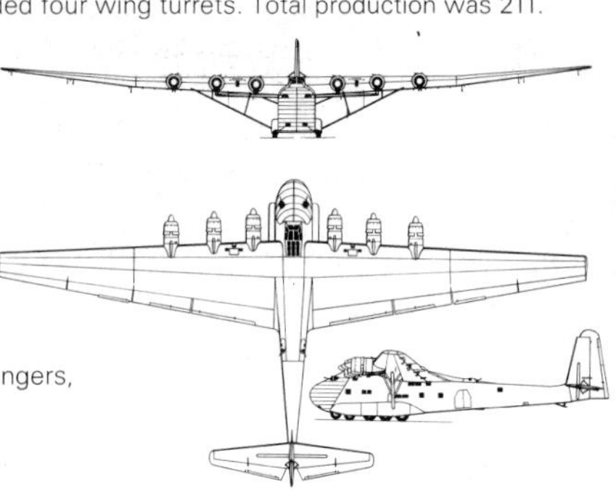

Specification: Messerschmitt Me 323E-2 Gigant short/medium-range heavy transport
Span: 55.00 m (180 ft 5.33 in)
Length: 28.50 m (93 ft 6 in)
Powerplant: 6×Gnome-Rhône 14R, 895 kW (1,200 hp) each
Armament: 2×20-mm cannon, 7×13-mm (0.51-in) machine-guns, and provision for a varying number of 7.92-mm (0.312-in) machine- guns
Payload: 7/11 flightcrew plus 120 passengers, or 60 litters and attendants, or freight
Max T/O weight: 45000 kg (99,206 lb)
Cruising speed: 140 mph at sea level
Operational range: 683 miles

Savoia-Marchetti S.M.82

First flown in 1938 as a development of the S.M.75 Marsupiale with a larger and deeper fuselage for greater capacity, the S.M.82 was Italy's largest and best transport aeroplane of World War II. The large fuselage allowed a great diversity of loads, including a dismantled fighter or various type of light vehicle. The type began to enter service early in 1940, 12 being on strength in June when Italy entered the war. In 1941 a bomber version was deployed, but this saw only limited service, and total S.M.82 production amounted to some 400 aircraft. After the Italian armistice, 50 aircraft operated under German control largely in the Baltic region, and 30 worked with the Allies. Post-war survivors were re-engined with 906-kW (1,215-hp) Pratt & Whitney Twin Wasp radials, remaining in service to the early 1960s.

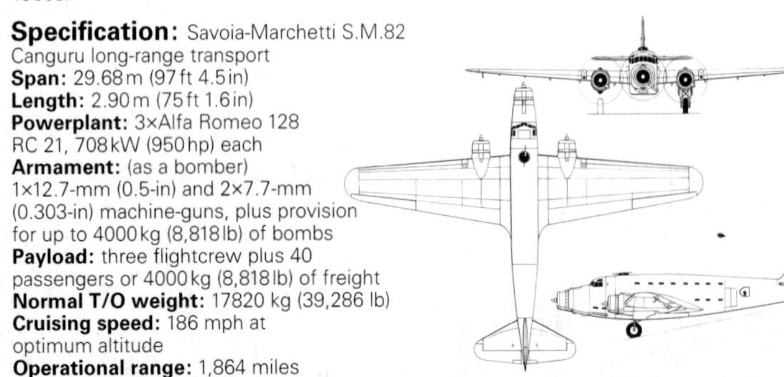

Specification: Savoia-Marchetti S.M.82 Canguru long-range transport
Span: 29.68 m (97 ft 4.5 in)
Length: 2.90 m (75 ft 1.6 in)
Powerplant: 3×Alfa Romeo 128 RC 21, 708 kW (950 hp) each
Armament: (as a bomber) 1×12.7-mm (0.5-in) and 2×7.7-mm (0.303-in) machine-guns, plus provision for up to 4000 kg (8,818 lb) of bombs
Payload: three flightcrew plus 40 passengers or 4000 kg (8,818 lb) of freight
Normal T/O weight: 17820 kg (39,286 lb)
Cruising speed: 186 mph at optimum altitude
Operational range: 1,864 miles

Tupolev TB-3

The ANT-6 was one of the first aircraft to reveal that the USSR had moved into the forefront of aeronautical endeavour by the late 1920s, and was designed from 1925 as the prototype of the TB-3 heavy bomber. The ANT-6 had much in common with the huge ANT-14 transport, and was powered initially by four 447-kW (600-hp) Curtiss Conquerors for its first flight in December 1930 and then by a quartet of 544-kW (730-hp) BMW VIs. The TB-3 was authorized in February 1931, and up to 1937 817 aircraft followed with engines varying from the 533-kW (715-hp) M-17F to the 723-kW (970-hp) M-34RN. Between 1939 and 1941 about 170 TB-3/M-17Fs were converted to G-2 civil transports, while 80 aircraft had already been transformed into military transports with roles such as glider towing, paratroop dropping and the delivery of light armoured vehicles.

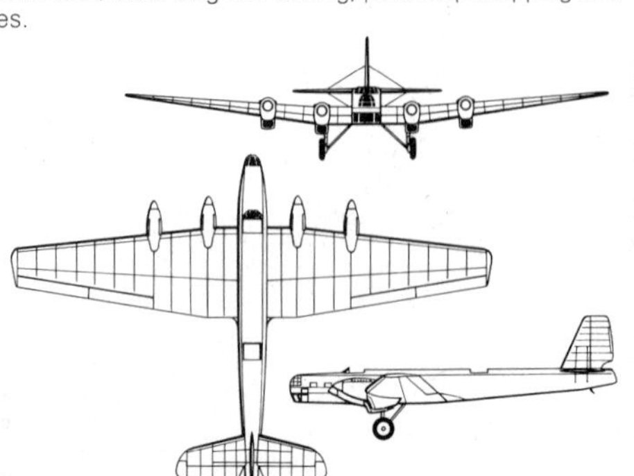

Specification: Tupolev TB-3/AM-34RN medium/long-range transport
Span: 40.50 m (132 ft 10.5 in)
Length: 25.30 m (83 ft 0 in)
Powerplant: 4×M-34RN, 723 kW (970 hp) each
Payload: four flightcrew plus more than 7000 kg (15,432 lb) of freight
Max T/O weight: 22000 kg (48,501 lb)
Maximum speed: 179 mph at 13,125 ft
Operational range: 1,940 miles

Hawker Siddeley Andover

he Andover was developed from the Avro 748 airliner to meet an RAF requirement for TOL transport able to operate in the trooping, paratrooping, airdropping, freighting and asevac roles. Development centred on more powerful engines driving larger-diameter ropellers, a longer fuselage with an upswept tail to allow the incorporation of a rear-loading beaver' ventral ramp/door, and a hydraulic kneeling arrangement in the landing gear to allow he hold floor to be adjusted to any truckbed height. The first Andover C.Mk 1 flew in July 965 and 31 were built, serving with three squadrons (one each at home, in the Persian Gulf nd in the Far East). Seven were later modified as navaid calibration aircraft (four Andover :.Mk 3s and three Andover E.Mk 3As), and six modified HS 748 Series 2 airliners were lelivered as Andover CC.Mk 2 VIP transports, two of them for The Queen's Flight.

Specification: Hawker Siddeley (Avro) Andover C.Mk 1 47-eat short-range tactical transport
Span: 29.95 m (98 ft 3 in)
Length: 23.75 m (77 ft 11 in)
Powerplant: 2×Rolls-Royce Dart RDa.12 Mk 201C, 2420 kW 3,245 shp) each
Payload: 44 troops, or 30 paratroops or 18 litters and five seated casualties plus three attendants, or 6691 kg 14,750 lb) of freight
Max T/O weight: 20185 kg (44,500 lb)
Max speed: 302 mph at 15,000 ft
Operational range: 374 miles with maximum payload

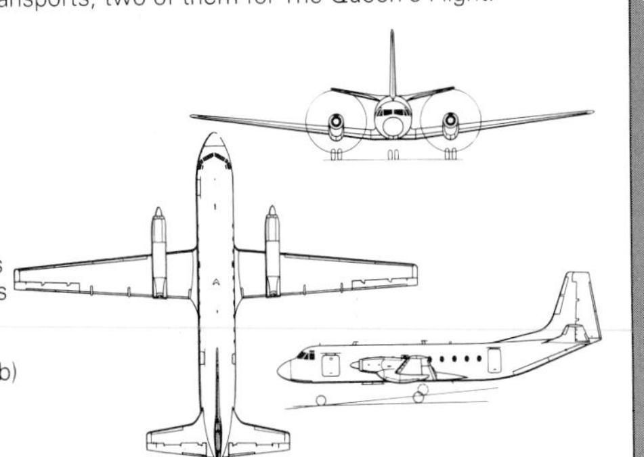

Shorts Belfast

The largest transport yet developed in the UK, the Belfast stemmed from an RAF requirement for a strategic freighter. The design originated with the Britannic, a 1957 Shorts proposal for a high-winged Britannia derivative that was then recast as the SC.5 with a larger fuselage and Tyne turboprops on a wing increased in span by 4.88 m (16 ft). The type was selected as the RAF's strategic freighter in January 1959, and the prototype flew in January 1964 with multi-wheel landing gear, a high wing and an upswept rear fuselage to permit the incoporation of a ventral ramp/door arrangement for the straight-in loading of bulky and long items such as battle tanks and surface-to-air missiles. Production amounted to only 10 Belfast C.Mk 1s which served with No.53 Squadron until the mid-1970s.

Specification: Shorts Belfast C.Mk 1 156-seat medium-range strategic transport
Span: 48.40 m (158 ft 9.5 in)
Length: 41.58 m (136 ft 5 in)
Powerplant: 4×Rolls-Royce Tyne RTy.12 Mk 101,4272 kW (5,730 shp) each
Payload: 150 troops or 36288 kg (80,000 lb) of freight
Max T/O weight: 104463 kg (230,300 lb)
Max speed: 346 mph at 28,000 ft
Operational range: 1,000 miles with a 35154-kg (77,500-lb) payload

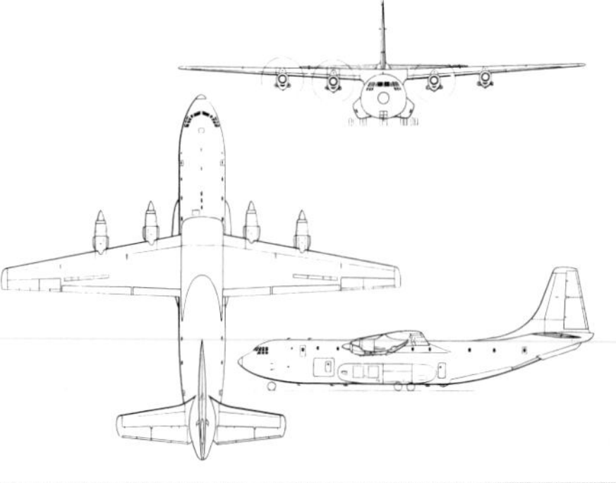

Lockheed Hercules

Still the classic tactical airlifter of our times despite the fact that it first flew in August 1954, the Hercules was ordered for RAF service in the mid-1960s and first flew with the US designation C-130K in October 1966, paralleling the USAF's C-130H. The 66 Hercules C.Mk 1s supplanted the Handley Page Hastings and Blackburn Beverley in RAF service, and have since become the RAF's sole tactical airlifters in the hands of Nos 24, 30, 47 and 70 Squadrons based at RAF Lyneham. A single aeroplane was converted to Hercules W.Mk 2 weather reconnaissance standard, and the others have been or are being upgraded: 30 aircraft stretched greatly to C-130H-30 standard are designated Hercules C.Mk 3, six are tankers designated Hercules C.Mk 1K, and 24 standard transports are designated Hercules C.Mk 1P as they are equipped with the refuelling probes to be installed on all Hercules.

Specification: Lockheed Hercules C.Mk 1 99-seat medium-range tactical transport
Span: 40.41 m (132 ft 7 in)
Length: 30.10 m (98 ft 9 in)
Powerplant: 4×Avco Lycoming T56-A-15, 3661 kW (4,910 shp) each
Payload: 92 troops, or 62 paratroops, or 74 litters plus two attendants, or 20280 kg (45,900 lb) of freight
Max T/O weight: 79380 kg (175,000 lb)
Max speed: 368 mph at optimum altitude
Operational range: 2,430 miles with maximum payload

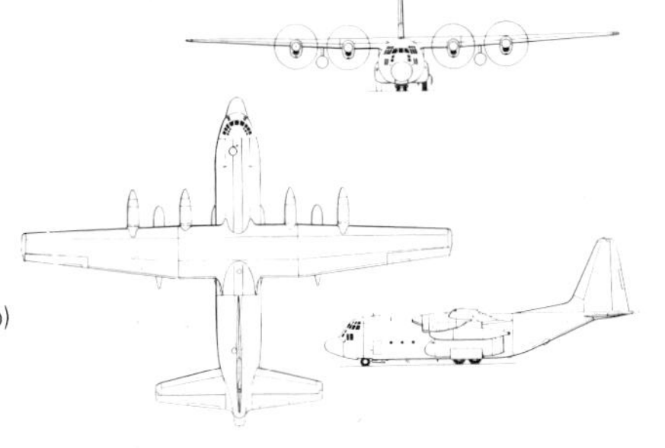

Lockheed TriStar

The TriStar is unusual amongst modern airlifters in being an airliner by origin. The first L-1011 was flown in December 1970, and the type was then produced in basic L-1011-1, extended-range L-1011-100, improved take-off L-1011-200 and long-range L-1011-500 variants. As airlines started to phase it from service, the RAF decided to adopt the type for conversion as a tanker and freighter, resulting in three military variants with underfloor tankage for transfer fuel. The four TriStar K.Mk 1s and two TriStar KC.Mk 2s are ex-British Airways L-1011-500s converted for the tanker and tanker/freighter roles, the latter with a freight door measuring 3.56 m (11 ft 8 in) by 2.64 m (8 ft 8 in) and seating for 194, while the three TriStar K.Mk 2s are ex-Pan American L-1011-500 aircraft modified approximately to K.Mk 1 standard with about 4536 kg (10,000 lb) less transfer fuel.

Specification: Lockheed TriStar K.Mk 1 207-seat long-range heavy transport and inflight-refuelling tanker
Span: 50.09 m (164 ft 6 in)
Length: 50.05 m (164 ft 2.5 in) excluding probe
Powerplant: 3×Rolls-Royce RB211-524B4, 22680 kg (50,000 lb) st each
Payload: 204 passengers or 44500 kg (98,110 lb) of freight, plus provision for 175974 litres (38,810 Imp gal) of transfer fuel
Max T/O weight: 245000 kg (540,000 lb)
Max speed: 600 mph at 35,000 ft
Operational range: 4,835 miles with maximum payload

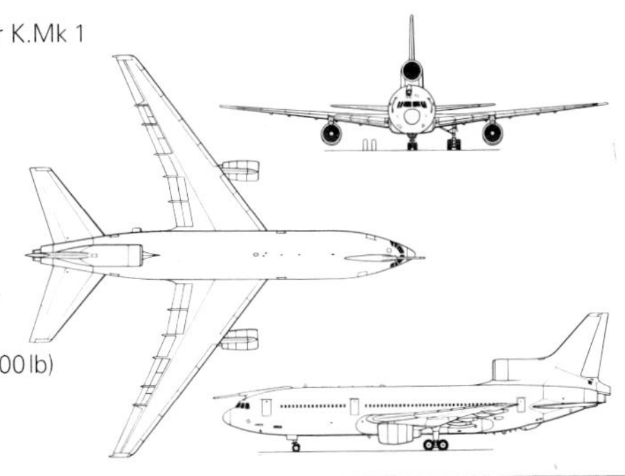

Handley Page Hastings

The Hastings took over from the Avro York as the RAF's standard long-range transport, and first flew in May 1946 and a low-wing monoplane with retractable tailwheel landing gear and a large cargo door in the port side of the rear fuselage. Production of the Hastings C.Mk 1 totalled 100, and some of these were revised to Hastings C.Mk 1A standard with additional tankage. In 1950 there appeared the Hastings C.Mk 2 with more-powerful engines, extra fuel capacity and a larger tailplane, set lower on the fuselage: production amounted to 43 aircraft plus three basically similar Hastings C.Mk 4s with VIP interiors. There were also Hastings Met.Mk 1 and T.Mk 5 meteorological and bombing trainer versions, and the type had been phased out by 1968 after serving with 14 squadrons (12 at home, one in the Middle East and one in the Far East).

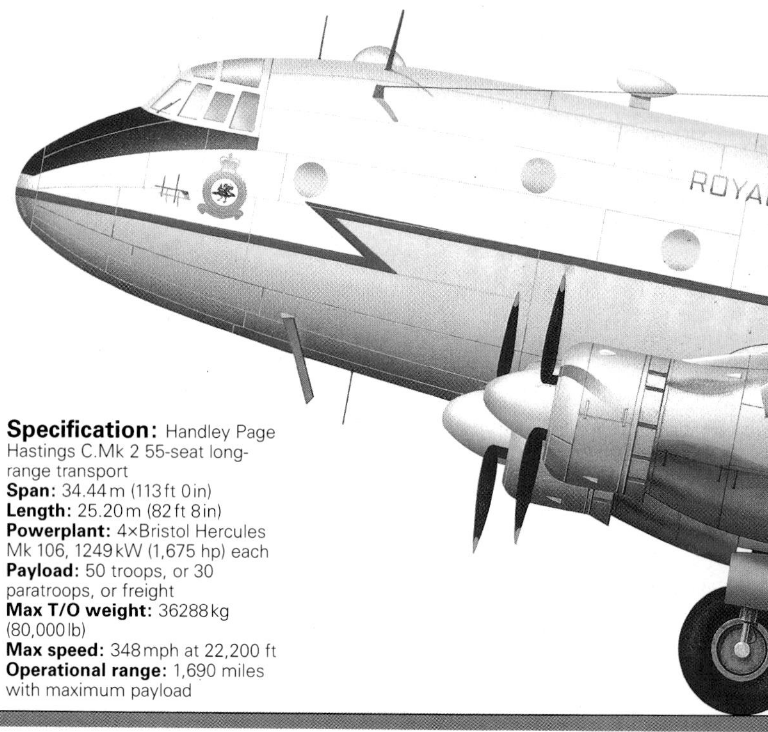

Specification: Handley Page Hastings C.Mk 2 55-seat long-range transport
Span: 34.44 m (113 ft 0 in)
Length: 25.20 m (82 ft 8 in)
Powerplant: 4×Bristol Hercules Mk 106, 1249 kW (1,675 hp) each
Payload: 50 troops, or 30 paratroops, or freight
Max T/O weight: 36288 kg (80,000 lb)
Max speed: 348 mph at 22,200 ft
Operational range: 1,690 miles with maximum payload

Avro York

Though designed in 1942 and first flown in July of that year, the York did not begin to enter full-scale service until after World War II as the UK relied on American transports during the war. The York was technically a low-risk design as it used the same flying surfaces, engines and tailwheel landing gear as the Lancaster bomber, married to a new rectangular-section fuselage. On the third prototype the standard Lancaster tail was supplemented by a third vertical surface, and this became standard on the 253 production York C.Mk 1 transports that began to enter full squadron service in 1945. Nine Transport Command squadrons finally operated the type, which began to leave service as the Hastings was introduced, but which did not finally disappear until 1957. The three versions of the York C.Mk 1 were all-passenger, all-freight, and mixed passenger/freight.

Specification: Avro York C.Mk 1 29-seat long-range transport
Span: 31.09 m (102 ft 0 in)
Length: 23.93 m (78 ft 6 in)
Powerplant: 4×Rolls-Royce Merlin Mk 24 or Mk 502, 1208 kW (1,620 hp) each
Payload: 24 passengers or 4536 kg (10,000 lb) of freight
Max T/O weight: 30845 kg (68,000 lb)
Max speed: 298 mph at 21,000 ft
Operational range: 2,700 miles

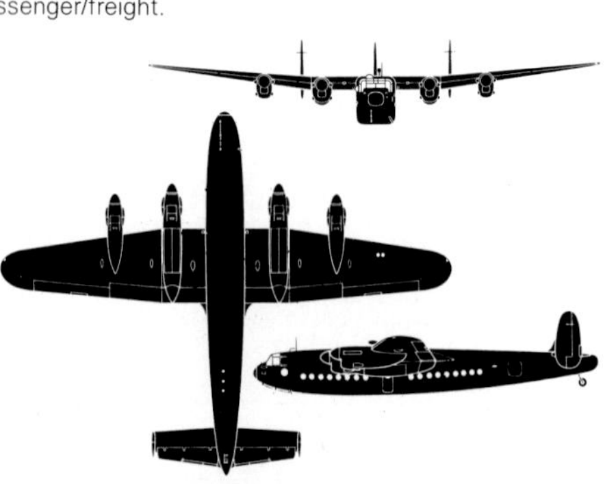

Vickers Valetta

The Valetta was designed as the military version of the Viking airliner, and by comparison with the civil type featured a strengthened floor, large loading doors on the port side of the fuselage, revised landing gear with longer-stroke oleos, and an altered fuel system for a different mark of Hercules radial. The first production Valetta C.Mk 1 flew in January 1948, and the type entered service in the trooping, paratrooping, airdropping, freighting, casevac and glider-towing roles. The 213 Valetta C.Mk 1s were complemented by 10 Valetta C.Mk 2 15-passenger VIP transports and 40 Valetta T.Mk 3 navigation trainers with a row of astrodomes above the fuselage; 18 were later modified to Valetta T.Mk 4 radar trainers. The Valetta served with 13 squadrons (four at home, six in the Middle East and three in the Far East), and was withdrawn as a transport in December 1966.

Specification: Vickers Valetta C.Mk 1 38-seat medium-range tactical transport
Span: 27.20 m (89 ft 3 in)
Length: 19.18 m (62 ft 11 in)
Powerplant: 2×Bristol Hercules Mk 230, 1473 kW (1,975 hp) each
Payload: 34 troops, or 20 paratroops, or 20 litters plus two attendants, or freight
Max T/O weight: 16556 kg (36,500 lb)
Max speed: 258 mph at 10,000 ft
Operational range: 360 miles with 34 troops

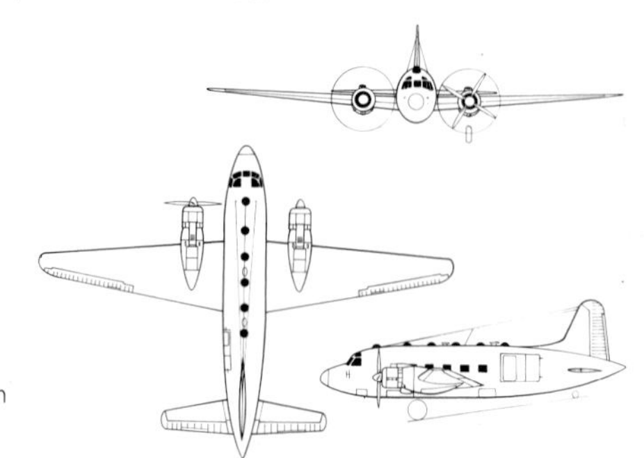

This Handley Page Hastings wears the markings of No. 24 Squadron, a Colerne-based transport unit. The Hastings equipped 11 Transport Command squadrons, and single units in the Middle and Far East. It also saw service as a meteorological and radar reconnaissance platform, for training V-bomber crews and even for gathering Elint.

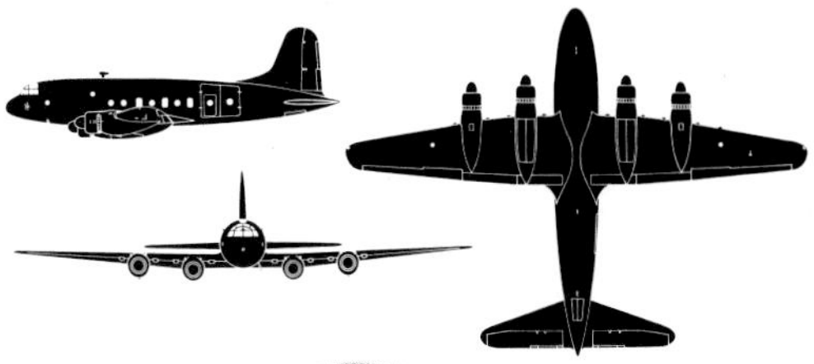

Blackburn Beverley

The Beverley was a developed version of the General Aircraft Limited G.A.L.60 Universal Transport, a design originated in 1946 and flown in 1950. General Aircraft then merged with Blackburn, which continued to develop the design with more powerful Centaurus radials in place of the original Hercules units for better performance. The Beverley proper first flew in June 1953 as a massive pod-and-boom type with fixed tricycle landing gear and a large tail with endplate vertical surfaces. Accommodation for 94 was provided in the boom, and access to the hold was provided by clamshell rear doors, which could be omitted for the air-drop of large loads. The type had virtually STOL performance, and production amounted to 47 aircraft that served with five squadrons (three at home, one in the Middle East and one in the Far East). The type was withdrawn in 1968.

Specification: Blackburn Beverley C.Mk 1 98-seat medium-range heavy transport
Span: 49.38 m (162 ft 0 in)
Length: 30.30 m (99 ft 5 in)
Powerplant: 4×Bristol Centaurus Mk 273, 2125 kW (2,850 hp) each
Payload: 94 troops, or 70 paratroops, or 20412 kg (45,000 lb) of freight
Max T/O weight: 61236 kg (135,000 lb)
Max speed: 238 mph at 5,700 ft
Operational range: 460 miles with maximum payload

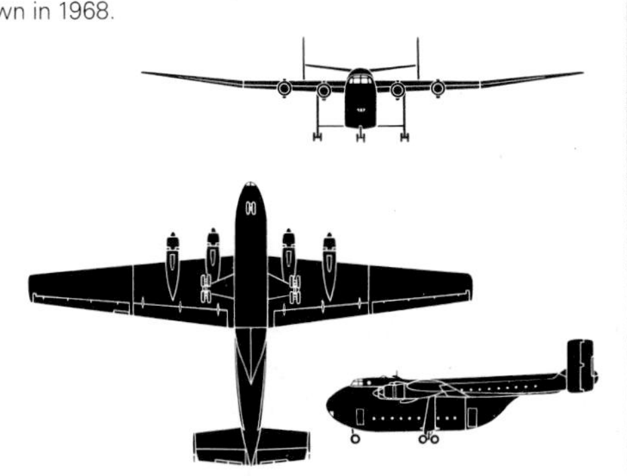

Scottish Aviation Pioneer

The Pioneer resulted from a 1945 requirement for a STOL communications aeroplane, and appeared in a high-wing monoplane powered by a 179-kW (240-hp) de Havilland Gipsy Queen 34 engine. This failed to secure an RAF order but was then produced as the civil Pioneer I four-seater, and so paved the way for the Pioneer II with considerably more power. This first flew in June 1950 and was fitted with full-span leading-edge slats plus trailing-edge Fowler flaps to provide a take-off distance of 68.5 m (75 yards) and a landing run of 60.35 m (66 yards). The Pioneer II was accepted for service as the Pioneer CC.Mk 1 communications and casevac aeroplane, and 40 were delivered for service in areas such as Cyprus, Aden and Malaya. There were four Pioneer squadrons (one at home, one in the Middle East and two in the Far East), and the Pioneer was finally withdrawn in the 1970s.

Specification: Scottish Aviation Pioneer CC.Mk 1 five-seat short-range STOL light transport
Span: 15.16 m (49 ft 9 in)
Length: 10.46 m (34 ft 4 in)
Powerplant: 1×Alvis Leonides Mk 502/4, 388 kW (520 hp)
Payload: four passengers
Normal T/O weight: 2631 kg (5,800 lb)
Max speed: 145 mph at 1,500 ft
Operational range: 300 miles with maximum payload

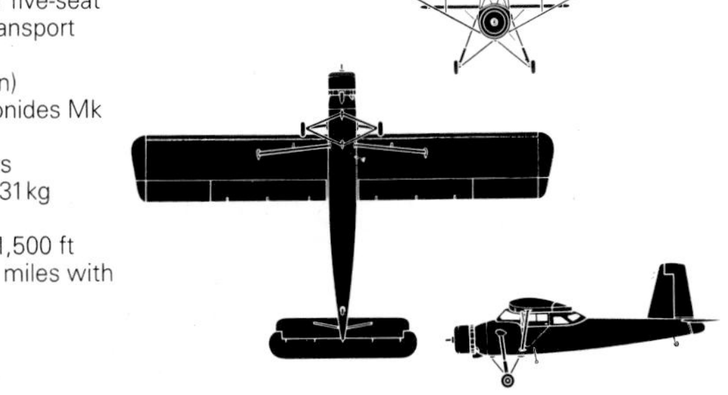

Hawker Siddeley Argosy

An Armstrong Whitworth/Hawker Siddeley Argosy of the RAF Benson Wing, which consisted of Nos 114 and 267 Squadrons. Some of these aircraft wore a desert camouflage scheme, and were affectionately known as chocolate bombers. The Argosy equipped two home-based transport units, and single squadrons in Aden, Cyprus and the Far East. A single calibration squadron also used the Argosy.

The Argosy was the military counterpart to the A.W.650 civil transport, and after development as a replacement for the Vickers Valetta, first flew in March 1961, some 27 months after the civil prototype. The type was based on a circular-section fuselage ending in upward/downward-opening rear 'crocodile doors' for straight-in loading and air-drops; when the type was used for paratrooping the volume inside the doors was used for kit stowage. The wing accommodated the four turboprops and the forward end of the twin booms that supported the tailplane and twin vertical surfaces, and the robust tricycle landing gear allowed operations from semi-prepared surfaces. Production for the RAF totalled 56 aircraft, these serving with six squadrons (three at home and one each in Cyprus, Aden and the Far East) before the type was withdrawn in 1975 as an economy measure.

Hawker Siddeley Comet

The Comet 1 was the world's first turbojet-powered airliner when it entered service with BOAC in May 1952, and from it was developed the Comet 2 with Rolls-Royce Avon axial-flow rather than de Havilland Ghost centrifugal-flow engines. In January and April 1954 two Comet 1s were lost, and airline confidence in the type plummeted. The RAF therefore took 10 Comet 2s with the square windows whose failures had caused the crashes after explosive decompression. With their window frames reinforced, the aircraft entered service with No. 216 Squadron as Comet C.Mk 2s, thereby becoming the world's first jet-powered military transports. From 1962 the Squadron also received five Comet C.Mk 4s with round windows, a longer fuselage for 94 passengers at a maximum weight of 73483 kg (162,000 lb), and 4763-kg (10,500-lb) Avon RA.29 engines for a speed of 542 mph.

Specification: de Havilland Comet C.Mk 2 49-seat medium-range transport
Span: 35.00 m (114 ft 10 in)
Length: 29.26 m (96 ft 0 in)
Powerplant: 4×Rolls-Royce Avon Mk 117/118, 3334 kg (7,350 lb) st each
Payload: 44 passengers
Max T/O weight: 54432 kg (120,000 lb)
Max speed: 480 mph at 40,000 ft
Operational range: 2,500 miles with maximum payload

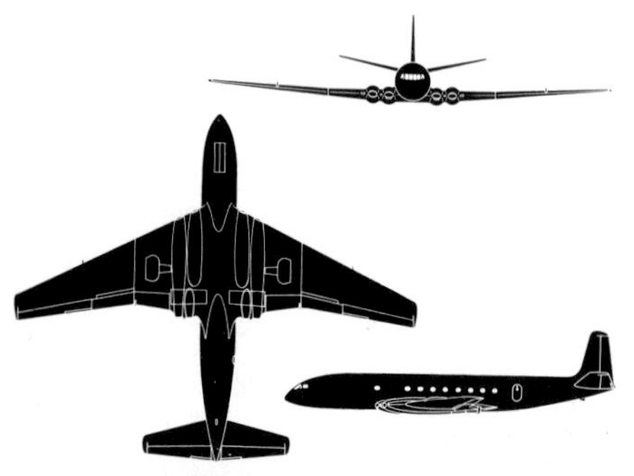

Scottish Aviation SA Twin Pioneer

The Twin Pioneer was, as its name suggests, the twin-engined larger brother of the Pioneer, and first flew in June 1955 as a 16-passenger civil transport. The RAF decided to order the type in 1956, initially contracting for 20 Twin Pioneer CC.Mk 1s equivalent to the baseline civil variant. The order was later increased to 39 aircraft, of which the last seven were delivered as Twin Pioneer CC.Mk 2s with a number of forgings and castings in place of original fabricated sheet metal and machined components. The last three introduced 477-kW (640-hp) Leonides Mk 531s that were then retrofitted to existing aircraft. With slats and flaps, the Twin Pioneer has the same type of STOL performance as the Pioneer, needing an area only 275 m (300 yards) long and 30.5 m (100 ft) wide for safe operation.

Specification: Scottish Aviation Twin Pioneer CC.Mk 1
19-seat short-range STOL light transport
Span: 23.32 m (76 ft 6 in)
Length: 13.79 m (45 ft 3 in)
Powerplant: 2×Alvis Leonides Mk 514, 410 kW (550 hp) each
Payload: 16 passengers, or 11 troops, or nine paratroops, or freight
Armament: 2×7.7-mm (0.303-in) machine-guns, plus provision for up 2×454-kg (1,000-lb), or 4×227- or 113-kg (500- or 250-lb) bombs
Normal T/O weight: 6623 kg (14,600 lb)
Max speed: 165 mph at 2,000 ft
Operational range: 398 miles with maximum passenger load

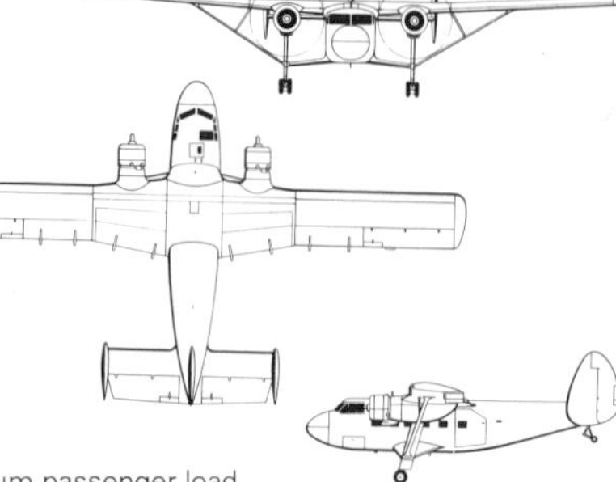

pecification: Hawker Siddeley rmstrong Whitworth) Argosy C.Mk 1 3-seat medium-range tactical transport
pan: 35.05 m (115 ft 0 in)
ength: 27.18 m (89 ft 2 in)
owerplant: 4×Rolls-Royce Dart RDa.8 Ak 101, 1998 kW (2,680 shp) each
ayload: 69 troops, or 54 paratroops, or 8 litters plus attendants, or 13154 kg 29,000 lb) of freight
Aax T/O weight: 46720 kg (103,000 lb)
Aax speed: 268 mph at 20,000 ft
)perational range: 345 miles with naximum payload

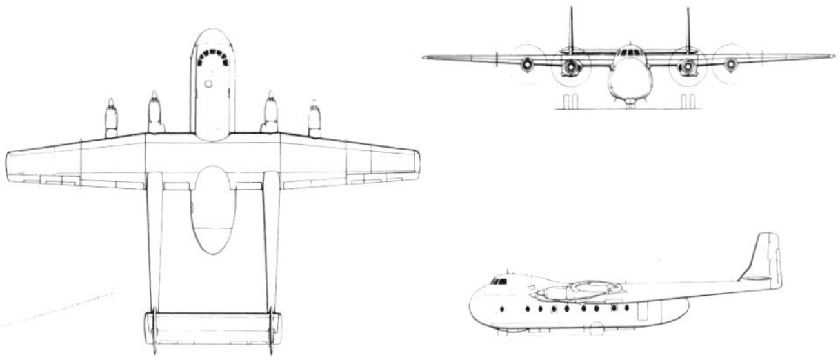

Bristol Britannia

Because of development delays the Britannia failed to secure the commercial success which it should have enjoyed, but was a classic turboprop-powered airliner that also had a significant career as a military transport. The Britannia C.Mk 1 was ordered in January 1956 and first flew in December 1958, production batches of six, four and 10 resulting in 20 mixed passenger and freight aircraft based on the civil Series 250 but fitted with a strengthened floor, rearward-facing seats and provision for the carriage of litters. Three ex-civil Britannia 252s were also delivered as crew trainers. The Britannia C.Mk 1s were operated by Nos 99 and 511 Squadrons of RAF Transport Command (later Air Support Command) until the mid-1970s, when the UK's apparently declining need for long-range transport led to their withdrawal.

Specification: Bristol Britannia C.Mk 1 119-seat long-range strategic transport
Span: 43.37 m (142 ft 3.5 in)
Length: 37.87 m (124 ft 3 in)
Powerplant: 4×Rolls-Royce (Bristol Siddeley) Proteus Mk 255, 3314 kW (4,445 shp) each
Payload: 113 troops, or 53 litters plus six attendants, or 16965 kg (37,400 lb) of freight
Max T/O weight: 83915 kg (185,000 lb)
Max speed: 360 mph at optimum altitude
Operational range: 4,268 miles with maximum payload

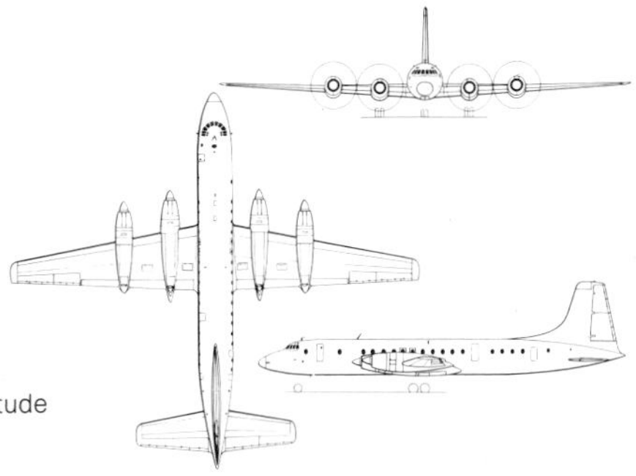

BAe (Vickers/BAC) VC10

The VC10 airliner was not a commercial success, but was clearly a considerable technical achievement offering long-range capability into comparatively small airfields. This persuaded the RAF to procure 14 of the type for a genuinely global airlift capability, the VC10 C.Mk 1 being ordered from September 1961 in batches of five, six and three as a variant of the standard VC10 with the powerplant and fin fuel tank of the Super VC10. Other features of the VC10 C.Mk 1, which first flew in November 1965, are a large cargo door in the port side of the forward fuselage, rearward-facing passenger seats, a strengthened floor, an inflight-refuelling probe and, in the tail cone, an Artouste auxiliary power unit to make the type fully independent of ground support facilities. The VC10 C.Mk 1s serve with No.10 Squadron based at RAF Brize Norton.

Specification: British Aerospace (Vickers/BAC) VC10 C.Mk 1 long-range strategic transport
Span: 44.55 m (146 ft 2 in)
Length: 40.74 m (133 ft 8 in) excluding probe
Powerplant: 4×Rolls-Royce Conway Mk 301, 9888 kg (21,800 lb) st each
Payload: 150 passengers, or 76 litters plus six attendants, or 26762 kg (59,000 lb) of freight
Max T/O weight: 146513 kg (323,000 lb)
Max speed: 580 mph at 30,000 ft
Operational range: 3,668 miles with maximum payload

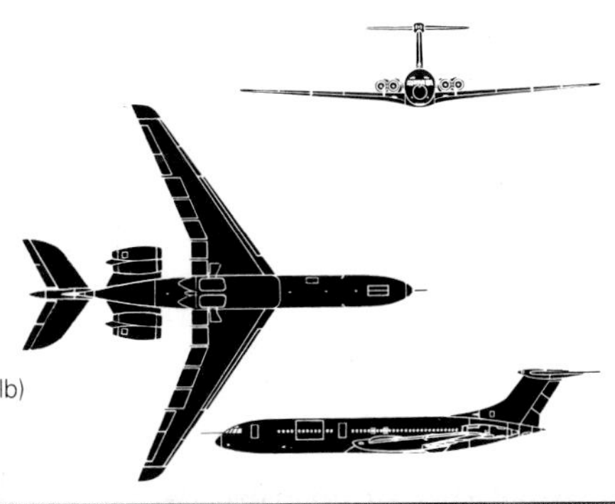

Douglas C-124 Globemaster II

The C-74 began life in World War II as a major development of the C-54 to provide the USAAF with a long-range heavy transport featuring a pilot and co-pilot in separate side-by-side cockpits. Deliveries of 14 aircraft were made between October 1945 and April 1947, and with four 2610-kW (3,500-hp) R-4360-49 radials the type could carry 125 troops or 25214 kg (55,586 lb) of freight. The C-124 was a radical development with a much larger fuselage accessed by clamshell chin doors and an inbuilt ramp. The YC-124 flew in November 1949 and was followed by 204 C-124As with 2610-kW R-3350-20W radials and by 243 C-124Cs with more power, additional fuel capacity, weather radar and wingtip combustion heaters for fuselage heating and deicing of the flying surfaces. The last aircraft was delivered in 1955, and the type passed to reserve service in the early 1960s.

Specification: Douglas C-124C Globemaster II eight-crew long-range personnel and freight transport
Span: 53.09 m (174 ft 2 in)
Length: 39.62 m (130 ft 0 in)
Powerplant: 4×Pratt & Whitney R-4360-63A, 2833 kW (3,800 hp) each
Payload: 200 troops, or 127 litters plus attendants, or 31072 kg (68,500 lb) of freight
Max T/O weight: 88225 kg (194,000 lb)
Max speed: 271 mph at sea level
Operational range: 4,030 miles with a 11964-kg (26,375-lb) payload

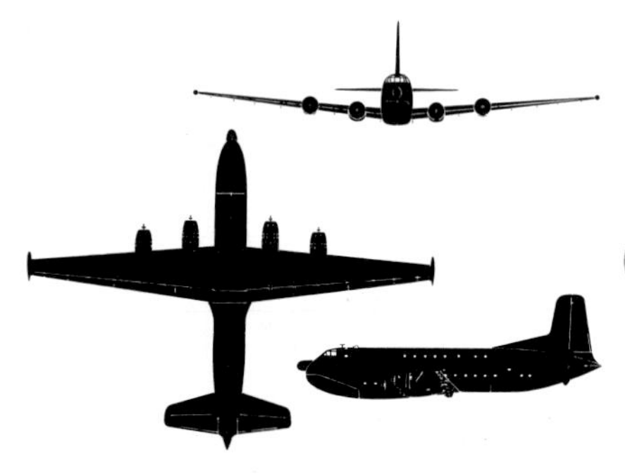

Douglas C-54 Skymaster

After its overly complex DC-4E airliner prototype Douglas turned its design attentions to a more practical unpressurised airliner, the DC-4A. This was overtaken by World War II and the 24 initial aircraft were taken over on the assembly line as C-54 26-seat military transports. Powered by 1007-kW (1,350-hp) R-2000-3 radials, the first of these flew in March 1942. Next came the militarised C-54A, of which 196 were built with 962-kW (1,290-hp) R-2000-7 engines, a freight door, a strengthened floor, and provision for 50 troops or freight. The 190 C-54Bs had integral wing tanks and provision for litters, the 294 C-54Ds had 1007-kW R-2000-11s, the 105 DC-4Es had more fuel and a convertible passenger/freight interior, and the 149 C-54Gs had 1081-kW (1,450-hp) R-2000-9s. There were many conversions to other roles in the period up to 1960, when most transports had disappeared from service.

Specification: Douglas C-54D Skymaster four-crew medium-range personnel and freight transport
Span: 35.81 m (117 ft 6 in)
Length: 28.60 m (93 ft 10 in)
Powerplant: 4×Pratt & Whitney R-2000-11, 1007 kW (1,350 hp) each
Payload: 50 troops or 14742 kg (32,500 lb) of freight
Max T/O weight: 33113 kg (73,000 lb)
Max speed: 275 mph at 20,000 ft
Operational range: 3,100 miles with a 6350-kg (14,100-lb) payload

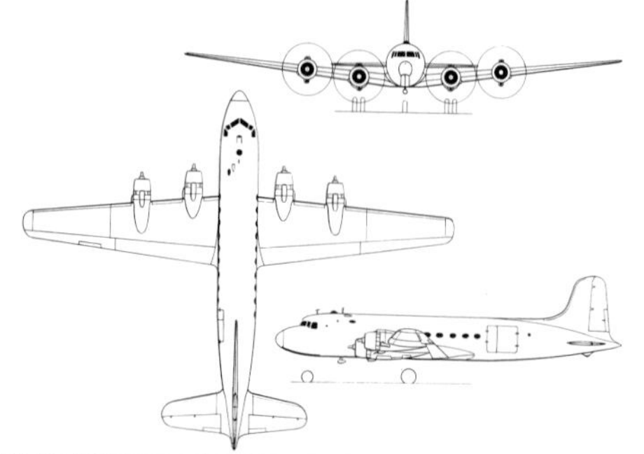

Boeing C-97 Stratofreighter

This was a transport based aerodynamically and structurally on the B-29 heavy bomber. The first of three XC-97 prototypes flew in November 1944, and these were followed by six generally similar YC-97s with Wright R-3350 radials before the advent of three YC-97As with features of the B-50 such as a taller fin and R-4360 radials. This set the pattern for the production series that started with the C-97A, of which 50 were built with R-4360-27 engines. Then came 14 C-97Cs with a strengthened cabin floor, and three earlier aircraft modified as C-97D flying command posts. Subsequent production centred on the KC-97 inflight-refuelling tanker series, of which about 160 were later modified as C-97G pure transports and C-97K tanker transports for the Strategic Air Command mission support role. There were also conversions to several other roles.

Specification: Boeing C-97G five-crew long-range personnel and freight transport
Span: 43.05 m (141 ft 3 in)
Length: 33.63 m (110 ft 4 in)
Powerplant: 4×Pratt & Whitney R-4360-59, 2610 kW (3,500 hp) each
Payload: 96 troops, or 69 litters plus attendants, or freight
Max T/O weight: 79380 kg (175,000 lb)
Max speed: 375 mph at optimum altitude
Operational range: 4,300 miles

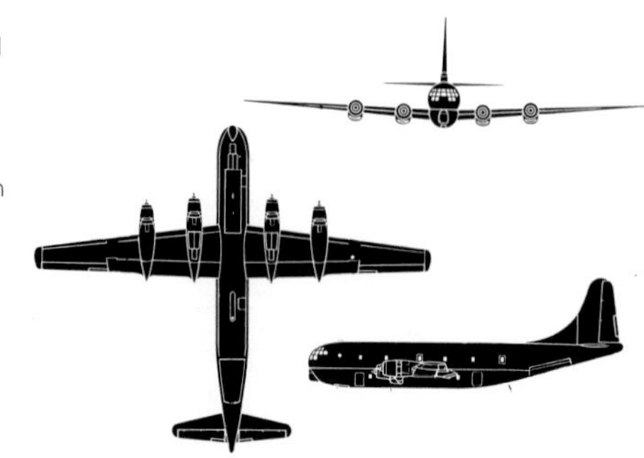

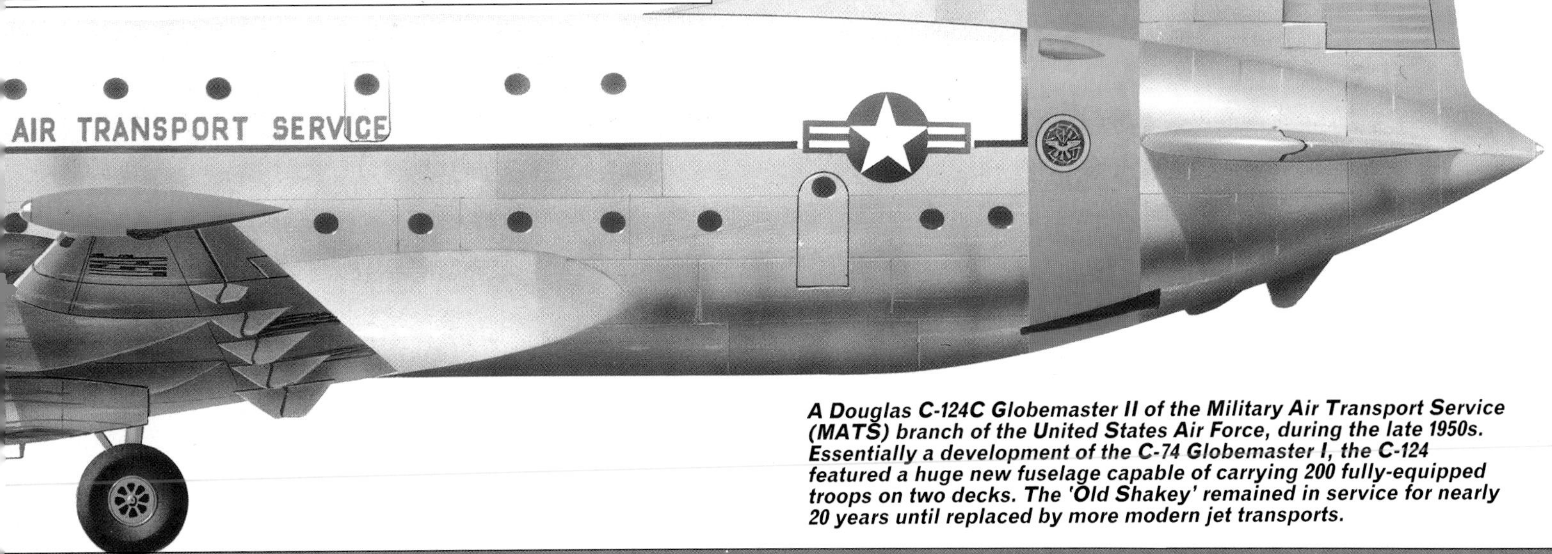

A Douglas C-124C Globemaster II of the Military Air Transport Service (MATS) branch of the United States Air Force, during the late 1950s. Essentially a development of the C-74 Globemaster I, the C-124 featured a huge new fuselage capable of carrying 200 fully-equipped troops on two decks. The 'Old Shakey' remained in service for nearly 20 years until replaced by more modern jet transports.

Douglas C-117 Skytrooper

This relatively little known aeroplane was a derivative of the C-47 for use as a staff transport. Towards the end of World War II the US Army felt that less spartan accommodation was appropriate for more important staff officers, and in 1944 and 1945 there appeared 17 C-117As with an airline-type interior seating 21 passengers. With the exception of this interior, an unreinforced floor and no freight-loading side doors, the aircraft were otherwise identical to the C-47B. The last C-117A was delivered in December 1945, and was the last new military variant of the DC-3 to be built. The designation C-117B was given to 11 C-117As with their engine high-blowers removed, and the designation C-117C was allocated during 1953 to 11 VC-47 transports after overhaul and revision to C-117B standard.

Specification: Douglas C-117A two/three-crew short/medium-range staff transport
Span: 28.96 m (95 ft 0 in)
Length: 19.66 m (64 ft 6 in)
Powerplant: 2×Pratt & Whitney R-1830-90C, 746 kW (1,000 hp) each
Payload: 21 passengers
Max T/O weight: 13608 kg (30,000 lb)
Max speed: 230 mph at 12,500 ft
Operational range: 1,600 miles

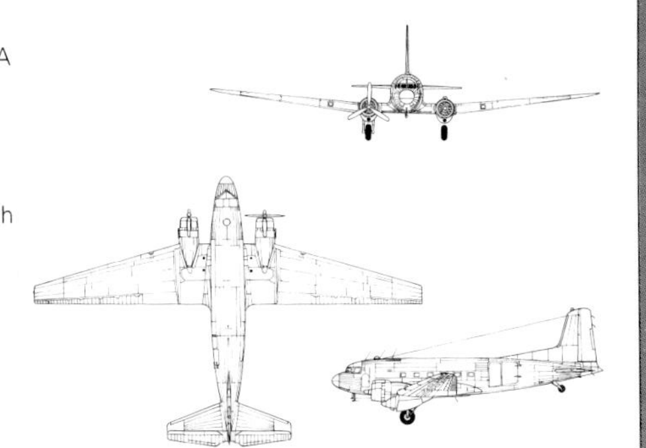

Douglas C-118 Liftmaster

This was the military equivalent of the DC-6A airliner, itself a development of the DC-4 that first flew in February 1946 after development with pressurised accommodation and greater payload under the military designation XC-112A. Military procurement started with a single C-118 (the 29th DC-6) as a 25-seat/12-bunk Presidential transport with the name *The Independence*. For personnel and logistic transport the USAF then bought 101 examples of the DC-6A with its fuselage stretched by 1.52 m (6 ft) by comparison with that of the DC-6. These aircraft were delivered between 1951 and 1955, and were bolstered by 40 similar R6D-1s loaned by the US Navy. The aircraft were used by the Military Air Transport Service (later Military Airlift Command) on the US forces' important transatlantic and transpacific routes. Some aircraft were modified as MC-118A aeromedical and VC-118A staff transports.

Specification: Douglas C-118A Liftmaster four/five-crew medium/long-range personnel and freight transport
Span: 35.81 m (117 ft 6 in)
Length: 32.18 m (105 ft 7 in)
Powerplant: 4×Pratt & Whitney R-2800-52W, 1864 kW (2,500 hp) each
Payload: 74 troops, or 60 litters plus attendants, or 12247 kg (27,000 lb) of freight
Max T/O weight: 48535 kg (107,000 lb)
Max speed: 307 mph at optimum altitude
Operational range: 2,925 miles with maximum payload

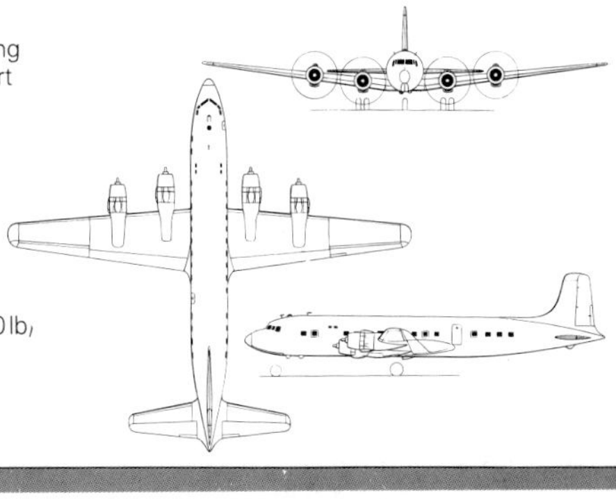

Douglas C-133 Cargomaster

This impressive aeroplane resulted from a 1952 requirement for a heavy strategic freighter. There was no prototype, the first of 35 C-133A production aircraft serving in this role after its first initial during April 1956. The type was powered by 4474-kW (6,000-shp) T34-P-3 turboprops and revealed the need for a dorsal fin extension. Later production aircraft had more power in the form of T34-P-7W or -7WA turboprops for greater take-off weight, from the eighth aeroplane onward a 'beaver tail' rear fuselage shape was introduced to improve local airflow, and the last three had clamshell rear doors to facilitate loading of lengthy items such as complete intermediate-range and intercontinental ballistic missiles. Further production resulted in 15 C-133B aircraft with 5592-kW (7,500-shp) T34-P-9W or -9WA turboprops and the clamshell rear doors.

Fairchild C-82 and C-119

Designed from 1941 as a specialised military freighter with twin booms supported the tail unit so that the central nacelle could have a large uninterrupted hold terminating in rear clamshell doors, the Packet first flew in September 1944 as the XC-82. There followed production of 220 C-82A aircraft with two 1566-kW (2,100-hp) R-2800-34 radials, glider-towing capability and accommodation for 42 paratroops; three similar C-82Ns were built by North American. The design was then revised with more power and the cockpit relocated into the forward fuselage contours, and after this had been tested as the XC-82B production was authorised as the C-119B with the fuselage widened by 0.356 m (14 in). Some 55 such aircraft were followed by 303 improved C-119Cs, 212 C-119Fs with ventral fins, and 480 C-119Gs with different propellers. There were also several updated variants culminating in the C-119L.

Specification: Fairchild C-119C four-crew short/medium-range troop and freight transport
Span: 32.385 m (109 ft 3 in)
Length: 26.37 m (86 ft 6 in)
Powerplant: 2×Pratt & Whitney R-4360-20, 2610 kW (3,500 hp) each
Payload: 62 troops or freight
Max T/O weight: 33566 kg (74,000 lb)
Max speed: 281 mph at 18,000 ft
Operational range: 1,770 miles

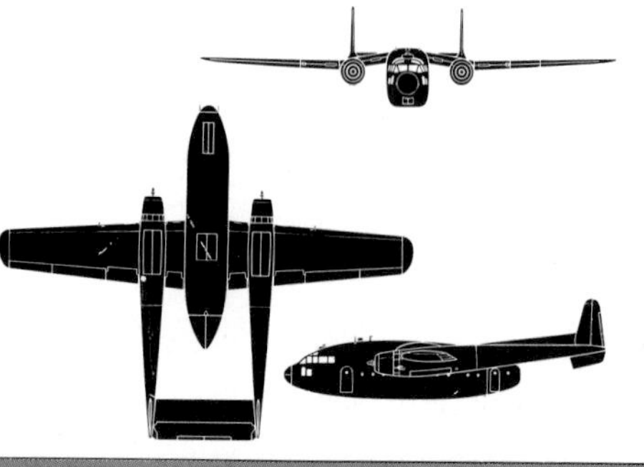

Lockheed C-121 Constellation

In 1948 the USAF ordered the L-749 version of the Constellation airliner, and nine C-121A and one VC-121B aircraft were powered by 1864-kW (2,500-hp) R-3350-75 radials. There followed 33 C-121Cs equivalent to the L-1049 Super Constellation with 2610-kW (3,500-hp) R-3350-34 engines and the fuselage lengthened by 6.35 m (20 ft 10 in) for the carriage of more payload at higher speed over longer range. A similar model was ordered by the US Navy as the R7V-1, and 32 of these aircraft with R-3350-91 radials were later transferred to the USAF with the designation C-121G, some remaining in service up to the 1970s with Air National Guard units. Many of these aircraft were later modified as staff transports with the basic designation VC-121, and larger numbers still were procured with the RC- and EC-121 designations for the Elint and airborne early warning roles respectively.

Specification: Lockheed C-121G Constellation four/five-crew long-range personnel and freight transport
Span: 37.49 m (121 ft 0 in)
Length: 35.41 m (116 ft 2 in)
Powerplant: 4×Wright R-3350-91, 2610 kW (3,500 hp) each
Payload: 72 troops or freight
Max T/O weight: 65772 kg (145,000 lb)
Max speed: 368 mph at 20,000 ft
Operational range: 2,100 miles

Specification: Douglas C-133A Cargomaster 10-crew long-range freight and personnel transport
Span: 54.76 m (179 ft 8 in)
Length: 48.01 m (157 ft 6 in)
Powerplant: 4×Pratt & Whitney T34-P-7WA, 4846 kW (6,500 shp) each
Payload: 368.1 m^3 (13,000 cu ft) of freight or 200 passengers
Max T/O weight: 127915 kg (282,000 lb)
Max speed: 331 mph at optimum altitude
Operational range: 3,795 miles with a 21319-kg (47,000-lb) payload

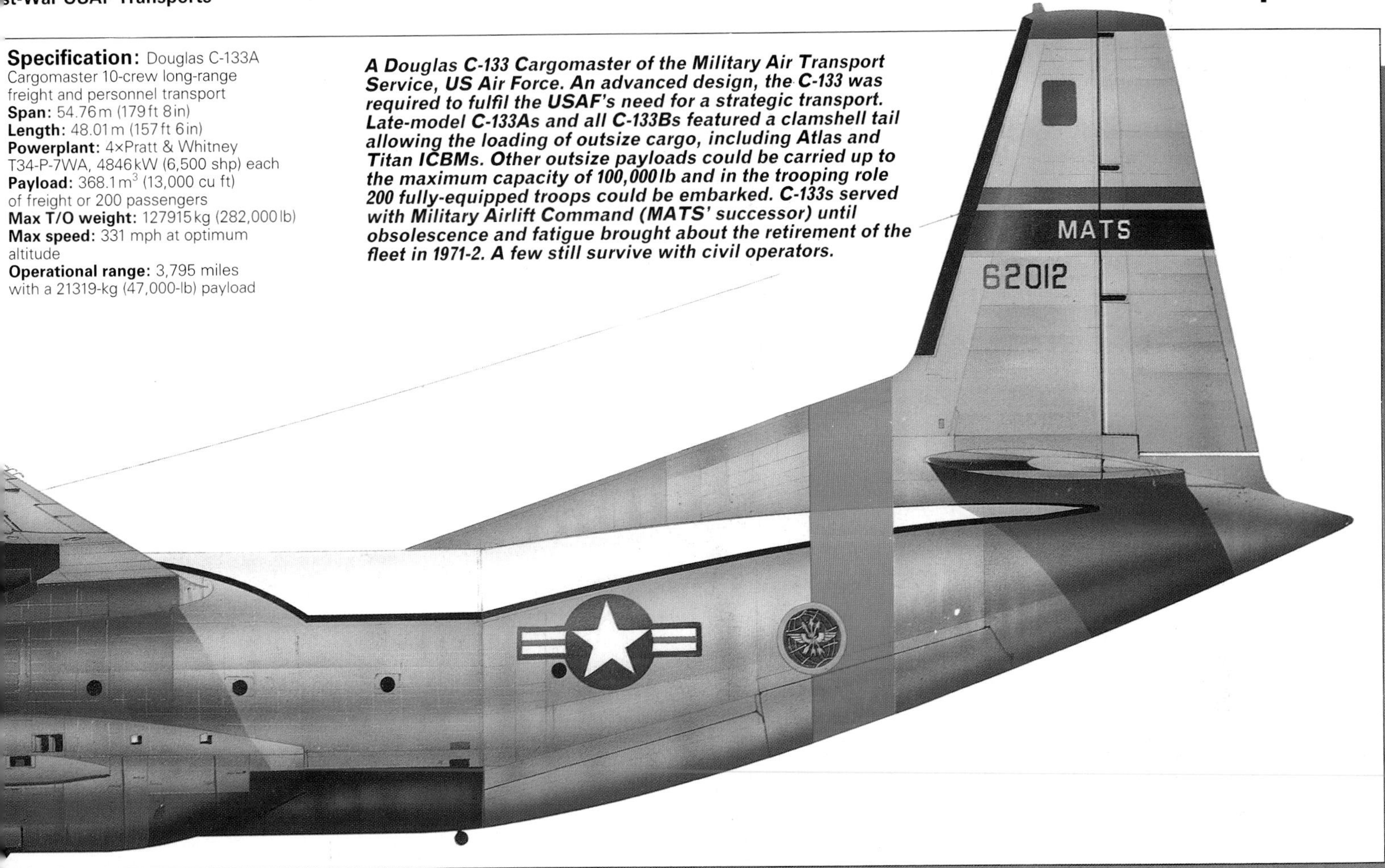

A Douglas C-133 Cargomaster of the Military Air Transport Service, US Air Force. An advanced design, the C-133 was required to fulfil the USAF's need for a strategic transport. Late-model C-133As and all C-133Bs featured a clamshell tail allowing the loading of outsize cargo, including Atlas and Titan ICBMs. Other outsize payloads could be carried up to the maximum capacity of 100,000 lb and in the trooping role 200 fully-equipped troops could be embarked. C-133s served with Military Airlift Command (MATS' successor) until obsolescence and fatigue brought about the retirement of the fleet in 1971-2. A few still survive with civil operators.

MATS

62012

Fairchild C-123 Provider

From its CG-18 cargo glider Chase developed the YC-122 powered transport, of which one YC-122 and two YC-122As were produced with two R-2000-11 radials. One YC-122A became the sole YC-122B with R-1820-101 radials, and the nine YC-122Cs were similar. The same path was followed with the CG-20. The prototype was engined with two R-2800-83 radials and flew in October 1949 as the XC-123A; a second machine was flown as the XC-123A with four J47 turbojets in podded pairs, but did not progress past this stage. The production contract for 300 C-123Bs finally went to Fairchild, and these began to enter service in 1955 with a large dorsal fin. Later conversions were 10 C-123Hs with two Fairchild J44-R-3 booster turbojets under the wings for arctic operations, and 183 C-123Ks with two 1293-kg (2,850-lb) thrust General Electric J85-GE-17 booster turbojets for improved all-round performance.

Specification: Fairchild C-123B Provider two-crew short/medium-range troop and freight transport
Span: 33.53 m (110 ft 0 in)
Length: 23.09 m (75 ft 9 in)
Powerplant: 2×Pratt & Whitney R-2800-99W, 1715 kW (2,300 hp) each
Payload: 61 troops, or 50 litters and six seated casualties plus attendants, or freight
Max T/O weight: 27216 kg (60,000 lb)
Max speed: 245 mph at optimum altitude
Operational range: 1,470 miles

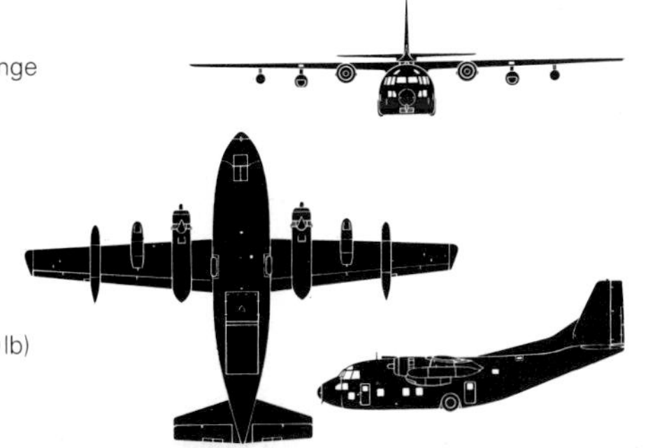

Northrop C-125 Raider

First flown in December 1946, the N-23 Pioneer was a STOL tri-motor transport designed for the commercial market. The type had fixed tailwheel landing gear and full-span ailerons and flaps, and after winning a 1947 USAF competition for a short-field tactical transport the N-32 version was ordered in small numbers as the YC-125. The batch of 23 aircraft comprised no more than a service trials batch, and deliveries from 1950 were of 13 YC-125A aircraft configured for the light assault role and 10 YC-125B aircraft configured for the Arctic rescue role with hold fittings for 20 litters, and provision for skis instead of wheels. The YC-125A had only a short operational career before the aircraft were relegated to ground use as maintenance training airframes at Shepherd Air Force Base up to 1955.

Specification: Northrop YC-125A Raider two-crew short-range STOL troop and freight transport
Span: 26.38 m (86 ft 6.5 in)
Length: 20.45 m (67 ft 1 in)
Powerplant: 3×Wright R-1820-99, 895 kW (1,200 hp) each
Payload: 32 troops or 5443 kg (12,000 lb) of freight
Max T/O weight: 18552 kg (40,900 lb)
Max speed: 207 mph at optimum altitude
Operational range: not recorded

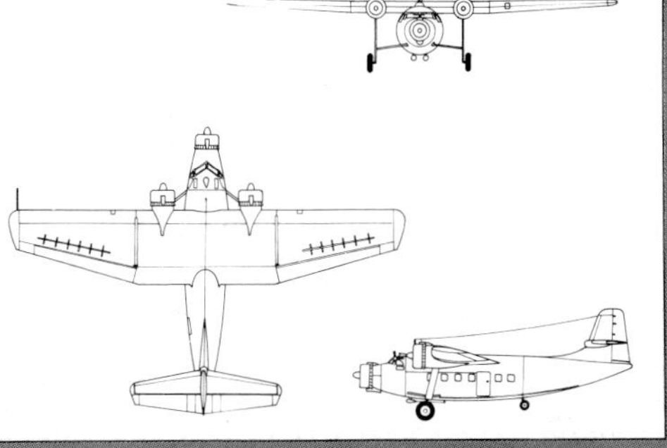

Convair C-131 Samaritan

The USAF procured 472 examples of the CV-240, 340 and 440 series of airliners in nine main variants. The pure transport versions were the C-131 (26 CV-240s with accommodation for 37 passengers or more often 27 litters plus attendants in the aeromedical role, and powered by 1864-kW/2,500-hp R-2800-99W radials), the C-131B (36 CV-240/340 hybrids for 48 passengers but often used as electronic test-beds, and powered by R-2800-99Ws or -103Ws), and the C-131D (27 CV-340s for 44 passengers and powered by R-2800-52Ws); the same C-121D designation was also used for six CV-440s. The USAF also operated ex-US Navy R4Y variants with the designations C-131F and C-131G, and there were also several VC-131 staff transport variants with improved soundproofing. These included the VC-131H, of which there were two equivalent to the CV-580 with 2796-kW (3,750-shp) Allison T56-A-9 turboprops.

Specification: Convair C-131B Samaritan four-crew short-range personnel and freight transport
Span: 32.11 m (105 ft 4 in)
Length: 24.13 m (79 ft 2 in)
Powerplant: 2×Pratt & Whitney R-2800-99W, 1864 kW (2,500 hp) each
Payload: 48 passengers or freight
Max T/O weight: 21319 kg (47,000 lb)
Max speed: 293 mph at optimum altitude
Operational range: 450 miles

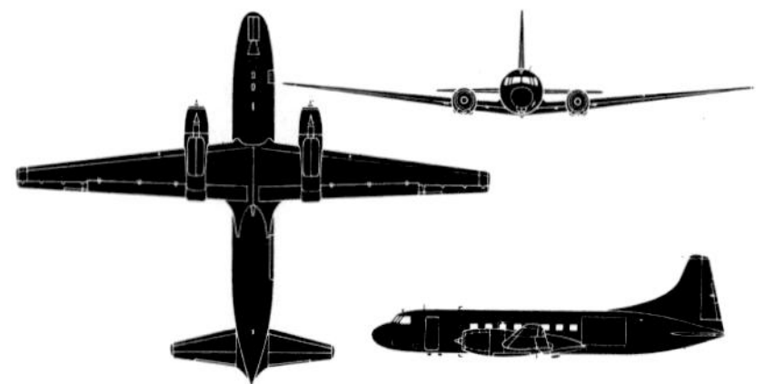

Lockheed C-130 Hercules

Development of the Hercules was started in 1951 to meet a USAF requirement for a turboprop-powered tactical transport, and the first of two YC-130 prototypes flew in August 1954 with blunt-nosed fuselage and 2423-kW (3,250-shp) T56-A-1 engines driving three-bladed propellers. The type was clearly a winner, and production was ordered of the C-130A model with a revised weather-radar nose and 2796-kW (3,750-shp) T56-A-1A (later -9) turboprops. In the pure transport role these 216 aircraft were followed by 145 C-130Bs with greater fuel capacity and 3020-kW (4,050-shp) T56-A-7s driving four-bladed propellers, 428 longer-range C-130Es with provision for two 5148-litre (1,360-US gal) underwing tanks in place of the earlier variants' 1703-litre (450-US gal) tanks, and 142 C-130Hs with 3661-kW (4,910-shp) T56-A-15s.

Specification: Lockheed C-130E Hercules four-crew short/medium-range troop and freight transport
Span: 40.41 m (132 ft 7 in)
Length: 29.79 m (97 ft 9 in)
Powerplant: 4×Allison T56-A-7A, 3020 kW (4,050 shp) each
Payload: 92 troops or freight
Max T/O weight: 79380 kg (175,000 lb)
Max speed: 384 mph at optimum altitude
Operational range: 2,420 miles with maximum payload

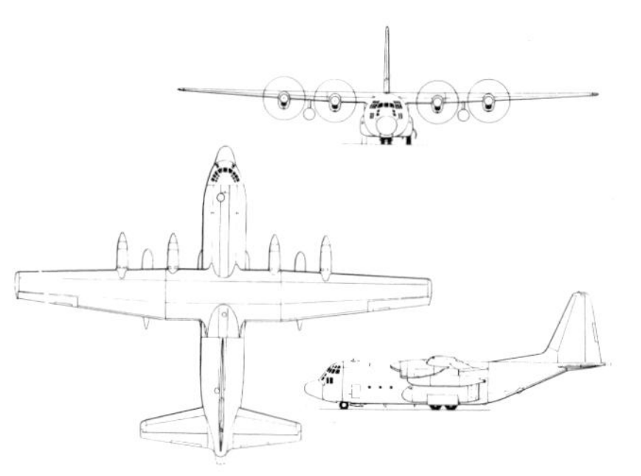

Boeing C-135 Stratolifter

Developed with the KC-135A Stratotanker from the Model 367-80 private-venture prototype, this was essentially the military counterpart to the Model 707 airliner, but was built in only modest numbers as the USAF's transport needs were (or were about to be) met by other types including the KC-135A that could double in this role with 80 seats or 37649 kg (83,000 lb) of freight. C-135 production of 48 aircraft was undertaken pending delivery of the C-141 StarLifter, the first 18 being C-135As with 6237-kg (13,750-lb) thrust J57-P-59W turbojets and the last 30 C-135Bs with 8165-kg (18,000-lb) thrust TF33-P-5 turbofans and a larger tailplane. Both variants lacked the KC-135's boom system, but retained structural provision for its retrofit. With the advent of the StarLifter the C-135s were converted into other forms for a host of alternative command and electronic roles.

Specification: Boeing C-135 four/five-crew long-range personnel and freight transport
Span: 39.88 m (130 ft 10 in)
Length: 41.53 m (136 ft 3 in)
Powerplant: 4×Pratt & Whitney J57-P-59W, 6237 kg (13,750 lb) st each
Payload: 126 troops or 40370 kg (89,000 lb) of freight
Max T/O weight: 134719 kg (297,000 lb)
Max speed: 585 mph at 30,000 ft
Operational range: not recorded

Lockheed C-141A StarLifter

The StarLifter was the first all-jet strategic transport to enter service after development to a 1960 requirement for a logistic airlifter to modernise the Military Air Transport Service (later Military Airlift Command). The type adhered to the basic design formula pioneered by the Lockheed Hercules with a rectangular-section hold, rear ramp/door, high wing and main landing gear units in external blisters though modified with a swept configuration, a T-tail and turbofan engines. The first C-141A flew in December 1963 and proved all that the USAF had demanded of the design. Production totalled 284 aircraft, the last of these being delivered in December 1966. The type entered regular service in April 1965, and was soon so much the workhorse of the airlift across the Pacific to supply the US forces in Vietnam that the C-97 and C-124 were retired, and the C-135 allocated to other tasks.

Specification: Lockheed C-141A StarLifter four-crew long-range freight and personnel transport
Span: 48.79 m (160 ft 1 in)
Length: 44.20 m (145 ft 0 in)
Powerplant: 4×Pratt & Whitney TF33-P-7, 9526 kg (21,000 lb) st each
Payload: 32136 kg (70,847 lb) of freight, or 154 troops, or 123 paratroops
Max T/O weight: 143610 kg (316,600 lb)
Max speed: 571 mph at 25,000 ft
Operational range: 4,080 miles

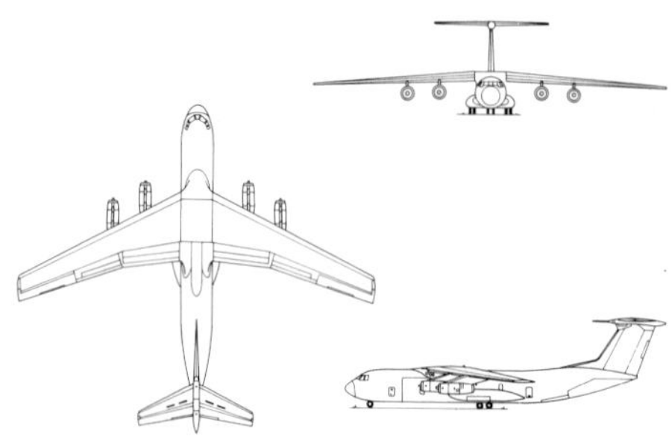

ockheed TriStar

he TriStar is unusual amongst modern airlifters in being an airliner by origin. The first L-1011 vas flown in December 1970, and the type was then produced in basic L-1011-1, extended-ange L-1011-100, improved take-off L- 1011-200 and long-range L-1011-500 variants. As irlines started to phase the type out of service, the RAF decided to adopt it for conversion s a tanker and freighter, resulting in three military variants with underfloor tankage for ransfer fuel. The four TriStar K.Mk 1s and two TriStar KC.Mk 2s are ex-British Airways -1011-500s converted for the tanker and tanker/freighter roles, the latter with a freight door neasuring 3.56 m (11 ft 8 in) by 2.64 m (8 ft 8 in), while the three TriStar K.Mk 2s are ex-Pan merican L-1011-500 aircraft modified approximately to K.Mk 1 standard with about 4536 kg 10,000 lb) less transfer fuel.

pecification: Lockheed riStar K.Mk 1 207-seat long-range eavy transport and inflight-efuelling tanker
pan: 50.09 m (164 ft 6 in)
ength: 50.05 m (164 ft 2.5 in)
owerplant: 3×Rolls-Royce RB211-524B4, 22680 kg (50,000 lb) t each
ayload: 204 passengers or 44500 kg (98,110 lb) of freight, plus rovision for 175974 litres (38,810 mp gal) of transfer fuel
Max T/O weight: 245000 kg (540,000 lb)
Max speed: 600 mph at 35,000 ft
Operational range: 4,835 miles

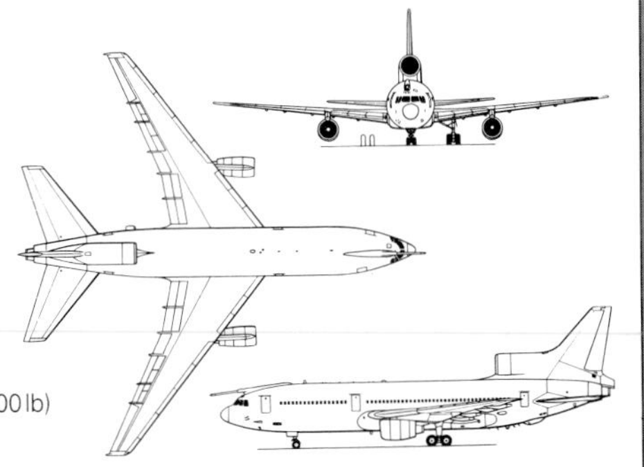

Douglas DC-8

The DC-8 prototype first flew on 30 May 1958, initiating a successful family of airliners, which although never rivalled the Boeing 707 for popularity was bought in considerable numbers for long-distance sectors. With the advent of noise regulations, many DC-8s had their original JT3D engines replaced by fuel-efficient and quiet CFM56 turbofans, these re-engined aircraft being designated in the 70 Series. Military use is very limited, although France, Spain, Peru and Thailand fly the type. These mainly fulfil a long-range passenger or VIP transport function, although one French aircraft is used for the collection of signals intelligence.

Specification: Douglas DC-8 Series 50 189-seat long-range passenger/freight transport
Span: 43.41 m
Length: 45.87 m
Powerplant: 4×Pratt & Whitney JT3D-3 turbofans, 8165-kg thrust each
Payload: maximum of 179, passengers or cargo in cabin
Max T/O weight: 142884 kg
Max speed: 932 km/h
Operational range: 9205 km

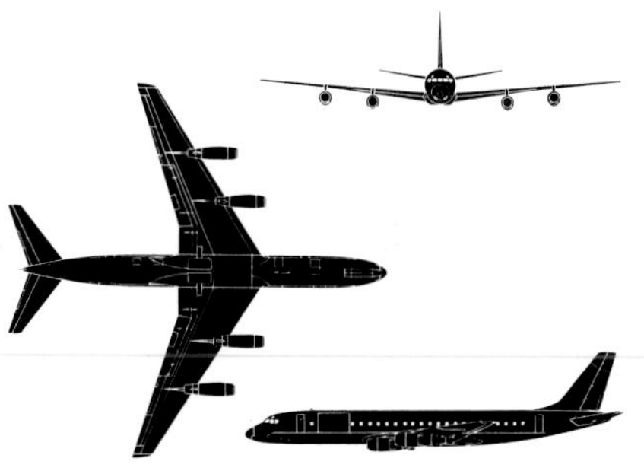

McDonnell Douglas KC-10A Extender

Based on the civil Douglas DC-10-30, the KC-10A Extender is a dual-role tanker/transport, with a refuelling boom and triple-point drogue refuelling capability if required. The main cabin is left clear for the carriage of either passengers or cargo, configurations being easily changed. In the transport role it is frequently used to transport high-value cargoes worldwide, including nuclear weapons. Using both its talents simultaneously it can deploy tactical aircraft over long distances, hauling support equipment and personnel in addition to providing fuel. The aircraft first flew on 12 July 1980, and 60 have since been ordered for Strategic Air Command, serving with the 2nd BW, 22nd ARW and 68th ARG.

Specification: McDonnell Douglas KC-10A Extender long-range transport/tanker
Span: 50.40 m
Length: 55.35 m
Powerplant: 3×General Electric CF6-50C2 turbofans, 23814 kg thrust each
Payload: 76843 kg and some passengers
Max T/O weight: 267620 kg
Max speed: 982 km/h
Operational range: 7033 km

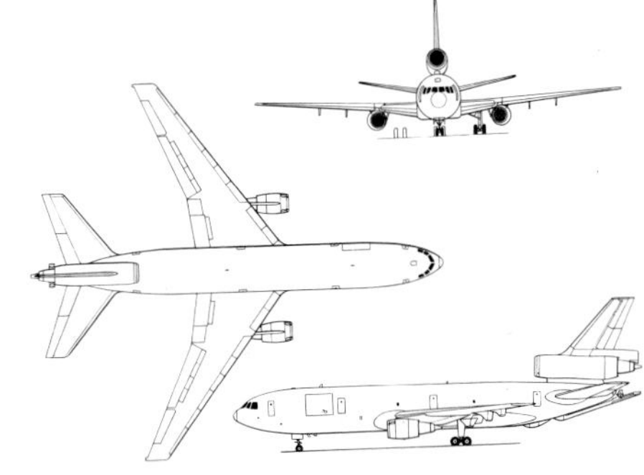

McDonnell Douglas C-17

Due to enter service in the early 1990s after a first flight in 1990, the C-17 is a conventionally configured military transport with 14-wheel landing gear and advanced features such as winglets for improved cruise performance, a large proportion of composites in the structure, and STOL airfield performance to allow the delivery of major loads into front-line airstrips after long-range delivery flights: as such the type can be used for strategic and tactical missions. The hold is accessed by a rear ramp/door, and is 26.52 m (87 ft 10 in) long including the 5.79-m (19-ft) rear ramp; the width and height are 5.49 m (18 ft) and 4.11 m (13 ft 6 in) respectively. The hold floor is fitted with roller conveyors, and its roof with a cargo winch. The C-17 has a major airdrop capability for 102 paratroops or a single-platform load of 24945 kg (55,000 lb).

Specification: McDonnell Douglas C-17 105-seat long-range heavy transport
Span: 50.29 m (165 ft 0 in)
Length: 52.02 m (170 ft 8 in)
Powerplant: 4×Pratt & Whitney F117 (PW2037), 17055 kg (37,600 lb) st each
Payload: 144 passengers, or 102 paratroops, or 78110 kg (259,000 lb) of freight
Max T/O weight: 259455 kg (572,000 lb)
Max speed: 512 mph
Operational range: 2,765 miles with maximum payload

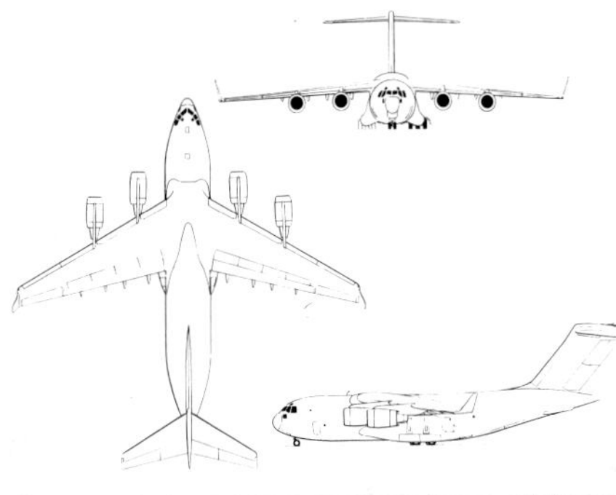

Lockheed C-5 Galaxy

Designed as a strategic transport able to operate into and out of poor airfields, the C-5A first flew in June 1966 and soon proved itself an able transporter of equipment such as complete missile equipments, tanks and large-calibre artillery. In configuration the Galaxy adheres to the modern concept with 28-wheel landing gear, a high wing carrying the four purpose-designed TF39-GE-1 turbofans, and an upswept tail for provision of a ventral loading ramp/door that is complemented by a hinging nose for through loading. The main hold is 36.91 m (121 ft 1 in) long, 5.79 m (19 ft) wide and 4.11 m (13 ft 6 in) high, and is served by powered freight handling systems. There is also accommodation in two upper-deck compartments for 90 passengers. The 50 C-5Bs have revised wings, greater power and a number of systems improvements, and 77 C-5As have been revised to this standard.

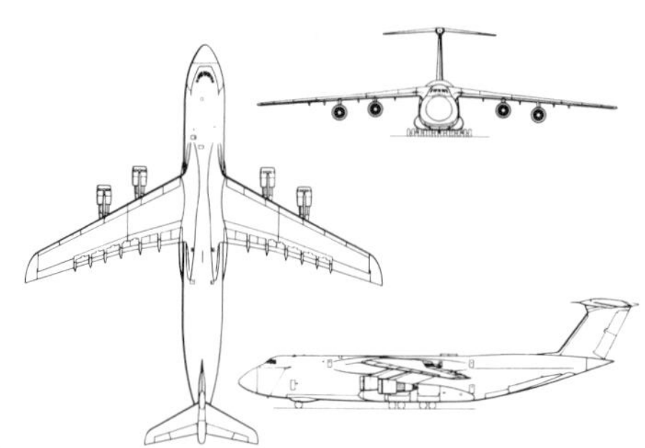

Specification: Lockheed C-5B Galaxy 370-seat long-range heavy transport
Span: 67.88 m (222 ft 8.5 in)
Length: 75.54 m (247 ft 10 in)
Powerplant: 4×General Electric TF39-GE-1C, 19504 kg (43,000 lb) st each
Payload: 90 passengers (standard) and 118390 kg (261,000 lb) of freight or 370 passengers
Max T/O weight: 379663 kg (837,000 lb)
Max speed: 571 mph at 25,000 ft
Operational range: 3,400 miles with maximum payload

Antonov An-72/An-74 'Coaler-A/B'

The An-72 first flew in December 1977 as a STOL-capable turbofan replacement for the An-26 turboprop-powered tactical transport, and uses the 'Coanda effect' for its high lift: the twin high-set engines are well clear of the debris which can cause problems on dirt airfields, and they exhaust over the titanium upper surface of the wings and their double- and triple-slotted flaps. The high-set tail allows the use of a rear ramp/door for access to the hold, which is 9.0 m (29 ft 6.25 in) long, 2.1 m (6 ft 10.75 in) wide and 2.2 m (7 ft 2.5 in) high: a movable 2500-kg (5,511-lb) capacity winch aids freight movement. The An-74 is a version optimised for arctic operations with alternative wheel/ski landing gear, a fuselage lengthened for weather radar, a revised wing spanning 2.9 m (9 ft 6 in) more than that of the An-72, and specialised de-icing and electronic equipment.

Specification: Antonov An-74 'Coaler-B' 35-seat short-range light STOL transport
Span: 31.90 m (104 ft 7.9 in)
Length: 28.70 m (94 ft 1.9 in)
Powerplant: 2×Lotarev D-36, 6500 kg (14,330 lb) st each
Payload: 32 passengers or 10000 kg (22,046 lb) of freight
Max T/O weight: 34500 kg (76,059 lb)
Max speed: 342 mph at optimum altitude
Operational range: 715 miles with maximum payload

Antonov An-124 Ruslan 'Condor'

The An-124 was designed in the 1970s as successor to the An-22 in the same basic roles, but is an altogether more capable aeroplane with a powerplant comprising four large turbofans. The type began to enter service in 1986, and amongst its military freighting capabilities is the ability to lift an entire SS-20 missile. The hold is 36.0 m (118 ft 1.5 in) long, and its width and height are 6.4 m and 14.4 m (21 ft and 14 ft 5 in) respectively. The type is designed for through-loading with a rear ramp/door and hinging nose, and stowage of freight is facilitated by two 10000-kg (22,046-lb) capacity longitudinally travelling gantries and two 5000-kg (11,023-lb) capacity transversely moving winches. There is a flightdeck separate from the compartment for a small number of passengers, in military service the manpower associated with the embarked freight load.

Specification: Antonov An-124 Ruslan 'Condor' 94-seat long-range heavy transport
Span: 73.30 m (240 ft 5.8 in)
Length: 69.50 m (228 ft 0.2 in)
Powerplant: 4×Lotarev D-18T, 23425 kg (51,642 lb) st each
Payload: 88 passengers and 150000 kg (330,693 lb) of freight
Max T/O weight: 405000 kg (892,872 lb)
Max speed: 537 mph at 39,370 ft
Operational range: 2,796 miles with maximum payload

The Lockheed C-5 Galaxy took over from the An-22 the honour of being the largest aircraft in the world, but has now lost it to the An-124 and the new six-engined An-225. The Galaxy was designed as a strategic military freighter, able to operate out of even the poorest airfields, and capable of carrying the largest items of military equipment. It entered service in 1971, after a first flight in June 1968.

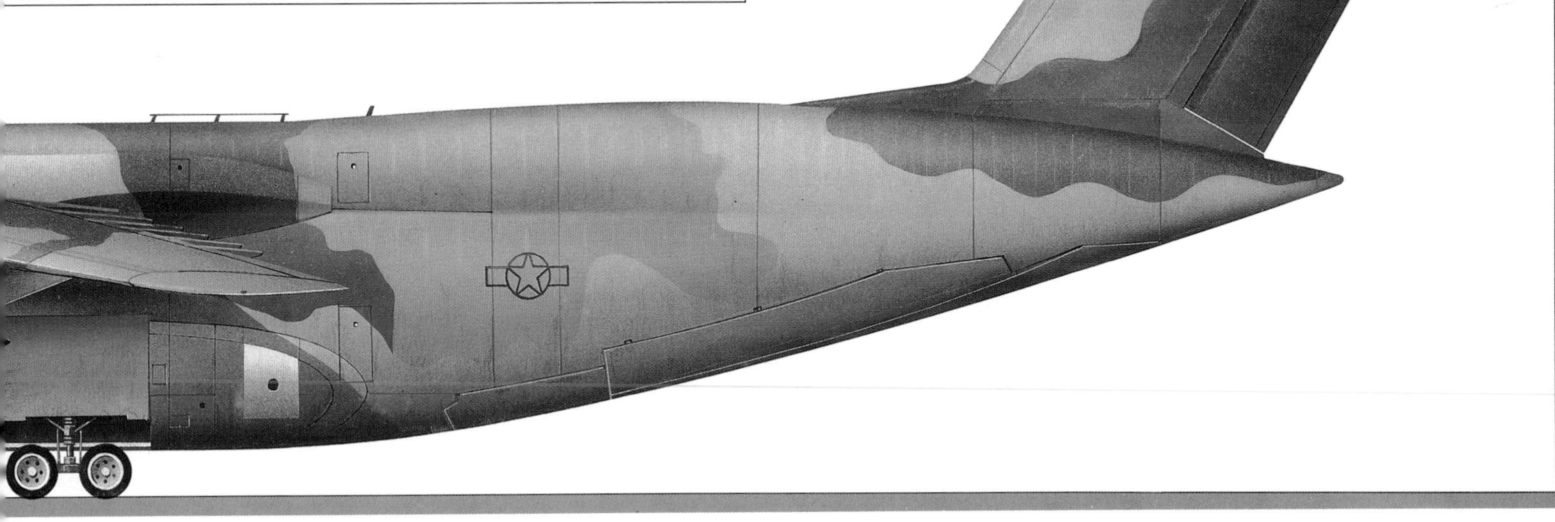

BAe (Vickers/BAC) VC10 C.Mk 1

The VC10 was planned as competitor to the Boeing 707 and McDonnell-Douglas DC-8 in the turbofan-powered intercontinental airliner role, the British hoping in vain that their design's large wing and low landing speed would encourage sales to airlines operating into smaller international airports that might not be prepared to extend their runways to cater for the American airliners. The first flight was made in June 1962. Civil sales were poor, so a military sale of 14 aircraft was doubly welcome. This VC10 C.Mk 1 was needed for a number of long-range tasks, and combined the fuselage of the VC10 with the basic powerplant and fuel system of the Super VC10, backward-facing seats, a large freight door in the port side of the forward fuselage, and a measure of local strengthening for the military version's harsher operating conditions.

Specification: BAe VC10 C.Mk 1
155-seat long-range heavy transport
Span: 44.55 m (146 ft 2 in)
Length: 48.36 m (158 ft 8 in) excluding probe
Powerplant: 4×Rolls-Royce Conway Mk 301, 9888 kg (21,800 lb)
Payload: 150 passengers, or 78 litters plus attendants, or 24494 kg (54,000 lb) of freight
Max T/O weight: 146512 kg (323,000 lb)
Max speed: 580 mph at optimum altitude
Operational range: 3,900 miles with maximum payload

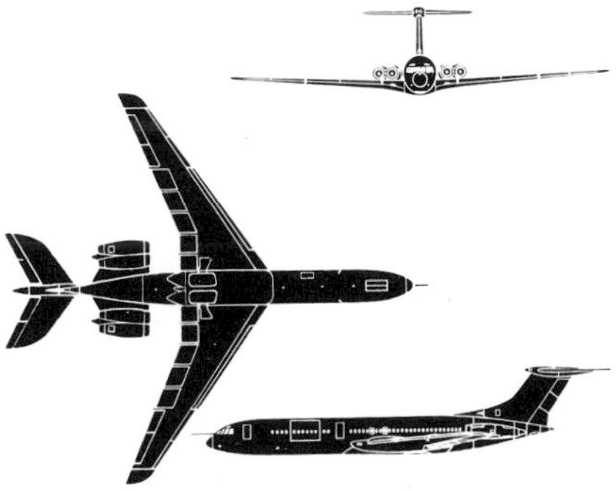

Boeing 707

The Boeing 367-80 was a company-funded prototype which spawned the extensive C-135 tanker/transport family and the slightly larger 707 airliner series. The latter was to become the most important airliner of its day, revolutionising long-distance travel. With its good range and internal capacity, several air arms purchased the type for long-range passenger/cargo transport and for the carriage of VIPs, while several nations have equipped the type for intelligence-gathering and inflight-refuelling. Notable military users include Argentina, Australia, Brazil, Canada, Iran, and West Germany. For many years Boeing 707s provided the President of the United States with his transport, designated C-137C, and the USAF still maintains a small fleet for VIP use.

Specification: Boeing 702-320
long-range passenger/cargo transport
Span: 44.42 m
Length: 36.61 m
Powerplant: 4×Pratt & Whitney JT37D-7 turbofans, 8618 kg thrust each
Payload: up to 219 passengers in high-density arrangement or 40325 kg of cargo
Max T/O weight: 151318 kg
Max speed: 974 km/h
Operational range: 5834 km

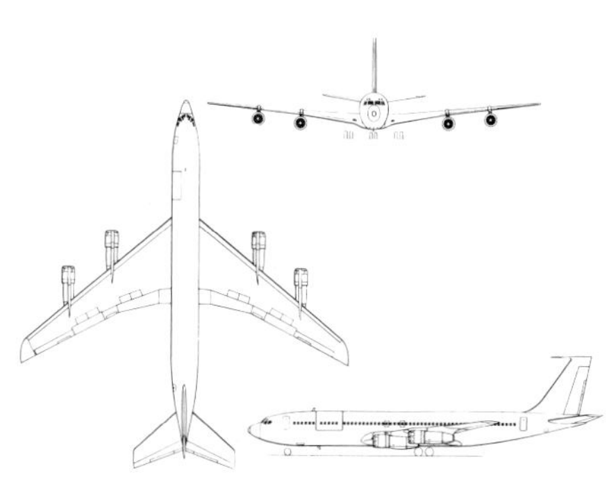

Antonov An-22 Antei 'Cock'

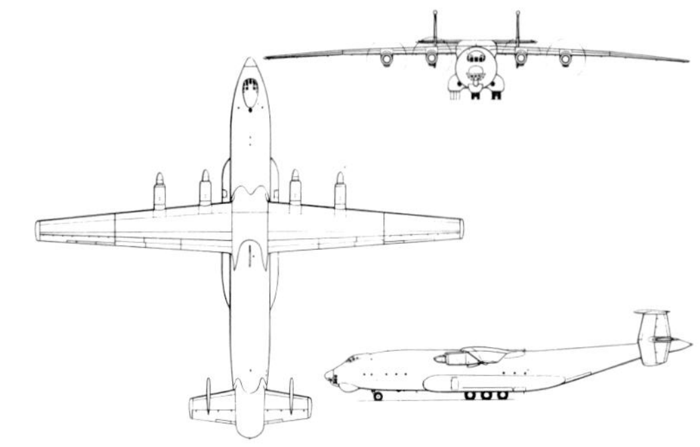

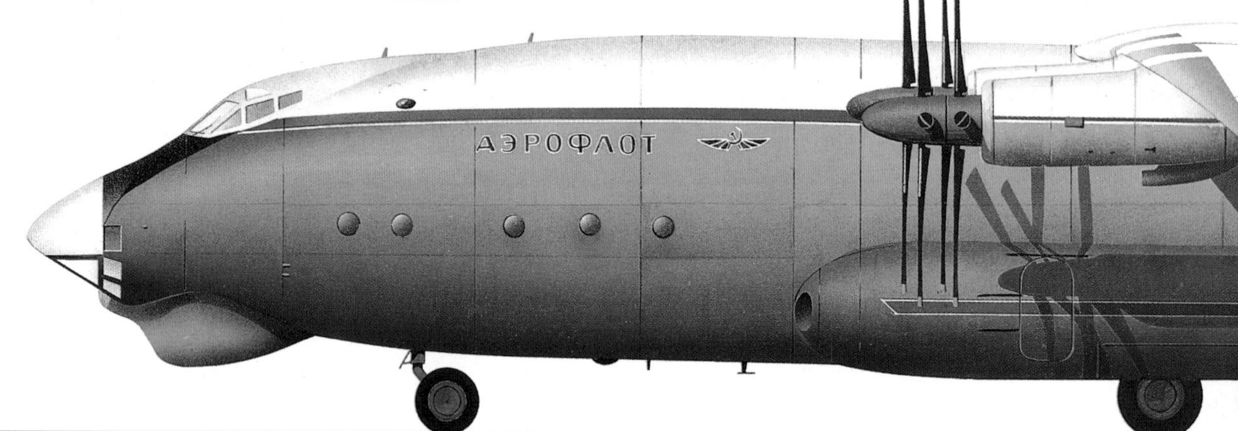

Specification: Antonov An-22 Antei 'Cock' 35-seat long-range heavy transport
Span: 64.40 m (211 ft 4 in)
Length: 57.92 m (190 ft 0 in)
Powerplant: 4×Kuznetsov NK-12MA, 11185 kW (15,000 shp) each
Payload: 29 passengers and 80000 kg (176,350 lb) of freight
Max T/O weight: 250000 kg (551,160 lb)
Max speed: 460 mph at optimum altitude
Operational range: 3,107 miles with maximum payload

Boeing 747

Replacing the Boeing 707 as the world's standard long-range transport, the 747 offered even greater internal capacity and economy, but the capacity has proved rather more than the average needs of military forces. The airframe did provide the basis for the E-4 command post, but in the military transport role Iran was the only purchaser, buying 16 in pre-revolutionary days. Other governments, notably Saudi Arabia, employ the aircraft in a quasi-military role, while the US military places many contracts with airlines for troop and cargo transport. Nineteen Pan Am 747s have been converted to act in time of emergency as military transports under the designation C-19.

Specification: Boeing 747-200B long-range heavy transport
Span: 59.64 m
Length: 70.51 m
Powerplant: 4×Pratt & Whitney JT9D-7 or GE CF6-50 of above 20000 kg thrust each (dependent on model)
Payload: up to 516 passengers or up to 113000 kg of cargo
Max T/O weight: 365142 kg
Max speed: 969 km/h
Operational range: 9624 km

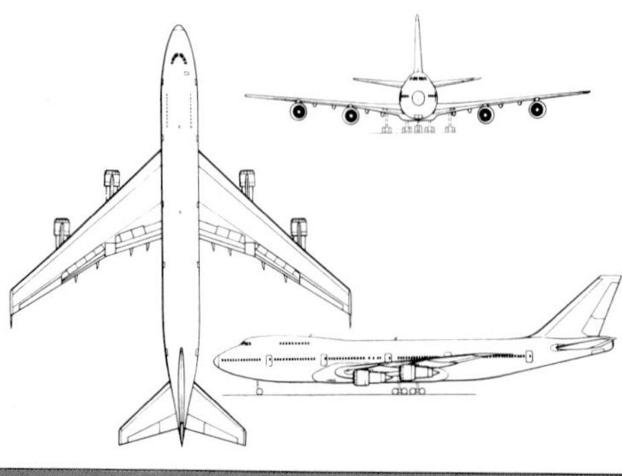

Ilyushin Il-76 'Candid'

The Il-76 was first flown in March 1971 as successor to the An-12. In common with other Soviet transports, the type has civil as well as military roles, and adheres to the standard high wing/upswept tail design formula with 20-wheel landing gear for off-runway capability. The hold is 20.0 m (65 ft 7.5 in) long, and its width and height are 3.40 m (11 ft 1.75 in) and 3.46 m (11 ft 4.25 in) respectively. The hold floor has roller conveyors, and the roof is fitted with two travelling gantries able to accommodate two 3000-kg (6,614-lb) or four 2500-kg (5,511-lb) cranes. The main variants, in addition to the baseline Il-76, are the Il-76T with additional fuel and higher weights, and the Il-76TD with improved D-30KP-1 turbofans, together with the similar but specifically military Il-76M and Il-76MD variants with a twin 23-mm cannon turret in the tail.

Specification: Ilyushin Il-76M 'Candid-B' 148-seat long-range heavy transport
Span: 50.50 m (165 ft 8 in)
Length: 46.59 m (152 ft 10.5 in)
Powerplant: 4×Soloviev D-30KP, 12000 kg (26,455 lb) st each
Payload: 140 passengers, or 90 paratroops, or 40000 kg (88,183 lb) of freight
Max T/O weight: 170000 kg (374,780 lb)
Max speed: 528 mph at optimum altitude
Operational range: 3,107 miles with maximum payload

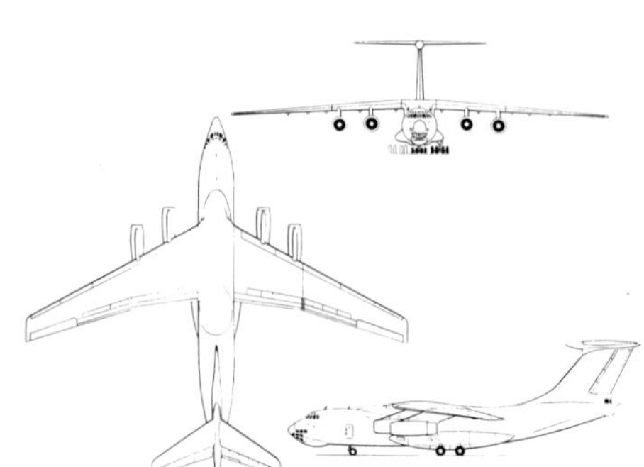

When first flown in February 1965 as the world's largest freighter, the An-22 was planned for twin roles: support of the Siberian resources-exploitation programme, and strategic freighting for the armed forces. As such the type was designed with 14-wheel landing gear able to cope with off-runway operations, and with the classic modern transport configuration using a high wing (with anhedralled outer sections) and an upswept tail with endplate vertical surfaces. The cargo hold is 33.0m (108ft 3in) long and has a square section 4.4m (14ft 5in) wide and high. Straight-in access to the hold is provided by a rear ramp/door, and movement of freight is eased by the provision of four overhead gantries and two 2500-kg (5,511-lb) capacity winches. There is a small passenger compartment between the flight deck and the main hold.

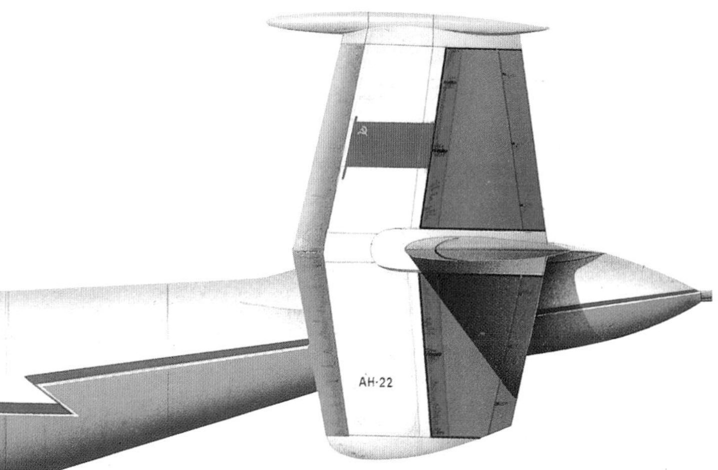

The gigantic turbo-powered Antonov An-22 Antei, dubbed 'Cock' by NATO, is now being replaced in service by the even larger turbofan-engined An-124 Ruslan. Large numbers remain in service with Aeroflot, the national airline, and with the Soviet Military Transport Aviation Force, or VTA. An-22s have visited Britain on several occasions, most recently collecting supplies for earthquake-stricken Armenia, although they are by no means regular visitors.

Lockheed C-130 Hercules

Still being produced in quantity nearly 25 years after its first flight in August 1954, the Hercules pioneered the modern concept of an airlifter with multi-wheel landing gear (retracting into external fairings in the case of the main units) for soft-field capability, a high-set wing carrying the engines, an upswept tail, and a ventral ramp/door for straight-in access to the basically rectangular hold 3.13m (10ft 3in) wide and 2.81m (9ft 2.75in) high. In the freight role the Hercules has been produced in many constantly up-engined variants (notably the C-130A, C-130B, C-130E and C-130H) and, in the C-130H-30 model, a fuselage stretch of 4.57m (15 ft) to improve capacity by lengthening the hold from 12.22m (40ft 1.75in) to 16.79m (55ft 1.25in). There are also special versions fitted with ski landing gear and other winter equipment.

Specification: Lockheed C-130H-30 Hercules 133-seat medium/long-range medium transport
Span: 40.41m (132ft 7in)
Length: 34.37m (112ft 9in)
Powerplant: 4×Avco Lycoming T56-A-15, 3362kW (4,508shp) each
Payload: 128 troops, or 92 paratroops, or 97 litters, or 17974kg (39,626lb) of freight
Max T/O weight: 79380kg (175,000lb)
Max speed: 374 mph
Operational range: 2,487 miles with maximum payload

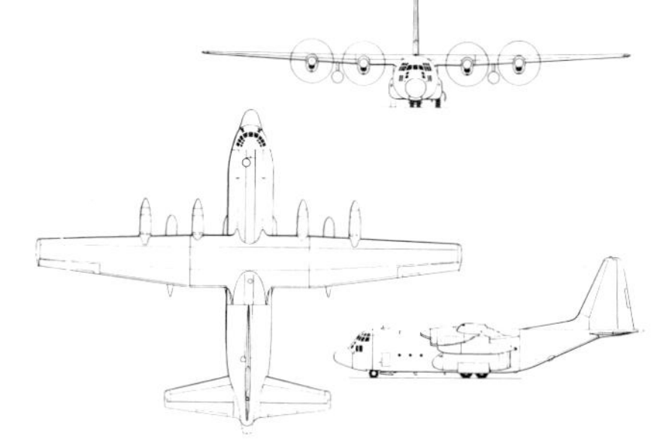

Lockheed C-141 StarLifter

The C-141 is the US Air Force's logistics transport, and first flew in 1963 as that service's first turbofan-powered airlifter. The type was designed for operations into and out of paved airfields and the layout is conventional, a rear ramp/door giving access in the C-141A initial version to a hold 21.33m (70 ft) long, 3.11m (10ft 2.5in) wide and 2.77m (9ft 1in) high for a maximum payload of 32136kg (70,847lb). In service, however, it was discovered that the C-141A's hold was full before the weight limit had been reached, and in 1977 Lockheed flew the first C-141B whose fuselage was stretched by 7.11m (23ft 4in) with plugs fore and aft of the wings to increase payload volume by 61.48 m^3 (2,171 cu ft) and allow the loading of 13 rather than 10 standard pallets. All 270 surviving aircraft were then upgraded to C-141B standard.

Specification: Lockheed C-141B StarLifter four-seat long-range logistics transport
Span: 48.74m (159ft 11in)
Length: 51.29m (168ft 3.5in)
Powerplant: 4×Pratt & Whitney TF33-P-7, 9526kg (21,000lb) st each
Payload: 42877kg (94,525lb) of freight
Max T/O weight: 155580kg (343,000lb)
Max speed: 566 mph at optimum altitude
Operational range: 2,935 miles with maximum payload

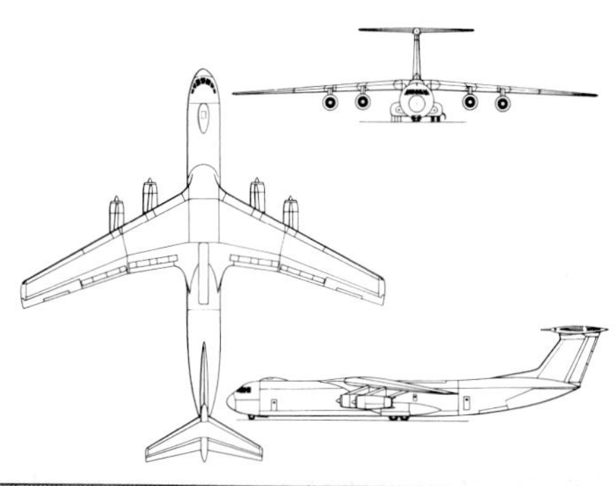

DHC-5 Buffalo

The Buffalo was developed from the Caribou as a turboprop-powered tactical and utility transport meeting a US Army requirement and capable of STOL performance. The type first flew in April 1964 and has the classic airlifter configuration, though with conventional landing gear whose main units retract into the rear of the engine nacelles, and has a high T-tail and ventral ramp/door accessing a hold 9.58 m (31 ft 5 in) long, 2.69 m (8 ft 9 in) wide and 2.08 m (6 ft 10 in) high. Only four examples were built of the DHC-5 with 2125-kW (2,850-shp) General Electric T64-10 turboprops and a 5080-kg (11,200-lb) payload, the first main variant being the DHC-5A with 2278-kW (3,055-shp) CT64-810-1 turboprops and a 6124-kg (13,500-lb) payload. The most important variant, however, is the DHC-5D with considerably more power for the longer-range movement of a heavier load.

Specification: de Havilland Canada DHC-5D Buffalo 44-seat short-range light/medium STOL assault transport
Span: 29.26 m (96 ft 0 in)
Length: 24.08 m (79 ft 0 in)
Powerplant: 2×General Electric CT64-820-4, 2336 kW (3,133 shp) each
Payload: 41 troops, or 34 paratroops, or 8164 kg (18,000 lb) of freight
Max T/O weight: 22316 kg (49,200 lb)
Max speed: 290 mph at 10,000 ft
Operational range: 691 miles with maximum payload

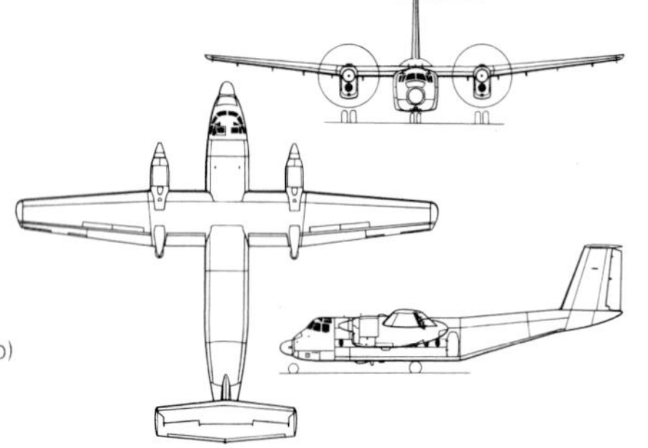

Lockheed C-130 Hercules

Still in production nearly 25 years after its first flight in August 1954, the Hercules pioneered the modern tactical transport concept with multi-wheel landing gear (retracting into external fairings in the case of the main units), a high-set wing carrying the powerful turboprop engines, an upswept tail, and a ventral ramp/door for straight-in access to the basically rectangular hold 3.13 m (10 ft 3 in) wide and 2.81 m (9 ft 2.75 in) high; the ramp also facilitates the air drop of heavy parachute loads and paratroops. As an assault transport the Hercules has been produced in several variants with more powerful engines (notably the C-130A, C-130B, C-130E and C-130H) and, in the C-130H-30 model, a fuselage stretch of 4.57 m (15 ft) to lengthen the hold from the standard 12.22 m (40 ft 1.75 in) to 16.79 m (55 ft 1.25 in), and so enable the carriage of 128 troops or 98 paratroops.

Specification: Lockheed C-130H Hercules 98-seat medium-range medium assault transport
Span: 40.41 m (132 ft 7 in)
Length: 29.79 m (97 ft 9 in)
Powerplant: 4×Avco Lycoming T56-A-15, 3362 kW (4,508 shp) each
Payload: 92 troops, or 64 paratroops or 19686 kg (43,400 lb) of freight
Max T/O weight: 79380 kg (175,000 lb)
Max speed: 384 mph at optimum altitude
Operational range: 2,487 miles with maximum payload

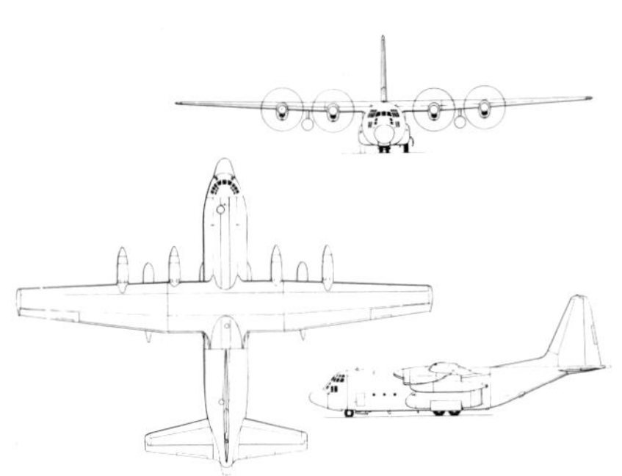

McDonnell Douglas C-17

Due to make its first flight in 1990, the C-17 is a conventionally configured military transport with 14-wheel landing gear and advanced features such as winglets for improved cruise performance, a large proportion of composites in the structure, and STOL airfield performance to allow the delivery of major loads into front-line airfields after long-range delivery flights: as such the type can be used for both strategic and tactical missions. The hold is accessed by a rear ramp/door under an upswept T-tail, and is 26.52 m (87 ft 10 in) long including the 5.79-m (19-ft) rear ramp; the width and height are 5.49 m (18 ft) and 4.11 m (13 ft 6 in) respectively. The hold floor is fitted with roller conveyors, and its roof with a cargo winch. In the assault role the C-17 has a major airdrop capability for 102 paratroops or a single-platform load of 24945 kg (55,000 lb).

Specification: McDonnell Douglas C-17 105-seat long-range heavy assault transport
Span: 50.29 m (165 ft 0 in)
Length: 52.02 m (170 ft 8 in)
Powerplant: 4×Pratt & Whitney F117 (PW2037), 17055 kg (37,600 lb) st each
Payload: 144 passengers, or 102 paratroops, or 78110 kg (259,000 lb) of freight
Max T/O weight: 259455 kg (572,000 lb)
Max speed: 512 mph at optimum altitude
Operational range: 2,765 miles with maximum payload

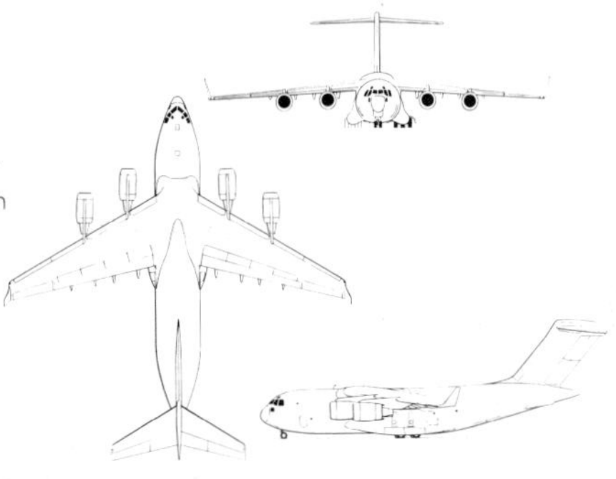

Shorts Skyvan

In the later 1950s Shorts was approached by F.G.Miles Ltd with the proposal that the two companies should collaborate on a development of the latter's H.D.M.106 Caravan light transport, itself a pod and twin boom derivative of the M.57 Aerovan pod and boom transport fitted with a high aspect ratio wing of the type developed in France by Hurel Dubois. Shorts bought the concept from Miles but then turned to a more capable notion with the Hurel Dubois wing married to a rectangular-section fuselage with a rear ramp. The SC.7 prototype first flew in January 1963 with 291-kW (390-hp) Continental GTSIO-520 piston engines, but the Skyvan Series 1 introduced Turbomeca Astazou II turboprops, changed in Series 3 aircraft to TPE331s. Military versions were the Skyvan Series 3M and the Skyvan Series 3M-200 cleared for a 6804-kg (15,000-lb) maximum weight.

Specification: Shorts Skyvan Series 3M 24-seat short-range light assault transport
Span: 19.79 m (64 ft 11 in)
Length: 12.60 m (41 ft 4 in)
Powerplant: 2 x Garrett TPE331-201, 533 kW (715 shp) each
Payload: 22 troops, or 16 paratroops, or 2722 kg (6,000 lb) of freight
Max T/O weight: 6577 kg (14,500 lb)
Max speed: 203 mph at 10,000 ft
Operational range: 240 miles with a 2268-kg (5,000-lb) payload

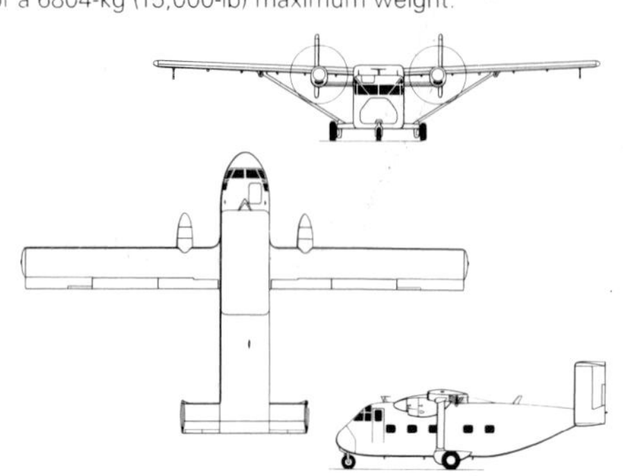

Douglas DC-6

he DC-6 was developed after World War II as a more powerful, larger and pressurized uccessor to the DC-4/C-54 Skymaster series, and initially flew during February 1946 in its -112 military form. The first of 175 DC-6s entered service in April 1947 with a length of 0.66 m (100 ft 7 in) and 1789kW (2,400hp) R-2800-CA15 radials for the carriage of 86 assengers. Subsequent models were the DC-6A Liftmaster freighter (77 built with trengthened floors and two upward-opening doors), the generally similar DC- 6B airliner 286 built), and the DC-6D convertible freighter with windows so it could be reconfigured for assengers. The DC-6 and DC-6B have faded out as airliners, but some have been revised s freighters with larger doors and, in a small number of aircraft, swing tails.

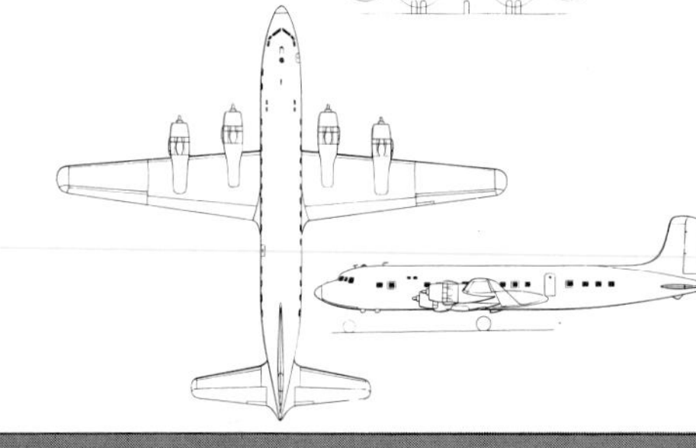

pecification: Douglas DC-6A ftmaster three/four-crew medium eight transport
pan: 35.81m (117ft 6in)
ength: 32.18m (105ft 7in)
owerplant: 4×Pratt & Whitney -2800-CB16 Double Wasp, 789kW (2,400hp) each
ayload: 12786kg (28,188lb) of eight
lax T/O weight: 48534kg 07,000lb)
ruising speed: 315mph at ptimum altitude
perational range: 2,925 miles ith maximum payload

Lockheed L-188 Electra

In 1954 American Airlines called for a short/medium-range turboprop domestic airliner of greater capacity than the Vickers Viscount, and Lockheed eventually won orders for its 100-seat L-188 from American and Eastern Airlines (75 aircraft in all). The L-188 was the only US turboprop airliner to achieve production status, the prototype flying in December 1957 and the L-188A variant entering service in January 1959. Two early aircraft were lost to structural/powerplant problems, and by the time a fix had been produced in 1961 airline confidence in the L-188A and longer-range L-188C had been lost in favour of the new jetliners. Production totalled 177, many going to Central and South American airlines. A large proportion has been converted for freighting with a special door ahead of the wing on the port side.

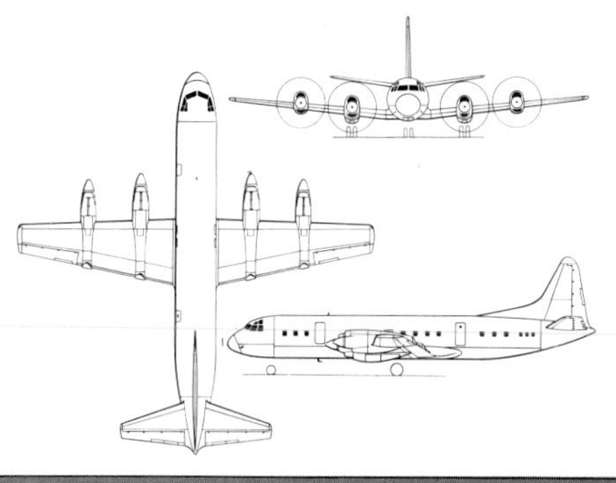

Specification: Lockheed L-188A Electra two/three-crew medium passenger and freight transport
Span: 30.18m (99ft 0in)
Length: 31.81m (104ft 6in)
Powerplant: 4×Allison 501-D13, 2796ekW (3,750ehp) each
Payload: 98 passengers or 12020kg (26,500lb) of freight
Max T/O weight: 52618kg (116,000lb)
Cruising speed: 405mph at 22,000ft
Operational range: 2,200 miles with maximum payload

Shorts Belfast

'he Belfast was developed to meet an RAF requirement for a strategic heavy freighter, and rst flew in January 1964 with a high wing, ventral access to the pressurized hold, and anding gear in external fuselage blisters. Only 10 aircraft were built, all going to the RAF as Belfast C.Mk 1s. The Belfast was retired from service use in September 1976, and five of hem were then revised by Marshall of Cambridge as civil freighters, receiving certification March 1980 and subsequently proving themselves admirable freighters for the carriage of utsize loads into and out of all types of airfield. The Belfast also possesses notable range vith a sizeable payload, a figure of about 3,860 miles being quoted with a 10000kg 22,046lb) payload.

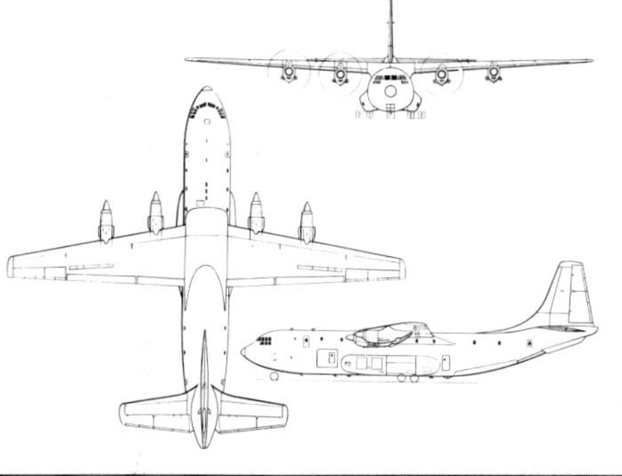

pecification: Shorts Belfast hree/four-crew heavy freight ransport
pan: 48.41 (158ft 10in)
ength: 41.58m (136ft 5in)
owerplant: 4×Rolls-Royce Tyne Ty.12 Mk 515/10, 4276ekW ,730ehp) each
ayload: 37376kg (75,000lb) of reight and 19 passengers
Max T/O weight: 104325kg 240,000lb)
ruising speed: 330mph at 4,000ft
perational range: 980 miles with aximum payload

Transall C-160

The C-160 was developed in the late 1950s and early 1960s to meet the requirements of the French and West German air forces for a tactical transport, and is typical of its breed with blistered main landing gear units, a high wing and ventral access to the payload compartment. The first of three prototypes flew in February 1963, and production totalled 175 aircraft. Four of these were later converted to C-160P standard for French domestic air mail services: the aircraft were modified to allow 13500kg (29,761lb) letters to be loaded or unloaded in 12 minutes. The C-160Ps operate between Paris and Bastia with a regularity of 98% carrying 1.8 million letters per night. In 1977 an improved version was flown, and six of these have been bought by Indonesia for its inter-island transmigration programme.

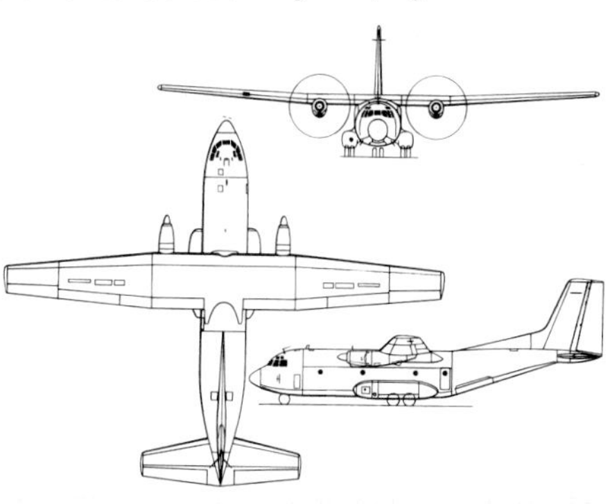

Specification: Transall C-160P three-crew medium freight (mail) transport
Span: 40.00m (131ft 3in)
Length: 32.40m (106ft 3.5in)
Powerplant: 2×Rolls-Royce Tyne RTy.20 Mk 22, 4550ekW (6,100ehp) each
Payload: 16000kg (35,273lb) of freight
Max T/O weight: 51000kg (112,434lb)
Cruising speed: 306mph at 26,245ft
Operational range: 730 miles with maximum payload

Lockheed L-100 Hercules

Though the Hercules is better known as a military transport, it was also developed in a civil version as the Model 382. The first L-100 (Model 382B) is a commercial counterpart to the C-130E and flew in April 1964 with 3020-ekW (4,050-ehp) Allison 501-D22 turboprops and a fuselage length of 29.79m (97ft 9in). This version was followed in 1968 by the L-100-20 (Model 382E) with -D22A engines and a fuselage stretch of 2.54m (8ft 4in), and then in 1970 by the L-100-30 (Model 382G) with a further fuselage stretch of 2.03m (6ft 8in). Slightly more than 100 L-100s have been delivered, proving themselves admirable freighters in areas of poor surface transport and/or adverse climate, and there is still the possibility of an L-100-50 with a further stretch of 6.09m (20ft).

Specification: Lockheed L-100-30 Hercules three-crew medium freight transport
Span: 40.41m (132ft 7in)
Length: 34.37m (112ft 9in)
Powerplant: 4×Allison 501-D22A, 3489ekW (4,680ehp) each
Payload: 23183kg (51,100lb) of freight or, in some circumstances, 128 passengers
Max T/O weight: 70308kg (155,000lb)
Cruising speed: 362mph at 20,000ft
Operational range: 1,570 miles with maximum payload

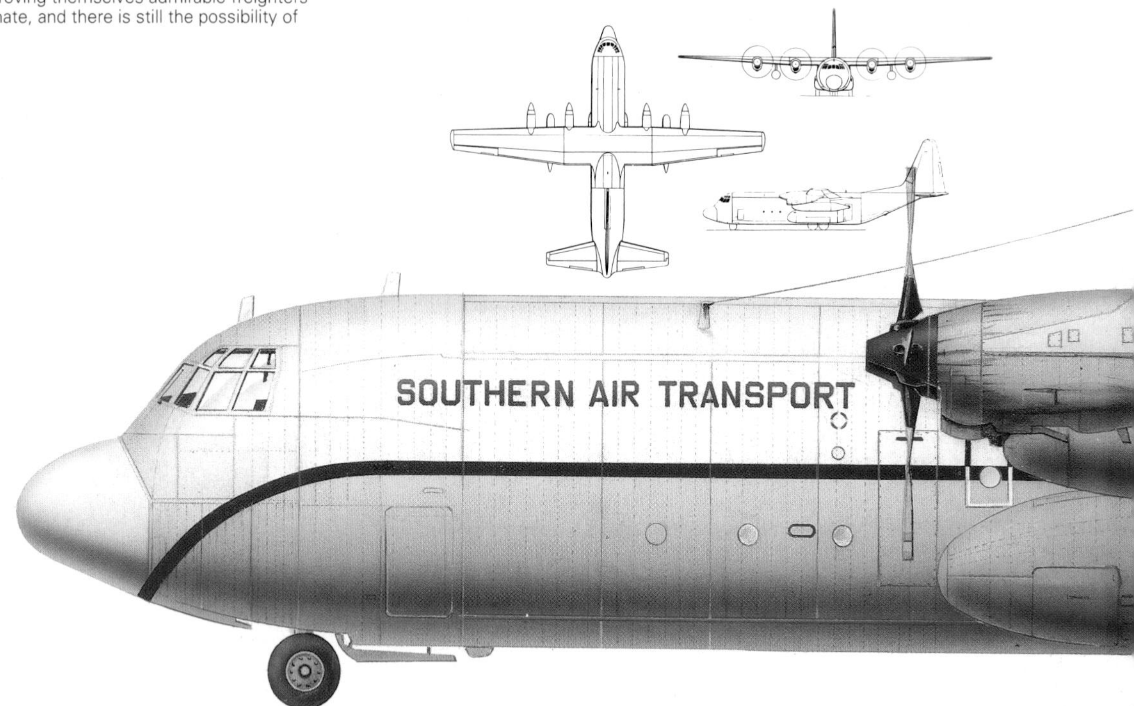

Aero Spacelines Guppy

The Guppy is a Boeing 377 Stratocruiser/C-97 development with a bulged upper-fuselage lobe, and was conceived for carriage of large items (loaded through a swinging tail section) for the US space programme. Flown in 1962, the B-377PG Pregnant Guppy had 2610kW (3,500hp) R-4360 radials, an inside height of 6.2m (20ft 4in) and a fuselage stretch of 5.08m (16ft 8in). In 1965 came the B-377SG Super Guppy with 5219ekW (7,000ehp) T34-P-7WA turboprops, span and length increased by 4.57 and 9.4m (15ft and 30ft 10in) respectively, and an inside height of 7.62m (25ft). The 1967 B-377MG Mini Guppy had piston engines plus a longer and wider fuselage. Next came the 1970 Guppy-101 with Allison turboprops and a swinging nose, and the final model was the 1970 B-377SGT Guppy-201, which first flew in August 1970.

Specification: Aero Spacelines B-377SGT Guppy-201 three/four-crew outsize freight (aircraft component) transport
Span: 47.62m (156ft 3in)
Length: 43.84m (143ft 10in)
Powerplant: 4×Allison 501-D22C, 3662ekW (4,912ehp) each
Payload: 24494kg (54,000lb) of freight
Max T/O weight: 77112kg (170,000lb)
Cruising speed: 253mph at 20,000ft
Operational range: 505 miles with maximum payload

Antonov An-12

The An-12 is the freighter counterpart to the An-10 Ukraina passenger transport. The An-12 was planned for military use with a rear gun turret and ventral access to the freight compartment, and first flew in 1958. The An-12 has a larger tail and greater fuel capacity than the An-10, but lacks otherwise standard features such as hold pressurization and an integral rear loading ramp: the freight compartment is accessed by upward-folding left and right doors plus a rear door hinged at the back so that its front lifts. The An-12BP military variant entered service in 1959, and was soon followed by a 'civilianized' Aeroflot version. The first true civil version was the An-12B that appeared in 1965 with a trim fairing in place of the gun turret. About 225 were built, serving as Aeroflot's main freighter up to the mid-1980s.

Specification: Antonov An-12B five-crew medium freight transport
Span: 38.00m (124ft 8in)
Length: 37.00m (121ft 4in)
Powerplant: 4×Ivchyenko AI-20K, 2985ekW (4,000ehp) each
Payload: 20000kg (44,092lb) of freight, plus 14 passengers in a pressurized compartment
Max T/O weight: 61000kg (134,480lb)
Cruising speed: 416mph at optimum altitude
Operational range: 2,235 miles with maximum payload

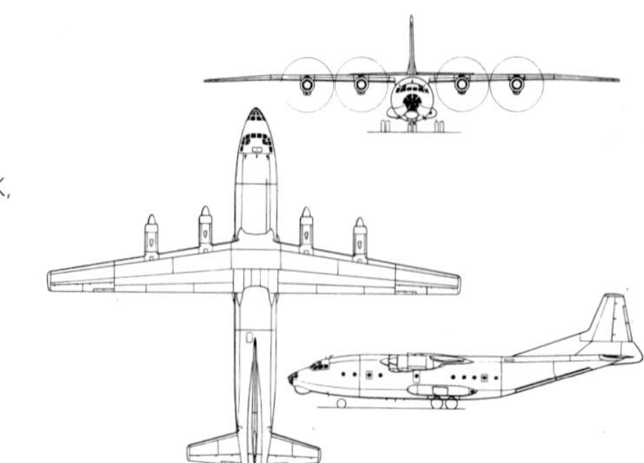

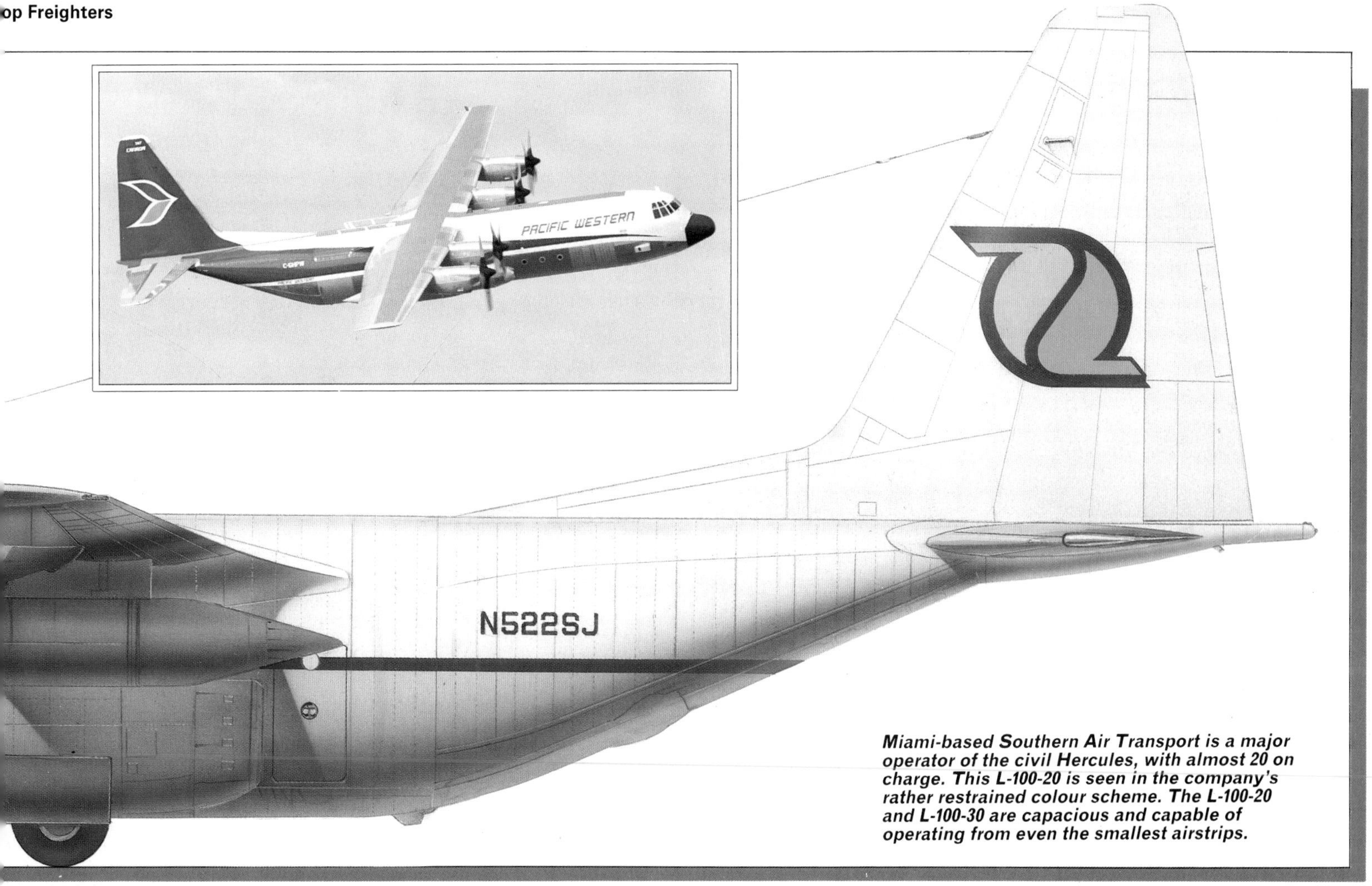

Miami-based Southern Air Transport is a major operator of the civil Hercules, with almost 20 on charge. This L-100-20 is seen in the company's rather restrained colour scheme. The L-100-20 and L-100-30 are capacious and capable of operating from even the smallest airstrips.

Antonov An-22 Antei

A logical development of the An-12's design philosophy for the carriage of much larger loads over greater ranges, the An-22 first flew in February 1965 and was at the time the world's largest aircraft. The type was designed for military and civil use, in the latter role providing Aeroflot with the capability to fly massive resources-exploitation equipment into poor fields such as those found in Siberia. The hold cross section was fixed at 4.4 m (14 ft 5.25 in) square, and there are four overhead travelling cranes for movement of the freight loaded through the two-part ventral door: the forward part is an integral ramp of variable height, and the rear part a rear-hinged unit that opens upward to facilitate loading. As in the An-12, the hold is unpressurized. Production was less than 200 aircraft.

Specification: Antonov An-22 Antei five/six-crew heavy freight transport
Span: 64.40 m (211 ft 3.5 in)
Length: 57.90 m (189 ft 11.5 in)
Powerplant: 4×Kuznetsov NK-12MA, 11185 ekW (15,000 ehp) each
Payload: 80000 kg (176,367 lb) of freight, plus 29 passengers in a pressurized compartment
Max T/O weight: 250000 kg (551,146 lb)
Cruising speed: 398 mph at optimum altitude
Operational range: 3,107 miles with maximum payload

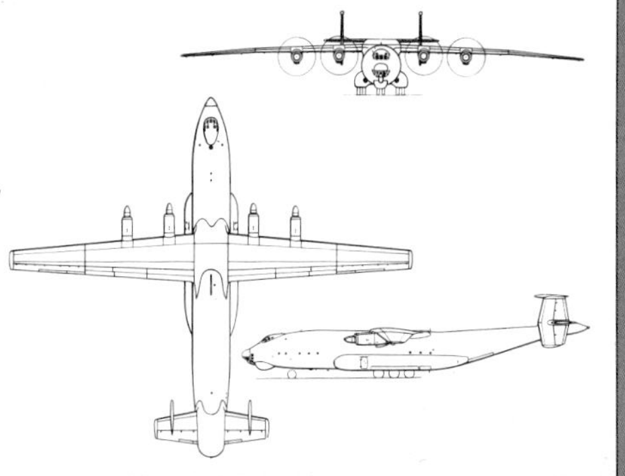

Armstrong Whitworth **AW.650 Argosy**

The Argosy was designed to meet a 1955 British military specification for a medium-range freighter, and was originally schemed with twin turboprops and a pod-and-narrow twin boom layout to provide unhindered loading/unloading access to the cargo compartment. By 1956 military interest had waned and the company began to see civil possibilities for a four-engine freighter. The first aeroplane flew in January 1959, and of the first 10 Argosy Series 100s with 1506 ekW (2,020 ehp) Dart Mk 526 turboprops seven were bought by a US airline with military contracts, the other three going to British European Airways. The only other civil aircraft were the seven Argosy Series 200s, of which the first flew in March 1964 with uprated engines, a larger payload bay accessed by bigger doors, and a revised wing of failsafe structure.

Specification: Armstrong Whitworth AW.650 Argosy Series 200 three/four-crew medium freight transport
Span: 30.05 m (115 ft 0 in)
Length: 26.44 m (86 ft 9 in)
Powerplant: 4×Rolls-Royce Dart Mk 532/1, 1662 ekW (2,230 ehp)
Payload: 14515 kg (32,000 lb) of freight, or 89 passengers
Max T/O weight: 42185 kg (93,000 lb)
Cruising speed: 280 mph at 18,000 ft
Operational range: 485 miles with maximum payload

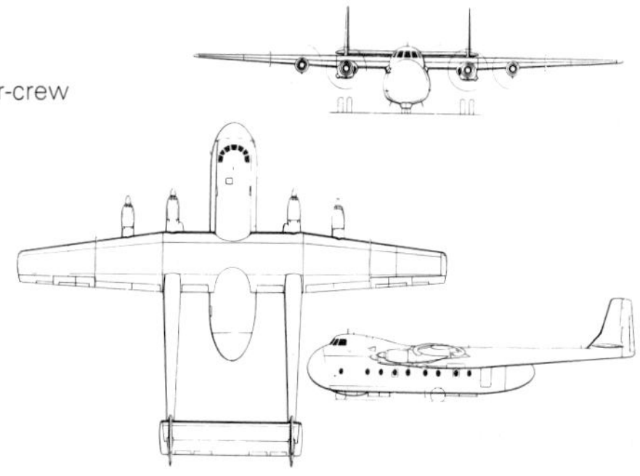

Vickers Vanguard

The Vanguard was essentially a scaled-up version of the Viscount produced to meet a BEA requirement for a 100-seat successor. The new Vickers 870 offered no design problems, but was delayed by disagreement between the two launch customers about specific layout: BEA wanted a high wing while Trans-Canada Air Lines wanted a low wing of the type finally agreed for the revised Vickers 950. This first flew in January 1959 and, though a good example of its type, found itself obsolete by comparison to the new jetliners. Sales were therefore limited to BEA (six Vickers 951s and 14 higher-weight Vickers 953s) and TCA (23 Vickers 952s with beefed-up structure). The aircraft enjoyed only limited service as airliners, several being adapted to freighting after conversion to the Merchantman standard with a port-side forward freight door.

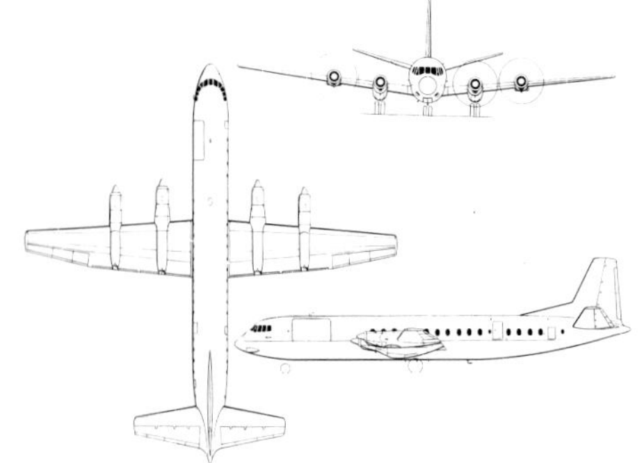

Specification: Vickers Type 952 Merchantman two/three-crew medium freight transport
Span: 36.15 m (118 ft 7 in)
Length: 37.45 m (122 ft 10.5 in)
Powerplant: 4×Rolls-Royce Tyne RTy.11 Mk 512, 4134 ekW (5,545 ehp) each
Payload: 19505 kg (43,000 lb) of freight
Max T/O weight: 66448 kg (146,500 lb)
Cruising speed: 425 mph at 20,000 ft
Operational range: 1,830 miles with maximum payload

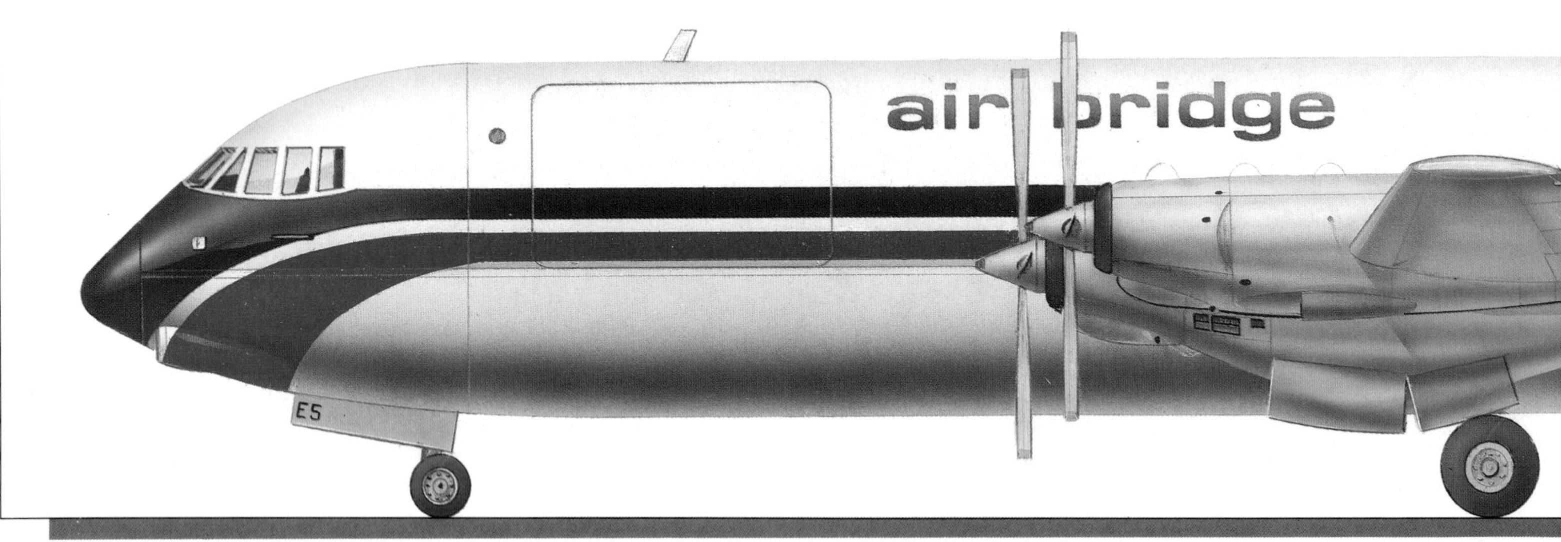

Canadair CL-44D4

When the Royal Canadian Air Force issued a 1956 requirement for a long-range transport, Canadair responded with several variants of the Bristol Britannia with lengthened fuselage and wings plus four powerplant options. The RCAF selected the Bristol Orion turboprop, but when this was cancelled it opted for the Tyne for its 12 CC-106 Yukons, which had the company designation CL-44-6. The first of these flew in November 1959 as the company sought a market for its CL-44D4 civil variant with a side-hingeing tail to facilitate the loading of long items. The swinging tail is hydraulically actuated to open or close the freight compartment in 90 seconds. Production totalled 27, including three converted to Canadair 400 (CL-44J) standard with a fuselage stretched by 4.62 m (15 ft 2 in) to increase accommodation to 214 passengers.

Specification: Canadair CL-44D4 three-crew medium freight transport
Span: 43.37 m (142 ft 3.5 in)
Length: 41.65 m (136 ft 8 in)
Powerplant: 4×Rolls-Royce Tyne RTy.12 Mk 515/10, 4273 ekW (5,730 ehp) each
Payload: 29995 kg (66,128 lb) of freight, or 178 passengers
Max T/O weight: 95256 kg (210,000 lb)
Cruising speed: 386 mph at 20,000 ft
Operational range: 2,875 miles with maximum payload

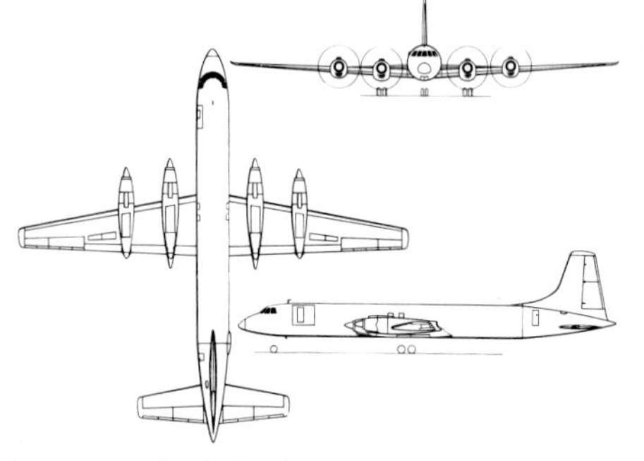

Conroy/Canadair CL-44-O

One Canadair CL-44D4 turboprop transport was bought from The Flying Tiger Line by the Conroy Aircraft Company of Santa Barbara, California. With the active co-operation of Canadair, Conroy then modified this CL-44D4-2 for the carriage of Rolls-Royce RB.211 turbofans and their nacelles from the UK to California for the Lockheed L-1011 TriStar airliner programme. This modification to CL-44-O Airlifter standard involved the removal of the fuselage above floor level and its replacement with a larger and unwindowed upper lobe that provided an interior height of 4.24 m (13 ft 11 in). The CL-44-O was first flown on 26 November 1969, and was used successfully if unspectacularly in its outsize freight role.

Specification: Conroy CL-44-O Airlifter three-crew medium freight transport
Span: 43.37 m (142 ft 3.5 in)
Length: 41.65 m (136 ft 8 in)
Powerplant: 4×Rolls-Royce Tyne RTy.12 Mk 515/10, 4273 ekW (5,730 ehp) each
Payload: 28349 kg (62,500 lb) of freight
Max T/O weight: 95256 kg (210,000 lb)
Cruising speed: 325 mph at 20,000 ft
Operational range: no data available

Operated by East Midlands Airport based Air Bridge Carriers this Vickers Vanguard Merchantman carries Elan logos and is flown on behalf of the latter company for its express parcel service. The aircraft entered service a couple of years ago to replace the Armstrong Whitworth Argosy previously in use.

Curtiss Commando

The Curtiss-Wright CW-20T was designed as a pressurized airliner for service with US operators. With a payload of 36 passengers and 3719 kg (8,200 lb) of freight, the type offered distinct advantages over the Boeing 247 and Douglas DC-3 when it first flew with endplate vertical tail surfaces in March 1940. The type was then modified with conventional tail surfaces, but was not produced in civil form as the USA was approaching its entry to World War II. The CW-20 was ordered for the USAAF as the C-46 Commando and for the US Navy as the R5D, production up to 1945 amounting to 3,182 aircraft. After World War II many of these military transports were converted to civil use as Super 46Cs and C-46Rs, a useful number remaining in service to this day.

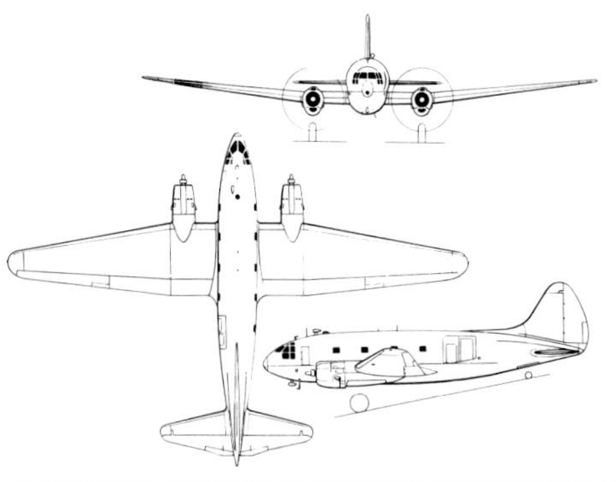

Specification: Curtiss Commando two/three-crew light passenger and freight transport
Span: 32.92 m (108 ft 0 in)
Length: 23.27 m (76 ft 4 in)
Powerplant: 2×Pratt & Whitney R-2800-51MI Double Wasp, 1491 kW (2,000 hp) each
Payload: 62 passengers or 7983 kg (17,600 lb) of freight
Max T/O weight: 21770 kg (48,000 lb) as a freighter
Cruising speed: 187 mph at 7,000 ft
Operational range: 1,170 miles with 2585 kg (5,700 lb) payload

Douglas Dakota

There are no words to exaggerate the importance of this classic aeroplane in the development of modern air transport. The world's first air transport of genuinely modern concept, the 14-passenger Douglas Sleeper Transport of 1935 and 21-passenger DC-3 of 1936 were successors to the DC-1 and DC-2, and appeared with the full range of features comprising low-wing all-metal stressed-skin construction, variable-pitch propellers, retractable landing gear and trailing-edge flaps. The 430 purely civil aircraft and 149 impressed aircraft built before World War II were soon overtaken in importance by 10,047 military transports produced in various C-47, C-53, C-117, Dakota and R4D variants, and production ended with 28 post-war DC-3Ds. Many thousands of these were converted for civil use after the War, several hundreds remaining in service mostly as freighters.

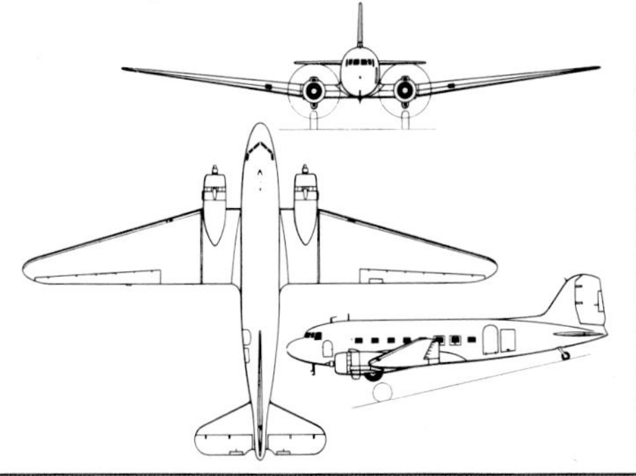

Specification: Douglas Dakota three-crew light transport
Span: 28.96 m (95 ft 0 in)
Length: 19.66 m (64 ft 5 in)
Powerplant: 2×Pratt & Whitney R-1830-90 Twin Wasp, 895 kW (1,200 hp) each
Payload: 36 passengers or 3003 kg (6,620 lb) of freight
Max T/O weight: 12701 kg (28,000 lb)
Cruising speed: 170 mph at 6,000 ft
Operational range: 350 miles with maximum payload

Boeing KC-135A/E/Q Stratotanker

Stemming from the same Model 367-80 prototype that led to the Boeing 707 jet airliner, the turbojet-powered KC-135A was designed as a tanker to provide the USAF's strategic bombers with global reach. The KC-135A offered high speed and great fuel capacity for transfer via the Boeing Flying Boom system, and first flew in August 1956, first deliveries beginning just three months later against orders for an eventual 820 aircraft. Each aeroplane is capable of carrying 118105 litres (25,980 Imp gal) of fuel for self-use or transfer. Some 128 are now being revised to KC-135E standard by reskinning of the wing undersurfaces and re-engining with ex-airline Pratt & Whitney JT3D-3B turbofans. Some 56 basic aircraft were modified to KC-135Q standard with provision for the special JP-7 fuel used by the Lockheed SR-71A 'Blackbird' reconnaissance platform.

Boeing KC-135R Stratotanker

The KC-135R first flew in August 1972 and is a radical updating of the KC-135A to maintain the type's service life until well into the next century: some 630 conversions are planned. Like the KC-135E, the KC-135R has reskinned wing undersurfaces, strengthened landing gear with anti-skid brake units, a larger tailplane, various systems improvements (including updated electric, hydraulic and flight-control systems), a new turbofan powerplant for completely transformed take-off and flight performance, an APU, and a total fuel capacity 92210 kg (203,285 lb), 6124 kg (13,500 lb) more than the KC-135A. The net result is an aeroplane able to transfer 150 per cent more fuel than the KC-135A at a radius of 4627 km (2,875 miles) yet able to operate safely from shorter runways at higher weights.

Specification: Boeing KC-135R Stratotanker four-crew inflight-refuelling tanker
Span: 39.88 m (130 ft 10 in)
Length: 41.53 m (136 ft 3 in)
Powerplant: 4×CFM International F108-CF-100, 9979 kg (22,000 lb) st each
Payload: transfer fuel (see above)
Max T/O weight: 146284 kg (322,500 lb)
Cruising speed: 530 mph at 30,500 ft
Operational range: not revealed

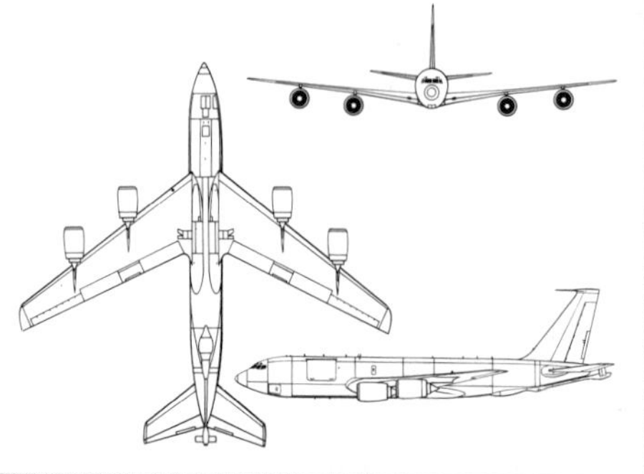

Boeing 707 Tanker/Transport

The 1980s have seen a considerable surge in the importance attached to inflight-refuelling, and in 1982 Boeing modified a Model 707 airliner to demonstrate the capabilities of such a tanker/transport conversion with a refuelling system comprising one centreline hose-and-drogue and two underwing HDU units. Boeing also offered a conversion with the standard Flying Boom and an additional 18927 litres (5,000 US gal) of fuel, allowing the transfer of 55792 kg (123,000 lb) at a radius of 1610 km (1,000 miles). Initial customers for production-standard aircraft were Saudi Arabia (the KE-3 variant with CFM56 turbofans) and Iran, later conversions with just the two underwing HDUs being undertaken by various contractors for Australia, Brazil, Canada, Israel, Morocco and Spain, with Italy a strong possibility to join these countries.

Specification: Boeing Model 707 Tanker/Transport five-seat inflight-refuelling tanker and long-range transport
Span: 44.42 m (145 ft 9 in)
Length: 46.61 m (152 ft 11 in)
Powerplant: 4×Pratt & Whitney JT3D-7, 8618 kg (19,000 lb) st each
Payload: transfer fuel (see above), or alternatively passengers or 40324 kg (88,900 lb) of freight
Max T/O weight: 151318 kg (333,600 lb)
Max speed: 605 mph at 25,000 ft
Operational range: 3,625 miles with 36287-kg (80,000-lb) payload

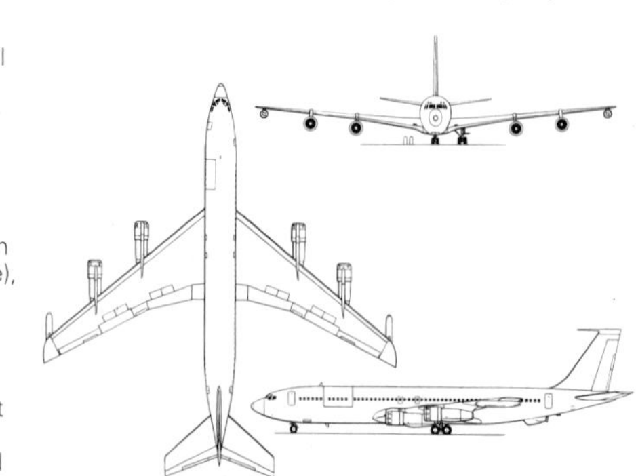

pecification: Boeing
-135A Stratotanker four-crew
light-refuelling tanker with long-
nge transport capability
an: 39.88 m (130 ft 10 in)
ngth: 40.99 m (134 ft 6 in)
werplant: 4×Pratt & Whitney
7-P-59W, 6237 kg (13,750 lb) st
ch
yload: transfer fuel (see above),
alternatively 80 passengers or
650 kg (83,000 lb) of freight
ax T/O weight: 143338 kg
16,000 lb)
ax speed: 585 mph at 30,000 ft
erational range: 1,150 miles to
fload 54432 kg (120,000 lb) of fuel

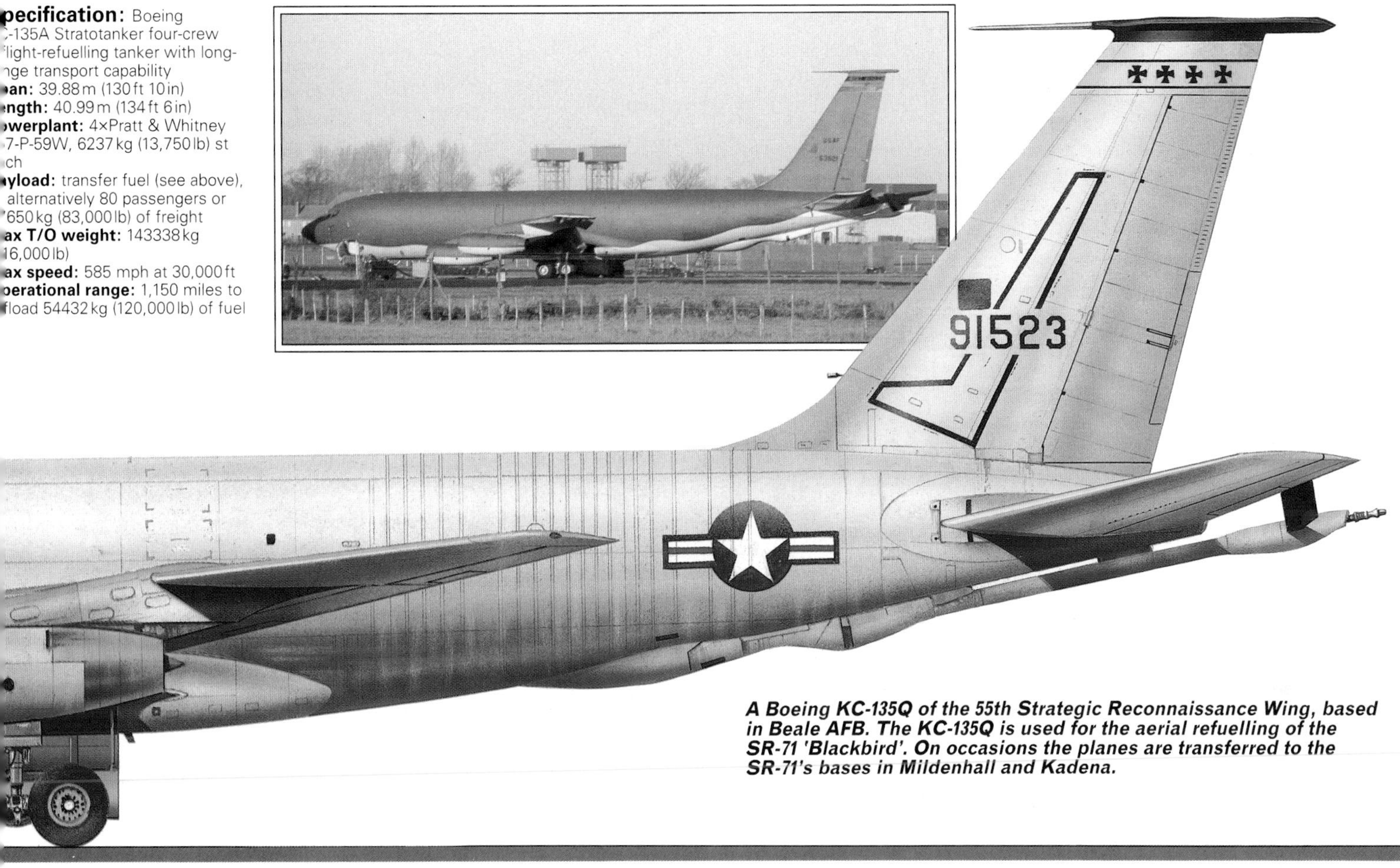

A Boeing KC-135Q of the 55th Strategic Reconnaissance Wing, based in Beale AFB. The KC-135Q is used for the aerial refuelling of the SR-71 'Blackbird'. On occasions the planes are transferred to the SR-71's bases in Mildenhall and Kadena.

Douglas KA-3 Skywarrior

Though developed as a massive carrierborne strategic bomber, the Skywarrior was employed in that basic role for only a comparatively short time before changing US priorities dictated its relegation to other roles, most notably electronic warfare and inflight refuelling. In these roles the Skywarrior found its metier, and the US Navy must have regretted that A-3 production had been limited to 280 airframes. The two most important tanker versions were the EKA-3B and KA-3B, both produced by conversion of the main Skywarrior production variant, the A-3B. The EKA-3Bs were combined ECM and tanker aircraft with ECM gear in the forward portion of the bomb bay and the HDU unit under the rear portion, while the KA-3Bs were dedicated tankers with additional fuel in the bomb bay for a total capacity of 19025 litres (5,026 US gal), of which two-thirds could be transferred.

Specification: Douglas KA-3B Skywarrior three-seat carrierborne and land-based inflight-refuelling tanker
Span: 22.10 m (72 ft 6 in)
Length: 23.37 m (76 ft 4 in)
Powerplant: 2×Pratt & Whitney J57-P-10, 4763 kg (10,500 lb) st each
Payload: 12681 litres (3,350 US gal) of transfer fuel
Max T/O weight: about 37195 kg (82,000 lb)
Max speed: 610 mph at 10,000 ft
Operational range: about 2,100 miles

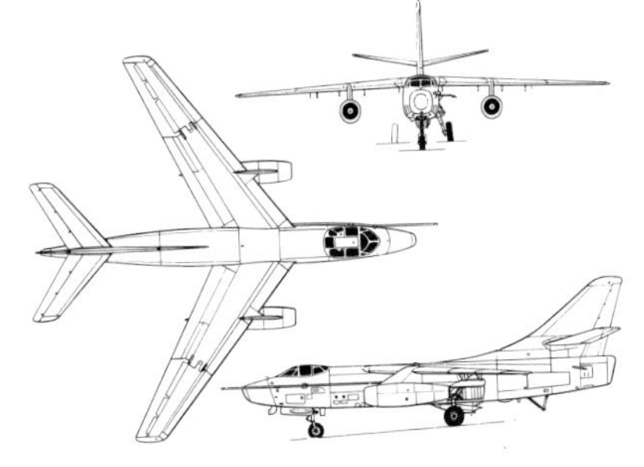

Grumman KA-6D Intruder

All other factors permitting, a tanker conversion of a current combat aeroplane offers considerable advantages in terms of performance compatibility and equipment/spares commonality. This latter is particularly important in carrierborne types, and for this reason the US Navy moved quite rapidly towards a tanker conversion of its A-6A Intruder strike/attack type. The prototype conversion first flew in May 1966, and subsequently 71 A-6As were converted to KA-6D configuration with an underfuselage HDU and up to five external tanks for the transfer of 9526 kg (21,000 lb) of fuel immediately after take-off or 6804 kg (15,000 lb) of fuel at a radius of 463.5 km (288 miles). The KA-6D is fitted with TACAN, can be used in emergencies as a bomber, and has a third string to its bow as it can serve as an air-sea rescue co-ordination aeroplane.

Specification: Grumman KA-6D Intruder two-seat carrierborne inflight-refuelling tanker
Span: 16.15 m (53 ft 0 in)
Length: 16.69 m (54 ft 9 in)
Powerplant: 2×Pratt & Whitney J52-P-8A, 4218 kg (9,300 lb) st each
Payload: 11356 litres (3,000 US gal) of transfer fuel
Max T/O weight: 27500 kg (60,616 lb)
Max speed: 685 mph at sea level
Operational range: about 1,075 miles

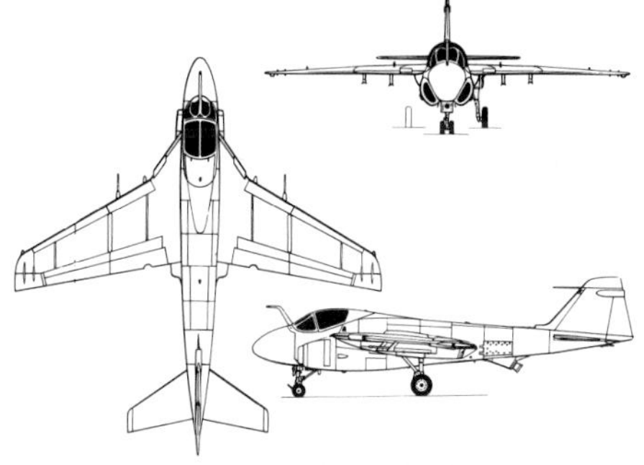

British Aerospace VC10

In 1978 it was announced that the RAF was considering the purchase of ex-airline VC10s for conversion to the tanker role. Ultimately nine aircraft were bought, the five VC10s and four Super VC10s being revised for compatibility with the basic VC10 C.Mk 1 and fitted with inflight-refuelling equipment to become VC10 K.Mk 2s and VC10 K.Mk 3s respectively. Each variant is fitted for remotely controlled three-point refuelling with a Flight Refuelling Mk 17 HDU in the lower rear fuselage, and two Flight Refuelling Mk 32/2800 HDUs under the wings. The VC10 K.Mk 2 has a length of 48.36 m (158 ft 8 in) and a standard fuel capacity of 81486 litres (17,925 Imp gal) boosted by the addition of five tanks in the fuselage for transfer fuel. The longer VC10 K.Mk 3 has a standard capacity of 88032 litres (19,365 Imp gal) supplemented by the five fuselage tanks.

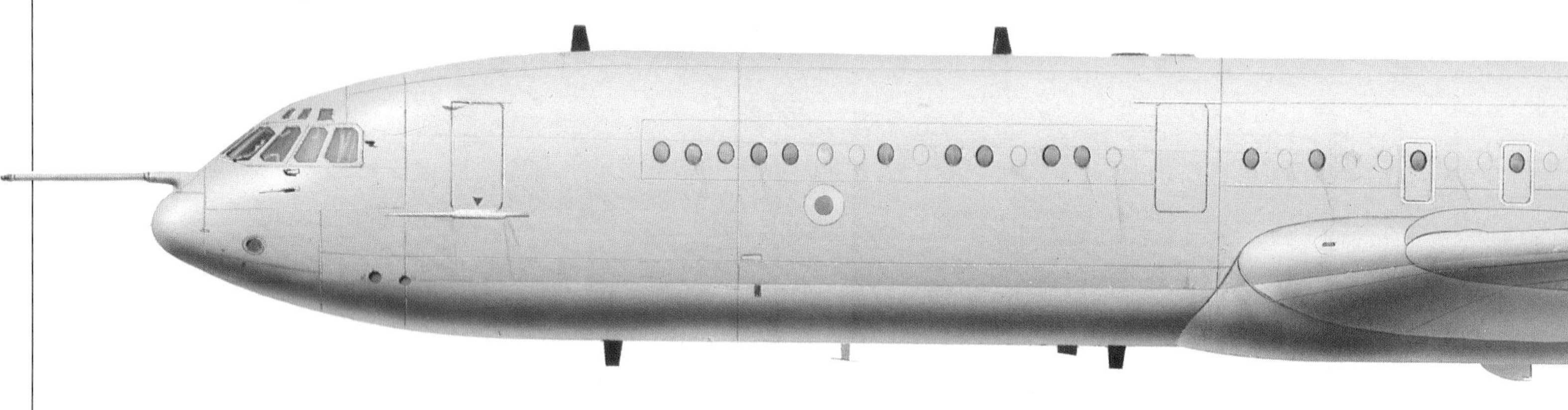

British Aerospace Victor

The first Victor B.Mk 1 bomber converted to a Victor B(K).Mk 1 tanker flew in July 1964, and the programme was then pressed ahead with all possible speed when the RAF's Valiant tankers had to be grounded for structural reasons. The first six aircraft to enter service from 1965 had only two Flight Refuelling Mk 20B underwing HDUs, the following 10 Victor B(K).Mk 1s and 14 Victor B(K).Mk 1As having an additional Mk 17 HDU in the rear of the bomb bay. From 1968 these two types were redesignated Victor K.Mk 1 and Victor K.Mk 1A, which were supplemented and then replaced by 24 Victor K.Mk 2s with revised avionics and reduced span. Fuel is accommodated in 10 wing, seven fuselage, two bomb bay and two non-jettisonable underwing tanks, and totals 72168 litres (15,875 Imp gal). Like many other such tankers, the Victor K.Mk 2 can itself be refuelled in flight.

Specification: British Aerospace (Handley Page/Hawker Siddeley) Victor K.Mk 2 four/five-seat inflight-refuelling tanker
Span: 34.44 m (113 ft 0 in)
Length: 35.03 m (114 ft 11 in)
Powerplant: 4×Rolls-Royce Conway Mk 201, 9344 kg (20,600 lb) st each
Payload: typically 45360 kg (100,000 lb) of transfer fuel
Max T/O weight: 107955 kg (238,000 lb)
Max speed: 610 mph at 40,000 ft
Operational range: 4,900 miles

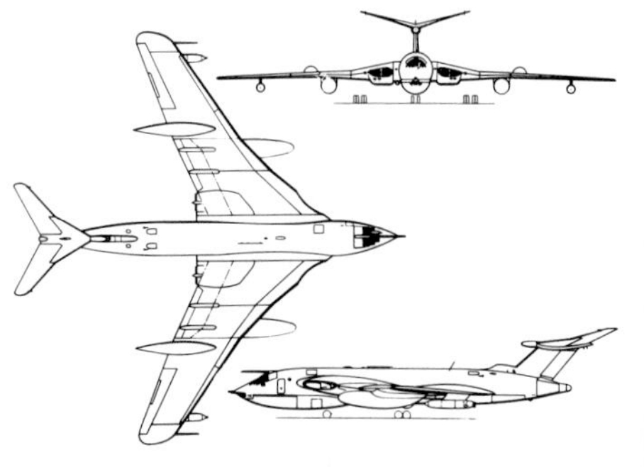

Ilyushin Il-76 'Midas'

Though for many years inferior to the West in flight-refuelling capability, the USSR has recently made strenuous efforts to remedy this imbalance, initially with modified bombers but recently with the 'Midas', an important development of the Il-76 'Candid' logistic transport and currently known only by its NATO reporting name. The type began to enter service in 1987, and the only revealed details are the fact that it is a three-point tanker with a centreline HDU in the lower fuselage and two underwing HDUs. The standard Il-76 has some 81820 litres (18,000 Imp gal) of fuel carried in integral wing tanks, and this could be supplemented by significant quantities of additional transfer fuel in the hold, which normally accommodates up to 40000 kg (88,183 lb) of freight.

Specification: Ilyushin Il-76 'Midas' five-seat inflight-refuelling tanker
Span: 50.50 m (165 ft 8 in)
Length: 46.59 m (152 ft 10.5 in)
Powerplant: 4×Soloviev D-30KP 12000 kg (26,455 lb) st each
Payload: unknown quantity of transfer fuel
Armament: 2×23-mm cannon in tail turret
Max T/O weight: 170000 kg (374,780 lb)
Max speed: 528 mph at optimum altitude
Operational range: 3,107 miles

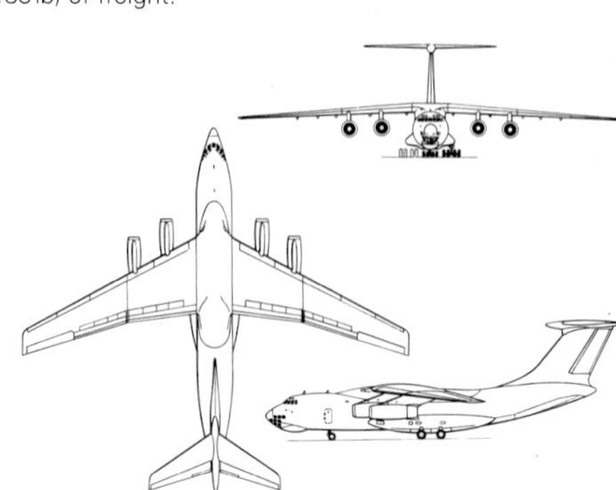

pecification: British
erospace (Vickers/BAC) VC10
Mk 3 4+17-seat inflight-refuelling
nker
pan: 44.55 m (146 ft 2 in)
ength: 52.32 m (171 ft 8 in)
xcluding refuelling probe
owerplant: 4×Rolls-Royce
onway Mk 550B, 9888 kg
1,800 lb) st each
ayload: 86364 kg (190,400 lb) of
ansfer fuel
lax T/O weight: 146513 kg
23,000 lb)
ruising speed: 425 mph at 30,000 ft
perational range: 3,900 miles
ith maximum payload

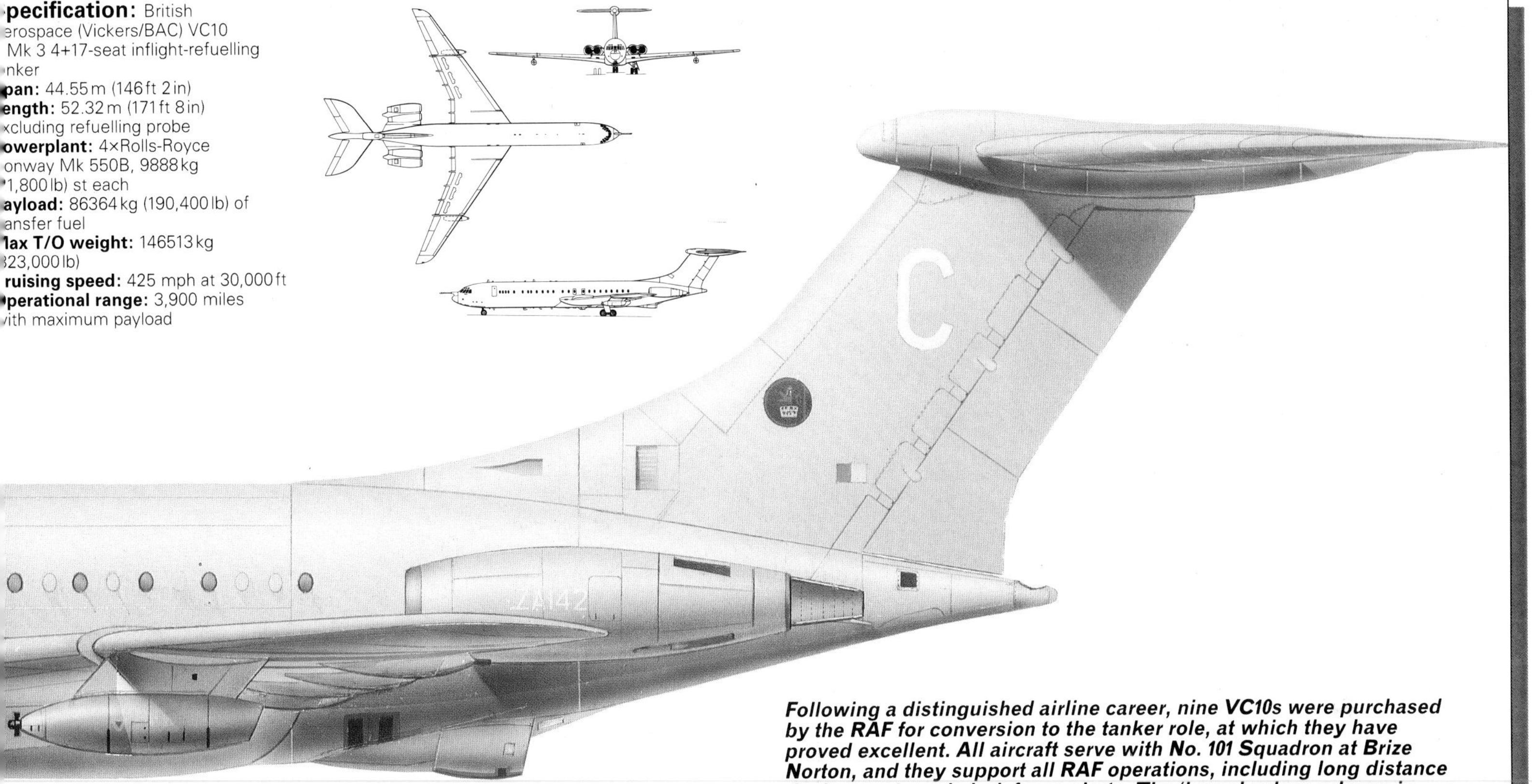

Following a distinguished airline career, nine VC10s were purchased by the RAF for conversion to the tanker role, at which they have proved excellent. All aircraft serve with No. 101 Squadron at Brize Norton, and they support all RAF operations, including long distance deployments and air defence alerts. The 'hemp' colour scheme is fleet-wide and minimises conspicuity in the sky and on concrete aprons.

Lockheed HC-130 Hercules

The Hercules is one of the most versatile aircraft currently in service and has been developed into a multitude of variants other than its primary long-range tactical transport form. Comparatively little known amongst these roles, but of particular importance, is the inflight refuelling of helicopters. This is a difficult task well suited to the comparatively low speed but great stability of the Hercules. The variant involved is the HC-130P, a designation applied to HC-130Hs converted with a pair of underwing HDUs and their associated plumbing. The HC-130H can be fitted with two 6184-litre (1,800-US gal) tanks in the hold, and this capability is retained in the HC-130P, which can transfer 22000 kg (48,500 lb) of fuel at a radius of 575 miles. The type is also capable of inflight recovery of parachuted payloads.

Specification: Lockheed HC-130P Hercules 10/12-seat inflight-refuelling tanker
Span: 40.41 m (132 ft 7 in)
Length: 29.79 m (97 ft 9 in)
Powerplant: 4×Avco Lycoming T56-A-15, 3355 kW (4,500 shp) each
Payload: transfer fuel (see above)
Max T/O weight: 70310 kg (155,000 lb)
Max speed: 384 mph at optimum altitude
Operational range: 2,487 miles

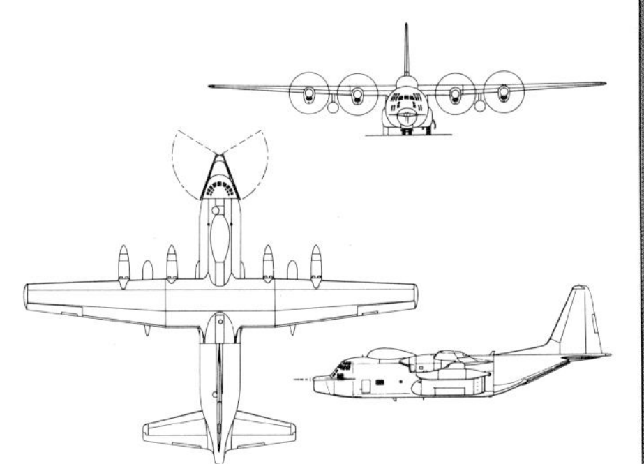

Lockheed KC-130 Hercules

In addition to the specialist helicopter-refuelling HC-130, there are four more conventional KC-130 tanker versions of the Hercules. Developed for the US Marine Corps as the GV-1 but redesignated in 1962, the KC-130F is a variant of the C-130B with 3661-kW (4,910-shp) engines, two underwing HDUs and extra tankage in the fuselage. The KC-130H is a C-130H variant very similar to the US Marine Corps' KC-130R but exported to six countries including Brazil, Israel, Saudi Arabia and Spain. The KC-130R has 3363-kW (4,508-shp) T56-A-15 turboprops, greater weights, and additional fuel capacity in the form of two 5148-litre (1,360-US gal) underwing tanks and a removable 13627-litre (3,600-US gal) in the cargo compartment. A British version is the Hercules C.Mk 1K with four 4091-litre (900-Imp gal) tanks in the hold plus a Mk 17B HDU on the rear ramp.

Specification: Lockheed KC-130F Hercules inflight-refuelling tanker
Span: 40.41 m (132 ft 7 in)
Length: 29.79 m (97 ft 9 in)
Powerplant: 4×Avco Lycoming T56-A-16, 3661 kW (4,910 shp) each
Payload: transfer fuel (see above)
Max T/O weight: 61235 kg (135,000 lb)
Max speed: 380 mph at 30,000 ft
Operational range: 1,000 miles to transfer 14061 kg (31,000 lb) of fuel

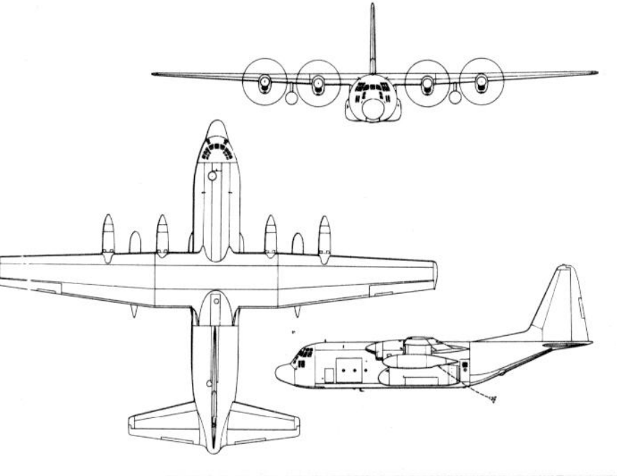

Chapter 11

FLYING BOATS

Heinkel He 115

Efficient both as a minelayer and a torpedo-bopmber, the He 115 was a twin-engine, twin-float mid-wing monoplane of all-metal monocoque construction. It first flew in 1936 and by 1940 the He 115B was in service as a minelayer, being equipped to carry a single 920-kg (2,028-lb) magnetic mine; aircraft of Kustenfliegergruppen 106 and 506 flew frequent mining sorties off the UK's east and south coasts. Later in 1940 the He 115C appeared with increased armament, and one sub-variant featured reinforced floats to permit landing on ice and frozen snow. The C-4 was a dedicated torpedo attack version, this variant being flown on several occasions against the famous North Cape convoys.

Arado Ar 196

One of the most widely-used and efficient small twin-float seaplanes of World War II, the Ar 196 became operational with the Kriegsmarine in 1939, serving aboard most of Germany's major fleet units. An agile aircraft with fairly heavy armament, it was employed for maritime patrol and reconnaissance, later serving not only with shore-based coastal squadrons but for sea-search duties with German commerce raiders in distant oceans. Of predominantly metal construction, only the rear fuselage was fabric-covered, and the Ar 196 could also carry small bombs under the wings for use on anti-submarine patrols. Production was also undertaken in France and the Netherlands, a total of 493 aircraft being completed in all factories.

Specification: Arado Ar 196A-3 2-seat reconnaissance floatplane
Span: 12.40 m (40 ft 9.5 in)
Length: 11.00 m (36 ft 0.5 in)
Powerplant: 1×BMW 132K, 723 kW (970 hp)
Armament: 2×20-mm cannon and 3 or 4×7.9-mm (0.312-in) machine-guns, plus 2×50-kg (110-lb) bombs
Max speed: 193 mph at 13,125 ft
Operational range: 665 miles

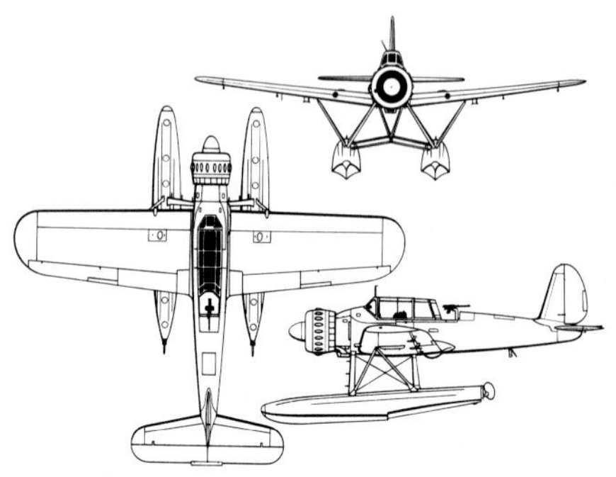

Heinkel He 59

Dating back to the years of Germany's clandestine military planning, the twin-engine He 59 biplane originated in 1930 as a torpedo-bomber with interchangeable wheel and twin-float undercarriage. By World War II the He 59C was performing a variety of duties, including coastal reconnaissance, air-sea rescue and bombing training. The D and E followed in the training role, and the N was a navigation trainer. The seaplanes saw widespread service in the early war years, carrying assault troops in the invasion of the Netherlands, laying mines off the UK's coast, and engaging in convoy shadowing and air-sea rescue in the Channel during the Battle of Britain. He 59s equipped about six *Gruppen* before being replaced by Do 18s and Do 24s.

Specification: Heinkel He 59B-2 4-seat general-purpose floatplane
Span: 23.70 m (77 0ft 9 in)
Length: 17.40 m (57 ft 1 in)
Powerplant: two BMW VI 6.0 ZU, 492 kW (660 hp) each
Armament: 3×7.9-mm (0.312-in) machine-guns, plus up to 1000-kg (2,205-lb) of bombs or 1×torpedo
Max speed: 137 mph at sea level
Operational range: 950 miles

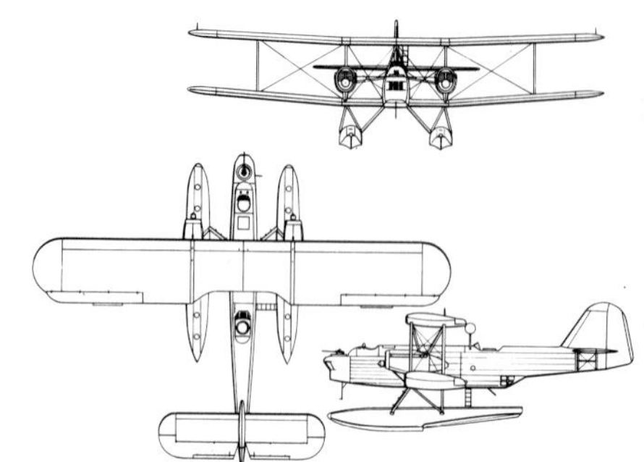

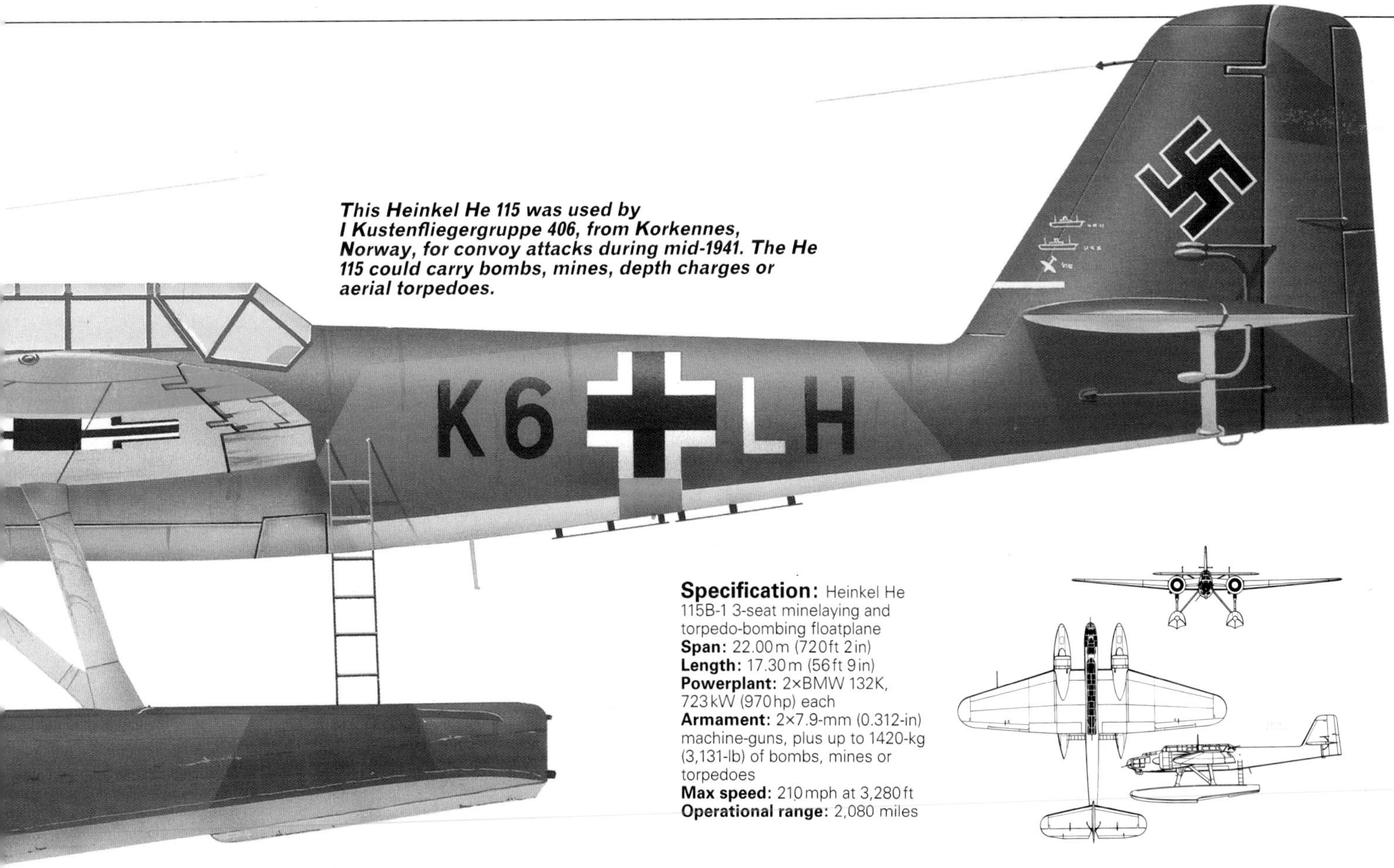

This Heinkel He 115 was used by I Kustenfliegergruppe 406, from Korkennes, Norway, for convoy attacks during mid-1941. The He 115 could carry bombs, mines, depth charges or aerial torpedoes.

Specification: Heinkel He 115B-1 3-seat minelaying and torpedo-bombing floatplane
Span: 22.00 m (720 ft 2 in)
Length: 17.30 m (56 ft 9 in)
Powerplant: 2×BMW 132K, 723 kW (970 hp) each
Armament: 2×7.9-mm (0.312-in) machine-guns, plus up to 1420-kg (3,131-lb) of bombs, mines or torpedoes
Max speed: 210 mph at 3,280 ft
Operational range: 2,080 miles

Dornier Do 18

A direct descendant of the distinguished Wal (whale) family of inter-war commercial flying boats, the tandem-twin engine Do 18 parasol monoplane first flew in 1935. At the outbreak of war the Do 18D was being replaced by the Do 18G-1 in the maritime reconnaissance role, and a similar unarmed trainer with dual controls was designated Do 18H. Production ran out in 1940 when many Do 18G-1s were modified for air-sea rescue work under the designation Do 18N-1. Do 18s were frequently encountered over the North Sea in the early months of the war and over the English Channel, particularly during the Battle of Britain. Production totalled about 100 Do 18s, of which some 70 were Do 18Gs.

Specification: Dornier Do 18G-1 4-seat maritime reconnaissance flying boat
Span: 23.70 m (770 ft 9.25 in)
Length: 19.37 m (63 ft 7 in)
Powerplant: 2×Junkers Jumo 205D, 656 kW (880 hp) each
Armament: 1×20-mm cannon and 1×13-mm (0.51-in) machine-gun, plus 100-kg (220-lb) of bombs
Max speed: 166 mph at 6,560 ft
Operational range: 2,175 miles

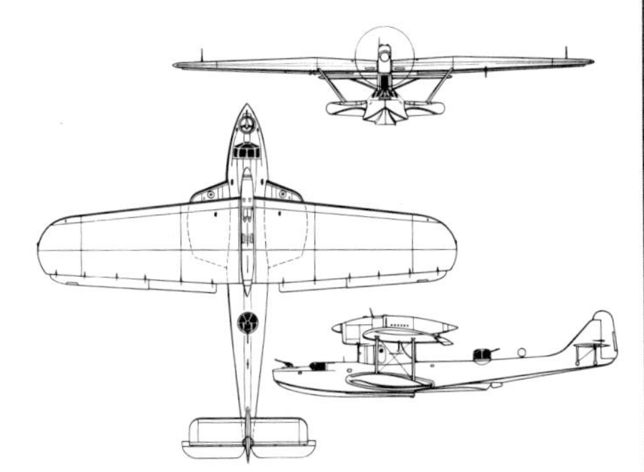

Dornier Do 24

Extending the successful parasol-wing flying boat formula, the Do 24 trimotor first flown in July 1937 and a production manufacturing licence was negotiated with the Dutch. A small number of German-built Do 24Ks was delivered to the Luftwaffe. After the invasion of the Netherlands, Dutch production continued, and the French CAMS company also joined the manufacturing programme. Maritime duties were largely confined to the air-sea rescue role (the Do 24N-1) and to maritime reconnaissance and transport duties (Do 24T-1 and T-2). Production of all versions amounted to about 255, examples finding their way into service with the RAAF, the Swedish air force, the Spanish air-sea rescue service and the French navy.

Specification: Dornier Do 24T-1 5/6-seat maritime reconnaissance and transport flying boat
Span: 27.00 m (880 ft 7 in)
Length: 22.00 m (72 ft 4 in)
Powerplant: 3×BMW-Bramo Fafnir 323R-2, 746 kW (1,000 hp) each
Armament: 1×20-mm cannon and 2×7.9-mm (0.312-in) machine-guns, plus up to 12×50-kg (110-lb) bombs
Max speed: 211 mph at 9,845 ft
Operational range: 2,920 miles

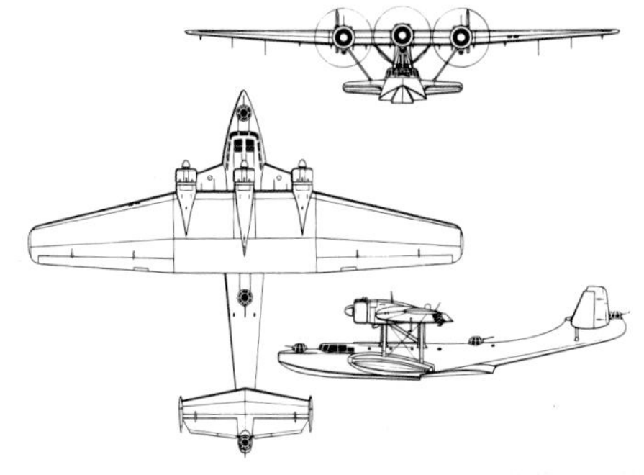

Kawanishi H8K 'Emily'

This Kawanishi H8K2 Model 12 is of the 801st Kokutai, based at Yokohama. Despite being built in small numbers, the 'Emily' earned a reputation as the most outstanding flying-boat of the war.

Aichi E13A 'Jake'

Produced to meet a 1937 requirement, the single-engine twin-float Aichi E13A1 'Jake' was a low-wing floatplane that served with the JNAF throughout the Pacific war, being present at the Pearl Harbor, Coral Sea and Midway battles. Though employed primarily for reconnaissance and anti-shipping operations, for which the sub-variant E13A1b with airborne search radar was developed, the E13A1 was also extensively used for coastal patrol, shipping escort and air-sea rescue duties. A trainer version, the E13A1-K with dual controls, was produced, as were specialist anti-submarine, night patrol and anti-patrol boat derivatives.

Specification: Aichi E13A1 'Jake' 2-seat reconnaissance and anti-shipping floatplane
Span: 14.50 m (47 ft 7 in)
Length: 11.30 m (37 ft 1 in)
Powerplant: 1×Mitsubishi Kinsei 43, 805 kW (1,080 hp)
Armament: 1×7.7-mm (0.303-in) machine-gun, plus up to 250-kg (551-lb) of bombs; 1×20-mm cannon added in anti-ship role
Max speed: 234 mph at 7,155 ft
Operational range: 1,300 miles

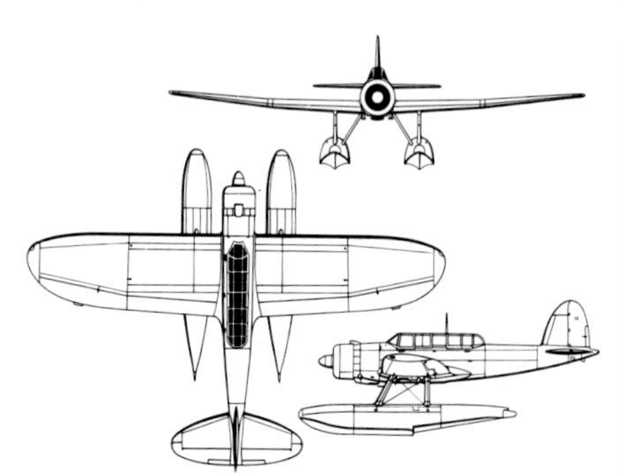

Kawanishi H6K 'Mavis'

A design that owed much to contemporary American commercial flying boats, the Japanese Type 97 four-engine parasol flying boat was a very large aeroplane of exceptionally graceful lines. First flown in July 1936 the aircraft entered naval service in 1938 as the H6K2, and by the date of Pearl Harbor the H6K4 had been standardised in production; capable of carrying two 800-kg (1,764-lb) bombs or torpedoes on wing-strut racks, 66 of this type were in service and became extremely active both in the reconnaissance, bomber and transport roles. A final version, the H6K5 with more powerful engines, was introduced before preference switched to the H8K series in 1943 when 217 H6Ks had been built.

Specification: Kawanishi H6K5 'Mavis' 9-seat maritime reconnaissance and bomber flying boat
Span: 40.00 m (1310 ft 2.75 in)
Length: 25.63 m (84 ft 0.75 in)
Powerplant: 4×Mitsubishi Kinsei 51 or 53, 969 kW (1,300 hp) each
Armament: 1×20-mm cannon and 4×7.7-mm (0.303-in) machine-guns, plus up to 1600-kg (3,528-lb) of bombs or 2×torpedoes
Max speed: 239 mph at 13,125 ft
Operational range: 4,210 miles

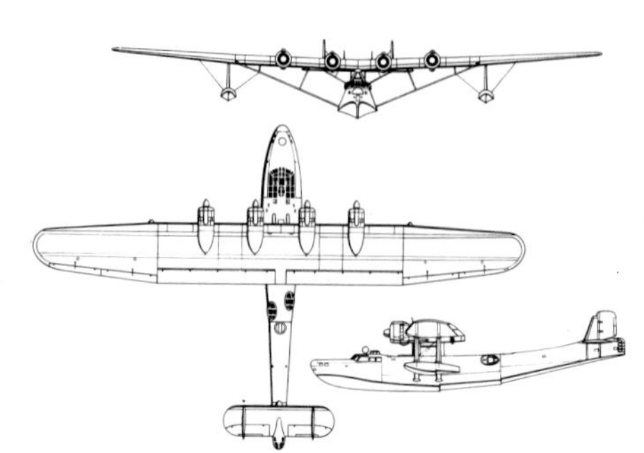

ecification: Kawanishi
2 'Emily' 9-seat maritime
onnaissance, bomber and 64-
transport flying boat
n: 38.00 m (1240ft 8in)
gth: 28.13m (92ft 4in)
verplant: 4×Mitsubishi MK4Q
ei 22, 1379kW (1,850hp) each
Armament: 5×20-mm cannon and 5×7.7-mm (0.303-in) machine guns, plus up to 1600-kg, (3,527-lb of bombs and depth charges or 2×torpedoes
Max speed: 290mph at 16,405ft
Operational range: 4,460 miles

Among wartime reconnaissance flying boats, the Japanese H8K was unequalled by those of any other combatant air force in performance, armament and handling qualities. Of cantilever wing configuration with four engines, the prototype first flew in January 1941, and production H8K1s were flown in action (a bombing attack on Oahu Island) just 14 months later. The basic design was progressively improved with increased power and armament, and by 1943 the H8K2 was in full scale production. Of outstandingly clean design, the boat featured shoulder-set wings with retracting stabilising floats at the wing tip, and bow, dorsal, beam and tail gun positions. Total production reached 167.

Blohm und Voss BV 138

Of unique configuration, the three-engine BV 138 flying boat featured foreshortened hull, high wing and twin tail booms. The prototype flew in July 1937 but possessed poor handling qualities both in the air and on the water, requiring complete redesign. Some BV 138As were pressed into service as transports for the 1940 Norwegian campaign, but in June 1941 BV 138Bs commenced their intended duties on maritime reconnaissance, based in Norway; thereafter they flew constant patrols over the North Sea and Arctic waters; they were prominent in shadowing the famous North Cape convoys, and the later BV 138MS carried mine-exploding hoops, while the radar-equipped BV 138C-1 flew anti-submarine sorties.

Specification: Blohm und Voss BV 138B-1 5-seat long-range maritime reconnaissance flying boat
Span: 26.94m (88ft 4.5in)
Length: 19.85m (65ft 1.5in)
Powerplant: 3×Junkers Jumo 205D, 656kW (880hp) each
Armament: 2×20-mm cannon, 1×15-mm cannon and 1×7.9-mm (0.312-in) machine-gun, plus 4×150-kg (331-lb) depth charges
Max speed: 180mph at sea level
Operational range: 2,410 miles

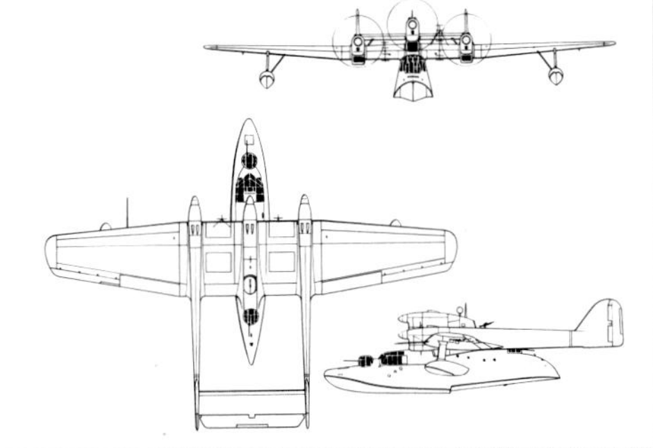

Blohm und Voss BV 222

Of striking proportions, the six-engine BV 222 flying boat was conceived before tHE World War II for North Atlantic commercial operation, the first prototype being flown in September 1940. It was followed by eight further prototypes, all of which featured defensive armaments. All served with Lufttransportstaffel See 222 in the Mediterranean on transport duties between Italy and North Africa; two were shot down by Allied fighters. Prototypes V2 to V5 were intended for maritime reconnissance with *Hohentweil* search and *Neptun* rear warning radar. The last prototype (V9) became the BV 22C-09 and was followed by the production C-010 to C-013; the next four examples were abandoned before completion.

Specification: Blohm und Voss BV 222C 11/14-seat reconnaissance and 110-man transport flying boat
Span: 46.00m (150ft 11in)
Length: 36.99m (121ft 4.5in)
Powerplant: 6×Junkers Jumo 207C, 746kW (1,000hp) each
Armament: 3×20-mm cannon and up to 12×13-mm (0.51-in) machine-guns
Max speed: 242mph at 16,405ft
Operational range: 3,790 miles

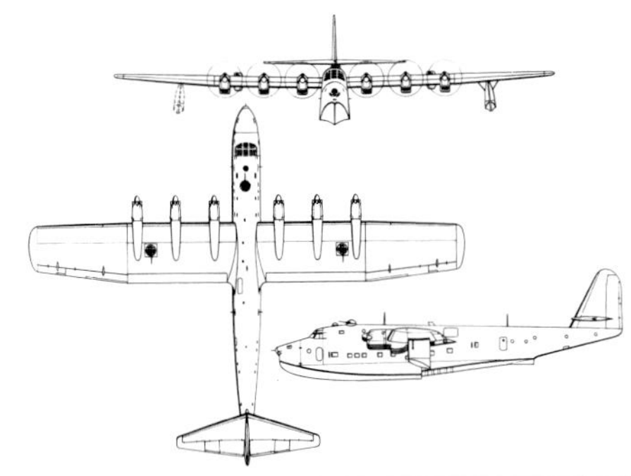

CRDA CANT Z.501 Gabbiano

Of unusual design, the small single-engine CANT Z.501 Gabbiano (Gull) parasol monoplane flying boat of all-wood construction was first flown in 1934, but by the time of Italy's entry into the war in June 1940 no fewer than 202 examples were in service. Their principal role was defined as reconnaissance bomber, external racks for bombs being incorporated in the underwing struts between wings, floats and hull. Another unusual feature was the location of a gun position in the rear of the engine nacelle above the wing. The boats were employed in all manner of coastal duties including anti-submarine patrols and air-sea rescue work and were frequently encountered by the RAF, particularly in the Aegean.

Specification: CRDA CANT Z.501 Gabbiano 4/5-seat light reconnaissance and bomber flying boat
Span: 22.50 m (730 ft 9.75 in)
Length: 14.30 m (46 ft 11 in)
Powerplant: 1×Isotta Fraschini Asso XI R2 215, 671 kW (900 hp)
Armament: 2 or 3×7.7-mm (0.303-in) machine-guns, plus up to 640-kg (1,411-lb) of bombs
Max speed: 171 mph at 8,200 ft
Operational range: 1,490 miles

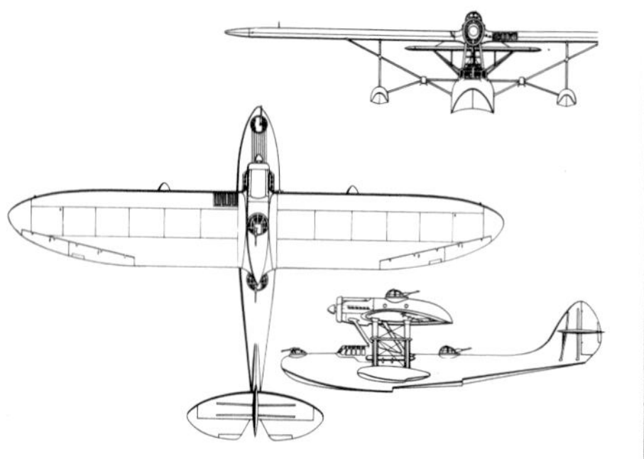

CRDA CANT Z.506B Airone

Italy's most important water-borne aircraft in World War II, the twin-float Z.506B Airone (Heron) trimotor was an efficient reconnaissance and torpedo bomber which earned universal praise for its pleasant handling both in the air and on the water. Numerous production batches appeared and by the date of Italy's entry into the war about 100 Z.506s were in service with the Regia Marina. Most used variant was the Series XII, and another version, the Z.506S (Soccorsio, or Aid), was an air-sea rescue variant also used by the Luftwaffe in the Mediterranean. Airone floatplanes took part in operations to occupy the Greek islands in 1941, and were later employed in coastal reconnaissance and anti-submarine patrols.

Specification: CRDA CANT Z.506B Airone Serie XII 54-seat torpedo, bomber and reconnaissance floatplane
Span: 226.50 m (86 ft 11.5 in)
Length: 19.24 m (63 ft 1.5 in)
Powerplant: 3×Alfa Romeo 126 RC.34, 559 kW (750 hp) each
Armament: 1×12.7-mm (0.5-in) and 3×303-in) machine-guns, plus up to 1200-kg (2,646-lb) of bombs or 1×800-kg (1,764-lb) torpedo
Max speed: 227 mph
Operational range: 1,245 miles

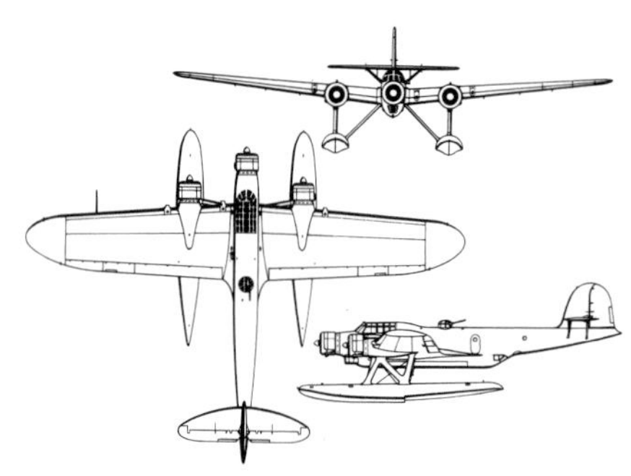

Junkers Ju 52/3mW

One of the anachronisms of World War II was the widespread use made by Germany of the ageing Ju 52/3m trimotor transport, a former peacetime airliner with corrugated skin and fixed landing gear. Many of these were manufactured to incorporate provision for interchangeable wheel and twin-float undercarriage; when equipped with floats the aircraft was designated the Ju 52/3mW. These aircraft were so successfully used in the 1940 Norwegian campaign that the Dutch Fokker company was ordered to produce large numbers of floats, these being applied to Ju 52/3mg4e, g5e, g7e and g8e variants as the need arose; they were widely employed as 18-man transports, not only in Norway but in the Mediterranean and Black Sea.

Specification: Junkers Ju 52/3mg7eW 3-crew transport floatplane
Span: 29.21 m (950 ft 10 in)
Length: 19.00 m (62 ft 4 in)
Powerplant: 3×BMW 132T, 619 kW (830 hp) each
Armament: 1×13-mm (0.51-in) and 2×7.9-mm (0.312-in) machine-guns
Max speed: 163 mph
Operational range: 930 miles

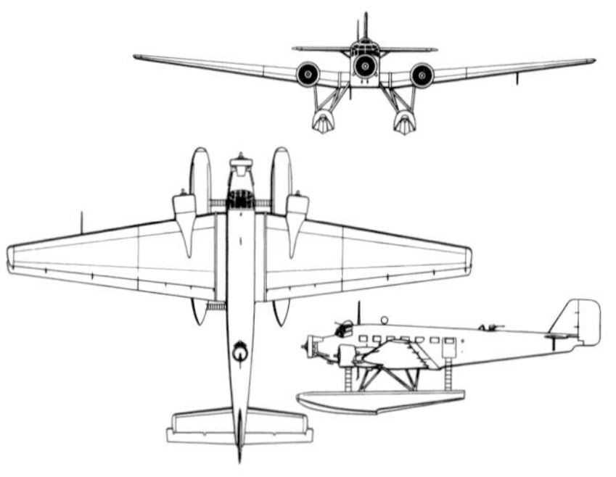

IMAM Ro.43

Developed before World War II from the land-based Meridionali Ro.37*bis* light reconnaissance aircraft, the Ro.43 became the Italian navy's standard shipborne aircraft in the fleet reconnaissance role, serving in fairly large numbers aboard most major warships. Of central-float configuration, with small balancing underwing floats, the two-seat biplane featured gull and inverted-gull wings, so that the pilot's forward line of vision above the fuselage was unrestricted by the top wing. On Italy's entry to the war 105 Ro.43s were in service, and the type continued to serve throughout the war despite poor performance. The Ro.44 was a single-seat fighter derivative.

Specification: IMAM Ro.43 2-seat reconnaissance floatplane
Span: 11.60 m (380 ft 4.75 in)
Length: 9.71 m (31 ft 10.25 in)
Powerplant: 1×Piaggio P.XR, 522 kW (700 hp)
Armament: 2×7.7-mm (0.303-in) machine-guns
Max speed: 186 mph at 8,200 ft
Operational range: 932 miles

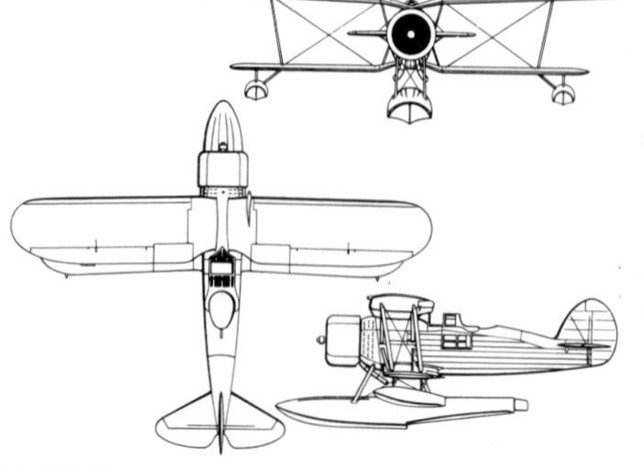

ikorsky S-38

ne amphibious Sikorsky S-38, derived from the earlier S-36, was first flown on 25 June 928. Of unusual configuration, with a central hull with eight-passenger cabin carrying a rut-braced parasol wing with twin outrigger booms supporting the tailplane and twin fins, e S-38 was designed for the Caribbean and South American services of NYRBA and Pan merican. The initial S-38A model, powered by 306 kW (410 hp) Wasps, was superseded by e 10-passenger up-engined S-38B, of which 75 were built, and the similarly-powered 4-seat S-38C. In addition to NYRBA and Pan Am, S-38s were operated by American irlines, Canadian Airways, Colonial Western Airways, Curtiss Flying Service, Inter-Island irways of Hawaii, Northwest Airways, and Western Air Express, as well as by the US Navy nd private owners, some remaining active until after World War 2.

pecification: Sikorsky S-38B
mphibian airliner
pan: 21.84 m (71 ft 8 in)
ength: 12.27 m (40 ft 3 in)
owerplant: 2×Pratt & Whitney
Vasp, 317 kW (425 hp) each
ayload: 10 passengers
lax T/O weight: 47540 kg
0,480 lb)
ruising speed: 103 mph
ange: 500 miles

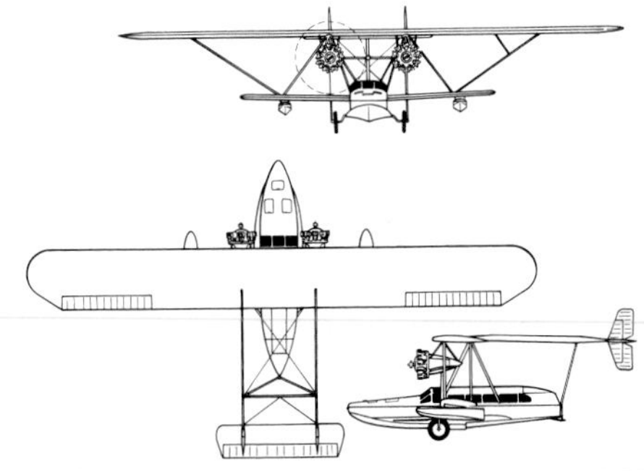

Sikorsky S-40

The growth of flying boat services in the Caribbean and Latin America forged with Consolidated Commodores and Sikorsky S-38s prompted Pan American to order its first four-engined flying boat in 1930. Retaining the successful airframe formula of the S-38, at the time of its first flight in 1931 the S-40 was the largest aeroplane ever built in the USA. It was designed to carry 24 passengers over a range of 950 miles or 40 passengers on shorter stage lengths up to 500 miles. Three were built, named *American Clipper*, *Caribbean Clipper* and *Southern Clipper*, beginning the PAA *Clipper* tradition which continues today. The Sikorsky S-40s operated mostly in the Caribbean. They were requisitioned by the US Navy after Pearl Harbor and used for transport and training until finally withdrawn from use in 1943.

Specification: Sikorsky S-40
flying boat airliner
Span: 34.75 m (114 ft 0 in)
Length: 23.37 m (76 ft 8 in)
Powerplant: 4×Pratt & Whitney R-1860 Hornet B, 429 kW (575 hp) each
Payload: 40 passengers
Max T/O weight: 15422 kg (34,000 lb)
Cruising speed: 115 mph
Range: 50 miles

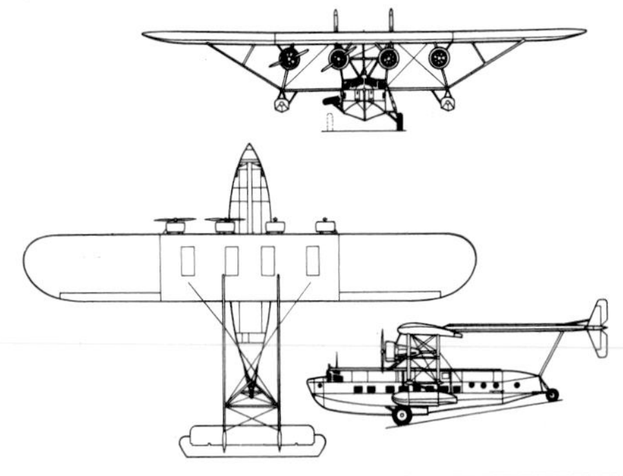

Sikorsky S-42

Shortly after the S-40 entered service, Pan American began seeking an even longer-range lying boat, for which requirement the Martin M-130 and Sikorsky S-42 were designed. The all-metal S-42 first flew on 29 March 1934 and quickly set 10 world records for payload to height and speed in its class. Although it was unable to match the M-130 for range, PAA ordered 10 S-42s, the first of which entered service in April 1935 on the airline's San Francisco-Hawaii service. PAA's S.42s, which included four S-42B models with long-range fuel tanks for Pacific and planned Atlantic routes, also operated on the New York-Bermuda, Miami-South America, Seattle-Alaska and Manila-Hong Kong routes. They usually operated n 32-passenger configuration although 40-seat day travel and 14-passenger overnight sleeper cabin layouts were also available.

Specification: Sikorsky S-40A
flying boat airliner
Span: 41.285 m (114 ft 2 in)
Length: 20.62 m (67 ft 8 in)
Powerplant: 4×Pratt & Whitney Hornet, 596 kW (800 hp) each
Payload: 40 passengers
Max T/O weight: 17237 kg (38,000 lb)
Cruising speed: 170 mph
Range: 1,200 miles

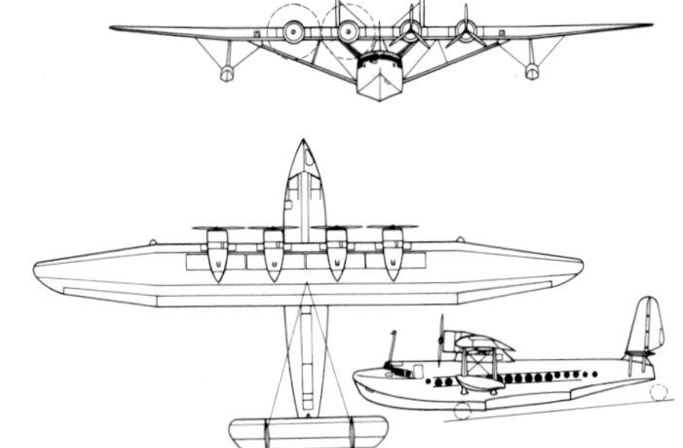

Sikorsky S-43

Unlike its immediate predecessor, the S-43 was an amphibian – the largest aircraft of that type ever built when it first flew in 1935. Styled by designer Michael Gluhareff along the elegant lines of the S-42, the S-43 Mini Clipper was powered by Pratt & Whitney Hornet radial engines. This, and the Wright Cyclone-engined S-43W, had single fins and rudders; the S-43B and S-43WB variants, similarly powered by P&W or Wright engines, had twin fins and rudders. Pan American was the major commercial operator of the aircraft, flying S-43s and S-43Bs on its Latin American routes. Other customers for the aircraft included Air France, which flew them in North Africa, Inter-Island Airways of Hawaii, the Dutch overseas carrier KNILM, and airlines in Chile, China, Norway and the USSR. The US Navy bought 11 S-43s for use as utility transport under the designation JRS-1, and the US Army operated four as OA-8s/OA-11s. Among private operators was Howard Hughes, whose S-43 is believed to be still in existence.

Specification: Sikorsky S-43
amphibian airliner
Span: 26.215 m (86 ft 0 in)
Length: 15.60 m (51 ft 2 in)
Powerplant: 2×Pratt & Whitney S1EG Hornet, 559 kW (750 hp) each
Payload: 40 passengers or 1347 kg (2,970 lb) of freight
Max T/O weight: 8845 kg (19,500 lb)
Cruising speed: 177 mph
Range: 775 miles

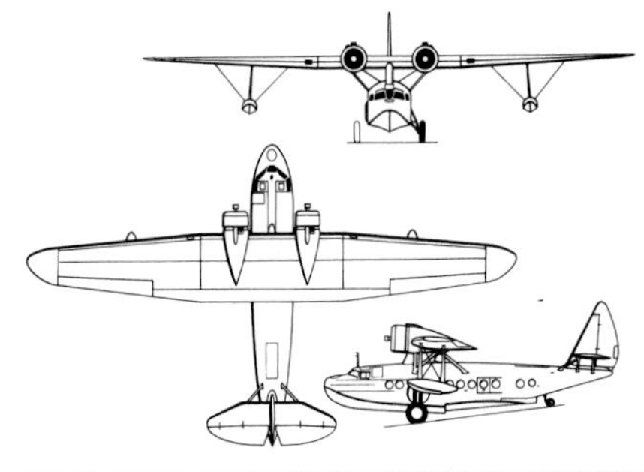

Dornier Do X

In 1926 Dr Claude Dornier conceived the idea of a large flying boat to carry 100 or more passengers over transatlantic routes. When it first flew on 21 October 1929, carrying a crew of ten, 150 passengers and nine stowaways, the Do X was the largest aircraft in the world, powered by 12 Siemens-Bristol Jupiters mounted in tandem-pair 'power eggs' driving tractor/pusher propellers. Cooling difficulties with these engines led to substitutions of Curtis Conquerors. On 2 November 1930 the Do X left Friedrichshafen bound for New York by way of Calshot, England, and Lisbon, where a fire severely damaged one wing. It was rebuilt and after further repairs on the Canary Islands the Do X made a leisurely passage to Brazil and along the South American coastline to New York, arriving nearly 10 months after leaving Germany. The Do X never entered regular service with Deutsche Lufthansa, and was destroyed by Allied bombing during World War 2.

Specification: Dornier Do X flying boat airliner
Span: 48.00 m (157 ft 5.75 in)
Length: 40.00 m (131 ft 4.75 in)
Powerplant: 12×Curtiss Conqueror, 447 kW (600 hp) each
Payload: 100 pasengers
Max T/O weight: 56000 kg (123,457 lb)
Cruising speed: 118 mph
Range: 1,056 miles

Boeing 314

In July 1936 Pan American Airways contracted with Boeing for six flying boat airliners capable of flying the North Atlantic non-stop. The Boeing 314 flew on 7 June 1938, and was then the largest civil aircraft in existence. It used the wings and four 1118 kW (1,500 hp) Wright Cyclone radial engines of the Boeing XB-15 bomber, mated to a spacious fuselage with cabin accommodation for 74 day or 40 overnight sleeper passengers. PAA's *Yankee Clipper* inaugurated North Atlantic passenger flights on 28 June, flying from New York to Southampton via Newfoundland. PAA subsequently ordered six improved Model 314As, the first flying on 20 March 1941. Three of these were transferred to BOAC, one being used by Churchill for his wartime transatlantic journeys. Two Boeing 314s were destroyed during the war, and a third in 1947. The remainder were sold post-war to independent operators and finally withdrawn from service and scrapped in 1950-51.

Specification: Boeing 314A long-range flying boat airliner
Span: 46.33 m (152 ft 0 in)
Length: 32.31 m (106 ft 1 in)
Powerplant: 4×Wright R-2600 Double Cyclone, 1193 kW (1,600 hp) each
Payload: 77 passengers or 3967 kg (8,745 lb) of freight
Max T/O weight: 37422 kg (82,500 lb)
Cruising speed: 175 mph
Range: 3,000 miles

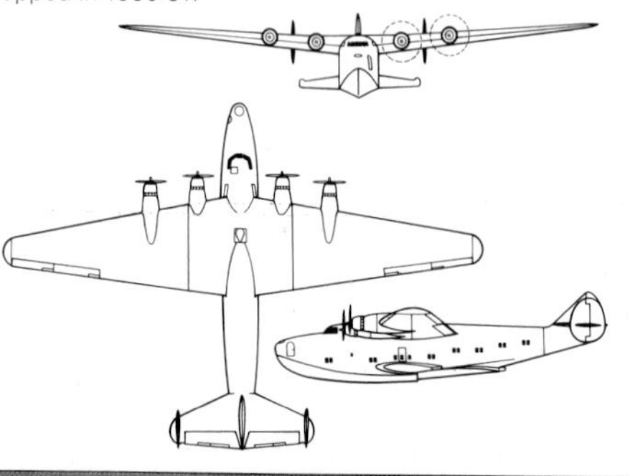

Consolidated Commodore

The Consolidated Model 16 Commodore was first flown in 1929. It was designed to meet the requirements of the newly established New York, Rio, and Buenos Aires line (NYRBA), which planned to link the principal cities of North, Central and South America. Based on the US Navy's Consolidated XPY-1, the Commodore was a strut-braced parasol wing flying boat. The first three aircraft were configured for 18 passengers and three crew; the subsequent Models 16-1 and 16-2 carried 22 and 30 passengers respectively. Commodore *Flagship Buenos Aires* made route-proving flights in the summer of 1929. NYRBA inaugurated its Miami-Buenos Aires service in February 1930. In August of that year Pan American took over NYRBA and subsequently operated 14 Commodores on routes which included the longest over-water service of the time, from Jamaica to Panama City. PAA's Commodores continued to fly Caribbean services until the mid-1940s.

Specification: Consolidated Model 16 Commodore flying boat airliner
Span: 30.48 m (100 ft 0 in)
Length: 18.795 m (61 ft 8 in)
Powerplant: 2×Pratt & Whitney Hornet B, 391 kW (525 hp) each
Payload: 16-30 pasengers depending on model
Max T/O weight: 7983 kg (17,600 lb)
Cruising speed: 108 mph
Range: 1,000 miles

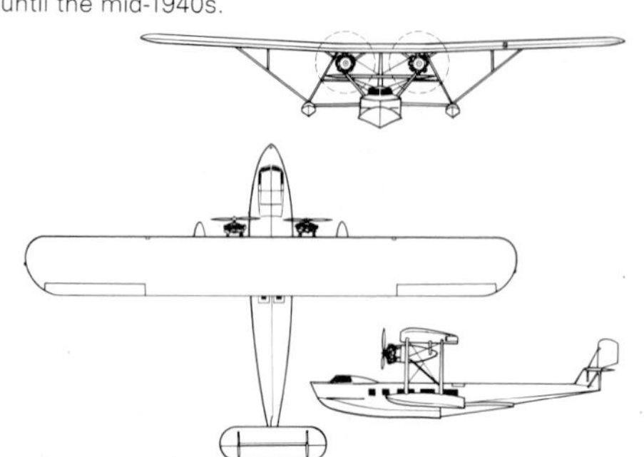

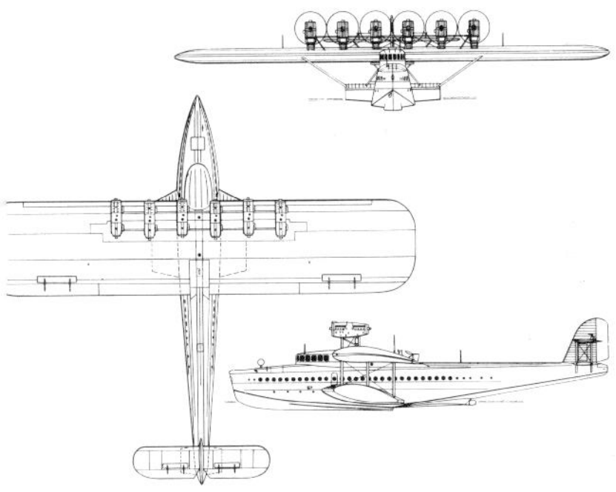

Three examples of the Dornier Do X were built, but none entered regular commercial service. The second and third aircraft were powered by Fiat engines, which proved no more successful than the Jupiters or Conquerors fitted to the prototype.

Dornier Do J Wal

One of the most successful 1920s flying boats, the Do J Wal (Whale) was designed in 1922, but in order not to infringe the restrictions laid on Germany by the Treaty of Versailles an Italian company, Construzioni Meccaniche Aeronautiche SA (CMASA), was set up at Pisa to build the aircraft. The Wal was powered by two engines mounted back-to-back, and proved popular as a passenger craft. Orders came quickly coming from operators in Brazil, Colombia, Spain and Germany. CASA of Spain began production of a military variant in 1928, the Dutch company Netherlands Aviolanda also built the Wal, while Dornier itself manufactured developed versions between 1931-36. In May Deutsche Lufthansa put the Wal into service flying airmail between Europe and South America, recovering and catapult launching the aircraft aboard pre-positioned depot ships. Wals made 328 South Atlantic crossings in DLH service.

Specification: Dornier Do J Wal flying boat transport and airliner
Span: 22.50 m (73 ft 10 in)
Length: 17.25 m (56 ft 7.25 in)
Powerplant: 2×Rolls-Royce Eagle IX, 268 kW (360 hp) each
Payload: 8-10 pasengers
Max T/O weight: 5700 kg (12,565 lb)
Cruising speed: 87 mph
Range: 1,350 miles

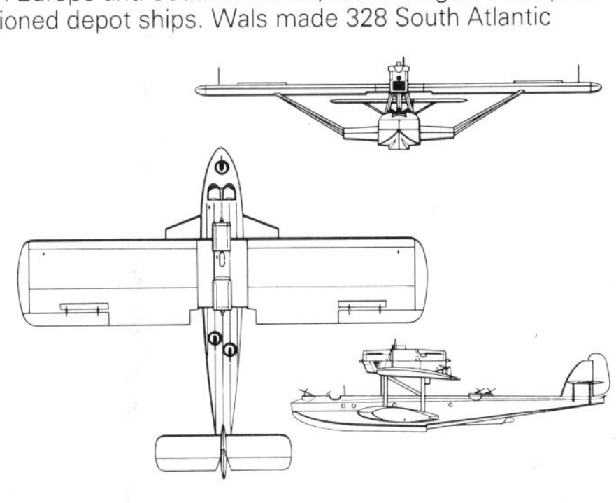

Dornier Do 18

The Do 18 was ordered by Deutsche Lufthansa in 1934 to replace the Wal and was of similar configuration, though greatly refined aerodynamically. The prototype, was powered by two Junkers Jumo 5 diesel engines mounted back-to-back and first flew on 15 March 1935. Four further DLH aircraft, powered by Jumo 6C engines and named *Zyklon, Aeolus, Pampero* and *Zephir* were designated Do 18E. The sole Do 18F, first flown on 11 June 1937, was a specially-equipped version with a larger wing. It established a straight-line nonstop distance record for seaplanes between 27-29 March 1938 flying 8392 km (5,214 miles) in 43 hours. With a crew of two pilots and a radio operator, the Do 18s were used for high-speed transatlantic mail flights, and like the earlier Wals could be catapult-launched from ships.

Specification: Dornier Do 18D flying boat transport
Span: 23.70 m (77 ft 9 in)
Length: 19.25 m (63 ft 2 in)
Powerplant: 2×Junkers Jumo 6C, 447 kW (600 hp) each
Payload: mail
Max T/O weight: 10000 kg (22,046 lb)
Cruising speed: 137 mph
Range: 2,174 miles

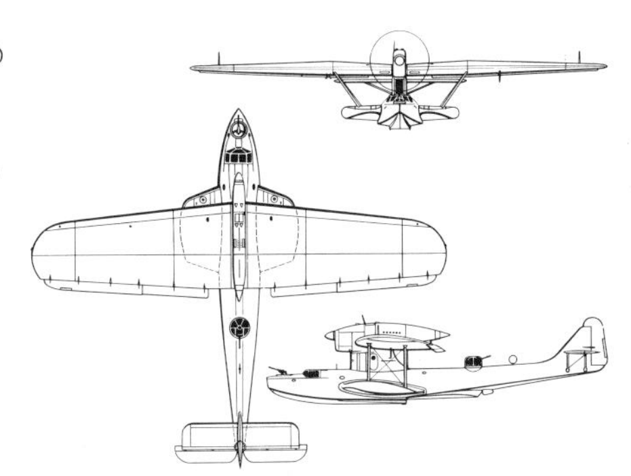

Short S.23 'C' class

Specification: Short S.23 flying boat airliner
Span: 34.75 m (114 ft 0 in)
Length: 26.82 m (88 ft 0 in)
Powerplant: 4×Bristol Pegasus XC, 686 kW (920 hp) each
Payload: 24 passengers or 3556 kg (7,840 lb) of freight
Max T/O weight: 19732 kg (43,500 lb)
Cruising speed: 165 mph
Range: 760 miles

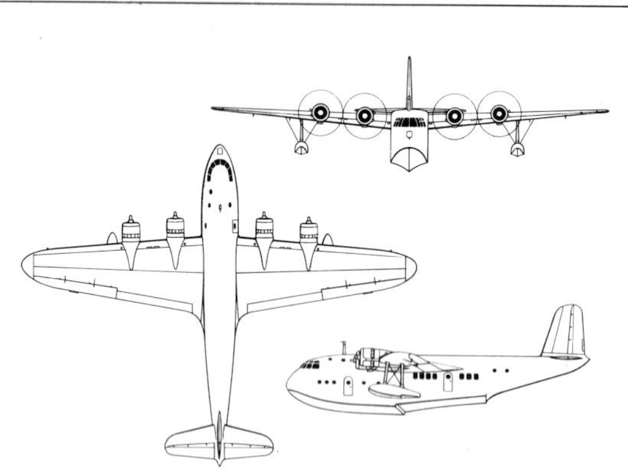

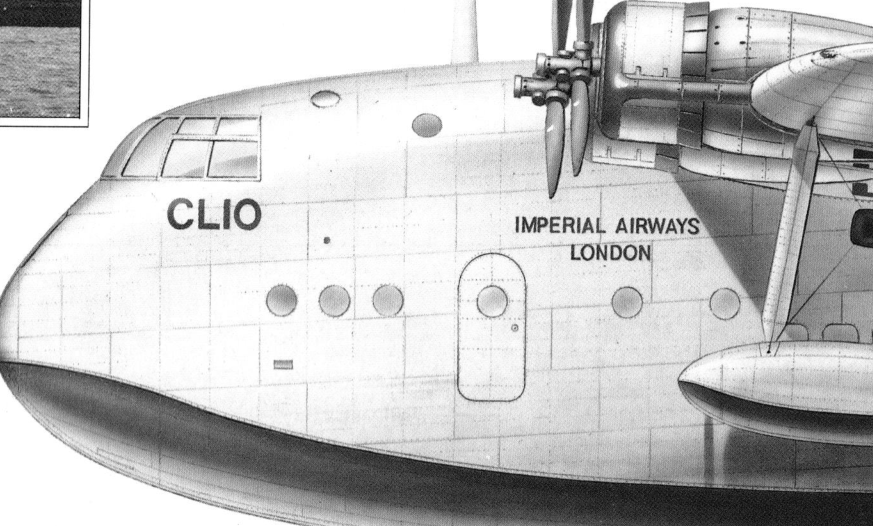

Dornier Do 26

Following experimental flights across the North Atlantic in 1937-38 using the Blohm und Voss Ha 139A four-engined seaplane, Deutsche Lufthansa began negotiations with Dornier for a high-speed flying boat capable of flying non-stop from Lisbon to New York. The resultant Do 26 first flew on 21 May 1938. An elegant gull-winged craft with retractable stabilising floats beneath its wings, the Do 26A was powered by four engines, mounted back-to-back in pairs driving tractor and pusher propellers. The aircraft carried a crew of four. Two Do 26As were completed and made a brief series of mail flights across the South Atlantic before the outbreak of war caused services, and completion of a third aircraft, to be abandoned.

Specification: Dornier Do 26A flying boat transport
Span: 30.00 m (98 ft 5.25 in)
Length: 24.60 m (80 ft 8.5 in)
Powerplant: 4×Junkers Jumo 205C, 447 kW (600 hp) each
Payload: 900 kg (1,984 lb)
Max T/O weight: 20000 kg (44,092 lb)
Cruising speed: 193 mph
Range: 5,592 miles

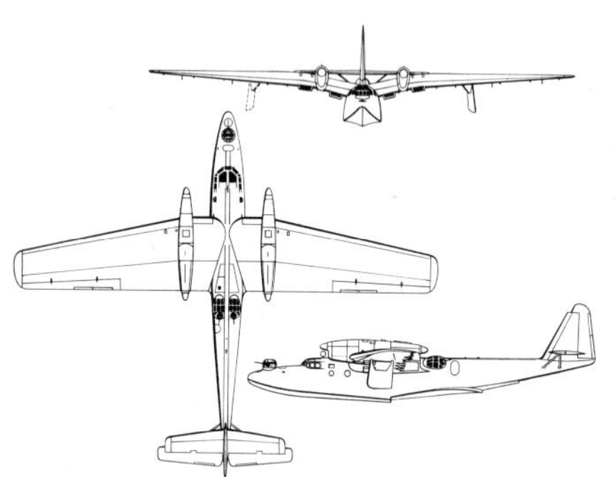

Martin M-130

Designed for Pan American's trans-Pacific routes, the first Martin M-130. *China Clipper*, flew on 30 December 1934 and made the inaugural return airmail flight from San Francisco to Manila between 22 November and 6 December 1935, breaking 19 international records on the five-day journey which staged via Honolulu, Midway, Wake Island and Guam. The all-metal M-130 was the first US-built flying boat to use airfoil-shaped sea wings or sponsons to provide water stability and serve as additional fuel tanks and lifting surfaces. PAA's two other M-130s, *Philippine Clipper* and *Hawaii Clipper*, entered service on 9 December 1935 and 2 May 1936 respectively, *Hawaii Clipper* operating the first passenger service in October 1936. This aircraft disappeared without trace between Guam and Manila on 28 July 1938. The remaining M-130s flew some 10,000 hours each with PAA until 1942, when they were taken over by the US Navy for military duty. Neither survived the war.

Specification: Martin M-130 long-range flying boat airliner
Span: 39.62 m (130 ft 0 in)
Length: 27.70 m (90 ft 10.5 in)
Powerplant: 4×Pratt & Whitney R-1830 Twin Wasp, 596 kW (800 hp) each
Payload: 43 passengers
Max T/O weight: 23702 kg (52,252 lb)
Cruising speed: 157 mph
Range: 3,200 miles

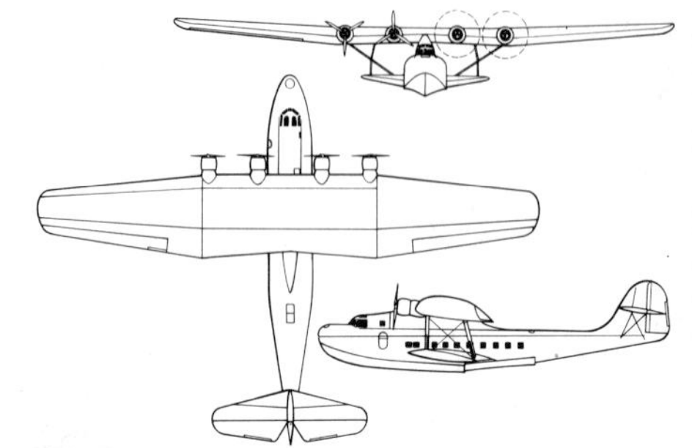

The Short S.23 was a major technical advance in flying boat design, featuring an all-metal structure with monocoque hull, tapered cantilever wing with electrically actuated flaps, variable-pitch propellers, a sleeping cabin, a promenade lounge and a steward's pantry. Imperial Airways ordered 28 before the 'C' class flagship *Canopus* first flew on 4 July 1936. It entered service on the Alexandria-Brindisi route on 31 October that year, followed by the remainder of the order. From 5 March 1937 'C' class flying boats operating from Hythe took over the Imperial routes formerly operated by landplanes from Croydon, eventually linking England with Australia, East Africa, Egypt, Malaya and South Africa. Three additional S.23s were delivered to Qantas Empire Airways in 1938 joining three previously transferred from the Imperial fleet. Despite the loss of eight boats in fatal crashes in their first two years of operation, the S.23 was among the most successful pre-war commercial airliners. Thirteen 'C' class boats survived wartime service, including later S.30 and S.33 variants, being retired in December 1947.

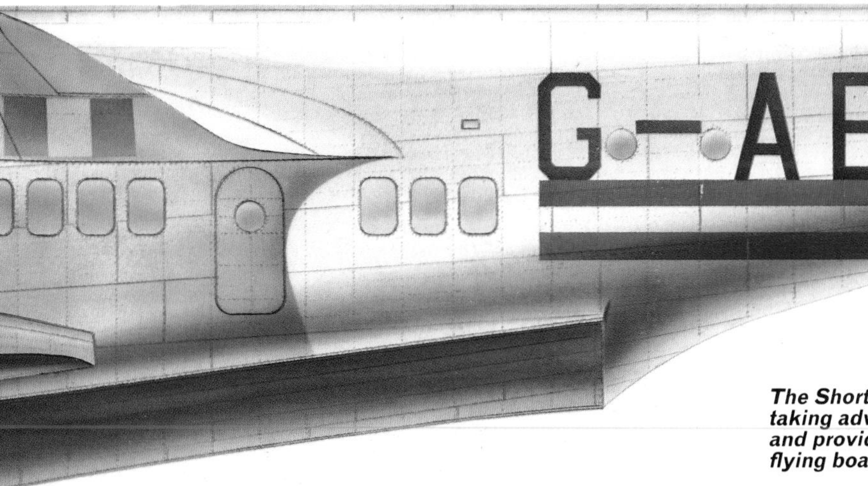

The Short C-Class boats ushered in a new era for British flying boats, taking advantage of the latest advances in aeronautical technology, and providing the basis for the later G-Class and military Sunderland flying boats.

Short S.8 Calcutta

Designed in 1927 for the Mediterranean sector of Imperial Airways' route to India and first flown on 21 February 1928, the Calcutta was the first flying boat with an all-metal stressed skin hull to go into commercial service. The first Calcutta (*City of Alexandria*) flew a number of British passenger flights before inaugurating the Mediterranean service between Genoa and Alexandria on 16 April 1929, and was soon joined by sister ships *City of Athens* and *City of Rome*, the latter being lost with all hands off Spezia in October 1929. Two further Calcuttas were built for Imperial, and one each for the Breguet company in France and for the French Navy. By mid-1932 the four surviving Calcuttas had completed nearly half a million trouble-free miles over the Mediterranean and Nile regions. Three examples of the enlarged 16-passenger Short S.17 Kent, powered by four 413 kW (555 hp) Jupiter engines, were built for Imperial Airways in 1931, serving on the Brindisi-Alexandria route.

Specification: Short S.8 Calcutta flying boat airliner
Span: 28.35 m (93 ft 0 in)
Length: 20.35 m (66 ft 9 in)
Powerplant: 3×Bristol Jupiter XIF, 403 kW (540 hp) each
Payload: 15 passengers
Max T/O weight: 10206 kg (22,500 lb)
Cruising speed: 7 mph
Range: 650 miles

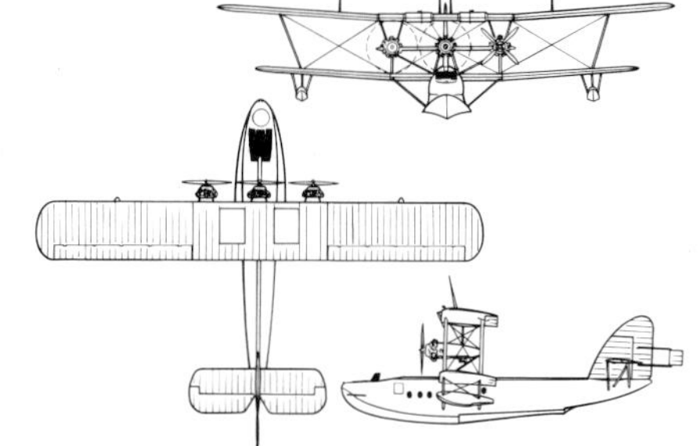

Short S.26 'G' class

Although it bore a strong family likeness to the S.23 flying boat, the S.26 was a much larger craft, developed to meet Imperial Airways' need for a long-range flying boat to operate mail services across the Atlantic. *Golden Hind* made its maiden flight in June 1939 and was delivered on 24 September, followed by sister ships *Golden Fleece* and *Golden Horn*. Plans for commercial transatlantic services were abandoned at the outbreak of World War 2, And all three 'G' class boats were transferred to the RAF for maritime reconnaissance duties, during which *Golden Fleece* was destroyed in June 1941. Late that year the two remaining S.26s were transferred to BOAC as 40-passenger transports, and on 9 January 1943 *Golden Horn* crashed into the River Tagus after an engine fire. In the last years of war *Golden Hind* flew commercial services between Mombassa and Ceylon, and in peacetime between Poole Harbour and Cairo, finally sinking in a gale in May 1945.

Specification: Short S.26 long-range flying boat airliner
Span: 40.94 m (134 ft 4 in)
Length: 30.89 m (101 ft 4 in)
Powerplant: 4×Bristol Hercules IV, 1029 kW (1,380 hp) each
Payload: 40 passengers
Max T/O weight: 33340 kg (73,500 lb)
Cruising speed: 180 mph
Range: 3,200 miles

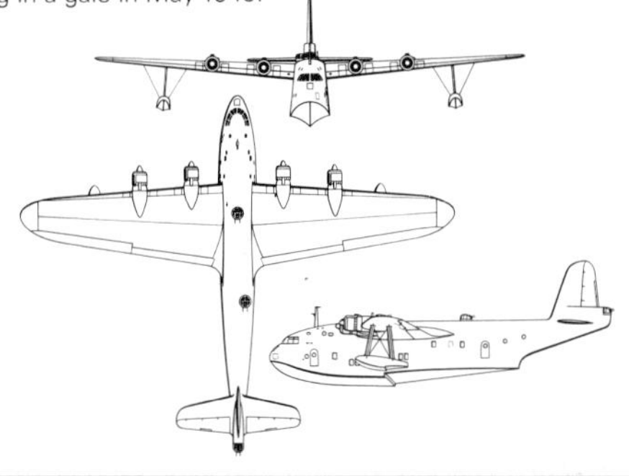

Boeing (Bureau of Aeronautics) TB

From the Martin-developed T3M version of the Curtiss SC torpedo-bomber, itself a navy design with an upper wing of shorter span than the lower and provision for one torpedo semi-recessed into the lower fuselage, the US Navy's Bureau of Aeronautics evolved an improved version retaining the same basic configuration, including large radiators on the sides of the forward fuselage just forward of the lower wing leading edges, but with equal-span wings and a revised nose accommodating the same Packard 3A-250 inline engine as used in the T3M. The type could be operated as a landplane on a four-wheel chassis or, more frequently, as a twin-float seaplane. Production of the only three aircraft was entrusted to Boeing with the designation TB-1, and these aircraft were all delivered by June 1927. The retrospective designation XTB-1 was allocated to the first machine for its part in the initial test programme from April 1927.

Specification: Boeing TB-1 three-seat torpedo-bomber
Span: 16.15 m (53 ft 0 in)
Length: 12.45 m (40 ft 10 in)
Powerplant: 1×Packard 3A-2500, 574 kW (770 hp)
Armament: 1×7.62-mm (0.3-in) machine-gun plus provision for 1×789-kg (1,740-lb) torpedo carried under the fuselage
Max T/O weight: 4439 kg (9,786 lb)
Max speed: 115 mph at sea level
Operational range: not recorded

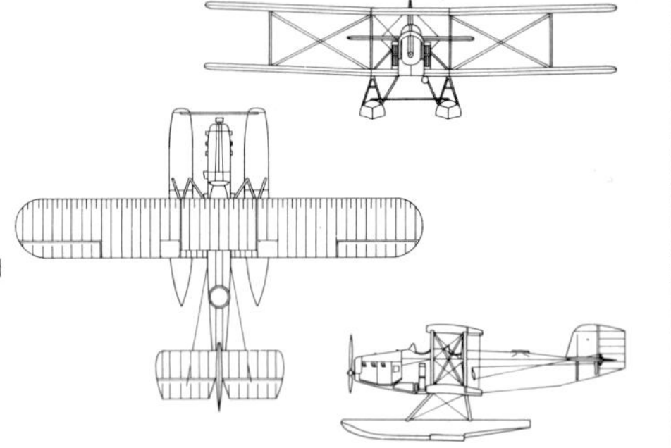

Vought O3U and SU Corsair

The O3U was introduced in 1930, and while essentially similar to the O2U-4 it had slight increases in the sweep and dihedral of the lower wing, and was fitted for the Grumman-developed amphibious float. Some 87 of this initial version were produced, and next came 29 O3U-2s with the Wright R-1690-A Hornet radial, a strengthened fuselage and a revised tail: the aircraft were redesignated SU-1s shortly after entering service. The 76 O3U-3s were similar to the O3U-2s apart from their 410-kW (550-hp) R-1340-12 engine. Next came 65 O3U-4s with the R-1690-42 engine: the aircraft were delivered as 45 SU-2s, and 20 SU-3s with low-pressure tyres suitable for soft-field operations by the US Marine Corps. The sole XO3U-5 was an engine test-bed, and finally came 32 examples of the O3U-6 with an enclosed cockpit and NAC cowling over the engine: 16 were delivered with the R-1340-12 and the other 16 with the R-1340-18.

Specification: Vought SU-4 Corsair two-seat scout aeroplane
Span: 10.97 m (36 ft 0 in)
Length: 8.37 m (27 ft 5.5 in) as a landplane
Powerplant: 1×Pratt & Whitney R-1690-42 Hornet, 447 kW (600 hp)
Armament: 3×7.62-mm (0.3-in) machine-guns
Max T/O weight: 2161 kg (4,765 lb)
Max speed: 167 mph at sea level
Operational range: 680 miles

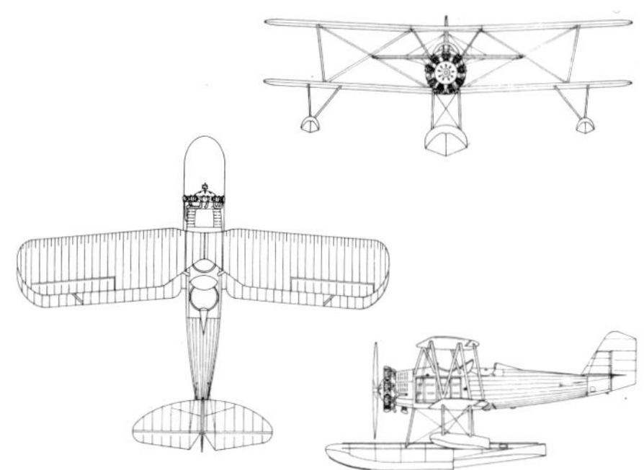

Curtiss SOC Seagull

First flown in April 1934, the Seagull outlasted its proposed successor, the SO3C Seamew monoplane and, serving on every US carrier, battleship and cruiser of the 1930s proved to be one of the most distinguished inter-war biplanes. The type resulted from a 1933 requirement for a scout and observation type stressed for catapult launches. The XO3C-1 prototype was an amphibian with wheels retracting into the central float, but this feature was abandoned in the production variants which had alternative wheel or float landing gear. Production started with the SOC-1, of which 135 were built with the 447-kW (600-hp) R-1340-18 radial and enclosed cockpits. The 40 SOC-2s were landplanes with the R-1340-22 radial, while the 83 SOC-3s and 44 SON-1s from the Naval Aircraft Factory were similar apart from their interchangeable landing gear. Aircraft fitted with arrester gear were suffixed A.

Specification: Curtiss SOC-3 two-seat scout and observation aeroplane
Span: 10.97 m (36 ft 0 in)
Length: 9.47 m (31 ft 1 in) as a floatplane
Powerplant: 1×Pratt & Whitney R-1340-22 Wasp, 447 kW (600 hp)
Armament: 2×7.62-mm (0.3-in) machine-guns
Max T/O weight: 2492 kg (5,495 lb)
Max speed: 161 mph at 5,000 ft
Operational range: 859 miles

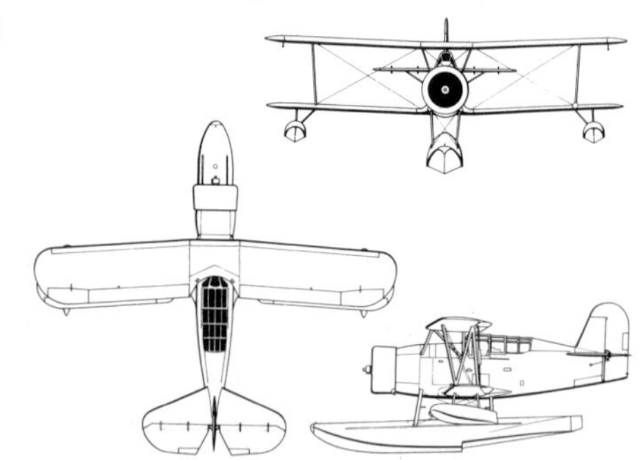

Naval Aircraft Factory N3N

Designed as a primary trainer for the US Navy in 1934, and outwardly similar to the Consolidated NY-2 and NY-3 then in service, the N3N featured an all-metal primary structure covered with fabric except along the fuselage sides, which had removable alloy panels. The XN3N-1 prototype flew in August 1935 with a 164-kW (220-hp) Wright J-5 radial, an obsolescent engine that was still stocked in considerable numbers. The prototype was evaluated as a landplane and floatplane, resulting in an order for 179 N3N-1s. Single XN3N-2 and XN3N-3 prototypes were used to evaluate the 179-kW (240-hp) R-760 engine that was then used in the last 20 N3N-1s and retrofitted in the earlier aircraft. There followed 816 N3N-3s with a revised tail and modified landing gear, and the N3Ns were amongst the navy's most important wheel- and float-equipped primary trainers throughout the later 1930s.

Specification: Naval Aircraft Factory N3N-3 two-seat primary trainer
Span: 10.36 m (34 ft 0 in)
Length: 7.77 m (25 ft 6 in)
Powerplant: 1×Wright R-760-2 Whirlwind 7, 175 kW (235 hp)
Armament: none
Max T/O weight: 1266 kg (2,792 lb)
Max speed: 126 mph at sea level
Operational range: 470 miles

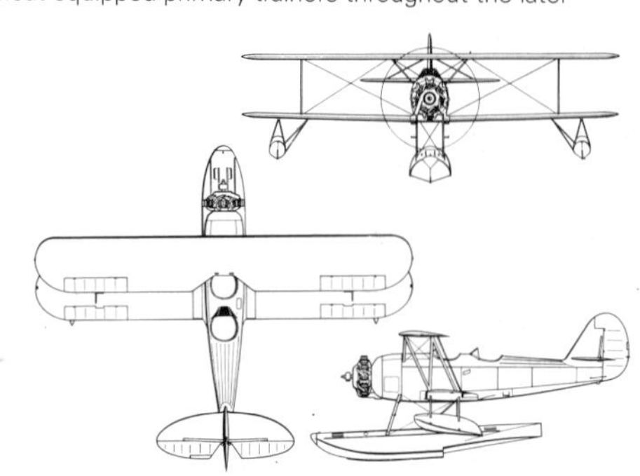

Supermarine Stranraer

The Stranraer was the last of Supermarine's series of classic biplane flying-boats. The type was originally named the Southampton Mk V, but had little in common with earlier Southamptons but its general configuration. The type was renamed Stranraer in August 1935, shortly after the first boat had flown with Pegasus IIIM radials driving two-blade wooden propellers, changed in production aircraft to Pegasus X radials driving three-blade metal propellers. The RAF ordered 23 of the type (batches of 17 and six), and these began to enter service from December 1936. Production was completed in March 1939 in the UK, though Canadian licensed production of 40 similar aircraft by Vickers lasted until 1941. In RAF service the Stranraer was flown by four squadrons, some boats remaining in service up to 1940 when they were replaced by Saro Lerwicks and Short Sunderlands.

Specification: Supermarine Stranraer six-seat general reconnaissance flying-boat
Span: 25.91 m (85 ft 0 in)
Length: 16.71 m (54 ft 10 in)
Powerplant: 2×Bristol Pegasus X, 652 kW (875 hp) each
Armament: 3×7.7-mm (0.303-in) machine-guns plus provision for up to 454 kg (1,000 lb) of bombs carried under the wings
Max T/O weight: 8618 kg (19,000 lb)
Max speed: 165 mph at 6,000 ft
Operational range: 1,000 miles

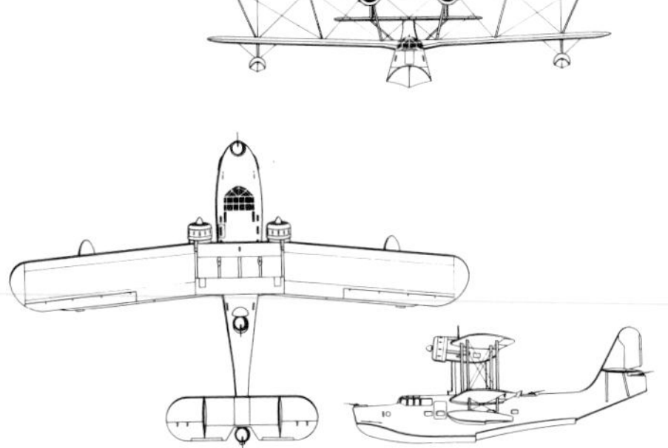

Saro Lerwick

The Lerwick was the second monoplane flying-boat ordered for the RAF, and was an advanced all-metal type intended as the medium-range partner to the long-range Short Sunderland. The first example flew in 1938, and production amounted to 21 aircraft which were delivered between 1939 and May 1941. The type served only with No.4 Operational Training Unit and No.209 Squadron, the latter flying the Lerwick between December 1939 and May 1941, replacing the Short Singapore Mk III and being replaced after only a short career by the altogether more successful Consolidated Catalina. There was little wrong with the outright performance and good armament of the Lerwick, but as an aeroplane the type had several handling deficiencies including lateral instability and difficult stall characteristics. The type was declared obsolete in 1942 after several accidents.

Specification: Saro Lerwick six-seat general reconnaissance flying-boat
Span: 24.63 m (80 ft 10 in)
Length: 19.39 m (63 ft 7.5 in)
Powerplant: 2×Bristol Hercules II, 1120 kW (1,375 hp) each
Armament: 7×7.7-mm (0.303-in) machine-guns plus provision for up to 907 kg (2,000 lb) of bombs carried under the wings
Max T/O weight: 15060 kg (33,200 lb)
Max speed: 216 mph at 4,000 ft
Operational range: not known

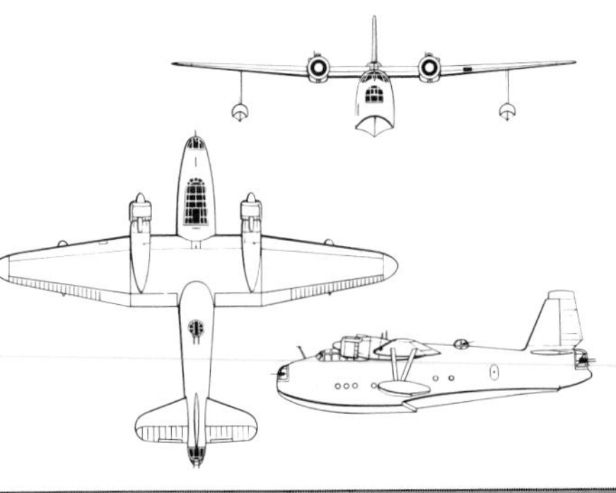

Supermarine Walrus

Developed ultimately from the Seagull III, the Walrus was first flown in June 1933 as the Seagull Mk V, differing from its nominal predecessor in most important aspects but the overall configuration and provision of amphibian landing gear. The type was received by Australia as the Seagull Mk V, but three months after the RAF had ordered the type in May 1935 the name Walrus was allocated. The Walrus Mk I had a metal hull and was powered by the 462-kW (620-hp) Pegasus IIM2, and most of the variant were delivered to the Fleet Air Arm. The main RAF version was the Walrus Mk II, which was used by seven home and four Middle Eastern air/sea rescue squadrons, and also by a single mine-spotting squadron. This type was built mainly by Saro up to 1944 with a wooden hull and other modifications, and entered RAF service in 1941.

Specification: Supermarine Walrus Mk II four-seat air/sea rescue amphibian
Span: 13.97 m (45 ft 10 in)
Length: 11.45 m (37 ft 7 in)
Powerplant: 1×Bristol Pegasus VI, 578 kW (775 hp)
Armament: 2×7.7-mm (0.303-in) machine-guns plus provision for up to 345 kg (760 lb) of bombs carried under the wings
Max T/O weight: 3226 kg (7,200 lb)
Max speed: 124 mph at sea level
Operational range: 600 miles

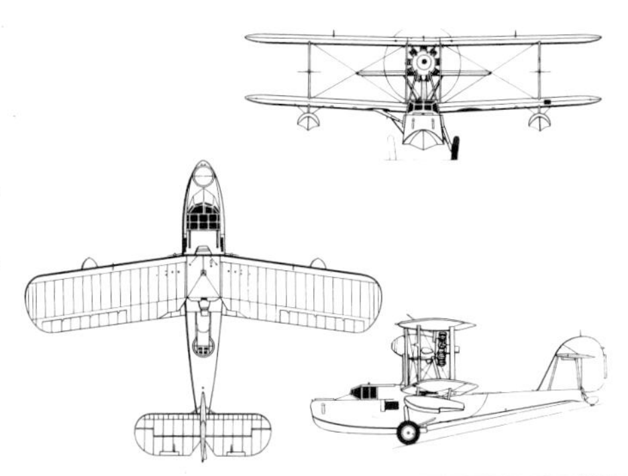

Consolidated Catalina

The success of the PBY in US service prompted a British evaluation of the type, and in 1939 the PBY-5 variant was ordered as the Catalina Mk I that began to enter service in 1941. The type was just as effective in British service, and orders (including Lend-Lease deliveries) then flowed thick and fast. For RAF service the 91 Mk Is were followed by 223 improved Catalina Mk IBs, seven Catalina Mk IIs (PBY-5s built by the Naval Aircraft Factory), 36 Catalina Mk IIAs transferred from the Royal Canadian Air Force, 11 Catalina Mk III amphibians, 97 Catalina Mk IVAs in the general reconnaissance role, and 190 Catalina Mk IVB Canadian-built boats used mainly in the air-sea rescue role. The Catalina was used by 24 RAF squadrons, nine of them home-based Coastal Command units.

Specification: Consolidated Catalina Mk IB eight/nine-seat general reconnaissance flying-boat
Span: 31.70 m (104 ft 0 in)
Length: 19.86 m (65 ft 1.75 in)
Powerplant: 2×Pratt & Whitney R-1830-S1C3-G Twin Wasp, 895 kW (1,200 hp) each
Armament: 6×7.7-mm (0.303-in) machine-guns plus provision for up to 907 kg (2,000 lb) of bombs carried under the wings
Max T/O weight: 12283 kg (27,080 lb)
Max speed: 190 mph at 10,500 ft
Operational range: 4,000 miles

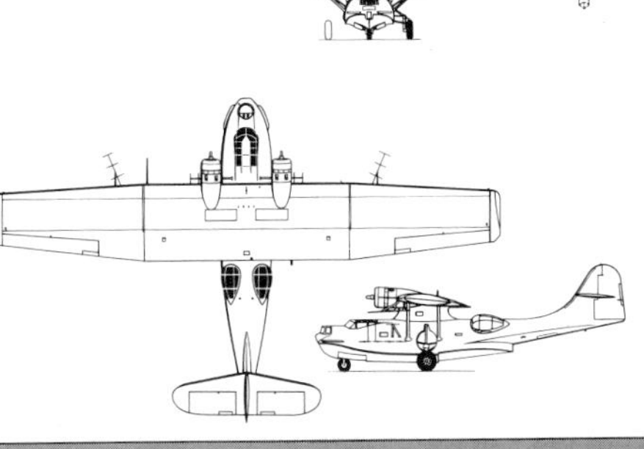

Short Singapore

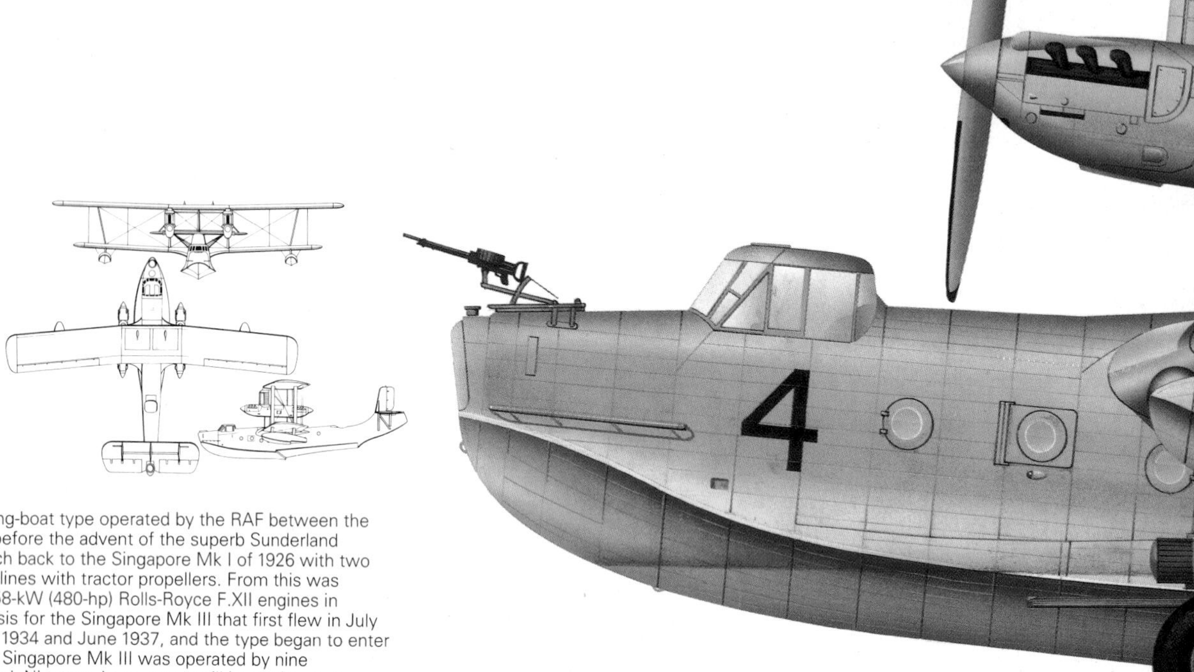

Specification: Short Singapore Mk III six-seat general reconnaissance flying-boat
Span: 27.40 m (90 ft 0 in)
Length: 19.50 m (64 ft 2 in)
Powerplant: 2×Rolls-Royce Kestrel VIII and 2×Rolls-Royce Kestrel IX, 544 kW (730 hp) each
Armament: 3×7.7-mm (0.303-in) machine-guns plus provision for 907 kg (2,000 lb) of bombs carried under the wings
Max T/O weight: 14288 kg (31,500 lb)
Max speed: 145 mph at 2,000 ft
Operational range: 1,000 miles

The Singapore was the most important flying-boat type operated by the RAF between the world wars, and was the last biplane boat before the advent of the superb Sunderland monoplane. The origins of the design stretch back to the Singapore Mk I of 1926 with two 485-kW (650-hp) Rolls-Royce Condor IIIA inlines with tractor propellers. From this was developed the Singapore Mk II with four 358-kW (480-hp) Rolls-Royce F.XII engines in tandem push/pull pairs. This formed the basis for the Singapore Mk III that first flew in July 1934. Some 39 aircraft were built between 1934 and June 1937, and the type began to enter service with No.230 Squadron in 1935. The Singapore Mk III was operated by nine squadrons, all but three of them home-based. Nineteen boats were still in service at the beginning of World War II, and these had been phased out by December 1941.

Felixstowe F.5

The F.5 marked the culmination of British flying-boat design in World War I, and was a linear descendant of the F.2A, F.2C and F.3 though itself too late for service in the 'Great War'. The F.5 first flew in May 1918, and though based on the F.3 had a wing of greater span and revised section. A number of other improvements were worked into the design. However, to ease manufacture a number of F.3 components were retrospectively incorporated and this had the effect of adding so much weight that the performance of the F.5 was slightly inferior to that of the F.3. Though the design emanated from the Seaplane Experimental Station at Felixstowe, production was entrusted to five commercial airframe manufacturers, and the type equipped a maximum of nine squadrons until replaced by the Supermarine Southampton in 1925. The USA produced an F.5L version with Liberty 12 inline engines.

Specification: Felixstowe F.5 four-seat general reconnaissance flying-boat
Span: 31.60 m (103 ft 8 in)
Length: 15.01 m (49 ft 3 in)
Powerplant: 2×Rolls-Royce Eagle VIII, 280 kW (375 hp) each
Armament: 4×7.7-mm (0.303-in) machine-guns plus provision for up to 417 kg (920 lb) of bombs carried under the wings
Max T/O weight: 5753 kg (12,682 lb)
Max speed: 88 mph at 2,000 ft
Operational endurance: 7 hours

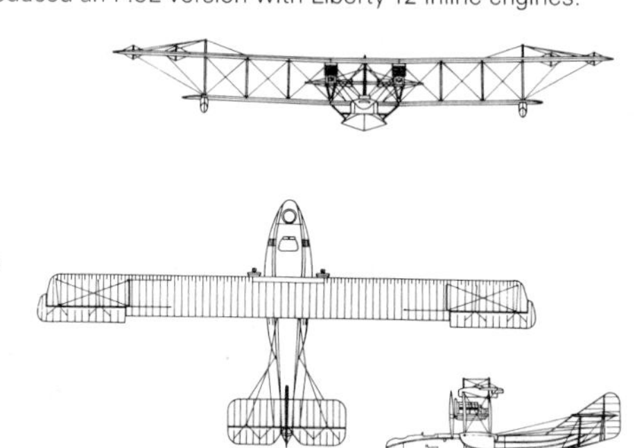

Supermarine Southampton

Despite its two open pilot's cockpits and ungainly engine disposition the Southampton served for some 12 years, longer than any other RAF flying-boat but the great Sunderland. The type was a military development of the civil Swan and first flew in 1925 as a replacement for the Felixstowe F.5. Production totalled 66 machines, the first 24 being Southampton Mk Is with a wooden hull and 350-kW (470-hp) Napier Lion Vs. There followed the metal-hulled main variant, namely the Southampton Mk II of which 42 were built. Southamptons entered service in August 1925 and equipped a total of five squadrons. The type did much to prove the utility of the flying-boat in the exacting task of maritime reconnaissance, and was finally retired in September 1937. There were also a number of experimental developments including the Mk X with three radial engines.

Specification: Supermarine Southampton Mk II five-seat general reconnaissance flying-boat
Span: 22.86 m (75 ft 0 in)
Length: 15.58 m (51 ft 1.5 in)
Powerplant: 2×Napier Lion V, 374 kW (502 hp) each
Armament: 3×7.7-mm (0.303-in) machine-guns plus provision for up to 499 kg (1,100 lb) of bombs carried under the wings
Max T/O weight: 6895 kg (15,200 lb)
Max speed: 108 mph at sea level
Operational range: 930 miles

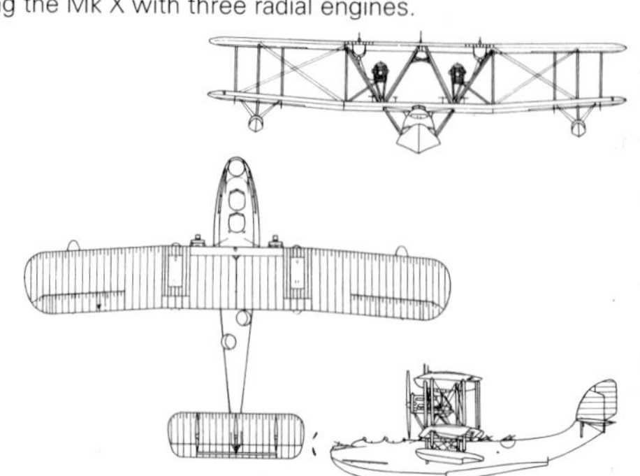

Seven squadrons used the Short Singapore Mk III, an example of which is seen here on its beaching trolley. The Singapore equipped seven squadrons, three of them based overseas.

Blackburn Iris

The Iris served with just a single squadron between 1930 and 1934, and was in its time the RAF's largest flying-boat. The design was started in 1924, and the Iris Mk I prototype first flew in September 1926 with three Condor inlines and a wooden hull/superstructure combination. This became the Iris Mk II when a metal hull was fitted. The Iris Mk III for the RAF first flew in November 1929, and introduced a metal superstructure, considerable internal revision and aerodynamically refined engine nacelles. Three production boats were ordered, the crash of one of these resulting in an order for a fourth of the type with a revised bow position accommodating a 37-mm COW cannon. These made a number of remarkable long-distance flights, and the three surviving boats were fitted with 615-kW (825-hp) Rolls-Royce Buzzard IIMS inlines to become Iris Mk V boats late in their careers.

Specification: Blackburn Iris Mk III five-seat general reconnaissance flying-boat
Span: 29.57 m (97 ft 0 in)
Length: 20.54 m (67 ft 4.75 in)
Powerplant: 3×Rolls-Royce Condor IIIB, 503 kW (675 hp) each
Armament: 3×7.7-mm (0.303-in) machine-guns plus provision for up to 907 kg (2,000 lb) of bombs carried under the wings
Max T/O weight: 13154 kg (29,000 lb)
Max speed: 118 mph at sea level
Operational range: 470 miles

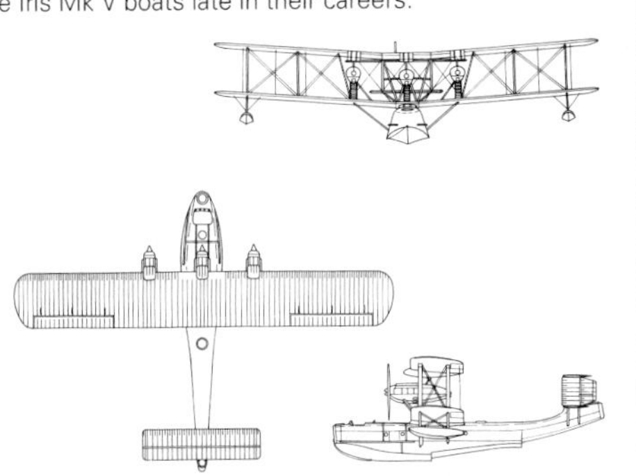

Short Rangoon

The Rangoon was a comparatively simple development of the civil Calcutta, a type designed for Imperial Airways' sectors such as the crossing of the Mediterranean and the route up the Nile to Lake Victoria. The type was the first production boat with an all-metal hull, and its reliability recommended it as a general reconnaissance boat for the RAF. The first Rangoon flew in September 1930, and production totalled six with specialised military gear (gun rings and bomb racks) as well as features such as fresh water stowage for the type's planned Middle Eastern use. The Rangoon entered service during 1931 with No.203 Squadron at Basra in Iraq, where its ability to take off on only two engines was a great asset, but in 1935 it was reallocated to No.210 Squadron based at Gibraltar. In July 1936 the boats were replaced by Short Singapores.

Specification: Short Rangoon five-seat general reconnaissance flying-boat
Span: 28.35 m (93 ft 0 in)
Length: 20.36 m (66 ft 9.5 in)
Powerplant: 3×Bristol Jupiter XIF, 403 kW (540 hp) each
Armament: 3×7.7-mm (0.303-in) machine-guns plus provision for up to 454 kg (1,000 lb) of bombs carried under the wings
Max T/O weight: 10206 kg (22,500 lb)
Max speed: 115 mph at optimum altitude
Operational range: 650 miles

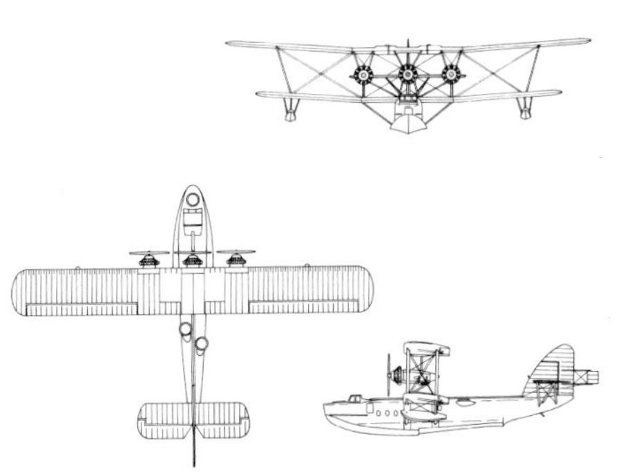

Short Sunderland

The Sunderland was the UK's finest flying-boat of World War II, and one of the greatest such aircraft of all time. The type was a military version of the 'C' class Empire type, and on its initial flight during October 1937 was the first British boat with a power-operated defensive turret. The type equipped a maximum of 28 squadrons in a service career that spanned the period from the summer of 1938 to May 1959. Production totalled 739 including 90 Sunderland Mk Is with 753-kW (1,010-hp) Bristol Pegasus XXIIs and five or seven machine-guns; 43 Sunderland Mk IIs with 794-kW (1,065-hp) Pegasus XVIIIs and a twin-gun dorsal turret instead of the two beam guns; 456 Sunderland Mk IIIs with ASV.Mk III or, in Sunderland Mk IIIA, ASV.Mk IIIA radar; and 150 Sunderland Mk Vs with different engines and ASV.Mk VIC radar with antennae in radomes under the wingtips.

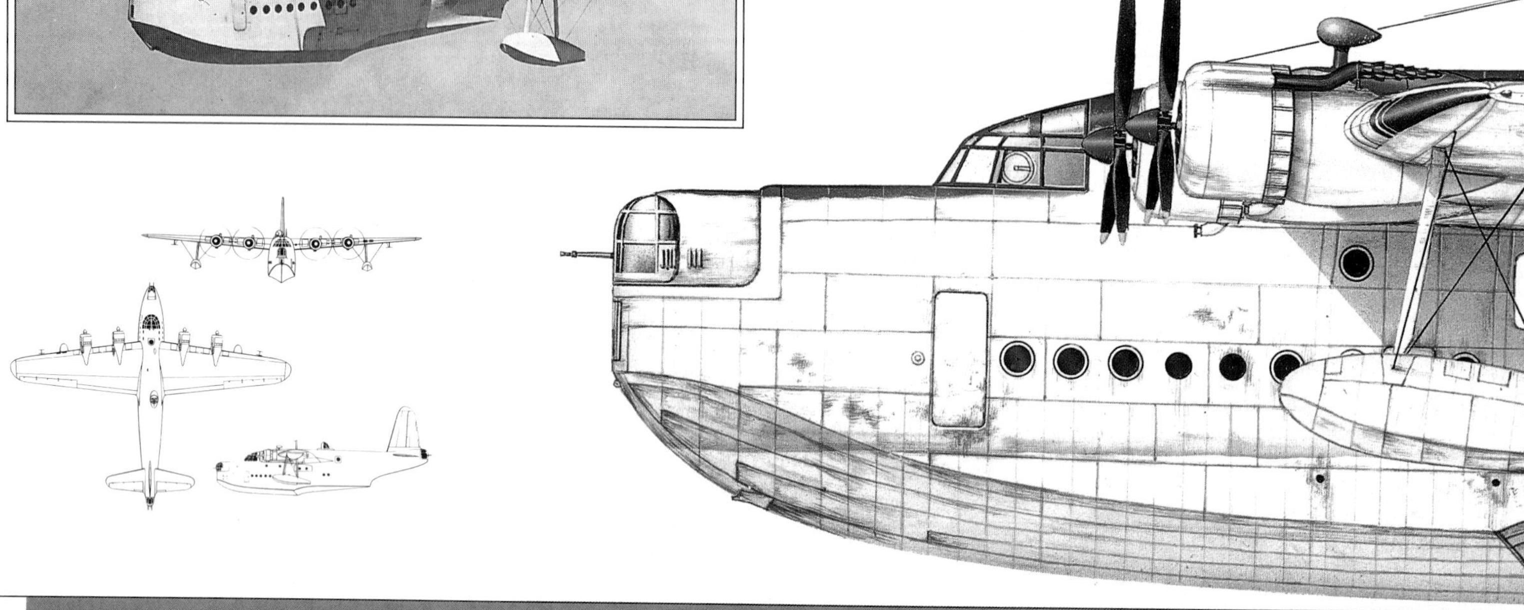

Saro Cloud

The Cloud was evolved from the Cutty Sark to meet a civil requirement and was developed in flying-boat and amphibian forms. The type first flew in 1931, and in it the RAF saw a comparatively cheap and tractable type on which the novice flying-boat pilot could cut his waterplane teeth before moving on to the service's larger boats. The cabin had been designed with eight passengers in mind, and this provided volume that could also be used for the training of flying-boat navigators, thereby giving the Cloud a double value to the service. The RAF ordered 16 of the amphibian model, and these began to enter service in August 1933 with Seaplane Training Squadron at Calshot. The last Cloud was delivered in June 1935, and before the type was withdrawn in the later 1930s it had also served with the School of Air Pilotage and No.48 Squadron.

Specification: Saro Cloud eight-seat training amphibian
Span: 19.51 m (64 ft 0 in)
Length: 15.28 m (50 ft 1.5 in)
Powerplant: 2×Armstrong Siddeley Serval V (Double Mongoose), 253.5 kW (340 hp) each
Armament: generally none, but provision was made for 2×7.7-mm (0.303-in) machine-guns plus 4×22.7-kg (50-lb) bombs carried under the wings
Max T/O weight: 4309 kg (9,500 lb)
Max speed: 118 mph at optimum altitude
Operational range: 380 miles

Blackburn Perth

The Perth was essentially an improved Iris, and was introduced to service in 1934. Like the Iris Mk III boats reworked to Mk V standard, the Perth was powered by Buzzard inline engines but also introduced a number of other more modern features such as an enclosed cockpit and long-distance facilities such as a galley, canteen and sleeping berths. The last Iris Mk V was sometimes designated Mk VI when carrying the 37-mm nose cannon, and the Perth was akin to this standard in having the same type of nose armament. The first Perth flew in October 1933, and production totalled just four aircraft, the last differing from its predecessors in having two rather than three gravity tanks in the upper wing. The last boat was retired in 1938, by which time the aircraft had been replaced in service by Southamptons.

Specification: Blackburn Perth five-seat general reconnaissance flying-boat
Span: 29.57 m (97 ft 0 in)
Length: 21.34 m (70 ft 0 in)
Powerplant: 3×Rolls-Royce Buzzard IIMS, 615 kW (825 hp) each
Armament: 1×37-mm cannon and 3×7.7-mm (0.303-in) machine-guns plus provision for 907 kg (2,000 lb) of bombs carried under the wings
Max T/O weight: 14742 kg (32,500 lb)
Max speed: 132 mph at sea level
Operational range: 1,300 miles

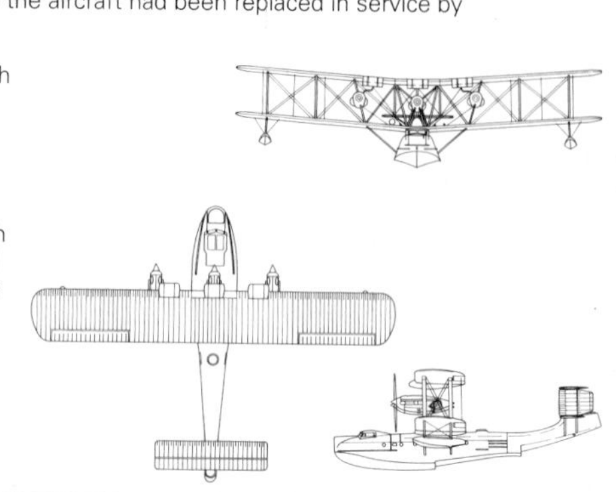

Specification: Short Sunderland Mk V 10-seat general reconnaissance and anti-submarine flying-boat
Span: 34.36 m (112 ft 9.5 in)
Length: 26.01 m (85 ft 4 in)
Powerplant: 4×Pratt & Whitney R-1830 Twin Wasp, 895 kW (1,200 hp) each
Armament: 2×12.7-mm (0.5-in) and 10×7.7-mm (0.303-in) machine-guns plus provision for up to 2250 kg (4,960 lb) of bombs carried internally
Max T/O weight: 29482 kg (65,000 lb)
Max speed: 213 mph at 5,000 ft
Operational range: 2,980 miles

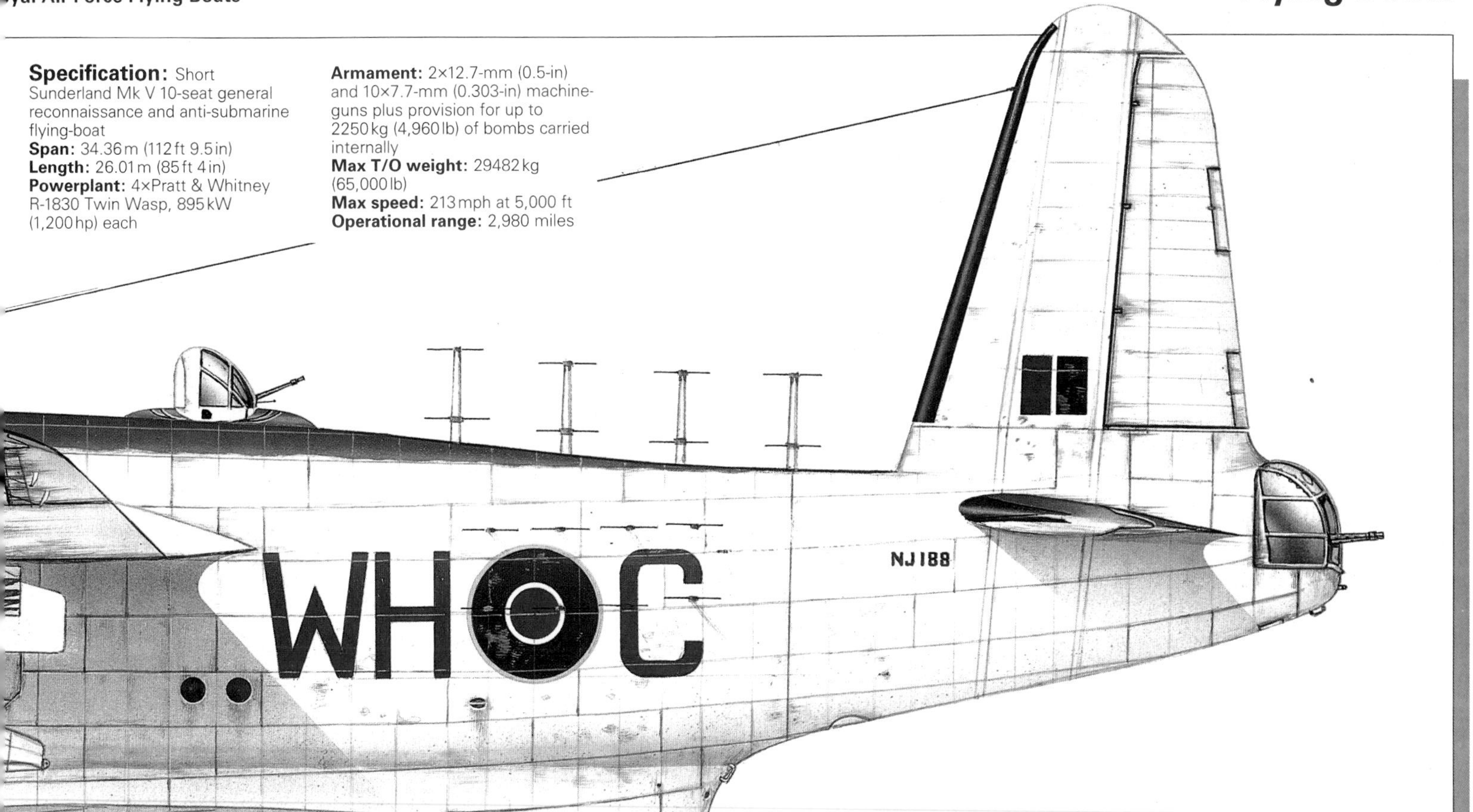

A Short Sunderland of No. 228 Squadron, RAF Coastal Command, based at Gibraltar. No. 228 was one of the first Sunderland squadrons and scored the RAF's first U-boat kill, in January 1940.

Supermarine Scapa

The Scapa was introduced to service in August 1935 as a modernised and re-engined derivative of the Southampton. This origin is betrayed by the fact that the type was known as the Southampton Mk IV when it appeared in 1932. The hull was provided with less angled sides to create more internal volume, the pilots were located side-by-side in a single enclosed cockpit rather than one behind the other in two open cockpits, the airframe was all-metal with fabric-covered flying surfaces (the Southampton having fabric-covered wooden wings and a metal fuselage/hull), and for a useful reduction in drag the powerplant was re-arranged as two Kestrel engines on the upper wing rather than two Lions mid-way between the wings. Production of 14 aircraft was completed by the end of 1935, and these boats served with a total of four squadrons up to 1938.

Specification: Supermarine Scapa five-seat general reconnaissance flying-boat
Span: 22.86 m (75 ft 0 in)
Length: 16.15 m (53 ft 0 in)
Powerplant: 2×Rolls-Royce Kestrel IIIMS, 391 kW (525 hp) each
Armament: 3×7.7-mm (0.303-in) machine-guns plus provision for up to 454 kg (1,000 lb) of bombs carried under the wings
Max T/O weight: 7276 kg (16,040 lb)
Max speed: 141.5 mph at 3,280 ft
Operational range: 1,100 miles

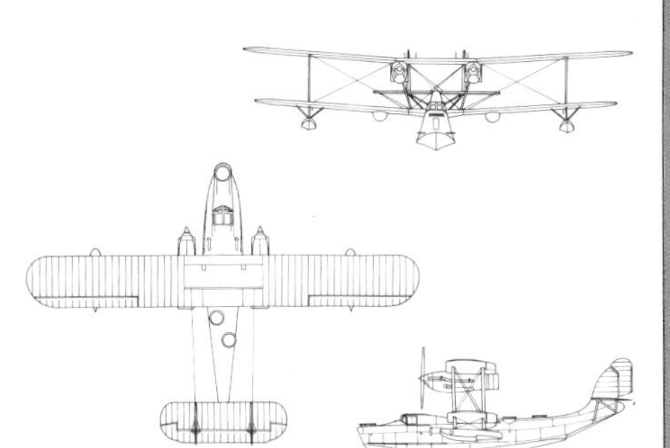

Saro London

The London was introduced to service in 1936, and was one of the RAF's last operational biplanes in World War II. The type was developed to a 1931 reconnaissance requirement and first flew in 1934. The type was ordered into production during 1935, and the first 10 aircraft were designated London Mk I with two 559-kW (750-hp) Pegasus III radials each in a polygonal nacelle on the upper wing and driving a two-blade propeller. The type was then improved as the London Mk II with more-powerful engines in circular nacelles and driving four-blade propellers, and production of this variant totalled 38. The type equipped a total of four squadrons, and of these three (one in the Mediterranean and two in the UK) were still operational with 29 boats at the beginning of World War II. The London was finally retired only in mid-1941.

Specification: Saro London Mk II six-seat general reconnaissance flying-boat
Span: 24.38 m (80 ft 0 in)
Length: 17.31 m (56 ft 9.5 in)
Powerplant: 2×Bristol Pegasus X, 686 kW (920 hp) each
Armament: 3×7.7-mm (0.303-in) machine-guns plus provision for up to 907 kg (2,000 lb) of bombs carried under the wings
Max T/O weight: 8346 kg (18,400 lb)
Max speed: 142 mph at sea level
Operational range: 1,740 miles

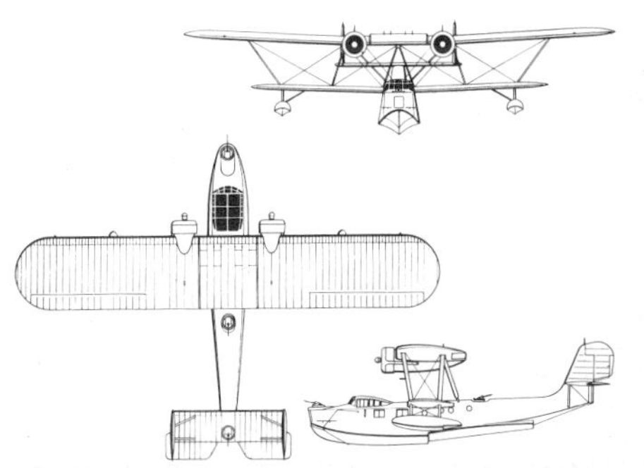

Chapter 12
CIVIL AIRCRAFT

Junkers F13

First flown in June 1919, the F13 was derived from the J 10 (CL I) close-support aeroplane of World War I and was the world's first purpose-built all-metal commercial aeroplane to enter service. The first example spanned 14.47 m (47 ft 5.75 in), was powered by a 119-kW (160-hp) Mercedes D.IIIa inline and featured an open cockpit for the two pilots plus an enclosed four-passenger cabin, but production aircraft had an enclosed cockpit and greater power, initially a 138-kW (185-hp) BMW IIIa inline. The type's metal structure with corrugated duraluminum skinning made for great reliability with minimal maintenance, and the F13 remained in production up to 1932. More than 350 examples were built in 70 variants on wheel, ski and float landing gears and powered by a host of engine types delivering up to 268 kW (360 hp). The most common engine was the 156-kW (210-hp) Junkers L-5.

The corrugated skin of the Junkers F13 proved incredibly strong and led Junkers to adopt the same construction for a series of airliners, culminating in the Ju 52 trimotor. The aircraft was the first all-metal commercial airliner, and was available with a series of powerplants and various types of undercarriage. Many of the 350 built served with Lufthansa, where they proved popular with passengers and crew alike.

Specification: Junkers F13a medium-range airliner
Span: 17.75 m (58 ft 2.75 in)
Length: 9.60 m (31 ft 6 in)
Powerplant: 1×BMW IIIa, 138 kW (185 hp)
Payload: two flightcrew plus four passengers or freight
Max T/O weight: 1730 kg (3,814 lb)
Max speed: 110 mph
Operational range: 404 miles

Armstrong Whitworth A.W.XV

The A.W.XV resulted from a 1930 Imperial Airways' requirement for a four-engined landplane to operate on the route between Kisumu in Kenya and Cape Town in South Africa: the winning design had to be capable of operating from small airfields, maintaining 9,000 ft on three engines with a 1361-kg (3,000-lb) payload, cruising at 185 km/h (115 mph) and covering at least 645 km (400 miles) without refuelling. The resulting A.W.XV was of mixed wood/metal construction with a thick wing set high on the capacious fuselage, and trim tailwheel landing gear of the fixed type. There was no prototype, the first of eight machines flying in June 1932. These enjoyed eventful careers in Africa, Europe and the Indian subcontinent, being notable for their comfort rather than their speed.

Specification: Armstrong Whitworth A.W.XV medium-range airliner
Span: 27.43 m (90 ft 0 in)
Length: 21.79 m (71 ft 6 in)
Powerplant: 4×Armstrong Siddeley Serval III, 253.5 kW (340 hp) each
Payload: three flightcrew plus 9-17 passengers or 2495 kg (5,500 lb) of freight
Max T/O weight: 9526 kg (21,000 lb)
Cruising speed: 118 mph at 9,000 ft
Operational range: 640 miles

Handley Page H.P.42

The H.P.42 was designed for Imperial Airways' European and eastern routes, with emphasis placed on reliability and comfort with small payload rather than high speed and heavy payload. The H.P.42 was of all-metal construction with fabric-covered flying surfaces and rear fuselage: the wings had Warren truss rather than wire bracing, and the inner portions of the lower wings were angled upwards so that their spars passed over rather than through the spacious cabin. The first example flew in November 1930, and eight aircraft were built in two versions: four H.P.42Es for the airline's eastern routes with 365-kW (490-hp) Jupiter XIFs and six (later 12) plus 12 passengers respectively in the forward and aft cabins separated by 14.16 m^3 (500 cu ft) of baggage and mail; and four H.P.42Ws for European operations with 18 plus 20 passengers separated by 7.08 m^3 (250 cu ft) of baggage volume.

Specification: Handley Page H.P.42W short/medium-range airliner
Span: 39.62 m (130 ft 0 in)
Length: 27.36 m (89 ft 9 in)
Powerplant: 4×Bristol Jupiter XBFM, 414 kW (555 hp) each
Payload: four flightcrew plus 38 passengers or freight
Max T/O weight: 13381 kg (29,500 lb)
Cruising speed: 100 mph
Operational range: 500 miles

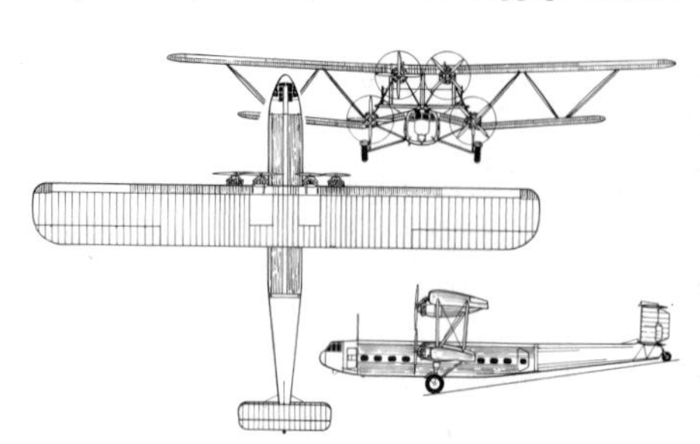

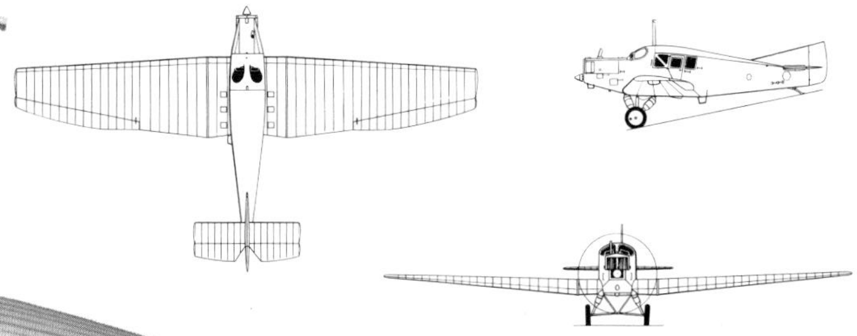

de Havilland D.H.86

Bearing a clear relationship with the elegant D.H.84 Dragon, the D.H.86 was de Havilland's first four-engined airliner and designed to meet a 1933 QANTAS requirement for an airliner to operate the Singapore-to-Brisbane sector of the Imperial route between England and Australia. De Havilland's traditional wood structure with fabric covering was used, the four engines being located on the lower wing of the biplane cellule. The first prototype flew in January 1934, the only modification required being a widening of the nose to accommodate two rather than one pilot from the fifth aeroplane onward. Production encompassed 32 basic D.H.86s, 20 improved D.H.86As for Imperial Airways' European routes, and 10 D.H.86Bs with small fixed fins on the tailplane for improved directional stability.

Specification: de Havilland D.H.86B short/medium-range airliner
Span: 19.66 m (64 ft 6 in)
Length: 14.05 m (46 ft 1 in)
Powerplant: 4×de Havilland Gipsy Six, 149 kW (200 hp) each
Payload: two flightcrew plus 10 passengers or freight
Max T/O weight: 4649 kg (10,250 lb)
Cruising speed: 142 mph
Operational range: 800 miles

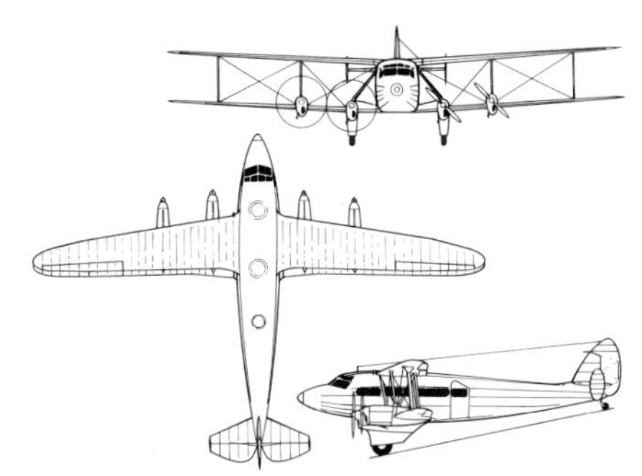

Boeing 247

Marking a revolution in airliner design and construction, the first Model 247 flew in February 1933 with all-metal construction in a low-wing cantilever monoplane layout with twin-radial powerplant, retractable landing gear, pneumatic de-icing boots on all leading edges and enclosed accommodation. Sixty were ordered by Boeing Air Transport, soon to become part of United Air Lines, and another 15 were ordered by other airlines and individuals. Most in-service aircraft were later retrofitted to Model 247D standard with low-drag NACA engine cowlings, controllable-pitch propellers and a rearward- rather than the original forward-sloping windscreen. Designed to meet the requirement of a single airline, the Model 247 proved too small for the needs of other airlines at a time of rapidly growing air traffic, and it also lacked the trailing-edge flaps that soon became standard.

Specification: Boeing 247D medium-range airliner
Span: 22.56 m (74 ft 0 in)
Length: 15.72 m (51 ft 7 in)
Powerplant: 2×Pratt & Whitney Wasp S1H-1G, 410 kW (550 hp) each
Payload: three flightcrew plus 10 passengers or freight
Max T/O weight: 6192 kg (13,650 lb)
Cruising speed: 189 mph at 8,000 ft
Operational range: 745 miles

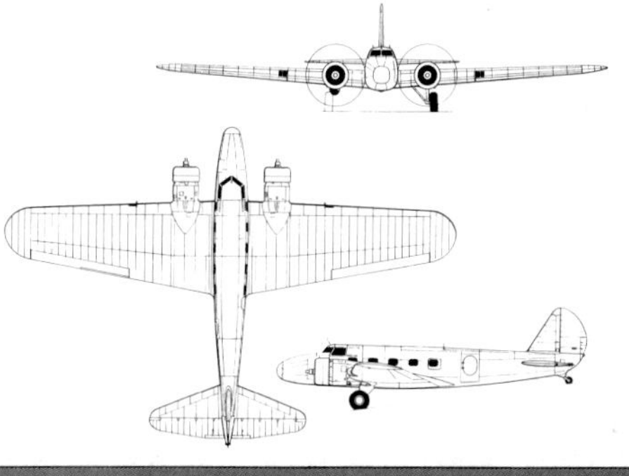

Ford 4-AT and 5-AT Tri-Motor

Serving more than 40 years as an effective transport, the Tri-Motor was a classic airliner of the late 1920s developed from the unsuccessful Ford 3-AT, itself evolved from the 2-AT Pullman designed by William Stout. From its predecessor the 3-AT inherited a high-wing cantilever monoplane layout of metal with corrugated metal skinning, but had three uncowled radials in place of the 2-AT's single Liberty inline. The 4-AT was a considerable improvement on the 3-AT and first flew in June 1926 with 149-kW (200-hp) Wright J-4 Whirlwind radials for a crew of two and eight passengers. Some 82 4-ATs with different engines and up to 12 passengers were followed by 117 5-ATs with a wing increased in span by 1.17 m (3 ft 10 in), greater power and more seating. Small numbers of variants and conversions were also produced with designations up to 13-A.

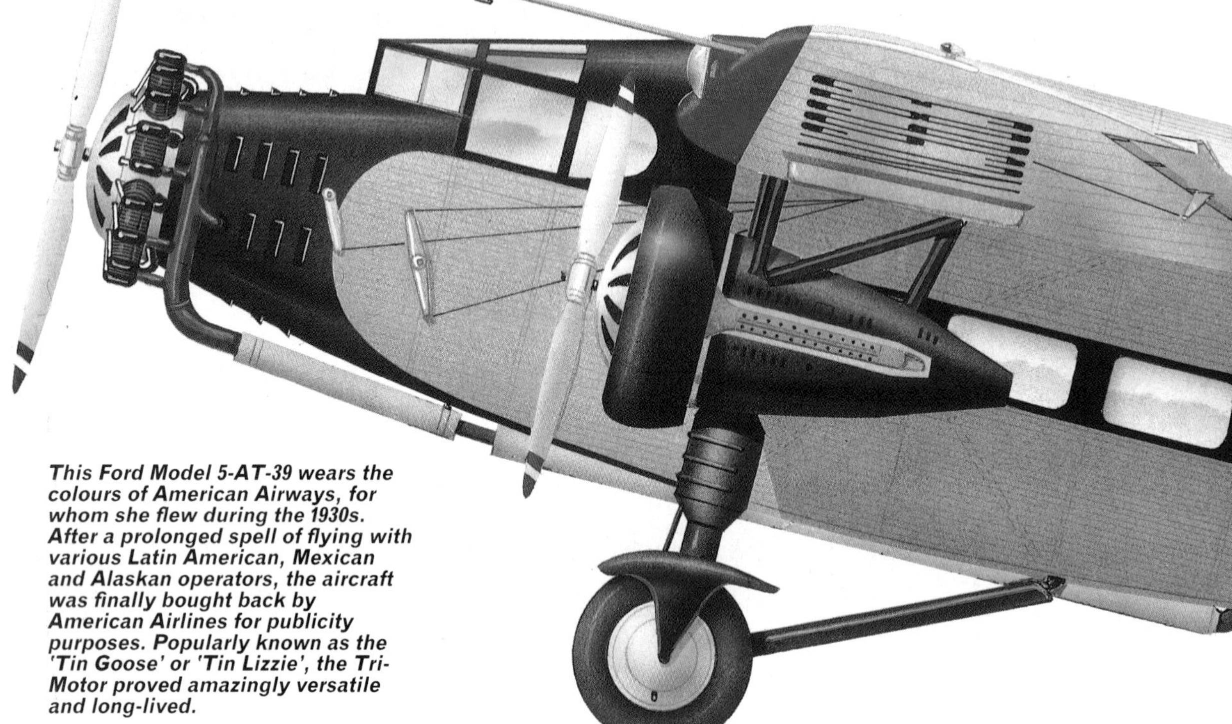

Specification: Ford 5-AT-D Tri-Motor short/medium-range airliner
Span: 23.72 m (77 ft 10 in)
Length: 15.32 m (50 ft 3 in)
Powerplant: 3×Pratt & Whitney Wasp SC-1, 313 kW (420 hp) each
Payload: two flightcrew plus 17 passengers or 782 kg (1,725 lb) of freight
Max T/O weight: 6123 kg (13,500 lb)
Cruising speed: 122 mph
Operational range: 550 miles

This Ford Model 5-AT-39 wears the colours of American Airways, for whom she flew during the 1930s. After a prolonged spell of flying with various Latin American, Mexican and Alaskan operators, the aircraft was finally bought back by American Airlines for publicity purposes. Popularly known as the 'Tin Goose' or 'Tin Lizzie', the Tri-Motor proved amazingly versatile and long-lived.

Curtiss T-32 (CW-4) 'Condor II'

In 1928 the US Army released the design of the B-2 twin-engine bomber for use as the basis of an airliner that became variously known as the Model 53, Condor CO and Condor 18. This fixed-gear biplane carried 18 passengers on two 466-kW (625-hp) Curtiss GV-1570 inlines, but only six were built. Yet, at the time the Boeing 247 was marking the beginning of a new airliner era, the company retained the same basic formula for the so-called 'Condor II' biplane with single rather than twin vertical tail surfaces, radial engines and retractable landing gear. The first example flew in January 1933, and production amounted to only 21 aircraft finished as luxurious 12-berth night sleepers. Ten improved AT-32 aircraft were later built with variable-pitch propellers and NACA cowlings rather than Townend rings, and 10 T-32s were improved to this standard as T-32Cs.

Specification: Curtiss T-32 'Condor II' medium/long-range airliner
Span: 24.99 m (82 ft 0 in)
Length: 14.81 m (48 ft 7 in)
Powerplant: 2×Wright R-1820F Cyclone, 537 kW (720 hp) each
Payload: three flightcrew plus 12 passengers or 1452 kg (3,200 lb) of freight
Max T/O weight: 7938 kg (17,500 lb)
Cruising speed: 167 mph
Operational range: 716 miles

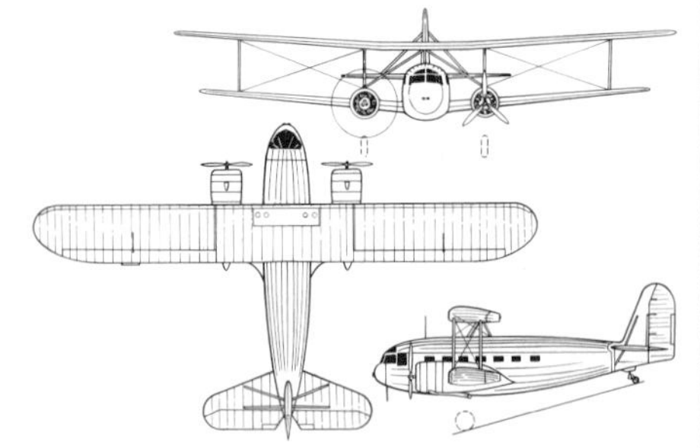

Douglas DC-2

Faced with a need to replace its obsolescent Fokker airliners, but located behind rival United Air Lines in the order queue for the Boeing 247, TWA in August 1932 issued a specification for an all-metal three-engined airliner able to seat 12 passengers. Douglas responded with a twin-engined design and convinced Charles Lindbergh, TWA's technical adviser, of the design's performance and safety features. The DC-1 prototype flew in July 1933 with Cyclone radials, immediately creating a favourable impression with its high flight and low landing speeds resulting from its use of trailing-edge flaps. The production version was the DC-2 with more powerful engines and the fuselage lengthened by 0.61 m to seat 14. The type was also operated by air forces under a number of designations, and total production was 198 including five licence-built aircraft.

Specification: Douglas DC-2 medium/long-range airliner
Span: 25.91 m (85 ft 0 in)
Length: 18.89 m (61 ft 11.75 in)
Powerplant: 2×Wright SGR-1820F52 Cyclone, 652 kW (825 hp) each
Payload: three flightcrew plus 14 passengers or freight
Normal T/O weight: 8419 kg (18,560 lb)
Cruising speed: 190 mph at 8,000 ft
Operational range: 1,000 miles

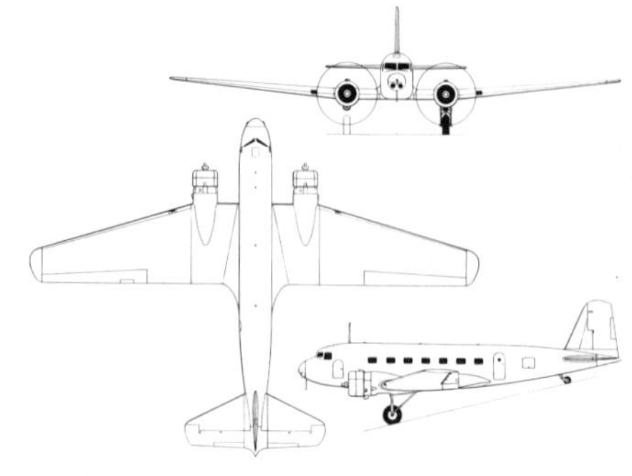

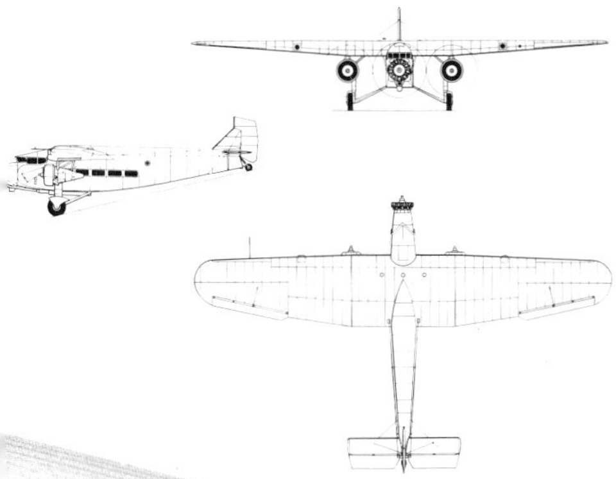

Douglas DC-3

In 1934 American Airlines requested Douglas to develop a transcontinental sleeper transport combining the spaciousness of the 'Condor II' with the speed and economy of the DC-2. This paved the way for a stretched and widened version of the DC-2, known as the Douglas Sleeper Transport with the powerful new SGR-1820-G for 28 day or 14 night passengers. The first DST flew in December 1935, and 40 were built including DST-As with Pratt & Whitney Twin Wasps. Far more popular was the dedicated unconvertible transport known as the DC-3, of which 539 (including 149 impressed by the military) were built before World War II as DC-3s with Cyclones, DC-3As with Twin Wasps and convertible DC-3Bs. After the war 28 civil aircraft were built, but the main production was of 10,047 military aircraft plus about 2,500 more built by licensees. The DC-3 and C-47 Dakota still serve in some numbers.

Specification: Douglas DC-3A medium/long-range airliner
Span: 28.96 m (95 ft 0 in)
Length: 19.65 m (64 ft 5.5 in)
Powerplant: 2×Pratt & Whitney Twin Wasp S1C3-G, 895 kW (1,200 hp) each
Payload: four flightcrew plus 21-32 passengers or 2041 kg (4,500 lb) of freight
Normal T/O weight: 11431 kg (25,200 lb)
Cruising speed: 207 mph at 8,500 ft
Operational range: 2,125 miles

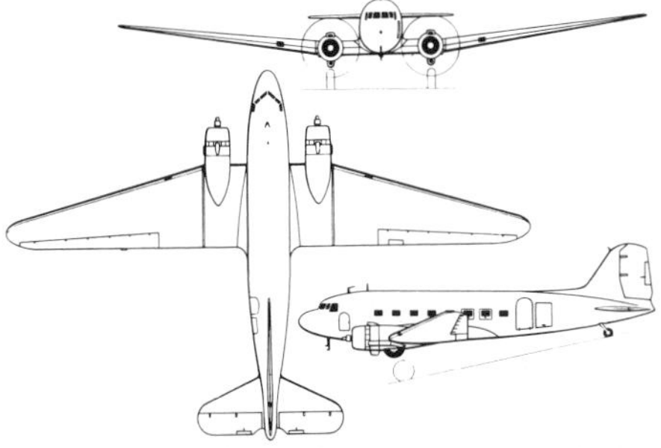

Farman F.60 Goliath

The Goliath was numerically the most important airliner of the 1920s, more than 60 being delivered. The type originated in the FF.60 prototype bomber of 1918. This had bluff fuselage contours that facilitated the conversion to airliner layout with four- and eight-passenger nose and amidships cabins separated by the open cockpit. In this guise the Goliath first flew in January 1919 with 171.5-kW (230-hp) Salmson/Canton-Unné 9Z radials of the type used in early production aircraft. The F.60 entered service in March 1920, and later developments included the F.60bis with 224-kW (300-hp) 9Az radials, the F.61 with 224-kW Renault 12Fe inlines, the F.63bis with 283-kW (380-hp) Gnome-Rhône Jupiter 9A radials and others with Maybach, Lorraine-Dietrich and Armstrong Siddeley Jaguar engines, culminating in the 1929 F.169 with Jupiter 9Akx engines.

Specification: Farman F.63bis short-range airliner
Span: 26.50 m (86 ft 11.25 in)
Length: 13.90 m (45 ft 7 in)
Powerplant: 2×Gnome-Rhône Jupiter 9A, 283 kW (380 hp) each
Payload: two flightcrew plus 12 passengers or freight
Max T/O weight: 5395 kg (1,894 lb)
Cruising speed: 94 mph at 6,560 ft
Operational range: 249 miles

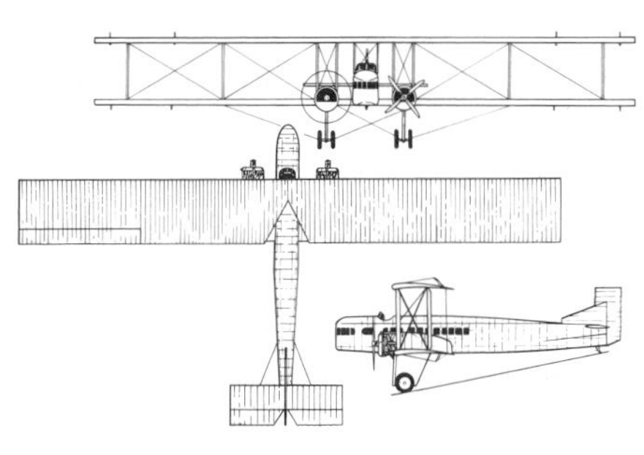

Junkers W33 and W34

The W33 and W34 appeared in 1926 and, being closely related to the F13, were built on the same production line. The two types were structurally similar in all respects except their engines and spans: the W33 was powered by a 231-kW (310-hp) Junkers L-5 inline and spanned 17.75 m (58 ft 2.75 in), while the W34 used any of several radials, initially a 313-kW (420-hp) Gnome-Rhône Jupiter VI but later a number of engines in ratings up to 492 kW (660 hp). A longer and less humped fuselage was introduced, and in conjunction with more power this increased payload capacity as well as improving performance. The W33 was generally used as a freight or mail transport, but could be fitted with six passenger seats, while the W34 was used for passenger operations. Production totalled 199 W33s and 1,791 examples of the W34 and its K43 reconnaissance bomber derivative.

Specification: Junkers W34he medium-range airliner
Span: 18.48 m (60 ft 7.5 in)
Length: 10.27 m (33 ft 8.3 in)
Powerplant: 1×BMW 132A, 492 kW (660 hp)
Payload: two flightcrew plus six passengers of 4.8 m³ (169 cu ft) or freight
Max T/O weight: 3200 kg (7,055 lb)
Cruising speed: 145 mph
Operational range: 560 miles

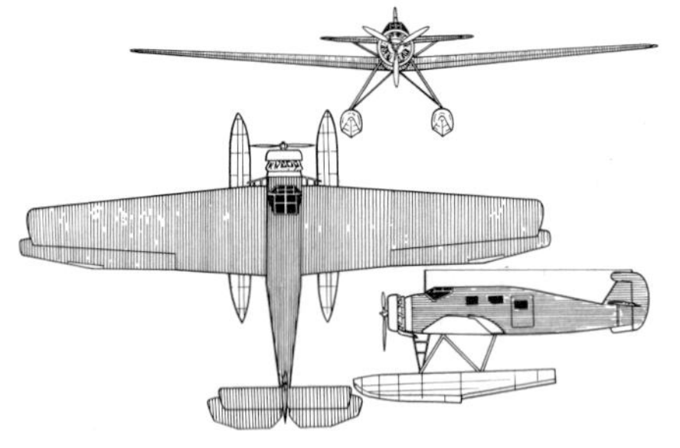

Junkers Ju 52

Descent from the F13 is evident from even a cursory glance at the Ju 52's fixed landing gear, low-wing monoplane layout and corrugated skinning. Designed as a transport and first flown in October 1930 with a 596.5-kW (800-hp) Junkers L-88 inline, the type had the patented Junkers 'double-wing' auxiliary flying surfaces doubling as flaps and ailerons and, though intended mainly as a freighter, could be fitted out as an airliner. Only six Ju 52 aircraft were built before the Ju 52/3m variant was introduced in April 1932 with three 391-kW (525-hp) Pratt & Whitney Hornet (BMW 132) radials. Carrying the same payload as the Ju 52 at higher speed, this was built in large numbers for civil and, increasingly, military use. The main civil variants were the Ju 52/3m ce, de, fe and ge with different engines.

Specification: Junkers Ju 52 medium-range airliner
Span: 29.00 m (95 ft 1.75 in)
Length: 18.30 m (60 ft 0.5 in)
Powerplant: 1×Junkers L-88, 634 kW (850 hp)
Payload: three flightcrew plus 17 passengers or 16.7 m³ (590 cu ft) of freight
Max T/O weight: 6600 kg (14,550 lb)
Cruising speed: 121 mph at sea level
Operational range: 932 miles

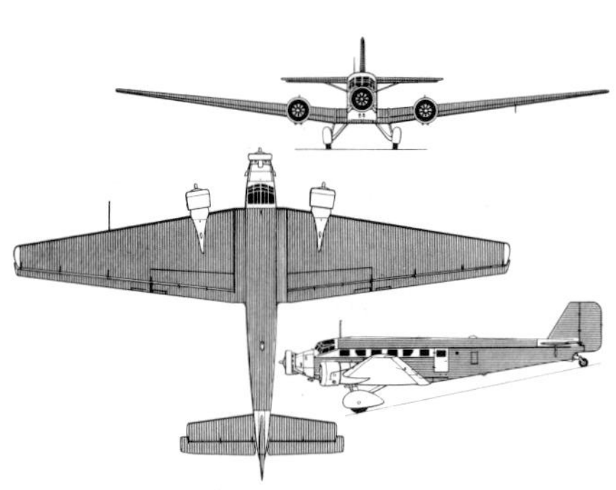

Fokker F.VII

After producing five F.VII cantilever high-wing monoplanes each with a single 268-kW (360-hp) Rolls-Royce Eagle inline, Fokker decided to produce a refined version as the F.VIIA, retaining the combination of steel-tube fuselage and plywood wing spanning 19.30 m (63 ft 3.75 in), but fitted with radial or inline engines in the 261- to 391-kW (350- to 525-hp) power range. A 298-kW (400-hp) Liberty inline was used for the first flight in March 1925. Fokker made 44 F.VIIAs, and others were licence-built. For the 1925 Ford Reliability Tour of the USA the company converted an F.VIIA with three 179-kW (240-hp) Whirlwinds, and so successful was the type that production of the F.VII-3m was launched, with the 164-kW (220-hp) Armstrong Siddeley Lynx as an alternative engine. The F.VIIB-3m introduced a larger-span wing and greater power, and the 74 Dutch-built aircraft were complemented by many licence-built machines.

Specification: Fokker F.VIIB-3m medium-range airliner
Span: 21.71 m (71 ft 2.75 in)
Length: 14.50 m (47 ft 7 in)
Powerplant: 3×Wright J-6 Whirlwind, 224 kW (300 hp) each
Payload: two flightcrew plus 10 passengers or 1080 kg (2,381 lb) of freight
Max T/O weight: 5300 kg (11,684 lb)
Max speed: 129 mph
Operational range: 746 miles

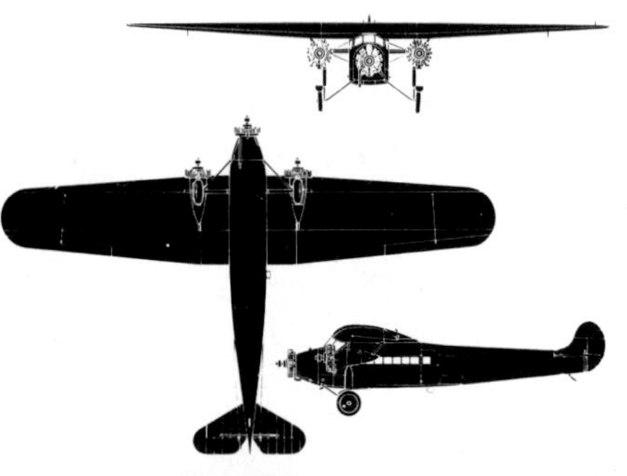

Focke-Wulf Fw 200 Condor

In the late 1930s strenuous efforts were made to bridge the North Atlantic with a landplane airliner. The goal remained unachieved before World War II, but the aeroplane that came closest to success was the Fw 200, schemed in 1936 as an all-metal low-wing monoplane with accommodation for 26 passengers. The Fw 200 V1 prototype flew in July 1937 with 652-kW (875-hp) Pratt & Whitney Hornet radials, and was followed by a personal aeroplane for Hitler and eight medium-range Fw 200As with the BMW 132G-1 radial: these latter went to Lufthansa (four) and to Danish Air Lines and the Syndicato Condor of Brazil (two each). The V1 was revised as the long-range Fw 200S-1, which in August 1938 made an unrefuelled crossing from Berlin to New York in 25 hours. The sole Fw 200B-1 had the 634-kW (850-hp) 132Dc radials, and three Fw 200B-0 2s had the 619-kW (830-hp) 132H.

Specification: Focke-Wulf Fw 200A Condor medium-range airliner
Span: 32.84 m (107 ft 8.9 in)
Length: 23.85 m (78 ft 3 in)
Powerplant: 4×BMW 132G-1, 537 kW (720 hp) each
Payload: four flightcrew plus 26 passengers or freight
Max T/O weight: 14600 kg (32,187 lb).
Cruising speed: 208 mph
Operational range: 901 miles

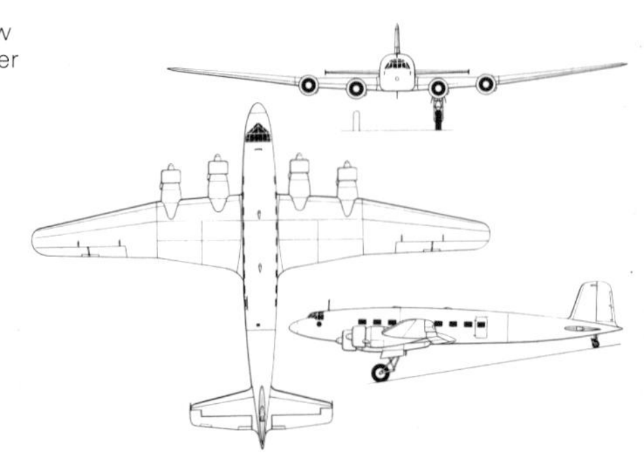

Vickers Viscount

irst flown as the V630 on 16 July 1948 to meet a British European Airways requirement for 32-passenger airliner, the prototype Viscount operated the world's first passenger-carrying urboprop services between London, Paris and Edinburgh in the summer of 1950. The lesign was subsequently enlarged to seat 40-53 passengers and powered by four 1,540-shp Rolls-Royce RDa3 Dart 505 turboprops as the production Viscount 700 which was ertificated in April 1953 and became a great sales success for Britain, making significant dvances into the North American market where Capital Airlines and Trans Canada Airlines ecame major customers. The Viscount 802, developed for BEA, featured a fuselage engthened by 3ft 10in, 65-71 seat cabin and 1,742shp Dart 510 engines. It first flew on 27 July 1956 and was succeeded by a range of higher powered 800-series Viscounts, culminating in the Viscount 810 with 1,990shp Dart 525s. Viscounts are still in passenger ervice in the UK with British Air Ferries, Guernsey Airways and Virgin Airways.

Specification: Vickers Viscount 810
Span: 28.57m (93ft 8½in)
Length: 26.03m (85ft 5in)
Height: 8.15m (26ft 9in)
Wing area: 89.46m² (963sqft)
Passenger capacity: 65-71
Empty weight: 18853kg (41,565lb)
Payload: 6577kg (14,500lb)
Maximum take-off weight: 32885kg (72,500lb)
Cruising speed: 350mph
Service ceiling: 25,000ft
Maximum range: 1,760 miles
Production total: (all models) 444

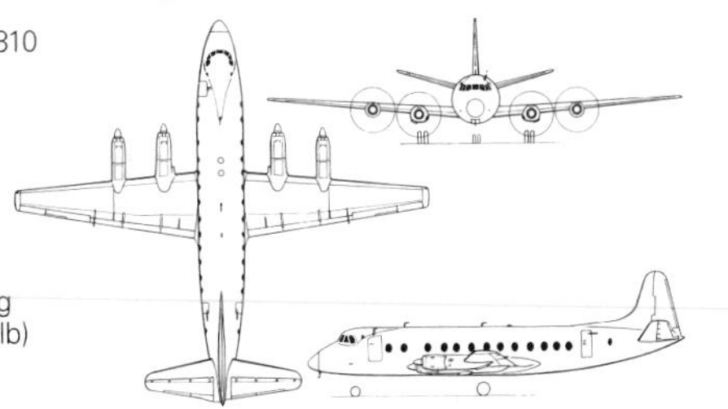

Ilyushin Il-18

The prototype 75-seat Ilyushin Il-18 named *Moskva,* first flew on 4 July 1957. After 20 aircraft had been built, passenger capacity was increased to 84 and four 4,000-shp Ivchyenko AI-20 turboprop engines adopted as standard on the production Il-18B. The Il-18 first entered Aeroflot service on 20 April 1959. Subsequent versions included the 80-100-passenger Il-18V and the Il-181/Il-18D, which had a maximum capacity of 122 and was powered by 4,250shp AI-20M engines. The Il-18D entered service during 1965, as did the Il-17Ye, which was similarly powered but had lower fuel capacity. The Il-18 was the first post-war Soviet airliner to have performance comparable to its Western contemporaries. Production ceased in 1970, the aircraft seeing service with airlines and military operators throughout the Soviet Bloc as well as in Africa, Asia, the Middle East and Cuba.

Specification: Ilyushin Il-18D
Span: 37.40m (122ft 8½in)
Length: 35.89m (117ft 9in)
Height: 10.15m (33ft 4in)
Wing area: 140m² (1,507sqft)
Passenger capacity: 80-122
Empty weight: 34999kg (77,160lb)
Payload: 13499kg (29,762lb)
Maximum take-off weight: 63998kg (141,093lb)
Cruising speed: 388mph
Maximum speed: 426mph
Service ceiling: 32,800ft
Maximum range: 4,040 miles
Production total: 800 approx

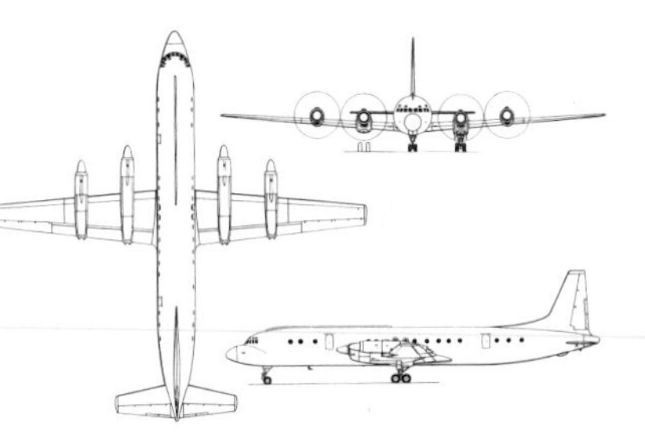

Breguet 763 Provence

Developed from the 1949 Breguet 761 prototype and popularly known as the *Deux Ponts* because of its capacious double-decker cabin, the Breguet 763 first flew on 20 July !951. It was powered by four 2,400-hp Pratt & Whitney R2800-CA18 Double Wasp piston engines and accommodated 59 tourist class passengers on its upper deck and 48 second-class passengers below, or up to 135 in all-economy seating. Twelve aircraft were delivered to Air France, which named them *Provence* and operated them principally on North African routes and occasionally on Paris-London services. Six were later converted to mixed car/cargo/passenger configuration as the *Universal.* The Deux Ponts retired from commercial service on 31 March 1971. Six were taken over by the French air force, which also operated four Breguet 765 Sahara heavy-duty military transport variants.

Specification: Breguet 763 Provence
Span: 42.98m (141ft 0½in)
Length: 28.94m (94ft 11½in)
Height: 9.65m (31ft 8in)
Wing area: 218.3m² (2,350sqft)
Passenger capacity: 107
Empty weights: 32241kg (71,080lb)
Payload: 14696kg (32,400lb)
Maximum take-off weight: 51599kg (113,758lb)
Cruising speed: 209mph
Maximum speed: 231mph
Service ceiling: 22,310ft
Maximum fuel range: 2,740 miles
Production total: 17

Sud-Est SE161 Languedoc

The SE161 Languedoc was a wartime development of the Bloch 161, which had flown in 1940 just before the Franco-German Armistice. Planned production for Lufthansa was delayed by French patriots within the SNCASE company, the first SE161 not flying until 17 September 1945. Air France ordered 40 Languedocs, powered initially by four 1,150-hp Gnôme-Rhône 14N radial engines, but these were later replaced on all production aircraft by 1,200-hp Pratt & Whitney Twin Wasps. The Languedoc entered service in May 1946 on routes from Paris to Algiers, Casablanca and most European capitals. Five aircraft were delivered to the Polish Airline LOT, and 60 to the Armée de l'Air and Aéronavale, several of which saw service as flying testbeds and launch vehicles for the Leduc experimental ramjet aircraft. Following retirement between 1949-52 some of Air France's Languedocs were sold to Air Liban, Misrair and the Spanish carrier Aviaco.

Specification: SE161 Languedoc
Span: 29.38m (96ft 4¾in)
Length: 24.24m (79ft 6¾in)
Height: 5.13m (16ft 10in)
Wing area: 111.27m² (1.197sqft)
Passenger capacity: 33
Empty weight: 12650kg (27,890lb)
Payload: 3923kg (8,650lb)
Maximum take-off weight: 22940kg (50,576lb)
Cruising speed: 233mph
Maximum speed: 273mph
Service ceiling: 23,620ft
Maximum fuel range: 1,988 miles
Production total: 100

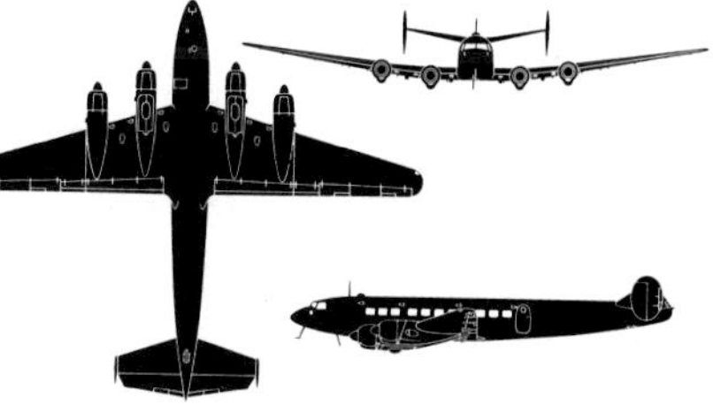

Lockheed Constellations

Specification: Lockheed 1049G Super Constellation
Span: 37.49 m (123 ft 0 in)
Length: 35.50 m (116 ft 2 in)
Height: 7.54 m (24 ft 9 in)
Passenger capacity: 69-92
Maximum take-off weight: 62368 kg (137,500 lb)
Cruising speed: 305 mph
Maximum speed: 370mph
Service ceiling: 22,300 ft
Maximum range: 4,810 miles
Production totals: 049/749: 233. **1049:** 579. **1649:** 44

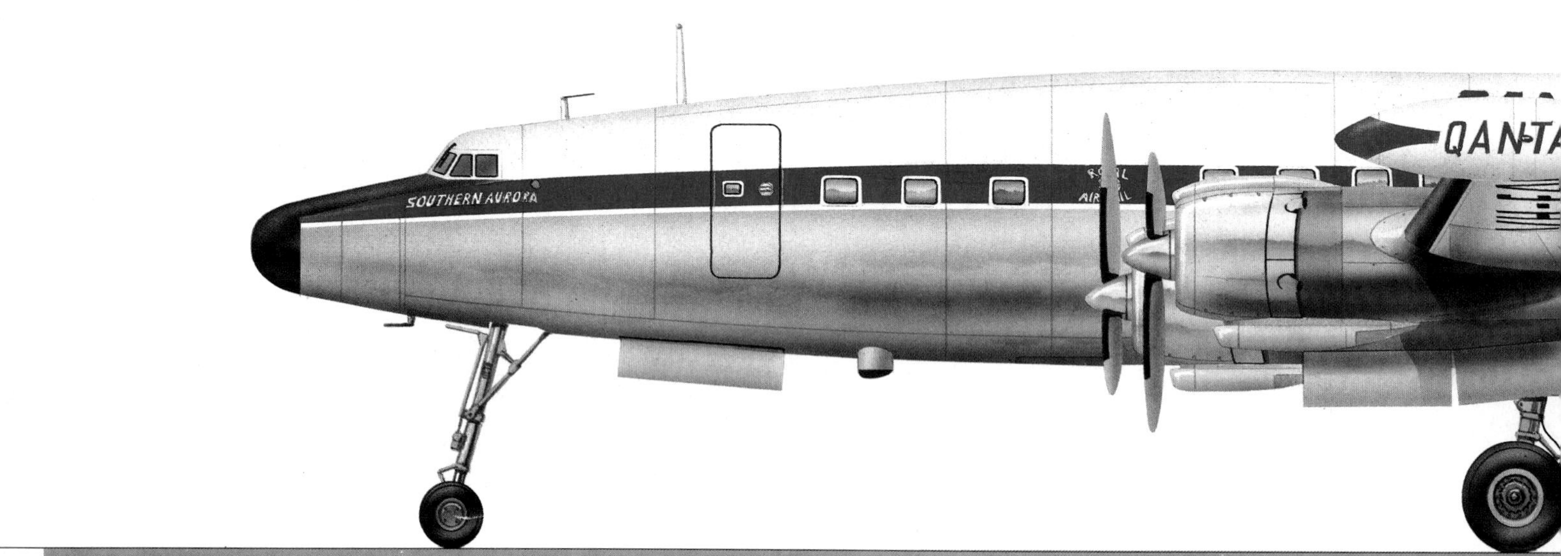

Douglas DC-4 Skymaster

The DC-4 was first conceived in 1935 and a prototype DC-4E was flown on 7 June 1938, but it bore little resemblance to the production C-54 Skymaster military transport which had its maiden flight on 14 February 1942. The later aircraft was virtually a new design, with a lighter airframe, entirely new wing, single fin and rudder in place of the DC-4E's triple fins, and four 1,100-hp Pratt & Whitney R-2000-3 radial engines. In addition to 1,236 military C-54 Skymasters of various marks, 79 DC-4s were manufactured after World War II. Many surplus USAF Skymasters were converted to civilian use, forming the mainstay of many US and overseas long-haul passenger and cargo services before purpose-built transports became available. The DC-4M North Star developed by Canadair was a pressurised version powered by four 1,725hp Rolls-Royce Merlin engines. It was used by the Royal Canadian Air Force, Trans Canada Airlines and BOAC, which called the aircraft Argonaut. A car-ferry version of the DC-4 developed by Aviation Traders Ltd in 1961 was known as the Carvair.

Specification: Douglas C-54D/DC
Span: 35.81 m (117 ft 6 in)
Length: 28.60 m (93 ft 10 in)
Height: 8.38 m (27 ft 6 in)
Wing area: 135.63 m^2 (1,460 sq ft)
Passenger capacity: 44-86
Empty weight: 17236 kg (38,000 lb)
Payload: 6395 kg (14,100 lb)
Maximum take-off weight: 33112 kg (73,000 lb)
Cruising speed: 203 mph
Maximum speed: 275 mph
Service ceiling: 22,300 ft
Maximum fuel range: 3,100 miles
Production total: 1,315

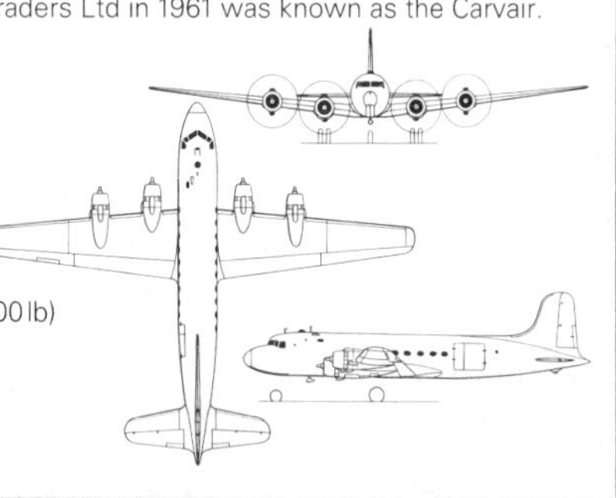

Martin 2-0-2, 4-0-4

The Martin 2-0-2, first flown on 22 November 1946, was the first post-war twin-engined airliner to be certified in the United States. Like the Convair 240 it was intended as a DC-3 replacement and similarly powered by two 2,400hp Pratt & Whitney R2800-CA18 Double Wasp radial engines, but its 36-seat passenger cabin was unpressurised. Thirty-three were built, the first of 25 for Northwest Airlines entering service in October 1947. The 2-0-2 was succeeded in production by the stretched and pressurised 40-seat Model 4-0-4. Sixty of these were delivered to Eastern Airlines, 41 to TWA and two to the US Coast Guard before production ended in 1953. Many redundant Martins were later sold off to 'third level' airlines in the USA and Latin America and some 4-0-4s were converted into corporate transports.

Specification: Martin 4-0-4
Span: 28.43 m (93 ft 3½ in)
Length: 22.73 m (74 ft 7 in)
Height: 8.66 m (28 ft 5 in)
Wing area: 80.26 m^2 (864 sq ft)
Passenger capacity: 40
Empty weight: 13211 kg (29, 126 lb)
Payload: 5303 kg (11,692 lb)
Maximum take-off weight: 20366 kg (44,900 lb)
Cruising speed: 280 mph
Maximum speed: 312 mph
Service ceiling: 29,000 ft
Maximum range: 2,600 miles
Production totals:
2-0-2: 33
4-0-4: 103

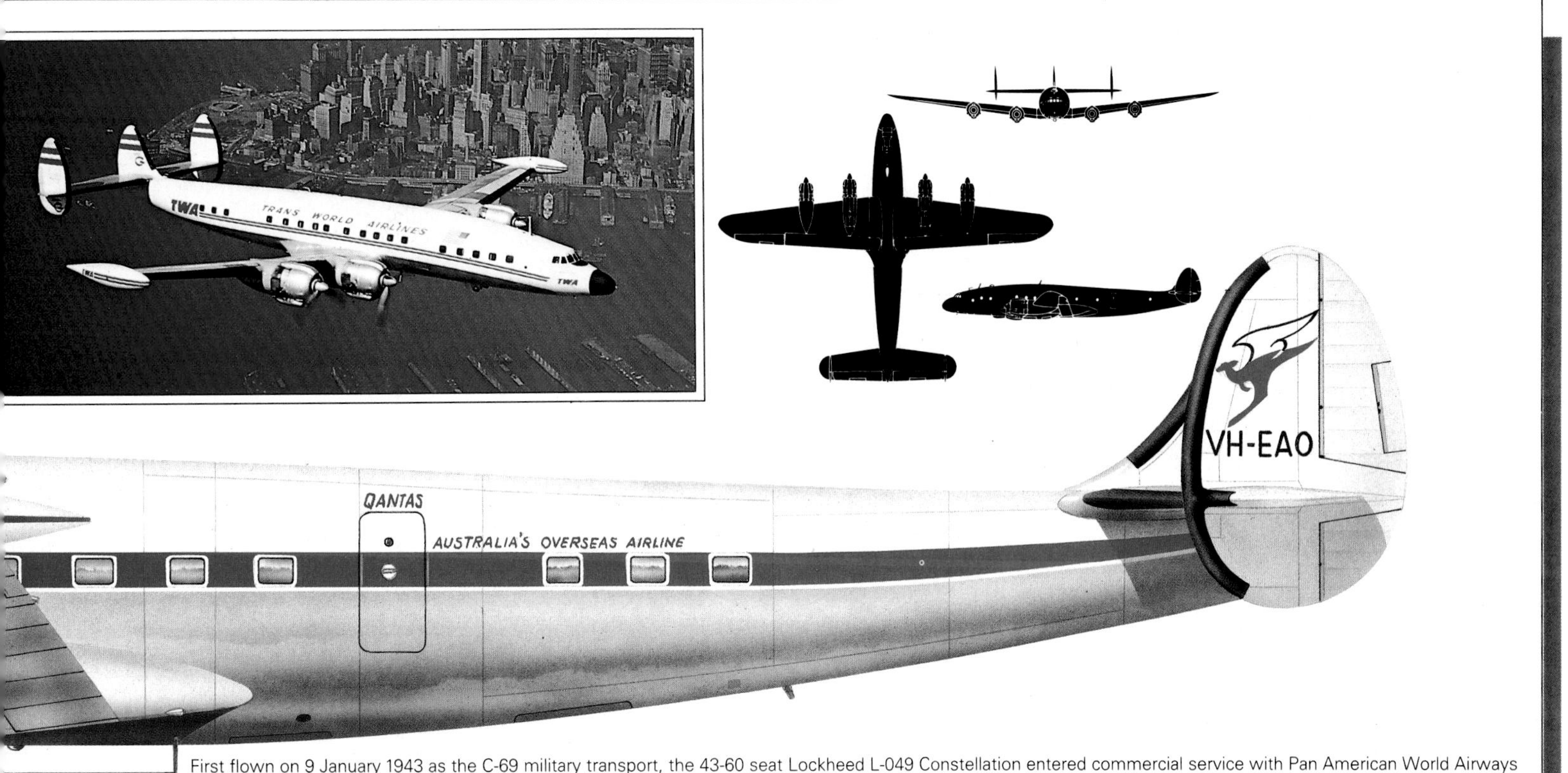

First flown on 9 January 1943 as the C-69 military transport, the 43-60 seat Lockheed L-049 Constellation entered commercial service with Pan American World Airways and Trans World Airways in early 1946. It was powered by four 2,200-hp Wright R3350 Duplex Cyclone piston engines, and also served with Air France, BOAC, KLM and Panair do Brasil. Increased passenger accommodation, engine power and range was provided by the L-649 and L-749 Constellation, from which was developed the L-1049 Super Constellation. This featured an 18 ft 4 in fuselage stretch and entered service with Eastern Airlines on 17 December 1951. Like its predecessors the Super Constellation was developed through several versions, culminating in the tip-tanked 3,400 hp R3350-powered L-1049G 'Super G' and 109-seat passenger/cargo L-1049H models. The ultimate Constellations development was the L-1649A Starliner. First flown in 1956, it featured an entirely new high-aspect ratio wing with greatly increased fuel capacity which made nonstop Transatlantic flights possible in either direction.

Convair 240, 340, 440, 580, 640

Seeking a post-war DC-3 replacement, American Airlines issued a specification in early 1945 which resulted in a 30-seat prototype Convair Model 110 flying on 8 July 1946. Before it could be developed the need for greater passenger capacity inspired the Convair 240, which was built on production jigs and made its maiden flight on 16 March 1947. This was a 40-seat pressurised aircraft powered by two 2,400-hp Pratt & Whitney R-2800-CA18 Double Wasp engines. It entered service with American Airlines on 1 June 1948 and was succeeded in production by the Convair 340 with 2,500-hp engines, a 4 ft 6 in longer fuselage and 44-seat cabin, and the further improved radar-equipped Convair 440 Metropolitan, which had a 52-seat cabin. Turboprop conversions of the Convairliner series developed by independent modifiers and the manufacturer are designated CV-540 (3,060-shp Napier Eland engines);

Specification: Convair 440
Span: 32.10 m (105 ft 4 in)
Length: 24.84 m (81 ft 6 in)
Height: 8.58 m (28 ft 2 in)
Passenger capacity: 44-52
Payload: 5822 kg (12,836 lb)
Maximum take-off weight: 22543 kg (49,700 lb)
Cruising speed: 289 mph
Service ceiling: 24,900 ft
Maximum range: 1,930 miles
Production totals:
240 incl military: 590
340 incl military: 329
440: 181

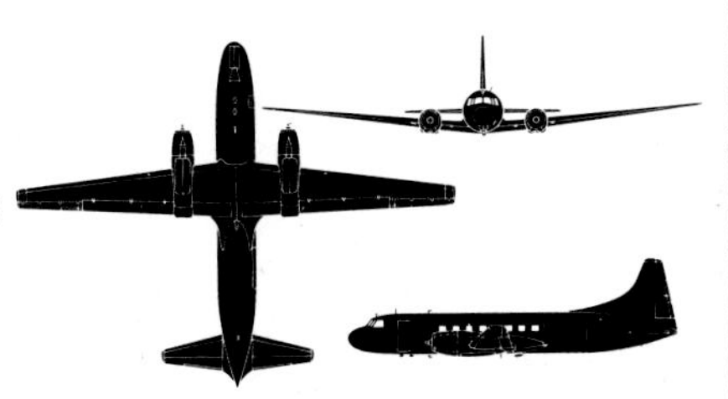

Boeing 377 Stratocruiser

The Boeing 377 Stratocruiser had its origins in the C-97 military transport which combined the wings, engines, tail unit and undercarriage of the B-29 Superfortress bomber with a new 'double bubble' fuselage. The Stratocruiser, powered by four 3,500-hp Pratt & Whitney R-4360-B3 Wasp Major piston engines, first flew on 8 July 1947 and entered service with Pan American World Airways on North Atlantic 'Presidential' routes two years later. American Overseas Airlines, Northwest Orient Airlines, United Airlines and British Overseas Airways Corporation also operated the Stratocruiser on long-haul routes, on which its two-deck pressurised cabins with single and double berth sleeping accommodation brought new standards of comfort in the pre-jet era. The Stratocruiser later provided the inspiration for Aero Spacelines Corporation's Guppy and Super Guppy oversize cargo aircraft.

Specification: Boeing 377 Stratocruiser
Span: 43.05 m (141 ft 3 in)
Length: 33.62 m (110 ft 4 in)
Height: 11.65 m (38 ft 3 in)
Wing area: 164.34 m^2 (1,769 sq ft)
Passenger capacity: 61
Empty weight: 37874 kg (83,500 lb)
Payload: 10722 kg (23,640 lb)
Maximum take-off weight: 67131 kg (148,000 lb)
Cruising speed: 340 mph
Maximum speed: 375 mph
Service ceiling: 32,000 ft
Maximum range: 4,200 miles
Production total:
(civilian models) 56

Bristol 175 Britannia

The Bristol Britannia was intended to meet British Overseas Airways Corporation's requirements for a 32-36 passenger piston-engined Medium Range Empire airliner, but major design changes resulted in the 90-seat, Bristol Proteus 625 turboprop-powered prototype, which first flew on 23 December 1953. The production Britannia 102, popularly known as the 'Whispering Giant', entered service with BOAC on 1 February 1957, operating the London-Johannesburg route. The long-range Britannia 300 series, with 10 ft 3 in fuselage stretch, four 4,120 shp Proteus 755 engines and accommodation for 99-133 passengers, began flying BOAC nonstop London-New York services on 19 December 1957. BOAC's Britannia 312s were the first turbine-powered airliners to operate transatlantic routes. Britannias were also ordered by Aeronaves de Mexico, Canadian Pacific, Cubana, El Al, Ghana Airways and RAF Transport Command.

Specification: Bristol Britannia 312
Span: 43.35 m (142 ft 3 in)
Length: 37.87 m (124 ft 3 in)
Height: 11.43 m (37 ft 6 in)
Wing area: 192.76 m^2 (2,075 sq ft)
Passenger capacity: 99
Empty weight: 39915 kg (88,000 lb)
Payload: 12700 kg (28,000 lb)
Maximum take-off weight: 83914 kg (185,000 lb)
Cruising speed: 357 mph
Maximum speed: 397 mph
Service ceiling: 24,000 ft
Maximum fuel range: 5,760 miles
Production total: 85

Douglas DC-6

First flown as the experimental XC-112A on 15 February 1946, the Douglas DC-6 retained the wing of the C-54 Skymaster but featured a pressurised fuselage lengthened by 6 ft 9 in, enlarged tail surfaces and four 2,100-hp R-2800-CA15 Double Wasp engines. Standard accommodation was for 48-52 passengers, with seats for up to 86 in high density configuration. American Airlines operated the first DC-6 service on its New York-Chicago route in April 1947. The all-cargo DC-6A Liftmaster which appeared in September 1949 had a further 5 ft fuselage stretch, 2,400 hp engines with water-methanol injection, reinforced cabin floor and upward opening freight doors. The DC-6B was similar but with cabin accommodation for 54/102 passengers. The last of the DC-6 series, a DC-6B for JAT Aerotransport of Jugoslavia, was delivered on 17 November 1958. Military DC-6s were designated C-118 (USAF) and R6D (US Navy).

Specification: Douglas DC-6B
Span: 35.81 m (117 ft 6 in)
Length: 32.18 m (105 ft 7 in)
Height: 8.73 m (28 ft 8 in)
Wing area: 135.91 m^2 (1,463 sq ft)
Passenger capacity: 54-102
Empty weight: 25109 kg (55,357 lb)
Payload: 11142 kg (24,565 lb)
Maximum take-off weight: 48534 kg (107,000 lb)
Cruising speed: 307 mph
Maximum speed: 360 mph
Service ceiling: 29,000 ft
Maximum fuel range: 4,720 miles
Production total: (all models) 704

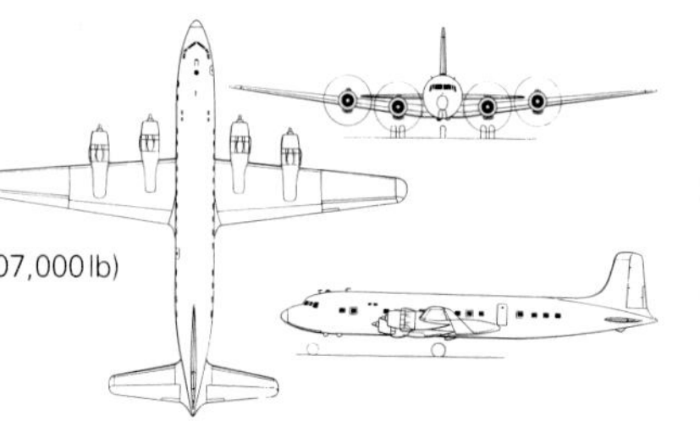

Douglas DC-7

The DC-7 was spurred by American Airlines' desire for an aircraft to compete against TWA's long-range Super Constellations. Using the wings and tail surfaces of a DC-6B, Douglas stretched the fuselage by 3 ft 4 in, and installed 3,250 hp Wright R-3350 Turbo Compound engines. The DC-7 prototype flew on 18 May 1953, by which time 58 had been ordered by American, Delta, National and United Airlines. American operated the first DC-7 service nonstop from Los Angeles to New York on 29 November 1953. The DC-7B was a more powerful long-range version flown by Pan American World Airways on transatlantic routes and also by American, Continental, Delta, Eastern Air Lines, National, Panagra and South African Airways. Final development was the DC-7C Seven Seas which had a 10 ft increase in wing span with additional fuel tanks in the centre section, 3 ft 6 in fuselage stretch enabling up to 105 passengers to be carried and 3,400 hp engines. DC-7Cs were operated by Alitalia, BOAC, KLM, PAA, Sabena, SAS, Swissair and TAI of France.

Specification: Douglas DC-7C
Span: 38.86 m (127 ft 6 in)
Length: 34.21 m (112 ft 3 in)
Height: 9.70 m (31 ft 10 in)
Passenger capacity: 105
Empty weight: 33004 kg (72,763 lb)
Payload: 9752 kg (21,500 lb)
Maximum take-off weight: 68463 kg (143,000 ft)
Cruising speed: 345 mph
Maximum speed: 405 mph
Service ceiling: 21,700 ft
Maximum fuel range: 5,640 miles
Production total: (all models) 338

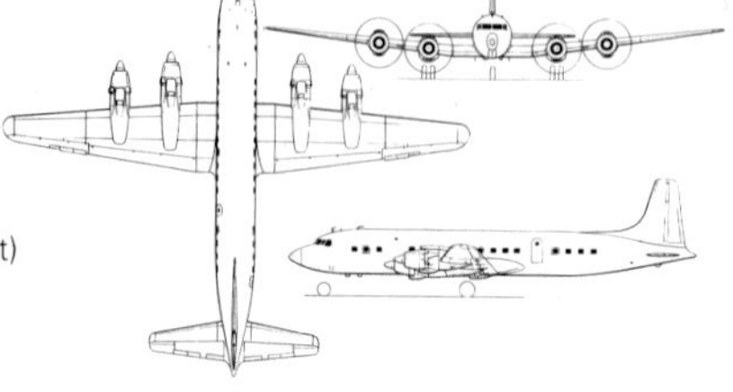

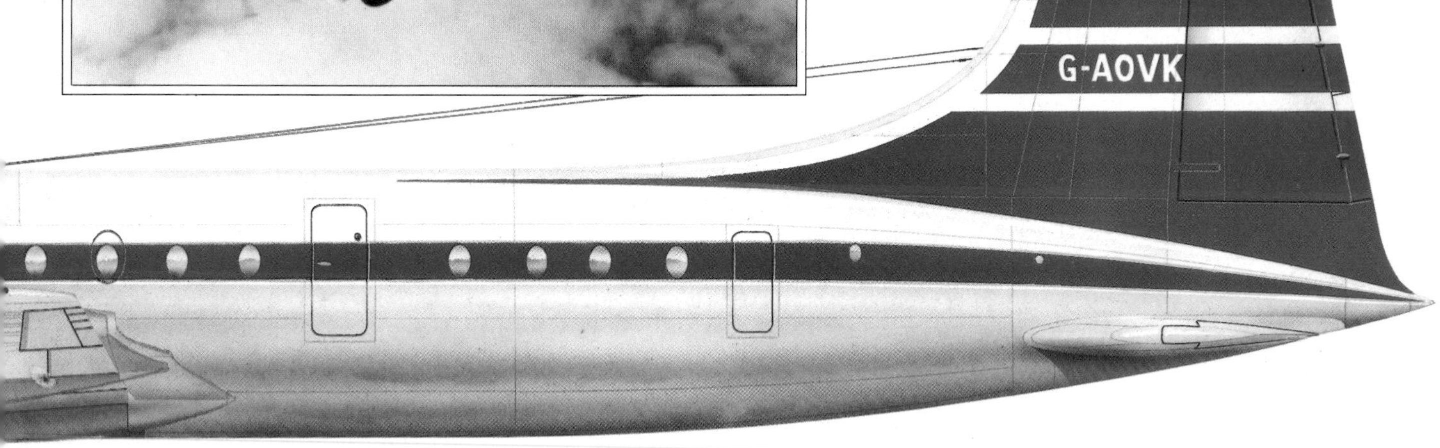

Lockheed L-188 Electra

The Lockheed L-188 was designed to an American Airlines requirement for a medium range airliner for US domestic routes. Orders for 144 had been received when the prototype, powered by four 3,730-shp Allison 501-D13 turboprops, first flew on 6 December 1957. The L-188A Electra entered service on Eastern's New York-Chicago route on 12 January 1959. The L-188C model had increased fuel capacity. Electras were ordered by Braniff, National Airlines, Northwest Orient, Pacific Southwest and Western Airlines in the United States, KLM in the Netherlands, Cathay Pacific and Garuda in the Far East and Ansett-ANA, Trans Australian Airlines and TEAL in Australasia. Hampered by two fatal accidents early in its career which resulted in extensive structural modifications, the aircraft had a relatively short production run and was retired from first-line service by 1975, although many continued to serve as cargo carriers. The P-3 Orion maritime patrol aircraft is based on the Electra airframe.

Specification: Lockheed L-188A Electra
Span: 30.17m (99ft 0in)
Length: 31.83m (104ft 5½in)
Height: 9.98m (32ft 9in)
Wing area: 120.77m² (1,300sqft)
Passenger capacity: 66-98
Empty weight: 26036kg (57,400lb)
Payload: 10353kg (22,825lb)
Maximum take-off weight: 51255kg (113.000lb)
Cruising speed: 373mph
Maximum speed: 448mph
Service ceiling: 28,400ft
Maximum range: 2,770 miles
Production total: 170

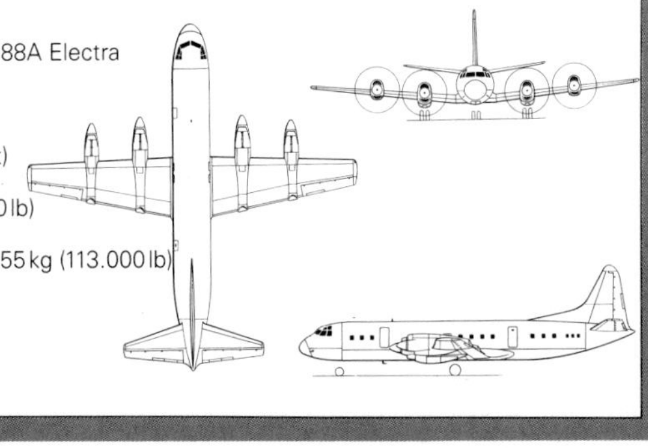

Airspeed AS57 Ambassador

Designed to meet Brabazon Committee Type IIA specification for a medium-range airliner, the prototype Airspeed AS57 Ambassador first flew on 10 July 1947. British European Airways ordered 20 47-passenger Ambassador 2 production variants powered by two 2,625-hp Bristol Centaurus 661 18-cylinder twin row radial piston engines. Known as the Elizabethan in BEA service, the aircraft began operating London-Paris services on 13 March 1952. Three more Ambassadors were built for Butler Air Transport in Australia. The last BEA Elizabethan flight was made on 30 July 1958, after which its aircraft were sold to charter companies such as BKS Air Transport and Dan-Air, and as executive transports to King Hussein of Jordan, the Decca Navigator Company and Shell Aviation. No airworthy Ambassadors survive.

Specification: Airspeed AS57 Ambassador
Span: 35.05m (115ft 0in)
Length: 24.99m (82ft 0in)
Height: 5.74m (18ft 10in)
Wing area: 111.48m (1,200sqft)
Passenger capacity: 47-55
Empty weight: 16467kg (36,304lb)
Payload: 5282kg (11,645lb)
Maximum take-off weight: 24947kg (55,000lb)
Cruising speed: 260mph
Maximum speed: 312mph
Service ceiling: 34,450ft
Maximum fuel range: 1,200 miles
Production total:
23

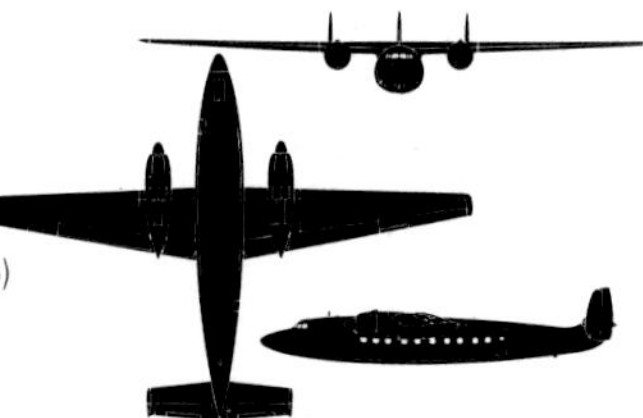

Beech Model 60 Duke

The Duke was Beech's first pressurised general-aviation aeroplane when it flew in December 1966 to fill the gap between the Baron and the Queen Air. Intended as a luxurious four/six-seater with high levels of equipment as standard, the Duke also found an application in the executive transport market. The Duke is similar in layout to other Beech twin-props, but being larger than the generally similar Baron, has stronger landing gear and more powerful engines. The cabin pressurisation system can be set to provide the equivalent of 10,000ft up to a height of 24,800 ft. Improved models are the A60 and B60 introduced in 1971 and 1974 respectively: the former allows a 23-kg (50-lb) increase in take-off weight, and the latter has a slightly larger cabin and greater fuel capacity.

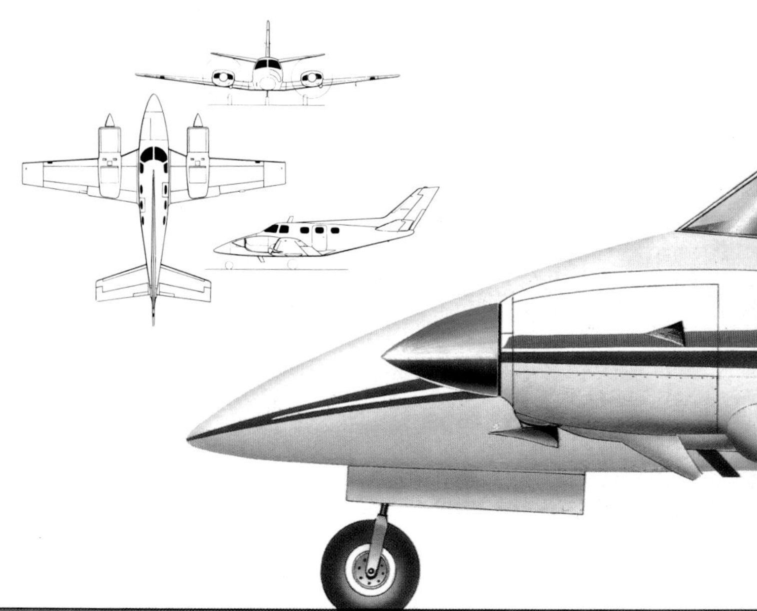

EMBRAER EMB-121 Xingu

With a wing and fuselage based on those of the larger EMB-110P2 Bandeirante and EMB-120 Brasilia respectively, the EMB-121 Xingu was planned as a small T-tailed type able to carry a small number of passengers over moderate ranges in great pressurised comfort. The Xingu naturally bears a strong similarity to other members of its Brazilian family, and the prototype first flew in October 1976, with production aircraft following just over six months later. There are currently three versions of the Xingu, namely the EMB-121A Xingu I with two PT6A-28 turboprops, the EMB-121A1 Xingu II with 559-kW (750-shp) PT6A-125 turboprops, and the EMB-121V Xingu III with 634-kW (850-shp) PT6A-42 turboprops and a fuselage lengthened by 0.89m (2ft 11in) for the greater comfort of an unchanged number of passengers, though the cabin can be arranged in a 'club' layout for seven passengers.

Specification: EMBRAER EMB-121A Xingu I 2+9-seat pressurised executive transport
Span: 14.45m (47ft 5in)
Length: 12.25m (40ft 2.25in)
Powerplant: 2×Pratt & Whitney Canada PT6A-28, 507kW (680shp) each
Max T/O weight: 5670kg (12,500lb)
Cruising speed: 280 mph at optimum altitude
Range: 1,411 miles with 780-kg (1,720-lb) payload

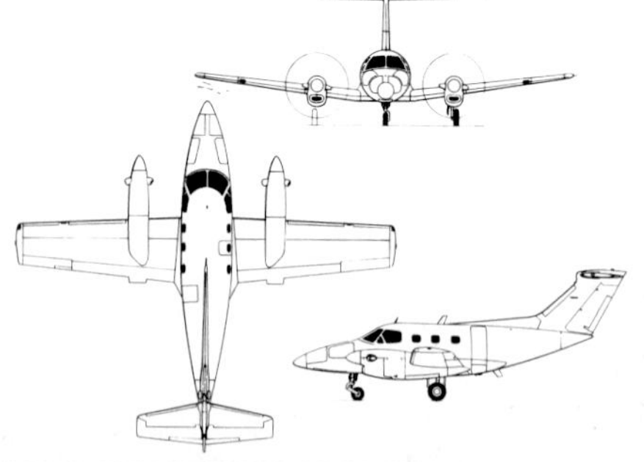

Beech King Air 200

The Model 90 King Air was developed as a pressurised Queen Air with turboprop power, and flew as a civil prototype in January 1964. The 10-seat King Air A90 began to reach customers later in 1964: this basic series has reached the King Air E90 mark, the later Super King Air F90 combining the fuselage of the Model 90 with the wings and tailplane of the Model 100 and Model 200. The Model 100 King Air was introduced in 1969 with a 15-seat fuselage and a wing derived from that of the Model 99 Airliner, while the B100 has Garrett TPE331-6-252B rather than PT6A-28 turboprops. The Model 200 Super King Air of 1972 has a longer-span wing, a T-tail and more fuel for the 634-kW (850-shp) PT6A-41 engines. The Super King Air B200 of 1981 has PT6A-42s, the Super King Air 300 has 783-kW (1,050-shp) PT6A-60As, and the 12/19-passenger King Air Exec-Liner has 820-kW (1,100-shp) PT6A-65Bs.

Specification: Beech Super King Air B200 2+8/10-seat pressurised executive transport
Span: 16.61m (54ft 6in)
Length: 13.34m (43ft 9in)
Powerplant: 2×Pratt & Whitney Canada PT6A-42, 634kW (850shp) each
Max T/O weight: 5670kg (12,500lb)
Cruising speed: 325 mph at 25,000ft
Range: 2,334 miles

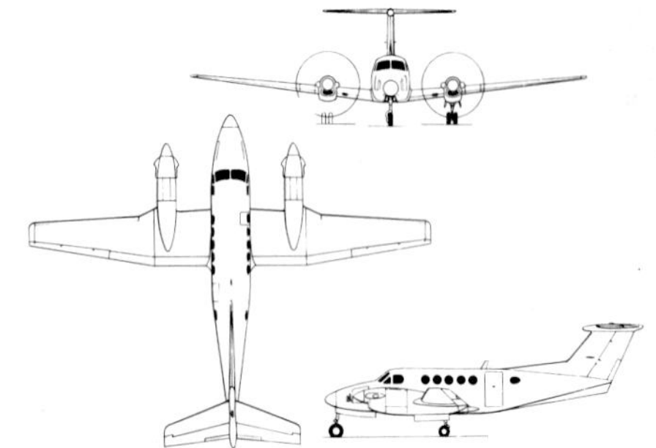

Stylish lines made the Duke an attractive proposition for purchasers requiring a pressurised luxury 4/6-seat transport. High altitude performance gives the type good range and speed capabilities for its size, a fact exploited by over 600 customers, mostly in the United States. The Duke was not a great success overseas, with only a few European purchasers. This example wears Austrian markings.

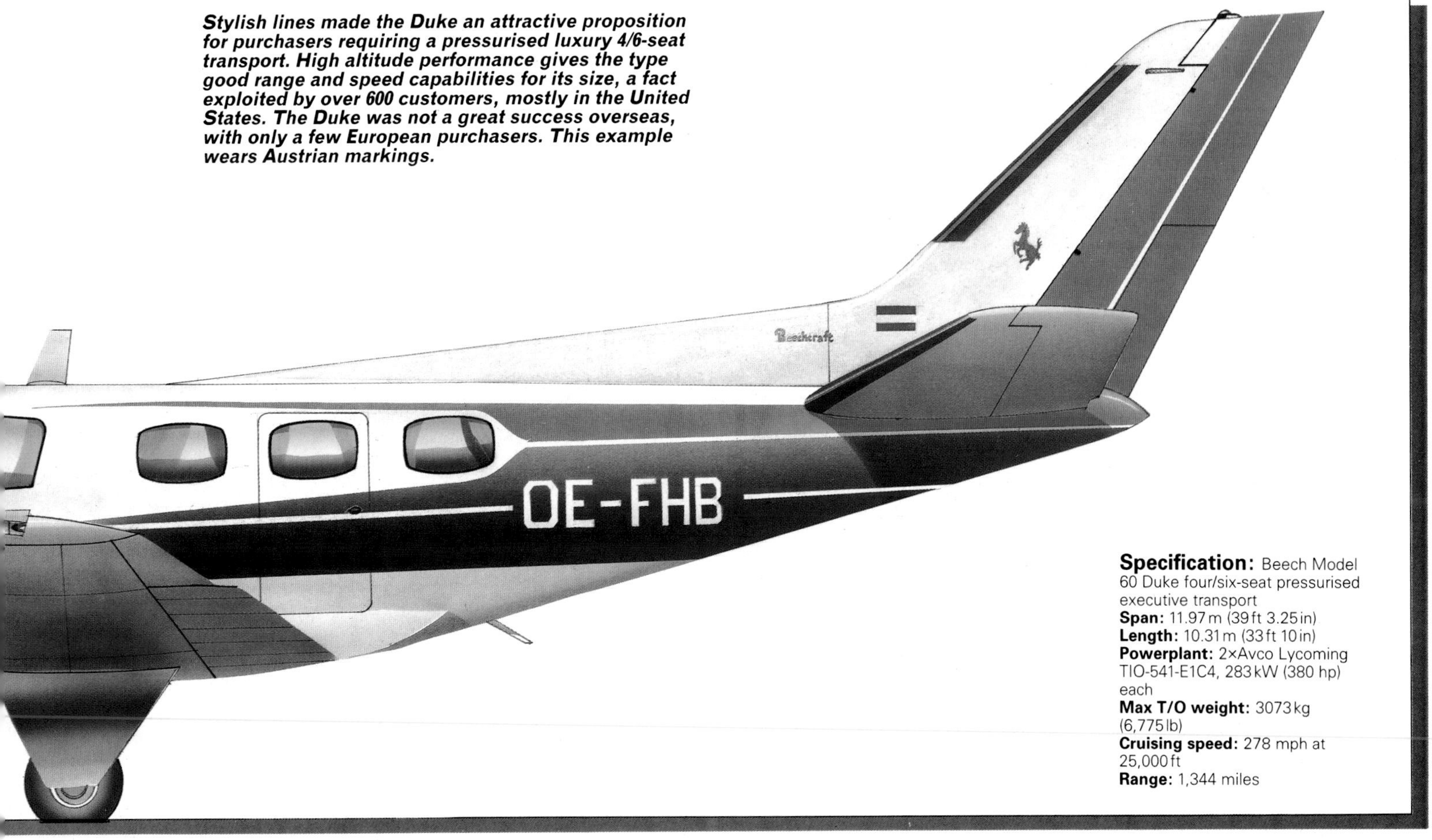

Specification: Beech Model 60 Duke four/six-seat pressurised executive transport
Span: 11.97 m (39 ft 3.25 in)
Length: 10.31 m (33 ft 10 in)
Powerplant: 2×Avco Lycoming TIO-541-E1C4, 283 kW (380 hp) each
Max T/O weight: 3073 kg (6,775 lb)
Cruising speed: 278 mph at 25,000 ft
Range: 1,344 miles

Beech Model 99 Executive

The Model 99 was designed in response to the company's appreciation of growing US commuter traffic in the 1960s, and first flew in July 1966 as precursor of the Model 99 Airliner, at that time Beech's largest production aeroplane with provision for a crew of two and up to 15 passengers carried on the power of two 410-kW (550-shp) PT6A-20 turboprops. The design was modelled on that of the Queen Air with a comparatively longer fuselage and twin wheels on each unit of the electrically retractable tricycle landing gear. Beech also offered the Model 99 Executive with a number of optional seating arrangements for corporate use. Similar versions were offered of the A99 and improved B99 with 507-kW (680-shp) PT6A-27 engines, and of the C99 introduced in 1980 with flat-rated PT6A-34 engines.

Specification: Beech Executive C99 2+15-seat pressurised executive transport
Span: 13.98 m (45 ft 10.5 in)
Length: 13.58 m (44 ft 6.75 in)
Powerplant: 2×Pratt & Whitney Canada PT6A-36, flat-rated at 533 kW (750 hp) each
Max T/O weight: 5126 kg (11,300 lb)
Cruising speed: 287 mph at 8,000 ft
Range: 1,048 miles

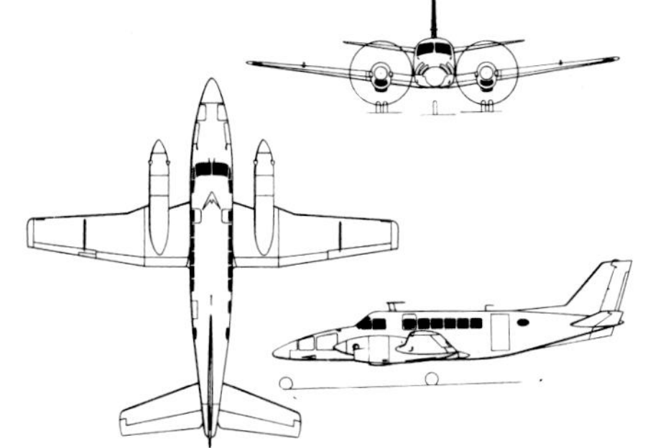

Beech Starship 1

First flown in August 1983 in the form of an 85 per cent scale version developed by Scaled Composites Inc, the Starship 1 is an extremely advanced executive transport offering operating economy, high performance and considerable comfort through the use of composite construction and canard configuration with pusher engines driving five-blade propellers of composite structure. The substantial rear-mounted wing is swept back 24° 24' at quarter-chord and ends in large vertical surfaces, while the foreplanes are interconnected with the flaps to sweep between 4° forward and 30° back as a means of countering pitch moment changes. Full-scale flight trials began in February 1986 with the first of six pre-production Starship 1s, and the type is due for FAA certification in 1989 with deliveries beginning later in the same year.

Specification: Beech Starship 1/2+11-seat pressurised executive transport
Span: 16.60 m (54 ft 4.75 in) for wing and 7.58 m (24 ft 10.5 in) for foreplanes
Length: 14.05 m (46 ft 1 in)
Powerplant: 2×Pratt & Whitney Canada PT6A-67A, 895 kW (1,200 shp) each
Max T/O weight: 6464 kg (14,250 lb)
Cruising speed: 387 mph at 35,000 ft
Range: 2,506 miles

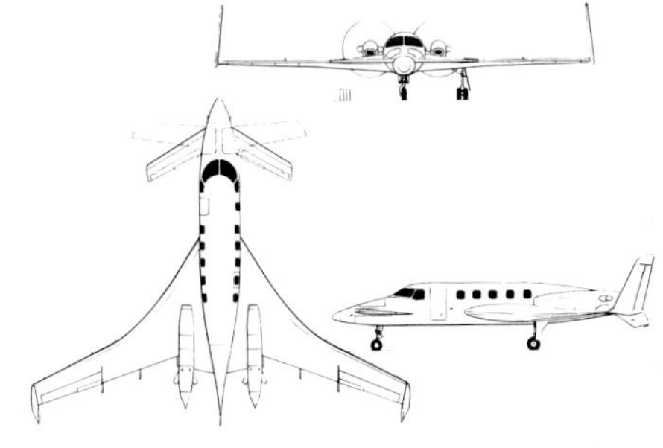

MU-2, Marquise and Solitaire

The PA-31T Cheyenne was first flown in October 1973 as a variant of the Pressurised Navajo with 462-kW (620-shp) PT6A-28 turboprops, though this model was redesignated Cheyenne II with the advent in 1978 of the PA-31T-1 Cheyenne I with 373-kW (500-hp) PT6A-11 engines. Though intended mainly for commuter work, the Cheyenne also proved successful in the corporate market. This success was extended by the 1981 advent of the PA-31T-2 Cheyenne IIXL with PT6A-135s flat-rated to 462 kW (620 shp) and a fuselage stretched by 0.61 m (2 ft). With the PA-42 Cheyenne III of 1980 the company introduced a much improved development with greater span, a longer fuselage, a T-tail and 537-kW (720-shp) PT6A-41s. There followed the Cheyenne IIIA with PT6A-61s, and the Cheyenne IV (now Cheyenne 400) with counter-rotating Garrett TPE331-14 turboprops flat-rated to 746 kW (1,000 shp).

Specification: Piper PA-42 Cheyenne IIIA 6/11-seat pressurised executive transport
Span: 14.53 m (47 ft 8 in) over tiptanks
Length: 13.23 m (43 ft 4.75 in)
Powerplant: 2×634-kW (850-shp) Pratt & Whitney Canada PT6A-61, flat-rated to 537 kW (720 shp) each
Max T/O weight: 5080 kg (11,200 lb)
Cruising speed: 358 mph at optimum altitude
Range: 2,366 miles

Piper PA-31/PA-42 Cheyenne

Mitsubishi began investigation of a high-performance executive twin in 1956, and the first of four prototypes flew in September 1963 as a pressurised high-wing monoplane with tiptanks and Turbomeca Astazou turboprops. The initial civil variants were the Astazou-powered MU-2A, the TPE331-powered MU-2B and similar MU-2D with integral tankage, the MU-2G with its fuselage stretched by 1.9 m (6 ft 2.75 in) and its main landing gear units in fuselage-side blisters, the MU-2J with more powerful engines, the short-fuselage MU-2K with MU-2J powerplant, the higher-weight MU-2L and MU-2M based on the MU-2J and MU-2K respectively, and the similar MU-2N and MU-2P with slower-turning propellers for reduced noise. With 533- or 496-kW (715- or 665-shp) TPE331-10-501M engines respectively, these last two are marketed in the USA as the Marquise and Solitaire.

Specification: Mitsubishi MU-2M 2+6/12-seat pressurised executive transport
Span: 11.94 m (39 ft 2 in)
Length: 10.13 m (33 ft 3 in)
Powerplant: 2×Garrett TPE331-6-251M, 540 kW (724 shp) each
Max T/O weight: 4750 kg (10,472 lb)
Cruising speed: 340 mph at 20,000 ft
Range: 1,680 miles

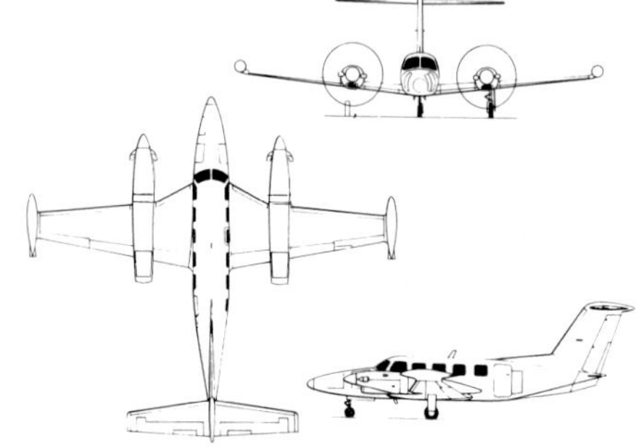

Cessna Model 441 Conquest

Announced in late 1974 as a high-speed pressurised executive transport with a low-mounted wing based on that of the Model 404 Titan, the Model 441 was then revised with a wing of greater span for higher aspect ratio, and flown with this wing in August 1975. By the time that deliveries began in 1977 the name Conquest had been given to the type. The Model 441 was Cessna's first turboprop aeroplane, the specific variant of the TPE331 being specially developed for this application and providing the bleed-air pressurisation that allows cruise at altitudes up to 35,000 ft. Marketing was made difficult by the crash of an early production aeroplane, resulting in a grounding of all Conquests until a revised tail unit had been produced, and since 1983 the type has been known as the Conquest II when the Model 425 Corsair was redesignated Conquest I.

Specification: Cessna Model 441 Conquest II 5/11-seat pressurised executive transport
Span: 15.04 m (49 ft 4 in)
Length: 11.89 m (39 ft 0.25 in)
Powerplant: 2×Garrett TPE331-8-401S/402S, 474 kW (635.5 shp) each
Max T/O weight: 4468 kg (9,850 lb)
Cruising speed: 298 mph at 35,000 ft
Range: 2,638 miles

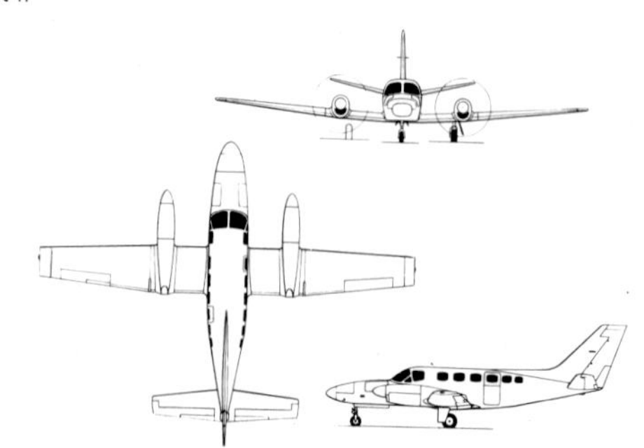

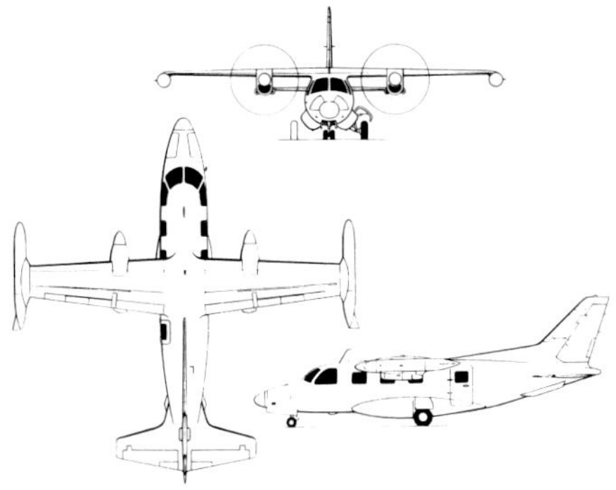

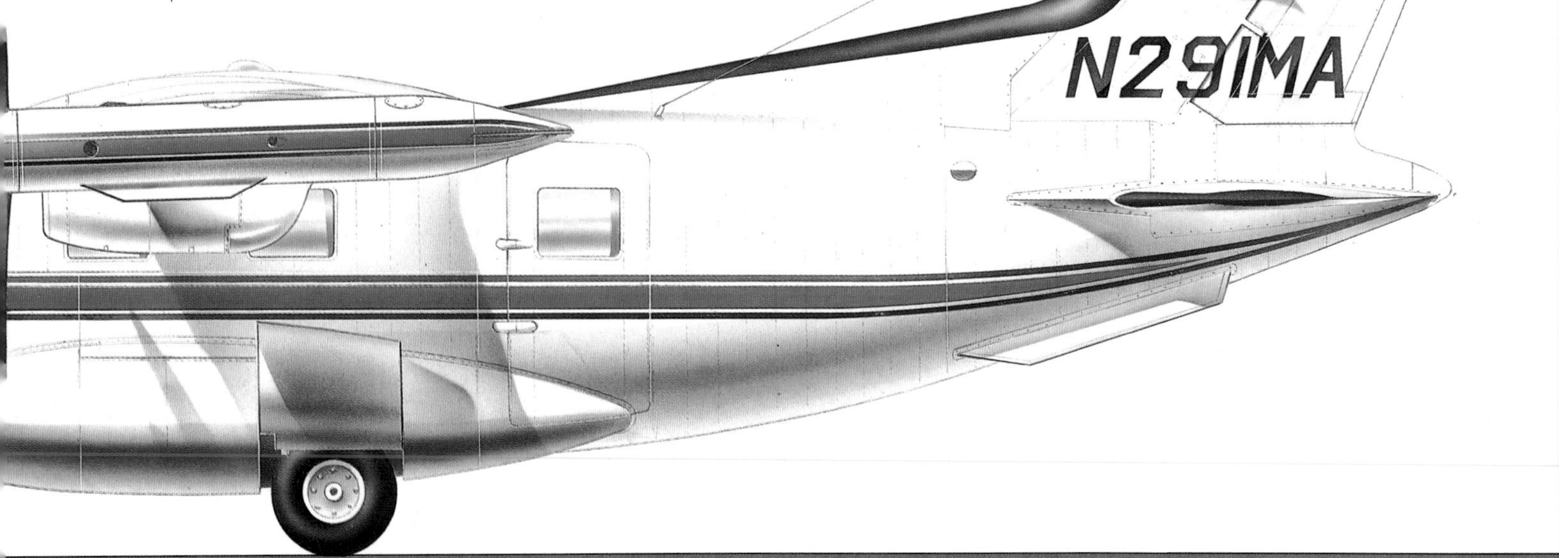

Mitsubishi recommenced aircraft manufacture in the 1950s with licence production of US types, but by the end of the decade had their own design for a twin-turboprop executive transport. The resulting MU-2 was built in considerable numbers in steadily advancing variants, culminating in the Marquise and Solitaire for the US market. All variants exhibit high cruising speed and turboprop economy.

Aero/Rockwell/Gulfstream Commander

The high-wing twin Commanders originated with Aero Design and Engineering, were bought by North American (later Rockwell) and finally resold to Gulfstream American. First came the 1952 five/seven-seat Commander 520, followed in 1954 by the Commander 560, and in 1955 by the Commander 560A and Commander 680 Super. In 1958 there came the four-seat Commander 500 (later Shrike Commander and then Shrike Commander Esquire), but there was greater interest in the larger aircraft, leading to the 1963 Grand Commander (later Courser Commander) and the 1964 turboprop-powered Turbo Commander (later Hawk Commander and then Turbo Commander 681, complemented by a Turbo Commander 690 and similar Commander 685 with piston engines). In 1980 the 690 was replaced by the Jetprop Commander 840 and Jetprop Commander 980 that led to Gulfstream's Commander Jetprop 840, 900, 980 and 1000 series.

Specification: North American (Rockwell) Hawk Commander 1/2+5/9-seat pressurised executive transport
Span: 14.22 m (49 ft 0.5 in)
Length: 13.52 m (44 ft 4.25 in)
Powerplant: 2×Garrett TPE-43BL, 451 kW (605 shp) each
Max T/O weight: 4264 kg (9,400 lb)
Cruising speed: 278 mph at optimum altitude
Range: 1,315 miles

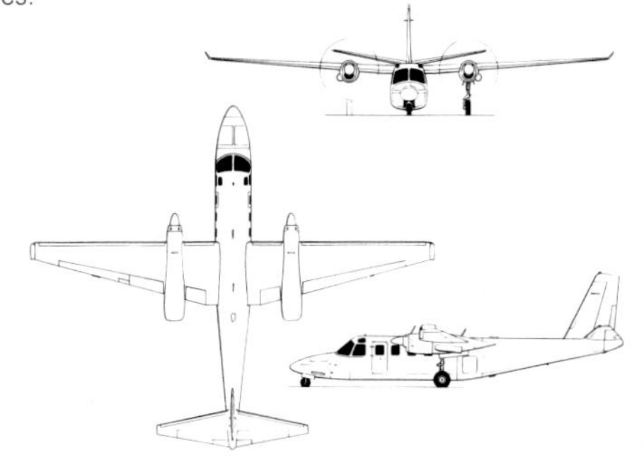

Cessna Model 414/421

The Model 421 first flew in October 1965, and was designed to supersede the Model 411 which it resembled in most features other than its Air Research pressurisation and air conditioning in a failsafe fuselage. Deliveries began in May 1967. In 1970 Cessna introduced the Model 421B with a longer nose for extra avionics and baggage volume, increased span and strengthened landing gear: this variant was delivered in Golden Eagle passenger and Executive Commuter forms, the latter a convertible 10-seat passenger/freight transport. In 1976 came the Model 421C in the same variants, but with a larger vertical tail and integral wing tankage rather than tiptanks. The Model 414 of 1968 combined the fuselage of the Model 421 with the wing of the Model 401, and led to improved Model 414 II, Model 414A, Chancellor II and Chancellor III versions with an increasing number of optional packages.

Specification: Cessna Model 421C Golden Eagle six/eight-seat pressurised executive transport
Span: 12.53 m (41 ft 1.5 in)
Length: 11.09 m (41 ft 4.5 in)
Powerplant: 2×Continental GTSIO-520-N, 280 kW (375 hp) each
Max T/O weight: 3379 kg (7,450 lb)
Cruising speed: 221 mph at 25,000 ft
Range: 1,710 miles

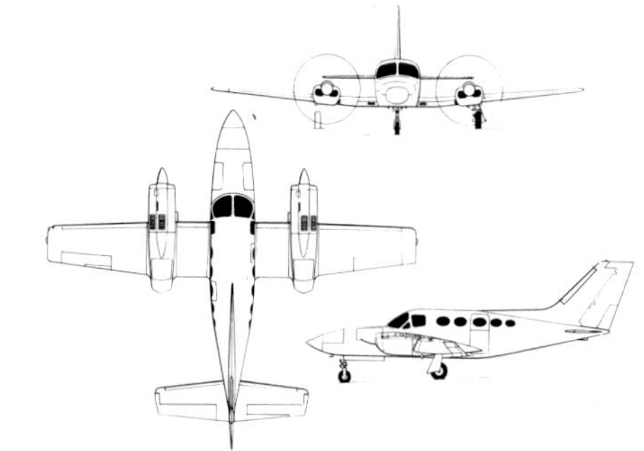

Cessna Model 404 Titan

The Model 404 may be considered the piston-engined equivalent to the turboprop-powered Model 441 Conquest, and shares with this later aeroplane the unusual feature, for a Cessna type, of a dihedral tailplane. The first Model 404 flew in February 1975 and deliveries began in October 1976. Customers were highly pleased with the type's operating economy, which offered an improvement of 30 per cent or more in ton/miles per gallon over the Model 402. The initial two variants were the Titan Ambassador passenger transport (including an executive version) and the Titan Courier convertible 10-passenger/freight transport. Ultimately seven variants were offered, the three in the Ambassador line being the basic Titan Ambassador and the more flexible Ambassador II and Ambassador III with factory-installed equipment and avionics packages.

Specification: Cessna Model 404 Titan Ambassador 1/2+8-seat pressurised executive transport
Span: 14.12 m (46 ft 4 in)
Length: 12.04 m (39 ft 6.25 in)
Powerplant: 2×Continental GTSIO-520-M, 280 kW (375 hp) each
Max T/O weight: 3810 kg (8,400 lb)
Cruising speed: 188 mph at 20,000 ft
Range: 2,119 miles

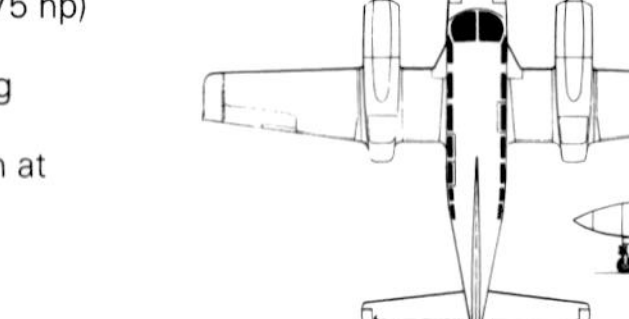

Piaggio P.180 Avanti

One of the most exciting executive transports to have appeared in recent years, the Avanti is superficially more conventional than the Starship, 1 but again makes extensive use of composites and has an unusual configuration. The type has a rear-mounted straight wing in the mid-position, and accommodates the two pusher engines: the other lifting surfaces are the straight canard foreplanes and the swept tailplane located at the top of the vertical tail. The combination of flapped canards and conventional tailplane makes for excellent field performance and very precise trimming, a fact that helps reduce cruise drag significantly, while the aft position of the wing leaves the cabin unobstructed. It is expected that the type will be certificated early in 1989, with deliveries of production aircraft beginning in the same year.

Specification: Piaggio P.180 Avanti 2+5/7-seat pressurised executive transport
Span: 13.84 m (45 ft 4.9 in)
Length: 14.17 m (46 ft 5.9 in)
Powerplant: 2×Pratt & Whitney PT6A-66, 634 kW (850 shp) each
Max T/O weight: 4770 kg (10,516 lb)
Cruising speed: 460 mph at optimum altitude
Range: 2,073 miles

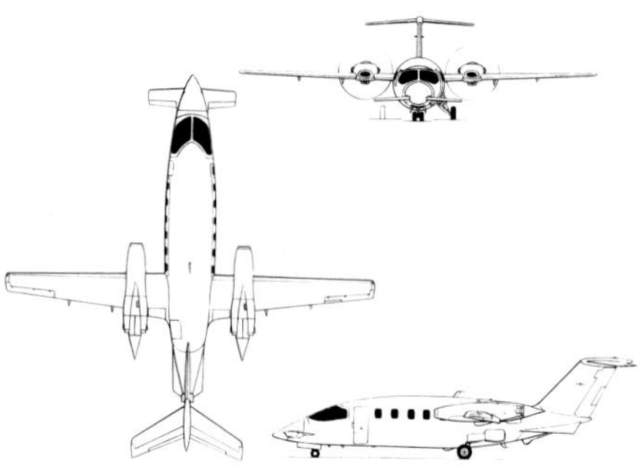

Fairchild (Swearingen) Merlin

Swearingen Aviation Corporation was taken over by Fairchild in 1979, but began the design of its Merlin IIA executive transport in 1964, marrying a new pressurised fuselage to the wing of the Queen Air and the landing gear of the Twin Bonanza. The first prototype flew in April 1965 and deliveries began in 1966. This initial version was powered by 410-kW (550-shp) Pratt & Whitney Canada PT6A-20 turboprops, while the Merlin IIB switched to 496-kW (665-shp) TPE331-1-151Gs. The following Merlin III had 626-kW (840-shp) TPE331-303Gs, a fuselage lengthened by 0.62 m (2 ft 0.5 in), and Swearingen-designed wings, landing gear and tail unit. The Merlin IV was essentially an executive version of the long-fuselage Metro 20-passenger commuterliner, while later variants were the 8/11-seat Merlin IIIC with 671-kW (900-shp) TPE331-10U-503Gs, and the 13/16-seat Merlin IVC.

Specification: Fairchild (Swearingen) Merlin IIIA 2+6/9-seat pressurised executive transport
Span: 14.10 m (46 ft 3 in)
Length: 12.85 m (42 ft 2 in)
Powerplant: 2×Garrett TPE331-3U-303G, 701 kW (904 hp) each
Max T/O weight: 5670 kg (12,500 lb)
Cruising speed: 325 mph at 16,000 ft
Range: 1,968 miles

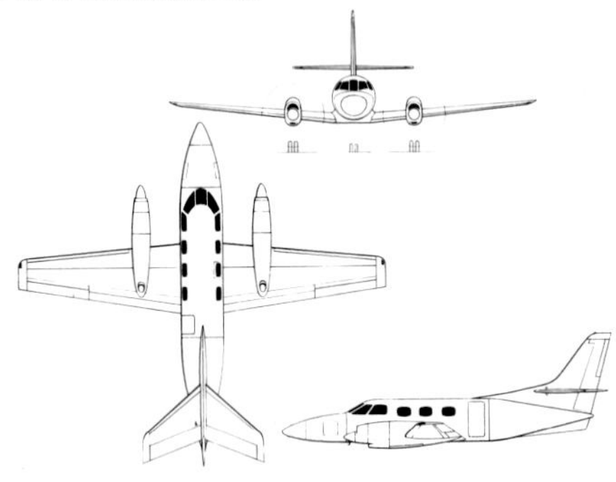

Piaggio P.166

Based conceptually on the P.136-L amphibian, the P.166 first flew in November 1957 and is particularly notable for its high-set gull wings and 254-kW (340-hp) Avco Lycoming GSO-480 pusher engines, the latter set in the angles of the wings. The type has a substantial fuselage accommodating the retractable tricycle landing gear and large high-set empennage, and among its attributes are good field performance and substantial range; the latter can be increased with the aid of detachable wingtip tanks. The initial P.166 was soon joined by the P.166B with fuel-injected engines, the P.166C with a redesigned central fuselage for a five-person cabin and main landing gear units that retract into lateral blisters, the P.166-BL2 with 283-kW (380-hp) IGSO-540-A1H engines and more fuel, and the definitive P.166-DL3 with an overall improvement in performance provided by a turboprop powerplant.

Specification: Piaggio P.166-DL3 1+5/9-seat pressurised executive transport
Span: 14.69 m (48 ft 2.5 in) over tiptanks
Length: 1.88 m (39 ft 0 in)
Powerplant: 2×Avco Lycoming LTP101-600, 447 kW (599 shp) each
Max T/O weight: 4300 kg (9,480 lb)
Cruising speed: 250 mph at 10,000 ft
Range: 1,264 miles

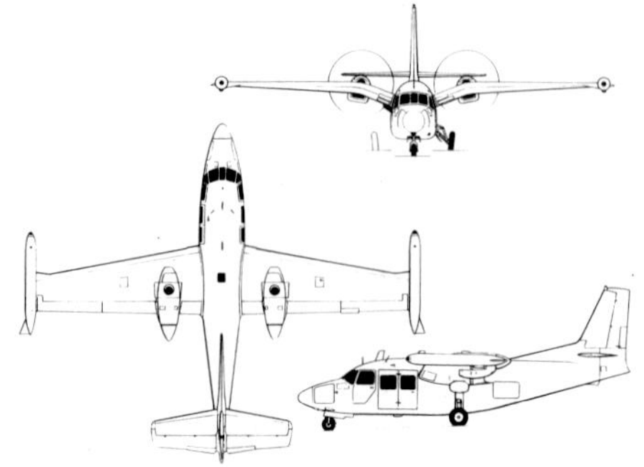

Saunders ST-27

Developed from the de Havilland DH.114 Heron 2 feederliners, powered by four piston engines, the ST-27 featured a stretched fuselage to increase passenger capacity and was powered by two PT6A turboprops. The prototype first flew in Manitoba, Canada on 28 May 1969. Thirteen conversions for customer airlines in Canada and Colombia followed. Shortage of used Heron airframes prompted plans to build the aircraft from scratch, and a prototype ST-27B was flown on 17 July 1974. This aircraft differed from the ST-27 in having increased fuel capacity, a larger fin and rudder, interior improvements and a maximum take-off weight of 6577-kg (14,500-lb). The first production standard ST-28 flew on 12 December 1975, but financial difficulties stopped production in 1976.

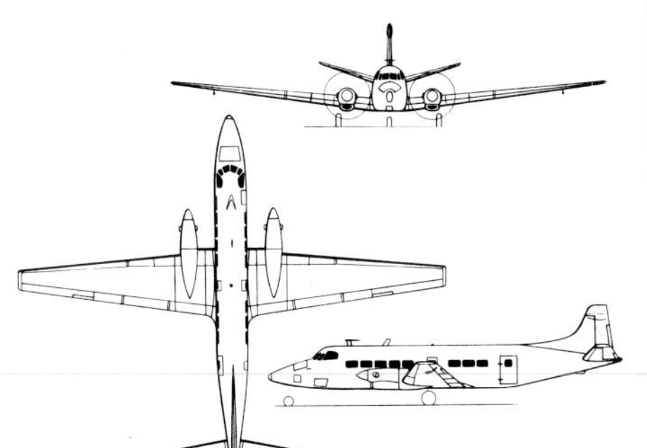

Specification: Saunders ST-27 feeder liners
Span: 21.79 m (71 ft 6 in)
Length: 18.24 m (59 ft 10 in)
Powerplant: 2×Pratt & Whitney Canada PT6A-34, 559-kW (750-shp) each
Payload: 23 passengers or 1912-kg (4,216-lb) of freight
Max T/O weight: 6123 kg (13,500 lb)
Cruising speed: 229 mph at 10,000 ft
Range with max payload: 817 miles

Shorts 330

Originally known as the SD3-30, the Shorts 330 was derived from the Skyvan STOL utility transport, employing that aircraft's outer wing panels and twin-finned tail unit mated to a longer fuselage with retractable tricycle undercarriage and accommodation for 30 passengers in an unpressurised cabin. The first prototype made its maiden flight from Belfast on 22 August 1974, a week after launch orders were received from Command Airways, New York and Canadian carrier Time Air, which operated the first Shorts 330 passenger service on 24 August 1976. The current model is the Shorts 330-200. A military tactical transport version designated Shorts 330-UTT and an all-freight Sherpa variant is also available. Eighteen Sherpas, designated C-23A, are in service with the USAF.

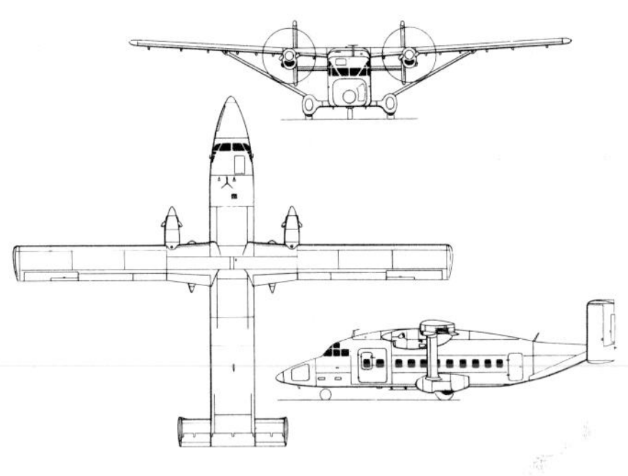

Specification: Shorts 330-200 commuterliner
Span: 22.76 m (74 ft 8 in)
Length: 17.69 m (58 ft 0.5 in)
Powerplant: 2×Pratt & Whitney Canada PT6A-45R, 893-kW (1,198-shp) each
Payload: 30 passengers or 2653-kg (5.850-lb) of freight
Max T/O weight: 10387 kg (22,900 lb)
Cruising speed: 219 mph at 10,000 ft
Range with max payload: 544 miles

Shorts 360

Shorts announced this stretched 36-seat development of the Model 330 on 10 July 1980, and the prototype first flew, six months ahead of schedule, on 1 June 1981. The Shorts 360 differs from the 330 in having a fuselage lengthened by 0.91 m (3 ft), a new low-drag rear fuselage with sweptback single ventral tail, strengthened outer wing panels and lift struts, and increased baggage capacity. The first production Shorts 360 entered commercial service with the US carrier Suburban Airlines on 1 December 1982. The current Shorts 360 Advanced was introduced in late 1985. The Shorts 360-300 is a further refined version featuring six-bladed propellers, new engine nacelles, cambered lift struts, interior improvements and enhanced 'hot and high' performance. First deliveries of this model were made to Philippine Airlines in March 1987.

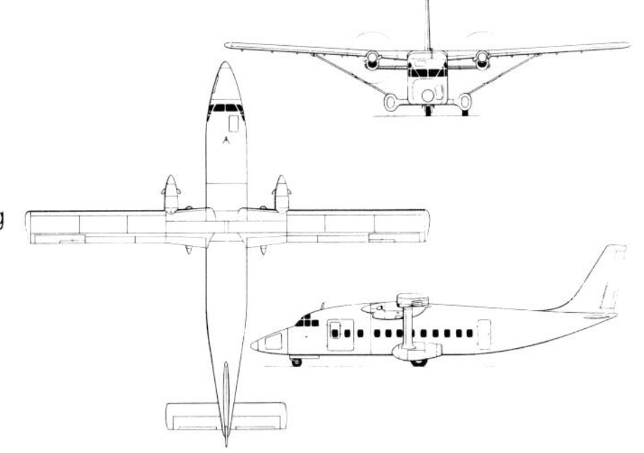

Specification: Shorts 360 commuterliner
Span: 22.81 m (74 ft 10 in)
Length: 21.59 m (70 ft 10 in)
Powerplant: 2×Pratt & Whitney Canada PT6A-65AR, 1062-kW (1,424-shp) each
Payload: 36 passengers or 3184-kg (7,020-lb) of freight
Max T/O weight: 11999 kg (26,453 lb)
Cruising speed: 244 mph at 10,000 ft
Range with max payload: 259 miles

Fairchild Metro

The Metro series of turboprop commuter aircraft was originally developed by the Swearingen company, which flew the first prototype on 26 August 1969. Early customers were Air Wisconsin and Mississippi Valley Airlines. A 12-seat corporate transport version, the Merlin III, first flew on 22 September 1970. Development was taken over by Fairchild Industries, which introduced the improved Metro II/Merlin IVA in 1975. These had larger cabin windows and structural changes and were powered by two 701-kW (940-shp) Garrett TPE331-3UW turboprops. The current Metro III differs from earlier models in having a 3.05-in (10-ft) increase in span, new engine cowlings, higher gross weight and more powerful TPE331-11U engines. All-cargo Expediter and corporate Merlin IVC versions are available.

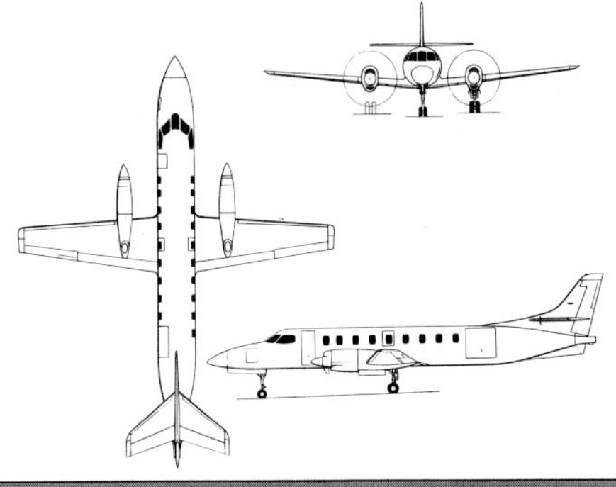

Specification: Fairchild Metro III commuterliner
Span: 17.37 m (57 ft 10 in)
Length: 18.09 m (59 ft 4.25 in)
Powerplant: 2×Garrett TPE331-11U, 820-kW (1,100-shp) each
Payload: 20 passengers or 2214-kg (4,880-lb) of freight
Max T/O weight: 72570 kg (16,000 lb)
Cruising speed: 320 mph at 12,000 ft
Range with max passengers: 1,000 miles

BAe Jetstream 31

Developed from the earlier Turboméca Astazou-engined Handley-Page HP.137 Jetstream, but with Garrett TPE331 turboprops driving new high-technology Dowty Rotol four-bladed propellers, the prototype Jetstream 31 first flew on 28 March 1980. The Jetstream 31 has achieved great popularity with commuter airline operators, particularly in the USA where it captured 60 per cent of its class market in 1987. The Jetstream 31 is offered in a variety of configurations for commuter, executive shuttle, corporate transport and special missions applications. Deliveries of the improved Jetstream Super 31 with 761-kW (1,020-shp) TPE331-12 engines will begin during 1988.

The Jetstream 31 was one of the great success stories of the Eighties and sold well, especially in North America. The Canadian operator uses the Jetstream primarily as a commercial executive jet.

Aérospatiale/Aeritalia ATR-42

Avions de Transport Régional was formed in November 1981 by Aérospatiale of France and Aeritalia of Italy to co-develop the ATR-42 twin turboprop regional transport aircraft. The first prototype made its maiden flight from Toulouse on 18 August 1984, the second on 31 October. A production standard aircraft was first flown on 30 April 1985. Manufacture involves Aeritalia (the fuselage, the tail and the hydraulic, air-conditioning and pressurisation systems) and Aérospatiale (the wings, flight deck, cabin and electrical systems, and the final assembly). Military freighter and search-and-rescue versions are planned. The 72-passenger ATR-72 launched in 1985 is expected to fly for the first time in September 1988.

Specification: ATR-42 regional transport
Span: 24.57 m (80 ft 7.5 in)
Length: 22.67 m (74 ft 4.5 in)
Powerplant: 2×Pratt & Whitney Canada PW120 or PW121, 1454 kW (1,950 shp) each
Payload: 42-50 passengers or 5227-kg (11,523-lb) of freight
Max T/O weight: 16700 kg (36,816 lb)
Cruising speed: 309 mph at 17,000 ft
Range with max passengers: 743 miles

Antonov An-28

Originally designated An-14M, the An-28 prototype was first flown in September 1969 as turboprop development of the piston-engined Antonov An-14, powered by two 604-kW (810-shp) Isotov TVD-850 engines. The An-28 was designed to replace An-2 biplanes on Aeroflot's short routes, where good STOL characteristics are required. The aircraft features a high aspect ratio wing with automatic leading-edge slats and a novel spoiler system which automatically deploys a spoiler on the upper surface of the opposite wing to a failed engine, preventing excessive yaw and wing drop. In February 1978 an agreement was signed with WSK-PZL Mielec of Poland for exclusive production of the An-28, the first of which flew on 22 July 1984. Production is expected to peak at 200 aircraft per year to meet Aeroflot's future needs.

Specification: PZL Mielec An-28 short-range light transport
Span: 22.07 m (72 ft 5 in)
Length: 13.10 m (72 ft 11.75 in)
Powerplant: 2×PZL Rzeszow TVD-10S, 716 kW (960 shp) each
Payload: 17 passengers or 2000 kg (4,409-lb) of freight
Max T/O weight: 6500 kg (14,330 lb)
Cruising speed: 217.5 mph at 9,845 ft
Range with max payload: 348 miles

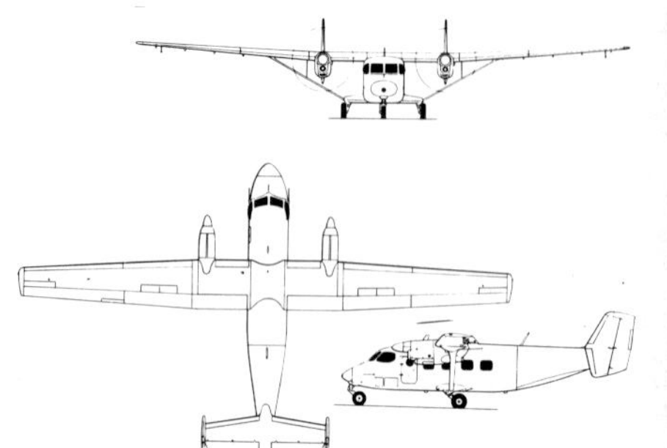

Specification: British Aerospace Jetstream 31 short-range commuterliner
Span: 15.85 m (52 ft 0 in)
Length: 14.37 m (74 ft 1.5 in)
Powerplant: 2×Garrett TPE331-10, 626-kW (840-shp) each
Payload: 19 passengers or 1805-kg (3,980-lb) of freight
Max T/O weight: 6950 kg (15,322 lb)
Cruising speed: 303 mph at 15,000 ft
Range with max payload: 776 miles

Beechcraft 99 Airliner

Development of the Beech 99 began during 1965, using the wings of the Beech 65/80 Queen Air executive aircraft mated to a longer fuselage with 15-seat cabin and two 410-kW (550-shp) Pratt & Whitney Canada PT6A-20 turboprops. The prototype first flew in December 1965, and the first customer delivery was made on 2 May 1968 to Commuter Airlines of Chicago. Subsequent 199, A99A and B99 models introduced 507-kW (680-shp) PT6A-27 engines, increased baggage capacity, an external luggage pannier and many internal improvements. Production was halted in 1975 but restarted in May 1979 with the improved Beech C99 Commuter, deliveries of which began on 30 July 1981, after which the aircraft's name was changed to C99 Airliner. Production of this aircraft was terminated during 1987.

Specification: Beechcraft C99 Airliner short-range commuterliner
Span: 13.98 m (45 ft 10.5 in)
Length: 13.58 m (44 ft 6.75 in)
Powerplant: 2×Pratt & Whitney Canada PT6A-36, (715-shp) each
Payload: 15 passengers or 1474-kg (3,250-lb) of freight
Max T/O weight: 5126 kg (11,300 lb)
Cruising speed: 282 mph at 8,000 ft
Range with max payload: 666 miles

Beechcraft 1900 Airliner

First flown on 3 September 1983, the Beechcraft 1900 is the largest model in the company's range, bearing some commonality with the Super King Air series of turboprop executive aircraft. FAA certification of the 1900 was granted. On 22 November 1983, since when the aircraft has entered service with 10 regional airlines in the USA. The company offers the 1900 in 19-seat Airliner and 12-seat Exec-Liner configurations. It is also in service with the US Air National Guard as the C-12J, and with the Egyptian air force which uses it for maritime surveillance and Elint missions.

Specification: Beechcraft 1900C airliner short-range commuterliner
Span: 16.6 m (54 ft 5.75 in)
Length: 16.2 m (53 ft 1.5 in)
Powerplant: 2×Pratt & Whitney Canada PT6A-65B, 820-kW (1,100-shp) each
Payload: 42-50 passengers or 2041-kg (4,500-lb) of freight
Max T/O weight: 7530 kg (16,600 lb)
Cruising speed: 295 mph at 8,000 ft
Range with max fuel: 915 miles

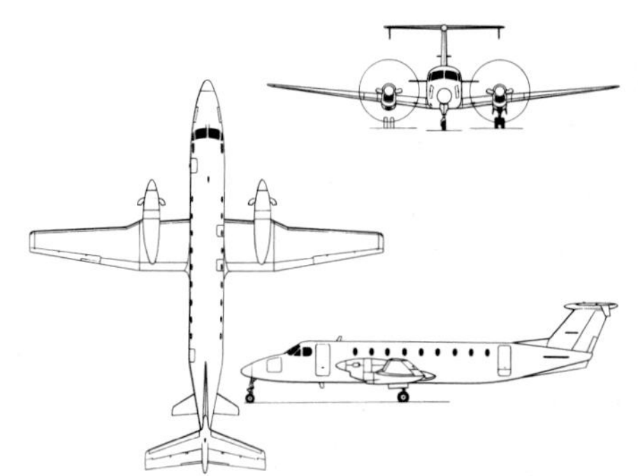

DHC-8 Dash 8

The DHC-8 Dash 8 was designed to fill the gap in de Havilland Canada's range of STOL airliners between the Twin Otter and Dash 7, and first flown on 20 June 1983. The initial production version, the Dash 8 Series 100, entered service on 19 December 1984. In commuter form it accommodates 36/39 passengers, while in corporate form it seats 17/24 passengers. A prototype of the 50/56-seat Dash 8 Series 300 is expected to enter commercial service in the course of 1988. In addition to serving commercial operators the Dash 8 is also used by the Canadian Armed Forces for navigation training and transport duties as the CT-142/CC-142. Two specially-equipped versions will be delivered to the USAF for use as airborne data-link relay aircraft.

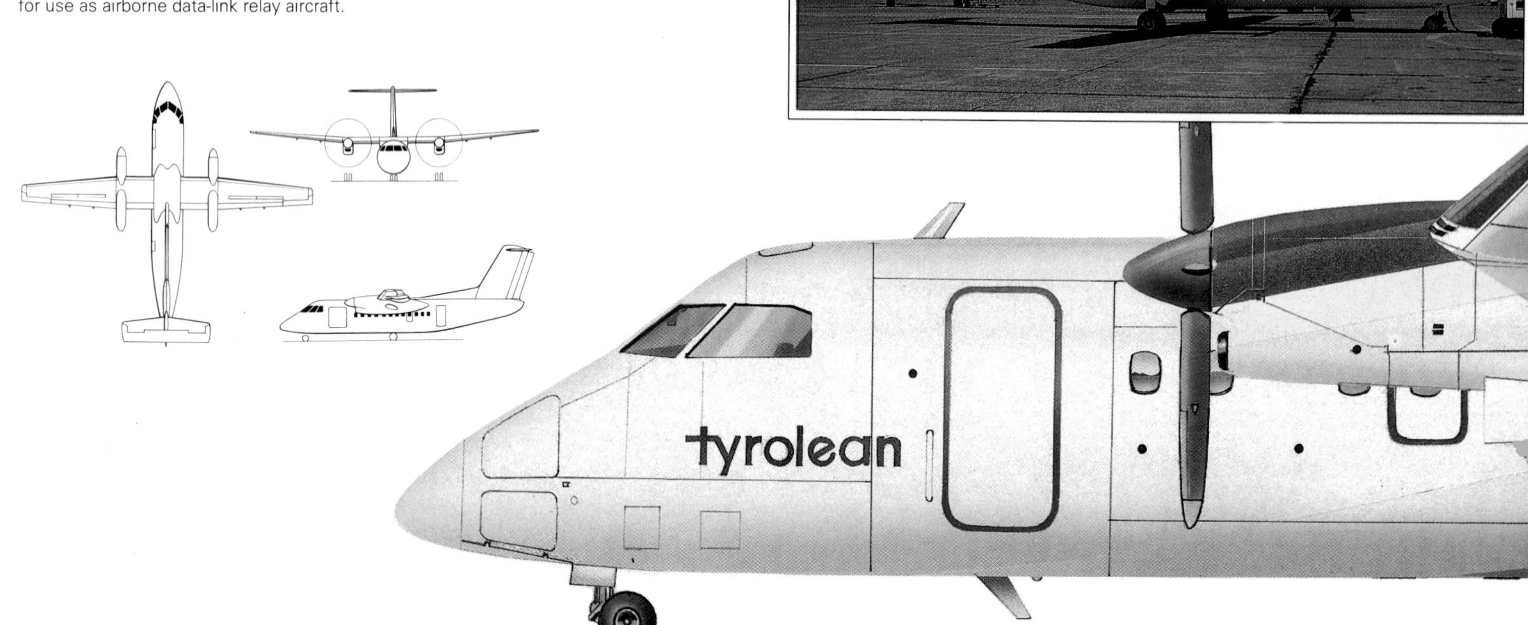

DHC-6 Twin Otter

Evolved from the single piston-engined Otter, the prototype 20-seat DHC-6 Twin Otter STOL transport first flew on 20 May 1965. Customer deliveries of the Twin Otter 100 with 432-kW (579-shp) Pratt & Whitney Canada PT6A-20 began in July 1968. The improved Twin Otter 200 with longer nose and increased baggage capacity appeared in April 1968, followed a year later by the current Twin Otter 300 which features a 454-kg (1,000-lb) increase in gross weight and more powerful engines. The Twin Otter has proved most versatile, operating on wheels, skis and floats in a variety of roles from commuter airline operations and cargo carrying to maritime surveillance, search and rescue and Polar exploration. Production is due to finish in 1988 after delivery of the 844th aircraft.

Specification: De Havilland Canada DHC-6 Twin Otter 300
Span: 19.81 m (65 ft 0 in)
Length: 15.77 m (51 ft 9 in)
Powerplant: 2×Pratt & Whitney Canada PT6A-27 462-kW (620-shp) each
Payload: 20 passengers or 1941-kg (4,280-lb)
Max T/O weight: 5670 kg (12,500 lb)
Cruising speed: 210 mph at 10,000 ft
Range with max payload: 115 miles

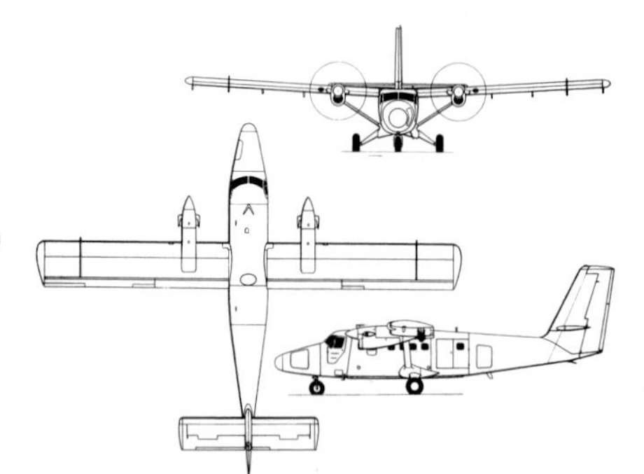

DHC-7 Dash 7

Development of the de Havilland Canada DHC-7 Dash 7 quiet STOL airliner began in 1972. The first pre-production prototype made its maiden flight on 27 March 1975, and the aircraft entered commercial service on 3 February 1978. The Dash 7 was designed to operate with full loads of 48-54 passengers from rough airfields as short as 610 m (2,000 ft), deriving its remarkable STOL performance from an aerodynamic lift system of double-slotted flaps and slow-turning four-bladed propellers. Production versions include the passenger-carrying Series 100, all-cargo Series 101, the higher gross weight Series 140 and the increased fuel capacity Series 151. The Dash 7 is currently the only aircraft approved for operation from London's dockland STOLport. Production of the Dash 7 is expected to be completed during 1988.

Specification: De Havilland Canada DHC-7 Dash 7 Series 100 transport
Span: 28.35 m (93 ft 0 in)
Length: 24.54 m (80 ft 6 in)
Powerplant: 4×Pratt & Whitney Canada PT6A-50, 835-kW (1,120-shp) each
Payload: 54 passengers or 5284-kg (11,650-lb) of freight
Max T/O weight: 19959 kg (44,000 lb)
Cruising speed: 261 mph at 15,000 ft
Range with max payload: 795 miles

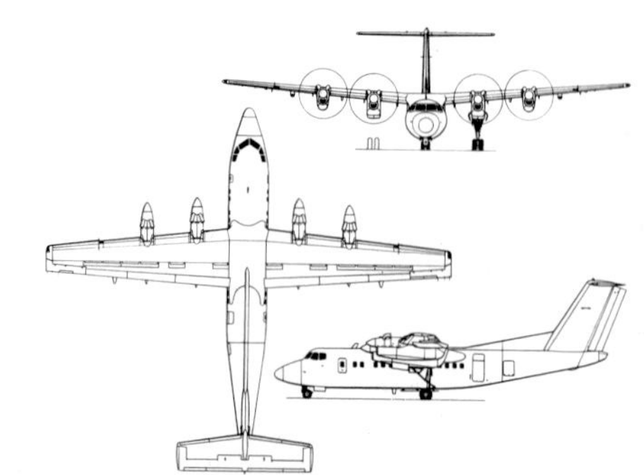

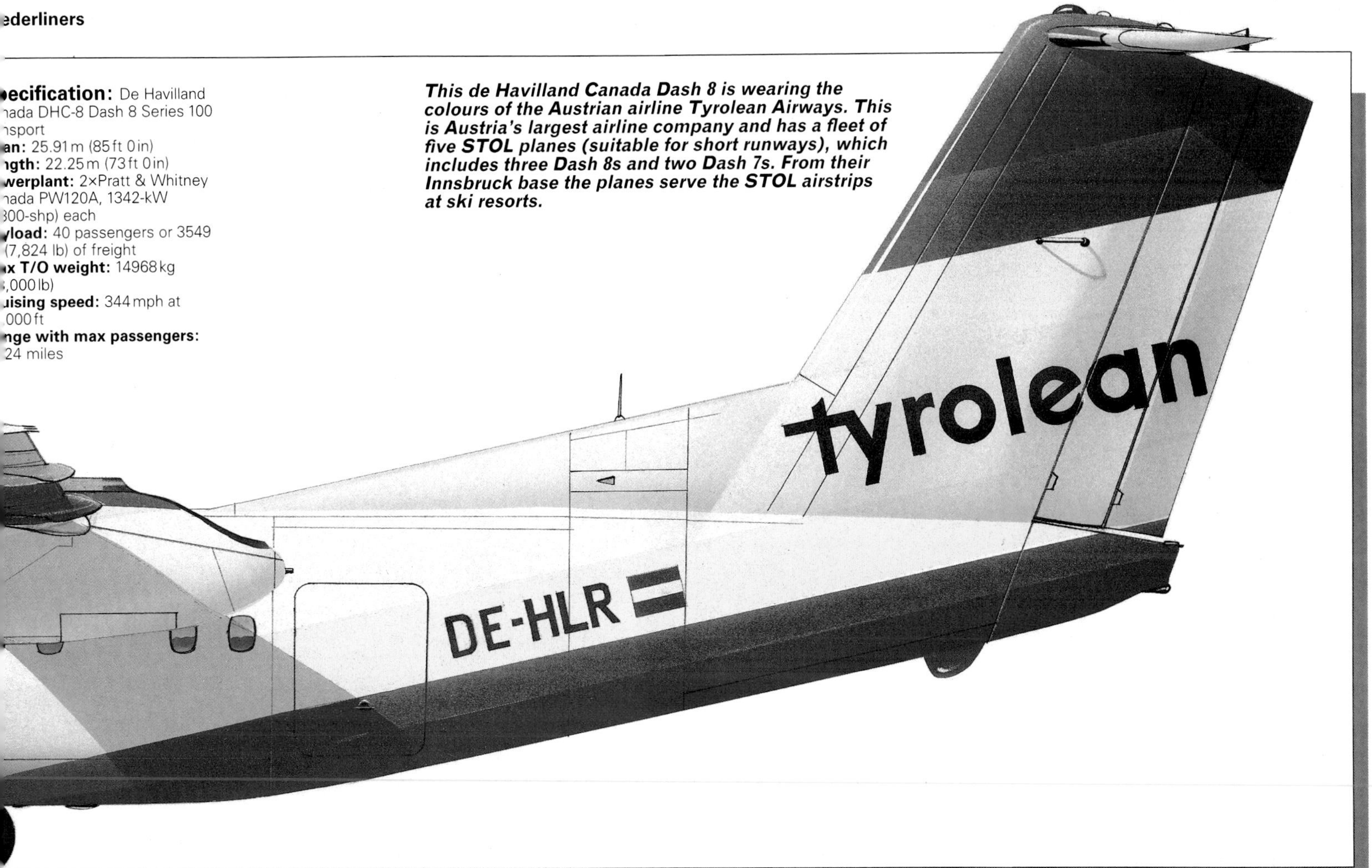

ecification: De Havilland
nada DHC-8 Dash 8 Series 100
nsport
an: 25.91 m (85 ft 0 in)
ngth: 22.25 m (73 ft 0 in)
werplant: 2×Pratt & Whitney
nada PW120A, 1342-kW
300-shp) each
yload: 40 passengers or 3549
(7,824 lb) of freight
x T/O weight: 14968 kg
,000 lb)
uising speed: 344 mph at
000 ft
nge with max passengers:
24 miles

This de Havilland Canada Dash 8 is wearing the colours of the Austrian airline Tyrolean Airways. This is Austria's largest airline company and has a fleet of five STOL planes (suitable for short runways), which includes three Dash 8s and two Dash 7s. From their Innsbruck base the planes serve the STOL airstrips at ski resorts.

Fokker F27 Friendship

The prototype F27 Friendship first flew on 24 November 1955. Production was by Fokker NV (Netherlands) and under licence by Fairchild Industries (USA). The first examples from each flew on 23 March and 15 April 1958 respectively. West Coast Airlines and Aer Lingus were the first commercial users. Significant variants included the Mk 100 with two Rolls-Royce Dart 514 turboprops; the Mk 200 with Dart 532-7s; the Mk 300 Combiplane with strengthened floor and cargo door; and the Mk 500 with a 1.5 m (4.92 ft) fuselage stretch. Apart from these, all variants had identical external dimensions and seating for 48. Fairchild introduced the long-fuselage FH-227 and FH-227B in 1965. Maritime patrol and F27M military transport versions were developed in the Netherlands. Production of the F227 ended with delivery of two aircraft to the Royal Thai navy in 1987.

Specification: Fokker F27-200
Friendship transport
Span: 29.00 m (95 ft 1.75 in)
Length: 23.56 m (77 ft 3.5 in)
Powerplant: 2×Rolls-Royce Dart
532-7R, 1681-kW (2,255-shp) each
Payload: 44 passengers or
4690-kg (10,340-lb) of freight
Max T/O weight: 20410 kg
(44,996 lb)
Cruising speed: 298 mph at
20,000 ft
Range with max payload: 1,286
miles

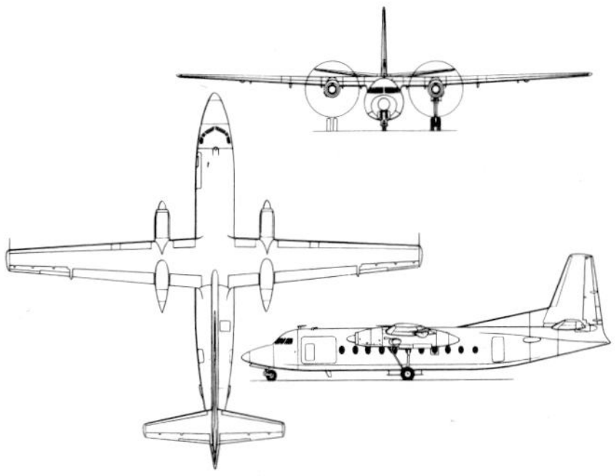

Saab 340

Developed jointly by Saab-Scania of Sweden and Fairchild Aircraft Corporation of the USA to meet both federal Aviation Administration and European Joint Airworthiness Requirements certicification standards, the pressurised Saab-Fairchild SF-340 was first flown in Sweden on 25 January 1983. Production SF-340A aircraft entered passenger service on 14 June 1984. In November 1985 Fairchild withdrew from the project. The aircraft is now known as the Saab 340A and is in service with commuter airlines in the USA, Australasia, Europe and South America. A corporate/executive transport version is also available.

Specification: Saab 340A
regional transportr
Span: 21.44 m (70 ft 4 in)
Length: 19.72 m (64 ft 8.5 in)
Powerplant: 2×General Electric
CT7-5A2, 1294-kW (1,735-shp) each
Payload: 35 passengers or
3440-kg (7,585-lb) of freight
Max T/O weight: 12371 kg
(27,275 lb)
Cruising speed: 316 mph at
15,000 ft
Range with max passengers: 932
miles

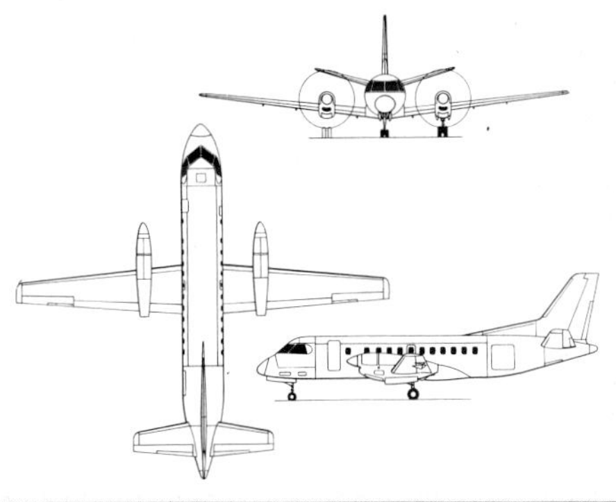

British Aerospace 125

The first versions of this very successful business jet had Bristol Siddeley Viper turbojets and standard six-seat cabins. The first modifications came when the then Hawker Siddeley company introduced the HS 125 Series 600. This variant had a stretched fuselage with executive accommodation for eight to 14 passengers (in high-density layouts), uprated Viper 601-22 engines, a taller fin and a dorsal fin fuel tank. In 1976 the first turbofan-engined version came out: the HS 125 Series 700, with Garrett TFE731 engines. The current production BAe 125 Series 800 has increased wing span, reprofiled outer airfoil section, curved windscreen, an extended dorsal fuel tank, and an 'all-glass' EFIS-equipped flight deck.

Canadair Challenger

In 1976 Canadair acquired rights to the LearStar 600 business jet designed by the late William P. Lear. After a major redesign the first prototype, renamed Challenger 600, flew on 8 November 1978, powered by two Avco Lycoming ALF 502L-2 turbofans of 3402kg (7,500lb) st each. The prototype Challenger 601 first flew on 10 April 1982. This version is powered by General Electric CF34-1A turbofans and features wingtip winglets, which are also retrofittable to the Model 600. In addition to serving with corporate owners, Challengers are also operated by the Canadian Armed Forces, Luftwaffe, Royal Malaysian Air Force and the Republic of China. The latest model Challenger 601-3A has uprated CF34-3A engines for better 'hot-and-high' performance and a fully integrated digital flight management system.

Specification: Canadair Challenger 601 executive transport
Span: 19.61m (64ft 4in)
Length: 20.85m (68ft 5in)
Powerplant: 2xGeneral Electric CF34-1A 4146kg (9,140lb) st each
Passenger capacity: up to 19
Max T/O weight: 19550kg (43,100lb)
Max speed: 529mph
Range: 3,960 miles

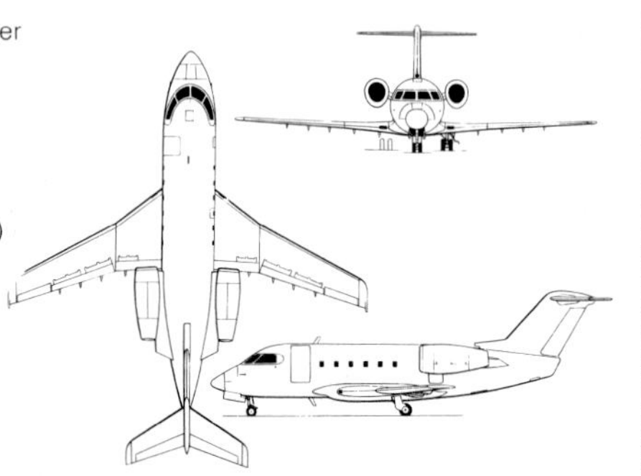

Cessna Citation I and II

In October 1968 the Cessna Aircraft Company announced plans to develop a six/eight-seat business jet: the Fanjet 500. Renamed Citation, the prototype flew on 15 September 1969. Unusual among business jets it had an unswept wing and relatively unsophisticated systems. The improved Model 501 Citation I, introduced in December 1976, featured uprated JT15D-1A turbofans and increased wingspan. The Model 550 Citation II had a 1.14m (45in) fuselage stretch, an increase in wingspan and JT15D-4 engines, and is produced alongside the improved Citation S/II, which has a new wing airfoil section and numerous refinements. Fifteen Citation S/IIs serve as naval flight officer trainers with the US Navy under the designation T-47A.

Specification: Cessna Citation S/II executive transport
Span: 15.91m (52ft 2.5in)
Length: 14.39m (47ft 2.5in)
Powerplant: 2xPratt & Whitney Canada JT15D-4B, 1134kg (2,500lb) st each
Passenger capacity: 7-10
Max T/O weight: 6849kg (15,100lb)
Max speed: Mach 0.721
Range: 2,300 miles

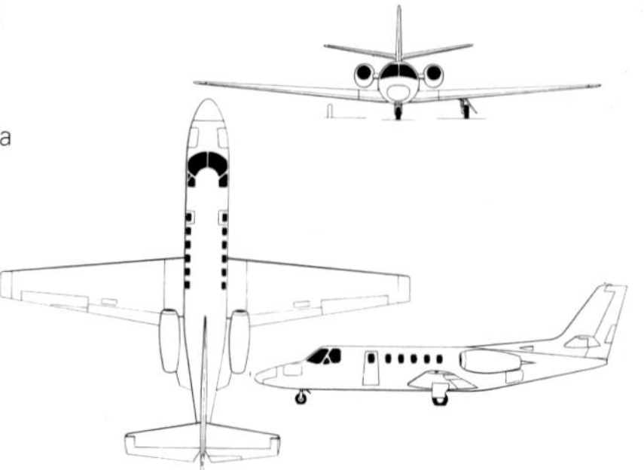

Specification: BAe 125-800 executive transport
Span: 15.66m (51ft 45in)
Length: 15.59m (51ft 2in)
Powerplant: 2xGarrett TFE731-5R, 1950kg (4,300lb) st each
Passenger capacity: 8-14
Max T/O weight: 12428kg (27,400lb)
Max speed: Mach 0.87
Range: 3,455 miles

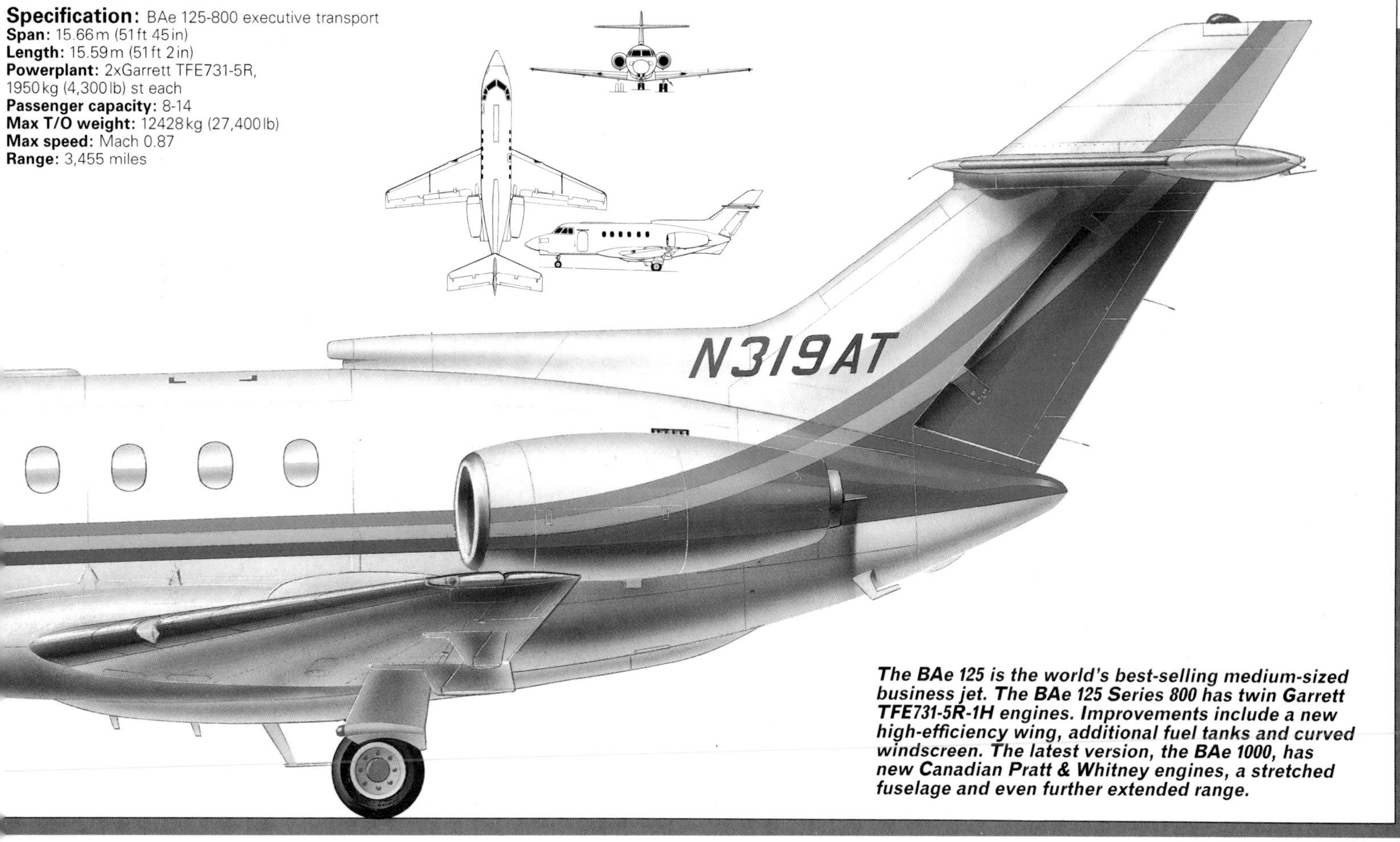

The BAe 125 is the world's best-selling medium-sized business jet. The BAe 125 Series 800 has twin Garrett TFE731-5R-1H engines. Improvements include a new high-efficiency wing, additional fuel tanks and curved windscreen. The latest version, the BAe 1000, has new Canadian Pratt & Whitney engines, a stretched fuselage and even further extended range.

Cessna Citation III

Though it shares the same name, the Cessna 650 Citation III has little in common with the straight-wing Citation I/II business jets. Designed to meet demand for a high-speed medium-size corporate transport business jet with intercontinental range, the prototype Citation III first flew on 30 May 1979. The aircraft features a swept wing of NASA-developed supercritical section, a swept T-tail and a circular-section fuselage providing an 8/11 seat pressurised cabin with stand-up headroom. FAA certification was obtained on 30 April 1982, with customer deliveries beginning in the following spring.

Specification: Cessna Citation III corporate transport
Span: 16.31m (53ft 6in)
Length: 16.90m (55ft 5.5in)
Powerplant: 2xGarrett TFE731-3B, 1656kg (3,650lb) st each
Passenger capacity: 8-15
Max T/O weight: 9979kg (22,000lb)
Max speed: Mach 0.851
Range: 2,700 miles

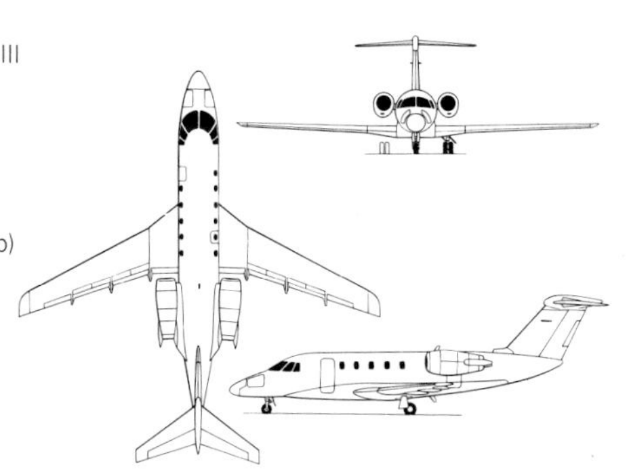

Dassault Falcon 10/100

First flown on 1 December 1970, the prototype Dassault Falcon 10 (Mystère 10) was originally known as the Minifalcon, being essentially a scaled-down version of the Falcon 20 with less-powerful General Electric CJ610 turbofans. Production versions are powered by Garrett TFE731 turbofans, the first such aircraft making its maiden flight on 30 April 1973 and customer deliveries beginning in November of that year. The current production Falcon 100 is externally similar but features an increase in maximum take-off weight, an additional cabin window on the starboard side, extended rear baggage compartment and a Collins EFIS CRT-based flight deck. A Falcon 10 is being test flown with an experimental wing constructed from carbon fibre composite materials.

Specification: Dassault-Breguet Falcon 100 executive transport
Span: 13.08m (42ft 11in)
Length: 13.87m (45ft 6in)
Powerplant: 2xGarrett TFE731-2, 1465kg (3,230lb) st each
Passenger capacity: 6-8
Max T/O weight: 8754kg (19,300lb)
Max speed: Mach 0.87
Range: 2,165 miles

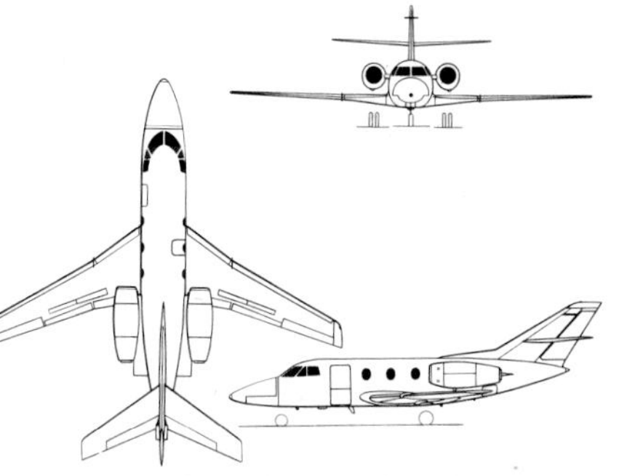

Learjet 55/56

Development of this enlarged Learjet was announced in 1977. It had new wing design, lacking the familiar Learjet tiptanks but incorporating NASA-developed Whitcomb winglets, originally used on the Learjet 28/29 Longhorn, few of which were manufactured. The prototype of the Learjet 50 series first flew on 19 April 1979 and introduced a fuselage of greater depth, providing improved cabin space and headroom. Three production versions were announced, all essentially similar save for weights and range. The Learjet 55B, also produced in two long-range versions, has an EFIS-equipped flight deck. The Learjet 55C, to be introduced during 1988, has ventral Delta-Fins conferring handling performance improvements.

Dassault Falcon 20/200

The prototype Mystère 20 first flew on 4 May 1963, and was powered by two Pratt & Whitney JT12A-8 turbojets, replaced on production aircraft by General Electric CF700 turbofans. Successive improvements in fuel capacity and engine power rating were introduced with the Falcon 20C, 20D and 20E models. The Falcon 20F (1977-83), featured additional fuel capacity and improvements to the flaps and leading-edge high-lift devices. The current production Falcon 200 was introduced in 1981 as the Falcon 20H. It has advanced EFIS avionics, increased fuselage fuel tank capacity, redesigned wing root fairings, an automatic wing slat-extension system and Garrett ATF-3-6A-4C turbofans, which also power the Falcon 20G version in service with the US Coast Guard as the HU-25A Guardian.

Specification: Dassault-Breguet Falcon 200 executive transport
Span: 16.32m (53ft 6.5in)
Length: 15.50m (51ft 0in)
Powerplant: 2xGarrett ATF3-6A, 2359kg (5,200lb) st each
Passenger capacity: 8-12
Max T/O weight: 19515kg (32,000lb)
Max speed: Mach 0.865
Range: 2,880 miles

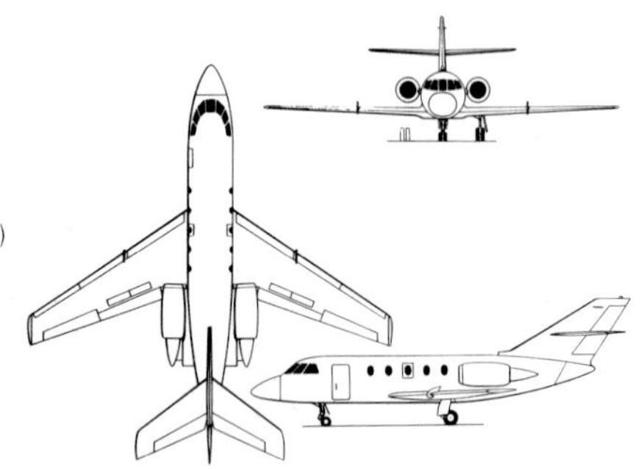

Dassault Falcon 50/900

The Falcon 50 was launched in May 1974 as a long-range three-engined business jet. It has the cabin cross-section and passenger capacity of the Falcon 20, but is otherwise an entirely new design, featuring a stretched fuselage to provide greater fuel and baggage capacity, and new wing and tail surfaces. The prototype first flew on 7 November 1976, and after a redesign of its wing, resumed testing on 6 May 1977. Two other prototypes and a demonstrator were also built. The Falcon 900 is an intercontinental-range aircraft of similar configuration to the Falcon 50, but larger to seat 19 passengers and is powered by three Garrett TFE731-5A turbofans of 2041kg (4,500lb) st each.

Specification: Dassault Falcon 50 executive/corporate transport
Span: 18.86m (61ft 10.5in)
Length: 18.50m (60ft 8.5in)
Powerplant: 3xGarrett TFE731-3, 1678kg (3,700lb) st each
Passenger capacity: 8-12
Max T/O weight: 18497kg (40,780lb)
Max speed: Mach 0.86
Range: 4,030 miles

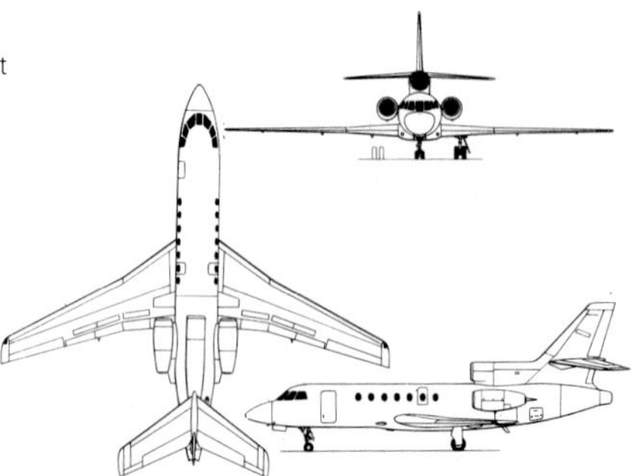

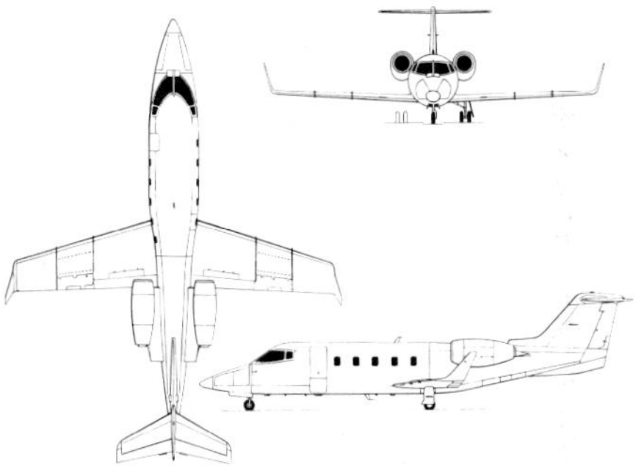

Specification: Learjet 55B executive transport
Span: 13.34 m (34 ft 9 in)
Length: 16.79 m (55 ft 1 in)
Powerplant: 2xGarrett TFE731-3, 1678 kg (3,700 lb) st each
Passenger capacity: 4-8
Max T/O weight: 9752 kg (21,500 lb)
Max speed: 549 mph
Range: 2,590 miles

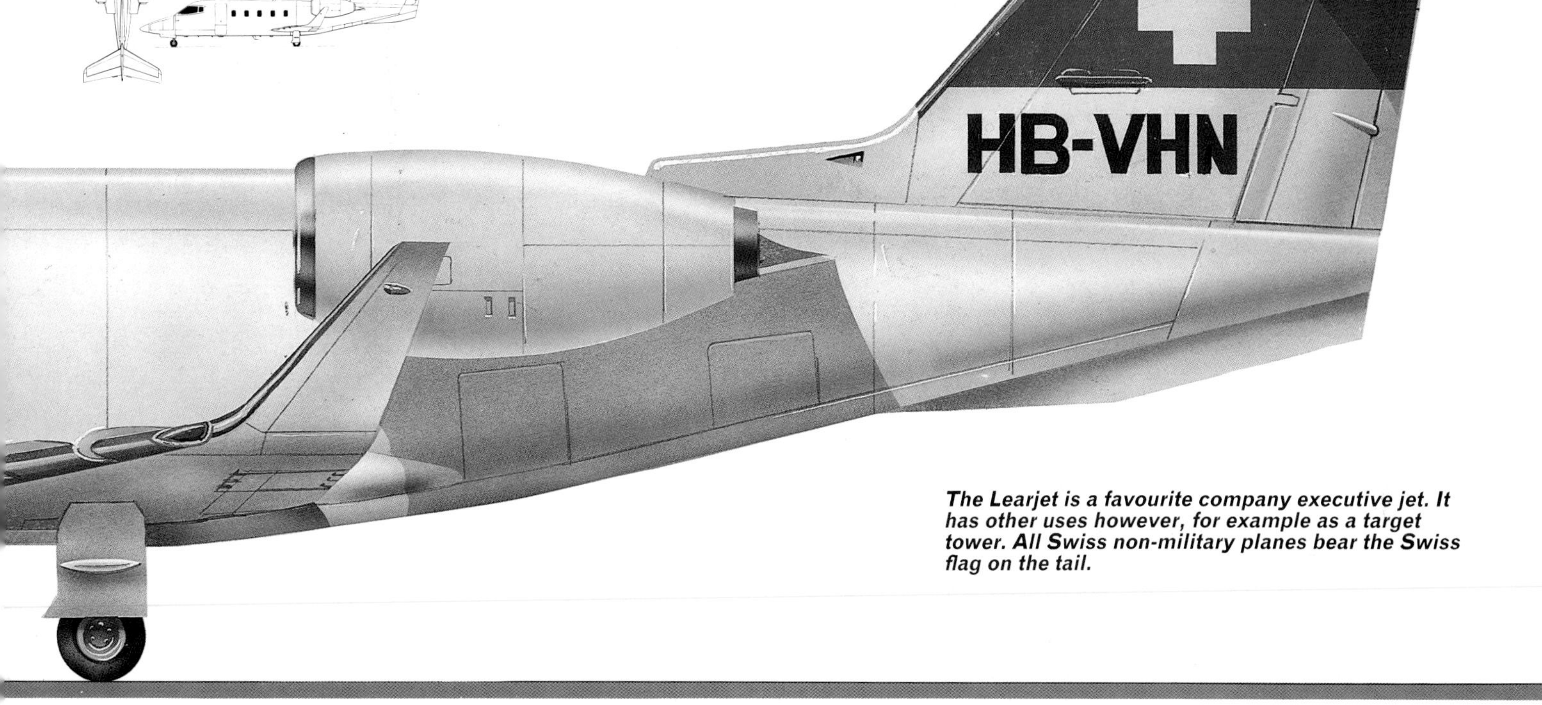

The Learjet is a favourite company executive jet. It has other uses however, for example as a target tower. All Swiss non-military planes bear the Swiss flag on the tail.

Gulfstream II, III and IV

Grumman Aircraft Corporation began development of the twin-jet Gulfstream II in May 1965. The first production model flew on 2 October 1966. It was powered by two 5171 kg (11,400 lb) st Rolls-Royce Spey Mk 511-8 turbofans and seated 10-19 passengers. In 1978 wingtip fuel tanks became available on the Gulfstream IITT, extending range by 14 per cent. In September 1978, Grumman sold the rights to Gulfstream American, who developed the Gulfstream III, with a stretched fuselage, revised nose profile, new supercritical wing with Whitcomb winglets and increased fuel capacity. The latest Gulfstream IV has a redesigned wing, longer fuselage, an all-digital flight deck and fuel-efficient Rolls-Royce Tay turbofans.

Specification: Gulfstream IV corporate transport
Span: 23.72 m (77 ft 10 in)
Length: 26.92 m (88 ft 4 in)
Powerplant: 2xRolls-Royce Tay Mk 610-8, 5634 kg (12,420 lb) st each
Passenger capacity: 10-19
Max T/O weight: 32522 kg (71,700 lb)
Max speed: Mach 0.88
Range: 4,950 miles

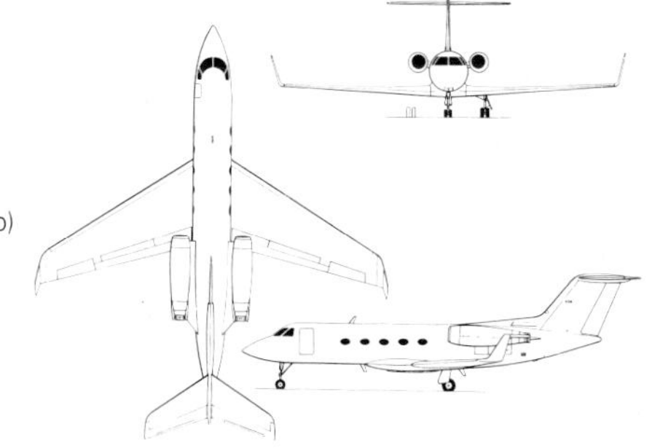

IAI Westwind

In 1968 Israeli Aircraft Industries took over production of the US-designed seven-passenger Aero Commander 1121 Jet Commander business jet from Rockwell International, renaming the General Electric CJ610 turbojet-engined aircraft the Commodore Jet. New production deliveries continued from Israel, where the IAI-developed Model 1123 Westwind was first flown on 28 September 1970. This featured a lengthened fuselage, uprated CJ610-9 engines and wingtip fuel tanks. It was superseded in 1975 by the Model 1124 Westwind I which was powered by two Garrett AiResearch TFE731-3 turbofans. The current production version is the Model 1124A Westwind II which first flew on 11 December 1979. It features a new Sigma wing airfoil section, NASA winglets and improvements in hot-and-high take-off performance, range and fuel economy.

Specification: IAI Westwind II executive/corporate transport
Span: 13.65 m (44 ft 9.5 in)
Length: 15.93 m (52 ft 3 in)
Powerplant: 2xGarrett TFE731-3, 1678 kg (3,700 lb) st each
Passenger capacity: 7-10
Max T/O weight: 10660 kg (23,500 lb)
Max speed: Mach 0.80
Range: 3,340 miles

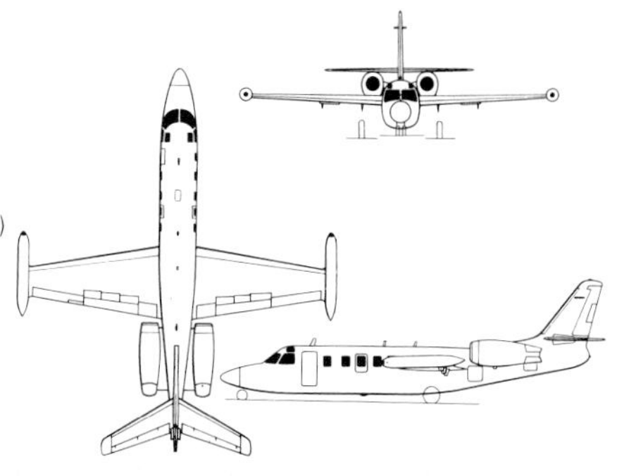

Learjet 20 and 30 series

William P. Lear began development of the original Lear Jet in 1959. The prototype first flew on 7 October 1963 and was the first true personal jet, offering comfortable accommodation combined with fighter-like performance. Deliveries of the General Electric CJ610-1 turbojet-powered Learjet 23 began in late 1964. Various improvements and refinements were incorporated in the Learjet 24D, which was subsequently developed by the Gates Learjet Corporation that acquired the Lear company in 1970. The Learjet 25 featured a 1.27 m (50 in) fuselage stretch, increasing standard passenger capacity to eight. The current production Learjet 35A and 36A were developed from the Model 25, with a 0.33 m (13 in) increase in fuselage length and a 2 ft extension to each wingtip, with Garrett TFE731 turbofan powerplants. The prototype, then known as the Model 26, first flew on 4 January 1973. The most recently announced development is the Learjet 31, with no tiptanks, but with winglets and ventral Delta-Fin strakes to enhance stability.

Specification: Learjet 35A executive transport
Span: 12.04 m (39 ft 6 in)
Length: 14.83 m (48 ft 8 in)
Powerplant: 2xGarrett TFE731-2, 1588 kg (3,500 lb) st each
Passenger capacity: 4-6
Max T/O weight: 8301 kg (18,300 lb)
Max speed: 542 mph
Range: 2,590 miles

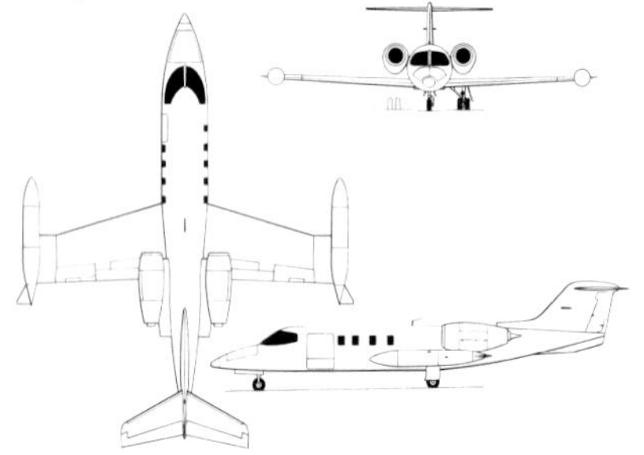

Lockheed JetStar

Development of the Lockheed Model 1329 JetStar began in 1956 to meet a US Air Force requirement. Two prototypes were each powered by two British-made Bristol Siddeley Orpheus turbojets of 2200 kg (4,850 lb) st each, but a four-engine configuration using 1089 kg (2,400 lb) st Pratt & Whitney JT12A-6s was adopted for the first production aircraft, which flew on 2 July 1960. The JetStar 8 with 1497 kg (3,300 lb) st JT12A-8 engines was introduced after 80 of the earlier JetStar 6s had been built. In 1973 the AiResearch Aviation Company began a modification programme which involved replacing the JT12A turbojets with four Garrett AiResearch TFE731-1 turbofans offering greater fuel economy and much reduced noise levels. Customer interest in the AiResearch JetStar 731 prompted Lockheed to restart production of a similarly-powered JetStar II, which also featured aerodynamic and systems refinements. The first JetStar II flew on 18 August 1976, and the 40th and last was delivered in 1980.

Specification: Lockheed JetStar II executive/corporate transport
Span: 16.59 m (54 ft 5 in)
Length: 18.41 m (60 ft 5 in)
Powerplant: 4xGarrett TFE731-3, 1678 kg (3,700 lb) st each
Passenger capacity: 6-12
Max T/O weight: 20185 kg (44,500 lb)
Max speed: 547 mph
Range: 3,190 miles

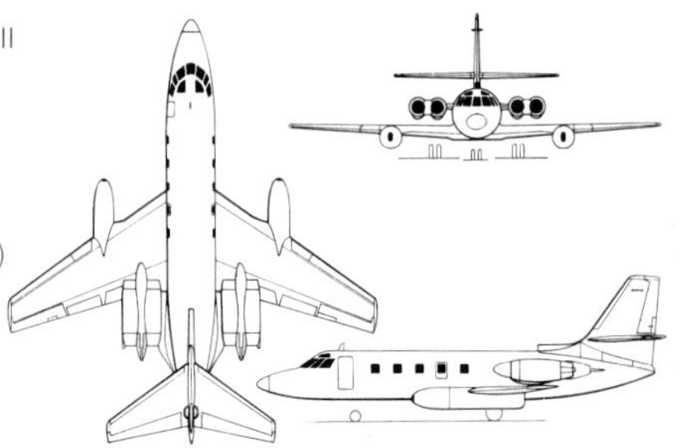

Mitsubishi Diamond

Mitsubishi Heavy Industries of Japan first flew the prototype of the MU-300 light business jet on 29 August 1978, subsequently shipping this and another aircraft for certification in the USA, where production Diamond Is were to be assembled from Japanese-manufactured components by Mitsubishi in San Angelo, Texas. Deliveries commenced in May 1983. The Diamond IA delivered from January 1984 incorporated uprated JT15D-4D engines for improved 'hot-and-high' performance, and higher operating weights. Further improvements were featured in the Diamond II which first flew on 20 June 1984. In 1985 Beech Aircraft acquired all rights to this aircraft, now known as the Beech Model 400 Beechjet. The first, assembled from Japanese-manufactured components, was delivered in June 1986.

Specification: Beechjet 400 executive transport
Span: 13.26 m (43 ft 6 in)
Length: 14.76 m (48 ft 5 in)
Powerplant: 2xPratt & Whitney Canada JT15D-5, 1315 kg (2,900 lb) st each
Passenger capacity: 7
Max T/O weight: 7158 kg (15,780 lb)
Max speed: 531 mph
Range: 2,190 miles

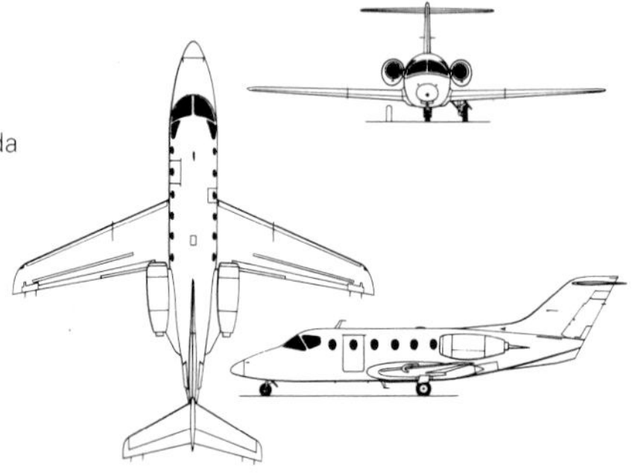

Rockwell Sabreliner Series

Like the Lockheed JetStar, the North American Sabreliner was developed to meet a USAF requirement, and the prototype first flew on 16 September 1958. Initial commercial models were similar to the military T-39. The first civil version was the Sabreliner 40, powered by two 1361 kg (3,000 lb) st Pratt & Whitney JT12A-6A turbojets and seating 7-9 passengers. The Sabreliner 60 featured a fuselage 0.965 m (38 in) longer to accommodate 10 passengers, and was powered by uprated JT12A-8A engines. The Sabreliner 75 featured a deeper fuselage with square cabin windows. CF700-2D turbofans were installed on the improved Sabreliner 75A which appeared in 1973. The Sabreliner 65 with a new supercritical wing and TFE731 engines was first flown on 29 June 1977 and was the last model produced by Rockwell, who sold the rights to the Sabreliner Corporation in 1983. Plans for new versions have been announced.

Specification: Rockwell Sabreliner 75A executive/corporate transport
Span: 13.61 m (44 ft 8 in)
Length: 14.38 m (47 ft 2 in)
Powerplant: 2xGeneral Electric CF700-2D, 2041 kg (4,500 lb) st each
Passenger capacity: up to 10
Max T/O weight: 10433 kg (23,000 lb)
Max speed: 563 mph
Range: 1,970 miles

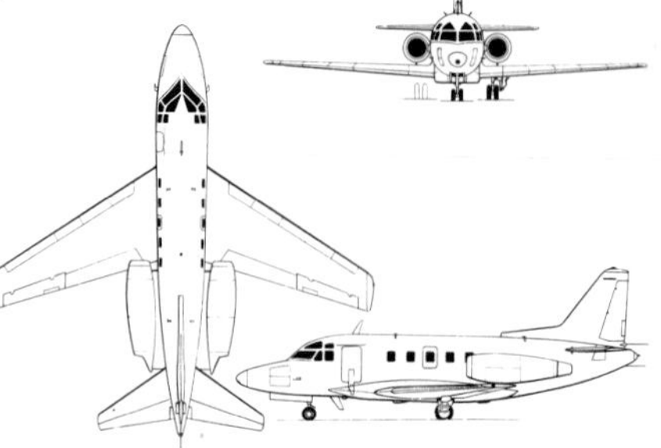

Douglas DC-8

The DC-8 was announced in 1955 and flown in May 1958. This was later than the rival Boeing 707, but sales were pursued with options such as variable weights and powerplants. The DC-8 Srs 10 had JT3C turbojets, and was followed by the Srs 20 with JT4As for enhanced field performance, the long-range Srs 30 with JT4As, the Srs 40 with Rolls-Royce Conway turbofans and the Srs 50 with JT3D turbofans. In 1965 there appeared the Super 60 variant with fuselage length options: the Super 61 stretched by 11.18 m (36ft 8in) for 259 passengers, and the Super 62 stretched by 2.03m (6ft 8in) for 189. The Super 62 also introduced a new wing, and the Super 63 had the fuselage of the Super 61 with the wing of the Super 62. There were freighter and convertible freighter variants, and the Super 60 series can be retrofitted with the CFM56 turbofan as the Super 70 series. Production totalled 555.

Specification: Douglas DC-8 Series 50 long-range jetliner
Span: 43.41m (142ft 5in)
Length: 45.87m (150ft 6in)
Powerplant: 4×Pratt & Whitney JT8D-1, 7718kg (17,000lb) st each
Payload: 179 passengers or 15586kg (34,360lb) of freight
Max T/O weight: 147420kg (325,000lb)
Cruising speed: 580 mph at 30,000ft
Operational range: 7,000 miles with maximum payload

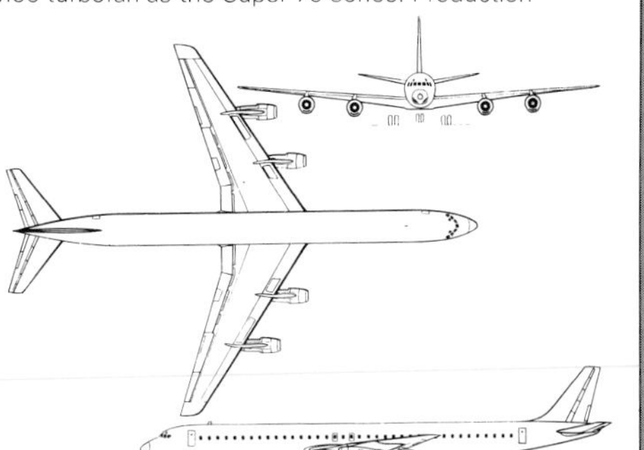

Tupolev Tu-124

Though it resembles the Tu-104 closely, the Tu-124 was a completely different aeroplane with only the most limited of commonality. The design originated in 1958, to meet an Aeroflot requirement for a smaller airliner capable of operation from unprepared airstrips. This placed great emphasis on good field performance (provided by double-slotted flaps and wing-mounted airbrake/spoiler/lift-dumper surfaces) and on sturdy landing gear, and when the prototype flew in June 1960 it was powered by purpose-designed turbofans. Production totalled about 150 up to 1966, and the initial version could seat 44 passengers when it entered service in 1962. By 1963 the standard model was the Tu-124B with seating for 56. The only other variants were the Tu-124K and Tu-124K2 VIP aircraft: the Tu-124K seated 4+8+24 in its three cabins, and the Tu-124K2 seated 22.

Specification: Tupolev Tu-124 short-range jetliner
Span: 25.55m (83ft 9.5in)
Length: 30.58m (100ft 4in)
Powerplant: 2×Soloviev D-20P, 5400kg (11,905lb) st each
Payload: 56 passengers or 6000kg (13,228lb) of freight
Max T/O weight: 38000kg (83,774lb)
Cruising speed: 540 mph at optimum altitude
Operational range: 760 miles with maximum payload

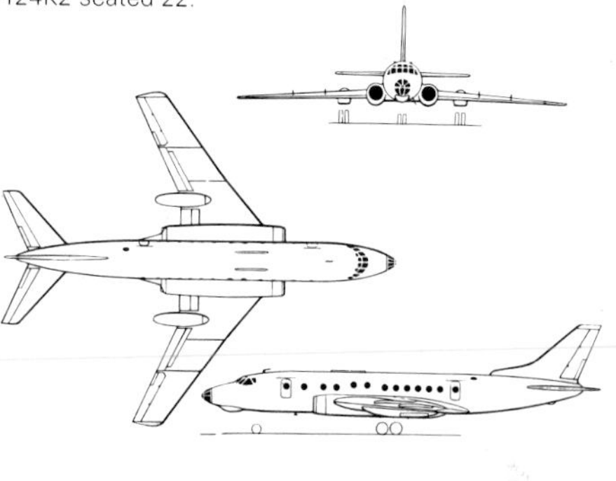

Tupolev Tu-134

The Tu-124's lack of operating economy and austere accommodation made export sales all but impossible. To remedy this fact Tupolev was instructed to produce a new airliner comparable with the Tu-124, but offering economy and comfort comparable to those of Western airliners. The resultant design was first designated Tu-124A as it used basically the same wings, fuselage and landing gear as the Tu-124 married to the fashionable rear engine/T-tail combination, but had been redesignated Tu-134 by the time it first flew, in about 1963. The type entered service in 1967 with 72 seats, and from 1970 the standard model was the Tu-134A with a lengthened 80-seat fuselage and thrust-reversing turbofans. Later variants (probably conversions) were the Tu-134B with a forward-facing flightdeck, the Tu-134B-1 for 90 passengers, and the Tu-134B-3 for 96 passengers. Production totalled about 520.

Specification: Tupolev Tu-134A short/medium-range jetliner
Span: 29.00m (95ft 1.75in)
Length: 37.05m (121ft 6.5in)
Powerplant: 2×Soloviev D-30-2, 6800kg (14,991lb) st each
Payload: 84 passengers or 8200kg (18,078lb) of freight
Max T/O weight: 47000kg (103,616lb)
Cruising speed: 558 mph at 27,890ft
Operational range: 1,175 miles with maximum payload

Vickers VC10

In the later 1950s BOAC ordered the Boeing 707, but also demanded the creation of a British airliner able to use existing 'hot-and-high' airports which, felt the airline, would not see the traffic growth to merit extension of their runways to cater for the DC-8 and Model 707. Thus was born the VC10 with rear-mounted turbofans, a T-tail and a large wing featuring slats and Fowler flaps. The VC10 first flew in June 1962, in a programme leading towards the BOAC order for 35, with options on another 10. The availability of more powerful Conways also allowed Vickers (BAC from February 1960) to create the transatlantic-range Super VC10 with 187 seats in a longer fuselage. But BOAC's changes of order made it difficult for BAC to proceed effectively, and these two great partners were produced to the extent of only 32 VC10s and 22 Super VC10s.

Specification: Vickers VC10 long-range jetliner
Span: 42.72m (140ft 2in)
Length: 48.36m (158ft 8in)
Powerplant: 4×Rolls-Royce Conway Mk 540, 9240kg (20,370lb) st each
Payload: 151 passengers or 18038kg (39,769lb) of freight
Max T/O weight: 142430kg (314,000lb)
Cruising speed: 568 mph at optimum altitude
Operational range: 5,040 miles with maximum payload

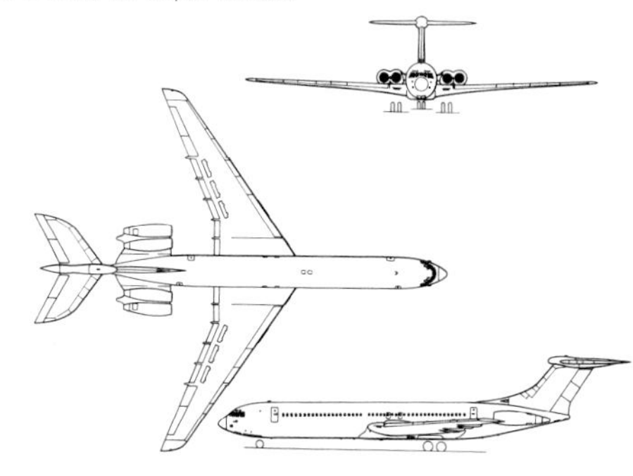

Sud-Est S.E.210 Caravelle

The Caravelle was the world's first short-range jetliner. Resulting from a 1951 French requirement that produced eight submissions, the Caravelle was originally planned round three SNECMA Atar turbojets (one in the fin and two on the fuselage sides) but then recast for a pair of more powerful Rolls- Royce Avons, the forward fuselage and flightdeck of the Comet, and a ventral airstair. The first Caravelle flew in May 1955, and the 282 production aircraft included 20 Caravelle Is with Avon RA.26 engines, 12 Mk IAs with Avon Mk 526 engines, 78 higher-weight Mk IIIs with Avon Mk 527 engines, 53 Mk VINs with silencer-equipped Avon Mk 531s, 63 Mk VIRs with reverser-equipped Avon Mk 533s, 22 Mk 10Bs with Pratt & Whitney JT8D-7 turbofans, 20 Mk 10Rs with thrust reversers, six Mk 11Rs with a longer fuselage and five Mk 12s with JT8D-9 engines and seating for 140.

Specification: SNCASE S.E.210 Caravelle III short-range jetliner
Span: 34.30 m (112 ft 6 in)
Length: 32.01 m (105 ft 0 in)
Powerplant: 2×Rolls-Royce Avon Mk 527, 5171 kg (11,400 lb) st each
Payload: 80 passengers or 8400 kg (18,519 lb) of freight
Max T/O weight: 46000 kg (101,411 lb)
Cruising speed: 500 mph at 32,81 ft
Operational range: 1,056 miles with maximum payload

Avro Canada C-102 Jetliner

Developed at about the same time as the British Comet, the Jetliner was planned for North American inter-city sectors, and was based on the concept of a conventional airliner of the times, but using wing-mounted pairs of turbojets rather than piston engines for greater speed, comfort and smoothness. The fuselage was of the same 3.05-m (10-ft) diameter as that of the Comet, and the wing section was the same as that of the Avro Lancaster bomber with simple split flaps. Advanced features were the integral tankage and the flying controls (hydraulically boosted rudder and ailerons, and aerodynamically tab-operated elevators). Work began in 1949, and the prototype first flew in August 1949. Despite considerable enthusiasm from potential buyers, no orders were placed as the Jetliner was too advanced for its period.

Specification: Avro Canada C-102 Jetliner short/medium-range jetliner prototype
Span: 29.89 m (98 ft 1 in)
Length: 24.61 m (80 ft 9 in)
Powerplant: 4×Rolls-Royce Derwent 5/17, 1633 kg (3,600 lb) st each
Payload: 40-52 passengers plus baggage and freight
Max T/O weight: 29484 kg (65,000 lb)
Cruising speed: 430 mph at 30,000 ft
Operational range: about 1,240 miles with maximum payload

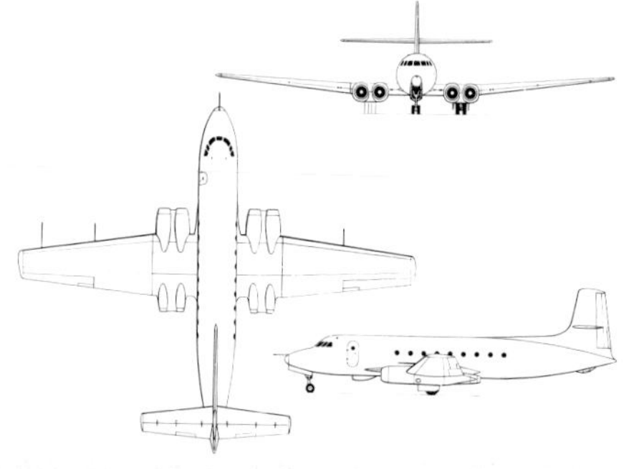

BAC One-Eleven

The origins of this pioneering T-tailed jetliner with rear-mounted turbofans lie with the Hunting H.107, a 32-seat project of 1956. Hunting was bought by the British Aircraft Corporation, which developed the type as the 59-passenger BAC.107 and finally as the 80-seat BAC.111 that flew as a One-Eleven Series 200 in August 1963 with two 4722-kg (10,410-lb) Spey Mk 506 turbofans. Certification followed in May 1964, and BAC announced the Series 300 with greater payload/range and 5171-kg (11,400-lb) Spey Mk 511s, and the Series 400 for the US market. Later developments were the 119-seat Series 500 and the 'hot-and-high' Series 475, produced by CNIAR in Romania as the Series 495 and Series 560. The One-Eleven has a remarkably sturdy airframe, and many surviving aircraft are being re-engined with Rolls-Royce Tay turbofans.

Specification: British Aircraft Corporation One-Eleven Series 500 short/medium-range jetliner
Span: 28.50 m (93 ft 6 in)
Length: 32.61 m (107 ft 0 in)
Powerplant: 2×Rolls-Royce Spey Mk 512DW, 5692 kg (12,500 lb) st each
Payload: 119 passengers or 11983 kg (26,418 lb) of freight
Max T/O weight: 47401 kg (104,500 lb)
Cruising speed: 541 mph at 21,000 ft
Operational range: 1,705 miles with maximum payload

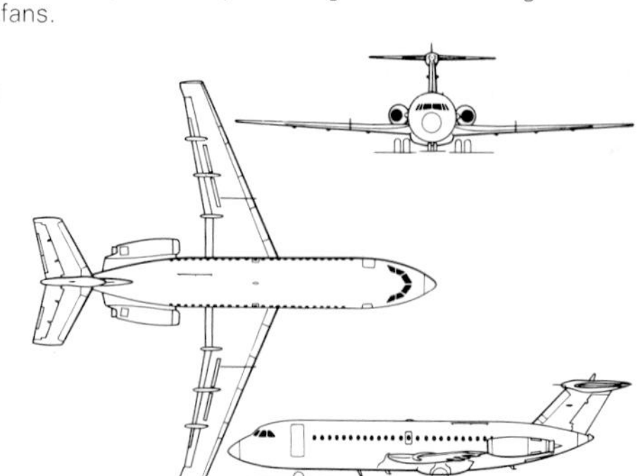

Alitalia became one of the largest operators of the Caravelle, with a peak strength of 21 aircraft during 1965. After its withdrawal from scheduled services, this aircraft was used for charter work, and was finally sold in Latin America.

Boeing 707

The Model 707 is possibly the most important airliner ever developed, and with the DC-8, set today's pattern of global air transport. The Model 367-80 prototype was entirely company-funded and first flew in July 1954. Initial sales were of the smaller KC-135 tanker version to the US Air Force, and the first civil variant was the 121/179-seat transcontinental Model 707-120 with 5897-kg (13,000-lb) JT3C-6 turbojets; a subvariant was the Model 707-138 for Qantas. Later variants were the 'hot-and-high' Model 707-220 with 7167-kg (15,800-lb) thrust JT4A-4/5s, the 131/189-seat intercontinental Model 707-320 with 7938-kg (17,500-lb) JT4A-11 turbojets and the Model 707-420 with 7484-kg (16,500-lb) Rolls-Royce Conway Mk 505 turbofans. The suffixes 'B' and 'C' indicate aircraft fitted with turbofans and convertible passenger/cargo interiors respectively. Total production was 917.

Specification: Boeing 707-320C long-range jetliner
Span: 44.42 m (145 ft 9 in)
Length: 46.61 m (152 ft 11 in)
Powerplant: 4×Pratt & Whitney JT3D-7, 6818 kg (19,000 lb) st each
Payload: 189 passengers or 42229 kg (93,098 lb) of freight
Max T/O weight: 151315 kg (333,600 lb)
Cruising speed: 605 mph at 25,000 ft
Operational range: 3,630 miles with 36287-kg (80,000-lb) payload

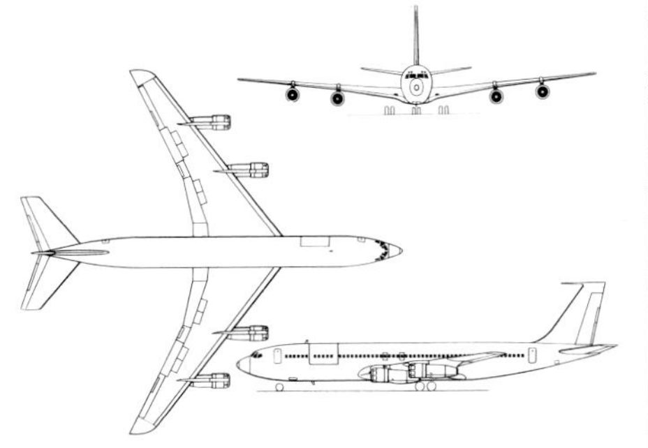

Boeing 720

Despite its exterior likeness to the Model 707, the Model 720 is structurally a completely different aeroplane, tailored to short/medium-range operations, with a fuselage 0.51 m (1 ft 8 in) longer than that of the 'short-body' Model 707-138, a lighter structure, less fuel, different engines, full-span leading-edge flaps and extended chord on the leading edges of the inner wing panels. The last increased sweep and reduced thickness/chord ratio, and offered such advantages that it was adopted for later Model 707s. The Model 720 first flew in November 1959 and was produced in smaller quantities (154 aircraft) than the Model 707. In 1960 Boeing produced the Model 720B with the same 8165-kg (18,000-lb) thrust Pratt & Whitney JT3D-3 turbofans as used in the 'B' series of Model 707s, conferring useful improvements in the cruise economy and range of the aircraft so fitted.

Specification: Boeing 707-020 medium/long-range jetliner
Span: 39.88 m (130 ft 10 in)
Length: 41.68 m (136 ft 9 in)
Powerplant: 4×Pratt & Whitney JT3C-7, 5443 kg (12,000 lb) st each
Payload: 165 passengers or 16783 kg (37,000 lb) of freight
Max T/O weight: 92081 kg (203,000 lb)
Cruising speed: 600 mph at 25,000 ft
Operational range: 3,005 miles with maximum payload

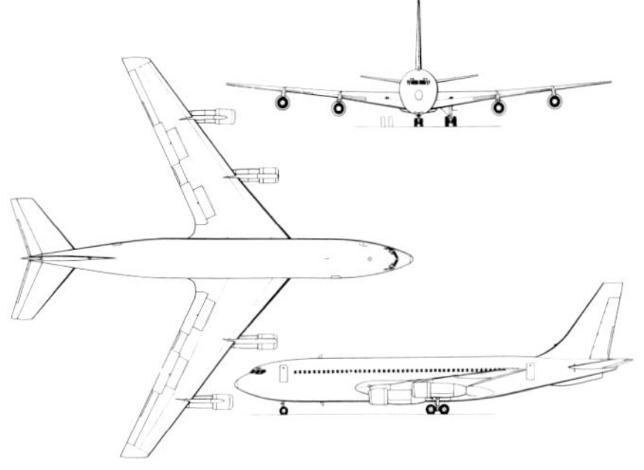

Tupolev Tu-104

Specification: Tupolev Tu-104A short/medium-range jetliner
Span: 34.54 m (13 ft 4 in)
Length: 38.85 m (127 ft 5.5 in)
Powerplant: 2×Mikulin AM-3, 6750 kg (14,881 lb) st each
Payload: 70 passengers or 9000 kg (19,841 lb) of freight
Max T/O weight: 76000 kg (167,549 lb)
Cruising speed: 559 mph at optimum altitude
Operational range: 1,647 miles with maximum payload

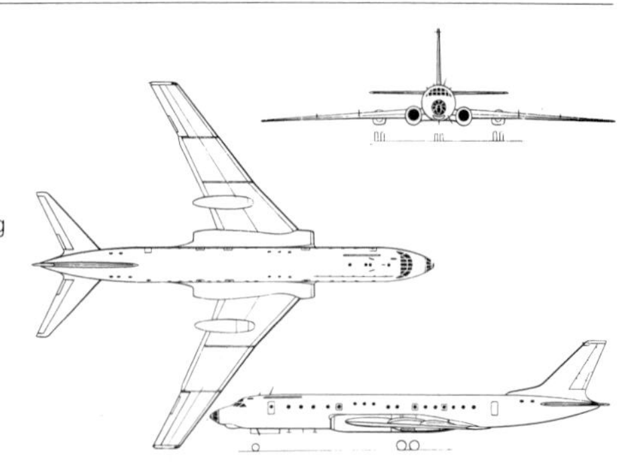

Although little known today, the Tu-104 was the world's second jetliner to enter service. The design was basically that of the Tu-16 'Badger' bomber with a larger fuselage mounting a revised nose landing gear unit, and with the wing in the low- rather than mid-set position. The Tu-104G prototype flew in June 1955, and the 48-seat initial version began to enter service in 1956, later examples having the AM-3M rather than lower-rated AM-3 engine. In 1958 the Tu-104A introduced seats for 70 passengers in the same fuselage, while the Tu-104B had a longer fuselage for 100 passengers. The adoption of the AM- 3M-500 engine in 1959 allowed a production switch to the Tu-104C and Tu-104D versions of the Tu-104A and Tu-104B respectively, and when production ended in 1960 about 210 aircraft had been delivered.

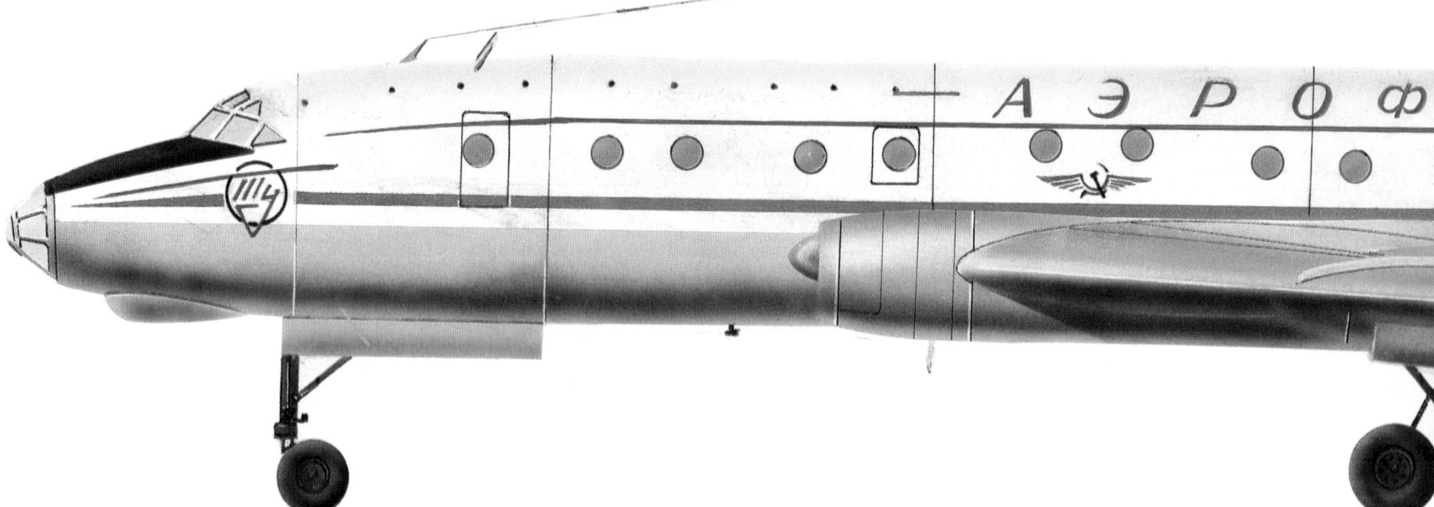

Convair CV-880

The CV-880 was developed to compete with the Boeing 707 and Douglas DC-8, the company's premise being that there would be demand for an airliner with smaller capacity than the two others but notably better performance, especially in speed. The type was initially called the Model 22 with the names 'Skylark' and then 'Golden Arrow', but the designation was then altered to CV-600 and then to CV-880 by the time the prototype first flew in January 1959. Like the Boeing 707, the CV-880 had low-set wing of 35° sweep, fitted with double-slotted trailing-edge flaps, but a considerably slimmer fuselage with accommodation of between 88 and 110 passengers. That Convair had seriously miscalculated was proved by orders for only 48 of the transcontinental CV-880, plus another 17 for the intercontinental CV-880M (Model 31) with additional fuel and other refinements.

Specification: Convair CV-880 long-range jetliner
Span: 36.58 m (120 ft 0 in)
Length: 39.42 m (129 ft 4 in)
Powerplant: 4×General Electric CJ805-3, 5080 kg (11,200 lb) st each
Payload: 110 passengers or 10500 kg (23,150 lb) of freight
Max T/O weight: 83689 kg (184,500 lb)
Cruising speed: 615 mph at 20,000 ft
Operational range: 3,200 miles with maximum payload

Convair CV-990 Coronado

Even before the first flight of its CV-880, Convair had begun to appreciate that a higher capacity would aid sales, and therefore began design of the Model 30 based closely on the Model 22. It was at this point that the major disadvantage of the Model 22's slim fuselage and five-abreast seating really became apparent: to raise seating to a maximum of 149 the fuselage was lengthened by 3.01 m (9 ft 10.5 in), and other developments were turbofan engines, full-span leading-edge flaps on the larger but thinner wings, and the adoption of aerodynamic 'bullets' on the trailing edges to reduce transonic drag. The first example of what had become the CV-990 flew in January 1961, and production totalled a mere 37. Refinement of in-service aircraft produced the CV-990A with features such as Krueger leading-edge flaps and revised engine pylons.

Specification: Convair CV-990A Coronado long-range jetliner
Span: 36.58 m (120 ft 0 in)
Length: 42.43 m (139 ft 2.5 in)
Powerplant: 4×General Electric CJ805-23B, 7280 kg (16,050 lb) st each
Payload: 149 passengers or 11992 kg (26,440 lb) of freight
Max T/O weight: 114761 kg (253,000 lb)
Cruising speed: 615 mph at 20,000 ft
Operational range: 3,800 miles with maximum payload

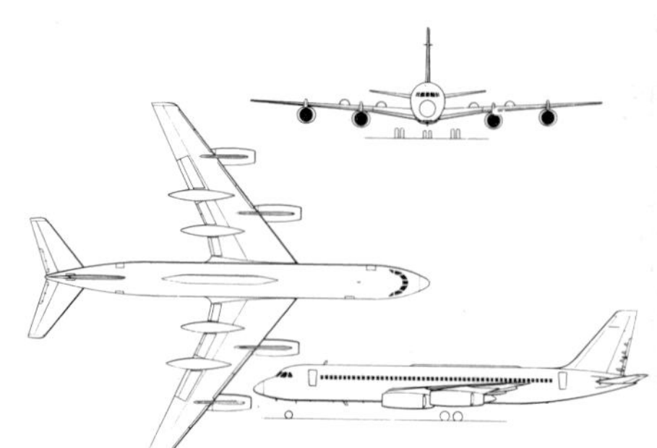

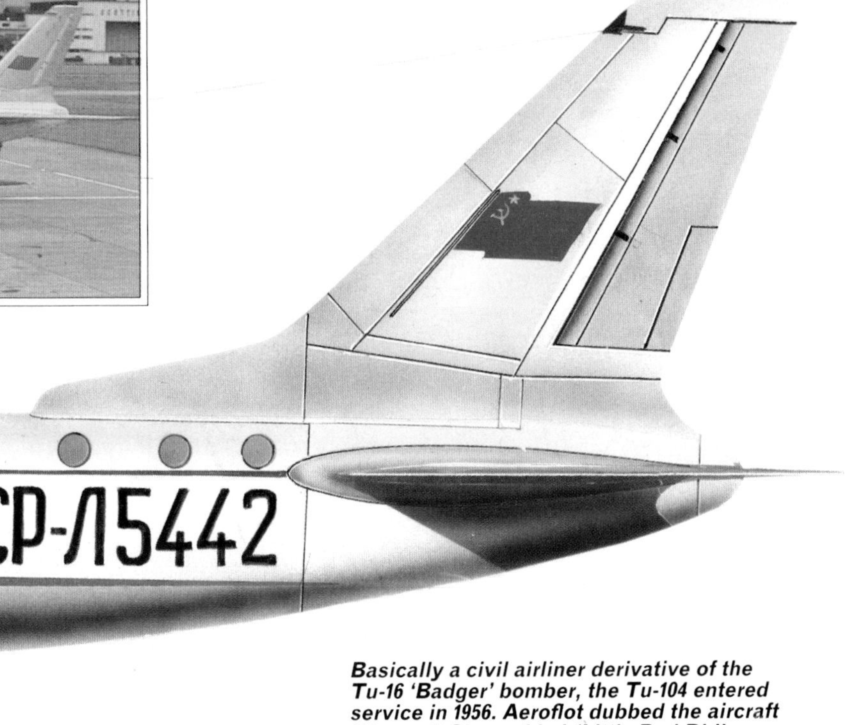

Basically a civil airliner derivative of the Tu-16 'Badger' bomber, the Tu-104 entered service in 1956. Aeroflot dubbed the aircraft 'Krasnyii Shapochka' (Little Red Riding Hood) and used most of the 200 built, with small numbers going to the Czech airline CSA and to the Soviet air force.

Dassault Mercure

Capitalizing on its success with the Mystère/Falcon series of business jets, Dassault sought to provide a competitor to the Boeing 737 in the short-range airliner market. The Mercure resembled the Model 737 in overall layout and its turbofan powerplant, and had wings swept at 25° with leading-edge slots and slats plus triple-slotted trailing-edge flaps. The fuselage was 5 cm (2 in) wider than that of the Model 737, providing accommodation options between 100 and 162. A French government loan was secured for 56 per cent of the launch costs while Dassault covered 14 per cent itself and lined up risk-sharing partners in the European aerospace industry to cover the balance. The first Mercure flew in May 1971, but the type failed to secure more than 10 orders, and these had served with Air Inter since 1974, with the French government meeting a proportion of the running costs.

Specification: Dassault Mercure short-range jetliner
Span: 30.56 m (100 ft 3 in)
Length: 34.84 m (114 ft 3.5 in)
Powerplant: 2×Pratt & Whitney JT8D-15, 7031 kg (15,500 lb) st each
Payload: 162 passengers or 16200 kg (35,714 lb) of freight
Max T/O weight: 56500 kg (124,559 lb)
Cruising speed: 575 mph at 20,000 ft
Operational range: 690 miles with maximum payload

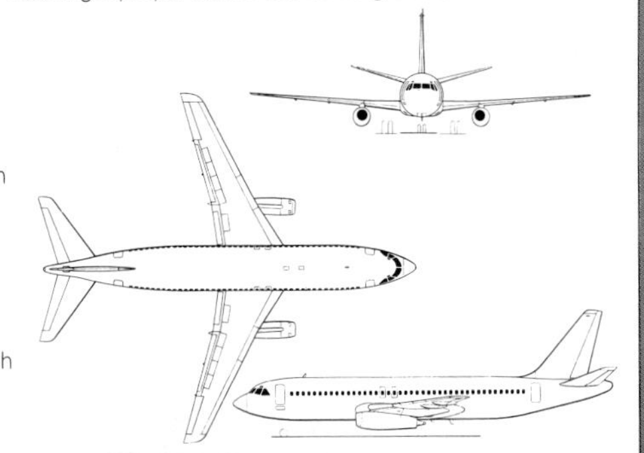

De Havilland D.H.106 Comet

The Comet was the world's first jetliner, with a design history stretching back to 1943. The first ideas were for a tailless design, later recast as a conventional but advanced aeroplane, to carry 32 passengers across the North Atlantic at high altitude. This Comet was ordered by BOAC and the first example flew in July 1949. The Comet 1 (9 built) entered service in May 1952, and later came the Comet 1A with greater power and weight (15), the 44-seat Comet 2 with Rolls-Royce Avons (15) and the proposed 78-seat Comet 3 with more fuel and uprated Avon RA.16 engines. Then two metal-fatigue crashes grounded the existing aircraft and led to order cancellations, losing the UK its four-year jetliner lead. In 1958 there appeared the revised 81-seat Comet 4 with Avon Mk 524 engines (28 built), followed by the 99-seat Comet 4B (18) and finally by the long-range Comet 4C (28).

Specification: de Havilland D.H.106 Comet 1A medium-range jetliner
Span: 35.05 m (115 ft 0 in)
Length: 28.35 m (93 ft 0 in)
Powerplant: 4×de Havilland Ghost 50 Mk 2, 2268 kg (5,000 lb) st each
Payload: 44 passengers
Max T/O weight: 52164 kg (115,000 lb)
Cruising speed: 490 mph at 40,000 ft
Operational range: about 2,000 miles with maximum payload

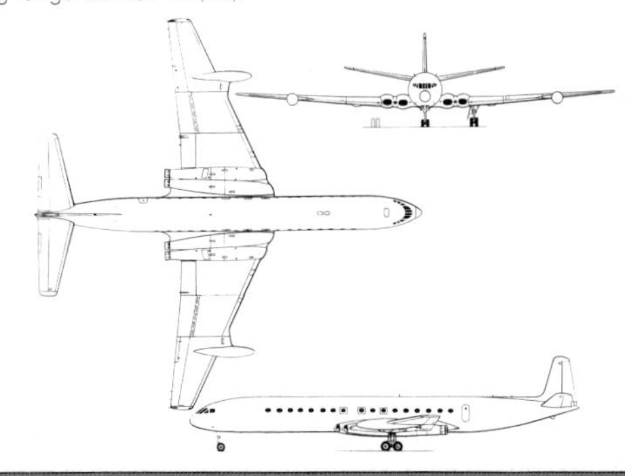

Airbus A300

Airbus Industrie, with partners in Belgium, France, West Germany, the Netherlands, Spain and the United Kingdom, was established in 1970 to develop a twin-engined large-capacity 'European Airbus'. The prototype Airbus A300 first flew on 28 October 1972, and the first production A300B2 on 28 June 1973. The standard powerplant for the Airbus was the 52,000 lb st General Electric CF6-50 turbofan, with the Pratt & Whitney JT9D-59 available to customer option. Current production model is the A300-600. It differs from the earlier A300 2/B4 in having a longer fuselage with increased capacity, A310 rear fuselage section and tailplane, all-digital two-crew flight deck with fly-by-wire controls, and improved handling and payload/range performance.

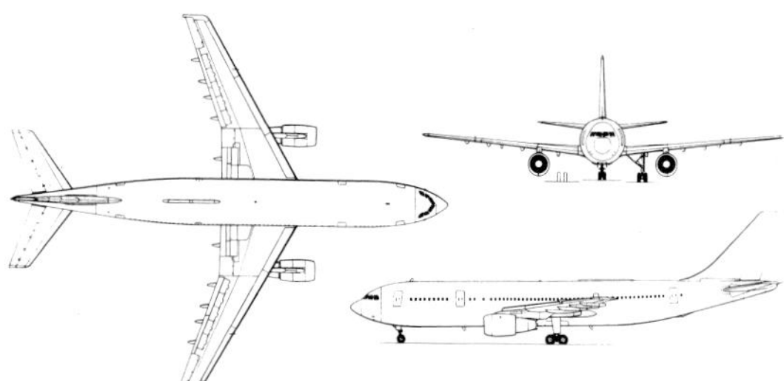

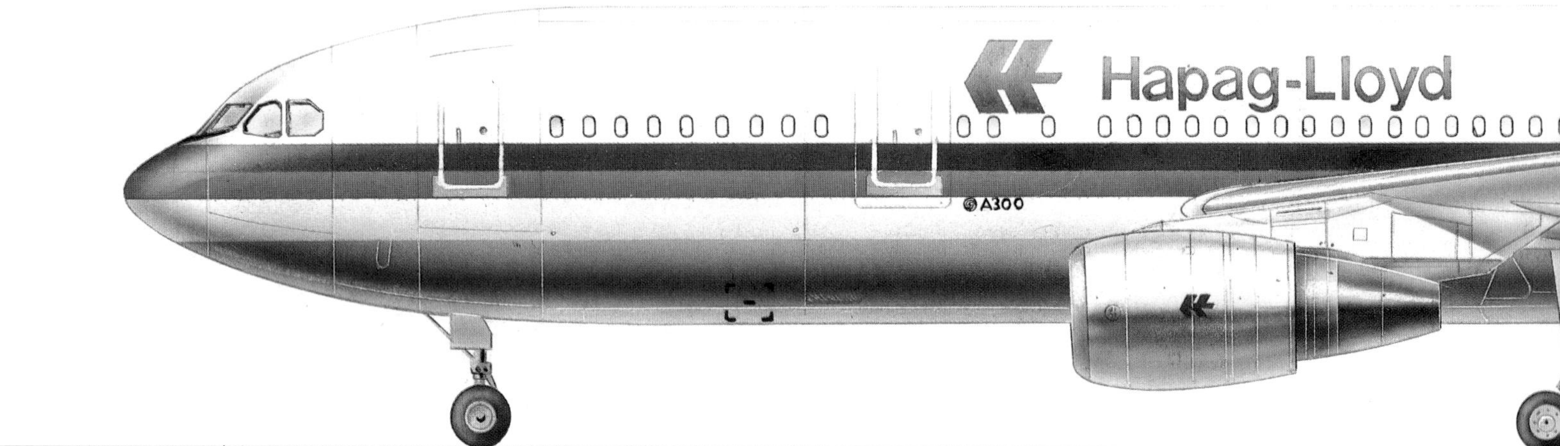

Airbus A310

The Airbus A310, which first flew on 3 April 1982, differs from the A300 series in having a shorter fuselage, advanced technology wings and tail surfaces, a digital two-crew cockpit and common engine pylons enabling General Electric CF6-80C2A2, Pratt & Whitney JT9D-7R4E1 or PW4152 turbofans to be installed. The A310 entered service with Lufthansa on 12 April 1983. The basic version is the A310-200, available in convertible passenger/cargo or all-freight models. The A310-300 extended-range version first flew on 8 July 1985 and entered service with Swissair on 17 December 1985. This model introduced as standard drag-reducing 'winglets', and has an additional fuel tank in the tailplane which also functions as a 'trim tank'.

Specification: Airbus A310-200
Span: 43.91 m (144 ft 1¼ in)
Length: 46.65 m (153 ft 1 in)
Height: 15.79 m (51 ft 10 in)
Wing area: 219 m² 2,360 sq ft
Passenger capacity: 210-250
Payload: 33293 kg (73,400 lb)
Maximum take-off weight: 138598 kg (305,560 lb)
Cruising speed: Mach 0.80
Service ceiling: 41,000 ft
Maximum range: 3,950 nm
Production total: (orders at 1 Jan 1988) 155+

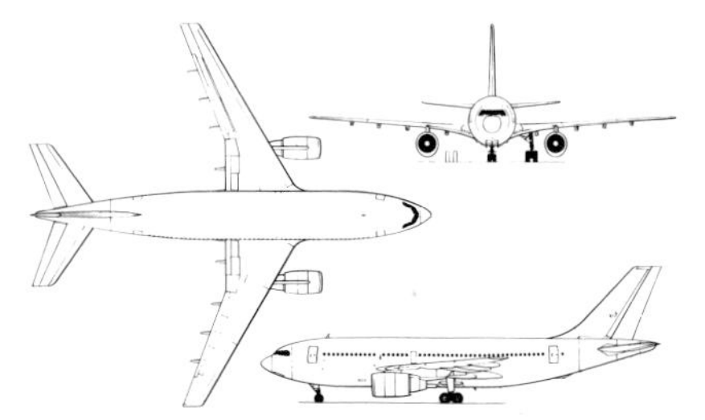

Boeing 727

The Boeing 727 was launched in December 1960, five years after the company began design studies for a short/medium-range jet airliner. Eastern and United airlines each ordered 40 aircraft. The prototype 727 flew on 9 February 1963 and the aircraft flew its first commercial service on 1 February 1964. Initially powered by three 14,000 lb st Pratt/Whitney JT8D-1 turbofans, the Boeing 727-100 accommodated 131 passengers, and was also offered in passenger/cargo and 'Quick Change' variants. The 727-200, with a 20-ft fuselage stretch and seats for 189 passengers, first flew on 27 July 1967 and entered service with Northeast Airlines on 14 December. Final versions were the Advanced 727-200 with increased fuel capacity, a succession of more powerful JT8D-25/17/17R engines rates at up to 17,400 lb st and 'Superjet' wide-body style cabin interiors; and the all-cargo 727-200F.

Specification: Boeing 727-200
Span: 32.91 m (108 ft 0¼ in)
Length: 46.68 m (153 ft 2 in)
Height: 10.36 m (34 ft 0 in)
Wing area: 157.93 m² 1,700 sq ft
Passenger capacity: 163-189
Payload: 19413 kg (42,800 lb)
Maximum take-off weight: 95027 kg (209,500 lb)
Cruising speed: 495 knots
Maximum speed: 549 knots
Maximum range: 2,555 nm
Production total: (all models 1,832)

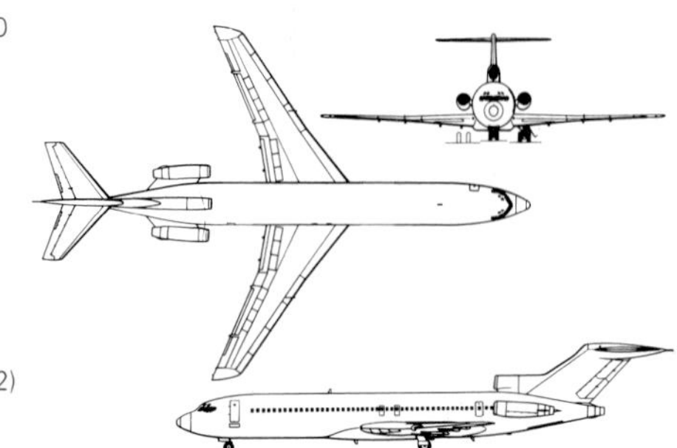

ecification: Airbus A300-600
n: 44.83 m (147 ft 1¼ in)
th: 54.07 m (177 ft 5 in)
ht: 16.62 m (54 ft 6 in)
g area: 260.12 m² 2,800 sq ft
enger capacity: 267-375
oad: 43571 kg (96,060 lb)
imum take-off weight:
16 kg (363,800 lb)
sing speed: 472 knots
imum speed: Mach 0.82
ice ceiling: 40,000 ft
imum range: 4,340 nm
duction total:
l orders at 1 Jan 1988 310

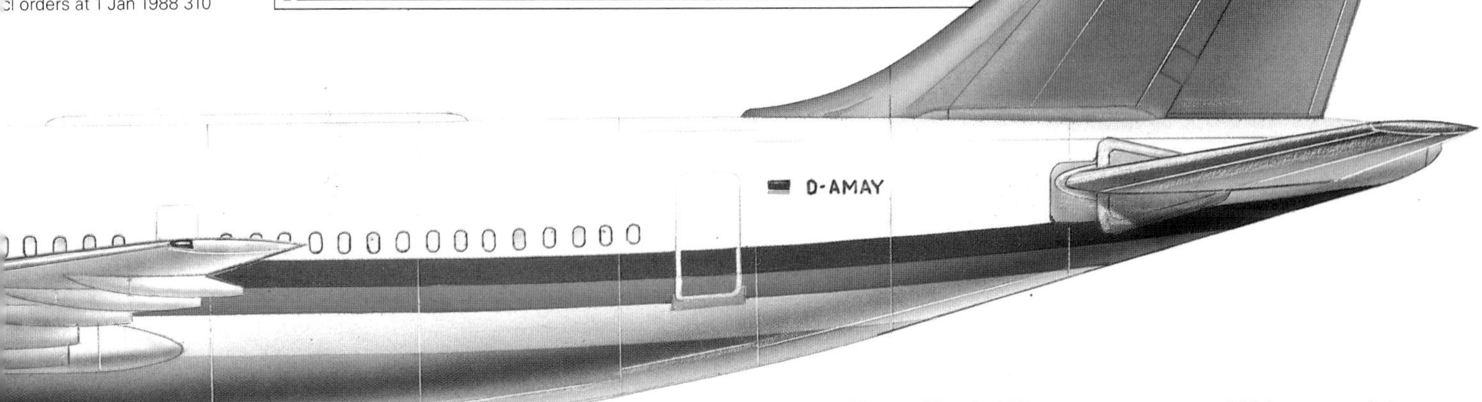

Hapag Lloyd of Hanover owns several Airbuses, mainly A310s, but also two A300s. These quiet, economical and adaptable wide-bodied transports are used mainly for Mediterranean charter flights. An A300B4 is shown here.

Boeing 737

First flown on 9 April 1967, the twin-engined Boeing 737 'Baby Boeing' became the world's best-selling airliner in March 1988 when orders exceeded 2,000. The original 100-seat 737-100, powered by 14,000 lb st Pratt & Whitney JT8D-7 turbofans, and 119/130 passenger 737-200 with 6-ft fuselage stretch and uprated engines, have been succeeded by Advanced 737-200 with improved flaps and leading edge slats, 15,500 lb st JT8D-15 engines and enhanced braking and anti-skid systems. Most recent variants are the 737-300, which features a 110-149 seat cabin in lengthened fuselage and fuel efficient 20,000 lb st CFM International CFM56-3B turbofans; the similarly powered 737-400 with a further fuselage stretch to accommodate 168 passengers, and the short-body 110-130 passenger 737-500, scheduled to fly in mid-1995.

Specification: Boeing 737-300
Span: 28.87 m (94 ft 9 in)
Length: 33.40 m (109 ft 7 in)
Height: 11.04 m (36 ft 3 in)
Wing area: 105.44 m² 1,135 sq ft
Passenger capacity: 110-149
Empty weight: 31479 kg (69,400 lb)
Payload: 16828 kg (37,100 lb)
Maximum take-off weight: 62822 kg (138,500 lb)
Cruising speed: 460 knots
Maximum speed: Mach 0.84
Maximum range: 2,590 nm
Production total: 2,028

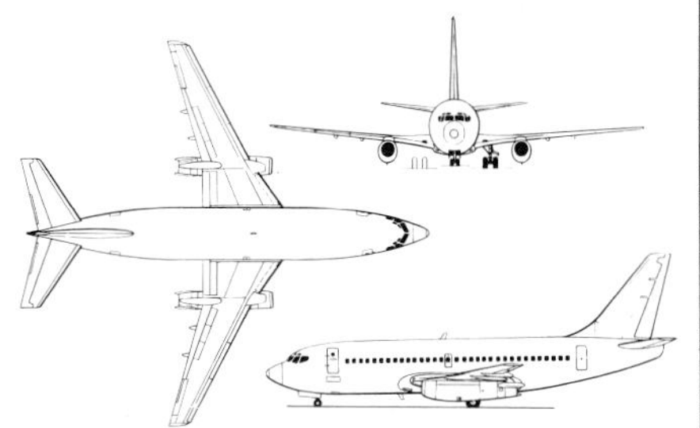

Boeing 747

Launched on 13 April 1966 with an order for 21 aircraft from Pan American, the Boeing 747 was the original 'Jumbo' jet, more than doubling the passenger and cargo capacities of contemporary transports. The prototype first flew on 9 February 1969 and the aircraft entered service in January 1970. Passenger versions include the 747-100B and -200; 747SP lighter weight, short-bodied long-range version of the 747-100; and 747-300, which features an extended upper deck providing increased passenger accommodation and crew rest areas. Engine options for all models include a variety of 50,000 lb st-class turbofans such as the General Electric CF6-50/80, Pratt & Whitney JT9D, and Rolls-Royce RB211-524 series. The latest version of the aircraft is the 747-400, an advanced long-range version of the 747-300 with 598,000 lb st-class engines, two-crew all-digital flight deck, tailplane fuel tank, and winglets.

Specification: Boeing 747-200B
Span: 59.63 m (195 ft 8 in)
Length: 70.66 m (231 ft 10 in)
Height: 19.32 m (63 ft 5 in)
Wing area: 520.95 m² (5,500 sq ft)
Passenger capacity: 452-516
Payload: 64818 kg (142,900 lb)
Maximum take-off weight: 377840 kg (833,000 lb)
Cruising speed: 522 knots
Service ceiling: 45,000 ft
Maximum range: 6,600 nm
Production total: 837

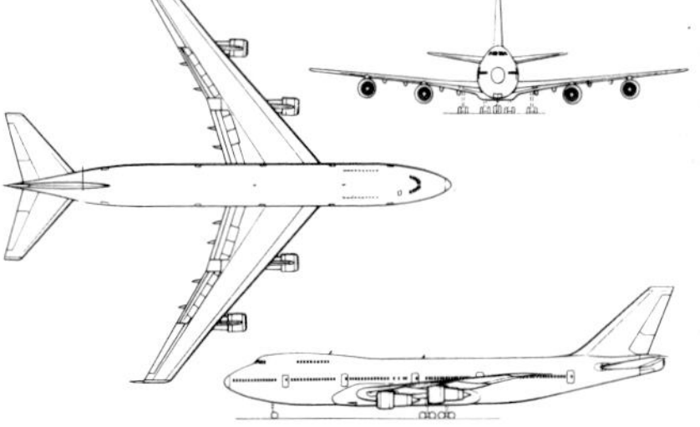

Boeing 757

Development of the advanced technology Boeing 757 short/medium-range airliner began in 1978 and the prototype flew on 19 February 1982; commercial services with launch customers Eastern Air Lines and British Airways commenced in January and February 1983. The 757 is a twin-engined design which retains the 'narrow body' cross-section of the Boeing 707/727/737 series. Powerplant options include Pratt & Whitney PW 2037 and 2040 or Rolls-Royce 535C and 535E turbofans in the 37,400-41,700 lb st class. The 757 features an advanced 'all glass' cockpit with electronic flight instrument systems using colour CRI displays. Three models are currently available: the 757-200 passenger transport; 757PF Package Freighter, a windowless cargo aircraft by United Parcel Service in the USA; and the 757-200 Combi, which can carry two standard cargo containers and 123-167 passengers.

Specification: Boeing 757-200
Span: 38.04 m (124 ft 10 in)
Length: 47.32 m (155 ft 3 in)
Height: 13.56 m (44 ft 6 in)
Wing area: 185.24 m^2 (5,500 sq ft)
Passenger capacity: 178-239
Maximum take-off weight: 113397 kg (250,000 lb)
Cruising speed: Mach 0.80
Maximum speed: Mach 0.86
Maximum range: 3,820 nm
Production total: (mid-1987) 132

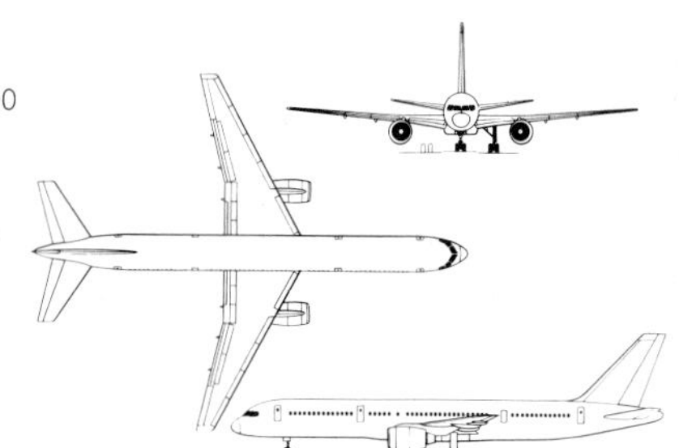

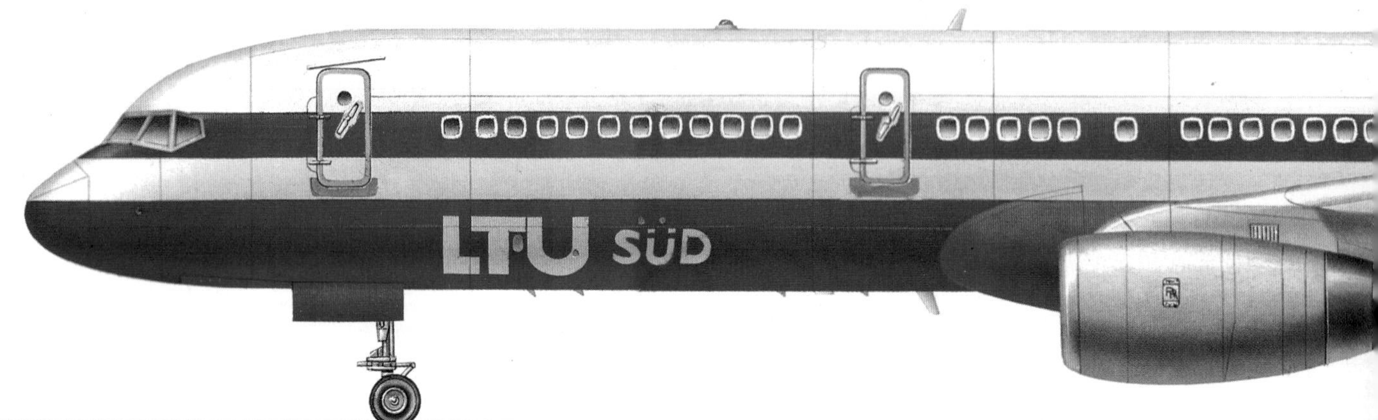

Boeing 767

Development of this wide-body advanced technology twin turbofan airliner began on 14 July 1978. First flown on 26 September 1981, the basic 767-200 was offered with Pratt & Whitney JT9D-7R4D or General Electric CF6-80A turbofans. Medium-range and higher gross weight variants of the basic model are available, as well as the extended range 767-200ER. The 767-300 which appeared in January 1986 has a fuselage 20 ft 1 in longer than that of the -200 series, accommodating 269 passengers. It entered service with Japan Airlines in September 1986. Deliveries of Rolls-Royce RB211-524D4D-engined 767-300s to British Airways will begin in 1989. Deliveries of the 767-300ER extended range variant began in 1988 to American Airlines.

Specification: Boeing 767-200ER
Span: 47.57 m (156 ft 1 in)
Length: 48.51 m (159 ft 2 in)
Height: 15.84 m (52 ft 0 in)
Wing area: 283.34 m^2 (3,050 sq ft)
Passenger capacity: 216-290
Payload: 16533 kg (36,450 lb)
Maximum take-off weight: 156488 kg (345,000 lb)
Cruising speed: Mach 0.80
Maximum range: 5,365 nm
Production total: (mid-1987) 176

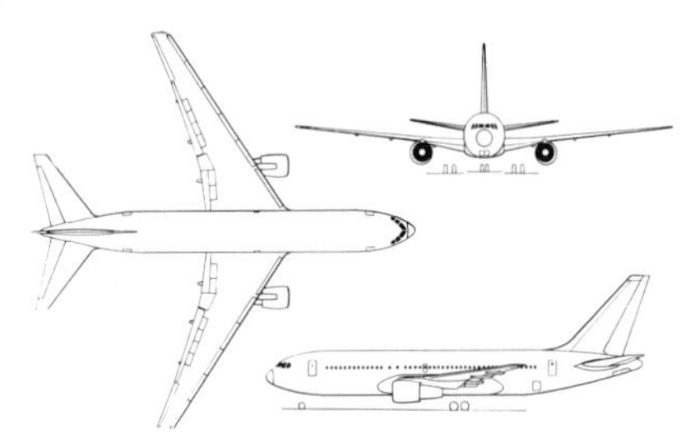

British Aerospace 146

First flown on 3 September 1981, the BAe 146 is a high-winged, short-range transport noted for its low external noise level which enables it to operate day and night into environmental sensitive airports, particularly in the United States. The BAe is powered by four pod-mounted 6,970 lb st Avco Lycoming ALF502R-5 turbofans. The 82-93 seat BAe 146 Series 100 entered service with the British carrier Dan-Air on 27 May 1983, and also serves with The Queen's Flight. The series 200, first flown on 1 August 1982, entered service with Air Wisconsin in June 1984. It features a stretched fuselage 7 ft 10 in longer than that of the BAe 146-100, with increased underfloor cargo volume, while the Series 300 is 15 ft 8½ in longer, with more spacious accommodation for 100 passengers. All versions are available as BAe 146-QT Quiet Trader all-freight aircraft.

Specification: BAe 146-200
Span: 26.33 m (86 ft 5 in)
Length: 28.60 m (93 ft 10 in)
Height: 8.61 m (28 ft 3 in)
Wing area: 77.29 m^2 (832 sq ft)
Passenger capacity: 111
Payload: 10477 kg (23,100 lb)
Maximum take-off weight: 42183 kg (93,000 lb)
Cruising speed: 383 knots
Maximum speed: Mach 0.70
Maximum range: 1,476 nm
Production total: 109

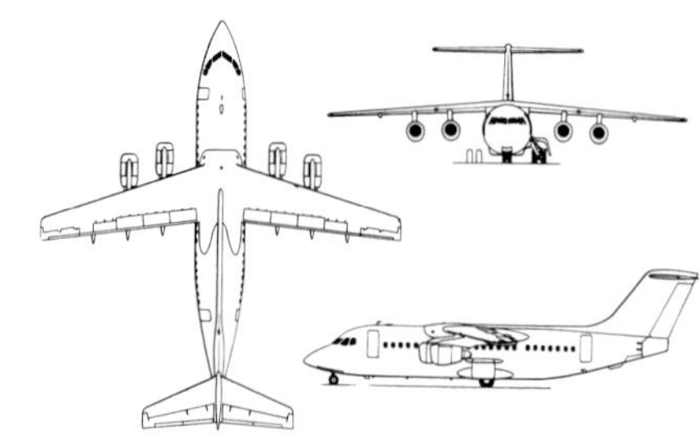

Both the LTU and its charter subsidiary LTU Süd use Boeing 757s. Some LTS planes are painted a very bright blue; others, such as the 757-205 (ER) pictured here, have the typical red and white LTU livery. The ER is one of the long-distance versions of the Boeing 757.

McDonnell Douglas *MD-80 Series*

The DC-9 twin jet short-haul airliner's potential for 'stretching' has been fully exploited since the 72-90 passenger 12,000 lb st Pratt & Whitney JT8D-5 powered DC-9-10 prototype first flew on 25 February 1965. Eastern Air Lines ordered the 97-115 seat Series 30 which had a 14 ft 11 in fuselage stretch, increased wingspan with triple slotted flaps, and uprated engines. In November 1967 the first 125-passenger DC-9-40 flew, while the Series 50 introduced in 1974 had a fuselage 27 ft 7 in longer than the original DC-9 and could seat 139. The MD-81 (formerly DC-9 'Super 80') announced in 1977 is 14 ft 3 in longer still, with greater wingspan, and is powered by two 18,500 lb st JT8D-209 turbofans. Other current variants in the MD-80 series include the 'hot and high' MD-82, which is being assembled in China and the United States; the long-range MD-83; short fuselage MD-87 with 20,000 lb st JT8D-217C engines; and the 142-seat MD-88.

Specification:
McDonnell Douglas MD-81
Span: 32.86 m (107 ft 10 in)
Length: 45.05 m (147 ft 10 in)
Height: 9.04 m (29 ft 8 in)
Wing area: 117.98 m^2 (1,270 sq ft)
Passenger capacity: 172
Payload: 17953 kg (39,580 lb)
Maximum take-off weight: 63502 kg (140,000 lb)
Cruising speed: Mach 0.76
Maximum speed: Mach 0.80
Maximum range: 1,565 nm
Production total: (including orders for MD-80 series at 1 Jan 1988) 867

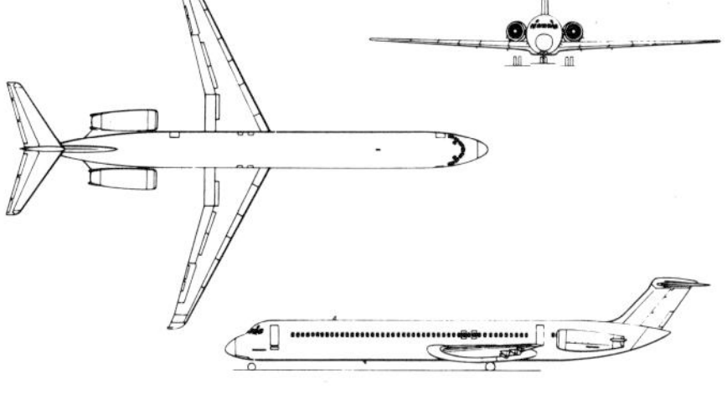

McDonnell Douglas *DC-10/MD-11 Series*

The DC-10 was developed to meet the short, medium and long-range needs of US trunk carriers, sharing with the rival Lockheed L-1010 TriStar a novel engine configuration with two underwing pods and the third engine mounted at the base of the fin. The first DC-10 Series 10 flew on 29 August 1970, the type entering service with launch customer American Airlines a year later. Powerplant for the first model was the 40,000 lb st General Electric CF6-6D. Intercontinental capability was introduced with the DC-10 Series 30 which first flew on 21 June 1972, initial deliveries going to KLM and Swissair. Other models include the DC-10-30ER, with further increased range, the -30CF convertible passenger/cargo aircraft, the dedicated all-cargo Series 30F and the intercontinental Series 40, powered by three Pratt & Whitney JT9D-20 or -59A engines. The MD-11 is an advanced derivative of the DC-10, featuring a fuselage 18 ft 7 in longer than that of the DC-10-30, aerodynamic improvements including winglets, all-digital two crew flight deck, GE CF6-80 or P&W PW4000 series turbofans and restyled passenger cabins. Deliveries will commence in 1990.

Specification: McDonnell Douglas DC-10-30
Span: 50.39 m (165 ft 4 in)
Length: 55.34 m (181 ft 7 in)
Height: 17.70 m (5829 ft 1 in)
Passenger capacity: 208-380
Maximum take-off weight: 251742 kg (555,000 lb)
Cruising speed: 498 knots
Maximum speed: Mach 0.88
Service ceiling: 33,400 ft
Maximum range: 5,950 nm
Production total: DC-10 380

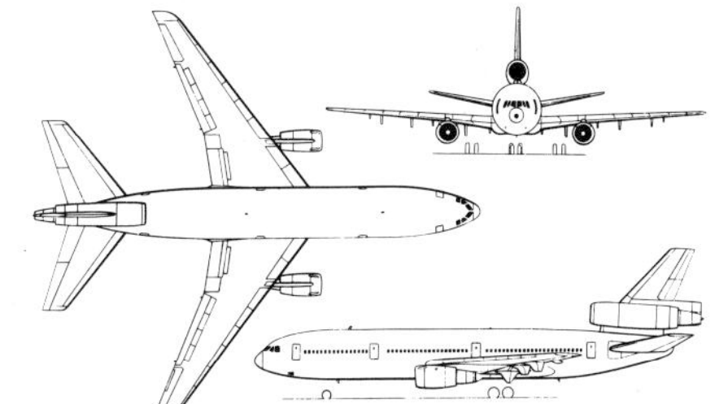

Ilyushin Il-62 'Classic'

Similar in appearance to the British Vickers VC10, the Ilyushin Il-62 was the first long-range jet airliner to go into production in the Soviet Union. The prototype, powered by four 16,356 lb st Lyulka AL-7 turbojets, first flew in January 1963. Production aircraft were powered by 23,150 lb st Kuznetsov NK-8-4 turbofans, entering service on internal routes in March 1968, with intercontinental services beginning on 15 September between Moscow-Montral. Aeroflot exclusively operate the improved, longer range Il-62M which appeared in 1970. The Il-62M is powered by 24,250 lb st Soloviev D-30KU turbofans with clamshell thrust reversers, and has a fin fuel tank, spoilers for roll control, provision for containerised cargo and updated flight deck. Final production version was the Il-62MK with increased seating capacity, and strengthened airframe for longer fatigue life.

Specification: Ilyushin Il-62M
Span: 43.20 m (141 ft 9 in)
Length: 53.12 m (174 ft 3½ in)
Height: 12.35 m (40 ft 6¼ in)
Wing area: 279.62 m² (3,010 sq ft)
Passenger capacity: 163-198
Payload: 22997 kg (50,700 lb)
Maximum take-off weight: 164996 kg (363,757 lb)
Cruising speed: 486 knots
Maximum speed: Mach 0.846
Service ceiling: 40,000 ft
Maximum range: 4,963 nm
Production total: 135+

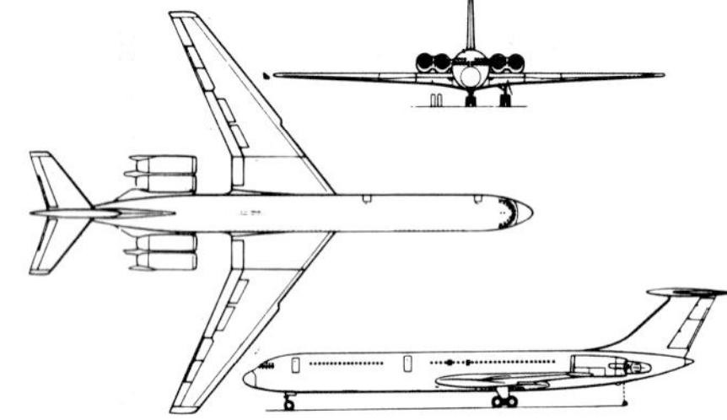

Ilyushin Il-86 'Camber'

The prototype of the Soviet Union's first wide-body turbofan airliner flew on 22 December 1976, but the production standard Il-86 did not enter service with Aeroflot until 26 December 1980, flying internal routes between Moscow and Tashkent. The aircraft is powered by four podded 28,660 lb st Kuznetsov NK-86 turbofans, the first Soviet jet airliner to adopt such a 'conventional' configuration, and is unique among contemporary large civil transport in having self-contained boarding stairs, dispensing with the need for airport 'airbridges'. Passengers board from ground level and stow their own baggage on the lower deck before ascending internal staircases to one of three cabins, each with nine-abreast seating. A long-range derivative, designated Il-96-300, is expected to fly in 1990, but is so extensively redesigned that it bears only a superficial similarity to the Il-86.

Specification: Ilyushin Il-86
Span: 48.06 m (157 ft 8¼ in)
Length: 59.53 m (195 ft 4 in)
Height: 15.79 m (51 ft 10 in)
Wing area: 319.94 m² (3,444 sq ft)
Passenger capacity: 350-375
Payload: 42002 kg (92,600 lb)
Maximum take-off weight: 205997 kg (454,150 lb)
Cruising speed: 512 knots
Maximum range: 2,480 nm
Production total: approx 55-60

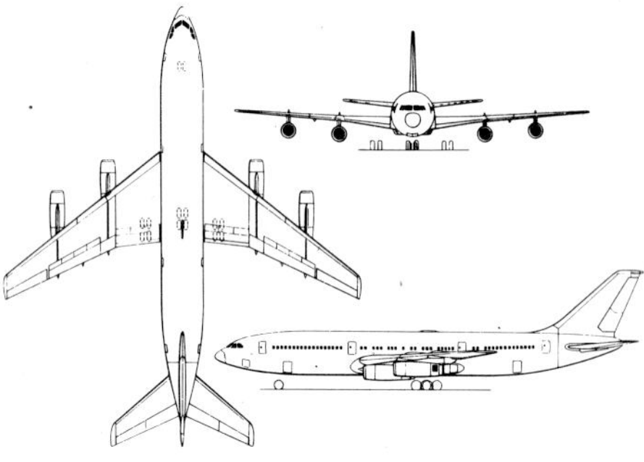

Lockheed L-1011 TriStar

The Lockheed L-1011 was designed to meet American Airlines' requirements for a 'trijet airbus', for which AA eventually selected the Douglas DC-10. But Eastern Air Lines and TWA became launch customers for the TriStar, which first flew on 17 November 1970, powered by three Rolls-Royce RB211-22B turbofans. Developed versions included the extended range L-1011-100, delivered initially to Cathay Pacific, the L-1011-200 'hot and high' variant with 48,000-50,000 lb st RB211-524 or -524B engines for British Airways, Gulf Air and Saudia, and the L-1011-500 with fuselage 13 ft 6 in shorter than other TriStar models, for which British Airways was launch customer. Late-model TriStar 500s incorporated an advanced-technology, longer-span wing with active ailerons. The last L-1011 was manufactured in August 1983.

Specification: Lockheed TriStar 500
Span: 50.08 m (164 ft 4 in)
Length: 50.05 m (164 ft 2½ in)
Height: 17.00 m (55 ft 9½ in)
Wing area: 328.95 m² (3,541 sq ft)
Passenger capacity: 246-300
Maximum take-off weight: 224980 kg (496,000 lb)
Cruising speed: 420 knots
Maximum speed: 473 knots
Service ceiling: 43,500 ft
Maximum payload range: 3,743 nm
Production total: 250

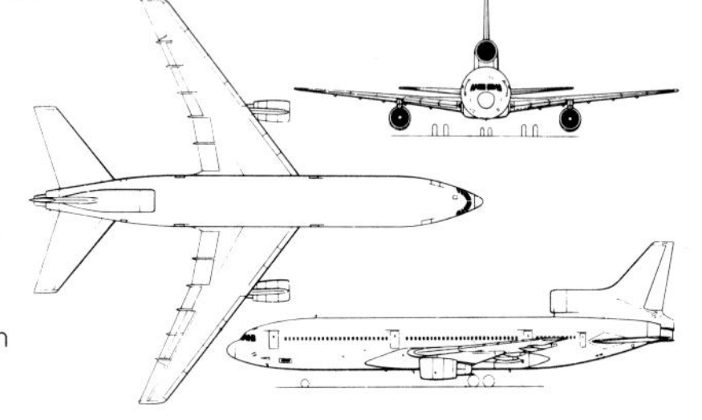

Tupolev Tu-1541

This Soviet tri-jet equivalent of the Boeing 727 first flew on 4 October 1968 and entered service with Aeroflot on 9 February 1972, eventually replacing the Tu-104 jet and Il-18 and An-10 turboprops on domestic and some international routes. Initially powered by three 20,950-lb Kuznetsov NK-8-2 turbofans, the Tu-154 (NATO code named 'Careless') has been developed through the similarly-powered Tu-154A, Tu-154B, Tu-154B-2 and all-freight Tu-14C versions to the current Tu-154M, which has 23,150 lb st Soloviev D-30KU-154-II turbofans similar to those powering the Ilyushin Il-62M. This model also has redesigned tail surfaces, increased spoiler area and revised passenger cabin configuration. It entered Aeroflot service in December 1984 and is also operated by Balkan Bulgarian Airlines, CAAC, Cubana, LOT and Syrianair. An all-cargo version of the Tu-154B is designated Tu-154C.

Specification: Tupolev Tu-154B
Span: 37.55 m (123 ft 2½ in)
Length: 47.89 m (157 ft 1¾ in)
Height: 11.39 m (37 ft 4¾ in)
Wing area: 201.40 m² (2,168 sq ft)
Passenger capacity: 128-169
Payload: 19998 kg (44,090 lb)
Maximum take-off weight: 95997 kg (211,640 lb)
Cruising speed: 486 knots
Maximum speed: Mach 0.9
Service ceiling: 39,000 ft
Maximum payload range: 1,483 nm
Production total: (all models) 600+

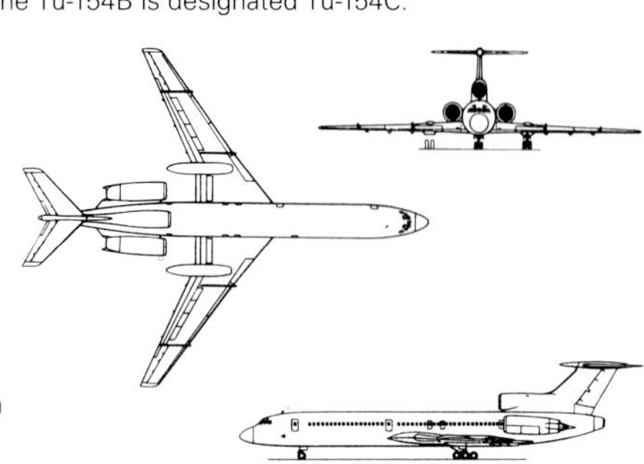

A

B

C

D

AIRCRAFT A–Z

M

N

P

R

S

AIRCRAFT A–Z

T

U

V

W

Y

Z